STUDIES IN THE CONTRACT LAWS OF ASIA V: ENDING AND CHANGING CONTRACTS

Studies in the Contract Laws of Asia V

Ending and Changing Contracts

Edited by

MINDY CHEN-WISHART

Provost's Chair Professor, National University of Singapore

Former Dean, Emerita Professor, Visiting Professor, Faculty of Law, University of Oxford

Emerita Fellow, Merton College, Oxford

DORA NEO

Associate Professor, Faculty of Law, National University of Singapore

STEFAN VOGENAUER

Managing Director, Max Planck Institute for Legal History and Legal Theory, Frankfurt

OXFORD
UNIVERSITY PRESS

OXFORD
UNIVERSITY PRESS

Great Clarendon Street, Oxford, OX2 6DP,
United Kingdom

Oxford University Press is a department of the University of Oxford.
It furthers the University's objective of excellence in research, scholarship,
and education by publishing worldwide. Oxford is a registered trade mark of
Oxford University Press in the UK and in certain other countries.

Published in the United States of America by Oxford University Press
198 Madison Avenue, New York, NY 10016, United States of America.

British Library Cataloguing in Publication Data
Data available

Library of Congress Control Number: 2025948939

ISBN 978–0–19–899581–4

DOI: 10.1093/oso/9780198995814.001.0001

Printed and bound by
CPI Group (UK) Ltd., Croydon, CR0 4YY

The manufacturer's authorised representative in the EU for product safety is
Oxford University Press España S.A. of Parque Empresarial San Fernando de Henares,
Avenida de Castilla, 2 – 28830 Madrid (www.oup.es/en or product.safety@oup.com).
OUP España S.A. also acts as importer into Spain of products made by the manufacturer.

FSC www.fsc.org
MIX
Paper | Supporting responsible forestry
FSC® C013604

To my parents Peter and Jean Chen, and my sons James, Zachary, and Max, whose encouragement to embark on this project brought me back to my origin: Luodong, Dunedin, Oxford, Singapore, Asia.

Mindy Chen-Wishart

To Rick with much appreciation

Dora Neo

To Johannes Benedikt Vogenauer

Stefan Vogenauer

Foreword

I am delighted and honoured to have been asked to write this foreword to the penultimate volume of the *Studies in the Contract Laws of Asia* series. I have long been a fan of the series. My enthusiasm is best evidenced by the fact that I contributed a chapter to the first volume and have since sought to emulate the series in a run of edited books on Asian private international law, albeit under a different publisher. I believe that I am not alone in my admiration.

What have I found so inspiring about the *Studies in the Contract Laws of Asia*?

A key element must be that the series is firmly rooted in empiricism. There are two broad approaches to writing about principles of Asian contract law. One is a magisterial, top-down approach (methodology A) exemplified by the Principles of Asian Contract Law (PACL) project mentioned in the introduction to this present volume. The other is an organic, bottom-up approach (methodology B) wherein participants contribute chapters on contract law as practised in their respective Asian jurisdictions. Similarities and differences in the chapter accounts are catalogued, with the strengths and weaknesses of the legal principles considered being identified through a comparative process.

Methodology A proposes to come up with a code of principles which reflects what the project participants believe contract law in Asia should (but may not yet) be. However, methodology A inevitably runs up against possibly unanswerable philosophical issues. Thus, what makes the principles espoused 'Asian' in nature? If the principles discerned are supposed to reflect what contract law should be, why do those principles have to be qualified as 'Asian' rather than advocated as 'universal' in scope? The difficulty is that, in a sense, methodology A seeks to derive what 'ought' to be Asian contract law from what the law currently 'is' within Asia. In deciding which contractual principles ought to be championed and which downplayed, difficult choices will have to be made. To be authoritative, the criteria for such choices must not be purely subjective, dependent on a majority vote or even the consensus view among the persons taking part in the top-down exercise. If that is the case, how exactly does one settle on the objective criteria for such choices, and what (if anything) is 'Asian' about them? I acknowledge methodology A's potential of producing harmonized principles of Asian law. But much like the road to Ithaca, the way will possibly be long and fraught with challenge.

In contrast, the *Studies in the Contract Laws of Asia* series adopts methodology B, which is more modest in its ambitions. The bottom-up approach is intended to yield a comparative study, grounded on the laws of selected Asian jurisdictions as they are. It will be left to students, academics, lawyers, legislators, judges, and lay persons to make use of the resulting product as they see fit. As the introductory chapter to this book observes, that usage will typically be (i) to facilitate the harmonization of contract law among two or more Asian states or (ii) to initiate a dialogue between Asian and non-Asian jurisdictions on how shared legal problems might be addressed. The existential question of what is 'Asian' about Asian contract law is thereby neatly finessed. Employing methodology B, the series has managed to publish five comprehensive volumes in the short span of less than a decade. Along the way, the series has established itself as a pioneer of the bottom-up approach.

A corollary to the series' inductive approach is that the series is eminently pragmatic. Contributors are not given free rein to say whatever they wish on a topic of contract law. For each volume in the series, the editors have come up with specific questions and hypothetical problems, which contributors are supposed to answer. For example, the template of questions and problems which the participants in this book had to address may be found in section IV of the introductory chapter. It is easy for legal writers (and their readers!) to lose themselves in a sea of legal speculation with little feel for how such abstract notions can be deployed to resolve the contractual disputes that trouble our everyday lives. It will be seen from the template that, by comparison, this series prioritizes a careful analysis of the concrete.

This does not mean that theoretical considerations are sacrificed or that the series is primarily intended for practitioners. Far from it. For me personally, the most valuable components of the series are the final chapters of each volume (including that by Professor Hugh Beale for this book). In those concluding chapters, the contract principles in the individual jurisdiction chapters are rigorously and critically examined, not only as among themselves but also by comparison with the contract laws of leading common law and civil law jurisdictions. True congruences are noted, false analogies are pointed out, and innovations are recognized. Attempts are made to explain how outliers or glaring anomalies have arisen as a matter of history or otherwise. Possible trajectories for future development are mooted. It is this profound engagement with the body of Asian contract laws that raises the series to another level, not merely as a work for practitioners or academics but as something for everyone concerned to know and understand what is happening in Asian contract law today.

I congratulate the editors and contributors of the publication of the fifth volume in the *Studies in the Contract Laws of Asia* series. I look forward to the publication of the sixth book to complete the series in the near future.

Anselmo Reyes
Kyoto
20 April 2025

Acknowledgements

We are extremely grateful for all the support we received in producing volume V of the *Studies in the Contract Laws of Asia*. Once again, we have benefited from generous institutional funding from two institutions: the EW Barker Centre for Law and Business at the Law Faculty of the National University of Singapore (NUS) and the Max Planck Institute for Legal History and Legal Theory in Frankfurt (mpilhlt). The superbly professional staff of the EW Barker Centre organized and hosted a two-day colloquium in August 2019, at which all the contributors to this volume presented their first drafts.

We are deeply indebted to those who participated in this event. It was opened by Justice Andrew Phang of the Supreme Court of Singapore; his welcome address is reproduced, in revised and updated form, in Chapter 2 of this volume. Helpful and thoughtful comments on the draft contributions were then provided by our Singaporean colleagues Sandra Booysen, Christian Hofmann, Pearlie Koh, Jeremiah Lau, Kelry Loi, Yip Man, Yeo Tiong Min, Irina Sakharova, Alvin See, Benjamin Wong, and Tan Zhong Xing.

After—often substantial—revision, the papers entered the editorial process, which was expertly steered by Vera Mark, with the support of Victoria Hooton (both mpilhlt). We were particularly delighted and honoured that Justice Anselmo Reyes of the Singapore International Commercial Court kindly agreed to contribute the foreword to this volume. Warm thanks are also due to the professional and efficient team at Oxford University Press for seeing the book through to publication.

Our greatest debt, however, is to our contributors. We were able to rely on them when we had to completely revise the timeline for this volume. The COVID-19 pandemic of 2020 hit just a week or two before their final manuscripts were due. When the historical significance of this 'unforeseen supervening event' became clear, we decided to pause the project: given that 'changing circumstances' is one of the two main themes of this book, we wanted to give the authors an opportunity for updating and expanding the papers so as to see to what extent, if any, Asian contract laws would respond to what was arguably the biggest global challenge in recent memory. We are most grateful for the patience and dedication of everyone involved, and it is great to see that the volume can be published with largely the original cast of authors, albeit much later than originally planned.

At the time of writing these acknowledgments, we are already preparing the sixth, and final, volume of the *Studies of the Contract Laws of Asia*, which will deal with public policy and illegality in contract law. It continues to be a privilege to collaborate with so many outstanding colleagues across a multitude of jurisdictions in Asia, and we remain grateful for this opportunity.

Mindy Chen-Wishart
Dora Neo
Stefan Vogenauer

Table of Contents

INDIA: ENDING CONTRACTS

INDONESIA: CHANGING CIRCUMSTANCES

INDONESIA: ENDING CONTRACTS

JAPAN: CHANGING CIRCUMSTANCES

JAPAN: ENDING CONTRACTS

KOREA: CHANGING CIRCUMSTANCES

KOREA: ENDING CONTRACTS

MALAYSIA: CHANGING CIRCUMSTANCES

MALAYSIA: ENDING CONTRACTS

MYANMAR: CHANGING CIRCUMSTANCES AND ENDING CONTRACTS

PHILIPPINES: CHANGING CIRCUMSTANCES

PHILIPPINES: ENDING CONTRACTS

SINGAPORE: CHANGING CIRCUMSTANCES

SINGAPORE: ENDING CONTRACTS

TAIWAN: CHANGING CIRCUMSTANCES

TAIWAN: ENDING CONTRACTS

THAILAND: CHANGING CIRCUMSTANCES

THAILAND: ENDING CONTRACTS

VIETNAM: CHANGING CIRCUMSTANCES

VIETNAM: ENDING CONTRACTS

CONCLUSIONS

Table of Cases

AUSTRALIA

CHINA

GERMANY

HONG KONG

INDIA

INDONESIA

JAPAN

KOREA

MALAYSIA

MYANMAR

NEW ZEALAND

PHILIPPINES

SINGAPORE

SPAIN

TAIWAN

THAILAND

UNITED KINGDOM

VIETNAM

Table of Legislation

INTERNATIONAL INSTRUMENTS

NATIONAL LEGISLATION

Australia

China

France

Germany

Indonesia

Italy

Japan

Korea

Malaysia

Myanmar

Netherlands

Philippines

Russia

Singapore

Spain

Switzerland

Taiwan

United Kingdom

United States

Vietnam

EUROPEAN UNION

Contributors

AHN Tae-Yong
The Law Office of Tae-Yong Ahn

Hugh BEALE
KC (Hon), FBA, Emeritus Professor, School of Law, University of Warwick, Coventry; Senior Research Fellow, Harris Manchester College; Visiting Research Fellow at the Institute of European and Comparative Law and Visiting Professor, University of Oxford

Gary F BELL
Secretary General of the International Academy of Comparative Law; Associate Professor, Faculty of Law, National University of Singapore

Adrian BRIGGS
KC, Emeritus Professor of Private International Law, Faculty of Law, University of Oxford

Ma Ngina Teresa CHAN-GONZAGA
Associate Dean for Academic Affairs, Ateneo de Manila University School of Law

Lei CHEN
Chair in International Arbitration and Chinese Law, Durham Law School, Durham University

Tsung-fu CHEN
Chair Professor and former Dean, Department of Law, College of Law, National Taiwan University, Taipei

Mindy CHEN-WISHART
Provost's Professor of Law, National University of Singapore; former Dean, Visiting and Emerita Professor, Faculty of Law, Oxford University, Emerita Fellow at Merton College, Oxford University, Visiting Research Fellow at the Institute of European and Comparative Law, Chair Professor at National Chengchi University

May Fong CHEONG
Associate Professor, School of Private and Commercial Law, Faculty of Law & Justice, University of New South Wales, Sydney; Adjunct Professor, Faculty of Law, Multimedia University

Michael Anthony C DIZON
Senior Lecturer and Co-director of Research and Innovation, Curtin Law School, Curtin University

DO Giang Nam
Vice Dean of the Faculty of Private Law, University of Law, Vietnam National University, Hanoi

Stephen HALL
Professor, Faculty of Law, The Chinese University of Hong Kong; Fellow, C W Chu College, The Chinese University of Hong Kong

HERLIANA
Associate Professor, Faculty of Law, Gadjah Mada University, Indonesia; Director of the Centre for Intellectual Property, Competition Law, and Dispute Settlement (CICODS)

Sheng-Lin JAN
Emeritus Professor, National Taiwan University; Adjunct Chair Professor, National Chengchi University

Akira KAMO
Professor, Graduate Schools for Law and Politics, University of Tokyo,

KWON Youngjoon
Justice, Supreme Court of Korea (current); Professor, Seoul National University (previous)

Nadnaphas LEAKPECH
Lecturer, Faculty of Law, Thammasat University, Bangkok

Yin Harn LEE
Senior Lecturer, University of Bristol Law School; Director, LLM in Law, Innovation and Technology, University of Bristol

Kelvin FK LOW
Professor, Faculty of Law, The University of Hong Kong

Chitra NARAYAN
Advocate, Madras High Court; Mediator and Arbitrator

Dora NEO
Associate Professor, Faculty of Law, National University of Singapore

Andrew PHANG
Senior Judge, Supreme Court of Singapore; Distinguished Professor of Law, Yong Pung How School of Law, Singapore Management University; Distinguished Honorary Professor of Law, Faculty of Law, National University of Singapore; Visiting Professor of Law, University of Reading; formerly, Justice of the Court of Appeal, Supreme Court of Singapore

Munin PONGSAPAN
Associate Professor and Director of Centre for Legal Sociology, Legal History and Legal Philosophy; Former Dean, Faculty of Law, Thammasat University, Bangkok; Co-chief Editor of Thai Legal Studies

Eriko TAOKA
Professor, College of Law and Politics, Rikkyo University, Tokyo

Chee Ho THAM
Professor, Yong Pung How School of Law, Singapore Management University

TRAN Kien
Associate Professor; Senior Lecturer, the Faculty of Private Law, University of Law, Vietnam National University, Hanoi

R Yashod VARDHAN
Senior Advocate, High Court of Madras, Arbitrator and Mediator

Stefan VOGENAUER
Managing Director, Max Planck Institute for Legal History and Legal Theory, Frankfurt am Main

WANG Lei
Professor, Research Center of Civil and Commercial Jurisprudence, Renmin University of China; School of Law, Renmin University of China

Zhicheng WU
Associate Professor, Research Center of Civil and Commercial Jurisprudence, Renmin University of China; School of Law, Renmin University of China

Abbreviations

AB	*Algemeene Bepalingen van Wetgeving voor Nederlandsch-Indië* (General Provisions of Legislation for the Dutch East Indies of 1846)
ALBL	Act on Land and Building Leases of 1991 (Japan)
art	article
BE	Buddhist Era
BGB	*Bürgerliches Gesetzbuch* (German Civil Code)
BGH	*Bundesgerichtshof* (German Federal Court of Justice)
BW	*Burgerlijk Wetboek* (Dutch Civil Code of 1838)
CCA	Consumer Contract Act (Japan)
CCC	Chinese Civil Code
CCR 2009	Consumer Protections (Fair Trading) (Cancellation of Contracts) Regulations 2009 (Singapore)
CESL	Common European Sales Law
ch	chapter
CISG	United Nations Convention on Contracts for the International Sale of Goods
CLA	Civil Law Act 1956 (Malaysia)
CNY	Chinese yuan
COVID-19	coronavirus disease 2019
CPFTA	Consumer Protection (Fair Trading) Act 2003 (Singapore)
CUP	Cambridge University Press
D&G	Dolce & Gabbana
DCFR	Draft Common Frame of Reference
DDA	Delhi Development Authority
DLO	District Lands Officer (Hong Kong)
FCA	Frustrated Contracts Act (Singapore)
GDP	gross domestic product
HKU Press	Hong Kong University Press
IBRA	Indonesian Bank Restructuring Agency
ICA	Indian Contract Act 1872
ICAC	Independent Commission against Corruption (Hong Kong)
ICC	Indonesian Civil Code; International Chamber of Commerce
IMF	International Monetary Fund
INDRA	Indonesian Debt Restructuring Agency
IS	*Indische Staatsregeling* (Dutch Colonial Constitution)
JCC	Japanese Civil Code
KIKO contract	Knock-in, Knock-out contract (Korea)
KCC	Korean Civil Code
MAC clause	Materially Adverse Change clause
MCA	Malaysian Contracts Act
MYR	Malaysian ringgit

n	note
NBW	*Nieuw Burgerlijk Wetboek*
NHA	National Housing Authority (Philippines)
OFCC	Old French Civil Code 1804
Ord	Ordinance (Hong Kong)
OUP	Oxford University Press
PACL	Principles of Asian Contract Law
para	paragraph
PCC	Philippine Civil Code
PECL	Principles of European Contract Law
PHP	Philippine peso
PICC	UNIDROIT Principles of International Commercial Contracts
RMB	Renminbi
RSFSR Civil Code	Civil Code of the Russian Soviet Federative Socialist Republic of 1964
s	section
SARS	Severe Acute Respiratory Syndrome
SGA	Sale of Goods Act 1930 (India); Sale of Goods Act 1979 (Singapore)
SGA 1982	Supply of Goods Act 1982 (Singapore)
SOGA	Sale of Goods Act 1957 (Malaysia)
SPC	Supreme People's Court of the People's Republic of China
SRA	Specific Relief Act 1963 (India)
TCC	Taiwanese Civil Code
TCCC	Thai Civil and Commercial Code
THB	Thai baht
UCC	Uniform Commercial Code (United States)
UCTA	Unfair Contract Terms Act 1977 (Singapore)
UK	United Kingdom
UNIDROIT	International Institute for the Unification of Private Law
US	United States of America
USSR	Union of Soviet Socialist Republics
VCC	Vietnamese Civil Code
VIAC	Vietnam International Arbitration Centre

1

Introduction

*Mindy CHEN-WISHART, Dora NEO, and Stefan VOGENAUER**

I. Genesis and Objectives of the Project

This project has resulted in part from the experience of Mindy Chen-Wishart on the Principles of Asian Contract Law (PACL) project,[1] initially as a representative of Singapore, but later as a joint chief editor.[2] The PACL experience revealed a glaring gap in the Asian literature of the sort that has underwritten the European efforts at harmonization which have borne fruit in the Principles of European Contract Law (PECL), the Draft Common Frame of Reference (DCFR), and the Common European Sales Law (CESL).[3] While there is a long history of comparative contract law studies in Europe, along with concerted efforts to encourage regional harmonization of the contract laws, in the lingua franca of English, the same cannot be said of Asia. Regional integration within Asia, for various historical and socio-political reasons, has not been a priority for many Asian jurisdictions.[4] Consequently, the bulk of the literature in the field of contract law is confined to texts and commentaries aimed at domestic audiences and in the local language. This 'Tower of Babel' poses inevitable obstacles to communication and understanding of each other's laws. With increasing global focus on the rising power and emerging markets of Asia and an increasing interest within Asia to harmonize their contract laws, the gaps need to be addressed.

This project has two main aims: to facilitate conversations *between* Asian jurisdictions, and between them and 'Western' jurisdictions, by providing (in a common language—English—since there is no obvious lingua franca in Asia) up-to-date and scholarly literature on the contract laws of many Asian jurisdictions and on comparative Asian contract law. This will lay the groundwork for those interested in exploring the possibility of regional harmonization within the commercial law sphere of Asia. It will also open up the channels of communication between contract law academics, policymakers, lawmakers, and practitioners in Asia and those in the 'West', with great potential for enhancing mutual understanding and fruitful collaborations. The project may also promote the development and teaching of courses on comparative Asian contract law in law schools worldwide.

* Parts I–III of this chapter are based on and borrow from M Chen-Wishart, D Neo, and S Vogenauer, 'Introduction' in M Chen-Wishart, A Loke, and B Ong (eds), *Studies in the Contract Laws of Asia, vol V: Ending and Changing Contracts* (OUP 2016) 1.

[1] S Han, 'Principles of Asian Contract Law: An Endeavor of Regional Harmonization of Contract Law in East Asia' (2013) 58 Villanova Law Review 589.

[2] Mindy Chen-Wishart is no longer involved with the PACL.

[3] For an overview, see G Dannemann and S Vogenauer, 'Introduction: The European Contract Law Initiative and the "CFR in Context" Project' in G Dannemann and S Vogenauer (eds), *The Common European Sales Law in Context: Interactions with English and German Law* (OUP 2013) 1–20.

[4] For example, Han (n 1) 591, has described the current relationship between China, Japan, and Korea as being 'politically cold, but economically warm'.

Mindy Chen-Wishart, Dora Neo, and Stefan Vogenauer, *Introduction* In: *Studies in the Contract Laws of Asia V: Ending and Changing Contracts*. Edited by: Mindy Chen-Wishart, Dora Neo, and Stefan Vogenauer, Oxford University Press.
 DOI: 10.1093/oso/9780198995814.003.0001

To these ends, there will be six titles in this series on the contract law regimes of key Asian jurisdictions and their comparative dimension, with each thematic volume addressing core legal issues that are encountered by contract lawyers in all jurisdictions. These are:

I. *Remedies for Breach of Contract* (published in 2016)
II. *Formation and Third Party Beneficiaries* (published in 2018)
III. *Contents of Contracts and Unfair Terms* (published in 2020)
IV. *Invalidity* (published in 2022)
V. *Ending and Changing Contracts* (published in 2026)
VI. *Public Policy and Illegality.*

In each volume, there are typically two contributions per jurisdiction directed to a fairly detailed brief provided by the editors. These include 'issues to be addressed' and hypotheticals involving commonly encountered problems. In addition, a concluding chapter analyses the contributions from a comparative perspective and draws out the common themes and theoretical underpinnings of the convergences and divergences revealed.

Most Asian countries have private law systems transplanted from European legal systems, sometimes as a legacy of colonialism, sometimes consciously imported by local elites. Thus, English law provides the common law roots of the legal systems in Singapore, India, Malaysia, Hong Kong, and Myanmar, while Germany's civil law model forms the basis of the contract laws in Japan, Korea, Taiwan, and, to a somewhat lesser extent, China and Thailand. Indeed, some jurisdictions are the result of 'double transplants'. For example, Thailand has adopted many Japanese provisions, while Myanmar and Malaysia have imported the Indian Contract Act. In addition, Vietnamese contract law has been greatly influenced by the French Civil Code of 1804, while Indonesian contract law is a copy of pre-1992 Dutch law, which was itself an adaptation of French law. The Philippines combines a Spanish legal legacy with more recent influences from US-American contract law. Consequently, this project will not only bring Asian voices into the international comparative law scholarship but also yield insights into the phenomenon of 'legal transplant'. Asia is the perfect laboratory for investigating how laws, developed in one jurisdiction, are interpreted and mutated after they are transplanted into another jurisdiction.

II. The Asian Jurisdictions Covered in This Volume

This volume examines the contract laws of thirteen Asian jurisdictions: China, Hong Kong, India, Indonesia, Japan, Korea, Malaysia, Myanmar, the Philippines, Singapore, Taiwan, Thailand, and Vietnam. The two main topics for each jurisdiction are:

(i) changes of circumstances subsequent to the making of a contract which make performance of the contract impossible, more difficult, economically less attractive, or pointless for one or both parties;
(ii) the termination of a contract by one of the parties for the breach of the other.

Asia is a vast region with almost fifty states. It is impossible to cover all these jurisdictions within the scope of this project. Instead, we focus on a representative sample of countries selected from the dynamic economies in East, Southeast, and South Asia. These are all countries whose legal systems have long-standing historical ties with either the English common law or the European civil law traditions. A few have borrowed from each other's jurisprudence. The largest economies by population size in East Asia are represented by the chapters on India, China, Indonesia, Japan, and the Philippines, while smaller jurisdictions are represented by the chapters on Singapore, Hong Kong, Taiwan, and Malaysia.

The juxtaposition of the contract laws of China, Hong Kong, and Taiwan presents an interesting study of contrasts between three territories with close political, cultural, and economic ties, yet very different legal traditions. The legal systems of Hong Kong and Taiwan are heavily influenced by their colonial histories, yielding a common law and a civil law system, respectively. In contrast, the Chinese Contract Law 1999 was the product of mixed reception drawing from civil law and common law jurisdictions as well as international restatements such as the United Nations Convention on Contracts for the International Sale of Goods (CISG), the UNIDROIT Principles of International Commercial Contracts (PICC), and the PECL. As it was supplemented by the Judicial Interpretations of the Supreme People's Court, there is the evolution of a genuinely hybrid civil and common law system. The new Chinese Civil Code, which came into force on 1 January 2021, has reinforced these developments.

India, the largest country in South Asia, is important not only economically but also historically as the test bed for many codifications of the common law, which were subsequently exported to other British colonies, including Malaysia, Myanmar, and Sri Lanka, or inherited on independence in Pakistan and Bangladesh. The contract law of the Philippines reflects its colonial history in being a hybrid of Spanish civil law and Anglo-American law of the United States. Thailand, one of the few states in the region that was never colonized by a Western power, has a contract law that reflects the legal influences of French, German, and Japanese civil law.

Indonesia—the fourth largest population in the world and the most populous Muslim majority country in the world—presents a bewildering picture. Three systems operate simultaneously: the indigenous (adat) laws of different ethnic groups, different varieties of Islamic contract law, and the Civil Code of 1847. The latter is a direct transplant from the 1838 Dutch Civil Code, which itself was very closely modelled on the French Civil Code of 1804. Today, the Indonesian Civil Code is still in the Dutch language, although 98 per cent of lawyers and judges do not understand Dutch or French and although Dutch contract law itself was substantially reformed in 1992,[5] as was the French contract law in 2016.

The socio-economic diversity of the selected Asian jurisdictions represented in this volume is reflected in Table 1.1, representing the situation in 2024, the year for which the latest comprehensive data is available. It will be evident that this volume represents the contract laws governing more than three-and-a-half billion people (ie nearly half the world population), with an average gross domestic product (GDP) per capita of US$ 22,904.20, above the world average of US$ 13,664.00.

[5] GF Bell, 'Formation of Contract and Stipulations for Third Parties in Indonesia' in M Chen-Wishart, A Loke, and S Vogenauer (eds), *Studies in the Contract Laws of Asia, vol II: Formation and Third Party Beneficiaries* (OUP 2018) 365, 365–69.

Table 1.1 Population and GDP per capita of subject jurisdiction

Country/territory	Population size (2023)	GDP per capita (2023) (US$)
China	1,408,975,000	13,303.10
Hong Kong	7,524,100	54,107.00
India	1,450,935,790	2,696.70
Indonesia	283,487,931	4,925.40
Japan	123,975,371	32,475.90
Korea (South)	51,751,065	36,238.60
Malaysia	35,557,673	11,867.30
Myanmar	54,500,091	1,359.30
Philippines	115,843,670	3,984.80
Singapore	6,036,860	90,674.10
Taiwan[a]	23,400,220	34,060.00
Thailand	71,668,011	7,345.10
Vietnam	100,987,686	4,717.30
Total	3,734,643,468 (45.87% of the world population of 8,142,056,45)	
Average		$22,904.20 (world average: $13,664.00)

Sources: [a] National Statistics Republic of China (Taiwan)], <http://eng.stat.gov.tw> accessed 25 February 2025; Statista, <https://www.statista.com/statistics/727592/gross-domestic-product-gdp-per-capita-in-taiwan/?srsltid=AfmBOor0zZvLiaWJd7pOQcavjt-T4z3e8wHmhZDZoXq1wRmA3D6bBITu> accessed 23 January 2026.

III. Methodology

The PACL experience revealed certain particularities with legal scholarship in the countries covered in this project if compared to Europe and, specifically, the UK. These include a different level of proficiency in written scholarly and legal English, a different structure of interpersonal relationships (being more hierarchical and loyalty-based), and a different style of scholarship (leaning more towards doctrinal exposition rather than policy and theoretical discussions). We put in place a number of measures to meet these challenges. First, we put a tremendous amount of effort into finding contributors with the combination of skills needed. We relied on personal contacts and recommendations. As would be expected, there was some unevenness in the contributions we received for the first volume, which we then worked extremely hard to iron out in the editorial process. This challenge has lessened with each volume of this project.

Secondly, contributors received very detailed terms of reference with the aim of providing sufficient guidance to ensure that the chapters cover the same issues and address the same themes to enable fruitful comparisons. At the same time, we sought to encourage our authors to explore issues that have been the subject(s) of particular attention or controversy and to address the normative dimensions that may inform law reform in their jurisdictions. Contributors were also provided with a short reading list on comparative materials to get a feel of the issues that are generally discussed in these contexts in the European and global settings; the hope was that this material would help the authors approach their own legal systems with various different models in mind. Given the confines of this volume, the aim is not to provide an exhaustive account of the law in each jurisdiction but to give an outline of the shape and form of the law and a taster of some of the issues that preoccupy that legal system.

Thirdly, this volume, like the preceding volumes, was facilitated by a colloquium involving all the contributors and editors as well as invited commentators, practitioners, and judges. The first draft was submitted by the contributors six weeks before the colloquium to enable the editors to review and revert, with 'talking points' for each contributor to address at the colloquium. This allowed the editors to highlight common issues, unusual features of the particular law, gaps in the papers, and areas for further explanations. This gave contributors time to consider how to respond at the colloquium and gave notice of what would need to be addressed in redrafting their papers.

Fourth, at the colloquium, each contributor addressed his or her 'talking points', followed by a commentator's remarks and open discussion. The colloquium yielded fruitful comparisons, raised further questions for consideration, and generally facilitated a better sense of the common endeavour. We also had a dedicated session on the publication process to impress on contributors the substantial revisions that would be necessary in most cases. After the colloquium, the editors wrote again to each contributor with detailed comments on the draft and suggestions for revision.

Lastly, once the second drafts had been submitted, the editors reviewed and reverted again on any issues still outstanding and worked to resolve them with the contributors. In respect of some papers, this turned out to be a very significant enterprise. In these ways, we sought to craft as good a representation of the contract law of each jurisdiction as we could.

The chapter on Myanmar contract law merits special mention: it has been excised from the work of Professors Adrian Briggs and (now also, Lord) Andrew Burrows of the Oxford Law Faculty, *The Law of Contract in Myanmar* (OUP 2017),[6] with their kind permission. The work is a major project of the Oxford–Burma/Myanmar Law Programme, instituted to assist Myanmar law schools and the wider community in the aftermath of the end of military rule and the introduction of democratic reforms after 2011. It is the first book to look in detail at Myanmar contract law, which clearly self-identifies as a common law system. The authors relied primarily on the Myanmar Contract Act 1872 (which is essentially identical to the Indian Contract Law Act of 1872 and regarded as a codification of the English common law) and on the relevant Burmese/Myanmar case law. They sought to identify, read, and understand all the reported decisions on contract of the courts of Burma/Myanmar since the enactment of the 1872 Act until about 1968, after which the Myanmar law reports are in the Burmese language only. The authors' research and writing was primarily carried out in Oxford using the facilities of the Bodleian Law library and electronic databases in addition to short teaching visits to Yangon, where they spoke with members

[6] Freely available at <www.law.ox.ac.uk/sites/default/files/migrated/briggsburrowsbook_-_thelawofcontractinmyanmar.pdf> accessed 25 February 2025.

of the law faculty, practitioners, and judges about the Myanmar law of contract.[7] We are pleased that Professor Briggs builds on their work in this collection of Asian contract law.

IV. Guidance Provided to Chapter Contributors

For ease of exposition, discussion of each jurisdiction is typically divided into two chapters—the first dealing with changes of circumstances, and the second dealing with termination for breach. In the case of Myanmar, the author combined both areas of discussion into a single chapter. We sent the contributors the following terms of reference:

> Contract parties are entitled to performance in accordance with the terms of the contract. Apart from variations or discharge *agreed between the parties*, there are two main circumstances when a party may be permitted to depart from the agreed terms. First, when change of circumstances after contract formation makes performance more difficult or impossible, and second, when the other party repudiates or breaches the original terms. In both these circumstances, the law must balance the concern to preserve predictability and legal certainty with that of fairness to both parties. It will also determine what principles should guide any claim for damages, restitution, or loss.
>
> In exploring these issues, we hope you will engage with the current critiques and debates taking place in your jurisdiction and the possible direction of development.
>
> In particular, please:
>
> - Highlight any *similarities* or *differences* you think are especially notable between your law and the laws of other Asian jurisdictions.
> - Analyse and comment on the *principles/interests/values/policies* that underlie your law.
> - It is most important that you *give examples* to illustrate your points.
>
> Notes:
> We have covered:
> - contractual remedies in Volume I,
> - contract formation and third party beneficiaries in Volume II,
> - contractual interpretation and the regulation of unfair terms in Volume III, and
> - mistake, fraud, misrepresentation, duress, undue influence, and unconscionability in Volume IV.
>
> You may have to refer to any of these topics in your contribution in order to set the law in your jurisdiction into its proper context, but please try to avoid overlaps and repetition as much as possible.
>
> In your respective papers, please cover the following issues, although it need not be in the order presented here.
>
> Please give a very *brief* introduction to the historical background to the modern law of contract in your jurisdiction.

[7] See <www.law.ox.ac.uk/the-myanmar-law-of-contract/myanmar-law-contract> accessed 25 February 2025.

Paper I: Change of Circumstances

1. When, if ever, are contract parties relieved from or entitled to adapt their contractual obligations because a change of circumstances after contract formation has made performance of the contract impossible, more difficult, economically less attractive, or pointless for one or both parties?
   1.1 Are there specific doctrines dealing with such changes of circumstances? Or are these cases resolved via established doctrines of contract law that originally had a different and more limited function (eg mistake; supplementary interpretation or implication of terms; *laesio enormis* or other means of policing the content of the contract)?
   1.2 What are the tests used by the courts to distinguish between relevant and irrelevant changes of circumstances?
2. Do parties tend to use contractual clauses allocating the risk with a view to potential supervening circumstances (eg indexation clauses, *force majeure* clauses, hardship clauses)? Do the courts respect such clauses?
3. What are the legal consequences if a change of circumstances is regarded as relevant?
   3.1 Is a contract necessarily brought to an end by a qualifying change of circumstances?
   3.2 If so, to what extent does restitution and/or loss apportionment follow if the contract has been (partially) performed?
   3.3 Can the party that relies on the change of circumstances terminate the contract? Can it claim damages?
   3.4 Can the court or one of the parties adapt the contract to the changed circumstances, and which factors guide the adaptation?
   3.5 Are the parties under a duty to renegotiate?
4. What are the theoretical justifications for the legal response (eg good faith, lack of consent)?
5. How would your jurisdiction decide the following hypotheticals?[8]
   5.1 In 1567, Abraham enters into a contract for an unlimited period of time with farmer Bill under which Abraham promises to build and maintain an irrigation channel from which Bill may extract water at a fixed price. By 2018, inflation and the rise in the cost of maintenance and labour have made the price wholly inadequate. Abraham's successors in law ask for an increase in the price that would provide them with adequate compensation. Alternatively, they wish to terminate the contract.
   5.2 In 2015, Citi Corporation receives a loan from Drive Bank. The interest rate is fixed at 10 per cent for five years. In the 20 years preceding the agreement, the rate of inflation had been relatively stable within a range of 1 to 6 per cent. In 2017, the economic situation begins to destabilize and inflation rises to 50 per cent. Drive Bank requests adjustment or, alternatively, termination of the contract.
   5.3 Easy leases business premises from Frugle for a fixed period of 15 years. Shortly after the contract has been concluded, a nearby military airport is unexpectedly shut down for political reasons. The government invests an enormous amount of public funds in order to improve the commercial infrastructure in the area. As a

[8] In order to facilitate comparison with European jurisdictions, the hypotheticals to be addressed in Paper I are based on Scenarios 1, 2(a), 4, 5, 7, and 11 of E Hondius and HC Grigoleit (eds), *Unexpected Circumstances in European Contract Law* (CUP 2011) 175–80.

result, Easy's profits are 500 per cent of what could reasonably have been expected at the time of making the contract. At the same time, the rental value of comparable business premises in the area rises to 500 per cent of the agreed rental price. Frugle requests that the rental price should be adjusted accordingly or, alternatively, that the agreement should be terminated.

5.4 Builder George agrees to refurbish the cellar of Han, the owner of a restaurant. The work is scheduled to start one month after the agreement. Before the work begins, the restaurant is completely destroyed by a storm that is much more violent than any other previous storm in the region. However, the cellar remains fully intact. Han immediately informs George of the situation and asks him not to start work. George insists on rendering performance because he has set aside two weeks to carry out the work and has already purchased the necessary materials. Is Han required to pay the contract price or, alternatively, to compensate George for his loss?

5.5 Gina books a room for the weekend at H Hotel in X City, the capital of country Z. However,

(i) the exhibition she intended to visit is cancelled at the very last moment;
(ii) a terrorist group declares that it plans to launch attacks on tourists in X;
(iii) an unforeseeable strike by airport personnel prevents Gina from travelling to X before Sunday afternoon;
(iv) the inauguration proceedings of the new head of state of Z that were scheduled for Saturday are cancelled. Gina had booked a room overlooking the street where the inauguration procession was supposed to pass by. Due to the inauguration, the rental price of the room was ten times higher than the regular price.

Can Gina cancel the booking?

5.6 Kris sells his family home to Leila at 70 per cent of its market value. Both parties assume that Leila will dedicate it to cultural use by the general public. However, this assumption is not expressly set out in the contract. After the sale, Leila changes her mind and gives the house to one of her sons instead. Can Kris claim the difference between the agreed price and the market value or, alternatively, restitution of the house?

Paper II: Termination of Contract

1. In what circumstances are contract parties entitled to withhold or discontinue their own performance?

1.1 Are there specific rules under which certain types of breach or non-performance always (or never) entitle the innocent party to terminate?

1.2 In the absence of specific rules, is there a general standard on the kind of breach or non-performance that is required?

- Does the effect of the breach, eg its seriousness, play a role?
- Does the nature of the term broken matter?
- Is intention necessary or relevant?
- Is the manner of the breach relevant?
- Does it matter whether the innocent party is a consumer or a business?

1.3 Is termination only available if the party in breach has been given a second chance, ie an opportunity to provide 'supplementary performance' (performance at a later date, cure, repair, etc), and has not done so? When is the innocent party not required to provide such an opportunity?

2. Do the courts respect termination clauses, both in standard terms and if individually negotiated?
3. How would your jurisdiction decide the following hypotheticals?[9]
   3.1 Car Machinery & Co appoint Traders Ltd as sole distributors of their car panel presses for a period of five years. Clause 7(b) of the agreement provides that 'Distributors shall send their representatives to visit all six large car manufacturers in the country at least once in every week for the purpose of soliciting orders for car panel presses. Failure to comply with this obligation shall entitle Car Machinery to terminate the agreement with immediate effect.' Traders Ltd miss two visits to car manufacturers in the second month of the contractual period. Is Car Machinery entitled to terminate the agreement?
   3.2 Prime Ltd sells a piece of land to Devil Corp. Under the terms of the contract, Devil pays a 10 per cent deposit, the remainder of the sum being due at 5:00 pm on 30 September, time being 'of the essence'. According to Clause 12, failure to meet the deadline would result in the deposit being forfeited and the agreement being terminated. Devil is ten minutes late in tendering the completion money and Prime refuse performance. Can Devil sue for specific performance, arguing that Prime's reliance on the clause is unreasonable in some way?
   Would the result be different if the contract did not include Clause 12?
   3.3 Seven Seas, an importer of seafood, sells two tons of mussels to Big Chef restaurant chain. After one ton has been delivered it turns out that the concentration of cadmium in the mussels is 2 per cent above the concentration permitted by national food regulations. Can Big Chef terminate the contract?
   3.4 Coco, a famous architect, agrees with David that he will landscape the garden in her next development. He is due to start work on 1 December. For David, this is an important opportunity to make his name as a landscape gardener. On 1 October, she tells him that she is no longer interested because the development will not include a garden after all. David has already purchased materials. He estimates that his future earnings will be 10 per cent lower because he will not be able to benefit from having worked with Coco. Can he insist on doing the work? Can he bring an action for breach of contract?
4. How does a party terminate a contract? Is it necessary to involve a court?
5. When, if ever, can an entitlement to termination be lost (eg breach by the party who wishes to terminate, lapse of time)?
6. What is the effect of termination?
   6.1 What happens to the contract?
   6.2 What happens to any benefits conferred in performance of the contract up to the point of termination? Does it matter whether the future and past performances can be separated from each other?

[9] In order to facilitate comparison with European jurisdictions, the hypotheticals to be addressed in Paper II are based on *L Schuler AG v Wickman Machine Tools Ltd* [1974] AC 235 (HL) (Hypothetical 3.1); *Union Eagle Ltd v Golden Achievement Ltd* [1997] AC 514 (PC) (Hypothetical 3.2); BGH, 8 March 1995, BGHZ 129, 75 (applying art 49 CISG) (Hypothetical 3.3); *Hochster v De la Tour* (1853) 2 E & B 678 (QB) (Hypothetical 3.4); and *Sumpter v Hedges* [1898] 1 QB 673 (CA) (Hypothetical 7).

6.3 What is the relationship between any claims for restitution and damages following termination?

6.4 Can the court give the party in breach additional time for performance?

7. How would your jurisdiction decide the following hypothetical?
Bob contracts to build a house for Sue for the price of $100,000. After doing a third of the work he abandons the job, leaving behind material worth $15,000 which Sue later uses to finish the works. Can Bob claim the value of the work done or of the materials?

V. Chapter Overviews

This volume covers thirteen jurisdictions in twenty-five chapters (**Chapters 3–27**). These are preceded by the present introductory chapter and the address delivered by Justice *Andrew PHANG* at the colloquium that brought together all the contributors to this volume in Singapore (**Chapter 2**). The country reports are followed by comparative conclusions drawn by *Hugh BEALE* (**Chapter 28**). His survey highlights the similarities and differences observed across the jurisdictions covered in this book and how they relate to the European source jurisdictions from which the Asian contract laws are derived. However, the chapters on the thirteen jurisdictions are interesting individually for the light they shed on commonly occurring questions as well as the values which underpin the approach taken for their resolution. Valuable comparative insights, whether on legal transplantation or legal culture, can also be obtained by reading different combinations of the chapters. It will be for our readers to decide how to best tackle these chapters, depending on their specific interest in the contract laws of Asia; some suggestions to this effect were made in the introduction to the first volume of *Studies in the Contract Laws of Asia*.[10]

In **Chapter 3**, *WANG Lei* analyses **the law relating to change of circumstances in China.** Under Article 533 Chinese Civil Code (CCC), where there are substantial changes in the basic conditions of a contract after the conclusion of the contract and continuing performance of the contract will cause obvious unfairness to one party, the adversely affected party may renegotiate with the other party. The change in conditions must be substantial and unforeseeable by the parties. If the negotiation fails within a reasonable period, the parties may request the people's court or an arbitration institution to modify or terminate the contract. The tribunal must refer to the actual situation of the case, and the modification or termination must be in accordance with the principle of fairness. If a party requests modification, the court cannot terminate the contract instead. If a party requests termination, the court can determine whether modification is the better option.

Force majeure is defined in the CCC to mean objective conditions which are unforeseeable, unavoidable, and insurmountable. The CCC provides that a party who is unable to perform the contract due to *force majeure* shall be exempted from liability in whole or in part according to the effect of the *force majeure* and that the parties may rescind the contract if the purpose of the contract cannot be achieved due to *force majeure.*

Termination of a contract for *force majeure* discharges future primary obligations. When the obligation to perform is severable, parts of the contract which have been wholly

[10] Chen-Wishart, Loke, and Ong (n *) 20.

performed can be severed from the remainder, and they are to be treated as separate contracts. There can be an apportionment of losses between the parties based on the principle of restitution. If one party has done much more than the other by the time of the change of circumstances, the party who received more benefit should pay for the benefit or return it. Reasonable restitution is determined by how much of the contract has been performed and by the severability of the performance.

Parties sometimes use automatic adaptation clauses in their contract to allocate risks with potential supervening circumstances in mind. But contractual clauses that directly exclude the application of the doctrine of change of circumstances are rare in China and will not be enforceable by the courts because of the mandatory nature of the rules on change of circumstances.

Obstacles to performance caused by the COVID-19 pandemic are analysed according to the rules of *force majeure*, the doctrine of changed circumstances, and the possibility of statutory rescission. The Supreme People's Court issued special guidelines for the hearing of such cases, for instance, that courts should take into full consideration the impact of the pandemic and matters such as the causal relationship between the pandemic and the failure to perform the contract.

In **Chapter 4**, *Lei CHEN* and *Zhicheng WU* explain **the termination of contracts in Chinese law**. The CCC is the main source of law, although specific rules on termination can also be found in other specialized statutes. Under the CCC, a contract can be terminated by consent of the parties in two ways: if the parties reach a consensus through negotiation (Article 562(1)); and where there is a clause in the contract specifying permissible causes of termination and one of these causes occurs (Article 562(2)). Although it may seem from a textual reading of the Article 562(2) that the courts will support an aggrieved party's exercise of the right to terminate if a cause for termination stipulated in the contract is satisfied, this may not always be the case. The court will decide whether to support the termination claim by applying the principles of good faith to assess the seriousness and effect of the breach on the aggrieved party's purpose in making the contract.

A contract can also be terminated by operation of law under two sets of rules. The first is the statutory right of termination which arises in the circumstances set out in Article 563 CCC. These include a failure to achieve the purpose of the contract due to an event of *force majeure*, an anticipatory breach by the other party, and the scenario where a party who has delayed performance of its principal obligation fails to perform within a reasonable time after the demand by the other party. The second is court-ordered termination, where the court has the discretion to terminate a contract (i) in response to a change of circumstances (discussed in Chapter 3) and (ii) upon the request of either contracting party, including the contract breaker, where the contract breaker fails to perform his non-pecuniary obligation in circumstances where the contract cannot be realized, such as where it is legally or practically impossible to perform the contract or where the subject matter of the obligation is unsuitable for enforcement (Article 580 CCC). The availability of court-ordered termination at the request of the contract breaker is an unusual feature of Chinese law, designed to break a deadlock between the contracting parties and reflecting the high value placed on societal interests in China. Under Article 564 CCC, the right of termination will be extinguished at the end of the time limit established by the contract or the applicable statute. Where no time is specified, the right will be extinguished one year from the time that the right holder knew or ought to have known of the cause for termination, or within a reasonable time after the right holder receives a notice from the other party enquiring whether he would like to exercise the right.

Upon termination, the rights and duties stipulated in the contract no longer bind the parties. There have been debates about whether contractual termination is retroactive, but the result is of no practical significance as Chinese courts have adopted a flexible approach to this question depending on the type of contract concerned. Article 566(1) CCC provides for restitution after termination of the contract, although the rules are not clear, and Article 566(2) provides that the contract breaker should bear liability for breach of contract.

In **Chapter 5**, *Stephen HALL* looks at the law on **changed circumstances and contract variation in Hong Kong**. This closely follows the relevant rules and principles of English law. The courts, therefore, attach great weight to the principles of freedom and bindingness of contract. As a corollary, they expect the parties to act responsibly enough to provide in the agreement itself for the consequences of any circumstances arising after the conclusion of the contract; if a party has not done so, the law will not, as a general rule, come to its rescue by modifying or terminating the contract. Typically, therefore, the parties to commercial contracts include a *force majeure* clause into their agreement. Such a clause expressly releases them from their obligations, either permanently or temporarily, if an extraordinary supervening event occurs. The courts give effect to these clauses according to their terms. Whether they apply or not, and what their legal effects are, is entirely a matter of their interpretation.

Where no such clause has been inserted, an unanticipated supervening circumstance is best accommodated by consensual variation of the contract. This may, however, give rise to problems with regard to the doctrine of consideration if the variation results in a party making a concession, while the other party only promises to do no more than it was originally required to do. The courts acknowledge that sufficient consideration exists if the first party derives a mere 'practical benefit' from the variation.

In the absence of a consensual variation, the law of Hong Kong has developed only very limited tools to deal with supervening circumstances. Initially, it only responded to events where the subject matter of the contract ceased to exist through no fault of either party. Here, the continuing existence of the subject matter of the contract was considered to be an implied condition of the effectiveness of the contract. Thus, a contract for renovations to a building was held to be terminated, and the parties were automatically relieved from any further obligations, where the building under repair had collapsed, without fault of either party and without either of the parties having assumed the risk. After World War II, the automatic termination of contracts was extended to situations where performance did not become physically impossible but was rendered unlawful by subsequent legal change, such as an embargo on payments to a New York bank account imposed by the United States government.

Today, the response to supervening circumstances no longer relies on a theory of implied terms. The contract will be automatically terminated if it has been frustrated. This is the case if a contractual obligation can no longer be performed because the circumstances have rendered the obligation impossible or 'a thing radically different' from the obligation undertaken in the contract, and neither of the parties was at fault or had assumed the risk of these circumstances. It is not sufficient that the change in circumstances simply makes performance of a contractual obligation much more onerous for one of the parties. In such cases of mere hardship, the courts refuse to terminate the contract and, *a fortiori*, to modify or amend the contract with a view to restoring the contractual equilibrium. Whether a supervening change in the commercial context amounts to a frustration of the contract depends, on the one hand, on the interpretation of the contractual term that stipulates the obligation of the party that cannot perform and, on the other, on the extent to which the changed circumstances change the character of the obligation so as to impose an obligation of a different kind from that contemplated in the agreement.

This is very much a decision that depends on the individual circumstances of each case, as can be seen in the case law. For example, a contract to sell generic goods, such as 100 tons of a certain metal, was held not to be frustrated by floods and transportation difficulties in China because the seller could have sourced the metal elsewhere. Also, a five-day delay of the obligation to perform an exchange contract due to an unanticipated closure of the Hong Kong futures exchange did not sufficiently change the character of the obligation so as to frustrate the contract. Yet, an exceptionally long delay of five years in the sale of a house, caused by the failure of the relevant district official to issue a certificate, which turned the modest gain expected by one of the parties into a substantial loss, transformed the performance of the bargain into something radically different from what had been undertaken by the parties. Another contract that was held to be frustrated concerned the building of flats. It specified that time was of the essence. Building work had commenced, but a major landslip had destroyed the foundation works and required the issuance of new building permissions. Moreover, the builder had incurred a major commercial loss. The contract was automatically terminated even though it would have been possible to recommence building work and finish it more than two years after the time stipulated in the contract.

In **Chapter 6**, *Kelvin FK LOW* explores the **termination of contracts in Hong Kong.** On this issue, too, the law of the former Crown Colony has largely tracked that of England, with an even stronger emphasis on freedom of contract and commercial certainty. The right to terminate a contract for breach depends on the classification of the term that was breached. The aggrieved party is only entitled to terminate if the term is a condition. If it is a warranty, the aggrieved party can only claim damages. A third category, that of intermediate or innominate terms, is acknowledged but practically irrelevant. Whether a term classifies as a condition or warranty depends on its construction. Where the intentions of the parties are not clear, the courts assume that the classification turns on the seriousness of the consequences of the breach. In instalment contracts, for example, whether a breach of the obligation to pay a single instalment on time is considered to be sufficiently serious to entitle the innocent party to terminate depends on the ratio which the breach bears to the contractual value as a whole and the degree of probability that such a breach will be repeated.

The parties have three options to ensure that the party aggrieved by a breach of a particular term is entitled to terminate the contract. First, they may expressly designate the term as a 'condition'. However, this may not generate the desired result if the court, in a given case, does not apply the clause to breaches that have only the most trivial consequences because it believes that the parties cannot reasonably have intended to give a right of termination in such cases and thus interprets the word 'condition' in a non-technical sense. It appears that no such cases have been reported in Hong Kong, but the Court of Final Appeal has cited with cautious approval an English decision that reached this outcome.

Secondly, the parties may explicitly provide that a breach of the term in question will give rise to a right of termination. Such express termination clauses are widely used, and the courts generally respect them, even if they are set forth in standard terms. In contrast to

English law, the courts have not construed such clauses in such a way that they do not apply to trivial breaches.

Thirdly, the parties may indicate their intention to create a contractual right of termination by using established wording to this effect. They may, for example, use the phrase 'time is of the essence' to express that a right to terminate shall arise immediately if performance of an obligation is delayed. In the absence of such wording, the general rules on termination apply, so it is a question of construction whether the parties intended the term setting forth the time of performance to be a condition (that entitles the innocent party to terminate the contract in the event of late performance) or a warranty (that only gives rise to damages). This will depend on how serious the consequences of the breach would appear at the time of making the contract. In contracts for the sale of land, for example, the term specifying the time of performance is always regarded as a condition.

Once a relevant breach occurs, the contract is not terminated automatically. The innocent party may elect to do nothing. It may also affirm the contract and thereby actively keep the contract alive, while losing the right to terminate. Finally, the party may 'accept the repudiation' of the party in breach and thereby terminate the contract. It does not have to involve a court to do so. It simply has to communicate to the party in breach that it treats the contract as at an end. The aggrieved party may do so immediately and does not have to give the party in breach an additional period of time to render performance unless that party stands to forfeit property if the contract is terminated and may apply to the courts for discretionary relief. The law of Hong Kong also acknowledges termination based on anticipatory breach: if non-performance of a contractual obligation on time would be sufficiently serious to entitle the aggrieved party to terminate the contract, the party may already terminate before the due date if it becomes clear that the other party will not perform on time.

The effect of termination is that the contractual obligations of both parties come to an end prospectively. Only certain ancillary terms intended by the parties to survive termination continue to apply. Separately, the innocent party may bring a claim in damages against the other party for loss caused by the breach. This will only cover damages for loss in respect of future obligations if there was a breach of a condition, not if there was a breach of an express termination clause. Restitution of money paid, goods delivered, or services provided can only be claimed under the law of unjust enrichment.

In **Chapter 7**, *Chitra NARAYAN* and *R Yashod VARDHAN* discuss the **law on change of circumstances in India.** Under section 56 of the Indian Contract Act 1872 (ICA), where there is a change in circumstances beyond the contemplation of the parties after the contract is made which renders performance impossible, or unlawful, by reason of some event which the promisor could not prevent, the contract becomes void. Impossibility would encompass physical and legal impossibility and also practical impossibility. The court will assess objectively whether the change in circumstances is so fundamental as to strike at the root of the contract as a whole and cause it to be frustrated. The intention of the parties is irrelevant: they would not be absolved from performance even if they had made their bargain on the footing that a particular thing or state of things would continue to exist, and that foundation then in fact ceased to exist. A contract would not be frustrated merely because performance had become more onerous. Further, where one of the parties had undertaken an absolute obligation to perform a particular act, the defence of impossibility would not be available. A temporary impossibility in performance would frustrate the contract only if time was of the essence of the contract. The doctrine of frustration does not apply to completed transfers of immovable property.

Sections 31–33 of the ICA cover events that are provided for in the contract or, although not provided for, could reasonably be contemplated by the parties. Provisions for *force majeure* are governed by section 32, which provides that contingent contracts to do or not to do anything if an uncertain future event happens cannot be enforced by law unless and until that event has happened and that such contracts become void if the event becomes impossible. The scope and applicability of the provisions in a *force majeure* clause must be carefully construed to see if the clause is activated. The situations in sections 31–33 have been understood as being mutually exclusive from those in section 56, but the Supreme Court of India has stated that sections 32 and 56 are both relevant to determining if a contract is frustrated. Where a supervening event was, or could reasonably have been, contemplated by the parties to the contract, the courts will not intervene to hold the contract frustrated as, in such cases, the parties ought to have allocated their risks in the contract for such eventuality. Therefore, section 32 of the ICA can be used to identify the boundaries of section 56 and the doctrine of frustration under Indian law. It is not clear whether an event which falls outside of a *force majeure* clause in a contract can cause the contract to be frustrated.

Where a contract has been frustrated, restitution may be available under section 65 of the ICA, which applies generally to void contracts. Where a contract *becomes* void, any person who has received an advantage under such agreement must restore it or compensate the person from whom he received it. If the advantage has been utilized or cannot be restored, the party must make compensation for the advantage retained, based on the value of the advantage in money terms.

Despite the severe and unprecedented nature of the COVID-19 pandemic, the principle that a contingency affecting performance must be provided for in the contract in order to be available to the parties continued. In the absence of such provisions, the risk will generally lie where it falls.

In **Chapter 8**, *R Yashod VARDHAN* and *Chitra NARAYAN* explore the **Indian law on termination of contracts**. Under the ICA, the innocent party has the option of ending the contract where the other party has refused to perform or disabled himself from performing his promise in its entirety (section 39). The contract also becomes voidable at the option of the innocent party where the promisor has prevented the innocent party from performing his promise (section 53) or has failed to perform his obligations within the specified time allowed for performance where time is of the essence of the contract (section 55). Under section 39, the innocent party has the right to claim damages for breach of contract even where he has agreed to the continuance of the contract after the breach. Similarly, paragraph 3 of section 55 allows an innocent party who has accepted late performance to claim compensation for the loss caused by the delay, provided that he gives notice of his intention to claim damages at the time that he accepts the late performance. Despite the language of section 39 allowing termination where there is a refusal to perform, or disablement from performance of, a promise 'in its entirety', the courts have applied the test of whether the breach was of a stipulation that was essential to the main purpose of the contract. In cases of performance in instalments, the courts have interpreted section 39 by adopting the approach taken in English case law, considering first a quantitative factor (ie the ratio that the breach bears to the contract as a whole) and, second, the degree of probability that the breach will be repeated. The prevention of the innocent party's performance by the other party under section 53 must be intentional. This could arise from the non-performance of a prior reciprocal obligation by the other party or by some other act of that party. Section 53 expressly provides that where the affected party elects to rescind the contract, he is entitled to compensation for any loss sustained from non-performance of the contract. As regards time clauses under section 55, a mere stipulation that time is of the essence will not necessarily make it so. The court must read this clause together with other provisions of the contract and construe the contract to ascertain whether such an inference is justified.

Under section 27 of the Specific Relief Act 1963, rescission of a contract that was voidable or terminable will not be allowed where the breach of contract has been condoned or waived by the innocent party. A party could also lose his right to terminate by not terminating the contract within the period of limitation, or by a change of circumstances since the making of the contract on account of which the parties cannot be restored to their earlier position, or by the creation of third-party rights, or when a part of the contract is sought to be rescinded and that part is not severable from the rest of the contract.

Where a voidable contract has been rescinded at the option of one party, two consequences follow under section 64 of the ICA. First, the other party to the contract need not perform any promise under the contract in which he is a promisor, and second, if the party rescinding the contract has received a benefit from another party under such contract, he must restore the benefit to the person from whom it was obtained. Under section 75 of the ICA, a person who rightfully rescinds a contract is entitled to compensation for any damage which he has sustained through the non-fulfilment of the contract.

In cases involving termination of contracts to which the state is a party, the courts will apply constitutional law principles of fairness and equality of treatment, as well as the proportionality principle, in reaching their decision.

In **Chapter 9**, *Gary F BELL* outlines the approach to **changed circumstances in Indonesia.** It very much follows the contract laws of the Netherlands and France before their respective reforms in 1992 and 2016. This is hardly surprising as the Indonesian Civil Code (ICC) closely follows the old civil codes of those countries. As a consequence, relief for supervening events is only provided in very rare instances.

First, the narrow doctrine of *force majeure* applies: the debtor is relieved of his or her obligation if performance has become impossible. The event causing the impossibility must have been 'external' to the debtor (ie he must not have been responsible for it), and it must have been unforeseeable and 'irresistible' (ie he could not have prevented it). The debtor does not have to pay damages; the contract is 'resolved', and both parties are put back in their original position. Because the requirements of the doctrine are so stringent, there are hardly any court decisions in which relief has been granted on its basis.

Secondly, if performance is not impossible but has become extremely burdensome for the debtor, a strict application of the ICC does not offer relief to the debtor, who has to perform. There are, however, legal scholars who suggest that the doctrine of *force majeure* should also apply in such cases of 'subjective impossibility'. The courts have not followed this suggestion, but they sometimes choose a more pragmatic route. They rely on equity and good faith, which they take to provide them with a broad discretion in adapting contracts to achieve justice in the case at hand. It is suggested that this is a more appropriate result because the doctrine of *force majeure* only provides for complete exoneration of the debtor, whereas an adaptation of the debtor's obligation normally leads to a fairer outcome. Ultimately, however, a reform of the ICC along the lines of the revised Civil Codes of France and the Netherlands would be advisable. Codifying a more clearly defined solution for cases of hardship would increase certainty and predictability in commercial transactions.

In **Chapter 10**, *HERLIANA* explains the **Indonesian regime on terminating contracts**. It broadly follows the model of the French Code civil of 1804, under which a 'resolutory' or 'void condition' is implied in every reciprocal contract. According to this, the creditor of an obligation may turn to the court to request termination if the debtor has not performed, although the creditor has at least twice put him on notice to perform. The court will order termination if the non-performance or malperformance is 'sufficiently serious', 'significant', or 'fundamental'. This is normally the case if the breach concerns an essential element of the contract, that is, an element that is characteristic for the type of contract in question. If the court grants termination, it declares the contract void. As a result, both parties are released from their obligations and have to return everything they have received. Their position should be as if the contract had never existed. The creditor may also request damages if the relevant requirements—most importantly, fault on the part of the debtor—are met.

However, the court may also rely on the principle of good faith to modify the contract and thus, for example, reduce the price to be paid by the debtor. More commonly, the judge may, at the request of the debtor, grant an additional period of time for performance of up to one month.

The parties may flesh out the precise mechanism for bringing the contract to an end in a specific termination clause. While some authors are of the view that such a clause can validly allow for unilateral termination, others maintain that the requirement to involve a court is mandatory.

In **Chapter 11**, *Eriko TAOKA* discusses the **Japanese law on change of circumstances**. This doctrine is derived from the application of good faith (Article 1(2) Japanese Civil Code (JCC)). Accordingly, a party to a contract is entitled to amend or cancel the contract if (i) a circumstance that constitutes a foundation or purpose of the contract has changed after the formation of the contract; (ii) the change of circumstance was unforeseeable to both parties at the formation of the contract; (iii) the change of circumstance occurred due to a reason not attributable to either of the parties (eg natural disaster or change of law), and the risk of it was not allocated to either party; and (iv) the enforcement of the original contract is deemed significantly inequitable to one of the parties in the light of good faith. This may happen because (a) a purpose of the contract has become disrupted (as distinct from impossibility); (b) one's performance of the contract has become economically 'impossible', where a party's cost of performance significantly outweighs the benefit that it expects from the contract; or (c) where the values of the reciprocal contractual performances have become economically imbalanced to such a degree that it would be significantly inequitable to one of the parties in light of good faith. An example is presented by the post-World War II cases of leases with options to purchase made before the war, where the market price had increased significantly over 10 to 20 years.

Cancellation of the contract is an effect of a qualifying change of circumstances. Cancellation has retrospective effect, requiring restitution, unless it is a continuous contract, when cancellation only has prospective effect. No damages claims are available.

There remains much uncertainty about the possibility of judicial amendments to the contract and a potential duty of the parties to renegotiate: how does it relate to cancellation of the contract? Is the amendment at a party's initiative or the court's? Must the parties accept a reasonable amendment? What if one party refuses? No Supreme Court case has amended a contract, although one decision accepts this as a possible outcome. At lower-court level, amendments have been awarded, but the tendency is to do so only when both parties have opted for this rather than for cancellation. Relevant factors in determining an amendment would include the existence of any administrative guidance for the price adjustment at issue; any profits each party originally expected; the potential influence of the price adjustment on each of the parties; and other factors the parties took into account to determine the original contract price.

As for renegotiation, it is a long-standing practice in Japan to insert a contractual term obliging the parties to negotiate in good faith to adjust the price where the price has become unreasonable due to an increase or decrease in associated costs, and changes in law, values of the currency, and other economic situations. Even in the absence of these, a duty to negotiate may be imposed on parties in a long-term contractual relationship based on the principle of good faith. Arguments have been made that a duty to negotiate both contradicts and supports the bindingness of contracts. Again, there is uncertainty over when a duty to negotiate is imposed and how it relates to a right to cancel or amend the contract.

An attempt to incorporate the doctrine of change of circumstances into the 2017 amendment to the JCC failed because the Legislative Council was unable to reach consensus on the legal effects of the doctrine, and there were concerns that the floodgates would be opened. Practitioners' opposition outweighed academics' appeal for a carefully qualified doctrine in the new amended Civil Code. There were no reported cases of change of circumstances arising from the COVID-19 pandemic, perhaps because of the parties' wide use of negotiation terms and the government's encouragement to parties to negotiate during the pandemic.

In **Chapter 12**, *Akira KAMO* discusses the **Japanese law on termination** (called 'cancellation'), which is allowed (i) on completion of the purpose of the contract (although certain contracts may be automatically terminated in certain circumstances); (ii) by agreement of the parties; (iii) by the parties' agreement in specified circumstances, unless disallowed by law (eg being a contravention of good faith or unilaterally prejudicial to consumers); (iv) by provisions of the JCC (eg cancellation of a sales contract by the buyer waiving or the seller refunding double the earnest money); (v) because of the nature of the contract (eg for work or mandate), although compensation should be paid; and (vi) for breach of contract.

In respect of (vi) breach, the law before the 2017 reform of the JCC allowed cancellation immediately (a) for delay where time is of the essence, especially in commercial contracts, (b) for impossibility in whole or in substantial part attributable to the debtor; (c) for serious non-performance in certain types of nominate contracts; and (d) when the purpose of the contract was frustrated by the debtor's *partial* non-performance. Cancellation is also permitted for all breaches (aside from impossibility) after the expiration of a reasonable time for a second chance at performance.

After the JCC came into effect in 1898, Japanese law began to be influenced by German legal scholarship before the modernization of the German law of obligations in 2002. This included a tripartite categorization of non-performance and five categories of grounds for cancellation of the contract, although the JCC had adopted a unitary concept of non-performance for both damages and cancellation. It also required fault, which was subsequently criticized as inconsistent with the CISG. Again, the requirement of fault was sidestepped in relation to the sale of specific property by way of a reinterpretation of an article to impose strict liability but only yielding reliance damages. All these were re-examined.

Legal developments via judicial decisions include relaxation of the need to make a demand and to give a reasonable period for a second chance to perform, allowing partial cancellation of divisible contracts, and restricting cancellation of leases of immovables.

The 2017 reform made four major changes. First, it stipulated that the debtor's fault is not a prerequisite for cancellation of contract. Secondly, it barred cancellation if the debtor's failure to perform an obligation upon expiration of the additional period of time is considered 'minor' in light of the purpose of the contract and the common sense in the transaction. Thirdly, it allowed immediate cancellation (i) where performance of the obligation in whole is impossible; (ii) where the debtor clearly expresses the intention to refuse to perform the obligation in whole; (iii) where performance of a part of the obligation is impossible or where the debtor clearly expresses the intention to refuse to perform a part of the obligation, and the purpose of the contract cannot be achieved by performance of the remaining part of the obligation; (iv) where, due to the nature of the contract or a manifestation of intention by the parties, the purpose of the contract cannot be achieved unless the obligation is performed at a specific time on a specific date or within a certain period of time, and if the debtor has failed to perform the obligation at that time or that period lapses; or (v) if the debtor does not perform the obligation, and it is obvious that the debtor is unlikely to perform the obligation to the extent necessary to achieve the purpose of the contract, even if the creditor makes a demand for performance within a reasonable time. Fourthly, the 2017 reform introduced partial cancellation where the contract is quantitatively divisible.

The right to cancel will be lost if the buyer of goods fails to notify the seller of any defects within one year. But, if the sale is between merchants, the buyer must notify without delay upon receipt. The creditor must give clear notice of the intention to cancel, which is effective when it is communicated to the breaching party. The creditor, who must give a second chance, can make a demand and give notice of cancellation at the same time. Commercial contracts for sale of goods where time is of the essence are automatically cancelled on the expiration of the time without due performance.

Cancellation relieves both parties from further performance or acceptance thereof. Terms intended to operate after cancellation (eg concerning dispute resolution) continue to operate after cancellation. Cancellation also has retroactive effect, and any performance rendered is subject to restoration: in kind, if possible, in money if not. Restoration should include interest on money, the natural or legal fruits of non-money, and the user value of property. An exception is made for certain continuous contracts (eg leases, employment) for which there has been *quid pro quo*. Third-party rights are protected. The creditor can claim damages for breach.

The right to cancel can be lost by waiver, the passing of five years for making a claim, failure to answer the debtor's question as to whether the contract will be cancelled, or if the creditor, knowing of his or her right to cancel, intentionally or negligently causes significant damage to the object of contract, or makes it impossible to return the object, or converts the object into another kind of property by processing or alteration.

In **Chapter 13**, *KWON Youngjoon* discusses the **Korean law of change of circumstances**, developed under the rubric of the good-faith principle (Article 2 Korean Civil Code (KCC)), which would relieve a contracting party if the circumstances underlying the contract significantly change, by giving the options of terminating, rescinding, or modifying the contract. One expression of the inevitable compromise between the values of voluntariness and fairness is to change the allocation of future risks between the parties. Contractual termination or modification is allowed (i) where a statute expressly permits; (ii) where the contract permits (eg *force majeure* clauses, which are narrowly interpreted); and (iii) where demanded by the principle of good faith. Category (iii) was originally denied by the Supreme Court in the 1950s, not clearly accepted in principle until 2007, and only applied to grant relief in 2020, although the reasoning is open to challenge. There were two unsuccessful attempts to legislate on the change of circumstances in 2003 and 2014.

The traditional approach requires (i) an *ex post* significant change of the underlying fundamental circumstances, (ii) that this was not foreseeable by the party seeking relief and not attributable to either party, and (iii) that enforcement would violate the principle of trust and good faith under Article 2. In 2017, a Supreme Court decision dropped the attributability requirement, regarding it as merged in the unforeseeability requirement, and concretized the violation of the principle of trust and good faith by reference to substantial imbalance between the parties and frustration of the purpose of the contract.

On a finding of relevant change of circumstances, the parties can terminate prospectively, in the case of continuing the contract, or rescind the contract retrospectively. There is no clear duty to renegotiate, although it is recognized in Article 6:111(2) PECL. Neither does the Supreme Court recognize a power to modify the contract, as it was proposed in 2003 and 2014.

In **Chapter 14,** AHN *Tae-Yong* examines the **Korean law on termination** with a distinctly theoretical or normative approach. Here, we merely summarize the law. First, he distinguishes termination from *exceptio*, under Article 536 KCC, where a party can suspend its own performance if the other has not rendered prior performance as stipulated or will not render concurrent performance; the concern is fairness and reciprocity. In contrast, termination is a response to a breach of contract. There is disagreement over whether fault is required before termination is permitted. The Supreme Court has established that termination is only permitted for breach of 'a major obligation to the extent that the obligation is necessary and indispensable to the attainment of the purpose of the contract and, without its performance, the purpose of the contract cannot be achieved and the terminating party would not have entered into the contract'. This is analogous to the consequentialist approach set out in the English case of *Hong Kong Fir Shipping.*[11]

The innocent party must tender its own performance before it can terminate for the other's breach, unless in a variety of situations, it is clear that the other party cannot or will not perform. For delayed or incomplete performance, even if the breach is material, the innocent party must make a demand to the breaching party and grant a reasonable time within which to perform (Article 544 *Nachfrist* notice). This is not required for impossibility of performance or delayed performance where time is of the essence. While the international trend is to not require a *Nachfrist* notice for a 'fundamental breach', an unstable concept, the result is not so different.

Termination retroactively extinguishes the contract, according to the 'direct effect theory'. Its effects include the requirement of mutual restitution (Article 548 KCC), the right of the innocent party to damages for breach, and the protection of third-party interests acquired from the contract in good faith. The creditor loses the right to terminate where (i) the debtor has asked the creditor to make his or her intention as to termination clear

[11] *Hong Kong Fir Shipping Co Ltd v Kawasaki Kisen Kaisha Ltd* [1962] 2 QB 26 (CA).

within a reasonable time and that time passes; (ii) the creditor is at fault in having destroyed, converted, or made unsuitable for restitution the thing that he or she received under the contract; or (iii) the creditor has led the debtor to believe that he or she would not terminate the contract. A contract terminated by reliance on a contractual termination clause and an agreement to terminate a contract are assumed to have the same effect unless stipulated otherwise.

Korean law also recognizes non-retroactive termination, an example being a contract of continuous performances for a certain period, such as a lease. The contract is only dissolved for the future, with damages available to the terminating party.

In **Chapter 15**, *Yin Harn LEE* and *May Fong CHEONG* explain the **Malaysian law on change of circumstances.** The relevant provision is section 57(2) of the Malaysian Contracts Act 1950 (MCA), which is essentially a re-enactment of section 56 of the ICA, set out earlier. The Malaysian courts consider section 57(2) to be the statutory embodiment of the doctrine of frustration. It envisages two sets of circumstances in which a contract will be discharged for frustration: where performance of the contract becomes (i) impossible or (ii) unlawful. When considering the applicable legal principles, the Malaysian courts have tended to cite English authorities rather than refer directly to the language of the statute. The test for frustration in Malaysia is based on the English House of Lords decision of *Davis Contractors Ltd v Fareham UDC*: where a contractual obligation has become impossible to perform because the circumstances in which performance is called for would render it a thing radically different from that which was undertaken by the contract.[12] Further, the event must occur after the formation of the contract and must not be due to the conduct of the parties. These requirements would be satisfied where the subject matter of the contract no longer existed or has been removed from the control of the relevant party; or where the performance of the contract has been rendered unlawful by a change in the law. However, a contract would not be frustrated merely because performance of the contract has become more onerous for one or both parties. The Malaysian courts have not directly discussed cases where the purpose of the contract no longer existed, although it was still physically possible to perform the contract, but the authors suggest that the Malaysian courts may be slow to adopt the concept of frustration of purpose.

Section 33 of the MCA (equivalent to section 32 of the ICA), which provides for contingent contracts, is often discussed together with section 57(2). It is not clear whether the Malaysian courts regard both sections as reflecting the doctrine of frustration. The authors are of the view that section 33 should not be regarded as doing so. There have been cases where both sections were applied to the same fact situation. For example, where an agreement for the sale of land was subject to the approval of the Foreign Investment Committee, but approval could not be obtained, the contract was seen to be void for two alternative grounds: first, because this was a contingent contract under which the contingent event became impossible under section 33(b); and second, and in the alternative, because the refusal of approval amounted to a supervening event which rendered the transaction impossible under section 57(2).

Where a contract has been frustrated in Malaysia, there are two potential statutory routes for dealing with its effects. The first is section 66 of the MCA (equivalent to section 65 of the ICA), the general restitutionary provision when a contract is discovered to be void or

[12] [1956] AC 696, 728–29.

becomes void. This is the preferred approach of the Malaysian courts. The second is via sections 15 and 16 of the Civil Law Act, which are essentially re-enactments of sections 1 and 2 of the UK Law Reform (Frustrated Contracts) Act 1943, based on the prevention of unjust enrichment.

In **Chapter 16**, *May Fong CHEONG* and *Yin Harn LEE* discuss the law of **termination of contracts in Malaysia**. The governing statute is the MCA 1950, which (as mentioned above) is essentially a re-enactment of the ICA. The Malaysian courts' willingness to engage in innovative interpretation of the relevant statutory provisions rather than to adhere to their strict language has allowed the Malaysian position on termination of contracts to track the English position fairly closely. Section 40 of the MCA is the main statutory provision dealing with termination for breach. It allows a party to a contract to terminate the contract where the other party either refuses to perform or disables himself from performing. The Malaysian courts have acknowledged that this corresponds to the English position relating to anticipatory breach, where an absolute refusal to perform is required before the innocent party can treat himself as discharged. Malaysian courts have also read into section 40 the principle that a party to the contract would also be entitled to terminate the contract where the other party has committed a 'fundamental breach', meaning a serious breach. In order to assess the seriousness of the breach, the courts have adopted the English law approach of classifying terms into conditions, warranties, and innominate terms. The Malaysian courts have sometimes used the term 'total failure of consideration' to refer to a situation wherein a breach would be serious enough to entitle to termination, but such language is undesirable as it appears to run counter to the Malaysian courts' own case law on fundamental breach. Under section 56(1) of the MCA, where time is of the essence of a contract and the promisor does not perform at the stipulated time, the contract becomes voidable at the option of the other party, meaning that he can put an end to the contract, just as in section 40. Whether time is of the essence of a contract is a matter of construction of the contract, and the court should consider the conduct and dealings of the parties in making this determination.

Contractual clauses entitling the parties to terminate the contract upon the occurrence of specified events are commonly used and recognized by the courts in Malaysia. There is no requirement of a serious breach of contract, and the courts have upheld clauses that allow the parties to terminate the contract at any time without giving any reason.

The innocent party's decision whether to terminate or to affirm the contract can be communicated expressly or by implication to the other party. A party seeking to terminate the contract will typically give notice to that effect to the other party, but this could be implied by conduct. The innocent party's right to terminate a contract for breach will be lost once he affirms the contract.

When a contract has been terminated for breach, both parties are discharged from the performance of future obligations, but all past rights and obligations arising under the contract prior to termination will still subsist, and the parties will still be liable for any breach of these past obligations. The combined operation of sections 65 and 66 of the MCA means that the termination of a contract for breach will give rise to concurrent obligations on the parts of both parties to make restitution to each other for any benefits that have been received under the contract. To the extent that these sections allow the party in breach to claim restitution, this represents a departure from the English position. The innocent party who has rescinded the contract will also have the option to claim compensatory damages pursuant to section 76 of the MCA.

In **Chapter 17,** *Adrian BRIGGS* explains that **the law of Myanmar** makes no provision **for change of circumstances** after the contract is made, unless the contract becomes 'impossible' (factually or legally) or illegal to perform, which the promisor 'could not prevent'. At that point, section 56 of the Myanmar Contract Act 1872 treats the contract as void (it is automatically unenforceable), but restitution or compensation is required of any benefits conferred up to that point (section 65).

'Impossibility' is tightly construed; it does not include cases of frustration of the original purpose of the contract, nor where it merely becomes more onerous, or expensive, to perform. The effect of temporary interruptions depends on the extent of their impact on the precise contract. In cases of partial impossibility, the contract is void, but the court may order specific performance of the part that is still performable; if the unperformable part is small, compensation should be ordered for it, and if the unperformed part is a considerable portion of the whole, or does not admit of compensation in money, the plaintiff must relinquish it if they seek specific performance of the performable part (sections 13–15 of the Myanmar Specific Relief Act 1877). Likewise, in cases of supervening illegality, care is needed to compare the precise obligations with the precise extent of the illegality which has supervened.

Parties are empowered to expressly provide for unusual events in their contract, including contracting out of section 56 of the Contract Act; rescind the old contract and make a new one about a similar subject matter, but on varied terms (section 62); and agree that part performance can discharge the whole contract (section 63).

The **Myanmar law on termination** appears at odds with the common law of England: certain breaches entitle the aggrieved party to *rescind* the contract, which then becomes void (triggering the mutual restitution of benefits (sections 64 and 65 of the Contract Act)), and claim damages. However, it is consistent with the codification in India and Malaysia and with most Asian civil law systems (although no provision is made for 'warning or last chance' as can be encountered in some civilian systems).

The innocent party can end (terminate or rescind) the contract if the other party has indicated, sufficiently clearly and unambiguously, that it refuses to perform its side of the contract (section 39 of the Contract Act) or has prevented the innocent party from performing its promise (section 53) when the contract becomes 'voidable'. Damages for breach are available despite the contract being declared 'void', 'voidable', or 'rescinded'. Neither party has a further obligation to perform. Any liquidated damages clause remains enforceable.

Despite the wording of section 39 of the Contract Act, which suggests that *any* deviation from the contractual obligation yields a right to end the contract, and a lack of Myanmar judicial authority to the contrary, a threshold of seriousness must be required. This is implied by the provision stating that the contract can only be ended for delay where time is 'of the essence' (section 55), whether expressly or impliedly; otherwise, only damages are available.

In **Chapter 18,** *Ma Ngina Teresa CHAN-GONZAGA* explores the ramifications of a **change of circumstances under the law of the Philippines.** For a long time, the Philippine rules on supervening events closely followed those of Spanish law, with its traditionally strong emphasis on the bindingness of contracts. As a result, a party could only be released from a contractual obligation that had become physically or legally impossible without the party being at fault, as in the case of *force majeure*. If the supervening event merely created unforeseen difficulties, performance was not excused. However, the New Civil Code of 1950 (PCC) introduced two new provisions.

The first, Article 1267 PCC, allows for a release if the contract was for a future performance; and there is an unforeseeable change in circumstances which renders performance extremely difficult, but not impossible; and neither party is at fault. The rule is based on the principle of *rebus sic stantibus*; that is, it is assumed that the intention of the parties cannot extend to a scenario where conditions have radically and drastically changed beyond what was contemplated at the time of concluding the contract. In such cases, the contract is said to lose its 'basis', similar to cases of 'failure of cause'. It is not entirely clear whether the provision only applies to contractual obligations 'to do' something or whether it also covers other types of contractual performance.

The second rule, Article 1250 PCC, deals with cases where an 'extraordinary inflation or deflation' intervenes after the conclusion of the contract. If such an event has been certified by the Central Bank, the party who has to perform a monetary obligation has to provide the value, rather than the contractual amount, of the currency at the time of making the contract.

Both provisions are applied restrictively by the courts. Article 1250 PCC has never been successfully pleaded and claims for a release from a contractual obligation under Article 1267 PCC rarely succeed. In those instances, however, the courts have sometimes gone beyond the remedy provided in the provision. Rather than merely releasing a party from its obligation, they proceeded to amend an obligation arising from the contract. In doing so, they invoked their equitable jurisdiction, which allows them to modify certain contractual obligations, such as the 'equitable reduction' of 'iniquitous or unconscionable' penalty clauses provided for in Article 1229 PCC. The courts have also relied on their equitable jurisdiction, as well as on the broad duty to act in good faith set forth in Article 19 PCC, in the very rare cases where they saw fit, as was held in one decision of the Supreme Court, to 'adjust the rights of parties in accordance with the circumstances obtaining at the time of rendition of the judgment, when these are significantly different from those existing at the time of generation of those rights'.

In Chapter 19, *Michael Anthony C DIZON* explains that the law on **ending contracts in the Philippines** is marred by terminological confusion. The concepts of 'termination' and 'rescission' are often employed loosely and interchangeably. They both involve a party bringing a contract to an end as a response to the other party being in breach. The correct approach is to limit the use of 'termination' to those scenarios where this is done with prospective effect so that the contract remains in force until the moment of termination and the parties are only released from their future obligations from this moment onwards. Vested rights or benefits received by the parties under the contract are not affected by its termination. In contrast, the 'rescission' of a contract has retrospective effect. The contract is dissolved from the beginning (*ab initio*). It is treated as if it had never been concluded. As a result, all obligations arising under it are fully extinguished, and the parties are restored to their original positions. They have to make mutual restitution of everything they received under the contract. The use of the term 'rescission' in this context was only introduced by the PCC. Its predecessor, the Spanish Civil Code of 1889, still used the French-inspired notion of 'resolution'. The change in terminology is particularly unfortunate because the PCC also speaks of 'rescission' in the context of contracts that may be 'rescinded' by a party because the contract is defective (and thus 'rescissible') due to external, equitable grounds that cause economic harm to this party or a third party.

Be that as it may, 'rescission' is now one of the remedies for breach of contract provided for in the PCC. Its Article 1191 requires that the breach be of a reciprocal obligation. Reciprocal obligations arise from the same cause and are correlative of each other to the extent that the performance by one party of its obligation is designed to be the equivalent and the condition for the performance by the other party of its own obligation, with one party being the creditor and the other the debtor. Moreover, the breach must not just be slight or casual but 'substantial' or 'fundamental'. These terms appear to be used synonymously. The test is whether, in light of the attendant circumstances, the object of a party in entering into the contract has been defeated because an essential term of the contract has been breached. It is not relevant whether the party in breach acted with fault. A simple breach is sufficient if the parties have included an 'automatic rescission clause' in their contract which stipulates that the aggrieved party has a right to rescind the contract upon the type of breach in question.

Finally, a valid rescission requires that the aggrieved party give notice to the other party that it rescinds the contract. Thereafter, the first party has the choice between simply treating the contract as rescinded, and acting accordingly without involving a court, or bringing an action for rescission in the courts. In practice, the aggrieved party will normally opt for 'extrajudicial' over 'judicial rescission' unless it has already made performances and needs the court to order restitution.

In all cases of judicial rescission, the courts have the discretionary power to grant the party in breach a 'grace period' or 'second chance' to perform its obligation. However, they will only order the fixing of a grace period in very limited circumstances and when the party in breach is willing to comply. At this stage, the courts might also filter out breaches that would normally give rise to rescission because they are technically 'substantial', but ultimately not serious, or breaches where the party in breach acted without fault or even in good faith.

As was said above, a successful rescission extinguishes the reciprocal obligations between the parties *ab initio*, and each party must return what it received under the contract. If restitution is impossible because a third party has acquired rights in the object of the contract, the aggrieved party may claim damages from the person responsible for the transfer. As a general rule, the party that is the victim of a substantial breach can either rescind the contract or elect the alternative remedy of specific performance. In either event, it can also claim damages under the general regime for damages in the PCC. If both parties were in breach, 'the liability of the first infractor shall be equitably tempered by the courts. If it cannot be determined which of the parties first violated the contract, the same shall be deemed extinguished, and each shall bear his own damages' (Article 1192 PCC).

In **Chapter 20**, *Dora NEO* discusses the **Singaporean law applicable to change of circumstances** after contract formation that change the balance of advantages and burdens assumed at formation. The common law doctrine of frustration applies where the supervening event occurred without the fault of either party and renders performance of the obligation radically or fundamentally different from what had been agreed in the contract. The latter is assessed on a multi-factorial approach. Frustration is based on construction of the contract, and its scope is narrow. Examples include (i) destruction of the subject matter of the contract unless the risk was allocated to one party, (ii) death or incapacity of a party where performance is personal, (iii) supervening illegality of contractual performance, (iv) unavailability of the contractual subject matter, (v) impossibility of the specified method of performance, (vi) failure of a specified or contemplated source of the contractual subject matter (partial failure is less certain), (vii) impossibility of purpose assumed by both parties, and (viii) delay if it falls outside the contractual risk allocation.

There is no frustration if (i) the parties have allocated the risk of change of circumstances to one of the parties, (ii) the change of circumstance is foreseeable or (iii) self-induced by the plaintiff, and (iv) the change of circumstance merely makes performance impracticable, unless the change of circumstances is truly exceptional. The effect of frustration is to discharge the contract for the future. The benefits and burdens from part-performance up to that point are regulated by the Frustrated Contracts Act 1959, based on the prevention of unjust enrichment rather than loss sharing.

The parties may provide for any change of circumstances by the use of *force majeure* clauses. Their application will depend on the construction of the clause. Other terms, such as price adjustment clauses, would also respond to a change of circumstances. A party may also resort to the general law to seek relief from the contract in the face of change of circumstances, for example, by the law of implied terms and the interpretation of express terms.

The COVID-19 pandemic has been found to be a frustrating event in situations where it caused a radical change in the parties' obligations. In Singapore, the COVID-19 (Temporary Measures) Act 2020, introduced on 17 April 2020, deals with, inter alia, the economic hardship associated with the pandemic by providing temporary relief for inability to perform certain types of contracts. It deals with situations that would not amount to frustration or be dealt with by *force majeure* clauses.

In **Chapter 21**, *Chee Ho THAM* discusses the law on **termination for breach in Singapore**. A party may withhold its own performance if (i) the preconditions to its performance are unfulfilled; (ii) the conditions permitting termination stipulated in the contract are fulfilled; or (iii) the other party has committed a repudiatory breach (namely, (a) anticipatory renunciation, (b) breach of a condition (but not a warranty), or (c) breach of an 'implied warranty' with sufficiently serious consequences). Categories (ii) and (iii) may overlap.

In consumer contracts, consumers are given wider powers to end the contract for the business party's breach, and mutual restitution is required. There is no general duty to give a second chance to perform, subject to consumers' right to rescind only after repair or replacement has become impossible.

Where (ii) or (iii) (b) are relied upon by a seller to terminate a sale of land, it is subject to the buyer's 'equitable proprietary interest' in the land arising from the equitable doctrine of conversion that makes the buyer a beneficiary under a constructive trust. In essence, relief may be granted against the forfeiture of an interest in land under a contract of sale where the breach is of a provision as to payment, where time is of the essence.

Termination for (iii) ends the contract prospectively. There is no general duty of mutual restitution, although restitution for unjust enrichment may be available in limited circumstances (eg total failure of consideration) or a claim for *quantum meruit*. This would be netted off where the innocent party claims damages. The party in breach cannot claim for its part performance. The effect of termination for (ii) depends on the contractual term.

Singapore has accepted Lord Reid's dicta in the Scottish case of *White and Carter (Councils) Ltd v McGregor*,[13] stating that an innocent party may only affirm the contract

[13] [1962] AC 413, 430–31 (HL, on appeal from the Court of Session).

in the face of anticipatory renunciation and go on to recover the contract price if it can be shown it has a 'legitimate interest' in performing the contract and does not require the defendant's cooperation. Silence may, in certain circumstances, amount to affirmation.

An exercise of the power to terminate or affirm (if permitted), clearly communicated, is irreversible. The power to terminate may be lost before it has been exercised because (i) it was given up or (ii) the contract was brought to an end for some other reason before it was exercised, for example, by frustration.

In **Chapter 22**, *Tsung-fu CHEN* explores the pedigree of **Taiwanese law on changes of circumstances** that occur after the conclusion of the contract. Under Articles 225 and 266 Taiwanese Civil Code of 1929 (TCC), a party is released from its obligation to perform if performance has become impossible after the conclusion of the contract, and the impossibility cannot be attributed to it. The other party is similarly released from its obligation to render counter-performance. As a result, the contract is automatically extinguished, and none of the parties is liable for damages. If the other party has already fully or partially rendered counter-performance, it may reclaim what it has performed under the rules of unjustified enrichment. If the party whose obligation has become impossible receives compensation or who has a claim for compensation against a third party (eg an insurer), the other party may demand the compensation received or an assignment of the claim against the third party. In this scenario, the contract is not extinguished, and the obligation of the other party to render counter-performance continues to exist. Since the first party is automatically released from its obligations, there is no need for *force majeure* clauses as are typically found in common law systems. If at all, such clauses tend to be included in international contracts, and they only become relevant if the impossibility is attributable to one of the parties.

Moreover, as early as 1941, and as a direct consequence of the turmoil caused by World War II, the Taiwanese legislature permitted judicial adjustments of the contractual rights and obligations of the parties if their legal relationship had become 'obviously unfair' due to an unexpected, war-related change of circumstances. A revised version which includes subsequent changes not caused by war was inserted in the TCC in 2000. The relevant provision, Article 227-2, is generally viewed as an emanation of the overarching principle of good faith. Additionally, the Code contains special rules permitting similar judicial interventions in agricultural and other leases.

The general rule in Article 227-2 TCC has five requirements. First, there must have been a change of the 'objective circumstances' that prevailed when the contract was concluded. Such changes are frequently linked to economic developments, such as inflation or depression, but they may also relate to other events, including war, natural disaster, and revolution. It is not entirely clear whether the rule also covers so-called changes of the 'subjective circumstances'. These occur where the parties shared a mistaken assumption as to the underlying basis of their transaction when making the contract, for example, as to the texture of the ground when the contract involved the extraction of rocks. A legislative proposal to follow the example of Germany and explicitly include such 'shared errors in motive' failed. Academic opinion is divided, and the case law oscillates between rejection and adoption of the broader approach. Secondly, the change of circumstances must have been unexpected and unforeseeable to both parties. Thirdly, it must have occurred after the conclusion and before the performance of the contract. Fourthly, it must not have been attributable to either of the parties. Fifthly, the change must have rendered the performance of the original contractual obligations 'obviously unfair'. This must include an extraordinary distortion of the contractual equilibrium that goes far beyond the ordinary contractual risk assumed by the parties, taking into account the losses of one of the parties and the gains obtained by the other. In applying the fifth requirement, the courts adopt a restrictive approach. This can be seen from the case law dealing with the consequences of the restrictions imposed during the COVID-19 pandemic. In the vast majority of decisions, the courts refused to grant a remedy because the changes did not surpass the ordinary contractual risk or did not cause extraordinary losses and/or gains.

If the requirements of Article 227-2 TCC are met, the parties are not under a duty to renegotiate. The disadvantaged party may immediately apply to the court to have the contract amended to the effect that the contractual equilibrium is restored. This may lead to an increase or a reduction of the price to be paid so that the amount is appropriate, but it may also lead to other alterations of the original obligations of the parties. If an adaptation is not possible, the court may terminate the contract. The contract is then extinguished, and the disadvantaged party may claim damages for its actual loss (hence, not the positive interest) and restitution of any performances rendered. This is also the case if the contract contains a clause dealing with changing circumstances, such as an indexation clause. Such clauses cannot exclude the application of Article 227-2 TCC. The courts have held that they are only valid to the extent that the relevant change of circumstances has been foreseeable and is in line with the ordinary course of events. Where the change is extraordinary and unforeseeable, however, the disadvantaged party may claim for amendment of the contract.

In **Chapter 23**, *Sheng-Lin JAN* presents the law on **ending contracts in Taiwan.** It distinguishes between the mechanisms of termination and rescission. The former typically applies to long-term contracts and has merely prospective effect. The latter is normally relevant in 'one-off' transactions and has retrospective effect. The right to terminate or rescind a contract may be based on a statutory rule or a contractual clause. Termination and rescission clauses are valid and enforceable unless they are standard terms in consumer contracts and unilaterally favour the business supplier of the clause.

The provisions on termination and rescission in the TCC are complex. Under the general regime, a party has a right to terminate or rescind a contract if the other party was (i) in breach; (ii) at fault; and, in some scenarios, (iii) did not cure the breach, although it was given a reasonable 'grace period' to do so. If the breach merely concerned an ancillary obligation, such as a duty of information or assistance, it must have been so significant that the contractual purpose cannot be achieved any longer. In contrast, any breach is sufficient if a primary contractual obligation was concerned. This includes cases of non-performance because of impossibility, delay, and non-conformity. In either event, the breach must have occurred: a mere anticipatory breach does not entitle the aggrieved party to terminate or rescind the contract. The lapse of a grace period is only relevant in two scenarios. In cases of non-conformity that can be remedied, the innocent party may not terminate or rescind the contract unless it has stipulated a reasonable *Nachfrist* during which the other party may cure the defect, and this period has lapsed without the defect being cured. The same requirement applies if performance has been delayed and the contract is not a 'fixed transaction' (ie its purpose can only be achieved by performance at a specific, 'fixed' time). Thus, in both cases, the party in breach is given a 'second chance' to perform. Finally, a party may not rescind a contract if it has been at fault for the other party's breach by destroying or damaging the subject matter of the contract.

A party may unilaterally terminate or rescind a contract if the relevant requirements are met. It does not have to involve a court. However, the TCC specifically provides the courts with the power to give the party in breach additional time for performance if its circumstances so demand, and this would not substantially prejudice the interests of the aggrieved party. As a consequence of a valid termination of the contract, the contract ceases to exist, and both parties are released from their respective obligations for the future. As a result of a valid rescission, the contract is treated as if it has never existed, and the parties must also return any performances that have been rendered. A claim for termination or rescission does not preclude a claim for damages.

However, there are also many special rules governing the termination or rescission of specific types of contract. These have slightly diverging requirements and effects, and they take precedence over the general regime. In a contract for the sale of goods, for example, the buyer may rescind for defective performance, although the seller was not at fault, and without having to stipulate an additional grace period. As a corollary, the buyer's claim is subject to a very short limitation period. Similarly, in lease contracts and contracts for work, a defective performance entitles the aggrieved party to rescind the contract even if the seller, lessor, or contractor was not at fault. The requirement of fault is also dispensed with in certain consumer contracts where the business is in breach. In leases and service contracts entered into for an indefinite period of time, each party may terminate the contract at any time. This is also the case in contracts of mandate, but if the termination by one of the parties causes a loss in the other party, the party terminating the contract is, as a general rule, liable for damages. Yet another remedy is available in sales contracts if the buyer receives defective goods and a rescission would cause loss on the part of the seller that significantly outweighs the buyer's loss. Here, the buyer may only claim a reduction of the price.

In **Chapter 24**, *Munin PONGSAPAN* explains **the law on change of circumstances in Thailand**. There is no general provision in the Thai Civil and Commercial Code (TCCC) that comprehensively deals with change of circumstances. Under section 219 TCCC, the debtor is relieved from performance if this becomes impossible because of a circumstance for which he is not responsible that occurs after the formation of the contract. Impossibility of performance must be definite and permanent. It must be distinguished from hardship, such as difficulties of performance due to financial difficulties or political unrest. Section 205 TCCC provides that the defendant is not in default where he is unable to perform due to a circumstance for which he is not responsible. The obligation to perform is suspended until the circumstance has passed. Contractual interpretation can be used as a tool to decide whether a situation is one of impossibility of performance or merely one of hardship. This would involve finding the true intention of the parties and applying the principle of good faith.

In cases of reciprocal contracts, where the debtor is relieved from liability because of impossibility, the effects of the counter-performance are as follows. Sections 370 and 371 TCCC apply to contracts that have the object of transferring ownership of a specific thing. If impossibility of performance occurs after the ownership has been transferred from the seller to the buyer, the buyer who is the owner of the lost or totally damaged property will have to bear the loss, meaning that he will have to pay the full price despite the loss or destruction. Section 372 TCCC applies to all other types of contracts that do not fall under sections 370 and 371. Under section 372, if an obligation becomes impossible to perform due to a cause not attributable to either party, the debtor has no right to receive the counter-performance. This means that, for example, where the debtor was hired to do work and the work was destroyed before it was completed, the debtor will not be entitled to demand any remuneration from the creditor despite having done some or most of the work. To avoid this extreme outcome, it is normal practice for contracts, such as hire of work contracts, to be divided into several phases so that the debtor can receive payment upon the full completion of each phase even if subsequent phases are impossible to complete. Where the circumstances temporarily prevent the debtor from performing the obligation, according to section 369 TCCC, the debtor will not be able to receive the counter-performance. This reflects the principle of withholding performance.

There is no comprehensive legislation in Thailand to deal with the COVID-19 pandemic. Most contracting parties have to rely heavily on the general provisions of the TCCC to determine their contractual rights and duties. As the effects of the pandemic were largely temporary and mostly did not render performance impossible, section 205 TCCC applied, in many cases, to excuse debtors from being in default during the pandemic. However, under section 369 TCCC, a debtor who was unable to fulfil his obligation on time would not have been able claim counter-performance. Employment contracts were governed by separate legislation, which set out special rules for the payment of wages.

In **Chapter 25**, *Nadnaphas LEAKPECH* discusses **termination of contracts in Thailand.** The provisions concerning termination of contract set out in the TCCC are modelled largely on the JCC of 1896 and, to a lesser extent, on the German Civil Code of 1900. Under Thai law, a contract can be terminated in two main ways: (i) by the consent of both parties and (ii) unilaterally, where one party has the right to terminate the contract. In termination by consent, one party makes an offer to terminate the contract, and the other party accepts such offer, expressly or impliedly. In unilateral termination, the right to terminate may arise under the terms of the contract, or it can be derived from statutory provisions that apply either to specific types of contracts or to contract law generally. Section 387 TCCC sets out the general principle for termination of contracts, providing that if one party does not perform the obligation, the other party may fix a reasonable period and notify him to perform within that period. If he does not perform within that period, the other party may rescind the contract. A party can rescind the contract without notification where there is a fixed time or period for performance of the contract and the other party has not performed within that time (section 388) or where performance becomes wholly or partly impossible by a cause attributable to the debtor (section 389).

The right to terminate the contract will only arise where there is a material breach or a material non-performance by the contract breaker. While termination under section 389 requires the debtor to be at fault, sections 387 and 388 do not refer expressly to fault. There is a debate among Thai scholars as to whether the fault of the debtor is required in order for the contract to be terminated under these sections. While it can be implied from a decision of the Supreme Court[14] that fault is not relevant in contractual termination, this is not conclusive.

Where there is no time limit specified within which the right of termination has to be exercised, section 393 TCCC sets out a procedure whereby the other party can fix a reasonable period and notify the right holder to invoke the right to terminate within such period,

[14] Case No 8605/2552 (2009).

failing which the right to terminate will be lost. Under section 394 TCCC, the right to terminate will also be lost if the person asserting the right has, by his own act or default, made it more difficult to make restitution when the contract was rescinded—which could be seen as an implied waiver of the termination right.

In order to terminate the contract for breach, the aggrieved party must declare his intention to the other party (section 386(1) TCCC) expressly or impliedly. The effects of termination are set out in section 391 TCCC. Upon termination, the parties are discharged from the contract retroactively; that is, the contract is cancelled from the beginning. The parties must be restored to their pre-contractual position, and each party must return all the benefits that he has received under the contract to the other party.

In **Chapter 26**, *DO Giang Nam* shows how the law on **supervening circumstances in Vietnam** has developed considerably with the enactment of the Vietnamese Civil Code 2015 (VCC 2015). The Code continues to emphasize the principle of bindingness of contract, or *pacta sunt servanda*, as set forth in its Article 3(2). However, it stipulates that a party may be released from its contractual obligations if an event occurs after the conclusion of the contract that makes the performance by this party either impossible or severely more onerous. For the first scenario, the VCC 2015 retains the long-established doctrine of *force majeure*. The party will not be liable for damages if it was not at fault because the event was objectively beyond its control, unforeseeable, and insurmountable (Articles 351(2) and 156 no 1 VCC 2015).

For the second scenario, the legislator introduced a new provision after extensive consultation (Article 420 VCC 2015). The drafters drew inspiration from the PICC, the PECL, and German law. The new rule codifies the doctrine of change of circumstances, which is seen as an emanation of the principle of good faith. It applies if the subsequent change of circumstances (i) is so fundamental that it distorts the contractual equilibrium in such a manner that (a) performance of the contract will cause serious damage to one of the parties and (b) the parties would not have concluded the contract, or would have concluded it with a completely different content, if they had foreseen the change; (ii) is objectively beyond the control of the disadvantaged party; (iii) could not have been reasonably foreseen at the time of making the contract; and (iv) cannot be mitigated in its effects by the disadvantaged party.

In the event of a fundamental change of circumstances, the disadvantaged party may request the other party to renegotiate the contract within a reasonable time period. Negotiations must be conducted in good faith, and a party violating this duty might be liable for damages. If the parties do not agree on a modification of the contract, either of them may request the court to (i) terminate the contract at a specified date so that both parties are released from performing any further obligations from this date or (ii) adapt the contract with a view to restoring the balance of the rights and obligations so that they meet the new, changed circumstances. However, in contrast to the solution under the PICC, the choice between these remedies is not at the discretion of the court. The court has to conduct a cost–benefit analysis and may only adapt the contract where the disadvantaged party's loss resulting from termination would exceed the expenses of this party for performance under the adapted contract. Article 420 VCC 2015 thus establishes a hierarchy of remedies: renegotiation must precede court intervention, and if the court intervenes termination normally takes precedence over adaptation of the contract. This solution is a response to the two main concerns that were voiced against the introduction of the doctrine of change of circumstances during the legislative process. The primacy of renegotiations helps to protect, as far as possible, the principle of bindingness of contract. The preference for termination over adaptation addresses the supposed lack of judicial expertise in rewriting contracts for the parties.

In **Chapter 27**, *TRAN Kien* covers the law on **termination of contracts in Vietnam**. This is governed by a complex, comprehensive, and sometimes confusing set of rules in the VCC 2015 and other pieces of legislation. They employ the concept of 'termination' in a broad fashion, so as to refer not only to instances where one or both parties actively 'terminate' the contract as a consequence of a breach or by mutual agreement, but also use it for many, if not all, other cases where the contract is brought to an end and the parties are discharged from performing. A contract is, for example, considered as 'terminated' if performance has occurred, has been waived, or has become impossible because the subject matter of the contract or one of the parties has ceased to exist after the making of the contract. It is also 'terminated' where the duration of a contract has expired and the contract has not been (fully) performed. Moreover, the various statutory regimes provide seemingly contradictory answers to the question whether the unilateral ending of a contractual relationship as a consequence of a breach can be categorized as a 'remedy', as is the case in many other jurisdictions. Finally, there are two mechanisms available to a party aggrieved by a breach to bring the contract to an end: 'cancellation' and 'unilateral termination of performance' (with the latter being called 'suspension of performance' in the Code governing commercial contracts).

Cancellation and unilateral termination have similar requirements. First, there must be a breach of contract, that is, late, partial, or defective performance. If the contract contains a clause that this particular breach entitles the aggrieved party to cancel or unilaterally terminate the contract, the party may do so. In the absence of such a clause, the breach has to be 'serious'; that is, the innocent party must be 'unable to achieve the purpose of entering into the contract'. The test for commercial contracts is phrased somewhat differently but is essentially similar. Here, the breach has to be 'fundamental'; that is, it has to cause 'damage' to the other party to the extent that the other party cannot achieve the purpose for which the contract was originally entered into. A party is not entitled to cancel or unilaterally terminate a contract before performance is due even if the other party has declared that it will not perform its obligations (anticipatory breach). Fault of the party in breach is not required or, according to some, presumed. The innocent party is not obliged to give the party in breach a 'second chance' to perform.

Secondly, the party who wishes to cancel or unilaterally terminate the contract does not have to involve a court. It simply has to give notice to the other party. The notice can be in writing, verbal, or by relevant conduct, and it must be received by the other party.

With regard to their legal effects, however, cancellation and unilateral termination differ considerably. The former leads to the contract being terminated retrospectively: the contract is deemed to have been ineffective *ab initio*, the parties are not required to perform their mutual obligations, and they have to return anything they have received under the contract (if performance in kind is impossible, the monetary value has to be restored). The latter leads to the contract being terminated prospectively: the parties do not have to continue to perform their obligations from the moment that the party in breach has received the notice of the innocent party; a party that has already performed an obligation may demand reimbursement for its performance. In both scenarios, penalty clauses and dispute resolution clauses continue to be operative, and the innocent party is entitled to bring a separate claim for damages.

Overall, **Chapters 3–28** not only introduce the diversity and commonalities between the contract law regimes of the different Asian jurisdictions but also aim to enhance the conversations between the Asian jurisdictions and the rest of the world.

2

On Comparative Analysis as Well as Ending and Changing Contracts

*Andrew PHANG**

I. Introduction

It is a great privilege and honour to be invited to speak to such an august body of legal scholars.[1] I look forward very much to seeing all the papers that will be presented in this conference, both now and when they are ultimately in print. I have already purchased the previous volumes in this series[2] and have not only been educated immensely by them but also enjoyed them tremendously. I realize that this might sound odd to the layperson, but as legal scholars, I think you can understand the pleasure that one can derive from a work that is full of scholarship as well as ideas.

I should say that, when I was in legal academia, it occurred to me that it would be really wonderful to have a book on Commonwealth contract law. I never got round to getting such a project off the ground.[3] As it has turned out, however, most contract textbooks today—regardless of the jurisdiction from which they emanate—do, in fact, embody substantive discussions of cases (where relevant) from other Commonwealth jurisdictions. This conference has gone one step further—by bringing together under one roof the contract laws that derive from the common law and civil law traditions (or even a hybrid of both). More importantly, it showcases *Asian* contract law—a subject that is of immense interest across

* All views expressed are personal views only and do not reflect in any way the views of the Supreme Court of Singapore, the Singapore Management University, the National University of Singapore, or the University of Reading.

[1] This was a Welcome Address delivered at a conference on the *Studies in the Contract Laws of Asia, vol V: Ending and Changing Contracts*, which was held on 15 August 2019 at the Faculty of Law, National University of Singapore. The original address was published in [2021] 4 Malayan Law Journal clv, although this chapter is quite different inasmuch as I have added a substantial Postscript that not only reviews the chapters in the book but also takes into account relevant developments and provides further thoughts as well as reflections on both themes considered in the original address and separate issues not hitherto considered. I am grateful to LexisNexis Southeast Asia and the Malayan Law Journal for their permission to reproduce the original address as well as to Professor Yihan Goh SC, then Dean of the Yong Pung How School of Law of the Singapore Management University, for his helpful comments and suggestions. Professor Goh was subsequently appointed a Judicial Commissioner, then Judge of the Supreme Court of Singapore. He is presently a Deputy Attorney-General of Singapore. All errors, however, remain mine alone. Although this Welcome Address was delivered some time ago, it still retains its relevance today, as the Postscript explains.

[2] M Chen-Wishart, A Loke, and B Ong (eds), *Studies in the Contract Laws of Asia, vol I: Remedies for Breach of Contract* (OUP 2016); M Chen-Wishart, A Loke, and S Vogenauer (eds), *Studies in the Contract Laws of Asia, vol II: Formation and Third Party Beneficiaries* (OUP 2018). And since the conference, see also M Chen-Wishart and S Vogenauer (eds), *Studies in the Contract Laws of Asia, vol III: Contents of Contracts and Unfair Terms* (OUP 2020); M Chen-Wishart, S Vogenauer, and H Sono (eds), *Studies in the Contract Laws of Asia, vol IV: Invalidity* (OUP 2022).

[3] For a very recent—and far more modest attempt—see A Phang and Y Goh, 'Contract Law in Commonwealth Countries: Uniformity or Divergence?' (2019) 31 Singapore Academy of Law Journal 170.

Andrew Phang, *On Comparative Analysis as Well as Ending and Changing Contracts* In: *Studies in the Contract Laws of Asia V: Ending and Changing Contracts*. Edited by: Mindy Chen-Wishart, Dora Neo, and Stefan Vogenauer, Oxford University Press. © Andrew Phang 2026. DOI: 10.1093/oso/9780198995814.003.0002

the globe. That the proceedings will be published in English will make the resulting work of even more importance in terms of its dissemination worldwide. Before I turn briefly to the themes of the present conference proper, let me touch on a more general point that also represents the underlying spirit of this conference and which flows, in fact, from what I have just said.

II. The Importance of Comparative Analysis

I would like, first, to emphasize a point that I have been making with increasing frequency lately.[4] And it is so important that I should mention it again briefly—although the more astute amongst you would notice that I had alluded to it (at least indirectly) right at the commencement of my address. Indeed, the point which I am going to speak of is even more needful in a conference of this nature. And it has to do with the importance of a *comparative outlook*.

It is almost trite to say that the world we live in has changed. With the advent of technology, the world is a much smaller place. This interconnectedness is exemplified by the increased (and increasing) internationalization as well as globalization which are now the norm. And it is this outlook that characterizes the approach which the Singapore courts adopt (especially with regard to novel or controversial areas of the law). Put simply, the search is (as Lord Goff of Chieveley put it in his justly famous as well as influential Maccabaean Lecture in Jurisprudence)[5] the *search for principle*. This entails the Singapore courts searching across all common law jurisdictions for the *principles* that are most appropriate to Singapore from the perspectives of both logic and local conditions (with the caveat that there ought not to be local or indigenous development merely for its own sake; for that would be mere parochialism).[6] Indeed, the Singapore courts are able to do this because of, as mentioned earlier, the advent of technology that has made comparative work more accessible. Hence, the development of the principles of Singapore common law and equity is one that has a *comparative outlook*.

Such a comparative outlook is crucial to the development of the contract laws of Asia in at least three ways. First, insofar as the development of the common law of contract of a particular jurisdiction is concerned, comparative analysis is important in the development of the law. Indeed, this is a point which I have just made with specific reference to the development of contract law in Singapore. Secondly, jurisdictions which derive their law of contract from the common law can (and ought to) learn from those which derive their law of contract from the civil law.[7] Thirdly (and which is a point closely related to the second), all Asian jurisdictions ought to try to work towards a *convergence* of their systems. Indeed, this conference represents an initial step in this direction. It is to be hoped that *an Asian Contract*

[4] See generally (in the specific context of the law of remedies) A Phang, 'The Law of Remedies: The Importance of Comparative and Integrated Analysis' (2016) 28 Singapore Academy of Law Journal 746, 748–51.

[5] R Goff, 'The Search for Principle' (1983) 69 Proceedings of the British Academy 169 (reprinted in W Swadling and G Jones (eds), *The Search for Principle—Essays in Honour of Lord Goff of Chieveley* (OUP 1999) 313–29).

[6] See generally A Phang, 'Recent Developments in Singapore Contract Law—The Search for Principle' (2011) 28 Journal of Contract Law 1.

[7] This is not, of course, a problem for those rare jurisdictions which derive their law of contract from a hybrid system of both common law and civil law.

Code might ultimately materialize.[8] That this is not a mere pipe dream is evidenced by, for example, the UNIDROIT Principles of International Commercial Contracts (PICC),[9] the Principles of European Contract Law (PECL),[10] and the Restatement (Second) of the Law of Contracts.[11]

Let me now turn to the themes of the present conference.

III. On Ending and Changing Contracts: Some General Thoughts

It used to be said that there are only two sure things in life—death and taxes.[12] This was true when I was much younger. Times have changed. The latter is now at least potentially avoidable—particularly with good tax planning and shrewd placement of wealth in appropriate tax havens. However, one thing has not—and will not—change. And that is death. For human beings, it marks the end of physical life. That having been said, even *contracts* have, in the final analysis, a fixed life span—an *end*. As the old saying goes, it is all a matter of time. Hence, whilst we are excited (or at least some are) with the 'birth' (or formation) of a contract, we must also be cognisant of the situations when it might end. This is important not only in order to anticipate the actions that must be taken at the very end but also to facilitate planning for such eventualities at the beginning, when a contract is in the process of being drafted.

It is also important to know how contracts end or terminate because parties will want to know what their 'inheritance' is—or, more accurately, what the consequences are and how they may (or may not) be able to move on after the contract has had a decent 'burial'.

Then there is the other main theme of this conference, and that brings to mind another given in life—that the only certain thing in life is that life is uncertain and, because of that, *change* is inevitable. And so also with contracts. Put simplistically, when and how can contracts be changed? What are the requirements before the change passes legal muster?

All that I have said thus far may make it sound as if the end of contracts or the changing of them is a simple affair. Nothing could be further from the truth. As I recently had occasion to observe at a hearing, one cannot premise a legal argument (in court at least) based purely on the mantra, 'It all depends on the facts of the case.' If that were the case, law schools would be redundant, for legal rules and principles—the normative part of the law—would be wholly unnecessary. And so, in the situation I just mentioned, it was (and, in fact, is) imperative to begin with the normative base—the *legal* rules and principles, which are *then applied* to the relevant facts of the case concerned. Looked at in this light, an even cursory

[8] cf the separate project to create a *Principles of Asian Contract Law* (see H Beale in the Foreword to Chen-Wishart, Loke, and Ong (n 2) viii).

[9] Published in 1994.

[10] First published in 2000.

[11] For the United States of America, and which was completed in 1979. Reference may also be made to H McGregor, *Contract Code (Drawn Up on Behalf of the English Law Commission)* (Giuffrè Editore and Sweet & Maxwell 1993) as well as (and much more recently) A Burrows, *A Restatement of the English Law of Contract* (OUP 2016) (a second edition of this last-mentioned work was published in 2020).

[12] The latter is not an apparent favourite with lawyers: see H Monroe, *Intolerable Inquisition? Reflections on the Law of Tax* (Steven & Sons 1991) 1. Reference may also be made to the Singapore High Court decision of *ABD Pte Ltd v Comptroller of Income Tax* [2010] 3 SLR 609 [1].

examination of the legal rules and principles applicable to the termination or end of contracts or their change demonstrates numerous actual as well as potential difficulties. And I am here speaking only from the perspective of the common law.

IV. Some Brief Specific Perspectives: Discharge by Breach of Contract and Discharge by Frustration

1. Introduction

Indeed, as I was reflecting on which specific perspectives to make brief observations upon, I was literally overwhelmed. This entire area of the law of contract is—as I alluded to earlier—very diverse and extremely complex. It is not perhaps an ideal approach, but I thought that I would just briefly mention two major doctrines that deal with the end of a contract—discharge by *breach of contract* and discharge under the doctrine of *frustration*. They are quite different legal modes by which a contract ends and raise a great many interesting issues. They also illustrate some of the general themes which I have referred to earlier in this address. However, before proceeding to consider these two doctrines, I should note that a contract could also end simply (and naturally) by *performance* of the terms of the contract by the parties or, alternatively, by the *agreement* of the said parties. I also note that contracts can also be *changed*, for example, by *varying* an existing agreement[13] or by way of *novation*.

2. Discharge by Breach of Contract

Turning, first, to *discharge by breach of contract*, this is, in fact (as has been observed in a decision of the Singapore Court of Appeal),[14] 'a confused and confusing area of contract law'. A breach of contract entitles the innocent party to recover damages from the party in breach as of right. The recoverability and quantum of damages will be subject to the common law rules on damages (in relation to remoteness, mitigation, and quantification). That having been said, not every breach will—in addition—entitle the innocent party to elect to treat the contract as discharged. In this regard, there are important *practical* consequences inasmuch as if the innocent party elects to treat the contract as discharged when it is not in fact legally justified in doing so, it will *itself* be in breach of contract. This raises the important issue as to when the innocent party is legally justified or entitled to elect to treat the contract as discharged (that is, to terminate the contract) as a result of the other party's breach of contract.

May I digress a little at this juncture to say that when I had to first lecture on this topic as a legal academic decades ago, I discovered that the two tests as to when the innocent party

[13] Which necessarily brings into play the doctrine of consideration (and all the related difficulties that that doctrine entails). See also one of Professor Treitel's Clarendon Lectures, GH Treitel, *Some Landmarks of Twentieth Century Contract Law* (Clarendon Press 2002).

[14] *RDC Concrete Pte Ltd v Sato Kogyo (S) Pte Ltd* [2007] 4 SLR(R) 413 [88].

is legally entitled to elect to treat the contract as discharged, whilst superficially clear, were, on a closer examination, potentially at odds with each other. This was due to the fact that these two approaches embodied different theoretical underpinnings and that there were, in fact, historical reasons that resulted in these two conceptually different approaches. As a result, I found that the topic of discharge by breach of contract was one of the most difficult topics to lecture on in law school—on a par, in my view, with the law relating to contractual illegality. This is not the time and the place to elaborate on the various issues and difficulties surrounding the law relating to discharge by breach of contract, and a brief snapshot will have to suffice. There is a more detailed elaboration in a joint essay I co-wrote with Professor Yihan Goh, the then Dean of the Singapore Management University School of Law, a few years ago.[15]

Put simply, there are (as I have already mentioned) two tests that the courts employ in ascertaining whether or not the innocent party can elect to treat itself as discharged from the contract as a result of a breach by the other party of one or more of the terms of the contract concerned.

The first is what has been popularly termed as the 'condition-warranty approach', which was elaborated upon in the oft-cited English Court of Appeal decision of *Bentsen v Taylor, Sons & Co (No 2)*.[16] The material portion reads thus:

> There is no way of deciding that question except *by looking at the contract in the light of the surrounding circumstances*, and then making up one's mind whether the intention of the parties, as gathered from the instrument itself, will best be carried out by treating the promise as a warranty sounding only in damages, or as a condition precedent by the failure to perform which the other party is relieved of his liability.[17]

The second is the '*Hong Kong Fir* approach',[18] which was elaborated upon in *Hong Kong Fir* itself, as follows:

> The test whether an event has this effect or not has been stated in a number of metaphors all of which I think amount to the same thing: does the occurrence of the event *deprive the party who has further undertakings still to perform of substantially the whole benefit which it was the intention of the parties as expressed in the contract* that he should obtain as the consideration for performing those undertakings?[19]

From a conceptual perspective, both tests are quite *different*. The 'condition-warranty approach' focuses on the nature of the term breached, whereas the '*Hong Kong Fir* approach' focuses on the actual consequences of the breach. However, it should be noted that these two

[15] A Phang and Y Goh, 'Encounters with History, Theory and Doctrine: Some Reflections on Discharge by Breach of Contract' in S Degeling, J Edelman, and J Goudkamp (eds), *Contract in Commercial Law* (Thomson Reuters 2016) ch 12.

[16] [1893] 2 QB 274.

[17] [1893] 2 QB 274, 281 (emphasis added).

[18] The '*Hong Kong Fir* approach' draws its terminology from the leading English Court of Appeal decision of *Hong Kong Fir Shipping Co Ltd v Kawasaki Kisen Kaisha Ltd* [1962] 2 QB 26.

[19] [1962] 2 QB 26, 66 (emphasis added).

tests are not necessarily inconsistent with each other, although they might be, depending on the particular factual matrix concerned.

There are, in fact, *historical reasons* that resulted in these two *conceptually different* approaches as embodied in the two tests just mentioned. To elaborate (albeit by way of the briefest of summaries), in a joint essay I have already referred to,[20] my co-author and I suggested that what was in substance what we now know as the '*Hong Kong Fir* approach' was the original approach adopted by the courts in an era when the focus was on the effects or the nature and consequences of the breach (which was due, in part at least, to the focus of the courts on the substantive fairness of transactions, as opposed to the more modern (and objective) will theory of contracts, which focuses on the intentions of the contracting parties).

By the time the UK Sale of Goods Act was enacted in 1893, the relevant case law had in fact developed in a manner which centred on an examination of the importance the contracting parties placed on the terms concerned. It appeared to embody the (quite different) condition-warranty approach and it was this particular approach that was incorporated into the Sale of Goods Act—thus marginalizing the *consequentialist* approach until it was resurrected once again by Lord Diplock in the *Hong Kong Fir* case.[21]

If the brief historical account just set out is correct, it would explain why the 'condition-warranty approach' and the *consequentialist* approach were different tests until they were integrated in the *Hong Kong Fir* case itself.

Not surprisingly, the law appears to be in a state of flux in many Commonwealth jurisdictions.[22] In Singapore, however, an attempt was made to develop a uniquely local set of jurisprudence and principles that seeks to cut the legal Gordian Knot by attempting to reconcile both these tests. The leading decision in this regard is that of the Singapore Court of Appeal in *RDC Concrete Pte Ltd v Sato Kogyo (S) Pte Ltd*.[23] However, given the *conceptually different* approaches as embodied in *the very nature of the tests themselves*, a *perfect* integration was impossible, especially where the factual matrix was such that the application of the respective tests would give rise to *different* results. In this last-mentioned situation, normative guidance is required as to which test ought to be applied first and what the legal effect would be on the test that is (if at all) to be applied next. In this regard, the court in *RDC Concrete* discussed the various tests as well as how they are to be applied,[24] summarizing the legal position in Table 2.1.[25]

[20] Phang and Goh (n 15) 263–67.

[21] [1962] 2 QB 26.

[22] See eg A Phang, 'Doctrine and Fairness in the Law of Contract' in J Young and R Lee (eds), The Common Law Lecture Series 2008–2009 (Faculty of Law, The University of Hong Kong 2010) 17–100, 41–61 (and the decisions from the various jurisdictions cited therein, including Australia, Canada, and Hong Kong). And for a recent essay with regard to the Malaysian context, see D Fung, '*Berjaya Times Square* Revisited: What's in a Name?' [2019] Journal of the Malaysian Judiciary 169. See also MF Cheong and YH Lee, 'Termination of Contracts: The Position under Malaysian Contract Law', ch 16 in this volume, 320, on the termination of contracts under Malaysian contract law. And insofar as the Singapore position is concerned, see CH Tham in, 'Termination under Singapore Law', ch 21 in this volume, 435.

[23] [2007] 4 SLR(R) 413.

[24] See generally [2007] 4 SLR(R) 413 [90]–[113].

[25] [2007] 4 SLR(R) 413 [113].

Table 2.1 Situations entitling an innocent party to terminate the contract at common law

Situation	Circumstances in which termination is legally justified	Relationship to other situations
I Express reference to the right to terminate and what will entitle the innocent party to terminate the contract		
(1)	The contractual term breached clearly states that, in the event of certain event or events occurring, the innocent party is entitled to terminate the contract.	None—it operates *independently of all other* situations. In other words, situations (2), (3)(a), and (3)(b) (ie all the situations in II, below) are *not* relevant.
II *No* express reference to the right to terminate and what will entitle the innocent party to terminate the contract		
(2)	The party in breach *renounces* the contract by clearly conveying to the innocent party that it *will not perform its contractual obligations at all.* *Quaere* whether the innocent party can terminate the contract if the party in breach *deliberately* chooses to perform its part of the contract in a manner that amounts to a *substantial breach.*	None—it operates *independently* of *all other* situations. In other words, Situation (1) is *not* relevant. Situations (3)(a) and (3)(b) are *not* relevant.
(3)(a)	'Condition-Warranty Approach'—the party in breach has breached a *condition* of the contract (as opposed to a *warranty*).	Should be applied *before* the '*Hongkong Fir* Approach' in Situation (3)(b). Situation (1) is *not* relevant. Situation (2) is *not* relevant.
(3)(b)	'*Hongkong Fir* Approach'—the party in breach that has committed a breach, the *consequences* of which *will deprive the innocent party of substantially the whole benefit which it was intended that the innocent party should obtain from the contract.*	Should be applied only *after* the 'Condition-Warranty Approach' in Situation (3)(a) *and* if the term breached is *not* found to be a *condition.* Situation (1) is *not* relevant. Situation (2) is *not* relevant.

Source: Author.

The Singapore Court of Appeal subsequently provided, in *Man Financial (S) Pte Ltd v Wong Bark Chuan David*,[26] a similar summary in *non*-tabular/diagrammatic form, as follows:

> 153 As stated in *RDC Concrete*, there are four situations which entitle the innocent party (here, the appellant) to elect to treat the contract as discharged as a result of the other party's (here, the respondent's) breach.
>
> 154 The *first* ('Situation 1') is where the contractual term in question clearly and unambiguously states that, should an event or certain events occur, the innocent party would be entitled to terminate the contract (see *RDC Concrete* at [91]).

26 [2008] 1 SLR(R) 663.

155 The *second* ('Situation 2') is where the party in breach of contract ('the guilty party'), by its words or conduct, simply *renounces* the contract inasmuch as it clearly conveys to the innocent party that it will not perform its contractual obligations at all (see *RDC Concrete* at [93]).

156 The *third* ('Situation 3(a)') is where the term breached (here, Clause C.1) is a *condition* of the contract. Under what has been termed the 'condition-warranty approach', the innocent party is entitled to terminate the contract if the term which is breached is a condition (as opposed to a warranty): see *RDC Concrete* at [97]. The focus here, unlike that in the next situation discussed below, is not so much on the (actual) consequences of the breach, but, rather, on the *nature of the term* breached.

157 The *fourth* ('Situation 3(b)') is where the breach of a term deprives the innocent party of substantially the whole benefit which it was intended to obtain from the contract (see *RDC Concrete* at [99]). (This approach is also commonly termed the '*Hongkong Fir* approach' after the leading English Court of Appeal decision of *Hongkong Fir Shipping Co Ltd v Kawasaki Kisen Kaisha Ltd* [1962] 2 QB 26; see especially *id* at 70.) The focus here, unlike that in Situation 3(a), is not so much on the nature of the term breached, but, rather, on the *nature and consequences of the breach.*

158 Because of the different perspectives adopted in Situation 3(a) and Situation 3(b), respectively (as briefly noted above), which differences might, depending on the precise factual matrix, yield different results when applied to the fact situation, this court in *RDC Concrete* concluded that, as between both the aforementioned situations, the approach in Situation 3(a) should be *applied first*, as follows (*id* at [112]):

> If the term is a *condition*, then the innocent party would be entitled to terminate the contract. *However*, if the term is a *warranty* (instead of a condition), then the court should nevertheless proceed to apply the approach in Situation 3(b) (*viz*, the *Hongkong Fir* approach) [emphasis in original].[27]

As I alluded to earlier, there is no perfect method of integrating the two tests. Indeed, that the approach suggested above in *RDC Concrete* still required refinement was demonstrated in the subsequent Singapore Court of Appeal decision of *Sports Connection Pte Ltd v Deuter Sports GmbH*.[28] Owing to constraints of space, it will suffice, for the present, to set out a summary of the legal position, in which the court in *Sports Connection* added a *very limited exception* to the principles laid down in *RDC Concrete*, observing as follows:

> We would therefore reaffirm the approach laid down in *RDC Concrete* for the reasons set out above, subject to the *extremely limited exception* that, where the term itself states *expressly (as well as clearly and unambiguously)* that *any* breach of it, *regardless* of the seriousness of the consequences that follow from that breach, will *never* entitle the innocent party to terminate the contract, then *the court will give effect to this particular type of term* (*viz*, a warranty *expressly* intended by the parties).[29]

[27] [2008] 1 SLR(R) 663 [153]–[158] (emphases in the original text).

[28] [2009] 3 SLR(R) 883.

[29] [2009] 3 SLR(R) 883 [57] (emphases in the original text). In addition to the decisions already referred to, reference may be made to the (also) Singapore Court of Appeal decision of *Alliance Concrete Singapore Pte Ltd v Comfort Resources Pte Ltd* [2009] 4 SLR(R) 602.

I have spent some time to describe how the Singapore courts have dealt with the thorny issues centring on discharge by breach of contract to illustrate a number of points of *general interest as well as potential application* to participants in the present conference.

The first is that *theoretical and historical approaches* are often necessary in order to work out the *doctrinal problems* in a thorny area of law (here, discharge by breach of contract). The second is that whilst a *comparative approach* is often useful, where an area of law is in too much of a state of flux across jurisdictions, the court concerned (here, in the *RDC Concrete* case) might have no option but to strike out on its own. This is not to state that doctrine, theory, and history are unimportant. Quite the contrary. As I have sought to demonstrate, an historical understanding was required to understand why two conceptually different approaches resulted, and a conceptual approach was necessary in order to understand why a *perfect* integration of these approaches was *not* possible and that a composite test that *prioritized* the *application* of the two tests was one that was best able to achieve (potentially at least) a *just and fair result* based on the facts at hand. Thirdly, whilst the Singapore approach towards the issue of discharge by breach of contract is by no means the final word in this thorny area of contract law, it remains a possible legal framework that could be considered by the courts of other jurisdictions, thus underscoring, once again, the signal importance of a comparative approach.

Let me now turn briefly to the doctrine of discharge by *frustration*.

3. Discharge by Frustration

The doctrine of discharge by frustration concerns another way by which the contract may be ended or terminated.[30] However, unlike discharge by breach of contract, the doctrine of frustration applies by *operation of law*. Put simply, whilst contractual obligations are generally absolute, the doctrine of frustration could automatically discharge all parties to the contract *by operation of law* where, through no fault of *either* party, an *external* catastrophic event has occurred or supervened *after*[31] the formation of the contract, thus so drastically altering the contractual arrangements agreed upon between the parties that to insist upon continuation of performance would, in effect, be to hold the parties to a *radically or fundamentally* different contract altogether.

Whilst the basic idea underlying the doctrine of frustration is relatively easy to state, it is by no means a doctrine without difficulties. However, putting the various difficulties to one side for the moment, what is interesting about the doctrine of frustration (particularly in the context of the present conference) is the fact that this doctrine at common law might have its roots in the civil law. In the leading English decision of *Taylor v Caldwell*,[32] Blackburn J, in addition to relying upon portions of the law of Justinian's *Digest*, quoted from a treatise which he had written when in practice, the relevant portion of which is, in fact, an English

[30] See also generally, A Phang, 'Frustration in English Law—A Reappraisal' (1992) 21 Anglo-American Law Review 278. And insofar as the Singapore position is concerned, see D Neo, 'Contractual Obligations and Change of Circumstances in Singapore', ch 20 in this volume, 417.

[31] The issue of timing is crucial as the legal position might otherwise possibly be one of common mistake instead (see eg A Phang and Y Goh, *Contract Law in Singapore* (Wolters Kluwer Law & Business 2012) 644). Reference may now be made to A Phang and Y Goh, *Contract Law in Singapore* (2nd edn, Wolters Kluwer Law & Business 2021) 730.

[32] (1863) 3 B & S 826.

translation of the work of the eminent French jurist, Pothier.[33] And the learned judge observed, more generally, thus:

> Although the Civil law is not of itself authority in an English Court, it affords great assistance in investigating the principles on which the law is grounded.[34]

Once again, the importance of *comparative analysis* comes clearly to the fore. In addition to the comparative aspect that I have just noted, there remain a number of difficult areas pertaining to this particular doctrine. Constraints of time preclude a detailed analysis, and it will suffice, for present purposes, to just mention them briefly here. The first relates to the issue of *increased costs* and, in particular, whether, despite the traditional view (at least under the common law) that increased costs should not suffice to result in a successful invocation of the doctrine, that doctrine might possibly be triggered if the increased costs are so extreme as to be 'astronomical'.[35] That, of course, assumes that a clear line can be drawn between mere increased costs (which are to be expected in everyday life), on the one hand, and astronomical costs, on the other.

Another difficulty relates to the role of *foreseeability*.[36] In this regard, the view by Professor Treitel to the effect that there is no reason why the doctrine of frustration should be excluded unless the alleged frustrating event is either actually foreseen or where there is a *sufficiently high* degree of foreseeability[37] is one that has much, in my view, to commend itself.[38]

Then there are the principles relating to the interpretation of *force majeure* clauses.[39] Yet another difficulty relates to the issue of *self-induced frustration*[40]—in particular, whether negligent conduct ought to constitute self-induced frustration[41] and also whether, in a situation where a party has entered into a number of contracts with a number of parties and a supervening event results in him being unable to satisfy all of the contracts, he may elect to

[33] C Blackburn, *A Treatise on the Effect of the Contract of Sale; on the Legal Rights and Property and Possession in Goods, Wares and Merchandize* (William Benning & Co 1845) 173. But cf C Macmillan, '*Taylor v Caldwell* (1863)' in C Mitchell and P Mitchell (eds), *Landmark Cases in the Law of Contract* (Hart Publishing 2008) ch 6, 193–95 (citing WW Buckland, 'Casus and Frustration in Roman and Common Law' (1932–33) 46 Harvard Law Review 1281). See also AWB Simpson, 'Innovation in Nineteenth Century Contract Law' (1975) 91 Law Quarterly Review 247, 271. But it should be noted that Professor Simpson also refers (at 270) to the earlier decision of *Hall v Wright* (1858) El Bl & El 746, 765 which, in his view, 'may well have been' the 'immediate source of the device [of the implied condition] used' in *Taylor v Caldwell* (1863) 3 B & S 826; interestingly, Pothier's views are also considered in this case, albeit not by all the judges. And on the influence of Pothier generally, see PS Atiyah, *The Rise and Fall of Freedom of Contract* (Clarendon Press 1979) 399–400. Reference may also be made to DM Walker, *The Oxford Companion to Law* (Clarendon Press 1980) 973 (and, in particular, to the entry entitled 'Pothier, Robert Joseph').

[34] (1863) 3 B & S 826, 835.

[35] See the House of Lords decision of *Tsakiroglou & Co Ltd v Noblee Thorl GmbH* [1962] AC 93, 118 and 128–29, per Lord Reid and Lord Hodson, respectively. See also Phang (n 30) 286–89.

[36] Phang (n 30) 289–94.

[37] See generally E Peel, *Treitel on the Law of Contract* (14th edn, Sweet & Maxwell 2015) para 19-078. Reference may now be made to E Peel, *Treitel on the Law of Contract* (15th edn, Sweet & Maxwell 2020) para 19-085.

[38] Phang (n 30), especially 293. Though cf now CH Tham and ZX Tan, 'Frustration' in ABL Phang (ed), *The Law of Contract in Singapore*, vol 2 (2nd edn, Academy Publishing 2022) ch 19, 1592–606.

[39] Phang (n 30) 294–95 as well as Phang and Goh, *Contract Law in Singapore* (2012) (n 31) 671–78 (and for the latter work, see now the new edition (also referenced at n 31) 758–67).

[40] See generally Phang (n 30) 295–308. Reference may also be made to the Privy Council decision (on appeal from the Supreme Court of Nova Scotia) of *Maritime National Fish v Ocean Trawlers Ltd* [1935] AC 524 and the English Court of Appeal decision of *The Super Servant Two* [1989] 1 Lloyd's Rep 148; affirmed [1990] 1 Lloyd's Rep 1.

[41] Phang (n 30) 297–99.

perform some of the contracts and claim that the others have been frustrated by the supervening event.

In respect of the latter, the question is whether, where a party is in danger of breaching one or more of the contracts in a situation where it is unable to fulfil its obligations to all contracting parties because of a supervening event, that party ought to be allowed to avail itself of the doctrine of frustration in order to escape possible contractual liability (a situation that arose in the English Court of Appeal decision in *The Super Servant Two*[42]).[43] In this last-mentioned regard, Professor Treitel was of the view that the party concerned ought to be able to avail itself of the doctrine of frustration,[44] and support for this view lies in the notion of fairness—as that party was not responsible for the supervening event, it ought, in all fairness, to be permitted to utilize the doctrine of frustration to escape liability; it would not be fair to fix it with responsibility by classifying its choices as to which contractual obligations it wished to fulfil as acts of self-induced frustration. However, as I have observed elsewhere:

> The arguments against Professor Treitel's views are, however, equally persuasive and take us back to the basic difficulty already considered in some detail in the context of the issue of increase in costs: that the party concerned entered into his contracts taking the risk, as all businessmen must, that he would, if a supervening event occurred, be placed in precisely the dilemma the defendants found themselves in *The Super Servant Two*; this being the case, the party ought to accept contractual lability for breach of contract.[45]

Indeed, in *The Super Servant Two* itself, Hobhouse J (as he then was and at first instance) refused to follow Professor Treitel's view, holding that there had been self-induced frustration.[46] The learned judge's decision was affirmed by the English Court of Appeal.[47] I have considered this decision in more detail elsewhere[48] and will therefore not repeat my views here, save to say that one at least partial solution to the dilemma in which the defendants found themselves in *The Super Servant Two* may lie in the concept of *prorating*.[49]

Another interesting (albeit highly specific) issue that arises is whether a contract for the sale of land can be frustrated. I mention this case specifically because a leading decision emanates from the Singapore Court of Appeal. This is the decision in *Lim Kim Som v Sheriffa Taibah bte Abdul Rahman*,[50] which held that the doctrine of frustration could (and did,

42 [1989] 1 Lloyd's Rep 148; affirmed [1990] 1 Lloyd's Rep 1. See also n 39.
43 Phang (n 30) 299–308.
44 Peel, *Treitel on the Law of Contract* (2015) (n 37) para 19-088 (and at para 19-095 in the latest edition, also referenced at n 37).
45 Phang (n 30) 299.
46 [1989] 1 Lloyd's Rep 148, 158.
47 [1990] 1 Lloyd's Rep 1.
48 Phang (n 30) 299–308.
49 ibid 305–308. See now also (and generally) Tham and Tan (n 38) 1606–29.
50 [1994] 1 SLR(R) 233; reversing [1992] 1 SLR(R) 375. This decision was followed by the Malaysian Court of Appeal in *Lee Seng Hock v Faimah bte Zain* [1996] 3 MLJ 665 (though cf the Malaysian High Court decision of *Yeo Siew Kiow v Nyo Chu Alang* [1997] 5 MLJ 313, where the *Lim Kim Som* case was not cited) and the Singapore High Court decision of *Win Supreme Investment (S) Pte Ltd v Joharah bte Abdul Wahab* [1996] 3 SLR(R) 583, and was distinguished in *Tay Ah Poon v Chionh Hai Guan* [1996] 2 SLR(R) 553 (reversed [1997] 1 SLR(R) 596. See also A Phang, 'Frustration of Contracts for the Sale of Land in Singapore' (1995) 44 International & Comparative Law Quarterly 443 and M Hwang, 'Does Compulsory Acquisition Frustrate a Contract for the Sale of Immovable Property? *Lim Kim Som* Revisited' [2000] Singapore Journal of Legal Studies 379.

in this case) apply to a contract for the sale of land. This continues to be the position in Singapore, notwithstanding subsequent Privy Council authority to the contrary.[51]

If I may, I would like to conclude this very brief discussion of the doctrine of frustration by paying tribute to a couple of legal titans in the law of contract. All of us, common and civil lawyers alike, are familiar with the immense breadth of scholarship of Professor Sir Guenter Heinz Treitel QC (to which I have, in fact, already made brief reference).[52] In addition to his magisterial textbook on the law of contract, his treatise, entitled *Frustration and Force Majeure*,[53] is (in the context of the doctrine of frustration) the first port of call—again, for common and civil lawyers alike. Indeed, two of the themes in his Clarendon Lectures[54] also correspond to two of the themes in the present conference—agreements to vary contracts as well as the various types or categories of terms. Professor Treitel sadly passed away on 14 June 2019.[55] It is a great loss to the legal profession. Barely one month later, on 15 July 2019, we lost Professor Brian Coote, who hailed from New Zealand and whose work (especially in, albeit not limited to, the law relating to exception clauses[56] and which certainly includes discharge by frustration) has been cited by both legal academics and courts alike.[57] Although I never met Professor Treitel personally (and with whom I had only the briefest of correspondence), I did meet with Professor Coote, whom I found to be an extraordinarily kind man.[58] I will miss him.

V. Conclusion

Many thanks once again for your kind invitation to speak today. I do wish you all the very best in this conference and look forward very much to reading your papers both now as well

[51] See the Privy Council decision (on appeal from the Court of Appeal of Barbados) in *E Johnson & Co (Barbados) Ltd v NSR Ltd* [1997] 1 AC 400.

[52] See nn 37 and 44.

[53] (2nd edn, Sweet & Maxwell 2004) (see now the 4th edn, Sweet & Maxwell 2022 by Professor Edwin Peel). There were, of course, numerous other works, including his contributions to *Chitty on Contracts* and *Carver's Carriage by Sea*. See also his Clarendon Lectures, which were published as *Some Landmarks of Twentieth Century Contract Law* (n 13), as well as my review essay of the same in A Phang, 'On Architecture and Justice in Twentieth Century Contract Law' (2003) 19 Journal of Contract Law 229.

[54] Treitel, *Some Landmarks of Twentieth Century Contract Law* (n 53).

[55] And see the obituary in *The Times*, 21 June 2019, 51. See also the very recent (as well as interesting) article by E McKendrick, 'Doctrine and Discretion in the Law of Contract Revisited' (2019) 7 Chinese Journal of Comparative Law 1, which revisits Professor Treitel's inaugural lecture given at the University of Oxford in 1980 (see GH Treitel, *Doctrine and Discretion in the Law of Contract* (Clarendon Press 1981)). And see now also F Reynolds, 'Guenter Heinz Treitel, 28 October 1928–14 June 2019' (2020) 19 Biographical Memoirs of Fellows of the British Academy and A Burrows, 'Professor Sir Guenter Treitel (1928–2019)' in J Goudkamp and D Nolan (eds), *Scholars of Contract Law* (Hart Publishing 2022) ch 11.

[56] See his seminal treatise, *Exception Clauses* (Sweet & Maxwell 1964).

[57] See eg (and only in the Singapore context) the Singapore High Court decision of *Emjay Enterprises Pte Ltd v Skylift Consolidator (Pte) Ltd* [2006] 2 SLR(R) 268 [11], [21], [22], [28], and [29] as well as the Singapore Court of Appeal decisions of *Sun Technosystems Pte Ltd v Federal Express Services (M) Sdn Bhd* [2007] 1 SLR(R) 411, [24] and *Family Food Court (a firm) v Seah Boon Lock* [2008] 4 SLR(R) 272 [36] and [48]. And see A Phang, 'Contract as Assumption—The Scholarship and Influence of Professor Brian Coote' (2011) 27 Journal of Contract Law 247, where it was observed (at 254) that 'even a cursory search revealed that Coote's work had been cited by the courts of no fewer than seven jurisdictions (viz, England, Canada, Australia, New Zealand, Hong Kong, Singapore and even the Turks and Caicos Islands (in this last instance, via the Judicial Committee of the Privy Council))'.

[58] Phang (n 57) 263–64. And see now also P Watts, 'Emeritus Professor Brian Coote, CBE, FRSNZ, Obituary' (2019) 36 Journal of Contract Law 1 and S Waddams, 'Professor Brian Coote (1929–2019)' in Goudkamp and Nolan (n 55) ch 13.

as the final versions, which will appear in print in the not too distant future. May I also wish all our overseas visitors a very pleasant stay in Singapore.

VI. Postscript

Not long after this Welcome Address was delivered in late 2019, a most unexpected—and tragic—event unfolded early the next calendar year, which changed the entire face of the world for the succeeding three years or so. This was the COVID-19 pandemic, which literally turned the whole world (including many contractual arrangements) upside down—thus (with not a little irony) underscoring the utter importance of the subject matter of the conference itself as contracts were sought to be ended or changed as a result of the pandemic. As the editors of the present volume also point out, this tragic pandemic was also responsible in large part for the delay in the publication of the book itself—and, in my respectful view, rightly so in order to ensure that this book was not only up to date but also (and perhaps more importantly) relevant to its readers.

As I reflected on the contents of my address that was delivered some time ago, a few main lessons struck me, and I shall endeavour to elaborate upon them briefly in the remainder of this Postscript.

The first is that certain concepts as well as ideas will remain—even with the passage of time. They provide the foundations upon which the law in a particular area of the law of contract can be developed with both stability as well as (where applicable) the requisite creativity and flexibility to initiate further developments as well as modifications and/or refinements. Hence, much of the address in relation to the relevant core legal principles has stood the test of time.

Indeed, this is very much the methodology of the common law. At key points, there will be a decision that consolidates the law and lays down guiding legal rules and principles, which will then be applied in so-called 'routine' or 'easy' cases until such time as there is a need to either discard or modify that decision in light of changed circumstances and/or changed reasoning. Insofar as the law relating to discharge by breach of contract is concerned, the decision in *RDC Concrete* (dealt with in some detail above) serves the aforementioned function and, during the close to two decades since it was decided, continues to be applied in the Singapore courts.[59] It also bears mentioning that *RDC Concrete* was included in volume 2 of *A Compendium of Singapore–China International Commercial Cases Curated for Their Relevance to the Belt and Road Initiative*[60]—a publication which was coordinated by the Singapore Judicial College and the China National Judges College[61]

[59] And see generally CH Tham, 'Discharge by Breach' in ABL Phang (ed) *The Law of Contract in Singapore*, vol 1 (2nd edn, Academy Publishing 2022) ch 17. See also eg (for cases decided after 2022), *Carlsberg South Asia Pte Ltd v Pawan Kumar Jagetia* [2023] SGHC(A) 29 [95]; *PT OKI Pulp & Paper Mills v Sunrise Industries (India) Ltd* [2023] SGHC(A) 38 [118]; *Builders Hub Pte Ltd v JP Nelson Equipment Pte Ltd* [2023] SGHC 120 [54]; *Government of the City of Buenos Aires v HN Singapore Pte Ltd* [2023] SGHC 139 [88]; *Ho Chee Kian v Ho Kwek Sin* [2024] 3 SLR 888; *ICOP Construction (SG) Pte Ltd v Tiong Seng Civil Engineering (Pte) Ltd* [2024] SGHC(A) 1 [257]; *Wong Ben v The WatchFund Ltd* [2024] SGHC 110 [108]–[110]; and *Dabbs, Matthew Edward v AAM Advisory Pte Ltd* [2024] SGHC 260, especially [24].

[60] (LexisNexis Singapore 2020). The English language version of the case is to be found at 193, whilst the Chinese language version of the headnote is to be found at 270 (together with commentary (in the Chinese language) by Professor Yihan Goh SC (at 273)).

[61] Who comprised the chief editors.

in order to curate international commercial cases from both the Singapore and the Chinese courts that are relevant to the Belt and Road Initiative. It was also discussed by the commentator of the case[62] in the aforementioned publication at a case forum between both these colleges.[63]

In contrast, however, to the law relating to discharge by breach of contract, the law relating to the doctrine of frustration in the Singapore context had—in the wake of the COVID-19 pandemic—witnessed a *legislative overlay* that served to obviate what might have (potentially at least) been a 'messy' situation in the courts. Constraints of space preclude an even cursory discussion. However, there is an excellent overview not only of the decisions under the common law[64] and the Frustrated Contracts Act,[65] which arose as a result of the pandemic, but also of the COVID-19 (Temporary Measures) Act 2020[66] by Professors Chee Ho Tham and Zhong Xing Tan in a major local contract law textbook,[67] which the interested reader can refer to.

In a related vein, a number of more general (as well as important) lessons also remain. For example, one of the major themes mentioned in my Welcome Address related to the importance of comparative analysis. Insofar as one aspect of comparative analysis is concerned, I have recently elaborated on the importance of *comparative common law*.[68] More importantly perhaps (and in the context of *the present book*), the chapters therein (which I have now had the opportunity to read) have in fact *underscored the vital importance of comparative analysis*. For instance, insofar as comparative common law is concerned, I found the relevant essays in the present volume fascinating in as much as they provide a veritable treasure trove of comparative material. This is especially important in the context of the law relating to discharge by breach of contract, which, as I have already alluded to above,[69] is still generally in a state of flux. However, even as between common law and civil law jurisdictions, there was still some similarity in terms of (not surprisingly) basic concepts such as that of fault (on the part of the party in breach of contract). There were also some similarities in relation, for example, to the concept of a fundamental change in circumstances (which in the common law context is embodied in *Hong Kong Fir*).[70] This last-mentioned point in fact segues into the law relating to frustration and *force majeure*. And, perhaps not surprisingly, this particular area of the law of contract demonstrates—as the chapters in this volume also illustrate—much more similarity not only in conceptual basis but also even in the content of the substantive law. Again, this is not surprising in light of the civil law roots of the common law doctrine of frustration, which were considered briefly earlier in the present chapter.[71] Quite apart from the practical uses of comparative analysis

[62] Viz, Professor Yihan Goh SC, the then Dean of the Yong Pung How School of Law, Singapore Management University (see also at n 60).

[63] Case Forum: Singapore–China International Commercial Cases (held on 1 November 2021).

[64] To which reference may now also be made to the Singapore Court of Appeal decision of *QBE Insurance (Singapore) Pte Ltd v Relax Beach Co Ltd* [2023] 2 SLR 655.

[65] See the Frustrated Contracts Act 1959 (Rev edn, 2020).

[66] Act No 14 of 2020. As the title of this Act itself suggests, the measures therein were intended to be only temporary until after the COVID-19 pandemic had been brought under control.

[67] Tham and Tan (n 38) 1629–40.

[68] A Phang, 'The Importance of Comparative Common Law—A View from Singapore' [2023] Journal of Business Law 538.

[69] See the text at n 22.

[70] [1962] 2 QB 26 and discussed in more detail above.

[71] See the text at nn 32–34.

which I have just referred to, on a personal level, I found all the chapters in the present volume to be—if I may be permitted to use the same term once again—simply fascinating. As I have observed in the context of legal history,[72] there is a sense in which there is simple beauty to be discerned as one absorbs as well as reflects upon the kaleidoscope of the many different laws described and analysed in the present book.

Another major theme mentioned in my Welcome Address related to the important roles that theory and/or history play in the development of the law of contract. Indeed, I referred there to *RDC Concrete* as an illustration. Since this conference, I have in fact developed this theme in two further articles, and the interested reader is referred to them for more detailed argumentation as well as illustrations.[73]

Finally, I would like to consider—briefly—the concept of what I have elsewhere termed '*a living legacy*'.[74] For reasons that will become apparent in a moment, this would, in my view, be an appropriate way in which to conclude the present chapter. In concluding my Welcome Address, I paid tribute to two giants of contract law who had then recently passed away—Professor Guenter Heinz Treitel QC and Professor Brian Coote. And some time prior to their passing, we had also lost Professor Patrick Selim Atiyah, who passed away on 30 March 2018.[75] Since the Address was delivered, we have (very unfortunately) lost two more giants in the law of contract. Sadly, Professor Michael Philip Furmston, who was best known as the author of *Cheshire, Fifoot, and Furmston's Law of Contract*,[76] was suddenly taken from us during the early hours of 28 June 2020.[77] Then, on 27 May 2023, that doyen of Canadian contract law, Professor Stephen Waddams, passed away.[78] I have since written an essay paying tribute to Professor Furmston, Professor Treitel, Professor Coote, and Professor Patrick Selim Atiyah. This was published in 2022 (and before Professor Waddams was also sadly taken from us).[79] A recent tribute to Professor Stephen Waddams appeared in the *Contract and Commercial Law Review*.[80] All these giants of contract law left behind

[72] A Phang, 'Review Article: On Beauty, Scholarship, and Function—The Lessons from, and Importance of, Legal History in the Development of the Law of Marine Insurance' [2023] Singapore Journal of Legal Studies 420.

[73] A Phang, 'The Importance of Theory and History in Understanding and Developing the Common Law of Contract—Some Preliminary Reflections' (2023) 1 Contract and Commercial Law Review 67 and, by the same author, 'The Importance of Theory and History in Understanding and Developing the Common Law of Contract—Some Further Preliminary Reflections' (2024) 4 Singapore Law Journal 1.

[74] A Phang, 'Giants of Contract Law—Some Personal Reflections' (2022) 2 Singapore Law Journal 1.

[75] Professor Atiyah was, of course, a leading scholar in the law of torts as well. See generally J Goudkamp, 'Patrick Selim Atiyah, 5 March 1931–30 March 2018' (2020) 19 Biographical Memoirs of Fellows of the British Academy 149 as well as, by the same author, 'Professor Patrick Atiyah (1931–2018)' in Goudkamp and Nolan (n 55) ch 14; also 'Professor Patrick Atiyah (1931–2018)' in J Goudkamp and D Nolan (eds), *Scholars of Tort Law* (Hart Publishing 2019) ch 11.

[76] Presently in its seventeenth edition (OUP 2017). Professor Furmston was working in earnest on the eighteenth edition when he passed away suddenly.

[77] A Phang, 'Obituary—Professor Michael Philip Furmston. 1 May 1933–28 June 2020' (2020) 36 Journal of Contract Law 201. See also A Phang, 'Theory as Practice and Practice as Theory—The Integrated and Integral Contract Scholarship of Professor Michael Furmston' (2014) 31 Journal of Contract Law 12.

[78] Professor Waddams was the author of many works, the foremost of which was his magisterial treatise on the Canadian law of contract: see SM Waddams, *The Law of Contracts* (8th edn, Thomson Reuters 2022), For a remembrance of Professor Waddams from the Faculty of Law of the University of Toronto see <www.law.utoronto.ca/news/in-memoriam-university-professor-stephen-waddams> accessed 14 March 2025. Indeed, Professor Waddams was not only a leading doctrinal contract scholar but also a learned contract theorist (see eg SM Waddams, *Principle and Policy in Contract Law: Competing or Complementary Concepts?* (CUP 2011)) as well as an eminent legal historian (see eg SM Waddams, *Law, Politics and the Church of England: The Career of Stephen Lushington 1782–1873* (CUP 1992)).

[79] Phang (n 74).

[80] JD McCamus, 'Stephen Waddams (1942–2023)' (2024) 2 Contract and Commercial Law Review 69.

a legacy of scholarship that will stand the test of time. More than that, as I concluded in the essay I have just referred to, there were also important *life lessons* to be learnt from the lives of the various giants of contract law:

> These included, first, the need to have hobbies and personal interests outside the law. A second lesson was the need to eschew procrastination—in particular, as in the law of contract generally, an objective test is applied to ascertain whether gratitude has been shown and, in this regard, one should be quick to demonstrate this tangibly rather than hiding it under a bushel. Thirdly, there is no substitute for perseverance and sheer hard work—this is evident from the lives and careers of all the scholars considered in the present essay, for none of them achieved success the easy way. A fourth lesson is that life, whilst unpredictable, is (paradoxically) not random—we are where we are for a purpose and it is our duty to fulfil that purpose (whatever it may be) to the best of our ability. The final—and most important—lesson is that we need to possess *humanity and humility*. Indeed, these have been the hallmarks of all *truly* great persons. Put simply, *people* matter more than wealth or status and it is only by possessing (and demonstrating) the qualities of humanity and humility that we can touch other lives for the better—thus establishing a 'living legacy' beyond our own physical lives.[81]

[81] Phang (n 74) 51–52 (emphases in the original text).

3

Change of Circumstances in China's Civil Legislation and Judicial Practice

WANG Lei

I. Introduction

In this complex and rapidly changing society, the principles that determine the legal effect of a change of circumstances are of great importance and help to allocate the risk of supervening events between the contracting parties, especially in relation to contracts that last for a long period of time. The doctrine of change of circumstances in China's civil legislation is a combined product of the civil law system and the common law system. This chapter will explore how the doctrine of change of circumstances operates in China's civil legislation and practice and examine the applicable principles through comparative and empirical legal methodologies.

II. Evolution of the Doctrine of Change of Circumstances in China's Civil Legislation: A Comparative Legal Methodology

1. Striking a Balance between the Interests of the Contracting Parties and Good Faith

The doctrine of change of circumstances is a concrete manifestation of the principle of good faith in the performance of a contract. From the perspective of contract law, the doctrine of change of circumstances applies to a significant change after the formation of the contract which is not due to the fault of either party and which makes the contract impossible to perform or makes performance obviously unfair. In such circumstances, the parties may request that the contract be changed or dissolved.

Article 8(1) of the 1999 Contract Law of the People's Republic of China (Contract Law of China) stipulated that: 'A lawfully established contract shall be legally binding on the parties thereto, each of whom shall perform its own obligations in accordance with the terms of the contract, and no party shall unilaterally modify or terminate the contract.' However, based on the principle of good faith, the contract may be modified or terminated in cases of a relevant change of circumstances. In such cases, the interests of the parties should be rebalanced. This is an exception, based on the principle of contractual justice, to the principle of the sanctity of contracts. It should be noted that the Contract Law of China and the various interpretations thereof are discussed in this chapter in order to provide a holistic historical, legal context. These provisions were superseded by the Chinese Civil Code (CCC) in 2020.

Wang Lei, *Change of Circumstances in China's Civil Legislation and Judicial Practice* In: *Studies in the Contract Laws of Asia V: Ending and Changing Contracts*. Edited by: Mindy Chen-Wishart, Dora Neo, and Stefan Vogenauer, Oxford University Press. DOI: 10.1093/oso/9780198995814.003.0003

Parties may sometimes use contractual clauses that allocate risk with potential supervening circumstances in mind (eg indexation clauses, *force majeure* clauses, hardship clauses). Hein Kötz is of the view that such clauses take precedence over the general rules on change of circumstances.[1] For example, Article 1195 of the new French Civil Code (2016) covers change of circumstances, and a popular casebook on European contract law states: 'The non-mandatory nature of Article 1195 [of the French Civil Code] allows the parties to modify or exclude the application of their provisions.'[2] In contrast, in China, contract clauses that directly exclude the application of the doctrine of change of circumstances are rare and will not be respected by the courts because of the mandatory nature of the rules on change of circumstances, which are based on contractual justice and not contractual freedom. Contracts between private individuals cannot prevail over the mandatory rules on change of circumstances. But if the contract itself already incorporates a clause providing for the automatic adaptation of the contract (eg a clause providing for automatic indexation of the price if unexpected hyperinflation occurs), then a request for renegotiation is not admissible. An automatic adaptation clause does not exclude the application of the doctrine of change of circumstances but determines its consequences in advance.

2. Change of Circumstances in China's Legislation

Before the promulgation of the Contract Law of China in 1999, there was a pioneering judgment that created the doctrine of change of circumstances in judicial practice. This case is commonly referred to as 'the dispute involving gas meter parts in a purchase and sale contract'.[3] However, despite the landmark nature of this judgment, the principle of change of circumstances was not incorporated into the Contract Law of China. Opponents to the doctrine considered that it would mainly apply to situations of unfairness caused by economic changes so that if this doctrine were adopted in the legislation, it could weaken both the motivation of contracting parties to avoid risks in the transaction and their ability to cope with risks and failures. Furthermore, it is hard to differentiate between changes of circumstances and commercial risks. This could encourage speculation and increase instability of contracts, which might eventually reduce the dynamism of the commodity market and endanger the safety and stability of commerce. In addition, it was felt that the vague, generalized, and loose principles of the doctrine of change of circumstances might lead to an abuse of judicial power with regard to modification of contracts.[4] However, abuse of judicial power is always a risk and should not prevent the recognition of a useful and fair principle.[5] Therefore, Article 26 of Interpretation II of the Supreme People's Court of

[1] H Kötz, *European Contract Law* (G Mertens and T Weir trs, 2nd edn, OUP 2017) 280.

[2] H Beale, B Fauvarque-Cosson, J Rutgers, and S Vogenauer, *Cases, Materials and Text on Contract Law: Ius Commune Casebooks for the Common Law of Europe* (3rd edn, Hart Publishing 2019) 1218.

[3] *Wuhan Gas Company v Chongqing Instrument Factory* (1996) The People's Republic of China Supreme People's Court Gazette, vol 2 (gas meter assembly line technology transfer contract, gas meter parts purchase and sale contract dispute). NB In this chapter, names of cases as well as titles of books or of contributions to edited volumes, of articles, and of journals that are originally written or published in Chinese are given in an English translation by the author.

[4] SUN Lihai (ed), *Selection of Legislative Materials for Contract Law of the People's Republic of China* (Law Press 1999) 163.

[5] Rousseau, *Emile: Education*, vol 2 (LI Pingyi tr, The Commercial Press 1978) 551.

Several Issues Concerning the Application of the Contract Law of the People's Republic of China (Article 26 of Interpretation II), which was later superseded by the CCC, incorporated the doctrine of change of circumstances into Chinese law for the first time in 2009. Article 26 of Interpretation II stipulated:

> Where any major change which is unforeseeable, is not a business risk, and is not caused by a *force majeure* occurs after the formation of a contract, if the continuous performance of the contract is obviously unfair to the other party or cannot realize the purposes of the contract and a party files a request for the modification or rescission of the contract with the people's court, the people's court shall decide whether to modify or rescind the contract under the principle of fairness and in light of the actualities of the case.[6]

In addition, Article 23 of the Interpretation of the Supreme People's Court on the Relevant Issues Concerning the Application of the Law for Trying Cases on Disputes over Contracts for the Sale of Commodity Houses stipulated:

> Where the contract for the sale of commodity houses stipulates that the buyer shall make the payment by means of guaranteed loans . . . If the contract on guaranteed loans for commodity houses fails to be concluded due to any reason for which neither party shall be liable, thus causing the contract for the sale of commodity houses unable to be implemented continuously, the party concerned may request rescission of the contract, and the seller shall refund the accepted money for purchase of the house and the interest thereof or the deposit to the buyer.[7]

The author believes that this Article 23 embodies the application of the principle of change of circumstances to contracts for the sale of commodity houses. If, for example, a buyer is unable to obtain a mortgage for a commodity house due to the enactment of new housing market policies, a contract which requires payment by a secured loan cannot be performed and thus can be terminated.

Upon the enactment of the CCC in 2020, the doctrine of change of circumstances became covered by Article 533 CCC (see section II.4). These rules were further refined in 2023 by Article 32 of the Interpretation by the Supreme People's Court of Several Issues Concerning the Application of General Provisions of the Book on Contract in the CCC (Article 32 of the Interpretation of the CCC).

3. The Principle of Change of Circumstances Should Be Narrowly and Strictly Applied

The doctrine of change of circumstances may lead to changes to the rights and obligations that were agreed to by both parties in the contract. It is an exception to the principle of freedom of contract because the decision whether and how to modify the contract lies with

[6] The preceding paragraph is taken from a translation of the statute on the Chinalawinfo Pkulaw Database <www.pkulaw.com/english?way=topGuid> accessed 30 April 2024.

[7] For the source of the translation of the preceding paragraph, see Pkulaw Database (n 6).

the court. This is distinct from frustration, where the contract automatically comes to an end if the court finds that the contract is frustrated. Changing contracts due to a change of circumstances is also an exception to the principle that parties must strictly abide by the contract. Therefore, the doctrine should be narrowly applied and should be subject to stringent constitutive requirements.

The constitutive elements of the doctrine of change of circumstances, which are also the specific tests for the application of the doctrine of change of circumstances, may be summarized as follows:

(i) There must be a change of circumstances in the sense of a change in the foundation (ie the objective basis) of the contract. The change of circumstances must be a radical or fundamental change from the original circumstances. 'Whether or not an event can be described as fundamental very much depends on the facts and circumstances of the particular case. It is an exercise in judgment and a question of degree.'[8]

(ii) The change of circumstances must occur after the contract is made and before performance is completed. If the change of circumstances occurred before the conclusion of the contract, it is the changed circumstances that constitute the objective basis for the establishment of the contract, unless the party was not aware of the change because of a mistake.

(iii) The change of circumstances must not be foreseen by the two parties; that is, it must be beyond their expectations. If it is expected by the parties, they should assume or assign the liabilities accordingly. There must be a total failure of both parties' expectations. Unlike the CCC, Article 6.2.2 of the UNIDROIT Principles of International Commercial Contracts 2010 (PICC) in its definition of hardship emphasizes only the relevance of the disadvantaged party's expectations but not those of both parties: 'There is hardship where . . . the events could not reasonably have been taken into account by the disadvantaged party at the conclusion of the contract.'

(iv) The parties must not be responsible for the change of circumstances. As John Cartwright says: 'It is clear that the change of circumstances must be outside the parties' control. It must have occurred "without default of either party".'[9] Otherwise, it is not a case of change of circumstances but will usually constitute a breach of the contract by that party.

(v) The originally intended legal effect of the contract must be altered in an unfair way or to an unfair extent due to the change of circumstances.[10] To some extent, the unfairness or an excessively onerous performance will simply be one element to be considered when deciding whether or not there has been a fundamental alteration to the equilibrium of the contract.

[8] S Vogenauer (ed), *Commentary on the UNIDROIT Principles of International Commercial Contracts* (2nd edn, OUP 2015) 816.

[9] J Cartwright, *Contract Law: An Introduction to the English Law of Contract for the Civil Lawyer* (2nd edn, Hart Publishing 2013) 256.

[10] *Chengdu Pengwei Industry Co Ltd v People's Government of Yongxiu County of Jiangxi Province and Office of the Leading Group for the Administration of Sand Mining of Poyang Lake of Yongxiu County* (2010) The Supreme People's Court Gazette, vol 4.

In sum, when we determine whether a relevant change of circumstances has occurred under Chinese law, we apply the constitutive elements approach of the civil law system. No one constitutive elements is conclusive; all of the five requirements listed above must be satisfied.

The purpose of the doctrine of change of circumstances is to correct a state of serious imbalance of interests between the parties. The legal effect of the application of the doctrine is that a 'negotiation obligation' is generated; that is, the party suffering may request the other party to renegotiate the contents of the contract.[11] The people's court actively guides the parties through the process of renegotiation and changing the contract. If the renegotiation fails, it is resolved by the court's judgment.[12] The duty to renegotiate is inherently uncertain and unenforceable. Renegotiation is not a true duty in civil law systems because a refusal to renegotiate will not lead to liability but only to other consequences, such as modification or termination, which reflect judicial intervention rather than the freedom of the contracting parties. If the subject matter of the duty to renegotiate is unfit for compulsory performance, the other party is likely to refuse to renegotiate.

Article 580 of the CCC stipulates:

> Where a party fails to perform the non-monetary obligations or its performance of non-monetary obligations fails to satisfy the terms of the contract, the other party may request it to perform it except under any of the following circumstances: ... (2) the subject matter of the obligation is unfit for compulsory performance or the performance expenses are excessively high.

In such cases, the parties may request the people's court to modify the contract. Then, the contract will be kept alive, although on revised terms. Finally, the parties may request the people's court to terminate the contract.

The application of the doctrine of change of circumstances must be based on an adversarial lawsuit and be filed by the contractual parties, and the type of judgment handed down is an action of formation but not an action of performance.[13] On 27 April 2009, the Notice of the Supreme People's Court on Correctly Applying the Interpretation II of Several Issues Concerning the Contract Law of the People's Republic of China so as to Serve the Primary Objectives of the Party and the State, No 165 [2009] of the Supreme People's Court stated that for the change of circumstances from Article 26 of Interpretation II,

> [t]he people's courts at all levels must accurately understand and prudently apply [the doctrine of change of circumstances]. If the aforesaid interpretation really needs to be applied to recognize a relevant change of circumstances to a case according to the special conditions, it shall be subject to the examination of the higher people's court, and be submitted to the Supreme People's Court for examination where necessary.[14]

[11] Igarashi Kiyoshi, 'Changes in Circumstances, Contract Adjustments, and Reintervention Obligations' in LIANG Huixing (ed), *Civil and Commercial Law*, vol 15 (Law Press 2000); HAN Shiyuan, 'Research on the Principles of Change of Circumstances' (2000) 4 Chinese and Foreign Law 435–455.

[12] *Guiding Opinions of the Supreme People's Court on Several Issues Concerning the Trial of Civil and Commercial Contract Dispute Cases under the Current Situation* (7 July 2009) Fa Fa [2009] No 40, art 4.

[13] PENG Fengzhi, *Study on the Principles of Change of Circumstances* (Wunan Book Publishing Company 1986) 60.

[14] For the source of the translation of the preceding paragraph, see Pkulaw Database (n 6).

As an uncertain legal concept, the doctrine of change of circumstances is difficult to define precisely, and the boundaries between a change of circumstances and commercial risks are difficult to draw. There is inevitably a margin of uncertainty and a degree of vagueness surrounding the five constitutive requirements of a change of circumstances. What tests are used by the courts to distinguish between relevant and irrelevant changes of circumstances? The author believes that this should depend on the dynamic balancing of a range of factors based on the particular facts of each case: the type of risk of significant changes, the timing of the occurrence of the risk,[15] the predictability and the degree of impact of the risk, the cause of the risk, the possibility of risk prevention, the length of duration of performance, whether the contractual obligations are continuing in nature, whether a party delays performance or commits other kinds of breach of contract,[16] the type of contract, and the nature of the transaction. No one factor is conclusive. Here, the dynamic balancing of factors is highly similar to the 'multifactorial approach' in common law[17] in that both seek to give guidance on this issue. The dynamic balancing of factors in the doctrine of change of circumstances involves the application and combination of dynamic systems theory and the balance of interests. Article 3 of the Guiding Opinions of the Supreme People's Court on Several Issues Concerning the Trial of Cases of Disputes over Civil and Commercial Contracts under the Current Situation, No 40 [2009] of the Supreme People's Court, issued by the Supreme People's Court on 7 July 2009, also stated:

> The people's courts shall reasonably distinguish between change of circumstances and commercial risks. Commercial risks are inherent in business activities, such as changes in supply and demand and price changes not reaching the level of abnormal changes. The change of circumstances is not a risk that is inherent in the market system and cannot be foreseen by the parties when they entered into their contract. When deciding whether a major objective change is a change of circumstances, the people's court shall take into account such factors as whether the type of risk is one that is unforeseeable taking a common sense approach, whether the degree of risk is far beyond the reasonable expectation of a normal person, whether the risk can be prevented and controlled, and whether the nature of the transaction falls within the usual scope of 'high risk and high return', and distinguish between the change of circumstances and commercial risks in the specific cases in combination with the specific situation of the market.[18]

4. The Unity Model of *force majeure* and Change of Circumstances

Force majeure in the Contract Law of China was mainly stipulated in Articles 94(1), 117, and 118, which provided as follows:

[15] *Chen Bin v Zhang Jinshan* and other housing sales contract disputes (2014) Kunming Intermediate People's Court of Yunnan Province, Kunmin Yichangzi No 85.

[16] *Big Zong Group Co Ltd, Zong Xijin v Huaibei Shenghuo Mining Co Ltd, Huaibei Shenghuo Real Estate Development Co Ltd, and Guoyang Shenghuo Real Estate Development Co Ltd* (2016) The Supreme People's Court Gazette, vol 6 (equity transfer dispute).

[17] H Beale, *Chitty on Contracts*, vol 1, *General Principles* (30th edn, Thomson Reuters (Legal) Limited 2008) para 019.

[18] For the source of the translation of the preceding paragraph, see Pkulaw Database (n 6).

> Article 94: The parties to a contract may terminate the contract under any of the following circumstances: (1) it is rendered impossible to achieve the purpose of contract due to an event of *force majeure*; . . .
>
> Article 117: A party who is unable to perform a contract due to *force majeure* is exempted from liability in part or in whole in light of the impact of the event of *force majeure*, except as otherwise provided by law. Where an event of *force majeure* occurs after the party's delay in performance, it is not exempted from such liability. For the purposes of this Law, *force majeure* means any objective circumstances which are unforeseeable, unavoidable, and insurmountable.
>
> Article 118: If a party is unable to perform a contract due to an event of *force majeure*, it shall timely notify the other party so as to mitigate the losses that may be caused to the other party, and shall provide evidence of such event of *force majeure* within a reasonable period.[19]

Under these provisions, *force majeure* applied where there were objective circumstances under which the contract might be terminated directly or a party might be exempted from liability. The current provisions on *force majeure* set out in Articles 590, 180, and 563(1) CCC achieve a similar effect.

Article 26 of Interpretation II excluded *force majeure* from the doctrine of change of circumstances. As seen in the earlier discussion, the doctrine of change of circumstances only applied where the change was 'not caused by a *force majeure*'. It is very hard to differentiate *force majeure* from change of circumstances. A *force majeure* means any objective circumstance that is unforeseeable, inevitable, and insurmountable. There might sometimes be confusion as to whether a situation is a *force majeure* or a change of circumstances. If this is the case, it is for the party affected by these events to decide which remedy to pursue.

Article 323 of the first draft of the CCC, published on 5 September 2018, continued to insist on the exclusion of *force majeure* from the provisions on change of circumstances. However, Article 323 of the second draft of the CCC, published on 4 January 2019, no longer prevented a *force majeure* situation from falling within the doctrine of change of circumstances. A similar approach was adopted in Article 533 of the finalized version of the CCC, published on 28 May 2020, which combined the two doctrines:

> After the conclusion of the contract, if the basic conditions of the contract have undergone substantial changes that were not foreseeable when the parties entered into the contract and are not commercial risks, and the continuing performance of the contract will cause obvious unfairness to one party, the adversely affected party may renegotiate with the other party. If the negotiation fails within a reasonable period, the parties may request the people's court or an arbitration institution to modify or terminate the contract.
>
> The people's court or arbitration institution shall refer to the actual situation of the case, and modify or terminate the contract in accordance with the principle of fairness.[20]

A *force majeure* event is usually a natural disaster or social anomaly that cannot be foreseen, avoided, or overcome, which can lead to the inability to fulfil a contract. A change of

[19] For the source of the translation of the three preceding paragraphs, see Pkulaw Database (n 6).

[20] For the source of the translation of the two preceding paragraphs, see Pkulaw Database (n 6).

circumstances does not usually result in the non-performance or impossibility of performance of a contract, but performance of the contract in the new circumstances may result in unfairness (eg performance may have become extremely expensive or excessively onerous) or it may no longer be possible to achieve the purpose of the contract. Under the CCC, where there is a change of circumstances, the affected party may request for renegotiation, and if that fails, the parties may file an action to modify or terminate the contract in order to be partially or wholly exempted from liability. The CCC adopts a unity model for *force majeure* and change of circumstances, a conscious legislative choice that reflects 'Chinese elements'. A change of circumstances, including one caused by *force majeure*, may result in a party becoming unable to perform a contract, or it may result in a major change in the basis of the transaction.

A more detailed analysis of Article 533 CCC is as follows.

First, it expands the scope of application of the doctrine of change of circumstances. '*Force majeure* and the doctrine of change of circumstances are not entirely different; rather, there is an overlap.'[21] Article 533 no longer simply excludes *force majeure* from the doctrine of change of circumstances but instead expands the scope of application of the doctrine, thereby changing the basis of the legislation from a dual model to one of unity.

Secondly, through the doctrine of change of circumstances, *force majeure* can lead to different outcomes that support the transaction. Previously, according to Article 94(1) and Articles 117–118 of the Contract Law of China, the function of *force majeure* was mainly to bring the contract to an end or reduce and exclude the liabilities of the defaulting party. *Force majeure* liberated the parties from contractual deadlock. Now, however, *force majeure* does not necessarily lead to contract failure. Article 533 CCC gives *force majeure* a new function, that of supporting the transaction by stipulating the process of renegotiation, modification, or termination of the contract. Accordingly, *force majeure* no longer necessarily causes failure of the transaction, but by rebalancing the interests of the parties, the court can make the transaction 'return to life'. 'In the case of *force majeure*, the parties should be allowed to choose the legal effect of *force majeure* or change of circumstances.'[22] Under the CCC, a change of circumstances will not necessarily lead to a termination of the contract. Article 533 CCC is notably situated in Chapter 4 (Performance of Contracts) and not in Chapter 7 (Termination of Contractual Rights and Obligations).

Thirdly, it places limits on who can file a complaint prompted by a change of circumstances. Article 533 CCC grants the right to apply to change the contract to the adversely affected party rather than to both parties. Similarly, Article 6.2.3 (Effects of hardship) PICC stipulates:

> (1) In case of hardship the disadvantaged party is entitled to request renegotiations. . . .
> (2) The request for renegotiation does not in itself entitle the disadvantaged party to withhold performance.
> (3) Upon failure to reach agreement within a reasonable time either party may resort to the court.

[21] HAN Shiyuan, '*Force Majeure, Change of Circumstances and Dissolution of Contracts*' (2014) 11 Law Application 61.

[22] WANG Liming, 'Discussion on Several Issues Concerning the System of Change of Circumstances: Comment on Article 323 of the Civil Code Contracts (Second Draft)' (2019) 3 Law and Business Research 3.

Fourth, the objective constitutive requirements of the doctrine of change of circumstances are stricter under the new CCC. One of the constitutive requirements is modified from a major change in 'the objective situation after the conclusion of the contract' stipulated by Article 26 of Interpretation II to significant changes of 'the basic conditions of the contract' stipulated by Article 533 CCC. This further reflects the original purposes of the doctrine of change of circumstances to encourage transactions and to maintain the binding force of existing transactions.

Fifth, it creates the option of renegotiation. Applying the doctrine of change of circumstances is to release both parties from the obligations which they originally agreed to perform. The adversely affected party is entitled to request renegotiation in good faith, and naturally he should indicate the grounds on which the request is based. Article 533 CCC does away with the constitutive requirement of 'cannot achieve the purpose of the contract'. Logically, if 'the objectives of the contract cannot be realized due to *force majeure*', the case will be dealt with according to Article 563 CCC, which provides that the parties to a contract may terminate the contract under certain circumstances. Under Article 563(1), this includes where 'it is rendered impossible to achieve the purpose of contract due to an event of *force majeure*'.

Sixth, as opposed to Article 26 of Interpretation II, Article 533 CCC adds a rule of renegotiation; that is, the adversely affected party may ask the other contracting party to renegotiate the contract and thereby strengthens the cooperation of the contract parties. Some Chinese contract law scholars have discussed whether renegotiation is a true obligation.[23] Others have suggested that the legislation should require the adversely affected party to request renegotiation without undue delay and strengthen the requirement for the parties to negotiate in good faith. Renegotiation is not a true obligation because it cannot be enforced. Upon failure of a negotiation, the court could modify or terminate the contract at its discretion so that the contracting party is subject to a 'forced' adjustment mechanism, and the result may not reflect his or her will; the law does not impose any liability for breach of the obligation to renegotiate.[24] It is obvious that an agreed adjustment of the contract by the two parties is preferable to an adjustment fixed by the court. The contracting parties are the best decision-makers for contractual matters. Judicial termination or modification is a last-resort remedy. The probability of judicial intervention would encourage the parties to renegotiate if they have an interest in maintaining the contract under conditions of their own choosing.

Finally, in China, the application of the doctrine of change of circumstances does not automatically bring the contract to an end, unlike the position in the common law doctrine of frustration, where the contract is terminated at the time of the changed circumstances. It should be noted that the only remedy for a change of circumstances resulting in frustration at common law is termination of the contract. The court at common law has no power to adjust the terms of the contract to reflect the changed circumstances. The civil law system takes a different position, which is the same as that set out under Article 6.2.3 (Effects of hardship) PICC and Article 6:111(3) of the Principles of European Contract Law (PECL): 'This power for the court to modify a contract can be found in all continental

[23] ZHANG Suhua and NING Yuan, 'On the Right of Re-negotiation in the Principle of Changing Situations' (2019) 3 Tsinghua Law 144–57.

[24] WANG Liming (n 22) 1.

legal systems that address such issues.'[25] The court can intervene in the arrangements after the failure of renegotiation. The failure may be caused by the other party's refusal to renegotiate. Or the renegotiation may have taken place but failed to produce an agreement within a reasonable time.

In China, how does the court determine whether to modify or terminate the contract in order to restore its equilibrium? According to Article 32 of the Interpretation of the CCC, if a party requests modification, the court cannot terminate the contract instead. If a party requests termination, the court can determine whether modification is the better option. Subject to these two conditions, the court can direct the parties to resume renegotiations with a view to reaching agreement on the adaption of the contract. If the performance of the contract is impossible, achieving the purpose of the contract is impossible, or the modification cannot eliminate imbalances of interests, the court should terminate the contract.[26] In order to encourage transactions, the court should give preference to modification: 'This [modification of the contract] is the more likely solution in the majority of cases.'[27] When it comes to modification of the contract in order to take into account the new circumstances, the court can increase or decrease[28] the payments under the contract, change the object of the payment, or delay or periodize the performance of the contract. Here, encouragement of the transaction and the nature of the contract are the more important factors.

Should there be a fair distribution of the losses (eg reliance losses) between the parties after the termination of the contract? Or should we let the loss lie where it falls? Should the loss caused by the change of circumstances be divided equally between the parties? We have consensus on the legal nature of the consequences of termination. It is not a remedy for breach of contract, and there is no claim for damages for breach of contract.[29] At most, there is an apportionment of the reliance losses between the parties. Of course, this may be different in the case of some commercial contracts. Article 566 CCC provides a framework for distribution of losses:

(1) After the termination of a contract, obligations shall cease if the contract has not yet been performed; if the contract has been performed, a party may, in accordance with the circumstances of performance or the nature of the contract, request the other party to restore such party to its original state or adopt other remedial measures, and such party shall have the right to demand compensation for losses.
(2) If a contract is terminated due to breach of contract, the party with the right of termination may request the party in breach to bear liability for breach of contract, unless otherwise agreed upon by the parties.[30]

Termination of a contract discharges future primary obligations, but it does not disturb past performance. When the obligation to perform is severable, parts of the contract which have been wholly performed can be severed from the remainder, and they are to be treated

[25] Kötz (n 1) 289.
[26] This is similar to the position under the German Civil Code, s 313(3).
[27] Vogenauer (n 8) 821.
[28] *Chengdu Pengwei Industry Co Ltd v People's Government of Yongxiu County of Jiangxi Province and Office of the Leading Group for the Administration of Sand Mining of Poyang Lake of Yongxiu County* (n 10).
[29] WANG Liming, *Study on Contract Law* (3rd edn, Renmin University Press 2018) 390.
[30] For the source of the translation of the two preceding paragraphs, see Pkulaw Database (n 6).

as separate contracts. If the contract was one where each party had already performed his obligations to an equal degree, then termination does not create difficulties in this respect. If one party has done much more than the other by the time of the change of circumstances, the law of restitution could assist. The party who received more benefit should pay for the benefit or return it.[31] So reasonable restitution is determined by how much of the contract has been performed and by the severability of the performance.

III. Application of the Doctrine of Change of Circumstances: Typological Case Analysis

The case law method and empirical analysis can help to clarify the constitutive requirements and the consequences of applying the doctrine of change of circumstances. In China's civil judicial practice, the doctrine of change of circumstances is commonly applied to matters such as adjustment of government policies, drastic changes in socio-economic circumstances, and soaring prices. Whether a matter amounts to a relevant change of circumstances or is merely a commercial risk depends on the contractual agreement and the dynamic balancing of interests from the perspectives of predictability, responsibility, and consequences. The doctrine of change of circumstances fundamentally deals with the roles of the market and the government in the process of resource allocation. Ultimately, it is the court that does the resource allocation in response to government action.

1. The Impact of Environmental Protection Policies on Contract Performance

The adjustment of environmental protection policies may constitute a change of circumstances. In one case, a contractor requested termination of a contract relating to land for breeding pigs. The people's court agreed because the local government had banned certain breeding upstream of the sources of drinking water. This meant that the purpose of the contract could not be achieved:

> 'The administrative actions of the government are significant changes that cannot be foreseen by the parties when concluding a contract, and the protection of the water source is related to the public interests and the health of the people', 'in the principle of fairness and the purpose of conserving resources and protecting the ecological environment', and therefore the aforementioned contract should be terminated.[32] Here, the basis for the termination of the contract was a change of circumstances. It was necessary to adjust or terminate the contract according to the 'fairness principle'.

In another case, the Changzhou Municipal People's Government adjusted the policies of energy conservation and emission reduction according to the requirements of the Jiangsu

[31] Cartwright (n 9) 257–60.
[32] Civil Judgment No 946, No 194, e11, Intermediate People's Court of Huanggang City, Hubei Province.

Provincial People's Government's Opinions on Further Strengthening Pollutant Emission Reduction Work, which required Xindong Company's power plant to dismantle coal-fired boilers by the end of June 2012. Thus, significant changes in the objective circumstances made Xindong's original desulfurization project for coal-fired boilers meaningless; the purpose of the contract could not be achieved. This change was unforeseen by the parties, and it was not part of ordinary business risk. Although contract law and the relevant judicial interpretations do not clearly stipulate that changes to government policies amount to a change of circumstances, if the changes mean that the contract cannot be performed or the purpose of the contract cannot be achieved, then they should be considered to fall under the doctrine of change of circumstances incorporated (at the time) in Article 26 of Interpretation II. Xindong Company claimed that its contract termination was not a breach of contract but the result of a change of circumstances, which had sufficient factual and legal bases in this case. The court agreed.[33] In this case, we find that the doctrine of change of circumstances played a defensive role, making it such that one party was not in breach because his obligation had already been discharged.

Can stoppages relating to environmental protection constitute *force majeure*? In one case, the defendant, a real estate company, insisted that it was not liable for the delayed performance of a contract to construct a house, work on which was stopped by government policies due to heavy air pollution. The court did not support this argument. The court of first instance held that, based on the 'green principle', the defendant should pay full attention to the relationship between seasonal climate rules and construction and anticipate relevant policies and stoppage risks. The court of second instance pointed out that the defendant already knew or ought to have known that 'the government has increased the intensity of pollution control in recent years'. Here, the judgment of the court of second instance correctly indicated that a rational person should know of stoppages related to environmental protection, based on the green principle and in light of the facts of government management. Therefore, the defendant could have foreseen the relevant policies and risks, and there was no *force majeure*.[34]

In another leading case, due to unforeseen changes in the natural environment, the purpose of the contract could not be achieved. In performing a sand extraction contract, Pengwei Company encountered a rare low water level which had not been seen for 36 years. This natural disaster made it impossible for sand dredgers to continue their operations in the sand mining lots, and the sand mining therefore ended. As a result, the purposes of the contract were not fulfilled, and huge losses were incurred by Pengwei Company. This objective change of situation was unforeseeable to Pengwei Company and the Sand Mining Office when the contract was concluded, and Pengwei Company's losses were not caused by a commercial risk. If performance of the contract had been continued, the balance of interests between the parties would have been obviously unfair, and the doctrine of change of circumstances could therefore be applied.[35]

[33] *Changzhou Xindong Chemical Development Co Ltd v Jiangsu Zhengtong Hongtai Co Ltd*, Supreme People's Court (2015) Mintizi No 39 (dispute about a construction contract and technology entrustment development).

[34] Civil Judgment of Zhengzhou Intermediate People's Court of Henan Province (2018) Yu 01 Min Zhong 7987. Quoted from HE Jian, 'Green Principles and Law and Economics' (2019) 2 Chinese Law 117.

[35] *Chengdu Pengwei Industry Co Ltd v People's Government of Yongxiu County of Jiangxi Province and Office of the Leading Group for the Administration of Sand Mining of Poyang Lake of Yongxiu County* (n 10).

2. The Impact of a Soaring 'State Price' on Contract Performance

The doctrine of change of circumstances may be applied to soaring contract prices during contract performance. In a contract for the supply of parts for gas meters, the price of aluminium ingots, the main raw material for the production of such parts, increased during the contract due to a change of circumstances that was unforeseen by the parties. When the contract was concluded, the state price of aluminium ingots was Chinese yuan (CNY) 4,400–4,600 per ton. Subsequently, it increased to CNY16,000 per ton, and the price of the aluminium was raised from CNY23.085 to CNY41. If the instrument factory had still been required to supply parts for gas meters according to the original contract, it would obviously have been unfair, and such disputes should be dealt with fairly and reasonably by applying the doctrine of change of circumstances.[36] Of course, whether it is obviously unfair to continue to perform the contract not only depends on a comparison of the price at the time of the contract with the price at the time of performance but also on whether the contract price fluctuation was foreseeable when the parties concluded the contract. The primary cause of the change of circumstances in this case was the rare situation of a soaring 'state price', which was an unforeseen policy risk and not an increase in the usual market price, which would be a business risk.

In a dispute over a purchase contract, Xinlong Company had stated its intention to purchase wind turbines at a comprehensive cost of CNY4,520/kw. The alleged unforeseen risk was the wind turbine price crash after the conclusion of the contract. However, Xinlong Company knew the actual rather than the desired contract price at the time of contracting so that there was no unforeseen situation. If Xinlong Company continued to perform the contract, it would not increase the performance cost expected at the time of conclusion of the contract. The fact that it was possible to obtain the subject matter of the contract from other sources for a lower price after the time of the contract did not mean that it could breach the contract and disturb the normal order of the transaction, so there was no obvious unfairness in this case. As a merchant in the market, Xinlong Company should have predicted that the price of wind turbines would fluctuate and affect the interests of the parties as a normal phenomenon of the market. Xinlong Company was an entity specializing in wind power generation and should have been able to foresee and value the price fluctuation to some extent and assume the corresponding business risks.[37]

3. The Impact of New Policies in the Housing Market on Contract Performance

The implementation of new real estate policies in the housing market may constitute a relevant change of circumstances. The main challenge in cases related to new real estate policies in trial practice is to determine the legal effect of such new policies on sales contracts for houses.

There are cases where sellers do not want to perform their house sales contracts, for example, when housing prices have risen sharply. The exact details of an increase of housing

[36] *Wuhan Gas Company v Chongqing Instrument Factory* (n 3).

[37] *Shenzhen Wind Power Technology (Group) Co Ltd v Wuyuan Xinlong Shunde Wind Power Co Ltd* (2015) Supreme People's Court Min Er Zhong Zi No 88 (trading contract dispute).

prices may be beyond the foresight of the parties, but such a rise is still a normal business or commercial risk. Therefore, there is no sufficient legal basis for adjusting the transaction price on the grounds that housing prices have risen sharply and that it would be unfair to require performance of the contract. The fact that housing prices have risen sharply does not amount to a change of circumstances. Therefore, the seller has no legal basis for requesting adjustment of the transaction price. If the seller sells the house to another buyer for a higher price and effects the change of registration, the original buyer has the right to request the seller to compensate him for the loss of his interest in the rise in value of the house, and the seller cannot actually obtain the gain from the increase in the price of the house.

4. The Impact of Other Significant Changes on Contract Performance

In judicial practice, it is strictly forbidden in contracts for construction projects to provide that the contractor bears any and all risks. Adjustments to the overall planning of the construction area by the government may constitute a change of circumstances or *force majeure*. Other illustrations of potentially relevant changes of circumstances in various different contexts include: abnormal fluctuation of the price of construction materials, the Severe Acute Respiratory Syndrome (SARS) outbreak, the COVID-19 pandemic and related prevention and control measures, financial crises, prohibition of profit-making by the military (to stop the military's external paid services by Notice of the Central Military Commission), earthquakes, rare natural environmental changes (such as the water level of Poyang Lake having dropped too low because of a natural disaster so that it was difficult to transport sand carriers to the mining area, which in turn affected the realization of the right to sand mining), and other significant or fundamental changes in circumstances. There may also be interactions between the various causes of change of circumstances, such as the 'soaring prices of building materials' being caused by 'environmental shutdown orders from the government'.

As to obstacles to the fulfilment of contracts caused by the COVID-19 pandemic and related prevention and control measures, the relevant applicable legal principles are the rules of *force majeure*, the doctrine of change of circumstances, and the possibility of statutory rescission. These principle always must be analysed systematically.[38] The Supreme People's Court of China issued three Guiding Opinions on Several Issues of Properly Hearing Civil Cases concerning the COVID-19 pandemic. The main judicial positions are as follows.

When applying laws for contractual disputes directly caused by the pandemic or pandemic prevention and control measures, the people's courts shall handle the disputes by taking into full consideration the impact of the pandemic on different regions, industries, and cases; the causal relationship between the pandemic or pandemic prevention and control measures and the failure to perform the contract; and their causative potency. A party that fails to perform a contract due to the pandemic or pandemic prevention and control measures shall, subject to the provisions on *force majeure*, be partially or wholly exempted from liability according to the degree of impact of the pandemic or pandemic prevention and control measures. If a party finds it difficult to perform a contract due to the pandemic

[38] WANG Lei, 'Measures for Prevention and Control of the COVID-19 Pneumonia Pandemic Provided by Civil and Commercial Law' (2020) 3 Journal of Southwest University of Political Science & Law 45–58. WANG Yi, 'COVID-19 Pneumonia Pandemic, Force Majeure and Change of Circumstances' (2020) 3 Law Science 36–48.

or pandemic prevention and control measures, the parties concerned may renegotiate the contract. If continuing performance of the contract makes it obviously unfair to one party, and the party requests to change the performance period, performance method, or price of the contract, the people's court shall, based on actual conditions of the case, decide whether to support such a request. If a party requests to dissolve the contract because the purpose of the contract cannot be achieved, the people's court shall support such a request.

On 21 November 2018, the 'The Great Show' by Dolce & Gabbana (D&G) suddenly became a trending topic because the D&G designers and executives were accused of insulting China and Chinese people. At the rehearsal of 'The Great Show' held by the world's top-line luxury brand in Shanghai, the Chinese team of models was the first to announce its refusal to appear at the show. A group of invited stars including Chen Kun, Zhang Ziyi, and Wang Junkai all successively proclaimed that they would not attend 'The Great Show'. As a result, the event, which was originally to be held at 8 pm on 21 November 2018 at the Shanghai World Expo Center, had to be cancelled. Subsequently, D&G was boycotted by a great many Chinese people, from a large number of stars to thousands of netizens. From the perspective of contract law, the D&G designers had engaged in the serious behaviour of insulting China, which was a significant change, unforeseen at the time of contracting and not a business risk. Chinese domestic actors terminated their endorsement contracts based on change of circumstances. Every contract is based on the parties' assumption that the circumstances under which it is concluded will not change too much. If the basic conditions of the endorsement contracts change significantly, insisting on strict adherence to the contracts and requiring Chinese actors to continue performance of the endorsement contracts is obviously unfair to them, and according to general life experience, would seriously damage their good image in the minds of their audiences.

On 11 August 2019, Versace listed Hong Kong and Macau as independent countries on the back of some of its T-shirts. Soon afterwards, large numbers of the world's top-line luxury brands like Givenchy, Coach, and Valentino were exposed for similar conduct. Famous actors like Yang Mi, Liu Wen, Guan Xiaotong, and Jackson Yee quickly made statements to terminate their endorsement contracts with these luxury brands one after another. Some commentators worried about the extortionate damages that may be claimed against these actors. The author is of the view that their obligations were discharged because of the application of the doctrine of change of circumstances. So there was no right to claim damages. Further, the author feels that only the actors can invoke termination in such circumstances, but the luxury brands cannot do so.

IV. The Special Relationship between New Real Estate Regulatory Policies and Change of Circumstances

Under the policies of property purchase limits (legal capacity to buy commodity houses in cities) and maximum loan limits (housing mortgage loan), the phenomenon of 'demanding refunds from developers' appeared in many cities across China. This must be analysed in terms of a change of circumstances. New real estate regulatory policies constitute a change of circumstances rather than *force majeure*.

According to Article 2 of the Opinions on the Cases of Housing Purchase Contract Disputes Affected by the Market Regulation Policy (Trial) implemented on 21 April 2011 by the Zhejiang Higher People's Court, due to the direct influence of regulatory policies such as maximum loans, property purchase limits, and property purchase bans, performance of the abovementioned contracts for the purchase of commodity houses became impossible. Such policies should be considered 'circumstances for which the parties cannot be held responsible'. The parties' request to terminate the contract may be supported by the people's court unless the parties have come to a special agreement.

According to Article 6 of the Opinions by the Zhejiang Higher People's Court, if it is indeed impossible to perform the contract concluded before the implementation of the control policy due to the subsequent property purchase limits or prohibition, the parties may request the termination of the contract, and the seller should return the purchase price or the deposit to the buyer. If the seller sues or brings a counterclaim against the buyer for the buyer to perform the contract, or to assume liability for breach of contract, or fails to return the deposit to the buyer, it is not supported by the people's court; but if the seller requests the buyer to bear the reasonable expenses for the contract, it may be supported appropriately by the people's court.

New real estate regulatory policies which constitute a change of circumstances may also affect the relevant intermediation contract. This would occur when a contract for the purchase of real estate was facilitated by a broker under an intermediation contract, and the purchase contract is subsequently terminated because of a change of circumstances. What then happens to the relevant intermediation contract?

On one hand, in respect of the necessary expenses actually incurred in intermediation activities, Article 964 CCC states: 'Where the middleman fails to cause the conclusion of the contract, he will have no claim for the remuneration. However, he may, in accordance with the contract, seek payment by the principal of necessary expenses incurred for intermediary activities.' According to the interpretative method used in civil law (ie *argumentum a fortiori*), Article 964 CCC stipulates that when a middleman fails to facilitate the establishment of contracts, he can request clients to pay the necessary expenses actually incurred. When a contract for the purchase of real estate is terminated due to the influence of regulatory policy, the contract has nonetheless been established, and it is appropriate and without question that the middleman has the right to request payment of the necessary expenses actually incurred.

On the other hand, in terms of remuneration for intermediation, Article 963 CCC states: 'Where a middleman contributes to the conclusion of a contract, the client shall pay remuneration in accordance with the agreement.' This must be read together with Article 964, set out above, which stipulates: 'Where the middleman fails to cause the conclusion of the contract, he will have no claim for the remuneration.' Where a contract for the purchase of real estate is terminated due to the influence of regulatory policy, it is not clear from the text of the legislation whether Article 963 CCC would cover this situation. The author thinks that it does not. If the client was still required to pay remuneration according to the strict method of interpretation, the balance of interests would be broken. Although a contract for the purchase of real estate has been established, it has nonetheless been terminated afterwards. The expected contractual purposes of the parties could not be fulfilled. The middleman's right to claim compensation should be supported to an appropriate extent rather than requiring payment in full. It can be seen that the principle of contractual fairness and the balance of interests should be used to provide a purposive, narrower interpretation of Article 963(1) CCC. The scope of application of that paragraph should be limited to the establishment of the contract by the middleman; it cannot include the circumstances in which the contract is terminated due to matters that cannot be attributed to either of the parties.

V. The Hypotheticals

In this section, I analyse the hypothetical problems posed by the editors by applying the relevant provisions of the CCC.[39]

1. Abraham and Bill

In 1567, Abraham enters into a contract for an unlimited period of time with farmer Bill under which Abraham promises to build and maintain an irrigation channel from which Bill may extract water at a fixed price. By 2018, inflation and the rise in the cost of maintenance and labour have made the price wholly inadequate. Abraham's successors in law ask for an increase in the price that would provide them with adequate compensation. Alternatively, they wish to terminate the contract.

According to Article 563 CCC, a contract requiring continuous performance of an obligation for an indefinite period of time may be terminated by a party at any time, provided that the other party is notified within a reasonable time. Therefore, Abraham's successors in law have the right to terminate the contract by giving reasonable notice.

2. Citi Corporation and Drive Bank

In 2015, Citi Corporation receives a loan from Drive Bank. The interest rate is fixed at 10 per cent for five years. In the 20 years preceding the agreement, the rate of inflation had been relatively stable within a range of 1 to 6 per cent. In 2017, the economic situation begins to destabilize, and inflation rises to 50 per cent. Drive Bank requests adjustment or, alternatively, termination of the contract.

The soaring rate of inflation can be regarded to be in the nature of a financial crisis. It is not a commercial risk and was not expected by the parties at the time of the contract. Under Article 533 CCC, as Drive Bank is adversely affected so that continuing performance of its contractual obligations under these changed circumstances would be obviously unfair, it has the right to request the people's court or arbitration institution to adjust the interest rate or to terminate the contract.

3. Easy and Frugle

Easy leases business premises from Frugle for a fixed period of 15 years. Shortly after the contract has been concluded, a nearby military airport is unexpectedly shut down for

[39] The fact scenarios for the hypotheticals in this section are taken from M Chen-Wishart, D Neo, and S Vogenauer, 'Introduction', ch 1 in this volume, 7–8.

political reasons. The government invests an enormous amount of public funds in order to improve the commercial infrastructure in the area. As a result, Easy's profits are 500 per cent of what could reasonably have been expected at the time of making the contract. At the same time, the rental value of comparable business premises in the area rises to 500 per cent of the agreed rental price. Frugle requests that the rental price should be adjusted accordingly or, alternatively, that the agreement should be terminated.

The closure of the military airport and the enormous investment by the government constitute a change of circumstances which couldn't be anticipated by Easy or Frugle at the time of the contract. It would be unfair to require Frugle to continue with the agreed rent under the original contract. Easy's unexpected good fortune needs to be shared with Frugle. Given Easy's 500 per cent increase in profits and the 500 per cent increase in the rental value of comparable business premises, Frugle could have also enjoyed a higher rent on his premises. What should be increased but is not would amount to a loss. According to Article 533 CCC, Frugle has the right to require the people's court or arbitration institution to increase the rental price or terminate the contract.

4. George and Han

Builder George agrees to refurbish the cellar of Han, the owner of a restaurant. The work is scheduled to start one month after the agreement. Before the work begins, the restaurant is completely destroyed by a storm that is much more violent than any other previous storm in the region. However, the cellar remains fully intact. Han immediately informs George of the situation and asks him not to start work. George insists on rendering performance because he has set aside two weeks to carry out the work and has already purchased the necessary materials. Is Han required to pay the contract price or, alternatively, to compensate George for his loss?

The violent unprecedented storm constitutes *force majeure*, which has made it impossible to achieve the purpose of the cellar refurbishment contract. According to Article 563 CCC, Han has the right to terminate the contract and is not required to pay the contract price. But Han should compensate George for his partial loss in accordance with the principle of fairness. It would be unfair for George to fully bear the unfortunate and unexpected consequences.

5. Gina and H Hotel

Gina books a room for the weekend at H Hotel in X City, the capital of country Z. However,

(i) the exhibition she intended to visit is cancelled at the very last moment;
(ii) a terrorist group declares that it plans to launch attacks on tourists in X;
(iii) an unforeseeable strike by airport personnel prevents Gina from travelling to X before Sunday afternoon;
(iv) the inauguration proceedings of the new head of state of Z that were scheduled for Saturday are cancelled. Gina had booked a room overlooking the street where

the inauguration procession was supposed to pass by. Due to the inauguration, the rental price of the room was ten times higher than the regular price.

Can Gina cancel the booking?

Situations (ii) and (iii) constitute a change of circumstances under Article 533 CCC, and applying that article, it would be unfair to require Gina to continue with the contract in those situations. Gina can therefore cancel the bookings. Whether situations (i) and (iv) would constitute a change of circumstances under Article 533 depends on the significance of the exhibition and the inauguration, based on the standard of a reasonable person. I am of the view that situation (iv) would constitute a change of circumstances under Article 533 but situation (i) would not. This is because in situation (i), visiting the exhibition was only Gina's individual purpose for contracting. However, in situation (iv), the inauguration ceremony was a grand festival in X City, and the rental of the room to watch the inauguration procession was not just Gina's individual purpose. Cancellation of the inauguration was out of a reasonable person's expectation.

6. Kris and Leila

Kris sells his family home to Leila at 70 per cent of its market value. Both parties assume that Leila will dedicate it to cultural use by the general public. However, this assumption is not expressly set out in the contract. After the sale, Leila changes her mind and gives the house to one of her sons instead. Can Kris claim the difference between the agreed price and the market value or, alternatively, restitution of the house?

The contract cannot be rescinded under Article 563 CCC because cultural use is not expressly stated as the purpose of the contract. Kris therefore cannot claim the difference between the agreed price and the market value or, alternatively, restitution of the house.

VI. Conclusion

Strict adherence to the contract is fundamentally important to the principle of contractual freedom. The doctrine of change of circumstances is a manifestation of good faith that balances the interests of the contracting parties. The doctrine of change of circumstances was developed from scratch in China, through landmark cases, judicial interpretations of special types of contracts (eg contracts for the sale of commodity houses), judicial interpretations of all types of contracts, and the legislative provisions of the CCC. Being an exception to the principle of abiding by the contract, the doctrine of change of circumstances should be narrowly applied.

In order to understand the operation of the doctrine of change of circumstances, two separate questions must be answered: first, what constitutes a relevant change of circumstances that would justify the application of the doctrine; and secondly, what are the consequences when the doctrine of change of circumstances applies? The assessment of whether the doctrine of change of circumstances applies should be carried out by a dynamic balancing of factors. The doctrine of change of circumstances in the CCC unites *force majeure* and a change of circumstances. Article 533 CCC stipulates that upon a change of circumstances, the adversely affected party cannot automatically withdraw or escape from the contract. Instead, the contract should be renegotiated, modified, or terminated. This means that *force majeure* no longer inevitably causes the failure of the transaction but, through a rebalancing of the interests of the parties, may make the transaction 'return to life'. This gives *force majeure* a new function of supporting transactions.

In general, situations and the attendant risks are rapidly changing in modern societies. Chinese society finds itself in a period of transitional change. In China's civil judicial practice, many disputes about change of circumstances are caused by adjustments of government policies. The doctrine of change of circumstances is a mechanism for the sharing of uncontrollable risks, and its application can deal at a fundamental level with the roles of the market and the government in the process of resource allocation.

The encouragement of transactions is a fundamental principle and can be said to be the basis of the unity model of change of circumstances and *force majeure*, the strict constitutive requirements of change of circumstances, and the preference for modification over termination of the contract. The dynamic balancing of factors is the test used by Chinese courts to distinguish between relevant and irrelevant changes of circumstances. The dynamic balancing of factors is very similar to the 'multifactorial approach' in common law, both of which belong to the case law method and indicate the direction in which the law relating to change of circumstances is likely to develop.

4

Termination of Contract in Chinese Law

Lei CHEN and Zhicheng WU

I. Introduction

A contract can be terminated in several ways. First, it will come to an end when the contract has been fully performed by the parties (discharge by performance). Secondly, where there has been a sufficiently serious breach of contract by one party, the party not in breach (the 'innocent party') may choose to terminate the contract (termination by breach). Finally, a contract that has not been fully performed can be terminated by consent. Chinese law incorporates two types of termination by consent in the Chinese Civil Code (CCC).[1] The first type is where the parties reach a consensus to bring an existing contract to an end (consensual termination by a new agreement). The second type is where the requirements for termination set out in the contract are fulfilled, and the innocent party exercises the right of termination according to the contract terms (consensual termination according to a prior clause). The focus of this chapter will be on termination by breach and termination by consent.

While every breach of contract gives rise to a right to claim damages for the loss suffered by the innocent party, not every breach of contract entitles the innocent party to terminate the contract. The innocent party can either affirm the contract or terminate it. Under Chinese law, whether the innocent party can terminate the contract depends largely on the consequences of the breach. Where the consequences of the breach are sufficiently serious, amounting to the non-fulfilment of the contract purpose, the courts will allow termination at the request of the innocent party.[2] Conversely, where the consequences of the breach are not serious, the court will not grant termination, and the innocent party will be confined to a remedy in damages.

Chinese law generally places a considerable premium on judicial supervision of the right to terminate. For example, even where the parties agree that the buyer can terminate the contract if there is a delayed performance by the seller, the contract may not be necessarily discharged when there is a delayed performance. The court has the discretion whether to terminate the contract at the buyer's request. The test is whether such a delayed performance is a fundamental breach, thus leading to the non-fulfilment of the contractual purpose. In practice, Chinese courts often resort to two general principles to curtail discharge by agreement, namely, the principles of good faith[3] and prohibition of abuse of rights.[4] This will be examined in detail when discussing the hypotheticals in section VII.

[1] Chinese Civil Code, art 562.
[2] Chinese Civil Code, art 563(1) item 4.
[3] Chinese Civil Code, art 7.
[4] Chinese Civil Code, art 132.

Lei Chen and Zhicheng Wu, *Termination of Contract in Chinese Law* In: *Studies in the Contract Laws of Asia V: Ending and Changing Contracts*. Edited by: Mindy Chen-Wishart, Dora Neo, and Stefan Vogenauer, Oxford University Press.
 DOI: 10.1093/oso/9780198995814.003.0004

Many provisions of the CCC governing contract termination were modelled on the United Nations Convention on Contracts for the International Sale of Goods (CISG), the Principles of International Commercial Contracts (PICC), and European continental civil codes.[5] Further, many doctrines in Chinese law will be familiar to Western jurists, such as good faith, change of circumstances, and prohibition of abuse of rights. Nonetheless, it is necessary to examine how these transplanted doctrines have been shaped in practice by Chinese values. One way to examine this is through the lens of how Chinese courts prioritize conflicting norms, for example, whether to enforce an agreed termination provision in a contract or to limit party autonomy by reference to principles of good faith and fairness. The following discussion will begin by introducing the sources of law and the types of contract termination. Subsequently, the exercise, extinction, and consequences of a right of termination will be discussed. Next, the Chinese law position will be elaborated on through addressing the hypotheticals. Finally, a conclusion will be provided.

II. Sources of Law

1. Chinese Civil Code

There is no general part in the CCC governing the law of obligations. The Book on Contracts forms the most sizable book of the CCC, containing 526 articles (Articles 463–988) which make up more than 40 per cent of the total 1,260 articles in the Code.[6] General rules of contractual termination lie in Part 1 ('General Rules') of Book 3 ('Book on Contracts') of the CCC, specifically, Articles 557 and 562–567 of Chapter 7 ('The coming to an end of contractual rights and duties'). Article 557 confirms that termination is an incident of the coming to an end of a contractual relationship. Article 562 governs termination by consent (either by agreement or under a prior clause), Article 563 governs termination by operation of law, Article 564 governs the duration of the right of termination, Article 565 governs the methods of exercising the right of termination, and Articles 566 and 567 govern the consequences of termination. Provisions in other chapters are also relevant. Article 528 connects the right to withhold performance and the right of termination. Article 533 deals with the relationship between change of circumstances and termination. Article 580 covers court-ordered termination where specific performance shall not be awarded.

Part 1 of the Book on Contracts provides general rules of contract law which are, in principle, applicable to all types of contracts. Part 2 of the Book on Contracts lays down rules of 19 nominate contracts. Rules of termination are expressly stated in the contract of sale,[7] contract of loan,[8] contract of lease,[9] contract of financial lease,[10] contract for work,[11]

[5] L Chen and LA DiMatteo, 'History of Chinese Contract Law' in LA DiMatteo and L Chen (eds), *Chinese Contract Law: Civil Law and Common Law Perspectives* (CUP 2017) 3–28.

[6] L Chen, 'Continuity and Change: Some Reflections on the Chinese Civil Code' (2021) 29 Asia Pacific Law Review 287.

[7] Chinese Civil Code, arts 597, 610, 631–634.

[8] Chinese Civil Code, art 673.

[9] Chinese Civil Code, arts 711,716, 722, 724, 729–731.

[10] Chinese Civil Code, arts 752–756, 758.

[11] Chinese Civil Code, arts 772, 778, 787.

construction contract,[12] technology contract,[13] mandate contract,[14] contract for property service,[15] and partnership contract.[16] One can also find rules of contractual termination outside the Book on Contracts, in the Books on General Provisions,[17] Property Rights,[18] and Personality Rights.[19]

2. Other Statutes

Special rules on contractual termination can also be found in statutes other than the CCC. The Trust Law 2001 states the scenarios where the beneficiary and the settlor may terminate the trust.[20] The Enterprise Bankruptcy Law 2006 empowers the insolvency office-holder to terminate the insolvent company's executory contracts.[21] The Insurance Law 2015 contains many provisions involving contractual termination in various contexts.[22] Similarly, the Labour Law 2018[23] and the Tourism Law 2018[24] have such provisions. When land is involved, contractual termination of a contract to grant usufructuary rights is expressly mentioned in the Rural Land Contract Law 2018[25] and the Urban Real Estate Administration Law 2019.[26]

Although there are specific termination provisions relating to nominate contracts or contained in other statutes, the CCC is the only place in Chinese law that systematically sets out the law of contractual termination. The following sections will therefore focus predominantly on the provisions of the Code, in particular those in Part 1 of the Book on Contracts.

III. Termination by Consent

Article 562 CCC contains two paragraphs dealing with contract termination by consent of the parties. Paragraph 1 states: 'The parties may terminate a contract if they reach a consensus through negotiation.' Paragraph 2 states: 'The parties may agree upon the cause for contractual termination by one party. When the cause occurs, the party holding the right of termination may terminate the contract.' While both paragraphs refer to consensual termination, the core difference between the two is that the former does not involve any right of termination whereas the latter does.

12 Chinese Civil Code, art 806.
13 Chinese Civil Code, art 857.
14 Chinese Civil Code, arts 928, 933.
15 Chinese Civil Code, arts 940, 946, 948.
16 Chinese Civil Code, arts 976–978.
17 Chinese Civil Code, arts 136, 199.
18 Chinese Civil Code, art 384.
19 Chinese Civil Code, art 1022.
20 Trust Law 2001, arts 50–51.
21 Enterprise Bankruptcy Law 2006, art 18.
22 Insurance Law (2015 Amendment) arts 15, 16, 27, 32, 37, 47, 50–54, 58.
23 Labour Law (2018 Amendment) arts 24–32.
24 Tourism Law (2018 Amendment) arts 63, 65–68.
25 Rural Land Contract Law (2018 Amendment) arts 25, 26, 42, 64.
26 Urban Real Estate Administration Law (2019 Amendment) arts 16, 17.

1. Consensual Termination by a New Agreement

Article 562(1) is quite plain. Two points should be addressed here. First, not all types of contracts can be terminated by agreement. A contract that is void *ab initio* has no binding effect, and therefore there is no contractual relationship to terminate. In contrast, a contract that is voidable but not yet rescinded can be terminated because a legal relationship exists before rescission.[27] The same logic applies to the case of a contract whose validity is pending, also known as an 'effect-to-be-determined contract',[28] exemplified by a contract entered into by a party with limited capacity.[29] This type of contract is not valid until it is ratified. While the Code states that such a contract cannot be unilaterally terminated,[30] it does not forbid termination by agreement during the period validity is pending. Secondly, termination does not necessarily eliminate any and all liability for breach of contract. Thus, where parties have reached a consensus to end the contract but do not make clear their intentions about whether any pre-existing breach of contract would be waived, the default position taken by the Supreme People's Court (SPC) is that the contract breaker cannot raise the counterparty's agreement to terminate the contract as a defence in an action of breach of contract.[31]

2. Consensual Termination Pursuant to a Contractual Clause

Article 562(2) CCC states that parties can include a clause in the contract stipulating permissible causes of termination. Such causes can include a party's act of breach as well as an objective event not attributable to any party. The list of causes stipulated in the contract may be fine-tuned to balance the parties' interests and may be different from the list of causes triggering the right of termination by operation of law as articulated in Article 563 CCC.[32]

The most crucial point here is the judicial approach regarding the binding effect of termination clauses. Must a court support the aggrieved party's exercise of the right to terminate as long as a cause for termination stipulated in the contract is satisfied? The answer seems to be in the affirmative based on a textual interpretation of the Code. However, the SPC expressed a different view in a milestone Trial Minute[33] in 2019 saying that the court

[27] YAO Mingbin, 'Normative Structure of Consensual Rescission of Contract' [2021] 1 Chinese Journal of Law 71 [姚明斌：《基于合意解除合同的规范构造》，《法学研究》2021年第1期].

[28] H Jiang, 'The Making of a Civil Code in China: Promises and Perils of a New Civil Law' (2021) 95 Tulane Law Review 777.

[29] Chinese Civil Code, art 145.

[30] Chinese Civil Code, art 136(2).

[31] Enforcement of the Civil Code Group of the Supreme People's Court (ed), *Understanding and Applying the Book on Contracts of the Chinese Civil Code, vol 1* (People's Court Press 2020) 633 [最高人民法院民法典贯彻实施工作领导小组主编：《中华人民共和国民法典合同编理解与适用（一）》，人民法院出版社2020年版，第633页].

[32] WANG Liming (ed), *Commentaries of the Chinese Civil Code: Book on Contracts: General Rules* (Renmin UP 2020) 470 [王利明主编:《中国民法典释评·合同编·通则》,中国人民大学出版社2020年版,第470页].

[33] *Minutes of Civil and Commercial Trials for All Courts Nationwide* (Supreme Court Issuance No 254, 2019). A Trial Minute is an official document issued by Chinese courts after an internal formal conference containing a set of judge-made rules articulated in a detailed way to interpret relevant legislation. A Minute issued by the Chinese Supreme Court somewhat resembles a Judicial Interpretation, though the right of issuance of the former is not limited to the Supreme Court but applies to lower courts as well. A Supreme Court Minute is generally regarded as less binding in judicial practice compared to a Judicial Interpretation.

shall not automatically support the aggrieved party's claim to terminate the contract pursuant to a contractually stipulated ground of termination. Rather, the court ought to follow the principle of good faith to determine the seriousness of the breach and the effect of the breach on the aggrieved party's purpose in making the contract. If the breach is obviously minor and does not negatively affect the aggrieved party's realization of the purpose of the contract, then the court ought not to support the aggrieved party's termination claim, even if the contractually stipulated event of termination is satisfied.[34]

IV. Termination by Operation of Law

There are two sets of rules for contractual termination by operation of law in China. The first provides a right of termination exercisable by the aggrieved party, hence named 'statutory right of termination'. The second provides a mechanism under which a party may apply to a court for the exercise of its discretion to terminate the contract, hence named 'court-ordered termination'.

1. Statutory Right of Termination

(a) Comparative overview

The core provision on the statutory right of termination by operation of law is Article 563, which provides:

> The parties to a contract may terminate the contract under any of the following circumstances:
> (1) where it is rendered impossible to achieve the purpose of the contract due to an event of *force majeure*;
> (2) where prior to the expiry date of performance, the other party expressly states, or indicates through its conduct, that it will not perform its principal obligation;
> (3) where the other party delays performance of its principal obligation, and fails to perform within a reasonable period after the demand;
> (4) where it is rendered impossible to achieve the purpose of a contract due to the delayed performance of the obligations or other breach of contract by the other party;
> (5) other circumstances as provided by law.
> A contract requiring the successive performance of the obligations without a term may be terminated by a party at any time, provided that the other party is notified within a reasonable period.[35]

One may find placing Chinese law in the comparative spectrum somewhat difficult. Leaving aside the ground of anticipatory breach there are two main approaches regarding grounds

[34] *Minutes of Civil and Commercial Trials for All Courts Nationwide* (Supreme Court Issuance No 254, 2019) art 47.
[35] For an English translation of the CCC, see L Chen and others (eds), *The Civil Code of the People's Republic of China: English Translation* (Brill 2021) <https://doi.org/10.1163/9789004468283>.

of termination in comparative law. One is the fundamental non-performance approach, which gives the aggrieved party a right of immediate termination. The other is the concept of *Nachfrist*, which gives the aggrieved party a right of termination after a demand to remediate a breach followed by the lapse of a reasonable time, no matter whether the breach is fundamental or not.[36] Article 563 CCC takes a mixed approach in the sense that (i) it adds a consequentialist limit to the fundamental breach approach,[37] by requiring a 'failure to achieve the purpose of the contract' (roughly equivalent to frustration of purpose) in items 1 and 4, and (ii) it adds the nature of the term breached to the ground of *Nachfrist* in item 3 by stating that *Nachfrist* is only applicable to the breach of a principal obligation and not generally applicable to all types of obligations, a position also recognized in judicial practice.[38]

(b) Frustration of purpose

To understand item 1, the core constituent element is that it is 'impossible to achieve the purpose of the contract'. While this must be 'due to an event of *force majeure*', *force majeure* itself is not determinative. Impediments to performance caused by *force majeure* may trigger a number of consequences. These include not only termination of contract[39] but also exemption of liability for breach,[40] suspension of limitation periods,[41] passing of risk,[42] and change of circumstances.[43] It follows that where a non-performance due to *force majeure* does not hinder the realization of the purpose of the contract, parties cannot rely on this event to terminate the contract.[44] The predominant view is that the right of termination in this scenario arises in relation to all types of non-performance, including non-delivery, delay, or defective performance.

The second part of item 4 further clarifies the pivotal role of frustration of purpose in that where the factor making it impossible to realize the purpose of the contract is not a *force majeure* event but a party's act of breach, the right of immediate termination arises, regardless of the type of term or the nature of duty breached.[45]

(c) Anticipatory breach

To constitute an anticipatory breach triggering a right to terminate, the duty breached must be a principal one. Anticipatory breach takes two forms: where the contract-breaker (i) expressly repudiates performance before the obligation becomes due or (ii) impliedly

[36] J Kleinschmidt, 'Art 9:301: Right to Terminate the Contract' in N Jansen and R Zimmermann (eds), *Commentaries on European Contract Laws* (OUP 2018) 1295–300.

[37] While the term 'fundamental breach' is not expressly stated in art 563, it is nevertheless widely adopted among Chinese academics and practitioners: *Tianjin Boyue Technology Development Ltd v Tianjin Zhicheng Zhongda Technology Ltd* [2021] Tianjin City High People's Court, JMZ No 772.

[38] *Qinyang City Supply and Marketing Cooperatives v Qinyang City Yubei Resource Recycling Ltd* [2021] Henan Province Jiaozuo City Intermediate People's Court, Y08MZ No 3863.

[39] *Ma Zhaolun v Henan Yousi Education Consulting Ltd* [2021] Henan Province High People's Court, YZMZ No 714.

[40] Chinese Civil Code, art 590.

[41] Chinese Civil Code, art 194.

[42] Chinese Civil Code, art 832.

[43] Chinese Civil Code, art 533.

[44] *Zhang Li v Li Guohui* [2022] Guangdong Province Shaoguan City Intermediate People's Court, Y02MZ No 2240.

[45] See generally ZHAO Wenjie, 'A Commentary on Article 94 of Contract Law (Termination)' [2019] 4 The Jurist 175 [赵文杰：《合同法第94条（法定解除）评注》，《法学家》2019年第4期].

repudiates by its conduct, conveying the message that it will not perform when the obligation becomes due.

In practice, it is easy for a judge to find repudiation if a party expressly manifests the intent not to or no longer to perform to the counterparty.[46] The difficult question is how to ascertain implied repudiation. While cases of repudiation implied in fact (ie presumed repudiation) may not always be clear, the CCC lists situations where repudiation is implied in law (ie constructive repudiation). Article 527 gives the party who should perform first a right to withhold performance. It states:

> The party who is required to perform first may suspend its performance if it has conclusive evidence showing that the other party is under any of the following circumstances:
> (1) where its business operations have seriously deteriorated;
> (2) where it has engaged in the transfer of assets or withdrawal of funds for the purpose of evading debts;
> (3) where it has lost its business creditworthiness;
> (4) where there is any other circumstance which causes or may cause it to lose its ability to perform.
> Where a party suspends performance without conclusive evidence, it shall be liable for breach of contract.

This provision is followed by Article 528, which states:

> If a party suspends its performance in accordance with the aforementioned provision, it shall promptly notify the other party. If the other party provides appropriate assurance for its performance, the party shall resume performance. After performance was suspended, if the other party fails to regain its ability to perform and fails to provide appropriate assurance within a reasonable period of time, such failure shall be seen as non-performance of its principal obligation, and the suspending party may terminate the contract and demand that the breaching party bear the liability for breach of contract.

From these provisions, one can see the functional connection between the right of termination and the right to withhold performance in the context of anticipatory breach, a position also recognized in judicial practice.[47]

(d) *Nachfrist*

In Chinese law, where there is a delay in the performance of a principal obligation and such delay does not render it impossible to realize the purpose of the contract, *Nachfrist* comes into play; that is, the aggrieved party (usually the creditor) may make a demand to the contract-breaker saying that if proper performance is not provided within a specific period of time, the contract will be terminated.

[46] *PICC Health Insurance Co Ltd v Beijing Hankun Traditional Chinese Medical Treatment Hospital Ltd* [2022] Beijing City No 3 Intermediate People's Court, J03MZ No 6522.

[47] *Jiaxin Zhonghong Machineries Leasing Ltd v Jiaxin Gengyu Commerce Exhibition Ltd* [2023] Zhejiang Province Jiaxin City Intermediate People's Court, Z04MZ No 259.

The demand does not have to take any specific form, though in practice it is often made in writing. To have the effect of *Nachfrist*, the demand must be made after a delayed performance. A demand made as a warning in advance before the due date of the obligation does not count. Such a demand should at least mention the obligation involved, the additional time period given for performance, and the consequence of failing to perform in time (ie contractual termination). The additional time period given must be reasonable, and this is a matter for the courts to assess. In a construction case, the defendant builder delayed the construction work, which was supposed to be finished by August 2021. The claimant made a demand to the defendant on 28 December 2021, giving the builder a period of 5 days to finish construction. The court recognized the legal effect of such notice, albeit short, and consequently that of the contractual termination, showing its friendly attitude towards the right-holder.[48]

(e) Miscellaneous provisions

As explained in section II of this chapter, Article 563 CCC is not the only provision governing the issue of contractual termination in Chinese law. Provisions exist in other parts of the Code (predominantly the Part on nominate contracts of the Book on Contracts) as well as in other statutes. One significant provision will be highlighted here. This is the newly inserted paragraph 2 in Article 563, which provides: 'A contract requiring the successive performance of the obligations without a term may be terminated by a party at any time, provided that the other party is notified within a reasonable period.' This is a welcome provision as the dichotomy of one-off contracts and long-term contracts is widely recognized in Chinese legal academia, the latter exemplified by contracts of loan, lease, safekeeping, warehousing, mandate, partnership, and supply of water and energy (namely, electricity, gas, and heating).[49]

2. Court-Ordered Termination

There are two scenarios where the court has the discretion to terminate a contract upon the request of a party. The first is a topic that was hotly debated throughout the codification process, namely, court-ordered termination upon the request of the contract-breaker. The second is court-ordered termination as a response to change of circumstances, which is covered in another chapter in this volume.[50]

(a) Relief for contract-breaker

Court-ordered termination at the request of the contract-breaker is a two-step process: the first is the application of a contract-breaker, and the second is the court's exercise of judicial discretion on whether to award an order to terminate the contract. The contract-breaker does not have any right of termination but is only in a position to present a petition to the

[48] *Liu Hui v Wang Cuixia* [2023] Beijing City No 1 Intermediate People's Court, J01MZ No 2896.

[49] *Chengzhou Xinyuan Water Conservancy Ltd v Chengzhou Waterworks Ltd* [2023] Chengzhou City Intermediate People's Court, X10MZ No 184.

[50] See WANG Lei, 'Change of Circumstances in China's Civil Legislation and Judicial Practice', ch 3 in this volume, 52–59.

court; satisfying the constituent requirements to present the petition does not guarantee a result in favour of the contract-breaker.

The application step is provided in Article 580 CCC, which states:

> Where a party fails to perform the non-pecuniary obligations or its performance of the non-pecuniary obligations fails to satisfy the terms of the contract, the other party may request it to perform unless any of the following circumstances occurs:
> (1) where it is legally or practically impossible to perform;
> (2) where the subject matter of the obligation is unsuitable for enforcement or the performance expenses are excessively high;
> (3) where the debtor fails to request performance within a reasonable period of time.
> If any of the aforementioned circumstances results in the purpose of the contract not being realised, the court or arbitral tribunal may terminate the contract upon the request of either party, without affecting the liability for breach of contract.

Thus, to be an eligible applicant, the contract-breaker must have committed a breach of a non-pecuniary obligation[51] which has caused frustration of the purpose of the contract, and the contract-breaker must actively apply to the court for an order to terminate the contract.[52]

The second step is the court's decision. Interestingly, six months before the entire mechanism was formally set out in the Code, the SPC had already decided on the factors that judges ought to consider when a contract-breaker applies for termination. Specifically, the 2019 SPC Trial Minutes say:

> A contract-breaker does not have the right to terminate the contract unilaterally. However, when parties come to a deadlock regarding the performance of some types of long-term contracts, it is against both parties' interest for the court to disallow the contract-breaker to terminate the contract by bringing such an action. Based on this prerequisite, where all the following conditions are met, the court shall support the contract-breaker's claim:
> (1) the contract-breaker was not in bad faith when committing breach;
> (2) it is obviously unfair to order specific performance against the contract-breaker;
> (3) it is against the principle of good faith for the aggrieved party to insist on the contract-breaker's specific performance.
> The order of termination does not diminish or extinguish the contract-breaker's liability for breach of contract.[53]

[51] Contract law holds a legal fiction that a pecuniary obligation is seen as always capable of being performed (Chinese Civil Code, art 579), which is in stark contrast to the mindset of insolvency law as otherwise a company in financial distress would never be in a position where it is unable to pay its debts (Enterprise Bankruptcy Law 2006, art 2).

[52] HUANG Wei (ed), *Commentaries of the Book on Contracts of the Chinese Civil Code* (Law Press 2020) 273–74 [黄薇主编:《中华人民共和国民法典合同编释义》,法律出版社2020年版,第273–274页].

[53] *Minutes of Civil and Commercial Trials for All Courts Nationwide* (Supreme Court Issuance No 254, 2019) art 48.

The SPC reaffirmed such a test after the promulgation of the Code,[54] which has been followed by lower courts.[55]

(b) Milestone case

The CCC and the SPC Trial Minutes allow the contract-breaker to request contract termination in order to address the phenomenon of contract deadlock. A leading Xinyu case,[56] though decided before the enactment of the CCC, explains what contract deadlock entails. The claimant, Xinyu Company, a developer and operator of a retail mall, concluded a sale and purchase agreement with the defendant for a shop unit in the mall. Purchasers of shop units were permitted to enter into possession before title transfer had been registered. Subsequently, the new management team of Xinyu Company decided to change the type of business to be operated in the mall.

Consequently, Xinyu Company offered to buy back the shop unit from the defendant. However, the defendant asked for a price of around renminbi (RMB) 6.6 million, while she had bought the unit from Xinyu for only RMB368,184. The market value was appraised at RMB531,700 by an accredited property valuer. As such, Xinyu Company sued to terminate the purchase agreement on the ground of the change of circumstances. Xinyu Company asserted that all the 150 shop units in the retail mall had been bought back by Xinyu since the business had been reconceptualized by the new management board, except for two units, including the defendant's unit. The original purpose of operating the boutique shop area in the mall under the new layout plan could no longer be fulfilled. The defendant challenged the termination of the contract and refused to vacate the premises. This situation resulted in a contract deadlock, as the innocent party, the defendant, did not want to take legal action to terminate the contract whereas the defaulting party, Xinyu Company, wished to terminate.

The court of first instance supported the termination request made by the defaulting party, Xinyu Company. The reasoning was that it would be a social waste if such a deadlock continued to exist. The shop unit held by the defendant was just one of 150 units in the mall. Most unit purchasers agreed to return the units to Xinyu Company to reconceptualize the business style. The sooner the defendant vacated the premises, the less waste it would generate. Guided by the principles of good faith and fairness, the court of first instance held that when the cost of performance outweighed the benefits to be obtained for the performance of the contract, specific performance was out of the question. In addition, the court reasoned that shop unit purchasers needed to consider and follow the collective decision of the majority. Therefore, the court ordered the contract to be terminated and the defaulting party to pay compensatory damages. The order for termination was affirmed by the court of second instance.

The Xinyu case is a landmark case in that it challenged the age-old doctrine that only the innocent party can request contract termination before the court. Given the growing

[54] Enforcement of the Civil Code Group of the Supreme People's Court (ed), *Understanding and Applying the Book on Contracts of the Chinese Civil Code, vol 2* (People's Court Press 2020) 741 [最高人民法院民法典贯彻实施工作领导小组主编：《中华人民共和国民法典合同编理解与适用（二）》，人民法院出版社2020年版，第741页].

[55] *Shandong Baoan Real Estate Development Ltd v Cui Chengqi* [2023] Shandong Province Weihai City Intermediate People's Court, L10MZ No 229; *Zibo Zichuan Ganglian Material Ltd v Building & Installing Engineer Co Ltd of China Railway 12th Bureau Group* [2023] Shandong Province Zibo City Intermediate People's Court, L03MZ No 1307.

[56] *Xinyu Ltd v Feng Yumei* [2016] Supreme Court Gazette issue 6 (2 June 2016).

number of contract deadlock cases which the Chinese courts faced when the CCC was being drafted, and prompted by the reasoning of the Xinyu case, the final version of the CCC allows the contract-breaker in very exceptional circumstances to request the court to terminate the contract. However controversial it may be, such a rule is driven by the high premium placed on societal interests in China.

The downside of this rule is that it risks affecting the contractual equilibrium between the creditor and the debtor. If the rule is easily invoked, it may raise the floodgates for debtors to leave their contracts. Does this rule pay sufficient regard to the performance interest of contract creditors? The effect of the rule is to place the overall societal interest ahead of the creditor's interests. Therefore, to avoid potential abuse by contract debtors, this rule should be applied with caution. One might argue that it is up to a court to exercise its jurisdiction as to whether to order termination, based on the individual circumstances of each case. But discretion given to the courts comes with a price, namely that of uncertainty. It is suggested that Chinese courts need to be cautious not to apply this discretion too broadly.

The scope of application of the SPC Trial Minutes and the CCC differs. According to the SPC document, a contract-breaker may only request termination of long-term contracts, but these do not necessarily need to involve non-pecuniary obligations, whereas the CCC only addresses the non-performance of non-pecuniary obligations, but the contracts do not necessarily have to be long-term contracts. While overlapping in some instances, these two situations are sometimes inconsistent. For example, during the COVID-19 pandemic, many small business owners struggled to survive. If a lessee of a commercial lease for a term of three years defaults only half a year after the commencement date because it becomes insolvent, the lessee may wish to request a contract termination before the court. In this instance, the facts involve the non-performance of a pecuniary obligation, that is, rental payment. Therefore, the second paragraph of Article 580 CCC cannot be invoked. The situation is likely to fall under the SPC Trial Minutes, although the question may arise as to whether a three-year contract is a long-term contract. It is expected for the legislature to incorporate the SPC Trial Minutes approach in order to synthesize the two rules in the foreseeable future.

V. The Exercise and Extinction of the Right of Termination

1. Exercise

The arising of a right of termination does not automatically generate the effect of contractual termination; an additional act must be done to achieve the result of termination. To exercise the right of termination, the right-holder only needs to send a notice to the counterparty in the contractual relationship; the right-holder does not have to bring an action.[57] There is no formality requirement regarding the notice, whether oral or written, instantaneous or non-instantaneous.[58] Notably, if the right-holder does bring an action instead of sending a notice, it also counts as an effective exercise of the right of termination.[59]

[57] Chinese Civil Code, art 565(1).
[58] *Chen Yongfei v Yu Lepeng* [2022] Zhejiang Province High People's Court, ZMZ No 1310.
[59] Chinese Civil Code, art 565(2).

2. Extinction

Article 564 CCC provides that the right of termination is extinguished in two types of cases, one where the law provides for, or the parties have agreed upon, a time limit for exercising the right and the other where the relevant statutory provisions and contractual stipulations are silent on the issue of extinction. These share one thing in common: lapse of time. In the former type of case, the right is automatically extinguished if no right-holder exercises it before the time limit expires.[60] In the latter type of case, the right ends (i) if it is not exercised within one year from the date when the right-holder knows or ought to have known about the cause for termination or (ii) if the right-holder receives a notice from the other party asking whether the right-holder would like to exercise the right of termination, and the right-holder fails to respond within a reasonable time.[61]

Article 564 does not make clear whether a right of termination might end *before* the time of expiry provided for in the article. The mainstream view is that one could lose a right of termination before it expires on the basis that a right of termination, like a right of rescission, can be expressly or impliedly waived. A typical example is where the right-holder knows about the cause for termination, yet still carries on to perform the contract or to ask the counterparty to make specific performance.[62] A persuasive view is that the court should be cautious when assessing the party's genuine intent as these acts do not necessarily amount to an implied waiver of the right of termination.[63]

VI. Consequences of Termination

The CCC contains two main sources of law regarding the consequences of termination. Article 566 addresses consequences not stipulated in the contract, whereas Article 567 deals with consequences stipulated in the contract. The first consequence of contractual termination is that rights and duties stipulated in the contract no longer bind the parties. Notably, there have been debates about whether contractual termination is retroactive. Recent judgments show that the practical value of such a debate is undermined by the courts' flexible position when dealing with different types of contracts. Where the contract in question is a one-off contract, the courts have said that termination is retroactive and use this to justify why restitution should be a legal response to termination.[64] Where the terminated contract is a long-term, executory, or partly executory one, the courts have said that termination is not retroactive. Hence, past performance and future performance should be treated differently because the former in principle does not trigger restitution.[65]

60 Chinese Civil Code, art 564(1).

61 Chinese Civil Code, art 564(2).

62 WANG (n 32), citing Chinese Civil Code, art 152(1) item 3.

63 LU Qing, *On the Termination of Contract* (Law Press 2022) 173–75 [陆青：《合同解除论》，法律出版社2022年版，第173–75页].

64 *Xu Tingde v Linyi Yishui Hongxin Mall Ltd* [2021] Shandong Province Linyi City Intermediate People's Court, L13MZ No 3740.

65 *Tu Zhengui v Suiyang Anjie Motor Carriage of Goods Ltd* [2021] Guizhou Province Zunyi City Intermediate People's Court, Q03MZ No 10651.

1. Restitution

The rules of restitution that apply after termination of a contract are not clear. Article 566(1) states:

> After the termination of a contract, performance shall cease if the contract has not been performed; if the contract has been performed, a party may, in accordance with the circumstances of performance or the nature of the contract, request the other party to restore such party to its original state or adopt other remedial measures, and such party shall have the right to demand compensation for losses.

The fact that the word 'restitution' and the phrase 'restitution of unjust(ified) enrichment' are not mentioned in the text above has led to a debate among contract and restitution lawyers regarding what kind of 'absence of basis' is included in Article 985 CCC.[66] It undoubtedly includes impaired consent transfers, which are more relevant to rescission as opposed to termination. The difficult case, however, concerns what English lawyers call 'qualified consent'[67] or 'qualified intent'.[68] Suppose, for example, that the defendant agrees to paint the claimant's house for a lump sum payment. Having received payment in advance, the defendant decides to breach the contract. The claimant elects to terminate the contract and seeks restitution from the defendant. Does this count as an unjustified enrichment claim? A detailed exploration of the codification process and Chinese contract lawyers' treatment of subsidiarity reveals the position that restitution of unjustified enrichment is indeed a response to contractual termination so that defences to unjustified enrichment (eg change of position,[69] bona fide purchase,[70] and illegality[71]) also apply in the present scenario.[72]

2. Compensation

Article 566(2) states: 'If a contract is terminated for breach, the party with the right of termination may request the contract-breaker to bear liability for breach of contract, unless otherwise agreed upon by the parties.' Two issues will be addressed. The first is the interpretation of the phrase 'liability for breach of contract'. While the legislature uses the phrase 'liability for breach for contract' rather than the term 'compensation' as in the preceding

[66] Article 985 is the general provision regarding restitution of unjustified enrichment. It provides that:

> Where a party is unjustifiably enriched without a legal basis at the expense of another, the aggrieved party has the right to claim for restitution of the enrichment acquired by the enrichee, except where:
> (i) the performance was made to discharge a moral obligation;
> (ii) an obligation was discharged before the due date; or
> (iii) an obligation was discharged which the performer knew did not exist.

[67] A Burrows, *The Law of Restitution* (3rd edn, OUP 2011) 86.

[68] C Mitchell, 'Unjust Enrichment' in A Burrows (ed), *English Private Law* (3rd edn, OUP 2013) 1055.

[69] Chinese Civil Code, art 986.

[70] Chinese Civil Code, arts 987, 988.

[71] Chinese Civil Code, art 157; *Minutes of Civil and Commercial Trials for All Courts Nationwide* (Supreme Court Issuance No 254, 2019) arts 32–34.

[72] Z Wu and W Swadling, 'Unjustified Enrichment in the Chinese Civil Code: Questions from the Common Law' (2021) 29(2) Asia Pacific Law Review 402, 413–15.

paragraph, the predominant view nevertheless is that they are essentially referring to the same thing so that the phrase 'liability for breach of contract' ought to be interpreted narrowly in the sense of not covering remedies which are inherently contradictory to termination, such as specific performance, repair, redoing, and replacement.[73] The second issue is the measurement of damages: whether the contract-breaker shall pay reliance interest or expectation/performance interest. A textual interpretation of Article 584 CCC leads to the answer being expectation interest subject to foreseeability.[74]

3. Contractual Clauses

Contractual termination in principle extinguishes the rights and duties stipulated in the contract in question, except for three types of stipulations. The first type are clauses in relation to the final settlement of accounts and liquidation, the validity of which are not infected by the contractual termination.[75] The second type are clauses relating to dispute settlement, such as clauses providing for the choice of court, choice of law, arbitration, etc.[76] The third type are security clauses outside of but ancillary to the terminated contract. Article 566(3) provides that after the termination of the principal contract, the security provider continues to be liable for the debtor's non-performance, unless otherwise stipulated in the security contract.

VII. Hypotheticals

1. Car Machinery & Co and Traders Ltd

In the case of missed inspection appointments, whether Car Machinery & Co is entitled to terminate the agreement after Traders Ltd missed two stipulated visits depends on the seriousness of the breach under Chinese law.[77]

Article 562(2) CCC provides for consensual termination under a prior clause. As a matter of principle, parties can include a clause in the contract stipulating the cause of termination. If the situation that arises falls under the termination clause, the innocent party is entitled to terminate the contract. Therefore, Car Machinery & Co is entitled to terminate the contract.

[73] L Chen, Specific Performance as a Contractual Remedy in Chinese Courts: An Empirical Study (2019) 7(1) The Chinese Journal of Comparative Law 95–123; XIE Hongfei and ZHU Guangxin (eds), *Commentaries of the Civil Code: Book on Contracts: General Rules, vol 2* (China Legal Publishing House 2020) 213 [谢鸿飞、朱广新主编：《民法典评注：合同编·通则》（第2册），中国法制出版社2020年版，第213页].

[74] Article 584 provides:

> Where a party fails to perform its obligations under the contract or its performance fails to satisfy the contract, thereby causing losses to the other party, the amount of compensation for losses shall be equal to the losses caused by the breach of contract, including the benefits receivable after the performance of the contract, provided that it does not exceed the probable losses caused by the breach that has been foreseen or ought to be foreseen when the party in breach concludes the contract.

[75] Chinese Civil Code, art 567.

[76] Chinese Civil Code, art 507.

[77] The fact scenarios for this and the other hypothetical situations discussed in this section VII are taken from M Chen-Wishart, D Neo, and S Vogenauer, 'Introduction', ch 1 in this volume, 9–10.

If Traders Ltd challenges the termination by Car Machinery & Co before a Chinese court, the court will most likely refer to Article 47 of the SPC 2019 Trial Minutes. Here, the court will examine whether the degree of breach of contract is significantly minor and whether it affects the fulfilment of the purpose of the contract, guided by the doctrine of good faith. If the breach is significantly minor and does not affect the fulfilment of contract purposes, the court will not support the termination request.

In the present case, one question is whether Traders Ltd's two missing visits amount to a fundamental breach. The failure of visits occurred in the second month of a five-year contract. The defaulting party could have been given an opportunity to remedy it by negotiation, such as by making two additional visits in the following four years and ten months. The court would likely hold that it would be unreasonable on the ground of good faith to terminate the contract where Traders Ltd failed to make only two required visits. Under the contract clause, there should be at least 1,560 required visits for the contract period. In proportion to this, the two missing visits may be viewed as a minor breach. Given the above analysis, more likely than not, a Chinese court will not support contract termination.

2. Prime Ltd and Devil Corp

In the hypothetical case concerning a land sale and purchase agreement, Devil is ten minutes late in paying the purchase price even though there is a contractual stipulation that time is of the essence and that failure to meet deadline would result in termination of the contract. The starting point is that a contractual stipulation that time is of the essence in relation to a particular contractual obligation demonstrates that timely performance is at the heart of the contract. The context may reveal that the particular piece of land to be sold is highly sought after in the property market.

Therefore, Prime Ltd is entitled to terminate the contract pursuant to Clause 12. But what would a Chinese court rule if Devil argues that Prime Ltd's reliance on the clause is unreasonable? Again, under Article 47 of the 2019 SPC Trial Minutes, a Chinese court would examine whether a ten-minute delay in tendering the money is a fundamental breach which frustrates the contract purpose. Some Chinese courts may not grant contract termination but award Prime Ltd damages occasioned by the delayed performance.

Chinese law aims to produce fair outcomes in cases where judges and arbitrators tailor the remedy to suit the facts of the case. However, this can result in uncertainty which can make it difficult for parties to predict the likely outcome of litigation.

If Clause 12 was not included in the contract, it is more likely that the Chinese courts would not grant contract termination. This is because termination by agreement will not be applicable, and the only ground of termination would be termination by operation of law. According to items (3) and (4) of Article 563(1) CCC, a party may terminate the contract where the other party delays the performance of its principal obligation and fails to perform within a reasonable period after the demand or where it is impossible to achieve the purpose of the contract due to the delayed performance of the obligations or other breach of contract by the other party.[78]

[78] Chinese Civil Code, art 563(1) item 1.

In the present scenario, the court would hold that a ten-minute delay in making payment is a minor breach. More to the point, good faith is relevant under Chinese law. Applying a 'reasonable man test', if the ten-minute delay can be explained away with an excusable reason, it can be said that Devil acted in good faith. On the other hand, if Prime Ltd decided to terminate the contract because it wished to sell the land to a subsequent buyer who offered a higher purchase price, it would be acting in bad faith. As such, Chinese courts would not order termination of the contract. Therefore, a Chinese court needs to consider all the facts and circumstances of the individual case to produce a fair outcome.

3. Seven Seas and Big Chef

Under Chinese law, if the quality requirement is not specified, performance shall be rendered under the mandatory state standard.[79] In the third hypothetical scenario, where Seven Seas provides mussels with a cadmium concentration exceeding the national food regulation by 2 per cent, the crux of the issue is whether this amounts to a fundamental breach. Generally, a small-scale deviation from the contractual standard may be remedied by damages or price reduction instead of termination. However, this case concerns food safety. It is necessary to refer to the relevant food safety law provisions. According to Articles 34 items 2 and 55 of the Food Safety Law (2021 Amendment), all restaurant operators are prohibited from serving food containing materials that exceed the mandatory state standard of food safety, and an administrative penalty will be imposed for a violation of this rule.[80]

In this scenario, supplying mussels with a cadmium concentration that is 2 per cent over the permitted mandatory state standards will be considered a fundamental breach. Consequently, Big Chef can terminate the contract under Chinese law.

4. Coco and David

In the scenario of the landscaping agreement, before the time fixed for performance under the contract, Coco informs David that she will not perform her obligations. This is an anticipatory breach of contract pursuant to Article 563(1) item 2 CCC. It gives David, the innocent party, an immediate right to terminate the contract and seek compensatory damages before the due date of performance under Article 578 CCC.[81]

Chinese law is silent on whether the innocent party must terminate the contract when there is an anticipatory breach or whether the innocent party can choose to affirm the contract instead. The use of the word 'may' in Articles 563 and 578 implies that the innocent party has a choice between seeking a remedy immediately or affirming the contract and waiting for the performance. Therefore, repudiation by Coco does not necessarily terminate the contract. An innocent party may choose to affirm the contract and insist on performance.

79 Chinese Civil Code, art 511 item 1.

80 Food Safety Law (2021 Amendment) art 125.

81 Chinese Civil Code, art 578: 'Where one party explicitly expresses or indicates by its conduct that it will not perform its obligations under a contract, the other party may request it to bear the liability for the breach of contract before the due date of the performance.'

However, the innocent party's choice is limited by the need to avoid waste arising from the principle of good faith and the duty to mitigate losses.[82] Although there is no express rule under Chinese law that the creditor must terminate merely because upholding the obligations would cause wasteful performance, the statutory ambiguity offers Chinese courts a great deal of discretion. In order to avoid wasteful performance, Chinese courts may refuse a specific performance order under the principle of good faith.[83] The CCC explicitly states that the parties must observe the principle of good faith in their civil activities.[84] Breach of the principle of good faith may bar the creditor from affirming the contract.[85]

Coco clearly intends to repudiate the contract. She claims that the next development does not include a garden. If this is true, repudiating the contract to avoid waste would be acting in good faith under Chinese law. However, if Coco has no genuine justification to repudiate, it would not be easy to find her acting in good faith.

On David's side, assuming his estimation of his loss of future earnings is proven by relevant evidence, he will have a 'legitimate interest' to justify the affirmation of the contract.[86] However, under Chinese law, the doctrine of good faith carries more weight than the 'legitimate interest test' in determining whether the innocent party should terminate the contract in such circumstances. Chinese courts would conduct a cost–benefit analysis—whether the wastefulness of the victim's continuing performance outweighs its performance interest in earning the contract price. If so, a court ruling would most likely terminate the contract.

5. Bob and Sue

The fifth hypothetical is a typical fundamental breach scenario because the contract's purpose cannot be realized due to Bob's abandonment of the contract before the contracted building work is completed. The central issue is the remedies when the contract is terminated.

First, can Bob claim the value of the work done? Unlike English law,[87] Chinese law does not distinguish between entire and divisible obligations in the CCC. However, Article 531(1) CCC provides for partial performance. It states, 'a creditor may reject the debtor's partial performance unless the partial performance does not harm the creditor's interest'.[88] Under Chinese law, there is a conceptual difference between partial and full performance. The contract creditor can refuse the partial performance by the contract debtor but a partial performance can also be accepted when it does not harm the creditor's interest. For example, suppose A loans B a sum of RMB10,000, with liquidated damages set at 20 per cent of the unpaid amount. B pays back RMB1,500 when the debt is due but defaults on the remaining amount. A should not refuse to take RMB1,500 and claim the full loan and the

[82] Chinese Civil Code, art 591.

[83] L Chen and LA DiMatteo, 'Inefficiency of Specific Performance as a Contractual Remedy in Chinese Courts: An Empirical and Normative Analysis' (2020) 40 Northwestern Journal of International Law and Business 275.

[84] Chinese Civil Code, art 7.

[85] L Chen, 'Availability of Specific Remedies in Chinese Contract Law' in M Chen-Wishart, A Loke, and B Ong (eds), *Studies in the Contract Laws of Asia, vol I: Remedies for Breach of Contract* (OUP 2016) 21.

[86] *White and Carter (Councils) Ltd v McGregor* [1962] AC 413 (HL).

[87] *Sumpter v Hedges* [1898] 1 QB 673.

[88] Chinese Civil Code, art 531.

liquidated damages unless there is a compelling reason to convince the court that accepting RMB1,500 would harm A's interest.

In this scenario, Sue may choose to accept a partial performance done by Bob. In this instance, Bob has rendered some performance to recover something for services rendered, albeit inadequately. There could be a remedy *in quantum meruit* under English law. In a similar vein, under Chinese law, where Sue accepts a partial performance, Bob is entitled to payment of the value of work done in the form of deductions from the damages sought by Sue.

If Sue does not accept the partial performance, whether Bob can recover the value of the building work he has done hinges on a single test, namely, whether it would harm Sue's interest if she accepted partial performance. Common sense dictates that if only a third of Bob's building work is done, this leaves the building unfinished. Sue, the building owner, cannot leave it in an unfinished state forever. The only sensible solution under such circumstances would be to complete the building by finding another builder. Therefore, Sue can argue that her interest would have been harmed if she had accepted the partial performance. The performance interests of Sue lie in the completion of the building to be built. There is no logical space for a *quantum meruit* remedy. Hence, Sue is entitled not to accept the partial performance, and Bob cannot recover the value of the work done.

Generally, whether a builder can recover the value of work done in an uncompleted construction under Chinese law is fact-sensitive. In this hypothetical, it is about building a single house. More likely than not, the Chinese court will not allow Bob to recover the value of the uncompleted work given the above analysis. What if Bob is contracted to build a complex of six buildings and has partially performed by completing two buildings? In this context, it is more likely that the Chinese court will award the value of work done to the builder. Specifically, in a lump sum construction contract, the relevant factors are how much work has been done, the quality of work done, whether the builder or building owner is a breaching party, and whether it is necessary to appoint a specialist appraiser. In short, Chinese law supports the recovery of partial work done by the builder where it involves multiple buildings.

Next, we turn to whether Bob can claim the value of the materials used by Sue. He can clearly do so under Chinese law. The reason is straightforward: Bob still holds the title of the building materials left over on the site. According to Article 238 CCC, Bob may claim damages, largely equal to the value of the building materials, when his property right has been infringed upon.[89]

VIII. Conclusion

Under Chinese law, termination appears less important in the remedial regime than in common law. Termination is seen as a remedy of last resort. This differs from English law, where termination is a significant remedy, though not necessarily easy to invoke. There is a difficult policy issue to balance. Should the remedial regime aim to encourage parties

[89] Chinese Civil Code, art 238: 'Where an infringement of a property right causes loss to the right holder, the right holder may claim damages in accordance with law, or request to bear other civil liabilities in accordance with law.'

to continue their relationship, or should it encourage parties to escape from a deal when things go wrong and to seek an alternative transaction elsewhere? Chinese law appears to lean towards the former model by (i) giving greater emphasis to remedies that enable the parties to maintain their relationship (such as cure of performance and price reduction)[90] and (ii) giving the courts significant judicial discretion to decide whether or not the breach justifies termination.[91] The difficulty with this approach is that it results in uncertainty and unpredictability. Nonetheless, a clear rule that provides certainty may be inflexible when it comes to achieving a fairer outcome which takes into account the specific circumstances of each case. This is particularly important in Chinese law, where societal collective interest (as shown in the Xinyu case) and good faith are prevailing values upheld by the Chinese courts.

There is, therefore, a need to strike a balance between the interest in certainty and the need to produce fair and just solutions where the rules are applied to individual fact situations. Chinese law appears to lean towards the fairness end of the spectrum.

[90] L Chen, 'Damages and Specific Performance in Chinese Contract Law' in DiMatteo and Chen, *Chinese Contract Law* (n 5) 378–80.

[91] It should be noted that in exceptional circumstances, a contract-breaker is allowed to request contract termination before the courts and, in such a case, termination appears to be an easily invoked remedy. Nonetheless, it is worth noting that not all the situations under art 580 will be treated so permissively by the courts: see Chinese Civil Code, art 580(2).

5

Contract Terms in Hong Kong

Changed Circumstances and Variation

Stephen HALL

I. Historical and Jurisprudential Context

Contracts made in Hong Kong are creatures of the common law, and the common law is an essentially customary legal system. What this means—since 1842, when China ceded the island to the United Kingdom, through to the 1997 acquisition of sovereignty functions by Beijing, and on to the present day—is considered in an earlier volume of this series.[1] For the reasons there discussed, and absent any further radical alterations to Hong Kong's constitutional and legal arrangements imposed by or at the behest of the powers on the Chinese mainland, it is likely that Hong Kong's courts will continue to cleave closely to the English common law including as it relates to contracts and commercial matters. Departures can be expected only where a rule of the English common law is clearly at odds with the customs, traditions, and reasonable expectations of the Hong Kong community or where the powers currently in control of Hong Kong and the Chinese mainland perceive or imagine a possible threat to their political security.

In the realm of contracts, the twin principles of freedom and sanctity of contract became firmly established as meta-principles in the nineteenth century. The classically liberal spirit of English contract law was famously encapsulated in 1875 by Sir George Jessel MR:

> if there is one thing which more than another public policy requires it is that men of full age and competent understanding shall have the utmost liberty of contracting, and that their contracts when entered into freely and voluntarily shall be held sacred and shall be enforced by Courts of justice.[2]

II. Consensual and Non-consensual Variation

Unanticipated circumstances arising after the conclusion of a contract can make its performance unexpectedly uneconomic, difficult, or even impossible. The factors producing such changed circumstances are potentially very wide-ranging. They can include destruction of the contract's subject matter, currency inflation, price and exchange-rate

[1] S Hall, 'Contract Terms in Hong Kong: Incorporation, Interpretation, Implication, and Unfair Terms' in M Chen-Wishart and S Vogenauer (eds), *Studies in the Contract Laws of Asia, vol III: Contents of Contracts and Unfair Terms* (OUP 2020) 62, 62–65.

[2] *Printing and Numerical Registering Co v Sampson* (1874–75) LR 19 Eq 462, 465 (Ch).

Stephen Hall, *Contract Terms in Hong Kong: Changed Circumstances and Variation* In: *Studies in the Contract Laws of Asia V: Ending and Changing Contracts*. Edited by: Mindy Chen-Wishart, Dora Neo, and Stefan Vogenauer, Oxford University Press. © Stephen Hall 2026. DOI: 10.1093/oso/9780198995814.003.0005

fluctuations, goods and labour shortages, resignation or incapacity of key personnel, industrial strikes and civil disturbances, domestic and foreign legal regulations, official bureaucratic delays, war and armed conflict, natural disasters, new technologies, and even fashion and consumer tastes.

1. Consensual Variation

The emergence of such supervening circumstances will sometimes motivate the party on whom the unexpected burden falls to seek a variation of the contract in order to restore the equilibrium of costs and benefits originally anticipated by the parties at the time of contracting.

The parties always remain free to agree a variation to their contract, whether in response to changed circumstances or otherwise. As with contract formation, a variation of contract must be the result of an agreement accompanied by both contractual intention and consideration. These requirements have been surveyed in a previous volume of this series.[3]

The requirements of agreement and intention in contract variation are very similar to those that apply in contract formation. Indeed, it has been observed that 'the requirements for a variation derive from the law governing contract formation'.[4] Over the last three decades, however, the requirement of consideration has seen the emergence of some important differences between the formation and variation of contracts.

In the context of contract variation, consideration is less likely to take the form of a transparent bargain than it does in contract formation. Thus, when forming a new contract, the typical commercial dynamic is that one party more or less explicitly requests a benefit for himself (eg a money price) in exchange for a benefit to the counterparty (eg the sale of goods or the supply of a service). When agreeing a variation of contract, however, the dynamic is often somewhat different and the bargain aspect less apparent. This is because a contract variation is an attempt to readjust legal relations within an established contractual framework, typically as the result of changed expectations or circumstances.

Nevertheless, commercial contract variations are generally agreed because both parties see some benefit to themselves in making the adjustment. More often than not, consideration for a variation consists of a mutual abandonment of existing rights and/or the conferment of new benefits by each of the parties on each other.[5] Where this occurs, the contract variation is supported by full legal consideration.

The first requirement of consideration is that it be either a *new* benefit to the promisor or a *new* detriment to the promisee. In order for something to be a 'benefit' in the full legal sense it must be something new, that is, something to which the promisor is not already legally entitled at the time he makes his promise.[6]

[3] L Ho, 'Contract Formation in Hong Kong' in M Chen-Wishart, A Loke, and S Vogenauer (eds), *Studies in the Contract Laws of Asia, vol II: Formation and Third Party Beneficiaries* (OUP 2018) 206, 220.

[4] S Wilken and K Ghaly, *The Law of Waiver, Variation, and Estoppel* (3rd edn, OUP 2012) 13; *Greenhouse v Paysafe Financial Services Ltd* [2018] EWHC 3296 (Com Ct) [13].

[5] *Re William Porter & Co Ltd* [1937] 2 All ER 361 (Ch).

[6] For example, in *Collins v Godefroy* (1831) 1 B & Ad 950, 109 ER 1040 (KB) (attendance at court in answer to subpoena not good consideration for promise to pay for attendance because promisee already legally obliged to attend).

Difficulty arises where the variation results in a party making a concession—either by promising to give more or accept less than the contract stipulates—in exchange for the other party's promise to do no more (or perhaps even less) than the contract requires. In the classical conception of consideration, a concession thus made is *nudum pactum* (a 'naked agreement' unclothed by consideration); the agreement to vary is thus contractually void and the contract remains unvaried.[7] However, by the early 1990s, in both England and Hong Kong[8] the common law came to recognize that a 'practical benefit' or the avoidance of a 'disbenefit' could serve as sufficient consideration supporting such a contract variation.

For the past 25–30 years, the common law rule in Hong Kong may thus be stated as follows. Full legal consideration is still needed for contract formation and can also support variation of a subsisting contract. For variation of a subsisting contract, consideration is still required and may take the truncated form of a 'practical benefit' accruing to the promisor. This raises an obvious question as to how full legal consideration differs from practical benefit.

There is a common thread running through the English and Hong Kong practical benefit cases since the early 1990s.[9] Where the promisor makes a concessionary promise concerning the terms of a subsisting contract, the promise will be supported by consideration where, as a result of making the promise, he protects an existing advantage that might otherwise be in jeopardy. This existing advantage might, for instance, be the avoidance of trouble, inconvenience, or expense (eg finding an alternative subcontractor or another paying occupant of premises) or the avoidance of liquidated damages (eg for late performance under a contract with a third party). Thus conceived, the initial formulation by which the promisor obtains a 'practical benefit' or avoids a 'disbenefit' are two ways of expressing the same idea. Whatever form the practical benefit takes, however, it is not constituted merely by the promisee's performance of his subsisting obligations or the promisor's avoidance of the trouble, inconvenience, or expense of enforcing those obligations; there must be some existing advantage over and above mere performance of the promisee's subsisting obligations.[10]

Practical benefit thus lacks the character of full legal consideration because it does not consist of a *new* benefit to the promisor. Although practical benefit is insufficient to support contract formation, it is capable of providing consideration for a concessionary promise varying a subsisting contract.

[7] *Stilk v Myrick* (1809) 2 Camp 317, 170 ER 1168 (KB).

[8] *Williams v Roffey Bros & Nicholls (Contractors) Ltd* [1991] 1 QB 1, 16, [1990] 1 All ER 512, 522 (CA, Eng); *UBC (Construction) Ltd v Sung Foo Kee Ltd* [1993] 2 HKLR 207, [1993] 2 HKC 458 (HC, HK).

[9] *Williams v Roffey Bros & Nicholls (Contractors) Ltd* (n 8); *UBC (Construction) Ltd v Sung Foo Kee Ltd* (n 8); *Re Selectmove Ltd* [1995] 2 All ER 531, [1995] 1 WLR 474 (CA, Eng); *Tam Moon Tong v Lucky Dragon Restaurant Ltd* (unreported, DCCJ 1706/2001, 15 August 2001) (DC, HK); *Bank of China (Hong Kong) Ltd v Cosan Ltd* [2006] HKCU 1407 (unreported, HCA 1600/2004, 18 August 2006) (CFI); *Chong Cheng Lin Courtney v Cathay Pacific Airways Ltd* [2011] 1 HKLRD 10 (CA, HK); *MWB Business Exchange Centres Ltd v Rock Advertising Ltd* [2016] EWCA Civ 553, [2017] QB 604, [2016] 2 Lloyd's Rep 291 (CA, Eng) (appeal allowed on other grounds, *Rock Advertising Ltd v MWB Business Exchange Centres Ltd* [2018] UKSC 24, [2019] AC 119, [2018] 4 All ER 21 (SC, UK) [18]).

[10] See further S Hall, *Ho and Hall's Hong Kong Contract Law, vol 1* (7th edn, LexisNexis Butterworths 2025) 162–175.

2. Non-consensual Variation

Unless the contract confers on one of the parties a power unilaterally to vary the contract, a unilateral decision or notification to vary it will not be effective.[11] A contract may confer a unilateral power of variation but only if this is clearly expressed.[12] Where the contract does clearly give one of the parties a power unilaterally to vary the contract, that power must not be exercised 'dishonestly, for an improper purpose, capriciously or arbitrarily'[13] or 'irrationally or perversely'.[14]

Where the counterparty resists efforts to vary the subsisting contract, a question arises as to whether he is legally required to negotiate and agree a variation or submit to a juridically mandated variation.

The common law in Hong Kong continues to respond to these supervening circumstances in the classically liberal mode of Sir George Jessel MR by respecting the parties' 'utmost liberty of contracting'. In other words, and subject to one important exception, the common law refrains from imposing on the parties any obligation to renegotiate, vary, or terminate their contract by reason of supervening circumstances. Thus, the common law in Hong Kong includes nothing in the nature of a *révision pour imprévision* in French administrative contracts or similar to that recently allowed by the French Code civil.[15]

Rather, the common law regards the parties' individual freedom of contract as involving a corresponding personal responsibility to construct their agreement for themselves in such a way as to provide for the consequences of supervening circumstances. The courts' task is, in principle, simply to ascertain and enforce the intentions of reasonable persons in the position of the parties as objectively manifested *at the time of concluding their contract*. A failure by the parties themselves to make provision for supervening events generally means that the contract is to be enforced notwithstanding that such events result in unanticipated hardship or difficulty.

We shall see, however, that the common law is not entirely without means of responding to the impact of unanticipated supervening circumstances on contractual relations.

III. Frustration: Impossibility or 'Radical Transformation'

The modern doctrine of frustration is the one unambiguous exception to the common law's hands-off approach to supervening events.

1. Pre-modern Doctrine

The common law originally took a rigid stance against modifying the binding force of contracts even in cases of impossibility of performance resulting from supervening events. In

[11] *Jebsen & Co Ltd v Asia Furniture* [1982] HKC 218, 223 (HC, HK).
[12] *Kwan Ka Man Blanche v Esprit Retail (Hong Kong) Ltd* [2004] 4 HKC 378 (CFI) [33].
[13] *Nash v Paragon Finance plc* [2001] EWCA Civ 1466, [2002] 2 All ER 248, [2002] 1 WLR 685 (CA, Eng) [32].
[14] *Chan Kam Yau v Hong Kong University of Science and Technology* [2007] HKCU 2129 (unreported, DCCJ 4016/2002, 21 December 2007) (DC, HK).
[15] Code civil, art 1195.

the English Civil War of the 1640s, a tenant under a lease was held off the property for three years by the presence of an invading foreign army. This was an event for which neither he nor the landlord had made any provision in the lease agreement. The tenant refused to pay rent during the period he was out of possession, and the landlord sued to recover. The court ruled in favour of the landlord and is reported to have observed:

> [T]hough the whole army had been enemy aliens, yet he ought to pay his rent. And this difference was taken, that where the law creates a duty or charge, and the party is disabled to perform it without any default in him, and hath no remedy over, there the law will excuse him . . . but when the party by his own contract creates a duty or charge upon himself, he is bound to make it good, if he may, notwithstanding any accident by inevitable necessity, because he might have provided against it by his contract. And therefore if the lessee covenant to repair a house, though it be burnt by lightning, or thrown down by enemies, yet he ought to repair it.[16]

The seventeenth-century reasoning was that because contractual obligations are voluntary, the contracting parties are free to make such provision as they choose for the occurrence of future events. If they fail to do so, then the parties remain bound to perform in accordance with their agreement. Contractual obligations were absolute.

2. Early Modern Doctrine

After some two centuries had passed and England had developed a much more complex society and economy, the rigidity of this doctrine of absolute contract no longer accorded with changed community customs and expectations. A case in 1857 served as a prelude to the abandonment of absolute contract. A vessel was moored at Port Philip in Australia when 17 of its 36 crew members refused to work and were imprisoned. The master of the vessel, on behalf of the owners, offered several of the remaining crew members an additional payment over and above their contracted wages if they were to assist in taking the ship to Bombay with a crew of only 19. The crew members accepted and helped take the vessel to Bombay. The owners refused to make the additional payment and argued, in accordance with well-established authority,[17] that the crew were already contractually bound to take the vessel to Bombay and that the owners therefore received no consideration for the promise to pay extra. The court held for the crew members on the basis that the depletion of the crew rendered the vessel unseaworthy, thereby terminating the contract as unreasonably dangerous to life: 'If [the crew] were not bound to go, they were free to make a new contract: and the master was justified in hiring them on the best terms he could make.'[18]

It was not long before absolute contract was unambiguously abandoned. In 1861, a music hall and pleasure gardens had been hired for four non-consecutive days and nights over a period of two months for the purpose of staging a series of entertainments. After the agreement was concluded, but before the first night's performance, the music hall was

16 *Paradine v Jane* (1647) Aleyn 26, 27, 82 ER 897 (KB).
17 *Stilk v Myrick* (n 7).
18 *Hartley v Ponsonby* (1857) 7 E & B 872, 878, 119 ER 1471, 1473 (QB).

destroyed by fire. The plaintiff hirers unsuccessfully sought to recover preliminary expenses of printing and advertising and other expenses necessarily incidental to the engagement.[19] The court relied on passages from Justinian's Digest and Pothier in support of its view that a debtor is freed from his obligation if the subject matter of the contract perishes without his fault and without having himself assumed the risk. This approach may have justified the adoption of a general rule of law similar to *force majeure* in some civilian systems. However, the court chose to tread a more familiar common law path by implying a term, based on the parties' presumed intentions, that the whole contract was contingent upon the music hall continuing to exist at the time the entertainments were to be provided. When it ceased to exist through no fault of either party and without allocation of risk, the contract automatically terminated in accordance with the implied term and both parties were released from any further obligations. Four years later, a contract to install machinery in a factory was automatically terminated by operation of an implied term when the factory, without fault by either party, burnt down.[20]

The same approach was subsequently adopted in Hong Kong to automatically terminate a contract for renovations to a building where, without fault of either party, a neighbouring house collapsed, thereby dragging down and destroying the building under repair; the continuing existence of the building was an implied condition of the contract's effectiveness and both parties were automatically relieved from any further obligations.[21]

In short order, it was recognized in England that a contract to perform services which can only be rendered by one of the parties personally will be automatically terminated by an implied term if that party dies or by illness or accident is rendered incapable of performing his obligations.[22] It was subsequently decided that, where the parties agreed that a contract is to be performed in only one way but that mode of performance is subsequently rendered impossible without fault by either party, the contract will be terminated by an implied term.[23]

The failure of the parties' contractual common purpose can also result in frustration. In a celebrated case involving the coronation processions for King Edward VII,[24] the defendant agreed to hire from the plaintiff a suite of rooms from which to view the processions that had been scheduled for 26 and 27 June 1902. The agreed price for two days' hire was £75. The defendant paid £25 upon concluding the contract, with the balance of £50 to be paid on 24 June. On the morning of the 24th, it was announced that the King was unwell and that the processions were cancelled. The defendant refused to pay the £50 balance, and the plaintiff sued. The court held for the defendant. The agreement resulted in a 'licence to use rooms for a particular purpose' (ie the viewing of the coronation processions), which purpose was 'regarded by both contracting parties as the foundation of the contract'.[25] The

[19] *Taylor v Caldwell* (1863) 3 B & S 826, 122 ER 309, [1861–73] All ER Rep 24 (QB).

[20] *Appleby v Myers* (1866–67) LR 2 CP 651, [1861–73] All ER Rep 452 (Exch).

[21] *The Wai Lee Firm v Ku Chung Ming* (1911) 6 HKLR 146 (SC, HK).

[22] *Stubbs v Holywell Railway Co* (1867) LR 2 Ex 311 (Exch) (death terminating a contract of employment); *Robinson v Davison* (1871) LR 6 Ex 269 (Exch) (contract for an eminent pianist to perform terminated by her succumbing to a dangerous illness).

[23] *Nicholl & Knight v Ashton, Eldridge & Co* [1901] 2 KB 126, [1900–03] All ER Rep 928 (CA, Eng) (parties agreed that cargo was to be transported only aboard a named vessel; when that vessel ran aground en route to collect the cargo, contract automatically terminated).

[24] *Krell v Henry* [1903] 2 KB 740, [1900–03] All ER Rep 20 (CA, Eng).

[25] *Krell v Henry* [1903] 2 KB 740, 750, [1900–03] All ER Rep 20, 23 (CA, Eng).

parties understood that the processions were a 'state of things' essential to the achievement of the contract's purpose, and there was an implied condition terminating the contract should the processions fail to materialize.

Conversely, where the 'state of things' was not truly essential to the contract's performance, its non-occurrence would not terminate the contract. This may be illustrated by another of the coronation decisions made by the same court, and on the same day, as the procession case. Among the events announced to mark the coronation was a royal naval review at Spithead on 28 June 1902. As with the procession in London, the review was cancelled because of the King's illness. Unfortunately, the defendant had already chartered a vessel from the plaintiff 'to take out a party . . . for the purpose of viewing the naval review and for a day's cruise round the fleet'. Although he had paid a deposit, the defendant did not turn up on 28 June or pay the balance of the agreed hire, and the plaintiff sued for breach of contract. The court held that the contract had not been frustrated and found for the plaintiff, observing that the chartered vessel 'had nothing particular to do with the review of the fleet except as a convenient carrier of passengers to see it; and other ships suitable for carrying passengers would have done equally as well'.[26]

Automatic termination was then extended to situations where performance of the contract was rendered unlawful by supervening official regulation, once again on the basis that a term was implied based on the parties' presumed intentions.[27]

3. Modern Doctrine

The implied-term theory of frustration was born, flourished, declined, and fell over a generous human lifespan of 93 years. There were two landmarks in the decline and fall. In the first of these, a contract to import goods into the United Kingdom was terminated by supervening war-time legislation banning the importation of those goods. The court eschewed the implied-term theory and observed that:

> [W]hen frustration occurs, it is automatic, and . . . its legal effect depends not on the intention of the parties or even on their knowledge as to the event, but on its occurrence in such circumstances as to show it to be *inconsistent with the further prosecution of the adventure*.[28]

The second landmark concerned a contract to build public housing in a post-war economic environment of labour and materials shortages.[29] The houses were completed much later than agreed, and at a financial cost to the builders that transformed their anticipated profit

[26] *Herne Bay Steam Boat Co v Hutton* [1903] 2 KB 683, 691 (CA, Eng).

[27] *Metropolitan Water Board v Dick, Kerr and Co Ltd* [1918] AC 119, [1916–17] All ER Rep 122 (HL) (contract to construct a reservoir automatically terminated when the British government used its war-time powers to stop the work); cf *Nam Sun Trading Co v Andersen, Meyer & Co Ltd* (1951) 35 HKLR 113 (SC, HK) (Hong Kong contract for sale of goods, stipulating that deposit and final payment was to be made in United States dollars to a New York bank account, frustrated by an embargo on such payments imposed by the United States government).

[28] *Denny, Mott & Dickson Ltd v James B Fraser & Co Ltd* [1944] AC 265, 276, [1944] 1 All ER 678, 683 (HL) (emphasis added).

[29] *Davis Contractors Ltd v Fareham Urban District Council* [1956] AC 696, [1956] 2 All ER 145 (HL).

into a substantial loss. The builders sought to have the contract recognized as terminated for frustration, in order to make an alternative *quantum meruit* claim. The builders were unsuccessful, but the court took the opportunity to reformulate the basis for frustration at common law. What was required, according to Lord Reid, was not an implied term but a more subtle exercise in ascertaining 'the true construction of the terms which are in the contract, read in light of the nature of the contract and of the relevant surrounding circumstances when the contract was made'. The question then becomes 'whether the contract which they did make is, on its true construction, *wide enough to apply to the new situation*: if it is not, then it is at an end'.[30] Lord Radcliffe's approach was very similar. He regarded a frustration as occurring 'whenever the law recognises that, without default of either party, a contractual obligation has become incapable of being performed because the circumstances in which performance is called for would *render it a thing radically different from that which was undertaken by the contract*'.[31]

These two landmarks effectively established the foundations of the modern common law doctrine of frustration. No longer reliant on a theory of implied term, frustration now operates as a general rule of law that automatically terminates the contract. In practical terms, the new radical-transformation theory requires four elements.

First, the parties' contractual adventure must be correctly identified. This will involve an accurate interpretation of the contract, having regard to both its express and implied terms.[32]

Then it will it be necessary to ascertain that, secondly, neither party has assumed the risk of the supervening event. Notwithstanding some formulations that emphasize the unforeseeability of the supervening event, there is no inflexible rule that a foreseeable risk which is not provided for in the contract will always mean that one of the parties was intended to bear the risk. Rather, the consequences of the occurrence of a foreseen or foreseeable risk which is not covered by the terms of the contract will depend on the facts of each case. In particular, where there is a custom or usual practice that one of the parties is to bear the risk of the supervening event, the silence of the contract on the point probably indicates the parties' intention that the custom or usual practice should prevail. Where there is no such custom or usual practice, the silence of the contract probably indicates that the parties really had no intention one way or the other and simply hoped that the problem would not materialize.[33] In the former situation, there will probably be no frustration, while in the latter there probably will be. It is more likely that the contract will be interpreted in such a way as to allocate the risk to a party where the contract assigns responsibility for a particular task to that party and a foreseeable supervening event prevents fulfilment of the responsibility;[34] in such a case, the contract will not be frustrated. This is not to say that the foreseeability or otherwise of the supervening event is irrelevant:

[30] [1956] AC 696, 720–21, [1956] 2 All ER 145, 153–54 (emphasis added).

[31] [1956] AC 696, 729, [1956] 2 All ER 145, 160 (emphasis added).

[32] For the interpretation and implication of contractual terms under the law of Hong Kong, see Hall (n 1) 68–78.

[33] *Ocean Tramp Tankers Corp v V/O Sovfracht (The Eugenia)* [1964] 2 QB 226, [1964] 1 All ER 161, [1963] 2 Lloyd's Rep 381 (CA, Eng).

[34] *Jan Albert (HK) Ltd v Shu Kong Garment Factory Ltd* [1990] 1 HKLR 317, [1989] 2 HKC 156 (CA, HK) (contract to export goods from mainland China to Germany not frustrated by reason of defendant exporter's failure to secure export permits from mainland China authorities because the contract, properly interpreted, allotted the risk of such failure to defendant).

> The only relevance of it being 'unforeseen' is this: If the parties did not foresee anything of the kind happening, you can readily infer they have made no provision for it: whereas, if they did foresee it, you would expect them to make provision for it.[35]

Finally, it will be necessary to establish that, thirdly, the supervening events and circumstances are not the fault or choice of either party,[36] and, fourthly, the events render achievement of the contractual adventure impossible or (to express essentially the same idea in other words) make further performance of the contract something radically different than that which the parties agreed. It is the fourth element that most clearly distinguishes the newer radical-transformation theory from the older implied-term theory and which opens the door to a potentially somewhat broader material scope for the termination of contracts on grounds of frustration. In particular, it is sometimes asserted that a contract has been frustrated because the general commercial context within which the contract was concluded has changed to a significant extent. An assertion of this sort is likely to be made when, due to circumstances outside the parties' control, an expected profit is transformed into a loss.

The potential for such an assertion was glimpsed in the post-war public housing case that finally marked the fall of the implied-term theory.[37] The plaintiffs' costs on the construction contract, produced by a shortage of building materials and labour, were higher than they had anticipated. The net result was that the contract took almost three times longer to complete than had been agreed, and the agreed price of £92,425 was not enough to cover the builders' actual costs of around £110,000. The plaintiffs' claim was that the contract had been frustrated by the shortage of materials and labour and the attendant increase in costs and time required for completion. On the facts, the court rejected the plea of frustration, but Lord Reid said:

> It may be that delay could be of a character so different from anything contemplated that the contract was at an end, but in this case, in my opinion, the most that could be said is that the delay was greater in degree than was to be expected. It was not caused by any new and unforeseeable factor or event; the job proved to be more onerous but it never became a job of a different kind from that contemplated in the contract.[38]

The radical-transformation theory of frustration thus makes termination of a contract theoretically possible for a change in an agreement's commercial context if that change was produced by an unanticipated delay of such a character as to impose an obligation 'of a different kind from that contemplated in the contract'. However, as the facts of the post-war public housing case itself indicate, it will be no easy matter to establish that a delay of the type identified by Lord Reid has occurred. For instance, the unanticipated closure in October 1987 of the Hong Kong futures exchange did not frustrate an exchange contract:

[35] *Ocean Tramp Tankers Corp v V/O Sovfracht (The Eugenia)* (n 33) (Lord Denning MR).

[36] *J Lauritzen AS v Wijsmuller BV* (*The Super Servant Two*) [1990] 1 Lloyd's Rep 1 (CA, Eng) (contract to charter either one of two named vessels not frustrated by reason of one of the vessels sinking and the owner choosing to assign the surviving vessel to honour a contract with a third party).

[37] *Davis Contractors Ltd v Fareham Urban District Council* (n 29).

[38] [1956] AC 696, 724, [1956] 2 All ER 145, 156.

> There was no unforeseen event which made the performance of the contract between the parties impossible. The market was closed for five days but then re-opened and the plaintiff acting in accordance with the terms of the contract proceeded to liquidate the defendant's account.[39]

However, a delay may exceptionally 'be of a character so different from anything contemplated' and of such far-reaching consequences that it transforms performance of the bargain into something radically different from that which was undertaken by the parties. In 2004, with a view to recovering about Hong Kong dollars (HK$)160,000 owed by the owner of the house, the chargee-vendor of a village ('ting') house in Hong Kong agreed to sell the house to a purchaser for HK$3.9 million. The purchaser was aware that the vendor was selling as chargee. The ting was subject to the Hong Kong government's New Territories Small House Policy.[40] Under Hong Kong law, the transaction could not be completed until a premium and fees were paid to the government in accordance with a demand note issued by an official known as a District Lands Officer (DLO). The premium was calculated by law as a percentage of the property's market value, and the contract of sale obliged the vendor to pay the premium. Despite repeated requests and reminders over a period of almost five years, during which time the market value of the land had greatly increased, the DLO failed to notify the amount of premium and fees payable. It was not until June 2009 that the DLO finally issued a demand note. The premium and fees were set at almost HK$3 million, which would have made it impossible to recover more than a fraction of the owner's debt. In September 2009, the chargee sought to rescind the agreement and return the purchaser's deposit, but the purchaser insisted on completion. In October 2010, the DLO increased the premium and some other fees, this time to more than HK$5 million (ie substantially more than the agreed purchase price, eliminating the prospect of recovering any part of the owner's debt, and resulting in the vendor's loss on the transaction). The purchaser commenced proceedings for specific performance or damages. Among the defences raised by the vendor was that the agreement had been frustrated.

The court agreed with the vendor. The consequence of the delay was that the vendor's anticipated recovery of its secured debt would have been transformed into a substantial loss. As the court emphasized, however, not every delay that results in a commercial loss will also result in frustration. The DLO's delay was caused by neither of the parties (and in spite of the vendor's efforts to avoid it), was of an extraordinary duration, and was unforeseen at the time of making the agreement. Because the transaction was a chargee-vendor sale, the usual allocation of risk whereby such a delay would ordinarily fall on the vendor did not apply: an ordinary vendor assumes the business risk of adverse delays and market fluctuations unless the contract provides otherwise because he is engaged in an ordinary market activity in which he knows that risk of loss is involved. A chargee-vendor, by contrast, is seeking merely to recover a secured debt and, as the court observed, '[a]t worst, the proceeds of sale may not

[39] *Chine Kit Ltd v Chu Kong-shing* [1990] HKCU 188 (unreported, HCCL 26/1988, 24 September 1990) (HC, HK).

[40] Under this policy, 'an adult male indigenous villager in the New Territories (being a descendant in the male line from a resident in 1898 of a recognised village) is entitled, once in his lifetime, to build a small ['ting' or 'ding'] house, up to 700 square feet in area and 3-storey high, in the village for himself on a piece of land owned by him or assigned to him by the Government at a concessionary rate': *Chan Yau v Chan Calvin* [2014] 5 HKLRD 304, [2014] 6 HKC 634 (CFI) [2].

enable him to recover his debt . . . [b]ut he would not land himself in personal liability'.[41] The exceptional circumstances of the delay operated to frustrate the contract by transforming its performance into something radically different from that which the parties undertook.

Where the contract stipulates an essential deadline, it will usually be an essential component of the contractual adventure. Accordingly, where a supervening event results in a delay that makes it impossible to meet an essential deadline, the contract will be frustrated. This principle is clearly illustrated by a case involving one of Hong Kong's worst natural disasters. On the night of 18 June 1972 near the University of Hong Kong, there was a major landslip that destroyed a block of flats called Kotewall Court,[42] some nearby dwellings, and the building site for a new block of flats called University Heights. Sixty-seven people were killed by the landslip, and the foundation works for University Heights were completely destroyed. There were at least 24 contracts of sale for flats in University Heights, and the purchasers sought to enforce their agreements. These contracts stipulated that the building had to be completed by no later than 24 May 1974 and that time was of the essence. As a result of the landslip, and given that the foundation works were completely lost and new official building approvals would be required, the earliest date it would be possible to complete the building was 1 October 1976. Consequently, the court held, the contracts were automatically terminated by the landslip, notwithstanding that it remained possible to recommence construction work and eventually erect a block of flats on the University Heights site.[43]

Perhaps more significantly, the University Heights case identified another basis upon which the contracts were frustrated. The scale of destruction wrought on the building site was such that it caused the total loss of all the work that had been done on the building's foundations. This represented a major commercial loss in 1972 of about HK$2 million. The court accepted that the scale of this loss, combined with the unforeseen and unforeseeable nature of its cause, rendered performance of the contract into a thing radically different from that which was agreed, and to have held the builders to the contract in these circumstances would have been unjust.

A more recent and succinct formulation of the modern common law doctrine postulates that an application of frustration requires a 'multi-factorial approach' and that the relevant factors will include:

> [1] the terms of the contract itself, its matrix or context, [2] the parties' knowledge, expectations, assumptions and contemplations, in particular as to risk, as at the time of contract, at any rate so far as these can be ascribed mutually and objectively, and then [3] the nature of the supervening event, and [4] the parties' reasonable and objectively ascertainable calculations as to the possibilities of future performance in the new circumstances.[44]

41 *Cheung Lai Kit v Rich Prosper Ltd* [2014] HKCU 906 (unreported, HCA 972/2011, 10 April 2014) (CFI) [75].

42 Henry Litton QC, a former Chairman of the Hong Kong Bar Association and a future member of the Hong Kong Court of Appeal and Court of Final Appeal, was among those rescued from the wreckage of Kotewall Court. He was rescued by Mr Leung Shiu-kay, a firefighter who was decorated by the Governor of Hong Kong for his conspicuous bravery in the Kotewall Court operations. Mr Leung died in 1980 at the age of 33 while fighting a fire on the island line of Hong Kong's Mass Transit Railway.

43 *Wong Lai-ying v Chinachem Investment Co Ltd* [1980] HKLR 1 (PC, HK).

44 *Edwinton Commercial Corp v Tsavliris Russ (Worldwide Salvage and Towage) Ltd (The Sea Angel)* [2007] EWCA Civ 547, [2007] 2 All ER (Comm) 634, [2007] 2 Lloyd's Rep 517 (CA, Eng) (Rix LJ) [111] (numbering added).

As far as contracts for the sale of goods are concerned, section 9 of the Hong Kong Sale of Goods Ordinance (Cap 26) provides: 'Where there is an agreement to sell specific goods, and subsequently the goods, without any fault on the part of the seller or buyer, perish before the risk passes to the buyer, the agreement is thereby avoided.' A contract to sell simply a quantity of apples is not a contract to sell specific goods; it is a sale of generic goods, and the seller will bear the risk of the goods perishing before ownership has passed to the buyer unless he can show that the contract was frustrated according to common law principles. For instance, a contract for the sale of 100 tons of antimony metal was held not to be frustrated by floods and transportation difficulties in China on the basis that the contract properly construed did not require the metal to originate from any particular source, and the vendor could have acquired it from sources outside China.[45] On the other hand, a contract to sell all the apples currently stored in a particular warehouse is a contract for specific goods, and their perishing is potentially covered by section 9.

4. Severe Acute Respiratory Syndrome and COVID-19

In 2003, Hong Kong was subjected to an epidemic of Severe Acute Respiratory Syndrome (SARS) that had spread to the territory from the Chinese mainland.

The SARS epidemic gave rise to an issue of frustration before Hong Kong's District Court.[46] A residential tenancy agreement stipulated that the defendant was to be the tenant of a flat for a period of two years commencing August 2002. There were numerous SARS infections in the high-rise building that included the flat. Learning of the building's infections, the defendant moved out of the flat on 29 March 2003 and stayed with relatives. On 31 March, the Health Department issued an order to isolate the building (and other buildings in the same estate) for a period of ten days, and the residents were evacuated to other locations for their safety. On 24 April, the defendant wrote to the plaintiff landlord terminating the tenancy agreement. When the plaintiff sued for breach of the agreement, the tenant pleaded that it had been frustrated on 31 March by the isolation order. The defence failed. Noting that the circumstances in which the doctrine of frustration can be applied to leases were 'exceedingly rare' to the point of being unprecedented, the court observed that the period of the isolation order was 'quite insignificant in terms of the overall use of the premises'.[47] According to the court, the SARS outbreak did not 'significantly change the nature of the outstanding contractual rights or obligations from that which the parties could reasonably have contemplated at the time of the execution of the tenancy agreement'.[48] Thus, although occupation of the flat was rendered unlawful for a period of ten days (out of two years), the isolation order did not transform the lease into a bargain radically different than that to which the parties had agreed.

At the time of writing, the world had recently been afflicted by the Coronavirus Disease 2019 (COVID-19) pandemic. In order to deal with the public health emergency perceived to have resulted from the pandemic, the Hong Kong government adopted a range of legal

[45] *Euramin SA v Shangxiang Minmetals Ltd* [1997] HKCU 455 (unreported, HCA 10274/1994, 25 March 1997) (HC, HK).

[46] *Li Ching Wing v Xuan Yi Xiong* [2004] 1 HKLRD 754, [2004] 1 HKC 353 (DC, HK).

[47] ibid [10]–[11].

[48] ibid [11].

and administrative measures that significantly disrupted the ordinary conduct of economic and social life.[49] However, no legislation was adopted adjusting the law on frustration to the contingencies of the pandemic. This left Hong Kong's courts to deal with any issues of contract frustration arising from the pandemic in accordance with common law principles. At the time of writing there were several such cases recorded, all involving an unsuccessful defence by tenants that a commercial lease had been frustrated and all resulting in summary judgment for the landlord.

In June 2019, a provider of flexible work spaces for rental to customers took a lease on premises in a prestigious commercial building in central Hong Kong.[50] The tenants began operating their business from the leased premises in September 2019, but by February 2020 the tenants asserted that demand for rented flexible workspaces and access to the leased premises had sharply declined as a combined result of the pandemic and the widespread public demonstrations mounted by the (since suppressed) pro-democracy social movement. The tenants quickly fell into serious arrears of rent and other financial obligations under the lease. When the landlord commenced proceedings to recover sums contractually owed, the tenants maintained that the lease had been frustrated because the effects of the pandemic and demonstrations had fundamentally changed the nature of the tenants' obligations in ways that were not contemplated at the time the lease was concluded. The defence failed on the basis that the tenants' obligations under the lease were to pay rent and observe the other terms of the lease, and there had been no change in the 'nature' of these obligations notwithstanding that the pandemic and social disruptions 'must have rendered [their] business operation more onerous and not profitable'.[51] This was held to be insufficient to frustrate the contract because the 'doctrine of frustration is not to be lightly invoked to relieve contracting parties of the normal consequences of imprudent commercial bargain or commercial risk'.[52] The landlord was awarded summary judgment.

A very similar case subsequently arose from the lease of shop premises, in a prime shopping area popular with tourists and Hong Kong locals, for the purpose of operating a business retailing certain beauty equipment and hair products.[53] The lease was concluded for a period of three years from August 2019. The tenants' business was adversely impacted by the Hong Kong government's decision, early in 2020 and in reaction to the pandemic, to tighten border controls and suspend transport services with the Chinese mainland, impose a 14-day quarantine requirement on persons entering Hong Kong from the Chinese mainland, and close all beauty salons (not including the tenants' retail business) for 73 days. The total number of visitors arriving in Hong Kong declined by 99 per cent compared to the corresponding period in the previous year. According to the tenants, these unforeseen developments affected their business so severely that they rendered it 'physically and commercially impossible' to meet their obligations under the lease.[54] In February and March 2020, the tenants ceased operating their business and vacated the leased premises so that the landlord might resume possession, but the landlord maintained that the lease remained

[49] Most measures were adopted under section 8 of the Prevention and Control of Disease Ordinance (Cap 599) and under the Prevention and Control of Disease Regulation (Cap 599A).

[50] *The Center (76) Ltd v Victory Serviced Office (HK) Ltd* [2020] HKCFI 2881, [2020] HKCU 4037 (CFI).

[51] ibid [39].

[52] ibid; furthermore, the fact that the tenants refused to vacate the premises while simultaneously maintaining that the contract had been frustrated was evidence of their lack of good faith in the frustration defence (ibid).

[53] *Sunbroad Holdings Ltd v A80 Paris HK Ltd* [2021] HKCFI 1422, [2021] 5 HKC 394 (CFI).

[54] ibid [51].

in force in accordance with its terms. Relying heavily on the recent judgment in the workspaces case,[55] the court rejected the frustration defence on the basis that the pandemic did not fundamentally change the nature of the outstanding contractual rights and obligations from that which the parties had reasonably contemplated at the time of the lease's conclusion. In the court's view, the parties intended that the tenants were to be permitted to operate a shop retailing certain beauty equipment and hair products, and there was 'no restriction preventing the [tenants] from doing just that'.[56] The court relied on the SARS case[57] to suggest in obiter that, even if the tenants' retail business had been closed for the same duration as Hong Kong's hair salons, there would still have been no frustration because 73 days was not a 'significant portion of the remainder of the lease term' of two years.[58] The landlord was awarded summary judgment.

In a more recent case,[59] tenants leased commercial shop premises from June 2012 to May 2021. The premises were in an area of Hong Kong popular with tourists and overseas visitors and from which the tenants operated a retail business in luxury jewellery and watches and other upmarket goods. With the arrival in Hong Kong of the COVID-19 pandemic and the government's regulatory reaction, the tenants' business suffered a sharp decline. In August 2019 and periodically thereafter, the tenants requested a 50 per cent reduction in rent, but the landlord refused. In February 2020, the tenants began defaulting on their rent and other obligations under the lease, and in March they gave the landlord cheques representing 50 per cent of the rent for February and March. Between April and July 2020, the tenants made further payments to the landlord in part satisfaction of their contractual obligations. In June 2020, the tenants informed the landlord of their intention to cease business operations on the leased premises the following month, but the landlord rejected the tenants' repudiation and maintained that the lease remained binding until May 2021. In November 2020, the tenants attempted to return the keys of the premises, but the landlord rejected the keys and reaffirmed its view that the lease remained binding. In March 2021, the landlord commenced legal proceedings against the tenants, claiming outstanding rent and other expenses. It was part of the tenants' defence that the lease had been frustrated by COVID-19.

The court noted that the tenants' obligations under the lease included the payment of monthly rent and other outgoing expenses and charges. These obligations were not conditional on the tenants' business performance, sales turnover, or even their use of the premises. On the contrary, the tenants expressly agreed to pay rent 'without any deduction and not to exercise any right or claim to withhold rent or other claim to set off'. The court was also of the view that the tenants had not shown how the pandemic specifically altered any of the parties' contractual rights and obligations as contemplated at the time of its execution. In this connection, the court pointedly remarked:

> What aggrieves the [tenants] is more of a general complaint that the pandemic—or more precisely, its economic effect as reflected in the decrease in the number of tourists

55 *The Center (76) Ltd v Victory Serviced Office (HK) Ltd* (n 50).
56 *Sunbroad Holdings Ltd v A80 Paris HK Ltd* (n 53) [62].
57 *Li Ching Wing v Xuan Yi Xiong* (n 46).
58 *Sunbroad Holdings Ltd v A80 Paris HK Ltd* (n 53) [58], [62].
59 *Holdwin Ltd v Prince Jewellery and Watch Co Ltd* [2021] HKCFI 2735, [2021] HKCU 4494 (CFI).

> and overseas visitors in Hong Kong—is said to have made the [tenants'] business at the Premises financially untenable. This is a common problem faced by retailers in Hong Kong during the Covid-19 pandemic.
>
> However, one has to recognise that ensuring the financial viability of the [tenants'] business was not the purpose of the Lease nor could it be reasonably suggested that was what the parties had contemplated at the time of entering the Lease. Unless such purpose constituted a part of the parties' contractual arrangement, that surely cannot be the case otherwise any supervening event which might materially impair the [tenants'] business could be a frustrating event (e.g., global events which threaten supply chains, cross-border travel, economic crises, etc to think of a few). It is therefore a *non sequitur* to say that the pandemic significantly changed the nature of the Lease or the parties' rights and obligations.[60]

The court was therefore of the view that the parties' contractual obligations, as properly identified, had not been negatived or transformed by the pandemic and the defence of frustration failed.[61] The landlord was awarded summary judgment.

In a factually very similar case,[62] and similarly involving leases of premises for the retail sale of luxury watches, the tenants took a somewhat different tack in mounting their frustration defence. The tenants maintained that the effects of the government's response to the pandemic were such as to defeat the parties' common purpose in concluding the lease.[63] The court took the view that the appropriate way to formulate any common purpose that might exist would be that the leased premises were to be 'commercially viably operated as luxury watch retail stores'.[64] However, having regard to the way business is customarily conducted, the court held that no such common purpose could be said to exist:

> To say that commercial viability of the business on the Premises is part of the common purpose of the [leases] is another way of saying that both parties agreed to take risks over the lack thereof. Given the landlord's wholesale lack of control over such business, it is simply difficult to see how, objectively speaking, the landlord can be taken to have agreed to bear such risks.[65]

As there was no radical or fundamental change to the nature of the rights or obligations established by the lease, the frustration defence failed and summary judgment was awarded to the landlord.

The same tenant timepiece retailers, in a factually similar case with a different landlord,[66] were unable to persuade the Hong Kong Court of Appeal to overturn summary judgment in the landlord's favour; once again the tenants could not establish that a commercial lease

60 ibid [35(4)]–[35(5)].

61 Furthermore, the fact that the tenants continued operating their business from the leased premises for six months after the arrival of the COVID-19 pandemic and offered to perform their obligations on the basis of a 50 per cent rent reduction was evidence of their lack of good faith in the frustration defence (ibid [42]).

62 *The One Property Ltd v The Swatch Group (Hong Kong) Ltd* [2022] HKCFI 362, [2022] HKCU 601 (CFI).

63 *Krell v Henry* (n 24).

64 *The One Property Ltd v The Swatch Group (Hong Kong) Ltd* (n 62) [17(b)], [18] (emphasis omitted).

65 ibid [21(c)].

66 *Vember Lord Ltd v The Swatch Group (Hong Kong) Ltd* [2023] HKCA 371, [2023] HKCU 1120 (CA, HK).

to operate a retail business in watches resulted in any 'common commercial purpose' that might have been frustrated by the pandemic or the government's measures resulting in a collapse in the number of foreign visitors and tourists to Hong Kong.

IV. *Force majeure*: Express Contractual Provision

It is not uncommon for commercial contracts to include a clause that expressly releases (permanently or temporarily) the contracting parties from their obligations upon the occurrence of an extraordinary supervening event. Such a provision is usually referred to as a *force majeure* clause.[67] If the parties have agreed a *force majeure* clause, the contract will not be frustrated by an event that falls within the scope of the clause. Instead, the consequences of the event will be regulated by the terms of the contract itself.[68] However, in order to avoid frustration the parties must have intended to make provision for the event that actually occurred.

In the University Heights case,[69] the contracts stipulated:

> [S]hould *any unforeseen circumstances* beyond the Vendor's control arise whereby the Vendor becomes unable to sell the [apartment] to the Purchaser . . . the Vendor shall be at liberty to rescind this Agreement forthwith and to refund to the Purchaser all instalments of purchase price paid by the Purchaser . . . and upon such rescission and upon repayment of the instalments of purchase price this Agreement shall become null and void . . . and neither party hereto shall have any claim against the other in respect thereof.

The purchasers argued that this clause made provision displacing the general rule automatically terminating contracts for frustration but that the vendor had not exercised its stipulated right to rescind and that the contracts therefore remained in force. The court acknowledged that the clause was indeed wide enough to cover the landslip. However, in interpreting a clause which is said to have anticipated the frustrating event, the question is not whether the words employed are in some general sense wide enough to cover the event. Indeed, the more general the words, the more likely they are to cover a broader range of events. The correct test is, instead, whether the general words are sufficient to support an inference that the parties intended to make provision for the *event that actually occurred.* The court held that the clause did not save the contracts from frustration precisely because its language was too general; it did not manifest an intention to provide for the specific event that made it impossible for the parties to achieve their contractual adventure.

Similarly, in the luxury jewellery case,[70] the lease contained a lengthy *force majeure* clause headed 'Suspension of Rent in Case of Fire Etc', which provided in part as follows:

> If the Premises or the Building or any part thereof shall at any time during the Lease be destroyed or damaged or become inaccessible owing to the fire water storm typhoon defective

67 *Force majeure*, from French: overwhelming force, fundamental force, superior force.
68 *Aircraft Purchase Fleet Ltd v Compagnia Aerea Italiana SpA* [2018] EWHC 3315 (QB) [110].
69 *Wong Lai-ying v Chinachem Investment Co Ltd* (n 43) (emphasis added).
70 *Holdwin Ltd v Prince Jewellery and Watch Co Ltd* (n 59) (emphasis added).

> construction white ants earthquake subsidence of the ground or any calamity or causes beyond the control of the [landlord] so as to render the Premises unfit for commercial use or inaccessible [*sic*] . . . or if any time [*sic*] during the continuance of this Lease the Premises or the Building shall be condemned as a dangerous structure or a demolition order or closing order shall become operative in respect of the Premises or the Building *then the rent hereby reserved or a fair proportion thereof according to the nature and extent of the damage sustained or order made shall be suspended* until the Premises or Building shall again be rendered accessible and fit for commercial use . . . . Nothing in this Section shall be construed as requiring the [landlord] to repair or reinstate the Premises if in its opinion it is not reasonably economical or practicable so to do.

When the landlord commenced proceedings to recover outstanding rent under the lease, the tenants raised the *force majeure* clause as a defence and argued inter alia that the clause had been triggered by the COVID-19 pandemic and that the agreed rent obligations had been suspended. This defence failed on the basis that the ordinary and natural meaning of the words employed in the *force majeure* clause indicated that the clause was 'premised upon physical damage' to the premises and was not intended to cover a decline in business resulting from the pandemic.[71]

Where, however, the parties have unambiguously expressed themselves, a *force majeure* clause will be given effect according to its terms. As Hong Kong's Court of Final Appeal has observed:

> Like any other contractual provision, a *force majeure* clause is to be given a fair reading in its factual matrix. Of course since contracts are made to be performed, clauses invoked to remove or modify obligations of performance ought at least in general to receive a strict construction. Such a construction means that any ambiguity would be resolved against the party seeking to rely on the clause. But that is not to say that such clauses, made within the freedom of contract, are to be viewed with hostility. It is not for the courts to encourage or discourage such clauses. Whether or not such a clause is to be included in a contract must be left to the parties freely to negotiate. . . . a strict construction does not mean a jaundiced construction.[72]

Each case will, therefore, turn on its own set of facts, including the language employed in the contract. In Australia, a lease permitting a neon advertising sign to be erected on the premises included a clause stipulating that the unpaid balance of the rental was due if the lessee's 'interest' in the premises was 'extinguished'. The Queensland government compulsorily acquired the premises, thereby extinguishing the lessee's interest. The court held that the contract was not frustrated as it had anticipated the compulsory acquisition, and the parties' obligations were to be governed by the clause.[73]

[71] ibid [51].
[72] *Goldlion Properties Ltd v Regent National Enterprises Ltd* (2009) 12 HKCFAR 512, [2009] 5 HKC 67 (CFA) (Bokhary PJ and Chan PJ) [6].
[73] *Claude Neon Ltd v Hardie* [1970] Qd R 93 (FCSC, Queensland).

V. Frustration: Consequences

A frustrating event automatically discharges a contract; neither party is required to make an election between discharging or affirming the contract upon the occurrence of the event.[74]

Until 1942, the position at common law was that all rights and obligations accruing after the frustration were terminated but that all rights and obligations accruing up to that time remained unaffected. In another of the coronation cases, the plaintiff hired a room from which to view the coronation processions for King Edward VII. The agreed price was £141, payable immediately. The plaintiff paid, however, only £100 upon conclusion of the agreement. Before he could pay the balance, the procession was cancelled due to the King's ill health. When the plaintiff sued for the return of the £100, he was unsuccessful; he was also required to pay the additional £41 because the entire sum was due and owing prior to the frustrating event.[75] In another case, the plaintiff agreed to install machinery in the defendant's factory. While the installation work was still in progress, the factory and partially installed machinery were destroyed by fire. The plaintiff could recover nothing because, under the terms of the contract, he was not entitled to any payment until the job was complete and the frustration had terminated all rights which had not yet accrued.[76]

The harshness of the common law position was ameliorated in 1942. An English company agreed to sell machinery to a Polish company. The contract was made in July 1939, and the machinery was to be delivered to Poland three to four months later. The agreement was that the Polish company would make an advance payment of £1,600 immediately and the balance of £3,200 upon delivery. In fact, the Polish company made an advance payment of only £1,000. Before any of the machinery could be delivered the German army invaded Poland in early September 1939, the United Kingdom declared war on Germany, and the contract was frustrated. The Polish company sued for the return of the £1,000 advance payment. The Polish company was able to recover its £1,000 and was relieved of any obligation to pay the £600 shortfall in the advance payment. The earlier position was overruled, but only to the extent that there had been a total failure of consideration for its actual and promised advance payment; the Polish company had received nothing in exchange for the payment.[77]

The following year, the United Kingdom Parliament enacted legislation that reformed the law concerning the consequences of frustration.[78] In 1948, the English statutory reforms were faithfully transposed to Hong Kong; these can now be found in the Law Amendment and Reform (Consolidation) Ordinance (Cap 23).[79] Whether a contract has been frustrated remains to be established according to the common law. The principal reforms effected by the Ordinance are embodied in section 16(2) (sums paid or payable before the frustrating event) and section 16(3) (obtaining a valuable benefit before the frustrating event).

Under section 16(2) of the Ordinance, the rule is that sums paid before the frustrating event are refundable, and sums payable before that event cease to be payable. This reverses the common law rule. The legislative rule is, however, subject to an important proviso. The

74 *Wong Lai-ying v Chinachem Investment Co Ltd* (n 43); *Cheung Lai Kit v Rich Prosper Ltd* (n 41).
75 *Chandler v Webster* [1904] 1 KB 493 (CA, Eng).
76 *Appleby v Myers* (n 20).
77 *Fibrosa Spolka Akcyjna v Fairbairn Lawson Combe Barbour Ltd* [1943] AC 32, [1942] 2 All ER 122 (HL).
78 Law Reform (Frustrated Contracts) Act 1943.
79 Ord, s 16.

party to whom such sums have been paid may retain an amount not greater than the expenses actually incurred by him in connection with his actual or anticipated performance of the contract. Similarly, he may claim such expenses up to, but not exceeding, any expenses incurred in connection with his actual or anticipated performance of the contract before the contract was frustrated. The court has a wide discretion to permit such claims ('if it considers it just to do so having regard to all the circumstances of the case').[80]

Under section 16(3) of the Ordinance it is possible for a party to recover for a partial performance which has, before the discharge by frustration, conferred a valuable benefit on the other party. A payment of money covered by section 16(2) is not within the ambit of section 16(3). In assessing an award under section 16(3), the court undertakes a two-stage process: (i) it must be satisfied of the existence of a valuable benefit gained by one party as a result of the other party's performance under the contract; (ii) it must then be established what is the just sum to award in all the circumstances of the case (with the upper limit of the award being the value of the benefit conferred).[81]

The Ordinance also importantly makes provision for the severance of non-frustrated parts of a contract.[82]

VI. Practical Applications

How might these principles of frustration work in a range of hypothetical scenarios?[83]

Let us first hypothesize that George agrees with Han to refurbish the cellar of Han's restaurant, with the work to commence in one month's time. Before the work begins, the restaurant is completely destroyed by a storm that is much more violent than any previous storm in the region. However, there is no damage to the cellar. Han immediately informs George of the new situation and asks him not to start work. George nevertheless insists on rendering performance because he has set aside two weeks to carry out the work and has already purchased the necessary materials. George now wishes to know whether Han is obliged to pay the contract price or, alternatively, compensate George for his losses.

The refurbishment contract will remain in force unless it can be proved that the contract is not, on its true construction, 'wide enough to apply to the new situation' or that the circumstances created by the supervening storm would render the agreement 'a thing radically different from that which was undertaken by the contract'. This requires, first, identifying the scope of the contractual adventure by interpreting the contract's terms. The task of interpretation can take account of any 'state of things' understood by the parties, at the time of making their agreement, as essential to the contract's performance. Having regard to the fact that the cellar was part of a restaurant at the time the agreement was made, it is probable that reasonable persons in the shoes of George and Han would have understood that the existence of the restaurant was a 'state of things' essential to the contract's performance.

[80] *Gamerco SA v ICM/Fair Warning (Agency) Ltd* [1995] 1 WLR 1226 (QB) (interpreting the equivalent provision in the Law Reform (Frustrated Contracts) Act 1943).

[81] *BP Exploration Co (Libya) Ltd v Hunt (No 2)* [1982] 1 All ER 925, [1979] 1 WLR 783 (QB) (interpreting the equivalent provision in the Law Reform (Frustrated Contracts) Act 1943).

[82] Ord, s 17(4).

[83] The fact scenarios of the hypotheticals described in section VI are taken from M Chen-Wishart, D Neo, and S Vogenauer, 'Introduction', ch 1 in this volume, 8.

Secondly, the contract does not appear to have allocated the risk of the storm to either party, and there would not appear to be any custom or usual practice allocating the risk of the supervening event. It would not be difficult to establish, thirdly, that the unforeseen storm did not occur as the result of the fault or choice of either party. Fourthly, given that the existence of the restaurant was a 'state of things' essential to the contract's performance, it would be relatively simple to establish that the restaurant's complete destruction renders achievement of the contractual adventure impossible or makes further performance of the contract something radically different than that which the parties agreed. It is therefore likely that the storm frustrated and automatically terminated the contract.

At common law, George would be unable to recover either his expectation or reliance losses. Legislation improves his position somewhat. George may now claim such expenses up to, but not exceeding, any expenses incurred in connection with his actual or anticipated performance of the contract before the contract was frustrated. The court has a wide discretion to permit such claims ('if it considers it just to do so having regard to all the circumstances of the case').

Let us next assume that Gina reserves a room for the weekend at a hotel and that the contract of reservation does not permit Gina to cancel unilaterally. However, Gina now wishes to cancel her reservation because:

(i) the inauguration proceedings of a public official that were scheduled for Saturday are cancelled. Gina had reserved a room overlooking the street along which the inauguration procession was planned to pass. The room's rental was ten times the usual rate because of the procession;
(ii) the exhibition that Gina intended to visit is cancelled at the very last moment;
(iii) a terrorist group declares that it plans to launch attacks on tourists in the city where the hotel is located;
(iv) an unforeseeable strike by airport personnel prevents Gina from travelling, before Sunday afternoon, to the city where the hotel is located.

Whether Gina can unilaterally cancel her reservation in situation (i) will depend on whether, at the time of making the contract of reservation, the hotel was aware that the procession was essential to the contractual adventure. If the hotel was or ought reasonably to have been aware of the essential importance of the procession to Gina, the contract was automatically terminated upon the procession's cancellation. The fact that the rental was ten times the usual rate will probably serve as strong evidence, if needed, from which the hotel's knowledge may be inferred.

Gina probably cannot unilaterally cancel her reservation in situation (ii). Even if the hotel was aware that Gina's intention was to visit the exhibition, it is most unlikely that the exhibition was a state of things essential to the contract's performance. The reserved room probably had nothing particular to do with the exhibition except as a convenient place to reside while making the visit, other hotels serving that purpose equally well.

Gina can probably unilaterally cancel her reservation in situation (iii). A change of circumstances that renders performance of the contract unreasonably hazardous to life will automatically terminate the contract.

Whether Gina can unilaterally cancel her reservation in situation (iv) will depend on whether she contractually assumed the risk of the strike occurring. If Gina assumed the risk, the contract of reservation will remain in force and she will not be free unilaterally to cancel the reservation. Conversely, if Gina did not assume the risk, the contract of reservation will be automatically terminated by the strike and she may cancel the reservation. The hypothetical scenario stipulates, perhaps improbably, that the strike by airport personnel was 'unforeseeable'. If the risk of the strike occurring truly was unforeseeable (eg because such strikes were unlawful or unprecedented in the place it occurred), then it will be easier to infer that neither party intended the contract to allocate risk and the contract was automatically terminated. If, on the other hand, the strike risk was foreseeable but the contract simply made no express provision for the contingency, then the parties will be taken to have contracted that the risk will lie where it customarily does in such situations; in this case, it would almost certainly lie with Gina, who would have assumed the customary risk of such occurrences. Only if there is no custom in such situations would the contract be automatically terminated by the strike.

Finally, let us hypothesize that Kris sells his house to Leila at 70 per cent of its market value. In making the contract of sale, both parties assume that Leila will dedicate the property's use to the general public for cultural purposes. However, this assumption is not expressly set out in the contract. After the sale, Leila changes her mind and gifts the house to her son. Can Kris claim the difference between the agreed price and the market value or, alternatively, restitution of the house?

The contract of sale is not frustrated. The doctrine of frustration will operate only if there has been a supervening event (ie an event arising between the making of the contract and its performance) that renders the agreement 'a thing radically different from that which was undertaken by the contract' and that was not the fault or choice of either party. Even if the assumed post-sale purpose of the house is a 'state of things' essential to the contractual adventure, its non-occurrence was the choice of one of the parties. Kris's remedy at common law, if any, would be for breach of contract (that the assumed post-sale purpose of the house is not expressly set out in the contract document is not necessarily dispositive).[84]

VII. Impossibility: Mistake

A common mistake at common law occurs when each party makes the same error about some fact or circumstance fundamental to the contract such that achievement of the contractual adventure is rendered impossible. There are five conditions that must be satisfied in order to establish a common mistake: (i) there must be a common assumption as to the existence of a state of affairs; (ii) there must be no warranty by either party that that state of affairs exists; (iii) the non-existence of the state of affairs must not be attributable to the fault of either party; (iv) the non-existence of the state of affairs must render performance of the contract impossible; (v) the state of affairs may be the existence, or a vital attribute, of the consideration to be provided or circumstances which must subsist if performance of the contractual adventure is to be possible. Where a common mistake is established, the contract is void.[85]

[84] Hall (n 1) 65–77.

[85] *Great Peace Shipping Ltd v Tsavliris Salvage (International) Ltd* [2002] EWCA Civ 1407, [2003] QB 679, [2002] 4 All ER 689 (CA, Eng) [76].

Common mistake functions in a way similar to frustration in that the error must be of such a nature as to render performance of the contractual adventure impossible. However, the error renders the contract void (ie a nullity from the outset) rather than terminated. More importantly, however, mistake cannot apply to facts or circumstances that arise after conclusion of the contract. There was, for instance, no operative mistake where a plaintiff remittance agent advanced Hong Kong cash to a defendant customer in the disappointed expectation and belief that a third party would transfer an equivalent sum in Philippine currency to the plaintiff; the plaintiff 'was not acting under any mistake of fact, but on what turned out to be his misprediction that what had always happened in the past (that is, that the banknotes would arrive safely) would happen again on this occasion'.[86] Mistake is therefore not available as a response to a post-contractual change of circumstances.

VIII. Hardship Falling Short of Impossibility: Interpretation

Unless post-contractual events render achievement of the contractual adventure impossible or make further performance of the contract something radically different than that which the parties agreed (with the effect of frustrating and automatically terminating the contract), the general rule is that the contract can be lawfully adjusted or terminated only by agreement of the parties. Lord Loreburn succinctly stated the orthodox common law position more than a century ago:

> [A] court can and ought to examine the contract and the circumstances in which it was made, not of course to vary, but only to explain it, in order to see whether or not from the nature of it the parties must have made their bargain on the footing that a particular thing or state of things would continue to exist.[87]

It is nevertheless possible that, in certain circumstances, modern common law principles of contract interpretation will reveal what the parties intended to occur in the event of changed circumstances disturbing the equilibrium of costs and benefits originally anticipated by the parties at the time of contracting.

In a recent United Kingdom Supreme Court case involving 21 holiday chalets at a leisure park in Wales that were leased between 1977 and 1991 on terms expiring in 2073, the lessees had agreed to pay an annual service charge. At the time the leases were granted, the United Kingdom was experiencing high rates of price inflation. For the first year of the term, the charge was a fixed sum of £90; then it escalated at a compounding rate of 10 per cent each succeeding year. This arrangement obviously had the potential eventually to impose a very substantial and ever-escalating financial obligation on the lessees as the years rolled by.[88] The lessees sought, inter alia, to have the term interpreted such that they were obliged to pay only a fair proportion of the lessor's costs, subject to a ceiling of £90 in the first year with the ceiling increasing at a compounding rate of 10 per cent in each succeeding year. This interpretation was argued to be in accordance with modern common law principles of contract

[86] *Patel's Wall Street Exchange Ltd v SK International* [2005] 2 HKLRD 551 (CFI) [37].
[87] *FA Tamplin Steamship Co Ltd v Anglo-Mexican Petroleum Products Co Ltd* [1916] 2 AC 397, 403 (HL).
[88] For a lease granted in 1977, the service charge would be more than £4,000 by 2017.

interpretation. These principles require that where the ordinary meaning of the words in a contract document is ambiguous or where it leads to an interpretation that reasonable persons in the position of the parties could not possibly have intended, then it is necessary to depart from the ordinary meaning and search for another that most accords with what reasonable persons in the position of the parties probably intended the contract to mean having regard to their background knowledge in making the agreement.[89]

A majority of the Supreme Court decided that the escalation clause could not bear the meaning that the lessees sought to impose on it. Lord Neuberger, the Supreme Court's president, said:

> Quite apart from the fact that the effect of [the escalation clause] appears clear in each lease as a matter of language, I am far from convinced by the commercially-based argument that it is inconceivable that a lessee would have agreed a service charge provision which had the effect for which the respondent contends, at least in the 1970s and much of the 1980s. Although I would have expected most solicitors to have advised against it, and imprudent though it undoubtedly has turned out to be (at least so far), a lessee could have taken the view that a fixed rate of increase of 10% per annum on a fixed initial service charge, at a time when annual inflation had been running at a higher rate for a number of years (well over 10% per annum between 1974 and 1981, indeed over 15% per annum for six of those eight years; although it was less than 10% per annum after 1981), was attractive or at least acceptable.

The Court reached this conclusion even after Lord Neuberger took the opportunity to articulate a number of general 'factors' to be considered in applying modern principles of contract interpretation, including the following[90]:

> [I]n some cases, an event subsequently occurs which was plainly not intended or contemplated by the parties, judging from the language of their contract. In such a case, if it is clear what the parties would have intended, the court will give effect to that intention.[91]

It therefore appears that had the text of the price escalation clause been less clear, and had the economic conditions at the time of concluding the contracts been different, the Court would have been more receptive to an interpretation argument along the lines advanced by the lessees. Neither the text of the clause nor the circumstances prevailing at the time the leases were granted could lead the Court to conclude that it was 'inconceivable' that reasonable persons in the position of the parties would have understood the clause to mean anything other than what it plainly said.

Where a contract is for an unlimited period of time, it is possible that a court could be somewhat more inclined to interpret the contract as conferring a right of unilateral termination on one or both of the parties. In 1929, a water company and a hospital authority in England concluded a contract by which the hospital would purchase water at a fixed rate of

[89] Hall (n 10) 256.
[90] *Arnold v Britton* [2015] UKSC 36, [2015] AC 1619, [2016] 1 All ER 1 [35], Lord Sumption and Lord Hughes agreeing.
[91] ibid [22].

7 pence per 1,000 gallons 'at all times hereafter' (the rate was changed to 2.439 pence upon the introduction of decimal currency in 1967). By 1975, the normal rate for the purchase of water had risen to 45 pence. The 1929 contract effectively replaced a 1909 statutory obligation on the company to supply water to the hospital at a non-fixed rate to be determined by arbitration in case of dispute. The court held that the company could terminate the contract. Having regard to the circumstances in which the contract was made, including the extant non-fixed nature of the price, the parties intended that there would be a right of termination and the phrase 'at all times hereafter' was intended to mean 'at all times hereafter during the subsistence of the agreement'.[92]

These principles of interpretation establish a framework within which common law courts may, in very narrow circumstances, restore the equilibrium of costs and benefits anticipated by the parties at the time of contracting that has been disturbed by unforeseen supervening events. The framework remains, however, closely tethered to the parties' objectively ascertained intentions at the time of contracting and is very far from resembling anything in the nature of a *révision pour imprévision*. On the contrary, as Lord Neuberger cautioned, 'there is no principle of interpretation which entitles a court to re-write a contractual provision simply because the factor which the parties catered for does not seem to be developing in the way in which the parties may well have expected'.[93]

IX. Practical Applications

How might these principles work in a range of hypothetical scenarios?[94]

Let us assume, first, that in the sixteenth century Abraham enters into a contract for an unlimited period of time with farmer Bill under which Abraham promises to build and maintain an irrigation channel from which Bill may extract water at a fixed price. Inflation and the rise in the cost of maintenance and labour have made the agreed price wholly inadequate. In 2018, Abraham's successors in law ask for an increase in the price that would provide them with adequate compensation. Alternatively, they wish to terminate the contract.

Secondly, let us assume that in 2015 Citi Corporation receives a loan from Drive Bank. The interest rate is fixed at 10 per cent for five years. In the 20 years preceding the agreement, the annual rate of inflation had been relatively stable within a range of 1–6 per cent. In 2017, the economic situation begins to destabilize and the annual inflation rate rises to 50 per cent. Drive Bank now requests adjustment or, alternatively, termination of the contract.

Finally, we may assume that Easy leases business premises from Frugle for a fixed period of 15 years. Shortly after the contract has been concluded, a nearby military airport is unexpectedly decommissioned. The government invests enormous public funds to improve the commercial infrastructure in the area. As a result, Easy's profits are five times greater than could reasonably have been expected at the time of making the contract. At the same time, the rental value of comparable business premises in the area increases by five times the

92 *Staffordshire Area Health Authority v South Staffordshire Waterworks Co* [1978] 3 All ER 769, [1978] 1 WLR 1387 (CA, Eng).

93 *Arnold v Britton* (n 90) [41].

94 The fact scenarios for the hypotheticals described in this section are taken from M Chen-Wishart, D Neo, and S Vogenauer, 'Introduction', ch 1 in this volume, 7–8.

agreed rent. Frugle requests that the rent should be adjusted accordingly or, alternatively, that the agreement should be terminated.

The common law principles regulating these three scenarios are essentially the same. Each of them involves one party's expectation of either an adjustment to consideration (in the form of a service charge, interest, or rent) or the contract's termination. The adjustment or termination would be in response to a change of circumstances for which the contract made no provision and which substantially disturbed the equilibrium of costs and benefits originally anticipated by the parties at the time of contracting. Such a disturbance is not per se sufficient to render achievement of the contractual adventure impossible or (to express essentially the same idea in other words) make further performance of the contract something radically different than that which the parties agreed. Consequently, none of these scenarios would automatically terminate the contract for frustration.

The common law includes nothing in the nature of a *révision pour imprévision*, and whether it is possible to adjust the parties' obligations in order to restore their equilibrium of costs and benefits will depend on whether such was their intention at the time of contracting. The court itself will not impose an adjustment on the parties, even if they now agree to such an imposition; it is simply not the courts' function to revise contracts.

Rather, a court must be satisfied that the parties themselves, at the time of contracting, would have intended an adjustment of their obligations or a termination of contract in the event of the new circumstances arising. If they did, then a court will give effect to that intention *but only if it is clear what the parties would have intended in the new circumstances.* This is essentially a matter of contract interpretation, but 'there is no principle of interpretation which entitles a court to re-write a contractual provision simply because the factor which the parties catered for does not seem to be developing in the way in which the parties may well have expected'.[95] Certainly, the imprudence of an agreement provides no basis for adjusting its terms.

There would appear to be nothing in the circumstances of the second and third agreements (the loan and the lease) that would make it inconceivable that the parties did not intend the contracts to bear their plain meaning. On the contrary, the long-term interest rate environment that prevailed at the time of making the second (loan) agreement indicated that the parties were making an agreement that was already generous to the lender. There is no evidence that the parties intended a variation in the event that rising interest rates would make the agreement less advantageous to the lender or displacing the expectation that each party would bear the customary risk of interest rate fluctuations. Further militating against a variation of the agreed interest rate is the loan agreement's relatively short duration. Similarly, the third (lease) agreement appears to contain nothing indicating the parties' intention to vary the rent in the event of a change in market rents, each party apparently accepting that he would bear the customary risk of any such changes. The fact that the agreement has a medium-length time limit would likely further militate against any variation of the contract.

The only potentially material difference with the first (service charge) agreement is that it is of unlimited duration. This makes it somewhat more likely that the contract could be interpreted in such a way as to confer a right of termination on A, subject to giving reasonable

[95] *Arnold v Britton* (n 90) [41].

notice. However, if there is nothing in the language of the contract or the circumstances surrounding its conclusion upon which such an intention could reasonably be inferred (such as the existence of price inflation at the time of contracting or the contract's replacement of a previous legal obligation to adjust the price), the contract would probably not be unilaterally terminable.

6

Termination of Contracts in Hong Kong

*Kelvin FK LOW**

I. Introduction

Among the many 'gifts' conferred upon Hong Kong by its British colonial masters, none is more valued than that of the rule of law, widely regarded as essential to Hong Kong's status as one of Asia's foremost financial centres. Nevertheless, Hong Kong's beginnings as a British colony and the earliest contracts agreed upon were unpromising. After the Opium Wars, Hong Kong was ceded to the United Kingdom; as frequent Chinese criticism points out, this happened under the first of many unequal treaties imposed upon China, triggering a century of humiliation. But even if one ignores such complaints, it is undeniable that Hong Kong's early days were marked by many dubious—if not outright illegal—agreements. Among the earliest contracts concluded in Hong Kong were the first auctions of land on Hong Kong island, which were held on 14 June 1841,[1] shortly after Captain Charles Elliot took possession of the island on behalf of the Crown on 26 January 1841. Although Western sources often point to the so-called Convention of Chuenpi as the basis of Elliot's actions and acknowledge that the Convention was never ratified by either the British or the Chinese government,[2] it is probably a misnomer to even describe this as a preliminary agreement. In truth, no agreement had been reached when Elliot took possession of Hong Kong island,[3] and the Treaty of Nanking, which provided for the cession, was only ratified on 26 June 1843. Not only were the auctions thus at least improper if not outright illegal, but also it is not entirely clear that these contracts would have satisfied ordinary English principles of contract law.[4] Under the terms announced on 1 May 1841, it was not clear what precisely the purchasers were bidding for in terms of the estate of the land. Although the subject of the bidding was rent, the precise estates purchased were not settled until well after the ratification of the Treaty of Nanking,[5] even though Elliot had dangled the carrot of a potential freehold fee simple estate to entice merchants to bid.[6] No proper grants[7] were made pursuant to these 'contracts' until at least 1844, after a Land Committee set up by the

* I am grateful to Professor Hugh Beale for his invaluable advice on writing for a comparative law audience and to Assistant Professor Jing Hui for his research assistance. The usual caveats apply.

1 R Nissim, *Land Administration and Practice in Hong Kong* (5th edn, HKU Press 2022) 3.

2 ibid.

3 H Mao, *The Qing Empire and the Opium War: The Collapse of the Heavenly Dynasty* (J Lawson, C Smith, and P Lavelle, CUP 2016) 195–97.

4 Contracts for the sale of land must satisfy the minimum of three Ps, being parties, property, and price, in order to be sufficiently certain, and 'property' in this context requires both 'the identity of the land which is to be sold and the estate which is to be granted' to be established: E Cooke, S Bridge, and M Dixon, *Megarry & Wade: The Law of Real Property* (9th edn, Sweet & Maxwell 2019) 608.

5 Nissim (n 1) 9.

6 ibid 5.

7 ibid 6.

Kelvin FK Low, *Termination of Contracts in Hong Kong* In: *Studies in the Contract Laws of Asia V: Ending and Changing Contracts*. Edited by: Mindy Chen-Wishart, Dora Neo, and Stefan Vogenauer, Oxford University Press.
 DOI: 10.1093/oso/9780198995814.003.0006

first Governor of Hong Kong, Sir Henry Pottinger, to investigate all claims to land had rendered its report.[8]

After this inauspicious start, principles of English common law came to be gradually transplanted and adapted to local needs from 5 April 1843, beginning with the Charter of the Colony of Hong Kong, through the Application of English Law Ordinance 1966, and culminating in Article 8 of the Basic Law, regarded as Hong Kong's mini-Constitution. Under the latter provision, the rules of the common law and equity are preserved despite the resumption of sovereignty over Hong Kong by China, which follows the civil law tradition. For the most part, Hong Kong contract law is indistinguishable from its English counterpart. Both the judiciary and the legislature generally follow English developments. In particular, Hong Kong contract law reflects, and perhaps even emphasizes, the hard-nosed character of English common law that is thought to be favoured by the international business community. The presence of foreign Non-Permanent Judges on the apex of the judicial hierarchy, previously dominated by sitting and former Law Lords and Justices of the UK Supreme Court,[9] also ensures the continued influence of English law in Hong Kong. As a small jurisdiction, it lacks the body of case law necessary to chart its own path in all issues, and the result is that, even where a local textbook exists, English cases dominate the table of cases.[10] Rightly or wrongly, the conservatism of both the judiciary and the legislature stems in part from the mindset that, lacking natural resources, Hong Kong's continued success depends on its appeal to the international business community. Much of Hong Kong's latter-day success as a British colony is attributable to such fortuitous circumstances as the Californian gold rush[11] and the victory of the communists in the Chinese Civil War,[12] which triggered the relocation of capital from Shanghai to Hong Kong. 'The spectacular economic growth seen in the 1970s and 1980s in Hong Kong . . . resulted largely from historical and geopolitical factors.'[13] Even today, external circumstances continue to play an important role in Hong Kong's fortune as it prospers as 'a parasitic economy that has benefitted hugely from the constraints on freedoms in China by acting as an entrepôt and running the only international capital market on Chinese soil'.[14] Hong Kongers also underappreciate the contribution of their own entrepreneurial spirit[15] and indefatigable industry,

[8] ibid 10.

[9] Of the fourteen Non-Permanent Judges from other jurisdictions at the time of writing in 2020, nine were from the United Kingdom, four from Australia, and one from Canada. By 2023, at the time of final revisions, the number of overseas Non-Permanent Judges had fallen to ten. One, Lord Millett, passed away. The UK representatives who were sitting UK Supreme Court judges—Lord Reed and Lord Hodge—resigned (see Victor Dawes, 'UK Judges' Exit Is Disappointing, But Hong Kong Judicial Independence Will Continue to Be Upheld' *South China Morning Post* (Hong Kong, 30 March 2022)), so did Justice Spigelman from Australia before them (see Gary Cheung, Jeffie Lam, and Jack Lau, 'Veteran Australian Judge James Spigelman Resigns from Hong Kong's Top Court, Citing National Security Law' *South China Morning Post* (Hong Kong, 18 September 2020). In the past, there was greater diversity among the Non-Permanent Judges.

[10] For contract law, see eg S Hall, *Ho & Hall's Hong Kong Contract Law* (6th edn, LexisNexis Butterworths 2022).

[11] E Sinn, *Pacific Crossing: California Gold, Chinese Migration, and the Making of Hong Kong* (HKU Press 2013).

[12] S Tsang, *A Modern History of Hong Kong* (IB Tauris 2004) 161–79.

[13] JD Wong, 'Between Two Episodes of Social Unrest below Lion Rock: From the 1967 Riots to the 2014 Umbrella Movement' in MHK Ng and JD Wong (eds), *Civil Unrest and Governance in Hong Kong: Law and Order from Historical and Cultural Perspectives* (Routledge 2017) 97, 105.

[14] D Webb, 'Freedom and the Future of China' (*High Table Talk*, Chi Sun College, University of Hong Kong, 30 October 2018) <https://webb-site.com/articles/chisun.asp> accessed 6 September 2019.

[15] Tsang (n 12). Note also that the phenomenon of nimble manufacturers in modern China imbued with a so-called Shanzhai (山寨) culture, sometimes regarded as embodying iterative innovation (see A Chubb, 'China's *Shanzhai* Culture: "Grabism" and the Politics of Hybridity' (2015) 24 Journal of Contemporary China 260, 267–70), employs a term that first developed that alternative meaning in Hong Kong: see L Wang, 'The Three Buzzwords: 山寨 (Shanzhai), 雷 (Lei), and 囧 (Jiong)' in Y Li and W Li (eds), *The Language Situation in China*

which has been dubbed the 'Lion Rock spirit'.[16] However, many Hong Kong residents, particularly those within the business and legal communities, are wont to overemphasize the importance of the English common law in general and its emphasis of commercial certainty over vague notions of good faith and fairness in particular.

It is often forgotten that corruption was endemic in Hong Kong throughout most of its colonial history in spite of the common law,[17] a problem that the colonial government only began to seriously tackle with the establishment of the Independent Commission against Corruption (ICAC) in 1974.[18] Likewise, racist laws that were also a feature of much of colonial rule, epitomized by the Peak District (Residence) Ordinance,[19] which prohibited any Chinese from residing in any area on Hong Kong island above the 788 feet contour, are mostly regarded as a distant memory.[20] Part of the fear of ambiguity in the law stems from 'one country, two systems', the epitome of uncertainty to many Hong Kongers, which stoked anxiety from the moment the Sino-British Joint Declaration was concluded.[21] The introduction of the Law of the People's Republic of China on Safeguarding National Security in the Hong Kong Special Administrative Region (commonly referred to as the Hong Kong national security law) following the notorious—and often violent—mass protests over a bill intended to introduce rendition of some criminal offenders to the mainland has led to a loss of confidence in 'one country, two systems' by many Hong Kongers.[22] An overemphasis on

(De Gruyter 2014) 249, 250. The original meaning of the Chinese word, 山寨, literally means mountain fortress. Many of the small, nimble, factories of Hong Kong were built in the mountainous areas of Hong Kong, hence the evolution of the alternative meaning.

16 After the RTHK television series, *Below the Lion Rock* (獅子山下), which took its name from Lion Rock (獅子山) in Kowloon Country Park, a mountain that bears a resemblance to a crouching lion. Even though it is less famous internationally than the Peak, Hong Kong residents feel a greater affinity to Lion Rock: see Rachel Blundy, 'Lion Rock Spirit Still Casting Its Spell on Hong Kong' *South China Morning Post* (Hong Kong, 22 April 2017).

17 I Scott and T Gong, *Corruption Prevention and Governance in Hong Kong* (Routledge 2019) 29–41.

18 ibid 44–56. Nor was the Prevention of Corruption Ordinance (Cap 201) modelled on English legislation. Instead, it and the ICAC were modelled on Singapore's Prevention of Corruption Ordinance (Ord 39 of 1960) and Singapore's Corrupt Practices Investigation Bureau. Both the Singapore Ordinance and Bureau were established by a Singapore government then already granted full internal self-governance though not yet fully free of British colonization as a part of Malaysia (1963), much less fully independent (1965).

19 Ord 4 of 1904. The Ordinance permitted the Governor-in-Council to exempt any Chinese from its operation, but the first Chinese to be exempted from the Ordinance, Sir Robert Hotung, was actually Eurasian, being of Dutch-Chinese parentage.

20 The Peak District (Residence) Ordinance was abolished in 1946.

21 Famously, Prime Minister Margaret Thatcher was thus confronted by Hong Kong's own Iron Lady, then journalist Emily Lau at a press conference: 'Prime Minister, two days ago you signed an agreement with China promising to deliver over 5 million people into the hands of a communist dictatorship. Is that morally defensible, or is it really true that in international politics the highest form of morality is one's own national interest?' See K Nakazawa, 'Hong Kong Iron Lady's Nightmare Scenario Comes True' *Nikkei Asian Review* (2 July 2020). These anxieties famously led to the pre-1997 mass emigration: see R Skeldon, 'Emigration and the Future of Hong Kong' (1990) 63 Pacific Affairs 500. Many of these migrants came to be known as 'astronauts', or 太空人, because they continued to work in Hong Kong despite 'settling' abroad for various reasons, including discrimination against Chinese. The clever expression 'felicitously combines the English meaning of a person who spends time in space, that is, an airplane, with a Cantonese play on words around "empty wife," "home without a wife" (in Hong Kong), or "house without a husband" (at the destination)': see R Skeldon, 'Reluctant Exiles or Bold Pioneers: An Introduction to Migration from Hong Kong' in R Skeldon (ed), *Reluctant Exiles? Migration from Hong Kong and the New Overseas Chinese* (ME Sharpe 1994) 3, 11.

22 See generally C Chan and F de Londras (eds), *China's National Security: Endangering Hong Kong's Rule of Law?* (Hart Publishing 2020). For the rendition saga, see eg A Chen, 'A Perfect Storm: Hong Kong—Mainland Rendition of Fugitive Offenders' (2019) 49 Hong Kong Law Journal 419; J Chan, 'Ten Days That Shocked the World: The Rendition Proposal in Hong Kong' (2019) 49 Hong Kong Law Journal 431; C Chan, 'Demise of One Country, Two Systems: Reflections on the Hong Kong Rendition Saga' (2019) 49 Hong Kong Law Journal 447. This loss of confidence has led to a new wave of mass emigration: see M-Y Kan, L Richards, and PW Walsh, 'The Migration Intentions of British National (Overseas) Status Holders in Hong Kong' (Migration Observatory, University of Oxford, 2 December 2021) <https://migrationobservatory.ox.ac.uk/resources/briefings/the-migrat

the laissez-faire economic policies of the British colonial government,[23] often referred to as 'positive non-intervention', likely an exaggeration,[24] has also led to a hesitance on the part of all bodies of government to intervene in commercial arrangements except in the most egregious of instances. So far as the Legislative Council is concerned, the domination by business interests of the functional constituency, which comprises half of the Legislative Council, ensures that commercial certainty is enshrined as a sacred cow. The same interests dominate the Election Committee, comprised of 1,200 persons, that 'elects' the Chief Executive of the Special Administrative Region. The most obvious cases of the dominance of business interests over these branches of government are in the context of the political challenges to pass the Minimum Wage Ordinance[25] and the Competition Ordinance[26] as well as how business interests shaped the resulting legislation.[27] Indeed, it is clear that the judiciary also place great emphasis on notions of freedom of contract and commercial certainty, possibly more so than in other common law jurisdictions, most notably in their extremely conservative application[28] of the Unconscionable Contracts Ordinance,[29] which was modelled on section 52A of the Australian Trade Practices Act.[30]

This chapter will examine how Hong Kong contract law has largely followed orthodox English contract law principles in relation to rights of termination for breach or

ion-intentions-of-british-national-overseas-status-holders-in-hong-kong> accessed 6 April 2023; cf AKT Chan and others, 'Hong Kong's New Wave of Migration: Socio-Political Factors of Individuals' Intention to Emigrate' (2022) 10 Comparative Migration Studies 49.

[23] Most famously by the Nobel Prize-winning economist, Milton Friedman, for which see eg M Friedman, 'The Real Lesson of Hong Kong' *National Review* (31 December 1997) 36.

[24] cf CW Chan, *The Myth of Hong Kong's* Laissez-Faire *Economic Governance: 1960s and 1970s* (Hong Kong Institute of Asia-Pacific Studies 1998). See also AJ Bradbrook, 'The Future of Domestic Rent Control in Hong Kong' (1977) 7 Hong Kong Law Journal 321, which opens with the line, 'It is anomalous that Hong Kong, a bastion of free enterprise in South-East Asia, possesses wide-ranging domestic rent control legislation which dates back 56 years.' It is perhaps even more ironic that rent control was only abolished after reunification with the communist mainland: see SH Goo and A Lee, *Land Law in Hong Kong* (5th edn, LexisNexis 2022) 795–801. It is also notable that the textile industry, the main driver of the economy during Hong Kong's period of rapid industrialization, was subjected to textile export quotas, such as that which featured in the famous Privy Council decision of *AG of Hong Kong v Daniel Chan Nai-Keung* [1987] 1 WLR 1339. The earliest quotas were in relation to textile exports to the United Kingdom and were only nominally 'voluntary' on the part of the then colony since agreement was secured only under threat of unilateral import quotas: see VK Aggarwal, *Liberal Protectionism: The International Politics of Organized Textile Trade* (University of California Press 1985) 54–63.

[25] Cap 608, passed in 2011.

[26] Cap 619, passed in 2012.

[27] For the Minimum Wage Ordinance (Cap 608), see eg MYH Wong, 'The Politics of the Minimum Wage in Hong Kong' (2014) 44 Journal of Contemporary Asia 735. For the Competition Ordinance (Cap 619), see eg TK Cheng, 'Sherman vs. Goliath? Tackling the Conglomerate Dominance Problem in Emerging and Small Economies—Hong Kong as a Case Study' (2017) 37 Northwestern Journal of International Law & Business 35 and KHF Kwok, 'The New Hong Kong Competition Law: Anomalies and Challenges' (2014) 37 World Competition 541.

[28] See eg *Shum Kit Ching v Caesar Beauty Centre Ltd* [2003] 3 HKLRD 422. See the criticisms of its application in MF Cheong and K Ding, 'From Unconscionability to Unfairness: A Critique of Hong Kong's Unconscionable Contracts Ordinance with Australian Developments' (2018) 35 Journal of Corporation Law 118; S Lo, 'Limitations in the Regulation of Unfair Marketing Practices in Hong Kong' (2008) 7 Journal of International Business & Law 77, 87–90; L Mason, 'Consumers and Unfair Contract Terms: Inadequate Legal Protection and Suggestions for Reform' (September 2014) <www.hk-lawyer.org/content/consumers-and-unfair-contract-terms-inadequate-legal-protection-and-suggestions-reform> accessed 6 June 2019; cf CA Ong and S Leung, 'The Unconscionable Contracts Ordinance Revisited' (2001) 9 Asia Pacific Law Review 187. But see now *Chang Pui Yin v Bank of Singapore* [2017] 4 HKLRD 458.

[29] Cap 458; cf S Hall, 'Contract Terms in Hong Kong: Incorporation, Interpretation, Implication, and Unfair Terms' in M Chen-Wishart and S Vogenauer (eds), *Studies in the Contract Laws of Asia, vol III: Contents of Contract and Unfair Terms* (OUP 2020) 62, 89–90.

[30] Law Reform Commission of Hong Kong, *Report on Sale of Goods and Supply of Services* (1990) 27–37.

non-performance, with a particular emphasis on commercial certainty and freedom of contract. It will first examine the general principles upon which a right of termination will arise, including the possibility of contractually providing for such a right, before considering how such a right is exercised and finally outlining the effects of termination.

II. The Right to Terminate a Contract

The circumstances under which one contracting party, the aggrieved party, may either withhold or discontinue their performance in the face of breach or non-performance by their counterparty are broadly similar to those in English law. A distinction is traditionally drawn between the mere right to withhold performance and the right to terminate the contract altogether. The former depends upon the interdependence or independence of the respective promises under an executory contract. Where mutual promises are independent of each other, non-performance of a promise by one contracting party would not excuse the other party from performance. Where mutual promises are interdependent, depending on the contractual order of performance, they are either concurrent conditions or else the performance of the earlier promise is a condition precedent to the performance of the later promise. This broad categorization of the possible relationships between mutual promises was recognized by the Court of Appeal in *Bilwide Ltd v Chung Chun Kwai*.[31] As is the case in English law, 'the question whether covenants are to be construed as dependent or independent falls to be decided in accordance with the intention of the parties collected from the instrument as a whole, and the surrounding circumstances'.[32] In English law, it has been observed that the courts are generally reluctant to classify promises as independent unless the intention of the parties to that effect are clear or if there is precedent to that effect for a particular category of contracts.[33] It has been suggested that this will also be the case in Hong Kong.[34] Although no Hong Kong court appears to have clearly affirmed the judicial preference for interdependence of mutual terms over independence, one of the English leading cases in support of this proposition, *Jones v Barkley*,[35] was cited with approval by the Hong Kong Court of Final Appeal in *Lau Suk Ching Peggy v Ma Hing Lam*[36] in holding that concurrent obligations to complete a sale and purchase agreement of shares were interdependent. So far as precedents are concerned, the most notable rule in English law as to the independence of terms is that a tenant's covenant to pay rent is independent of a landlord's covenant to repair and other obligations.[37] This rule has been applied in numerous Hong Kong cases[38] even though it puts tenants in an extremely unenviable position.

[31] [1993] HKEC 340.

[32] ibid [20], citing *Kidner v Stimpson* (1918) 35 TLR 63.

[33] E Peel, *Treitel: The Law of Contract* (15th edn, Sweet & Maxwell 2020) para 17-021, citing *Kingston v Preston* (1773) Lofft 194 and *Jones v Barkley* (1781) 2 Dougl 648, 689.

[34] Hall (n 10) para 15-10, citing Peel (n 33) para 17-021.

[35] (1781) 2 Dougl 648.

[36] (2010) 13 HKCFAR 226 [57].

[37] *Taylor v Webb* [1937] 2 KB 283. See also *Edge v Boileau* [1885] 16 QB 117 (quiet enjoyment).

[38] *Charmway Development Ltd v Long China Engineering Limited* [2001] 3 HKC 515 [18]–[19]; *Golden Sunrise Ltd v Lee Kwok Hung* [2005] 1 HKC 466 [37]–[39], [41] (Court of Appeal); *Ridge Ltd v Golden Castle Ltd* [2005] HKEC 1611 [13] (Court of Appeal); *Chan Nuen Heung v Forever Brilliant Ltd* [2007] HKEC 1771 [38]–[39]; *Worldwide Flight Services Holdings SA Royal Caribbean Cruises Ltd v Kai Tak Cruise Plaza Ltd* [2018] HKCFI 1639 [10]; *Lui Tso Chung* (呂祖仲) *v Ding Wai Hong* (丁煒雄) [2018] HKCFI 2083 [21].

Although the right to withhold performance is notionally distinct from the right to terminate, the rules relating to both often give rise to confusion. In *Mariner International Hotels Ltd v Atlas Ltd*,[39] the parties entered into a contract for the sale and purchase of all the shares in a British Virgin Islands company, Crest Inc, for HK$1.07 billion. Crest Inc's only assets were all of the shares of a Hong Kong company, Ocean Time Investments Ltd, which in turn owned land in Tsuen Wan upon which a hotel was being constructed. The court regarded the 'commercial reality' of the contract as one for the sale and purchase of the hotel.[40] Under the terms of the agreement, completion of the purchase was 'conditional upon', inter alia, the vendor procuring the 'practical completion' of the hotel by 30 June 1998, and time was of the essence. On 30 June 1998, the hotel was not in a state so as to satisfy the meaning of the expression 'practical completion', which the court construed to mean the completion of works that are free from patent defects other than those which are trifling, and the purchaser declined to complete, alleging repudiatory breach on the part of the vendor. Although the vendor's lawyers advanced an argument to the effect that its obligation to secure practical completion of the hotel was not one the breach of which automatically gave rise to a right to terminate the contract, this argument was rejected by the Court of Final Appeal on the basis that the obligation was a condition precedent to completion. There are passages in the judgment which appear to confuse the contingent and promissory senses of the expression 'condition'.[41] But ultimately, the conclusion that the vendor was in repudiatory breach—which meant that the right to terminate arose in favour of the purchaser—turned on the contractual stipulation that time was of the essence.[42] Accordingly, it was not the classification of the obligation to secure 'practical completion' of the hotel as a condition precedent which gave rise to the right to terminate but the failure to comply with that same obligation within the contractually stipulated time that did so.[43]

1. Basic Rules on Termination

The right to terminate a contract for breach or non-performance generally turns on quite different considerations than the mere right to withhold performance. Historically, prior to the English Court of Appeal decision of *Hong Kong Fir Shipping Co Ltd v Kawasaki Kisen Kaisha Ltd*,[44] which introduced the category of intermediate or innominate terms, contractual terms were classified by common law courts as either conditions or warranties. A condition is a term the breach of which will entitle the aggrieved party to terminate the contract, whereas a warranty is a term the breach of which will not. For the most part, classification into either condition or warranty turned on the seriousness of the consequences of breach. Just as this historical two-fold classification is most readily reflected in the classification of the implied terms in the English Sale of Goods Act 1979,[45] the same structure

[39] (2007) 10 HKCFAR 1.
[40] ibid [2].
[41] ibid [26] (Bokhary PJ) [62]–[63] (Chan PJ); cf SJ Stoljar, 'The Contractual Concept of Condition' (1953) 69 Law Quarterly Review 485; GH Treitel, '"Conditions" and "Conditions Precedent"' (1990) 106 Law Quarterly Review 185.
[42] *Mariner International Hotels Ltd v Atlas Ltd* (n 39) [30].
[43] cf Treitel (n 41) 188–89.
[44] [1962] 2 QB 26.
[45] Cap 54.

can be found in the Hong Kong Sale of Goods Ordinance.[46] Since the decision of *Hong Kong Fir* introduced the category of intermediate or innominate terms, from which no obvious answer follows as to the availability of the right to terminate upon breach, difficult questions have been raised as to the classification exercise. Are there now three categories of terms—conditions, warranties, and innominate terms? Or has the category of innominate terms replaced the category of warranties? The availability of the right to terminate for breach of an innominate term depends upon the seriousness of the breach. In *Hong Kong Fir* itself, Diplock LJ expressed the view that a breach was sufficiently serious if it had the effect of depriving the innocent party 'of substantially the whole benefit which it was the intention of the parties as expressed in the contract that he should obtain as the consideration for performing those undertakings'.[47] In Hong Kong, the existence of this third category of contractual terms has been acknowledged by the Court of Final Appeal in *Mariner International Hotels Ltd v Atlas Ltd*,[48] but as we shall see, this category is almost never invoked. When a term is implied by statute, it may be explicitly classified within one of the three categories. For example, the Sale of Goods Ordinance classifies the terms it implies as either conditions or warranties.[49] Just as judicial precedent also helpfully classifies terms, most notably in setting out that time is of the essence (ie a condition) in particular contracts in England,[50] Hong Kong case law serves the same purpose.[51] Otherwise, the classification of terms turns essentially on the intentions of the parties,[52] as divined by the courts ex post.

In England, a leading text suggests that there is 'a general requirement of substantial failure'.[53] The classification of terms into conditions, warranties, and innominate terms is relegated to the role of an exception to the requirement of substantial failure.[54] A Hong Kong text appears to suggest a similar approach, albeit without assigning the role of general principle to one and exception to the other. Rather, they are both regarded as different types of qualifying breaches that would entitle the innocent party to terminate the contract.[55] The so-called 'general principle' laid down in *Treitel* is certainly not universally adopted among English texts.[56] So far as Hong Kong is concerned, the practical insignificance of the category of innominate terms and the courts' repeated emphasis on commercial certainty and the parties' intentions implies that, to the extent that any general principle can be enunciated, it is the parties' intentions that serves that role, with the seriousness of the breach playing the subservient role of assisting the courts in divining that intention where it may not otherwise be clear.

[46] Cap 26.

[47] [1962] 2 QB 26 70.

[48] (2007) 10 HKCFAR 1 [26] (Bokhary PJ) [62]–[63] (Chan PJ).

[49] cf Sale of Goods Ordinance (Cap 26), ss 14, 15, 16, and 17.

[50] *Bunge Corporation New York v Tradax SA* [1981] 1 WLR 711 (strict time stipulations in commercial contracts).

[51] *Lee Gee Kee v Chong Kai Tai* [1996] 1 HKC 105 (stipulations as to time in a sale of land), reversed on another ground in *Chong Kai Tai Ringo v Lee Gee Kee* [1997] HKLRD 461.

[52] (2007) 10 HKCFAR 1 [62]–[63] (Chan PJ).

[53] Peel (n 33) para 18-032.

[54] ibid para 18-041–18-057.

[55] Hall (n 10) para 18-7–18-23.

[56] cf H Beale and others, *Chitty on Contracts* (34th edn, Sweet & Maxwell 2021) 1984–92; J Beatson, A Burrows, and J Cartwright, *Anson's Law of Contract* (31st edn, OUP 2020) 146–55; M Chen-Wishart, *Contract Law* (7th edn, OUP 2022) 509–18; E McKendrick, *Contract Law: Texts, Cases, and Materials* (10th edn, OUP 2022) 747–82; M Furmston, *Cheshire, Fifoot & Furmston's Law of Contract* (17th edn, OUP 2017) 206–13.

2. Termination for Delay in Performance

In Hong Kong law, whether or not an innocent party may terminate a contract for delay turns on the question of whether time is 'of the essence' of the contract. If time is of the essence, then punctuality is a condition. This otherwise simple rule is somewhat complicated by the differences in treatment of time stipulations at law and in equity. The common law regarded time stipulations as conditions whereas equity did not. The modern position is that the equitable rule generally prevails (ie time is not of the essence) unless the parties either stipulate that time is of the essence or the nature of the subject matter of the contract or the surrounding circumstances show that time should be regarded as being of the essence. Where time is explicitly provided to be of the essence, the position is clear, if apparently harsh, as demonstrated by the Privy Council decision of *Union Eagle Ltd v Golden Achievement Ltd*,[57] a case on appeal from Hong Kong which served as a model for one of the hypothetical scenarios set forth by the editors of this volume.[58] A sale and purchase agreement for a flat specified that completion was to take place before 5 pm on 30 September 1991. As is customary, 10 per cent of the purchase price was paid as a deposit. The purchaser tendered the purchase price ten minutes after 5 pm, after the vendor declared the contract repudiated and the deposit forfeited. The purchaser's suit for specific performance failed. Often cited in English texts as authority for the harsh treatment of time stipulations when made of the essence as a matter of English law, the decision quintessentially reflects Hong Kong values. The purchaser's suit failed not only before the Privy Council but also at every level of court,[59] although Godfrey JA dissented in the Court of Appeal. In doing so, the lower courts in Hong Kong were merely following established local authority. Famously, in the earlier case of *World Ford Development Ltd v Ip Ming Wai*,[60] Litton JA (as he then was) remarked that '[g]enerally speaking, there is no elasticity in punctuality'. That case also involved a sale of land where time was made of the essence. Performance was likewise late, although by a larger measure of time, 24 minutes. The result, however, was the same and presaged the decision of the Privy Council in *Union Eagle Ltd v Golden Achievement Ltd*. Indeed, the position appears to be the same in Hong Kong with respect to contracts for the sale of land even if time is not explicitly made of the essence by the parties, in contrast with the position in English law.[61] According to Godfrey JA in *Wong Wai Chi, Ann v Cheung Kwok Fung, Wilson*:

> In these provisional agreements for sale and purchase in today's secondary market in Hong Kong, everybody does, usually, proceed on the footing that time is to be of the essence, and that a purchaser who refuses or fails to sign the agreement, if it is available for signature on the specified date, and there is no blame to be attributed to the vendor, will be held to be in repudiatory breach of the agreement. . . . Of course, each case must depend on its own facts. But in the absence of special circumstances, it will usually be the case that a provisional agreement for sale and purchase in the common form in use in Hong Kong

[57] [1997] AC 514.

[58] See the 'Prime and Devil' scenario set out in M Chen-Wishart, D Neo, and S Vogenauer, 'Introduction', ch 1 in this volume, 9.

[59] cf [1995] HKLY 242 (High Court), [1996] 1 HKC 349 (Litton VP and Ching JA, Godfrey JA dissenting).

[60] [1994] 2 HKLR 1, 10.

[61] *Urban 1 (Blonk Street) Ltd v Ayres* [2014] 1 WLR 756.

> will be treated as one of which time is of the essence, although no express provision in that behalf is contained in the agreement.[62]

Accordingly, it would appear that *Union Eagle Ltd v Golden Achievement Ltd* would likely have been decided in the same way even if the contract in the case did not explicitly make time of the essence. Hence, the variation of the hypothetical set forth by the editors of this volume where, unlike *Union Eagle Ltd v Golden Achievement Ltd*, time is not explicitly made of the essence, would not affect the case's resolution.

Where time is not of the essence as a matter of construction of the contract, the position in Hong Kong is the same as that in English law. An innocent party who has been subjected to unreasonable delay under such circumstances may give notice to the party in breach, thus making time of the essence. As Deputy Judge Gill observed in *Joy & Peace.com Inc v Topshow Consultants Ltd*:

> Of course a contract for due performance which expresses no time limit is not a charter for unreasonable delay. If undue delay can be established, the aggrieved party is entitled to give notice, calling for performance within a reasonable period of time; what is reasonable will depend on the facts and circumstances. Once that period has expired without performance then the aggrieved party can sue for breach. In this case there is evidence of delay but not undue delay. More importantly, there was no notice from the plaintiff calling for performance which preceded its announcement that there was a breach giving it the right to rescind.[63]

In that case, the parties had entered into an agreement for the sale and purchase of 25 per cent of the vendor's shares in a company called Chinakids Holdings Ltd. The purchase price of US$800,000 was expressed to be payable by 20 March 2000, but the agreement contained no date for the transfer of the shares, which were to be allotted after a reorganization of the Chinakids group so that Chinakids Holdings Ltd could be listed on the Growth Enterprise Market in Hong Kong. By 2 May 2001, no shares had been transferred pursuant to the agreement as the reorganization had not been completed. The purchaser claimed that the vendor was in breach of its obligation to deliver the shares within a reasonable time and that such breach was repudiatory in nature, and thus purported to terminate the agreement. It thereupon sued to recover the purchase price and sought summary judgment. It seems clear from the judgment that the court had elided two quite separate issues: first, whether the vendor was in breach at all; secondly, whether the purchaser would be entitled to terminate the agreement if the vendor had been in breach. This is perhaps most obvious in the court's conclusion, in the paragraph immediately after the above quote:

> In the circumstances I am not satisfied that this is a case for reading into the agreement an implied obligation by the defendant to perform within a reasonable period of time, namely

[62] [1996] 3 HKC 287, 290. See also *See To Keung v Sunny Way Ltd* [2005] 4 HKC 535 [57]; *KSDY International Co Ltd v Honway (China) Ltd* [2006] HKCU 515 [51].

[63] [2002] 2 HKC 143 [26].

> a few weeks. It follows that by not having performed by 2 May 2000 it was not in breach and the plaintiff was not entitled to rescind.[64]

Nevertheless, the expression of the view that a notice following undue delay may suffice to make time of the essence for a stipulation which was not such as a matter of construction is an accurate statement of Hong Kong law.

3. Agreed Rights of Termination

There are a number of methods for the parties to agree upon rights of termination. First, they may classify particular terms (or even all terms) as conditions. Secondly, instead of labelling particular terms as conditions, they may explicitly provide for the right to terminate for breach of those terms. Finally, they may provide explicitly that timely performance is of the essence.[65] The strategy of classifying terms as conditions entails an element of risk, as demonstrated in *L Schuler AG v Wickman Machine Tool Sales Ltd* (on which another of the hypothetical scenarios used for this volume is based, albeit with a twist).[66] In 1963, the appellants appointed the respondents as sole distributors of their car panel presses for 4.5 years. By Clause 7(b), the contract provided that '[i]t shall be [a] condition of this agreement that (i) [the respondents] shall send its representatives to visit' the six largest UK motor manufacturers 'at least once in every week' to solicit orders for panel presses. Clause 7(b) was the only clause of the contract described as a condition, but Clause 11 set out a right to terminate the agreement on the part of either party for the other's material breach and subsequent failure to remedy the same within 60 days of being required to do so in writing. Leaving aside breaches that had been waived or excused, out of 240 visits required under Clause 7(b), only 212 were made, a shortfall of 28 over a period of six months. The appellant argued that it was entitled to terminate the contract for the breaches, contending that as Clause 7(b) was a condition, it had the right to do so however trivial the consequences of the breach. A majority of the House of Lords disagreed and found in favour of the respondents, holding that the term 'condition' was ambiguous[67] and did not mean that any breach, however trivial, of Clause 7(b) carried with it the right to terminate. As Lord Reid remarked:

> The fact that a particular construction leads to a very unreasonable result must be a relevant consideration. The more unreasonable the result the more unlikely it is that the parties can have intended it, and if they do intend it the more necessary it is that they shall make that intention abundantly clear.

L Schuler AG v Wickman Machine Tool Sales Ltd has been cited with approval by the Hong Kong Court of Final Appeal in *Building Authority v Appeal Tribunal (Buildings) (ENM*

[64] ibid [27]. The reference to 2 May 2000 in this quotation appears to be a typographical error since the rest of the judgment refers to 2 May 2001.

[65] See section II.2.

[66] [1974] AC 235; this served as model for the 'Car Machinery & Co v Traders Ltd' scenario in M Chen-Wishart, D Neo, and S Vogenauer, 'Introduction', ch 1 in this volume, 9.

[67] cf Treitel (n 41).

Holdings Ltd),[68] but with the caveat of also approving the limitations imposed on such a construction recently laid down by the UK Supreme Court in *Arnold v Britton*.[69]

Since the House of Lords in *L Schuler AG v Wickman Machine Tool Sales Ltd* decided that the labelling within a contract of a term as a 'condition' did not necessarily have the effect of entitling the aggrieved party to terminate the contract in the event of its breach, especially if the effect of such an interpretation would lead to a very unreasonable result, well-drafted contracts have tended to avoid the risk of 'condition' being interpreted in a non-technical sense by explicitly providing for the right to terminate the contract.[70] Explicit termination clauses are generally respected regardless of whether they are individually negotiated or included as part of standard terms. This is because, although standard term contracts are subject to some statutory control in Hong Kong,[71] such scrutiny does not extend to control over termination clauses. There is only limited scope for the courts to 'read down' such clauses in a manner similar to *L Schuler AG v Wickman Machine Tool Sales Ltd*.[72] This was what the House of Lords and the English Court of Appeal, respectively, did in the case of *Antaios Compania Naviera SA v Salen Rederierna AB (The Antaios)*[73] and *Rice (t/a Garden Guardian) v Great Yarmouth Borough Council*.[74] In *The Antaios*, a three-year time charter included a clause which provided that:

> failing the punctual and regular payment of the hire *or on any breach of this charter party* the owners shall be at liberty to withdraw the vessel from the service of the charterers without prejudice to any claim they (the owners) may otherwise have against the charterers [emphasis added].

When a dispute arose between the parties, arbitrators decided against the shipowners, holding that 'any other breach of this charter party' meant a repudiatory breach. Lord Diplock, delivering the leading judgment, famously remarked that 'if detailed semantic and syntactical analysis of words in a commercial contract is going to lead to a conclusion that flouts business commonsense, it must be made to yield to business commonsense'.[75] In *Rice (t/a Garden Guardian) v Great Yarmouth Borough Council*, a four-year agreement between the claimants and the defendant local authority for the former to maintain the latter's sports facilities provided that the latter could terminate the contract for breach of any of the claimants' obligations under the contract. When the local authority sought to terminate the contract pursuant to the contractual provision, the English Court of Appeal rejected a literal construction of the clause as visiting 'the same draconian consequences upon any breach, however small, of any obligation, however small'[76] that 'flies in the face of commercial common sense'.[77]

68 (2018) 21 HKCFAR 194.
69 [2015] AC 1619.
70 See eg *Lombard North Central plc v Butterworth* [1987] QB 527 (England); *Union Eagle Ltd v Golden Achievement Ltd* (n 57).
71 Most notably Control of Exemption Clauses Ordinance (Cap 71) s 8(1).
72 [1974] AC 235.
73 [1985] AC 191. Contra *BNP Paribas v Wockhardt EU Operations (Swiss) AG* [2009] EWHC 3116 (Comm); 132 Con LR 177.
74 [2003] TCLR 1.
75 [1985] AC 191 201.
76 [2003] TCLR 1 [22].
77 ibid [24].

However, the UK Supreme Court has recently cast a moderating eye over both *L Schuler AG v Wickman Machine Tool Sales Ltd* and *Antaios Compania Naviera SA v Salen Rederierna AB (The Antaios)* in *Arnold v Britton*.[78] Delivering the leading judgment, Lord Neuberger PSC remarked:

> [C]ommercial common sense is not to be invoked retrospectively. The mere fact that a contractual arrangement, if interpreted according to its natural language, has worked out badly, or even disastrously, for one of the parties is not a reason for departing from the natural language. Commercial common sense is only relevant to the extent of how matters would or could have been perceived by the parties, or by reasonable people in the position of the parties, as at the date that the contract was made. Judicial observations such as those of Lord Reid in *Wickman Machine Tools Sales Ltd v L Schuler AG* [1974] AC 235, 251 and Lord Diplock in *Antaios Cia Naviera SA v Salen Rederierna AB (The Antaios)* [1985] AC 191, 201, quoted by Lord Carnwath JSC at para 110, have to be read and applied bearing that important point in mind.

It should come as no surprise that the Hong Kong courts, long enamoured of commercial certainty over vague notions of fairness or reasonableness, have warmly embraced the retreat to certainty in *Arnold v Britton*,[79] though Lord Neuberger's status as a sitting overseas Non-Permanent Judge of the Court of Final Appeal and that court's extensive links to the English bench may also have contributed to the enthusiasm.[80]

Even before *Arnold v Britton* was decided, however, the Hong Kong courts demonstrated reluctance to moderate the construction of such clauses. *Rice (t/a Garden Guardian) v Great Yarmouth Borough Council* was distinguished by the Court of First Instance in *Secretary for Justice v Yu's Tin Sing Enterprises Co Ltd*,[81] which concerned a three-year contract between the defendant and the Director of Cultural and Leisure Services of the Hong Kong Government for the provision of cleansing and supporting services for leisure venues in the Kowloon East district. Clause 15 of the contract obliged the defendant to pay a minimum wage and set maximum working hours for its staff. Clause 15.5 provided that the government may terminate the contract for breach of the relevant promissory obligations (found in Clause 15.1 and 15.2). The contract contained many separate termination clauses for other obligations undertaken by the defendant. Some were unrelated to Clause 15 but clause 16 repeated the defendants' obligations under Clause 15 ('16.1 The Contractor agrees and undertakes to perform the Contract in accordance with the terms as set out in Clause 15 of Special Conditions of Contract') and the government's right to terminate ('16.2 . . . the Government may at any time terminate the Contract forthwith if the Contractor is in breach of all or any of the commitments set out in clause 16.1'). Clause 25(a) further provided the government the right to terminate the contract if 'the Contractor

[78] [2015] AC 1619, especially [19] (Lord Neuberger).

[79] See eg *Smart Essence Development Ltd v Hong Kong Housing Authority* [2016] HKEC 951 [46]; *Win Glories Ltd (紳榮有限公司) v Majorluck Ltd (集旺有限公司)* [2018] 1 HKLRD 63 [37]; *Joe Zhixiong Zhou v Saif Partners II LP* [2018] HKCFI 357 [49]; *Win Glories Ltd v Majorluck Ltd* [2018] HKEC 814 [31]; *Building Authority v Appeal Tribunal (Buildings) (ENM Holdings Ltd)* (n 68) [54]; *Baynard Ltd v Secretary for Justice* [2019] HKEC 1135 [58]; cf *Maeda Kensetsu Kogyo Kabushiki Kaisha v Bauer Hong Kong Ltd* [2018] HKEC 2373 [20]–[26].

[80] The leading judgment in *Building Authority v Appeal Tribunal (Buildings) (ENM Holdings Ltd)* (n 68) was jointly delivered by Lord Collins.

[81] [2008] HKEC 1506.

shall fail to carry out the whole or any part of the Services or neglect to observe or perform any of the terms and conditions of the Contract'. The Court of First Instance distinguished *Rice (t/a Garden Guardian) v Great Yarmouth Borough Council* on the basis that 'there was no characterisation of any particular term as a condition or indication which terms were to be considered so important that any breach would justify termination'.[82] In *Secretary for Justice v Yu's Tin Sing Enterprises Co Ltd*, by contrast, Clause 15.5 explicitly stipulated the right to terminate for '**any** breach of clause 15.1 and 15.2'.[83] *Secretary for Justice v Yu's Tin Sing Enterprises Co Ltd* essentially provides the template for drafters to avoid the consequences of *Rice (t/a Garden Guardian) v Great Yarmouth Borough Council*, at least in Hong Kong. Instead of simply establishing a universal right to terminate for any breach as was the case in *Rice*,[84] simply spill a bit more ink and fell a few more trees by repeatedly reproducing the right over and over again ad nauseam throughout the contract with respect to every promissory term, at least if it is only concerned to secure the right to terminate. Accordingly, for the car panel hypothetical scenario set forth by the editors of this volume, based on *L Schuler AG v Wickman Machine Tool Sales Ltd* but slightly modified, the outcome would be the converse of the case because the agreement in the hypothetical employed an express right to terminate rather than the ambiguous label of 'condition'. Such a strategy, though, may not be regarded by commercial parties as providing a sufficiently comprehensive remedy, owing to differences in rights to recover for loss of bargain depending on whether termination follows from the courts' characterization of a clause as a condition or an express right to terminate.

4. Seriousness of the Breach

In England, the concept of an intermediate/innominate term was introduced by the English Court of Appeal in *Hong Kong Fir Shipping Co v Kawasaki Kisen Kaisha Ltd*.[85] Such intermediate/innominate terms differ from the traditional binary classification of the common law in that their breach neither automatically permits nor forbids the innocent party from terminating the contract. The right to terminate depends instead on the seriousness of the breach, and an innocent party will only be able to terminate a contract for breach of an intermediate term if he can show that the particular breach deprived him of substantially the whole benefit which it was intended that he should obtain from the contract. Although the concept of such intermediate/innominate terms has been accepted by the Hong Kong courts, and citations of *Hong Kong Fir Shipping Co v Kawasaki Kisen Kaisha Ltd* can readily be found, actual cases in which a contractual term has been held to be such a term are few and far between. One of the few contractual terms which the Hong Kong courts have independently and consistently held to be an intermediate/innominate term is an 'as is' clause in a contract for the sale of land. The leading case is *Homyip Investment Ltd v Chu Kang Ming Trade Development Co Ltd*,[86] in which the dispute arose out of a provisional sale and

[82] ibid [48].
[83] ibid [49] (emphasis in the original).
[84] But note that such a universal right was also provided in the contract in *Secretary for Justice v Yu's Tin Sing Enterprises Co Ltd* (n 81) via Clause 25(a).
[85] [1962] 2 QB 26.
[86] [1995] 2 HKC 458.

purchase agreement of land in Tai Po. The property was a two-storey residential house with two bedrooms on the first floor. In each of the bedrooms, the vendor had constructed a false ceiling, thereby creating a loft between the false ceiling and the pitched roof. Access to this loft was by way of a staircase located on the staircase landing on the first floor, which itself led to a further landing, and two doors were constructed which led into the loft areas so created. When the purchaser's mortgagee's surveyor discovered the loft, suspicions arose as to whether the loft was an illegal structure contrary to the Buildings Ordinance as the approved building plans only referred to the building as a two-storey house.[87] When the purchaser raised a requisition requiring the vendor to produce evidence to demonstrate that the loft was approved by the Building Authority, the vendor removed the staircase leading to the loft, the staircase landing at loft level, and the doors leading to the added loft areas. It also replied to the requisition stating, 'the alleged forming and use of an additional storey together with the staircase leading thereto and the openings made for access in connection therewith has been discontinued and reinstated'. When asked for a clarification, the vendor's solicitors replied that none was necessary in light of a further inspection of the property by the purchasers. The main dispute between the parties was whether or not the requisition was satisfactorily answered or whether or not the vendor had failed to show good title to the property. Secondarily, however, assuming the vendor had satisfactorily showed good title, the purchaser alleged that the vendor had breached Clause 4 of the agreement, which provided that the property was sold on an 'as is' basis. In the circumstances, Cheung J found for the purchaser in the main dispute, rendering the secondary question moot. Nevertheless, the court briefly discussed the significance of Clause 4 by way of obiter. Observing that it was indisputable that the clause had been breached (by the removal of the staircase, additional staircase landing, and doors leading to the loft area), Cheung J accepted the submissions of the vendor's lawyer that Clause 4 was an intermediate/innominate term. The court further agreed that, as the property had been purchased without inspection and the purchaser had not been aware of the loft at the time the agreement was executed, '[t]he physical state and condition inside was simply of no concern'. Accordingly, if it had been relevant, the removal of the staircase would not have the effect of substantially depriving the purchaser of the whole benefit which it was intended it should obtain from the contract.

Grandco (Holdings) Ltd v Harbour Wealth Co Ltd[88] concerned another sale of land in Tai Po. As was the case in *Homyip Investment Ltd*, the property was purchased on an 'as is' basis. However, unlike *Homyip Investment Ltd*, in addition to an unauthorized loft, the vendor had filled in a rear sloping garden in order to level it, which was a further unauthorized alteration. Although the gradient of the slope was slight, being only 6 degrees, because of the size of the garden, its lowest point was some 5.6 feet lower than the highest point. When requisitions were raised as to the loft and the garden, the vendor reinstated the loft and garden to their original states. This reinstatement of the garden to its original sloping state meant that the purchaser was unable to build a swimming pool in the rear garden, which led the purchaser to treat the contract as repudiated. The vendor sought to rely on *Homyip Investment Ltd* to argue that the 'as is' clause was an intermediate term and the existence of a gradient in the garden did not substantially deprive the purchaser of the whole benefit which it was intended it should obtain from the contract. In *Grandco (Holdings) Ltd*,

[87] Cap 123.
[88] [2000] HKEC 367.

however, Deputy Judge To found that the breach was sufficiently serious as to amount to a repudiatory breach. *Homyip Investment Ltd* was distinguished on two grounds. First, the court noted that the purchaser in that case had entered into the contract without inspecting the property. Secondly, as the text of the 'as is' clause was not referred to in the judgment, its authority was limited. It is not entirely clear how the text of the clause is relevant to determining the seriousness of the breach as opposed to whether there has been a breach in the first place, but the inspection of the property beforehand and the purchaser's intended use of the garden, which was frustrated by its reinstatement, appears to have played a significant role to the difference in outcome between the two cases.

It is undoubtedly the case that the category of innominate/intermediate terms introduced by *Hong Kong Fir Shipping Co v Kawasaki Kisen Kaisha Ltd* is part of Hong Kong law, albeit only in a minor role. Whilst the scarcity of cases is explicable in part by Hong Kong's relatively small body of case law and defensive drafting on the part of its lawyers, judicial conservativism is also a contributing factor.

The question of the seriousness of a breach is perhaps more significant in relation to instalment contracts. According to *Chinluck Properties Ltd v Casil Clearing Ltd*,[89] citing *Maple Flock Co Ltd v Universal Furniture Products (Wembley) Ltd*,[90] the right to terminate is dependent upon two chief considerations: first, the ratio which the breach bears to the contract as a whole in quantitative terms, and secondly, the degree of probability or improbability that such a breach will be repeated. The case concerned a loan of HK$330m, by instalments, for the purposes of developing land in Peng Chau. The refusal to pay out some HK$80m was considered by the Court of First Instance to affect a significant quantity of the whole loan, being approximately 25 per cent of the total amount to be lent. Therefore, for the hypothetical scenario set by the editors of this volume, in which one ton of mussels out of two tons contracted for is delivered by a seafood importer to a restaurant chain with a cadmium concentration 2 per cent above that permitted by national food regulations,[91] it is likely that the restaurant will be able to terminate the contract. Although the concentration of cadmium appears to only be marginally above the permitted levels, suggesting that the probability of a repeated breach is not high, the instalment in breach amounts to half of the contract quantity.

5. Limitations on Rights of Termination

Similarly to English law, in Hong Kong law there is no formal system of notice such as the French *mise en demeure* or the German *Nachfrist* before a contracting party may treat its counterparty as being in default and exercise its right to terminate. Limitations on an innocent party's rights of termination are few and far between. Some of these are probably not even true limitations on the right to terminate, such as the so-called 'prevention principle'. In *Kensland Realty Ltd v Whale View Investment Ltd*,[92] the Hong Kong Court of Final Appeal held that where the party in breach committed a repudiatory breach only because

[89] [2004] HKEC 916 [77].
[90] [1934] 1 KB 148.
[91] For the detailed fact scenario of this hypothetical ('Seven Seas and Big Chef'), see M Chen-Wishart, D Neo, and S Vogenauer, 'Introduction', ch 1 in this volume, 9.
[92] (2001) 4 HKCFAR 381.

of the other party's earlier breach of contract, a 'prevention principle' would operate to preclude the party who was originally in breach from terminating the contract by accepting the repudiation. The case concerned the sale and purchase of shop premises in Mongkok for HK$55m. The relevant contract was a sub-sale which required the purchaser to split payment by way of cheques or cashier's orders as the vendor required upon settlement. The contract provided for settlement to occur between 10 am and 1 pm on 2 September 1997 and explicitly provided that time was of the essence. It was, however, silent on how much notice the vendor was required to give with regard to the details of the split payment. Despite earlier requests to do so, the vendor only provided notice at 11:13 am, with a correction at 11:48 am, leaving the purchaser with 72 minutes to arrange for eight cheques and two cashier's orders. Appeals for an extension of time were rejected. The purchaser finally presented the cheques just after 1 pm and the two cashier's orders arrived at 1:06 pm. The vendor sought to terminate the contract on the basis of the purchaser's repudiatory breach. In the circumstances, the Court of Final Appeal held that, given the silence of the contract on this issue, there must be an implied term that reasonable time be given so as to permit the purchaser to arrange the split payments. Drawing upon 'the long-established legal principle that a person is not permitted to take advantage of his own wrong',[93] Ribeiro PJ, delivering the leading judgment, fashioned a 'prevention principle'. In the contractual context, Ribeiro PJ observed that this principle was restrained by two limitations:

> First, it is necessary to show the relevant party's 'wrong' involves his breach of the contract in respect of an obligation owed to the other party. . . .
>
> The second limitation on the operation of the principle is a causation requirement. It is necessary to show that the contractual rights or benefits which the party in question is seeking to assert or claim arise as a direct consequence of that party's prior breach.[94]

Bokhary PJ delivered a separate judgment concurring with Ribeiro PJ, and reached the same conclusion using the same authorities but without employing the same label of 'prevention principle'. It is doubtful if it was necessary to identify any 'prevention principle' to reach the result. The case could have been analysed on the entirely orthodox basis that the purchaser's express obligation to make a split payment within the contractually stipulated time was conditional upon the vendor's implied obligation to give reasonable notice as to the details of such payment. Having failed to do so, the vendor could not therefore complain of the purchaser's breach. Simply put, the vendor's breach excused the purchaser's breach of a dependent obligation. In these circumstances, all remedies would be unavailable to the vendor, not merely termination for repudiatory breach.

In truth, there are even fewer limitations on the right to terminate under Hong Kong law than under English law, reflecting Hong Kong law's preference for commercial certainty. This is best shown in some key omissions when Hong Kong passed its Sale of Goods (Amendment) Ordinance[95] in October 1994. Although broadly following the UK amendments of the same year,[96] not only did Hong Kong retain the implied term of

[93] ibid [91].
[94] ibid [94]–[95].
[95] Ord 85 of 1994.
[96] The *Report on Sale of Goods and Supply of Services* (1990) of the Law Reform Commission of Hong Kong (n 30) was drafted in light of the Joint Report by the Law Commission and the Scottish Law Commission, *Sale and Supply of Goods* (Law Com No 160, Scot Law Com No 104, 1987).

'merchantable quality' in section 16(2) of its Sale of Goods Ordinance rather than adopt the new implied term of 'satisfactory quality' in section 14(2) of the English Sale of Goods Act 1979—because 'it is familiar and has a well-known minimum content with a flexible periphery'[97]—it also did not follow the English amendments, found in section 15A of the English Act, that limited the rights of non-consumers to reject goods non-compliant with conditions implied under sections 13–15 of the English Sale of Goods Act 1979 if the breach is so slight that it would be unreasonable for the buyers to reject them. Indeed, it is evident from the Report of the Law Reform Commission of Hong Kong that this proposed amendment was not even considered. Although it is impossible to divine the cause of this omission, it is perhaps unsurprising that the amendment would detract from commercial certainty.

Hong Kong does not have an equivalent to the UK Consumer Rights Act 2015 and its Unconscionable Contracts Ordinance,[98] modelled on section 52A of the Australian Trade Practices Act,[99] does not deal specifically with rights to terminate.

6. Second Chances

Hong Kong law does not generally permit extra time for performance. The only exception relates to circumstances where the obligor stands to forfeit property if the contract is terminated. Although the jurisdiction was originally equitable, in certain contracts, the power to grant relief has been statutorily enshrined, most notably in relation to forfeitures of leases of land. For such cases, relief is available under section 21F of the High Court Ordinance[100] or section 69 of the District Court Ordinance[101] (where the landlord is proceeding by action for non-payment of rent), section 69B of the District Court Ordinance (where the landlord has exercised his right otherwise than by action for non-payment of rent), or section 58 of the Conveyancing and Property Ordinance[102] (which applies generally in respect of all covenants and regardless of how the landlord is exercising his right of forfeiture). It may appear somewhat bizarre that the District Court but not the High Court has a specific power to provide relief where the landlord has proceeded by way of self-help. However, the omission to provide for a specific power to the High Court produces no gap in the law given the generality of section 58 of the Conveyancing and Property Act, which section 21F(10) explicitly provides is not excluded by its terms. In England, the general equitable power to provide relief was restricted by the House of Lords in *Scandinavian Trading Tanker Co AB v Flota Petrolera Ecuatoriana (The Scaptrade)*[103] to cases where a proprietary or possessory right is to be forfeited, a position endorsed by the Privy Council hearing an appeal from Hong Kong in the above-mentioned *Union Eagle Ltd v Golden Achievement Ltd.*[104]

97 Law Reform Commission of Hong Kong (n 30) 7.
98 Cap 458.
99 Law Reform Commission of Hong Kong (n 30) 27–37.
100 Cap 4.
101 Cap 336.
102 Cap 219.
103 [1983] 2 AC 694.
104 [1997] AC 514.

7. Termination before Performance Is Due

If, before the date stipulated for performance is due, it becomes clear that the other party will not perform—either because he has communicated an intention not to perform or has become unable to perform—then, provided the obligation due is one of sufficient seriousness that non-performance on the date due will entitle the innocent party to terminate the contract, the innocent party may terminate the contract forthwith and sue for damages. It is not necessary for the innocent party to wait for the due date of performance before bringing its action for damages. The classic English case of *Hochster v de la Tour*,[105] which established this proposition for what is commonly called anticipatory breach, was applied in Hong Kong as early as 1962 by Mills-Owen J in *C Itoh & Co Ltd v Wing On Cheong Emporium Ltd*.[106] Under two contracts for the sale of textile goods which had been varied, the defendant buyer was obliged to take delivery in March 1960 of certain goods manufactured by the plaintiff seller in Japan. Under a third contract, which was also varied, the defendant buyer was to take delivery of a further quantity of goods in June 1960. At the defendant buyer's request, the plaintiff seller withheld shipment of the goods under the first two contracts. However, on 10 June 1960 the plaintiff seller wrote to the defendant buyer stating its intention to ship the goods under all three contracts by the end of the month and required the defendant buyer to take delivery of the goods upon their arrival in Hong Kong. The defendant buyer replied the following day indicating that it refused to take delivery until October. As Mills-Owen J observed,

> it appears to me the plaintiff company could have treated the reply of the defendant company as an anticipatory breach and need not have actually shipped the goods but could immediately have enforced its remedies.[107]

More recently, in *Crowning Success Ltd v Brightland Corp Ltd*,[108] the same principle was set out by the Court of Appeal in relation to the sale of commercial premises on the 45th floor of the Convention Plaza in Wanchai. The Court also further clarified that under Hong Kong law, upon acceptance of a repudiatory anticipatory breach, the innocent party need not remain ready and willing to perform up until the date of performance. The premises under dispute, known as unit C, were sold for HK$14.8m with completion due on 22 July 2005. At the time the agreement was concluded, the 45th floor had not yet been partitioned, but a floor plan signed by a certified architect showed the location of the unit, its dimensions and shape, and stated its saleable area to be 144.42 m^2. Inspection of the unit was permitted by the vendor at 1 pm on the day of completion. Upon inspection, it was discovered that the unit was smaller than contractually stipulated (by some 200 ft^2) and had a different configuration than the contractual stipulation. The excluded area also deprived the purchaser of a sea view, which commands a significant premium. Accordingly, at 4:40 pm, the purchaser sought to terminate the agreement and seek the return of all monies it had already paid. The vendor sought originally to argue that the purchaser had 'jumped the gun' by prematurely

105 (1853) 2 E&B 678.
106 [1962] HKLR 1. See also *A-Mayson Development Co Ltd v Betterfit Ltd* [1992] 2 HKC 533.
107 *C Itoh & Co Ltd v Wing On Cheong Emporium Ltd* (n 106) 6.
108 [2010] HKEC 494.

seeking restitution when the vendor should have been given until midnight to rectify its default but abandoned this and sought instead to rely on the case of *Camberra Investment Ltd v Chan Wai-tak*[109] to demonstrate that, in order to be able to terminate a contract for repudiatory breach, an innocent party had to be able and willing to perform its own concurrent and dependent obligations. Distinguishing that case, Le Pichon JA remarked:

> It is unarguable but [*sic*] that the vendor was in no position to deliver the property it had agreed to assign. On the findings of the judge, this is a clear case of anticipatory breach by the vendor. The *Camberra* principle can have no application to the present case and is irrelevant.[110]

Therefore, in the hypothetical scenario set forth by the editors of this volume in which a garden designer is engaged by a famous architect for her next development,[111] the designer will be able to bring an action for breach of contract immediately upon being informed by the architect that she has abandoned a garden for the project. His ability to sue to recover his estimated loss of future earnings will depend on his ability to prove this loss to the satisfaction of the courts. Nevertheless, he should be able to recover at least the cost of the purchased materials as a reliance loss.

III. The Process of Termination

A repudiatory breach, whether actual or anticipatory, does not automatically terminate a contract. As Asquith LJ famously remarked in *Howard v Pickford Tool Co Ltd*,[112] '[a]n unaccepted repudiation is a thing writ in water', cited with approval by Lord Hoffmann NPJ in the Court of Final Appeal in *Ji Shan International Investment Ltd v Resources Main Enterprises Ltd*.[113] Quoting Lord Steyn in *Vitol SA v Norelf Ltd (The Santa Clara)*,[114] the Hong Kong Court of Appeal in *Chao Keh Lung v Don Xia* explained:

> An act of acceptance of a repudiation requires no particular form: a communication does not have to be couched in the language of acceptance. It is sufficient that the communication or conduct *clearly and unequivocally* conveys to the repudiating party that that aggrieved party is treating the contract as at an end.[115]

As is apparent from the above quote, an innocent party need not involve the court in order to terminate the contract by accepting the repudiatory breach. Indeed, the innocent party is free to keep the contract alive and perform its own contractual obligations provided it can do so without the cooperation of the party in breach. Thus, in *Torvan Shipping Ltd v*

[109] [1989] 1 HKLRD 568.
[110] [2010] HKEC 494 [15].
[111] For this hypothetical fact scenario ('David and Coco'), see M Chen-Wishart, D Neo, and S Vogenauer, 'Introduction', ch 1 in this volume, 9.
[112] [1951] 1 KB 417, 421.
[113] [1999] 1 HKC 12, 15.
[114] [1996] AC 800, 810–11.
[115] [2004] 2 HKLRD 11 [41] (emphasis added by Cheung JA).

Gilman & Company Ltd,[116] the Hong Kong Court of Appeal held that a seller of unascertained goods, being rolls of paper, was unable to sue for price when the buyer indicated that it would refuse to accept future deliveries and withdrew its assent to future appropriation of goods to the contract. For much the same reason, in the hypothetical scenario of the famous architect and the garden designer,[117] the designer will not be able to insist on doing the work since doing so will require the architect's cooperation. The controversial proposition proposed by the House of Lords in *White & Carter (Councils) Ltd v McGregor*[118] that the party in breach may restrict the innocent party to a claim in damages where the latter did not have a legitimate interest in performing the contract was briefly considered by the Hong Kong Court of Appeal in *Ricoh Hong Kong Ltd v Wallbanck Brothers Securities (Hong Kong) Ltd*[119] but found to be unsubstantiated by the party in breach and hence inapplicable in a judgment dealing with costs.

IV. Loss of Right to Terminate

Generally, the right to terminate may only be lost through affirmation. As Ma CJHC (as he then was) explained in *Diamond Jubilee Investment Ltd v Chan Yiu Chung Sidney*:

> In the absence of contractual provisions to the contrary, the general rule is that there is no duty on an innocent party to accept a repudiatory breach, either within a reasonable time or at all. No question of reasonableness or mitigation arises. Quite simply, when a repudiatory breach occurs, the innocent party either can affirm the contract or accept the repudiation thereby bringing it to an end. I would add here that the principle in *Johnson v Agnew* [1980] AC 367 whereby in a sale of land an innocent party even can wait until trial before making an election whether to claim damages for breach or claim specific performance (thereby affirming the contract), is a classic illustration of the existing common law position.[120]

Delay per se is therefore irrelevant. As Rogers VP clarified in *Cheung Ching Ping v Allcom Ltd*:

> Insofar as it was argued . . . that there was a limit to the length of time which an innocent party may take before deciding whether to accept repudiation or affirm the contract, it seems to me that the matter really revolves upon whether the delay is consistent only with an affirmation of the contract or, put in another way, the circumstances surrounding the delay dictate that the innocent party must have affirmed the contract or, at least, give rise to a condition where the party in default could raise an estoppel.[121]

116 [1977] HKLR 460; cf *Fuji Xerox (Hong Kong) Ltd v Vigers Hong Kong Ltd* [2007] HKEC 2382. See also *White & Carter (Councils) Ltd v McGregor* [1962] AC 413, 428–30.

117 Referred to at the end of section II.7 of this chapter.

118 [1962] AC 413.

119 [2016] 3 HKLRD 134 [6]. See also *Shum Kit Ching v Caesar Beauty Centre Ltd* (n 28); *Fuji Xerox (Hong Kong) Ltd v Vigers Hong Kong Ltd* (n 116).

120 [2010] 1 HKLRD 638, 645–46.

121 [2010] 2 HKLRD 324, 330–31.

In order to establish such an estoppel, sometimes called estoppel by waiver, however, 'three elements [had] to be established by the party relying on it'.[122] These are, according to Ma CJ in *Hua Tyan Development Ltd v Zurich Insurance Co Ltd*:

> [F]irst, a clear and unequivocal representation by the person said to have waived rights [i.e. the innocent party], whether by words or conduct, that the representor's legal rights will not be insisted upon; secondly, reliance by the representee [i.e. the party in breach] on the representation; and thirdly, that it would be inequitable for the representor to go back on the representation.[123]

If an innocent party chooses to affirm the contract, then the contract remains 'alive', which carries significant consequences. As Ribeiro PJ explained in *Kensland Realty Ltd v Whale View Investment Ltd*,[124] '[w]hen an innocent party elects to keep a contract alive in this manner, it remains alive for the benefit of both parties. . . . The innocent party is therefore bound to perform his obligations under the contract.' This carries the obvious danger that the innocent party may itself subsequently be found to also be in breach of its obligations. Where the original breach was merely anticipatory in nature, this breach may also excuse the party originally in anticipatory breach from its obligations. A similar result could follow a frustrating event following an unaccepted anticipatory breach. The Hong Kong Court of Appeal in *Link Brain Ltd v Fujian Finance Co Ltd*[125] quoted Lord Ackner in *Fercometal SARL v Mediterranean Shipping Co SA (The Simona)* with approval:

> When A wrongfully repudiates his contractual obligations in anticipation of the time for their performance, he presents the innocent party B with two choices. He may either affirm the contract by treating it as still in force or he may treat it as finally and conclusively discharged. There is no third choice, as a sort of via media, to affirm the contract and yet to be absolved from tendering further performance unless and until A gives reasonable notice that he is once again able and willing to perform. Such a choice would negate the contract being kept alive for the benefit of both parties and would deny the party who unsuccessfully sought to rescind, the right to take advantage of any supervening circumstance which would justify him in declining to complete.[126]

V. Effect of Termination

The effect of termination is to bring to an end most of the contractual obligations on both parties prospectively, though the party in breach would remain liable for damages for loss caused by this breach. However, ancillary terms within the contract intended by the parties to survive termination will continue to apply. Historically, as a matter of English law, it was considered that there existed a so-called 'doctrine of fundamental breach' which prevented exclusion clauses from surviving such breaches. Prior to the House of Lords decision in

[122] *Hua Tyan Development Ltd v Zurich Insurance Co Ltd* (2014) 17 HKCFAR 493 [18].
[123] ibid.
[124] (2001) 4 HKCFAR 381 [85].
[125] [1990] 2 HKLR 353, 366.
[126] [1989] AC 788, 805.

Photo Production Ltd v Securicor Ltd,[127] this was true also of Hong Kong law,[128] but it was quickly abandoned following that decision.[129] In civil law terms, termination as a matter of contract law resembles *Kündigung* or *résiliation* rather than *Rücktritt* or *résolution*, but with an important caveat. *Rücktritt* or *résolution*-like retrospective effects, which carry restitutionary consequences, operate instead alongside contractual principles through the law of unjust enrichment *after* the contract is terminated, provided the elements of a claim in unjust enrichment can also be established.

1. Damages for Loss in Respect of Future Obligations

The availability of damages for loss in respect of future obligations following termination depends in part on how the right to terminate arises. In English law, termination pursuant to an express contractual right to do so does not expose the party in breach to liability for damages for losses arising from non-performance of future obligations whereas termination for breach of a condition does, even if the term is a condition by express provision and would not be so in its absence. *Financings Ltd v Baldock*,[130] authority for the former proposition, has been applied in Hong Kong in relation to both leases of land in *Hop Woo Cheung Enterprises Ltd v Intergroup Industries Ltd*[131] and a hire purchase agreement of a motor vehicle in *Hang Seng Finance Ltd v Liu Kwok Man*.[132] Although *Lombard North Central plc v Butterworth*,[133] authority for the latter proposition, was cited in *Okachi (Hong Kong) Ltd v Nominee (Holding) Ltd*, it was cited for a different proposition. Nevertheless, it is likely that the Hong Kong courts will follow English law.[134] Accordingly, tremendous care must be exercised in terminating contracts, for where a contract may be terminated both because it is repudiatory in nature and because of an express contractual right to terminate, relying upon the latter to terminate will preclude a claim for loss in respect of future obligations.[135] An innocent party who wishes to terminate for the other party's breach is thus forced to choose between two evils: (i) litigation in order to establish that the other party's breach is repudiatory in character, entailing the risk that it would itself be in repudiatory breach should the court disagree; or (ii) foregoing a claim for loss of bargain in respect of future obligations in return for the certainty of lawful termination.

2. Restitution for Unjust Enrichment

Hong Kong contract law, like English law, does not favour parties seeking restitution as termination operates entirely prospectively. It is convenient to treat the payment of money

[127] [1980] AC 827.

[128] *The Hong Kong and Kowloon Wharf and Godown Co Ltd v Bank Negara Indonesia* [1980] HKLR 161.

[129] *The Yien Yieh Commercial Bank Ltd v Kwai Chung Cold Storage Co Ltd* [1987] HKEC 90. See also *Carewins Development (China) Ltd v Bright Fortune Shipping Ltd* (2009) 12 HKCFAR 185 [68].

[130] [1963] 2 QB 104.

[131] [1982] HKC 436.

[132] [1991] HKEC 321.

[133] [1987] QB 527.

[134] [2006] HKCA 436, [2007] 1 HKLRD 55. It is significant that the position in Australia is consistent with that in England: see *Gumland Property Holdings Pty Ltd v Duffy Bros Fruit Market (Campbelltown) Pty Ltd* (2008) 234 CLR 237 [58].

[135] *Phones 4U Ltd (in administration) v EE Ltd* [2018] EWHC 49 (Comm), [2018] 1 Lloyd's Rep 204.

separately from the provision of goods or services. Property rights, including in money, that have been transferred pursuant to the contract do not revest. Where money has been paid, in principle it is only recoverable if there has been a 'total failure of consideration'; that is, the innocent party has not received any part of what it contracted for. Modern Hong Kong law analyses such claims following the analytical framework of modern restitution claims: '(i) Was [the defendant] enriched? (ii) Was the enrichment at the plaintiffs' expense? (iii) Was the enrichment unjust?'[136] However, the difficulties in establishing 'total failure of consideration' may be avoided if the court can be persuaded that the contract was a divisible contract.[137] Unless the money was paid as a deposit or was payment for work done by the other party,[138] the same is true for the party in breach upon termination of the contract.[139]

If the innocent party has performed its obligations in relation to goods or services fully, its remedy lies in an action for price. If performance is only partial, then it may possibly recover in either *quantum valebant* (goods) or *quantum meruit* (services).[140] Where the contract is for a lump sum, the party in breach will not be able to recover in restitution for benefits received by the other party unless those benefits could have been returned but were not. The classic case is *Sumpter v Hedges*,[141] on which one of the hypotheticals for this volume was based, where a builder was employed to construct a house for a lump sum of £565.[142] Abandoning the job midway when he ran out of money, the builder left some materials behind which the owner used to finish the works. The builder's claim failed with regard to the value of the work done but succeeded in respect of the value of the materials. *Sumpter v Hedges* has been applied in Hong Kong[143] in *Marvel Harvest Ltd v Wing Tung On Construction Co Ltd*[144] and *Brainchild Productions Ltd v Kam Kwong Design Company (a firm)*.[145]

3. Relationship between Damages and Restitution

An innocent party would have to elect between damages for expectation loss and a claim for restitution for the two remedies are alternative and inconsistent.[146] A claim for damages for expectation loss seeks to put the innocent party in the position it would have been in had

[136] *Takahashi v Cheng Zhen Shu* (2011) 14 HKCFAR 558 [26]. See also SB Gallagher, *The Law of Unjust Enrichment in Hong Kong* (2nd edn, LexisNexis 2021) 26–35.

[137] *Brainchild Productions Limited v Kam Kwong Design Company (a firm)* [1985] HKEC 189; *Teamways Ltd v WP Engineering Ltd* [2011] HKEC 390; *Prime View Inc Ltd v Asian Richly Ltd* [2017] HKEC 2084.

[138] *Hyundai Heavy Industries Co Ltd v Papadopoulos* [1980] 1 WLR 1129, cited with approval in *Polyset Ltd v Panhandat Ltd* (2002) 5 HKCFAR 234.

[139] *Dies v British & International Mining and Finance Corp Ltd* [1939] 1 KB 724, cited with approval in *Polyset Ltd v Panhandat Ltd* (n 138).

[140] *Lau Leung Wood v Standard Oil Co of New York* (1907) 2 HKLR 192, applying *Lodder v Slowey* [1904] AC 442. But see *Trident Engineering Co Ltd v Mansion Fire Engineering Co Ltd* (unreported), HCCT 3 & 6 of 1996, 15 June 2000, *Sunbury Co Ltd v May Design Ltd* (unreported), Construction List No Con 10 of 1990, 1 September 1992, and the discussion in Gallagher (n 136) 229–52.

[141] [1898] 1 QB 673.

[142] For the details of this hypothetical ('Bob and Sue'), see M Chen-Wishart, D Neo, and S Vogenauer, 'Introduction', ch 1 in this volume, 10.

[143] Albeit only in respect of denying the claim for benefits that cannot be returned, though it is likely that the Hong Kong courts will also apply the other principle established by the case.

[144] [1984] HKEC 320.

[145] [1985] KHEC 189.

[146] *Tang Man Sit v Capacious Investments Ltd* [1996] AC 514 (Hong Kong).

the contract been performed, whereas a claim for restitution seeks to put it in the position as if there was no contract.

VI. Conclusion

It will be evident that Hong Kong's common law rules on the termination of contracts track English common law extremely closely, perhaps more so than any other former British colony. Where it differs from English common law, it is almost always harsher, favouring commercial certainty over considerations of fairness. Hong Kong law's piquant prejudice in favour of certainty over fairness may justifiably be described as reflecting capitalism on steroids. This is the result of a confluence of factors. The Legislative Council is stacked with commercial interests. Defensive drafting is commonplace, and the courts are extremely conservative, for fear of affecting Hong Kong's status as an international financial centre. This conservatism is no doubt in part influenced by the exaggerated idea that the British had governed Hong Kong through 'positive non-intervention'. However, it is not entirely clear that this was the case, nor is it obvious that near absolute observance of commercial certainty at the expense of considerations of fairness is a requisite of success for international financial centres. Modern English common law tends to be more tempered and the courts more interventionist, but this does not appear to have harmed London's credentials as an international financial centre.

7

Changes in Circumstances and Their Impact on Contractual Obligations in India

*Chitra NARAYAN and R Yashod VARDHAN**

I. Introduction

In England, theories of construction of contracts and identification of the intention of the parties beyond the express terms of the contract justified the discharge of obligations under a contract where parties found, after the contract was made, that performance became impossible, or unlawful, or where the subject matter of the contract no longer existed, or where the state of affairs assumed to be the foundation of the contract did not happen or exist (though performance may be literally possible).[1] On these bases, the courts assumed a power to intervene in contracts and reframe obligations. These theories implied a term or exception in the contract to discharge performance. This predicament was avoided in the Indian Contract Act 1872 (ICA). In a series of provisions, the ICA acknowledges, as a rule of positive law, that circumstances could change so as to make performance impossible, or impact the manner of performance contemplated, and this would result in a discharge or recast of the obligations of parties.[2]

These provisions in the ICA compartmentalize the nature of the variations and prescribe outcomes to meet the new context. Specifically, the ICA categorizes the changed circumstances into those that are contemplated by the parties and those that are, in a manner of speaking, a turn of events that the parties did not anticipate. In the former category, governed by sections 31 to 33, fall events that are provided for in the contract or, though not provided for, could reasonably be contemplated by the parties. Provisions for *force majeure* that parties incorporate in contracts are addressed here. The latter type of events, which are of a nature that frustrate the contract, are addressed in section 56 of the ICA, as a part of provisions relating to the performance of contracts. In these cases, the court will adjudicate objectively if the change of circumstances is so fundamental that it discharges performance under the contract. In making this assessment, viz whether performance has become impossible, the courts in India have relied on judgments of the courts in England.

While these categories have been neatly labelled, and appear to be mutually exclusive, the question that arises is whether this should be so. The first set of circumstances, as stated, has been interpreted to cover situations that the parties could have reasonably contemplated at

* The authors gratefully acknowledge the assistance of Ms Gayathri Rajagopalan, Advocate, Madras High Court.

1 F Pollock and DF Mulla, *The Indian Contract Act* (2nd edn, Sweet & Maxwell 1909) 253.

2 The rule as to an agreement to do an impossible act is the same as in England: *Satyabrata Ghose v Mugneeram Bangur & Co* AIR 1954 SC 44 *(Satyabrata Ghose)*.

Chitra Narayan and R Yashod Vardhan, *Changes in Circumstances and Their Impact on Contractual Obligations in India* In: *Studies in the Contract Laws of Asia V: Ending and Changing Contracts*. Edited by: Mindy Chen-Wishart, Dora Neo, and Stefan Vogenauer, Oxford University Press. © Chitra Narayan and R Yashod Vardhan 2026.
DOI: 10.1093/oso/9780198995814.003.0007

the time of the contract. How burdensome is this responsibility, and what is the extent of prescience expected? In the latter category falls the difficult question of assessing if the contract has indeed been frustrated. In determining this, the courts have held that the contract would not be frustrated simply because it has become more onerous. How onerous should performance be to become regarded as 'impossible of performance'? What about commercial impossibility, and how would this be assessed? What is the figurative 'leap' that difficulties must take to render the contract impossible of performance?

II. The Analytical Framework

Unlike other provisions of the ICA, the origins of the rules relating to frustration of contract are not from English law.[3] Some years ahead of the ICA being enacted, in 1863, English courts considered the theory of implied terms in *Taylor v Caldwell*[4] to justify discharge in a contract where it had become physically impossible to perform the obligation. In 1872, the ICA, in the chapter setting out the rules for performance under the contract, took into account and provided for outcomes in an agreement to do an impossible act, or where performance of the obligations became impossible or illegal after the contract had been executed. The articulation of a specific rule on frustration in the statute, together with provisions on contingent contracts discharging or varying performance found in the ICA, has been definitive of the law of frustration in India, with certain distinctions that we will briefly enumerate.

The definitive judgment of *Satyabrata Ghose v Mugneeran Bangur & Co* (*Satyabrata Ghose*)[5] of the Supreme Court of India declared that section 56 of the ICA encompassed the whole of the law on frustration. Performance is discharged and the agreement is void if, at the time of the agreement, both parties or one party did not know of the circumstances that make performance impossible. Under this rule, performance is discharged where the performance becomes impossible or illegal after the execution of the contract. The section prescribes the outcome, and the scope of examination is limited to the gravity and magnitude of the change in circumstances that makes performance impossible. Foreseeability of the circumstances rendering the performance impossible is also addressed, and the matrix of sections provides that if the impossibility was foreseen, section 56 will not be applied.

Not surprisingly however, English cases have been relied on to understand how similar situations have been addressed and for identification of the principles and factors that would justify discharge of performance of the agreement on the notion of frustration or impossibility, including in situations of self-induced frustration. In *Satyabrata Ghose*, the Supreme Court of India formulated an analytical framework as to when the courts will intervene under section 56 of the ICA. The courts in India have also looked at various aspects of frustration in the context of different situations that have come up before them.

[3] Sir Frederick Pollock suggests that the rule has been formulated by the framers of the Act since there is no known source for this rule. Pollock and Mulla (n 1) 253.

[4] 122 ER 309 [1861–73] All ER Rep 24, (1863) 3 B&S 826.

[5] *Satyabrata Ghose v Mugneeram Bangur & Co* (n 2).

As to the effect of frustration, the rules set out in the ICA on restitution, which operate across all situations where a contract is or becomes void, apply to frustration of a contract as well. Section 56(3) also accommodates a situation where one person promises to do something that they are aware, or ought to be aware with reasonable diligence, is impossible or unlawful. Compensation is due from such a party to the promisee for loss arising from the non-performance of the promise. This provision for anticipated impossibility by one party alone, and its compensation, is at variance with the understanding of frustration, where both parties are unable to anticipate the situation beforehand. The provisions on the effect of frustration are also at variance with interpretations in English law on restitution and compensation, and with the present law in England, *viz* the Law Reform (Frustrated Contracts) Act 1943.

The existence of a separate set of rules in the ICA for contingencies that operate as conditions for performance or for permitting discharge have also defined the meaning and scope of frustration under section 56. If a contingency is contemplated or could reasonably be contemplated as impacting performance, it is sections 31 to 33 (relating to contingent contracts) that come into play, and the onus is on the parties to have provided for the outcome under the contract. Section 56 and the doctrine of frustration would not operate to the extent of contingencies provided for or contemplated. The situations provided in the two sets of rules—section 56 and sections 31 to 33—have been understood as being mutually exclusive. This has also led to the evaluation whether, despite terms for *force majeure* in the contract, impossibility can occur from causes not enumerated or contemplated in these terms. With this distinction in Indian law, several situations addressed in English cases as frustration would not be similarly treated in India. These aspects are considered in some detail below.

1. The Departure from English Law Embodied in Section 56 ICA

Section 56 of the ICA addresses discharge from performance under the agreement or contract as a result of supervening impossibility or illegality and reads as follows:

> S. 56. Agreement to do impossible act.—An agreement to do an act impossible in itself is void.
>
> Contract to do act afterwards becoming impossible or unlawful.—A contract to do an act which, after the contract is made, becomes impossible, or, by reason of some event which the promisor could not prevent, unlawful, becomes void when the act becomes impossible or unlawful.[6]
>
> Compensation for loss through non-performance of act known to be impossible or unlawful.—Where one person has promised to do something which he knew, or, with reasonable diligence, might have known, and which the promisee did not know, to be impossible or unlawful, such promisor must make compensation to such promisee for any loss which such promisee sustains through the non-performance of the promise.

[6] ICA, s 65.

Illustrations

(a) A agrees with B to discover treasure by magic. The agreement is void.
(b) A and B contract to marry each other. Before the time fixed for the marriage, A goes mad. The contract becomes void.
(c) A contracts to marry B, being already married to C, and being forbidden by the law to which he is subject to practice polygamy. A must make compensation to B for the loss caused to her by the non-performance of his promise.
(d) A contracts to take in cargo for B at a foreign port. A's Government afterwards declares war against the country in which the port is situated. The contract becomes void when war is declared.
(e) A contracts to act at a theatre for six months in consideration of a sum paid in advance by B. On several occasions A is too ill to act. The contract to act on those occasions becomes void.[7]

The section addresses two situations—impossibility of performance at the time the agreement was executed and impossibility or illegality arising after the execution of the agreement. The first paragraph in the section addresses the first stage. The agreement to do an act impossible in itself is void. A few aspects may be noticed in this paragraph: unlike the second paragraph, it does not address an agreement contemplating an act that is illegal. Such agreements, which are also void, are addressed separately in section 23 of the ICA dealing with contracts opposed to public policy. This is so because parties are presumed to know the law, notwithstanding that they did not, in fact, know that the act was illegal at the time of the agreement. The paragraph uses the expression 'impossible in itself', and this would mean that the action is impossible in the very nature of things[8] and not due to the fault of the person agreeing to do the act.[9]

The second paragraph addresses impossibility or illegality arising after the contract is executed but before or during performance. The reference to the illegality that has arisen is qualified with 'an event which the promisor could not prevent' which renders it unlawful. Notwithstanding that a similar qualification is not stated as regards the situation of impossibility in the earlier part of this paragraph, the section only covers impossibility arising without any attribution to the promisor.[10] The courts have categorized cases of self-induced frustration under section 39 of the ICA.[11] Again, the attempt has been to make neat categories of blameworthiness and blamelessness as to events causing impossibility.

The third paragraph addresses the consequences of the agreement where one person promises to do something which he knew, or with reasonable diligence might have known, to be impossible or unlawful. The promisor in such cases must compensate the promisee if any loss is sustained by the promisee on account of the non-performance of the promise. This paragraph, it is submitted, would also address the situation in paragraph 1, *viz* knowledge at the time of the agreement. This is for the reason that the impossibility or illegality addressed in this paragraph is something that was present at the time of making

[7] Based on a modified version of *Robinson v Davison* (1871) 1 LR 6 Exch 269.
[8] Pollock and Mulla (n 1) 253.
[9] W Stokes, *The Anglo-Indian Codes* (Clarendon Press 1887).
[10] *Boothalinga Agencies v VTC Poriaswami Nadar* AIR 1969 SC 110.
[11] *VL Narasu v PSV Iyer* 65 LW 1154.

the promise and is not a turn of events after the contract is made. The reference in this third paragraph to absence of knowledge on the part of the promisee that the agreement is unlawful is curious since the first paragraph does not address impossibility on account of illegality. Mistake or lack of knowledge as to the law is not a defence, and a mistake as to the law in force in India does not make the contract voidable.[12] Further, the availability of compensation in cases of frustration of contracts is limited to the circumstances provided in the third paragraph of section 56, and payment of compensation will not fall due in the event of the impossibility or illegality arising after contract formation.[13] The compensation, we submit, would be calculated on the basis of the expectation measure, as would be applicable for cases of breach.

All the Illustrations to section 56 of the ICA address physical and legal impossibility, and have not assisted in the understanding of the scope of the section. In the 1950s, two judgments of the Supreme Court defined the scope of section 56 and its relationship with the situations covered in section 32 of the ICA. Since then, these pronouncements have become the measure by which the very admissibility of frustration as a ground for discharge has been judged. In *Ganga Saran v Ram Charan Ram Gopal*,[14] the Supreme Court of India held that the courts in India would not, unlike the courts in England, have to look at the contract to determine if the parties had made their bargain on the footing that a particular thing or state of things would continue to exist and to absolve performance if that foundation ceased to exist. Sections 32 and 56 of the ICA, respectively, would determine if the contract was frustrated on their terms. In *Satyabrata Ghose*,[15] the court noted that the principles enunciated in various English decisions cannot be said to be uniform and that the differences need not concern Indian courts as section 56 laid down a rule of positive law:

> [T]he only doctrine we have to go by is that of supervening impossibility or illegality as laid down in section 56 of the Contract Act, taking the word "impossible" in its practical and not literal sense. . . . [S]ection 56 lays down a rule of positive law and does not leave the matter to be determined according to the intention of parties.[16]

The belief, knowledge, and intention of the parties are evidence,

> but evidence only on which the court has to form its own conclusion whether the changed circumstances destroyed altogether the basis of the adventure and its underlying object. . . . When such an event or change of circumstances occurs which is so fundamental as to be regarded by law as striking at the root of the contract as a whole it is the court which has to pronounce the contract to be frustrated and at an end.[17]

[12] ICA, s 21: 'Effect of mistakes as to law.—A contract is not voidable because it was caused by a mistake as to any law in force in India; but a mistake as to a law not in force in India has the same effect as a mistake of fact.'

[13] The case of *Firm Hussainbhoy Karimji v Haridas* AIR 1928 Sind 21 extends this paragraph to circumstances of supervening illegality as well. The aspect of illegality of the subject matter of the agreement being covered by s 21 was not considered in this case.

[14] AIR 1952 SC 9.

[15] AIR 1954 SC 44.

[16] ibid [10].

[17] ibid [16]. Incidentally, in their assessment of the scope of s 56, the authors Pollock and Mulla opined that the coronation cases would more appropriately fall within the scope of s 32: see Pollock and Mulla (n 1).

The court then proceeded to list a variety of factors to assess whether the contract was frustrated.[18] The test of frustration or impossibility is based on an objective assessment of the events and its effect on performance.

2. Exceptions to Section 56 ICA: Contingencies within Parties' Contemplation

Sections 31 to 33 of the ICA provide as follows:

> S. 31. 'Contingent contract' defined.—A 'contingent contract' is a contract to do or not to do something, if some event, collateral to such contract, does or does not happen.
> S. 32. Enforcement of contracts contingent on an event happening.—Contingent contracts to do or not to do anything if an uncertain future event happens, cannot be enforced by law unless and until that event has happened.
> If the event becomes impossible, such contracts become void.
> S. 33. Enforcement of contracts contingent on an event not happening.—Contingent contracts to do or not to do anything if an uncertain future event does not happen, can be enforced when the happening of that event becomes impossible, and not before.

Sections 31 to 33 deal with contracts that have contemplated and made provision for contingencies affecting performance of promises under the contract. The contingency in section 31 involves an event collateral to the contract. The contingency is therefore neither the promise nor the consideration but an event that relates to the promise or its due performance. Contingent contracts are not properly the subject matter of this chapter since they provide for the converse of the circumstances that are addressed here, namely, that performance is prescribed and will arise only upon the contingency provided for under the contract being met. Sections 31 to 33 address *force majeure* situations that are contemplated by the parties as affecting performance, as opposed to section 56 (excepting paragraph 3). In the cases detailed below, these provisions have been relied on for assessing whether parties could have contemplated the frustrating event, and where this could have been done, the courts have held that the parties ought to have allocated their risks in the contract for such eventuality, and the court will not intervene under section 56. Sections 31 to 33 of the ICA have thus worked to identify the boundaries of section 56 and the doctrine of frustration under Indian law.

3. The Judgments That Defined the Law on Frustration

In the case of *Satyabrata Ghose*, the defendant subdivided land owned by it for residential buildings. The plaintiff booked a plot on payment of a small advance. The sale deed for the land would be executed after the defendant put in roads and infrastructure for utilities. Several parts of the property under development were requisitioned for the war. The

[18] *Satyabrata Ghose v Mugneeram Bangur & Co* (n 2) [22]–[24].

defendant wrote to the allottees expressing its inability to carry on the development work and offered the allottees two options—to treat the contract as cancelled and to take back the advance paid or to execute the sale deed and take the land without the promised infrastructure, and failing exercise of these options within a time specified, the defendant would treat the agreement as cancelled. On application for a declaration by one of the allottees, the court held that the requisition orders were, by their nature, of a temporary character, though they would extend over the duration of the war and thereafter. Having regard to the nature and terms of the contract, the existence of war conditions at the time when it was entered into, the extent of work involved, and a total absence of any definite period of time agreed to by the parties within which the work was to be completed, it could not be said that the requisition order vitally affected the contract or made its performance impossible. The order of requisition did not affect the fundamental basis on which the agreement rested or strike at the roots of the enterprise.

Relying on section 32 of the ICA, the court added that:

> while all cases where the contract as a matter of construction contained, impliedly or expressly, a term according to which it would stand discharged on the happening of certain circumstances, are treated as cases of frustration under English law, in India they would be dealt with under section 32 of the Indian Contract Act which deals with contingent contracts.... [I]f the parties do contemplate the possibility of an intervening circumstance which might affect the performance of the contract, but expressly stipulate that the contract would stand despite such circumstance, there can be no case of frustration.

Though war as a condition defining performance was not expressly stipulated in the contract, the court concluded that it would have been in the contemplation of the parties, and the impact of the war on the ability of the parties to perform would not be a ground to discharge the contract on the ground of impossibility. Finally, the court observed that 'impossibility' in section 56 was not confined to physical impossibility but would also include 'practical impossibility'.

While *Satyabrata Ghose* set the legal framework for frustration under the ICA, *Alopi Pershad and Sons Ltd v Union of India* (*Alopi Pershad*)[19] has been definitive of the understanding of the meaning of the expression 'impossible' in Indian law. Here, the circumstances existing at the time when the terms of the contract were agreed on were claimed to be entirely displaced by reason of the war and the resulting increase in costs. Alopi Pershad contracted to supply *ghee* (clarified butter) before the war and had continued supplies during the war. A modification of the contract was negotiated three years after the war commenced. Alopi Pershad claimed thereafter that the terms of the contract would not be binding on them on account of the increase in prices of *ghee*, which was locked into a price for supply that was not commercially sustainable. The court, relying on the case of *British Movietonews Ltd v London and District Cinemas Ltd (British Movietonews)*,[20] responded

[19] AIR 1960 SC 588.

[20] *British Movietonews Ltd v London and District Cinemas Ltd* [1952] AC 166, 185 (Lord Simon):

> Parties to an executory contract are often faced, in the course of carrying it out, with a turn of events that they did not at all anticipate, for example, a wholly abnormal rise or fall in prices which is an unexpected obstacle to execution. This does not in itself get rid of the bargain they have made.

that 'There is no general liberty reserved to the courts to absolve a party from the liability to perform his part of the contract, merely because on account of an uncontemplated turn of events, the performance of the contract may become onerous.' Thus, while the power of the court to intervene when frustration occurs is based on the rules of positive law in the ICA, a tendency to rely on English precedents in interpreting the rule in section 56 has resulted in a particular view being taken on the scope of impossibility under the section which remains unchallenged till now.[21]

The claim in *Alopi Pershad* was one for variation of the contract and for payment of increased charges owing to war conditions. Evidence in this case had been placed on record that showed that the supplier was paying more to procure the ghee than the buyer was being charged under the contract. The reliance on the case of *British Movietonews* and the precedents considered there laid the foundation for the approach to be taken. The judgment threw up several possibilities for change in circumstances, without tethering these to the extent of impact in monetary terms. How badly would the contractor lose? Would performance be at the cost of its survival? These considerations, it would seem, are immaterial in determining impossibility. Would the decision have been different if the parties had not renegotiated the contract after the war started? We believe not.

Another important case which has articulated the scope of the doctrine of frustration or impossibility is the case of *Naihati Jute Mills Ltd v Khyaliram Jagannath*.[22] Here, the contract for the purchase of jute from Pakistan was regulated by import licensing. The purchaser agreed to provide an import licence to the supplier based on which the goods would be despatched. The contract also made provision for certain *force majeure* conditions (acts of God, war, break in relations between governments, requisition, interference by government, etc) in the event of which the time for provision of the import licence or opening of letters of credit would be extended by agreement. The applications made by the purchaser for the import licence were rejected by the authorities in India, and the suppliers claimed damages for non-provision of the import licence as undertaken in the contract. The court referred to the law on frustration as laid down in *Satyabrata Ghose* and said:

> The courts have no general power to absolve a part of performance of contract merely because performance has become more onerous on account of an unforeseen turn of events. The question would depend upon whether the contract which the appellants entered into was that they would make their best endeavours to get the license or whether the contract was that they would obtain it or else be liable for breach of that stipulation. . . . In such a case the doctrine of discharge by frustration cannot be available, nor that of an implied term that the existing state of affairs would continue at the date of performance. The reason is that where there is an express term the court cannot find on construction of the contract an implied term inconsistent with such express term.[23]

Since the purchasers had undertaken an absolute obligation to provide the licence, and to pay damages if this was not procured in the time agreed, the defence of impossibility

[21] *Ganga Saran v Ram Charan Ram Gopal (Firm)* (n 14); *Satyabrata Ghose v Mugneeram Bangur & Co* (n 2); *Alopi Pershad* (n 19).

[22] AIR 1968 SC 522.

[23] ibid [10].

of performance of the contract would not be available to them. The court also considered the question of the impact on the contract between the parties if an embargo on imports were imposed by the Indian government and held that the question would still be whether the appellants were relieved from liability for their failure to deliver the license. A contract is not frustrated merely because the circumstances in which it was made are altered. The court did not bring the obligation in the context of *force majeure* provisions in the contract, despite the likelihood of the refusal to grant the licence being in the contemplation of the parties.[24] Since the issues in obtaining the licence were factored in as a delaying and not a discharging event, the purchaser could not contend that the performance was discharged under sections 31 and 32 of the ICA. On the facts of the case, the refusal to grant the licence was due to a personal disqualification of the purchaser under the rules. The rule followed was that when there is an absolute obligation, the court will not find an implied term inconsistent with such express obligation. This may be distinguished (also considering the provisions of sections 31 and 33) from a situation where the impossibility that arose was beyond the parties' contemplation at the time the agreement was made.

On the interplay of other obligations relating to performance, such as performance within a stipulated time and time being of the essence, the Supreme Court held that if the performance of the contract is rendered unlawful either for a determinate period of time or for an indeterminate period of time, the contract would not stand discharged unless the ban on its performance existed on the day or during the time in which it has to be performed. This was a case against the same defendant in the case of *Satyabrata Ghose* filed by another allottee.[25] The contract was held not to be frustrated since it was entered into during the time of war, and no time was specified for laying the roads in the development contract. However, where time is of the essence of the contract, an order of injunction passed by the court restraining any action to be taken to complete the contract amounted to frustration of the contract.[26]

(a) Contract held not frustrated despite commercial difficulties

In the following situations, contracts were considered not to be frustrated despite commercial difficulties:

(i) a contract for collection of tolls at two toll gates for the duration of a year, where an order prohibiting transport of grain to the state resulted in the stoppage of a considerable amount, but not all, of the traffic;[27]

(ii) a contract for the supply of goods, where there was a diversion of the shipping route which might result in exorbitant costs, and the court held that physical impossibility of transportation must be shown for frustration;[28]

[24] Similarly, in *Alopi Pershad* (n 19), although the impact of war conditions should have been a factor that ought to have been taken in to account and provided for, the court did not make a reference to ss 31–33 of the ICA but chose to proceed under s 56 of the ICA.

[25] *Mugneeram Bangur v Gurbachan Singh* AIR 1965 SC 1523.

[26] *M/s Shanti Vijay & Co v Princess Fatima Fouzia* (1979) 4 SCC 602, 617.

[27] *President of the District Board, South Kanara v G Shantappa Naik* AIR 1925 Mad 907.

[28] *Karl Ettlinger v Chagandas & Co* AIR 1915 Bom 232.

(iii) a contract for the lease of salt manufacturing works, where the defendant's ability to perform was affected by a strike by local workmen which ought to have been anticipated;[29]

(iv) a contract for the collection of tolls, where some bridges on the toll route were washed away owing to a monsoon of exceptional severity during a few months of the one-year contract, in circumstances where the *ghat* ('hilly') region where the bridges were located were typically subject to severe monsoons and there was a provision in the contract which specified that the 'sales would be subject to all risks';[30]

(v) a contract for the supply of eucalyptus wood of a specified girth from certain identified plantations, where the plaintiff discovered, after the contract was executed, that the specified type of wood was not available in the plantations (it being his responsibility to ascertain the availability of such wood).[31]

(b) The core principles summarized

The following principles now frame the rules on discharge of a contract on account of impossibility:

(i) Sections 31 to 33 deal with cases where the contingency is provided for in the contract.

(ii) Sections 31 to 33 would also apply where a contingency could have been reasonably contemplated by the parties.

(iii) If a contingency under sections 31 to 33 arises, the contract would not be impossible of performance, and the outcome would be as provided in the contract, that is, allocation of risks under the contract.

(iv) Where time is not of the essence of the contract, a temporary impossibility of performance will not operate to frustrate the contract or discharge the obligations of parties.

(v) Where time is of the essence of the contract, a temporary impossibility will operate to discharge the obligations under the contract.

(vi) The expression 'impossibility' is not restricted to physical impossibility but includes practical impossibility, even where physical performance may be possible.

(vii) Impossibility will be found where the whole purpose or basis of the contract was frustrated by the intrusion or occurrence of an unexpected event or change of circumstances which was beyond what was contemplated by the parties.

(viii) A change in the law which operates to make the act agreed under the contract illegal will discharge performance under the contract.

(ix) A change in circumstances after the formation of the contract that makes performance of the contract more difficult or economically less attractive will not relieve the parties from their obligations under the contract or allow for variation of the contractual obligations. Consequently, if the event has a commercial implication

[29] *Hari Lakshman Joshi v The Secretary of State for India* AIR 1928 Bom 61.

[30] *Panakattan Sankaran v The District Board of Malabar* (1934) 39 LW 51, 54, relying on *Hirji Mulji v Cheong Yue Steamship Company Limited* 1926 AC 497.

[31] *Gwalior Rayon Silk Mfg (Wvg) Co Ltd v Shri Andavar & Co* AIR 1991 Ker 134.

on the contract, the performance will not become impossible, even if the commercial impact is severe or even a commercial loss.

4. Restitution

In all cases not falling under section 56(3) of the ICA, restitution is the only legal consequence of frustration, and this is governed by section 65 of the ICA. Section 65 addresses the effect of an agreement discovered to be void or a contract that subsequently becomes void:

> S. 65. Obligation of person who has received advantage under void agreement, or contract that becomes void.—When an agreement is discovered to be void, or when a contract becomes void, any person who has received any advantage under such agreement or contract is bound to restore it, or to make compensation for it to the person from whom he received it.

Section 65 obliges a party who has received an *advantage* under an agreement that is discovered to be, or becomes, void to restore it. If the advantage has been utilized or cannot be restored, the party must make compensation for it in monetary terms,[32] as spelt out in *Govindram Seksaria v Edward Radbone.*[33] That was a case where a substantial portion of the machinery for a refining plant had been supplied from Germany when the Second World War began and the contract became void. It was contended by the Custodian of Enemy Property that against the payment of 83,875 Reichmarks made by the appellant, the appellant had received goods of the value of 158,000 Reichmarks, and the difference constituted the advantage that had to be paid by the purchaser. The Privy Council held that the expression 'advantage' occurring in the section may appear to be a contradiction in terms since compensation connotes a measure of loss or damage and not the value of an advantage. However, making compensation for an advantage would mean valuing or quantifying in money terms the advantage retained. It was held that, on facts, the Custodian had not proved that any advantage had been received of a value greater than the price paid.

5. Inability to Perform in Part

Inability to perform a part of a contract and its effect are addressed in section 12 of the Specific Relief Act 1963. This section provides that a party to a contract shall not be directed to perform a part of the contract except in the circumstances provided in that section. The section sets out rules for assessing if a part of a contract can still be performed and when specific performance of such part will be directed.

32 We submit that the provisions relating to compensation in ss 73–75 of the ICA apply in the event of breach or avoidance, and would not cover frustration in s 56, the consequence of which is that the agreement is void or renders the contract void.

33 AIR 1948 PC 56.

6. Illegality Discharging Performance

In the case of illegality as a ground for discharging performance, the change in law must make the contract as a whole illegal. Frustration on account of a change in law was rejected in a case where land was sold by the government for the development of property into a hotel on the basis of tenders received, for which a certain floor area ratio (FAR) was stipulated for construction. The appellant, the successful bidder, delayed payments under the agreement, and the transfer of property after full payment was made two years after the agreed date. In the meantime, the master plan for the city was revised, reducing the FAR. Since the project could be implemented, though with a lower FAR, the revision was held to not frustrate the contract.[34] Under section 57 of the ICA, if the agreement has a set of reciprocal promises that are severable, with one set of promises being legal and another being illegal, the first set of promises would be legal and enforceable, while the second would be void. On the basis of this section, it has been held that the prohibition on forward contracts under the Securities Contracts (Regulation) Act 1956 would nevertheless allow separation of the ready leg of the contract[35] from the forward leg[36] of the contract. The first set of promises would constitute a binding contract.[37] Change in law following the contract was applied to hold that the contract was impossible of performance in the case of *Boothalinga Agencies v VTC Poriaswami Nadar*.[38]

Two important cases decided by the Supreme Court of India in recent times have reviewed the doctrine of frustration, on the ground of illegality and commercial impossibility, vis-à-vis contingencies provided in the contracts. In the first, *Delhi Development Authority v Kenneth Builders and Developers Private Limited*,[39] an agreement was entered into by Delhi Development Authority (DDA) and Kenneth for the joint development of land into a residential complex. The land was provided by the DDA and the project was to be developed by Kenneth. The contract stipulated that the land was provided on an 'as-is-where-is basis', and the developer was deemed to have satisfied itself of the correctness and sufficiency of all the materials in relation to its obligations under the contract. It was agreed that it would be the responsibility of the developer to obtain all clearances from all the relevant agencies. The project land had been classified as residential land in the city's master plan. However, when work on the project was started by the developer, it was found that the land abutted the Delhi Ridge, a protected area. The exact boundaries of the Ridge were not properly demarcated, and the project land had morphological similarity to the Ridge. Any developmental activity adjoining the Ridge required the permission of both the Ridge Management Board constituted to oversee its protection and the Supreme Court. The developer filed a writ petition, a public law remedy under the Constitution of India, for setting aside the tender/auction of the project and for declaration that the project was incapable of performance. The Supreme Court so declared and directed the return of the bid amount by the DDA to the developer on the ground that the performance of the contract was frustrated on account of the prohibition of the physical activity at the Ridge, which made performance

[34] *Ganga Retreat & Towers Ltd v State of Rajasthan* (2003) 12 SCC 91.
[35] Contract for purchase or sale of securities at an agreed price which is executed immediately.
[36] Agreement to transfer the same securities on the future date for a price agreed presently.
[37] *BOI Finance Ltd v Custodian* (1997) 10 SCC 488.
[38] AIR 1969 SC 110.
[39] (2016) 13 SCC 561.

impracticable. This judgment, passed in discretionary and summary proceedings, unravels the clear distinction made between illegality, impossibility, and contingencies contemplated by parties in the context of the ICA. Though the parties did not specifically identify the need for approval from the Ridge Management Board, the parties had contemplated that approvals would be required for the project, to be determined by the developer on his assessment of the property and to be obtained by him. This condition was a contingency contemplated by the parties and therefore outside the scope of section 56. The Supreme Court in this case departed from well-established principles distinguishing contingency and impossibility and equated the inability to obtain approval with impossibility. The parties ought to have contemplated this contingency, and where this approval could not be obtained, the consequences would follow on the basis of the terms of the contract.

In the second case, *Energy Watchdog v Central Electricity Regulatory Commission* (*Energy Watchdog*),[40] the respondents were thermal power-producing companies which had bid, and were selected by various State Electricity Distribution Utilities, to supply electricity on a long-term basis, based on tariffs proposed by the bidders. The tariffs for supply of electricity were finalized based on guidelines issued by a sectoral regulatory authority. Though the bidders could tender rates on an escalatable and a non-escalatable basis, the tenders were submitted and accepted on non-escalatable rates. The respondents had bid on the basis of the price of imported coal from Indonesia, which was the source of fuel for their power plants. Within a few years of the power purchase agreements, a change in policy in Indonesia resulted in the price of coal imports being increased to align with international prices, instead of the price that had prevailed for the last 40 years. The respondents filed petitions before the electricity regulator asking to be discharged from the power purchase agreements or, in the alternative, to develop a mechanism to restore the respondents to the same economic position that they were in prior to the occurrence of the change in law in Indonesia.

The contract in *Energy Watchdog* had an extensive provision on *force majeure*, which set out a list of circumstances that would operate and discharge performance or allow for delayed performance by the respondents. This clause also set out a list of factors that would be excluded from *force majeure*; this list also comprised any increase in cost of fuel. The Supreme Court held that provisions for *force majeure* in the contract would be governed by section 32 of the ICA, which deals with contingent contracts. The purchase and cost of coal was entirely a matter for the person who set up the power plant to bear. It was clear that the unexpected rise in the price of coal would not absolve the generating companies from performing their part of the contract for the very good reason that when they submitted their bids, this was a risk that they knowingly took. The court relied on *Treitel on Frustration and Force Majeure*[41] and referenced *Tennants (Lancashire) Ltd v C.S. Wilson & Co Ltd*,[42] in which it was held that the expression 'hinders the delivery' in a contract would only be engaged if there was not merely a question of a rise in price but a serious hindrance to the performance of the contract as a whole. Reliance was also placed on the case of *Peter Dixon & Sons Ltd v Henderson, Craig & Co Ltd*,[43] which considered impossibility in the context

40 (2017) 14 SCC 80.
41 In ibid 114, the Court refers to G Treitel, *Frustration and Force Majeure* (3rd edn, Sweet & Maxwell 2014) paras 12-034 and 15-158.
42 1917 AC 495 (HL).
43 (1919) 2 KB 778 (CA).

of the First World War. In that case, British ships were not available for freight during the First World War. Foreign ships could be obtained at an increased freight charge, but these ships were liable to be captured by the enemy or attacked. The Supreme Court noted that the ground of impossibility pleaded in that case was not limited to the question of securing foreign ships at an increased freight charge but turned on the aspect of such ships being liable to attack or capture. The court considered not just the contract in question but also that the whole trade had been 'dislocated' by this risk. This latter aspect was held to constitute a hindrance to, or prevention from, carrying out the contract.

The narrow considerations for concluding that the contract has been frustrated were reiterated in *Energy Watchdog*. The Supreme Court held that the fundamental basis of the contract was not dislodged, and there was no potentially frustrating event except the cost of fuel, as has been pointed out above. Alternative modes of performance were available, though at a higher price. Therefore, the increase in the cost of fuel would not lead to the contract as a whole being frustrated. The scope and applicability of the provisions in the *force majeure* clause would have to be carefully considered in the context of the other provisions of the contract. Thus, where the contract was a fixed-rate contract but made provision for payment of a higher rate to tide over a change-in-law event, it was held that the clause for price variation had to be construed narrowly and that a circular issued by the government providing for higher prices could not be interpreted as a change brought about by 'law'.[44]

7. Frustration and Transfers of Immovable Property

There is a clear difference between a completed conveyance and an executory contract. Once a valid conveyance for transfer of interest in land comes into existence, the rights of parties thereafter are governed by the provisions of the Transfer of Property Act 1882. Section 56 of the ICA does not apply to a completed transfer,[45] and English decisions on this point can have no relevance.

However, according to section 54 of the Transfer of Property Act 1882, an agreement for the sale of land, unlike a valid deed of sale, does not of itself create any interest in the property which is the subject matter of the contract. The obligations of parties under such an agreement to sell are, therefore, the same as in other ordinary contracts, and consequently, the frustration in the ICA is held applicable to such contracts.[46]

In the case of *Sushila Devi v Hari Singh*, the appellant owned lands in a village that she would give on lease for cultivation for a few years at a time. The tenant was selected by a process of tender. The respondent's tender was accepted. They had deposited, together with the tender, both earnest money and security for the payment of rent. Partition intervened and the lands became a part of Pakistan. Because of communal troubles, it was not possible for the respondents to go to the village in Pakistan to cultivate the land or to collect the rent from those who were cultivating the land. The respondents claimed frustration of the contract and sought return of the amount given as security deposit but not the earnest money.

[44] *South East Asia Marine v Oil India Ltd* (2020) 5 SCC 164.
[45] *Raja Dhruv Dev Chand v Raja Harmohinder Singh* AIR 1968 SC 1024.
[46] *Satyabrata Ghose v Mugneeram Bangur & Co* (n 2).

The court was of the view that as the lease deed had not been executed, the doctrine in section 56 of the ICA applied to this case, and the contract was frustrated.[47]

8. Contingency and Partial Performance

In *PC Varghese v Devaki Amma Balambika Devi*, an agreement to sell a piece of land was sought to be specifically performed at a time when the sale deed had not been executed by the sellers. The land was owned by members of a family, which included a minor. The agreement to sell set out the responsibility of the sellers to obtain the sanction of the court to sell the minor's share. This was not done. The sellers claimed that the sale was contingent on the sanction being obtained from the court, which had not been given yet. The court held that the condition of obtaining the sanction of the court for sale of the minor's share did not make the contract a contingent contract. The agreement did not provide that, in the event that permission to sell the minor's share was not obtained within the time set out, the agreement would become invalid or unenforceable. The contract could be performed by the sellers to the extent of their shares in the property. The decree of specific performance granted by the trial court was upheld.[48]

9. Impact of COVID-19 on Contracts

The government of India responded to the COVID-19 pandemic by imposing a complete lockdown for the entire country from March 2020 for 68 days, which was eased gradually. Containment zones were identified in which the incidence of COVID-19 was high and to which restrictions were imposed.

A few cases that have arisen following the impact of COVID-19 have been in the context of contracts for lease of premises. Since the tenants, who claimed a remission or waiver of rent because of the lockdown, intended to continue in occupation of the premises, the courts in each of these cases acknowledged that frustration would not apply, since none of the parties were claiming a discharge of their obligations under the agreement, and that the contractual relations would continue to hold. The Delhi High Court, in the cases before it, also acknowledged that in terms of the law as discussed above, frustration would not apply to a lease of immoveable property since these contracts were executed and not executory.

The courts have, however, addressed the issue of impact of COVID-19 on such contracts differently. In the case of *Ramanand v Dr Girish Soni*,[49] the Delhi High Court considered a case filed by tenants who had been evicted from the property following orders of the Rent Tribunal prior to the outbreak of COVID-19. In an appeal to the High Court, they had been permitted to remain in the property subject to their payment of a substantially higher rent (in comparison with the nominal amount paid earlier), pending final hearing of the appeal. In considering their application for suspension of rent during the lockdown period, the court recognized that although the question of whether COVID-19 had the effect of

[47] *Sushila Devi v Hari Singh* (1971) 2 SCC 288.
[48] *PC Varghese v Devaki Amma Balambika Devi* (2005) 8 SCC 486.
[49] AIR 2020 Del 80.

suspending the obligations of parties to pay rent would typically have to be considered by evaluating the provisions for *force majeure* to see if the particular situation had been covered, there was no contract or contractual terms which formed the basis of the occupation in this case. The court then proceeded to consider the claim for suspension of rent based on equitable considerations, *viz* by looking at the circumstances concerning the case, such as the nature of the property (commercial), the financial status of the party claiming remission, the amount of rent being paid (which was substantially lower than the market rate), and the contractual conditions, and rejected the application for suspension of rent for the duration of the lockdown.

In a case before the Madras High Court,[50] the petition for suspension of rental during the period of lockdown was made in respect of a shop that had been licensed by the government of Tamil Nadu. Here, the government, through an order, had directed the waiver of the rental for a duration of two months of the lockdown. The writ (a public remedy available against the government) sought waiver of rental for the entire duration of the lockdown, during which the petitioner's shop had to be shut down. The licence made no provision for *force majeure*. The court in this case held, through the application of provisions of the ICA relating to reciprocal obligations,[51] that if the government, as a party to the contract, had directed closure or in other words had not performed its prior reciprocal obligation to permit the operations of the shop, it could not in turn claim the licence fee. The court noted that the government had acknowledged the existence of *force majeure* conditions as a result of the lockdown when it waived the licence fees for a period of two months. Waiver was granted for the remaining duration of full lockdown, and permission was given to the petitioner to apply for remission in the licence fees for the duration when partial lockdown operated in the area.

In order to mitigate the long-term effects felt by micro, small, and medium enterprises on account of the lockdown, the government of India has issued an order applicable to contracts with the government of India or government companies, for a refund of 95 per cent of the performance security, earnest money, or liquidated damages forfeited by the enterprise as a result of default in performance where the period of completion was between 19 February 2020 and 31 March 2022.[52]

As section 56 of the ICA renders the contract void and exempts the parties from further performance, the emphasis by the Supreme Court in *South East Asia Marine Engineering and Construction Ltd v Oil India Limited*[53] on the scope and drafting of provisions in a contract that set outcomes for future uncertain events and provide for allocation of risks/mitigation of the effects of such events becomes important when we contemplate, additionally, changes brought about by climate change.

Even though the effect of COVID-19 and the complete lockdown was severe and unprecedented, the principle that a contingency affecting performance must be provided for in the contract in order to be available to the parties continues. In the absence of such provisions, the risk will lie where it falls.

[50] *R Narayanan v Government of Tamil Nadu* (2021) 2 CTC 49.
[51] ICA, ss 51 and 54.
[52] Ministry of Finance, 'Government Provides Big Relief to MSMEs for COVID-19 period; Fulfils Promise Announced in Union Budget 2023–24' <https://pib.gov.in/PressReleasePage.aspx?PRID=1896631#:~:text=The%20contractor%2F%20supplier%20should%20be,2020%20and%2031.03> accessed 14 June 2024.
[53] (2020) 5 SCC 164.

III. The Hypotheticals

1. Abraham and Bill

In 1567, Abraham enters into a contract for an unlimited period of time with farmer Bill under which Abraham promises to build and maintain an irrigation channel from which Bill may extract water at a fixed price. By 2018, inflation and the rise in the cost of maintenance and labour have made the price wholly inadequate. Abraham's successors in law ask for an increase in the price that would provide them with adequate compensation. Alternatively, they wish to terminate the contract.[54]

Given the fact that the contract was entered into prior to the coming into force of the ICA, it will be equity and not ICA that would apply, and this will not be treated as a case of mere economic hardship but one where the fundamental basis of the contract has been dislodged and Abraham's successors will be entitled to treat the contract as impossible of performance.

2. Citi Corporation and Drive Bank

In 2015, Citi Corporation receives a loan from Drive Bank. The interest rate is fixed at 10 per cent for five years. In the 20 years preceding the agreement, the rate of inflation had been relatively stable within a range of 1 to 6 per cent. In 2017, the economic situation begins to destabilize and inflation rises to 50 per cent. Drive Bank requests adjustment or, alternatively, termination of the contract.

Applying Indian law, Drive Bank cannot terminate the contract on account of the change in the rate of interest following the unusual inflation. Parties to the contract would be expected to contemplate changes to the economic situation and provide for interest linked to economic conditions. Economic hardship, however onerous, would not constitute impossibility under the ICA.[55]

3. Easy and Frugle

Easy leases business premises from Frugle for a fixed period of 15 years. Shortly after the contract has been concluded, a nearby military airport is unexpectedly shut down for political reasons. The government invests an enormous amount of public funds in order to improve the commercial infrastructure in the area. As a result, Easy's profits are 500 per cent of what could reasonably have been expected at the time of making the contract. At the same time, the rental value of comparable business premises in the area rises to 500 per cent of the agreed rental price. Frugle requests that the rental price should be adjusted accordingly or, alternatively, that the agreement should be terminated.

[54] The fact scenarios of the hypothetical situations in this section III are taken from M Chen-Wishart, D Neo, and S Vogenauer, 'Introduction', ch 1 in this volume, 7–8.

[55] *Alopi Pershad* (n 19).

Applying Indian law, the doctrine of frustration will not apply to the lease of land by Frugle to Easy since this is a concluded contract. Under section 108(e) of the Transfer of Property Act 1882,[56] the following conditions must be satisfied for the lease to become void: a rendering unfit or destruction of a material part of the property by fire, tempest, or flood; or violence of an army or of a mob, or other irresistible force, which is not the case here.

4. George and Han

George agrees to refurbish the cellar of Han, the owner of a restaurant. The work is scheduled to start one month after the agreement. Before the work begins, the restaurant is completely destroyed by a storm that is much more violent than any other previous storm in the region. However, the cellar remains fully intact. Han immediately informs George of the situation and asks him not to start work. George insists on rendering performance because he has set aside two weeks to carry out the work and has already purchased the necessary materials. Is Han required to pay the contract price or, alternatively, to compensate Georg for his loss?

The contract for refurbishment of the cellar has become impossible of performance under section 56 of the ICA, though it is not impossible in the physical sense since the cellar was left intact after the storm. The impossibility in this case arises from the fact that with the destruction of the restaurant, the basis of the contract for the refurbishment of the cellar was frustrated by the intrusion or occurrence of an unexpected event or change of circumstances which was beyond what was contemplated by the parties. Han is not required to pay George the contract price or compensate him for the loss, which is limited to the loss of profits anticipated and to the cost of the materials purchased. The ICA does not contemplate the payment of compensation in the event of frustration of the contract. Under section 65 of the ICA, since restitution is limited to the advantage received by the counter party, George would have been entitled to restitution had he commenced work on the cellar and to the extent of the costs of such work done.

5. Gina and H Hotel

Gina books a room for the weekend at H Hotel in X City, the capital of country Z. However,

(i) the exhibition she intended to visit is cancelled at the very last moment;
(ii) a terrorist group declares that it plans to launch attacks on tourists in X;
(iii) an unforeseeable strike by airport personnel prevents Gina from travelling to X before Sunday afternoon;

[56] Transfer of Property Act 1882, s 108(e):

> If by fire, tempest or flood, or violence of an army or of a mob, or other irresistible force, any material part of the property be wholly destroyed or rendered substantially and permanently unfit for the purposes for which it was let, the lease shall, at the option of the lessee, be void: Provided that, if the injury be occasioned by the wrongful act or default of the lessee, he shall not be entitled to avail himself of the benefit of this provision.

(iv) the inauguration proceedings of the new head of state of Z that were scheduled for Saturday are cancelled. Gina had booked a room overlooking the street where the inauguration procession was supposed to pass by. Due to the inauguration, the rental price of the room was ten times higher than the regular price.
Can Gina cancel the booking?

Gina can cancel the booking in situations (ii) and (iii). In situation (ii), the declaration by the terrorist groups that it will launch attacks on tourists in X makes it practically impossible for her to travel as to do so would be putting her life at risk. In situation (iii), the strike by the airport personnel makes it physically impossible for Gina to travel to X before Sunday afternoon, assuming that alternative means of travel do not exist, and if they did, they would get Gina to X only on or after Sunday afternoon, which is at the end of her stay. However, Gina cannot cancel the booking in situations (i) and (iv) of the hypothetical. In situation (iv), the inauguration proceedings for the head of state of Z scheduled for Saturday afternoon being cancelled would not make the performance of the contract an impossibility as this was an event, going by the premium rates and the choice of room, that the parties had in contemplation when the contract was signed and is a contingency that ought to have been provided for in the contract. In situation (i), the cancellation of the exhibition does not render impossible Gina's obligation to stay in the hotel, though if she were travelling for this purpose alone, this would have rendered her travel and stay at the hotel impractical or pointless. However, this is a contingency that does not relate to the obligations of the hotel and has no relevance to performance of the obligations under the contract. If Gina's travel was for the purpose of and contingent upon attending the exhibition, Gina ought to have provided for such contingency and allocated the risk of the exhibition not taking place in the contract.

IV. Conclusion

The relative bargaining capacities of the parties and the hardship that performance of a contract under changed circumstances would cause, while not a consideration under section 56 of the ICA, had been a part of the law of specific relief until recently. Section 20 of the Specific Relief Act 1963, until its abolition in 2018, gave the courts the discretion to deny the relief of specific performance of contracts where the performance of the contract would involve some hardship on the defendant that she did not foresee, or where the defendant entered into the contract under circumstances which, though not rendering the contract voidable, made it inequitable to enforce specific performance. The discretion under this section was vast, but we submit, perhaps justified given the deep inequalities caused by poverty and caste in India.

In the recent judgment of the Supreme Court in *Energy Watchdog*, the court approved the 'multi-factorial approach' as well as the test of 'radically different' to assess frustration as set out in the *Edwinton Commercial Corporation v Tsavliris Russ (Worlwide Salvage & Towage) Ltd (The Sea Angel).*[57] While giving a context-driven approach to the issue, the rigor for claiming frustration remains, both in the assessment of the contemplation of

[57] 2007 EWCA Civ 547, (2007) 2 Lloyd's Rep 517 (CA).

risk and in the emphasis that the obligations will be discharged only if performance in the new circumstances would be 'radically different' from what had been contemplated in the contract.

The role of impossibility in commercial contracts that are heavily negotiated is limited, if any role is played at all. The extensive *force majeure* clause in the *Energy Watchdog* case is an example. The clause was given full judicial consideration and not treated as a matter of impossibility in keeping with the statutory scheme providing for mutually exclusive spaces for contingency, as set out in sections 31 to 33 of the ICA and impossibility as set out in section 56. While acknowledging that impossibility was not in issue in the *Energy Watchdog* case since this was a contingency provided for in the contract, the position that prevails in India, and was reiterated in this case, is an unyielding standard that closes the door to a qualitative assessment of commercial impossibility or onerousness. We submit that the test introduced in *Alopi Pershad*[58] has resulted in subsuming all manner of onerousness under the head of 'economic hardship' that renders section 56 of the ICA inapplicable and allows change of circumstances to be taken into account only on a radical change in the contract. Under the law as it stands in India today, it will be the responsibility of parties to anticipate 'onerous situations' and allocate risks that would be more accommodating of commercial realities. The *Sea Angel* case, which the *Energy Watchdog* case considers, suggests a multi-factorial assessment that will serve us well.

The 'radically different' but temporary effects of COVID-19 have shown the fault lines in the positive rule of frustration in section 56 of the ICA. This rule proved inadequate to meet the needs of the situation. Since the remediation sought because of COVID-19 was exemption from performance for the period of the pandemic and not discharge, the provisions of section 56 proved to be inapplicable since the only outcome in section 56 is to make the contract void, which would not be an outcome which the parties prefer. The onus falls back on the parties to craft *force majeure* clauses that are wide enough to provide for eventualities that they cannot specifically anticipate.

[58] See section II.3.

8

Discharge of Performance and Termination of Contracts in India

*R Yashod VARDHAN and Chitra NARAYAN**

I. Introduction

The Indian Contract Act 1872 (ICA) is the primary law of contract in India. Sir Frederick Pollock, in the second edition of his commentary on the ICA,[1] published in 1909, lamented: 'One can only repeat that it [the ICA 1872] has remained unrevised longer than any codifying Act ought, and hope that the Legislative Department will not lose sight of the matter.' While his commentary has seen 17 editions, the law that is now 150 years old has undergone very limited amendments.

The rules made in 1872 governing termination of contracts and discharge of contractual obligations thus remain the same to this day, save for small changes.[2] These rules are not the subject of discrete treatment in the ICA but, to a large extent, are found in the chapter on 'Performance of Contracts'. The focus, as can be expected in a chapter on performance, is on the detailing of obligations to be met. The provisions are not granular but frugal in their enumeration of the circumstances warranting termination or discharge. Breaches of standards in performance are met with two broad consequences, the first being discharging performance of obligations by the promisee and the second entitling a party to terminate the contract. There are some provisions that stipulate standards for performance but are silent on the rights of the promisee in the event of a breach.[3]

Where one of the contracting parties is the state or its instrumentality, over which the state has deep and pervasive control, contract law has over time been infused with the principles of fairness and proportionality. This chapter is divided into two substantive parts, in addition to this introduction and the conclusion. The first part sets out the rules in Indian law for discharge and termination. The second part addresses the impact of constitutional and administrative law principles on termination of contracts to which the government is a party.

* The authors gratefully acknowledge the assistance of Ms Gayathri Rajagopalan, Advocate, Madras High Court.

1 F Pollock and DF Mulla, *The Indian Contract Act* (2nd ed, Sweet & Maxwell, 1909).

2 For instance, s 43 was amended to clarify that a promisee could compel 'any one or more' joint promisors to perform, instead of being able to 'compel any one' of such joint promisors.

3 See for instance ICA, ss 40, 46.

R Yashod Vardhan and Chitra Narayan, *Discharge of Performance and Termination of Contracts in India* In: *Studies in the Contract Laws of Asia V: Ending and Changing Contracts*. Edited by: Mindy Chen-Wishart, Dora Neo, and Stefan Vogenauer, Oxford University Press. © R Yashod Vardhan and Chitra Narayan 2026. DOI: 10.1093/oso/9780198995814.003.0008

II. Termination and Discharge

1. General

The specific obligations of parties with respect to performance of promises are introduced in the first section of Chapter IV of the ICA, 'Of the Performance of Contracts' (section 37):

> S. 37. Obligations of parties to contracts.—The parties to a contract must either perform, or offer to perform, their respective promises, unless such performance is dispensed with or excused under the provisions of this Act, or of any other law.

For certain categories of breach specified in the ICA, a right to terminate the contract is granted. There are certain other breaches that do not permit termination of the contract but discharge a party from performance of its obligations. The Specific Relief Act 1963 (SRA), which is a law relating to remedies (including remedies under contracts), sets out circumstances where a party to a contract can seek and obtain the remedy of rescission of the contract on standards distinct from those under the ICA.[4] The Sale of Goods Act 1930 (SGA), which is the law relating to sales of every kind of movable property other than actionable claims and money, may also be relevant where the contract in question is a sales contract. The SGA is based upon and is largely a reproduction of the English Sale of Goods Act 1893, and therefore, English authorities on interpretation of different sections, although not technically binding in India, have had great persuasive value.[5] Although the law in the UK is now consolidated in the Sale of Goods Act 1979, the law in India remains unamended.

2. Discharge of Performance of Obligations

The performance of obligations under a contract is discharged in the following circumstances:

(i) Under section 38 of the ICA, performance by the promisor is discharged where the promisee has refused to accept the promisor's offer of performance that was unconditional, made in accordance with the contract and of the whole of the promise. The provision also preserves the promisor's rights under the contract.

(ii) Performance is discharged in the following circumstances, where the contract consists of reciprocal promises, to be performed simultaneously, or sequentially: (a) under section 51 of the ICA, where the reciprocal promises are to be performed simultaneously, the promisor need not perform unless the promisee is ready and willing to perform her reciprocal promise; and (b) under section 54 of the ICA, in the case of performance of reciprocal promises to be performed sequentially, where the promisor of the promise that needs to be performed first fails to perform it. The promisor of the preceding obligation in such a case cannot claim performance of

[4] SRA, ss 27–29.
[5] *Consolidated Coffee Ltd v Coffee Board* (1980) 3 SCC 358.

the reciprocal promise and is bound to make compensation to the other party for any loss sustained by such non-performance on the basis of the expectation interest.

(iii) Non-performance of the promisor is excused if the promisee neglects or refuses to provide reasonable facilities for performance of the promise under section 67 of the ICA. Section 67 addresses an aspect of the promisee's obligations that impacts performance, similar to those addressed in section 54 and in section 53 (allowing for termination and considered later). However, this section is not included under the group of sections addressing reciprocal promises to which sections 51, 53, and 54 belong as the responsibility of the promisee under section 67 is more in the nature of a facilitation for performance.

The sections on discharge referred to above are typically rudimentary in their expression and do not address discharge of the contract. Rather, they discharge the performance under the contract. The question arises whether the discharge is permanent or only a deferral. The rules, on their own, do not put an end to the contract. Courts have, in situations allowing for discharge under these sections, relied on and incorporated rules on termination to determine the obligations of parties and closure under the contract. The essentiality of time and the seriousness of the unperformed reciprocal obligation have been used to justify putting an end to the contract.[6] Sections 39, 53, and 55 of the ICA, which are relevant in these contexts, are dealt with in the later paragraphs.

3. Voidable Contracts and Termination

The ICA distinguishes agreements and contracts, with the latter being a category of the former and enforceable by law.[7] Section 2(i) of the ICA defines a 'voidable contract' as an agreement which is *enforceable by law* at the option of one of the parties but not at the option of the other. In the use of the expression 'agreement', this definition applies where elements are present that vitiate the formation of a contract between the parties, but the agreement will nevertheless be enforceable as a contract upon the exercise of the option to enforce it by the party affected by the vitiating factor. In the rules governing termination, however, the right to terminate is variously described as 'put an end to the contract',[8] 'rescission',[9] and 'voidable'.[10] The use of the expression 'voidable' in the rules for termination evidently covers situations other than where the agreement is vitiated by formation defects in the manner addressed by section 2(i). The Calcutta High Court took the view that the difference in the language used in some provisions for termination was of consequence and that the right to restitution, available in section 64 of the ICA on rescission of a voidable contract, would not be available under provisions for termination that did not use the expression 'voidable'.[11] On appeal, the Privy Council held that the effect of both expressions

6 *MR Malhotra v Competent Builders Private Ltd* (2012) 192 DLT 295; *Norman J Hamilton v Umedbhai S Patel* (1979) 81 Bom LR 340; *Manokji Framji v Firm of Maniklal Pritamdas* AIR 1924 Sind 105; *Bank of India v Jamsetji AH Chinoy* AIR 1950 PC 90; *Ramachandra Narayan Nayak v Karnataka Neeravari Nigam Ltd* (2013) 15 SCC 140.

7 ICA, s 2(h)—an agreement enforceable by law is a contract.

8 ICA, s 39.

9 ICA, s 64.

10 ICA, ss 53–55.

11 *The International Film Co Ltd v Muralidhar Chatterjee* (1939) 44 CWN 11.

would be the same, and a party 'putting an end' to the contract would also be entitled to restitution under that section.[12]

(a) Termination on refusal to perform

Sections 39 and 55 of the ICA are the pivotal provisions in the chapter on performance, and reference is often made to the obligations in these provisions—to perform fully, and within the stipulated time—in order to determine outcomes under other sections in this chapter. The general rule under which a contract can be rightly rescinded is first contemplated in section 39. Sections 53 and 55 deal with special rules for contracts in which there are reciprocal obligations or where time is of the essence of their performance.[13] Termination as an outcome also arises under more than one rule in the chapter, for instance, where promises are to be performed simultaneously, but one of the parties is not ready or willing to perform. Section 39 provides:

> S. 39. Effect of refusal of party to perform promise wholly.—When a party to a contract has refused to perform, or disabled himself from performing, his promise in its entirety, the promisee may put an end to the contract, unless he has signified, by words or conduct, his acquiescence in its continuance.

The Illustrations to this section are as follows:

(a) A, a singer, enters into a contract with B, the manager of a theatre, to sing at his theatre two nights in every week during the next two months, and B engages to pay her 100 rupees for each night's performance. On the sixth night A wilfully absents herself from the theatre. B is at liberty to put an end to the contract.

(b) A, a singer, enters into a contract with B, the manager of a theatre, to sing at his theatre two nights in every week during the next two months, and B engages to pay her at the rate of 100 rupees for each night. On the sixth night A wilfully absents herself. With the assent of B, A sings on the seventh night. B has signified his acquiescence in the continuance of the contract, and cannot now put an end to it, but is entitled to compensation for the damage sustained by him through A's failure to sing on the sixth night.

As can be seen from the second Illustration above, a party can claim compensation for the loss thus occasioned despite acquiescing to the continuation of the contract after the breach. This principle is also found in section 55 of the ICA that permits a party to terminate the contract where time is of the essence and the promisor fails to perform their obligations in this time. Paragraph 3 of section 55 allows the promisee to waive the delay in performance, and to claim compensation for the loss caused by the delay, subject to the condition that notice of their intention to claim such compensation is given at the time of acceptance of the performance.

In a contract for exhibition of films, heavy rains damaged a portion of the theatre, which was ordered to be pulled down.[14] A distinction was drawn between impossibility in section

[12] *Muralidhar Chatterjee v International Film Co Ltd* AIR 1943 PC 34.

[13] *Mirza Javed Murtaza v UP Financial Corporation Kanpur* AIR 1983 All 234.

[14] *VL Narasu v PSV Iyer* 65 LW 1154; AIR 1953 Mad 300; (1952) 2 MLJ 832.

56 of the ICA and the ground of being 'disabled from performing' in section 39 of the ICA. The court, relying on *Bank Line Ltd v Arthur Capel & Co*,[15] held that section 56 would only apply to cases of frustration that arise without blame or fault from either party. Acts and omissions which result in self-induced frustration must be deliberate and intentional, not merely passive negligence. That section 39 refers to conduct that is more than just a failure to perform is clear from the language used in the section: 'refused to perform'. It should 'be of such a character that it might be fairly inferred therefrom that the promisor has no intention of performing the contract.... The conduct must be such as could be held to amount to repudiation.'[16] A mere breach will not entitle the innocent party to terminate. The Supreme Court[17] adopted the test set in *Freeth v Burr*[18] that for an act to be relied on as rescission, the act should be one amounting to abandonment or refusal by a party to perform and that repudiation of a contract is a serious matter, not to be lightly found or inferred. A challenge by the persons with the right to pre-emption regarding the valuation of the shares to be transferred, as occurred in this case, concerned the manner of performance, and it could not be said to be a case of repudiation.

Not every breach would justify termination, and the element of intention is important.[19] In *Sooltan Chand v Schiller*,[20] the claimants, after receiving certain instalments of linseed, while not refusing altogether to pay the price, sought adjustment of the price against claims towards excess refraction and empty bags. The Calcutta High Court clarified that the language used in section 39 'means to enact what was the law in England and the law here before the Act was passed, namely, that where a party to a contract refuses altogether to perform or is disabled from performing his part of it, the other side has a right to rescind it'. The application of this section to obligations for payment has also relied on English judgments[21] to conclude that failure to pay one of a series of payments would not, in the absence of a prospective refusal, discharge the other party from proceeding with the contract. The provisions of section 38(2) of the SGA provide an answer as to whether there is a repudiation of the whole contract in situations where payment and delivery is in instalments. This will have to be considered in context, based on the terms of the contract and the circumstances of the case.[22]

Section 39 of the ICA stipulates a refusal to perform, or a disablement from performing, a promise its entirety, and the first Illustration confirms this. We will not know whether A turned up for performance on the subsequent dates since her absence on one day was sufficient to justify the termination. The author, Whitely Stokes, took the view that under this section, a partial failure to perform rendered the whole contract terminable, even though the failure was such that damages would properly compensate for it.[23] Despite this language, the courts have tested the breach not on the ground of whether there was performance of the entirety of the promise but by examining whether the breach was of an essential

[15] [1919] 2 AC 435.
[16] *VL Narasu v PSV Iyer* (n 14) 1161.
[17] *Claude-Lila Parulekar v Sakal Papers P Ltd* (2005) 11 SCC 73; *Mishra Bandhu Karyalaya v Shivratanlal Koshal* AIR 1970 MP 261.
[18] (1874–1880) All ER Rep 751.
[19] *Rash Behary Shaha v Nrithya Gopal Nundy* (1906) 33 Cal 477, 491.
[20] (1878) 4 Cal 252, 255.
[21] *Freeth v Burr* (1874) LR 9 CP 2018; *Mersey Steel and Iron Co v Naylor, Benzon, and Co* (1884) 9 AppCas 434.
[22] SGA, s 38(2).
[23] W Stokes, *The Anglo-Indian Codes* (Clarendon Press 1887).

condition. This test was imported from section 12 of the SGA, which defines a condition as a stipulation essential to the main purpose of the contract, a breach of which gives the right to repudiate the contract, and this rule has been adopted generally for all contracts. The principles adopted also correspond to section 16(b) of the SRA, which bars the relief of specific performance if the party claiming such performance has breached an essential term of the contract. Where a 60 MW power plant was supplied under a contract which required the supply, erection, and commissioning of a 108 MW power plant, the capacity of the power plant was treated as an essential condition of the contract, breach of which justified repudiation of the contract.[24] In another case, the provision for maintenance services in a contract for installation of telecommunication facilities was held to be a warranty entitling the promisee only to compensation, and not termination, in the event of a breach. In this case, the damages ordered under the Consumer Protection Act 1986, however, was the amount of the contract price for the installation of the facilities.[25]

In cases of performance in instalments, section 39 of the ICA has been interpreted by adopting the twin test in *Maple Flock Company Ltd v Universal Furniture Products (Wembley) Ltd*[26] that 'in deciding whether there has been repudiation of a contract, regard must be had first, to the ratio quantitatively, which the breach bears to the contract as a whole, and secondly, the degree of probability or improbability that the breach will be repeated'.[27] In a contract for purchase of quicksilver to be delivered under a cost, insurance, and freight (CIF) contract in two consignments which were delayed by war, the purchaser refused to make payment on the bill of lading and other documents presented to him for the first instalment and insisted that payment would be made only on delivery at port. When the second instalment arrived at the port, the purchaser demanded delivery, which was refused on the ground that the contract had been cancelled by the purchaser's breach in respect of the first consignment. The court held that the reasons given by the purchaser in refusing the first consignment constituted a breach which the sellers might well expect to be repeated with regard to the second half of the instalment. The breach was a refusal to perform the contract to the extent of one half and so extensive that the seller was entitled to cancel the contract.[28] For goods deliverable by instalments, the breach in relation to one instalment does not by itself entitle rescission of other instalments. But where the breach is of such a type as satisfies the *Maple Flock* test in terms of the ratio of the breach and the likelihood that it would be repeated, the whole contract may be regarded as repudiated. This was the result in a case where issues with the quality of the cotton in two instalments which had been delivered entitled the defendant to refuse acceptance of the balance of the deliveries.[29]

The Illustration (b) in section 39 of the ICA, and the broad but sparse language employed in section 39, has enabled fact-centric determination of breach and a multifactorial test to assess the seriousness of the breach. The simple language and the avoidance of over-prescription has given room to the courts to interpret this section in the context of the facts of the case.

24 *Svenska Handelsbanken v M/s Indian Charge Chrome* (1994) 1 SCC 502.
25 *Indochem Electronic v Additional Collector of Customs, AP* (2006) 3 SCC 721.
26 [1934] 1 KB 148.
27 *M/s Shah.Moolchand Kesarimull v M/s Associated Agencies* AIR 1942 Mad 139, (1941) 54 LW 217>, 222.
28 ibid.
29 *Motilal Srinivas Sarda v The Netha Co-operative Spinning Mills Ltd* AIR 1975 AP 169. See also SGA, s 38 on delivery of goods in instalments.

The editors pose the following hypothetical situation:[30] Car Machinery & Co appoint Traders Ltd as sole distributors of their car panel presses for a period of five years. Clause 7(b) of the agreement provides that 'Distributors shall send their representatives to visit all six large car manufacturers in the country at least once in every week for the purpose of soliciting orders for car panel presses. Failure to comply with this obligation shall entitle Car Machinery to terminate the agreement with immediate effect.' Traders Ltd misses two visits to car manufacturers in the second month of the contractual period. Is Car Machinery entitled to terminate the agreement?

The clause for termination negotiated by the parties will be enforced. The agreement is for distribution of the panels, and the specification in the agreement that Traders Ltd, the sole distributor, visit all six large car manufacturers in the country at least once a week shows the intention of the parties to make this an essential condition of the contract. Given the nature of the obligations of Traders, and the importance of visiting the identified six large car manufacturers in performing the obligations, the failure to undertake these visits for two successive weeks will be a breach of an essential obligation of the contract. Additionally, in the light of two successive breaches Car Machinery would be justified in anticipating repeated breaches and would be entitled to terminate the contract.

Another hypothetical situation is as follows: Seven Seas, an importer of seafood, sells two tons of mussels to Big Chef restaurant chain. After one ton has been delivered, it turns out that the concentration of cadmium in the mussels is 2 per cent above the concentration permitted by national food regulations. Can Big Chef terminate the contract?

Big Chef will be entitled to terminate the contract under section 39 of the ICA. The contract contains an implied condition as to the quality of the goods or their fitness for purpose in accordance with section 16 of the SGA. Seven Seas, a regular importer of mussels, must have been aware or be deemed to be aware of the following, even in the absence of specific information being shared by Big Chef: (i) the mussels must be of a standard fit for consumption: (ii) the import and sale of mussels in the country must meet the national food regulations. On the basis that Seven Seas is a regular importer, Big Chef has relied on its experience and judgement that only mussels meeting the regulations will be imported by the former. The requirement that the mussels meet the regulations is a stipulation that is essential to the main purpose of the contract, that is, procurement for human consumption.

In a case where the defendant was not in a position to give possession of the property agreed to be sold, rescission was permitted under section 39 of the ICA.[31] In another case relating to a contract for the installation of low-tension load management systems within a period of 20 months, the appellant did not provide locations for the installations despite the significant lapse of time, and the respondent terminated the contract. The failure was held to be a fundamental breach justifying termination and a claim for damages for the entire contract—that is, the part performed and the part prevented from being performed.[32]

As noted, section 39 is a go-to section in cases of breach, given the generality in its language. It has not mattered that the section makes no provision for quality, extent of performance, or importance of the obligations to be performed. Despite this frugal wording,

[30] The fact scenarios for the two following hypothetical cases are taken from M Chen-Wishart, D Neo, and S Vogenauer, 'Introduction', ch 1 in this volume, 9.
[31] *Chaudhary Rambabu v Dilip Kumar* AIR 1981 MP 158.
[32] *Maharashtra State Electricity Distribution Co Ltd v Datar Switchgear Ltd* (2018) 3 SCC 133.

several dimensions—intention to abandon, seriousness of the breach, breach of essential conditions, and impossibility that is self-induced—have been incorporated by decisions into the section, and a variety of circumstances have thus come to be addressed under the section.

(b) Contract not performed in time

The second rule for termination addresses non-performance of a contract within a time fixed by the contract. The innocent party in such a case would be entitled to terminate the contract under the first paragraph of section 55 if the time fixed was of the essence of the contract. Under the second paragraph of section 55, if the time fixed was not of the essence of the contract, the contract does not become voidable for late performance, but the promisee is entitled to compensation from the promisor for any loss occasioned to him by the promisor's failure to perform within the fixed time. If, despite having the right to treat the contract as voidable on account of the promisor's failure to perform within the time fixed by the contract, the promisee accepts performance at some other time, the third paragraph of section 55 provides that the promisee cannot claim compensation for any loss occasioned by such failure, unless, at the time of acceptance, he gives notice to the promisor of his intention to do so. A related provision on time for performance is section 46 of the ICA, which sets out the obligations when time is not specified in the contract. In such cases, the promise must be performed within a reasonable time, which is a question of fact in each particular case.

Section 55 expressly stipulates that the provision of time for performance of obligations will not be final as to the time within which the performance should be undertaken unless such time is of essence. Consequently, the contract cannot be terminated if there is delay in performance where time is not of the essence of the contract (second paragraph of section 55).[33] In terms of tests to determine if 'time is of essence', some of the issues considered by courts are fixing responsibility for timely performance of the contract in the absence of a stipulation as to time (under section 46) and whether time should be determined not to be of essence despite being so specified (second paragraph of section 55).

For determining whether time is 'of essence' so as to entitle the promisee to terminate the contract on its breach, the test to be followed is the same as that followed by the English courts of equity, *viz* to ascertain whether in fact performance of the contract was meant to depend on the promise being fulfilled to the day or whether a day was named in order to secure performance within a reasonable time.[34] The Supreme Court held that a mere stipulation that time is of the essence will not make it so, and this has to be read with other provisions of the contract, which may on a construction of the terms exclude such inference. Provisions for extension of time and for payment of damages for delayed completion would ordinarily show that time was never intended by the parties to be of the essence. But time could be of the essence despite such clauses, on a consideration of other factors. Where a time was set for completion, with liquidated damages payable for delay, time was held to be of the essence on the basis that this contract was part of a larger contract that was time bound, and in turn linked to a foreign collaboration for erection of plant and machinery within a stipulated time.[35] In a case of a compromise where the creditor in whose favour the

[33] *Hind Construction Contractors v State of Maharashtra* (1979) 2 SCC 70.
[34] Stokes (n 23) 505.
[35] *NV Chowdary v Hindustan Steel Works Construction Ltd* AIR 1984 AP 110.

judgment was given agreed to accept in full satisfaction a lesser amount if paid within an agreed period, the agreement further being that on failure to pay, he would proceed with the execution without the judgment debtors being entitled to raise any objection, it was clear that the parties intended to make time of the essence.[36]

As regards contracts for transfer of immoveable property, the Privy Council in *Jamshed Khodaram Irani v Burjorji Dhunjibhai*[37] established two principles that have been followed by the courts in India in interpreting the first paragraph of section 55. Section 55, the Privy Council noted, embodied the rule in equity that time was not of the essence of the contract. Relying on *Stickney v Keeble*[38] and *Tilley v Thomas*,[39] the court held that:

> the special jurisdiction of equity to disregard the letter of the contract in ascertaining what the parties to the contract are to be taken as having really and in substance intended as regards the time of its performance may be excluded by any plainly expressed stipulation.[40] . . . But equity will not assist where there has been undue delay on the part of one party to the contract and the other has given him reasonable notice that he must complete within a definite time.[41]

The second principle established, despite the absence of any language in section 55 to this effect, was the presumption that time was not of the essence in contracts relating to sale of immovable property.

This view, that time was not of essence in contracts for transfer of immoveable property, has been subsequently reconsidered. A Constitution Bench of the Supreme Court[42] held that the presumption as to time not being of the essence in contracts for transfer of immoveable property may be displaced, and it may be inferred from the terms of the contract, the nature of the property, and the object in making the contract that it is to be performed within the time stipulated. In this case it was held that the stipulation for payment within 'a period of ten days only' was evidence of the intention to make time of the essence. The presumption regarding time not being of the essence was negated where the settlement agreement between disputing brothers provided for transfer of the land within 150 days, though extendable by another 10 to 20 days with the consent of both the parties but not more.[43] This was also the view in a case where the contract set an outer limit for the sale, and the sale was undertaken in view of the seller's need for funds.[44] Likewise, if the object of the agreement to purchase land is a commercial purpose (eg for construction of a factory), then the court would be strongly inclined to hold time as essential.[45] Time will be of the essence in

[36] *Kissen Gopal v Madan Lal* AIR 1937 Par 542.

[37] AIR 1915 PC 83, (1916) 43 IA 26.

[38] [1915] AC 386.

[39] LR 3 Ch App 61.

[40] *Jamshed Khodaram Irani v Burjorji Dhunjibhai* (n 37) 32, 33.

[41] ibid. See also *Gomathinayagam Pillai v Palaniswami Nadar* (1967) 1 SCR 227, AIR 1967 SC 868.

[42] *Chand Rani v Kamal Rani* (1993) 1 SCC 519 (a five-judge bench); *KS Vidyanadam v Vairavan* (1997) 3 SCC 1.

[43] *Narinder Kumar Malik v Surinder Kumar Malik* (2009) 8 SCC 743.

[44] *Suraj Singh v Smt Nathi Bai* AIR 1990 MP 323.

[45] *Citadel Fine Pharmaceuticals v Ramaniyam Real Estates P Ltd* (2011) 9 SCC 147; *Sriram Cotton Pressing Factory Pvt Ltd v KE Narayanaswami Naidu* AIR 1965 Mad 352, quoting E Fry and GR Northcote, *A Treatise on the Specific Performance of Contracts* (6th edn, Stevens and Sons 1921) 505 and SC Banerji (Banerjee), *The Law of Specific Relief in British India: Tagore Law Lectures, 1906* (2nd edn, R Cambray & Co 1917) 381.

mercantile contracts.[46] R owned a colliery and D agreed to transport the coal for two years at a specified rate. Disputes arose and R withheld payments, while D stopped the transportation. The court, holding R to be in breach, stated that in mercantile contracts, timely payment was an essential condition of the contract.[47]

Consider the following hypothetical: Prime Ltd sells a piece of land to Devil Corp. Under the terms of the contract, Devil pays a 10 per cent deposit, the remainder of the sum being due at 5:00 pm on 30 September, time being 'of the essence'. According to Clause 12, failure to meet the deadline would result in the deposit being forfeited and the agreement being terminated. Devil is ten minutes late in tendering the completion money and Prime refuses performance. Can Devil sue for specific performance, arguing that Prime's reliance on the clause is unreasonable in some way? Would the result be different if the contract did not include Clause 12?[48]

The hypothetical contract between Prime Ltd and Devil Corp, though for sale of land, is between two commercial entities, and accordingly, the presumption will be that the time provided under the contract would be of essence. The term of the contract stipulating the time to the hour for deposit by Devil Corp of the balance consideration for the land would fortify this intention. If the date or time was not adhered to, Devil being the defaulting party cannot sue for specific performance. The result would not be different if the contract did not include Clause 12. Section 16 of the SRA referred to above also bars specific performance where the party seeking it is itself guilty of breach of an essential term of the contract.

What then of contracts (i) where no time is mentioned, or (ii) time is mentioned but not of the essence, or even (iii) where time is of the essence but the contract is not terminated by the promisee despite delay? There are several views taken by the courts. The first view is that no notice is mandated and that the contract can be terminated on non-fulfilment of performance within a reasonable time, reasonableness being assessed based on the nature of the case. The provision for performance within a reasonable time as mandated by section 46 of the ICA would be an implied term of the contract.[49] The second view is that upon delay, notice issued by the promisee giving a reasonable time for performance will make time of the essence, with the promisee having the right to repudiate the contract if this time is not met.[50] A subsidiary view here is that the question of whether the time indicated in the subsequent notice would be of the essence of the contract would be a matter of construction to be derived from the reasonableness of the time given.[51]

The third view, taken in the case of *Claude-Lila Parulekar v Sakal Papers P Ltd (Claude-Lila Parulekar)*, was that if there was no stipulation in the contract as to time for

[46] *Balchandra Pandurang Rajandekar v Mahadeo Laximinarayan Shraogi* AIR 1947 Nag 193; *Mahabir Prasad Rungta v Durga Dutt* AIR 1961 SC 990.

[47] *Mahabir Prasad Rungta v Durga Datta* (n 46).

[48] The fact scenario for this hypothetical is taken from M Chen-Wishart, D Neo, and S Vogenauer, 'Introduction', ch 1 in this volume, 9.

[49] *Binda Prasad v Kishori Saran* AIR 1929 PC 195; *Dinkerrai Lalit Kumar v Sukhdayal Rambilas* AIR 1947 Bom 293; *Sat Prakash v Dr Bodhi Raj* AIR 1958 Punj 111; *Official Receiver, Calcutta High Court v Baneshwar Prasad Singh* AIR 1962 Pat 155; *HPA International v Bhagwandas Fatehchand Daswani* (2004) 6 SCC 537.

[50] *Mulla Badruddin v Tufail Ahmed* AIR 1963 MP 31; *Tadepalli Kuttumba Rama Sastry v Seetepalli Dahhina Murthy* AIR 1960 AP 178; *Jamshed Khoduram Irani v Burjorji Dhunjibhai* (n 37); *Pichai Moideen Rowther v Chathurbuja Das Kushal Das & Sons* AIR 1933 Mad 736; *Nannapaneni Subayya Chowdary v Garikapati Veerayya* AIR 1957 AP 307; *Andard Mount (London) Ltd v Curewell (India) Ltd* AIR 1985 Del 45; *Dau Alakhram v Mt Kulawati Bai* AIR 1950 Nag 238.

[51] *Tandra Venkata Subrahmanyam v Vegesana Viswanadharaju* AIR 1968 AP 190.

performance, it was not open to a party to unilaterally stipulate a time and then cancel the contract because of an alleged failure of the other party to act within the time stipulated. In the circumstances, the contract for sale of the shares to the appellants could not be avoided by reason of any alleged failure on the part of the appellants to pay the price fixed within the time fixed by the seller.[52] However, in *Hind Construction Contractors v State of Maharashtra*[53] (decided by a three-judge bench), followed in *Bangalore Development Authority v Syndicate Bank* and in *Kailash Nath Associates v DDA*,[54] the service of notice subsequently limiting time for completion and making time of the essence was upheld by the Supreme Court. If time was not of the essence of the contract or the stipulation as to the time fixed for completion ceased to be applicable by reason of waiver, then the only course open to the respondent was to fix a reasonable time for completion, making it the essence, and if the time fixed is reasonable and the appellant had failed to complete the work within the time so fixed, the respondent would be entitled to rescind the contract.

Claude-Lila Parulekar (decided by a two-judge bench) did not consider these judgments, including *Hind Construction Contractors*, as binding precedents of a larger bench. Further, the judgments in *Hind Construction Contractors, Bangalore Development Authority*, and *Kailash Nath* are to be preferred as they harmoniously construe the two sections dealing with time, section 46, which refers to completion within reasonable time where no time is specified, and section 55, which deals with the effect of time being of the essence of the contract. Termination would thus be possible, where time is not of the essence, only if the party has been given a second chance by stipulating a reasonable time for performance. The court could also give the party in breach additional time for performance where time is found not to be of essence of the contract.

If there is a provision for notice before termination, this requirement must be complied with before termination.[55]

(c) Prevention of performance

Prevention by one party of performance under the contract entitles the promisor to terminate the contract:

> S. 53. Liability of party preventing event on which the contract is to take effect.—When a contract contains reciprocal promises, and one party to the contract prevents the other from performing his promise, the contract becomes voidable at the option of the party so prevented; and he is entitled to compensation from the other party for any loss which he may sustain in consequence of the non-performance of the contract.

Under section 53, the prevention must be intentional and could arise from the non-performance of the prior reciprocal obligation or, it is submitted, by other actions of the

[52] *Claude-Lila Parulekar* (n 17) 97. The court appears to have followed the view of the English Courts in *Behzadi v Shaftesbury Hotels Ltd* [1992] Ch 1.

[53] *Hind Construction Contractors v State of Maharashtra* (n 33).

[54] *Bangalore Development Authority v Syndicate Bank* (2007) 6 SCC 711, 718. See also *Kailash Nath Associates v DDA* (2015) 4 SCC 136, applying the ratio from *Webb v Hughes* (1870) 10 LR Eq 281.

[55] *Rithwik Energy Generation Private Limited v Bangalore Electricity Supply Company Limited* (2018) 17 SCC 223.

promisee. Significantly, this situation makes express provision for compensation for loss sustained on account of the non-performance of the contract. Unlike section 54, which discharges performance on the failure of a prior reciprocal obligation, this section permits termination where performance is prevented. The language adopted in the section suggests that the contract could be terminated only if one party *prevents* the other party, as opposed to using the passive—the party *is prevented* from performance. However, in *State of Gujarat v A A Pathan*,[56] the land over which the overbridge was to be constructed under the contract was not provided to the contractor by the state due to an injunction granted by a court at the instance of a third party. It was held that the contractor could rescind the contract under section 53 and claim damages for the loss of profit caused. This ruling did not consider the decision of the Supreme Court in another case where it was held that if the performance was prevented not by the party but on account of an interim order granted in proceedings initiated by a third party, it would be a case of frustration under section 56 ICA and not a breach of contract.[57]

Notwithstanding that the language of section 53 allows for two outcomes—avoidance or specific performance by affirming the contract—the courts have applied the principle of constructive performance expounded in *Roberts v Bury Improvement Commissioners*.[58] Prevention by one party is constructively tantamount to the fulfilment of the contract by the other. The contract in question, a compromise decree, contained two provisions—that the claimant would take her late husband's nephew in adoption and that she would hold and enjoy certain properties without interference from the relatives of her late husband. Meanwhile, the nephew's marriage took place, thereby making him ineligible for adoption. The court held that on the claimant being prevented from fulfilling her part of the contract on account of the marriage of the nephew, the effect would be that she would be deemed to have performed her obligation, and the properties would be hers to enjoy as agreed.[59] The fiction of fulfilment of contract will not apply to claims arising out of termination of an employment contract as the law of employment contracts in India is separately codified, and section 14(c) of the SRA bars specific performance of contracts that are for personal service.[60]

A wrongful repudiation by one party does not of itself absolve the innocent party, if she sues on the contract, of establishing her right to recover by proving performance on her part of conditions precedent. If the innocent party insists on performance of the contract, the repudiation will be *brutum fulmen*; that is, the parties will be left with their rights and liabilities as before.[61]

In cases of wrongful termination, innocent parties can, instead of seeking damages, insist on specific performance of the contract under the SRA. Recent amendments to the SRA have introduced the performance interest in the case of breach of contracts through two changes. The discretion available to courts in granting specific performance of contracts has been removed, and specific performance of contracts is now the rule, subject to limited

[56] (2001) 42 (4) GLR 2915.
[57] *Shanti Vijay & Co v Princess Futura Fouzia* (1979) 4 SCC 602.
[58] (1969–70) 5 CPC 310. *Mackay v Dick* (1881) 6 AC 251 also relied on.
[59] *Makkineni Nagayya v Makkineni Bapamma* AIR 1958 AP 504; *Alagu Pillai v Veluchami* (1923) 45 MLJ 76; *Secretary, Department of Irrigation v Millars Machinery Company* 1985 KLT 1084.
[60] *Gayatri Balaswamy v ISG Novasoft Technologies Ltd* (2014) 5 LW 97.
[61] *Florrie Edridge v Rustomji Dhanjibhoy Sethna* AIR 1933 PC 233.

exceptions.[62] The distinction made earlier, regarding the rights to specific performance, between contracts involving moveable and immoveable property, has also been removed.

Where a breach is condoned or waived by a party, it is no longer open to that party to avoid the contract.[63] A party can also lose its right to terminate the contract by not acting to terminate it within the period of limitation, or by a change of circumstances since the making of the contract on account of which the parties cannot be restored to their earlier position,[64] or by the creation of third party rights,[65] or when a part of the contract is sought to be rescinded and that part is not severable from the rest of the contract.[66]

Apart from the provision of giving notice of reasonable time for performance under section 55 ICA, the provision of a second chance before termination of a contract has also been stipulated by a 2018 amendment to the SRA, in cases where the promisee proposes to obtain substituted performance of the contract in the event of a breach.[67]

(d) Rescission of contract by courts

The ICA does not mandate the involvement of courts for termination of a contract. An enabling provision is, however, found in section 27 of the SRA, under which persons (and not just the parties to a contract) *may* approach the courts to rescind a contract on the ground that the contract is voidable or terminable. However, the court may refuse to intervene under this section when third-party rights are involved. Section 27 also confers a right to approach the court to have a contract rescinded on equitable grounds and to balance the parties' interests, a remedy that is not available under the ICA.

4. Effect of Termination

Sections 64 and 73–75 of ICA address the rights of restitution and compensation following breach of contract and termination. Section 73 of the ICA entitles the innocent party to receive compensation from the party who has broken the contract.[68] This section has been

62 SRA, s 10: The specific performance of a contract shall be enforced by the court subject to the provisions contained in sub-s (2) of s 11, s 14, and s 16.

63 *Ganga Retreat and Towers Ltd v State of Rajasthan* (2003) 12 SCC 91. See also SRA, s 27(2)(a).

64 SRA, s 27(2)(b).

65 SRA, s 27(2)(c).

66 SRA, s 27(2)(d).

67 Specific Relief (Amendment) Act, s 20:

> Substituted performance of contract.—(1) Without prejudice to the generality of the provisions contained in the Indian Contract Act, 1872 (9 of 1872), and, except as otherwise agreed upon by the parties, where the contract is broken due to non-performance of promise by any party, the party who suffers by such breach shall have the option of substituted performance through a third party or by his own agency, and recover the expenses and other costs actually incurred, spent or suffered by him, from the party committing such breach. (2) No substituted performance of contract under sub-section (1) shall be undertaken unless the party who suffers such breach has given a notice in writing, of not less than thirty days, to the party in breach calling upon him to perform the contract within such time as specified in the notice, and on his refusal or failure to do so, he may get the same performed by a third party or by his own agency.

68 ICA, s 73:

> Compensation for loss or damage caused by breach of contract.—When a contract has been broken, the party who suffers by such breach is entitled to receive, from the party who has broken the contract, compensation for any loss or damage caused to him thereby, which naturally arose in the usual course of things from such breach, or which the parties knew, when they made the contract, to be likely to result from the breach of it. Such compensation is not to be given for any remote and indirect loss or damage sustained by reason of the breach.

held to be declaratory of the common law as to damages. Damages can be recovered only if the breach was the dominant or effective cause of the loss caused. If a sum is named in the contract as payable in the case of breach, the court will award reasonable compensation not exceeding the amount so named regardless of whether it is in the nature of liquidated damages or penalty. By enacting section 74 providing for a common principle applicable to stipulations in the nature of both liquidated damages and penalty, Indian law has sought to cut across the web of rules and presumptions under English common law.[69] The Madras High Court has clarified that under section 74, (i) unlike English law, a stipulation in the nature of a penalty is enforceable, as a ceiling, as in the case of a sum stipulated as liquidated damages; (ii) the primary test for distinguishing between liquidated damages and penalty clauses is whether, when tested at contract formation, the stipulated sum bears a reasonable correlation to anticipated loss, in which event it will be construed as a liquidated damages clause; (iii) a stipulated sum that bears such reasonable correlation to anticipated loss is considered as a genuine pre-estimate of loss; (iv) for purposes of enforcement, the two categories are treated differently—if the court concludes that the stipulated sum is a genuine pre-estimate of anticipated loss in case of breach, the sum would be ordered to be paid where the court also concludes that it is difficult or impossible to prove loss, but if it is concluded that the stipulated sum is by way of penalty, the person claiming such penalty would be required to prove loss accurately; (v) even if the court concludes that the stipulated compensation is a genuine pre-estimate of the loss, the party claiming is required to prove that loss was incurred as a result of the breach; (vi) if it is not difficult or impossible to prove loss, the person claiming liquidated damages is required to prove loss, including quantum of loss.[70]

Section 75 of the ICA entitles the person rightfully rescinding a contract to compensation for any damage sustained through non-fulfilment of the contract.[71]

Consider this hypothetical: Coco, a famous architect, agrees with David that he will landscape the garden in her next development. For David, the start of work on 1 December is an important opportunity to make his name as a landscape gardener. On 1 October, Coco tells him that she is no longer interested because the development will not include a garden after all. David has already purchased materials. He estimates that his future earnings will be 10 per cent lower because he will not be able to benefit from having worked with Coco. Can he insist on doing the work? Can he bring an action under the ICA for breach of contract?[72]

Coco has committed an anticipatory breach of the contract and refused to perform her obligations under the contract before they were due to be performed. Under section 9 of

[69] *Fateh Chand v Balkishan Dass* AIR 1963 SC 1405.

[70] *3i Infotech Limited v Tamil Nadu e-Government Agency* (2019) SCC OnLine Mad 33295.

[71] ICA, s 75:

> Party rightfully rescinding contract, entitled to compensation.—A person who rightfully rescinds a contract is entitled to compensation for any damage which he has sustained through the non-fulfilment of the contract.
>
> Illustration:
> A, a singer, contracts with B, the manager of a theatre, to sing at his theatre for two nights in every week during the next two months, and B engages to pay her 100 rupees for each night's performance. On the sixth night, A wilfully absents herself from the theatre, and B, in consequence, rescinds the contract. B is entitled to claim compensation for the damage which he has sustained through the non-fulfilment of the contract.

[72] The fact scenario for this hypothetical is taken from M Chen-Wishart, D Neo, and S Vogenauer, 'Introduction', ch 1 in this volume, 9.

the SRA, read with section 19(a) of the SRA, the contract can only be enforced against the parties to the contract. David cannot claim specific performance of the project, as originally agreed, as this would involve enforcement of the contract against the landowner, who is not a party to the contract. David can, however, claim compensation for losses incurred under section 75 of the ICA, including loss of profit under this contract, which Coco, being in the business, would reasonably be expected to know was the consequence of her breach. The compensation would, however, not include the loss on the purchase of the materials as he would have used it in the completion of the task in any event. In the alternative, David could sue for compensation for the loss incurred by buying the materials, subject to his ability to mitigate losses by putting the materials to use in another project. After categorizing losses that would arise from the breach of a contract into compensation that would protect the expectation interest (putting the party in as good a position as she would have occupied had the contract been performed) and compensation that would protect the reliance interest (putting the party in as good a position as she was in before the contract was made), the Supreme Court of India[73] held that a claimant cannot ordinarily recover compensation for both the expectation interest and the reliance interest. The claim of the party rescinding the contract must address one or the other—the claim for wasted expenditure or claim for damages—not both together as that would result in a windfall to the party.

Section 64 of the ICA is a recognition of the principle that there must be *restitutio in integrum* as a condition of rescission of a terminable contract. A person electing to end a contract terminable at her option is bound to return any benefit received under the contract but is entitled to set off any damages caused by the defaulting party's breach.[74] Section 64 of the ICA addresses the rights of the defaulting party to restitution, while section 75 of the ICA addresses the rights of the innocent party rescinding the contract.

Section 64 of the ICA sets out two consequences on the rescission of a contract: (i) the other party need not perform any promise under the contract in which she is the promisor; and (ii) any benefit received by the person rescinding the contract from the other party must be restored. If the contract has been substantially executed, the section does not exclude consideration transferred before rescission and it is submitted that this will also be regarded as a benefit derived by the rescinding party which may be liable to be restored. Restoration may not be ordered if performance in entirety (and not substantial performance) was the essential condition.

The editors pose another hypothetical: Bob contracts to build a house for Sue for the price of $100,000. After doing a third of the work he abandons the job, leaving behind material worth $15,000, which Sue later uses to finish the works. Can Bob claim the value of the work done or of the materials?[75]

Bob has committed a breach of the contract by not completing the work agreed to be performed. Sue has accepted the breach, rescinded the contract, and undertaken the performance of the work by another agency. Sue is required to restore the value of materials procured by Bob, which she has utilized. Bob will be entitled to make a claim for restitution of the value of the materials left at the site and utilized by Sue. Since Bob has completed only

[73] *Kanchan Udyog v United Spirits Ltd* (2017) 8 SCC 327.
[74] *Muralidhar Chatterjee v International Film Co Ltd* (n 12).
[75] The fact scenario for this hypothetical is taken from M Chen-Wishart, D Neo, and S Vogenauer, 'Introduction', ch 1 in this volume, 10.

a third of the work, which would not qualify as substantial completion, the actual value of the construction cannot be claimed by Bob. Section 64 of the ICA addresses benefits conferred by the defaulting party on the counterparty and allows them to be recovered on termination of the contract. Sue will be entitled to make a counter-claim for the loss suffered by her on account of the breach and will be entitled to set off any claim made by Bob for restitution against her counter-claim. Sue could have, in the alternative, not accepted the repudiation by Bob and given a notice to Bob to cure the breach. In the event of Bob's failure to perform, she could have got the work done through another agency or by her own agency and claimed the expenses, costs incurred, and compensation under section 20 of the SRA after adjustment for the amounts due to Bob.

United Access Services Licences (UASLs) executed by the government of India with telecom licensees, including the appellant, were set aside by the Supreme Court of India[76] on finding that the policy of the government to allot 2G spectrum licences on a first-come-first-serve basis was illegal. The appellant filed a claim before the statutory tribunal for telecom disputes for refund of the substantial non-refundable entry fee paid, of rupees (Rs) 14,549 million for 20 years, under contract (section 56: subsequent frustration on account of illegality read with section 65 of the ICA) and constitutional law, which was rejected on the ground of *in pari delicto est conditio defendentis.* Incidentally, in subsequent auctions of the 2G spectrum, the government decided to permit those applicants who had participated in the quashed auctions to set off the licence money paid in the prior, quashed auctions. The Supreme Court held that the principles of restitution would be subject to a defence of illegality and limited to those cases where the party claiming restitution itself was not *in pari delicto.* When the party claiming restitution is equally or more responsible for the illegality of a contract, they are considered *in pari delicto.* Finding that the appellant was *in pari delicto* with the relevant department of the government, the Court held that the appellant could not be rendered assistance for obtaining refund of the entry fee.[77] Refund permitted in the case of other licensees who were not at fault, but whose licenses were cancelled because of the illegalities committed by the government, was upheld.[78]

III. Contracts with the State or Its Instrumentality

In the public law sphere, the fairness of the conduct of the state was incorporated in judicial review of contracts where the state was a party, including in cases relating to termination of contracts. Article 14 of the Constitution of India[79] was included in the evaluation of the conduct of the contracting party and interpreted as striking at arbitrariness in state action and ensuring fairness and equality of treatment. Initially, review in the latter class of cases was restricted to state actions at the stage of calling for tenders.[80]

When the allottees of houses from an instrumentality of the state (over which the state exercised deep and pervasive control) challenged the unilateral increase in costs after the

[76] *Centre for Public Interest Litigation v Union of India* (2012) 3 SCC 1.

[77] *Loop Telecom and Trading Limited v Union of India* (2022) 6 SCC 762.

[78] ibid [72].

[79] Article 14: 'The State shall not deny to any person equality before the law or equal protection of the laws within the territory of India.'

[80] *Ramana Dayaram Shetty v International Airport Authority of India* (1979) 3 SCC 489.

contracts had been concluded, the Supreme Court refused to interfere, observing that once a lawful contract was entered into, it would be those terms that would govern the rights and obligations of the parties and not constitutional principles.[81]

In *Indian Oil Corporation Ltd v Amritsar Gas Service* (*Amritsar Gas Service*),[82] a dispute raised by a distributor of liquefied petroleum gas (LPG) upon termination of the gas distributorship granted by a state-owned petroleum corporation after receipt of certain complaints from consumers was referred to arbitration. The contract provided that the agreement was determinable by either party by giving 30 days' notice. The arbitrator held the state entity to be in breach of contract and directed restoration of the distributorship. Setting aside the restoration, the Supreme Court held that the contract, being determinable in nature, could not be specifically enforced in view of the bar in section 14 of the SRA, and compensation alone could have been awarded.[83]

It was almost a quarter-century after *Amritsar Gas Service* that the Supreme Court was once again confronted with the application of public law principles in the matter of cancellation of a gas distributorship contract by the same state-owned petroleum corporation. Upon the distributor taking up the task, a request was made to the public entity to transfer the distributorship to his spouse to comply with a particular contractual term. This was not acceded to, and the distributorship was terminated on the ground of breach. This time, the challenge to the termination was by way of a civil suit. In *Indian Oil Corporation Ltd v Niloufer Siddiqui* (*Niloufer*),[84] the Supreme Court distinguished the decision in *Amritsar Gas Service* on the ground that it was rendered in the context of arbitral proceedings and affirmed the order of the High Court directing the restoration of the terminated dealership, holding that given the unequal bargaining capacities, the contract was unconscionable as it gave the state entity an unfettered right to terminate the distributorship without providing any reasons, which violated Article 14 of the Constitution.[85]

The *Niloufer* judgment failed to consider the caution exercised by the Supreme Court in holding that the rule relating to vitiation of a contract on the ground of it being unconscionable cannot be applied to commercial transactions.[86] More recently, the Supreme Court, in reviewing the validity of arbitration agreements in commercial contracts by the state or government agencies, brought in the test of equality and arbitrariness in Article 14 of the Constitution that would be breached if the government agencies stipulated unilateral appointment of arbitrators by them when disputes arise.[87] While standard form contracts in commercial transactions have by and large been held to bind parties,[88] in public employment contracts, the scrutiny has been strict. Whether *Niloufer* will be restricted in its application as a precedent to public employment contracts remains to be seen.

Actions of the state under contracts have also been tested on the basis of the proportionality principle. An allotment of an industrial plot by a public undertaking was subject to the

[81] *Bareilly Development Authority v Ajai Pal Singh* (1989) 2 SCC 116.
[82] (1991) 1 SCC 533.
[83] ibid.
[84] *Indian Oil Corporation Ltd v Niloufer Siddiqui* (2015) 16 SCC 125.
[85] ibid.
[86] *Central Inland Water Transport Corporation Ltd v Brojo Nath Ganguly* AIR 1986 SC 1571.
[87] *Central Organisation for Railway Electrification v M/s ECI SPIC SMO MCML (JV) A Joint Venture Company* 2024 INSC 857.
[88] See eg *InterGlobe Aviation Ltd v N Satchidanand* (2011) 7 SCC 463, where a standard form contract of the airline excluding liability for delay was held to be valid.

condition that a certain percentage of the area should be constructed upon and commercial production commenced within a specified time. Delays in handing over possession and getting the building plans approved led to the time limit being breached, whereupon the authority terminated the contract and resumed the land. Observing that the law, and much less the contract, did not warrant compliance with the impossible, the Court, applying the principle of proportionality, held that where two remedies to enforce a contract were available to a state authority, the harsher remedy of resumption and forfeiture could not have been resorted to.[89] A power purchase agreement was entered into between a state entity and a private company for procurement of solar power. Owing to reasons beyond the control of the company, there were delays in the commissioning of the plant and compliance with the conditions subsequent could not be done within the time specified. The agreement was terminated as per the terms of the contract. In the case of *Madhya Pradesh Power Management Co Ltd v Renew Clean Energy (P) Ltd (Renew Clean Energy)*,[90] holding that the termination by the state entity was *not fair* in view of the substantial investment and reasons for the delay, the Supreme Court, while setting aside the termination, directed the company to pay liquidated damages instead.

IV. Conclusion

The 13th Report of the Law Commission of India, published in 1978, has been the only comprehensive review of the ICA to date. The Commission acknowledged the reliance on developments in common law, which have now become part of Indian law through court decisions. While recommending changes to other provisions to resolve conflicts in interpretation, the Commission's view was that the provisions on termination needed no changes.

Niloufer and *Renew Clean Energy* are cases where the application of constitutional law principles trumped the contractual terms and contract law. These decisions will lead to uncertainty in outcomes as to what would constitute reasonable or fair action would depend on the individual views and predilections of judges. Whether a breach committed by an individual can be dealt with differently merely on account of the fact that the other contracting party is the state is a question that is yet to be squarely raised and decided. Application of constitutional law principles to commercial contracts can, at best, only supplement and not supplant the contractual terms. Rather than applying this doctrine of fair dealing only to state actions piecemeal and at the discretion of the courts, India would do well to regulate unconscionable contracts by adopting fairness as an implied obligation in all contracts as has been done in certain other jurisdictions and as suggested by the 199th Report of the Law Commission of India on Unfair (Procedural and Substantive) Terms in Contract (August 2006).

Though the scheme for termination of contracts under the ICA is frugal and does not contain the more granular expositions of rules on termination obtaining in several jurisdictions, it has accommodated a wide variety of cases. The elaboration that these statutory sections received has come from English cases, often judgments relied upon by judges of

[89] *Managing Director HSIDC v Hari Om Enterprises* (2009) 16 SCC 208.
[90] *Madhya Pradesh Power Management Co Ltd v Renew Clean Energy (P) Ltd* (2018) 6 SCC 157.

English descent or training. The ICA provisions on termination and discharge have withstood the test of time, as can also be discerned from the absence of conflicts in interpretation by courts. A few aspects may, however, be noted. Specialized or sector-specific laws now regulate termination in contractual relations, which once relied only on the ICA.[91] Reliance on English authorities should be circumspect, given that several aspects of contract law in England are now governed by statutes.

[91] Consumer Protection Act 1986, Electricity Act 2003, Companies Act 2013, Insolvency and Bankruptcy Code 2016.

9

Change of Circumstances in the Indonesian Law of Obligations

Gary F BELL

I. Introduction

A short introduction to Indonesian contract law is contained in the second volume of this series,[1] and I highlighted six essential features in my contribution to the third volume.[2] It is worth repeating a few of these before proceeding, particularly for the benefit of those who have not had a chance to read either of these.

First, the Indonesian Civil Code (ICC) is in Dutch and, to this day, no official Indonesian version has ever been adopted by the legislator. Secondly, this in part explains why there is very little doctrine written on Indonesian contract law: Indonesian academics today rarely speak Dutch, and the few Indonesian lawyers fluent in Dutch are very knowledgeable but produce much less doctrine than they used to as most of them are now in their late seventies and early eighties.

Thirdly, there is in fact very little help to be found in jurisprudence. Most cases were not published until recently, and now that many cases are published, they are still not properly indexed and one can often find everything and its contrary in the decisions of Indonesian courts.[3] The reasons given for decisions are often not very clear or compelling. The Supreme Court (Mahkamah Agung) has not issued many clear guidelines in the field of contract law in the last two decades (or more).

Fourthly, the Civil Code in place in Indonesia is essentially the same (with a few modifications) as the 1838 Civil Code that was in place in the Netherlands before the reform of the Dutch Civil Code. In the field of contract law, most of the articles are a translation into Dutch of the 1804 French Civil Code, although a few articles were modified and a few were added, and some articles were interpreted slightly differently from the interpretations the French courts gave to the *Code Napoléon*.

Fifthly, the French reform of contract law came into force in 2016, and the ICC on contract is now orphaned as both its Dutch and French progenitors are no longer in force.

[1] GF Bell, 'Formation of Contract and Stipulations for Third Parties in Indonesia' in M Chen-Wishart, A Loke, and S Vogenauer (eds), *Studies in the Contract Laws of Asia, vol II: Formation and Third Party Beneficiaries* (OUP 2017) 365, 365–71.

[2] GF Bell, 'Contractual Interpretation and Protection against Unfair Terms in Indonesia' in M Chen-Wishart and S Vogenauer (eds), *Studies in the Contract Laws of Asia, vol III: Contents of Contracts and Unfair Terms* (OUP 2020) 135.

[3] '[Judges in Indonesia] have to reinvent the wheel from one case to the other and produce quite diverse decisions in similar cases': A Bedner, 'Indonesian Legal Scholarship and Jurisprudence as an Obstacle for Transplanting Legal Institutions' (2013) 5 Hague Journal on the Rule of Law 253, 253–56.

Gary F Bell, *Change of Circumstances in the Indonesian Law of Obligations* In: *Studies in the Contract Laws of Asia V: Ending and Changing Contracts*. Edited by: Mindy Chen-Wishart, Dora Neo, and Stefan Vogenauer, Oxford University Press.
 DOI: 10.1093/oso/9780198995814.003.0009

Sixthly, this chapter is only concerned with the contract law under the ICC and not with Islamic contract law or *adat* contract laws also in force in some respects in Indonesia—the contract law under the ICC is the main contract law; it is the law applicable to all commercial—except some Islamic banking and financing transactions.

Now, coming to changes of circumstances in Indonesian contract law, the question is: who bears the risk when unforeseen events make the performance of the contractual obligation of one party impossible or extremely onerous? The law in Indonesia deals with the matter in three ways.

First, in cases where the performance of an obligation has become objectively impossible (and some other conditions are fulfilled), the law applies the classic French/Dutch theory of *force majeure/overmacht*, also referred to in Indonesia as objective *force majeure* (*objectieve overmacht* in Dutch, *overmacht yang objektif* or *keadaan memaksa yang objektif* in Indonesian), and in most cases, the debtor (obligor) is relieved of his obligation and both parties are put back in the position they would have been had they not contracted.[4]

Secondly, if the performance of the obligation is not impossible but extremely onerous for the debtor, the situation becomes a bit less clear in Indonesian law. The ICC does not provide for such circumstances. The Code adopted the then French and Dutch classic position against what the French call the *imprévision* in civil and commercial contracts[5]—the ICC only contains provisions for relief in case the performance of the obligation becomes objectively impossible. If the performance is possible, it must be performed however onerous that performance (or the compensation in lieu of performance) may have become. However, some Indonesian academics have argued that in such cases, which they refer to as cases of subjective *force majeure* (*subjectieve overmacht* in Dutch, thus showing the influence of more recent Dutch developments), the ICC's rules on *force majeure* should be applied. This, however, in my view, would lead to an unsatisfactory result—the creditor (obligee) would bear the entire risk alone as the debtor would be completely exonerated for not performing (what the Code provides in cases of *force majeure*), which seems unfair given that the performance is not entirely impossible. It seems, however, that the very wide discretion Indonesian judges exercise in revising contracts on the basis of equity and good faith may have avoided this unsatisfactory result. This discretion allows the judges to adapt contracts when there is a change of circumstances—there have been judicial decisions which seem to have adapted the contract to achieve fairness in cases of changed circumstances but without necessarily elaborating a detailed theory relating to changed circumstances.

Thirdly, if the parties have provided for a clause in their contract relating to changes of circumstances—often referred to as a *force majeure* clause—then that clause will prevail over the legal rules mentioned above. In a sense, the rules above apply only to unforeseen

[4] This results from a resolution of the contract (a kind of avoidance *ab initio*). However, in a contract of successive performance, if part of the contract has been, in the past, mutually performed and the performance only became impossible at a later time, the contract is 'resiliated' (*résiliation du contrat*)—it remains valid for the period when it could be performed and avoided from the time at which performance became impossible.

[5] Until its reform in 2016, French law accepted the revision of contracts because of *imprévision* only in administrative law: an administrative contract (ie a contract with the state or a state entity) can be revised if there is a change of circumstances, even if the performance of the obligation is not objectively impossible. In Indonesia, however, contracts with the administration are not considered a separate category of contracts and there is no court like the French Conseil d'État with a separate jurisdiction over administrative contracts. Therefore, the category of administrative contracts and the acceptance of *imprévision* for such contracts are not relevant in Indonesia.

and unforeseeable events—events are not unforeseen when the parties have provided for them in their contract. These three categories will now be looked at in turn.

Before proceeding, it is important to state that the rules of Indonesian law on the first two legal categories—impossibility and hardship—are not rules of contract law but rules of obligations in general. The ICC articles on *force majeure* are in Book 3 'On Obligations', Chapter 1 'On Obligations in General', in section 3 'On Compensation for Costs, Damages and Interests for Breach of Obligations', not for breach of contract alone. Mr Satrio, the most prolific scholar on the Indonesian law of obligations, puts his discussion of the allocation of risks and of objective and subjective *force majeure* (*overmacht*) in his book on obligations in general,[6] not in his books on contract law.[7] It may well be that these rules apply mostly to contractual obligations but, conceptually, they may apply to any obligation.[8] It is important for common law lawyers to know that most of what will be explained below are rules of the law of obligations which also apply to contract law (except, of course, for the rules regarding contractual *force majeure* clauses, which are obviously only contractual).

A word should also be said about the terminology used in this chapter. Recent comparative law books in English have divided the two first categories above as cases of impossibility and cases of hardship. These categorizations are not known in Indonesian civil law. Table 9.1 shows the terminology used in the civil law tradition all the way to Indonesian law.

Table 9.1 *Force majeure* terminology

	Impossibility	**Hardship**
Roman law	*Vis major* (*force majeure*)	–
French law	*Force majeure*	*Imprévision* (unforseeability)
Dutch law	*Objectieve overmacht* (objective *force majeure*)	*Subjectieve overmacht* (subjective *force majeure*)
Indonesian law	*Overmacht*[a] *yang objektif* or *Keadaan memaksa*[b] *yang objektif* (objective *force majeure*)	*Overmacht yang subjektif* or *Keadaan memaksa yang subjektif* (subjective *force majeure*) or, alternatively, *Kepatutan* (equity) and *itikad baik* (good faith)

Note: [a] The Dutch term *overmacht*, sometimes in its old spelling found in the Code (*overmagt*), is often used in Indonesian doctrine and jurisprudence without a translation, as are the words *force majeure*. [b] Sometimes, other terms are used to translate *force majeure*, for example, *keadaan kahar*. Since the Code is in Dutch, not in Indonesian, the vocabulary in Indonesian is not legislatively settled. However, *keadaan memaksa* seems to be the translation most commonly used by scholars.

Source: Author.

[6] J Satrio, *Hukum Perikatan—Perikatan Pada Umumnya* [*The Law of Obligations—Obligations in General*] (Citra Aditya Bakti 1993) (hereafter Satrio, *Obligations*).

[7] J Satrio, *Hukum Perikatan—Perikatan Yang Lahir Dari Perjanjian—Buku I* and *Buku II* [*The Law of Obligations—Obligations Arising from Agreements—Book I* and *Book II*] (Citra Aditya Bakti 1994) (hereafter Satrio, *Contracts I* and Satrio, *Contracts II*).

[8] A concrete example would be an obligation arising from ICC, art 1359, by which one is obliged to return what has been given without being due. This is a legal, not a contractual, obligation. If the thing to be returned is destroyed by a *force majeure*, the general rules of obligations on *force majeure* would apply.

In an effort to be faithful to the law that I am describing, I will use the expression *force majeure* for cases of impossibility when referring to French law or *objective force majeure* or *objective overmacht* when referring to Indonesian law. For cases of hardship, I will use *imprévision* when referring to French law and classic Dutch and Indonesian law and subjective *force majeure* or *overmacht* when referring to more recent doctrinal developments in Dutch and Indonesian law. For convenience of comparison with other jurisdictions, I will name the two main parts of this chapter *Impossibility* and *Hardship*.

In this chapter, I will discuss whether the debtor can perform his obligation using the word 'perform' in English to translate the French, Dutch, and Indonesian terms '*exécuter*', '*uitvoeren*', and '*melaksanakan*'. It should be noted, however, that the civil law concept of '*exécution*' is wider than the common law concept of performance since, in French civil law, we talk of damages ('*réparation pécuniaire*') as '*exécution par équivalent*' (performance by equivalent).

I should also point out that I will use the terms 'debtor', 'debt', and 'creditor' in their civil law sense. A debtor (*pengutang* in Indonesian, nowadays sometimes referred to as an obligor in English) is someone who owes a debt (*utang* in Indonesian) or if you prefer an obligation, any obligation (not just the obligation to give money, as a debt is often defined in the common law). A creditor (*kreditor* or *orang yang memberi piutang* in Indonesian, nowadays sometimes referred to as an obligee in English) is someone who is owed a debt, an obligation (someone who has a *créance* in French or *piutang* in Indonesian, with no exact equivalent term in English). The obligation owed to the creditor can be any obligation and is not limited to obligations to pay money. In a contract of sale, the buyer is the debtor (obligor) of the obligation to pay and is also the creditor (obligee) of the obligation to give the thing sold. Similarly, the seller is the debtor (obligor) of the obligation to give the thing sold and also the creditor (obligee) of the obligation to pay—the obligation to give the thing sold is a debt because in civil law a debt is not restricted to a debt of money.

II. Impossibility (*vis major, force majeure, objectieve overmacht, keadaan memaksa yang objektif*)

1. Classic French and Dutch Theory of *force majeure* and *objectieve overmacht* before the Reform of Their Codes

As mentioned at the outset of this chapter, the relevant articles of the ICC on *force majeure* are taken directly from the old Dutch Civil Code (the *Burgerlijk Wetboek*, BW of 1838), which were a direct translation of the Old French Civil Code (OFCC). Table 9.2 shows the two most relevant articles of the OFCC and the ICC on change of circumstances with their English translations.

Table 9.2 Provisions on *force majeure*

Old French Civil Code (original)	Old French Civil Code (unofficial translation)[a]	Indonesian Civil Code (original)	Indonesian Civil Code (unofficial translation)[b]
Article 1147. Le débiteur est condamné, s'il y a lieu, au paiement de dommages et intérêts, soit à raison de l'inexécution de l'obligation, soit à raison du retard dans l'exécution, toutes les fois qu'il ne justifie pas que l'inexécution provient d'une cause étrangère qui ne peut lui être imputée, encore qu'il n'y ait aucune mauvaise foi de sa part.	**Article 1147.** A debtor shall be ordered to pay damages, in the proper circumstance, either on account of the non-performance of the obligation, or on account of the delay in performing, whenever he cannot establish that the non-performance was due to an external cause that cannot be imputed to him, provided, moreover, there is no bad faith on his part.	**Artikel 1244.** De schuldenaar moet, indien daartoe gronden bestaan, veroordeeld worden tot vergoeding van kosten, schaden en interessen, zoo dikwijls hij niet bewijzen kan dat het niet uitvoeren of het niet tijdig uitvoeren der verbindtenis voortkomt uit eene vreemde oorzaak, die hem niet kan worden toegerekend, al heeft er ook geene kwade trouw van zijne zijde plaats gehad.	**Article 1244.** If there [are grounds to do so] the debtor is to compensate for costs, damages and interests if he cannot prove [that the non-performance or late performance of the obligation arises from an extraneous cause],[c] for which he is not responsible and he was not acting in bad faith.
Article 1148. Il n'y a lieu à aucuns dommages et intérêts lorsque, par suite d'une force majeure ou d'un cas fortuit, le débiteur a été empêché de donner ou de faire ce à quoi il était obligé, ou a fait ce qui lui était interdit.	**Article 1148.** Damages are not due when, because of a *force majeure* or a fortuitous event, the debtor[d] either was prevented from giving or doing what he was obligated to give or did what he was forbidden to do.	**Artikel 1245.** Geene vergoeding van kosten, schaden en interessen heeft plaats, indien de schuldenaar door overmagt of door toeval verhinderd is geworden om iets te geven of te doen, waartoe hij verpligt was, of iets gedaan heeft hetwelk hem verboden was.	**Article 1245.** The debtor need not compensate for costs, damages or interests, if a [*force majeure/ overmacht*][e] or a [fortuitous event][f] prevented him from giving or doing [what he was obliged or did something that he was obliged not to do].[g]

Note: [a] In this chapter, I use an English translation for the Old French Civil Code as it was as of 1 July 2013, translated by DW Gruning <https://advocatetanmoy.com/wp-content/uploads/2019/12/french-civil-code.pdf> accessed 7 January 2025. [b] The Indonesian and English translations of the ICC that I use in this chapter are translations of the Dutch version of the ICC, which is the only version that is in force to this day. The original and the translations I use are available in a trilingual version of the Code at <www.academia.edu/29817835/Trilingual_Indonesian_Civil_Code> accessed 7 January 2025. [c] Whenever I modify a translation, because it seems inaccurate or in order to use the standardized translation of terms I use in this chapter (eg *force majeure*), I put my modifications in square brackets. The original words *vreemde oorzaak* were translated by 'unforeseen event', which is inaccurate. I am told that the words *het niet uitvoeren of het niet tijdig uitvoeren der verbindtenis voortkomt uit eene vreemde oorzaak* are more accurately translated as 'the non-performance or late performance of the obligation arises from an *extraneous* cause'. I have therefore modified the translation. The requirement that the *force majeure* or fortuitous event be unforeseeable is not found in the Code but in doctrine and jurisprudence. Besides, the requirement of unforeseeability would apply to both a *force majeure* and a fortuitous event (to the extent that there is a difference between the two), and therefore the fortuitous event should not be defined as unforeseeable, as opposed to the *force majeure*, which would be otherwise. [d] The English translation uses the word 'obligor-debtor', whereas the French original only used the word *débiteur*. As I mentioned above, the translators probably wanted to show that a debt in civil law (unlike in the common law) is not necessarily a debt of money since any obligation is a debt and any person who has any obligation is a debtor. For simplicity, I will use the word 'debtor' in its civil law sense. [e] The Dutch text of the ICC uses the word *overmagt*, which is the old spelling of *overmacht*, that is, *force majeure*. The English translation I use translated this word by 'Act of God', which is a common law concept. I therefore replaced 'Act of God' by the proper civil law concept of *force majeure* or *overmacht*. [f] The word *toeval*, translated as *hal yang terjadi secara kebetulan* or *hal yang tidak terduka* in Indonesian (which could be translated as 'something that happens by chance' or 'something that is not expected'), should be translated in English by 'fortuitous event', which is closer to the French *cas fortuit*. [g] I am told that this is a more accurate translation.

Source: Author.

As can be seen, the Old French Code and the ICC are essentially the same. As mentioned, these articles are in a section of the Code entitled 'On Compensation for Costs, Damages and Interests for Breach of Obligations'.[9] The first article states the liability of the debtor for non-performance or late performance of his obligation unless it arises from an extraneous cause (ie not caused by him), for which he is not responsible. Also, he must not have been acting in bad faith. The second article is to a similar effect: there is no liability for damages if a *force majeure* or fortuitous event causes the debtor not to perform his obligation to give, to do, or not to do.[10] The obligation which existed becomes extinguished because of the *force majeure*.[11]

These two articles of the OFCC, the BW, and the ICC were interpreted and, in the case of the ICC, continue to be interpreted as relieving the debtor of any liability when he could not perform his obligation because its performance was *completely* impossible. The conditions for this exoneration in French law (from the Code but also from doctrine and jurisprudence) are as follows:

- The *force majeure* or 'fortuitous event' must be *external*—not something for which the debtor is responsible or which is linked to him (eg his sickness);
- it must be *unforeseeable*;
- it must be *irresistible*—the debtor could not have prevented it; and
- it must have made the execution of the obligation *impossible*. The fact that an obligation has become very onerous is no excuse under these articles.[12]

The consequences of an impossibility due to a *force majeure* is that the obligation (the debt) is extinguished and the creditor cannot claim any compensation.[13] In a bilateral contract for service ('obligation to do'), where the service is prevented by a *force majeure*, the debtor of the service would be relieved of his obligation to provide the service and the creditor of that obligation would be entitled to no damages. Since this is a bilateral contract, the obligation to pay for the service would be without a cause (the obligation to provide the service being extinguished) and therefore the debtor of that obligation (the one seeking the service) would also be relieved of his obligation to pay (and can be reimbursed if he has paid through the *répétition de l'indu*—the getting back of what is not due, Article 1235 OFCC).

There are two other articles of the ICC which relate to cases where a thing is the object of an 'obligation to give' (as opposed to an 'obligation to do' or 'not to do') and the thing perishes because of a fortuitous event or a *force majeure* before it is transferred to the creditor (Table 9.3).

9 '*Section 4: Des dommages et intérêts résultant de l'inexécution de l'obligation*' in the OFCC and '*Van de vergoeding van kosten, schaden en interessen, voortpruitende uit het niet nakomen eener verbindtenis*' in the ICC.

10 Satrio, *Obligations* (n 6) 249.

11 ibid.

12 F Terré, P Simler, and Y Lequette, *Droit civil. Les obligations (Précis)* (11th edn, Dalloz 2013) para 582. In French, the four conditions rhyme: *externalité, imprévisibilité, irrésistibilité, et impossibilité*. Additionally, the debtor must be in good faith (OFCC, art 1148, which is the same as ICC, art 1245), but as good faith is presumed and the debtor is rarely found to be in bad faith, it is usually not listed as a formal condition.

13 Terré, Simler, and Lequette (n 12) para 583. There are however exceptions in the law for the *prêt à usage* (OFCC, art 1881), when the debtor was put in default (*mise en demeure*) (OFCC, arts 1138 and 1302). Also, a partial impossibility (of some obligations but not others) or a momentary impossibility would only provide partial (from the jurisprudence Req 26 July 1909 DP 1911.1.55, as mentioned in Terré, Simler, and Lequette (n 12) para 583) or momentary relief (eg Civ 3e, 22 February 2006, RDC 2006, 763, as mentioned in Terré, Simler, and Lequette (n 12) para 583).

Table 9.3 Provisions governing loss of contractual object

Old French Civil Code (original)	Old French Civil Code (translation)	Indonesian Civil Code (original)	Indonesian Civil Code (translation)
Article 1302. Lorsque le corps certain et déterminé qui était l'objet de l'obligation vient à périr, est mis hors du commerce, ou se perd de manière qu'on en ignore absolument l'existence, l'obligation est éteinte si la chose a péri ou a été perdue sans la faute du débiteur et avant qu'il fût en demeure. Lors même que le débiteur est en demeure, et s'il ne s'est pas chargé des cas fortuits, l'obligation est éteinte dans le cas où la chose fût également périe chez le créancier si elle lui eût été livrée. Le débiteur est tenu de prouver le cas fortuit qu'il allègue. De quelque manière que la chose volée ait péri ou ait été perdue, sa perte ne dispense pas celui qui l'a soustraite, de la restitution du prix.	**Article 1302.** When a certain and determined thing that was the object of an obligation is destroyed, or ceases to be a thing in commerce, or is lost in such a way that its existence is absolutely unknown, the obligation is extinguished if the thing has been destroyed or lost without the fault of the debtor, and before he has been put in default. Even when the debtor is in default, if he has not taken upon himself the risk of fortuitous events, the obligation is extinguished provided the thing would also have been destroyed in the hands of the creditor if it had been delivered to him. The debtor must prove the fortuitous event he alleges. No matter how a stolen thing has been destroyed or lost, its loss does not exonerate the person who has taken it from restituting its price.	**Artikel 1444.** In geval de zekere en bepaalde zaak, welke het onderwerp der overeenkomst uitmaakte, vergaat, buiten den handel der menschen geraakt, of verloren gaat, zoodanig dat men van derzelver bestaan te eenenmale onkundig is, vervalt de verbindtenis, mits de zaak vergaan of verloren zij buiten de schuld van den schuldenaar, en voor dat hij in de levering daarvan nalatig gebleven was. Zelfs dan wanneer de schuldenaar in gebreke is om eene zaak te leveren, en hij voor geene onvoorziene toevallen heeft ingestaan, is de verbindtenis vernietigd, indien de zaak op gelijke wijze bij den schuldeischer zoude vergaan zijn, ingeval dezelve aan hem ware geleverd geweest. De schuldenaar is gehouden het onvoorzeiene toeval, waarop hij zich beroept, te bewijzen. Op welke wijze ook eene ontvreemde zaak vergaan of verloren zij, ontslaat dit verlies dengene die deze zaak ontvreemd heeft geenszins van de verpligting om de waarde te vergoeden.	**Article 1444.** Where a certain and specific [thing] that constitutes the [object] of the agreement is destroyed, becomes unmerchantable, or is lost, to the extent that one is not aware whether or not the [thing] still exists, the obligation is [extinguished], insofar as the [thing] is destroyed or lost due to no fault of the debtor, and prior to [him being put in default[a] in] delivering the [thing]. [Even when the debtor is in default on delivering the thing, if he is not liable for fortuitous events, the obligation is extinguished] if the thing would have perished in a similar manner had it been delivered to the creditor. The debtor must prove the unforeseen event he asserts. Irrespective of the manner in which the goods are lost or destroyed, the individual who has [stolen the thing is] not relieved from the obligation to compensate the value thereof.

Table 9.3 Continued

Old French Civil Code (original)	Old French Civil Code (translation)	Indonesian Civil Code (original)	Indonesian Civil Code (translation)
Article 1303. Lorsque la chose est périe, mise hors du commerce ou perdue, sans la faute du débiteur, il est tenu, s'il y a quelques droits ou actions en indemnité par rapport à cette chose, de les céder à son créancier.	**Article 1303.** When a thing has been destroyed, or ceases to be a thing in commerce, or is lost without the fault of the debtor, he is bound to assign to his creditor any rights or actions for indemnity he may be entitled to with respect to that thing.	**Artikel 1445.** Indien de verschuldigde zaak zonder toedoen van den schuldenaar vergaan, buiten den handel der menschen geraakt of verloren is, is de schuldenaar gehouden, in geval hij eenige regten of vorderingen tot schadevergoeding betrekkelijk deze zaak heeft, die aan zijnen schuldeischer af te staan.	**Article 1445.** If the [thing] owed [is] destroyed, becomes unmerchantable or [is] lost through no fault of the debtor, the debtor is required, if he has any rights or claims for recourse related to [this thing], to assign them to the creditor.

Note: [a] It would take too long to explain here the classic process of putting in default in the French/Dutch/Indonesian civil law tradition. Suffice it to say that a debtor that has been put in default could only invoke a *force majeure* if the thing would have disappeared even if it had already been delivered. The relevance of the provisions on putting in default in Indonesia is, however, uncertain. ICC, art 1238, which explains how to put in default, has been declared 'no longer valid' (*tidak berlaku lagi*) by the *Circular of the Supreme Court No. 3 of 1963 on Not Considering the Civil Code as Legislation* (*Surat Edaran Mahkamah Agung Nomor 3 Tahun 1963 Tentang Gagasan Menganggap Burgerlijk Wetboek Tidak Sebagai Undang-Undang*). It is unclear whether or not the Court could exercise any such power to declare parts of the Civil Code invalid by a circular. Even if that circular was valid (which I doubt it was), it is unclear what the effect the invalidity of art 1238 would have on numerous other articles of the Code that require the debtor to be put in default. The circular is rather amateurish, and no thought was given to its consequences.

Source: Author.

2. *Force majeure* (*overmacht yang objektif*) in Indonesia, Unreformed

As seen above, Indonesian law is not different from the old French and Dutch law: when the execution of an obligation becomes objectively impossible because of a *force majeure*, the debtor is exonerated.

Satrio accurately points out that the real issue is who should bear the unforeseen risk of a loss: the debtor or the creditor.[14] He notes that there are different theories on changed circumstances and that there are two categories: the first one, the objective *force majeure/overmacht* discussed here, and the second, the subjective *force majeure/overmacht* discussed below.

The distinction is between an impossibility that is not related to the person of the debtor but is objective—ie no one could perform this obligation as the object of the sale, a specific and unique Picasso, has been destroyed by lightening—and an impossibility that is subjective—it might be objectively possible to perform the obligation to pay a loan in US dollars, but, because of a drastic unforeseeable drop in the value of the debtor's currency, the debtor is subjectively incapable of making the full payment in US dollars.

[14] His discussion of *force majeure/overmacht* is placed right after his discussion of the allocation of risks. Satrio, *Obligations* (n 6) ch 8, 233 on 'The issue of risk' and ch 9, 249 on 'The issue of *overmacht*'.

The objective *overmacht* (classic French *force majeure*) is very limited in its scope since it would in principle never apply to the delivery of generic goods or services. If I must deliver a ton of rice, the fact that the 50,000 tons of rice I own have been destroyed does not prevent me from buying new rice (however expensive) and delivering one ton. I might go bankrupt if I have to do this for all my clients, but the delivery of the rice is not objectively impossible. However, it could be said to be subjectively impossible—I may not have enough funds to buy new rice or to compensate you and therefore I cannot subjectively do it.[15] The same is true for the 'obligation to do', that is, to provide a service. Unless the service is *intuitu personae* (only this actor can play this role and he has been struck by lightning), one cannot invoke an objective *overmacht* when one can hire another service provider to provide the service even though it would be at exorbitant cost; but this could be a subjective *overmacht*.[16]

When an objective *force majeure* occurs, both proponents and opponents of the concept of subjective *force majeure* in Indonesia agree that there is a complete exoneration of the debtor. The obligation is simply extinguished and the creditor has no recourse. If the obligation of the debtor is part of a synallagmatic (bilateral) contract, the correlative obligations of the other contracting party are similarly extinguished as having no cause.

In the case of an obligation to do (eg an obligation to paint a house which has been destroyed by lightning), the painter (the debtor) is relieved of his obligation because of the *force majeure* and the owner of the house of his because his contractual obligation to pay the painter now has no cause. Therefore, even though the debtor's obligation is extinguished, the loss is in a sense his: he loses his profit on the paint job.

The situation in Indonesia should be different from the situation in France with respect to the obligation to transfer ownership of a thing in a contract of sale ('obligation to give'). In French law, the ownership of the thing sold is transferred immediately on the formation of the contract even though the transfer of possession occurs later[17] (of course, the parties can provide otherwise in their contract). In France, the thing sold, but not yet delivered, is therefore already owned by the buyer and in case of a *force majeure* the debtor is relieved of his obligation to deliver;[18] yet the buyer is not necessarily relieved of his obligation to pay since he already owned the thing sold and therefore his payment has a cause. However, following Dutch law (and German law), in Indonesia the contract of sale and the transfer of ownership are two different juridical acts and therefore ownership is not transferred automatically at the time of the sale but rather when the thing is physically delivered, unless the parties agree otherwise. Tables 9.4, 9.5, and 9.6 show the provisions under the ICC for transfer of ownership and the consequences of the loss of the contractual object.

[15] Satrio, *Obligations* (n 6) 257–58. *Force majeure* could apply to generic goods when there is a new embargo or a new ban on import—no other goods of the same kind could be imported.

[16] ibid 258.

[17] OFCC, art 1583: '[The sale] is perfect between the parties and the ownership is acquired as of right by the buyer with regard to the seller as soon as they have agreed on the thing and on the price, although the thing has not yet been delivered nor the price paid.' This article is still in force as special contracts (such as the contract of sale) were not the object of the French reform of contract law.

[18] OFCC, art 1302, which is ICC, art 1444 in Indonesia.

Table 9.4 Transfer of ownership

Indonesian Civil Code (original)	Indonesian Civil Code (translation)
Artikel 1458. Zij wordt gehouden tusschen de partijen voltrokken te zijn, zoodra deze het eens zijn geworden over de zaak en den prijs, hoewel ook de zaak nog niet mogt geleverd, noch de prijs betaald zijn.	**Article 1458.** The [sale] is deemed to have been concluded between the parties as soon as they [agree] on the subject matter and the price, notwithstanding that the [object] has not been delivered or that payment has not been made.
Artikel 1459. De eigendom van het verkochte goed gaat niet eer tot den kooper over, dan nadat de levering daarvan geschied is overeenkomstig Article 612, 613, en 616.	**Article 1459.** The ownership rights over the [object] sold do not transfer to the buyer until after delivery takes place in accordance with the provisions of articles 612, 613 and 616.

Source: Author.

In Indonesia, the buyer of a thing not yet delivered would therefore not normally own it and, unlike what would be the case in France, he should therefore probably not have to pay for it if it is destroyed by a *force majeure* before it is physically delivered—if he has already paid for it, he could be reimbursed. Table 9.5, which shows the article governing contracts of exchange illustrates this principle and, understandably, it does not have an equivalent in the OFCC:

Table 9.5 Nullification of contract upon loss of object

Indonesian Civil Code (original)	Indonesian Civil Code (translation)
Artikel 1545. Indien eene zekere en bepaalde zaak, welke men beloofd had in ruiling te geven, buiten schuld van den eigenaar is verloren gegaan, wordt de overeenkomst voor vervallen gehouden, en kan degene die van zijne zijde aan de overeenkomst voldaan heeft de teruggave van het in ruiling gegeven goed vorderen.	**Article 1545.** If an object, which has been promised for an exchange, is lost beyond the fault of the owner, then the agreement is deemed null and void and the party who has performed his obligation may claim for the object he has delivered in the exchange.[a]

Note: [a] See also for the same principle in the contract of rent, ICC, art 1553.
Source: Author.

However, the following article from the law of sale seems to contradict this presumption and to reaffirm the French position, at least with respect to objects that are certain and specific: the buyer is responsible from the time the contract is formed and should pay the price even if the thing is destroyed before it is delivered.[19]

[19] S Suharnoko, 'Contract Law in a Comparative Perspective' (2012) 2 Indonesia Law Review 104.

Table 9.6 Obligation to pay despite loss

Indonesian Civil Code (original)	Indonesian Civil Code (translation)
Artikel 1460. Indien de verkochte zaak in een zeker en bepaald voorwerp bestaat, is dezelver, van het oogenblik van den koop af, voor rekening van den kooper, hoewel de levering nog niet hebbe plaats gehad; en heft de verkooper het regt om den prijs te vorderen.	**Article 1460.** If the [thing] sold consists of [a certain and specific object], it falls under the liability of the buyer from the time of purchase, notwithstanding that delivery has not yet taken place; and the seller is entitled to demand the purchase price.

Source: Author.

This seems to contradict the Indonesian position that the buyer does not own the thing until it is delivered. However, Agri Chairunisa Isradjuningtias indicates that Article 1460 ICC has been interpreted restrictively so that the risk is ultimately borne by the seller rather than the buyer. The provision is interpreted as applying only to unique, irreplaceable goods specifically designated by the buyer (something quite rare in practice).[20]

On objective *force majeure* generally (including cases of sale), doctrine and jurisprudence also explain that the debtor must not by his fault have contributed to the *force majeure* and in the case of a thing being destroyed, he must have acted as 'a good family father' in preserving the thing owed.[21] In an Indonesian case, a transporter sought exoneration for failing to deliver the goods because they were seized by the army. The court held, however, that the transporter was at fault for not securing the proper documents before transporting the goods and therefore it could not invoke an *overmacht*.[22]

It is also clear that the debtor has the burden of proving the unforeseeability and the lack of contributory fault on his part.[23] The standard of proof of unforeseeability is an objective one—what needs to be proven is not whether the debtor could foresee (subjectively) but whether a reasonable person in his position could have foreseen the event.[24] However, because good faith is always presumed,[25] it is the creditor who has the burden of proving that the debtor acted in bad faith.[26]

Satrio also correctly points out that the Code does not define what constitutes a *force majeure*—indeed Articles 1244 and 1245 ICC mention extraneous cause, *force majeure/overmacht*, and fortuitous event without defining them. The fact that one is not responsible for the event and is not in bad faith does not make an event an *overmacht*.[27] We must turn to jurisprudence to know what qualifies as an *overmacht*.

20 AC Isradjuningtias, 'Force majeure (overmacht) dalam hukum kontrak (perjanjian) Indonesia' (2015) 1 Veritas et Justicia 136, 151–52. See also S Gautama and RN Hornick, *An Introduction to Indonesian Law—Unity in Diversity* (4th edn, Alumni 1983) 137.

21 Satrio, *Obligations* (n 6) 264–65: see ICC, art 1235. The 'good family father' ('*bon père de famille*') is the civil law equivalent of the reasonable man of the common law.

22 PT Surabaya, 8 August 1952, as quoted in Satrio, *Obligations* (n 6) 275 (Pengadilan Tinggi/High Court of Surabaya).

23 ICC, arts 1244 and 1444; Satrio, *Obligations* (n 6) 267–68.

24 Satrio, *Obligations* (n 6) 266.

25 ICC, art 1965: 'Good faith is always be presumed and the individual who files a claim alleging bad faith must prove it.'

26 ICC, art 1244. Satrio, *Obligations* (n 6) 268.

27 He gives the example of a person who cannot check into the hotel she reserved because of a train accident: this is not an *overmacht* (she can still pay) even though she is not responsible for the train accident and is not in bad faith. Satrio, *Obligations* (n 6) 252. This resembles Gina's scenario on which the editors asked us to comment

Satrio gives examples of cases where the court held that there was no *overmacht*. For example, a court ruled that big winds and waves that caused damage to goods transported by sea did not constitute an *overmacht* because a boat should have been strong enough to face such winds and waves. However, the court did admit that there could be cases where winds and waves are so extraordinarily strong that it could not be reasonably demanded (*redelijkerwijze niet geeist kondenden*) of the debtor to be prepared to face them.[28]

In another case, the beneficiary of a life insurance policy argued that her deceased husband had stopped paying insurance premiums because the Japanese occupation of Indonesia during the Second World War made payments to a Dutch company impossible. She argued the war was an *overmacht* and she therefore claimed benefits. The court stated correctly that if the war was an *overmacht* exonerating the husband from paying his premium, the consequence would be that the insurance company would also not have to perform its own obligations.[29] It is therefore not clear that this case defines what constitutes a *force majeure/overmacht*.

There was also no *overmacht* found in a case where a seller could not deliver a motorcycle because his usual supplier could not secure the import of a motorcycle due to new government regulations. The court held that the seller could get the motorcycle from another source.[30]

We therefore only have cases where it was held that there was no objective *overmacht* and no case where *overmacht* was found. This only allows for a negative definition of *overmacht*.

III. Hardship (*imprévision, subjectieve overmacht, overmacht yang subjektif*)

1. Classic French Rejection of *imprévision* (*overmacht yang subjektif*)

The classic French/Dutch doctrine and jurisprudence limited the cases of *force majeure* to what the Indonesian doctrine calls an objective *force majeure*—only in cases where it was absolutely and objectively impossible to perform was the debtor exonerated. That classic position has been legislatively abandoned through reforms of the Civil Code in both the

(for the details of this hypothetical, see M Chen-Wishart, D Neo, and S Vogenauer, 'Introduction', ch 1 in this volume, 8). One of the reasons Gina could not get to the hotel room she had reserved was that there was a strike at the airport. However, the real issue is whether it was still possible for Gina to pay for her hotel room—the performance of that obligation was certainly still possible and there was, therefore, no *force majeure*.

28 HgH, 17 September 1925, as quoted in Satrio, *Obligations* (n 6) 271 (Hogerrechtshof Batavia—High Court of Batavia (Jakarta)). The issue here is whether by saying it could not have been reasonably demanded (*redelijkerwijze niet geeist kondenden*) to be prepared to face such bad weather, the court is establishing a criterion for *force majeure* or is suggesting that the debtor only has to do its best effort as Satrio suggests—a subjective *force majeure*. But it did not seem to suffice in this case that the debtor did its best, and therefore the court did not seem to create a theory of subjective *force majeure*, which in any event, to use a common law expression, would have been *obiter dictum* in this case.

29 Panitia Untuk Menyelesaikan Pemulihan Hak (Dalam Tingkat Banding) 14 July 1951, as quoted in Satrio, *Obligations* (n 6) 274 (Commission to Settle the Recovery of Rights (Appeal Level), which was a judicial-like body established after the war). The Commission also stated that one cannot expect an insurance company to pay benefits when it received no premium.

30 PNI Jakarta 29 June 1955 no 1196/1954, as quoted in Satrio, *Obligations* (n 6) 277 (Pengadilan Negeri (Istimewa)—Special District Court of Jakarta).

Netherlands (in 1992) and France (in 2016). There has been no such legislative reform in Indonesia. Because the old French and Dutch law is still the law in Indonesia, and because the new Dutch model is nevertheless influential among some Indonesian academics, it is useful to briefly explain the classic position and the new position in France and the Netherlands.

The classic French position in French civil and commercial contract law (as opposed to administrative contract law)[31] is that, in cases of *imprévision* (unforeseeability) of changes of circumstances that fall short of an objective *force majeure* (ie short of an objective impossibility of performance), the debtor must fully bear the risk and the court will not intervene to reduce any hardship. The position was clearly stated by the French Supreme Court, the Cour de Cassation, in the 1876 case of the *Canal de Craponne*,[32] which rejected the theory of *imprévision* (revision in cases of hardship). The facts of the case are rather extreme. A contract was entered into in the sixteenth century by which the owner of an irrigation canal agreed to provide water in perpetuity to neighbouring lands in exchange of three *sous* (cents). Centuries of inflation had made that amount derisory and the successor owner asked the court to revise the contract. The Cour de Cassation decided that it could not revise a contract, no matter how inequitable it had become, because as the French Civil Code says, 'Agreements lawfully entered into have the force of law for those who have made them.'[33] The Court therefore had no power to revise the contract. The *Canal de Craponne* case was no doubt the inspiration for the scenario the editors have asked us to address in which, in 1567, Abraham undertook to provide water for a fixed price forever and in 2018, after centuries of inflation, Abraham's successors asked for an increase in price.[34] The classical position in French law would therefore hold that Abraham's successors cannot get an increase in price.

There has been doctrinal criticism of this position, but the outcome of the famous *Canal de Craponne* case remained unchanged in France until the reform of the Civil Code. Some decisions of the Cour de Cassation at one point seemed to adopt a more subjective approach to the concept of *force majeure*, but in a plenary session the Court reaffirmed the classic rejection of the theory of *imprévision* by holding that a medical sickness that subjectively prevented the debtor from performing his obligation was not a *force majeure* as measures could have been taken for when the debtor would be sick and, in any event, someone else could have performed the obligation (ie it was not an objective *force majeure*).[35]

It took an amendment to the French Civil Code to allow the courts to revise a contract that has become too onerous due to a change of circumstances. The following new article, which applies only to contractual obligations, came into force on 1 October 2016:

[31] See n 5.

[32] Cass civ 6 March 1876, D 1876.I.93, translated in H Beale, B Fauvarque-Cosson, J Rutgers, and S Vogenauer, *Ius Commune Casebook for the Common Law of Europe: Cases, Material and Text on Contract Law* (3rd edn, Hart Publishing 2019) 1213.

[33] OFCC, art 1134(1). In Indonesia we find the very same article at ICC, art 1338(1). It states the principle of Roman law: *pacta sunt servanda*.

[34] For the full fact scenario of this hypothetical, see M Chen-Wishart, D Neo, and S Vogenauer, 'Introduction', ch 1 in this volume, 7.

[35] Cass Ass plén 14 April 2006, D 2006, 1577 (Cour de cassation—Assemblée plénière). In that case however, the Court held that the serious aggravation of the sickness and the eventual death of the contracting party did constitute a *force majeure* because it was unpredictable.

Article 1195. – If a change of circumstances that was unforeseeable at the time of the conclusion of the contract renders performance excessively onerous for a party who had not accepted the risk of such a change, that party may ask the other contracting party to renegotiate the contract. The first party must continue to perform his obligations during renegotiation.
In the case of refusal or the failure of renegotiations, the parties may agree to terminate the contract from the date and on the conditions which they determine, or by a common agreement ask the court to set about its adaptation. In the absence of an agreement within a reasonable time, the court may, on the request of a party, revise the contract or put an end to it, from a date and subject to such conditions as it shall determine.[36]

2. The Dutch Position

The Dutch originally had the same provisions as the Indonesians still do on *overmacht*, and the *Canal de Craponne* case would not have been decided differently. However, there was pressure over time in the Dutch doctrine and jurisprudence to accept the concept of subjective *overmacht*, more so than in France. This may explain why, when a new book of the Civil Code on obligations came into force in 1992, the following article, which applies only to contractual obligations, was included:

Article 6:258 Unforeseen circumstances

1. Upon a right of action (legal claim) of one of the parties to an agreement, the court may change the legal effects of that agreement or it may dissolve this agreement in full or in part if there are unforeseen circumstances of such a nature that the opposite party, according to standards of reasonableness and fairness, may not expect an unchanged continuation of the agreement. The court may change or dissolve the agreement with retroactive effect.
2. The court shall not change or dissolve the agreement as far as the unforeseen circumstances, in view of the nature of the agreement or of common opinion, should remain for account of the party who appeals to these circumstances.
3. For the purpose of this Article, a person to whom a right or obligation from the agreement has passed, is equated with an original party to that agreement.[37]

Because of the many links between jurists in Indonesia and the Netherlands, Indonesian doctrine has been exposed to the concept of subjective *overmacht*.

[36] *The Law of Contract, the General Regime of Obligations, and Proof of Obligations—The new provisions of the Code civil created by Ordonnance no 2016-131 of 10 February 2016*, translated by J Cartwright, B Fauvarque-Cosson, and S Whittaker, translation commissioned by the Direction des affaires civiles et du sceau, Ministère de la Justice, République française <www.textes.justice.gouv.fr/art_pix/THE-LAW-OF-CONTRACT-2-5-16.pdf> accessed 7 January 2025.

[37] Civil Code of the Netherlands, translation by 'Dutch Civil Law' <www.dutchcivillaw.com/civilcodegeneral.htm> accessed 16 January 2026.

3. Subjective *force majeure*/*overmacht yang subjektif* in Indonesian Law

There is no doubt that the classic theory of *force majeure* is one of objective *force majeure* in Indonesia: the debtor is excused only if it is completely and objectively impossible to perform the obligation. In his excellent article on changes of circumstances in Indonesia, Taufiq Adiyanto writes:

> It is notable, in Indonesian contract law, the concepts of *force majeure* in Articles 1244, 1245 and 1444 of the ICC were interlinked, and commonly named as an all-or-nothing approach. This means if performance was entirely impossible due to a cause for which the debtor had no responsibility towards the obligation, the contractual obligation was terminated immediately. If, however, performance was fully possible, there was no *force majeure*. The judge generally [uses the] impossibility test to decide whether the circumstance was categorized as a *force majeure* rather than [a] test on the limits of culpability or imputability of risk.
>
> When dealing with the external cause which hampers the performance of a contract, Indonesian law at the present moment only has a solution under the principle of *force majeure* (1244, 1245 and 1444 ICC). Indonesian contract law does not have any explicit provisions which stipulate the change of circumstances particularly that do not amount to impossibility. The invocation of unexpected circumstances, aside from impossibility, to a binding contract, is not acceptable under the ICC unless there is an impossibility to perform. In other words, a party cannot be released from any obligations when the performance has become excessively burdensome.[38]

There has been pressure, mainly in Indonesian doctrine, to move towards acceptance of a less exacting theory of *force majeure*. As explained above, such a subjective *force majeure* theory would not require an absolute and objective impossibility of performance but a subjective one. The focus would no longer be on the impossibility but on the absence of fault—that is, whether the debtor made his best effort (no fault/best effort) and/or whether it would be reasonable and fair in the circumstances to require more of him (reasonableness/equity).

Satrio refers to Dutch authors from the beginning of the twentieth century to state that the subjective theory of *force majeure* has gained support in the jurisprudence.[39] This is presumably in Dutch jurisprudence as he does not refer to any Indonesian jurisprudence, even from the colonial era, which clearly accepted the theory of subjective *force majeure*.

> In [Hofmann's] opinion, a [subjective] *force majeure* exists if the debtor has made every effort—according to the standards applicable in the community concerned—in accordance with the contract.[40]

[38] T Adiyanto, 'Dealing with Unexpected Circumstances: Judicial Modification of Contract under Indonesian and Dutch Law' (2019) 5 Hasanuddin Law Review 102, 105.

[39] Satrio, *Obligations* (n 6) 259 cites LC Hofmann, *Het Nederlands Verbintenissenrecht, vol 1, Algemene leer der Verbintenissen* (4th edn, Wolters 1935) 60 and S van Brakel, *Leerboek van het Nederlandse Verbintenissenrecht, vol 1* (4th edn, Tjeenk Willink 1948) 122.

[40] My translation of Satrio, *Obligations* (n 6) 259 describing the views of Hofmann, an academic.

Satrio mentions that in the Netherlands the courts have often accepted a drastic increase in price as a subjective *force majeure*.[41] These cases all seem to have occurred after the First World War, a time of hyperinflation in Europe.[42]

The theory has also been endorsed by some academics in Indonesia. Taufiq Adiyanto gives a good account of the support it has received in academia.[43] He mentions, among others, the support that Soebekti, a famous scholar, gave to the theory.[44]

Satrio refers to this subjective *force majeure* theory as an 'effort theory' (*Teori Upaya*). The problem with this theory, as he rightly points out, is that it would transform every obligation of result into an 'obligation of means' (ie of best effort, like the obligation of the doctor to treat you, not to cure you), excusing the non-performance of any obligation the debtor made a best effort to perform.[45] This would destroy the essential distinction between 'obligations of means' and 'obligations of result', which is quite important in civil law and particularly important in commercial law where most obligations are obligations of result. For example, in a contract of sale, if the seller does not deliver goods of the agreed quality and quantity (an obligation of result), no matter how much she tried to deliver such goods, the buyer is entitled to specific performance of the contract or to damages. Accepting the concept of subjective *force majeure* would give the seller 'a best effort' defence completely exonerating her of her obligation even in a commercial sale.

Another problem with this theory, to which I have just alluded, is that in my view it does not lead to a satisfactory remedy. The ideal solution for cases of true hardship due to unforeseen circumstance would probably be that a court could revise the contract to ensure that the debtor performs to the extent that it is possible and fair. However, if the definition of *force majeure* is extended to include subjective *force majeure*, then hardship situations will have to fit into Articles 1244, 1245, and 1444 ICC. These articles provide only one remedy: the debtor's obligation is extinguished and need not be performed at all even though, in most cases of hardship, the debtor could probably perform his obligation in part. In a synallagmatic contract, the creditor would also be relieved of his obligation. The articles of the ICC do not provide for a revision of the obligations by the court. If the case of the *Canal de Craponne* (or the scenario of Abraham) were considered a case of subjective *force majeure*, then the contract would be 'resiliated' (voided for the future)[46] rather than renegotiated or adapted to take into account inflation—the provider of the water would no longer have any obligation at all to provide water. Is this really what the proponents of the subjective *force majeure* have in mind?

[41] Satrio, *Obligations* (n 6) 262, where he refers to the following cases: Hof Den Haag 8 December 1916, Rechtbank Dordrecht, 5 December 1917, Rechtbank den Haag, 15 April 1919, as mentioned in van Brakel (n 39) 124.

[42] German law also introduced the revision of contracts by the courts after the First World War (a period of hyperinflation) presuming that all contracts included a *clausula rebus sic stantibus*: RG 21 September 1920, RGZ 100, 129, 131; cf Beale and others (n 32) 1222–25. This is in contrast to the French position.

[43] Adiyanto (n 38) 107.

[44] R Soebekti, *Hukum perjanjian* (19th edn, Intermasa 2002) 56.

[45] Satrio, *Obligations* (n 6) 259–61. In civil law, an obligation of result is one that may only be excused by a *force majeure*—for example, the obligation of the seller to deliver the goods or of the buyer to pay—as opposed to an obligation of means, which only requires best efforts—such as the obligation of a doctor who must make the best effort to cure his patient but does not undertake to deliver specific results.

[46] For the notion of *résiliation*, see n 4.

There does not seem to have been any clear case (let alone a line of cases) by Indonesian courts recognizing a subjective *force majeure* and completely relieving the debtor of his obligations. This is particularly surprising as Indonesia experienced very drastic hyperinflation and currency devaluation during and after the Second World War and during and after the Asian Financial Crisis that started in 1997.

In an earlier volume of this series, I mentioned two cases as examples of Indonesian courts intervening to remedy hardships caused by changing circumstances.[47] In a 1953 case, someone had bought a piece of land before the Second World War at a certain price, the payment of which became due after the war, that is, after the market value had gone up multiple times due to hyperinflation. The buyer was willing to make what was by then a derisory payment (the contract price before hyperinflation) in exchange for the property and would immediately re-sell the property for an enormous profit. This was certainly not a case of objective *force majeure* since it was not impossible for the seller to surrender the property, even though it was extremely onerous to do so for such a derisory price. The court refused directly to amend the contract price, speaking only of a vague obligation to share some of the profits notwithstanding the fact that such an obligation was not explicitly stated in the contract or the law.[48] This seems to be a remedy tailored by the court to implement fairness, equity, and good faith. What the court did not do is declare a subjective *force majeure* and find the obligation of the seller (debtor of the obligation to give the land) to be extinguished.

In 1955, as related by Professor Gautama,

> the Supreme Court of Indonesia refused to allow land which had been pledged for Rp 50 prior to World War II to be redeemed for the same price, and instead fashioned its own formula of redemption. The Court noted that the price of gold had increased 30 times during the intervening years. 'Justice' it said 'required that the risk of currency fluctuations be born equally by the parties'.[49]

The Court did not declare a subjective *force majeure* and did not exonerate the seller from his obligation to surrender the land. The Court in that case therefore effectively modified the contract, which is a better result in cases of hardship caused by a change of circumstances than extinguishing all obligations.

It therefore seems that the Indonesian courts do not handle cases of hardship caused by a change of circumstances as cases of subjective *force majeure* (leading to the extinction of obligations) but rather by way of adapting the contracts for reasons of fairness and equity. In fact, this remedy in equity is widely available in Indonesian contract law and, in my view, is a better solution for cases of hardship caused by a change of circumstances than the solution available under the theory of subjective *force majeure*. It is based on the two articles of the ICC shown in Table 9.7.

[47] Bell (n 2) 150; cf S Vogenauer, 'Interpretation of Contracts and Control of Unfair Terms in Asia: A Comparison' in M Chen-Wishart and S Vogenauer (n 2) 477, 503.

[48] Case in the Mahkamah Agung (Supreme Court) 28 May 1953 No 62aK/Sip/1952 under the name of 'Jual-Beli Bersyarat' published in H.1953—2 & 3. Reported in part in Satrio, *Contracts II* (n 7) 170–72.

[49] S Gautama, *Indonesian Business Law* (Citra Aditya Bakti 1995) 85.

Table 9.7 Considerations of good faith and equity in the ICC and the OFCC

Indonesian Civil Code in Dutch (official version)	Unofficial Indonesian translation of the Civil Code	Unofficial English translation	Original French Civil Code
Artikel 1338. [alinea 3] Zij moeten te goeder trouw worden ten uitvoer gebragt. (BW 751, 1066, 1243v, 1266v, 1335v, 1363, 1603, 1611, 1646-3 1688, 1813; Civ 1134).	**Article 1338.** [alinea 3] Perjanjian harus dilaksanakan dengan itikad baik.	**Article 1338.** [paragraph 3] They [contracts] must be executed in good faith. (BW 751, 1066, 1243v, 1266v, 1335v, 1363, 1603, 1611, 1646-3, 1688, 1813; Civ 1134).	**Article 1134.** [alinéa 3]Elles [les conventions] doivent être exécutées de bonne foi.
Artikel 1339. Overeenkomsten verbinden niet alleen tot datgene hetwelk uitdrukkelijk bij dezelve bepaald is, maar ok tot al hetgeen dat, naar den aar van dezelve overeenkomsten, door de billijkheid, het gebruik of de wet, wordt gevorderd. (AB[a] 15; BW 1347, 1482, 1492, 1800v, 1817, 1819; Civ 1135).	**Article 1339.** Perjanjian tidak hanya mengikat apa yang dengan tegas ditentukan di dalamnya, melainkan juga segala sesuatu yang menurut sifatnya perjanjian dituntut berdasarkan keadilan, kebiasaan, atau undang-undang.	**Article 1339.** Agreements bind not only to what is explicitly set out in them, but also to everything which by the nature of the obligation is required by equity, customs, or laws. (AB 15; BW 1347, 1482, 1492, 1800v, 1817, 1819; Civ 1135).	**Article 1135.** Les conventions obligent non seulement à ce qui y est exprimé, mais encore à toutes les suites que l'équité, l'usage ou la loi donnent à l'obligation d'après sa nature.

Note: [a] AB stands for *Algemeene Bepalingen van Wetgiving voor Nederlandsch-Indië*, the General Provisions of Legislation for the Dutch East Indies.

Source: Author.

On the availability of revision of contracts for fairness and equity, I summarized the Indonesian position as follows:[50]

> Professor Gautama summarized the position in Indonesia as follows: 'A contract must be performed by the parties "in good faith". To ensure good faith, the judge in a civil suit has power to supervise the implementation of the contract, and to invoke *principles of reasonableness and justice* in doing so. In practice it means that a judge is free to deviate from the letter of the contract if such deviation is necessary to ensure good faith.'[51] It therefore seems that nowadays, the courts in Indonesia are no longer hesitant in applying the principle of good faith and are not bound by the letter of the contract.
>
> Satrio concludes to the same effect that 'It appears that several decisions in Indonesia indicate that the judge, based on equity [*kepatutan*] can change the basic rights and obligations of the contract without having to mention many reasons and that all that is necessary is the opinion of the court that the content of the contract is not fair.'[52]

[50] Bell (n 2) 151.
[51] Gautama (n 49) (emphasis in the original).
[52] My translation of Satrio, *Contracts II* (n 7) 230. See also Soebekti, who says that 'in Article 1338(3), the judge is empowered to oversee the performance of a contract so that the performance does not violate fairness or

> It is therefore now clear that in Indonesia, the courts are free to modify contracts if their content is not fair. Article 1339 does allow the court to 'find' equitable obligations not explicitly stated in the contract thus modifying the written contract.

My colleague Taufiq Adiyanto also states that the courts use the principle of good faith and equity to revise contracts when a hardship caused by a change of circumstances arises, rather than apply the theory of subjective *force majeure*.[53] The case of the *Canal de Craponne* (and the scenario of Abraham's successors) would today be decided in Indonesia by the court invoking the concepts of fairness and equity to modify the price. Therefore, in my view, a better remedy is now available in Indonesia through the courts' revision of contracts on the basis of equity, fairness, and good faith rather than through the theory of subjective *force majeure*. That is, if one believes that courts should indeed adapt contracts in cases of hardship and inequity.

Most of the hypothetical scenarios the editors wanted us to address[54] would today in Indonesian law lead to a possible revision of contract on the basis of equity, fairness, and good faith rather than through any theory of *force majeure*. Whether it is a case of sudden hyperinflation (Citi Corporation scenario); the case of a sudden five-fold increase in business and in the value of a lease due to government investment (Easy's leases of business premises from Frugle); the case of a contract to refurbish the cellar of a restaurant that has now been completely destroyed by a storm (Han's cellar); or Gina's ruined travel plans because of a cancelled conference, terrorist threats, an airport strike, and the cancellation of the president's inauguration, in all these instances there would be no *force majeure* as performance is still possible, but in Indonesia a court could review the contract on the basis of equity, fairness, and good faith.[55]

This power of the Indonesian courts to revise contracts on the basis of equity, fairness, and good faith might be one of the reasons why, even during the Asian Financial Crisis with runaway inflation and the Indonesian rupiah losing more than 80 per cent of its value against the US dollar, there were still almost no cases where a court invoked the theory of subjective *force majeure*. There was one case where the Supreme Court did characterize the consequences of the hyperinflation of the financial crisis as a case of subjective *force majeure*, but one case does not make a *jurisprudence constante*,[56] especially since this case can

justice': Soebekti (n 44) 41; and at 43: 'with the guidelines that all agreements must be implemented in good faith the judge is empowered to prevent an implementation that greatly offends a sense of justice' [my translation].

[53] Adiyanto (n 38) 108–09.

[54] The fact scenarios of these hypotheticals are set out in more detail in M Chen-Wishart, D Neo, and S Vogenauer, 'Introduction', ch 1 in this volume, 7–8.

[55] An additional scenario mentioned by the editors (Kris sells his family home to Leila) may be a problem in the common law but is not in civil law jurisdictions. If parties have set the price of the home at 70 per cent of its market value under the unwritten assumption that it would be dedicated to a cultural use by the general public, but the buyer changes her mind after the sale, then, in the common law, the parol evidence rule may pose a problem, but in the civil law, there is no such rule and one can look at the negotiations between the parties to find their true intent (cf Vogenauer (n 47) 499–503). In any event, a court in Indonesia always has the power to revise contracts on the basis of equity, fairness, and good faith. All this assumes that no third party has relied on the written contract to his detriment.

[56] Although 'jurisprudence' (what the common law would call 'case law') plays an important role in the development of the civil law, technically there is no *stare decisis* in civil law and one case, even of the Supreme Court, does not automatically create law (no binding precedent). For jurisprudence to become so convincing that it be followed, it must be *constante* (consistent, ie more than one case) or there must be clear signs that the Supreme Court fully considered the issue and its implications in future cases and used a particular case to send a clear signal as to the direction of the jurisprudence (eg through an *Assemblée plénière* in France, an institution that does not exist in Indonesia).

be distinguished in many respects—the contract had its own *force majeure* clause and the case was governed by more specific provisions of the Code.[57]

One must also see that when there is a major crisis leading to hardships for debtors, their difficulties are often not resolved through the private law of obligations. Colleagues who oppose the revision of contracts because of hardship often forget that the now very common regimes of protection from creditors and from bankruptcy (often referred to as 'Chapter 11' regimes)[58] are a form of revision of contracts under court supervision due to hardship. During the financial crisis of 1997, one of the so-called 'conditionalities' that the International Monetary Fund (IMF) imposed on Indonesia in return for loans was the adoption of a new bankruptcy law to introduce a debt restructuring and bankruptcy protection regime that would allow debtors suffering hardships to renegotiate and restructure their debts under court supervision.[59] This is a form of revision of contracts due to hardship but one that takes into account all debts to all creditors rather than looking at only one particular obligation or contract. This seems more efficient and fairer. When it comes to hardship, few contract laws take into account the presence of other creditors, with the notable exception of section 2-615 of the United States Uniform Commercial Code (UCC).[60]

In fact, during the Asian Financial Crisis, the situation was very dire in Indonesia—all the banks were insolvent and had to be nationalized, and a large number of (if not most) large enterprises and conglomerates were effectively insolvent as they were incapable of paying their debts. Solving this economic catastrophe was well beyond the capacity of any private law provision on hardship or subjective *force majeure*. The solution came through government and IMF-backed bodies created to renegotiate and restructure debts and restart the economy, namely the Indonesian Bank Restructuring Agency (IBRA)[61] and the Indonesian Debt Restructuring Agency (INDRA).[62] This explains why we have almost no court cases on subjective *force majeure* or revision of contract in equity due to hardship.

[57] Indonesian Supreme Court No 1787 K/PDT/2005 (*PT Pertamina (Persero) v PT Wahana Seno Utama*). It would be problematic to extend the decision in this case to other cases since, as mentioned, the contract had its own specific *force majeure* clause and the construction contract was affected by ICC, art 1610, which specifically prohibits the contractor from requiring a price increase even if the costs of labour and materials increase.

[58] Referring to Chapter 11 of Title 11 of the United States Uniform Commercial Code, which provides that an insolvent debtor may ask for court protection against its creditors and for the right to negotiate with its creditors, under court supervision, a deal which would reorganize the enterprise and usually reschedule and reduce its debts.

[59] This Indonesian regime for the postponement and renegotiations of debt liabilities and the avoidance of bankruptcy is now found in Law No 37 of 2004 on Bankruptcy and Suspension of Payments, arts 222–294.

[60] UCC, s 2-615 Excuse by Failure of Presupposed Conditions:

> Except so far as a seller may have assumed a greater obligation and subject to the preceding section on substituted performance: …
>
> (b) Where the causes mentioned in paragraph (a) affect only a part of the seller's capacity to perform, he must allocate production and deliveries among his customers but may at his option include regular customers not then under contract as well as his own requirements for further manufacture. He may so allocate in any manner which is fair and reasonable.
>
> (c) The seller must notify the buyer seasonably that there will be delay or non-delivery and, when allocation is required under paragraph (b), of the estimated quota thus made available for the buyer.

[61] *Undang-Undang Nomor 10 Tahun 1998 Tentang Perubahan Atas Undang-Undang Nomor 7 Tahun 1992 Tentang Perbankan* (Law No 10 of 1998, amending Law No 7 of 1992 on Banking) and Government Regulation No 17 of 1997.

[62] Keputusan Presiden (Keppres) RI *No 31 Tahun 1999 Tentang Pembentukan Badan Restrukturisasi Utang Luar Negeri Perusahaan Indonesia (Indonesian Debt Restructuring Agency)* (Presidential decree No 31 of year 1999 on the Formation of the Agency for the Restructuring of Indonesian Enterprises' Foreign Debts).

IV. Contractual *force majeure* Clauses

As the ICC states, 'Agreements lawfully entered into have the force of law for those who have made them.'[63] Parties are, of course, free to allocate the risk of future events however they want. Such contractual *force majeure* and hardship clauses prevail over the provisions of the Code.

Since Indonesia does not have provisions in its Code for hardship and subjective *force majeure*, it would be wise to provide for such situations in the contract. It should be noted that although such clauses are usually referred to as *force majeure* clauses in English, they are not about *force majeure*, as understood in the Old French, Old Dutch, and Indonesian Codes—these clauses are generally not mainly about objective *force majeure* but rather about subjective *force majeure* or hardship. When drafting such a clause in a contract governed by Indonesian law, foreign lawyers should be fully aware of the nomenclature and categories used in Indonesian civil law and not use boiler-plate common law clauses which inevitably lead to confusion and uncertainty in the Indonesian context.

V. What Happened during COVID-19?

This chapter was originally written in June 2020. Have there been legislative, doctrinal, or jurisprudential developments since then, especially in light of the COVID-19 pandemic?

Contrary to what was done in some other jurisdictions, the Indonesian Parliament and government did not adopt a special legislation or regulation[64] to deal with radical changes of circumstances caused by the COVID-19 pandemic. When COVID-19 made the performance of contractual obligations either impossible or extremely onerous (hardship), parties had to rely on the *force majeure* clauses they had in their contract. If the contract did not have a *force majeure* clause or if such a clause did not cover events similar to the COVID-19 pandemic but also did not (even implicitly) exclude the application of the general law of contract on changes of circumstances, the only recourse was to the general law of contract described above. Therefore, the only clear recourse remained the *force majeure* provision of the ICC, thus requiring an absolute impossibility to perform the obligation. There has not been any systematic recourse to the concept of subjective *force majeure/overmacht yang subjektif* (hardship) during the COVID-19 crisis, thus confirming that this concept is not yet clearly part of Indonesian law. It also seems that, even during the COVID crisis, there has not been any systematic recourse to the revision of contract on the basis of equity and good faith that I mentioned above.

[63] ICC, art 1338(1), which is the same as OFCC, art 1134(1).

[64] In an emergency, the President of Indonesia has the power to amend legislation such as the ICC (which is normally the exclusive prerogative of parliament) through a *Government Regulation in Lieu of Law* (*Peraturan Pemerintah Pengganti Undang-Undang*) commonly known as *Perppu*. Such *Perppu* must be approved at the next session of Parliament or cease to be law: see the Indonesian Constitution, art 22.

VI. A Need for Reform?

Should Indonesia reform the ICC by adopting a modern provision on hardship as now seems to be fashionable in civil law jurisdictions, in particular in the Netherlands and France, which found the provisions of their civil codes, similar to those of the ICC, unsatisfactory? There are two main reasons why it might be a good idea.

First, the efforts of some academic colleagues to push for the adoption by the courts of a theory of subjective *force majeure* is, in my humble view, and with all due respect, misguided. I understand and share the desire for a fairer resolution of the unfairness created by some radical changes of circumstances, but classifying such events as *forces majeures* does not lead to a just solution since the only remedy provided by the Code for a *force majeure* is a complete exoneration of the debtor, not an adaptation of the contract. A legislated remedy that is tailored to hardship situations, rather than complete impossibilities of performance, would be more efficient and would lead to fairer results.

Secondly, although the very broad discretion that the Indonesian courts exercise in revising contracts in equity and good faith does seem to take care of the issue of hardship, that discretion can be criticized as being too broad and as bringing lots of uncertainty in commercial transactions. It might be better to have a well-defined and delineated legislated remedy specific to cases of hardships as is now the case in the Netherlands and France.

However, very unfortunately, the reform of civil and contract law has not been a legislative priority in Indonesia and it is therefore very unlikely that a reform would be adopted in the near future.

VII. Conclusion

The provisions of the ICC on change of circumstances are not different from those of the BW and the OFCC. Indonesia is therefore stuck with old provisions that do not accomplish the contractual justice that academics and courts seem to want to achieve. Court decisions on 'impossibility' or objective *force majeure* are almost non-existent as the requirements and conditions are too exacting. The concept of subjective *force majeure*, though promoted by some academics, has not been accepted by the courts. Instead, cases of hardship are treated as all other cases in which the courts intervene to re-establish fairness and equity. This situation is less than satisfactory in that the discretion exercised by the courts leads to contractual uncertainty, especially since the courts in Indonesia do not have a high reputation when it comes to fairness and probity. It would be better to legislate a specific provision on hardship as has been done in the Netherlands and in France. However, it is unlikely that the ICC will be amended any time soon. In the meantime, I hope that this short summary of the law will be useful.

10

Termination of Contracts under Indonesian Law

HERLIANA

I. Introduction

Indonesia adopted the civil law system while under Dutch colonial rule and in doing so inherited much from the old Dutch *Burgerlijk Wetboek* of 1838 (BW), which in turn was modelled on the old French Code civil of 1804 (OFCC).

In 1846, the Dutch colonial government enacted the General Provisions of Legislation for the Dutch East Indies (*Algemeene Bepalingen van Wetgeving voor Nederlandsch-Indië*, AB). This was the first law to create legal pluralism, dividing the population in the East Indies[1] into three different groups: Europeans (which included Japanese), foreign Orientals (Chinese and Middle Eastern), and indigenous Indonesians.[2] Each group had its own law for private matters. Article 163 of the Dutch Colonial Constitution (*Indische Staatsregeling*, IS) ruled that the BW only applied to Europeans and those who were given the status of European (including Japanese). While for foreign Orientals, the AB and the IS applied—with the exception of articles concerning family law, marriage, and inheritance—indigenous Indonesians were not covered by these codes unless they had obtained the same status as Europeans by decision of the Governor-General.[3] Article 11 AB stipulated that for indigenous Indonesians, judges would apply religious law as well as customary or *adat* law. Consequently, during that period, contracts between indigenous Indonesians were governed by customary law.

The BW became the official civil code of Indonesia in April 1847 and continued to be applied after the 1945/1949 Indonesian independence as the Indonesian Civil Code (ICC) by force of section II of the Transitional Provisions of the 1945 Indonesian Constitution, which stipulated that all laws and regulations which were in force before the Indonesian independence should be applicable as long as they did not conflict with the Constitution. What, then, about the principle of non-discrimination, given the categorization of the population into groups under Dutch rule? Article 27 of the Indonesian Constitution stipulates that every Indonesian citizen is equal before the law and government. However, this article does not automatically abolish any grouping of the population. Rather, what is being eliminated is the spirit of discrimination. Consequently, in the area of private law, legal

[1] The terms 'East Indies' or 'Indies' refers to the islands in the Indonesian and Philippine archipelagoes.

[2] AB, art 4.

[3] The grounds on which one could obtain European status included, but were not limited to, being married to a Dutch national, obtaining Dutch education, or converting to Christianity.

Herliana, *Termination of Contracts under Indonesian Law* In: *Studies in the Contract Laws of Asia V: Ending and Changing Contracts*. Edited by: Mindy Chen-Wishart, Dora Neo, and Stefan Vogenauer, Oxford University Press.
DOI: 10.1093/oso/9780198995814.003.0010

pluralism remains in force without creating discrimination based on race. To unify all those pre-existing legal systems proved to be extremely difficult; the concept of having a different law for each group of the Indonesian population as previously applied by the Dutch was one of the main reasons.[4]

Indonesian courts played a significant role in overcoming the problems arising from the conflict of laws. For example, in 1956 the Jakarta District Court ruled that a sales contract between two Indonesians who were subject to different customary laws was governed by the ICC because the sale involved an item that was intended for use by all population groups and the contract site was Jakarta, which was considered a place for modern commerce and which was, in turn, governed by the ICC. According to Daniel S Lev, difficulties arose due to the distinction made by courts between big cities, types of contract, and the subject matters thereof.[5]

The efforts for the unification of law started during the Japanese occupation from 1942 to 1945.[6] However, no significant progress was made even after the Indonesian independence in 1945. The ICC continues to be enforced as follows:

(i) Book I, on marriage and divorce, applies to the European and Chinese population;
(ii) Book II, especially on inheritance, applies to the European and Chinese population;
(iii) Book II, on land rights, is no longer applicable since the enactment of the Agrarian Act 1960;[7]
(iv) Book III, on obligations (including contracts), applies to the entire Indonesian population, but it is not mandatory;
(v) Book IV, on evidence and prescription, applies to the entire Indonesian population.

Since the provisions of Book III are not mandatory, currently some contracts are still governed by *adat* law. This concerns, in particular, transactions made between Indonesians in rural areas. Van Vollenhoven[8] pointed out three features of a contract under *adat* law in Indonesia: communalism, a cash-and-carry principle, and concreteness.[9] According to Siombo, this is in line with Holleman's opinion, who posits that different customary laws are of a general nature, with common features as follows:[10]

(i) *Magis* (Magic): Religion and/or Spirituality
This feature is interpreted as a mindset based on religiosity and/or spirituality, namely, people's beliefs about the existence of something sacred. Before

[4] DS Lev, 'The Lady and the Banyan Tree: Civil-Law Change in Indonesia' (1965) 14 American Journal of Comparative Law 283, 287.

[5] ibid.

[6] ibid 283.

[7] This new Agrarian Act eliminated most of Book II, especially European land rights. It created new land rights applicable to all population groups. The drafters of the Act asserted that it was based on customary law.

[8] Cornelius van Vollenhoven was a legal scholar who, at the turn of the nineteenth to the twentieth century, introduced the term '*adat* law' among Dutch academics and politicians.

[9] Indonesian contract law was strongly influenced by *adat* law, namely, the rules that were developed following the customs regulating the daily lives of individual tribes in Indonesia. It is from this that van Vollenhoven drew the above-mentioned principles of communalism, cash-and-carry, and concreteness. S Hutabarat, 'Harmonisasi Hukum Kontrak dan Dampaknya Pada Hukum Kontrak Indonesia' (2016) 2 Veritas et Justitia 112, 118.

[10] MR Siombo, 'Hukum Adat' *Asas-asas Hukum Adat* (Universitas Terbuka 2014) 1, 16–18.

indigenous peoples came into contact with the colonizer's religion, this spiritual nature was manifested in a belief in supernatural things.

(ii) *Komunal* (Communal)
Customary law has the characteristics of communalism, meaning that it prioritizes common interests, while personal interests also include common interests.[11]

(iii) *Konkret* (Concrete)
Another characteristic of customary law is that it is clearly existing in a material or physical form.[12] This means that every legal relationship that occurs in society can be defined.[13]

(iv) *Kontan* (Cash)
This feature means that every performance is always accompanied by a counter-performance, which is given immediately. Performance and counter-performance are carried out together, at the same time.[14]

Contract law based on customary law is still applicable in Indonesia. In the 1950s, Supreme Court Justice Malikoel Adil argued that European private law could be transplanted to the Indonesian legal system if it did not violate customary law. Furthermore, he stated that customary law should be maintained as a positive source of law. The introduction of European private law should be guided by a rational theory of reception.[15] Similarly, Wirjono Prodjodikoro, a legal scholar, maintained that a new statute on contract law should not include European concepts which are unknown to local customary law. For example, in Indonesian customary law there are no consensual contracts but only real contracts, meaning that a right over a good may be created only upon actual transfer, whereas the ICC stipulates that a contract is made by way of a meeting of minds in which an offer meets an acceptance. Thus, the sources of contract law, according to Prodjodikoro, are customary law, something he calls a national sense of justice, and the international validity of certain legal rules. Lev offered quite a different opinion, saying that applying *adat* law concepts to modern contract law would impose severe restrictions on legal development. This is because the development of modern contract law was so complex that customary law was no longer suitable.[16]

The emergence of modern contract law was partly supported by the enactment of Law No 1 of 1967 concerning Foreign Investment and Law No 6 of 1968 concerning Domestic Investment. These investment laws resulted in contracts between Indonesians, as well as between Indonesians and foreign parties, becoming more frequent. During that period, contracts from foreign counterparts were simply translated into the Indonesian language. Not enough consideration was given to whether these were compatible with Indonesian contract law and its concepts. Instead, some ambiguous contract law

11 H Hadikusuma, *Pengantar Ilmu Hukum Adat Indonesia Edisi Revisi* (Mandar Maju 2014) 35.
12 ibid 35.
13 Siombo (n 10) 14.
14 ibid 14.
15 Lev (n 4) 302.
16 ibid 302.

principles have been re-interpreted to accommodate foreign concepts into Indonesian contract law.[17]

International contract law in Indonesia developed from a collection of contracts created by Indonesian parties and their foreign counterparts. Those contracts constitute a 'customary international contract law'. In the fields of investment, banking, capital markets, oil and gas, and many other areas, parties often deviate from the provisions set out in the ICC.

II. Termination of Contract

1. Discharge of Contractual Obligations and Termination

Contractual relationships sometimes do not go as well as planned. There are various circumstances that can hinder the performance of a contract by the debtor. In this situation, the creditor's interests need to be protected. One way to do this is by giving the creditor the right to terminate the contract. The termination of a contract is regulated in Article 1381 ICC under the title 'discharge of obligations' (*hapusnya perikatan*), which is translated from the Dutch *an het te niet gaan der verbindtenissen*. Indonesian contract law does not distinguish between termination and discharge of contractual obligations, both of which are mentioned in Article 1381:

> Obligations are discharged by: payment, offer of immediate payment followed by consignment or custody, renewal of the debt, set-offs or compensation, consolidation of debts, relief from a debt, the destruction of the goods that were owed, invalidity or nullification, operation of nullification conditions, and lapse of time.

The point in which discharge and termination of a contract differ is the conditions surrounding the ending of a contractual relationship. A discharge of contract takes place when the parties have already performed their obligations, while termination is an option in cases of non-performance, fraud, breach, or agreement to terminate.

In the event of non-performance, the aggrieved party may claim for invalidity (*kebatalan*) or nullification (*pembatalan*) of contract. The consequence of invalidity is one that the court is required to apply *ex officio*. In case of nullification the aggrieved party is required to file a lawsuit to nullify. According to Article 1381 ICC, nullification can be effected by implementing a nullification condition or by lapse of time.

Under the ICC, there is a difference between an invalid (void) and a challengeable (voidable) contract.[18] The consequence of invalidity is the obligation to restore the original state that existed prior to the conclusion of the contract (*restitutio in integrum*), while in

[17] S Hartono and others, *The Indonesian Law on Contracts*, Institute of Developing Economics (IDE) Asian Law Series No 10, IDE (IDE-JETRO) March 2001, Japan, 21–22. The ICC only provides the general principles of contract law in Indonesia; an unofficial English translation is available at <www.refworld.org/pdfid/3ffbd0804.pdf> accessed 18 December 2024. It should be noted that the two laws mentioned in this paragraph have been replaced by Law No 25 of 2007 concerning Investment.

[18] ICC, arts 1446, 1335 (respectively).

nullification cases, the court declares the contract effective for the period up to the date of judgment. In this case, the court may require the return of any performances that might remain. If such return is impossible, the court will award damages in the form of cost, profit, and potential loss as a result of breach.[19]

The concept of invalidity under the ICC is similar to that of *résolution* under the OFCC, in that it leads to a mutual restitution of benefits. However, in the 2016 reform of French contract law the retrospective nature was renounced due to impracticality. Under the revised French Civil Code, *résolution* is considered as a sanction for non-performance, regardless of whether or not the creditor has suffered a loss or the debtor is at fault.[20]

2. Entitlement of the Parties to Withhold or Discontinue Their Performance

The ICC does not expressly rule on whether a party can discontinue performance if the other party does not perform. However, for sale and purchase agreements Article 1478 ICC stipulates that the seller 'is not obligated to deliver the goods if the buyer has not paid the purchase price and if the seller has not granted him an extension of the period of payment'.

According to J Satrio, in a reciprocal contract, before the creditor requests the debtor to perform, the creditor himself must perform.[21] This implies that the debtor is allowed to discontinue his performance if the creditor has not performed. This is in line with the principle of *exceptio non adimpleti contractus*, which means that a party is excused from performing a contract if the other party has not fulfilled his obligations as set out in the contract. Furthermore, Riduan Syahrani states that *exceptio non adimpleti contractus* can be used as a defence by a debtor in a lawsuit to free himself from paying damages for breach of contract due to non-performance by the creditor.[22] If such argument is proven, no compensation has to be paid by the debtor.[23]

3. Types of Breach Justifying Termination

In France, Article 1184(1) OFCC stated:

> A condition subsequent is always implied in bilateral contracts for the event that one of two parties does not perform his undertaking.

19 ICC, art 1246 states: 'Compensation of costs, damages and interests that the creditor may claim comprises [compensation] of losses he had suffered and profits he would have enjoyed, subject to the limitations or modifications stipulated hereunder.'

20 H Beale, B Fauvarque-Cosson, J Rutgers, and S Vogenauer, *Cases, Materials and Text on Contract Law, Ius Commune Casebook for the Common Law of Europe* (3rd edn, Hart Publishing 2019) 983.

21 J Satrio, *Hukum Perjanjian* (Citra Aditya Bakti 1992) 134.

22 HR Syahrani, *Seluk Beluk dan Asas-Asas Hukum Perdata* (PT Alumni 2004) 242.

23 *Exceptio non adimpleti contractus* is also supported by the Supreme Court, which held that a debtor can discontinue his performance if the creditor fails to perform. See eg Supreme Court decision No 23/K/N/1999 in a dispute between PT Waskita Karya against PT Mustika Princess Hotel and Supreme Court decision No 704 K/Pdt.Sus/2012 in a dispute between PT Telkomsel against PT Prima Jaya Informatika.

> In that case, the contract is not avoided by operation of law [*de plein droit*]. The party towards whom the undertaking has not been fulfilled has the choice either to compel the other to fulfil the agreement when it is possible, or to request its *résolution* with damages.
>
> *Résolution* must be applied for in court, and the defendant may be granted time according to circumstances.

This provision was abolished in the revised French Civil Code of 2016. Even before the 2016 reform, French law recognized exceptions that allow the aggrieved party to unilaterally terminate a contract, provided that the contract includes such a right. The French Supreme Court, the Cour de cassation, in its decision of 13 October 1998, held that unilateral termination of a contract can be allowed if the counterparty has committed a serious breach.[24]

Indonesian law recognizes three types of breach, namely, failure to perform the obligation, failure to perform the contract in time, and performance that is different to what is agreed.[25] The implications of a breach of contract are as follows:

(i) The debtor is required to compensate the creditor for costs, damages, and interest (Article 1236 ICC).
(ii) The object of the contract becomes the creditor's liability. Liability of the debtor for failure by him to deliver the goods arises from the time of the non-performance (Article 1237 ICC).
(iii) In a bilateral contract, the creditor is entitled to terminate the contract, with or without asking for damages (Article 1266 (1)).

Similarly to French law, under the ICC it is only in a reciprocal contract that a creditor is given the right to terminate. The ICC is silent on the type of breach that gives rise to this right to terminate. Article 1266 states:

> A void [or resolutory] condition is deemed to have been included in reciprocal contracts for the case a party does not fulfill his obligation.
>
> In such case, the contract is not void by law, but voidance must be requested to the court.
>
> The request must also be made if the conditions of voidance concerning the non-fulfillment of an obligation [are] included in the contract.
>
> If the void condition is not included in the contract, the judge, considering the situation, upon the defendant's request, has the discretion to fix a time frame to fulfill such obligation, but such time frame may not exceed one month.

A 'void condition'—a concept that corresponds to the *condition résolutoire* in the OFCC—is a condition which, if met, causes the contract to become void, and restores the parties to a status as though the contractual obligations had never existed. Such void or resolutory condition does not delay the fulfilment of the obligation; it only obliges the creditor to return what he has received if a certain event occurs. The above article implies that termination of a contract is not achieved by a unilateral act of termination; it requires a lawsuit.

[24] H Kötz, *European Contract Law* (2nd edn, OUP 2017) 219.
[25] Satrio (n 21) 122.

Furthermore, the ICC states that the request must also be made even if a resolutory condition concerning the non-fulfilment of an obligation is included in the contract. If such a condition is not included, the judge has the discretion to fix a time frame to fulfil such obligations if requested by a party; however, such time frame may not exceed one month. This confirms that under the ICC, the means provided to the aggrieved party to terminate the contract are not self-executory. In confirming this, in the case *PT Dua Berlian v Lee Kum Kee*,[26] the Supreme Court held that a unilateral termination of contract is considered a tort. Furthermore, in the same decision the Court argued that immediate termination was improper conduct against the duty of care.

Article 1267 ICC states:

> The party against whom the obligation is not fulfilled may opt to compel the counterparty to fulfill the agreement where such fulfillment is still possible, or demand the termination of such agreement, with compensation of costs, damages and interests.

However, the principle of freedom of contract enables the parties to formulate their clauses as they wish. The parties may stipulate that specific provisions are to continue even after termination of the contract. This could be, for example, confidentiality obligations or settlement mechanisms to be used in the event of a dispute, such as arbitration. Thus, termination does not necessarily mean that all obligations cease altogether.

Both in France and Indonesia, the court has a discretion to determine whether a non-performance is sufficiently serious to grant termination. In this respect, a French court will examine the nature of the breach and whether it is an essential or non-essential non-performance. Economic context is one of many considerations that French courts will take into account.[27]

Similarly, in Indonesia, judges will usually look at whether the breach is significant or fundamental. The nature of a 'significant breach' is usually assessed by determining which element of the contract is breached. Indonesian judges will examine whether the breach concerns essential elements (*essentialia negotii*) of the contract. Each type of contract has its own essential components. The essential elements in each type of contract distinguish it from other types of contract. For example, the essential elements in a sale and purchase agreement are the goods and the price. Thus, a breach in respect to the goods or the price can lead to a termination of a contract.

In *Purwoko Jermmy v Ali Imran*,[28] the Supreme Court held that a contract was void because of a delay in performance by the contractor. This delay meant that the resolutory (or 'void') condition stipulated in the contract was met. At district court level, the claimant had requested the court to declare that the contract with the defendant was void on the grounds that the defendant—a housing developer—did not act professionally when he asked a third-party subcontractor to carry out several crucial works on the construction. In addition, the development of the houses was behind schedule. The breach committed by the contractor was categorized as essential and serious. The Supreme Court accepted

26 Supreme Court decision No 1284 K/Pdt/1998 of 18 December 2000.

27 Beale and others (n 20) 997.

28 Supreme Court decision No 455 K/Pdt/2013 of 23 October 2013.

this reasoning as the basis for terminating the contract. In this decision, the Court, due to the existence of a resolutory condition, did not grant an extension to the contractor. Had there not been a resolutory condition in the contract, the Court would have given such an extension under Article 1266 ICC, as a consequence of applying the resolutory condition implied by this article.

Under certain circumstances the parties can also provide further details of the contract, for example the place of performance, or a guarantee by the seller regarding certain qualities of the goods. These details are considered to be *accidentalia* elements. In addition, there is also the category of *naturalia* elements, which are those that are naturally contained in certain types of contract.

Judges will be very careful in deciding whether or not to terminate a contract. Generally speaking, only a breach in respect to an essential element or principle will be considered as a serious breach and therefore followed by termination. To determine whether a term is essential, judges will usually look at the recital clause. A recital clause serves as confirmation of how important certain terms and conditions are. It explains the intention of the parties and the purpose of the contract. Intention and purpose play important roles, especially when there is disagreement or dispute concerning a certain clause or the meaning of certain clauses. The interpretation of certain clauses, or the question whether these include specific rights and obligations, involves taking into account the intention and purpose. A recital clause may clarify, for example, that the seller of raw material or component parts must comply precisely with any given specifications. Thus, when the seller fails to comply with such specifications, the buyer has a legitimate reason to cancel the contract instead of only being entitled to claim damages.[29]

Suharnoko explains this requirement by giving the example of a buyer who is in the business of making high-tech component parts. Accordingly, his contracts will demand precise specifications since a small deviation would cause defective and substandard products.[30] In a situation like this, judges will pay more attention to the nature of the contract than to the intention of the parties or the effect of the breach. In this example, the judges would see specification as more crucial than the parties' intention.

A decision by the Sleman District Court[31] serves as a good practical example. In this case, the seller of a piece of real estate was not the rightful owner but rather had rented that property from another person. The court considered this a breach of *essentialia* since in a sales agreement the seller must be the rightful owner of the goods or the land in question. Consequently, the contract was terminated and the seller was ordered to return all payments he had received.

The impact of the termination of a contract varies. Only in rare circumstances do contracts provide that termination will result in a cancellation of the contract as if it had never existed. Mostly, termination will result in relieving the parties from performing future obligations. The party who breaches the contract is still liable for the breach. The main obligations of the party in breach are replaced by secondary obligations, such as to pay damages for the loss resulting from the breach.

29 Suharnoko, 'Contract Law in a Comparative Perspective' (2012) 2 Indonesia Law Review 117, 131.
30 ibid.
31 Sleman District Court decision No 104/Pdt.G/2006/Pn.Slmn of 17 January 2007 (copy on file with author).

4. A Second Chance for the Party in Breach

Under French law, if the judge refuses termination, he can grant the non-performing party a second chance to execute his obligations. Article 1228 of the revised French Civil Code of 2016 gives a judge the power to grant an additional period of time for performance. Article 1229, together with Articles 1343–1345 of the same Code, allows up to two years for money to be paid. In Indonesia, Article 1266 ICC states that if the agreement does not contain a resolutory condition, the judge, upon the defendant's request, has the discretion to grant an additional period to fulfil the obligations. While both French and Indonesian judges may give extra time for performance, in Indonesia such an extension can only be given for 30 days at the maximum, and it must be based on the request of the defendant (debtor).

In addition to this, under French law a judge may also make a judicial modification such as reducing the amount of money to be paid. Under French commercial law, the judge is also given the authority to modify a contract by adjusting the price. This is based on the principle of good faith. Likewise, the good-faith principle enshrined in Article 1338 ICC enables a judge to modify contractual clauses. This power to modify is also strengthened by the principle of equity, or propriety, which states that parties are not only bound by the obligations as stipulated in the contract but also by notions of justice, by customs, and by law.

In *Ny Boesono and R Boesono v Sri Setianingsih*,[32] the Supreme Court held that a monthly interest rate of 10 per cent in a loan agreement, even if expressly consented to, is considered an injustice. The claimant, a retired person in dire circumstances, had pledged his pension book to secure a loan from the defendant and subsequently claimed for termination. The Supreme Court was of the opinion that 10 per cent interest per month was too high and therefore reduced it to only 1 per cent. Such a reduction of interest rate is considered as one of the other measures judges can implement. The request of termination is only partially granted by way of reducing the interest to be paid.

Article 1226 of the French Civil Code, as revised in 2016, stipulates that when termination is unilateral, a notice to perform is necessary before termination can take place, except in cases of urgency. The creditor must give notice to the debtor and request him to perform within a reasonable time. The notice must also state that if the debtor fails to perform, the creditor has a right to terminate the contract. If the debtor still fails to perform after receiving the notice, the creditor is entitled to terminate the contract.[33]

Similarly, under Indonesian law, failure to perform contractual obligations does not automatically put a party in breach. The debtor must be given notice by the creditor, such notice containing the demand to perform. If the first notice goes without response, meaning the debtor still fails to perform, the creditor may send a second and a third notice. This is expressed in Article 1238 ICC, which states that:

> [t]he debtor shall be deemed in default, either by an order or other similar deed, or pursuant to the obligation itself, where such obligation stipulates that the debtor shall be in default, upon failure to deliver within the stipulated time period.

32 Supreme Court decision No 3431/K/Pdt/1985 of 4 March 1987.
33 Beale and others (n 20) 1011.

Furthermore, Article 1243 ICC provides that:

> [c]ompensation for costs, damages and interests for breach of an obligation only becomes obligatory if the debtor, after having been declared to be in default, remains in default, or in case of obligations where he must give or produce something, [and this] is only given after the lapse of a period of time.

The wording 'after having been declared . . . remains in default' indicates that the debtor is given a second chance to perform. It is the creditor's obligation to remind the debtor to perform in the form of a written notice. The creditor usually sends a third notice before he sues the debtor before the district court. Hence, in the event of non-performance, the contract does not automatically come to an end. The creditor can request the debtor to perform and can ask for damages. Satrio states that the notice is the way to bring the debtor in default.[34] Consequently, once the second or third chance to perform has lapsed, the debtor is now in a state of breach of contract, and the legal consequences of breach are triggered, such as the creditor requests performance, damages, termination of contract, or a combination of any of those measures.[35]

5. Contractual Termination Clauses

A contract may contain a clause regarding its termination that is individually negotiated by the parties. This may be an explicit resolutory condition clause which might stipulate: 'If A does not carry out its obligations in accordance with this contract, B may cancel the agreement.' If A is in breach of contract, B can unilaterally terminate the contract in line with the clause. A judge would be bound to respect such a clause due to the principle of *pacta sunt servanda*.

Even where the parties have not inserted an express resolutory condition in a contract, such a condition is, as mentioned above, deemed to exist in every reciprocal contract (Article 1266 ICC). However, there are two different opinions regarding the applicability of Article 1266 ICC. One view says that it is a mandatory provision which must be followed, while the other holds that it is a default rule and therefore can be deviated from. The former believes that the parties may not deviate from Article 1266 because a resolutory condition is the condition of the cancellation of a contract if one of the parties does not render performance.

In principle, there is freedom of contract, but in the context of a cancellation of the agreement as a result of non-performance, the contract must be subject to the provisions of Article 1266 ICC. As a matter of statutory language, this article appears to say that resolutory conditions are non-negotiable. Yet according to Subekti,[36] non-performance is not a condition that *does* cancel the contract but a condition that *may* cancel the contract. To be able to cancel, the injured party has to file a lawsuit demanding cancellation of the contract. The court's ruling is not a declaratory judgment which merely states that the contract is void.

[34] Satrio (n 21) 105.
[35] J Satrio, *Hukum Perikatan yang Lahir dari Undang Undang* (Citra Aditya Bakti 1993) 105.
[36] Subekti, *Hukum Perjanjian* (Intermasa 2002) 20.

Rather, it nullifies the contract with all the consequences. So the nullification of a contract must be based on a court decision. Only a judicial ruling can determine that a true non-performance has taken place, not the non-performance as such. The requirement of a court judgment has the consequence that nullification is not automatic.

However, those who believe that Article 1266 is a mere default rule argue that Book III of the ICC follows an 'open system', which means that parties to a contract are given the freedom to draft clauses as they wish, as long as they do not breach the principles of equity (propriety), customs, and laws.

An obligation with resolutory conditions is an obligation that depends on an event that is still going to happen or when it is still unclear if it is going to take place. It can be achieved either by postponing the starting time of the obligation or by terminating the obligation due to a certain event. In the first case, the obligation is only brought into existence if and when the event in question occurs. In the latter, an obligation that is existing will end or be cancelled if the intended event occurs. This kind of latter agreement is called an obligation with a condition.

6. The Hypotheticals

(a) Car Machinery & Co and Traders Ltd

Car Machinery & Co appoint Traders Ltd as sole distributors of their car panel presses for a period of five years. Clause 7(b) of the agreement provides that 'Distributors shall send their representatives to visit all six large car manufacturers in the country at least once in every week for the purpose of soliciting orders for car panel presses. Failure to comply with this obligation shall entitle Car Machinery to terminate the agreement with immediate effect.' Traders Ltd miss two visits to car manufacturers in the second month of the contractual period. Is Car Machinery entitled to terminate the agreement?[37]

In Indonesia, a breach of contract does not automatically terminate the contract. This is because when a debtor commits a breach, the creditor may file a lawsuit requesting full performance or asking for damages. In this case, where the distributor missed 2 out of 24 visits, this will not be sufficient reason to terminate the contract. The principles of equity which are manifested in the principle of good faith, appropriateness, and correctness will come into play.

(b) Prime Ltd and Devil Corp

Prime Ltd sells a piece of land to Devil Corp. Under the terms of the contract, Devil pays a 10 per cent deposit, the remainder of the sum being due at 5:00 pm on 30 September, time being 'of the essence'. According to Clause 12, failure to meet the deadline would result in the deposit being forfeited and the agreement being terminated. Devil is ten minutes late in tendering the completion money and Prime refuse performance. Can Devil sue for specific performance, arguing that Prime's reliance on the clause is unreasonable in some way? Would the result be different if the contract did not include Clause 12?

[37] The fact scenarios of the hypothetical cases discussed in this section are taken from M Chen-Wishart, D Neo, and S Vogenauer, 'Introduction', ch 1 in this volume, 9.

If the contract specifically mentions the time of performance, the party who fails to perform in a timely manner would be in breach of contract. However, a delay of ten minutes is unlikely to be considered a breach since it is insignificant. Even though the contract states that 'failure to meet the deadline would result in termination', the court will examine whether the creditor has a special interest in the timelines of performance. If that is the case, then it can be assumed that delayed performance is a fundamental breach. If Clause 12 were not included in the contract, the court would be even less likely to order termination on these facts.

(c) Seven Seas and Big Chef

Seven Seas, an importer of seafood, sells two tons of mussels to Big Chef restaurant chain. After one ton has been delivered it turns out that the concentration of cadmium in the mussels is 2 per cent above the concentration permitted by national food regulations. Can Big Chef terminate the contract?

The issue in this case is related to an *essentialia* element of the contract. The purpose of the purchase is that the mussels will be sold in the restaurant. Failure to comply with the requirements stipulated by national food regulations will render Big Chef unable to serve the mussels. The judge will likely rule for termination of the contract since this breach is significant.

(d) Coco and David

Coco, a famous architect, agrees with David that he will landscape the garden in her next development. He is due to start work on 1 December. For David, this is an important opportunity to make his name as a landscape gardener. On 1 October, she tells him that she is no longer interested because the development will not include a garden after all. David has already purchased materials. He estimates that his future earnings will be 10 per cent lower because he will not be able to benefit from having worked with Coco. Can he insist on doing the work? Can he bring an action for breach of contract?

A contract between Coco and David was made when they consented. Under Indonesian law, a unilateral termination of contract is against the law. Thus, Coco cannot withdraw from the agreement without David's consent. David may seek financial damages for whatever he already spent in order to fulfil his obligation. In this case, the judge will not likely order the performance of landscaping since Coco no longer needs that landscape work.

7. Bringing About Termination

French law, after the 2016 reform, allows immediate termination of contract if the parties agreed on this. A creditor can include the right to immediate termination in the contract; however, the debtor can still request the court to declare that such a termination is unjustified.[38] In contrast, Indonesian contract law does not expressly recognize a method to enable one party to a contract to free himself if the other party is in breach.

[38] Kötz (n 24) 229.

Article 1338(1) ICC stipulates that '[a]ll valid agreements apply to the individuals who have concluded them as law'. Paragraph (2) reads: 'Such agreements are irrevocable other than by mutual consent, or pursuant to reasons stipulated by the law.' The question is whether a party to a contract is bound by a contract until a stipulated time lapse? The answer is no. Here are the 'reasons stipulated by law' as mentioned in Article 1338(2):

(i) Article 1266(1) ICC (discussed above).
(ii) Article 1267 ICC, which reads: 'The party against whom the obligation is not fulfilled may opt to compel the counterparty to fulfill the agreement where such fulfillment is still possible, or demand the termination of such agreement with compensation of costs, damages and interests'.
(iii) Article 1335 ICC, which states that '[a]ny contract without a cause, or concluded pursuant to a fraudulent or prohibited cause, is not enforceable'.
(iv) Article 1611 ICC, which states (with regard to contracts to produce a work): 'The principal may, if he so desires, terminate the contract, even though the work has been commenced, provided that he compensates the contractor for all the costs and labour incurred and the profit that he would have gained'.
(v) Article 1646 of the ICC, which stipulates that '[a] partnership shall be dissolved for the following reasons: . . . (3) pursuant to the intent of several or one of the partners'.
(vi) Article 1813 ICC, which reads: 'A mandate shall terminate as follows: due to revocation of the mandate granted to the mandatary; due to termination of the mandate by the mandatary'.

As discussed above, Article 1266(2) stipulates that in case a party does not fulfil his obligation, the agreement is not void by law, but voidance must be requested from a court. Even though there is no uniform opinion in respect of whether Article 1266 is mandatory, it is common practice in Indonesia to seek termination of contract before a court since there is case law saying that unilateral termination (self-termination without involving a court) is considered unlawful.

In a case from 2014, the Supreme Court considered unilateral contract termination as against the applicable law,[39] holding that an action of the applicant terminating the contract unilaterally can be qualified as unlawful conduct because it is contrary to Article 1338 ICC, whose first two paragraphs were cited at the beginning of the present section. Furthermore, in 2016 the Supreme Court held that a unilateral cancellation of a construction contract is considered unlawful conduct.[40] This was based on the facts proven in the court proceedings: the claimant as the contractor was acting based on a warrant issued by the defendant to start the work (*Surat Perintah Mulai Kerja*).

Indonesian district courts often terminate a contract because of unlawful conduct of one of the parties. For example, they have cancelled contracts because they were written in a foreign language. This is contrary to Article 30 of Law No 24 of 2009 on Flag, Language and National Anthem, which requires the Indonesian language to be used in any Memorandum of Understanding or agreement involving Indonesian parties. The district court understood

[39] Supreme Court decision No 1051 K/Pdt/2014 of 12 November 2014.
[40] Supreme Court decision No 28 K/Pdt/2016 of 17 November 2016.

this provision as saying that all agreements using a foreign language are void as a matter of law (*batal demi hukum*). This interpretation was upheld by the Jakarta High Court.[41]As a result of such a constant interpretation, case law, or *Yurisprudensi*,[42] on the question was developed in the Supreme Court. However, the Court still made clear that termination requires a court judgment because 'unilateral termination of contract is considered as an unlawful conduct'.[43]

8. Loss of Entitlement to Termination

Under the ICC, the innocent party or the creditor may renounce his right to terminate but has to do so explicitly. However, in practice, when the creditor accepts a late performance or a performance other than what has been agreed, it can be assumed that the creditor waives his right to terminate the contract. In French law, the right to *résolution* may be renounced, and the court can exercise its discretion to refuse *résolution* to a party who has appeared to waive his right.[44]

If a period of time has been set in the contract, the lapse of that specified time will be considered as a waiver of the termination right. If no period of time has been agreed, the rule in the ICC applies. In Indonesia, all legal claims expire after 30 years.[45] Article 1946 ICC, concerning prescription (*daluwarsa*), states that such expiration serves as a means of acquiring something or being released from a contract, after the lapse of a specific time period, and pursuant to the requirements stipulated by the law.[46] This means that a party's entitlement to terminate a contract will be lost, irrevocably, after 30 years.

9. Effect of Termination

In general, the termination of a contract releases both parties from their obligations. Like in other jurisdictions, under the ICC, the effects are different for void and voidable contracts. The main difference is that while a void contract is invalid as of the date of conclusion and the aggrieved party is entitled to remedies, a voidable contract only becomes invalid as of the date of the judge's decision. The judge has to declare the contract void *ex officio*, even without the request of either party. In this context, the aggrieved party is entitled to receive compensation.

Under the revised French Civil Code of 2016, termination ends the contract (Article 1229), and restitution takes place under the conditions provided by Articles 1352–1352-9. Restitution in French law does not happen automatically; rather, it depends on whether

41 See eg in decision No 48/Pdt/2014/PT.DKI of 7 May 2014.

42 *Yurisprudensi* is similar to precedent in the common law system. Even though Indonesia is a civil law country, higher court decisions—especially Supreme Court decisions—are binding on lower court judges.

43 Supreme Court decision No 4/Yur/Pdt/2018. This reasoning originates from Supreme Court decision No 1051K/Pdt/2014 of 12 November 2014.

44 Beale and others (n 20) 1057.

45 ICC, art 1967.

46 See eg Jakarta Pusat District Court decision No 538/Pdt.G/2014/PN.JKT.PST of 3 July 2013: performance purported to be rendered on 11 November 2014 for a contract made in 1978 was rightfully rejected due to lapse of time.

termination in the specific case has retroactive effect or takes effect for the future only.[47] The shape restitution takes varies depending on the object of the contract. If a party received property from the other party before the contract is terminated, the receiving party must return it. If returning the property is impossible, the debtor shall pay a monetary amount corresponding to the current value, unless he has sold it. If the object is money, the receiving party will have to repay that sum with interest. In a service contract, the party who received the service has to pay the value of the service.[48]

Indonesian law, in contrast, does not have clear rules on restitution. The judge may not order the restoration of the original state without being requested by the aggrieved party. This is due to the principle of the 'passive judge' in civil procedure,[49] which means that the judge cannot determine the scope of the case, including what claim should be made—this is determined by the parties. In addition, *ultra petita* is not allowed under Indonesian civil procedural law; this is why a judge is not allowed to grant more than what the party requested, except in very rare circumstances.[50] If a contract is terminated because it has been declared void, everything is returned to its original state. Such restitution has the effect of cancelling the contract, as if it had never existed.

(a) The fate of the contract

After termination, the parties are no longer bound by future obligations but still liable for breaches that happened in the past, prior to termination. If the contract stipulates that certain obligations are to continue after termination, they will continue to apply. This can be shown, for example, in the existence of dispute resolution clauses where the parties chose arbitration.[51] It is a common principle in many jurisdictions that a termination of contract does not affect dispute settlement provisions.

(b) Benefits conferred before termination

The right to request the cancellation of an agreement, demand restoration, or even sue for compensation is the right for a party who feels disadvantaged or damaged, while those who have already received the disadvantaged or damaged party's performance must return it. The aggrieved party may, depending on the circumstances, be entitled to recover from a non-conforming party the expenses it incurred, additional costs, and lost profit.[52]

Indonesian contract law is predominantly built upon a fault-based system. Article 1243 ICC stipulates:

> Compensation for costs, damages, and interests for the breach of an obligation only becomes obligatory if the debtor, after having been declared to be in default, remains

[47] Beale and others (n 20) 1048.

[48] ibid 1049–50.

[49] Indonesian Civil Procedural Law, art 178(2) states that judges must assess every aspect of the lawsuit; they are prohibited to decide matters that are not in dispute or to grant more than what is asked by the defendant.

[50] Supreme Court decision No 556K/Sip/1971 of 9 November 1971; Supreme Court decision No 425 K/Sip/1975 of 15 July 1975; and Supreme Court decision No 964 K/Pdt/1986 of 1 December 1988 stated that *ultra petita* is allowed, provided it does not deviate from the facts and is in accordance with the material claim.

[51] Law No 30 of 1999 concerning Arbitration and Alternative Dispute Resolution, art 10, states that an arbitration agreement does not become void with the annulment or termination of the main contract.

[52] ICC, art 1234.

> in default, or in case of obligations where he must give or produce something, [such compensation] is only given after the lapse of a period of time.

If such non-performance is caused by *force majeure*, the breaching party is not obliged to compensate because there is no fault on his side.[53] The concept of good faith is also being used to determine whether fault exists. Article 1244 ICC stipulates that the debtor who is in breach of his obligation has to pay damages if he cannot prove that the non-performance or late performance is caused by an unforeseen event for which there is no fault on his side and the creditor cannot prove that the debtor was not acting in bad faith.[54]

(c) The relationship between claims for restitution and for damages

In the event of a breach of contract, French contract law allows the creditor to seek both *résolution* and damages. Damages are based on the loss suffered by the creditor as a consequence of a breach. If both parties are in breach, both of them are required to pay damages. It is possible for the judge to refuse termination and award compensation only.[55]

Under the ICC, the injured party may sue for damages, which may consist of costs, losses, and interests. Costs include all expenses incurred due to the breach. Loss means injury to the good or other object of the contract resulting from the breach. Interest refers to the lost profit suffered by the aggrieved party. The ICC imposes parameters for, and limitations on the amount of, damages that the aggrieved party may claim: (i) the injury must have been foreseeable at the time the contract was formed (Article 1247), (ii) the injury must be the direct result of the breach (Article 1248), and (iii) if the performance is to be in the payment of money, the court may award interest, which is calculated from the date on which the lawsuit is filed (Article 1250).

What if a party to a contract has been unjustly enriched at the expense of another party? In the revised Dutch Civil Code of 1992, unjustified enrichment is stipulated in Article 6:212(1), which says that:

> [a] person who has been unjustifiably enriched at the expense of someone else, for another reason than the reception of an undue performance, has to compensate the damage suffered by the other person as a result, but only to the amount of his enrichment.

The ICC does not recognize the doctrine of unjust or unjustified enrichment. It regulates the concept of payment without liability, as referred to in Article 1359, which states:

> Each payment presumes a debt; each payment which was not made pursuant to a debt may be reclaimed.
> With respect to gratuitous obligations which one has fulfilled voluntarily, there is no reclamation.

While some scholars argue that the concept of unjust enrichment has been accommodated in Article 1359 ICC, in fact unjust enrichment is not limited to payment of money

53 ICC, art 1245.
54 See GF Bell, 'Change of Circumstances in the Indonesian Law of Obligations', 188.
55 Beale and others (n 20) 1044.

or material. Thus, Article 1359 cannot be regarded as a general rule on unjust enrichment. There is a need to provide legal protection for someone whose rights are unjustly harmed. Therefore, a loss of one party due to the gain of the other party which is improperly obtained gives rise to the losing party seeking restitution. However, there is lack of precedent of judicial decisions dealing with the relationship between restitution and damages.

(d) Hypothetical scenario

Consider the following hypothetical scenario: Bob contracts to build a house for Sue for the price of $100,000. After doing one third of the work he abandons the job, leaving behind material worth $15,000, which Sue later uses to finish the works. Can Bob claim the value of the work done or of the materials?[56]

Indonesian law does not have a general rule on unjust enrichment. This case would likely be resolved using principles of moral and justice as well as equity. This case is similar to restitution for wrongs. Bob may file a lawsuit against Sue asserting that there has been a tort, but instead of seeking damages, Bob seeks restitution reflecting the gain Sue has enjoyed through the tort. Before Bob can recover any benefits from Sue, he must return the benefits he has received from Sue. If Bob is unable to give this counter-restitution, his claim will be barred.

[56] The fact scenario of this hypothetical case is taken from M Chen-Wishart, D Neo, and S Vogenauer, 'Introduction', 10.

11

Ending and Changing Performance under Japanese Law

Eriko TAOKA

I. Introduction

Under Japanese law, a party to a contract is entitled to either amend or cancel the contract if the following conditions are satisfied: (i) a circumstance that constitutes a foundation of the contract has changed after the formation of the contract, (ii) the change of circumstance was unforeseeable to both parties at the time of the formation of the contract, (iii) the change of circumstance has occurred due to a reason not attributable to either of the parties, and (iv) the enforcement of the original contract is deemed significantly inequitable to one of the parties in the light of good faith.[1] This rule is called the doctrine of changed circumstances in Japanese law. With the four above-listed requirements, this doctrine is intended to address a situation where the application of the principle of *pacta sunt servanda* would bring about an inequitable consequence to one of the parties in a contract because of a change of surrounding circumstances.[2] Accordingly, the doctrine is viewed as an exception to *pacta sunt servanda*. Although there is no express provision for the doctrine in the Japanese Civil Code (JCC),[3] it is unanimously recognized as a rule derived from the application of good faith (Article 1(2) JCC).[4]

After briefly outlining the historical development of the doctrine of changed circumstances, this contribution will explain the conditions of the doctrine and the discussions around these conditions and will present competing opinions as to the legal consequences of the doctrine's application. This chapter will also introduce discussions concerning the

[1] Masaaki Katsumoto, *Minpō ni okeru jijōhenkō no gensoku* [*The Principle of Changed Circumstances in the Civil Code*] (Yūhikaku 1926) 567; Tomohei Taniguchi and Kiyoshi Igarashi (eds), *Chūshaku minpō (13) hoteiban* [*Japanese Civil Law Annotated (13)*] (rev edn, Yūhikaku 2006) 71–74.

[2] Katsumoto, *Jijōhenkō* (n 1) 567; Hiroshi Suekawa, *Kēyaku sōron* [*Law of Contracts*] (Kōbundō 1932) 194; Sakae Wagatsuma, *Minpō kōgi (Saikenkakuron jōkan)* [*Lecture on Civil Law (Law of Contracts vol 1)*] (Iwanamishoten 1954) 25–26, 178; Kiyoshi Igarashi, 'Jijōhenkō no gensoku no saikentō' ['The Principle of Changed Circumstances Re-considered'] (1975) 8 Hōgaku kyōshitsu 37, 37; Mitsuru Nakayama, 'Jijōhenkō gensoku' ['The Principle of Changed Circumstances'] in Hiroshi Endō, Ryōhei Hayashi, and Hiroshi Mizumoto (eds), *Gendai kēyakuhō taikē (1)* [*Contemporary Contract Law System (1)*] (Yūhikaku 1983) 72; Taniguchi and Igarashi, *Chūshaku minpō* (n 1) 69; Hajime Nakamura, 'Jijōhenkō gensoku no gensokukitē an ni okeru mondaiten' ['Issues Concerning the Amendment Proposal of the Principle of Changed Circumstances'] in Takashi Tsuburaya (ed), *Shakai no henyō to minpōten* [*Changes in the Society and the Civil Code*] (Seibundoh 2010) 329.

[3] Act 89 of 1896. The express provision was not created upon the 2017 amendments to the Civil Code, either (Minpō no ichibu wo kaisē suru hōritsu [Civil Code (Law of Claims) Reform Act] (Act 44 of 2017)). For details, see section V.

[4] Katsumoto, *Jijōhenkō* (n 1) 466, 567.

Eriko Taoka, *Ending and Changing Performance under Japanese Law* In: *Studies in the Contract Laws of Asia V: Ending and Changing Contracts*. Edited by: Mindy Chen-Wishart, Dora Neo, and Stefan Vogenauer, Oxford University Press.
 DOI: 10.1093/oso/9780198995814.003.0011

doctrine during the process of revising the JCC in 2017, which will show the current understanding of the doctrine.[5] Example cases are presented in the pertinent places.

II. The Doctrine of Changed Circumstances in Japanese Law

1. Historical Development

The JCC does not contain an express provision concerning the doctrine of changed circumstances[6] because at the time of the creation of the JCC in 1896, the doctrine of *clausula rebus sic stantibus* had been all but forgotten in Western Europe: since the JCC was created by making references primarily to laws of France and Germany, topics not covered by the French Civil Code or German Civil Code at that time were naturally left out from the JCC.[7]

The introduction and development of the doctrine of changed circumstances in Japanese law owes much to Masaaki Katsumoto's studies on the historical development of the *clausula* doctrine, in particular, the doctrine of *Geschäftsgrundlage* in Germany in the late 1920s. While Katsumoto eventually opposed introducing the idea of *Geschäftsgrundlage* into Japanese law, he proposed the doctrine of changed circumstances.[8] The conditions of the doctrine he originally proposed were later clarified to become those as outlined at the beginning of this chapter. In one of the leading cases involving the doctrine, the Supreme Court of Judicature[9] allowed a seller to cancel the sales contract for land when the price control regulations enacted by the government after the conclusion of the contract rendered it uncertain whether and when the seller could acquire permission to transfer the ownership right to the buyer.[10] This case is the only one where the highest court of Japan granted relief due to changed circumstances. While there are other cases where parties attempted to invoke the doctrine of changed circumstances before the Supreme Court, they

[5] The Legislative Council Subcommittee to amend the Civil Code was established in 2009. The bill to amend the Civil Code was passed by the Diet in May 2017. The 2017 amendments are the first extensive reforms of the Code since its enactment in 1896. The amended Civil Code took effect on 1 April 2020.

[6] While there is no general provision for the doctrine of changed circumstances, there are special provisions representing the doctrine (Act on Land and Building Leases, arts 11, 32; Agricultural Land Act, art 21; Quarrying Act, art 7; Fidelity Guarantee Act, arts 3, 4, and 5; and Trust Act, art 150). For instance, the Act on Land and Building Leases (Act 90 of 4 October 1991) is a special law applicable to lease contracts for land for the purpose of owning buildings and lease contracts for buildings, and its art 11 provides that:

> when the rent becomes unreasonable, as a result of the increase or decrease in tax and other public dues relating to the land or the rise or fall of land prices or fluctuations in other economic circumstances, or in comparison to the rent on similar land in the vicinity, the parties may, notwithstanding the contract conditions, request future increases or decreases in the rent; provided however, that when special provisions exist to the effect that the rent will not be increased for a fixed period, those provisions apply.

The same rule is provided in relation to lease contracts for buildings, as well (art 32). These provisions represent the doctrine of changed circumstances in lease contracts.

[7] Taniguchi and Igarashi, *Chūshaku minpō* (n 1) 69; Supreme Court of Judicature 24 September 1920, 26 Minroku 1343 (stating that a contract must be performed and that a drastic change of the market price of the good at issue would not justify the repudiation of the performance of the contract).

[8] Katsumoto, *Jijōhenkō* (n 1) 54, 559, 799. Katsumoto rejected the introduction of the concept of *Geschäftsgrundlage* because it could allow a contract to be invalidated due to parties' subjective intentions, when such a case should be addressed as a case of mistake.

[9] The Supreme Court of Judicature was the forerunner of the Supreme Court of Japan. The former was abolished in 1947, and the latter was later established.

[10] Supreme Court of Judicature, 6 December 1944, 23 Minshū 613.

have been unsuccessful, which indicates the difficulty of satisfying the conditions of the doctrine.[11]

2. Conditions of the Doctrine of Changed Circumstances

The first condition of the doctrine of changed circumstances is that a circumstance which constitutes a foundational element of the contract has changed after the formation of the contract. In order to satisfy condition (i), the changed circumstance at issue must be expressly or implicitly shared by the parties as part of the foundation of the contract at issue.[12] This will be the case when the circumstance was used to determine the contract price (eg a market condition affecting the value of sales goods, the rental values of leased objects, or the cost of labour in relation to a construction contract). If a factual circumstance is shared by the parties as relating to the purpose of the contract, this circumstance is also considered a foundation of the contract.

A change of such a circumstance must happen after the formation of the contract in order for condition (i) to be met. If a situation changed prior to the formation of a contract, such a change would be addressed under the law of mistake (Article 95 JCC).[13]

Concerning condition (ii), the change of the circumstance at issue must be unforeseeable to both parties at the time of the contract; this is because parties are expected to allocate the risk of the occurrence of an event insofar as the risk is predictable. For example, in the case where a seller sold one of his two houses to a buyer on 21 November 1944 (ie during the Second World War) and later requested to cancel the contract because he lost the other house he owned due to an air attack, the Supreme Court rejected the application of the doctrine because losing the house should have been predictable to the seller, considering the state of the war at the time of the conclusion of the contract.[14] By examining the predictability of the change of circumstances, condition (ii) is intended to establish whether and how the parties allocated or should have allocated the risk associated with the circumstances in question.[15]

In order to satisfy condition (iii), the change in circumstances must have occurred due to a reason not attributable to either of the parties. Typical examples for this situation are changes caused by an event beyond the parties' control (eg war, natural disaster, or the enactment of a new law).[16] This condition is required because no one should be relieved from hardship for which he himself is responsible. If a party is responsible for the occurrence

[11] Supreme Court, 6 February 1951, 5(3) Minshū 36; Supreme Court, 12 February 1954, 8(2) Minshū 448; Supreme Court, 25 May 1956, 10 Minshū 566.

[12] Kiyoshi Igarashi, *Kēyaku to jijōhenkō* [*'Contracts and Changed Circumstances'*] (Yūhikaku 1969) 194.

[13] Taniguchi and Igarashi, *Chūshaku minpō* (n 1) 73; Minpō (Saikenhō) Kaisēkentō Īnkai (ed), *Shōkai saikenhō kaisē no kihon hōshin II kēyaku oyobi saiken ippan (1)* [*Commentaries on the Basic Policy on Amendments to the Law of Claims Contracts and Claims in General (1)*] (Shōjihōmu 2009) 390–91.

[14] Supreme Court, 28 January 1954, 8(1) Minshū 234.

[15] Katsumoto, *Jijōhenkō* (n 1) 25; Hiroyuki Kubo, *Kēzai hendō to kēyaku riron* [*Economic Changes and Contract Theory*] (Seibundoh 1992) 240; Taniguchi and Igarashi, *Chūshaku minpō* (n 1) 73; Hajime Nakamura, 'Kinji no "jijōhenkō no gensoku" ron no henyō to "jijōhenkō no gensoku" ron no zentei no henka ni tsuite' ['Recent Changes of the Doctrine of Changed Circumstances and Overall State of the Principle of Changed Circumstances'] (2009) 6 Meiji Law School Review 113, 132; Yoshio Shiomi, *Shin saikenhō* [*New Law of Claims*] (Shinzansha 2017) 107.

[16] Katsumoto, *Jijōhenkō* (n 1) 583–84; Taniguchi and Igarashi, *Chūshaku minpō* (n 1) 74.

of an event which has made the other party's performance of the obligation difficult, the former party is held responsible for that. In a situation where a change of circumstances (eg inflation) has occurred while a disadvantaged party (eg a seller of land) was in delay in performing her obligation, condition (iii) would not be satisfied. Although the inflation is not attributable to her, the delay is.[17]

Since condition (iii) is also intended to properly allocate the risk associated with the changed circumstance at issue, a risk could be deemed as a reason attributable to a party even if he was not responsible for the risk materializing insofar as the risk itself is considered to be within the scope of his control in the light of good faith. In the first hypothetical treated in section III, if Gina cancelled the hotel room reservation due to her getting sick, the cancellation would be deemed to have been caused by a reason attributable to her even if there was nothing that she could have done about getting sick.

Finally, condition (iv) requires that the enforcement of the original contract is deemed significantly inequitable to one of the parties in light of the good-faith principle. The following three categories are thought to satisfy this condition.[18]

The first category is (a) a case where a purpose of the contract has become disrupted. Since a party's direct purpose in entering into a contract is to receive another party's performance of an obligation, a disruption of the direct purpose of a contract means an impossibility of performance of a party's obligation. As the doctrine of changed circumstances does not cover an impossibility of performance, a disruption of the direct purpose of a contract is also outside the scope of the doctrine.[19] Therefore, cases categorized as (a) are those where a purpose of a contract *other* than the direct purpose has become disrupted.[20] A party's subjective expectation for the contract would not be considered a purpose of the contract unless his expectation is made known to and agreed with the other party as a purpose of the contract.[21] Although a party's expectation does not have to be expressly stated in the contract as a purpose of the contract, the contents of the contract have to be decided by taking into account the expectation.[22] Suppose that a lessee entered into a lease contract for land with the intention to operate a gas station thereon. After the conclusion of the contract, however, a third

[17] Supreme Court, 6 February 1951 (n 11); Supreme Court, 12 February 1954 (n 11); Supreme Court, 25 May 1956 (n 11); Ōsaka District Court, 15 February 1950, 1(2) Kaminshū 212; Kyoto District Court, 15 May 1952, 3(5) Kaminshū 645; Ōsaka High Court, 12 September 1969, 582 Hanrējihō 76; Taniguchi and Igarashi, *Chūshaku minpō* (n 1) 74. For opinions to the contrary, see Katsumoto, *Jijōhenkō* (n 1) 575 (arguing that the doctrine of changed circumstances should be applicable for the reason that the purpose of the doctrine is a fair allocation of the risk that is beyond the control of both parties); Yoshishige Kuroda, 'Jijōhenkō gensoku ni kansuru ichi kōsatsu' ['Some Thoughts on the Principle of Changed Circumstances'] (1967) 11(1) Aichigakuin Law Review 67, 70.

[18] Taniguchi and Igarashi, *Chūshaku minpō* (n 1) 74–76. The categorical analysis was learned from K Larenz, *Geschäftsgrundlage und Vertragserfüllung: die Bedeutung 'veränderter Umstände' im Zivilrecht* (Beck 1957) 89–107.

[19] Taniguchi and Igarashi, *Chūshaku minpō* (n 1) 71; Igarashi, 'Jijōhenkō saikentō' (n 2) 37; Nakayama, 'Jijōhenkō gensoku' (n 7) 75, 77. Impossibility of performance is covered by laws concerning contractual default (JCC, arts 542(1)(i) and (iii) and 415) or risk allocation (art 536). For opinions to the contrary, see Katsumoto, *Jijōhenkō* (n 1) 40–43 (arguing that a case of impossibility of performance can also be covered by the doctrine of changed circumstances because there is a fine line between a case of impossibility and one where the performance is still possible).

[20] Shūsei Ono, 'Mokuteki futōtatsu no fukken' ['Restoration of the Failure to Achieve the Purpose of the Contract'] (2009) 8(1) Hitostubashi Law Review 1, 25.

[21] Hiroshi Endō, 'Jijōhenkō ni yoru kaijo' ['Cancellation Based on Changed Circumstances'] in Kaoru Yunoki, Tomohei Taniguchi, and Ichiro Kato (ed), *Hanrei enshū (saikenhō 1)* [*Practice Case Law (Law of Claims 1)*] (Yūhikaku 1963) 270.

[22] Nakayama, 'Jijōhenkō gensoku' (n 2) 76; Igarashi, *Kēyaku* (n 12) 152–53; Ono, 'Mokuteki futōtatsu' (n 20) 24; Keizo Yamamoto, *Minpō kōgi IV kēyaku* [*Textbook on the Civil Code IV: Contracts*] (Yūhikaku 2005) 113.

party acquired a permit to run a gas station in close vicinity. As a result, the lessee was unable to acquire a permit for his gas station. The lessee was entitled to cancel the contract under the doctrine of changed circumstances because his purpose of running a gas station on the leased premises had been shared with the lessor, and the rent was calculated on that basis.[23]

The second category is (b) a case where one's performance of the contract has become economically 'impossible'. An economic impossibility is determined through weighing a party's cost of performance against the benefit that he expects from the contract. If the cost now significantly exceeds the benefit because of a change of a circumstances, the performance of his obligation is thought to have become economically impossible.[24] However, impossibility of performance is considered to be outside the scope of the doctrine of changed circumstances as the 'impossibility' in case (b) does not mean actual impossibility: it only means a situation where a party's cost of performing his obligation now exceeds the benefit he receives from the contract to a significant extent, albeit not to such a degree that it is considered materially impossible for him to perform the obligation.[25] The classification is made by taking into consideration whether the continuance of the contract is deemed appropriate.[26] If the answer is in the negative, the situation would be treated as a case of impossibility, and there would be no way of invoking specific performance. If the answer is in the positive, it would be covered by the doctrine of changed circumstances, although the dividing line is unclear.

In the last category, (c), the values of the performances in a contract have become economically imbalanced to such a degree that its performance would be significantly inequitable to one of the parties in the light of good faith. Although there is no specific criterion as to the degree of inequitability required, lower courts' decisions in cases involving the inflation after the Second World War can provide a rough idea for the benchmark. There are many cases involving lease contracts concluded before the Second World War with purchase options for agreed prices on the ending of the leases; the rents, therefore, were practically the payment of the purchase price in instalments, and the agreed purchase prices were calculated on the market values of the properties at the time of the contracts. After the war, when the lessees exercised their purchase options, courts applied the doctrine of changed circumstances in cases where the value of the land was now 23 times the contract price due to inflation over 20 years,[27] 36 times over 8 years,[28] and 40 times over 18 years.[29] In contrast, the fluctuation of the market value was not held significant enough to justify the application of the doctrine of changed circumstances where the value of the real estate increased 6 times over 7 years,[30] 4 times over 1 year,[31] and 4 times over 2 years.[32]

[23] Ōsaka High Court, 29 November 1978, 924 Hanrējihō 70.

[24] Minpō (Saikenhō) Kaisēkentō Īnkai, *Shōkai saikenhō kaisē* (n 13) 388–89.

[25] Takao Kanda, 'Rikōshōgai' ['Obstacles to Performance'] (1971) 22(2/3) Otaru University of Commerce Economic Law Review 311, 314.

[26] Nakayama, 'Jijōhenkō gensoku' (n 2) 76; Kubo, *Kēzai hendō* (n 15) 228–29.

[27] Kobe District Court, Itami Branch, 26 December 1988, 1319 Hanrējihō 139.

[28] Ōsaka District Court, 29 August 1959, 10(8) Kaminshū 1812.

[29] Fukuoka High Court, 9 December 1964, 23(12) Minshū 2471. Other cases where the doctrine of changed circumstances was applied: Tokyo High Court, 26 August 1955, 6(8) Kaminshū 1698 (147 times bigger in 10 years); Kanazawa District Court, 24 March 1956, 7(3) Kaminshū 341 (100 times larger in 9 years); Tokyo District Court, 26 November 1959, 210 Hanrējihō 27 (100 times larger in 6 years); Sapporo District Court, 30 July 1976, 851 Hanrējihō 222 (1333 times larger in 29 years).

[30] Supreme Court, 16 June 1981, 1010 Hanrējihō 43.

[31] Tokyo High Court, 20 April 1989, 1313 Hanrējihō 131.

[32] Tokyo District Court, 12 December 1989, 731 Hanrētaimuzu 19.

III. The Hypotheticals

1. Gina and H Hotel

Gina booked a room for the weekend at H Hotel in X City, the capital of country Z. However, she wishes to cancel the room because the inauguration proceedings of the new head of state of Z that were scheduled for Saturday are cancelled. Gina had booked a room overlooking the street where the inauguration procession was supposed to pass by.[33]

In this case, viewing the inauguration procession would be deemed a foundation of the room rental contract if the rental price was higher than usual because of the inauguration procession. (Condition (i) is satisfied.) Condition (iii) would also be satisfied because the cancellation of the procession is not attributable to either party. Condition (iv) would be satisfied as well because viewing the inauguration was shared as a purpose of the room rental contract, especially if it was the basis for calculating the rental. Therefore, Gina would be able to cancel the booking provided that condition (ii) is also met.

In contrast, where Gina wishes to cancel the booking because the exhibition she had intended to visit was cancelled at the very last moment, paying a visit to the exhibition is not likely to be considered a purpose of the room rental contract but rather merely her personal motivation to enter into the contract with H. Even if her motivation was made known to H, a customer's motivation behind the stay at a hotel is generally irrelevant to the hotel. Furthermore, none of the terms of the room rental contract between Gina and H was determined based on her expectation to visit the exhibition.

Where Gina was unable to travel to X City because of an unforeseeable strike by airport personnel, this instance is one where a purpose of the contract has become disrupted since a rental contract for a hotel room is intended for a customer to actually come and use the room. (Conditions (i) and (iv) would be satisfied.) Since the strike was unforeseeable for Gina and the hotel at the time of booking, and furthermore, the strike was not caused by a reason attributable to either of the parties, conditions (ii) and (iii) would be satisfied. By contrast, if Gina decided not to travel to X City because a terrorist group declares that they would launch attacks on tourists in X, whether condition (iv) is satisfied (ie whether a purpose of the room rental contract has been disrupted) would depend on the evaluation of the seriousness of the threat. If, for instance, the threat is grave enough for governmental authorities to issue a warning to not travel to Country Z, a purpose of the contract would be considered to have been disrupted, just like the airport strike example. However, if the societal function of City X remains intact (eg although police security checks in public places become stricter than usual, the government does not issue a warning to not travel to the country), the situation would be considered her voluntary choice not to travel rather than a disruption of a purpose of the contract.[34] If a reason for cancellation is her voluntary choice

[33] The fact scenarios for this and the other hypothetical situations discussed in this section are taken from M Chen-Wishart, D Neo, and S Vogenauer, 'Introduction', ch 1 in this volume, 7–8.

[34] When evaluating the seriousness of the danger to travel to a specific country, the risk evaluation by the governmental authority served as a benchmark. See eg Tokyo District Court, 28 January 2004, 1870 Hanrējihō 50: a customer made a contract with a travel agency for a tour around several countries. However, a warning against traveling to Turkmenistan, which was one of the countries scheduled to be visited in the tour, was issued by the Ministry of Foreign Justice due to the 9/11 terrorist attack. The customer was entitled to cancel the contract.

not to travel, the reason is also considered to be attributable to her, and therefore condition (iii) would not be satisfied either.

In Japan, the COVID-19 pandemic led to cases similar to Gina's booking contract. In one case, X attempted to cancel her wedding venue contract with a wedding company Y because of the risk of contracting COVID-19. X's cancellation was not justified by the doctrine of changed circumstances because the risk was not material enough, and therefore her cancellation was considered her voluntary choice.[35] By contrast, where X's cancellation was made after the government's declaration of state of emergency, the cancellation was considered to have been made because of a reason not attributable to X herself.[36]

2. George and Han

Builder George agreed to refurbish the cellar of Han, the owner of a restaurant. The work was scheduled to start one month after the agreement. Before the work began, the restaurant was completely destroyed by a storm that was much more violent than any other previous storm in the region. However, the cellar remained fully intact. Han immediately informed George of the situation and asked him not to start work. George insisted on rendering performance.

In this case, the fact that the renovation of the cellar was intended to ultimately benefit the restaurant would be considered to comprise a purpose of the renovation contract because the renovation was likely to enhance the operation of the restaurant. Since this purpose has been disrupted by an incident (ie the storm) that was not attributable to either party, conditions (i), (iii), and (iv) would be satisfied. Given the extraordinary severity of the storm, the unforeseeability condition (ii) would also be satisfied. Therefore, Han would be able to cancel the contract. Upon Han's cancellation, George, in principle, would not be entitled to claim against Han for compensation. Although some argue that in a case like this, the cost George incurred to purchase materials should be compensated by Han if the materials are of no use for other construction services George offers,[37] not much academic attention has been paid to whether losses a party has incurred prior to the change of circumstances should be allocated between the parties, and if so, how.[38]

[35] Tokyo District Court, 27 September 2021, 2534 Hanrējihō 70: at the time of X's cancellation in March 2020, the Japanese government had not yet issued a state of emergency. While Y's wedding venue was in Tokyo, there was a total of only 712 COVID-19 cases in Tokyo at that time. Although the Tokyo municipality government requested certain businesses to be closed shortly after X's cancellation, the wedding industry did not fall under this restriction. There were indeed several wedding receptions held at Y's venues on the day X was supposed to have hers.

[36] Nagoya District Court, 25 February 2022, LLI/DB Hanrēhisho. Since the issue in this case was whether Y's claim against X for damages was permissible for the reason that X's cancellation was made by a reason attributable to X, the doctrine of changed circumstances was not contested. The answer is in the negative.

[37] Ono, 'Mokuteki futōtatsu' (n 20) 25.

[38] Igarashi, *Kēyaku* (n 12) 18. As will be explained later in the main text, during the process of the recent amendments to the JCC, a proposal was made to enact an express provision for the doctrine of changed circumstances. In relation to the proposal, it was discussed whether compensation of losses should also be permissible under the doctrine. However, the proposal for creating an express provision of the doctrine itself was turned down (Materials 19–2 for the Legislative Council, Sub-Committee of the Civil Code (Law of Claims) 20 <www.moj.go.jp/content/000052602.pdf> accessed 5 July 2019).

3. Citi Corporation and Drive Bank

Citi Corporation received a loan from Drive Bank in 2015 with a fixed interest rate of 10 per cent for five years. In the 20 years preceding the agreement, the rate of inflation had been relatively stable within a range 1 to 6 per cent. In 2017, the economic situation began to destabilize, and inflation rose to 50 per cent.

The doctrine of changed circumstances would be inapplicable to a loan contract because an adjustment of the loaned amount or interest rate in response to inflation goes against the economic principle of nominalism as applied to an obligation to pay money.[39] Since adjusting one's obligation to pay money in response to an inflation rate potentially influences various contracts in the society, such an adjustment, if necessary, is thought to be better made by the administrative authority rather than the judicial system.[40]

4. Kris and Leila

Kris sold his family home to Leila at 70 per cent of its market value. Both parties assumed that Leila would dedicate it to cultural use by the general public. However, this assumption was not expressly set out in the contract. After the sale, Leila changed her mind and gave the house to one of her sons.

The doctrine of changed circumstances would not be applicable to this case because the possibility that the other party could change her mind after the contract should have occurred to Kris at the time he entered the contract, and therefore condition (ii) would not be satisfied.[41] This case, instead, would be dealt with by the Law of Mistake (Article 95 JCC) or rules for contractual default. If Leila implicitly assumed a contractual obligation to use the house only for a cultural use, Kris is entitled to cancel the contract due to her breach of this obligation (Article 542(1)(v) JCC). Such an obligation could be inferred from the fact that the price of the house was discounted. Alternatively, Kris could also try to rescind the contract on account of his mistake in motivation (Article 95 JCC).

[39] Masao Sanakata, *Kin yakkanron* [*Theory on Gold Clauses*] (Yūhikaku 1939) 447; Hiroyuki Kawachi, 'Kinsen saiken to mēmokushugi' ['Monetary Claims and Nominalism'] in Tsuneo Matsumoto and Yoshio Shiomi (eds), *Hanrei practice minpō II saiken* [*Case Law Practice, Civil Law II, Claims*] (Shinzansha 2010) 7; Supreme Court, 20 June 1961, 15(6) Minshū 1602; Supreme Court, 15 October 1982, 1060 Hanrējihō 76 (stating that a monetary obligation means that the debtor is required to pay the specified amount, except for a situation where an obligor is required to pay in a specific type of currency, such as gold coins, and that there is no justification in law to allow the amount of one's monetary obligation to be adjusted in response to a fluctuation of the value of the currency.

[40] Endō, 'Jijōhenkō ni yoru kaijo' (n 21) 283; Kuroda, 'Jijōhenkō gensoku' (n 17) 76; Kiyoshi Igarashi, *Kēyaku* (n 12) 157, 203–05; Eiichi Hoshino, *Minji hanrē kenkyū (2) saiken* [*Studies on Civil Law Cases (2) Claims*] (Yūhikaku 1972) 290–91. For opinions to the contrary, see Katsumoto, *Jijōhenkō* (n 1) 573, 629; Sōzō Komachiya, *Kahēkachi no hendō to kēyaku* [*Changes of the Value of the Currency and Contracts*] (Yūhikaku 1925) 191; Kikuo Ishida, 'Jijōhenkō no gensoku' (1969) 164 Hōgaku seminā 17, 19; Toshio Hironaka, 'Rippōbu no taiman to minjisaiban no arikata' (1974) 221 Hōgaku seminā 51.

[41] Sakae Wagatsuma, *Minpō sōsoku* [*Civil Law General*] (Iwanamishoten 1965) 240; Minpō (Saikenhō) Kaisēkentō Īnkai, *Shōkai saikenhō kaisē* (n 13) 150.

IV. Legal Effects of the Doctrine

As for the legal effects of the doctrine of changed circumstances, three consequences are proposed: cancellation, amendment, and/or duty to renegotiate the contract. Cancellation is unanimously agreed as a legal effect of the doctrine. However, a consensus has not yet been reached over whether to recognize an amendment of contract and/or a duty to renegotiate as legal effects. There is no consensus on how an amendment of or a duty to renegotiate the contract would operate, what the legal consequences of breaching such duty to renegotiate would be, or on the relationship between the three possible remedies.[42]

1. Cancellation

In the case where the doctrine of changed circumstances becomes applicable, a disadvantaged party may cancel the contract following the general rules of cancellation. In principle, upon a cancellation of a contract, the parties are required to each return the other to the situation they would have been in if there had been no contract (Article 545). If the contract is of a continuous nature, a cancellation only takes effect with regard to the portion that has not been performed yet.[43] When a cancellation is allowed, the other party is not entitled to claim for damages caused by the cancellation (see also the 'George and Han' scenario in section III).

2. Amendment of the Contract

Amendment of a contract by a court is often proposed in academic literature as a legal effects of the doctrine of changed circumstances. The justification for this is that it is reasonable to assume that the parties intend to maintain their contractual relationship as far as possible rather than dissolving it.[44] However, some scholars oppose this position, arguing that amending a contract can lead to unreasonable intervention by the courts into the parties' private autonomy.[45]

Among the scholars who argue for recognizing the amendment of a contract as one of the legal effects of the doctrine of change of circumstances, there are debates on the ways such amendments should operate. A general understanding is that a disadvantaged party acquires a right to request an amendment of the contract and may exercise this right against the other party rather than that the contract at issue is automatically amended should the doctrine of changed circumstances become applicable.[46] Recognizing a right to amend the contract would not be a problem because the right only allows a disadvantaged party to

[42] Taniguchi and Igarashi, *Chūshaku minpō* (n 1) 72, 89.

[43] Igarashi, *Kēyaku* (n 12) 182–83.

[44] ibid. Some also argue that the amendment of a contract should be recognized as a legal effect of the doctrine of changed circumstances because it can be justified as a partial cancellation of the contract. See eg Nakamura, 'Jijōhenkō gensoku' (n 2) 335.

[45] Masanobu Katō, *Shin minpō taikei I minpō sōsoku* [*New Civil Law System I Civil Code General*] (2nd edn, Yūhikaku 2005) 271; Tokyo District Court, 10 May 1961, 12(5) Kaminshū 1032.

[46] Taniguchi and Igarashi, *Chūshaku minpō* (n 1) 88; Yutaka Yamamoto, 'Jijōhenkō no gensoku, saikōshō gimu' (2010) 353 Hōgaku kyōshitsu 76, 79.

make a proposal to amend the contract. The contract would not be amended unless the other party voluntarily agrees with the proposal.[47]

Scholars favouring the amendment option also commonly argue that the possibility of amending the contract at issue should be explored first and that cancellation should be permitted only if an amendment is not feasible.[48] However, opinions vary as to whether an aggrieved party is required to opt for amending the contract if the amendment is objectively deemed reasonable. In terms of the legal proceedings, this raises the question whether a judge may favour amending the contract even when the disadvantaged party opts for cancellation. (i) Emphasizing that a judge is expected to identify and respect a reasonable person's intention in a given case, rather than the actual party's intention, some argue that a judge may amend the contract at issue if a reasonable person would prefer the amendment in the same situation as in a given case.[49] There is also an opinion supporting a judge's power to amend the contract without either party's request for the amendment, on condition that the parties are provided with an opportunity to renegotiate on their own and that the judge takes into account this negotiation process when amending the contract.[50] Others, in contrast, argue that (ii) the disadvantaged party should retain the choice between cancelling and amending the contract because, in light of the parties' private autonomy, a court should not have the authority to bind them to contractual terms different to the original ones without their consent.[51] Those scholars argue that the judge may only decline to cancel the contract in a situation where an aggrieved party opts for cancellation despite the fact that amending the contract is reasonable. This approach is intended to give priority to an amendment over a cancellation without going as far as forcing an aggrieved party to amend the contract against her will in court.[52]

The opinions described above also differ when it comes to the question whether a judge may amend the contract even if the other party, not the aggrieved party, does not consent to the proposed amendment insofar as the amendment is objectively viewed reasonable. Opinion (i) above naturally answers this question in the affirmative. Those supporting opinion (ii) above have different answers: Some argue (a) that an amendment may be made even when the other party wishes to cancel the contract insofar as the amendment is objectively deemed reasonable.[53] Some others argue (b) that amending the contract should not

[47] Kubo, *Kēzai hendō* (n 15) 242; Yamamoto, 'Jijōhenkō' (n 46) 79.

[48] Katsumoto, *Jijōhenkō* (n 1) 598, 611; Wagatsuma, *Saiken kakuron* (n 2) 27; Nakayama, 'Jijōhenkō gensoku' (n 2) 73; Endō, 'Jijōhenkō ni yoru kaijo' (n 21) 272–73; Igarashi, *Kēyaku* (n 12) 165; Eiichi Hoshino, *Minpō gairon IV* (Ryōshofukyūkai 1976) 23; Kubo, *Kēzai hendō* (n 15) 242; Nakamura, 'Jijōhenkō gensoku' (n 2) 333, 336.

[49] Taniguchi and Igarashi, *Chūshaku minpō* (n 1) 90; Ishida, 'Jijōhenkō no gensoku' (n 40) 19; Igarashi, 'Jijōhenkō saikentō' (n 2) 40; Kiyoshi Igarashi, 'Jijōhenkō no gensoku to kōikiso ron' ['The Principle of Changed Circumstances and the Doctrine of Geschäftsgrundlage'] (1978) 3 Jurisuto zōkan hōritsugaku no sōten 231; Kubo, *Kēzai hendō* (n 15) 243; Takashi Uchida, *Kēyaku no jidai* (Iwanamishoten 2000) 111; Kobe District Court, 26 December 1988 (n 27) (the court adjusted the price of the land in a sales contract despite the fact that a party invoking the doctrine of changed circumstances requested a cancellation).

[50] Yasuo Wada, 'Chōki kēyaku to jijōhenkō no gensoku' ['Long-term Contracts and the Principle of Changed Circumstances'] (1998) 1126 Jurisuto 240, 244.

[51] Yamamoto, *Minpō kōgi* (n 22) 109; Minpō (Saikenhō) Kaisēkentō Īnkai, *Shōkai saikenhō kaisē* (n 13) 399.

[52] Some courts' decisions can be explained based on this view. Tokyo High Court, 26 August 1955 (n 29); Kumamoto District Court, Yatsushiro Branch, 15 October 1955, 6(10) Kaminshū 2145; Tokyo District Court, 16 November 1959 (n 29) (allowing a party to cancel the contract taking into account that the other party had refused to amend the contract). Also, Tokyo District Court, 19 August 1959, 200 Hanrējihō 22; Tokyo High Court, 30 June 1987, 1243 Hanrējihō 34 (stating that requesting a cancellation without attempting to amend the price of the contract was not permissible).

[53] Minpō (Saikenhō) Kaisēkentō Īnkai, *Shōkai saikenhō kaisē* (n 13) 399 (proposing that a judge has the power to determine whether the amendment of a contract submitted by a party is reasonable).

be made even if the disadvantaged party opts for the amendment insofar as the other party opts for the cancellation because the latter should not be bound to a contract against her will.[54]

The courts' approach to the amendment of a contract remains unsettled. At the Supreme Court level, there is no case where the Court actually amended a contract as a result of the application of the doctrine of changed circumstances, although in one case the Court mentioned that the amendment could be made under the doctrine.[55] At the lower courts' level, while there are cases where judges adjusted contracts under the doctrine of changed circumstances,[56] opinions vary as to the relationship between cancellation and amendment of the contract. Overall, however, the general tendency seems close to opinion (ii) (b) above because courts tend to respect the parties' choices regardless of the different views on the relationship between cancellation and amendment. Some courts made it clear that contracts should be amended only when both of the parties opt for amendment rather than cancellation.[57] Other courts seem to have let the aggrieved party choose freely between the two effects.[58] Although there are some courts' opinions stating, at least as a matter of principle, that the contract at issue should be amended rather than cancelled insofar as the amendment is objectively reasonable,[59] it is rare for a court to actually amend the contract despite the fact that one of the parties opted for cancellation.[60] Instead, in cases where amending the contract is deemed objectively reasonable, but the aggrieved party insists on cancellation, courts often only take into account the feasibility of amending the contract and allow the cancellation only where a voluntary amendment is considered infeasible (eg where one of the parties has already refused to renegotiate prior to the case being presented before the court).[61]

As for the guiding factors for amending a contract, if an amendment only involves an adjustment of the contract price in response to a change of the market price or associated cost, the task of amendment would not be so complicated.[62] Courts that have made price

[54] Wagatsuma, *Saiken kakuron* (n 2) 27; Nakayama, 'Jijōhenkō gensoku' (n 2) 79.

[55] Supreme Court, 6 April 1956, 10(4) Minshū 342.

[56] Nagasaki District Court, 9 June 1952, 3(6) Kaminshū 791; Sendai High Court, 14 April 1958, 9(4) Kaminshū 666; Fukuoka High Court, 9 December 1964 (n 29); Sapporo District Court, 30 July 1976 (n 29).

[57] Sendai High Court, 14 April 1958 (n 56).

[58] There are cases where courts allowed cancellations upon requests by the aggrieved parties without discussing the possibilities of amending the contracts: Kanazawa District Court, 24 March 1956 (n 29); Ōsaka District Court, 29 August 1959 (n 28); and those where the aggrieved parties requested only amending the contracts and only the possibility of amendment was discussed (Ōsaka District Court, 20 October 1951, 18 Hanrētaimuzu 62); Tokyo District Court, 6 November 1959 (n 29).

[59] Nagasaki District Court, 9 June 1952 (n 56); Tokyo High Court, 26 August 1955 (n 29); Tokyo District Court, 19 August 1959 (n 52); Tokyo District Court, 26 November 1959 (n 29); Takamatsu High Court, 24 October 1960, 11(10) Kaminshū 2286; Ōsaka District Court, 30 June 1966, 370 Jurisuto 3 (stating that the cancellation should be permissible when the other party refused to amend the contract); Kobe District Court, Itami Branch, 26 December 1988 (n 27).

[60] Kobe District Court, Itami Branch, 26 December 1988 (n 27) is such a rare case among the cases cited in n 59.

[61] Nagasaki District Court, 9 June 1952 (n 56) (the aggrieved party only requested for cancellation. The court permitted the cancellation because the other party had refused to adjust the purchase price according to the inflation prior to the case being submitted before the court); Tokyo District Court, 19 August 1959 (n 52) (stating that the cancellation was not permissible, even though the changed circumstance was grave enough to invoke the doctrine of changed circumstances, because the aggrieved party had not attempted to renegotiate with the other party for amending the contract); Tokyo District Court, 26 November 1959 (n 29); Takamatsu High Court, 24 October 1960 (n 59) (permitting the cancellation as requested by the aggrieved party because an amendment proposed by the aggrieved party, which was later considered reasonable by the court, had been turned down by the other party).

[62] Most court decisions that amended contracts involve adjustments of rent in a lease contract for real estate or of the sales price for real estate (eg Ōsaka District Court, 20 October 1951 (n 58) (lease); Sendai High Court,

adjustments seem to take a 'reconciliation-like approach'[63] taking into account various factors, such as an administrative guidance for the price adjustment at issue, if there is any,[64] the prospect of the profits each party originally expected, the potential influence of the price adjustment on each of the parties, and other factors the parties took into account to determine the original contract price.[65]

3. Duty to Renegotiate

Since a duty to negotiate is an obligation to negotiate in good faith, it includes various obligations: initiate a negotiation, when necessary; respond to the initiation; make a proposal; respond to the proposal without delay; make an alternative proposal; respond to the alternative without delay; and provide information necessary for the negotiation.[66] A duty to negotiate can be imposed upon parties in contexts irrelevant to the doctrine of changed circumstance. Parties may also provide for the duty either expressly or implicitly in their contract.[67] Even in the absence of this, a duty to negotiate can be imposed upon the parties in a long-term contractual relationship based on the principle of good faith (Article 1(2) JCC).[68]

In Japan, it is a long-standing practice to insert a term in a contract to obligate the parties to negotiate in good faith for the purpose of adjusting the price in the event where the price has become unreasonable due to an increase or decrease in associated costs, changes in law,

14 April 1958 (n 56) (sale); Fukuoka High Court, 9 December 1964 (n 29) (sale); Sapporo District Court, 30 July 1976 (n 29) (sale); Kobe District Court, Itami Branch, 26 December 1988 (n 27) (sale)). Hiroyasu Ishikawa, '"Saikōshōgimu" ron no kōzō to sono rironteki kiso (2)' ['The Structure and Basis of the Doctrine of Renegotiation (2)'] (2001) 118(4) Journal of Jurisprudence Association 530, 615 (stating that the more complex the task of amending a contract becomes, the more necessary it becomes to encourage the parties' voluntary negotiations).

63 Takashi Uchida, 'Hanrē hihyō: Saihan hēsē 15-nen 10-gatsu 21-nichi' ['Case Review: The Supreme Court, 21 October 2003'] (2004) 121(12) Journal of Jurisprudence Association 147, 164.

64 An administrative guidance regarding the price adjustment in construction contracts was issued in order to deal with the rise of material costs caused by the oil shock in the 1970s. The guidance was referred to by courts to make price adjustments (eg Kobe District Court, 9 July 1982, 483 Hanrētaimuzu 109).

65 Supreme Court, 21 October 2003, 57(9) Minshū 1213; Supreme Court, 21 October 2003, 1844 Hanrējihō 50; Supreme Court 23 October 2003, 1844 Hanreijiō 54 (stating that the factors mentioned in the main text should be taken into account for adjusting the rent). These decisions address lease contracts between real estate developers and landowners. During the bubble economy, so-called 'sublease business schemes' were widely practiced. Under a sublease business scheme, a real estate developer helped a landowner acquire financing from a bank to erect an office building on the land, then rented the building from the owner for 15 to 20 years and subleased it to tenants. In the lease contract for land between the real estate developer and owner, there was a clause to guarantee an annual increase of the rent by a fixed percentage (a rent guarantee clause) because the value of real estate was believed to continue to rise. However, when the economic bubble burst, developers who became unable to pay the rents with the guaranteed increases brought cases before courts, attempting to invalidate the rent guarantee clauses. There were more than 100 such cases submitted to the Tokyo District Court alone (Uchida, *Kēyaku no jidai* (n 49) 114). Although the Supreme Court applied the Act on Land and Building Leases instead of the doctrine of changed circumstances to permit adjustments of the rents, these decisions are viewed as applications of the doctrine of changed circumstances under the guise of the Act (Takashi Uchida, 'Jijōhenkō to kēyaku no kōsokuryoku' ['Changed Circumstances and the Enforceability of Contract'] in Masanobu Kato (ed), *21 Sēki no nikkan minji hōgaku* [*Civil Law Jurisprudence in Japan and Korea in the 21st Century*] (Shinzansha 2005) 8–9).

66 Kazuhiko Matsui, 'Katē shikōteki hōsisutem to saikōshōgimu' ['The Process-Oriented Legal System and the Obligation of Renegotiation'] (1996) 115(1) Hitotsubashi Review 250, 264–66; Yamamoto, *Minpō kōgi* (n 22) 110. See also Ishikawa, '"Saikōshōgimu" ron no kōzō' (n 62) 614.

67 Tokyo District Court, 10 May 1961 (n 45); Tokyo High Court, 29 January 1981, 437 Hanrētaimuzu 112.

68 Ōsaka High Court, 23 February 1979, 580 Kinyūshōjihōmu 34; Tokyo High Court, 29 January 1981 (n 67); Tokyo District Court, 30 January 1981, 453 Hanrētaimuzu 129.

values of the currency, and other economic situations.[69] This practice can help contractual parties to solve their disputes outside the courts without invoking the doctrine of changed circumstance. However, the parties could still resort to the doctrine even if the contract at issue contains a term obligating them to renegotiate because such a duty would not force the parties to agree to amend the contract.[70]

Scholars arguing for a duty to renegotiate as one of the legal effects of the doctrine of changed circumstances justify the imposition of the duty as follows:[71] a party's right to claim for the performance of the other party's obligation transforms itself into his claim for the performance of an adjusted obligation for the reason that the performance of the original obligation has become extremely difficult under the changed circumstances. This transformed claim manifests as a request for a renegotiation and obligates the other party to renegotiate.[72]

Some of the proponents for the duty to renegotiate also attempt to change the nature of the doctrine of changed circumstances as well as the concept of contract. Traditionally, the doctrine of changed circumstances has been intended to rectify situations where the principle of *pacta sunt servanda* leads to inequitable consequences.[73] By dealing with situations beyond the parties' ability to predict, the doctrine governs situations outside the scope of the parties' private autonomy. The concept of contract presumed in this traditional line of thought is a static one: the contents of the obligations are determined at the time of the formation of the contract and are therefore unchangeable. Some scholars challenge this traditional view by introducing a duty to renegotiate into the doctrine of changed circumstances. According to those scholars, the doctrine is not a rule which works outside the scope of private autonomy but rather a rule that supports and facilitates parties' private autonomy; they argue that this is the case because the doctrine, through imposing a duty to renegotiate on the parties, is intended to let them exercise their private autonomy and to restore or rearrange the contractual order by themselves.[74] Based on this view, the

[69] Genichi Endo and Kazuaki Kinoshita, 'Torihiki jitsumu no henyō to torihiki kihon kēyaku' ['Changes in Contracting Practices and Standard Contract Forms'] (2017) 2142 Shōjihōmu 40; Zenichi Shishido, 'Nihon teki torihiki kankō no jittai to henyō' ['Japanese Contracting Practice and Its Changes'] (2017) 2142 Shōjihōmu 11. For example, for construction contracts, construction workers are advised to use standard form contracts prepared by the Central Council for Construction Business (Construction Business Act, art 35). The Central Council for Construction Business is an independent administrative committee established by the Act for the purpose of maintaining fair construction business practices. The standard forms prepared by the Council contain clauses that require the parties to negotiate for the purpose of adjusting the price (eg the standard form for public construction works, art 25). If the negotiation does not lead to an agreement, the contract provides that a party placing the order of the construction is required to inform the other party of the amount (art 25(3) and (7)). If the other party does not agree with the notified amount, the parties may file their case to mediation (art 52).
In a sales contract, it is common to provide the manner for adjusting the contract price. It is also equally common to provide a duty to faithfully negotiate in the event of so-called hardship, Kubo, *Kēzai hendō* (n 15) 205–16.

[70] Kubo, *Kēzai hendō* (n 15) 248–49; Tokyo District Court, 10 May 1961 (n 45); Tokyo High Court, 25 June 1973, 710 Hanrējihō 59; Yokohama District Court, 7 February 1975, 792 Hanrējihō 73; Tokyo High Court 29 January 1981 (n 67).

[71] Wagatsuma, *Saikenkakuron* (n 2) 26; Ishikawa, '"Saikōshōgimu" ron no kōzō' (n 62) 617–18; Kubo, *Kēzai hendō* (n 15) 246. See also Masaaki Katsumoto, 'Kigyō no torihiki hippaku to jijōhenkō no gensoku' ['Financially Difficult Situations of Companies and the Principle of Changed Circumstances'] (1974) 55 New Business Law Journal 6, 9.

[72] Minpō (Saikenhō) Kaisēkentō Īnkai, *Shōkai saikenhō kaisē* (n 13) 394.

[73] See also n 8 and accompanying main text.

[74] Matsui, 'Katē shikōteki hōsisutem' (n 66) 270–71; Kenji Yamamoto, 'Kēyakukōshōkankē no hōtekikōzō ni tsuite no ichikōsatsu (1) (2) (3)' ['Some Thoughts on the Legal Structure of Contractual Negotiation (1) (2) (3)'] (1989) 100(2) Minshōhō zasshi 198, 100(3) Minshōhō zasshi 387, 100(5) Minshōhō zasshi 808; Yutaka Yamamoto, 'Kēyakukihan no kakutoku to sono sētōka' ['Identification of Rules on Contracts and Their Justification'] (1991) 53 Shihō 218; Yutaka Yamamoto, 'Saikōshōgimuron ni tsuite' ['Concerning the Doctrine of Renegotiation'] (2006)

concept of contract is no longer static but rather fluid in the sense that 'contractual obligations are not finalized at the time of the formation of the contract, but rather changed and re-established through the parties' continuous negotiations'[75] even after the formation of the contract. Since a renegotiation, as well as an amendment of a contract, is a process of redefining the contractual obligations, the process is part of upholding a contract, in other words: the principle of *pacta sunt servanda*. In consequence, the doctrine of changed circumstance becomes a rule facilitating the *pacta sunt servanda* principle rather than an exception to it.[76]

A similar view is shared in the so-called relational contract theory. According to this theory, a contract and contractual obligations are not created by the parties' intentions alone. The social norms surrounding the contract also comprise part of the contract and are reflected in the parties' contractual obligations.[77] Among the social norms, those of particular importance are the principle of continuity, which states that the continuity of a contractual relationship should be valued, and the principle of flexibility, which requires a contract to be flexible and adaptable to changing environments.[78] According to this theory, a duty to renegotiate, and to amend a contract, has to be part of the legal effects of the doctrine of changed circumstances so that the doctrine represents these two principles—the principles of continuity and flexibility.[79] Since the relational contract theory also views the concept of contract as a fluid one, the doctrine of changed circumstances is viewed as a rule to support the *pacta sunt servanda* principle.

No consensus has been reached as to whether and how the duty to renegotiate can be part of the legal effects of the doctrine. One reason for this is that there is still ambiguity as to when such a duty is imposed upon parties instead of providing the aggrieved party a right to cancel the contract. Opinions also vary regarding the consequences of one's breach of the duty to renegotiate: some argue that a party breaching the duty to renegotiate loses his right to request an amendment and/or cancellation of the contract, while others argue that a party's breach of the duty to renegotiate only leads to a postponement of his exercise of the right to request an amendment and/or cancellation (which means he may still request an amendment or cancellation if the negotiations are unsuccessful). There is also a school of thought arguing that one party's breach of the duty to renegotiate gives the other party a right to claim damages if any loss or damage occurred due to the lagging negotiations.[80]

63(1) Kyūshū University Journal of Law and Politics 1; Tomohiro Yoshimasa, *Jijōhenkōhōri to Kēyakukihan* [*The Doctrine of Changed Circumstances and Rules on Contracts*] (Yūhikaku 2014) 74–75; Tomohiro Yoshimasa, 'Kēyakutēketsu go no jijōhendō to kēyakukihan no igi (1) (2)' ['A Change of Circumstances after the Contract and the Significance of the Rules on Contracts (1) (2)'] (2003) 128(1) Minshōhō zasshi 43, 128(2) Minshōhō zasshi 3.

[75] Yamamoto, 'Kēyakukōshōkankē (1)' (n 74) 220.

[76] Yamamoto, 'Kēyakukōshōkankē (3)' (n 74) 809; Matsui, 'Katē shikōteki hōsisutem' (n 66) 270–71; Yoshimasa, *Jijōhenkōhōri* (n 74) 74. Accordingly, this school of thought also attempts to substantiate the meanings of the duty of negotiation in order to prevent opportunistic behaviour in the negotiation process: see Ishikawa, '"Saikōshōgimu" ron no kōzō' (n 62); Osamu Morita, 'America ni okeru "saikōshōgimu" ron' ['Discussions on the Duty to Negotiate in American Law'] in Osamu Morita (ed), *Kēyakusekinin no hōgakuteki kōzō* [*The Legal Structure of Contractual Responsibilities*] (Yūhikaku 2006) 334; Yoshimasa, *Jijōhenkōhōri* (n 74) 171.

[77] Uchida, *Kēyaku no Jidai* (n 49) 62–69.

[78] ibid 63; Takashi Uchida, 'Sēdoteki kēyaku to kankēteki kēyaku' ['Systematic Contracts and Relational Contracts'] in Kōji Shindō and Takashi Uchida (eds), *Kēzokuteki kēyaku to shōjihōmu* [*Continuous Contracts and Commercial Legal Practice*] (Shōjihōmu 2006) 24.

[79] Uchida, *Kēyaku no jidai* (n 49) 112.

[80] Ishikawa, '"Saikōshōgimu" ron no kōzō' (n 62) 617–18.

Another argument involves the views towards the doctrine of changed circumstances. As was explained above, some proponents of the duty to renegotiate push forward the concept of a fluid contract. Those scholars also attempt to make the doctrine more relaxed so that its legal effects—a duty to renegotiate and an amendment of a contract, in particular—can play larger roles than they currently do.[81] However, caution is raised against relaxing the doctrine of changed circumstances for the sake of stability of the contract because a party's will, once expressed, should be faithfully observed, which is the basis of the contract as a legal system.[82]

V. Current State of the Doctrine: A Failed Attempt at Codification

During the discussion on the 2017 amendments to the JCC, the enactment of an express provision for the doctrine of changed circumstances was proposed, but this was eventually turned down.[83] One reason is that the members of the Legislative Council were unable to reach consensus on the legal effects of the doctrine as outlined above.[84] Another reason lies in the opposing views towards the doctrine as described above. Among the members of the Legislative Council, the lawyers in particular expressed strong concerns about making an express provision of the doctrine, arguing that this could lead to too many attempts by parties to plead the doctrine.[85] By contrast, the academics among Council members argued that such concerns can and should be addressed by clarifying the conditions of the doctrine.[86] However, the practitioners' reserved attitude towards the application of the doctrine persisted and took the form of attempts to make the conditions of the doctrine even stricter than those currently recognized in order to make sure that the doctrine would not be easily invoked.[87] Furthermore, the practitioners in the Legislative Council also opposed the idea of providing the amendment of a contract as one of the legal effects because, according to them, that would lead to a court's excessive intervention into parties' private autonomy.

The fact that the Legislative Council eventually gave up on creating an express provision for the doctrine is testament to the ambiguity of the contents of the doctrine despite the fact that its existence has been well established in Japanese law. One way of clarifying the contents of the doctrine would be to wait for more court decisions applying the doctrine. However, that would likely not happen in the near future because the prevalent contracting practice of inserting a term to negotiate in good faith into contracts would limit the role of the doctrine in the Japanese society. In fact, during the recent COVID-19 pandemic, those good-faith negotiation terms seem to have played a far more important role than the doctrine of changed circumstances.[88] The government's approach to potential disputes related to the doctrine of changed circumstances during the pandemic was also to issue various

[81] Uchida, 'Jijōhenkō' (n 65) 21.

[82] Nakamura, 'Kinji no "Jijōhenkō"' (n 15) 129; Shiomi, *Shin saikenhō* (n 15) 101, 103.

[83] Legislative Council, Subcommittee of the Civil Law (Law of Claims), minutes of the 75th Meeting on 30 July 2013 <www.moj.go.jp/shingi1/shingi04900189.html> accessed 5 July 2019.

[84] Materials 19-2 for the Legislative Council (n 38) 21.

[85] Legislative Council, Subcommittee of the Civil Code (Law of Claims), minutes of the 19th Meeting on 30 November 2012, 19–24 <www.moj.go.jp/shingi1/shingi04900056.html> accessed 5 July 2019.

[86] ibid 20, 27–30.

[87] Materials 82-2 for the Legislative Council, Subcommittee of the Civil Code (Law of Claims) 9–10 <www.moj.go.jp/content/000125960.pdf> accessed 5 July 2019.

[88] Hiroyasu Ishikawa, 'Pandemic ni yoru jijōhenkō to kēyaku no kaitē' ['Circumstances Changed by the COVID-19 Pandemic and Amendments of Contracts'] (2021) 72(1) Journal of Social Science 29, 35.

instructions that reminded the public of the importance of voluntary negotiations without specifying the manner of adjusting the contract prices in specific types of contracts.[89] Perhaps owing to this contracting practice, no court decision is officially reported where a dispute was caused by the pandemic and solved by the doctrine of changed circumstances. However, that does not negate the importance of the doctrine as a rule for the Japanese society. Although it is hardly ever applied in courts, the doctrine continues to provide the general guidelines as to the ways in which parties deal with unpredictable circumstances.

VI. Further Hypotheticals

In closing, this section will supply answers to the remaining two hypothetical situations proposed by the volume editors.[90]

1. Easy and Frugle

Suppose Easy leased business premises from Frugle for a fixed period of 15 years. Shortly after the contract had been concluded, a nearby military airport was unexpectedly shut down for political reasons. The government invested an enormous amount of public funds in order to improve the commercial infrastructure in the area. As a result, Easy's profits became 500 per cent of what could reasonably have been expected at the time of making the contract. At the same time, the rental value of comparable business premises in the area rose to 500 per cent of the agreed rental price.

The Act on Land and Building Leases contains a provision to respond to changes in the market values of the rental property (Article 11).[91] Frugle may request increase of the rent in response to the increase of the rental value in accordance with this article without having to resort to the doctrine of changed circumstances.

2. Abraham and Bill

In 1567, Abraham entered into a contract for an unlimited period of time with farmer Bill under which Abraham promised to build and maintain an irrigation channel from which

[89] Ministry of Justice, 'Shingata korona wirusu kansenshō no ēkyō wo uketa chintaishaku kēyaku no tōjisha no minasama e' ['For People Who Have Difficulty Performing Their Lease Contracts Because of the COVID-19 Pandemic'] <www.moj.go.jp/content/001320302.pdf> accessed 25 May 2020 (suggesting parties in lease contracts confer in good faith in the case where lessees have faced difficulties paying the rent); Ministry of Land, Infrastructure, Transport and Tourism, 'Shingata korona wirusu kansenshō ni kakaru taiō ni tsuite' ['Responses to the COVID-19 Pandemic'] <www.mlit.go.jp/common/001340555.pdf> accessed 31 March 2020 (concerning lease contracts for business purposes, such as running restaurants, and suggesting parties confer in good faith to cope with difficulties caused by the pandemic); Financial Services Agency, 'Chinryō no shiharai ni kakaru jigyōshatō e no hairyo ni tsuite' ['As for Consideration and Care for Tenants with Difficulties Paying the Rent'] <www.fsa.go.jp/news/r1/shouken/20200508_1.pdf> accessed 8 May 2020 (suggesting financial institutions confer in good faith with tenants in lease contracts the financial institutions maintain as part of their investment).

[90] The fact scenarios of these hypothetical cases are taken from M Chen-Wishart, D Neo, and S Vogenauer, ch 1 'Introduction', 7–8.

[91] See (n 6) for the text of this norm.

Bill could extract water at a fixed price. By 2018, inflation and the rise in the cost of maintenance and labour have made the price wholly inadequate. Abraham's successors in law ask for an increase in the price that would provide them with adequate compensation. Alternatively, they wish to terminate the contract.

The doctrine of changed circumstances would likely be inapplicable to this case because the inflation and rise in the cost of maintenance and labour in this example would happen in the natural course of events. If one wishes to enter into a contract the duration of which is potentially as long as 500 years, one should anticipate such changes of circumstances. According to the schools of thought that view the doctrine as a rule to facilitate parties' negotiations and voluntary amendments under changed circumstances, the conditions of the doctrine could be relaxed to govern a case like this example.[92] However, this is not the predominant view in Japan. A feasible way to open negotiations with Bill's successors would be for Abraham's successors to use a right to terminate the contract as an instigator because a continuous contract with an unspecified duration is, in principle, terminable at any time in Japanese law.[93] In a continuous contractual relationship, a justifiable reason for termination is often required by case law, and the fact that Abraham's successors would not be able to keep the contract without incurring losses would be seen as a justifiable reason for terminating the contract.[94] With the right to terminate the contract, Abraham's successors could negotiate the compensation with Bill's successors even though such a negotiation is not the consequence required by law.[95]

[92] Uchida, 'Jijōhenkō' (n 65) 21 (stating that if a long-term contract is reasonably crafted but does not specify the way to adjust the price in response to changes in the associated costs or market, the contract should be interpreted to mean that parties deliberately left the matter open to re-negotiation. Therefore, parties should be obligated to renegotiate and adjust the price under the doctrine of changed circumstances).

[93] Hiroyasu Nakata, *Kēzokuteki torihiki no kenkyū* [*Study on Continuous Transactional Relationships*] (Yūhikaku 2000) 134.

[94] A typical example of a justifiable reason for cancellation is the deterioration of the other party's financial status or behaviour by the other party that has damaged the trust between the parties. Situations where a party wishes to terminate the contract may also be taken into account. Hiroyasu Nakata, *Kēzokuteki torihiki* (n 93) 135–36; Tokyo District Court, 28 August 1987, 1274 Hanrējihō 98.

[95] Tokyo District Court, 13 April 1995, 675 Rōdōhanrē 13: This was a case where an employer, wishing to change some terms of the employment contract, offered his employee a new employment contract with the condition that the latter would be dismissed if she did not take the offer. The court stated that the employer was entitled to dismiss her upon her refusal to take the offer, provided that changing the terms of the existing employment contract was requisite for the employer's business operation to such a degree that the necessity for the changes exceeded the disadvantage the employee suffered because of the changes, and provided that there was an unavoidable reason that justified the employer's dismissal of the employee upon the latter's refusal to take the offer, and provided furthermore that the employer had made sufficient efforts to avoid the dismissal. Although an employer's right to dismiss his employee is subject to special restrictions under Japanese labour law, this case illustrates that the right to terminate a contract can serve as an impetus to renegotiate terms of the contract.

12

Termination of Contracts under Japanese Law

Akira KAMO

I. Introduction

1. An Overview of Termination of Contracts under Japanese Law

Once parties have entered a contract, they are bound by its terms. Termination of contract means that parties are released from the binding contract, and that requires a justification. The *Minpo*, the Japanese Civil Code of 1896 (JCC),[1] includes various provisions for the termination of contracts. Some of these were substantially revised by the Civil Code (Law of Obligations) Reform Act 2017 (2017 Reform).[2] It is essential to gain an overall picture of the termination of contracts and identify the rules governing breach of contract within this system.

(a) Termination on completion of the purpose of contract

First, a contract is terminated when its purpose is accomplished by the performance of the obligations. When a seller delivers goods conforming to the terms of the contract and the buyer pays the agreed price, both parties' contractual obligations are discharged (Article 473 JCC), resulting in termination of the sales contract. In the case of continuous contracts, such as lease (*chintaishaku*) or employment contracts (*koyo*), if the contract parties agreed a fixed term, expiration of that term brings the contract to an end (Articles 622 and 597(1) JCC), unless it is renewed by reference to the parties' express or implied intention or statutory provision.[3] When no fixed term is specified for a continuous contract, each party may

[1] *Minpo* [Civil Code] (Act No 89 of 1896). The Japanese Civil Code was enacted in two stages. The Parliament passed and promulgated Book 1 (General Provisions), Book 2 (Property Rights), and Book 3 (Obligations) of the Civil Code on 27 April 1896 (Act No 89 of 1896), and Book 4 (Family) and Book 5 (Succession) of the Civil Code on 21 June 1898 (Act No 9 of 1898). They together came into effect on 16 July 1898. As a result of the law reform in 2004, it was clarified that the Civil Code is one law in legislative form. For a historical overview of the Japanese Civil Code, see Y Yamashita, 'Formation of Contract in Japan' in M Chen-Wishart, A Loke, and S Vogenauer (eds), *Studies in the Contract Laws of Asia, vol II: Formation and Third Party Beneficiaries* (OUP 2018) 244 and M Okino, 'The Interpretation of Contracts under Japanese Law' in M Chen-Wishart and S Vogenauer (eds), *Studies in the Contract Laws of Asia, vol III: Contents of Contracts and Unfair Terms* (OUP 2020) 161–62.

[2] *Minpo no Ichibu wo Kaiseisuru Houritu* [Civil Code (Law of Obligations) Reform Act] (Act No 44 of 2017). The Act came into force from 1 April 2020. For the background of the 2017 Reform, see H Sono, L Nottage, A Pardieck, and K Saigusa, *Contract Law in Japan* (Wolters Kluwer 2019) 24–25; Okino (n 1) 162–63. See also A Kamo, 'Crystallization, Unification, or Differentiation? The Japanese Civil Code (Law of Obligations) Reform Commission and Basic Reform Policy' (2010) 24 Columbia Journal of Asian Law 171, 176–87.

[3] Several types of continuous contracts are presumed to be renewed after expiration of a fixed term (JCC, arts 619(1) and 629(1)), based on the presumed intention to renew the contract. Such contracts are not renewed if a party expresses a contrary intention.
From the early twentieth century, special legislation accumulated to protect the rights of the lessee of land or houses. These were combined in the Act on Land and Building Leases of 1991 (*Shakuchishakuyaho*, 'ALBL'), which provides that lease of land or buildings is deemed to be renewed upon expiration of a fixed term under

Akira Kamo, *Termination of Contracts under Japanese Law* In: *Studies in the Contract Laws of Asia V: Ending and Changing Contracts*. Edited by: Mindy Chen-Wishart, Dora Neo, and Stefan Vogenauer, Oxford University Press.
 DOI: 10.1093/oso/9780198995814.003.0012

in principle terminate the contract by giving notice to the other party, with termination taking effect after a reasonable period of time (Articles 617(1) and 627(2) JCC).[4]

(b) Termination without accomplishing the purpose of contract

A contract may be terminated without the parties having accomplished its purpose. The JCC contains 13 types of nominate contracts[5] and, for some of these, provides details on when a contract is automatically terminated by operation of law. In this respect, the legal characterization of the contract is of great practical significance.

Termination of a contract may also be effectuated by one or both of the contract parties. In this chapter, this type of termination is referred to as 'cancellation' (corresponding with the concept of *kaijo* under Japanese law). This may occur by the contracting parties' agreement to release each other from the contract, either by new agreement after the conclusion of the contract (*goi kaijo*) or by reference to a term in the original contract giving one or both parties the right to cancel the contract when a certain event occurs (*yakujo kaijo*).

Cancellation of contract is also permitted in accordance with statutory provisions (*hotei kaijo*). When a contract party fails to perform her obligation, the other party may cancel the contract under several conditions (Articles 540–548 JCC). In addition, regarding several types of nominate contracts, the JCC allows a contract party to cancel the contract without assuming a breach of contract (*nini kaijo*). Here, too, the legal characterization of the contract has practical importance.

2. Plan of This Chapter

After briefly discussing the automatic termination of contract by operation of law (section II), this chapter will explain how contracts are cancelled under Japanese law. First, cancellation by an agreement of the contracting parties is examined (section III). Secondly, statutory cancellation of a contract not based on breach of contract (voluntary cancellation) is explained (section IV). Then, cancellation for breach of contract or non-performance of obligation is investigated (section V). Comparing the original provisions of the JCC with the ones revised in the 2017 Reform sheds light not only on the legal developments in Japanese contract law but also on the characteristics of Japanese legal scholarship. After an examination of the requirements for a cancellation of contract, we move on to the effects of cancellation of contracts (section VI) and finally, when the right to cancel a contract is lost (section VII).

several conditions, and the lessor can refuse only when there is a justifiable reason (ALBL, arts 5, 6, 26, and 28). Since restrictions on the termination of lease may deter owners of land or buildings from renting out their property, the ALBL also establishes several types of lease contracts which are not subject to provisions on the renewal of lease contracts (ALBL, arts 22–25 and 38–40).

[4] To strengthen the legal status of the lessee of a land lease, the ALBL sets the minimum term of a land lease at 30 years (ALBL, art 3) and includes provisions for continuity protection of building leases without a fixed term (ALBL, arts 27(2) and 26(2), (3)).

[5] The concept of contract under Japanese law (*keiyaku*) has a broad scope and includes gratuitous contracts, such as gift (*zoyo*), loan for use (*shiyotaisyaku*), and mandate (*inin*), which are not regarded as contracts under common law.

II. Automatic Termination of Contract by Operation of Law

The JCC provides for some nominate contracts that a contract is terminated automatically when certain circumstances arise.[6] An example for this is the mandate (*inin*), a contract where one party (mandator) commissions the other party (mandatary) to perform a juristic or legal act, for example to conclude a contract (Article 643 JCC). The JCC provides that a mandate terminates (i) when a mandator or a mandatary dies, (ii) when a mandator or mandatary is subject to an order commencing bankruptcy proceeding, or (iii) when the family court declares a guardianship over the mandatary (Article 653 JCC). The rationale for this provision is that a mandate is based on a mutual relationship of trust between mandator and mandatary.[7] Thus, contract parties would have the intention to bring the mandate to an end when one of them dies.[8] The commencement of bankruptcy proceedings would undermine the basis of trust and thus of the mandate.[9] A person subject to guardianship (a ward) cannot perform a juristic or legal act by herself, and the mandator would not put trust in the guardian who could perform the juristic or legal act in lieu of a ward.[10]

Loss of property is also a ground for automatic termination for several types of contracts.[11] A lease (*chintaishaku*) is terminated when the whole leased property becomes unusable or unprofitable due to grounds such as destruction (Article 616-2 JCC). When a leased property is completely destroyed, the lessor can no longer make the property available for the borrower. In response to this, rent ceases to be incurred; thus, the lease comes to an end.[12]

[6] A loan for use (*shiyotaisyaku*), where a borrower has the right to use the property of a lender gratuitously and is obliged to return it (JCC, art 593), terminates when a borrower dies (JCC, art 597(3)). A loan for consumption (*shohitaishaku*), where a borrower borrows property (most typically money) and is obliged to return a thing of the same type, quality, and quantity to the lender (JCC, art 587), is terminated when it is made in writing and either of the parties receives an order commencing bankruptcy proceedings before the borrower receives the property from the lender (JCC, art 587-2(3), see section IV.2).
Although there is no express provision in the Civil Code, it is generally accepted that an employment contract is terminated when the employee dies (S Wagatsuma, *Saiken Kakuron, Chukan 2 (Minpo Kogi V3) [Special Part of the Law of Obligation, vol 2-2 (Lectures on the Civil Code, vol V-3)]* (Iwanamishoten 1962) 593; H Nakata, *Keiyakuho* [*Contract Law*] (new edn, Yuhikaku 2021) 501).

[7] K Ume, *Minpo Yogi, Makinosan, Saikenhen* [*Essence of the Civil Code, vol 3, Law of Obligations*] (33rd edn, Yuhikaku 1912) 754–55.

[8] Supreme Court, 22 September 1992, Kinyuhomujijo 1358, 55. This is the default rule. If the parties agreed to the contrary, the mandate continues and the heirs of the deceased step into her shoes (JCC, art 896). Article 506 of the Commercial Code (*Shoho*) also provides that a mandate of commercial transaction does not terminate upon the death of the principal.

[9] Ume (n 7) 755. However, bankruptcy of the mandator does not necessarily undermine the mutual relationship of trust between the parties. The Supreme Court held that on the bankruptcy of a limited liability company (mandator), its director (mandatary) does not lose her position (Supreme Court, 10 June 2004, Minshu 58 (5) 1178).

[10] Ume (n 7) 755.

[11] Before the 2017 Reform, a bilateral contract (eg a sales contract) may terminate automatically when the performance of obligation has become impossible due to grounds not attributable to either party, by application of a provision on allocation of risk of loss (JCC, former art 536(1)). For details, see section V.1(a)(2)(ii).

[12] JCC, art 616-2 should be applied by analogy to other types of contracts, such as loan for use (*shiyotaisyaku*) and bailment (*kitaku*) (Nakata (n 6) 191, 555).

III. Cancellation of Contract Based on Agreement of the Contract Parties

1. Agreement after Conclusion of Contract

Contract parties who have bound themselves in a contractual relationship are free to agree to release themselves from it. They can make a new agreement for cancellation independently of any breach of contract. No writing is required; a mere consensus of the parties is sufficient to bring a contract to an end.

Cancellation has retroactive effects only when the parties agree on this. Since a contract binds in principle only the parties who conclude it, an agreement of cancellation of contract has no retroactive effects with regard to third parties.[13]

2. Agreed Right of Cancellation

(a) Validity

The parties may insert clauses in their contract that grant one or both of the parties the right to cancel the contract unilaterally if certain events occur (eg financial difficulties of a contract party).[14] The validity of such clauses is judged by the general rules of contract law. If a cancellation clause violates mandatory law, it is void.[15] For example, the Consumer Contract Act (*Shohishakeiyakuho*, CCA) provides that when a contract between a consumer and a business trader includes a clause that grants the business trader the right of cancellation solely because the consumer has received a decision for commencement of guardianship (*koken*, Article 7 JCC), curatorship (*hosa*, Article 11 JCC), or assistance (*hojo*, Article 15 JCC), this clause is void (Article 8-3 CCA). This kind of cancellation clause would have stifling effects on the filing of petitions for guardianship, curatorship, or assistance, which is contrary to the objectives of law to protect those with disabilities.[16]

A cancellation clause is also void if it contravenes the principle of good faith (Article 1(2) JCC) or is against public policy (Article 90 JCC). In this respect, the CCA expressly provides for the nullity of clauses in consumer contracts:

[13] Nakata (n 6) 188; Sono and others (n 2) 141.

[14] A contract party exercises the right of cancellation by manifestation of intention to the other party (JCC, art 540(1): see section V.3(b)).

[15] Another example is a clause in a full-payout finance lease contract stipulating that the contract may be cancelled on the ground of a petition for commencement of civil rehabilitation proceedings. In a 2008 judgment, the Supreme Court held this to be void. The objective of civil rehabilitation proceedings is to maintain the whole property held by a debtor in financial difficulties and appropriately coordinate legal relationships between the debtor and her creditors based on a rehabilitation plan (Civil Rehabilitation Act, *Minjisaiseiho*, art 1). While a leased asset under a full-payout lease contract is significant of security, cancellation of the contract would take the asset away from debtor's estate. This is contrary to the objective of civil rehabilitation proceedings (Supreme Court, 16 December 2008, Minshu 62 (10) 2561). On the other hand, the validity of a cancellation clause for commencement of bankruptcy proceeding has not been judged by the Supreme Court, and there are conflicting academic opinions.

[16] Shohishacho Shohishaseidoka [Consumer Affairs Agency, Legal System Planning Division], *Chikujokaisetsu Shohishakeiyakuho* [*Commentary on the Consumer Contract Act*] (4th edn, Shojihomu 2019) 269–70.

> Article 10 (Nullity of Clauses Unilaterally Prejudicial to Consumers' Interests)
> A consumer contract clause is void if it deems a consumer's nonfeasance to manifest an intention to make an offer or accept an offer of a consumer contract, or if it otherwise restricts consumer's rights or expands consumer's obligations as compared to when statutory default rules are applied, unilaterally prejudicing the interests of the consumer in violation of the fundamental principle provided in Article 1(2) of the Civil Code.

This involves two steps in judging whether a consumer contract clause is void: (i) whether it restricts a consumer's rights or expands a consumer's obligations as compared to the statutory default rules and (ii) whether it prejudices the interests of the consumer in violation of the principle of good faith. In practice, Article 10 CCA has considerable significance for consumer transactions and there are numerous Supreme Court decisions on this provision.[17]

(b) Provisions in the Civil Code: Agreement on earnest money

The Civil Code contains several provisions which assume that parties of a sales contract have agreed on a right of cancellation even if they did not explicitly refer to cancellation of the contract.[18] Article 557(1) JCC[19] on earnest money (*tetsuke*) is of particular practical and theoretical importance. If a buyer pays earnest money, the buyer may cancel the contract by waiving the earnest money, or the seller may cancel the contract by reimbursing the buyer twice this amount before the counterparty commences to perform her obligation. A drafter of the Civil Code 1896 explained that Article 557 CC reflected a custom of earnest money in Japan.[20]

Article 557(1) JCC was criticized by legal scholars after the Second World War for weakening the binding force of contracts.[21] It was considered to reflect premodern Japanese society and legal practice, where the fundamental principle of Western contract law, *pacta sunt servanda*, was not appropriately understood and accepted. From the 1990s onwards, however, Article 557(1) JCC has been re-evaluated. It is pointed out that earnest money is used most typically for sales of immovables and is not unusual in contracts of valuable assets for parties to reserve a cancellation right; thus Article 557(1) JCC can be justified

[17] A recent example is a 2022 Supreme Court judgment concerning a clause in a housing lease that granted the immediate cancellation right of the lease to the company who guaranteed the lessee's obligations (Supreme Court, 12 December 2022, Minshu 76 (7) 1696). For restrictions on cancellation of lease of immovable, see section V.1(c)(3).

[18] Another example is an agreement on the redemption of immovables (*kaimodoshi*). A seller of immovable property may cancel the sale by refunding the price and costs of the contract paid by the buyer in accordance with a special agreement on redemption executed simultaneously with the contract for sale (JCC, art 579). This kind of agreement on redemption has long been employed for financial purposes in Japan. The Civil Code contains detailed provisions on redemption of immovables aimed to protect the seller-debtor (Ume (n 7) 545). JCC, art 579 originally stipulated that the amount paid for redemption was restricted to that of the sales price and the costs of the contract paid by the buyer. Because of this restriction, the agreement on redemption became unpopular as a method of granting credit, and other legal methods such as mortgage by transfer (*jototanpo*) have been developed in financial practice by case law. Although the 2017 Reform relaxed the restrictions on the redemption price by permitting parties to agree an amount exceeding the sales price, agreements on redemption of immovables are unlikely to become widespread again as a method of granting credit (Nakata (n 6) 345).

[19] JCC, art 557 is applied *mutatis mutandis* to other types of onerous contracts (JCC, art 559).

[20] Ume (n 7) 481–82.

[21] Most notably, S Kurusu, *Nihon no Tetsukeho [Law on Earnest Money in Japan]* (1964) 80(6) Hogakukyokaizasshi 719, reprinted in *Kurusu Saburo Chosakushu III [The Collected Works of Saburo Kurusu, vol 3]* (Shinzansha 2004) 215.

in modern legal practice.[22] In addition, there is doctrinal support for Article 557(1) JCC since the parties may restrict the binding effects of a contract by their consensus.[23] Thus, the criticism voiced against Article 557(1) JCC has recently been tempered, which illustrates a transition of thought in Japanese legal scholarship.[24]

IV. Statutory Rights of Cancellation Not for Breach of Contract (Voluntary Cancellation)

The JCC contains provisions for several nominate contracts that allow a party to cancel the contract at her discretion.[25] The rationales for these rights of voluntary cancellation are based on the nature of the relevant nominate contract. In this section, the voluntary cancellation of a contract for work (*ukeoi*) and mandate (*inin*) are examined.[26]

1. Contract for Work

(a) Provisions in the Civil Code

A contract for work is a contract where one of the parties (contractor) promises to complete specified work and the other party (client) promises to pay remuneration for the outcome of the work (Article 632 JCC). Article 641 JCC gives a client the right of voluntary cancellation:[27]

> Article 641 (Cancellation of Contract by Client)
> A client may cancel the contract for work at any time whilst the contractor has not completed the work by paying compensation for damages.

[22] M Yokoyama, *Minpo 557 Jo (Tetsuke) [Article 557 of the Civil Code (Earnest Money)]* in T Hironaka and E Hoshino (eds), *Minpoten no Hyakunen III* [*Centenary of the Civil Code, vol 3*] (Yuhikaku 1998) 334–35.

[23] Y Shiomi, *Keiyaku Kakuron I* [*Contract Law, Special Provisions, vol 1*] (Shinzansha 2002) 74.

[24] Y Shiomi, *Shin Keiyaku Kakuron I [New Series of Contract Law, Special Provisions, vol 1]* (Shinzansha, 2021) 94–96.

[25] Manifestation of intention to the debtor is required to cancel a contract (JCC, art 540(1): see section V.3.(b)).

[26] While the JCC does not require the written form for gratuitous contracts, it admits their voluntary cancellation. A donor may cancel the oral gift whose performance has not been completed (JCC, art 550). This rule induces parties to make a gift in a written form, which helps to make the contents of gift clear and prevent the reckless promise of a gift. See T Hironaka (ed), *Minpo Shuseian (Zensanhen) no Riyusho [Exposition of the Revised Draft of the Civil Code (Book I, II and III)]* (Yuhikaku, 1987) 528–29. JCC, art 593-2 (a loan for use) and art 657-2(2) (gratuitous bailment) are also justified on similar grounds.
A loan for consumption (*shohitaishaku*) is classified as a real contract and delivery of property (most typically, money) is required for formation. This has been criticized because it is impractical for financial institutions that an agreement on loan for use is not enforceable prior to delivery of money (Yamashita (n 1) 245). The 2017 Reform relaxed this prerequisite; a loan for consumption becomes effective based on the written agreement (JCC, art 587-2(1)). In this case, the borrower may cancel the loan before the delivery of property with payment of compensation to the lender (JCC, art 587-2(2)). It is meaningless that the borrower receives the unnecessary property and gives it back immediately (Nakata (n 6) 357). Voluntary cancellation right of a bailor (JCC, art 657-2(1)) is justified on the similar grounds.

[27] A contractor may also cancel the contract if a client receives an order commencing bankruptcy proceedings before the work is completed (JCC, art 642(1)) to avoid the risk of not being paid on completion (JCC, art 633) and may participate in the distribution of the bankruptcy estate with respect to the remuneration for the work already completed and expenses not included therein (JCC, art 642 (2)). The bankruptcy trustee may not claim for damages suffered from the cancellation of contract (JCC, art 642(3)).

Because an agreed work is usually carried out for the benefit of the client, it is meaningless that the contractor continues work which the client no longer wants. Thus, the client may cancel the contract any time before completion by the contractor, on payment of compensation to the latter.[28]

On the other hand, once a contractor has completed the work, the client may no longer cancel the contract at her discretion. In this regard, Article 634 JCC[29] deals with *partial* completion of the work:

> Article 634 (Remuneration in Proportion to Benefit Received by Client)
> In the following cases, if a client receives any benefit from the performance of any divisible portion of the outcome of the work that the contractor has already completed, that portion is deemed to be the completed work; in this case, the contractor may demand remuneration in proportion to the benefit to be received by the party ordering work:
> (i) if the contractor is no longer able to complete the work due to any grounds not attributable to the client; or
> (ii) if the contract for work is cancelled before the completion of work.

When the client cancels the contract in accordance with Article 641 JCC and has received any benefit from the performance of any divisible portion of the outcome of work that the contractor has already completed, the contractor may demand remuneration in proportion to the benefit received by the client.[30]

One of the problems concerning Article 634(ii) JCC is whether it applies where a client (or a contractor) has not cancelled the contract, for example, when a contractor abandoned building a house halfway through because of financial distress, but the client does not cancel the contract, instead concluding a contract with another contractor to erect the house. Some maintain that Article 634(ii) JCC can be applied by analogy and the contractor may demand remuneration in proportion to the work already done.[31] A different approach is expressed in a Supreme Court judgment,[32] holding that the contractor may claim for the value of construction materials provided by her but incorporated by a third party into the property of the client, who thus gains ownership of the materials, through the doctrine of specification (*kako*) (Article 246(2) JCC). The contractor may demand compensation for unjust enrichment against the client (Article 248 JCC).

(b) The hypotheticals

(1) Coco and David

Coco, a famous architect, agrees with David that he will landscape the garden in her next development. He is due to start work on 1 December. For David, this is an important

[28] Ume (n 7) 721–22.

[29] JCC, art 634 was introduced in the 2017 Reform aiming to codify judicial precedents. It was held that the work is deemed as partially completed, even before its perfection, if the performance of the contractor is divisible and the client enjoys the benefit from the partial performance; the client can cancel only the remaining part of contract (Great Court of Judicature, 30 April 1932, Minshu 11, 780. See also Supreme Court, 17 February 1981, Hanreijiho 996, 61).

[30] If the contractor may demand the partial remuneration pursuant to JCC, art 634(ii), this will leave little compensation of damages (JCC, art 641) to be claimed.

[31] O Kasai, '*634 Jo*' ['Article 634 CC'] in Y Yamamoto (ed), *Shin Chushaku Minpo (14)* [*New Series of Commentary on the Civil Code, vol 14*] (Yuhikaku 2018) 200.

[32] Supreme Court, 25 January 1979, Minshu 33(1) 26.

opportunity to make his name as a landscape gardener. On 1 October, Coco tells him that she is no longer interested because the development will not include a garden after all. David has already purchased materials. He estimates that his future earnings will be 10 per cent lower because he will not be able to benefit from having worked with Coco. Can he insist on doing the work? Can he bring an action for breach of contract?[33]

The contract between Coco and David is likely to qualify as a contract for work, and Coco may cancel the contract at her will at any time before David accomplishes his work (Article 641 JCC). When Coco cancels the contract, David can not insist on continuing his work, but he may claim for compensation of damages including the price of purchased materials and the amount of the agreed remuneration, from which the amount of expected costs is deducted.

(2) Bob and Sue

Bob contracts to build a house for Sue for the price of $100,000. After doing a third of the work he abandons the job, leaving behind material worth $15,000, which Sue later uses to finish the works. Can Bob claim the value of the work done or of the materials?

The construction contract between Bob and Sue is typical of a contract for work. If Sue has cancelled the contract expressly or implicitly, Bob may claim remuneration for the part of work completed if his performance is divisible and Sue enjoys the benefit from the partial performance (Article 634(ii) JCC). Even if Sue did not cancel the contract, Bob may claim proportional remuneration if the application by analogy of Article 634(ii) JCC is affirmed. Otherwise, Bob still may demand recovery for unjust enrichment from Sue since he lost the ownership of building materials by completing the construction work (Articles 246(2) and 248 JCC).

2. Mandate

Article 651 deals specifically with the cancellation of a mandate as follows:

(1) A mandate may be cancelled by either party at any time.
(2) In the following cases, a party that has cancelled a mandate pursuant to the preceding paragraph must compensate for damage suffered by the other party; provided, however, that this does not apply if there was a compelling reason for the termination:
   (i) if the party cancels the mandate at a time that is detrimental to the other party; or
   (ii) if the mandator cancels the mandate for which the purpose includes the interests of the mandatary (excluding the profit to be obtained exclusively by receiving remuneration).

As we have seen in section II, a mandate is based on a mutual relationship of trust between mandator and mandatary. Thus, whenever a party loses trust in the other, she may cancel the mandate.[34] Since the benefits which the other party expected from the mandate should be guaranteed, the party who cancels the mandate at a time that is detrimental to the other

[33] The fact scenarios for the hypotheticals discussed in this section are taken from M Chen-Wishart, D Neo, and S Vogenauer, 'Introduction', ch 1 in this volume, 9 and 10.
[34] Ume (n 7) 751.

party must compensate in damages, unless there are unavoidable grounds for cancellation (Article 651(2)(i) JCC). Furthermore, a mandator should pay compensation for loss caused by a cancellation of the contract if the mandatory was to receive non-monetary benefits from the mandate (Article 651(2)(ii) JCC).[35]

V. Statutory Rights of Cancellation for Breach of Contract

While voluntary cancellation is allowed only for specific types of nominate contracts, cancellation for breach of contract is permitted for all types of contracts[36] as a general remedy for the aggrieved party.[37] The grounds for cancellation of contract were substantially revised by the 2017 Reform. Comparing the original and the revised provisions, this section explores the legal developments with regard to the grounds for cancellation of contract (section V.1 and 2), then examines the requirements for exercising the right of cancellation (section V.3).

1. Legal Developments before the 2017 Reform

(a) Original provisions in the Civil Code 1896

(1) Cancellation with demand to perform obligation within a reasonable period of time

> Former Article 541 (Right to Cancel for Non-Performance such as Delayed Performance)
> In cases where one of the parties does not perform her obligation, if the other party demands performance of the obligation, specifying a reasonable period of time, but no performance is tendered during that period, the other party may cancel the contract.

In principle, the aggrieved party cannot cancel the contract immediately on breach but must give the breaching party a second chance to fulfill her obligations. It is only after the passing of an additional reasonable period of time without the breach being remedied that the aggrieved party is allowed to cancel the contract (former Article 541 JCC).

The former Article 541 JCC revised a provision of the Japanese Civil Code of 1890 (Old Civil Code), which was abolished as a result of enactment of the Civil Code of 1896 without

[35] These rules are based on judicial precedents (Supreme Court, 19 January 1981, Minshu 35 (1) 1) and were codified by the 2017 Reform.

[36] Hironaka (n 26) 519. The concept of cancellation for breach under Japanese law covers both bilateral contracts (eg sales) and unilateral contracts (eg gift). It has a wider scope than that under German law (*Rücktritt*), which only deals with bilateral contracts.

[37] Before the 2017 Reform, the former art 635 JCC prevented a client from cancelling the contract for work under which the contractor undertook to construct a building or other immovable structure on land, after completion by the contractor, even if the completed structure had serious defects. The rationale was that, otherwise, the contractor would be obliged to demolish the immovable structure, imposing a serious burden on the contractor and causing negative consequences on the national economy (Ume (n 7) 711–12). With the development of construction technology, however, this rationale is no longer persuasive. In 2002, the Supreme Court finally adopted the position that a client may require the contractor to pay the amount needed to have another constructor demolish the defective building and rebuild it (Supreme Court, 24 September 2002, Hanreijiho 1801, 77). Although the Supreme Court did not permit the client to cancel the contract, it accomplished the same goal by awarding compensation. The former art 635 JCC became a dead letter and was abolished by the 2017 Reform.

ever having come into effect. The Old Civil Code was drafted under the leadership of a French law professor, Gustave Emile Boissonade, and its provisions were coloured by the French legal tradition. Article 421(2) of the Old Civil Code (Book of Property) required the aggrieved party to file a petition to court in order to cancel the contract. The court then had a discretionary power to bestow an additional period of time for performance on the breaching party, considering the parties' circumstances. The Civil Code of 1896 made it unnecessary to file a petition to the court, but it employed an additional period of time for performance as a prerequisite for cancellation of contract. The underlying idea was that since cancellation is a drastic remedy, it is reasonable to give the breaching party a second chance to perform her obligations.[38]

Drafters of the Civil Code 1896 explained that the former Article 541 to be included therein covered all cases where a contract party fails to perform her obligations while performance is still possible, that is, all cases of delayed, incomplete, and defective performance. Impossibility of performance was regulated by the former Article 543 JCC.[39]

(2) Cancellation without demand to perform obligation (immediate cancellation)

(i) Delay where time is of the essence The Civil Code 1896 also included two provisions allowing immediate cancellation:

> Former Article 542 (Right to Cancel for Delayed Performance Where Time Is of the Essence)
> In cases where, due to the nature of the contract or manifestation of intention by the parties, the purpose of the contract cannot be achieved unless the obligation is performed at a specific time on a certain date or within a certain period of time, if one of the parties has failed to perform the obligation at the time that period lapses, the other party may immediately cancel the contract without making the demand referred to in the preceding Article.

If time is of the essence for performance, the subsequent performance is meaningless for the creditor, and thus immediate termination is allowed.[40] The aggrieved party must be able to show that performance precisely on time is regarded as essential to the contract based on the nature of the contract or the parties' agreement.

There has been one important special rule, Article 525 of the Commercial Code (*Shoho*):

> Article 525 (Cancellation for Delayed Performance in Sales Contract between Merchants Where Time Is of the Essence)
> In a sales contract between merchants where, due to the nature of the contract or manifestation of intention by the parties, the purpose of the contract cannot be achieved unless the obligation is performed at a specific time on a certain date or within a certain period of time, if one of the parties has failed to perform the obligation at the time that period lapses, the other party is deemed to cancel the contract unless she immediately demands that the breaching party perform the obligation.

[38] Hironaka (n 26) 519.
[39] ibid 520.
[40] ibid 519–20.

A sales contract between merchants is deemed to be cancelled where time is of the essence and there is a delay in performance. Here, an aggrieved party neither has to make a demand of performance to the breaching party nor manifest an intention to cancel (see section V.3(b)). It is vital for transactions between merchants to fix the legal status as soon as a breach has occurred and to prevent the aggrieved party from speculating unfairly at the risk of breaching party.[41]

(ii) Impossibility of performance

> Former Article 543 (Right to Cancel for Impossibility of Performance)
> If performance of the debtor's obligations has become impossible, in whole or in part, the creditor may cancel the contract; provided, however, that this shall not apply if the impossibility of performance is due to reasons not attributable to the debtor.

Since giving an additional period of time to the breaching party is pointless when performance of all her obligations have become impossible, the aggrieved party may cancel the contract immediately. Immediate cancellation for *partial* impossibility was considered to be permissible only when the *partial* impossibility is serious enough to justify immediate cancellation.[42]

Importantly, the former Article 543 JCC, unlike the former Article 541 JCC, required that the impossibility of performance be attributable to the debtor. The rationale was to exclude cases covered by provisions on allocation of risk of loss (the former Articles 534–536 JCC). There are three grounds for the impossibility of performance.[43] First, if the impossibility is attributable to the creditor, the creditor cannot cancel the contract. Secondly, if the impossibility of the performance was not attributable to either party (eg when the performance became impossible due to *force majeure*), the contractual relationship was regulated by the provisions on allocation of risk of loss in the former Article 536(1) JCC:

> Former Article 536 (Risk of Loss Allocated to Debtor)
> (1) Except in the cases provided for in the preceding two Articles, if the performance of any obligation has become impossible due to grounds not attributable to either party, the debtor does not have the right to receive performance in return.

While the debtor was exempted from the obligation, she lost the right to claim performance against the creditor. The contract was automatically terminated by operation of law.[44]

[41] H Tanikawa, '542 Jo, IV' ['Article 542, IV'] in T Taniguchi and K Igarashi (eds), *Shinpan Chushaku Minpo (13)* [*New Edition of Commentary on the Civil Code, vol 13*] (Yuhikaku 1996) 697–98.

[42] S Wagatsuma, *Saiken Kakuron, Jokan (Minpo Kogi V1)* [*Special Part of the Law of Obligations, vol 1 (Lectures on the Civil Code, vol V-1)*] (Iwanamishoten 1954) 173.

[43] Ume (n 7) 429–30; N Matsunami, K Niho, and M Niida, *Teikoku Minpo Seikai, Saiken* [*Authentic Interpretation of the Civil Code in the Empire of Japan, The Law of Obligations*] (Nihonhoritsugakko 1903) 890–91.

[44] Before the 2017 Reform, the former art 534 JCC included provisions which allocated the risk of loss to the creditor; where the purpose of a bilateral contract was the creation or transfer of rights in a specific property (eg sales contract), if the property had been lost or damaged due to reasons not attributable to the debtor, such loss or damage fell on the creditor. This was, however, criticized as being unfair to the creditor (buyer) since it was unlikely that she could manage the risk of loss before delivery of property. The former art 534 JCC was abolished by the 2017 Reform (see n 74).

Finally, where impossibility of performance was attributable to the debtor, the creditor could no longer enforce the right to performance but could release herself from the contractual relationship by cancelling the contract (the former Article 543 JCC).

(iii) The seriousness of non-performance Besides the former Articles 542 and 543 JCC, the Civil Code 1896 allowed immediate cancellation for serious non-performance in certain types of nominate contracts. For instance, where a seller sells property belonging to a third party, she must acquire the property from the third party to transfer to the buyer (former Article 560 JCC). Otherwise, the buyer may cancel the sales contract immediately (former Article 561 JCC) since the seller's failure to acquire the property is serious enough to justify immediate cancellation.[45]

Regarding lease contracts, Article 612 JCC, which was not amended in 2017, stipulates that a lessee may not assign her rights or sublet without approval of the lessor (Article 612(1) JCC). Violation of this allows the lessor to cancel the lease contract immediately (Article 612(2) JCC). Since there is a risk that the lessee who had once assigned her rights or sublet without the lessor's consent might repeat the same kind of violation, the type of violation is serious enough to justify immediate cancellation.[46]

(iv) Frustration of the purpose of contract by partial non-performance The Civil Code *before* the 2017 Reform contained provisions for certain types of contracts that allowed the aggrieved party to cancel the contract immediately when the other party *partially* failed to perform her obligations and the purpose of contract was frustrated by the *partial* non-performance. Most of these provisions were regarding seller's warranty[47] and were applied *mutatis mutandis* to other types of onerous contracts (Article 559 JCC).

The former Article 566(1) JCC provided that where the sales property was encumbered with the security right of a third party, the buyer could cancel the contract if she had not known of the encumbrance and could not achieve the purpose of the contract because of the encumbrance. This provision was also applied *mutatis mutandis* where the property sold had defects unknown to the buyer at the time of conclusion of contract (former Article 570 JCC).[48] A drafter of the Civil Code explained that since it was the seller's duty to supply the buyer with the property conforming to the terms of contract, the buyer was allowed to cancel the whole contract immediately if she could not achieve the purpose of contract by the property received.[49]

[45] Hironaka (n 26) 543.

[46] Ume (n 7) 654–55. Regarding restrictions on the cancellation of a lease of immovables pursuant to art 612(2) JCC, see n 70.

[47] Regarding a contract for work, the former art 635 JCC provided that a client may cancel the contract when there was any defect in the object of work performed and the purpose of the contract could not be achieved because of the defect, unless the object of the work performed was to construct a building or other immovable structure on land (see also n 36).

[48] In addition, the former art 563 JCC provided that in a sales contract where a seller could not transfer part of the right covered by the contract because the part of the right belonged to the third party, and this was unknown to the buyer, who would not have bought the rights if she had known the full facts, she could cancel the sales contract. This provision was applied *mutatis mutandis* to cases involving a shortage in the object of the sales contract made for a designated quantity and cases where part of the object was already lost at the time of the contract if the buyer did not know of the shortage or loss (former art 565 JCC).

[49] Ume (n 7) 498–99, 504, 507, 525–26.

(b) German influence and its reflection

While the Old Civil Code belonged to the French legal tradition, the Civil Code 1896 was drafted with reference to the laws of various jurisdictions, including the first and second drafts of the German Civil Code. Subsequently, German legal scholarship exerted a far-reaching influence on Japanese legal scholarship. Various German concepts and doctrines were introduced and provisions of the Civil Code that had origins distinct from German law were construed in a German way. This phenomenon was later called 'reception of doctrines' (*Theorienrezeption*).[50] Criticism of this academic attitude already existed in the 1920s. From the 1960s onwards, the consequences of 'reception of doctrines' were thoroughly re-examined by legal scholars.[51] Cancellation for breach of contract provides illustrative examples of such scholarly transition in Japan.

(1) Tripartite categorization of non-performance

First, a tripartite categorization of non-performance was introduced from German law: impossibility (*Unmöglichkeit*), delayed performance (*Verzug*), and imperfect performance or positive violation of obligations (*positive Forderungsverletzung*).[52] Based on this trichotomy, a prevailing view in legal scholarship divided grounds for cancellation of contract into five categories: (i) delayed performance in general, (ii) delayed performance where time is of the essence, (iii) impossibility of performance, (iv) incomplete performance which can be cured by subsequent performance, and (v) incomplete performance which cannot be cured by subsequent performance. Giving an additional period of time for remedying the breach of contract was required only for (i) and (iv).[53]

The tripartite categorization of non-performance derived from the uniqueness of the German Civil Code before its modernization in 2002. Regarding claims for damages, the German Civil Code originally included only provisions on impossibility of performance and delayed performance (former Articles 280 and 286 of the German Civil Code). Incomplete performance, which was not provided for in the German Civil Code, was considered to require a separate category of non-performance.

On the other hand, the JCC adopted a unitary concept of non-performance for claims for damages (former Article 415 JCC) and cancellation of contract (former Article 541 JCC). There was little need for establishing incomplete performance as a separate category. In the 1960s, research into the Japanese reception of German legal doctrines revealed no clear reason for giving absolute priority to the German trichotomy, and its necessity has been reconsidered in the academe.[54]

[50] Z Kitagawa, *Nihon Hogaku no Rekishi to Riron* [*History and Theories of Japanese Legal Scholarship*] (Nihonhyoronsha 1968) 25–26.

[51] See also Okino (n 1) 162.

[52] For the Japanese reception of the trichotomy of non-performance from German law, Kitagawa (n 50) 21–23; S Hayakawa, *Fukanzenriko, Sekkyokuteki Saikenshingai* [*Imperfect Performance, Positive Violation of Obligation (Positive Forderungsverletzung)*], in E Hoshino (ed), *Minpo Koza 4, Saiken Soron* [*Course of Lectures on the Civil Code, vol 4, General Part of Law of Obligations*] (Yuhikaku 1985) 54–60.

[53] Wagatsuma (n 42) 152.

[54] Hayakawa (n 52) 61–71. See also K Nakata, 'Performance and Monetary Remedies for Breach of Contract in Japan' in M Chen-Wishart, A Loke, and B Ong (eds), *Studies in the Contract Laws of Asia, vol I: Remedies for Breach of Contract* (OUP 2016) 111.

(2) Debtor's fault as a subjective requirement for cancellation

As we have seen, the former Article 543 JCC required for immediate cancellation that the impossibility be attributable to the debtor. After the enactment of the Civil Code, a view had prevailed in legal scholarship under German influence that the debtor's fault (*Verschulden*), a subjective requirement, was a prerequisite for any kind of cancellation for breach of contract.[55]

In the mid-1980s, however, a critical view emerged influenced by the United Nations Convention on Contracts for the International Sale of Goods (CISG). Accordingly, cancellation of contract is a remedy for a contract party to release herself from the contractual relationship when she can no longer expect to gain the benefits for which she entered the contract. Since cancellation is not considered a sanction against the debtor who failed to perform her obligations, the debtor's fault is not necessary as a prerequisite for cancellation. Even when the non-performance is not attributable to either of the parties, it is reasonable to allow the aggrieved party to cancel the contract if the non-performance has serious effects on her interests.[56]

(3) Seller's warranty as statutory liability

The JCC originally contained provisions on a seller's warranty that allowed the buyer to cancel the sales contract immediately. After the enactment of the Civil Code 1896, legal scholars inspired by German legal scholarship attached different meanings to these provisions, especially the former Article 570 JCC on delivery of defective property.[57]

It was pointed out that in a case of sales of a *specific* property the seller was released from her obligation by delivering the property even if it possessed defects. The underlying doctrine was that a *specific* property was the only thing of its kind that existed in the world and contract parties could not make an agreement that the seller was obliged to deliver a non-defective property.[58] The buyer could not require the seller to repair the defective property or deliver a substitute property free from defects, while she must make full payment. This unfairness led to the special strict liabilities imposed under the former Article 570 JCC. Unlike contractual liability, this was not premised on the seller's fault, while the scope of the seller's liability was limited to reliance damages and the buyer could not claim for expectation damages.[59] This view was later called 'statutory liability doctrine' and accepted widely in practice.

However, criticism of this statutory liability doctrine grew from the 1960s.[60] Critics cast doubt on the doctrinal distinction between *specific* and *non-specific* property. Even with a

55 Wagatsuma (n 42) 153, 173, 175.

56 Y Shiomi, *Saiken Soron I* [*General Part of Law of Obligations vol 1*] (2nd edn, Shinzansha 2003) 430–32.

57 A representative work was K Yunoki, *Urinushi Kashitanposekinin no Kenkyu* [*Study on Seller's Warranty on Defective Property*] (Yuhikaku 1963).

58 S Wagatsuma, *Saiken Kakuron, Chukan 1 (Minpo Kogi V2)* [*Special Part of the Law of Obligations, vol 2-1 (Lectures on the Civil Code, vol V-2)*] (Iwanamishoten 1957) 272.
To justify this doctrine, the former art 483 JCC was often cited (see Nakata (n 54) 125). It provided that the debtor was obliged to deliver a specific property on an 'as-is' basis as at the time when the delivery was due. This article has been considered a default rule and was not applied if the parties agreed to the contrary. Therefore, the traditional prevailing view had attached an exaggerated importance to this article. The 2017 Reform amended art 483 JCC to clarify that parties may agree otherwise and now it is considered not to justify the doctrine regarding sales of a specific property.

59 Wagatsuma (n 58) 271. See also Nakata (n 54) 125–26.

60 See eg the monumental work by Z Kitagawa, *Keiyaku Sekinin no Kenkyu* [*A Study on Contractual Liability*] (Yuhikaku 1963). See also Shiomi (n 23) 183–86.

sales contract of *specific* property, it would be possible for parties to make an agreement that the seller should deliver a non-defective property. If the seller delivered defective property, the buyer should be granted the same remedies as in a case of sales of *non-specific* property. This view, called the 'contractual liability doctrine', which was consistent with the position of the Civil Code drafters, became influential among legal scholars and there emerged judicial precedents which seemed to be favourable to it.[61] According to this view, issues related to a seller's warranty could be regulated by general provisions on claims for damages (former Article 415 JCC) and those on cancellation of contract (former Articles 541, 542, and 543 JCC), and the necessity of special provisions on a seller's warranty should be re-examined.

(c) Legal developments by judicial precedence

(1) Reasonableness of additional period of time and necessity of demand

Judicial precedents also played an important role in the 2017 Reform. Regarding the former Article 541 JCC, the Great Court of Judicature (*Taishinin*), the highest Japanese court until 1947, held that the aggrieved party was allowed to give the breaching party a relatively short period to complete the performance, assuming that the breaching party should have already prepared the performance for the most part.[62] Furthermore, it held that even if the aggrieved party did not specify an additional period of time, the aggrieved party could cancel the contract after a reasonable period of time had passed from the time of the demand of performance.[63] Thus, setting an additional reasonable period was understood in practice as just a matter of procedure, not a substantial requirement for cancellation of contract.[64]

Furthermore, it was also disputed whether contract parties could agree that no demand was required for a cancellation of the contract. The Supreme Court acknowledged the validity of such an agreement in the lease of immovables,[65] while it also imposed additional requirements for such cancellations (see section V.3). In legal scholarship, an immediate cancellation clause is considered valid, unless it violates mandatory law, is against public policy (Article 90 JCC), or contravenes the principle of good faith (Article 1(2) JCC).[66]

(2) Cancellation of contract for partial non-performance

Regarding cancellation of contract for partial non-performance, judicial precedents outside the scope of provisions in the Civil Code 1896 were established. When a debtor's contractual obligation was divisible and the debtor fulfilled her obligation only in part, the principle was that the creditor could cancel the remaining part of the contract. The cancellation of the contract as a whole was allowed only when the creditor could not achieve the purpose of contract from the partial performance.[67] When a debtor (eg a seller) performed

[61] Supreme Court, 26 January 1996, Minshu 50 (1) 155; Supreme Court, 1 June 2010, Minshu 64 (4) 953.

[62] Great Court of Judicature, 15 July 1924, Minshu 3, 362.

[63] Great Court of Judicature, 2 February 1927, Minshu 6, 133.

[64] For detailed analysis on judicial precedents, see O Morita, *Keiyaku Sekinin no Hogakutekikozo* [*Legal Structure of Contractual Liability*] (Yuhikaku 2006) 433–39.

[65] Supreme Court, 5 April 1962, Minshu 16 (4) 679; Supreme Court, 2 July 1965, Minshu 19 (5) 1153; Supreme Court, 21 November 1968, Minshu 22 (12) 2741.

[66] T Uchida, *Mino II, Saiken Kakuron* [*Civil Code II, Special Part of the Law of Obligations*] (3rd edn, Tokyodaigakushuppannkai, 2011) 91; Nakata (n 6) 208.

[67] Great Court of Judicature, 19 February 1925, Minshu 4, 64.

its principal duties (eg the duty to deliver sales goods), but failed to fulfill its ancillary duties (eg the duty to provide information about the sales goods), the creditor could cancel the contract only when this violation frustrated the purpose of contract.[68]

(3) Restriction on cancellation requiring the seriousness of non-performance

There were also legal developments that aimed to restrict cancellation of lease contract. After the Second World War, Japan suffered from a housing shortage, and the cancellation of a lease imposed a considerable burden on the lessee to find a new residence or business facilities. From the 1960s onwards, by a series of Supreme Court judgments, cancellation of a lease of immovable property was strictly limited to cases where the lessor could prove that the lessee's violation of an obligation constituted a collapse of the personal relationship of trust between parties.[69] In such cases, the lessee did not need to give the lessor an additional period of time for remedying the breach of contract[70] because the continuation of the lease was no longer desirable. Here, the seriousness of the manner of violation also afforded a ground for immediate cancellation.[71]

After the housing crisis had passed, the judicial precedents on the restriction of cancellation of lease of immovable property were maintained. This can be justified by protecting the parties' expectations for the continuity of the contract.[72] In cases of continuous contracts, contract parties make relation-specific investments and have expectations for the continuity of their contractual relationship, which should be protected in certain cases by way of restricting the cancellation of contract. It has been reported that at the lower court level, justifiable grounds are required for cancelling long-term distribution contracts or franchise contracts.[73]

2. 2017 Reform

(a) No subjective requirement

Against a backdrop of the recent shift of legal scholarship, the 2017 Reform adopted the position that the debtor's fault is not a prerequisite for cancellation of contract:

> Article 543 (Non-Performance Due to Grounds Attributable to Creditor)
> If non-performance of an obligation is due to grounds attributable to a creditor, the creditor may not cancel the contract under the preceding two Articles.

While a creditor may not cancel the contract when the debtor's non-performance is attributable to herself, she may cancel the contract even if non-performance was not attributable

[68] Supreme Court, 6 April 1967, Minshu 21 (3) 533.

[69] Supreme Court, 28 July 1964, Minshu 18 (6) 1220; Supreme Court, 21 April 1966, Minshu 20 (4) 720.

[70] Supreme Court, 20 February 1975, Minshu 29 (2) 99.

[71] The cancellation pursuant to art 612(2) JCC (see section V.1(a)(2)(iii)) was also restricted. Even when a lessee sublet without consent of the lessor, if the lessee could prove the circumstances that the lessee's violation of duties did not constitute the destruction of personal relationship of trust with the lessor, cancellation of the lease was not permitted (Supreme Court, 25 September 1953, Minshu 7 (9) 979).

[72] Uchida (n 66) 83–85, 244–45.

[73] Sono and others (n 2) 137–38.

to the debtor.[74] Unlike the former Article 543 JCC, the revised Article 542(1) JCC does not require for cancellation that the impossibility is attributable to the debtor.

As a result of the 2017 Reform, the provisions on risk allocation also needed to be revised:

> Article 536 (Risk of Loss Allocated to Debtor)
> (1) If the performance of an obligation becomes impossible due to grounds not attributable to either party, the creditor may refuse to perform counter-performance.

The creditor is granted the right to refuse performance under the revised Article 536(1) JCC. If the creditor wants to extinguish her obligations, she must resort to the right of cancellation.[75] In this way, the Civil Code demarcates cases covered by provisions on the allocation of risk of loss from those by provisions of cancellation.

(b) Cancellation with demand to perform an obligation within a reasonable period of time

While the reformed Civil Code maintained the general rules of cancellation under Article 541 JCC, a proviso was added:

> Article 541 (Cancellation with Demand to Perform of Obligation)
> In cases where one of the parties does not perform her obligation, if the other party demands performance of the obligation, specifying a reasonable period of time, but no performance is tendered during that period, the other party may cancel the contract; provided, however, that this does not apply if the non-performance of the obligation upon expiration of the period is regarded as minor in light of the purpose of contract and common sense in the transaction.

Thus, cancellation is not allowed if a party's failure to perform an obligation upon expiration of the additional period of time is considered 'minor' in light of the purpose of the contract and common sense in the transaction. Drafters of the 2017 Reform explained that the criterion of 'minor' non-performance under Article 541 JCC was more relaxed than that for immediate cancellation under Article 542(1)(v) JCC: the failure to 'achieve the purpose of the contract'.[76] Even when there remains the possibility that an aggrieved party could accomplish the purpose of the contract after the lapse of the additional period, she may cancel the contract unless the non-performance upon expiration of the period is judged as minor. Influenced by the prevalent understanding in practice that setting an additional period of

[74] T Tsutsui and H Muramatsu (eds), *Ichimon Itto Minpo (Saikenkankei) Kaisei* [*Questions & Answers on the Civil Code (Law of Obligations) Reform*] (Shojihomu 2018) 232.

[75] In addition, a new provision on allocation of risk of loss was introduced:

> Article 567 (Transfer of Risk of Loss)
> (1) If a seller delivers a property (which is limited to one that has been ascertained as the subject matter of the sale; hereinafter the same applies in this Article) to the buyer, and the property is lost or damaged after the time of the delivery due to any grounds not attributable to either party, the buyer may not demand cure of the non-conformity of performance, demand a reduction of the price, claim compensation for loss or damages, or cancel the contract, on the ground of the loss or damage. In such a case, the buyer may not refuse to pay the price.

Based on the criticism of the former art 534 JCC (see n 43), the rule was adopted that the risk of loss was transferred by delivery of property.

[76] Tsutsui and Muramatsu (n 74) 236.

time under Article 541 JCC is just a procedural requirement for the cancellation of contract (see section V.1(c)(1)), the 2017 Reform adopted the position that the aggrieved party may cancel the contract pursuant to Article 541 JCC irrespective of whether she may still gain the expected benefit from the contract. This rule may provide certainty for the aggrieved party about a possible cancellation and enable her to engage in a substitute transaction.

This explanation is, however, criticized by legal scholars since there is no clear reason for different criteria to be employed for cancellation under Article 541 JCC and under Article 542(1) JCC.[77] It is also proposed that both of the criteria can be subsumed under the superordinate concept of 'material breach of contract (material non-performance)'.[78] There is still no established view on the relationship between these criteria, and judicial precedents are expected to determine this point.

(c) Cancellation without demand to perform the obligation (immediate cancellation)

(1) Grounds for immediate cancellation

The grounds for immediate cancellation are now collectively stipulated in Article 542(1) JCC:

> Article 542 (Cancellation without Demand to Perform Obligation)
> (1) In the following cases, a creditor may immediately cancel the contract without making the demand referred to in the preceding Article:
> (i) where performance of the obligation in whole is impossible;
> (ii) where the debtor clearly expresses the intention to refuse to perform the obligation in whole;
> (iii) where performance of a part of the obligation is impossible, or where the debtor clearly expresses the intention to refuse to perform a part of the obligation, and if the purpose of the contract cannot be achieved by performance of the remaining part of obligation;
> (iv) where, due to the nature of the contract or a manifestation of intention by the parties, the purpose of the contract cannot be achieved unless the obligation is performed at a specific time on a certain date or within a certain period of time, and if the debtor has failed to perform the obligation at that time that period lapses; or
> (v) besides the cases set forth in the preceding subparagraphs, if the debtor does not perform the obligation and it is obvious that the debtor is unlikely to perform the obligation to the extent necessary to achieve the purpose of the contract, even if the creditor would make the demand referred to in the preceding Article.

Article 542(1)(i) JCC is the successor of the former Article 543 JCC. Impossibility of performance is judged in light of the cause of the claim, such as a contract, and of common sense in the transaction (Article 412-2(1) JCC).[79]

[77] M Yokoyama, 'Keiyaku no Kaijo [Cancellation of Contract]' 86(12) Horitsujiho 30, 33 (2014).

[78] Y Shiomi, *Shin Saiken Soron I* [*New Series of General Part of Law of Obligations, vol 1*] (Shinzansha 2017) 556–57.

[79] Impossibility of performance is not limited to cases of physical impossibility and can include cases where the costs of performance which a debtor should bear becomes disproportionately large in relation to the benefits that the creditor would gain from the contract (Shiomi (n 78) 285–87; Sono and others (n 2) 149).

Article 542(1)(ii) JCC is apparently influenced by a recent international trend in contract law (eg Article 72(1) CISG)[80] which relates to repudiation of performance and includes anticipatory repudiation of contract.[81] The intention to refuse performance must be so definite that it is unlikely to be overturned afterwards.[82]

Article 542(1)(iii) JCC stipulates that partial non-performance of obligations provides the basis for immediate cancellation only if it frustrates the purpose of the contract, which corresponds to judicial precedents before the 2017 Reform (see section V.1(c)(2)).

Article 542(1)(iv) JCC maintains the content of the former Article 542 JCC. Since Article 525 of the Commercial Code was not subject to the 2017 Reform, a sales contract between merchants where time is of the essence is in principle deemed to be cancelled by the debtor's failure to perform an obligation in time.

Article 542(1)(v) JCC functions as a catch-all provision covering cases where other subparagraphs of Article 542(1) JCC are not applicable. It shows that the criterion for immediate cancellation is whether the purpose of contract is achievable by tendering a delayed performance.

(2) Abolition of provisions for a seller's warranty

Regarding the nature of a seller's warranty, drafters of the 2017 Reform expressly supported the 'contractual liability doctrine' (see section V.1(b)(3) above).[83] With the revision of Article 542(1) JCC stipulating comprehensive grounds for immediate cancellation, most of the provisions relating to a seller's warranty were abolished.[84] The revised Articles 564 and 565 JCC allow a buyer to cancel a sales contract pursuant to Articles 541 and 542 JCC when a seller transferred property which did not conform to the terms of the sales contract.

(d) Cancellation of a part of the contract

With the 2017 Reform, a provision for partial cancellation of contract was introduced:

> Article 542 (Cancellation without Demand to Perform Obligation)
> (2) In the following cases, a creditor may immediately cancel a part of the contract without making the demand referred to in the preceding Article:
> (i) where performance of a part of the obligation is impossible; or
> (ii) where the debtor clearly expresses the intention to refuse to perform a part of the obligation.

Under Article 542(2) JCC, an aggrieved party cancels the contract only in part, thus frustration of the purpose of contract as provided in Article 542(1)(iii) JCC is not required. Partial cancellation is allowed only when the contract is quantitatively divisible, although Article 542(2) JCC does not expressly stipulate this.[85]

[80] Nakata (n 6) 211–12.
[81] ibid 211; Sono and others (n 2) 149.
[82] Tsutsui and Muramatsu (n 74) 76, 238.
[83] ibid 274–75.
[84] ibid 268. The former art 635 JCC on a contractor's warranty was also abolished (see n 46).
[85] Tsutsui and Muramatsu (n 74) 239.

(e) Hypotheticals

(1) Car Machinery & Co and Traders Ltd

Car Machinery & Co appoint Traders Ltd as sole distributors of their car panel presses for a period of five years. Clause 7(b) of the agreement provides that 'Distributors shall send their representatives to visit all six large car manufacturers in the country at least once in every week for the purpose of soliciting orders for car panel presses. Failure to comply with this obligation shall entitle Car Machinery to terminate the agreement with immediate effect.' Traders Ltd miss two visits to car manufacturers in the second month of the contractual period. Is Car Machinery entitled to terminate the agreement?[86]

Since Clause 7(b) stipulates clearly that Traders' failure to visit six car manufacturers once a week is the ground for immediate cancellation, the performance of this obligation is likely to be considered important in light of the purpose of contract.[87] Unless Clause 7(b) violates the principle of good faith (Article 1(2) JCC) or is against public policy (Article 90 JCC) (see section V.1.(c)(1)),[88] immediate cancellation is valid. Although cancellation of long-term distribution contracts can be restricted under Japanese law (see section V.1(c)(3)), Car Machinery may cancel the contract because Traders failed to perform its obligations in the second month of the contractual period and there is no reasonable expectation for continuity of the contract.

(2) Prime Ltd and Devil Corp

Prime Ltd sells a piece of land to Devil Corp. Under the terms of the contract, Devil pays a 10 per cent deposit, the remainder of the sum being due at 5:00 pm on 30 September, time being 'of the essence'. According to Clause 12, failure to meet the deadline would result in the deposit being forfeited and the agreement being terminated. Devil is ten minutes late in tendering the completion money and Prime refuses performance. Can Devil sue for specific performance, arguing that Prime's reliance on the clause is unreasonable in some way? Would the result be different if the contract did not include Clause 12?

Prime Ltd and Devil Corp both take the form of a company qualifying as merchant under Japanese law (Article 4(1) Commercial Code and Article 5 Company Act, *Kaishaho*). If the sales contract between Prime and Devil is interpreted as time being of the essence based on the contract provision regarding Devil's payment of the remaining sales price, the sales contract is deemed to have been cancelled when Devil failed to meet the deadline of tendering the completion money (Article 525 Commercial Code). In this case, the result would be the same even if the contract did not include Clause 12, because Prime does not need to manifest the intention of cancellation to Devil. Such an interpretation of the contract is employed when the contract provision regarding Devil's payment is considered reasonable

[86] The fact scenarios for this and the other hypothetical situations discussed in this section are taken from M Chen-Wishart, D Neo, and S Vogenauer, 'Introduction', ch 1 in this volume, 9.

[87] If based on other circumstances, Traders Ltd's failure to perform its obligation is interpreted as immaterial to the purpose of contract, the cancellation can be denied pursuant to the proviso of art 541 JCC, or an exercise of the cancellation right can be invalid as abuse of rights (JCC, art 1(3)).

[88] If, in contrast to the hypothetical scenario between Car Machinery and Traders, one of the contract parties is a consumer and the other is a business trader, there is a possibility that an immediate cancellation clause is nullified by art 10 CCA (see section III.2.(a)).

to both parties.[89] Otherwise, Prime may cancel the contract only when the requirements of Article 541 or Article 542(1) JCC are fulfilled.[90]

(3) Seven Seas and Big Chef

Seven Seas, an importer of seafood, sells two tons of mussels to Big Chef restaurant chain. After one ton has been delivered it turns out that the concentration of cadmium in the mussels is 2 per cent above the concentration permitted by national food regulations. Can Big Chef terminate the contract?

Seven Seas' obligations as a seller is to deliver mussels which meet national food regulations. Given that the contract between Seven Seas and Big Chef is quantitatively divisible, if Big Chef should give Seven Seas an additional reasonable period of time for tendering performance and this period expires without result, Big Chef may cancel a part of the contract (Article 541 JCC). When Seven Seas can no longer deliver mussels conforming to the terms of the contract or clearly expresses the intention to refuse to deliver such mussels, Big Chef may cancel the contract immediately (Article 542(2) JCC). Moreover, if delivery of two tons of mussels is necessary to achieve the purpose of the contract (for instance, Big Chef planned to have 'Big Chef's Mussel Festival 2023' requiring two tons of mussels and Seven Sea entered into the contract with Big Chef on the premise of this plan), Big Chef may cancel the contract as a whole with the demand to perform the obligation in an additional period of time (Articles 541 JCC) or immediately (Article 542(1)(iii), (v) JCC).

3. Requirements for Exercising the Right of Cancellation

(a) Notice of non-conformity of sales goods

In addition to Articles 541 and 542 JCC, a buyer must meet the following requirements for exercising the right of cancellation:[91]

> Article 566 (Limitation on Period of Warranty with Respect to Kind or Quality of Sales Goods)
> If property delivered by the seller to the buyer does not conform to the terms of the contract with respect to the kind or quality, and the buyer fails to notify the seller of the non-conformity within one year from the time the buyer becomes aware of it, the buyer may not demand cure of the non-conformity of performance, demand a reduction of the price, claim compensation for loss or damages, or cancel the contract, on the grounds of the non-conformity; provided, however, that this does not apply if the seller knew or did not know due to gross negligence, of the non-conformity at the time of the delivery.

[89] For example, the sales price was set low in exchange for a strict time for payment (see Supreme Court, 29 August 1969, Hanreijiho 570, 49).

[90] If, unlike the scenario in Prime Ltd and Devil Corp, at least one of the sales contract parties is not a merchant and the contract parties agreed that time is of the essence for payment of the remaining sales price, the aggrieved seller may cancel the contract immediately pursuant to art 542(1)(iv) JCC. Contract parties can make an agreement like Clause 12 that the contract is cancelled without manifestation of intention to the other party when certain events happen, unless it violates mandatory law, is against public policy (JCC, art 90), or contravenes the principle of good faith (JCC, art 1(2)) (see section V.3(b)).

[91] Article 566 JCC is applied *mutatis mutandis* to other types of onerous contracts (JCC, art 559).

When a seller delivers property to the buyer, she might consider performance to have been completed. It would place an undue burden on the seller if she had to preserve the relevant evidence for a long period of time in preparation for the potential pursuit of a warranty by the buyer. Therefore, Article 566 JCC requires the buyer to notify the seller that the property delivered does not conform to the terms of contract with respect to the kind or quality[92] within one year from the time the buyer becomes aware of its delivery.[93]

In a sales contract between merchants, the requirement of notification of non-conformity is stricter. A merchant buyer must inspect a sales property without delay upon receiving it (Article 526(1) Commercial Code). A buyer who discovers the non-conformity of the property with the terms of contract with respect to the kind, quality, or quantity must notify the seller immediately thereof. Even when it is impossible to immediately discover the non-conformity of the property, if the buyer discovers the non-conformity within six months from the time of its delivery, she must immediately notify the seller thereof. Otherwise, the buyer loses the remedy for the non-conformity (Article 526(2) Commercial Code), unless the seller knew of it (Article 526(3) Commercial Code). In the hypothetical involving delivery of mussels, Big Chef must inspect the mussels received without delay upon receipt and notify Seven Seas of the concentration of cadmium in them.

(b) The manner of cancellation

Unlike Article 421(2) of the Old Civil Code (Book of Property) (see section V.1(a)(1)), no involvement of the courts is necessary for the cancellation of the contract under the current Civil Code. Article 540(1) JCC provides that one of the contract parties exercises the right of cancellation by manifestation of intention to the other.[94] The manifestation of intention must be conclusive and may not be revoked (Article 540(2) JCC). It becomes effective at the time it reaches the addressee (Article 97(1) JCC).

Where the aggrieved party makes a demand for performance to the breaching party pursuant to Article 541 JCC, she can also manifest the intention of cancellation at the same time so that the lapse of an additional period brings the contract to an end. Moreover, the contract parties can agree that the contract is cancelled without manifestation of intention. The validity of this automatic cancellation clause is determined by considering whether it violates mandatory law, is against public policy (Article 90 JCC), or contravenes the principle of good faith (Article 1(2) JCC).[95]

A statutory exception to Article 540 JCC is Article 525 Commercial Code. A sales contract between merchants where time is of the essence for an obligation is deemed to be cancelled if the obligation is not performed on time. The aggrieved party does not need to manifest the intention of cancellation to the breaching party.

[92] Article 566 JCC does not apply where a sales good does not conform to the terms of the contract with respect to the quantity. Since inadequacy in quantity is usually obvious to the seller, there is little need to protect the seller (Tsutsui and Muramatsu (n 74) 284).

[93] Tsutsui and Muramatsu (n 74) 284. There is no need to protect a seller who knew or did not know due to gross negligence the non-conformity at the time of the delivery (proviso of JCC, art 566).

[94] If there are several holders of a cancellation right, manifestation of the intention of cancellation must be made by all the rights holders (JCC, art 544(1)). When there are several counterparties, the holder of the cancellation right must manifest intention to cancel the contract to all the counterparties (JCC, art 544(1)). If the right of cancellation is extinguished with respect to one of the rights holders or counterparties, it shall also be extinguished with respect to the other rights holders or counterparties (JCC, art 544(2)).

[95] Uchida (n 66) 91–92. It is pointed out that an automatic cancellation clause is qualified as a condition subsequent (JCC, art 127 (2)) (Nakata (n 6) 189).

VI. Effects of Cancellation

1. Extinction of Outstanding Obligations

As a result of cancellation of contract, obligations that have yet to be performed are extinguished.[96] Both parties are relieved from rendering performance to the other party and accepting performance from the other party.[97]

2. Obligation of Restoration

(a) Restoration to the position before conclusion of contract

(1) Effects between contract parties

(i) Retroactive effects

> Article 545 (Effects of Cancellation)
> (1) If one of the parties exercises the right of cancellation, each party assumes an obligation to restore the other party to the position before conclusion of contract; provided, however, that this may not prejudice the rights of a third party.

According to the prevailing view in legal scholarship, Article 545(1) JCC means that the cancellation of a contract has retroactive effects.[98] When a contract is cancelled, it is deemed not to have been formed. Any performance which has been rendered becomes subject to restoration. Where both parties are obliged to make restoration, their obligations must be fulfilled simultaneously (Articles 546 and 533 JCC).

In principle, restoration should be made in kind. When restoration in kind becomes impossible, the prevalent view is that the recipient must return the monetary value of the property.[99]

(ii) The scope of restoration If money was paid before cancellation, the recipient must repay the amount received and the interest which has accrued from the time of receipt (Article 545(2) JCC). If property other than money was delivered before cancellation, the recipient must return the property with its natural or legal fruits (Article 545(3)). In a 1976 judgment,[100] the Supreme Court held that in a case of cancellation of a sales contract, the buyer who has received delivery of a property is obligated to return to the seller the benefit of having used the property until the cancellation. Since cancellation of contract has retroactive effects, the contract parties are obliged to restore the property to a state as if

[96] Wagatsuma (n 42) 188; Nakata (n 6) 227.

[97] Clauses which are intended to operate after cancellation (eg dispute resolution) continue to operate after cancellation.

[98] Wagatsuma (n 42) 188. This view was adopted by the Judgment of the Supreme Court, 22 September 1959, Minshu 13 (11) 1451.

[99] For details see Nakata (n 6) 230–33.

[100] Supreme Court, 13 February 1976, Minshu 30 (1) 1. See also Supreme Court, 22 September 1959, Minshu 13 (11) 1451.

no delivery had been made under the contract. The Supreme Court, however, did not indicate the criteria for calculating the amount the recipient should pay for use of the property. Thus, it is not clear that a reduction in the value of the property would be included in the benefit of use of the property which should be returned.

(2) Effects with regard to third parties

The proviso of Article 545(1) JCC has been interpreted as protecting the rights of any third party by limiting the retroactive effects of cancellation.[101] The main example relates to sales contracts of immovables.[102] When such contracts are cancelled, the buyer is deemed not to acquire ownership in the immovables and so would not be able to transfer ownership to a subsequent third-party buyer. The proviso allows the third-party buyer to acquire ownership despite the retroactive effects of cancellation. Established judicial precedents also require the third-party buyer to have registered her rights in the immovables before cancellation.[103] The underlying idea is that those who are protected by the proviso of Article 545(1) JCC should implement necessary procedures to assert their rights against third parties.

(b) Exemption from restoration to the position before conclusion of contract

(1) Prospective effects

The Civil Code includes provisions for certain types of contracts that exempt the contract parties from the duty of restoration. Article 620 JCC provides that the cancellation of a lease (*chintaishaku*) only has prospective effects:

> Article 620 (Effects of Cancellation of Lease)
> If a lease is cancelled, the cancellation becomes effective solely toward the future. In such a case, the cancellation does not preclude a claim for compensation for loss or damage.

Parties of lease contracts do not have to return the benefit they received before the cancellation. The lessee is obliged to return the leased property in the condition it was received (Articles 601 and 621 JCC).[104]

Article 620 JCC is applied *mutatis mutandis* to employment contracts (*koyo*), mandates (*inin*), and partnerships (*kumiai*) (Articles 630, 652, and 684 JCC). These types of contracts have in common that the contractual relationship continues for some time. It is reasonable for parties of continuous contracts that restoration is unnecessary to the extent that conforming performances have been delivered.[105] For this reason, Article 620 JCC is also applied by analogy to other types of continuous contracts.

[101] Wagatsuma (n 42) 197.

[102] In case of the sales of movable property, an innocent third party may resort to art 192 JCC, which provides that a good-faith purchaser acquires the ownership of movable property by transaction with a non-owner.

[103] Supreme Court, 14 June 1958, Minshu 12 (9) 1449.

[104] Article 621 JCC provides that if any damage is caused to the leased property, the lessee should restore the property to the condition at the time of its receipt, unless the damage is caused due to any grounds not attributable to the lessee. However, any normal wear and any aging degradation of the leased property is excluded from the damage to be restored. This article was codified by the 2017 Reform, based on a judicial precedent (Supreme Court, 24 March 2011, Minshu 65 (2) 903).

[105] Wagatsuma (n 58) 484; Nakata (n 6) 429.

(2) Proportional remuneration
When a party of a continuous contract rendered a part of the service promised, but the other party did not pay for it, the other party should pay remuneration in proportion to the service provided. The relevant provision is Article 634(ii) JCC on contracts for work (see section IV.1(a)). Similar rules are provided for employment contracts (Article 624-2(ii) JCC), mandates (Article 648(3)(ii) JCC), and bailments (Articles 665 and 648(3)(ii) JCC).

3. Claim for Damages

Under the influence of French law, Article 424 of the Old Civil Code (Book of Property) allowed a party cancelling a contract to claim for damages. Drafters of the current Civil Code maintained this position.[106] Article 545(4) JCC provides that the exercise of the right of cancellation does not preclude claims for compensation for damages. According to the prevailing view, this enables the cancelling party to obtain the benefits from the contract by limiting the retroactive effects of cancellation.[107]

VII. Loss of Cancellation Rights

1. General Grounds for Loss of Right

The right of cancellation is extinguished in the event that there are general grounds for loss of the right.[108] For example, a waiver of the cancellation in advance is valid,[109] unless it violates mandatory law,[110] is against public policy (Article 90 JCC), or contravenes the principle of good faith (Article 1(2) JCC).

Although the right of cancellation is not a claim, a prevailing view in legal scholarship maintains that provisions on extinctive prescription of claims are applicable.[111] Thus, if a holder of a cancellation right does not exercise this right within five years from the time when she came to know that the right could be exercised, the right of cancellation is extinguished by prescription (Article 166(1)(i) JCC).

106 Hironaka (n 26) 522. In this respect, the drafters of the Civil Code expressly rejected the rules provided in the German Civil Code before the law reform of 2002, which required a contract party to choose between a claim for damages and a cancellation of contract (former arts 325(1) and 326(1) of the German Civil Code).

107 Wagatsuma (n 42) 188, 200.

108 For cancellation pursuant to art 541 JCC, there remains the possibility that the purpose of the contract is accomplished. If the breaching party delivers conforming performance after the lapse of an additional period and the aggrieved party can achieve the purpose of the contract by accepting the performance, the right of cancellation is extinguished because of fulfillment of its purpose.

109 Great Court of Judicature, 15 September 1904, Minroku 10, 1115. Wagatsuma (n 42) 207, 213.

110 Article 8-2 CCA nullifies clauses in consumer contracts that force a consumer to waive the right of cancellation.

111 Shiomi (n 78) 622; Nakata (n 6) 246.

2. Special Grounds for Loss of Cancellation Right

(a) Extinction of the right of cancellation by demand

The Civil Code sets forth two special provisions regarding the extinction of the right of cancellation. First, Article 547 JCC provides for cases where no time limit other than a general prescription period is set for the exercise of the right of termination. To resolve an unstable legal status,[112] the counterparty may specify a reasonable period of time and make a demand to the rights holder to give a definite answer as to whether she will cancel within that period of time.

If the rights holder manifests her intention to cancel the contract, the cancellation becomes effective (Article 540(1) JCC). If she answers that she does not intend to exercise the right of cancellation, the right is extinguished by waiver. If she does not provide a clear answer to the demand, the right of cancellation is extinguished pursuant to Article 547 JCC.

(b) Extinction of the right of cancellation by acts of rights holder

Secondly, Article 548 JCC provides that the cancellation right is extinguished if the rights holder intentionally or negligently causes significant damage to the object of contract, or makes it impossible to return the object, or converts the object into another kind of property by way of specification or alteration. For example, if the aggrieved party has significantly damaged the property, she cannot cancel the contract. A drafter of the Civil Code 1896 explained that in the cases provided in Article 548 JCC the rights holder is deemed to have waived the right of cancellation.[113] If the rights holder did not recognize at the time of her act that the right of cancellation had accrued, she does not lose the right of cancellation (proviso of Article 548 JCC).

VIII. Concluding Remarks

This chapter has examined the topic of termination of contracts under Japanese law. Based on the investigations in this chapter, three points should be noted from the viewpoint of comparative law.

First, it is essential to analyse the subject from a broad perspective. A comprehensive knowledge of termination of contracts is needed to understand cancellation for breach of contract. In this respect, the legal qualification of a contract has significance under Japanese law. If a contract qualifies as a certain type of nominate contract, special rules regarding the requirements and effects of termination apply. This might be overlooked if consideration is focused only on cancellation for breach of contract.

Secondly, it is important to view the legal system as a dynamic one. The attitude of Japanese law towards German law is a good example. Certainly, there was a period when Japanese scholars introduced German legal doctrines extensively in order to establish a logical framework of Japanese private law: the era of 'reception of doctrines' (see section V.1(b)).

[112] Hironaka (n 26) 532.
[113] Ume (n 7) 460–61.

This academic attitude was, however, severely criticized from the 1960s onwards, and now it is accepted that German law was just one of the mother laws for the JCC and there is no reason for giving absolute priority to German doctrines when interpreting provisions of the Civil Code. This transition in thought is important for understanding Japanese law.

Finally, it is fruitful to pay attention to the differences in the legal systems being compared. Sometimes Asian jurisdictions are divided into several groups, such as groups adhering to English, French, and German legal traditions. Although this is useful for cognitive purposes, the attitude towards mother laws varies from jurisdiction to jurisdiction and there are legal developments unique to each jurisdiction. Thus, it is more instructive for comparative purposes to elucidate the differences among jurisdictions assigned to the same group. Focusing on the differences expands and deepens insights into the dynamics of jurisdictions compared, and this promotes productive dialogue. This is one of the enduring contributions of comparative legal studies.

13

Change of Circumstances in Korean Law

KWON Youngjoon

I. Introduction

This chapter provides a general overview of the doctrine of change of circumstances under Korean law. It is a legal doctrine under which a contracting party may be exempted from the binding effects of the contract in question by being allowed to terminate, rescind, or modify the contract if the circumstances underlying the contract significantly change and the performance of the contract on an as-is-basis would be against the good-faith principle. The Korean Civil Code (KCC) does not have a provision expressly stipulating this doctrine. But it has been recognized by civil law scholars as one of the doctrines derived from the principle of trust and good faith as stipulated in Article 2 KCC.[1] This article stipulates that '[t]he exercise of rights and the performance of obligations shall be in accordance with the principle of trust and good faith'. This provision is highly comprehensive and abstract in nature and is thus called a general provision or blank provision in the sense that it gives a judge wide discretion in interpreting and applying it. Hence, it allows incorporating sub-principles such as the doctrine of change of circumstances. This doctrine has also been accepted explicitly by the Supreme Court of Korea since 2007. However, the scope of its applicability still remains to be clearly determined. The Supreme Court has rarely and only recently applied this doctrine to allow a party to terminate or rescind a contract, notwithstanding its general acceptance of the doctrine on the theoretical level. Such reluctance to grant relief is also found among the lower courts. Therefore, the theoretical and practical implications of the doctrine of change of circumstances for contract law are still considered one of the most intriguing yet unresolved issues. Against this backdrop, I will first give a general explanation on the background of the doctrine and then address its requirements and consequences. I will also examine some hypothetical cases posed by the editors to show how the doctrine might function in practice under Korean law.

II. General Explanation

1. Theoretical Background

It is widely accepted that a contract should be honoured and respected by the parties. The well-known maxim of *pacta sunt servanda* ('one should abide by an agreement')[2] stresses

[1] The first academic article on the doctrine of change of circumstances dates back to 1957: SON Joochan, 'Mookgabeondonggwa Sajeongbyeongyeongui Wonchic' ['Price Fluctuation and the Principle of Change of Circumstances'] (1957) 6 Beobjo Korean [Lawyers Association Journal] 38.

[2] On this notion, see generally R Zimmermann, *The Law of Obligations: Roman Foundations of the Civilian Tradition* (OUP 1990) 543, 576–82.

Kwon Youngjoon, *Change of Circumstances in Korean Law* In: *Studies in the Contract Laws of Asia V: Ending and Changing Contracts*. Edited by: Mindy Chen-Wishart, Dora Neo, and Stefan Vogenauer, Oxford University Press.
 DOI: 10.1093/oso/9780198995814.003.0013

the sanctity of the legally binding contract. This idea is intimately related to the concept of private autonomy. Under the influence of liberalism, which permeated classical contract law, the concept of the binding nature of a contract was deemed the flip side of the concept of private autonomy. One's legal fate should be determined by one's own will, and one should be bound by what one has voluntarily agreed to. Consequently, a contractual relationship is established at the time of the making of the valid contract and is, in principle, not subject to subsequent unilateral alteration or annulment unless the same parties agree to it.

However, there are cases where enforcing the contract on its face would put one party in a drastically disadvantageous position due to an *ex-post* change of circumstances surrounding the contract. Imposing an excessively onerous burden on a faultless party who never assumed or foresaw such an unanticipated risk at the time of contract seems unfair. Fairness of the contract, or equivalence of the contract, is another value that should be cherished as much as the binding force of a contract. To express this value, putting certain limits on private autonomy or on the principle of *pacta sunt servanda* seems inevitable.[3] The doctrine of change of circumstances is one of the means to set out proper limitations on the above principles, thereby drawing a boundary between the sanctity of the contract and paternalistic interventions to terminate or alter the contract. Such a boundary-drawing function of the doctrine can also be explained from the perspective of risk allocation as described further below.[4]

A contract concerns future obligations. Of course, some contracts may be performed simultaneously at the time of their making; however, in practice, there is usually a time gap between the making of a contract and its performance. Since the future is full of contingencies, contracting parties inevitably face future risks. Parties normally understand that circumstances underlying the contract may change between the time of the contract and the time of performance and assume these risks. Therefore, allocating risks becomes one of the central elements of a contract. In this sense, a contract is also a means to allocate future risks and contingencies.

However, there may be situations where contracting parties are silent about some future risks which were beyond their anticipation at the time of the contract. These risks remain unregulated by the contract. The doctrine of change of circumstances steps in at this juncture and allocates risks not specifically assigned to either party based on the good-faith principle. Of course, this doctrinal vehicle should not be abused since doing so may impact the principle of the sanctity of contract. Most of the time, a promisor assumes risks associated with performance. As such, a party is still bound to fulfil its contractual obligations even when performance becomes more onerous. The mere fact that the cost of performance has increased is not sufficient to excuse a party from its obligations. Even significant changes in the domestic or global economic situation do not necessarily justify judicial intervention since the economy tends to fluctuate over time.

However, not all risks are of the same kind; some are significant, while others are minor. Some are foreseeable, while others are not. In reality, parties are equipped with only limited

[3] JI Wonlim, *Minbeobgangeui* [*Lecture on Civil Law*] (16th edn, Pakyoungsa 2018) 1294.

[4] On this perspective under Korean law, see generally KWON Youngjoon, 'Wiheombaebooneui gwanjeomeseo bon sajeongbyeongyeongeui wonchik' ['The Doctrine of Change of Circumstances from the Perspective of Risk Allocation'] (2010) 51 Minsabeobhak [Civil Law Journal] 203, 203.

rationality. The limit of human capacity to foresee the future makes it impossible for them to assume any and all future risks in advance at the time of contract. Some risks eventuate that make performance excessively onerous, where both parties can hardly anticipate these risks, and where enforcing the contract does not do justice to one party. The need then arises for an *ex-post* risk allocation mechanism by virtue of law or the power of the judiciary, to modify the contractual framework that has failed to deal with such grave risks. This necessity becomes even clearer in a long-term contract, where the contractual relationship is vulnerable to a greater number of contingencies that may arise during the lengthy contractual term.

In this regard, the doctrine of change of circumstances, at least theoretically, carries significant meaning in contract law by creating meaningful tension between autonomy and paternalism as well as between the sanctity and fairness of the contract. Therefore, delving into the doctrine requires an in-depth contemplation of these values.

2. Taxonomy

The idea underlying the doctrine of change of circumstances broadly applies to cases in which contractual termination or modification is allowed on the basis of a change of circumstances surrounding the contract. The cases can be classified into three categories.

(a) Specific statutory provisions

Contractual termination or modification is allowed pursuant to certain specific statutory provisions. In the KCC, there are various provisions that fall into this category (see Articles 218, 286, 557, 627, 628, and 661). For example,

- Article 286 allows the parties to request an increase or decrease in the rent where the rent becomes unreasonable due to changes in the price of the land or an increase or decrease in taxes or burdens upon the land.
- Article 557 stipulates that the donor may rescind a contract of gift, if after the conclusion of a contract of gift the donor's property status has changed to his detriment and the donor's standard of living would become gravely affected by the performance of the contract of a gift.
- There are numerous provisions in other statutes where a similar idea is reflected. For instance, Article 252 of the Korean Civil Procedure Act provides a specific type of lawsuit to alter the original judgment of the court on periodical payment when a special situation occurs that greatly infringes the equilibrium between the parties as the situation forming the basis for computing such payments has been significantly changed.

(b) Specific contractual terms

Contractual termination or modification is allowed under certain specific terms of the relevant contract. Parties are free to create any terms or conditions in the contract (subject to mandatory provisions or public policy), including terms to deal with unanticipated risks. Generally, one of the parties agrees to assume such risks. For example:

- The MAC (Materially Adverse Change) clause is frequently used in the context of merger and acquisition transactions, and its significance has increased in practice.[5] It gives the purchaser the right to walk away from the transaction before the closing if certain events that are detrimental to the target company occur (eg insolvency or failure in obtaining administrative permission). What comprises these events is left to the contracting parties to decide.
- Provisions to deal with price fluctuations in the market are often inserted in large-scale construction contracts.
- The parties may include a *force majeure* clause to deal with an 'accident that the obligor was unable to anticipate or avoid despite exercise of utmost care and that occurs externally, ie beyond the obligor's control'.[6] As such, the debtor must be unable to anticipate or avoid the accident or event despite his or her exercise of utmost care; any accident or event that the debtor was able to anticipate or avoid cannot constitute a *force majeure* event.[7] A *force majeure* event is an accident occurring externally, that is, acts of God (including earthquakes and storms) or occurrences of a social or societal nature (including riots, war, and blockades) and excludes any personal reasons (such as financial status or absence of the obligor).[8]

The Supreme Court tends to limit the scope of *force majeure*. For example, the following were not regarded as *force majeure*: an embankment road was washed away by the highest rainfall in 50 years and a passenger walking on the road drowned;[9] the so-called International Monetary Fund (IMF) crisis (the nationwide recession in Korea in the late 1990s) and the resulting troubles in the supply of materials;[10] and cases where the project owner was still liable where building occupancy was delayed due to the builder's insolvency,[11] the late commencement of construction, or the need to excavate remains.[12]

(c) Modification in the absence of statutory or contractual provisions

Contractual termination or modification may be allowed despite the non-existence of any specific statutory provisions or specific contractual terms. This applies to cases where the doctrine of change of circumstances in a genuine sense is invoked under the umbrella of the good-faith principle. What I will address in this chapter is confined to the doctrine of change of circumstances in relation to cases in this category.

[5] JEONG Youngcheol, 'Giyeobinsoogeyaksang "Joongdaehan Akyeonghyang" Johange gwanhan Silmooyeongoo' ['Practical Review on the MAC Clause in the Merger and Acquisition Contract'] (2008) 26 Sangsabeobyeongoo [Studies on Commercial Law] 273, 278.

[6] YANG Changsoo and KIM Jaehyeong, *Minbeob I, Geyakbeob* [*Civil Code I, Contract Law*] (2nd edn, Pakyoungsa 2015) 413.

[7] Supreme Court Decision 2005Da59475, 59482, 54999 (23 August 2007); Supreme Court Decision 2008Da15940, 15957 (10 July 2008).

[8] YANG Changsoo and KIM Jaehyeong (n 6) 413.

[9] Supreme Court Decision 99Da53247 (26 May 2000).

[10] Supreme Court Decision 2001Da1386 (4 September 2002).

[11] Supreme Court Decision 2005Da59475, 59482, 54999 (23 August 2007).

[12] Supreme Court Decision 2008Da15940, 15957 (10 July 2008).

3. A Diachronic Overview of Legal Precedents

(a) The earlier strict attitude of the Korean Supreme Court

Korean courts have been relatively strict in their acknowledgment or application of the doctrine of change of circumstances. In the 1950s, the Supreme Court ruled that the doctrine of change of circumstances is not accepted in the interpretation of the KCC.[13] In one case, a purchaser of a forest paid the balance of the purchase price 14 years after the execution date of the sale and purchase agreement, but the price had increased about 202 times during that period due to sudden changes in economic conditions arising out of the Korean War and currency reforms. The Supreme Court ruled that even though the currency value had drastically changed between the making and the execution of the contract, and despite the resulting significant unfairness, the seller did not have a right of rescission on grounds of a change of circumstances.[14] For several decades, the Supreme Court refused either to acknowledge the doctrine itself or to apply it in favour of the party who asserted it.[15] In another case, the Supreme Court held that 'it cannot be assumed that there was a sufficient change of circumstances to allow rescission of a contract merely because nine years have passed since a sales contract was executed and because the market price has increased'.[16] However, a slight shift in the Supreme Court's stance on this issue had begun to emerge, with a change in tone and nuances that implicitly leaves a theoretical possibility for this doctrine to be applied if the facts of the case demand such conclusion.

(b) A series of legal precedents on guarantee contracts

In a series of cases between 1990 and 2000, the Supreme Court allowed termination of a continuing guarantee agreement based on the doctrine of change of circumstances.[17] All these cases concerned officers or employees guaranteeing the debt of the company they had worked for at the time of contract who subsequently retired. It was disputed that the change of circumstances (namely, their retirement from the company) should be the normative justification for them to either terminate the guarantee contract or be exempt from guarantee liability for the debts incurred after their retirement.

These cases are limited to a very specific set of facts. In particular, (i) the guarantor was an officer or employee of a company that was the main debtor; (ii) therefore, even without the guarantor, there existed a party who was liable for the relevant debt, that is, the main debtor company; and (iii) the guarantor, as the officer or employee of the main debtor company, would find it difficult to refuse a request to provide a guarantee for the company. In other words, the precedents take into account that, for one thing, it is necessary to reasonably

[13] Supreme Court Decision 4286Minsang231 (14 April 1955); Supreme Court Decision 4288Minsang234, 235 (10 March 1956).

[14] Supreme Court Decision 63Da452 (12 September 1963). This decision is explained in detail in BAEK Taeseung, 'Article 2' in KIM Yongdam (ed), *Jooseokminbeob (1)* [*Commentaries on the Civil Code (1)*] (4th edn, Korean Society of Judicial Administration 2010) 177–78.

[15] Supreme Court Decision 80Da1414 (22 April 1980); Supreme Court Decision 90Da19664 (26 February 1991); Supreme Court Decision 98Da45904 (3 September 1999); Supreme Court Decision 2001Da20165 (26 April 2002); Supreme Court Decision 2004Da11193 (20 August 2004).

[16] Supreme Court Decision 90Da19664 (26 February 1991).

[17] Supreme Court Decision 89Daka1381 (27 February 1990); Supreme Court Decision 95Da17533 (29 October 1996); Supreme Court Decision 98Da34911 (12 December 1998); Supreme Court Decision 99Da61750 (10 March 2000).

limit the responsibility of a person in the position of officer or employee of the main debtor company who finds it very difficult to refuse the request of their then employer and so in fact could not avoid providing a guarantee; and for another, the creditor can still seek performance of the main obligation from the main debtor company, which generally has greater financial resources than the guarantor officer or employee. The precedents concluded, in light of the characteristics and special circumstances of such a guarantee agreement, that if an officer or employee becomes the guarantor for the company, he shall not be held liable for the obligation of guarantee after his resignation from the position as officer or employee.

This line of decisions does not fall into the category of cases described in section II.2(c) as the conclusion results not from applying the doctrine of change of circumstances but from reasonably interpreting the contracting parties' intent with regard to the scope of the obligation of guarantee based on the principle of trust and good faith, considering the special circumstances.[18] If the doctrine of change of circumstances in the context of these cases had been applied to such precedent cases, the right of termination of the officer or employee might have not been acknowledged. That is because, in order for the principle of change of circumstances to apply, it would be necessary that the relevant party was not able to predict any change of circumstances. In this case, anyone could predict the circumstance that an officer or employee might resign from his or her position at the company. Therefore, the precedents cannot be construed as cases where the doctrine of change of circumstances in a pure or narrow sense was applied.

(c) Recognition of the doctrine in 2007

It was not until 2007 that the Supreme Court established a clear position by ruling that termination of a contract on grounds of a change of circumstances is recognized as an exception to the principle that the terms of a contract are to be respected. The requirements are that (i) a significant change of circumstances has occurred which could not have been anticipated by the parties at the time of execution of the contract, (ii) such change has occurred due to a cause not attributable to the party which seeks the right to terminate, and (iii) if the original binding force of the contract were recognized, it would lead to a consequence that would violate the principle of trust and good faith.[19] The Supreme Court further ruled that the term 'circumstances' in this context shall mean the objective circumstances underlying the contract, not a party's subjective or personal circumstances.

In the case in question, the plaintiff purchased land that the local government (the defendant) had released from the green belt, but later, the defendant designated the land as a public site and sought to expropriate the land. As a result, it was impossible for the plaintiff to develop buildings and it sought termination of the sales agreement and reimbursement of the purchase price on grounds of change of circumstances or the principle of trust and good faith. However, the Supreme Court found that the possibility of construction on the land was only the plaintiff's subjective purpose in purchasing the land and could not be viewed as an underlying condition of the sales agreement, thus refusing to apply the principle of change of circumstances or the principle of trust and good faith.

18 However, GWAK Yoonjik and KIM Jaehyeong, *Minbeobchongchick* [*General Provisions of Civil Law*] (9th edn, Pakyoungsa 2013) 79 introduce these cases as cases where the doctrine of the change of circumstances was applied.

19 Supreme Court Decision 2004Da31302 (29 March 2007).

(d) The actual application of the doctrine

It is one thing to acknowledge the doctrine of change of circumstances on a general level and another to actually apply it to a specific case. For a considerable period of time, it was difficult to find a Supreme Court decision where a claim or a defence based on the doctrine of change of circumstances succeeded. That is because should the doctrine be widely applied, it is likely to undermine the principle that the terms of a contract are to be respected, the fundamental principle of contract law which not only corresponds to the intent of the parties to the contract but also benefits transactions by promoting the legal stability of the contract. The doctrine of change of circumstances, which releases the contracting party from the binding force of the contract executed by his/her own will, conflicts with the fundamental principle of contract law. Therefore, a party's argument based on the principle of change of circumstances is rarely accepted by the courts' practice in Korea.[20]

However, there is one instance where this doctrine was invoked and applied.[21] This case concerned a lease of land where the lessee intended to build a display house, and the lessor was aware of the purpose of the lease contract. However, the lessee failed to obtain a permit for construction of the display house from the relevant authority. The lessee then rescinded the lease contract for the reason of change of circumstances. The lessor claimed that a failure to obtain the approval was not a sufficient cause to apply the doctrine of change of circumstances. The Supreme Court ruled that it amounted to frustration of the purpose of the contract and that it would be gravely inappropriate to retain the contractual relationship when there is significant imbalance between the contracting parties. While it is doubtful if the doctrine of change of circumstances could be applied to this case, especially considering that a failure to obtain the approval was something predictable at the time of the contract, this case is meaningful as the Supreme Court applied the doctrine of change of circumstances to discharge the contracting parties from the contractual obligations. This case also indicates that the Supreme Court began to take a more lenient position in applying this doctrine.

4. Efforts to Codify the Doctrine

So far, there have been two failed attempts to codify the doctrine in the KCC. In 2004, an amendment draft was composed by the Civil Code Amendment Committee of the Ministry of Justice. Some Committee members agreed that the doctrine of change of circumstances needed to be incorporated in the draft. At the time, there was no Supreme Court decision that clearly acknowledged the doctrine, but a majority of scholarly opinion was that the doctrine could be acknowledged. Draft Article 544–4 read:

> Either party may request for modification of a contract if there was a substantial change of circumstances that was not foreseeable to the contracting parties at the time of the execution of the contract, and if sustaining the contract as it stands is manifestly inappropriate. If agreement as to the modification of the contract is not reached within a reasonable time, then the party in question can rescind or terminate the contract.

20 KWON Youngjoon (n 4) 218.
21 Supreme Court Decision 2020Da254846 (10 December 2020).

However, the amendment draft that was submitted to the National Assembly of Korea was discarded due to the expiry of the legislative term of four years.

Another attempt was made by the newly constituted Civil Code Amendment Committee in 2014. Draft Article 538–2 KCC provided that:

> [e]ither party may request for modification of a contract or may rescind or terminate the contract if there was a substantial change of circumstances fundamental to the formation of contract that was not foreseeable to the contracting parties at the time of the execution of the contract, and if recognition of the binding power as prescribed in the contract would result in substantial imbalance between the parties or disallow the parties from achieving the intended purpose of the contract.

However, the amendment draft was not submitted to the National Assembly for review due to a backlog of legislative bills pending legislation.

III. Requirements

According to the Supreme Court ruling in 2007 (and subsequent others),[22] termination or rescission of a contract for change of circumstances requires that (i) the underlying fundamental circumstances of the contract have changed significantly; (ii) the change of circumstances occurred after execution of the contract; (iii) the parties to the contract were unable to anticipate such change of circumstances; (iv) the change of circumstances occurred due to a cause not attributable to the party who claims the termination right; and (v) if the original binding force of the contract were maintained, it would lead to a consequence that would violate the principle of trust and good faith. Most commentators, in general, also have provided analogous explanations with respect to the principle of change of circumstances. However, the above requirements were slightly modified in a Supreme Court decision of 2017. I will first provide an account of the traditional understanding of the requirements and then set out what has been modified in the 2017 decision.

1. The Traditional Approach to the Requirements

(a) *Ex-post* significant change of the underlying fundamental circumstances

There must be a significant change of circumstances that is excessively onerous and unforeseeable. In general, small-scale price fluctuations due to inflation do not satisfy this requirement since they are neither excessively onerous nor unforeseeable. This requirement is to be distinguished from the notion of impossibility in the sense that the performance is still regarded as possible but excessively onerous. However, the borderline between change of circumstances (or hardship) and impossibility is sometimes blurry.

Secondly, the change must relate to a circumstance that is fundamental to the establishment of a contract. This refers to a major change of circumstance that would make the

[22] Supreme Court Decision 2008Da44368 (24 June 2011); Supreme Court Decision 2012Da13637 (26 September 2013).

parties question the premises of the contract or agree a contract on terms different from the ones at issue. It should relate to the objective basis, as opposed to the subjective basis, of the contract. The latter refers to the subjective or personal expectations, reliance, or hope associated with the contract; the risk here lies with that specific party. Whether or not a certain circumstance is objective or subjective is a matter of contract interpretation.

Thirdly, the change must have occurred after the contract was made. If this change had already taken place at the time of the contract, and the parties had failed to take notice of this, it is not a matter of change of circumstance but rather a matter of mutual mistake. How mutual mistake is to be handled differs among jurisdictions. The Korean Supreme Court deals with this case by supplemental interpretation of contract (borrowing this idea of *ergänzende Auslegung* from German law),[23] which has priority over the application of the doctrine of change of circumstances.[24] This is because the intention of the parties, including even hypothetical intention, is to be taken into consideration prior to resorting to the notion of good faith, according to the notion of private autonomy.

(b) Unforeseeability and non-attributability

To qualify as a change of circumstance, the change must be something that the parties could not have anticipated at the time of the contract. The specificity and definitiveness of anticipation is a complicated issue, to be determined on a case-by-case basis. If the consideration of even the slightest possibility of contingencies were held to be 'anticipation', the scope of this would be too broad, rendering the doctrine of change of circumstances almost meaningless. On the other hand, if the anticipation requirement is only fulfilled if one can accurately foresee every detail of every contingency, then the scope would be too narrow and excessively enlarge the scope of the doctrine. The possibility of anticipation is not negated merely because a given risk is very unlikely to occur in reality. The low probability of risk does not mean that the risk could not be foreseen or assigned to one party or another.[25] An insurance contract is a typical example of risk allocation over a low probability risk.

Even when there are no explicit statutory or contractual provisions on the allocation of risk, the court will first endeavour to decide if the risk has been implicitly assumed by or allocated between the parties. In a more speculative contract that entails substantial risk of loss as well as expectation of significant gain, the parties are more likely to have allocated the risks in advance. For instance, a sale on the futures market is a speculative contract. Thus, one might easily assume that the parties have allocated the risks in advance. The same thing can be said of the Knock-in, Knock-out (KIKO) contract, which has been quite a controversial legal issue in Korea. The KIKO contract is a currency-hedging contract designed to reduce potential risks from foreign exchange rate fluctuations. Under a contract of this kind, an exporter could sell dollar earnings at a higher exchange rate to the bank when the currency fluctuates, thereby hedging the fluctuation risks. The bank incurs losses in return for contract fees. However, if the foreign currency strengthens against the Korean currency (won) over a specified limit, the exporters must sell the foreign currency at a lower rate, which leads to losses for the exporter and gains for the bank. Contrary to common expectations, the dollar soared dramatically in the wake of the global financial crisis, leading to

[23] Supreme Court Decision 2005Da13288 (23 November 2006).
[24] BAEK Taeseung (n 14) 184.
[25] MJ Trebilcock, *The Limits of Freedom of Contract* (Harvard University Press 1993) 128.

tremendous losses for exporters. Concerned exporters filed more than 110 cases, arguing the invalidity of their KIKO contracts on various grounds, including change of circumstances. In one case, the court decided that such a sharp rise in foreign currency amounted to a change of circumstances, thereby granting an exporter the right to terminate this contract,[26] but courts generally have been reluctant to accept this argument,[27] and the Supreme Court also upheld this line of decisions.[28] The KIKO contract was aimed at hedging or allocating risks arising from currency fluctuation. Therefore, an exporter signing this type of contract has already agreed to assume the risks at the time of contracting. In this case, there is no room for the doctrine of change of circumstances to intervene.

The change of circumstances must not be the fault of the party seeking relief. It is quite clear that one should not be allowed to benefit from one's own fault. The requirement of non-attributability manifests this idea. In general, attributability in the context of contract law refers to the intentional conduct or negligence of the party in non-performance. However, when unforeseeable contingencies arise, it is hardly imaginable to think that those contingencies are attributable to the contracting parties. If a party has created such contingencies, then it may well be said that these contingencies were foreseeable. For this reason, there has been criticism that this requirement is not necessary and can simply be reflected in the context of other requirements, in particular the requirement of unforeseeability.[29]

(c) Violation of the good-faith principle

Finally, there must be a violation of the principle of trust and good faith as stipulated in Article 2 KCC, which means that it would be grossly unfair if the original binding force of the contract was kept as it is. It is to ensure that strictly adhering to the original contract would be grossly unfair because one party suffers from an excessive and onerous burden that could not be justified even in the name of the sanctity of the contract. After all, law is about justice and fairness. If adhering to the contract is against justice and fairness, the law is responsible for providing an exit from such undue consequence. The good-faith principle, manifested in the form of the doctrine of change of circumstances, offers such an exit. However, this requirement does not provide concrete standards and thus is considered to be somewhat hollow and murky. There is no specific discussion on this requirement either in the legal precedents or in scholarly works. This implies that this requirement can only be determined with a specific set of facts on the table.

2. Changes in the Requirements

In 2017, the Supreme Court rendered a decision in which requirements for the application of the doctrine of change of circumstances were slightly modified.[30] A fitness club was forced to close due to severe financial difficulties. A club member sought compensation

[26] Seoul Central District Court Decision 2008Kahap3816 (30 December 2008).

[27] For example, Seoul Central District Court Decision 2008Kahap4262 (8 January 2009); Incheon District Court Decision 2009Kahap228 (9 March 2009); Seoul High Court Decision 2009Ra997 (21 August 2009).

[28] For example, Supreme Court Decision 2011Da53638, 53690 (26 September 2013).

[29] KWON Youngjoon (n 4) 238.

[30] Supreme Court Decision 2016Da249557 (12 June 2017).

for the loss due to the abrupt shutdown of the club. The club asserted that it had already terminated the contract based on the doctrine of change of circumstances as soon as it was closed and therefore was not liable for losses incurred afterwards. The lower courts as well as the Supreme Court did not accept such assertion. In doing so, the Supreme Court reiterated the requirements but in a different way.

First of all, there is meaningful change with regard to the requirement of attributability. It has been a long-standing position of the Korean Supreme Court that the change of circumstances must not be attributable to the party who claims the termination right. However, this requirement was subject to academic criticism, as I have mentioned earlier. The doctrine of change of circumstances is about allocating risks between contracting parties. Most of the risks associated with the contract are allocated *ex ante* through the contract either explicitly or implicitly. The doctrine of change of circumstances steps in only when risks that were never considered or allocated between the parties have been realized. However, reasonable parties would expect that the risks that are attributable to either of the parties should be borne by such party. In that regard, it might be said that there is generally an implicit agreement that the risk falls on the side of the party at fault. If such is the case, the risks attributable to one of the parties are not subject to the doctrine of change of circumstances. In practice, it would be difficult to imagine a case where a risk that was not foreseeable by the parties is a type of risk that can be attributed to one party. It would be senseless, for example, to discuss the attributability of the event of war, disaster, or economic crisis to either party of the contract.

From a comparative perspective, it should be noted that section 313 of the *Bürgerliches Gesetzbuch* (BGB, the German Civil Code), Article 6:111 of the Principles of European Contract Law (PECL), and Article III.—1:110 of the Draft Common Frame of Reference (DCFR), all of which contain provisions for the doctrine of change of circumstances, do not list non-attributability as one of the requirements for the application of the doctrine. Based on this observation, neither of the amendment drafts of the KCC in 2004 and 2014 required non-attributability in the provisions on change of circumstances. This requirement can be absorbed into that of unforeseeability and need not be an independent requirement. With the 2017 decision, the Supreme Court finally decided to discard this requirement in the application of the doctrine of change of circumstances.

Another noteworthy change that emerged in this decision is that the Supreme Court came up with two types of situation to which the doctrine of change of circumstances may be applied and, at the same time, eliminated the requirement of a 'violation of the good-faith principle'. Under Korean law, the doctrine of change of circumstances is considered a specific form of the good-faith principle, derived from Article 2 KCC. Therefore, it is redundant and somewhat awkward to set upon a requirement reiterating the violation of the good-faith principle. Rather, the true function of requirements is to give concrete shape to this abstract principle. The last requirement of a 'violation of the good-faith principle' failed to fulfil such function. In that regard, it makes sense that the Supreme Court discarded it and replaced it with more concrete requirements by suggesting two types of change of circumstances: substantial imbalance between the parties and frustration of the purpose of the contract.

It is noteworthy that these changes in the requirements were already suggested in the 2014 Civil Code amendment draft that was publicized before the 2017 decision. The above-mentioned changes of the abandonment of the non-attributability and good-faith requirements and the addition of categories of change of circumstances coincide exactly with the content of the amendment draft.

IV. Consequences

When the change of circumstances satisfies the above requirements, certain legal consequences come into being.

1. Duty to Renegotiate

The first legal consequence of applying the principle of change of circumstances one might come up with is the duty to renegotiate. In Korea, there has not been much discussion on this issue and therefore no consensus has been reached on the recognition of the duty to renegotiate. It would be ideal if parties could reach a new agreement that duly reflects the change of circumstances, which might be called an optimal contractual relationship. However, it is one thing to hope for such an optimal relationship and another to legally obligate parties to renegotiate. Renegotiation by nature is something that should be based on voluntary will, unless there are statutory or contractual provisions imposing a duty to renegotiate.[31] Further, imposing such an obligation often does not result in successful modification of the contract. One party generally benefits from the change of circumstances that results in the suffering of the other party. Smooth renegotiation and modification of the contract cannot be easily expected. Imposing the duty to renegotiate is likely to increase transaction costs without leading to a successful outcome.[32] Neither of the amendment drafts made in 2004 and 2014 acknowledge the duty to renegotiate in the wake of a change of circumstances. Meanwhile, looking at how international model laws deal with the duty to renegotiate, Article 6:111(2) PECL, for one, requires the parties to renegotiate before they demand modification or discharge of the contract. The aim is clear: to facilitate autonomous solutions between parties before seeking a remedy. The UNIDROIT Principles of International Commercial Contracts (PICC), on the one hand, and the DCFR, on the other hand, do not recognize a duty to renegotiate.

2. Modification

A second possible consequence, also debated controversially, is judicial modification, or at least judicial confirmation of the terms and conditions of the modification sought by the party. Voluntary modification by the parties is, of course, both possible and desirable. Whether or not judicial modification of a contract will be recognized as one of the legal consequences of applying the principle of the change of circumstances is not yet clear. There has been no Supreme Court decision so far in Korea that acknowledged judicial modification as one possible consequence.

[31] Supreme Court Decision 2008Da44368 (24 June 2011) deals with the interpretation of a renegotiation clause.
[32] KWON Youngjoon (n 4) 242.

There are two dimensions to the discussion on the acceptability of judicial modification in the context of the KCC. The first regards the feasibility of judicial modification within the current KCC, with no express provision. It may be possible, as can be seen in Germany, where there is no explicit ground contained in the BGB, but the German courts have developed this approach under section 242 BGB, which embodies the good-faith principle. In theory, this may be feasible in Korea as well. Yet, it seems too much of a stretch of the good-faith principle. The good-faith principle is the last resort and should be used in a moderate manner. Of course, the approach adopted by the German Reichsgericht is understandable as a response to hyperinflation in the aftermath of the First World War. Without such an extraordinary situation, judicial modification of the contract based on the good-faith principle does not seem either feasible or desirable.

The second dimension regards the feasibility of judicial modification at the level of legislation. It concerns the desirability of accepting judicial modification of a contract in the form of a statutory provision to resolve problematic situations caused by the change of circumstances. As the current KCC does not expressly allow judicial modification, and the good-faith principle does not provide the grounds for such judicial intervention, the issue of judicial modification is handed over to the legislature. It becomes, indeed, a matter of policymaking: whether or not it is desirable to allow the court to modify the terms of a contract that the parties agreed upon.

In the course of making the 2004 amendment draft, the Committee members unanimously agreed that a provision governing change of circumstances needed to be codified. The Committee also considered judicial modification as one of the possible remedies for a change of circumstances. However, this proposal was rejected by a narrow margin after some discussion. The main grounds for the rejection were that it might impair party autonomy and that it would unduly increase the courts' caseload. The draft provision, Article 544–4, does mention the possibility of modifying the contract. However, this refers to consensual modification reached by the parties. By contrast, the 2014 amendment draft introduced judicial modification as one of the possible remedies in Article 538–2. The problem with this provision is that it fails to address the relationship between the remedy for judicial modification and the remedy for termination or rescission. I suggest that the former be the primary remedy and the latter be only secondary. This is because reasonable parties may wish to maintain the contract with a bit of modification rather than terminating the contract altogether. In this scenario, the application for rescission will be rejected if judicial modification, the primary remedy, is the appropriate approach.

3. Termination or Rescission

It is clearly acknowledged by scholars that where the requirements are satisfied, the parties can terminate, in the case of a continuing contract, or rescind the contract. Although actual termination or rescission rarely takes place, its availability is evident. Most jurisdictions that recognize the doctrine of change of circumstances discharge a concerned party from his or her obligations. For instance, section 313 BGB expressly states that the disadvantaged party can terminate the contract if a modification is not possible or reasonable. Section 265 of the Restatement of Contracts (2d) in the USA states, with regard to frustration, that 'remaining duties to render performance are discharged unless the language or circumstances of the contract indicate the contrary'. The PECL, PICC, and DCFR all take similar, but still slightly different, approaches. In those model laws, it is the court, upon the request of parties, which ultimately determines the termination of the contract as well as its terms and conditions (Article 6111(3)(a) PECL; Article 6.2.3(4)(a) PICC; Article III—1:110 (2)(b) DCFR).

Termination here refers to putting an end to a continuing contract with non-retroactive effect (Article 550 KCC), while rescission here refers to putting an end to a contract in general with a retroactive effect (Article 548 KCC). In the case of rescission, each party should restore the other party to its original position (Article 548 KCC). Therefore, each party is required to return the goods or value that he or she has already received under the rescinded contract. In general, termination or rescission does not interfere with the right to claim damages (Article 551 KCC). However, a change of circumstances which was far beyond the control of the parties does not yield damages since the KCC requires a party's intention or fault with regard to non-performance for that (Article 390 KCC).

V. The Hypotheticals

1. Abraham and Bill

In 1567, Abraham enters into a contract for an unlimited period of time with farmer Bill under which Abraham promises to build and maintain an irrigation channel from which Bill may extract water at a fixed price. By 2018, inflation and the rise in the cost of maintenance and labour have made the price wholly inadequate. Abraham's successors in law ask for an increase in the price that would provide them with adequate compensation. Alternatively, they wish to terminate the contract.[33]

Several centuries have passed since the contract was made. It is probable that circumstances which were once the premise of the contract have dramatically changed over these centuries. From the given facts, it is clear that there has been inflation and a rise in the cost that consequently made the price wholly inadequate. The exact extent of the changes is not clearly described. Therefore, it is not clear how this case would be decided in Korean courts. There is a Supreme Court decision denying the application of the doctrine of change of circumstances to a case where the price soared, rising by about 202 times in 14 years.[34] This shows the strict attitude towards the application of this doctrine. However, the stance of the Korean Supreme Court has become more favourable towards the doctrine. Furthermore, if changes over several centuries were not within the boundary of the doctrine, it would become almost pointless. Therefore, it is possible that termination of the contract would be allowed if the changes are significant enough to justify the termination of the contract. Modification of the contract (ie increasing the price) is not likely to be accepted since there is no clear legal doctrine permitting this.

[33] The fact scenarios for this and the other hypothetical cases in this section V are taken from M Chen-Wishart, D Neo, and S Vogenauer, 'Introduction', ch 1 in this volume, 7–8.

[34] Supreme Court Decision 63Da452 (12 September 1963).

Another possible option is to resort to Article 689 KCC, which stipulates that each party may at any time rescind a contract of mandate for the future. A mandate is a contract under which one of the parties thereto has entrusted the other party with the management of affairs (Article 680 KCC). Maintaining an irrigation channel can fit into the category of a mandate contract. Abraham's successors in law can therefore terminate the contract based on Article 689.

2. Citi Corporation and Drive Bank

In 2015, Citi Corporation receives a loan from Drive Bank. The interest rate is fixed at 10 per cent for five years. In the 20 years preceding the agreement, the rate of inflation had been relatively stable within a range of 1 to 6 per cent. In 2017, the economic situation begins to destabilize and inflation rises to 50 per cent. Drive Bank requests adjustment or, alternatively, termination of the contract.

Given the strict stance towards the doctrine of change of circumstances, termination based on the doctrine is not likely to be recognized here. As mentioned above, there is a legal precedent where termination was denied, even when the price soared to a level of 202 times that at the time of the contract. In a relatively recent case, a bank and a systems operator concluded an online system supply and maintenance contract.[35] The bank was the consignee of the state-run lottery business and was to receive a flat fee from the state. The systems operator was to receive fees from the bank in proportion to the revenue of the lottery. At the time of contract, the bank's revenue was calculated by an accounting firm; however, in the end the bank had to pay 11 times more in fees than it originally anticipated. Even so, the bank's claim to terminate the contract based on the doctrine of change of circumstances was rejected by the courts, including the Supreme Court. It is therefore unlikely that termination would be allowed in this hypothetical case.

3. Easy and Frugle

Easy leases business premises from Frugle for a fixed period of 15 years. Shortly after the contract has been concluded, a nearby military airport is unexpectedly shut down for political reasons. The government invests an enormous amount of public funds in order to improve the commercial infrastructure in the area. As a result, Easy's profits are 500 per cent of what could reasonably have been expected at the time of making the contract. At the same time, the rental value of comparable business premises in the area rises to 500 per cent of the agreed rental price. Frugle requests that the rental price should be adjusted accordingly or, alternatively, that the agreement should be terminated.

Based on the case law presented above, termination under the doctrine of change of circumstances is not likely to succeed here. Changes due to governmental action are risks that are generally assumed and anticipated by the parties. This is even more so in a society where such governmental action or inaction happens frequently. In the leading case in 2007, the plaintiff purchased land with the expectation that the administrative restriction thereon would be lifted. On the contrary, it turned out that the land in question was about to be expropriated. The Supreme Court denied the application of the principle of change of circumstances.[35] Consistently, the conclusion is likely to be the same in this hypothetical case.

4. George and Han

Builder George agrees to refurbish the cellar of Han, the owner of a restaurant. The work is scheduled to start one month after the agreement. Before the work begins, the restaurant is completely destroyed by a storm that is much more violent than any other previous storm in the region. However, the cellar remains fully intact. Han immediately informs George of the situation and asks him not to start work. George insists on rendering performance because he has set aside two weeks to carry out the work and has already purchased the necessary materials. Is Han required to pay the contract price or, alternatively, to compensate George for his loss?

As suggested by the draft amendment of 2004, as well as the Supreme Court decision that followed in 2017,[36] change of circumstances can be categorized into 'substantial imbalance' and 'frustration of purpose'. However, most of the legal precedents in Korea so far have dealt with the former type. Since there are few cases on change of circumstances based on frustration of purpose, it is not easy to predict how Korean courts would react to this hypothetical case. If this is about a common mistake in the situation that already existed at the time of the contract, Korean courts are likely to apply a supplementary interpretation of a contract, a way of contract interpretation to fill the gap that the parties failed to incorporate into the terms and conditions of the contract.[37] If it is about contingencies that arise after the conclusion of the contract and frustrate the purpose of the contract, Korean courts apply the doctrine of change of circumstances. The cellar, which is the object of the contract, still remains intact. However, if it could be recognized that the purpose of refurbishing the cellar was to run the restaurant, the complete destruction of the restaurant would frustrate the purpose of the contract. A recent Supreme Court case acknowledged frustration of purpose as a ground for the rescission of the contract based on the doctrine of change of circumstances.[38] Given this case, it could also be said that the doctrine could be invoked in this hypothetical.

5. Gina and H Hotel

Gina books a room for the weekend at H Hotel in X City, the capital of country Z. However,

(i) the exhibition she intended to visit is cancelled at the very last moment;
(ii) a terrorist group declares that it plans to launch attacks on tourists in X;
(iii) an unforeseeable strike by airport personnel prevents Gina from travelling to X before Sunday afternoon;

[35] Supreme Court Decision 2004Da31302 (29 March 2007).
[36] Supreme Court Decision 2016Da249557 (12 June 2017).
[37] Supreme Court Decision 2005Da13288 (23 November 2006).
[38] Supreme Court Decision 2020Da254846 (10 December 2020).

(iv) the inauguration proceedings of the new head of state of Z that were scheduled for Saturday are cancelled. Gina had booked a room overlooking the street where the inauguration procession was supposed to pass by. Due to the inauguration, the rental price of the room was ten times higher than the regular price.

Can Gina cancel the booking?

As described above, there are two doctrinal possibilities. One is to resort to the change of circumstances doctrine. Since there is no similar case in Korea as of yet, it is not easy to predict the outcome. However, the 2017 Supreme Court decision clearly suggested the possibility of the application of the doctrine, and this might be the classic case where this doctrine can be applied. However, this could be a case of frustration of the subjective purpose of the contract, so termination is not allowed. The impossibility doctrine may not be applied to this case either. Paying for the hotel may be upsetting for Gina but it is not impossible. The notion of economic impossibility is discussed at a scholarly level.[39] But it has not been explicitly accepted by the Supreme Court. Even assuming that it is accepted, it is not clear from the fact of the hypothetical case whether this amounts to economic impossibility.

6. Kris and Leila

Kris sells his family home to Leila at 70 per cent of its market value. Both parties assume that Leila will dedicate it to cultural use by the general public. However, this assumption is not expressly set out in the contract. After the sale, Leila changes her mind and gives the house to one of her sons instead. Can Kris claim the difference between the agreed price and the market value or, alternatively, restitution of the house?

For Kris to be able to claim the difference between the agreed price and market value or restitution of the house, he needs to prove that the contract is either conditional or subject to avoidance due to mistake or fraud. If the lower price was conditioned upon Leila's dedication of the family home to cultural use by the general public, and if the clause expressing this condition could be construed to say that the difference could be claimed by Kris if such condition is not met, then Kris can claim the difference based on such terms and conditions of the contract. If Kris can prove that he erroneously believed in the Leila's good faith, then he can avoid the contract based on his mistake so long as the requirements in Article 109 KCC are met. If Leila deceived Kris, Kris can avoid the contract based on Article 110 KCC. In both cases, avoidance of the contract gives rise to restitution claim based on Article 741 KCC. However, as the facts state that Leila changed her mind only after the execution of a contract, it is less likely that this would constitute mistake or fraud, which requires erroneous belief or deceit at the time of the contract. The doctrine of change of circumstances is not likely to play a meaningful role either. Betrayal of belief that Leila would not change her mind is not likely to meet the high threshold of the requirements as set forth by the Korean legal precedents.

[39] See eg PARK Chanju, 'Gyeongjejeok Bulneunge Gwanhan Gaenyeomjeongripeu Pilyoseong' ['Necessity to Establish the Notion of Economical Impossibility'] (2009) 396 Ingweongwa Jeongeui [Human Rights and Justice] 6, 7.

14

Termination under Korean Law

AHN Tae-Yong

I. Introduction

It is said that one of the distinct features of the civil law tradition is its 'legal science'. Professor Merryman mentions 'the attitude' in the civil law tradition 'that definitions of concepts and classes express scientific truth', where the assumption is that 'the materials of the law . . . can be seen as naturally occurring phenomena, or data, from whose study the legal scientist can discover inherent principles and relationships'.[1] While other critics consider the same as deplorable 'conceptual jurisprudence',[2] Merryman rather positively considers that the culture of civil law holds central the logical integrity of the system and is not just for the achievement of 'functional utility' but for the pursuit of 'the embodiment of reality'.[3]

I begin this chapter with the above observation because the topic of termination would be a good place to demonstrate the 'legal science' or 'conceptual jurisprudence' of the civil law tradition. Although modern contract law tends to view termination mostly as a 'remedy' for non-performance, the civil law tradition treats termination as an integral part of the grand theory of contract; its requirements and effects make sense as the 'properties' of contract.

Merryman explains that, together with concepts, 'the work of legal science is carried on according to the methods of traditional formal logic'.[4] He says that legal science is peculiar in its 'high level of abstraction' in which 'the principles developed by legal scientists have been taken out of their factual and historical context, and are consequently lacking in concreteness' as 'the legal scientist is more interested in developing and elaborating a theoretical scientific structure than he is in solving concrete problems'.[5] Naturally, 'legal science attempts to be pure'; 'legal scientists deliberately focus their attention on pure legal phenomena and values, such as the "legal" value of certainty in the law, and exclude all others'.[6]

Merryman attributed this legal science to the creation of German scholars in the mid-to-late nineteenth century.[7] I vividly remember such an 'atmosphere' when I was a law student in Korea in the late 1980s to mid-1990s, as Korean law was under heavy influence of German jurisprudence. At that time the Korean Civil Code was barely over 30 years old, and scholars believed that their task was to make law more logical and scientific in the sense that it should be science that explains the empirical world by way of the principles.[8]

[1] JH Merryman, *The Civil Law Tradition* (2nd edn, Stanford University Press 1985) 62–63.
[2] ibid 64.
[3] ibid.
[4] ibid.
[5] ibid.
[6] ibid.
[7] ibid 61.
[8] Hegel, a consummate proponent of German Idealism, was one of the most influential theoreticians on the development of the legal science of German origin. He said: '[O]ur own phrase that "Reason is in the world" . . . means

Ahn Tae-Yong, *Termination under Korean Law* In: *Studies in the Contract Laws of Asia V: Ending and Changing Contracts*. Edited by: Mindy Chen-Wishart, Dora Neo, and Stefan Vogenauer, Oxford University Press.
DOI: 10.1093/oso/9780198995814.003.0014

The 'legal science' as described by Merryman exerted enormous influence on legal education and the mindset of the early generations of jurists of Korea.

Though I started from the same position, over the course of my legal practice I began to see the actual working of the law differently. The past several decades were a period of rapid social development and change in Korea. Although many pieces of legislation were introduced, the Civil Code remained fixed in letters. The law must catch up with reality while tending to its own desire for more sophistication. Empirical experiences pulled ahead of concepts and logic, which were subsequently busy appraising the new territories opened up for them. The Korean Civil Code exhibited a remarkable degree of flexibility and willingness to accommodate development and change, but this was not achieved by the dogmas of legal science. As Merryman points out, legal science tacitly admits the necessity of 'proper arrangement and manipulation' of the concepts.[9] Indeed, in many situations, the concepts and logic work like a *tool* for the administration of justice rather than a pure truth through which reality is embodied.

As will be seen in this chapter, complex forces are at work surrounding the concepts and logic which attempt to reinterpret, reformulate, rearrange, and even replace the existing state of the law. Such forces can include not only courts and scholars but also the public's demand and the breakthroughs in other jurisdictions.

II. Distinction with Suspension of Performance

Termination dissolves the contract and frees the parties from its obligations. A party terminating the contract forestalls the other party's claim while withholding its own performance. In this sense, termination seems to share the aspect of *exceptio non adimpleti contractus* (a defence which allows each party to a reciprocal contract to refuse the performance of an obligation under the contract). Some may think that *exceptio* is functionally an equivalent to termination, and indeed, in some jurisdictions, termination is not clearly distinguished from *exceptio*.[10] Professor Treitel, after comparing it with civil law, says that common law does not have a 'formal machinery of termination'.[11] Treitel notes that, in the common law tradition, the aggrieved party's defence of *exceptio* is not distinguished from his total abrogation of the contract.[12] Both are more or less treated under the same notion of termination.[13] In the civil law tradition, however, suspension of performance and termination are clearly distinguished.

The Civil Code of Korea provides for termination in Article 543 and for *exceptio* in Article 536. The first paragraph of Article 536 provides that 'a party of a reciprocal contract may withhold his own performance until the other party offers that party's performance'. This doctrine of *exceptio* consists of two elements—reciprocity and concurrence of

that Reason is the soul of the world it inhabits, its immanent principle, its most proper and inward nature, its universal': Georg Wilhelm Friedrich Hegel, *The Science of Logic*, § 24 n.

[9] ibid 64.
[10] GH Treitel, *Remedies for Breach of Contract—A Comparative Approach* (OUP 1988) 245, 300, 319.
[11] ibid 319, 334.
[12] ibid 245, 300, 319.
[13] ibid 300.

obligations. It is applicable only to a reciprocal contract, a contract under which one obligation is meant to be performed in exchange of the other. The assumption of Article 536(1) is that the reciprocal obligations are to be performed concurrently unless stipulated otherwise. When one obligation is to be performed reciprocally with but prior to the other obligation, the bearer of the first obligation may not invoke the doctrine of *exceptio*—he should perform first, in principle.

Termination under Korean law does not maintain any logical connection with the doctrine of *exceptio*, nor is it exclusively concerned with reciprocal contracts.[14] Termination and *exceptio* do not interact with each other except that *exceptio* informs the determination on whether a reciprocal contract is breached (once the defence of *exceptio* is established, there is no breach). To understand the conceptual gulf that exists between termination and *exceptio* in a civil law system like Korea, one should understand the life of a contract. A contract is alive even if there is a breach by a party. Even when the breach is serious or the performance has become impossible (by the debtor's fault), that fact alone does not end the contract.[15] It is conceptualized in Korean law that the contract holds on, in the face of the non-performance, to generate the inherent power to redress the situation, such as the right of specific performance or the right to damages.[16] A breached contract ends only when the contract is formally terminated.[17] In contrast, *exceptio* does not concern itself with the ending of a contract–its function is limited to ensuring fairness in exchange of performances.[18]

A recent *en banc* decision of the Korean Supreme Court can give us a taste of what termination really means vis-à-vis suspension of performance.[19] Here, the seller of real property made a contract to sell to party A. The price was to be paid in three instalments. The seller received the down payment and the middle payment, which together amounted to approximately 60 per cent of the total price. On the promised date of delivery in exchange for the final payment, the seller was unable to perform because of the existing lease on the property. The buyer A sent a notice to the seller to the effect that the contract would be terminated unless the seller complied with the contract (but instead of giving effect to this statement, the buyer preferred to have the contract fulfilled) and further discussed with the seller the matter of damages. Several months later, the seller resold the same property to a third party B for a higher price. The seller was indicted for criminal breach of trust.[20] The issue was whether the contract had already been terminated before the seller resold the property to B so that the seller was no longer obligated towards A. The lower court found that the contract was indeed terminated and so the seller was not guilty, but the Supreme Court disagreed. Even though the seller had breached the contract and the buyer went on to

[14] Some scholars attempt to define termination from the perspective of reciprocity. Jin-yung Chung, 'Non-Performance of Incidental Obligations and Termination—Supreme Court 2004Da67011 (14 July 2005)' (2005) 30 The Journal of Civil Law 213. See also Myung-Ji Son, 'Study on "Material" Breach for Statutory Termination' (2019) 89 The Journal of Civil Law 85. However, in Korean law, reciprocity is not a factor in termination; neither the Civil Code nor the case law requires it for termination.

[15] See eg Supreme Court 94Da15776 (25 October 1994).

[16] TY Ahn, 'Damages under Korean Law' in M Chen-Wishart, A Loke, and B Ong (eds), *Studies in the Contract Laws of Asia, vol I: Remedies for Breach of Contract* (OUP 2016) 165 n 4.

[17] See eg Supreme Court 66Da1183 (27 September 1966).

[18] The Supreme Court considers that the rationale of *exceptio* is the spirit of fairness and good faith. See eg Supreme Court 94Da31242 (24 February 1995).

[19] Supreme Court 2017Do4027 (17 May 2018) (*en banc*).

[20] Supreme Court 2016Do19308 (13 December 2018).

suspend his final payment, the contract was not yet legitimately terminated; the notice was treated as urging performance rather than a formal notice of termination (we will discuss the requirements of termination in section III). The seller was still bound by the contract[21] and, having received substantial payment, neglected his duty to take care of the property for the benefit of the intended buyer. The contract continued to exist despite the suspension of performance, whereas a legitimate termination would have altered the reality into something completely different—the non-existence of the contract.

III. Requirements of Termination

1. Non-performance

(a) Fault

In Korea, termination is one of the statutory remedies for the other party's non-performance. Fault is, in principle, a requirement to establish non-performance.[22] If so, should termination be allowed only when the debtor is at fault for non-performance? The positions of the jurisdictions and the scholars are divided.[23] In Korea, the mainstream opinion requires fault for termination,[24] which reflects the fact that the non-performance law of the Civil Code is founded on fault liability. Recently, the opposite view that termination should be permitted without the requirement of fault has gained force, and in the course of the discussion for an amendment of the Civil Code in 2004, the two sides clashed hard. At that time, the mainstream position prevailed.[25] But by the time the two sides collided again in 2013, the opposition had grown strong.[26] The 2013 proposal to amend the provisions on termination intentionally omitted any reference to the fault of the debtor as a requirement for termination.[27] The 'no fault' side argues that the purpose of termination is to free the parties from the bonds of the contract, rather than to pursue the liability of the non-performing party, so the requirement of fault that holds true for the remedy of damages is not necessary with respect to termination.[28] Further, the 'international trend' and in particular Germany's departure from the requirement of fault have been a considerable reinforcement for the position that fault should not be required for termination.[29]

[21] Supreme Court 84Do691 (21 August 1984).

[22] Korean Civil Code, art 390.

[23] See eg Young-Doo Kim, 'Termination under International Uniform Contract Laws and the Direction for Amendment of the Civil Code' (2008) 43 The Journal of Civil Law 35, 48; Dae-Kyung Kim, 'Comparative Law Study of Fault as Requirement of Termination' (2010) 45 Kyunghee Law Journal 67, 81–83; Jong-Geun Oh, 'Effect of Agreement to Terminate—Supreme Court 2005Da6341 (9 June 2005)' (2012) 59 The Journal of Civil Law 239, 252–53.

[24] Won-Lim Ji, *The Lecture on the Civil Law* (11th edn, Hongmun Publishing 2013) 1353–54; Duk-Soo Song, *The New Lecture on the Civil Law* (7th edn, Pakyoung Publishing 2014) 1346; Dae-Kyung Kim (n 23) 71, 73.

[25] Jae-Mok Lee, 'International Trend on Fault as Requirement of Termination and Discussion under Our Civil Code' (2006) 356 Human Rights and Justice 142–60, 158–59; Jin-Myung Chung, 'Termination of Contract and Its Effect: Reasons for Amendment and the Text of the Draft Amendment of the Civil Code' (2011) 55 The Journal of Civil Law 259–96; Dong-Hun Kim, 'Effect of Non-Performance—Termination of Contract: The Text of the Draft Amendment of the Civil Code' (2013) 65 The Journal of Civil Law 385, 391.

[26] Dong-Hun Kim (n 25) 391.

[27] Dong-Hun Kim (n 25) 388–89.

[28] Jin-Myung Chung, 'Termination of Contract and Fault' (1998) 51 The Journal of Comparative Civil Laws 5, 15–17; Dong-Hun Kim (n 25) 392.

[29] Young-Bok Park, 'Recent Discussion of Contract Liabilities in the West and the Contract Liabilities System of Our Civil Code' (1996) 13/14 The Journal of Civil Law 316; Young-Doo Kim, 'Termination of Contract and

The question of whether fault should be required for termination is tricky. For the 'no fault' side, the understanding of termination itself is different—termination is primarily to free the creditor from the contract with the non-performing debtor so as to allow him to enter into a new transaction with another party.[30] Most of the international model contract laws do not require fault for termination, and in their termination provisions, there is little hint of punishment for non-performance.[31] Nevertheless, since the debtor is usually disadvantaged by termination,[32] it may be desirable to require fault before permitting termination.

By a clever argument, the 'no fault' side made a landing on the black letters of the Civil Code, and although this is a bit technical, I will explain it briefly because this kind of submission of different versions of 'truth' is rather typical in the working of conceptual jurisprudence.

To terminate a contract for 'impossibility' (as opposed to 'delay') of performance, the Civil Code expressly requires fault of the debtor.[33] The fate of the contract when performance has become impossible through no fault of either party is dealt with by Article 537 of the Korean Civil Code, titled 'The Principle of Assumption of Risk by the Debtor': If performance of an obligation of one party in a reciprocal contract becomes impracticable due to a cause for which no party is responsible, that party [whose obligation is discharged] may not demand performance of the other party.

However, there is no equivalent of Article 537 with respect to delayed performance. So, unless we interpret Article 544 (on termination for delay) to not require fault, the contract whose performance is in delay through no fault of either party will continue with no means to end it.[34] The 'no fault' side argues that this shows that the intention of the Civil Code is that the contract should end for delay irrespective of the debtor's fault insofar as the notice of termination is preceded by a *Nachfrist* demand, that is, the demand to grant an extended period for fulfilment.[35] Fault is not required for termination because it is the lapse of the *Nachfrist* period that justifies termination.[36] (I am cautious with regard to this argument with the *Nachfrist* demand; we will discuss more later.)

Now the hitherto undefeatable position of 'fault' suddenly looks vulnerable: a chink in the armour is exposed. It at least reminds us that the problem of fault is not settled in the Civil Code. This kind of conceptual manoeuvring is what Merryman refers to as 'arrangement and manipulation' of the concepts, which is not only inevitable but also necessary for a system of conceptual jurisprudence to survive. We will see more examples in the following sections.

Fault of the Debtor' (2007) 35 The Journal of Civil Law 41, 42–43; Dong-Hun Kim (n 25) 391–92; Dong-Hun Kim, *Study on the Law of Obligations (II)* (Dong-Bang Publishing 2017) 288–89.

30 Hyung-Bae Kim, *The Particulars of the Law of Obligations (I)* (Pakyoung Publishing 1995) 268; Jin-Myung Chung (n 28) 17.

31 See eg the Principles of European Contract Law (PECL), art 9:305.

32 In the history of law, termination was perceived as a 'heavy weapon' and 'drastic remedy'; the general right to terminate was only slowly recognized. N Jansen and R Zimmermann, *Commentaries on European Contract Laws* (OUP 2018) 1287.

33 Korean Civil Code, art 546. Supreme Court 2000Da50497 (26 April 2002).

34 Hyung-Bae Kim (n 30) 267–68; Jin-Myung Chung (n 28) 23.

35 Hyung-Bae Kim (n 30) 264–65, 279–80; Dae-Kyung Kim (n 23) 72.

36 Jin-Myung Chung (n 28) 16; Soon-Goo Myung, 'Termination of Contract for Delay under the Civil Code and Its Comparative Law Characteristics' (1995) 12 Hanyang Journal of Law 429, 440–41 (in German law, a *Nachfrist* justifies termination).

(b) Breach of a major obligation

It is the established law of Korea that termination is only allowed for violation of a major obligation. Breach of an incidental obligation (I will use the term 'minor obligation' interchangeably) does not suffice. The Supreme Court has confirmed on many occasions that:

> to terminate a contract due to non-performance, the obligation concerned should be a major obligation to the extent that the obligation is *necessary and indispensable to the attainment of the purpose of the contract* and, *without its performance*, the purpose of the contract cannot be achieved and *the terminating party would* not *have entered into the contract*.[37]

Throughout this chapter, I will call this principle the 'unattainability of the purpose' standard. Note that the Korean Civil Code does not stipulate this standard as a general requirement of termination;[38] it is established by the case law. Nevertheless, this standard—the requirement of materiality of breach—is the pivot on which the whole structure of termination rests. Many Asian countries that adhere to the civil law tradition adopt similar standards as the top principle governing the law of termination.[39]

Although the orthodox scholarly position in Korea has categorized obligations into major and incidental ones by reference to their generic nature, it is now increasingly recognized that the courts' distinction between a major obligation and an incidental obligation in the context of termination is not an abstract categorization of obligations. Rather, the courts use the terminology to denote the concrete importance of an obligation after examining all relevant points of consideration in a given case.[40]

The distinction between a major obligation and an incidental one should be made by 'taking consideration of the reasonable intention of the parties as expressed at the time of the contract or clearly exhibited through the circumstances, including examination of the purpose and content of the contract and the consequence of the non-performance'.[41]

For example, when a party promises to pay a sum prior to the due date and then fails to do so, terminating the contract for that breach is not allowed if such promise was made as a favour.[42] However, when the buyer of the real property promises to discharge the seller's debt and tax, this is not incidental because *without that promise the seller would not have entered into the contract*.[43] No termination was allowed where the contractor was obliged to make and supply a video product but did not prepare a preview on the agreed date. The Supreme Court held that the obligation to prepare the preview was only an obligation incidentally involved in the process of fulfilling the main obligation.[44] Termination was allowed where the seller sold some shops in a building, also promising to ensure non-competition

37 Supreme Court 2004Da67011 (14 July 2005) (emphases added).

38 Though, the phrase itself is in use in other articles, eg art 545 (time of essence) and art 575 (warranty liability).

39 They include Cambodia, China, Japan (before 2017), Korea, Taiwan (for ancillary obligations only: see S-L Jan, 'Termination and Rescission under Taiwanese Contract Law', ch 23 in this volume, text at nn 12, 25), and Vietnam, among others.

40 Soo-Jeong Choi, 'Non-Performance That Gives Rise to Termination' (2002) 68 Justice 76, 80–84; Jin-Myung Chung (n 14) 213, 231–35; Dong-Hun Kim, 'Recent Case Law on Termination' (2007) 19 Kookmin Journal of Law 175, 184; Dong-Hun Kim (n 29) 302–03.

41 Supreme Court 97Ma575 (7 April 1997).

42 Supreme Court 93Da17966 (13 July 1993).

43 Supreme Court 93Da19108 (29 June 1993).

44 Supreme Court 96Da14364, 14371 (9 July 1996).

among the shopkeepers by enforcing the designated trade of each shop but later reneging on that promise by allowing certain shops to change trade. The Supreme Court held that the seller's obligation to ensure non-competition was a major obligation *without which the shopkeepers would not have entered into the contracts.*[45] The degree of non-performance is also relevant. In one case, the Supreme Court rejected the claim of termination where the amount not paid was only 2 per cent of the purchase price.[46]

Where the contract stipulated a separate remedy, other than termination, for breach of a particular obligation, the Supreme Court reasoned that those obligations were not the kind of obligations without which the parties would not have entered the contract.[47]

The standard of the 'unattainability of the purpose', which has long been the pillar of stability and predictability in this field, is under attack. Under the influence of comparative law studies, a trend of proposing alternative terms like 'material' or 'fundamental' is often observed.[48] The 2013 draft revision of the termination law managed to fend off those suggestions but settled on a format in which the 'unattainability of the purpose' is only a proviso.[49] Japan, a jurisdiction closely monitored by Korean scholars, recently revised its law of termination, in which the importance of the 'unattainability of purpose' is severely downgraded.[50] An alternative view proposes that termination should be allowed only when the creditor's obligation maintains 'subjective equivalence' with the debtor's obligation.[51]

However, none of those arguments sets out sufficiently clear terms.[52] Later on, I will discuss this problem further in relation to the *Nachfrist* requirement, but for now, I point out that the recent push for replacement of the 'unattainability of the purpose' standard overlooks its remarkable degree of intuitive comprehensibility, practical applicability, and steadiness in its core meaning. Although some scholars attack this standard,[53] the 'unattainability of the purpose' principle dynamically characterizes a breach as major or minor only after considering the totality of circumstances,[54] just as Lord Diplock refused to accept the argument that an obligation should be abstractly categorized as either condition or warranty in the *Hong Kong Fir Shipping* case.[55]

45 Supreme Court 2004Da67011 (14 July 2005).

46 Supreme Court 66Da626 (31 May 1966).

47 Supreme Court 93Da2766 (22 December 1994).

48 Kwang-Hyun Suk, 'Fundamental Breach under the CISG' (2006) 23 The Journal of Law 437, 437–38; Young-Doo Kim (n 23) 53; Dong-Hun Kim (n 29) 273–75, 287–88; Soo-Jeong Choi (n 40) 87–89; Jae-Mok Lee (n 25) 160.

49 It was said that the 'unattainability of the purpose' standard was 'passively' adopted in the draft revision. See Dong-Hun Kim (n 25) 394–95; Jae-Hyung Kim, 'The Draft of the Civil Code Reform on Termination of Contract, Assumption of Risk, and Change of Circumstances' (2014) 55 The Journal of Law 20. Several scholars voted against such format, arguing that the materiality should be placed as the main requirement of termination. Jae-Hyung Kim, 20.

50 Revised Japanese Civil Code, art 541. See Akira Kamo, 'Termination of Contracts under Japanese Law', chapter 12 in this volume, 250.

51 Jin-Myung Chung (n 14) 242.

52 See eg AB Cohen, 'Reviving Jacob and Youngs, Inc. v. Kent: Material Breach Doctrine Reconsidered' (1997) 42 Villanova Law Review 65, 67, 88–90 ('absence of focus' in 'material breach'); R Koch, 'The Concept of Fundamental Breach of Contract under the United Nations Convention on Contracts for the International Sale of Goods (CISG)' in Pace (ed), *Review of the Convention on Contracts for the International Sale of Goods (CISG)* (Kluwer Law International 1999) 177, 268 (determination of fundamental breach is 'arbitrary').

53 See eg Jin-Myung Chung (n 14) 235–37.

54 See eg Supreme Court 2011Da102301 (29 March 2012) (termination for a minor breach is possible if the purpose of the contract is derailed).

55 *Hong Kong Fir Shipping Co Ltd v Kawasaki Kisen Kaisha Ltd* [1962] 2 QB 26, [1961] EWCA Civ 7, [1962] 1 All ER 474.

(c) Offer of performance by the terminating party

Where two opposing obligations are to be performed reciprocally at the same time, one party cannot claim the other party's non-performance unless he offers performance of his own.[56] Although unstated in the letters of the law, this has been assumed by the Supreme Court on numerous occasions,[57] especially where the obligations of the parties are *reciprocal and concurrent*.[58]

For example, in a contract for the sale of real estate, the buyer's obligation to pay the purchase price is to be performed reciprocally and concurrently with the seller's obligation to transfer title (unless stipulated otherwise). To put the buyer into non-performance, the seller must offer the buyer all the documents necessary for the transfer of title and ask him to receive them in return for payment. Only then can the buyer fall into delay.[59]

A party can terminate a reciprocal contract without offering its own performance if: the other party has already expressed that he will not perform;[60] it is clear from the circumstances that the other party will not perform even if the terminating party should perform;[61] it is clear that even if the terminating party should offer his performance, the other party will not be able to perform within a reasonable time;[62] where the defect of the other party's performance is so grave that it could not be repaired or even if it could be repaired, it would take too much time to repair;[63] or the other party's corresponding obligation has become impossible to perform.[64]

2. Demand (*Nachfrist* Notice)

Article 544 of the Civil Code provides that for *delayed or incomplete*[65] performance, the terminating party must make a demand to the non-performing party and grant a reasonable time within which to perform. This is a crucial procedural requirement in termination, often called a '*Nachfrist* notice'. Without an appropriate demand, termination does not take effect.[66] Such a demand is not required when the contract is terminated for impossibility of performance.[67]

A demand made without specifying a reasonable period is still valid, in which case the party who made the demand can terminate after a reasonable time has passed.[68] There is no specific guidance from the case law on what is 'a reasonable period'. It will depend on the circumstances of each case; an impossibly short period would not be considered reasonable, but any working length of time would be acceptable.[69]

56 Supreme Court 97Da54604 (13 March 1998).
57 See eg Supreme Court 74Da355 (9 September 1975).
58 Supreme Court 94Da24565 (11 October 1994).
59 Supreme Court 91Da25703 (22 September 1992).
60 Supreme Court 94Da16083 (28 April 1995).
61 Supreme Court 93Da7204 (24 August 1993).
62 ibid.
63 Supreme Court 96Da16650 (23 August 1996).
64 Supreme Court 2000Da22850 (24 January 2003).
65 General applicability of art 544 is noted by the scholars. See eg Seung-Hyun Sung, 'Is Article 544 of the Civil Code Only for Delay?—A Theory for a New Understanding of Article 544' (2016) 36 The Journal of Law 257.
66 Supreme Court 70Da1342 (23 February 1971).
67 See Civil Code, art 546.
68 Supreme Court 94Da35930 (25 November 1994).
69 Supreme Court 78Da2496 (24 July 1979); Supreme Court 79Da1859 (15 January 1980).

An excessive demand that is made in bad faith is struck down as invalid. The Supreme Court has held, on many occasions, that when the demand for performance exceeds the performance due under the contract, it is only effective if the difference between the two is small or the difference was an error, but if the difference is considerable and the clearly expressed intention of the creditor is not to accept less than the demanded amount, the demand is invalid.[70]

In addition to the case of impossibility of performance, a demand is not required for termination when the contract stipulates that time is of essence (ie if the contract is not performed at a specific time or within a specific period, the purpose of the contract will become unattainable).[71] If the debtor has clearly expressed the intention not to perform by the due date, the creditor can terminate the contract even before the due date without making a demand.[72]

There are two theoretical issues that we should consider with respect to the requirement of a *Nachfrist* notice. Firstly, the fact that the breach is material does not necessarily exempt the terminating party from the requirement of a *Nachfrist* demand. If we consider that the policy concern of a *Nachfrist* notice is a 'second chance' or the procedure commensurate to termination as the 'last resort', this requirement should operate on top of the materiality of breach; it is not to be dispensed with on the account of it.

On this point, the position of Korean law is not entirely the same as the international trend of 'fundamental breach'. For example, Article 49(1) of the United Nations Convention on Contracts for the International Sale of Goods (CISG) provides that the buyer can terminate the contract without granting an additional period of performance if the breach is 'fundamental'. Other international model laws have followed suit.[73] Of course, the practical difference may not be as large as it may seem because the notion of 'fundamental breach' somehow addresses the need of a *Nachfrist* notice within itself. These international projects specify that in case of 'non-fundamental delay', a *Nachfrist* notice should be given before termination.[74] Thanks to terms like 'non-fundamental delay', we can deduce that 'fundamental breach' concerns time being 'of the essence'.[75] 'Fundamental breach' in certain international model laws also includes a deliberate refusal to perform.[76]

Where 'time is of the essence' and there is 'refusal to perform', Korean law also dispenses with a *Nachfrist* notice. However, the reasoning is very different. Under the international model laws, the corresponding demand is not required because the breach is 'fundamental', while in Korean law, the same is not required because requiring a *Nachfrist* notice in such circumstances would be unreasonable.[77] The practical result may look identical but, in terms of the efficiency and stability in administering the cases, there is a hefty cost to pay when the need of a *Nachfrist* notice is to be processed through the channel of 'fundamental'. The term 'fundamental' in the international model laws is highly debatable,[78] uncertain,

[70] Supreme Court 2004Da13083 (9 July 2004).
[71] Civil Code, art 545.
[72] Supreme Court 2014Da227225 (12 February 2015).
[73] PECL, art 9:301; Draft Common Frame of Reference (DCFR) art III.-3:502; UNIDROIT Principles of International Commercial Contracts (PICC) (2016) art 7.3.1.
[74] CIS, art 49(1); PECL, art 9:301(2); DCFR, art III.-3:503; PICC (2016) art 7.3.1(3).
[75] PECL, art 8:103; PICC (2016) art 7.3.1(2).
[76] PECL, art 8:103; DCFR, art III.-3:502(2); PICC (2016) art 7.3.1(2).
[77] See eg Dong-Hun Kim (n 25) 394 (requiring a *Nachfrist* notice for a major breach).
[78] M Will, 'Article 25' in CM Bianca and MJ Bonell (eds), *Commentary on the International Sales Law* (Giuffrè 1987) 209. See also Koch (n 51) 263.

and vague.[79] The term has become even more obscure in the international model laws subsequent to the CISG because it is by now seriously overburdened with control of a wide range of issues, even including equitable concerns like limitation of termination,[80] and as a result, its meaning is unstable and unintelligible. In Korean law, in contrast, such matters do not belong to the 'materiality' of breach as the core meaning of materiality does not deviate from 'unattainability of the purpose'.

Secondly, a *Nachfrist* notice is not, and should not be, an all-powerful *carte blanche* in termination. As mentioned earlier,[81] the trend of thinking is that a *Nachfrist* notice justifies termination, against which I have my reservations. A conspicuous development in this regard emerged in the Japanese Civil Code Reform Act of 2017, which revised the law of termination in a sweeping manner. Under the revised law, the creditor can terminate a contract unless the breach is 'insignificant'.[82] In this novel scheme, control by 'unattainability of the purpose', 'fundamental breach', or any equivalent principle, is relinquished. Fault, too, is dropped as the requirement for termination.[83] Termination is extraordinarily expedited. The only checkpoint is whether an additional period of performance is given before termination. In fact, the Japanese reform of termination is a case of the tenet that 'a *Nachfrist* notice justifies termination'.[84] Even the requirement of a *Nachfrist* notice can be dispensed with in certain circumstances, such as when 'the purpose of the contract is unattainable'.[85]

The traditional civil law approach with 'unattainability of the purpose' and the international model laws with 'fundamental breach' agree at least on one baseline—that termination should not be easily allowed and must pass a threshold of materiality. When this baseline is renounced, the practical result is that the creditor can terminate the contract for a minor breach (unless it is truly negligible) even though the purpose of the contract is still within reach. Further, the creditor would attempt to terminate the contract *immediately*, without giving any chance of further performance, if the purpose of the contract is at risk.[86] Here, the standard of 'unattainability of the purpose', the hitherto central pillar in restraining termination, is turned on its head and is given the role of a trigger for an express termination (rather than requiring a *Nachfrist*). There are considerable technical difficulties as well. The revised termination law of Japan introduces at least three distinctions of breach—that which hinders the purpose of the contract (terminable immediately), that which is not grave enough to hinder the purpose of the contract but is not 'insignificant' (terminable with an additional period of performance), and that which is 'insignificant'

[79] United Nations Conference on Contracts for the International Sale of Goods (1980), Official Records A/CONF.97/19, 206, 295–303, 329–330.

[80] For example, in PICC (2016) art 7.3.1 the term 'fundamental' considers a factor like 'the breaching party will suffer disproportionate loss'.

[81] See section III.1(a).

[82] Revised Japanese Civil Code, art 541. See also Akira Kamo, 'Termination of Contracts under Japanese Law', chapter 12 in this volume, 250. The Japanese word '*keibi* (軽微)' can also be translated as 'trivial'.

[83] Kamo (n 82) 249. Removing fault and materiality requirements at the same time is very serious. See eg Young-Doo Kim (n 23) 59 (recognizing the importance of the materiality standard especially when fault is not required).

[84] The first exhibition of this manifesto is contained in s 323 of the German Civil Code (BGB) (2002), which the revised Japanese Civil Code seems to follow closely. See also Myung-Ji Son (n 14) 110 (the Japanese reform of 2017 is affected by the German revision of 2002, which considers a *Nachfrist*, rather than the materiality, as the key to termination).

[85] Revised Japanese Civil Code, art 542.

[86] The previous 'purpose of contract' standard was deliberated but rejected to pave the way for a lower standard of 'insignificant'. Min-Hee Kwak, 'Change of Paradigm in Breach of Contract for Termination in the Revised Civil Code of Japan' (2018) 35 The Journal of Property Law 35, 45–46, 50.

(not terminable). Managing a system of termination stably while juggling with these distinctions would be a tall order.

Obviously, this scheme aims at creating a regime of 'easy termination'.[87] The proponents of this scheme are inspired by the international model laws,[88] and they often think that the CISG and the PECL would support the modern spirit and rationality in their scheme of the new termination law.[89] However, that is not the vision of the CISG and the PECL. The international model laws have been an inspiring force in the field of termination partly because they are willing to go the extra mile to maintain the continuity of the contract by restraining termination and providing for the mechanisms to mend the contractual relationship in crisis. With the backbone notion of 'fundamental breach'[90] and the offer of mechanisms like a possible cure after the due date,[91] the CISG views a contract not as 'a duel fought with deadly weapons' but as 'a relationship calling for cooperation and accommodation',[92] as pointed out by Professor Honnold, one of the leading authorities in formulation of the CISG. The CISG thinks highly of 'open lines of communication between the parties so that each knows what to expect from the other'.[93] The trend of accentuating the creditor's interest in the expedited dissolution of a contract is a divergent force from the original vision.[94]

IV. Effects of Termination

1. Retroactive Extinguishment

Article 548 of the Civil Code says that '[w]hen a party terminated the contract, each party is obliged to make restitution to the other party'. There are two major theories in Korea about

[87] ibid 37, 58.

[88] Kamo (n 82) 247 (decisive influence of the CISG on the Japanese reform of termination law); Min-Hee Kwak (n 86) 45–46 (influence of the CISG, PECL, PICC on the Japanese reform); R Zimmermann, 'The German Civil Code and the Development of Private Law in Germany' (2006) Oxford University Comparative Law Forum <https://ouclf.law.ox.ac.uk/the-german-civil-code-and-the-development-of-private-law-in-germany> accessed 23 February 2020 (influence of the CISG and PECL on the German reform); R Zimmermann, 'Breach of Contract and Remedies under the New German Law of Obligations' 48 *Saggi, Conferenze e Seminari* 44–47. Reproduced with permission of Centro di studi e ricerche di diritto comparator e straniero, diretto da MJ Bonell (2002) <www.cisg.law.pace.edu/cisg/biblio/zimmerman.html> accessed 23 February 2020 (similarities between the PECL and German revision of termination).

[89] See eg Min-Hee Kwak (n 86) 37, 46, 48, 61 (citing Japanese authorities such as Shiomi Yoshio).

[90] Will (n 78) 205 (separation of a non-fundamental and a fundamental breach is 'of cardinal importance'); L Graffi, 'Case Law on the Concept of "Fundamental Breach" in the Vienna Sales Convention' (2003) 3 Revue de droit des affaires internationales [International Business Law Journal] (Forum Europeén de la Communication, Paris) 338, 338–49 (fundamental breach is 'a milestone concept' since it is 'the necessary precondition for avoiding the contract'); A Lorenz, 'Fundamental Breach under the CISG', available at <www.cisg.law.pace.edu/cisg/biblio/lorenz.html> accessed 23 February 2020 (contract avoidance is not available for just any breach of contract; fundamental breach is a prerequisite).

[91] TY Ahn, 'Specific Performance and Cure under Korean Law' in Chen-Wishart, Loke, and Ong (n 1) 140, 154.

[92] J Honnold, *Uniform Law for International Sales under the 1980 United Nations Convention* (4th edn, Kluwer Law International 2009) 292. This is in agreement with the mainstream view in Korea (contract is a relationship of cooperation). See eg Yoon-Jik Kwak, *General Provisions of the Law of Obligations* (6th edn, Pakyoung Publishing 2003) 18.

[93] Honnold (n 92) 297.

[94] See eg Jae-Hyung Kim (n 49) 21 (referring to the two opposing trends of the CISG and the PECL, on one hand, and the German reform, on the other); Dong-Hun Kim (n 25) 393–95 (the 'purpose of contract' and 'fundamental breach' are to moderate the interests between creditor and debtor); Myung-Ji Son (n 14) 107–10 (the German and Japanese reforms are based on a line of thinking that is different from the central importance of the materiality requirement).

the interpretation of this article.[95] One theory argues that this article implies that the contract is *retroactively extinguished* by termination and, as a result, mutual restitution is required to return the parties' contractual relationship to the *status quo ante*, that is, the state before they entered into the contract. This theory is known as the 'Direct Effect Theory' and is the position of the mainstream scholarly opinion[96] and the courts.[97]

The other theory argues that the language of Article 548 does not necessarily presuppose retroactive extinguishment; instead, it imposes the obligation of restitution on each party as a way of liquidating the existing contractual relationship.[98] According to this theory, the contractual relationship, upon termination, *transforms* into a legal relationship specifically committed to liquidating what has transpired between the parties up to the time of termination.[99] Under this theory, the existing obligations cease to exist and the performances already made are to be restituted. This rearrangement takes place as of termination and its effect is for the future.[100] This theory is known as the 'Liquidation Theory' and is an important minority position.[101]

It appears that neither theory denies that termination aims to return the parties to the *status quo ante* before conclusion of the contract.[102] They differ greatly on whether this is to happen retroactively or non-retroactively.[103] Under the Direct Effect Theory, restitution is a logical result of the retroactive extinguishment, whereas compensation of damages for non-performance needs a separate positive ground because the contract itself, from which the right to damages derives, has disappeared retroactively.[104] In contrast, under the Liquidation Theory, the obligation of restitution arises from the theory's concept of 'transformation',[105] and the right to damages is better explained because the contract continues to maintain its life, albeit transformed.[106] Under the Direct Effect Theory, any third party who has acquired an interest based on the terminated contract would be affected by termination so that their protection becomes a particular concern. Under the Liquidation Theory, a third party cannot be affected by termination because termination under this theory does not attempt to rewrite the past.[107]

The Liquidation Theory has some attractive aspects, but it runs counter to the letter of the Korean Civil Code, which indicates that termination is intended to be retroactive.[108] The Civil Code expressly states that the right to damages is not affected by termination, that the third party's interest is protected despite termination, and that there exists another kind of dissolution of contract that has no retroactive effect (Article 550). Note that the CISG, the PECL, the Draft Common Frame of Reference (DCFR), and the UNIDROIT Principles of International Commercial Contracts (PICC), which all seem to take the

95 There are other theories, too, but the two mentioned here are most important. For the various theories, see eg Si-Young Oh, 'Effect of Termination and Its Legal Nature' (2012) 58 The Journal of Law 325.

96 Won-Lim Ji (n 24) 1363; Duk-Soo Song (n 24) 1359.

97 Supreme Court 75Da1394 (24 May 1977).

98 Hyung-Bae Kim (n 30) 289.

99 ibid 294–95, 297; Yong-Dam Kim, 'An Observation on Effect of Termination' (1960) Law and Administration 30.

100 Hyung-Bae Kim (n 30) 296.

101 ibid 289; Jin-Myung Chung (n 28) 23–25; Yong-Dam Kim (n 99) 30–31.

102 Hyung-Bae Kim (n 30) 297.

103 Duk-Soo Song (n 24) 1359.

104 Won-Lim Ji (n 24) 1365; Duk-Soo Song (n 24) 1367.

105 Yong-Dam Kim (n 99) 31.

106 Hyung-Bae Kim (n 30) 291, 311; Jin-Myung Chung (n 28) 25; Yong-Dam Kim (n 99) 30.

107 Hyung-Bae Kim (n 30) 298; Young-Doo Kim (n 23) 86.

108 Jong-Geun Oh (n 23) 253.

position of non-retroactive dissolution of contract, do not speak of protection of a third party. In contrast, the Korean Civil Code has an explicit provision for protecting a third party from the fallout of termination. With respect to termination pursuant to Article 550, which has no retroactive effect, the Civil Code does not bother to provide for the same, which indicates that the drafters of the Civil Code were conscious of the implications of retroactive and non-retroactive dissolutions of contract.

By virtue of retroactive extinguishment of contract by termination, where the seller of the land had permitted the buyer to begin construction of the building on the land before full payment, the buyer is obliged to demolish the building if the contract is later terminated unless the buyer has a separate right to use the land for construction.[109] When the shares in a company were transferred under a contract, ownership in the shares automatically returns to the seller when the contract is terminated, and the buyer is not able to exercise the rights of the shareholder.[110] When the creditor of a company acquired the company and set off his obligation to pay the purchase price against the company's existing debt to him, the company remains indebted to the creditor if the acquisition is terminated.[111]

Under the doctrine of retroactive extinguishment, when a contract for sale of real property is terminated after title is transferred, the ownership of the real property automatically returns to the seller without any further action.[112] Some scholars argue that the ownership should stay with the debtor after termination and the debtor is only obligated to return the property to the creditor,[113] but such version of termination is not accepted by the courts.

2. Restitution

As a result of the retroactive extinguishment of a contract following termination, the parties to the contract are obliged to return what they received or gained under the contract, and each party's legal status is restituted to that which had existed before the contract.[114]

It is important to understand that in a civil law jurisdiction like Korea, the right to restitution does not arise from breach of contract per se; it arises from termination. Restitution makes sense to compensate for the void created by the extinction of a validly existing legal cause.[115] Therefore, both parties, including the terminating party, bear the obligation of restitution.[116] The parties' obligations of restitution are to be performed reciprocally and concurrently.[117] In principle, all benefits that each party received or gained under the contract should be returned to the other party.[118] It is not even relevant whether a party had been aware of the cause for termination.[119] In other words, the fault of the non-performing party is not considered in determination of the scope of restitution.[120]

109 Supreme Court 87DaKa2895 (28 June 1988).
110 Supreme Court 2002Da29411 (10 September 2002).
111 Supreme Court 79Da1257 (26 August 1980).
112 Supreme Court 75Da1394 (24 May 1977).
113 See Si-Young Oh (n 95) 347 (summarizing the opinion of these scholars).
114 See eg Supreme Court 94Da33989 (28 April 1995).
115 Supreme Court 2017Da37324 (24 January 2018).
116 Supreme Court 94Da10061 (24 March 1995).
117 Civil Code, art 536.
118 Supreme Court 2013Da14675 (12 December 2013).
119 ibid.
120 Supreme Court 94Da10061 (24 March 1995).

The obligation of restitution is to be performed, in principle, even if its cost exceeds the value of the benefit to be returned.[121] If the return of the original benefit has become impossible 'in light of the social norm or the notion of transaction', the party should pay the value of the benefit at the time when the return became impossible.[122]

The benefit that a party gained through the use of a thing that he received under the contract should also be returned.[123] If the buyer's income resulted from his special efforts and ability, and could not ordinarily be obtained from the thing itself, such portion should be deducted from the amount returned.[124] The buyer should also be compensated the cost of repair or the increase of the value as the result of the improvement.[125]

Likewise, if a party received money under the terminated contract, he should return the money and the interest that accrued at the agreed rate or, in the absence of such rate, at the rate of 5 per cent per annum.[126]

3. Exceptions to Retroactive Effect

(a) Protection of third parties

Article 548(1) of the Civil Code, which provides for retroactive extinguishment as the effect of termination, has a proviso that termination shall not injure the interest of a third party. By virtue of this proviso, while termination completely expunges the contractual relationship, a third party's acquisition of an interest based on the terminated contract is protected.

For example, where the seller of property terminated the contract, but before such termination, the buyer re-sold the property to a third party who subsequently completed title transfer,[127] the termination of the contract between the seller and the buyer does not affect the acquisition of the property by the third party. Consequently, ownership of the property does not revert to the seller[128] (the seller must content himself with the current price of the property as restitution).

A third party who was aware of the possibility of termination when he acquired the interest is still protected[129] as the third party's position should not be subjected to the caprices of the terminating party. Further, the case law also protects a third party who acquired the interest after termination if he was not aware that the contract had already been terminated.[130]

(b) Compensation of damages

Article 551 of the Civil Code provides that termination of contract does not affect the terminating party's claim of damages. This is another important exception to the retroactive

121 Supreme Court 88Da*Ka*31866 (9 March 1990).
122 ibid.
123 Dong-Hun Kim (n 40) 186–90.
124 Supreme Court 2006Da26328 (8 September 2006).
125 Civil Code, art 203(2). See eg Supreme Court 99Da66564, 66571 (23 August 2002).
126 Civil Code, art 548(2). Supreme Court 2011Da50509 (26 April 2013). For a commercial contract, the rate is 6 per cent per annum: Commercial Code, art 54.
127 Supreme Court 2002Da33502 (11 October 2002).
128 Supreme Court 81DaKa1110 (23 November 1982).
129 Supreme Court 2008Da57746 (23 December 2010).
130 Supreme Court 2005Da6341 (9 June 2005).

effect of termination. If we carry the principle of retroactive extinguishment through to its logical end, any claim of damages for non-performance is not possible because the basis of the claim has been retroactively erased. Obviously, such position would encourage breach of contract as the aggrieved party would be discouraged from terminating the contract for fear of losing the right to damages. Article 551 is, thus, an inevitable exception to the retroactive effect of termination.[131]

The principles and the usual working of the law of damages, as explained in detail in volume I of this series, are also true in the situation of termination.[132]

4. Non-retroactive Termination

In addition to a termination that dissolves a contract retroactively, the Civil Code acknowledges a termination that dissolves a contract only for the future. In the Civil Code, these two forms of termination are clearly distinguished—the former is called *haejae* and the latter is called *haeji*.[133] For the purposes of this chapter, I will refer to the former as retroactive termination and the latter as non-retroactive termination.

The Civil Code gives us only a hint that non-retroactive termination should exist under Korean law. It simply says that in the case of non-retroactive termination, the contract is dissolved for the future and the terminating party may claim damages for non-performance.[134] Everything else is left to interpretation. In particular, the Civil Code is completely silent on which contracts are subject to non-retroactive termination. The widely accepted criterion is that a contract of continuous performances for a certain period is subject to non-retroactive termination.[135]

A good example of a contract subject to non-retroactive termination is lease.[136] The performance of lease is made continuously for the duration of the lease. When the lease is terminated, it is unreasonable to retroactively unwind the lease. The lessee has already enjoyed the lease up to the time of termination and the lessor has received or is entitled to receive the rent for that portion of the lease.[137]

The mere fact that the performance of a contract would take a long time does not set the contract to non-retroactive termination. For example, termination of the construction of a building is retroactive. It is because the contract consists of a single performance on each side—construction and payment, and we assume that a partial construction does not satisfy the contract.

What if the contractor, who did not complete the work, had delivered a meaningful amount of the work before termination? Isn't retroactive termination too harsh? The Supreme Court maintains that if the completed portion of the work is beneficial to the owner, the contractor may claim the price of his work although the contract is retroactively terminated. In one case, a software contractor completed 87 per cent of the development

[131] Duk-Soo Song (n 24) 1367; Jong-Geun Oh (n 23) 270–71.
[132] Supreme Court 2015Da59115 (15 April 2016): see Ahn (n 16) 165.
[133] Both *haejae* and *haeji* are a combination of two Chinese characters. Literally, *haejae* means 'unwind and remove', whereas *haeji* means 'unwind and cease'.
[134] Civil Code, arts 550 and 551.
[135] Won-Lim Ji (n 24) 1378; Duk-Soo Song (n 24) 1370.
[136] See eg Supreme Court 93Da61321 (22 November 1994).
[137] Supreme Court 96Da14616 (26 July 1996).

of the software when the contract was terminated by the owner, who was dissatisfied with the work. The Supreme Court recognized that the owner could make the software workable by supplementation and so granted the contractor the right to claim the price for the completed portion of the work.[138] Of course, this is a case of retroactive termination, but the reasoning of the Court approaches the rationale of non-retroactive termination—partial satisfaction of the contract.

V. Termination Provision in Contract and Agreement to Terminate

1. Termination Provision in a Contract

The parties to a contract may stipulate the requirements for a right to terminate and the consequences of termination. Whether such a stipulation refers to the statutory right to terminate, or is a reservation of an independent right to end the contract,[139] is a matter of contract interpretation.

The parties to a contract may stipulate the right to terminate in any manner they mutually agree. For example, they may agree that their contract may be terminated for a cause other than non-performance (eg termination after a lapse of a period) or a minor breach; or they may agree that the contract may be terminated without serving a demand of performance or giving an additional period of performance.[140] A contract may provide that party A may terminate the contract if party B violates any one of its obligations for any short span of time and that determination of breach of contract is completely at the discretion of party *A*,[141] provided that such termination provision can survive the fairness examination.

Unless stipulated otherwise, the contract terminated according to a termination provision of the contract is extinguished retroactively.[142] The fact that the contract stipulates a non-statutory right to terminate is not regarded as renunciation or exclusion of the statutory right to terminate unless the contract specifically says so.[143]

2. An Agreement to Terminate

An agreement to terminate an existing contract is recognized as a matter of party autonomy.[144] The Supreme Court has held that an agreement to terminate is a separate contract between the parties to end the existing contract, and therefore, there should be an offer and acceptance of the offer which match each other to generate the intended effect.[145] An agreement to terminate can be made implicitly as well as explicitly. An implicit agreement to terminate must meet a stricter test.[146]

138 Supreme Court 95Da7932 (30 July 1996).
139 Supreme Court 2014Da14429 (15 December 2016).
140 ibid.
141 Supreme Court 81Da89 (18 January 1983).
142 Supreme Court 2000Da9123 (9 June 2000).
143 Supreme Court 89DaKa14110 (27 March 1990).
144 Supreme Court 2010Da699 (29 July 2010).
145 Supreme Court 2010Da77385 (10 February 2011).
146 ibid.

Unless otherwise stipulated, an agreement to terminate extinguishes the existing contract retroactively.[147] As a practical matter, the parties who contemplate termination by an agreement are advised to agree on the consequences of termination. The court may interpret that the parties, by their agreement to terminate, which is silent on such issues as restitution or damages, agreed to forgo those issues.[148]

VI. Limitation on Termination

The Civil Code has two provisions concerning limitation on termination. In order to protect the non-performing debtor from the uncertainty of termination, Article 552 provides that the debtor may request the creditor to make clear its intention to terminate within a reasonable time, and if the time lapses without a notice of termination, the creditor loses the right to terminate.[149] Moreover, Article 553 provides that if the creditor is at fault in having destroyed, converted, or made unsuitable for restitution the thing that he received under the contract, the creditor forfeits the right to terminate.

In Korean law, the principle of good faith is particularly active in the limitation on termination. This limitation is known as 'the principle of forfeiture' in Korean law.[150] Basically, this principle says that when the creditor has caused the debtor to rely on the creditor's word or act that he would not terminate the contract or the debtor has a justifiable reason to believe so, the creditor may not terminate the contract against such reliance of the debtor.[151]

For example, in selling an office, the seller acquired the right to terminate when a cause of termination occurred. But the seller did not indicate his intention to terminate; instead, the seller tried to convince the buyer that the contract would be implemented and went on to receive the payment from the buyer and even demanded some damages. The Supreme Court held that the seller then may not choose to exercise the right to terminate later because the right to terminate was abandoned.[152]

VII. The Hypotheticals

I will now turn to the hypothetical scenarios proposed by the volume editors.[153]

1. Failure to Visit Once a Week

The first point to address under Korean law is whether the termination clause at issue in this scenario is a mere reminder of statutory termination (only a major/material breach is

[147] Supreme Court 95Da16011 (30 July 1996).
[148] Supreme Court 92Da4130 (23 June 1992).
[149] Supreme Court 2003Da41463 (8 December 2005).
[150] Supreme Court 94Da12234 (25 November 1994).
[151] Supreme Court 2009Da68941 (10 February 2011).
[152] Supreme Court 91Da8005 (14 May 1991). See also Supreme Court 93Da50130 (26 May 1995).
[153] For the fact scenarios of the hypothetical cases discussed in this section, see M Chen-Wishart, D Neo, and S Vogenauer, 'Introduction', ch 1 in this volume, 9–10.

subject to termination) or a stipulation of a separate right to end the contract (termination is to be effected in accordance with the contract's stipulation). This termination clause does not look like a mere repetition of termination in the Civil Code so that it should be given full effect. The remaining question is control of fairness. As explained in volume III of this series, there are many concerns of fairness that limit termination. For example, if the contract is a standard form contract, then a termination clause like this is not valid.[154]

2. Failure to Meet the Deadline by Ten Minutes

The 'time is of the essence' stipulation does not always mean the exact compliance to a minute. The meaning of this clause should be established by contract interpretation. Article 545 of the Civil Code provides that a 'time of the essence' stipulation is given effect when the purpose of the contract cannot be attained if the specified time is not strictly complied with. In this hypothetical, a mere ten-minute delay does not seem to work against the purpose of the contract. Because of the way Article 545 operates, the presence or absence of a 'time is of the essence' clause is not likely to produce absolutely diverging results under Korean law, except that the clause will better inform the court of the parties' emphasis on timely performance.

3. Delivery of Contaminated Seafood

Unless the contract contains a separate termination clause for this kind of situation, it is handled pursuant to the provisions of the Civil Code. First, it should be determined whether this non-performance has already frustrated the purpose of the contract or can be made good by the delivery of the conforming performance. If the timely delivery of seafood was such a controlling concern that the purpose of the contract is already frustrated, the buyer may terminate the entire contract. The Supreme Court (regarding the impossibility of performance) states that when a part of performance becomes impossible, the entire contract may be terminated if the purpose of the contract could not be attained by the remaining part of the performance.[155] If a delivery of the conforming performance should be an option in this situation, the buyer may not terminate the contract without making a demand for performance within a reasonable time.[156]

4. The Unwanted Garden

As explained earlier, termination is different from suspension of performance. Unless David formally terminates the contract for Coco's material breach, the contract maintains its effect. However, demanding Coco keep the garden plan as specific performance of the

[154] TY Ahn, 'Regulation of Unfair Terms under Korean Law' in M Chen-Wishart and S Vogenauer (eds), *Studies in the Contract Laws of Asia, vol III: Contents of Contracts and Unfair Terms* (OUP 2020) 224, 233.
[155] Supreme Court 94Da57817 (9 February 1996).
[156] See section III.2. on the *Nachfrist* notice.

contract would be unrealistic if what Coco has promised to David could be reduced merely to payment in exchange for his work (obviously, David desired this work to be an important opportunity to make his name as a landscape gardener, but that was not part of the contract). David may seek damages or termination with damages. It is established in the law of damages that the aggrieved party may seek compensation of either expectation interest or reliance interest.[157] If the expenditure is of a kind that is usually made in preparation of making and performing the contract, the amount should be compensated for, irrespective of whether the non-performing party knew or could have known it. An excess of the expenditure can be included in the damages only when the non-performing party knew or could have known such special circumstances.[158] As a matter of Korean law, it is unrealistic that David claims the damages of expectation interest for the loss of his future business opportunity.[159]

5. Incomplete Performance in a Contract for Work

A case of similar factual pattern is explained earlier in this chapter.[160] If the contractor, who did not complete the work, had delivered a meaningful amount of the work before termination and that portion of the work was beneficial to the owner, the contractor may claim the price of his work although the contract was terminated due to the non-completion of the work.[161]

VIII. Conclusion

As demonstrated in this chapter, termination in a civil law jurisdiction is a highly elaborate scheme that ends a contract. Termination is a formal action, procedurally strict, and drastic in its effect. Termination is not permitted for a cause less than the unattainability of the purpose of the contract, and once it is legitimately undertaken, termination retroactively extinguishes the contract so that the parties are to be restituted to the *status quo ante*. Termination is distinguished from all other remedies by its gravity: it dissolves a source of legal rights and obligations that has validly existed.

As we have seen in this chapter, this system of termination is constructed largely by a logical network of concepts.[162] At the same time, this structure is not airtight. The concepts themselves are the locus of interaction with the empirical data. They are constantly subjected to theoretical attempts at reinterpretation, reformulation, rearrangement, and

157 Supreme Court 2004Da51825 (25 January 2007).

158 Supreme Court 2001Da75295 (23 October 2003).

159 For any expectation interest to be protected in Korean law, it must be legally grounded, as well as individual, concrete, and direct. In this sense, expectation interest is also called a 'legal (*de jure*) interest', the opposite of which is a fortuitous, *de facto*, or indirect interest. An expectation interest is recognized when vesting of such interest is intended by the statutes or the contract (eg pricing was made in consideration of the expectation interest). See eg Supreme Court 2012Da15336 (23 July 2015). In this case, David's expectations do not seem to meet this standard.

160 See section IV.4 on non-retroactive termination.

161 Supreme Court 95Da7932 (30 July 1996).

162 Hegel said: 'Unless it is a system, a philosophy is not a scientific production.' Hegel, *The Science of Logic* (n 8) § 14.

replacement, that is, 'proper arrangement and manipulation'. The system is breathing through none other than the concepts themselves. We have also seen that when the lacunae in the logical flow are too serious, they have to be repaired by concessions and exceptions. Such 'adulteration' of the otherwise 'pure' system, which is inevitable, cannot be explained without considering the appeal to practical considerations.

Both the proponents of 'legal science', who adhere to it like a religion, and its opponents, who quickly dismiss it as a fantasy, assume a straw man—the pure version of legal science which assumes perfect (or almost perfect) governance of our empirical world through a limited number of abstract concepts and formal logic. Such legal science cannot exist in reality. Justice Holmes' admonition that 'general propositions do not decide concrete cases' is very true because concepts and logic are dead unless the action of interpretation is applied. However, it is also true that law is no longer freewheeling once concepts are laid down; the interpretation must negotiate with them to make its way, which results in increased probability of prediction in law.

My understanding of conceptual jurisprudence (for I do not like the phrase 'legal science' because of its mathematical connotation) is that, despite its many limitations and flaws, it still performs its most important function—the intelligibility of law. Conceptual jurisprudence in its pure version has been accused of serving the ideology of the legal priesthood. But, once we become free of the obsession with the 'eternal truth' in concepts and logic, conceptual jurisprudence can be understood as a form of transparency, though imperfect, that the law-administrator and the law-administered should be bound by the same set of rules that are universally intelligible at a fair degree. At least such was the spirit of civil law since the Napoleonic Code.

15

Change of Circumstances

The Position under Malaysian Contract Law

Yin Harn LEE and May Fong CHEONG

I. Introduction

The law governing contracts in Malaysia is the Contracts Act 1950 (Contracts Act),[1] which is essentially a re-enactment of the Indian Contract Act 1872 (Indian Contract Act). The Indian Contract Act is, in turn, a codification of the then-prevailing English legal principles relating to contracts.[2]

Under the contract law of Malaysia, the entitlement of parties to be discharged from their contractual obligations as a result of a change of circumstances is dealt with through the doctrine of frustration, as is the case in English law. Accordingly, this chapter proceeds as follows. Section II sets out the provisions of the Contracts Act that relate to frustration. Section III considers the courts' application of the doctrine of frustration to various fact situations. Section IV discusses *force majeure* clauses and their enforceability, while section V sets out the effects of frustration. Section VI takes a step back to consider the theoretical justifications for the doctrine of frustration. Section VII considers how the Malaysian courts[3] will address the various hypotheticals, and section VIII concludes this contribution. As this chapter will show, the Malaysian position on frustration tracks the English position fairly closely. In particular, sections 1 and 2 of the UK Law Reform (Frustrated Contracts) Act 1943, which deals with the consequences of frustration, have essentially been re-enacted by sections 15 and 16 of the Malaysian Civil Law Act 1956 (CLA).[4] However, several issues remain unresolved. The first is the extent to which the English concept of 'frustration of purpose' is applicable in Malaysian law. The second is the relationship between the doctrine of frustration and section 33 of the Contracts Act, which deals with contingent contracts. The third is whether the effects of frustrated contracts would be more appropriately dealt with under sections 15 and 16 of the CLA, or under the general provision relating to restitutionary claims as set out in section 66 of the Contracts Act, or both.

[1] Act 136.

[2] On the historical background of the Contracts Act, see MF Cheong and YH Lee, 'Specific Remedies and Money Awards in the Protection of the Performance Interest under Malaysian Contract Law' in M Chen-Wishart, A Loke and B Ong (eds), *Studies in the Contract Laws of Asia, vol I: Remedies for Breach of Contract* (OUP 2016) 326–30.

[3] The superior courts in Malaysia consist of the Federal Court (the apex court), the Court of Appeal, and two High Courts (one for the states of Peninsular Malaysia and one for the states of Sabah and Sarawak).

[4] Act 67.

Yin Harn Lee and May Fong Cheong, *Change of Circumstances: The Position under Malaysian Contract Law* In: *Studies in the Contract Laws of Asia V: Ending and Changing Contracts*. Edited by: Mindy Chen-Wishart, Dora Neo, and Stefan Vogenauer, Oxford University Press. © Yin Harn Lee and May Fong Cheong 2026. DOI: 10.1093/oso/9780198995814.003.0015

II. Frustration under the Contracts Act

The key provision of the Contracts Act dealing with supervening changes of circumstances is section 57(2), which states that:

> A contract to do an act which, after the contract is made, becomes impossible, or by reason of some event which the promisor could not prevent, unlawful, becomes void when the act becomes impossible or unlawful.

While the provision contains no express reference to the concept as such, the Malaysian courts have consistently held that section 57(2) is the statutory embodiment of the English doctrine of frustration.[5]

Another provision which is often discussed in conjunction with the doctrine of frustration is section 33, which deals with contingent contracts. Section 33 provides as follows:

> (a) Contingent contracts to do or not to do anything if an uncertain future event happens cannot be enforced by law unless and until that event has happened.
> (b) If the event becomes impossible, such contracts become void.

There is some debate as to whether, alongside section 57(2), section 33 should also be seen as reflecting the doctrine of frustration. This question is of more than semantic importance. If section 33 were to be understood as embodying the doctrine of frustration, then parties to a contract that has 'become void' due to the non-fulfilment of a contingent condition would be entitled to rely on the remedial provisions set out in sections 15 and 16 of the CLA, which were enacted specifically to deal with frustrated contracts, rather than the 'catch-all' restitutionary provision found in section 66 of the Contracts Act.[6]

There is authority from the Indian Supreme Court which supports the position that both sections 33 and 57(2) should be regarded as statutory embodiments of the doctrine of frustration.[7] To date, however, the Malaysian courts have yet to make a clear statement as to the relationship between section 33 and the doctrine of frustration, though there are several decisions in which both sections 33 and 57(2) have been applied to the same fact situation. The most significant of these is *National Land Finance Co-operative Society Ltd v Sharidal Sdn Bhd*.[8] The parties in this case entered into an agreement for the sale and purchase of land, which was expressed to be subject to the approval of the Foreign Investment Committee. When approval was refused, the plaintiff vendors contended that

[5] *Lee Seng Hock v Fatimah bte Zain* [1996] 3 MLJ 665, 673 (referring to '[t]he doctrine of frustration which has since received statutory recognition in s 57(2) of the Act'). See also *Ramli bin Zakaria v Government of Malaysia* [1982] 2 MLJ 257, 261; *Ho Weng Leong v Ng Kee Chin* [1996] 5 MLJ 139, 149; *Nga Sheau Sheau v United Merchant Finance Bhd* [2004] 4 MLJ 53, 64.

[6] See section IV. For a discussion of s 66 in the context of the effects of termination for breach of contract, see MF Cheong and YH Lee, 'Termination of Contracts: The Position under Malaysian Contract Law', ch 16 in this volume, 333–335.

[7] *Ganga Saran v Ram Charan Ram Gopal* 1952 AIR 9. See also C Narayan and RY Vardhan, 'Changes in Circumstances and Their Impact on Contractual Obligations in India', ch 7 in this volume, 143.

[8] [1983] 2 MLJ 211. See also *Nga Sheau Sheau v United Merchant Finance Bhd* (n 5). For a Federal Court decision that applied *National Land Finance Co-operative Society Ltd* on s 33, see *Detik Ria Sdn Bhd v Prudential Corp Holdings Ltd* [2025] 3 MLJ 22, 76–77. For a discussion of both cases, see MF Cheong, SM Choong and KJ Yong, *Contract Law in Malaysia* (Sweet & Maxwell, 2nd ed 2026) 441–443.

the agreement had become void. The Federal Court found in favour of the plaintiffs on two alternative grounds. First, the agreement between the parties was a contingent contract within the meaning of section 33 as it was conditional upon the approval of the Foreign Investment Committee. When approval was refused, the contingent event became impossible, making the agreement void under section 33(b). Second, and in the alternative, even if the requirement as to approval were to be regarded as a promissory—rather than contingent—condition, the agreement would still be void under section 57(2) as the refusal amounted to a supervening event which rendered the transaction impossible.

The better view, it is submitted, is that section 33 should not be seen as reflecting the doctrine of frustration. First, unlike section 57(2), section 33 does not speak of the impossibility of the contractual performance itself; it merely refers to the impossibility of the *event* on which performance is contingent. Second, it is well established that the doctrine of frustration 'is to be confined to very narrow circumstances . . . commercial bargains should not be lightly avoided or brushed aside merely upon a change of circumstances'.[9] An interpretation which brings the potentially large class of cases involving the non-fulfilment of a contingent condition within its scope would run counter to that principle. Third, in cases such as *National Land Finance*, the possibility that the contingent condition might not be fulfilled should be obvious to both parties; it is therefore open to them to address such risk through an express contractual provision.[10] Where the parties have chosen not to do so, it can be argued that they have accepted that the risk of non-fulfilment should lie where it falls.[11] In these circumstances, the doctrine of frustration should not intervene in the allocation of risk between the parties.

III. The Test for Frustration

Section 57(2) of the Contracts Act envisages two sets of circumstances in which a contract will be discharged for frustration. The first is where the contractual act has been rendered 'impossible' by a supervening event, while the second is where the act becomes 'unlawful' due to such an event.[12] The term 'impossible' is not defined in the Contracts Act itself. Because of this, the Malaysian courts have sought guidance from English authorities. In the vast majority of cases, they have applied the test formulated by the English House of Lords in *Davis Contractors Ltd v Fareham UDC*,[13] where it was held that:

[9] *Eastacres Development Sdn Bhd v Fatimah Mutallip* [2000] 7 MLJ 371. For an English authority to this effect, see *Tsakiroglou & Co Ltd v Noblee Thorl GmbH* [1962] AC 93.

[10] *Khau Daw Yau v Kin Nam Realty Development Sdn Bhd* [1983] 1 MLJ 335. See also V Sinnadurai, *Law of Contract* (4th edn, LexisNexis 2011) para 10.13.

[11] This proposition is not without controversy: see *Ocean Tramp Tankers Corporation v V/O Sovfracht ('The Eugenia')* [1964] 2 QB 226, 239, Lord Denning MR stating that:

> cases have occurred where the parties have foreseen the danger ahead, and yet made no provision for it in the contract . . . So here the parties foresaw that the canal might become impassable: it was the very thing they feared. But they made no provision for it. So there is room for the doctrine to apply if it be a proper case for it.

For a critique of this statement, see E Peel, *Treitel on the Law of Contract* (14th edn, Sweet & Maxwell 2015) para 19–080.

[12] *Standard Chartered Bank v Kuala Lumpur Landmark Sdn Bhd* [1991] 2 MLJ 251; *Cahaya Ideal v Orang-Orang Yang Mengenali Diri Sebagai 'Ponga' (Poongavanam a/l Vadivelu)* [1999] MLJU 125; *Yee Seng Plantations Sdn Bhd v Kerajaan Negeri Terengganu* [2000] 3 MLJ 699; *Holsten Marketing (M) Sdn Bhd v TSK Commodities Sdn Bhd* [2024] 3 MLJ 655.

[13] [1956] AC 696.

> Frustration occurs whenever the law recognises that without default of either party a contractual obligation has become incapable of being performed because the circumstances in which performance is called for would render it a thing radically different from that which was undertaken by the contract.[14]

One of the earliest Malaysian cases to apply this test was the Federal Court decision of *Ramli bin Zakaria v Government of Malaysia*.[15] This was subsequently accepted by the Court of Appeal in *Lai Kok Kit @ Sulaiman Lai bin Abdullah v MBF Finance Bhd*[16] as 'an accurate proposition governing the law of frustration'.[17]

The Malaysian courts have also emphasized that, for the doctrine of frustration to apply, the supervening event must occur *subsequently* to the formation of the contract.[18] In addition, the frustrating event must not be 'self-induced'; that is to say, it must not have arisen from the conduct of the parties themselves or those for whom the parties are responsible.[19] These principles are reflected in part in the language of section 57(2), which refers to 'an act which, *after the contract is made*, becomes impossible, or *by reason of some event which the promisor could not prevent*, unlawful'.[20] In general, however, the Malaysian courts have tended to cite English authorities in support of these propositions rather than referring directly to the language of the statute itself.[21]

1. Unavailability of Contractual Subject Matter

The Malaysian courts have consistently held contracts to have become impossible of performance where the subject matter of the contract no longer exists or has been removed from the control of the relevant party. In *Lee Seng Hock v Fatimah bin Zain*,[22] a contract for the sale and purchase of land was held to be frustrated where the land was compulsorily acquired by the government before it could be transferred to the purchaser.[23] Similarly,

[14] ibid 728–29; cf *Kung Swee Heng v Paritam Kaur* [1948] 1 MLJ 170.

[15] [1982] 2 MLJ 257.

[16] [2000] 3 MLJ 136.

[17] ibid 143. For other cases citing *Davis Contractors*, see *Khoo Than Sui v Chan Chiau Hee* [1976] 1 MLJ 25; *Kin Nam Development Sdn Bhd v Khau Daw Yau* [1984] 1 MLJ 256; *Lee Seng Hock v Fatimah bte Zain* (n 5); *Punca Klasik Sdn Bhd v All Persons in Occupation of the Wooden House Erected on a Portion of Land held under Grant No 26977 for Lot 4271 in the Township of Johor Bahru, Johor* [1996] 5 MLJ 92; *Eastacres Development Sdn Bhd v Fatimah Mutallip* (n 9); *Pacific Forest Industries Sdn Bhd v Lin Wen-Chih* [2009] 6 MLJ 293. See also *Guan Aik Moh (KL) Sdn Bhd v Selangor Properties Bhd* [2007] 4 MLJ 201.

[18] *Goh Yew Chew v Soh Kian Tee* [1970] 1 MLJ 138; *Standard Chartered Bank v Kuala Lumpur Landmark Sdn Bhd* (n 12); *Eastacres Development Sdn Bhd v Fatimah Mutallip* (n 9); *Malayan Banking Bhd v Premier Expand Sdn Bhd* [2013] 8 MLJ 32.

[19] *Goh Yew Chew v Soh Kian Tee* (n 18); *Dato' Yap Peng v Public Bank Bhd* [1997] 3 MLJ 484; *Yee Seng Plantations Sdn Bhd v Kerajaan Negeri Terengganu* (n 12); *Eastacres Development Sdn Bhd v Fatimah Mutallip* (n 9); *Maxisegar Sdn Bhd v Silver Concept Sdn Bhd* [2001] 6 MLJ 762; *BIG Industrial Gas Sdn Bhd v Pan Wijaya Property Sdn Bhd* [2018] 3 MLJ 326; *Anggerik 64 Sdn Bhd v Majlis Agama Islam Negeri Pulau Pinang* [2023] MLJU 814.

[20] Emphases added.

[21] These English authorities include *Ocean Tramp Tankers Corporation v V/O Sovfracht* (n 11); *J Lauritzen AS v Wijsmuller BV ('The Super Servant Two')* [1990] 1 Lloyd's Rep 1. See also *Maritime National Fish Ltd v Ocean Trawlers Ltd* [1935] AC 524.

[22] [1996] 3 MLJ 665.

[23] See also *Yeo Siew Kow v Nyo Chu Alang* [1997] 5 MLJ 313; *Hamdan bin Johan v FELCRA Bhd* [2012] 4 MLJ 785; *Apt Assoc Sdn Bhd v Adnan bin Ishak* [2016] MLJU 1858; *Gan Jin Sim @ Gan Gim Sim v Swi Chuan @ Nan Swu Chuan* [2017] 1 MLJ 794.

hire-purchase agreements relating to the sale of a vehicle have been held to be frustrated where the vehicle was subsequently seized by the custom authorities in circumstances which meant that the vendor was no longer able to pass good title to the purchaser.[24] In such cases, the Malaysian approach mirrors the position under English law.[25]

2. The Performance Is Rendered Unlawful by a Supervening Event

The Malaysian courts have also held contracts to be frustrated where their performance has been rendered unlawful by a change in the law.[26] In *JM Abdul Kader v Shaw Brothers Ltd*,[27] an agreement for a monthly tenancy was held to be frustrated by the retrospective operation of the Rent Restriction Ordinance. In *Lee Kin v Chan Suan Eng*,[28] a lease which provided for renewals of five years at a time was held to be frustrated by new legislation which permitted only annual renewals.[29]

However, the courts have also made it clear that not every change in the law which has the potential to affect the parties' performance of their contractual obligations can be regarded as a frustrating event. Much will depend on the nature of the change as well as its impact on the respective obligations of the parties. In *Dato Yap Peng v Public Bank Bhd*,[30] the plaintiffs, a linked group of companies, had provided various securities for loans granted to them by the defendant banks. Subsequently, the Central Bank issued an order whose effect was to impose a prohibition on the plaintiffs from dealing with their assets. The plaintiffs sought a declaration that the loan agreements had been frustrated by the order, arguing that, as they were unable to deal with any of their assets under the order, it was impossible for them to obtain a discharge of the securities which they had given to the defendants. This contention was ultimately rejected. The Court of Appeal held that, as the order contained a provision allowing the disposal of the assets with the approval of the Central Bank, it was for the plaintiffs to apply for and obtain that approval if they wished to obtain a discharge of the securities. The contract would only be frustrated if and when such an application had been made and rejected by the Central Bank.[31]

The courts have also held contracts to be frustrated where their performance has been rendered unlawful by the subsequent grant of an injunction which has the effect of prohibiting the performance in question. In *Shigenori Ono v Thong Foo Ching*,[32] a contract for the sale and purchase of land was held to be frustrated by an injunction which had

[24] *Public Finance Bhd v Ehwan bin Saring* [1996] 3 MLJ 331; *BBMB Kewangan Bhd v Tan Swee Heng* [2002] MLJU 330; cf *Ahmad Ismail v Malayan Motor Company* [1973] 1 MLJ 117.

[25] See eg *BP Exploration Co (Libya) Ltd v Hunt (No 2)* [1979] 1 WLR 783 (contract frustrated by compulsory acquisition of oil fields); *Morgan v Manser* [1948] 1 KB 184 (contract between variety artist and manager frustrated by conscription of artist).

[26] For English cases, see eg *Metropolitan Water Board v Dick Kerr & Co Ltd* [1918] AC 119 (contract frustrated by a notice given by the Ministry of Munitions which prohibited further work on the project); *Denny, Mott & Dickson Ltd v Fraser & Co Ltd* [1944] AC 265 (contract for the supply of timber frustrated by the coming into force of the Control of Timber (No 4) Order 1939, which prohibited the import of timber).

[27] [1940] 1 MLJ 270.

[28] [1933] 2 MLJ 197.

[29] cf *Mohamed v Ho Wai* (1961) 27 MLJ 7.

[30] [1997] 3 MLJ 484.

[31] In doing so, the court referred to the English case of *Dalmia Dairy Industries Ltd v National Bank of Pakistan* [1978] 2 Lloyd's Rep 223. See also *Tye Ong Kiat v Tan Guan Hoo* [1951] 1 MLJ 73.

[32] [1992] 1 MLJ 117.

been obtained by a third party in separate legal proceedings restraining the defendant from 'selling, disposing, renting, transferring or in any way dealing with' the property in question.

On other occasions, however, the courts have been known to differ as to the precise effect of an injunction, and in particular as to whether it is radical enough to frustrate the contract. This can be seen in a pair of cases arising from the same facts. In *Standard Chartered Bank v Kuala Lumpur Landmark Sdn Bhd*,[33] the defendant was to deliver a bank guarantee for the payment of Malaysian ringgit (MYR) 18 million to the plaintiff under the terms of a redemption agreement. Shortly before the due date for the delivery of the bank guarantee, the parties were served with an interim injunction obtained by another party in separate legal proceedings restraining them from proceeding with, completing, or acting in any manner whatsoever on the redemption agreement. The question which arose was whether the redemption agreement had been frustrated by the injunction.

At the High Court, Lim Beng Choon J answered this question in the affirmative. He held that the performance of the agreement in the present circumstances would amount to a radical change of its original terms and conditions, as the redemption agreement was intended to suspend the right of the plaintiff to institute foreclosure proceedings only if the defendant was able to deliver the bank guarantee within the time stipulated. In a subsequent application arising from the same facts, however, a different High Court judge, Anuar J, arrived at precisely the opposite conclusion.[34] Anuar J took the view that the only effect of the injunction was to delay the performance of the defendant's obligations under the redemption agreement. On this basis, he held that the plaintiff would suffer no detriment if the agreement were to be performed at a later date as it would still be entitled to the amount of MYR18 million as well as interest on that sum for the period of delay. In the interim, the plaintiff would still hold charges over the defendant's property as security. Because of this, the delay occasioned by the injunction did not have the effect of frustrating the contract. These two differing conclusions appear to stem from the two judges' different interpretations as to the degree to which the performance of the contract would become 'radically different' before triggering the doctrine of frustration.

3. The Performance Has Become More Onerous

The Malaysian courts have consistently held that a contract will not be frustrated merely because a supervening change of circumstances has rendered its performance more onerous for one or both parties. This principle is set out clearly in *Kin Nam Development Sdn Bhd v Khau Daw Yau*,[35] where the Federal Court held that the doctrine of frustration 'does not apply just because the promisor's obligation has become, because of change of circumstances, more onerous than what he has contracted for'.[36] Once again, this mirrors the English position. In *Davis Contractors*, the House of Lords had emphasized that '[i]t is not

33 [1991] 2 MLJ 251.
34 [1994] 2 MLJ 559.
35 [1984] 1 MLJ 256.
36 ibid 258. This was cited with approval by the Federal Court in *Pacific Forest Industries Sdn Bhd v Lin Wen-Chih* (n 17); cf A Phang, *Cheshire, Fifoot and Furmston's Law of Contract* (Singapore and Malaysian edition, Butterworths Asia 1994) 811–12, 823 (suggesting that this approach might be too restrictive).

hardship or inconvenience or material loss itself which calls the principle of frustration into play'.[37]

Applying this principle, the Malaysian courts have held the 1997 Asian Financial Crisis not to be a supervening event which gives rise to frustration.[38] This was the case in *Sentul Raya Sdn Bhd v Hariram a/l Jayaram*,[39] where the defendant housing developer argued that the contracts it had entered into for the sale and purchase of condominium units which it was to construct had been frustrated by the 1997 financial crisis, which it claimed had rendered the completion of the condominiums commercially impossible. This argument was rejected by the Court of Appeal, which held that '[t]he 1997 financial crisis merely made it more onerous or perhaps more expensive for the appellant to perform its obligations. It did not render the contract radically different'.[40]

It seems that a contract will not be frustrated where a party has a choice whether to perform that contract or another one. In *Kin Nam Development*, the defendant housing developer concluded contracts for the sale and purchase of all houses which it proposed to build before it had obtained approval for the conversion and subdivision of the land on which construction was to take place. This approval was subsequently granted but subject to a special condition that around 30 per cent of the houses were to be reserved for Bumiputera purchasers.[41] All of the purchasers were non-Bumiputera. Because of this, the defendant sought to argue that the contracts had been frustrated by the special condition. This contention was rejected by the Federal Court, which held that the special condition had not altered the substance of the defendant's contractual obligations towards the purchasers. The court noted that the defendant was still in a position to perform 70 per cent of its contracts, even though 'it may not be able to do justice when choosing which contracts it should perform'.[42] This means that where parties in the same position as the defendant in *Kin Nam Development* are able to perform *some*—but not all—of their contracts, they are precluded from relying on frustration as a ground for discharging any of these contracts.

4. Failure to Obtain Approval, Licence, or Permission

In a number of cases, frustration has been found where the parties have been unsuccessful in obtaining the approval of a third party which is required for the performance of their contractual obligations. In such cases, the rejection by the third party is usually characterized as a supervening event which renders performance impossible. Thus, an agreement entitling one party to cut and extract timber from land belonging to the other was held to be frustrated when the former failed to obtain the necessary permit from the Forests

[37] [1956] AC 696, 729.

[38] For an overview, see H Hunter, 'From Coronations to Sand Bans: Frustration and Force Majeure in the Twenty-First Century' (2011) 28 *Journal of Contract Law* 61, 64–67.

[39] [2008] 4 MLJ 852.

[40] ibid [13]. See also *Highceed Corp Sdn Bhd v Warisan Harta Sabah Sdn Bhd* [2000] 5 MLJ 337; *Eastacres Development Sdn Bhd v Fatimah Mutallip* (n 9); *Maxisegar Sdn Bhd v Silver Concept Sdn Bhd* (n 19); *Tai Kim Yew v Sentul Raya Sdn Bhd* [2004] 4 MLJ 227; *Chinaya a/l Ganggaya v Sentul Raya Sdn Bhd* [2008] 2 MLJ 468; *Balbeer Singh a/l Karam Singh v Sentul Raya Sdn Bhd* [2013] 9 MLJ 360; *Shishi Group Sdn Bhd v Mtrustee Bhd (as trustee for Pavilion REIT)* [2023] MLJU 913.

[41] 'Bumiputera' is a term used to describe people of Malay ethnicity and other indigenous peoples of Malaysia.

[42] The facts in this case are reminiscent of those in the English case of *J Lauritzen AS v Wijsmuller BV* (n 21). See also *Rajeswari Thedshanamurthy v Sentul Raya Sdn Bhd* [1983] 1 MLJ 88.

Department.[43] Similarly, an agreement for the rental of premises to be used as a karaoke and musical lounge was held to be frustrated by the landlord's failure to obtain conversion of the property's condition of use from residential to commercial.[44]

At the same time, there are also cases in which such failure has been treated not as a frustrating event but rather as the non-fulfilment of a contingent condition within the meaning of section 33 of the Contracts Act.[45] This leads to the contract 'becoming void' pursuant to section 33(b) rather than being discharged for frustration under section 57(2). A survey of both sets of cases shows no clear qualitative difference between those that have been decided under section 57(2) and those to which section 33 has been applied instead.

The better view, it is submitted, is that cases of this kind should be treated as falling within section 33 rather than section 57(2), for much the same reasons as those that have been cited in support of the position that section 33 should not be seen as reflecting the doctrine of frustration. This approach is also more consistent with the English authorities. In *Total Gas Marketing Ltd v Arco British Ltd*,[46] the House of Lords held a contract to be terminated when the contingent condition to which it was expressed to be subject failed to materialize; crucially, however, this was founded on the non-fulfilment of the contingent condition itself rather than the doctrine of frustration.[47] A similar view has also been expressed by leading Malaysian textbook author Visu Sinnadurai, who argues that the obtaining of the relevant approval, licence, or permission should be treated as a condition precedent to the performance of the parties' contractual obligations; because of this, no performance is due under the contract so long as the condition remains unfulfilled.[48]

5. 'Frustration of Purpose'

The English courts have been known to hold contracts to be frustrated where, although their performance is not technically impossible, the purpose of the contract has been so undermined by the supervening event that the parties should no longer be bound by it. This was the case in *Krell v Henry*,[49] where a contract for the hire of a flat for the purpose of viewing the coronation procession of King Edward VII was held to be frustrated by the cancellation of the procession.

To date, there has been no Malaysian case in which the concept of 'frustration of purpose' has been explicitly discussed. However, in *Semangat Positif Sdn Bhd v Pelantar Agresif (M) Sdn Bhd* (*Semangat Positif*),[50] the High Court did employ language which was reminiscent of it. In this case, the defendant rented out part of its property to the plaintiff to enable the latter to operate a fishing pond business. Subsequently, another part of the defendant's property was compulsorily acquired by the government of Malaysia for the purpose of

43 *Yong Ung Kai v Enting* [1965] 2 MLJ 98.

44 *Ho Weng Leong v Ng Kee Chin* (n 5). See also *National Land Finance Co-operative Society Ltd v Sharidal Sdn Bhd* (n 8); *Ng Kheng Yong @ Ng Tet Lai v Seng Hup Realty Sdn Bhd* [2004] 3 MLJ 477.

45 See *Halimah bte Abdul Rahman v Fatimah bte Abdullah* [1976] 2 MLJ 64; *Royal Selangor Golf Club v Anglo-Oriental (Malaysia) Sdn Bhd* [1990] 2 MLJ 163; *Rengamah a/p Rengasamy v Tai Yoke Lai* [1998] 5 MLJ 260; *Multi-Purpose Holdings Bhd v Ketua Pengarah Hasil Dalam Negeri* [1998] 5 MLJ 317.

46 [1998] 2 Lloyd's Rep 209.

47 See also *Hargreaves Transport Ltd v Lynch* [1969] 1 WLR 215.

48 Sinnadurai, *Law of Contract* (n 10) para 10.25.

49 [1903] 2 KB 740.

50 [2010] 7 MLJ 137.

constructing a rail link. As the structures that had been constructed by the plaintiff encroached upon the acquired land, they had to be demolished. The plaintiff claimed that it was no longer able to operate its fishing pond business and made a claim against the defendant for breach of contract. The defendant contended that the tenancy agreement between the parties had been frustrated. The High Court found in favour of the defendant, holding that:

> It was . . . not in dispute that the tenancy was for a fishing pond business. When part of the demised area was taken away by the third party, it became quite impossible for the plaintiff to continue its business. The whole purpose of the tenancy as was depicted in the tenancy agreement itself, was for the fishing rights. When the third party [ie the Government of Malaysia] came in, the essence of the agreement was lost.[51]

While the language used in this passage suggests some implicit recognition of frustration of purpose, it is still far from conclusive, and the outcome in *Semangat Positif* can readily be explained on the basis that the tenancy agreement was frustrated by the defendant's loss of control over the part of its land which was compulsorily acquired. There is also some difficulty reconciling frustration of purpose with the statutory language of the Contracts Act itself. After all, section 57(2) refers specifically to the impossibility of 'the act' which one of the parties has contracted to perform and not to its purpose. Simply because the purpose underpinning an act has become impossible of realization does not mean that the *act* itself has become impossible.

That the Malaysian courts will be slow to adopt frustration of purpose is also borne out by the case of *Philippine Center for Print Excellence Foundation Inc v Corporate Information Travel Sdn Bhd*.[52] The plaintiff here was an association carrying out business in the printing industry. To facilitate its members' attendance at a trade fair in Germany, it engaged the services of the defendant to make bookings of hotel rooms in Germany, which the defendant duly did. Subsequently, the trade fair was cancelled due to the COVID-19 pandemic, and the plaintiff sought to cancel the bookings and asked for a refund of the payments it had made to the defendant on the ground of frustration. The Sessions Court held that the doctrine of frustration was not applicable as the contract between the parties was merely for the booking of the rooms. The hotel rooms were available for the plaintiff's use for the duration of the booking, and the plaintiff's members remained free to travel to Germany as no COVID-19-related travel restrictions applied.

IV. *Force majeure* Clauses

Given the restrictive operation of the doctrine of frustration, *force majeure* clauses are often found in contracts, particularly those between commercial parties.[53] Such clauses allow parties to set out more precisely the kinds of events that would prevent one or both

[51] ibid [26].
[52] [2022] MLJU 3285.
[53] Phang, *Cheshire, Fifoot and Furmston's Law of Contract* (n 36) 605; Sinnadurai, *Law of Contract* (n 10) para 10.47.

parties from fulfilling their obligations under the contract as well as the effects of such an event.[54] These clauses have the advantage of yielding more certainty compared to the doctrine of frustration[55] and are routinely enforced by the Malaysian courts. In *Lai Mew Seng v Cosmopac Sdn Bhd*,[56] the High Court observed that 'if a contract contains a *force majeure* clause then that clause will generally govern the matter'.[57] In some cases, the courts have even intimated that matters could have been resolved to the greater satisfaction of the parties had they possessed the foresight to include an appropriately-worded clause of this kind.[58] The only exception is where the parties have sought to insert a *force majeure* clause into a statutorily prescribed standard-form contract which allows for no such provision. In such cases, the courts have held that the parties should not be allowed to circumvent the requirements of the statute by incorporating their own *force majeure* clauses.[59]

In most cases involving a *force majeure* clause, the only real question is whether, as a matter of construction,[60] the clause is broad enough to cover the event that has materialized.[61] In *Araprop Development Sdn Bhd v Leong Chee Kee*,[62] the parties entered into a contract for the sale and purchase of property under which the defendant vendor was to deliver vacant possession of the property to the plaintiff purchasers within 30 months from the date of the contract. The delivery of vacant possession was delayed by well over two years. The defendant argued that the late delivery was due to circumstances beyond its control, namely, the failure of its telephone and electricity contractors to complete their cabling works on time. It sought to rely on a clause of the sale and purchase agreement which exempted it from liability for the non-fulfilment of any term of the agreement where such fulfilment was prevented by acts of God; civil commotion; inclement weather; acts of war; strike loss; damage by fire, flood, or tempest; delay by the relevant authorities in granting any necessary sanctions or approvals; 'or other circumstances of whatever nature beyond the Vendor's control'.

The Court of Appeal, applying the *ejusdem generis* rule, held that the general phrase 'or other circumstances of whatever nature beyond the Vendor's control' should be given a restricted meaning and should be confined to circumstances similar in nature to those specifically enumerated by the preceding words. Accordingly, it held that the clause did not extend to delays caused by the fault of third-party subcontractors. This was especially

[54] H Beale, B Fauvarque-Cosson, J Rutgers, and S Vogenauer, *Cases, Materials and Text on Contract Law* (3rd edn, Hart Publishing 2019) 1250.

[55] E McKendrick, 'Force Majeure Clauses: The Gap between Doctrine and Practice' in A Burrows and E Peel (eds), *Contract Terms* (OUP 2007) 240.

[56] [1997] MLJU 11.

[57] ibid 38.

[58] *Finmark Consultants Pte Ltd v Development & Commercial Bank Bhd* [1994] 3 MLJ 192; *Teh Khem On v Yeoh & Wu Development Sdn Bhd* [1995] 2 MLJ 663; *Muhammad Radhieddeen bin Abdul Khalid v Saujana Triangle Sdn Bhd* [2017] MLJU 95. See also *JRI Resources Sdn Bhd v Varia Tenggara Sdn Bhd* [2013] MLJU 185; *Francis Yong Wing Kheong v Saujana Triangle Sdn Bhd* [2016] MLJU 1865; *Keiko Nakagawa v Saujana Triangle Sdn Bhd* [2016] MLJU 1867. See also *MITTI Power Cables Sdn Bhd v Leader Cable Industry* [2021] MLJU 496 [16] (making the same observation in relation to a consent judgment).

[59] *SEA Housing Corporation Sdn Bhd v Lee Poh Choo* [1982] 2 MLJ 31.

[60] Ordinary rules of commercial construction apply to *force majeure* clauses: see D Robertson, 'Force Majeure Clauses' (2009) 25 Journal of Contract Law 62, 63.

[61] *Hong Guan & Co Ltd v Jumabhoy & Sons Ltd* [1960] 1 MLJ 141; *Eastacres Development Sdn Bhd v Fatimah Mutallip* (n 9).

[62] [2008] 1 MLJ 783.

the case as the defendant had the option of terminating its contracts with the third-party subcontractors—and, presumably, hiring new ones—once it became obvious that they were unable to complete the works on time.[63]

Despite the utility of *force majeure* clauses, in practice, they are often inserted into contracts as standard 'boilerplate' provisions, without the parties having turned their minds towards the specific supervening events that might affect their ability to perform their contractual obligations. A typical example of a *force majeure* clause used in Malaysia is set out below:

> Neither party shall be liable for any delay in or failure of performance under this Agreement if such delay or failure is caused by acts of God, riots, war, strikes or other labor troubles, or any other events beyond the control of the parties affected.

This *force majeure* clause, like the one in *Araprop Development*, is framed in very general terms. Because of this, it is also unlikely to cover the kind of situation which materialized in *Araprop Development*. Parties seeking to make use of *force majeure* clauses should therefore be careful to specify, precisely, the potential supervening events that might prevent them from fulfilling their contractual obligations.

Finally, the COVID-19 pandemic has given rise to a few cases in which the key issue is whether the *force majeure* clause set out in the contract between the parties is broad or precise enough to capture the pandemic itself. In these cases, the courts seemed inclined to hold that the pandemic and its effects are covered even by a fairly generally-worded *force majeure* clause.[64]

V. Effects of Frustration

Section 57(2) of the Contracts Act provides that a contract which is frustrated 'becomes void' upon the occurrence of the frustrating event. This means that the contract, while initially valid, is discharged due to the frustrating event. The discharge occurs automatically, and both parties are released from performing the obligations which fall due after the frustrating event. The contract cannot be kept on foot at the option of either party, and neither the court nor the parties have the power to adjust the terms of the contract so as to fit the changed circumstances. In dealing with the economic consequences of frustrated contracts, two sets of provisions have been applied by the Malaysian courts. These are, respectively, sections 15 and 16 of the CLA and section 66 of the Contracts Act.

[63] For other cases on the construction of *force majeure* clauses, see *Tang Kham Thai v Langkah Cergas Sdn Bhd* [2005] 7 MLJ 605; *Malaysia Land Properties Sdn Bhd v Tan Peng Foo* [2014] 1 MLJ 718; *Platinum Nanochem Sdn Bhd v Mecpro Heavy Engineering Ltd* [2016] 11 MLJ 141.

[64] See eg *Sit Seng & Sons Realty Sdn Bhd v M Mohamed Ali* [2022] MLJU 315 (rejecting the plaintiff's claim for summary judgment on the ground that there was a triable issue as to whether the *force majeure* clause excused the defendant from the performance of their contractual obligations due to the pandemic); *Dato' Vijay Kumar Natarajan v Malaysia Airlines Berhad* [2021] MLJU 407 (striking out the plaintiff's claim for compensation for the cancellation of his flight tickets, on the ground that the defendant had made the cancellation in compliance with measures put in place by the government of Malaysia to contain the COVID-19 outbreak and that this was covered by the *force majeure* clause in the defendant's conditions of carriage). See also section IX in this chapter.

1. Sections 15 and 16 CLA

Sections 15 and 16 of the CLA are essentially re-enactments of sections 1 and 2 of the UK Law Reform (Frustrated Contracts) Act 1943. The relevant provisions of section 15 are as follows:

(1) Where a contract has become impossible of performance or been otherwise frustrated, and the parties thereto have for that reason been discharged from the further performance of the contract, subsections (2) to (6) shall, subject to section 16, have effect in relation thereto.

(2) All sums paid or payable to any party in pursuance of the contract before the time when the parties were so discharged (in this Act referred to as 'the time of discharge') shall, in the case of sums so paid, be recoverable from him as money received by him for the use of the party by whom the sums were paid, and, in the case of sums so payable, cease to be so payable:

Provided that, if the party to whom the sums were so paid or payable incurred expenses before the time of discharge in, or for the purpose of, the performance of the contract, the Court may, if it considers it just to do so having regard to all the circumstances of the case, allow him to retain or, as the case may be, recover the whole or any part of the sums so paid or payable, not being an amount in excess of the expenses so incurred.

(3) Where any party to the contract has, by reason of anything done by any other party thereto in, or for the purpose of, the performance of the contract, obtained a valuable benefit (other than a payment of money to which subsection (2) applies) before the time of discharge, there shall be recoverable from him by the said other party such sum (if any), not exceeding the value of the said benefit to the party obtaining it, as the Court considers just, having regard to all the circumstances of the case and, in particular –

(a) the amount of any expenses incurred before the time of discharge by the party benefited in, or for the purpose of, the performance of the contract, including any sums paid or payable by him to any other party in pursuance of the contract and retained or recoverable by that party under subsection (2); and

(b) the effect, in relation to the said benefit, of the circumstances giving rise to the frustration of the contract.

(4) In estimating, for the purposes of subsections (1) to (3), the amount of any expenses incurred by any party to the contract, the Court may, without prejudice to the generality of the said subsections, include such sum as appears to be reasonable in respect of overhead expenses and in respect of any work or services performed personally by the said party.

The relevant provisions of section 16 are as follows:

(3) Where any contract to which section 15 applies contains any provisions which, upon the true construction of the contract, is intended to have effect in the event of

circumstances arising which operate, or would but for the said provision operate, to frustrate the contract, or is intended to have effect whether those circumstances arise or not, the Court shall give effect to the said provision and shall only give effect to section 15 to such extent, if any, as appears to the Court to be consistent with the said provision.

(4) Where it appears to the Court that a part of any contract to which section 15 applies can properly be severed from the remainder of the contract, being a part wholly performed before the time of discharge, or so performed except for the payment in respect of that part of the contract of sums which are or can be ascertained under the contract, the Court shall treat that part of the contract as if it were a separate contract and had not been frustrated and shall treat section 15 as only applicable to the remainder of that contract.

There are relatively few cases in which these provisions have been applied.[65] The most notable of these is *National Land Finance*, the facts of which were set out in section II. After holding that the contract between the parties could be treated as being void for frustration, the Federal Court, applying section 15(2) of the CLA, ordered the vendor to return the deposit to the purchaser.[66]

A number of complex questions have arisen under English law as to the interpretation of the corresponding provisions of the UK Law Reform (Frustrated Contracts) Act. These include the assessment of the 'just sum' which a party who has incurred expenditure in the performance of their contractual obligations should be permitted to retain or recover as well as the identification and quantification of any 'valuable benefit' obtained by one party from the other.[67] Thus far, the Malaysian courts have yet to engage with these questions, though there are two cases whose facts might have lent themselves to such an analysis.

In the first of these cases, *United Asian Bank Bhd v Chun Chai Chai*,[68] the tenancy agreement entered into between the parties was held to be frustrated due to the landlords' inability to obtain electricity supply for the premises. By this time, the tenants had been in occupation of the premises for some six months and had paid to the landlords a deposit of MYR25,800 as well as rent amounting to MYR21,900. The High Court held that, as the tenancy agreement had been frustrated, the tenants were entitled to the return of all these sums pursuant to section 15 of the CLA. However, it did not engage in any consideration of whether the tenants' possession of the premises constituted a 'valuable benefit' within the meaning of section 15(3). This was despite the fact that the court, in dealing with the tenants' alternative claim for restitution at common law—rather than under the CLA—on the basis of total failure of consideration, had held that there was no such failure as the premises were otherwise fit for occupation and the tenants were not prevented from obtaining a temporary electricity supply from other sources.

The second case, *Yew Siew Hoo v Nikmat Maju Development Sdn Bhd*,[69] arose from the decision of the state government of Negeri Sembilan to designate and develop an Integrated

[65] The effect of s 15(2) was summarized in *Hong Leong Bank Bhd v Tan Siew Nam* [2014] 5 MLJ 34.
[66] See also *Koperasi Mahadaya Bhd v Koperasi Polis Diraja Malaysia Bhd* [2012] 2 MLJ 569.
[67] For English authorities to this effect, see *BP Exploration Co (Libya) Ltd v Hunt (No 2)* (n 25); *Gamerco SA v ICM/Fair Warning (Agency) Ltd* [1995] 1 WLR 1226.
[68] [1988] 2 CLJ (Rep) 502.
[69] [2014] 4 MLJ 413.

Pig Farming Area (IPFA) in a particular district. The defendant was the developer of the IPFA, and one of its obligations was to construct a central waste treatment plant to treat wastewater from the pig farms in the IPFA. The plaintiffs were operators of pig farms located outside the IPFA. They were permitted to continue their operations on condition that their farms were also connected to the treatment plant. The plaintiffs entered into tapping agreements with the defendant under which the plaintiffs would be allowed to connect to the plant for a fee. Subsequently, an outbreak of the Japanese encephalitis disease led the state government to ban the rearing and sale of pigs in the area occupied by the plaintiffs. At this point, the defendant had completed the construction of the treatment plant but had yet to put it into operation. The plaintiffs had already paid the defendant a portion of the fees due under the tapping agreements. The plaintiffs sought to recover these fees on the ground that the tapping agreements had been frustrated. However, the defendant contended that it should be allowed to retain the fees to set off the construction costs of the treatment plant.

At first instance, the High Court held that the tapping agreements were frustrated and exercised its discretion under section 15(2) of the CLA to allow the defendant to retain all the sums that had been paid to it by the plaintiffs as an allowance for the costs of construction it had incurred.[70] This was reversed by the Court of Appeal, which held that the costs of constructing the treatment plant had not been incurred by the defendant in the performance of its obligations under the tapping agreements. Rather, they arose from a separate and pre-existing obligation under the defendant's agreement with the state government in relation to the IPFA project. Accordingly, the defendant was not entitled to an allowance for its expenses pursuant to section 15(2), and the plaintiffs were able to recover the full sum paid. This was despite the defendant's claim that, in order to accommodate the tapping agreements, it had had to enlarge the size of the treatment plant beyond what would otherwise have been required. The Court of Appeal did note, however, that 'in order for s 15(2) to apply, the defendant bears the burden of proving that the expenses incurred by the defendant were for the performance of the [tapping agreements]'.[71] The implication of this is that the defendant had been unable to discharge its burden of proof. Future litigants seeking to rely on section 15(2) should therefore be mindful of the need to demonstrate that any expenses which they seek to recover are clearly linked to the performance of the contract in question.

2. Section 66 Contracts Act

In the vast majority of cases involving frustrated contracts, the Malaysian courts have tended to rely on section 66 of the Contracts Act rather than sections 15 and 16 of the CLA. Section 66 is something of a 'catch-all' restitutionary provision for any agreement that is 'discovered to be void' or that 'becomes void'. It provides that:

> When an agreement is discovered to be void, or when a contract becomes void, any person who has received any advantage under the agreement or contract is bound to restore it, or to make compensation for it, to the person from whom he received it.

70 There is no reported judgment of the first instance decision.

71 *Yew Siew Hoo v Nikmat Maju Development Sdn Bhd* (n 69) [14].

Section 57(2) of the Contracts Act states that a contract which has been frustrated 'becomes void'. It is on this basis that the Malaysian courts have held section 66 to be applicable to frustrated contracts. Some support for this can be found in Illustration (d) to section 66, which bears resemblance to Illustration (e) to section 57. The Illustration to section 66 refers to *A*, who contracts to sing for *B* at a concert, while the Illustration to section 57 refers to *A*, who agrees to act at *B's* theatre. In both Illustrations, *A*, who has received an amount in advance from *B*, falls ill and fails to perform. Illustration (e) to section 57 states that '[t]he contract to act on those occasions becomes void'. Illustration (d) to section 66 provides that '*A* is not bound to make compensation to *B* for the loss of the profits which *B* would have made if *A* had been able to sing, but must refund to *B* the MYR1,000 paid in advance'.

Although section 66 refers to the need for a party who has received an advantage under the contract to 'make compensation' to the party from whom it was received, the provision should be understood as being restitutionary in nature, and the term 'compensation' should be interpreted accordingly,[72] as held by the Privy Council in a case on the identically worded Indian counterpart to section 66.[73]

Accordingly, neither party may rely on section 66 to claim compensatory damages for the non-performance of obligations that fall due after the frustrating event. This is evident from the judgment in *Lee Seng Hock*, which concerned a contract for the sale and purchase of land. The plaintiff purchaser had paid a deposit amounting to 10 per cent of the purchase price at the time of the contract. Before the sale was completed, the land was compulsorily acquired by the government, and the defendant was awarded compensation in accordance with the Land Acquisition Act 1960.[74] The plaintiff brought a claim for the compensation that had been awarded to the vendor, less the balance of the purchase price due under the contract. This was rejected by the Court of Appeal, which held that, as the contract was frustrated by the compulsory acquisition of the land, the plaintiff was only entitled under section 66 to the return of his deposit.

Section 66 has been applied in a number of cases to order the refund of deposits paid under a contract which is subsequently frustrated.[75] In some cases, it has also been applied to compel the return of payments that have been made under a contract, where the courts have found—whether expressly or impliedly—that the party seeking restitution has received no part of the promised performance. A case in point is *BBMB Kewangan Bhd v Tan Swee Heng*,[76] where the parties entered into a hire-purchase agreement for a car. A year later, the car was seized by the Customs and Excise Department for an offence relating to customs duty. The High Court held that the hire-purchase agreement had been frustrated by the seizure and retention of the car. It also found that there had been a total failure of consideration for the purchaser as the purchaser was unable to enjoy quiet possession of the car, would not have the right to purchase the car at the time when the property was to pass, and had not received the car free from encumbrances in favour of any third party (in this case,

[72] *Lori (M) Bhd v Arab-Malaysian Finance Bhd* [1999] 3 MLJ 81; *Public Bank Bhd v Abdul Rashid bin Abdul Majid* [2012] 6 MLJ 348; *Lo Ga Lung v Diong Ching Diung* [2015] 1 MLJ 127.

[73] *Govindram Seksaria v Edward Radbone* (1948) 50 BOMLR 561. See also C Narayan and RY Vardhan, 'Changes in Circumstances and Their Impact on Contractual Obligations in India', ch 7 in this volume, 149.

[74] Act 486.

[75] *National Land Finance Co-operative Society Ltd v Sharidal Sdn Bhd* (n 8); *Eastacres Development Sdn Bhd v Fatimah Mutallip* (n 9). See also *Ho Weng Leong v Ng Kee Chin* (n 5) (restitution ordered of the advance payments, security deposit and water and electricity deposit, that had been paid).

[76] [2002] MLJU 330.

the custom authorities). Applying section 66, the High Court held that the purchaser was entitled to recover his deposit and all the monthly instalments which he had paid towards the purchase price of the car.[77]

The approach taken in these cases is consistent with the position under English common law, which allows recovery of payments made before the frustrating event only where there has been a *total* failure of consideration; no recovery is possible where the party seeking restitution has received any part of the performance due under the contract.[78] To date, the Malaysian courts have yet to engage with the more difficult question of whether recovery will be permitted under section 66 where the failure of consideration is only partial in nature. Again, there are a handful of cases in which this question could potentially have been raised on the facts. In *Semangat Positif*, the High Court noted that, although the plaintiff had made rental payments to the defendant under the tenancy agreement, and had incurred costs in constructing the fishing pond and other structures, there was also evidence that the plaintiff had earned substantial income during the subsistence of the tenancy. This would have been relevant to the assessment of any restitutionary claim brought under section 66. However, as no submissions had been made by either party on this point, the court simply allowed the benefits that had been obtained by each party to lie where they fell.[79]

The question of whether section 66 is applicable to cases involving partial failure of consideration will become much less significant if the courts were to stop applying that provision in future cases involving frustrated contracts and to rely exclusively on sections 15 and 16 of the CLA instead. This is discussed in the following section.

3. The Effect and Applicability of Both Provisions

As the preceding discussion shows, the provisions of the CLA that deal specifically with the consequences of frustration have been applied fairly infrequently. In the majority of cases, the Malaysian courts have preferred to rely instead on the 'catch-all' restitutionary provision in section 66 of the Contracts Act, and typically without articulating any specific reasons for preferring the latter over the former. It is not altogether clear why this should be the case, though it should perhaps be noted that the corresponding provisions of the UK Law Reform (Frustrated Contracts) Act have also generated very little in the way of case law.

The two sets of provisions differ in terms of their effect. Most notably, while section 66 requires a party who has received an advantage under the contract to restore it or make restitution for it to the other party, it does not allow that party to set off any expenses which it may have incurred in the course of performance against the sum to be returned. In contrast, section 15(2) expressly empowers the court to make orders relating to loss apportionment in order to take into account the parties' wasted expenditure. In addition, while it is currently unclear whether section 66 would apply in cases of frustration involving partial but

77 See also *Public Finance Bhd v Ehwan bin Saring* (n 24).

78 *Whincup v Hughes* (1870–71) LR 6 CP 78; *Fibrosa Spolka Akcyjna v Fairbairn Lawson Combe Barbour Ltd* [1943] AC 32. This is despite the preponderance of academic opinion to the contrary: see A Burrows, *The Law of Restitution* (3rd edn, OUP 2011) 330–34; G Virgo, *The Principles of the Law of Restitution* (3rd edn, OUP 2015) 325–29.

79 See also *Murugesan v Krishnasamy* [1958] 1 MLJ 92.

not total failure of consideration, sections 15(2) and (3) clearly dispense with the requirement of total failure.

It is submitted that it would be preferable for Malaysian courts to apply sections 15 and 16 consistently in all cases involving frustrated contracts, to the exclusion of section 66. First, sections 15 and 16 of the CLA were enacted to deal specifically with frustrated contracts, while section 66 of the Contracts Act is a general restitutionary provision applicable to all cases where an agreement is 'discovered to be void' or 'becomes void'. The ordinary rules of statutory interpretation, in particular the principle *generalia specialibus non derogant*, indicate that the former should take precedence over the latter. Sections 15 and 16 of the CLA are also more recent in time, having been enacted after the coming into force of the Contracts Act. Second, the English equivalents to sections 15 and 16 were enacted in order to remedy the defects of the common law in this area, which permitted recovery only where there had been total failure of consideration and did not provide a means by which losses incurred in the performance of the contract could be apportioned by the court. These defects are also present—or, in the case of non-recovery for partial failure of consideration, potentially present—within section 66. Because sections 15 and 16 have been designed to address precisely these issues, they should be treated as the only remedial provisions applicable in cases involving frustrated contracts.[80] This is also the position taken by Sinnadurai, who has argued that 'since the consequences of frustration are now dealt with by the CLA 1956, sections 57 and 66 of the Contracts Act are impliedly repealed insofar as they may be inconsistent with this subsequent legislation'.[81] There is some relatively recent authority to this effect: in *Hong Leong Bank Bhd v Tan Siew Nam*,[82] the Court of Appeal held that the first instance judge had erred in law in applying section 66 of the Contracts Act in isolation without reading it together with section 15 of the CLA.

VI. Theoretical Justifications

The English courts have advanced a number of different theoretical justifications for the doctrine of frustration over time.[83] The earliest of these is the 'implied terms' theory, which sought to justify the doctrine on the basis of an implied term that the contract would come to an end upon the occurrence of the supervening event.[84] This was eventually superseded by the theory that the doctrine of frustration is a device through which the court imposes on the parties the 'just and reasonable' solution which the changed circumstances require.[85] At present, the prevailing view, as articulated by Lord Radcliffe in *Davis Contractors*, is that the doctrine of frustration has its basis in the parties' lack of consent to the performance of their contractual obligations under radically changed circumstances.

To date, the Malaysian courts have not engaged to any significant degree with debates surrounding the theoretical basis for the doctrine of frustration. Given the courts' reliance

[80] *Goh Yew Chew v Soh Kian Tee* (n 18) 142 (Ali FJ holding that 'in the case of frustrated contracts the legislature in this country has in fact intervened by making provisions in section 15 of the Civil Law Ordinance 1956').

[81] Sinnadurai, *Law of Contract* (n 10) para 10.52. See also RR Sethu, 'The History, Impact and Influence of the Indian Contracts Act 1872' (2011) 28 Journal of Contract Law 31, 53.

[82] [2014] 5 MLJ 34.

[83] For an overview, see *National Carriers Ltd v Panalpina (Northern) Ltd* [1981] AC 675.

[84] *Taylor v Caldwell* (1863) 3 B&S 826.

[85] *Hirji Mulji v Cheong Yue Steamship Co Ltd* [1926] AC 497; *J Lauritzen AS v Wijsmuller BV* (n 21).

on *Davis Contractors*, however, they can be said to have impliedly adopted the 'lack of consent' rationale articulated in that case. In *Pacific Forest Industries*, the Federal Court referred expressly to the relevant passage from *Davis Contractors* which set out the 'radical change in obligation' test in the doctrine of frustration[86] and explained that:

> The Latin maxim *non haec in foedera veni* would apply, which literally means 'It was not this that I promised to do'. There must be such a change in the significance of the obligation that the thing undertaken would, if performed, be a different thing from that contracted for.[87]

VII. The Hypotheticals

This section sets out how the hypothetical scenarios proposed by the volume editors would be handled under Malaysian law.[88]

1. Abraham and Bill

The Malaysian courts have consistently held that a supervening event which renders the performance of an obligation more onerous than what was originally contracted for, but does not render the obligation impossible of performance or produce a radical change in the nature of the obligation within the meaning of *Davis Contractors*, will not give rise to a finding of frustration. This is especially the case where the obligation has become more onerous due to an unexpected economic crisis or financial hardship. Because of this, it is unlikely that a Malaysian court will hold that inflation and increased costs have rendered the obligations of Abraham's successors in law 'impossible of performance' or 'radically different' from those originally undertaken as they are merely required to continue maintaining the irrigation channel as they have done since 1567.

2. Citi Corporation and Drive Bank

The outcome of this hypothetical is likely to be the same as the previous one involving Abraham and Bill, and for the same reasons. A Malaysian court is likely to hold that the sudden rise in inflation has not rendered the parties' obligations 'radically different' or 'impossible of performance' but merely more unprofitable and onerous for Drive Bank. In *Sentul Raya*, the 1997 Asian financial crisis had left the defendant without sufficient financial resources to perform its contractual obligations, yet this was held not to be a frustrating event. On the facts of this hypothetical, Drive Bank appears to be in a much better position compared to the defendant in *Sentul Raya* as it is only required to bear with the fixed

[86] *Davis Contractors Ltd v Fareham UDC* (n 13) 728–29.
[87] *Pacific Forest Industries Sdn Bhd v Lin Wen-Chih* (n 17) 304.
[88] The fact scenarios for this and the other hypothetical situations discussed in this section can be found in M Chen-Wishart, D Neo, and S Vogenauer, 'Introduction', ch 1 in this volume, 7–8.

interest rate for a further three years, after which adjustment would presumably be permitted under the terms of the contract.

Even in the unlikely event that frustration is found, the effect of this would be to discharge the contract automatically, and Drive Bank would have no basis on which to seek adjustment of its terms.

3. Easy and Frugle

It is unlikely that a Malaysian court will hold that the contract between Easy and Frugle has been frustrated. The only effect of the change of circumstances is to make the contract a much better bargain for Easy than the parties could have anticipated. It is difficult to see how this, in itself, can be said to make the parties' obligations as lessor and lessee 'radically different'. Unlike the previous two hypotheticals, Frugle's contractual obligations cannot even be said to have become more onerous as a result of the changes to the local area; instead, it is only making less profit from the lease than it could otherwise have done. Even if frustration were to be found, Frugle would still not be entitled to adjust the rental price as the effect of frustration is to bring the contract to an end and discharge the parties from any future obligations under it.

4. George and Han

In this hypothetical, the refurbishment of the cellar remains physically possible because it has been left intact by the storm. Accordingly, George is likely to argue that his contractual obligations have not been rendered 'impossible' within the meaning of section 57(2), nor have they become 'radically different' in the *Davis Contractors* sense. If a Malaysian court were to adopt this line of reasoning, it is likely to find that the contract has not been frustrated and that George is correct to treat it as subsisting. George would therefore be entitled to claim the contract price for his performance.

The position might be different if Han could persuade the court to adopt the concept of frustration of purpose as developed through the English authorities. This would allow Han to argue that, although the refurbishment was still technically possible, the purpose for which the work was to be carried out had been frustrated by the destruction of the restaurant. However, this might be a difficult argument for Han to make as the Malaysian courts have yet to consider frustration of purpose, other than the few passages in *Semangat Positif* which appear to allude to the concept.

If the court could be persuaded to adopt the frustration of purpose approach, and to find that the contract between George and Han had indeed been frustrated, this would be very advantageous to Han. The contract would be discharged automatically, meaning that George would no longer be obliged to carry out the refurbishment and Han would no longer be obliged to pay the contract price. Even if George insisted on rendering performance, this might not entitle him to recover any payment from Han. While section 15(3) of the CLA does allow a party to a contract which is subsequently frustrated to seek restitution in relation to any 'valuable benefit' which the other party may have obtained under the contract, this only applies to benefits that have been conferred *before* the time of discharge. In this case, George would have chosen to carry out the refurbishment *after* the occurrence of the frustrating event and therefore after the time of discharge. The most George would be able to claim is the recovery of a 'just sum', pursuant to section 15(2) of the CLA, in relation to the cost of purchasing the necessary materials as he appears to have incurred this expense prior to the frustrating event.

5. Gina and H Hotel

(a) Cancellation of the exhibition

In a case of a standard hotel booking, the hotel's contractual obligations consist of the provision of a room and associated services, while the guest's obligation is to pay the agreed price for the room. It is unlikely that a Malaysian court would hold these obligations to be rendered 'impossible of performance' or 'radically different' by the cancellation of the exhibition, particularly as H Hotel might be unaware of Gina's intention to attend the exhibition. This conclusion is supported by the case of *Philippine Center for Print Excellence.*

(b) Terrorist activity

Even if Gina's concerns about a potential terrorist attack led her to avoid staying at H Hotel that weekend, it is unlikely that a Malaysian court would hold the contract to be frustrated. This is because Gina's obligation to pay the agreed price for her hotel room under the contract remains unaffected, whether she chooses to make use of the room or not. In *Mohamed v Ho Wai,*[89] a tenancy agreement was held not to be frustrated even though the tenant, along with all other persons living in the same neighbourhood, had been compelled to vacate the premises pursuant to emergency regulations enacted to address communist guerrilla activity throughout the state. In doing so, the High Court observed that such an agreement did not necessarily require the tenant to reside on the property.[90] Gina's case is arguably even weaker than that of the tenant in *Mohamed v Ho Wai,* for whom staying on the rental premises was not a lawful option.

(c) Airport strike

Once again, it is unlikely that a Malaysian court would hold the contract between Gina and H Hotel to be frustrated by the strike, for the same reasons as those discussed above. The fact that Gina is unable to avail herself of the room for the full duration of the booking does not render her or H Hotel's contractual obligations 'impossible of performance' or 'radically different' from those which they initially assumed.

(d) Inauguration proceedings

The outcome of this hypothetical will depend on whether Gina is able to persuade the court that first, it should adopt the English concept of frustration of purpose; and second, the purpose of the contract between Gina and H Hotel is to enable Gina to view the inauguration procession.

[89] (1961) 27 MLJ 7.

[90] See also the English case of *London and Northern Estates Co v Schlesinger* [1916] 1 KB 20.

Gina might find it difficult to persuade the court to apply the concept of frustration of purpose, for the same reasons as those given in the hypothetical relating to George and Han. In particular, H Hotel is likely to argue that both its and Gina's contractual obligations remain the same regardless of whether the inauguration proceedings are taking place. This is also supported by the decision in *Philippine Centre for Print Excellence*. If the court is prepared to take into account frustration of purpose, however, Gina will be able to argue that the purpose of the contract was to allow Gina to view the inauguration procession—particularly given that the rental price of the room is ten times higher than the regular price—and that this contractual purpose had been frustrated by the cancellation of the inauguration proceedings. If the court is prepared to accept this argument, then it will hold the contract to be frustrated, discharging Gina from any further obligations under the contract.

6. Kris and Leila

In this hypothetical, the parties' assumption that Leila would dedicate the house to cultural use by the general public was not expressly set out in the contract. Because of this, there is a prior question as to whether it can be treated as an implied term. If no such term is to be implied, then it is difficult to see how Kris can be said to have any contractual claim against Leila, much less one based on frustration.

Even if such a term were to be implied, it is unlikely that a Malaysian court would characterize Leila's decision to give the house to one of her sons as a frustrating event as frustration is usually understood to arise from a supervening event which is outside the control of both parties.[91] Instead it is much more likely to be treated as a breach of contract on Leila's part. Where this is the case, Kris will have a claim for damages against Leila for breach of contract but will not be entitled to seek restitution for the house.

VIII. Conclusion

The Malaysian approach towards change of circumstances that have an impact on the performance of contractual obligations closely mirrors the English position. While section 57(2) of the Contracts Act does not refer to frustration as such, the Malaysian courts have consistently held that it embodies the English doctrine of frustration and have applied the test set out in *Davis Contractors* in determining whether the changed circumstances have rendered performance to be so 'radically different' as to frustrate the contract. The only point at which the Malaysian position differs—or potentially differs—from the English position is that the Malaysian courts have yet to engage with the concept of frustration of purpose, and the recent case of *Philippine Center for Print Excellence* suggests they will be slow to adopt it. With regard to the relationship between the doctrine of frustration and section 33 of the Contracts Act, which deals with contingent contracts, we have argued that section 33 should not be treated as a provision governing frustrated contracts, due to both the language of that provision and the importance of ensuring that the doctrine of frustration is confined to a narrow class of cases. Following the discussion in section IV, we also conclude

[91] *BIG Industrial Gas Sdn Bhd v Pan Wijaya Property Sdn Bhd* (n 19).

that the Malaysian courts should apply sections 15 and 16 of the CLA, rather than section 66 of the Contracts Act, when dealing with the effects of frustrated contracts as sections 15 and 16 were enacted specifically to deal with issues arising from frustrated contracts. The difficulties which the Malaysian courts potentially face in applying section 66 to frustrated contracts, particularly in cases of partial failure of consideration, could be overcome if the courts were to rely exclusively on sections 15 and 16 instead. This would also enable the judicial development of distinctive concepts such as 'just sum' and 'valuable benefit' which are provided for in sections 15 and 16 to achieve a fairer distribution between the parties.

IX. Temporary Measures for Reducing the Impact of Coronavirus Disease (COVID-19) Act 2020

The Temporary Measures for Reducing the Impact of the Coronavirus Disease 2019 (COVID-19) Act 2020 (COVID-19 Act)[92] was enacted by the Malaysian Parliament to provide for certain temporary reliefs from the adverse effects of the COVID-19 pandemic. Part II of the COVID-19 Act relates to the performance of contractual obligations. In essence, it bars the enforcement of a contractual right against a defaulting party who is able to show that (i) there is an inability on their part to perform the relevant contractual obligation; (ii) the obligation arises from one of the categories of contracts specified in the Schedule to the COVID-19 Act; and (iii) the inability to perform is due to the measures prescribed, made, or taken under the Prevention and Control of Infectious Diseases Act 1988[93] to control or prevent the spread of COVID-19.[94] In *SN Akmida Holdings Sdn Bhd v Kerajaan Malaysia*,[95] the High Court emphasized that the burden is on the party relying on the COVID-19 Act to make out all the elements set out above. In particular, it stated that the party in question must identify the specific measure or measures said to have prevented the performance of the contractual obligation and to demonstrate the nexus between the measure and the inability to perform. A mere general statement by the party that its business had been affected by the pandemic and that preventive measures had been taken to curb its spread will not suffice. While there is no express legislative statement or judicial commentary on the relationship between the COVID-19 Act and the doctrine of frustration, one effect of these provisions is that parties who are unable to perform their contractual obligations due to the measures taken to control or prevent the spread of COVID-19 are much less likely to have to fall back on the doctrine of frustration in order to avoid liability for non-performance. Section 57(2) of the Contracts Act has been applied to contracts affected by the COVID-19 pandemic. In *MITTI Power Cables Sdn Bhd v Lender Cable Industry Bhd*,[96] the High Court applied the test of frustration in *Davis Contractors* and *Ramli bin Zakaria* and held that the consent judgment to pay money was not frustrated due to the pandemic. However, in *Lim Kee Sim v Loi Cheng Pheng*,[97] it was successfully argued that the contract was frustrated because the pandemic rendered it impossible for the vendor to fulfil the contractual obligations under the share sale agreement entered into by the parties.

[92] Act 829.
[93] Act 342.
[94] COVID-19 Act, s 7.
[95] [2021] MLJU 2449.
[96] [2021] MLJU 496.
[97] [2025] MLJU 107.

16

Termination of Contracts

The Position under Malaysian Contract Law

May Fong CHEONG and Yin Harn LEE

I. Introduction

The law governing contracts in Malaysia is the Contracts Act 1950 (Contracts Act),[1] which applies to both commercial and consumer transactions.[2] The Contracts Act is essentially a re-enactment of the Indian Contract Act 1872 (Indian Contract Act), which is in turn a codification of the then-prevailing English legal principles relating to contracts.[3]

This chapter proceeds as follows. Section II discusses the provisions of the Contracts Act that relate to termination for breach. Section III considers termination clauses. Sections IV and V deal respectively with the procedure for terminating a contract and the circumstances under which the right to terminate will be lost. Section VI sets out the legal effects of termination. Over the course of this discussion, it will become apparent that, while the Malaysian position on termination of contracts tracks the English position fairly closely, this owes much more to the Malaysian courts' innovative interpretation of the relevant statutory provisions than the strict language of the provisions themselves. As section VII of this chapter concludes, this approach is far from ideal, and the limitations of the statutory provisions on termination highlight the urgent need for reform of the Contracts Act in order to enable Malaysian contract law to keep pace with the legal developments elsewhere in the common law world.

II. Termination for Breach under the Contracts Act

The main statutory provision relating to termination for breach is section 40 of the Contracts Act. This provides as follows:

> Where a party to a contract has refused to perform, or disabled himself from performing, his promise in its entirety, the promisee may put an end to the contract, unless he has signified, by words or conduct, his acquiescence in its continuation.

[1] Act 136.

[2] See Sale of Goods Act 1957 (Act 382) and Consumer Protection Act 1999 (Act 599), respectively.

[3] On the historical background, see MF Cheong and YH Lee, 'Specific Remedies and Money Awards in the Protection of the Performance Interest under Malaysian Contract Law' in M Chen-Wishart, A Loke, and B Ong (eds), *Studies in the Contract Laws of Asia, vol I: Remedies for Breach of Contract* (OUP 2016) 325, 326–30.

May Fong Cheong and Yin Harn Lee, *Termination of Contracts: The Position under Malaysian Contract Law* In: *Studies in the Contract Laws of Asia V: Ending and Changing Contracts*. Edited by: Mindy Chen-Wishart, Dora Neo, and Stefan Vogenauer, Oxford University Press. © May Fong Cheong and Yin Harn Lee 2026. DOI: 10.1093/oso/9780198995814.003.0016

1. Anticipatory Breach

Taken on its face, section 40 envisages two sets of circumstances in which a party to a contract will be entitled to terminate it. The first is where the other party has 'refused to perform' their obligations under the contract, and the second is where the other party has 'disabled himself from performing' those obligations. Under section 40, the innocent party will then have the option either to terminate the contract and treat it as having come to an end or to affirm the contract and treat it as subsisting.

In this regard, section 40 mirrors the English position relating to 'anticipatory breach', a point which has been acknowledged by the Malaysian courts.[4] Under English law, an anticipatory breach will occur when, before performance is due, one party *either* 'repudiates' or 'renounces' the contract, by evincing an intention not to carry out its obligations when performance falls due,[5] *or* does or omits to do an act which disables it from performing its contractual obligations.[6] The Malaysian courts[7] have adopted the test set out in the English courts in determining whether a repudiation has occurred. In *Rasiah Munusamy v Lim & Sons Sdn Bhd*,[8] the Supreme Court referred to *Freeth v Burr*[9] and held that a mere refusal to perform is insufficient, but there must be an absolute refusal to perform for the other party to treat himself as discharged.

2. Fundamental Breach

Under English law, a party to a contract may also be entitled to terminate it when the other party has failed to render performance at the time when performance falls due, depending on the seriousness of the breach. While section 40 makes no express reference to this type of breach, the Malaysian courts have also read into section 40 the principle that a party to a contract will be entitled to terminate it and treat itself as discharged from further liability where the other party has committed a 'fundamental breach'. In *Hwa Chea Lin v Malim Jaya (Melaka) Sdn Bhd*,[10] Suriyadi J stated:

> In Malaysia, the terminology of fundamental breach, which is a concept of the common law, though not in exact term terms [*sic*] has become a creature of statute (see *Choo Yin Loo v Visuvalingam Pillay* (1930) 7 FMSLR 135). The relevant provision . . . is now enshrined in s 40 of the Act . . .
> (Henceforth, I shall maintain the terminology of 'fundamental breach' since I am fully satisfied that the provision of s 40 is the direct descendant of the common law concept).[11]

[4] *Choo Yin Loo v SK Visuvalingam Pillay* (1930) 7 FMSLR 135.
[5] *Hochster v De La Tour* (1853) 2 El & Bl 678.
[6] *Universal Cargo Carriers Corp v Citati* [1957] 2 QB 401.
[7] On the hierarchy of courts in Malaysia, see Cheong and Lee (n 3) 328.
[8] [1985] 2 MLJ 291.
[9] (1874) LR 9 CP 208, 214.
[10] [1996] 4 MLJ 544.
[11] ibid 551–52. See also *Arab-Malaysian Finance Bhd v Samian bin Sabin* [2003] 5 MLJ 403; *Tan Tien Sing v Grobina Resorts Sdn Bhd* [2005] 7 MLJ 590; *Damansara Realty Bhd v Bungsar Hill Holdings Sdn Bhd* [2011] 6 MLJ 464. See also *Ban Hong Joo Mines Ltd v Chen & Yap Ltd* [1969] 2 MLJ 83, 86 (referring to a breach which 'clearly went to the root of the contract'); *Syarikat Jaya v Star Publications (M) Bhd* [1990] 1 MLJ 31, 34 (referring to a breach which 'deprive[s] the plaintiffs of substantially the whole benefit of the contract').

It is true that, in English law, the concept of a 'fundamental breach' is more often associated with exemption clauses rather than termination as such. The term 'fundamental breach' was at one time used by the English courts to denote a breach that goes so much to the root of the contract that liability for it was incapable of being excluded by an exemption or limitation clause.[12] However, that concept has since been rejected by the House of Lords in *Suisse Atlantique Société d'Armement Maritime SA v NV Rotterdamsche Kolen Centrale*,[13] where Lord Reid stated that:

> General use of the term 'fundamental breach' is of recent origin and I can find nothing to indicate that it means either more or less than the well known type of breach which entitles the innocent party to treat it as repudiatory and to rescind the contract.[14]

The Malaysian courts' use of the term 'fundamental breach' to refer to a breach which is sufficiently serious to entitle the innocent party to terminate the contract is consistent with this definition.[15]

In *Damansara Realty Bhd v Bungsar Hill Holdings Sdn Bhd*,[16] the Federal Court observed that the distinction between a repudiation or anticipatory breach on the one hand, and a fundamental breach on the other hand, may not always be clear-cut, particularly where ongoing contracts are concerned. This was the case in *Damansara Realty*, which involved a property development agreement entered into between a development company and a landowner, under which the company was given development rights over the property for 15 years. The development company obtained some of the necessary regulatory approvals for the work to be done under the contract but had failed to commence any work even after 13.5 years into the contract period. The Federal Court found on the facts that it was the intention of the parties that the development work should be completed by the end of the 15-year period. The development company's delay in commencing work meant that this outcome had become virtually impossible. Because of this, its failure to commence work at a reasonable time amounted to a breach which entitled the landowner to terminate the contract. In stating this, the Federal Court acknowledged the difficulty of classifying the development company's breach as either a repudiation or a fundamental breach but also emphasized the importance of not being unduly concerned with questions of terminology. Richard Malanjum CJ (Sabah and Sarawak) stated that:

> the present case is more towards a situation where there has been a breach of a continuing promise. It is certainly a case of repudiation but also involves fundamental breach of an existing obligation which gives rise to the inevitable conclusion that the promise or bargain would not be fulfilled by or on the due date. . . .
>
> It is therefore our considered opinion that a termination in anticipation of an inevitable breach is recognised under our law. It may be termed as termination upon an anticipatory

[12] *Karsales (Harrow) Ltd v Wallis* [1956] 1 WLR 936; *Harbutt's Plasticine Ltd v Wayne Tank & Pump Co Ltd* [1970] 1 QB 447.

[13] [1967] 1 AC 361.

[14] ibid 397. See also *Photo Production Ltd v Securicor Transport Ltd* [1980] AC 827, 841–46.

[15] For an overview, see JW Carter, 'Fundamental Breach and Discharge for Breach under the Contracts Act 1950' (2011) 28 Journal of Contract Law 85. See also *Tan Kau Tiah @ Tan Ching Hai v Tetuan Teh Kim Teh, Salina & Co (a firm)* [2010] 3 MLJ 569 [49]–[50].

[16] [2011] 6 MLJ 464.

> breach (repudiation), or termination based upon a fundamental breach of an existing obligation (fundamental breach) . . . In both circumstances, the innocent party is entitled to treat the contract as having been repudiated and may rightly treat itself as having been discharged from the contract. The innocent party has the option to rescind the contract (ie rescission for breach) or to affirm the contract.[17]

3. Seriousness of the Breach

Section 40 itself does not expressly lay down a 'seriousness' threshold for a breach which entitles a contracting party to terminate. Instead, it merely speaks of one party's failure to perform their contractual promise 'in its entirety'. This is an expression amenable to a wide range of interpretations. On one end of the spectrum, a party to a contract could be said to perform their promise 'in its entirety' only where every single term has been complied with, such that even the breach of a very trivial term would entitle the other party to terminate. On the other hand, a failure to perform a promise 'in its entirety' might also be said to occur only where a party has failed to perform any part of the contract so that even the breach of a very serious term would not entitle the innocent party to terminate, provided that the party in breach had performed at least *some* of their contractual promises. However, as the discussion on fundamental breach indicates, the Malaysian courts have adopted an English-style 'seriousness' threshold in determining whether a breach of contract is one which entitles the innocent party to terminate it. In doing so, they have been able to avoid both of these extremes.

(a) Conditions, warranties, and innominate terms

In determining whether a breach of contract is sufficiently serious, the Malaysian courts follow the English approach of classifying contractual terms as either 'conditions', 'warranties', or 'innominate terms'. Under English law, every contractual term was traditionally seen as being classifiable, at the time of formation, as either a condition or a warranty.[18] A condition is an essential term, the breach of which entitles the innocent party to terminate the contract. A warranty, meanwhile, is a non-essential or subsidiary term, the breach of which does not entitle the innocent party to terminate but only to claim damages. Since the decision of the Court of Appeal in *Hong Kong Fir Shipping Co Ltd v Kawsaki Kisen Kaisha Ltd*,[19] English law has also recognized a third category of contractual term, known as the 'innominate term', which is not readily classifiable as either a condition or warranty at the time of formation. Whether the breach of such a term gives rise to a right of termination will depend on the consequences of the breach. If the effect of the breach is such as to deprive the innocent party of substantially the whole benefit under the contract, then the innocent party will be entitled to terminate the contract and treat themselves as discharged.

This approach to the classification of contractual terms has been adopted by the Malaysian courts. In *Ching Yik Development Sdn Bhd v Setapak Heights Development*

[17] ibid [64]–[66].
[18] Compare *Bettini v Gye* (1876) 1 QBD 183 with *Poussard v Spiers & Pond* (1876) 1 QBD 410.
[19] [1962] 2 QB 26.

Sdn Bhd,[20] a decision of the Court of Appeal, Gopal Sri Ram JCA, while not referring expressly to the terms 'condition,' 'warranty', and 'innominate term', laid down the following principles:

> Now, in every contract . . . there are, generally speaking, some terms that are of fundamental importance and others of less or minor importance . . . Where the term that has been flouted is fundamental to the contract, the innocent party is entitled to treat himself as being discharged from further obligations under it. But where the obligation that has been breached is only subsidiary or minor in nature, the innocent party may not treat himself as being free of his obligations under the contract, although he may sue and recover damages for the non-performance of the subsidiary term. . . .
>
> Another approach to the problem in cases that involve synallagmatic contracts is to look at the consequences of the breach of the term in question. If the breach is of such a nature that it goes to the root of the contract, then the term broken is fundamental in nature. On the other hand, if the consequences of the breach complained of are not serious in the sense that they do not go to the root of the contract, then the term in question is a subsidiary one entitling the innocent party to recover damages but not to treat the contract as being at an end.[21]

(b) 'Total failure of consideration'

In describing a breach which is serious enough to entitle the innocent party to terminate the contract, the Malaysian courts have sometimes had recourse to the language of 'total failure of consideration'. In *Damansara Realty*, the Federal Court considered this concept in relation to the words 'his promise in its entirety' in section 40 of the Contracts Act. Richard Malanjum CJ (Sabah and Sarawak) stated that:

> There is a total failure of consideration (and a failure to perform a promise in its entirety) where a reasonable and commercially sensible man would look upon the project of having little or no value at all. If the reasonable and commercially sensible man sees the performance of the contract of having some value, it should be taken that there has been no total failure of consideration and accordingly the promise has been performed in part. In the earlier instance, there is a right to terminate the contract, but not in the latter instance.[22]

In a sense, it is not difficult to see why the Federal Court should have equated the concept of a failure to perform a promise in its entirety with that of a total failure of consideration—a concept developed through the English law of restitution[23]—as both involve the non-performance of a contractual promise by a party to the contract. However, the proposition that the innocent party will be entitled to terminate the contract only where there has been

[20] [1996] 3 MLJ 675.

[21] ibid 681–83. See also *Abdul Razak bin Datuk Abu Samah v Shah Alam Properties Sdn Bhd* [1992] 2 MLJ 500, 506.

[22] [2011] 6 MLJ 464 [60]. See also *U TV Sdn Bhd v Comintel Sdn Bhd* [2017] 5 MLJ 292 [54]. See also *Berjaya Times Squares Sdn Bhd v M Concept Sdn Bhd* [2010] 1 MLJ 597, 609–10.

[23] *Fibrosa Spolka Akcyjna v Fairbairn Lawson Combe Barbour* [1943] AC 32, 48.

a total failure of consideration runs counter to much of the Malaysian courts' own case law on fundamental breach. Under English law, a failure of consideration will be total only where the innocent party has received *no* part of the promised performance at all. Where the innocent party has received even a trivial part of the promised performance, this will amount to a partial rather than a total failure of consideration.[24] Taken to its logical conclusion, this would mean that the innocent party would be entitled to terminate the contract only where the other party had performed no part of its contractual obligations at all. As discussed previously, while such an interpretation is available on the statutory language of section 40, at least in principle, this is not how the Malaysian courts have traditionally approached that provision.

In any event, it is not obvious that such a radical departure from the traditional approach was intended by the Federal Court in *Damansara Realty* at all. After appearing to link section 40 with total failure of consideration, the Federal Court then reverted to the more orthodox language of fundamental breach, stating that: 'The right of an innocent party to terminate a contract or treat itself as having been discharged from the contract is mainly premised on the ground of repudiation or fundamental breach.'[25] As discussed above, it ultimately held that the development company's prolonged and unreasonable delay in commencing work could be construed as either a repudiation of the contract or a fundamental breach, giving rise to a right to terminate on the part of the landowner. The decision in *Damansara Realty* is therefore entirely consistent with the orthodox approach. Because of this, it is not clear why the reference to total failure of consideration was thought necessary. It is submitted that the Malaysian courts should, in future, refrain from using the language of total failure of consideration in cases involving termination for breach as this could potentially lead to confusion.[26]

(c) Stipulations as to time

In addition to section 40, section 56 of the Contracts Act is relevant to termination for breach. Following section 56(1), the effect of a failure to render performance at a fixed time

[24] *Stocznia Gdanska SA v Latvia Shipping Co* [1998] 1 WLR 574, 588. In this sense, the definition of total failure of consideration articulated by the Federal Court in *Damansara Realty*, as being predicated on the value of the part performance to 'the reasonable and commercially sensible man', does not appear to be entirely consistent with the English authorities.

[25] [2011] 6 MLJ 464 [62].

[26] See also Carter (n 15) 95: 'I do not agree that s 40 is inapplicable if there is part performance, or . . . that it applies only if there is a "total failure of consideration".' Difficulties arising from *Berjaya Times Square Sdn Bhd v M Concept Sdn Bhd* (n 22), which applied the concept of total failure of consideration in considering s 40, which was further expounded in *Damansara Realty*, was acknowledged by the Federal Court in *Lim Swee Choo and Chiam Eng Huat @ Chiam Eng Hong v Ong Koh Hou @ Won Kok Fong* Civil Appeal Nos 02(f)-22-07/2024 (W) and 02(f)-23-07/2024 (W). In the broad grounds of judgment delivered on 8 April 2025, the Court stated at [23]:

> We agree with learned council for the Plaintiffs that this Court is duty bound to clarify the Malaysian position on the common law doctrine of total failure of consideration given the divergence in interpretation and approach taken by this Court in *Berjaya Times Square Sdn. Bhd. v. M Concept Sdn. Bhd.* and *Damansara Realty Bhd v. Bangsar Hill Holdings Sdn. Bhd. & Anor* departing from the original context in which the doctrine was initially restated by the House of Lords in *Stocznia Gdanska SA v. Latvian Shipping Co*' [Citations of cases omitted]. The Federal Court in *Lim Swee Choo* delivered its full judgment on 2 October 2025, see [2025] 6 MLJ 327. The Court at [74] clarified that 'the notion of total failure of consideration should not inform the interpretation of section 40'. For a discussion of *Berjaya Times Square*, *Damansara Realty* and *Lim Swee Choo*, see MF Cheong, SM Choong and KJ Yong, *Contract Law in Malaysia* (Sweet & Maxwell, 2nd ed 2026) 497–502.

in a contract where time is expressed to be of the essence is that the contract 'becomes voidable at the option of the promisee'. Under section 56(2), if there was no such intention expressed, the contract does not become voidable by the failure to render performance at the specified time; however, the promisee is entitled to compensation from the promisor for losses suffered by the said failure to perform.

While section 56(1) refers to a contract which 'becomes voidable at the option of the promisee'—in contrast to section 40, which provides that the innocent party may 'put an end to the contract'—Malaysian courts have generally understood section 56(1) as having essentially the same effect as section 40, namely, that it gives the innocent party the right to terminate the contract in cases where time has been made of the essence but the other party has failed to perform within the stipulated time.[27] In some instances, the Malaysian courts have also linked section 56(1) with section 40 and have characterized the failure to perform within the stipulated time as a breach of a condition[28] or a breach of a fundamental term.[29]

The classic statement of principle as to when time will be considered to be of the essence of the contract is set out in the judgment of Gill J in *Tan Ah Kian v Haji Hasnan*:[30]

> Firstly, time is of the essence of the contract where the parties expressly stipulate in the contract that it shall be so...
>
> Second, time is of the essence of the contract where it was not originally stated to be so but has been made so by one party by giving reasonable notice to the other, who has failed to perform the contract, with sufficient promptitude...
>
> Third, time is of the essence of the contract where from the nature of the contract or of its subject matter time must be taken to be of the essence of the agreement. A simple illustration of this rule would be the case of a sale of property which fluctuates in value with the passage of time.[31]

In *Damansara Realty*, the Federal Court expanded upon the first and third of these situations. It held that the fact that the contract contained a clause stating time to be of the essence did not *ipso facto* result in time being of the essence, nor did the fact that a contract did not contain such a clause mean that time was not intended to be of the essence. Instead, in determining whether time was of the essence in any given case, the court should consider the conduct and dealings of the parties. On the facts of this case, the Federal Court held that, even in the absence of an express clause to that effect, it was implicit from the property development agreement between the parties that time was of the essence as the development was to be commenced and completed within a 15-year period.

[27] On the statutory language of contracts that 'become voidable', see section V.

[28] *Eng Mee Yong v Letchumanan* [1979] 2 MLJ 212, 218; *Gan Hwa Kian v Shencourt Sdn Bhd* [2007] 4 MLJ 554 [12].

[29] *LSSC Development Sdn Bhd v Thomas a/l Iruthayam* [2007] 4 MLJ 1 [15]–[16], [22]; *Berjaya Times Squares Sdn Bhd v M Concept Sdn Bhd* (n 22) [27]; *BC Development Sdn Bhd v The Titular Roman Catholic Bishop of Malacca Johor* [2010] 5 MLJ 778 [29].

[30] [1962] MLJ 400.

[31] ibid 402. See also *Sharikat Eastern Plastics Industry v Sharikat Lam Seng Trading* [1972] 1 MLJ 21. On the second scenario, see *Mensa Mercantile (Far East) Pte Ltd v Eikobina (M) Sdn Bhd* [1989] 2 MLJ 170.

III. Termination Clauses

Malaysian courts generally recognize and enforce contractual clauses entitling the parties to terminate the contract upon the occurrence of a specified breach or breaches.[32] In *Dream Property Sdn Bhd v Atlas Housing Sdn Bhd*,[33] the Federal Court, enforcing an automatic termination clause which provided that the contract 'shall be treated as null and void and of no further effect' upon the defendant's breach, observed that such clauses are 'not novel or unusual in Malaysian contract law'.[34]

Unlike termination under section 40 of the Contracts Act, there is no 'seriousness' threshold for the operation of a contractual termination clause. In several cases, the courts have upheld clauses that allow the parties to terminate the contract 'at any time' or 'without giving any reason'. In *American International Assurance Co Ltd v Koh Yen Bee*,[35] the contract between the defendant insurance company and the plaintiff, one of its agents, stipulated that it 'may be terminated without giving any reason thereof . . . [b]y either party upon 15 days' notice in writing'. The majority of the Court of Appeal upheld the defendant's termination of the plaintiff (who had been the defendant's agent for 11 years) with a letter giving 15 days' notice of termination.[36] In *Chan Whye & Sons Contractors (suing as a firm) v Sarawak Shell Bhd*,[37] the contract was for an initial period of three years with an option for the defendant to extend it for a further year. The court upheld the defendant's notice to terminate following a clause which allowed the defendant to, 'at any time, terminate the Contract by written notice to [the plaintiff]'.

The following sections will set out how the hypothetical scenarios proposed by the volume editors would be treated under Malaysian law.[38]

1. The Hypotheticals

(a) Car Machinery & Co and Traders Ltd

There are a number of grounds on which Car Machinery might be entitled to terminate its contract with Traders. First, Car Machinery could rely on its contractual right to termination under Clause 7(b). The Malaysian courts are generally prepared to enforce termination clauses even where no breach has been committed by the other party, as occurred in *Koh Yen Bee* and *Chan Whye & Sons*.

Second, Car Machinery might terminate the contract pursuant to section 40 of the Contracts Act if Trader's breach could be regarded as a fundamental breach and the term breached by Traders could be construed as a condition. There is room to argue that the

[32] See *Associated Pan Malaysia Cement Sdn Bhd v Syarikat Teknical & Kejuruteraan Sdn Bhd* [1990] 3 MLJ 287 [44]; *Kredin Sdn Bhd v YTF Investments Sdn Bhd* [1998] 1 MLJ 46, 55; *Platinum Nanochem Sdn Bhd v Mecpro Heavy Engineering Ltd* [2016] 11 MLJ 141 [90].

[33] [2015] 2 MLJ 441.

[34] ibid [77].

[35] [2002] 4 MLJ 301.

[36] cf Mohd Noor Ahmad JCA's dissent (holding that a 15-days' notice was unreasonable and that the plaintiff should have been given 12 months' notice considering her length of service with the defendant) ibid 326. See also *Wong Pa Hock v American International Assurance Co Ltd* [2001] MLJU 688.

[37] [2003] 5 MLJ 68. See also *Anuiti Enterprise (M) Sdn Bhd v Cubic Electronics Sdn Bhd* [2006] 6 MLJ 565.

[38] The fact scenarios for the hypothetical situations discussed in the following can be found in M Chen-Wishart, D Neo, and S Vogenauer, 'Introduction', ch 1 in this volume, 9.

parties intended the term to be a condition going to the root of the contract[39] as the clause provides that Car Machinery would be entitled to terminate the contract if Traders failed to comply with its obligation to visit the six large car manufacturers every week.

It is possible, however, that the court might decline to construe the term in question as a condition, notwithstanding the parties' express stipulation. In *Damansara Realty*, the Federal Court emphasized that a contractual clause stating time to be of the essence did not *ipso facto* result in time being of the essence; instead, the court shall consider the surrounding circumstances. In light of the condition/warranty distinction, it is probable that the court might hold the term breached by Traders *not* to be a condition, despite the parties' express intention, but only an innominate term at best. However, Car Machinery would still be entitled to terminate the contract pursuant to section 40 if it could show that the breach committed by Traders had the effect of depriving it of substantially the whole of the benefit of the contract.

In summary, Car Machinery will be entitled to terminate the contract in reliance on the contractual right to terminate under Clause 7(b) or, alternatively, on the basis of section 40 of the Contracts Act if it is able to show that the term breached by Traders is *either* a condition *or* an innominate term whose breach results in sufficiently serious consequences.

(b) Prime Ltd and Devil Corp

A Malaysian court is likely to treat the contract between Prime and Devil as being one where time is of the essence. First, the parties have made an express stipulation to that effect in the contract itself. While *Damansara Realty* made it clear that the presence of such an express stipulation does not *ipso facto* result in time being of the essence, decided cases[40] show that the courts are usually prepared to find that it was the intention of the parties to make time of the essence where such clauses are incorporated into the contract. The contract between Prime and Devil also specifies the exact time by which payment is to be made and not merely the date for payment. The contract appears to be commercial in nature as both Prime and Devil are companies. As acknowledged in *Damansara Realty*, there is a *prima facie* acceptance that time will be of the essence for commercial contracts. These factors strengthen the argument that the parties intended time to be of the essence of the contract.

Because Devil has tendered the completion money after the time stipulated for performance, it seems very likely that a Malaysian court will hold that the contract has been terminated pursuant to Clause 12. As the Malaysian courts are generally prepared to recognize and enforce automatic termination clauses, there is therefore no room for Devil to argue that Prime's reliance on Clause 12 is unreasonable. As the contract has been terminated, Devil will not be able to sue for specific performance.

Even in the absence of Clause 12, the nature of the contract is such that the court is likely to find time to be of the essence, for the same reasons as those set out above. Because of this, Prime would still have a right to terminate the contract pursuant to section 56(1) of the Contracts Act.

[39] *Associated Pan Malaysia Cement Sdn Bhd v Syarikat Teknical & Kejuruteraan Sdn Bhd* (n 32) 291:

> It is open to the parties to a contract to make it clear . . . that a particular stipulation is to be regarded as a condition which goes to the root of the contract, so that it is clear that the parties contemplate that any breach of it entitles the other party at once to treat the contract as at an end.

[40] See eg *Abdul Rahim bin Syed Mohd v Ramakrishnan Kandasamy Wan* [1996] 3 MLJ 385, 405.

(c) Seven Seas and Big Chef

It is not obvious from the facts whether the contract between Seven Seas and Big Chef contains any express terms stipulating the permissible level of cadmium in the mussels supplied. Because this is a contract for the sale of goods, however, a term as to the quality or fitness of the goods supplied can be implied into the contract pursuant to section 16(1)(a) of the Sale of Goods Act 1957 (SOGA),[41] which provides that:

> Where the buyer, expressly or by implication makes known to the seller the particular purpose for which the goods are required, so as to show that the buyer relies on the seller's skill or judgment, and the goods are of a description which it is in the course of the seller's business to supply (whether he is the manufacturer or producer or not) there is an implied condition that the goods shall be reasonably fit for such purpose.

Given the nature of the parties' respective businesses, it seems very likely that a court will find Seven Seas to be aware of the purpose for which the mussels are required, namely, for consumption in Big Chef's restaurants. As Seven Seas is an importer of seafood, the mussels in this case are goods 'of a description which it is in the course of the seller's business to supply'. In light of this, the court is likely to construe the implied condition that 'the goods shall be reasonably fit' for the purpose for which they are required to include compliance with national food regulations. Because of this, it is likely that Seven Seas will be held to have breached the implied condition as to the 'reasonable fitness' of the mussels. Section 12(1) of the SOGA defines a 'condition' as 'a stipulation essential to the main purpose of the contract, the breach of which gives rise to a right to treat the contract as repudiated'. On its face, therefore, Big Chef would appear to have the right to terminate the contract.

However, section 38(2) of the SOGA may potentially limit Big Chef's ability to terminate the contract. This section provides that where there is non-delivery, or defective delivery of one or more instalments, of goods which are to be delivered by stated instalments and to be separately paid for, or the buyer refuses to take delivery of or pay for one or more instalments, it is a question in each case depending on the terms of the contract and the circumstances of the case, whether the breach of contract is a repudiation of the whole contract or whether it is a severable breach giving rise to a claim for compensation but not to a right to treat the whole contract as repudiated.

Whether section 38(2) is applicable will depend on the terms of the contract, particularly whether it stipulates that the mussels are to be delivered in stated instalments—presumably of one ton each—that are to be paid for separately. Assuming section 38(2) applies, then the English case of *Maple Flock Co Ltd v Universal Furniture Products (Wembley) Ltd*[42] may be relevant as its facts bear a close resemblance to the present hypothetical. The contract in *Maple Flock* involved the sale and purchase of 100 tons of rag flock, to be delivered in three loads of 1.5 tons per week. A sample drawn from one of the deliveries showed a contamination of 250 parts of chlorine in parts of the flock, well above the maximum allowed by the law then in force.

In *Maple Flock*, the English Court of Appeal laid down two tests to be considered in applying the English counterpart to section 38(2) of the SOGA. The first is the quantitative

41 Act 382.
42 [1934] 1 KB 148.

ratio which the breach bears to the contract as a whole, and the second is the degree of probability that the breach will be repeated. Applying these tests it held that the sellers' breach of contract did not amount to a repudiation. First, the quantitative ratio of the defective delivery was relatively small as it comprised only 1.5 tons out of a contract for 100 tons. Second, the probability of the breach being repeated was 'practically negligible' as the sellers' business was conducted carefully, and the defective delivery was an isolated instance out of 20 satisfactory deliveries that had already been made.

If it were to follow the approach in *Maple Flock*, a Malaysian court would likely reach the opposite conclusion on the facts of the present hypothetical. Here, the defective delivery related to one ton of mussels out of a contracted two tons, a much higher ratio compared to that in *Maple Flock*. There is also no evidence of Seven Seas having made satisfactory deliveries either prior or subsequent to the current breach for a similar finding that the probability of the breach being repeated as 'practically negligible'. Thus, the likelihood that Seven Seas will be found to have repudiated the contract, thus entitling Big Chef to terminate it, is much higher compared to *Maple Flock*.

(d) Coco and David

Coco is likely to have repudiated the contract when she informed David that she was no longer interested in David's services. Coco's refusal to proceed with the contract means that David has the option either of terminating the contract and treating it as having come to an end or affirming the contract and treating it as subsisting.

If David chooses the latter option, he is, in principle, entitled to insist on rendering performance. In *Teh Wan Sang & Sons Sdn Bhd v See Teow Chuan*,[43] the defendant tenant wrote to the plaintiff landlord purporting to terminate the tenancy agreement between the parties, which still had over a year left to run. Subsequently, the tenant vacated the premises, but the landlord refused to accept the tenant's repudiation and continued to seek the agreed rent from the tenant. The High Court held that the landlord was entitled to insist on the continuation of the contract notwithstanding the tenant's repudiation. Accordingly, the landlord was awarded arrears of rent from the tenant up until the point at which the landlord terminated the agreement by accepting a new tenant. Significantly, despite the High Court's reference to the English case of *White & Carter (Councils) Ltd v McGregor*,[44] the High Court at no point suggested that the landlord would be entitled to treat the contract as subsisting only if it had a 'legitimate interest' in performing the contract rather than terminating it and claiming damages for breach. This stands in contrast to *White & Carter (Councils)*, where the House of Lords held that the innocent party would not be able to affirm the contract if they had 'no legitimate interest, financial or otherwise', in performing the contract.[45]

In practice, however, David may face difficulties in performing his contractual obligations as he requires Coco's cooperation to give him access to the development before he can carry out any landscaping work. The High Court in *Teh Wan Sang* noted that there were not many cases in which an innocent party would be able to perform their own contractual obligations without the repudiating party's cooperation. If so, there seems little point

[43] [1984] 1 MLJ 130.
[44] [1962] AC 413.
[45] ibid 431.

for David not to terminate the contract. If David were to terminate the contract, he would be entitled to bring an action against Coco for anticipatory breach and sue for damages immediately.

IV. Procedure for Termination

As in English law, a repudiation or fundamental breach by one party to a contract does not have the effect of discharging the contract automatically. Instead, the innocent party must exercise their right of termination in order to bring the contract to an end. A party who does so is sometimes said to 'rescind' the contract or to exercise their right of 'rescission', though this terminology may potentially lead to confusion with cases where the contract has been rescinded on the basis of a vitiating factor such as coercion, fraud, misrepresentation, or undue influence.[46]

The innocent party's decision as to whether to terminate or to affirm the contract can be communicated either expressly or by implication. This was acknowledged by the Court of Appeal in *Mintye Properties Sdn Bhd v Yayasan Melaka*,[47] where Gopal Sri Ram JCA stated:

> For an election [between the termination or affirmation of the contract] to be effective and binding, the innocent party must by words or conduct communicate his decision to the contract breaker. In other words it may be express or implied from conduct.[48]

In practice, most parties seeking to exercise their right to terminate for breach will do so by giving notice to that effect to the other party. In keeping with the principles outlined in *Mintye Properties*, however, this is not the only means by which the decision can be communicated. In *Tan Hock Chan v Kho Teck Seng*,[49] the Federal Court held that the plaintiff had successfully exercised his option to terminate the contract following the defendant's repudiation when he commenced legal proceedings against the latter, even though he had not given prior express notice to the defendant of his intention to terminate.

There is no need for the innocent party to apply to the court for an order to terminate the contract, and in practice, parties rarely do so.[50] A case in which such an application was made is *Teh Khem On v Yeoh & Wu Development Sdn Bhd*.[51] In the course of his judgment, Peh Swee Chin FCJ commented on the unusual nature of the plaintiffs' application, observing that:

[46] MF Cheong and YH Lee, *Civil Remedies* (2nd edn, Sweet & Maxwell 2016) para 3.001–3.008. For an illustration of such confusion, see *Sik Hong Photo Sdn Bhd v Ch'ng Beng Choo* [2010] 5 AMR 110 (incorrectly stating that 'the fundamental breach entitled the innocent party to rescind the contract and to have the parties restored to a position where they will stand as if the contract had never been made, ie the return of property by way of *restitutio in integrum*').

[47] [2006] 6 MLJ 420.

[48] ibid [10].

[49] [1980] 1 MLJ 308.

[50] The Specific Relief Act 1950, s 34(1) allows '[a]ny person interested in a contract in writing' to sue to have it rescinded where, inter alia, the contract is 'voidable or terminable by the plaintiff'. However, this is not frequently used.

[51] [1995] 2 MLJ 663.

> The [plaintiff's] claim for rescission of contract for its breach could be considered by the court though it is unusual; unusual because a victim of a breach of contract usually terminates or rescinds the contract for breach before going to court, instead of asking for an order for such rescission for breach.[52]

V. Loss of Right to Terminate

The innocent party's right to terminate a contract for breach will be lost once they affirm the contract.[53] As in English law, the affirmation need not be express but may be inferred through the conduct of the party concerned. This was the case in *First Count Sdn Bhd v Wang Yew Logging & Plantation Sdn Bhd*,[54] where the parties entered into a contract under which the plaintiff was to fell, extract, and harvest timber logs from the defendant's timber concession. In breach of agreement, the defendant subsequently purported to impose a unilateral reduction of the monthly fee payable to the plaintiff. However, the plaintiff continued to carry out logging operations for the defendant for nearly 54 months after the reduction of the fee. The Court of Appeal held that, in doing so, the plaintiff had affirmed the contract and acquiesced in its continuation.[55]

VI. Effects of Termination

Once a contract has been terminated for breach, both parties are discharged from the performance of future obligations that have yet to fall due. However, all accrued rights and obligations arising under the contract will still subsist, and the parties will be liable for any breach of these past obligations.[56]

Following the termination of a contract, the parties will be able to avail themselves of the restitutionary remedies set out in sections 65 and 66 of the Contracts Act, and the innocent party will also have the option to claim compensatory damages pursuant to section 76.[57] As Carter has observed, these provisions can sometimes be difficult to navigate as they refer to contracts that are 'voidable', that 'become void', or have been 'rightly rescinded', rather than employing the language of 'termination'.[58] However, it is clear from the jurisprudence of the Malaysian and Indian courts that these expressions should be understood as referring to contracts that have been terminated for breach as well as contracts that have been rescinded on the basis of a vitiating factor.[59]

52 ibid 673.

53 Contracts Act, s 40 (providing that 'the promisee may put an end to the contract, *unless he has signified, by words or conduct, his acquiescence in its continuation*') (emphasis by the authors).

54 [2013] 4 MLJ 693.

55 See also *Sim Chio Huat v Wong Ted Fui* [1983] 1 MLJ 151. For a similar English case, see *Tele2 International Card Company SA v Post Office Ltd* [2009] EWCA Civ 9.

56 *Berjaya Times Squares Sdn Bhd v M Concept Sdn Bhd* (n 22).

57 See *Abdul Razak bin Datuk Abu Samah v Shah Alam Properties Sdn Bhd* (n 21) 508. See also *Poh Geok Sing v HB Enterprise Sdn Bhd* [2006] 1 MLJ 617 [13].

58 Carter (n 15) 93.

59 PS Tay, 'Mistake, Fraud and Misrepresentation in Malaysian Contract Law' in M Chen-Wishart, S Vogenauer, and H Sono (eds), *Studies in the Contract Laws of Asia, vol IV: Invalidity* (OUP 2022) 253; MF Cheong and YH Lee, 'Contracts Resulting from Threats and Unfair Exploitation: The Position under Malaysian Contract Law' in Chen-Wishart, Vogenauer, and Sono (this note) 271.

1. Restitution under Sections 65 and 66 Contracts Act

Section 65 deals with the consequences of the 'rescission' of a 'voidable contract'. It provides that:

> When a person at whose option a contract is voidable rescinds it, the other party thereto need not perform any promise therein contained in which he is promisor. The party rescinding a voidable contract shall, if he has received any benefit thereunder from another party to such contract, restore the benefit, so far as may be, to the person from whom it was received.

Section 66, meanwhile, deals with the obligations of a party who has received a benefit under an agreement that is subsequently 'discovered to be void' or a contract that 'becomes void'.[60] It provides that:

> When an agreement is discovered to be void, or when a contract becomes void, any person who has received any advantage under the agreement or contract is bound to restore it, or to make compensation for it, to the person from whom he received it.

As indicated previously, notwithstanding the language of these provisions, there is clear authority that they apply to contracts that have been terminated for breach. In *Muralidhar Chatterjee v International Film Co Ltd*,[61] a case on appeal from India, the Privy Council held that the Indian counterparts to sections 65 and 66 apply not only to contracts that have been rescinded on the basis of one or more vitiating factors but also to contracts that have been 'put at an end' within the meaning of the Indian equivalent of section 40. In doing so, the Privy Council highlighted the similarities between Illustration (a) to the Indian counterpart to section 40 and Illustration (c) to the Indian counterpart to section 66. Both Illustrations provide the same scenario in similar wordings of a singer, *A*, who agreed with the manager of a theatre, *B*, to sing at his theatre two nights in every week during the next two months for an agreed fee for each's night's performance. On the sixth night, the singer wilfully absents herself from the theatre. The last sentence of Illustration (a) states that the singer 'is at liberty to put an end to the contract' while Illustration (c) states that the singer 'in consequence, rescinds the contract. *B* must pay *A* for the five nights on which she had sung.' These Illustrations, the Privy Council held, 'cannot be made consistent with any other view' besides an interpretation that equates the phrase 'rescinds the contract' with 'putting an end to the contract'.

The interpretation in *Muralidhar Chatterjee* was subsequently confirmed by a differently constituted Privy Council in the Malaysian case of *Linggi Plantations Ltd v Jagatheesan*,[62] where Lord Hailsham stated that the words 'voidable' and 'rescinds' in section 65 are

[60] For a discussion of s 66 in the context of the effects of frustration, see YH Lee and MF Cheong, 'Change of Circumstances: The Position under Malaysian Contract Law', ch 15 in this volume, 311–313.

[61] AIR 1943 PC 34.

[62] [1972] 1 MLJ 89.

applicable to both cases of contracts brought to end due to vitiating factors and contracts terminated through repudiation or breach of fundamental terms.[63]

In *Yong Mok Hin v United Malay States Sugar Industries Ltd*,[64] the Federal Court expressly confirmed the applicability of section 66 to cases of termination for breach. Unlike section 65, section 66 does not contain any reference to the rescission of a voidable contract. However, the Federal Court was able to circumvent this linguistic difficulty by holding that section 66's reference to 'a contract [that] becomes void' includes 'voidable contracts which become void by rescission', including 'rescission' for breach.[65] In doing so, the court referred to the following observation from Pollock and Mulla's leading commentary on the Indian Contract Act: 'Whenever one party to a contract has the option of annulling it, the contract is voidable; and when he makes use of that option the agreement becomes void.'[66] While this exercise in interpretative creativity has been criticized,[67] it is justifiable by reference to Illustration (c) to section 66, which is *in pari materia* with its Indian counterpart as set out above.

The combined effect of sections 65 and 66 is two-fold. First, under section 65, an innocent party who has received any benefit from the other party under the contract is bound, upon terminating the contract, to 'restore the benefit, so far as may be', to that other party. Second, under section 66, 'any person' (including the party in breach) who has received any advantage under the contract is obliged to 'restore it, or to make compensation for it' to the party from whom it was received.[68] To put it another way, the termination of a contract for breach will give rise to concurrent obligations on the parts of both parties to make restitution to each other for any benefits that have been received under the contract.[69]

To the extent that sections 65 and 66 of the Contracts Act allow the party in breach to claim restitution, this represents something of a departure from the English position. The English courts have traditionally been unwilling to allow the party in breach to recover on a *quantum meruit* or *quantum valebant* basis for services provided or goods supplied under a contract that is subsequently terminated for breach.[70] One argument that has sometimes been made in support of barring the party in breach from claiming restitution is that to do otherwise would be to allow the party in breach to take advantage of their own wrongful act. Responding to this concern, Gopal Sri Ram JCA at the Court of Appeal in *Poh Geok Sing v HB Enterprise Sdn Bhd*[71] added the following qualification to the operation of section 65:

[63] ibid 92. See also *Kang Yoon Mook Xavier v Insun Development Sdn Bhd* [1995] 2 MLJ 91; *Berjaya Times Squares Sdn Bhd v M Concept Sdn Bhd* (n 22); *Code Focus Sdn Bhd v Tan Chee Hoe & Sons Sdn Bhd* [2013] 4 MLJ 59.

[64] [1967] 2 MLJ 9. See also G Cowper-Hill, 'Voidable Contracts under the Contracts (Malay States) Ordinance 1950' (1967) 9 *Malaya Law Review* 344.

[65] See also *Hsu Seng v Choi Soi Fua* [1990] 1 MLJ 300.

[66] MC Setalvad and RN Gooderson, *Pollock and Mulla on the Indian Contract and Specific Relief Acts: With a Commentary, Critical and Explanatory* (8th edn, NM Tripathi 1957) 383.

[67] V Sinnadurai, *Law of Contract, vol 1* (3rd edn, LexisNexis Butterworths 2003) para 12.30.

[68] As to whether s 66 applies to third parties, see *Badiaddin vin Mohd Mahidin v Arab Malaysian Finance Bhd* [1998] 1 MLJ 393.

[69] See Carter (n 15) 95.

[70] See eg *Sumpter v Hedges* [1898] 1 QB 673; *Bolton v Mahadeva* [1972] 1 WLR 1009. This is despite the preponderance of academic opinion to the contrary: A Burrows, *The Law of Restitution* (3rd edn, OUP 2011) 356–91; G Virgo, *The Principles of the Law of Restitution* (3rd edn, OUP 2015) 333–35. In contrast, the English courts have been somewhat more willing to allow claims for the restitution of money paid under the contract by the party in breach: see *Dies v British International Mining and Finance Corp Ltd* [1939] 1 KB 724.

[71] [2006] 1 MLJ 617.

> A contract breaker must pay damages to the innocent party. However, if he has made any payment under the contract (not being a true deposit for the purchase of movable or immovable property) the contract breaker is entitled to set off that payment against the damages he has to pay. However, he cannot seek to recover any benefit he may have conferred upon the innocent party where he is himself guilty of a breach of contract. Were it otherwise, a contract breaker will be in a position to take advantage of his own wrong. This is against principle and the policy of the law.[72]

While the Court's concern with not allowing the party in breach to take advantage of their own wrong is understandable, it is submitted that such an approach is not only inconsistent with the express wording of section 65 itself but also gives insufficient weight to the innocent party's right to claim damages for breach, which can be set off against any restitutionary claim made by the party in breach.[73] Indeed, as Burrows points out, far from allowing the party in breach to take advantage of their own wrong, denying restitution to the party in breach might well have the effect of giving the innocent party a windfall, leaving them in a much better position than if the contract had been performed.[74]

2. Compensatory Damages under Section 76 Contracts Act

Section 76 provides that:

> A person who rightly rescinds a contract is entitled to compensation for any damage which he has sustained through the non-fulfilment of the contract.

This is supported by an Illustration which bears a very close resemblance to Illustration (a) to section 40 and Illustration (c) to section 66 earlier referred to. The Illustration to section 76 states that when *B*, the manager of the theatre, rescinds the contract due to *A*'s wilful absence on the sixth night, '*B* is entitled to claim compensation for the damage which he has sustained through the non-fulfilment of the contract.'

In *Muralidhar Chatterjee*, the Privy Council held that the Indian counterpart to section 76 was applicable in a case where a contract had been terminated for breach. This was subsequently confirmed in the Malaysian context by the Federal Court in *Yong Mok Hin*.[75] Where a contract has been terminated for breach, therefore, the innocent party will be able to claim compensatory damages for the non-performance of the contract.[76]

In *Berjaya Times Squares Sdn Bhd v M Concept Sdn Bhd*,[77] the Federal Court indicated that an innocent party who has exercised their right to terminate a contract for breach is entitled to claim either restitution or compensatory damages, but not both, stating:

72 ibid [19].

73 See also RR Sethu, 'The History, Impact and Influence of the Indian Contracts Act 1872' (2011) 28 *Journal of Contract Law* 31, 56 (describing this as 're-writing the provisions of the Contracts Act').

74 See Burrows (n 70) 353, 357 (for an illustration of claims for work performed in a construction contract).

75 *Yong Mok Hin v United Malay States Sugar Industries Ltd* (n 64) refers specifically to s 75 of the Contracts Act instead of s 76, but given the context of the decision, this is almost certainly a typographical error. See also *Chye Fook v Teh Teng Seng Realty Sdn Bhd* [1989] 1 MLJ 308; *Hims Enterprise (M) Sdn Bhd v Ishak bin Subari* [1992] 1 CLJ 132.

76 On the principles applicable to the assessment of damages, see Cheong and Lee (n 3) 351–67.

77 [2010] 1 MLJ 597.

> [T]he innocent party has the alternative remedy of suing to recover monies paid under the contract to the guilty party. But he can *under no circumstances* have his money returned *and* claim damages.[78]

It is submitted, however, that there is no reason in principle why the innocent party should not be able to claim both restitution of any benefits conferred under the contract and compensatory damages for its non-performance, subject to the bar against double recovery. Such an interpretation would be more consistent with the legislative structure of sections 66 and 76, which are framed as independent provisions. Furthermore, there is no indication within the Contracts Act that these two provisions are to be treated as being mutually exclusive such that a claim under one provision would bar a claim under the other.

3. Hypothetical: Bob and Sue

Turning now to the remaining hypothetical scenario proposed by the volume editors,[79] one can say that Bob's abandonment of the building work is likely to be construed as either a repudiation or a fundamental breach of the contract between him and Sue, following the approach taken in *Damansara Realty*. This will entitle Sue to terminate the contract pursuant to section 40 of the Contracts Act. In this case, Sue's conduct is consistent with the termination—as opposed to the affirmation—of the contract as she has used the material left behind by Bob to complete the building work. This indicates that she has no expectation that Bob will return to carry out the work himself.

Once the contract has been terminated, the restitutionary provisions set out in sections 65 and 66 will come into play. Bob may be able to bring a claim for the value of the work done or for the value of the materials under either or both of these provisions. However, Bob may have difficulty demonstrating that the work he has done constitutes a 'benefit' or 'advantage' to Sue within the meaning of sections 65 and 66. In the case of *Poh Geok Sing*, the facts of which are very similar to this hypothetical, the judge at first instance directed an assessment of the construction work that had been partially done by the plaintiff and ordered the defendant to pay the assessed value. On appeal, however, the Court of Appeal held that it was not open to the judge to direct an assessment of the value of the work as there was no prior finding that the work constituted a benefit to the defendant.

However, Bob has a better chance of recovering the value of the materials pursuant to either section 65 or 66. As Sue had the choice as to whether or not to use these materials in the completion of the work, it would be difficult for her to deny that they constituted a 'benefit' or 'advantage' to her.[80] It should also be borne in mind that Sue will be entitled to claim compensatory damages from Bob pursuant to section 76 of the Contracts Act and will be entitled to set off that claim against any restitutionary claim made by Bob.

[78] ibid [20] (emphasis in original). See also Carter (n 15) 96.

[79] The detailed facts of this hypothetical situation can be found in M Chen-Wishart, D Neo, and S Vogenauer, ch 1, 'Introduction', 10.

[80] For a similar English case, see *Sumpter v Hedges* (n 70).

VII. Conclusion

The analysis of different aspects of Malaysian contract law in the *Studies in the Contract Laws of Asia* series highlights a strong recurring theme of the relationship between the Contracts Act and its original source jurisdiction, English law. In the first volume, *Remedies for Breach of Contract*, we observed the strong influence that is still exerted by the English common law and rules of equity over the Malaysian courts' interpretation of the Contracts Act and the Specific Relief Act 1950.[81] In the fourth volume, *Invalidity*, we highlighted the difficulties faced by the Malaysian courts in incorporating developments elsewhere in the common law world within the limited language of the Contracts Act. In contradistinction, in the present volume, we observe that the Malaysian courts have been able to interpret and apply the provisions of the Contracts Act that relate to termination for breach in a way that keeps pace with developments elsewhere in the common law world and meets the changing needs of commercial life in Malaysia. In particular, the analysis in section I shows that the courts have been able to accommodate common law concepts such as repudiation, the distinction between conditions and warranties, and the innominate terms approach by interpreting section 40 accordingly. Section V also shows how the courts have been able to reconcile terms such as 'put an end to the contract', 'rescinds', 'voidable contract', and 'contract becomes void' in order to bring the remedial provisions set out in sections 65, 66, and 76 into play. In doing so, the courts have been assisted by the Illustrations to the relevant provisions of the Contracts Act. This is in a sense a tribute to both the Malaysian courts' creative interpretation of the statutory provisions and the skill of the drafters of the Contracts Act, bearing in mind that, at the time the Indian Contract Act was drafted, concepts such as the distinction between conditions and warranties, repudiation, and the right to terminate for breach were not yet fully developed.[82]

Having said that, it is difficult to deny that the Contracts Act is an archaic piece of legislation. This chapter is perhaps the most vivid illustration of a statute that is very dependent on both the courts and legal practitioners keeping in mind the legislative purpose of the Contracts Act and having the willingness to interpret and apply it creatively when called for. This is not the ideal position for an important statute that lays out the core contractual principles forming the foundation for all commercial and consumer transactions. There is no better occasion to call for the reform of the Contracts Act, as highlighted by the linguistic limitations of the provisions of this statute in dealing with the important subject of termination of contracts.

[81] Act 137.
[82] Carter (n 15) 92–93.

17

Myanmar

Change of Circumstances and Termination of Contract for Breach

*Adrian BRIGGS, KC**

I. Change of Circumstances

1. Introduction

It is apparent that, by contrast with some (not all) of the civil law systems, there is no general power in Myanmar contract law for a court to alter the terms of the contract to provide for situations where facts and circumstances have changed since the contract was made or to reflect the fact that if the parties had known then what they know now, they would have contracted on materially different terms. If the parties agree to alter the terms, that is entirely a matter for them; but it is not until the contract becomes impossible (factually or legally) to perform that the Myanmar Contract Act 1872 (hereafter also referred to as the Contract Act or the 1872 Act) makes any provision for the change. Furthermore, if and when the test of impossibility is satisfied, the contract becomes void; it does not mutate into a contract on different terms. The remedial consequences of a contract's becoming void are the general ones set out in sections 64 and 65 of the Contract Act: neither Myanmar nor India has enacted (in the way that Malaysia has) a separate judicial power to apportion losses in the manner in which an English court could.

Everything turns on the meaning of 'impossible'. So far as one can tell from the case law, Myanmar has not diluted the meaning of impossible to include those cases in which the acts contracted for can still be performed but the purpose for which the contract was made is now lost or defeated. No case said, still less held, that 'frustration of purpose' was good enough to meet the requirements of section 56 (which are set out below). Even so, it is apparent that there are degrees of impossibility. Some local systems—Thai law, in particular—appear to be even stricter in their interpretation of what is impossible; others—Malaysia, and possibly also India—have been more prepared, by reflecting modern English case law, to accept that if the purpose of the contract has become impossible of performance, the contract has become void. All systems, it appears, have had to grapple with the same general issue; in Myanmar, neither the Contract Act nor the jurisprudence of the courts gives much support to the idea that a contract becomes void when its original purpose becomes impossible to achieve. Those legal systems which deal with unforeseen and unpleasant surprises

* Although this chapter is presented in the name of one of us only, its entirety is closely derived from A Briggs and A I Burrows, *The Law of Contract in Myanmar* (OUP 2017), a volume jointly written as part of the Oxford University Myanmar Law Programme and available at <www.law.ox.ac.uk/sites/default/files/migrated/briggsburrowsbook_-_thelawofcontractinmyanmar.pdf> accessed 9 April 2024.

Adrian Briggs, KC, *Myanmar* In: *Studies in the Contract Laws of Asia V: Ending and Changing Contracts*. Edited by: Mindy Chen-Wishart, Dora Neo, and Stefan Vogenauer, Oxford University Press. © Adrian Briggs 2026.
DOI: 10.1093/oso/9780198995814.003.0017

by giving a court power to find that it would be an exercise of bad faith to claim to enforce the contract according to its original terms did not appear to be particularly satisfied with the results. Whether Myanmar law could do anything reminiscent of this by relying on section 13(3) of the Burma Laws Act 1898 is unknown, but doubtful.

The parties may make an agreement—a special agreement, as the first reported case called it—to provide for certain unusual events which may occur during the life of the contract. There is no reason to doubt their effectiveness in law; but it is not possible to say whether they are much used in daily commerce.

2. Myanmar Statutory Law and the Available Case Law

A contract may be formed on the basis of a perfectly valid agreement but subsequently become (automatically) void because of subsequent impossibility or illegality. According to the Myanmar Contract Act, section 56, second paragraph, a contract becomes void where, after the contract is made, performance becomes impossible or illegal.[1] If a contract becomes void, in accordance with this provision, there is now no obligation to perform.

> 56. *Agreement to do impossible act.* An agreement to do an act impossible in itself is void.
> *Contract to do act afterwards becoming impossible or unlawful.* A contract to do an act which, after the contract is made, becomes impossible, or, by reason of some event which the promisor could not prevent, unlawful, becomes void when the act becomes impossible or unlawful.

At this point we are concerned with the second paragraph of section 56. (The 'Illustration', or example situation, given in the Act for the first paragraph of section 56 is an agreement to find treasure by magic.) It is also necessary to mention the final provision of section 2 of the Act, which relates to the second paragraph of section 56, and which provides as follows:

> 2. *Interpretation clause:* In this Act the following words and expressions are used in the following senses, unless a contrary intention appears from the context...
> (j) a contract which ceases to be enforceable by law[2] becomes void when it ceases to be enforceable.

(a) The first reported case

The first reported case to raise the issues considered in this part of the paper was *Mi Me v Nga On Gaing*;[3] and it tells us a surprising amount. Land had been leased to a tenant who agreed to pay 425 baskets of paddy by way of rent. The tenant expected to provide the paddy from the crop he would raise. When the rains failed the crop failed, and the tenant could not

[1] For example, *SKR Cama & Co v KK Shah* AIR 1916 LB 7; *JG Buchanan v SC Mall* AIR 1918 LB 46 (effect of Royal Proclamation against Trading with the Enemy of 5 August 1914. In the latter case the contract was governed by German law, but this was held to have no relevance to the effect of the Proclamation).

[2] This means that it ceases to be enforceable as a matter of substantive law, such as by a provision of the Contract Act, rather than because of some procedural objection, such as limitation: *Mahanth Singh v U Ba Yi* (1939) RLR 358, AIR 1939 PC 110, (1939) 66 Ind App 196.

[3] (1910) UBR 22.

pay or, at any rate, could not pay from his harvest. When the landlord refused the surrender of the lease, and demanded the rent, the tenant pleaded that section 56 and the drought rendered the lease, and hence the obligation to pay rent, void. The judge[4] rejected the tenant's plea. On its true construction the lease did not say or mean that rent was '425 baskets or such smaller amount as was produced in that season from the demised land'. It was not impossible to furnish the landlord with 425 baskets of paddy as there was plenty of rice in the world. It was not relevant that it might, in some sense, be 'impossible' for the tenant to perform for otherwise, all debtors who were unable to meet their liabilities would be able to claim that their contracts were void and their debts automatically dissolved. It was not relevant that the obvious purpose of the lease was to allow the tenant to grow paddy and pay rent, as both parties knew, and that this purpose had failed, or that the tenant would certainly not have taken the lease if he had known that the rains were going to fail. It was not relevant that the failure of the rains was a surprise for the parties; they could have made special provision for drought in the lease if they had wished.[5] It was not relevant that it may have been said to be harsh to hold the tenant to the bargain he had struck; there had been no undue influence in the making of the lease and there was no basis for judicial intervention. And the word 'frustration' was nowhere to be seen.

(b) Terminology

In many systems of the common law the effect of such supervening events is now referred to as the frustration of the contract, but the 1872 Act did not (and does not) refer to it in these terms. After all, the term 'frustration' was not part of the common law. English and other common lawyers tend to think of their doctrine of frustration as first established by a case decided in 1863, but the judgment in that case does not use the word 'frustration', and it is therefore no surprise that the draftsman of the Contract Act did not use it either.

The only reported decision in Myanmar prior to independence to mention (but not rely on) the (English) doctrine of frustration was a criminal appeal by sailors convicted of wrongfully refusing to join their ship. The ship's route would now take it through what had become a war zone, and the High Court refused to construe the promise of the sailors as being to sail through such waters; their conviction was overturned. There was a brief discussion whether their articles of seamanship had been frustrated, but this was unnecessary to the decision and really led nowhere; the case turned entirely on the construction of the sailors' articles and the effect of the criminal law.

It is true that in decisions after 1948 the courts certainly used the terminology of 'frustration' and discussed some of the English (and Indian) cases, especially in the context of contracts which had been affected by war and the civil turbulence which followed it. This reference to English material, however, appears to be purely narrative as the judgments then state that the applicable principle is 'enshrined' or 'embodied' in section 56, which is then applied according to its terms. So for example, when in 1940 the government made a contract, pursuant to an option which it had, to purchase in 1943 the assets of the Rangoon Telephone Company, the invasion and war, which destroyed the government and much of

[4] GW Shaw, CSI, Judicial Commissioner of Upper Burma. It is a remarkably learned judgment, making reference to the leading Indian textbooks as well as to the writings of Savigny, but then, Mr Shaw (as he then was) was a Scot.

[5] The tenant contended that there had been an oral variation to this effect; his evidence was decisively rejected by the Commissioner.

the assets of the company, rendered performance of the contract impossible; it therefore became void.[6] No doubt it is true that the land on which the ruined buildings were found could have been conveyed, but that was not the contract which had been made. Again, when a company contracted to import and sell oil to a purchaser but was unable to deliver the oil because supervening legislation allowed the government to refuse to issue the necessary licence, the performance of the contract became unlawful; the contract was therefore void.[7] By contrast, when a town was invaded by insurrectionists, this did not make the contract of lease impossible to perform, and the contract remained valid. The 'temporary phase' of short-term interruption to leasehold occupation of land was quite different from the effect of war on the contract of sale to the government.[8] But a monthly tenancy of a house may become void if the house is destroyed by fire with the result that the subject matter of the lease becomes non-existent.[9] It may be said that there are 'degrees of impossibility', but the courts have remained faithful to the plain wording of the Act.

The rule is therefore this: the parties to a contract cannot call upon each other to perform when an event of the kind described in the second paragraph of section 56 has occurred. We will therefore explore the effect of section 56 and will deal, briefly, at the end with alternative solutions—not alternative doctrines because there are none—to the problem.

(c) The automatic operation of section 56, second paragraph

The way in which the contract becomes void in the circumstances described by the second paragraph of section 56 is that it happens automatically.[10] No option is given to the parties; no decision needs to be taken by either of them. The contract becomes void and the only remaining questions are those which explain how the law deals with the consequences of that voidness. It is true that the parties can regulate the position in advance by making express provision in their contract that, in the event of something happening which would otherwise make the contract void, each party shall remain bound to perform: to put the point another way, the parties can contract out of these provisions of the Act. But where this has not been done, and the second paragraph of section 56 applies, the voidness of the contract is an automatic consequence of the event which rendered performance impossible or unlawful; it is not a matter of choice or election. It follows that the event which brings about this cataclysmic consequence must be a sufficiently serious one.

The supervening event must make the performance of the contract impossible. The rule obviously has no application to a case in which the contract has been fully performed but the enjoyment of the benefit obtained under the contract is prevented or taken away. If I buy a car and soon after the purchase the car is stolen, I cannot claim that performance of the contract is impossible, and that the contract of sale is void, for the contract has already been performed. By contrast, if I hire a car for a period of a year, the theft of the car makes it impossible for the party letting the car to me to perform his obligation to make the car available to me, and the contract may then have become void.[11]

[6] *Rangoon Telephone Co Ltd v Union of Burma* (1948) BLR 527 (HC).

[7] *U Than Tin v M Ba Ba* (1953) BLR 9 (SC). The court did go on to say that the commercial purpose of the contract had also been frustrated, but this does not alter its first conclusion that s 56 applied according to its terms.

[8] *Daw Pu v Ko Don* (1955) BLR 33 (HC).

[9] *Maung Kyaw Nyein v Maung Kyaw Kyaw* (1957) BLR 266 (HC).

[10] *KM Modi v Mohamed Siddique* (1947) RLR 423; *Rangoon Telephone Co Ltd v Union of Burma* (n 6).

[11] *Ah Htaung v Union of Burma* (1957) BLR 122 (HC) (grant of excise licence to produce alcoholic spirit was a completed contract, so effect of supervening insurgency did not render it void and allow the licensee to withhold payment, even though the licensee was prevented from enjoying the benefit of the licence. It might have been

(d) The seriousness of the supervening occurrence

Section 56 plainly does not mean that all unexpected occurrences after the making of the contract render the contract void. Rather, the occurrence must make the contractual performance impossible or unlawful. But what exactly is meant by impossibility or unlawfulness in this context? It is helpful to think of this in terms of the seriousness of the supervening occurrence. In assessing the degree of seriousness, and the impact which it has on the contract, it is helpful to deal separately with events and legislation.

(1) Supervening event

The Act illustrates subsequent impossibility with the example of an agreement to marry, after which (but before the actual marriage) one party goes mad. The contract becomes void as a result of this supervening event.[12] Perhaps a more practical example would be a contract made to let and hire a lorry or boat which is, without the fault of either party, stolen or destroyed before the date for delivery: the contract will, in principle at least (ie assuming that on its true construction it does not make provision for this occurrence), become void.[13]

However, if a contract merely becomes more onerous, or expensive, to perform, it will not be held to have become void.[14] Suppose a trader agrees to sell a quantity of Myanmar coffee beans to a Japanese importer for a fixed price and that some months after the contract is made, unseasonal weather damages the coffee crop, with the result that the trader now has to pay three times as much to obtain the coffee beans from local farmers to fulfil his contract. This does not make the contract of sale void, for the contract to sell coffee to the Japanese importer is not impossible to perform; it may be more financially onerous, perhaps very much more onerous, to perform, but that is not the same as being impossible to perform. A similar analysis would apply where it becomes more expensive for me to perform my contact with you because the government has raised the price of gas and electricity. If, by contrast, the trader had contracted to supply beans from a particular coffee estate in Shan state, but after the contract had been made, a cyclone destroyed all the coffee trees on the estate, it would be impossible to perform the act promised and the contract would become void. If a tenant has agreed to pay a rent for agricultural land in the form of a quantity of rice, and the failure of the rains means that she cannot raise a crop, the contract does not become void, even though it will be much more burdensome for her to perform it. The contract, on its true construction, does not say that a rent will be paid out of the crop which the tenant has been able to raise. The promise to pay was on a true construction absolute, and it remained fully enforceable: there is plenty of rice in the world, and it is a matter wholly personal to the tenant if she has difficulty in coming by it.[15] As to the proposition that it would be unconscionable to enforce it, there is no basis in law for such an argument.[16]

Other cases are more difficult because, although section 56 refers to the act becoming impossible, it may appear from the facts that that performance is 'partly possible': no longer

otherwise if the licence had required the licensee to open and run a liquor shop, but on a true construction the licensee had a privilege, not a duty, to produce alcohol).

[12] Illustration (b) to s 56.
[13] As will be shown below, if the supervening event could have been prevented by the exercise of reasonable care on the part of the owner, the contract may not become void after all.
[14] *Mi Me v Nga On Gaing* (n 3).
[15] ibid 24.
[16] ibid.

entirely possible but not completely impossible, either. If the thing to be sold and purchased is utterly destroyed so that a contract to sell ten tons of coffee beans from a particular estate cannot be performed at all because there is no coffee, not even a single bean, the contract will be made void. But what if the effect of the supervening event is that five tons of coffee beans are still available? Does one say that the act for which the contract provided is impossible because it is impossible to deliver ten tons? Or is it not impossible because some of the subject matter of the contract is still available and delivery is possible in part? It appears that the answer is that the contract has become void but that the court may decree specific performance of the part which is still performable.[17] This appears from sections 13–15 of the Specific Relief Act 1877, which provide:

> 13. *Contracts of which the subject has partially ceased to exist.* Notwithstanding anything contained in section 56 of the Contact Act, a contract is not wholly impossible of performance because a portion of its subject-matter, existing at its date, has ceased to exist at the time of the performance.
> 14. *Specific performance of part of contract where part unperformed is small.* Where a party to a contract is unable to perform the whole of his part of it, but the part which must be left unperformed bears only a small proportion to the whole in value, and admits of compensation in money, the Court may, at the suit of either party, direct the specific performance of so much of the contract as can be performed, and award compensation in money for the deficiency.
> 15. *Specific performance of part of contract where part unperformed is large.* Where a party to a contract is unable to perform the whole of his part of it, and the part which must be left unperformed forms a considerable portion of the whole, or[18] does not admit of compensation in money, he is not entitled to obtain a decree for specific performance. But the Court may, at the suit of the other party, direct the party in default to perform specifically so much of his part of the contract as he can perform, provided that the plaintiff relinquishes all claim to further performance, and all right to compensation either for the deficiency, or for the loss or damage sustained by him through the default of the defendant.

Suppose I make a contract to hire the public rooms of a hotel for the purpose of a business meeting but that the day before the meeting is to start a terrorist attack destroys one of the rooms, though leaving the other two intact. I may wish to argue that the hotel is in breach of its contract by failing to provide the rooms which I had booked and it had promised, but the hotel may seek to defend the claim by arguing that the attack made it impossible for the hotel to perform the act it had promised to perform, with the result that the contract has become void. Such cases are always difficult because each side of the argument has something to be said for it. If the contract had provided for an individual fee for each separate room, it would be possible to treat the contract as though it were three separate contracts but, where this is not possible, the answer to this question is hard to see. Illustration (e) to section 56 might be taken to indicate that the contract is valid as far as it can still be performed,[19] and

[17] *Rangoon Telephone Co Ltd v Union of Burma* (n 6) (where the government did not bring a suit under the Specific Relief Act: see at 536).

[18] It may be that 'or' needs to be read as 'and', with the consequence that specific relief will be refused if it would leave unperformed obligations whose non-performance could not be otherwise compensated in money.

[19] Illustration (e) to s 56 reads: 'A contracts to act at a theatre for six months in consideration of a sum paid in advance by B. On several occasions A is too ill to act. The contract to act on those occasions becomes void.'

void only to the extent that it cannot be performed,[20] but this is not an easy solution to accept if a single and undivided price was agreed for the entire package. It may be better to say that in these circumstances, the contract is void;[21] but that if a party, entitled by Specific Relief Act sections 14 and 15 as the case may be,[22] wishes to apply for specific performance of so much of the contract as could be performed, they may do so. The attraction of this is that it allows the parties to decide for themselves, in the light of events, whether to persist with performing a fragment of the contract. If it is objected that this seems intellectually incoherent (how can a void contract be decreed for specific performance?), the answer is that the 1877 Act gives the parties the right to decide whether to proceed with performance of the fraction of the contract which can still be performed.

The courts have sometimes chosen a form of words to serve as a test of what is required, such as the supervening event being one 'striking at the root of the contract'[23] or making it 'practically impossible to perform'; though found in the reported cases, these expressions do not appear to have added anything to (or taken anything away from) the plain words of the section. Even so, there are degrees of impossibility. The broad question is whether the supervening event is serious enough for the law to consider the contract to have become void. If, therefore, the event strikes at the root of the contract, and is quite outside what the parties contemplated when they made the agreement, section 56 will apply if the court feels able to say that performance of the contract has become impossible.[24] If the most that can be said is that the common object of the parties has been defeated, yet the contract still remains possible to perform, there is no case which holds that section 56 provides that the contract becomes void.[25] For section 56 to apply, the judge will have to hold, in express terms, that performance of the contract has become impossible. That will discourage relaxation in the rigour of the law.

(2) Supervening illegality

Let us return to our example of the Myanmar trader who has contracted to sell coffee to a Japanese importer. If, after the contract was made, the legislative authorities in Myanmar[26] were to prohibit the export of coffee, the contract would become void. A contract to do an act which has been made unlawful to perform becomes void.[27] There is a clear parallel between subsequent impossibility and subsequent unlawfulness: in each situation the performance contracted may be said to be impossible, whether physically or legally.

[20] *Rangoon Telephone Co Ltd v Union of Burma* (n 6).

[21] Cf *Mohamed Ismail v The King* (1940) RLR 468, AIR 1940 Ran 252 (contract to serve as seaman signed in times of peace became void when the outbreak of war made seamanship, though technically still possible, a far more hazardous exercise).

[22] That is, depending on the magnitude of the impossibility.

[23] *Rangoon Telephone Co Ltd v Union of Burma* (n 6); *Maung Kyaw Nyein v Maung Kyaw Kyaw* (n 9): the latter decision may in this respect be a little more open to finding a lease to be rendered void than was allowed in *Daw Pu v Ko Don* (n 8) (holding that dispossession by communist insurgency did not frustrate the lease because it would only be temporary).

[24] *Rangoon Telephone Co Ltd v Union of Burma* (n 6). The further conclusion of the court, that when the contract became void, the arbitration clause in it also became void, would now be considered to be inconsistent with the Arbitration Act 2016, s 18(a)(i).

[25] *U Than Tin v M Ba Ba* (n 7).

[26] The possible effect of legislation in Japan banning the import of coffee beans from Myanmar raises a question of private international law, which is dealt with in A Briggs, *Private International Law in Myanmar*, ch 5, point (46)(d).

[27] *U Than Tin v M Ba Ba* (n 7) (import of oil). See also Illustration (d) to s 56 (contract to take delivery of cargo at a port in a country which is now at war with Myanmar: contract becomes void).

However, supervening illegality may be more difficult to deal with than supervening physical impossibility, for something which is made illegal today may be made legal again tomorrow. Suppose a contract is made for the export of rice from Myanmar to a purchaser overseas but that disastrous weather causes Myanmar to impose legislation prohibiting the export of rice. Of course, no one can foretell the future, but it may be realistic to predict that the prohibition will be temporary and that when conditions return to normal the prohibition will be lifted.[28] In those circumstances, does section 56 apply?

The answer must depend, at least to begin with, on the interpretation of the contract. If the contract provides for delivery by a certain date, and it appears that this will be impossible because it will be unlawful, the contract will be made void. But if though the date for delivery was stated in the contract it cannot be said that time was of the essence of the contract—in other words, that it was a contract to deliver rice rather than to deliver rice on or before a certain date and that being even a day late would defeat the purpose of the contract—the supervening illegality may not make the contract void, though it would provide the seller with a lawful excuse for non-delivery on the date specified in the contract. So also with a contract for the carriage of goods by sea in circumstances in which it becomes impossible for the ship to take the course intended, say because an outbreak of war.[29] If the contract had provided specifically for carriage by that route and no other, it would become void. If it did not, but the cargo was perishable and could only be delivered if that route were taken, then again, the contract will have become void. But if the contract was not specific as to the route to be taken, it is unlikely that the supervening event will be held to make the contract void.

It follows in cases of supervening illegality that care is needed to compare the precise terms of the promises with the precise extent of the illegality which has supervened. If the law which has supervened, which appears at first sight to be broad and general in effect, does not actually prevent the lawful performance of the promise, the contract will not be affected by illegality and will not become void.[30]

There is a further difficulty where only a part of the contract is rendered illegal by supervening legislation. For example, the Urban Rent Control Act 1948 did not make existing leases void—that would have been completely contrary to the purpose of the Act as it would have made tenants homeless—but it did reduce the rent which could lawfully be charged, making it illegal to demand the sum originally agreed in the lease.[31] Though it became illegal to perform them according to the terms which had been agreed, the leases remained valid, with the rent provision altered by statute.[32] There is nothing wrong with saying that the original contractual rent provision became void, but it is perhaps not the best way to describe the legal result, which was that one term of a contract was altered by legislative force.

[28] *Hwe Ngwe Chew v The Official Receiver, High Court* (1959) BLR 12 (HC) (on whether the Urban Rent Control Act, which was enacted as a temporary measure which could be extended, rendered the contract void, held not).

[29] For insurgency being found to be a supervening event which makes the contract void, see *U Ba Thein v Chairman, State Timber Board* (1958) BLR 373 (HC) 373; *State Timber Board v Daw Thaung Yin* (1967) BLR 99 (CC).

[30] *VERM Krishnan Chettyar v MMK Subbiah Chettyar* (1949) BLR 56 (SC).

[31] There are many, many examples of the point being made: see for one, *Ko Than Nyunt v Maung Khin Myint* (1951) BLR 124 (HC).

[32] The court must have considered that the supervening illegality did not bring the case within the second para of s 56. The reason must have been that the supervening legislation was not intended to make the original leases void, and its effect was understood accordingly.

(e) Event not affecting the possibility of performing the act but still making the promise a very different thing from what was originally expected

Suppose I make a contract with a driver who will drive me and my family, and all our luggage, to the airport before we leave on holiday and that the driver knows that this is why I have arranged for his services. Suppose that on the day before we are to leave, the airline on which we are to fly goes out of business and that it is now not possible for me to fly out for my holiday: does this render the contract with the driver void? It is still entirely possible for the driver to take us and our luggage to the airport, and for me to pay him his fee, but it is clear to us both that the purpose for which I made the contract with him is now a purpose which cannot be fulfilled. The starting point, though, will be that the contract can still be performed and is for that reason not void.[33] The application of the very first decision[34] of the Myanmar courts on this issue is straightforward.

However, *if* the court is able to construe the contract as containing some unexpressed condition, written in invisible ink, the answer may be different. In a case in which seamen had signed articles of agreement to work on board a merchant ship, but then the outbreak of war meant that the ship was liable to be a target of enemy action, the court accepted that although the seamen and the ship could still sail, the seamen were not at fault in (and liable to criminal conviction for) refusing to sail. The circumstances had changed very dramatically, and either the terms of the articles did not include a promise to join the ship which was going to sail through a war zone or the change meant that the contract was really not the same contract at all, and it was to be regarded as having become void.[35] The court did not quite put it in these terms, but it was saying, in effect, that it would be just too harsh to interpret the promise of the seamen as one to work on board the vessel for the same reward in peacetime and in war and, on that basis, to hold them to have committed a criminal offence. And in effect, this is the basis on which a court decides whether a contract, still capable of being performed, should be held to have become void on the ground that circumstances have changed so dramatically that neither side should be expected to perform as though nothing had changed.

It can be seen that the power of the court to construe the contract, and to find that it contains terms or meaning which did not appear to be there, gives it power, if it wishes to use it, to find a solution which is more nuanced than the all-or-nothing rule in section 56.

(f) Responsibility or blame for the supervening event

According to the second paragraph of section 56, if the contract becomes unlawful because of something which the promisor 'could not prevent', it does not become void. In fact, the drafting of section 56 is curious in speaking of an event which the promisor could not prevent only in relation to supervening unlawfulness, but at this point we simply have to read section 56 as it should have been written so that the same point applies to subsequent impossibility as it does to subsequent unlawfulness. So if I make a contract to let my house to a tenant, or to sell my car to a buyer, the contract does not become void if I set fire to

33 *Mi Me v Nga On Gaing* (n 3).

34 ibid.

35 *Mohamed Ismail v The King* (n 21) (outbreak of war made going to sea as a seaman a significantly different thing, and the contract became void, even if the risk of war had been foreseen when the articles of agreement were signed. The case arose as a criminal prosecution under the Merchant Shipping Act, s 100; the fact that the contracts became void meant that an element of the criminal charge could not be established).

the house, or sell the car to a third party, before the contract of letting or sale is due to be performed; the same is true if the house is broken into and burned because I did not have proper security or the car is stolen because I left it unlocked when I parked it. In all these cases it may be true that it is no longer possible for me to perform the act which I promised to perform, but that is because of something which it was my responsibility to prevent; something for which I accepted the burden and risk. That will not relieve me of the obligation of performing or of paying compensation for failure to perform.

(g) Events which could have been, or which were, foreseen

If on its true construction the contract were to provide that a specified future event should occur which makes performance impossible or unlawful, the contract is not rendered void but remains valid and enforceable, with compensation being recoverable for failure to perform, the rule in section 56 will not apply to it.[36] A similar situation will arise if the contract makes provision for its discharge in the event of 'Act of God or *vis major*' except that in this case the question will be the interpretation of these contractual words.[37]

According to some authority, if an event occurs even though it could have been foreseen or was actually foreseen, but which is not dealt with (whether expressly or by implication) in the contract, the contract still becomes void.[38] For example, if a contract is made in circumstances in which one side or both foresee that legislation may be adopted to make it unlawful to perform the contract, the contract will still become void if and when that legislation is adopted, always assuming that the parties have not made provision for the risk in their contract. On the other hand, a contract for carriage by sea did not become void when there were monsoon storms at sea for the obvious reason that, even though the contract became impossible to perform, all parties knew perfectly well of the risk of such weather in the Bay of Bengal.[39] Everything appears to depend on the court's assessment of the intentions of the parties and the question whether they allocated or assumed the risk of a predictable disastrous occurrence.

(h) Alternative solution: Responding to the event by altering the terms of the contract

There are no alternative doctrines in the Contract Act for the problem to which section 56 is the legislative solution.

It was, however, suggested by lawyers in practice in Myanmar that in practice, there is an alternative strategy: to solve the problem by making a consensual alteration to the terms of the contract. In particular, if circumstances have changed, but not sufficiently dramatically to come within section 56, it is only by agreement to alter the terms of the contract that any relief may be found. (It is obviously more difficult for this to be done if the contract has become void, but it is always possible that the parties devise their own solution outside the formal structure of the 1872 Act; and if they do so and are content, no one is going to complain.)

36 *Rangoon Telephone Co Ltd v Union of Burma* (n 6).
37 On which, see *The State Agricultural Marketing Board v Aung Trading Co* (1966) BLR 252 (CC).
38 *Mohamed Ismail v The King* (n 21).
39 *The State Agricultural Marketing Board v Aung Trading Co* (n 37).

(1) Release from performance when the contract is rescinded or altered by agreement

There is no obligation to perform a contract which the parties have agreed to rescind. If A has agreed to perform a service for B, but A and B agree that the contract should be scrapped, treated as though it had never taken place, they are free to do so: who could have any greater right to do this than the parties themselves? Similarly, if they agree to scrap the original contract and replace it with another, who could possibly prevent them? As section 62 says:

> 62. *Effect of novation, rescission, and alteration of contract.* If the parties to a contract agree to substitute a new contract for it, or to rescind or alter it, the original contract need not be performed.

If parties to a contract agree that the original contract shall cease to bind them and shall be replaced by a new one, on terms which are similar or different, the effect of such an agreement is that the original obligation is rescinded by agreement and is not required to be performed because it has ceased to exist as an obligation at all;[40] it is replaced by the new contract which must now be performed. It does not matter whether the original contract has already been breached.[41]

The consensual substitution of one contract for another does not contradict the doctrine of consideration: even if the only significant change is that one party assumes a greater burden than before, the obligation of the other remaining unaltered, there is no room for the contention that there is a lack of consideration. As Illustration (b) to section 62 explains, if A owes $10,000 to B, but A and B agree that this debt should be replaced by a mortgage granted by A in favour of B for $5000, the new agreement extinguishes the old, which no longer has to be performed. It is that simple. The effect of the 1872 Act is that no consideration is needed to alter or vary the terms of an existing agreement: consideration is a requirement for the formation of a contractual relationship but not for the alteration of that relationship. The second effect is that when the original contract was rescinded by agreement, the original obligation to perform wholly disappeared. When the new contract was formed, there was no existing obligation, and the new contract may be seen to be supported by its own consideration.

It has been held that where parties make a contract upon certain terms, and then agree that one of those terms should be varied, the alteration will not fall within section 62 as there has not been, in substance, a complete rescission of the original contract.[42] It is hard to see that this can be correct for section 62 uses the word 'alter' alongside 'rescind' and the marginal note to section 62 also refers to the 'alteration' of a contract. Surely the point is this: if on a true construction of their acts the parties agreed that the entire contract should be set aside and replaced by another, this will count as a rescission of the original contract and creation of a new one; but if all they agreed was to alter or amend the terms of a contract

[40] *U San Ya v PRMPSPL Firm* AIR 1936 Ran 396. See also *AC Akhoon v A Habib* (1952) BLR 236 (SC) 246–47, which is not based on s 62 but is certainly consistent with it.

[41] One reason for this is that mediation may be a practical solution once there has been a breach; it would make such consensual resolution less helpful if it were too late to agree to a variation of the contract after it had been breached.

[42] *Messrs IAG Mohamed & Sons v The East Asiatic Co Ltd* (1958) BLR 524 (HC) (only one clause of the contract was varied by agreement, leaving the rest unaltered. This was therefore the only change in the obligation by which the parties were otherwise still bound).

which would otherwise remain the same, the original contract is not rescinded but continues to apply albeit in its amended form.

(2) Release from performance when the obligation is dispensed with or remitted by the promisee

We have just dealt with the case in which all the parties to a contract agree to replace it with another contract. It made sense that the law allows this to be done because if all those who have an interest in the contract agree, there is no need for the law to interfere. The next point deals with the case in which the party who has an interest in the benefit of another's performance deals with it in a way which causes no harm, but does only benefit, to the other. Once again, the law takes the view that it has no need to interfere.

If a promisor under a contract is obliged to perform an act, but the promisee chooses to release him from the obligation to perform, whether wholly or partially, the promisor is released from performance to that extent, and the failure to perform the original promise is justified.[43] According to section 63:

> 63. *Promisee may dispense with or remit performance of promise.* Every promisee may dispense with or remit, wholly or in part, the performance of the promise made to him, or may extend the time for such performance, or may accept instead of it any satisfaction which he thinks fit.

If the parties have made a contract, the result is a relationship made up, in terms of legal analysis, from duties and rights. For example, under a contract of lending and borrowing, the lender has a right to repayment of the sum loaned, with interest, if this has been lawfully agreed, and the borrower has a duty to repay the sum fixed by the contract on such date as the contract may specify. If it should happen that the borrower is unable to repay in full on the due date, he may approach the lender and ask for the time to repay to be extended, or for the sum required to be repaid to be reduced, or both. The lender may not agree; he is within his rights to insist on performance of the terms of the contract according to their strict letter. But if the lender is prepared to let the borrower pay less or take longer to pay, and accept this smaller or later payment as a full discharge of the debt, he is entitled to do that: it is his privilege to release the borrower from the strict duty to do what the borrower had promised to do.[44]

And what is true for a contract of lending and borrowing is equally true for other contracts. If a potter has promised to make 100 cooking pots for a customer for a fixed price, but it becomes clear that he will only be able to complete 80 of them before he runs out of money, he may ask his customer to allow him to deliver 80 pots rather than the full 100 which had been agreed. If the customer agrees and the potter delivers the 80 pots, his failure to supply the missing 20 is justified and cannot be seen to be a failure to perform.

Why would a lender or a customer agree to this? The immediate answer is perhaps that it is the lender's business, or the customer's business, and we have no right to ask them to explain themselves. But there may be good commercial reasons for being generous to a

[43] *Sakarchand Shamji v Ismail Hoosein* AIR 1931 Ran 189; *Ariff Moosajee Dooply v Dr T Chan Taik* (1950) BLR 227 (HC).

[44] See Illustrations (b) and (c) to s 63.

borrower or to the potter. The relationship between the parties may be one which has gone on a long time, and the expectation of future business may be a reason to be a little forgiving on this occasion. And if the lender refuses to allow the borrower a little flexibility and chooses instead to sue the borrower for performance of his obligation to pay in full, it will probably go badly for the lender. Legal proceedings may be slow, will be costly to bring, and by the time of judgment the borrower may have become bankrupt and unable to pay anything. There is therefore all the sense in the world in allowing the lender to let the borrower off part of the debt, and for the customer to let the potter off part of the obligation, and for the law to regard this as binding.

Of course, there has to be an overt letting off: if all that happens is that the creditor does not immediately press his claim but sits quietly by, this should not count as a dispensation, and section 63 will not apply because of it.[45] If a dispensation or letting off is the product of fraud or misrepresentation or coercion or undue influence, it should not be, and will not be, effective. For example, if the borrower lies about his financial difficulties, the lender's dispensation or remission will have been obtained by improper means. Now if consent to a contract is obtained by such means, the contract may be avoided. By parity of reasoning, a dispensation or remission of performance, or the acceptance of satisfaction, which is obtained by equivalent means, may be avoided, for the same reasons. The same is true if the acceptance of the payment is 'under protest', or 'without prejudice', or 'with full reservation of rights'.

If the creditor says that he will accept the (reduced) performance of the debtor as satisfaction of the debt, and the debtor performs, section 63 certainly comes into effect.[46] What is the position if the creditor says that he will accept a reduced performance, but the debtor does not actually pay or do anything at all? The early view of the Myanmar courts was that if the debtor does not even make a start in performing the (reduced) obligation which the creditor has stipulated for, the original contract remains in full effect. However, in coming to this conclusion the courts were treating the debtor as not having accepted or provided consideration for the creditor's offer,[47] drawing the conclusion that the creditor's offer was ineffective.[48] The error in the reasoning of the courts was to read section 63 as though it required a fresh contract, with proposal, acceptance, and consideration, to supersede the original one. The High Court[49] overruled these cases when it pointed out that section 63 simply required the creditor to state[50] that he would accept a reduced performance and that as soon as the creditor had made this statement, it took effect according to its terms. No question of acceptance, or of the presence or absence of consideration, arose.[51] The result

[45] *Pannalal Rangalal v Tin Tin U* (1954) BLR 19 (SC).

[46] *Sakarchand Shamji v Ismail Hoosein* (n 43); *Ariff Moosajee Dooply v Dr T Chan Taik* (n 43). The principle was even applied where the (reduced) payment was made in non-legal Japanese 'currency' (but to which the Japanese Currency (Evaluation) Act 1947 subsequently applied) during the years of the war. See also *Messrs Dawson's Bank Ltd v Ko Sin Sein* (1960) BLR 394 (HC): the payment and the acceptance were sufficient to satisfy s 63.

[47] *ALMS Subramoniem Chetty v Gangaya* (1907–08) LBR 365.

[48] *Maung Pu v Maung Po Thant* AIR 1928 Ran 144, (1928) ILR 6 Ran 191; *Sakarchand Shamji v Ismail Hoosein* (n 43); *Ma On Baw v VEPR Chettyar Firm* (1935) AIR 188 (Ran).

[49] *AKACTAL Chettyar v AKRMMK Firm* (1938) RLR 660, AIR 1939 Ran 84, following the decision of the Privy Council in *Chunna Mal Ram Nath v Mool Chand Ram Bhagat* (1928) 55 Ind App 154, AIR 1928 PC 99.

[50] As distinct from 'propose': there is no need to look for proposal and acceptance of it.

[51] *AKACTAL Chettyar v AKRMMK Firm* (n 49). The case is also authority for the proposition that s 63 allowed a third party (Debtor 3) to the agreement (made between the Creditor and Debtors 1 and 2, to accept reduced performance from Debtors 1, 2, and 3) to take advantage of it. No question of privity arose in connection with s 63. The case was approved and applied in *S Samuel v KRS Annamalay Chettyar* (1951) BLR 17 (HC).

is that the contract is altered; and if the reduced performance is itself not delivered, it will be that reduced obligation, not the original unreduced one, which forms the basis for legal proceedings.

The rule established by section 63 is in sharp distinction from the position in English law and is much more sensible.[52] The effect of section 63 is as though the right to receive performance from the debtor or the potter is treated as though it were a piece of intangible property.[53] If the owner of that intangible property—the lender or creditor or the potter's customer—wishes to give away or surrender all or some of that right, that property, as though it were a gift, the law does not stand in the way of a sensible decision, freely taken.

It follows that the variation of existing contracts is easily made; and that in practice this may be the response of the parties—if not of the strict law—to the problem caused by supervening impossibility or illegality in performance.

(i) Return and repayment when a contract has become void

According to the Contract Act *void contracts* are valid contracts which subsequently become void, most obviously because of subsequent impossibility or illegality.[54]

Section 65 of the Contract Act deals specifically with the restitution of benefits conferred under a void agreement or a contract that has become void. It reads as follows:

> 65. *Obligation of person who has received advantage under void agreement or contract that becomes void.* When an agreement is discovered to be void, or when a contract becomes void, any person who has received any advantage under such agreement or contract is bound to restore it, or to make compensation for it, to the person from whom he received it.

Though the effect of the second paragraph of section 56 is that, when such a supervening event takes place, there is no longer an obligation to perform, it is possible that some acts of performance had been undertaken before the date on which the contract became void. Section 65 means that a person who received any advantage under the contract before it became void is bound to restore it or to make 'compensation' for it. The fourth Illustration to section 65 demonstrates the point. If a singer is paid a sum of money to sing at a concert but contracts an illness which makes it impossible for her to perform, she has no obligation to compensate the impresario for the profits he will now fail to make but will be obliged to repay the advance payment.

In this respect, section 65 works reasonably well if the supervening event occurs before any performance has taken place: in the case of the singer, before she has sung the opening aria. If the supervening event occurs after, say, she has performed two of ten contracted-for concerts, section 65 appears to mean that she must reimburse the whole of the fee paid to her, but the impresario, who has received the advantage of two concerts' worth of performance will, in his turn, have to make compensation for what he has received.

52 And if there were any doubt about it, which there is not, the departure from the curious requirements of English law is deliberate: see the decision of the Privy Council on appeal from an Indian court in *Chunna Mal Ram Nath v Mool Chand Ram Bhagat* (n 49).

53 For the general proposition that contractual debts and other choses in action are (intangible) property, Transfer of Property Act 1882, ss 130–137; see also *Dawson's Bank Ltd v C Ein Shaung* (1951) BLR 300 (HC).

54 Contract Act, s 56, second para.

It is not hard to see how complications can arise, but even if there is no case law to provide the details, the statutory rule in section 65 is perfectly sensible as the basis for argument over the detail.

3. The Hypothetical Questions

(a) Abraham and Bill

In 1567, Abraham enters into a contract for an unlimited period of time with farmer Bill under which Abraham promises to build and maintain an irrigation channel from which Bill may extract water at a fixed price. By 2018, inflation and the rise in the cost of maintenance and labour have made the price wholly inadequate. Abraham's successors in law ask for an increase in the price that would provide them with adequate compensation. Alternatively, they wish to terminate the contract.[55]

To answer the question it would be necessary to assume (i) that the Contract Act 1872 claimed to apply to a contract concluded 300 years before it was drafted and in a pre-colonial society, (ii) the answer is to be found entirely in contract law and is unaffected by principles of property law, and (iii) it is possible to identify an individual as Abraham's 'successor' in the relevant sense and that someone can be identified as Bill's successor with the current benefit of the right to extract the water. The reference to 'assumption' in relation to (i) and (ii) is because there is no other basis on which one may proceed; (iii) seems likely to be rather challenging.

Subject to that, *Mi Me v Nga On Gaing* (1910) UBR 22 would support the conclusion that the terms of the contract remain enforceable as such; the argument that such a radical, albeit incremental, change of circumstance might render the contract void was neither raised nor ruled on in any later case.

(b) Citi Corporation and Drive Bank

In 2015, Citi Corporation receives a loan from Drive Bank. The interest rate is fixed at 10 per cent for five years. In the 20 years preceding the agreement, the rate of inflation had been relatively stable within a range of 1 to 6 per cent. In 2017, the economic situation begins to destabilize and inflation rises to 50 per cent. Drive Bank requests adjustment or, alternatively, termination of the contract.

The answer is the same: unless the contract is construed to contain a term which it does not appear to have, the obligations are not impossible to perform, and Drive Bank cannot ask the court to re-write the contract. In the absence of agreement between the parties to vary its terms, the contract is binding according to its terms.

(c) Easy and Frugle

Easy leases business premises from Frugle for a fixed period of 15 years. Shortly after the contract has been concluded, a nearby military airport is unexpectedly shut down for political reasons. The government invests an enormous amount of public funds in order to improve the commercial infrastructure in the area. As a result, Easy's profits are 500 per cent of

55 The fact scenarios for this and the other hypothetical situations discussed in this section are taken from M Chen-Wishart, D Neo, and S Vogenauer, 'Introduction', ch 1, 7–8.

what could reasonably have been expected at the time of making the contract. At the same time, the rental value of comparable business premises in the area rises to 500 per cent of the agreed rental price. Frugle requests that the rental price should be adjusted accordingly or, alternatively, that the agreement should be terminated.

The answer is the same: the good fortune of Easy is the other side of the coin of the misfortune of the tenant for whom the rains did not come. In the absence of a provision discerned by the court (but which we cannot see), or an agreement between the parties to vary the terms of the lease (for which there is no rational expectation), the lease is enforceable according to its terms.

(d) George and Han

Builder George agrees to refurbish the cellar of Han, the owner of a restaurant. The work is scheduled to start one month after the agreement. Before the work begins, the restaurant is completely destroyed by a storm that is much more violent than any other previous storm in the region. However, the cellar remains fully intact. Han immediately informs George of the situation and asks him not to start work. George insists on rendering performance because he has set aside two weeks to carry out the work and has already purchased the necessary materials. Is Han required to pay the contract price or, alternatively, to compensate George for his loss?

The contractual duty to refurbish, and to pay for the refurbishment, is not impossible to perform as the obligation of George is confined in its entirety to the cellar, which remains entirely intact. If a Myanmar court were to hold that performance of the contract had become impossible, because the 'commercial purpose' for which the contract had been made had been destroyed, it would go beyond any decision so far made, and so far, reported. If the contract is not void, Han is obliged to grant George access. If George has made an offer of performance, and this has not been accepted by Han, George does not lose his rights under the contract (Contract Act, section 38).[56] If on its true construction George has performed by tendering performance, he is entitled to the fee; if as a result of Han's breach of contract George is prevented from what he needs to do under the contract to be entitled to the fee, he may sue for compensation (sections 38 and 73).

(e) Gina and H Hotel

Gina books a room for the weekend at H Hotel in X City, the capital of country Z. However,

(i) the exhibition she intended to visit is cancelled at the very last moment;
(ii) a terrorist group declares that it plans to launch attacks on tourists in X;

[56] Section 38 is as follows:

> 38. *Effect of refusal to accept offer of performance.* Where a promisor has made an offer of performance to the promisee, and the offer has not been accepted, the promisor is not responsible for non-performance, nor does he thereby lose his rights under the contract. Every such offer must fulfil the following conditions: (1) it must be unconditional; (2) it must be made at a proper time and place, and under such circumstances, that the person to whom it is made may have a reasonable opportunity of ascertaining that the person by whom it is made is able and willing there and then to do the whole of what he is bound by his promise to do; (3) if the offer is an offer to deliver anything to the promisee, the promisee must have a reasonable opportunity of seeing that the thing offered is the thing which the promisor is bound by his promise to deliver.

(iii) an unforeseeable strike by airport personnel prevents Gina from travelling to X before Sunday afternoon; and
(iv) the inauguration proceedings of the new head of state of Z that were scheduled for Saturday are cancelled. Gina had booked a room overlooking the street where the inauguration procession was supposed to pass by. Due to the inauguration, the rental price of the room was ten times higher than the regular price.

Can Gina cancel the booking?

Of course not: the contract is not impossible to perform; and if Gina purports to cancel the booking, she will break her contract. Her contract with H Hotel appears to be fully and completely performable for Gina has no obligation to occupy the room, just a duty to pay for it (if she pays for it, she obtains a licence to use it). The proposition that performance of the contract is impossible, in any proper sense of the word 'impossible', is neither tenable nor correct. She made a contract, was not the victim of undue influence, and now regrets making it on the terms she did. Contractual freedom comes at a price.

It might also be suggested that the contract has been performed: that a licence to occupy the room has been granted to Gina, who may occupy the room, or not, as she chooses: there is some analogy with Ah Htaung's case.[57] But the obligations of the hotel are not yet completely performed: it has to provide a key, exercise its duties as innkeeper, provide room service, and so forth. So the analogy with Ah Htaung's case is not exact.

(f) Kris and Leila

Kris sells his family home to Leila at 70 per cent of its market value. Both parties assume that Leila will dedicate it to cultural use by the general public. However, this assumption is not expressly set out in the contract. After the sale, Leila changes her mind and gives the house to one of her sons instead. Can Kris claim the difference between the agreed price and the market value or, alternatively, restitution of the house?

No. Unless the court will read such a condition as to future use into the contract, there is nothing in the contract to complain about. The first, and perhaps the only point to be made is that any complaint by Kris should be directed to himself: he should have agreed on the terms he actually wanted. That having been said, the proposition that Leila can do this and get away with it is not intuitive. Section 31 of the Transfer of Property Act of 1882 may mean that the transfer to Leila can be undone.[58] The general issue, for both the Contract Act and the 1882 Act, may be that if the assumption is shared but not expressed, it may be incapable of supporting any argument by way of objection to Leila's behaviour.

[57] *Ah Htaung v Union of Burma* (n 11).

[58] Transfer of Property Act 1882, s 31:

> Subject to the provisions of section 12 on a transfer of property an interest therein may be created with the condition superadded that it shall cease to exist in case a specified uncertain event shall happen or in case a specified uncertain event shall not happen.
>
> *Illustrations:*
>
> (a) A transfers a farm to B for his life, with a proviso that, in case B cuts down a certain wood, the transfer shall cease to have any effect. B cuts down the wood. He loses his life interest in the farm.
>
> (b) A transfers a farm to B. provided that, if B shall not go to England within three years after the date of the transfer his interest in the farm shall cease. B does not go to England within the term prescribed. His interest in the farm ceases.

II. Termination

1. Introduction

The provisions of the Contract Act may appear, to an English reader unaware of the history of the law, rather odd. In response to certain kinds of non-performance—we will need to examine which kinds—the innocent party may rescind the contract, which becomes void. The statutory consequence, as it is for all void contracts and void agreements, is the return and repayment of what had been paid or transferred by way of performance. A claim for compensation for non-performance may be made notwithstanding the rescission of the contract, by virtue of section 75. No doubt accounting rules are capable of dealing with the relationship between the two.

How can it be, one may ask, that a contract can be rescinded and compensation claimed for non-performance? The question makes sense from the perspective of modern and uncodified systems of common law, but the Contract Act in India, Malaysia, and Myanmar is clear. What is also clear, as is revealed by the other chapters of this book, is that most local civilian systems adopt the same approach; what is also true is that it was only in the last 50 years that the uncodified common laws of England—and Hong Kong and Singapore, now appearing as local outliers—abandoned this analysis in favour of one which drew a linguistic distinction between the *rescission* of a contract which had been brought about by fraud, misrepresentation, or unlawful pressure and *termination* of a contract for breach, which in some sense left the contract sufficiently alive to generate and support a secondary right to damages for breach. In an uncodified common law system, the judges can do this if they wish to, and the systems which have reoriented their law on breach may proclaim their new faith with the zeal of the convert: good for them. The local systems which contain, or which derive their modern codes from, a nineteenth-century codification see it their own way. Their underlying reasons may not be congruent; but at this point their legal structures are strikingly similar.

A debate about terminology may be revealing but is essentially arid. Should, for example, systems distinguish between rescission and termination? Is 'termination' not preferable if one is trying to convey the sense that although the contract may have been ended, all that has actually been affected is the primary duty of the parties to perform, leaving the rest—and the history—of the contract unimpaired and still in legally valid existence? A moment's reflection shows this to be a thoroughly bad point. After all, in plain English, 'termination' has a variety of meanings, which makes it an inept choice for those promoting the cause of dogmatic and linguistic purity. The termination of a marriage is done without retrospective effect; the termination of a pregnancy certainly isn't. Those who criticize the use of 'rescission' (which conveys a clear sense of retrospective re-ordering), on the basis that 'termination' should have been used instead, ignore the complex ambiguity of their own language. The truth is that it does not matter what label is applied; what matters is the orientation and purpose of the legal remedies which are triggered by a certain event or non-event. A fixation with nomenclature is a pointless distraction.

Likewise, though legislation usually provides in detail for what may be done when a contract is broken, it may make different provision, or no provision, for the circumstances in which a party to a contract may invoke a pre-existing contractual term which, in the circumstances of performance or non-performance, may bring the contract to an agreed end.

Is that termination? If you wish, yes. Is it agreed termination? If you wish, yes. Is it the same kind of termination as that which may follow from breach? It depends; one must go back to the books and study the law. And that is the point: the task of the adult lawyer is to focus on the established detail of the law and, in particular, its relationship with the law governing non-performance. It is a distraction to waste time niggling over nomenclature in one's own language; it is positively insane to do it when working with translations made into and out of a foreign language with linguistic conventions all their own.

All systems examined in this volume accept that there are some non-performances which allow the innocent party to put some sort of end to the continuing life of the contract and others which do not. The techniques by which they do so are similar (although nothing in Myanmar law resembles the 'warning or last chance' principle encountered in some civilian systems): they involve questions about the importance of the term broken and about the seriousness of the breach. They certainly diverge on points of detail. Some systems have created an elaborate structure within which to locate the answer; others get by with rather less in the way of apparatus. Myanmar is one of those which has little supplementary detail, but it is surprising what can be teased out of the Contract Act if one is prepared to admit that its drafters knew when to prescribe and when to stand back, and to respect them for it.

2. Myanmar Statutory Law and the Available Case Law

Let us proceed to set out the structure and the detail of the law.

(a) The duty to perform

The point of departure is the general definition of performance in section 37 of the Act:

> 37. *Obligations of parties to contracts.* The parties to a contract must either perform, or offer to perform, their respective promises, unless such performance is dispensed with or excused under the provisions of this Act, or of any other law.

The rest of this part of the Contract Act proceeds on the basis that the duty to perform has arisen: if it has not, because (for example) the other party is not ready to perform yet the promises were required to be performed simultaneously (section 51), or because performance is not due until the opposite party has performed (section 54), then there is no obligation to perform and so nothing to withhold.

(b) Putting an end to the contract because of a refusal to perform

The Contract Act allows a party to put an end to, or terminate, or rescind, the contract on the ground that the other party has indicated by word or deed, sufficiently clearly and sufficiently unambiguously,[59] that he refuses to perform his side of the contract. According to section 39:

[59] *EE Master v Garrett & Taylor Ltd* AIR 1931 Ran 126: the dramatic remedy made available to the promisee does not arise if the language is less than plain.

> 39. *Effect of refusal of party to perform promise wholly.* When a party to a contract has refused to perform, or disabled himself from performing, his promise in its entirety, the promisee may put an end to the contract, unless he has signified, by words or conduct, his acquiescence in its continuance.

A rule closely related to section 39 applies when a party is prevented from performing by the other party preventing the event on which performance is due. According to section 53:

> 53. *Liability of party preventing event on which the contract is to take effect.* Where a contract contains reciprocal promises, and one party to the contract prevents the other from performing his promise, the contract becomes voidable at the option of the party so prevented; and he is entitled to compensation from the other party for any loss which he may sustain in consequence of the non-performance of the contract.

The law on putting an end to a contract on account of the other party's failure or refusal to perform, or (which is to say the same thing) on the rescission of the contract for breach, which is framed by these two sections of the Act, can be broken down into a number of points, which are explained below.

(c) The power to put an end to the contract, or not, lies with the promisee

It is obviously sensible that the law allows a party to put an end to the obligations of performance which were created by the contract if the other party has dug in his heels and refused, and still refuses, to perform.[60]

Section 39 makes it clear that the decision to put an end to the contract is taken by the party who is not in breach. A contract is not brought to an end by the breach or refusal of the party who refuses to perform but by the decision of the promisee, whom we will sometimes refer to as the 'innocent party', to accept that it is time to put an end to the contract. We may say that the innocent party has an option[61] to put an end to the contract,[62] even though there may be circumstances in which there may be an option but there is in practice not much of a choice to be made: for example, if in a contract to sell oil or a car, the seller has used the oil, or has sold and delivered the car to another person, there is not much point in the buyer insisting that the seller make delivery in accordance with his promise. In such circumstances the seller may have disabled himself from performing his contractual obligation, and the only practical way forward is for the buyer to put an end to the contract and claim such compensation for the loss caused by the breach of contract as the law may allow or the contract may provide. Even so, it is important to realize that it remains his choice to put an end to the contract.

60 *Pannalal Rangalal v Tin Tin U* (n 45).

61 It is an option, not an obligation: *Etbari v Bellamy* AIR 1938 Ran 207. The option to put an end to the contract may be exercised by the promisee if the promisor has announced in advance his refusal to perform even if the date for performance has not yet arrived: *Abdul Razak v U Paw Tun Aung & Co* (1950) BLR 258 (SC), but the option is entirely with the promisee (in that case, the pledger, who promises to redeliver): see at 268.

62 For further illustration, *G Kyi Maung v Morrison & Co* AIR 1933 Ran 399, (1933) ILR 11 Ran 506 (refusal of buyer to accept a milling notice was a repudiation which permitted, but did not oblige, the seller to put an end to the contract).

(d) The terminology used by the Act

The language used in section 39 is clear and precise when it speaks of the promisee putting an end to the contract. It would make no difference for it to have referred to the promisee terminating the contract: each expression conveys the sense that the contract is a valid one but that the promisee has despaired of, or tired of waiting for, the promisor to fulfil his obligation and that he is done with it.

Section 53 refers to the breach as rendering the contract 'voidable'. The link is then made from section 53 to sections 64, 65, and 75, where the innocent party is said to have the option to 'rescind' the contract because it is voidable as a result of the other party's non-performance. This means that the party who has not received the performance he expected is entitled to treat the contract—which was perfectly good and valid as a source of obligation—as voidable. Judged from the structure and thought processes of the modern and uncodified common law, this is problematic.

The process of putting an end to a contract because of a failure by the promisor to perform was traditionally referred to in common law systems as the 'rescission' of the contract, and the Contract Act reflects that. If there is a superficial problem, it is that the same terminology, of voidable contracts, and rescission, is deployed in the context of contracts formed on the basis of consent that was not free and for which section 19 offers the option of rescission.

There would be a risk of confusion if this terminology were to appear to elide rescission of a contract because consent to it was not free, as where the contract was induced by fraud, misrepresentation, coercion, or undue influence,[63] with the putting of an end to the contract because of its breach. The two are not the same because the latter does not treat the parties as though the contract was flawed from the beginning. Where a voidable contract is rescinded under section 19 there is, of course, no inherent right to compensation for non-performance, albeit that the second paragraph of section 19 allows the victim of fraud or misrepresentation to insist that the contract shall be performed and he be put in the position as though the representations had been true. Where, by contrast, the contract is rescinded for non-performance, and is treated as voidable in that sense, compensatory damages for loss resulting from non-fulfilment of the contract can be awarded.[64] Section 53 says so, and section 75 underlines the point:

> 75. *Party rightfully rescinding contract entitled to compensation.* A person who rightly rescinds a contract is entitled to compensation for any damage which he has sustained through the non-fulfilment of the contract.

Section 75 is there because if rescission had simply made the contract void, there would be no obvious cause of action for claiming or ordering compensation for loss caused by breach of that contract.[65] It is perfectly clear that the approach of the 1872 Act is decisively different from that of the common law as generally understood today. This is made crystal clear by a

[63] Contract Act, s 19.

[64] *Muralidhur Chatterjee v International Film Co Ltd* (1943) 70 Ind App 35. Sir George Rankin, who delivered the judgment of the Board, had earlier been Chief Justice of the High Court of Calcutta.

[65] The single Illustration to s 75 is of rescission of a contract for non-performance and not rescission on grounds of lack of free consent. It is therefore a 'rescission for breach' provision.

decision of the Privy Council on an appeal from Calcutta,[66] which is taken to be reliable[67] as to Myanmar law also and in which the court said this:

> The right of one party upon refusal by the other to perform the contract is described indifferently by the Act as a right to 'put an end to' or 'rescind' it; and Illustration (c) [to Section 65] plainly imports that this right is either that of 'a person at whose option the contract is voidable' (Section 64) or is such that by the exercise of it the contract 'becomes void' (Section 65). Of these two propositions it is to be observed that they are not mutually exclusive, whether or not each involves the other...
> From these sections it must be conceded that, as language is used in this Act, the right to treat a contract as voidable and to rescind it may be accompanied by a right to recover damages for the wrongful act which grounds the right of rescission. The ordinary notion of an English lawyer that the right to recover damages must be based upon a valid and subsisting contract, and that a plaintiff could not declare upon a contract as being void, cannot be taken as a guide to the use of the words 'void' and 'voidable' in the Indian Statute.

One sees in the 1872 Act a distinctive principle of practical law. When the party who has been given the option to do so elects to say about the not-yet performed contract, 'Okay, that's enough; I'm ending it now', the contract is no longer something alive, to be performed as such. Instead, it simply becomes part of the background by reference to which compensation, or payment, or repayment, or return (according to the particular facts) will be ordered in accordance with the preferences of the plaintiff and the relevant provisions of the Act. It is unnecessary to conceptualize this as the contract being kept alive in order to provide a basis for compensation. The 1872 Act does that, referring back to the contract, whether void or otherwise, for the data needed to calculate what the law requires to be paid.

(e) The nature or extent of non-performance which allows the promisee to put an end to the contract

It would not be correct to read section 39 as though it said and meant that as soon as there is the smallest breach—the slightest shortcoming in the performance of the promisor—the promisee may pounce on it and put an end to the contract. This point is admittedly tricky because it involves accepting that section 39 does not mean what it may, on one reading, appear to say. We may as well start with this point, though in doing so we should be aware that questions concerning section 39 have not troubled the courts, either before or after independence (from which it may be deduced that it is, to lawyers in Myanmar, perfectly clear what it means).

(1) How great, or how bad, must the failure to perform actually be?

Section 39 speaks of the promisor refusing to perform 'his promise in its entirety'. We must be careful with the meaning of this expression. Of course, in the example given earlier, of the seller who sells the contract goods to someone else, the promisor will now not be able to perform any of his promise: his behaviour means he will perform zero per cent of his promise: his conduct has made it entirely impossible for him to perform, as one might

[66] *Muralidhur Chatterjee v International Film Co Ltd* (n 64) [17] and [20].
[67] There is no trace of the point having arisen in any reported Myanmar case.

say. But section 39 may still apply if the promisor has performed part of his promise. The Illustrations to section 39 (reproduced under section 75) refer to a singer who agrees to sing twice a week for eight weeks and fails to perform after the end of the third week. The Illustrations say that the manager of the theatre is entitled to put an end to the contract, and this must be taken to be the law. It would not be correct to say that the singer has entirely failed to perform her promise: she has performed six concerts, after all, precisely as the contract required her to. If this is nevertheless a case in which she 'has refused to perform . . . her contract in its entirety', it would be because she has not performed the entirety, the whole 100 per cent, of her contract. In other words, a single breach of contract would mean that she has not entirely performed her contract, and the promisee would be entitled to put an end to the contract.

This requires further analysis. A singer who fails to turn up and perform is one thing; it does not follow that a single failure to perform a promise of a contract which contains many promises will allow the promisee to pounce on a trivial or minor breach and rescind the contract there and then. It cannot be correct that a promisee, who now wishes that he had not made the contract which he did make, can seize on the smallest imperfection in the promisor's performance to escape from the continuing obligations which the parties, by their contract, had created. It must be a requirement of the law that the failure of performance by the promisor be serious, even if we lack (as we do lack) authority in the form of Myanmar judicial decisions for this conclusion. If it is not serious enough, there will still be a right under section 73 to claim compensation for loss caused by the breach, but there will be no right to rescind the contract. What section 39 is concerned with is a refusal to perform one of the central terms of the contract or a refusal to perform a promise which affects a vital part of the contract.

Take the case of an employee who works for a commercial organization. Suppose she breaches her duty to serve her employer faithfully by divulging confidential information to a rival company but in every other respect performs the duties of her employment. In this case the refusal to perform, the breach, is of a central term of the contract; the breach is one which strikes at the heart of the contract. In such a case there is no doubt that section 39 will allow the promisee employer to bring the contract of employment to an end. If by contrast an employee, who is required to report for work at 8 o'clock every morning, arrives 15 minutes late on one occasion, it is technically accurate to say that he has failed to perform the entirety of his contract of employment; it is equally clear that in such a case section 39 does not allow the employer to rescind (ie put an end to) the contract.

Some have considered it helpful to use the language of a 'repudiatory' breach to convey the true sense and meaning of section 39: it may suggest a decision to treat the contract, or the promise, or both, with complete disrespect. Others propose 'renunciation' of the contract: a party treats the contract as something by which he no longer considers himself to be bound or obliged. Both may be thought to capture the essence of the distinction between breaches which are not so serious and breaches which are really serious. But the invention and multiplication of terminology can be dangerous. Section 39 does not use the language of 'repudiation' or 'renunciation'; and nor does it require bad faith, disrespect, or contemptuous behaviour to be shown on the part of the promisor. Neither—significantly—does the case law. However, it is necessary to find a way to identify the kind of breach which is serious enough to trigger this remedy. The idea that the failure to perform is a 'refusal' as opposed to a mere failure, that the breach is fundamental and goes to the very heart and essence of the contract, is the gist of it. But even if these words had been written into section 39, the evaluation of the facts in relation to them would be, as the other systems showed, just as tricky.

(2) Cases where it is not known how serious the refusal to perform will be

It may be that one way to avoid the uncertainty which may result from section 39, which arises from the fact that it is not designed to encompass every single failure to perform, is for the parties to include in their contract an express statement of the promises or terms whose breach will, or the breaches which will, entitle the promisee to rescind the contract. In the context of employment, or of contracts of personal or professional service, this makes excellent sense.

Suppose, however, that this has not been done and that the impresario, in whose theatre the singer had promised to perform, does not know, on the basis of one night's absence, whether this marks the start of an indefinite period of non-performance or is just a short-term, temporary, interruption in normal service. What is he supposed to do when the next concert may be only 24 hours away? In the Rangoon of 1872 he can hardly make a phone call or send a text to find out what is going on. Suppose the owner of goods which are to be carried by road or sea discovers that the carrier company has not arrived at the agreed time and that it is impossible to tell whether the carrier is just running a little late or that it is simply not going to come: what is he to do? Suppose the limousine which is supposed to get me to Yangon airport does not appear at the agreed time: is the breach of the promise to arrive on time one which allows me, there and then, to put an end to the contract and make alternative plans? Or does the law require me to wait and see how serious the breach really turns out to be, how late the driver is, and risk missing my flight by doing so?

There are various answers to the question. The first has to be that, in those cases in which it is not realistic or sensible to expect me to wait and see, I am entitled to act to put an end to the contract. We need to use common sense as our guide. If the carpenter who has agreed to come to my house this morning to repair the door has not arrived precisely on time, no one would suggest that I can rescind (ie put an end to) the contract: if I claim to have done so when he arrives 30 minutes late, he will be entitled to say that my refusal to allow him onto the premises to do the work is a refusal by me to perform my side of the contract. Cases like this can, in the end, only be resolved by negotiation or by a judge. But if I have perishable goods, or have a customer who will sue me if I fail to deliver the goods that I have promised to deliver to him on time, or I have a flight to catch, it would be silly to suggest that I am required to wait and see whether the lorry or the vessel will appear. And if I have an audience of ticket holders, who will be demanding reimbursement and trashing my reputation for putting on excellent performances if I have no singer in place for the night after tomorrow, of course I can terminate the contract while the situation can still be salvaged.

The second raises a more general question about the effect of dates in contracts, which is examined under the next point.

(3) The terminology of conditions, warranties, and innominate terms

The law on putting an end to the contract, contained in section 39, appears to be based on a judgment that the non-performance is of a kind which justifies this response by the promisee. There would be another way of addressing the issue whether the case is one in which the contract may be rescinded or put to an end, which would be to identify the particular term of the contract which had been broken as one which would always allow, or may allow, or would in no circumstances allow, the promisee to end the contract. This tripartite division of terms, which was wholly unknown in 1872, is well established in other common law jurisdictions, with the nomenclature of *conditions* (terms which, if broken, will always allow the innocent party to put an end to the contract), *warranties* (terms which, if broken, will never allow the innocent party to put an end to the contract), and *innominate terms* (terms which do not have a name and which may or may not justify an end being put to the contract, the decision in the particular case depending on the seriousness of the consequences of the breach). This description of terms is not found in the Contract Act,[68] although the terminology of conditions and warranties[69] plays a significant part in the Sale of Goods Act 1930.

An advantage of this scheme may lie in the opportunity which it gives the parties to know in advance, at least where the term broken will be a condition or warranty, whether a breach of that term will be one which allows the contract to be rescinded. The designation of a term of the contract as a condition or a warranty would be one over which the parties, in principle at least, would have control; and if the parties were to designate a term as a condition, they would immediately know what the consequences of its breach would be. But this technique of common-law contract law is not part of the Contract Act and is not yet, so far as one can tell from the case law, part of Myanmar contract law. It follows that the question whether, in any case of non-performance, section 39 allows the contract to be rescinded (or put to an end) is to be answered in accordance with the law which we have set out above: is the breach, in the circumstances in which it has come about, serious enough to justify the innocent party in putting an end to the contract. No greater elaboration of the law will achieve anything of measurable value: 'serious enough' is the best test.

(f) Breach by failure to perform on time

A contract will often provide for a promise to be performed on a certain date or at a certain time, and the question naturally arises whether the other party is entitled not to perform his promise if the first promisor fails to perform on the date specified. According to section 55:

> 55. *Effect of failure to perform at fixed time in contract in which time is essential.* When a party to a contract promises to do a certain thing at or before a specified time, or certain things before certain specified times, and fails to do any such thing at or before the specified time, the contract, or so much of it as had not been performed, becomes voidable at the option of the promisee, if the intention of the parties was that time should be of the essence of the contract.
>
> *Effect of such failure where time is not* essential. If it was not the intention of the parties that time should be of the essence of the contract, the contract does not become voidable by the failure to do such thing at or before the specified time; but the promisee is entitled to compensation from the promisor for any loss occasioned to him by such failure.
>
> *Effect of acceptance of performance at time other than that agreed upon.* If, in the case of a contract voidable on account of the promisor's failure to perform his promise at the time

[68] Although it does appear to have been folded into the Act in India and (most strikingly) in Malaysia.

[69] The original provisions of the Contract Act 1872, which dealt with contracts for the sale of goods in ss 76–123 (deleted on the making of the Sale of Goods Act 1930), made extensive use in this context of the term 'warranty' but did not use 'condition', still less 'innominate term', as a type of contract term.

> agreed, the promisee accepts performance of such promise at any time other than that agreed, the promisee cannot claim compensation for any loss occasioned by the non-performance of the promise at the time agreed, unless, at the time of such acceptance, he gives notice to the promisor of his intention to do so.

If the failure of the promisor to perform on time is one which allows[70] the promisee to rescind (ie to put an end to) the contract, and he does so, then as with cases falling under section 39, the promisee is no longer required to perform his own promises. If this is not the case, then the promisee remains liable to perform his own promises but may sue for compensation for any loss which he has sustained by reason of the lateness in performance. Two immediate questions therefore arise. The first is whether the contract is one for which the date of performance was unusually critical; the second is to examine the effect, on the obligations of the promisee, of the promisor not performing on time. The promisee must, at the least, be excused from the immediate obligation to perform.

(1) Is the time or date of performance critical?

In many contracts the date specified for performance will not be treated as a term which, if not complied with, will allow the other party to rescind (ie put an end to) the contract. This often comes as a surprise to ordinary people (and to some lawyers), but the explanation is easy enough. The practical circumstances of life are such that although the parties may provide in their contract a date or time for performance, this may become unachievable because the train was late, the post was unreliable, the traffic was at a standstill, the power went down, or even because the promisor was not as diligent as she might have been. If, however, the failure of the promisor to meet the precise date stipulated in the contract were to mean that she had failed to perform her promise in its entirety, her lateness may be considered to be a breach which allows the other party to rescind (ie put an end to) the contract as well as claiming compensation for any loss or damage caused by the breach.

Section 55 explains why this is not so and shows that a stipulation as to time occupies a special place in general contract law. A contract may become voidable—liable to be rescinded—if time was intended by the parties to be essential to the contract or (as it may otherwise be said) 'of the essence of the contract', which in this context must mean that it was essential to this particular promise. Although the notion of time being essential, or of the essence, has been in use in the common law for a very long time, its meaning is a little elusive. It means that time is of such significance that non-compliance with that timing allows the other party to put an end to the contract. The reasoning which is used to explain it is, therefore, circular.

In fact, the rule does not depend on there being an express stipulation in the contract that time is to be of the essence but upon the intention of the parties being to this effect.[71] It will depend on the express words of the contract, the nature of the contract itself, and on the surrounding circumstances.[72] If the contract provides for penalties to be applied

[70] It does not oblige: *B Dey v LJ John alias JJ Lynch* (1900-02) LBR 21.

[71] *Maung Wala v Mg Shwe Gun* AIR 1924 Ran 57 (if seller is ready and willing to tender performance on the due date, but the buyer behaves in such a way as to make this impracticable, this will extend time for performance and will mean that time is no longer of the essence); *U Jama v Ma Bi* (1966) BLR 278 (CC).

[72] Which may include the behaviour of the parties as an indication of how urgent they seem to have regarded the date of performance as being, even in contract for the sale of land: *U Han v U Thi* (1959) BLR 278 (HC).

in the event of failure to perform on the stipulated date, that fact may well indicate that time was of the essence.[73] As indicated above, in commercial and shipping cases, as well as in cases involving being driven to the airport, timely performance may very well be important, and the notion that the party who had expected performance on a particular date should wait around for an indefinite period, not knowing whether performance will be late or non-existent, is not a sensible one. Outside the context of commercial contracts time is not generally essential, but there are certainly many cases in which it still is. A contract for the delivery of flowers to my mother on her birthday is one in which the precise date for performance is crucial. Even if I do not inform the florist that the date is of central importance, he probably does not need to be told. But otherwise, the law generally takes the view that dates in contracts are aspirational rather than strict pledges.

(2) Consequences of failure to perform on time if time is essential

If the contract is one in which time is of the essence, a failure to perform on time, or a refusal to perform on time, will allow the promisee to rescind the contract. Section 75 will also allow the party who rescinded the contract to sue for damages in respect of loss caused by the non-fulfilment of the promise. It will also follow, as a matter of logic and of law, that his obligation to perform any promises of his own is at an end: it is not that he has a lawful excuse for non-performance but that he has no obligation to perform any more.

(g) The promisee's options

If the promisor has brought himself within the range of conduct to which section 39 applies, the promisee is at liberty to rescind or not to rescind.

(1) Exercising the option to rescind the contract

First, she may exercise her option to rescind or put an end to the contract. If this is done, the promises which the contract obliged each party to perform no longer require performance: when a contract is rescinded for breach, there is no longer any question of either party requiring the other to perform what was promised. On rescission the contract becomes void; the Privy Council made the point precisely, noting that this meant that the position under the Contract Act was distinct from the position under the English common law as then (and now) understood.[74] A claim for compensation may still be brought by the innocent party in accordance with sections 73 and 75, and if the contract contained a term which fixed in advance, or 'liquidated' the damages which would be payable on breach,[75] that term would remain operative. As explained above, it is not wholly easy to reconcile this with the idea that the contract has become void, but that appears to be how the Contract Act deals with the matter.

As to benefits conferred under a contract that has been rescinded for breach, section 64 provides that the party rescinding (ie the party who is not in breach) must make restitution

[73] *AKRMMK Chidambaram Chettyar v Khoo Hwa Lam* (1950) BLR 98 (SC); *U Htan Hmat v Daw Gon* (1957) BLR 73 (HC).

[74] *Muralidhur Chatterjee v International Film Co Ltd* (n 64) (decision of the Privy Council on appeal from the High Court of Calcutta).

[75] If by contrast the contract provided that on the occurrence of certain events a sum of money would be paid, as will sometimes be provided for when a relationship such as commercial distribution is terminated, this is not a liquidated damages clause but a term providing for a particular kind of performance on the occurrence of certain events. It will not be operative if the promisee exercises his option under s 39 to put an end to the contract.

to the contract-breaker of benefits received under the contract.[76] And to ensure that an innocent party can equally have restitution of benefits it has conferred on the party in breach, section 65 will apply in line with the proposition that, once rescinded, the contract becomes void:

> 64. *Consequences of rescission of voidable contract.* When a person at whose option a contract is voidable rescinds it, the other party thereto need not perform any promise therein contained in which he is promisor. The party rescinding a voidable contract shall, if he has received any benefit thereunder from another party to such contract, restore such benefit, so far as may be, to the person from whom it was received.[77]
> 65. *Obligation of person who has received advantage under void agreement or contract that becomes void.* When an agreement is discovered to be void, or when a contract becomes void, any person who has received any advantage under such agreement or contract is bound to restore it, or to make compensation for it, to the person from whom he received it.

That provides one form of remedy when the contract is rescinded for breach. If, however, the party who suffers loss caused by non-fulfilment claims damages as well, relying on section 75 to do so, the adjustment, by way of set-off or giving credit, will take place according to ordinary principles.[78]

(2) Exercising the option to not rescind the contract

Alternatively, the promisee may refuse to agree or to accept that he should now rescind the contract.[79] Although it may seem a strange thing to do if it is simply impossible for the promisor now to perform his promise, there may be other cases in which it makes more sense. Suppose in a contract of employment it is provided that an employee must be given two months' notice to bring the employment relationship to an end and also that an annual bonus payment will be made to every employee at the end of the year. Suppose that the employer tells the employee that he is being dismissed from the employment: perhaps the employer wishes to deprive this employee of the right to what would otherwise be a substantial bonus payment. The employee may refuse to accept that the contract should be brought to an end and may continue to insist that he retains his status and rights as employee until the end of the period of notice which the employer would have had to give if the employer were to have complied with the terms of the contract.[80]

There may be special cases, such as agency, in which a refusal by the principal to treat the agent as agent does automatically bring the agency to an end, whether or not the agent chooses to put an end to the contract.[81] But agency is a special case, and even here the agent retains his remedies for breach of contract.[82] Similarly, if the manager of the national

76 *Muralidhur Chatterjee v International Film Co Ltd* (n 64).
77 See s 75.
78 *Muralidhur Chatterjee v International Film Co Ltd* (n 64) [23].
79 *B Dey v LJ John alias JJ Lynch* (n 70).
80 For present purposes, it is assumed that the contractual terms of the employment contract discussed at this point are consistent with the Employment and Skills Development Law 2013 and the Employment Contract Template published on 28 August 2017 (or that if they are not, they have been submitted to and approved by the Township Labour Office for the individual case).
81 Contract Act, s 201.
82 Contract Act, s 205.

football team is wrongly sacked in circumstances which plainly breach his contract of service, he can hardly point to section 39 and say that he declines to exercise his option to rescind the contract, with the consequence that he will be picking the team for Sunday's international match: that would be absurd, and whatever else the common law is, it is never absurd. The correct analysis is that he is no longer the manager but that he may continue to claim the benefits of his contract until the termination of the contract according to its terms. Of course, if the national association says that the manager refused to perform his contract to manage the team successfully and that the correct analysis is that the national association exercised *its* right under section 39 to put an end to the contract, the dispute between the parties will be principally resolved on the question of interpretation of the promises created by the contract and, hence, on the question of which of the two committed a section 39 breach.

If the promisee makes it clear that she is not exercising the option to put an end to the contract, then as the option has been set aside by the promisee in this way, it is lost and gone; it cannot be brought back if the promisee changes her mind at a later date. In the Illustrations[83] to section 39, if the singer who had absented herself from two performances, returns to the theatre and continues to sing, the option which the impresario had to put an end to the contract is lost by deliberate non-exercise, and though the singer may be liable to pay compensation for the loss caused by her absence, the contract will continue in effect.

3. The Hypothetical Question

(a) Car Machinery & Co and Traders Ltd

Car Machinery & Co appoint Traders Ltd as sole distributors of their car panel presses for a period of five years. Clause 7(b) of the agreement provides that 'Distributors shall send their representatives to visit all six large car manufacturers in the country at least once in every week for the purpose of soliciting orders for car panel presses. Failure to comply with this obligation shall entitle Car Machinery to terminate the agreement with immediate effect.' Traders Ltd miss two visits to car manufacturers in the second month of the contractual period. Is Car Machinery entitled to terminate the agreement?[84]

One cannot say for sure. There will be (has already been) a failure by Traders Ltd to perform the promise in its entirety, and at first sight section 39 might appear to give Car Machinery the right to put an end to the contract by rescinding it. One may be reluctant to say that this is the answer, but the first Illustration to section 39 does say that:

[83] Though the Illustrations are technically not part of the sections of the Act, they have been provided by the legislature as being helpful in the working and application of the Act and are to be understood accordingly; rejecting them as repugnant to the section would be justified only in the very last resort: see to this effect *Mahomed Syedol Ariffin v Yeoh Ooi Gark* (1916) LR 43 Ind App 256, AIR 1916 PC 242 (decision of the Privy Council on appeal from the Court of Appeal of the Straits Settlements). A rather less respectful view of the Illustrations was given in *Myingyan Municipality v Maung Po Nyun* AIR 1930 Ran 173, (1930) ILR 8 Ran 320, but the Privy Council decision was not referred to by, and presumably not cited to, the High Court, which gave no reasons of its own to justify its opinion.

[84] The fact scenarios of this and the other hypothetical cases discussed herein are taken from M Chen-Wishart, D Neo, and S Vogenauer, 'Introduction', ch 1, 9–10.

> (a) A, a singer, enters into a contract with B, the manager of a theatre, to sing at his theatre two nights in every week during the next two months, and B engages to pay her 100 rupees for each night's performance. On the sixth night A wilfully absents herself from the theatre. B is at liberty to put an end to the contract.

and that may be equivalent to the situation described in the hypothetical. But as we said, the consequences of the singer's breach in nineteenth-century Rangoon are very much more serious than Traders' failure to make a couple of visits.

(b) Prime Ltd and Devil Corp

Prime Ltd sells a piece of land to Devil Corp. Under the terms of the contract, Devil pays a 10 per cent deposit, the remainder of the sum being due at 5:00 pm on 30 September, time being 'of the essence'. According to Clause 12, failure to meet the deadline would result in the deposit being forfeited and the agreement being terminated. Devil is ten minutes late in tendering the completion money and Prime refuse performance. Can Devil sue for specific performance, arguing that Prime's reliance on the clause is unreasonable in some way?

Would the result be different if the contract did not include Clause 12?

Section 55 is likely to mean that the contract is voidable by Prime Ltd, and that is the whole answer. Nothing in the Specific Relief Act of 1877 allows the answer given by section 55 to be overridden. Section 74 also provides for the enforcement of agreements to pay a specific sum in the event of breach; and in the absence of any broad and general jurisdiction to re-write contracts—and of course there is none—Devil cannot obtain specific performance of a contract which is now void.

If Clause 12 were not there, the second paragraph of section 55 would mean that the contract was not voidable by reason of late tender of payment, but if there has been loss caused to Prime, it can recover compensation.

(c) Seven Seas and Big Chef

Seven Seas, an importer of seafood, sells two tons of mussels to Big Chef restaurant chain. After one ton has been delivered, it turns out that the concentration of cadmium in the mussels is 2 per cent above the concentration permitted by national food regulations. Can Big Chef terminate the contract?

The answer appears to be yes: section 39 would tend to suggest that this was permitted. Sale of Goods Act 1930 would allow the buyer to reject the goods, and at that point it is much easier to see that Big Chief may put an end to, or rescind, the contract: the breach is a very serious one, and Big Chef cannot be expected to wait and see if Seven Seas can improve its performance.

(d) Coco and David

Coco, a famous architect, agrees with David that he will landscape the garden in her next development. He is due to start work on 1 December. For David, this is an important opportunity to make his name as a landscape gardener. On 1 October, she tells him that she is no longer interested because the development will not include a garden after all. David has already purchased materials. He estimates that his future earnings will be 10 per cent lower because he will not be able to benefit from having worked with Coco. Can he insist on doing the work? Can he bring an action for breach of contract?

Section 39 will allow him to put an end to the contract, and insofar as he suffers financial loss from the non-fulfilment of the contract, section 75 will allow him to recover compensation. The rules for the assessment of damages, governed in general by section 73, may not allow him to recover for losses which are the indirect consequences of the breach, so his loss of earnings—as distinct from the loss of fee from Coco, which is recoverable—may not be recoverable.

As to whether he could instead refuse to put an end to the contract, it is true that the option lies with him. But it would require the court to see this as a contract whose obligations it would enforce by specific performance, and section 21 of the Specific Relief Act would strongly suggest that this is not a contract which would be decreed for specific performance. This is because it is a contract for the non-performance of which compensation in money is an adequate relief; it is also a contract which runs into such minute or numerous details, or which is so dependent on the personal qualifications or volition of the parties, or otherwise from its nature is such that the Court cannot enforce specific performance of its material terms (Specific Relief Act 1877, section 21).[85]

(e) Bob and Sue

Bob contracts to build a house for Sue for the price of $100,000. After doing a third of the work he abandons the job, leaving behind material worth $15,000, which Sue later uses to finish the works. Can Bob claim the value of the work done or of the materials?

Sue is entitled to rescind the contract. Section 64 requires her to restore to Bob any benefit she has received under the contract, which will certainly extend to the unused materials but will not require her to account for unquantifiable work done. Insofar as Bob's non-fulfilment of the contract has left her worse off than she would have been if he had done the job he promised to do, section 75 allows her to obtain compensation.

4. Closing Considerations

To conclude, let us consider some further questions, starting with: how does a party terminate a contract? Is it necessary to involve a court?

Termination is effected by communication to the other party; there is no need for judicial involvement. According to section 66:

> 66. *Mode of communicating or revoking rescission of voidable contract.* The rescission of a voidable contract may be communicated or revoked in the same manner, and subject to the same rules, as apply to the communication or revocation of a proposal.

[85] The fact scenarios of this and the other hypothetical cases discussed herein are taken from M Chen-Wishart, D Neo, and S Vogenauer, 'Introduction', ch 1, 7–8.
enforced: (a) a contract for the non performance of which compensation in money is an adequate relief; (b) a contract which runs into such minute or numerous details, or which is so dependent on the personal qualifications or volition of the parties, or otherwise from its nature is such that the Court cannot enforce specific performance of its material terms; (c) a contract the terms of which the Court cannot find with reasonable certainty.

But if the contract itself provides that in the event of breach the party can treat the contract as at an end without the need to give notice to the other, then no notice need be given.[86]

Next to consider is the question of when, if ever, an entitlement to termination can be lost (eg breach by the party who wishes to terminate, lapse of time)?

According to section 39, this right may be lost if he has signified, by words or conduct, that he acquiesces in the continuance of the contract. That is probably sufficient to deal with most of the cases which it is realistic to consider.

Finally: what is the effect of termination? What happens to the contract? What happens to any benefits conferred in performance of the contract up to the point of termination? Does it matter whether the future and past performances can be separated from each other? What is the relationship between any claims for restitution and damages following termination? Can the court give the party in breach additional time for performance?

As explained above, the contract is voidable, and on rescission it comes to an end with prospective *and* retrospective effect. Benefits must in principle be returned, but a party who has suffered loss by reason of the non-fulfilment of the contract may obtain damages by way of compensation under section 75. These are not alternative remedies, but arithmetic will make the necessary adjustment so that section 75 simply deals with the difference between where the plaintiff is now and where she would have been if the contract had been fulfilled. The idea of giving, or having to give, additional time for performance (a feature of some civilian systems) does not appear to have any basis in the Act.

86 *Pannalal Rangalal v Tin Tin U* (n 45).

18

Revision of Contracts in the Philippines

The Ramifications of a Change of Circumstances

Ma Ngina Teresa CHAN-GONZAGA

I. Introduction

Fundamental to most legal traditions and systems is the principle that obligations stemming from contracts have the force of law as between parties and must be complied with in good faith by those who enter into such. Philippine contract law is no different.

Philippine contract law's historical antecedents are decidedly Spanish and, because of that, obviously Roman in origin too. The Philippines was under Spanish rule since the 1500s and, as was the case for other Spanish colonies, the application of laws was roughly in the following order: (i) latest laws enacted specifically for the colonies, (ii) the *Recopilación de las Indias*, (iii) the *Novisima*, (iv) the *Nueva*, (v) the *Leyes de Toro*, (vi) the royal Castilian ordinances, (vii) the *Ordenamiento de Alcala*, (viii) the *Fuero Juzgo*, and (ix) the *Partidas*.[1] A codification of civil laws in Spain was not undertaken until 1889, but soon after such was promulgated in July of that year, a royal decree was issued extending the application of the Spanish Civil Code to the Philippines. Case law has since resolved that the Code became effective in the Philippines on 7 or 8 December 1889.[2]

While Spanish sovereignty would last less than a decade hence,[3] the Civil Code—being of a non-political nature—survived American colonization, Japanese wartime occupation, and even the eventual establishment of the Philippine Republic in 1946. It is true that President Manuel Roxas called for the drafting of a Civil Code in 1947, but even the Code Commission established for this purpose conceded that approximately 57 per cent of the articles in this Civil Code—styled the 1950 New Civil Code—are derived from the Spanish Code.[4]

Contract law forms part of the law on obligations, and Article 1156 of the Civil Code identifies it as one of the items in an exclusive list of 'sources of obligation', the others being law, delict, quasi-delict, and quasi-contracts. Article 1305 of the Civil Code defines it, a little simplistically, as the 'meeting of minds between two persons whereby one binds himself, with respect to the other, to give something or to render some service'.

[1] RF Balane, *Civil Law Florilegium: Essays on the Philippine Variant of the Civil Law Tradition* (University of the Philippines College of Law 2012) 54.

[2] ibid 58–59, citing *Mijares v Nery* [1904] GR No 1380, and *De la Rama v De la Rama* [1907] GR No 1056.

[3] The Philippine revolution started in 1896 and Spain ceded its claim to the Philippine Islands to the Americans in the 1899 Treaty of Paris.

[4] Balane (n 1) 61; NR Malolos and TC Martin, *Report of the Code Commission on the Proposed Civil Code of the Philippines* (Domerte Book Supply 1951).

Ma Ngina Teresa Chan-Gonzaga, *Revision of Contracts in the Philippines* In: *Studies in the Contract Laws of Asia V: Ending and Changing Contracts*. Edited by: Mindy Chen-Wishart, Dora Neo, and Stefan Vogenauer, Oxford University Press.
 DOI: 10.1093/oso/9780198995814.003.0018

For the most part, contracts in the Philippines are consensual. Mutuality is a recognized characteristic of contracts, and the law prohibits unilateral modification of contractual provisions.[5] Any indication therefore that one party seeks to elude compliance with clauses and terms previously freely entered into is necessarily and understandably met with disapprobation and censure.

Indeed, that contracts are to be treated as having the force of law between parties is not just mandated at statutory level in the civil law tradition but constitutionally supported as well. The Philippine Constitution of 1987, in (deceptively) absolute language, pronounces that '[n]o law impairing the obligation of contracts shall be passed'.[6] That said, there are obviously accepted exceptions to the requirement of compulsory and strict observance. The constitutional provision, while seemingly categorical, has always yielded to police power measures that are legislatively enacted.[7] These acts of Congress are usually extraordinary measures intended to afford relief to a significant segment of society.[8]

Moreover, while Article 1315 of the Civil Code embodies the principles of mutuality and consensuality, it also provides that parties are bound not only by what is stipulated but also to all consequences in keeping with, among other things, good faith.[9] Indeed, it can be argued that all provisions that result in statutory relief, as well as those that allow for judicial intervention in cases of change of circumstances, are grounded in the basic principles of equity and good faith as well as the rule of construction, which maintains that the greatest reciprocity of interests should be upheld when dealing with onerous contracts.[10] The Supreme Court, on occasion, has modified contracts if it deemed that the situation called for an exercising of its equity jurisdiction; to 'balance the equities' as it were, in determining the relief to be handed down so as to render full justice to all parties.[11]

II. When Change of Circumstances Results in Impossibility

Civil law has provided for exceptions to the strictness of contracts including the release of an obligor (ie the debtor) when the failure to fulfil the obligation is due to the impossibility of performance or the loss of the thing due without fault on the part of the obligor, such as those traced to the occurrence of a fortuitous event or *force majeure*.

The Philippine statutory pronouncements on this matter set out the rules: that a person is excused from responsibility for those events which could not be foreseen or which, though foreseen, were inevitable; that the obligation shall be extinguished should a prestation

[5] Civil Code of the Philippines (Civil Code), art 1308. The contract must bind both contracting parties; its validity or compliance cannot be left to the will of one of them. For an online version of the Civil Code, see <www.officialgazette.gov.ph/1949/06/18/republic-act-no-386> accessed 1 February 2024.

[6] Philippine Constitution of 1987, art III (The Bill of Rights) s 10.

[7] *Rutter v Esteban* [1953] GR No L-3708; *Del Rosario v De los Santos* [1968] GR Nos L-20589-90.

[8] *Rutter v Esteban* (n 7); *Del Rosario v De los Santos* (n 7).

[9] Civil Code, art 1315: 'Contracts are perfected by mere consent, and from that moment the parties are bound not only to the fulfilment of what has been expressly stipulated but also to all the consequences which, according to their nature, may be in keeping with good faith, usage and law.'

[10] JBL Reyes, 'Revision of Contracts in View of Supervening Events' in RF Balane (ed), *J.B.L. Ipse Loquitur: A Collection of Essays and Lectures* (University of the Philippines Law Complex 2002) 72.

[11] *Agcaoili v Government Service Insurance System* [1988] GR No L-30056; *Reyes v Lim* [2003] GR No 134241; *Hulst v PR Builders, Inc* [2007] GR No 156364.

(ie the object of the obligation)[12] become impossible without the fault of the obligor; that the obligation to deliver a determinate thing[13] shall be extinguished if it is lost without the fault of the debtor; and that the debtor in obligations to do shall also be released when the prestation becomes impossible without his fault.

These provisions of the Civil Code in particular address the situations mentioned:

> Article 1174. Except in cases expressly specified by the law, or when it is otherwise declared by stipulation, or when the nature of the obligation requires the assumption of risk, no person shall be responsible for those events which could not be foreseen, or which, though foreseen, were inevitable.
>
> Article 1262. An obligation which consists in the delivery of a determinate thing shall be extinguished if it should be lost or destroyed without the fault of the debtor and before he has incurred in delay. . . .
>
> Article 1266. The debtor in obligations to do shall also be released when the prestation becomes legally or physically impossible without the fault of the obligor.

When the obligation consists of the delivery of something determinate, positive law provides that such obligation is necessarily extinguished if the object is lost or destroyed after the obligation is entered into and the obligor is neither at fault nor guilty of any delay. This of course does not apply if there is a legal provision (eg insurance law) or a contractual stipulation that provides for the contrary or when the nature of the obligation itself accounts for the obligor assuming the risk of loss.[14] Liability is also not escaped even in cases of fortuitous events when the obligation to give[15] is one which pertains to a generic thing as courts have had the occasion to remind litigants that *genus nunquam perit*—a generic item never perishes, unless of course traffic in the entire *genus* becomes illegal and therefore the obligation becomes legally impossible.[16]

Article 1266 of the Civil Code in particular provides for the obligor's release in case of the supervening impossibility of the prestation, whether legal or physical, without ascribable fault. Legal impossibility here refers to the prohibition of an act because of the passage of a law which takes place after the establishment of the obligation, while physical impossibility refers to the situation where 'the act by reason of its nature cannot be accomplished'.[17] The impossibility in this case is one which appears after the making of the obligation and will result in the extinguishment or extinction of the debtor's obligation (subject to the restitution of that which may have already been received). The debtor is released and does not incur any liability for the non-performance of the contracted prestation rendered impossible.[18]

[12] Derived from the simplistic language of art 1156 of the Civil Code, there are three possible prestations: to give, to do, or not to do.

[13] Under Philippine law, the term 'determinate' is akin to 'specific', as opposed to 'generic'. The first sentence of art 1460 of the Civil Code provides that 'a thing is determinate when it is particularly designated or physically segregated from all others of the same class'.

[14] Civil Code, art 1262(2): 'When by law or stipulation, the obligor is liable even for fortuitous events, the loss of the thing does not extinguish the obligation, and he shall be responsible for damages. The same rule applies when the nature of the obligation requires the assumption of risk.'

[15] cf n 12.

[16] RF Balane, *Jottings and Jurisprudence in Civil Law (Obligations and Contracts)* (Central Book Supply Inc 2020) 400; Civil Code, art 1263, which provides: 'In an obligation to deliver a generic thing, the loss or destruction of anything of the same kind does not extinguish the obligation.'

[17] ET Rabuya, *Obligations and Contracts* (Rex Book Store 2019) 314.

[18] ibid 315.

All the aforementioned provisions in this section are direct derivations from pre-existing provisions in the Spanish Civil Code. A novel rule, however, was introduced in the Philippine Civil Code:

> Article 1264. The courts shall determine whether, under the circumstances, the partial loss of the object of the obligation is so important as to extinguish the obligation.

This provision makes judicial determination a factor in establishing the possible avoidance of an obligation in case there is disagreement between the parties. Moreover, it must be noted that, textually, the provision gives the courts the authority to extinguish the obligation, not to change or modify its terms. To date, there has been no case brought before the Supreme Court in reliance of this particular article.

III. When Change of Circumstances Results in Difficulty of Performance

A more complex issue, however, arises when the supervening event, or the change of circumstances, does not exactly qualify as a fortuitous event nor lead to a complete impossibility—legal or physical—of performance.

As the pre-eminent Philippine jurisconsult[19] and former Supreme Court Justice, Jose BL Reyes, put it: '[I]n the absence of general principles established by statute, an individual obligor can hardly expect remedy for his particular case, even if desperate, if the same is not covered by the remedial laws. What then?'[20]

1. The Pre-1950 Situation

The strict standard prior to the promulgation of the Civil Code was that bargains which turned out to be luckless due to supervening events were not exempt from performance. This is perhaps best shown in the 1949 case of *Reyes v Caltex (Philippines) Inc*, which was decided right before the Code came into effect:

> Where a person by his contract charges himself with an obligation possible to be performed, he must perform it, unless its performance is rendered impossible by the act of God, by the law, or by the other party, it being the rule that in case the party desires to be excused from performance in the event of contingencies arising, it is his duty to provide therefor in his contract. Hence, performance is not excused by subsequent inability to perform, by unforeseen difficulties, by unusual or unexpected expenses, by danger, by inevitable accident, by the breaking of machinery, by strikes, by sickness, by failure of a party to avail himself of the benefits to be had under the contract, by weather conditions, by financial stringency, or by stagnation of business. Neither is performance excused by the

[19] A term used by former University of the Philippines College of Law Dean Raul C Pangalangan to describe Justice Reyes. RC Pangalangan, 'Foreword' in Balane (n 10) iii.

[20] Reyes (n 10) 63.

> fact that the contract turns out to be hard and improvident, unprofitable or impracticable, ill advised, or even foolish, or less profitable, or unexpectedly burdensome. (17 C. J. S., 946–948).
> In the absence of a statute to the contrary, conditions arising from a state of war in which the country is engaged, will not ordinarily constitute an excuse for non-performance of contract; and impossibility of performance arising from the acts of the legislature and the executive branch of government in war time does not, without more, constitute an excuse for non-performance. (17 C. J. S., 953, 954.)[21]

That said, the early Supreme Court also had occasion to show an inclination towards equity despite positive law. In the 1928 case of *Labayen v Talisay-Silay Milling Co, Inc*, the Supreme Court grappled with the question of whether one may obligate himself to do something which, when accomplished, will 'prove to be dangerous to life and property'. It answered in the negative; and while the obligation here—to build a railroad across some perilous terrain—was not technically impossible, the Supreme Court, citing Manresa's *Codigo Civil Español*, absolved the obligor from damages and said that not to sanction an exception would 'run counter to public policy and the law by forcing the performance of a contract undesirable and harmful'.[22]

2. Statutory Changes Brought About by the New Civil Code of the Philippines

The two Civil Code provisions—Articles 1250 and 1267—that primarily deal with this matter are both new provisions; that is, these did not have counterparts in the Spanish Civil Code applicable in the Philippines prior to 1950.

(a) Difficulty of performance

Under the Civil Code, Article 1267 is the main article that deals with change of circumstances and is more general and broader in language and application than Article 1250:

> Article 1267. When the service has become so difficult as to be manifestly beyond the contemplation of the parties, the obligor may also be released therefrom, in whole or in part.

While it may perhaps be argued, as Senator Arturo M Tolentino does, that the principle of good faith may be relied upon in cases dealing with unforeseen changes even in the absence of positive law,[23] the Supreme Court has also had occasion to remark that without this article, a party would:

> remain bound by its contract under the theretofore prevailing doctrine that performance therewith is not excused 'by the fact that the contract turns out to be hard and improvident, unprofitable, or unexpectedly burdensome', since in case a party desires to be excused from

[21] *Reyes v Caltex (Philippines) Inc* [1949] GR No L-1802.
[22] *Labayen v Talisay-Silay Milling Co, Inc* [1928] GR No L-29298.
[23] AM Tolentino, *Commentaries and Jurisprudence on the Civil Code of the Philippines, vol 4* (Central Law Book Publishing 1991) 348.

> performance in the event of such contingencies arising, it is his duty to provide therefor in the contract.[24]

Article 1267 of the Civil Code supplements the rule that impossibility of performance excuses the obligor. In their report, the Code Commission pointed out that 'the intention of the parties should govern and if it appears that the service turns out to be so difficult as to have been beyond their contemplation, it would be doing violence to that intention to hold the obligor still responsible'.[25]

Jurisprudence (ie case law) and commentaries have loosely referred to the principle embodied in this article as one based on 'frustration of enterprise' or 'frustration of the commercial object'; or as 'relative impossibility', 'moral impossibility'; or as the 'theory of imprevisibility'; or, more ubiquitously, as the 'doctrine of unforeseen events'.[26]

The basis for Article 1267 of the Civil Code is largely recognized to be the principle of *rebus sic stantibus*—that is, the position that 'contracts which involve successive performances or for performances over a long period of time are to be understood in the context of conditions prevailing at the time they were entered into'—a qualification of the perceived harshness of the rule of *pacta sunt servanda*.[27] Professor Ruben F Balane observes that parties to contracts generally come to an agreement in light of present conditions (ie at the time of the contract's perfection) and, where one obligor's undertaking is spread out over time, on the assumption that conditions will only be subject to the common and normal changes (which they must anticipate and take into consideration). Hence, if conditions are radically and drastically altered beyond their contemplation, 'the contract loses its basis due to a reason akin to failure of cause'.[28]

(1) Elements of Article 1267

There are four requisites for this article's application, which authorities like Tolentino have summarized[29] and which have subsequently been concurred in and cited by the Supreme Court in *Tagaytay Realty Co v Gacutan*:

1. '[T]he event or change in circumstances could not have been foreseen at the time of the execution of the contract';
2. 'it makes the performance of the contract *extremely difficult but not impossible*';
3. 'it must not be due to the act of any of the parties'; and
4. 'the contract is for a future prestation' (ie work carried out successively or over a long period of time).[30]

With respect to the non-foreseeability of the change, it is not enough that none of the parties anticipated the difficulty; it is necessary to establish that such difficulty could not have

24 *Occeña v Jabson* [1976] GR No L-44349, citing *Reyes v Caltex (Philippines) Inc* (n 21).

25 EL Paras, *Civil Code of the Philippines Annotated* (Rex Book Store 2016) 402; Malolos and Martin (n 4) 133.

26 Balane (n 16) 404; Tolentino (n 23) 347–48; DP Jurado, *Comments and Jurisprudence on Obligations and Contracts* (Rex Book Store 2010) 295; Paras (n 25) 444; and JC Vitug, *Civil Law* (Rex Book Store 2006) 89.

27 Balane (n 16) 404.

28 ibid 404–05.

29 ibid 410. See also Tolentino (n 23) 348.

30 *Tagaytay Realty Co v Gacutan* [2015] GR No 160033, citing Tolentino (n 23) 347–48 (emphasis added).

been anticipated.[31] Claims of financial struggles and difficulty in meeting obligations due to an economic emergency like the 1997 Asian currency crisis;[32] or to a political shift after the assassination of former Senator Benigno Aquino Jr in 1983 or the EDSA Revolution (People Power Revolution), which saw the ouster of former president Ferdinand Marcos Sr in 1986;[33] or to the increase in the price of oil and the accompanying global escalation of the prices of basic commodities have not met with any success.[34]

It is not enough that the performance is beyond the contemplation of the parties; it must turn out to be *extremely* difficult.[35] The change of circumstances must also not be such as to bring about impossibility of performance; otherwise, as earlier discussed, it is Article 1262 (loss of thing due) or Article 1266 (impossibility of performance) which will govern. Article 1267 only applies in case the change of circumstances brings about 'extreme difficulty'. This distinction, however, has sometimes been confused since plaintiffs seeking to elude liability often cite as alternative grounds the possibility of relief under Article 1262 or Article 1266, and Article 1267.

The Supreme Court has also contributed to the blurring of lines in its disposal of issues in cases.[36] In *Osmeña III v Social Security System of the Philippines*, for instance, the Supreme Court—in declaring a supervening merger to have effected changes in circumstances—said that fulfilment of the obligations that each party had agreed to undertake was now 'legally impossible', thereby giving the impression that it was properly the subject of Article 1266. But in the immediately succeeding line, it talked of how the total or partial release is allowed when the service has become so difficult as to be manifestly beyond the parties' contemplation.[37] In addition, the Supreme Court, in the *Huibonhoa v Court of Appeals* case, opined that even if there was indeed a fortuitous event, the petitioner chose the wrong remedy—reformation of contract[38]— and should have availed herself of rescission 'in order that the court could release her from performing her obligation under [Articles] 1266 and 1267 of the Civil Code'.[39]

Justice Reyes posits that the statutory adoption of the principle of *rebus sic stantibus* or the basis-of-transaction doctrine is only an expansion of the exonerative rule dealing with fortuitous events 'but projected from the sphere of physical or legal impossibility into the

[31] Paras (n 25) 445.

[32] *Iloilo Jar Corporation v Comglasco Corporation/Aguila Glass* [2017] GR No 219509. See also *Comglasco Corporation/Aguila Glass v Santos Car Check Center Corporation* [2015] GR No 202989; *Lepanto Ceramics, Inc v Lepanto Ceramics Employees Association* [2010] GR No 180866.

[33] *Philippine National Construction Corporation v Court of Appeals* [1997] GR No 116896.

[34] *Occeña v Jabson* (n 24).

[35] *Magat Jr v Court of Appeals* [2000] GR No 124221.

[36] Balane (n 16) 405.

[37] *Osmeña III v Social Security System of the Philippines* [2007] GR No 165272.

[38] The reformation of a contract is a remedy rooted in equity but also expressly provided for in the Civil Code, to wit:

> Article 1359. When, there having been a meeting of the minds of the parties to a contract, their true intention is not expressed in the instrument purporting to embody the agreement, by reason of mistake, fraud, inequitable conduct or accident, one of the parties may ask for the reformation of the instrument to the end that such true intention may be expressed.

According to the Supreme Court in *Banico v Stager* [2020] GR No 232825, citing *Makati Tuscany Condominium Corp v Multi-Realty Dev't Corp* [2018] GR No 185530 and *Toyota Motor Philippines Corporation v Court of Appeals* [1992] GR No 102881, 'in an action for reformation, the court does not attempt to make another contract for the parties but the instrument is made or construed to express or conform to their real intention'. For further information, see MAC Dizon, 'Contract Terms in the Philippines: Incorporation, Interpretation, Implication, and Unfair Terms' in M Chen-Wishart and S Vogenauer (eds), *Studies in the Contract Laws of Asia, vol III: Contents of Contracts and Unfair Terms* (OUP 2017) 308, 328–31.

[39] *Huibonhoa v Court of Appeals* [1999] GR No 95897.

field of practical and economic impossibility', which may account for the intimate link between articles dealing with both fortuitous events and supervening (but not necessarily fortuitous) events that result in a change of circumstances.[40]

(2) Scope of Article 1267

There exists a school of thought which posits that, since Article 1267 of the Civil Code speaks of a 'service', real obligations with a prestation to give—such as cases involving the delivery of a determinate thing[41] or to pay rentals[42]— are not within its reach.[43] In the latest case, decided in 2017, where Article 1267 was invoked, this is in fact the position that the Supreme Court takes:

> To evade responsibility, Comglasco explained that by virtue of Article 1267, it was released from the lease contract. It cited the existing global and regional economic crisis for its inability to comply with its obligation.
> Comglasco's position fails to impress because Article 1267 applies only to obligations to do and not to obligations to give. . . .
> Considering that Comglasco's obligation of paying rent is not an obligation to do, it could not rightfully invoke Article 1267 of the Civil Code. Even so, its position is still without merit as financial struggles due to an economic crisis is not enough reason for the courts to grant reprieve from contractual obligations.[44]

However, because of a few cases of note where the Supreme Court did grant reprieve, there is also the view that, while Article 1267 employs the term 'service', when one takes into account the reasons behind its enactment, it should be understood to refer to the 'performance' of any kind of obligation, that the Article's operation is not confined solely to obligations to do.[45]

The 1994 case of *Naga Telephone Co, Inc (NATELCO) v Court of Appeals*, decided *en banc*, is central to this stance. NATELCO was a telephone company rendering telephone services in Naga City, while Camarines Sur II Electric Cooperative, Inc (CASURECO II) was a corporation operating electric power services. They entered into a contract in 1977 for the use by NATELCO of CASURECO's electric light posts. In consideration therefore, NATELCO agreed to install, free of charge, ten telephone connections for the use by CASURECO. After ten years, CASURECO filed an action for reformation of the contract with damages on the grounds that, inter alia, it was too one-sided in favour of NATELCO and that after more than a decade of NATELCO's use, the cables strung by them on the posts had become much heavier with the rise in subscribers, worsened by the fact that their employees bore holes through the posts, which weakened the latter during typhoons. The court of first instance observed that the contract had indeed become unfair to CASURECO because of subsequent events, even if it had been fair to both parties at perfection. The trial

[40] Reyes (n 10) 70.
[41] *Development Bank of the Philippines v Clarges Realty Corporation* [2016] GR No 170060.
[42] *Iloilo Jar v Comglasco* (n 32).
[43] Paras (n 25) 444.
[44] *Iloilo Jar v Comglasco* (n 32).
[45] Jurado (n 26) 296; Balane (n 16) 420. See also RE Agpalo, *Obligations and Contracts* (Rex Book Store 2008) 222.

court concluded that, while it could not, strictly speaking, make another contract for the parties in an action for reformation, it could order that the contract be reformed to abolish the inequities therein, for reasons of justice and equity. The Court of Appeals affirmed this, albeit on different grounds, one of which was that Article 1267 was supposedly applicable to afford CASURECO relief. NATELCO went to the Supreme Court disputing this as the contract did not involve the rendition of a service or a personal prestation, nor was it for a future service with future unusual change.[46] The Supreme Court, however, ruled in favour of the article's application, thus:

> Article 1267 speaks of 'service' which has become so difficult. Taking into consideration the rationale behind this provision, the term 'service' should be understood as referring to the 'performance' of the obligation. In the present case, the obligation of private respondent consists in allowing petitioners to use its posts in Naga City, which is the service contemplated in said article. Furthermore, a bare reading of this article reveals that it is not a requirement thereunder that the contract be for future service with future unusual change. According to Senator Arturo M. Tolentino, Article 1267 states in our law the doctrine of unforeseen events. This is said to be based on the discredited theory of rebus sic stantibus in public international law; under this theory, the parties stipulate in the light of certain prevailing conditions, and once these conditions cease to exist the contract also ceases to exist. Considering practical needs and the demands of equity and good faith, the disappearance of the basis of a contract gives rise to a right to relief in favour of the party prejudiced.[47]

NATELCO thus seemingly operationally defines the word 'service' in Article 1267 as having the wider sense of 'performance of obligation'. This arguably can embrace all obligations, including real ones 'to give'.[48] This position was also taken in the 2016 case of *Spouses Poon v Prime Savings Bank*,[49] where the Supreme Court, while denying the theory that the closure of a party's business was a fortuitous or an unforeseen event that rendered the lease agreement *functus officio*, conceded the presence of the second *Tagaytay Realty Co* requisite, that is, that the change makes the performance of the contract extremely difficult but not impossible:

> The law speaks of 'service'. This term should be understood as referring to the performance of an obligation or a prestation.... In a reciprocal contract such as the lease in this case, one obligation of respondent as the lessee was to pay the agreed rents for the whole contract period. It would be hard-pressed to complete the lease term since it was already out of business only three and a half years into the 10-year contract period. Without a doubt, the second and the fourth requisites mentioned above are present in this case.

It bears noting that in setting forth the *Tagaytay Realty Co* requisites, the Supreme Court does not use the word 'service' but the phrase 'performance of the contract'. Cases

[46] *Naga Telephone Co, Inc (NATELCO) v Court of Appeals* [1994] GR No 107112.
[47] ibid (emphases added).
[48] Balane (n 16) 420.
[49] *Spouses Poon v Prime Savings Bank* [2016] GR No 183794.

subsequent to *NATELCO* and *Spouses Poon*, however, reverted back to the narrow definition of service as an obligation 'to do'. Indeed, the two most recent cases to rule on Article 1267 claims do not in any manner make reference to *NATELCO*, *Tagaytay Realty Co*, or *Spouses Poon*.[50]

The foregoing notwithstanding, the Philippine Constitution of 1987 ordains that 'no doctrine or principle of law laid down by the [Supreme Court] in a decision rendered *en banc* or in division may be modified or reversed except by the [Supreme Court] sitting *en banc*'.[51] This would mean that the prevailing doctrine with respect to the coverage of Article 1267 would be the *NATELCO* case where 'service' would cover any 'performance of an obligation'.

(3) Outcome when Article 1267 is found to be germane

The other notable issue relating to Article 1267 which has been tackled by the Supreme Court is what a party is entitled to if a change of circumstances is regarded as relevant. In the case of *Occeña v Jabson*, where a property developer wanted a modification of the terms of its subdivision contract with landowners, the Supreme Court dismissed the complaint for failure to state a cause of action, ratiocinating that:

> The Civil Code authorizes the release of an obligor when the service has become so difficult as to be manifestly beyond the contemplation of the parties *but does not authorize the courts to modify or revise the subdivision contract between the parties or fix a different sharing ratio from that contractually stipulated with the force of law between the parties....* The cited article does not grant the courts this authority to remake, modify or revise the contract or to fix the division of shares between the parties as contractually stipulated with the force of law between the parties, so as to substitute its own terms for those covenanted by the parties themselves. Respondent's complaint for modification of contract manifestly has no basis in law and therefore states no cause of action.[52]

Interestingly, in the aforementioned case of *NATELCO*, the Supreme Court 'released' the obligor because the service had become so difficult as to be manifestly beyond the contemplation of the parties, but it did not stop with such release. It insisted simply that the *Occeña* ruling is not applicable in this case since, unlike the plaintiff's complaint in *Occeña*, the allegations in the instant case properly made out a cause of action under Article 1267, albeit without expressly mentioning said article. The Supreme Court declared the parties free from their correlative obligations under the contract and then added:

> However, our disposition of the present controversy does not end here. We have to take into account the possible consequences of merely releasing the parties therefrom: petitioners will remove the telephone wires/cables in the posts of private respondent, resulting in disruption of their service to the public; while private respondent, in consonance with the

[50] *Development Bank of the Philippines v Clarges* (n 41) 48. See also *Iloilo Jar v Comglasco* (n 32); *Comglasco v Santos* (n 32).

[51] Philippine Constitution of 1987, art VIII, s 4(3). See also *Firestone Ceramics v Court of Appeals* [2000] GR No 127245.

[52] *Occeña v Jabson* (n 24) (emphasis added).

> contract will return all the telephone units to petitioners, causing prejudice to its business. *We shall not allow such eventuality.*[53]

It then adopted the order of the court of first instance for NATELCO to pay CASURECO for the use of its posts and for CASURECO to pay NATELCO monthly dues for all its telephone connections. The peculiar circumstances of the case supposedly behoved the Supreme Court to exercise its *equity jurisdiction*, otherwise basic and essential services to the public would be disrupted.[54]

(b) Extraordinary inflation or deflation

Article 1250 of the Civil Code provides that:

> [i]n case an extraordinary inflation or deflation of the currency stipulated should supervene, the value of the currency at the time of the establishment of the obligation shall be the basis of payment, unless there is an agreement to the contrary.

Article 1250, in effect, states that the value—not the amount—of the currency at the time of the constitution of the contract should be used for reckoning payment in case there is extraordinary inflation or deflation, a revaluation or adjustment in value (to consider the purchasing power of the stated amount) being necessary unless the parties provided otherwise.

This provision was born of experience. When the Second World War ended, there was an inordinate number of legal contests brought about by debts and obligations contracted during the belligerent Japanese occupation of the Philippines.[55] The military war notes (derisively called 'Mickey Mouse money'[56] then) issued by the occupying force depreciated to an alarming extent towards the end of the war and became totally worthless after liberation.[57] Inflation saw the prices of basic commodities shoot up to levels still considered sky high even by today's standards.[58]

Disputes abounded regarding the proper resolution of contracts that had been entered into during the occupation and which remained unpaid after liberation, especially since the notes were no longer legal tender after the re-establishment of the Philippine government.[59] The question of how much had to be paid in Philippine currency was the subject of necessary valuation.[60]

Recalling the silence of the law then, the Code Commission years later observed that in the event of another war, the rights and obligations of creditor and debtor ought to be equitably adjusted: 'For lack of an express provision on the question, there is a great deal of uncertainty and confusion as a result of contracts entered into or payments made during the last war. It is thought that the foregoing rule provides a just solution for cases.'[61]

[53] ibid (emphasis added).
[54] *NATELCO v Court of Appeals* (n 46).
[55] Jurado (n 26) 261–63.
[56] *Cuyugan v Dizon* [1947] GR No L-208; *Aurrecoechea v Kabankalan Sugar Co, Inc* [1948] GR No L-551; *Morales v Ventanilla* [1949] GR No L-1617; *Chua Kay v Lim Chang* [1956] GR No L-5995.
[57] Tolentino (n 23) 304.
[58] Jurado (n 26) 261–63.
[59] Tolentino (n 23) 304.
[60] ibid.
[61] Balane (n 16) 354; Malolos and Martin (n 4) 132–33.

It has to be pointed out though that in the seven decades since the Civil Code took effect, there has been no instance where the Supreme Court has recognized the adjustment of any currency value under Article 1250, though not for lack of trying on the part of litigants seeking revaluation. There have been cases which reached the Supreme Court with petitioners attempting to argue for the article's application, to no avail. But there have been a few noteworthy pronouncements or observations made by the Supreme Court in the disposition of these cases.

(1) What it means to be 'extraordinary'

While the Civil Code does not expressly define what makes inflation or deflation 'extraordinary', the Supreme Court has, in a couple of cases, cited with approval the definitions proffered by legal commentators. In the case of *Filipino Pipe and Foundry Corporation v NAWASA*, the Supreme Court quoted Tolentino and stated that extraordinary inflation exists:

> when there is a decrease or increase in the purchasing power of the Philippine currency which is unusual or beyond the common fluctuation in the value of said currency, and such decrease or increase *could not have reasonably been foreseen* or was *manifestly beyond contemplation* of the parties at the time of the establishment of the obligation.[62]

The Supreme Court refused to consider the happenstance in that case as extraordinary as it was merely a decline in the peso's purchasing power or, as put by the Court, simply 'a universal trend that has not spared our country'.[63]

The Supreme Court also saw fit in the *Filipino Pipe and Foundry Corporation* case to recount what happened to the Deutschmark in the 1920s as an example of what rendered inflation 'extraordinary':

> In early 1921, the value of the German mark was 4.2 to the U.S. dollar. By May of the same year, it had stumbled to 62 to the U.S. dollar. And as prices went up rapidly, so that (sic) by October 1923, it had reached 4.2 trillion to the U.S. dollar! (Bernardo M. Villegas & Victor R. Abola, Economics, An Introduction [Third Edition]).[64]

In the case of *Hahn v Court of Appeals*, the Supreme Court outlined the meaning of extraordinary inflation or deflation of currency as 'any uncommon decrease or increase in the purchasing power of currency which the parties could not have reasonably foreseen and which has been due to war or the effects thereof, or any other unusual *force majeure* or fortuitous event'.[65]

[62] *Filipino Pipe and Foundry Corporation v National Waterworks and Sewerage Authority* [1988] GR No L-43446, citing Tolentino (n 23) 304 (emphases added).

[63] *Filipino Pipe and Foundry Corporation v National Waterworks and Sewerage Authority* (n 62).

[64] ibid.

[65] *Hahn v Court of Appeals* [1989] GR No 55372.

(2) Elements of Article 1250

Cases have made pronouncements on the parameters of Article 1250's application. *Equitable PCI Bank v Ng* recapitulated what the Supreme Court felt was needed to be shown for extraordinary inflation or deflation to affect an obligation:

1. '[T]hat the obligation was contractual in nature';
2. 'that there was an official declaration of extraordinary inflation or deflation from the [Central Bank of the Philippines (Bangko Sentral ng Pilipinas or 'BSP')]'; and
3. 'that the parties expressly agreed to consider the effects of the extraordinary inflation or deflation'.[66]

That the article only applies to contractual obligations, not extra-contractual ones, is a view that is shared by commentators and which has been upheld by the Supreme Court in a number of cases.[67] It does not apply to damages arising from torts or from other sources of obligation, such as the government's exercise of the power of eminent domain (ie the taking of private property for public use after paying just compensation). In the case of *Velasco v Manila Electric Co*, which involved a tort claim, the Supreme Court seized on the text of the provision to support the proposition that this only applies to contracts and that the usage of the words 'currency stipulated' meant obligations where a particular currency has been identified by mutual agreement as the medium of payment.[68]

Equitable PCI's requirement of an official government declaration for the article to be operative is also a reiteration of earlier pronouncements such as that in *Commissioner v Burgos*, where Acting Chief Justice Claudio Teehankee concurred in the result but admonished that the applicability of Article 1250 should be considered mere *obiter* since it may not be invoked without a proper declaration by competent authorities.[69] In the case of *Huibonhoa*, the Supreme Court said that for Huibonhoa to escape liability by reason of a fortuitous event, she must prove that inflation was the sole and proximate cause of the loss or destruction of the contract (or in this case, the delay in constructing a building).[70]

This is a fair and reasonable condition. However, this case also lamented that Huibonhoa 'even failed to prove by evidence, documentary or testimonial, that there was an extraordinary inflation from July 1983 to February 1984', making it seem that the petitioner did not just need to show the role extraordinary inflation played in her particular case but must also prove its actual occurrence. In another case, the Supreme Court also declared that supervening extraordinary inflation or deflation is never assumed; and that it requires the party petitioning for Article 1250 to provide the factual basis for its application.[71] It is, however, posited that there is no need for a case-to-case establishment of the supervening extraordinary inflation or deflation since an official government declaration must have been

[66] *Equitable PCI Bank v Ng* [2007] GR No 171545.

[67] Balane (n 16) 355. See also *Nepomuceno v City of Surigao* [2008] GR No 146091; *Commissioner of Public Highways v Burgos* [1980] GR No L-36706.

[68] *Velasco v Manila Electric Co* [1971] GR No L-18390.

[69] *Commissioner of Public Highways v Burgos* (n 67): Justice Teehankee's concurring opinion. See also *Telengtan Brothers and Sons v United States Lines, Inc* [2006] GR No 132284.

[70] *Huibonhoa v Court of Appeals* (n 39).

[71] HS de Leon and HM de Leon Jr, *Comments and Cases on Obligations and Contracts* (Rex Book Store 2014) 342, citing *Singson v Caltex Philippines, Inc* [2000] GR No 137798.

issued for the article to apply in the first place and the courts can take judicial notice of such declaration.

Moreover, the final requisite of an express agreement to consider the effects of the extraordinary inflation or deflation is admittedly confusing, and the Supreme Court's observations in the few cases that dealt with Article 1250 have not been very edifying.

In *Equitable PCI*, a case which involved dollar-denominated loans and the question of what date's exchange rate ought to prevail, the Supreme Court denied application of the article and said, inter alia, that there was no agreement in the contract to recognize the effect of any extraordinary inflation and that there did not appear to be any stipulation either in the promissory note or loan agreement.[72]

In a slightly earlier case, *Telengtan Brothers and Sons v United States Lines, Inc*, one of the parties contended that judicial notice must be taken of succeeding devaluations of the peso against the dollar, 'tantamount to an extraordinary inflation'.[73] The Supreme Court observed that:

> Lest it be overlooked, Article 1250 of the Code, as couched, clearly provides that the value of the peso at the time of the establishment of the obligation shall control and be the basis of payment of the contractual obligation, unless there is '*agreement to the contrary*.' It is only when there is a contrary agreement that extraordinary inflation will make the value of the currency at the time of payment, not at the time of the establishment of obligation, the basis for payment.

This would have been enough, but the Supreme Court also saw fit to hark back to the case of *Mobil Oil Philippines, Inc v Court of Appeals*, which was unclear in its language:

> The Supreme Court, in [the *Mobil Oil Philippines, Inc* case], formulated the same rule in the following wise:
>
> In other words, an agreement is needed for the effects of an extraordinary inflation to be taken into account to alter the value of the currency at the time of the establishment of the obligation which, as a rule, is always the determinative element, to be varied by agreement that would find reason only in the supervention of extraordinary inflation or deflation.[74]

Citing these cases, a few authors have taken this to mean that for extraordinary inflation or deflation to affect an obligation, the parties must stipulate and agree to recognize the effects of such supervening event.[75] Otherwise, the value at the time of payment controls.

The majority of commentators, however, hew to the arguably better view that under Article 1250, should there be established an extraordinary inflation or deflation, the basis for payment is the value at the time the obligation was incurred, unless there is a contrary agreement.[76]

[72] *Equitable PCI v Ng* (n 66).
[73] *Telengtan Brothers v United States Lines* (n 69).
[74] ibid. See *Mobil Oil Philippines, Inc v Court of Appeals* [1989] GR No L-58122.
[75] Rabuya (n 17) 265–66. See also de Leon and de Leon Jr (n 71) 327.
[76] Paras (n 25) 402; Balane (n 16) 361.

(3) The actual situation: A non-operational provision

Rather than requiring that the parties expressly agree to consider the effects of the extraordinary inflation or deflation, perhaps the better interpretation is that Article 1250 of the Civil Code will necessitate a revaluation or adjustment when certain requisites apply, including that 'there exists no stipulation to the contrary'.[77] It is when the parties do not want the value of the currency at the time of the establishment of the obligation as the basis of payment that they should expressly stipulate on another basis.[78]

As mentioned, however, Article 1250 has never been rendered operational. Indeed, it would appear that it would take a war or an equally disastrous economic event to trigger its application. Moreover, Tolentino believes that even without Article 1250's express inclusion in the Code, the solution would remain the same:[79]

> To determine payment when there has been great fluctuation in the value of currency, we can resort, considering the circumstances of each particular case, to the principle of *good faith*. . . .
>
> Debts in money, in case of inflation, or devaluation of currency, are considered as *debts of value*. . . . When the currency is devalued in terms beyond what could have been reasonably foreseen by the parties, *the doctrine of unforeseen risks can be applied*, and the effects of the devaluation should not be borne by the creditor alone. The revaluation of the credit in such cases must be made, according to the principles of *good faith* and in view of the circumstances of each particular case, recognizing the real value of the credit as in consonance with the intent of the parties.[80]

The extraordinariness of the inflation or deflation, if it has resulted in difficulty of performance manifestly beyond the contemplation of the parties, could also arguably be considered as falling within the purview of Article 1267.

IV. The Hypotheticals

1. Abraham and Bill

In 1567, Abraham enters into a contract for an unlimited period of time with farmer Bill under which Abraham promises to build and maintain an irrigation channel from which Bill may extract water at a fixed price. By 2018, inflation and the rise in the cost of maintenance and labour have made the price wholly inadequate. Abraham's successors in law ask for an increase in the price that would provide them with adequate compensation. Alternatively, they wish to terminate the contract.[81]

It can be argued that the price cannot be increased without Bill's (or his heirs') consent. The agreement on the fixed price is binding upon the parties, and the rise in the cost

[77] Vitug (n 26) 77.

[78] EL Pineda, *Obligations and Contracts* (Central Book Supply Inc 2009) 250.

[79] Tolentino (n 23) 303–04.

[80] ibid (emphases added).

[81] The fact scenarios of this and the other hypothetical situations discussed in this section are taken from M Chen-Wishart, D Neo, and S Vogenauer, 'Introduction', ch 1 in this volume, 7–8.

of maintenance and labour would not justify any unilateral increase of the agreed price. Abraham and his successors would be presumed to have assumed the risk of unfavourable developments.

While Abraham's successors might be able to make a case under Article 1267 of the Civil Code, it bears noting that mere inconvenience, unexpected impediments, increased expenses, or even pecuniary inability to fulfil an engagement will not relieve the obligor from an undertaking that it has knowingly and freely contracted. They will need to show that conditions are radically and drastically altered beyond contemplation and that it is extremely difficult for them to maintain the upkeep.

Abraham's successors can also make a case that even if a period was not fixed, the circumstances are such that a period was intended, and consequently they can go to court and have the latter fix the duration thereof. This is allowed by Article 1197 of the Civil Code, which directs the court in such cases to determine the period as may have been contemplated by the parties.[82]

2. Citi Corporation and Drive Bank

In 2015, Citi Corporation receives a loan from Drive Bank. The interest rate is fixed at 10 per cent for five years. In the 20 years preceding the agreement, the rate of inflation had been relatively stable within a range of 1 to 6 per cent. In 2017, the economic situation begins to destabilize and inflation rises to 50 per cent. Drive Bank requests adjustment or, alternatively, termination of the contract.

The supervening inflation would not justify any upward adjustment of the agreed price or stipulated interest rates. Article 1250 could potentially be at play but unless the requisites are present (eg the official declaration of extraordinary inflation), there can be no relief for Drive Bank under this article. Article 1267 may also not be appropriate here as this only involves a loan agreement which is being met by the borrower. Drive Bank may have to bear the loss of what turned out to be a bad bargain unless it included a clause on material adverse change in the loan contract.

3. Easy and Frugle

Easy leases business premises from Frugle for a fixed period of 15 years. Shortly after the contract has been concluded, a nearby military airport is unexpectedly shut down for political reasons. The government invests an enormous amount of public funds in order to improve the commercial infrastructure in the area. As a result, Easy's profits are 500 per cent of what could reasonably have been expected at the time of making the contract. At the same time, the rental value of comparable business premises in the area rises to 500 per cent of

[82] Civil Code, art 1197:

> If the obligation does not fix a period, but from its nature and the circumstances it can be inferred that a period was intended, the courts may fix the duration thereof.
> The courts shall also fix the duration of the period when it depends upon the will of the debtor.
> In every case, the courts shall determine such period as may under the circumstances have been probably contemplated by the parties. Once fixed by the courts, the period cannot be changed by them.

the agreed rental price. Frugle requests that the rental price should be adjusted accordingly or, alternatively, that the agreement should be terminated.

The lease contract will not be terminated nor the price adjusted. The agreement on the rental price is binding upon the parties. It does not appear that the supervening events have made it manifestly difficult for either party to fulfil their contractual obligations, which therefore makes Article 1267 inapplicable here. In *Ledesma v Javellana*, the Supreme Court declined to modify the terms of the renewal of a contract despite the lessor's claim that renewing it at the same price would cause injustice due to the change in existing economic conditions. The Supreme Court sympathized with the situation but observed that it was 'unable to remedy what turned out to be a bad bargain in which they had entered into [*sic*]'.[83]

4. George and Han

Builder George agrees to refurbish the cellar of Han, the owner of a restaurant. The work is scheduled to start one month after the agreement. Before the work begins, the restaurant is completely destroyed by a storm that is much more violent than any other previous storm in the region. However, the cellar remains fully intact. Han immediately informs George of the situation and asks him not to start work. George insists on rendering performance because he has set aside two weeks to carry out the work and has already purchased the necessary materials. Is Han required to pay the contract price or, alternatively, to compensate George for his loss?

Han would have to bear the loss in this case. In order that fortuitous events may relieve obligors of their obligations, it must be established that the event rendered it impossible for the obligors to perform their obligations in the normal manner. The object of the contract here is the refurbishment of the cellar, which does not appear to have been affected or destroyed by the storm. Han cannot cite the destruction of the restaurant as basis for refusing to pay George. Han's obligation here is to deliver a generic thing (ie money), which would not be extinguished by the loss or destruction of the restaurant, there being no stipulation or agreement between the parties that the payment for George's services would be sourced from the revenues of Han's restaurant business. As between the two, Han should bear the loss.

5. Gina and H Hotel

Gina books a room for the weekend at H Hotel in X City, the capital of country Z. However,

(i) the exhibition she intended to visit is cancelled at the very last moment;
(ii) a terrorist group declares that it is to launch attacks on tourists in X;
(iii) an unforeseeable strike by airport personnel prevents Gina from travelling to X before Sunday afternoon;

[83] *Ledesma v Javellana* [1983] GR No L-55187.

(iv) the inauguration proceedings of the new head of state of Z that were scheduled for Saturday are cancelled. Gina had booked a room overlooking the street where the inauguration procession was supposed to pass by. Due to the inauguration, the rental price of the room was ten times higher than the regular price.

Can Gina cancel the booking?

Gina bears the loss resulting from the three first incidents. These are all unfortunate but between the two parties, where the state of affairs is not due to the acts of the other party, Gina bears the loss. However, she may be able to make an argument for cancellation in the case of the inauguration. She may justify cancelling her hotel booking if she is able to establish that she booked accommodations at H Hotel primarily so that she could view the inauguration proceedings (which is why she agreed to pay a higher rental price) and that H Hotel, in charging higher rentals, was aware of this. Under these circumstances, Gina would be able to argue that her motive determined the 'cause' of her contract with H Hotel such that the negation of the motive resulted in the negation of the 'cause' for the contract.

In a few cases, the Supreme Court has conceded that the motive of the parties may be regarded as *causa* when it predetermines the purpose of the contract.[84] In *Uy v Court of Appeals*, a case that saw the National Housing Authority (NHA) cancelling a contract over lands that were found not suitable for housing, the Supreme Court said that quality of the land was an implied condition for the NHA to enter into the contract. On the part of the NHA, therefore, the motive was the cause for its being a party to the sale. Accordingly, the Supreme Court held that the NHA was justified in cancelling the contract.[85]

6. Kris and Leila

Kris sells his family home to Leila at 70 per cent of its market value. Both parties assume that Leila will dedicate it to cultural use by the general public. However, this assumption is not expressly set out in the contract. After the sale, Leila changes her mind and gives the house to one of her sons instead. Can Kris claim the difference between the agreed price and the market value or, alternatively, restitution of the house?

Kris can neither claim the difference between the agreed price and the market value of the family home nor demand the restitution of the house on account of Leila's supposed breach of the 'assumed' condition. When the terms of a written contract are clear and leave no doubt upon the intention of the parties, the literal meaning of its stipulations shall control. Here, the condition that Leila would dedicate the house to cultural use is not expressly provided in the contract and thus, it is not likely that Philippine courts would give effect to this alleged condition, especially if Leila denies that this condition was ever agreed or formed a material part of the contract. Furthermore, the inadequacy of the agreed price would not affect a contract, except as it may indicate a defect in consent.

84 *Liguez v Court of Appeals* [1957] GR No L-11240.
85 *Uy v Court of Appeals* [1999] GR No 120465.

V. Sanctioned Revisions and a Partiality for Parity

While the responses given to the hypotheticals above—which for the most part lean towards the parties not being able to find relief—are objective and probable given the state of the positive law, it is also noteworthy that the Civil Code can be said to show a bias, if you will, for the principle that there should ideally be a balance between the prestations such that when equilibrium is lost through *force majeure* or unforeseen events, justice and equity demand the chance for relief.[86]

There are provisions—some already discussed at length—that allow equitable revision or modification of contracts through judicial relief. Some Civil Code provisions which allow for such alterations or modifications include (emphases added):

> Article 1191. The power to rescind obligations is implied in reciprocal ones, in case one of the obligors should not comply with what is incumbent upon him.
>
> The injured party may choose between the fulfillment and the rescission of the obligation, with the payment of damages in either case. He may also seek rescission, even after he has chosen fulfillment, if the latter should become impossible.
>
> *The court shall decree the rescission claimed, unless there be just cause authorizing the fixing of a period.*
>
> This is understood to be without prejudice to the rights of third persons who have acquired the thing, in accordance with articles 1385 and 1388 and the Mortgage Law.
>
> Article 1229. The judge shall *equitably reduce the penalty* when the principal obligation has been partly or irregularly complied with by the debtor. Even if there has been no performance, the penalty may also be *reduced by the courts if it is iniquitous or unconscionable.*[87]
>
> Article 1469. In order that the price may be considered certain, it shall be sufficient that it be so with reference to another thing certain, or that the determination thereof be left to the judgment of a special person or persons.
>
> Should such person or persons be unable or unwilling to fix it, the contract shall be inefficacious, unless the parties subsequently agree upon the price.
>
> *If the third person or persons acted in bad faith or by mistake, the courts may fix the price.*
>
> Where such third person or persons are prevented from fixing the price or terms by fault of the seller or the buyer, the party not in fault may have such remedies against the party in fault as are allowed the seller or the buyer, as the case may be.[88]

Moreover, as previously discussed, Article 1250 will alter the basis of payment. Case law on Article 1267, *NATELCO v Court of Appeals* to be specific, has shown that, while it only speaks of 'release' and not modification, courts can provide for relief akin to modification in the exercise of their equitable jurisdiction. Indeed, Justice Reyes had already expressed dissatisfaction with the Supreme Court's resolution of the *Occeña* case:[89]

86 Reyes (n 10) 73.

87 This is a provision under the Civil Code's Section on 'Obligations with a Penal Clause'.

88 This is a provision under the Title on 'Sales'.

89 *Occeña v Jabson* (n 24), where the Supreme Court said that art 1267 'does not grant the courts this authority to remake, modify or revise the contract or to fix the division of shares between the parties as contractually stipulated with the force of law between the parties, so as to substitute its own terms for those covenanted by the parties themselves'.

> Considering that the other Articles of the Code empower the courts to 'equitably reduce' penal clauses (Art. 1229) and liquidated damages (Art. 2227) even if stipulated, 'if iniquitous or unconscionable'; and to regulate rentals of rural lands under the provisions of Article 1680, why could not the [Supreme] Court also determine [in the *Occeña* case] if the landowner's share in the price of the lots to be sold had become 'iniquitous and unconscionable' under the new circumstances and if so, order it reduced to a just proportion that would be in consonance with equity and good faith?[90]

VI. Conclusion

As pointed out at the beginning of this chapter, the fundamental rule under Philippine law is still the tenet that the provisions of a contract have the force of law and must be complied with in good faith. Most contracts drawn up in modern transactions would invariably have clauses that cover *force majeure* and material adverse changes as well as clauses that provide for sanctions in case of breach. Experienced contract lawyers would ensure that *force majeure* clauses are operationally defined as comprehensively—and narrowly drawn—as possible to the extent that it can be done within the limits and requisites already provided by statutory and case law.[91]

Penalty clauses are also widely used and are regulated by a few provisions in the Civil Code, the most important one being Article 1226, the first paragraph of which provides:

> Article 1226. In obligations with a penal clause, the penalty shall substitute the indemnity for damages and the payment of interests in case of noncompliance, if there is no stipulation to the contrary. Nevertheless, damages shall be paid if the obligor refuses to pay the penalty or is guilty of fraud in the fulfillment of the obligation.

Most cases reaching the courts on penal clauses deal with either the factual issue of breach or the possibility of cutting the contracted liquidated damages since Article 1229 of the Civil Code allows judges discretion for the equitable reduction of the penalty when (i) 'the principal obligation has been partly or irregularly complied with' or (ii) 'it is iniquitous or unconscionable'.

If there were no provisions for fortuitous events and penal clauses, then the doctrine of frustration of enterprise would possibly be more utilized in disputes. The paucity of cases reaching the Supreme Court in reliance on Articles 1250 and 1267 may very well be due in part to the accepted constraints of the principle that contracts have the force of law as between parties.

It is true that Article 1250 of the Civil Code has never been successfully pleaded in any case, that less than one-quarter of all Article 1267 cases reaching the Supreme Court since the Civil Code was enacted into law were argued successfully, and that the last time that happened was nearly two decades ago. However, the state of Philippine contract law and jurisprudence—viewed as a whole—as well as the arc followed by case law and the language of the Supreme Court in its decisions on relevant cases shows that it has come a long way from the uncompromising tenor of pre-1950 *Reyes v Caltex*.

[90] Reyes (n 10) 84.
[91] Civil Code, art 1174; *Juan F Nakpil & Sons v Court of Appeals* [1986] GR No L-47851.

As shown earlier, the Civil Code has numerous provisions that allow for judicial resolution and relief in the interest of justice and equity. Indeed, as Justice Reyes has pointed out,

> the Civil Code, more than its predecessor, the Spanish Code of 1889, leans in favour of the recognition of the principle that onerous contracts establish an equilibrium of proportionality (not necessarily an equality) between the respective prestations of the parties and when such contemplated equilibrium is lost by fortuitous causes, the debtor should, in justice, be entitled to relief.[92]

In addition, for better or worse, Philippine courts have not shown themselves totally averse to the exercise of equity jurisdiction and do so supposedly 'to prevent unjust enrichment and to ensure restitution'.[93] An oft quoted definition in cases where such jurisdiction is called into play is as follows:

> Equity jurisdiction aims to do complete justice in cases where a court of law is unable to adapt its judgments to the special circumstances of a case because of the inflexibility of its statutory or legal jurisdiction. Equity is the principle by which substantial justice may be attained in cases where the prescribed or customary forms of ordinary law are inadequate.[94]

The Supreme Court itself has had the occasion to exercise such jurisdiction. In *Agcaoili v Government Service Insurance System*, where it ordered a contract modified, it declared that it may 'adjust the rights of parties in accordance with the circumstances obtaining at the time of rendition of judgment, when these are significantly different from those existing at the time of generation of those rights' and pronounced that such adjustment was entirely consistent with the principle that 'in the exercise of rights, a person must act with justice, give everyone his due, and observe honesty and good faith'.[95]

Indeed, even the prevailing *en banc* decision involving Article 1267, the *NATELCO* case, is one where the Supreme Court exercised equity jurisdiction. Because of this, one can venture an opinion that a change of circumstances that results in unfair disparity between contracting parties can trigger the possibility of invoking the courts' equity jurisdiction, in addition to the legal remedies that are covered by positive law.

Be that as it may, it bears pointing out that Philippine contract law is still fundamentally of the civil law tradition and codified. The function of equity should be supplementary when there is remedial inadequacy on the part of positive law. It cannot violate statutory directives, nor can it create causes or rights of action. Too much reliance on equity jurisdiction can be unsettling and can undercut reliance on conventional contracts.

A balance must therefore be struck on this matter and prudence exercised by the courts when modifying or altering contractual agreements in light of extreme change of circumstances. Ideally, clarificatory measures and parameters for the application and treatment of the relevant provisions should be legislated and made part of positive law, not the subject of judicial legislation.

[92] Reyes (n 10) 73.

[93] *Reyes v Lim* (n 11); *Regulus Development, Inc v Antonio dela Cruz* [2016] GR No 198172.

[94] *Reyes v Lim* (n 11). See also *Enrile v Sandiganbayan* [2016] GR No 213847; *Viva Shipping Lines, Inc v Keppel Philippines Mining, Inc* [2016] GR No 177382.

[95] *Agcaoili v Government Service Insurance System* (n 11) citing Civil Code, art 19.

19

Rescission of Contracts in the Philippines

Ending Performance and Extinguishing Obligations

Michael Anthony C DIZON

I. Introduction

There are a number of express causes for ending contracts and extinguishing obligations under Philippine contract law. Rescission for breach of contract is one of them. Rescission of a contract is an available remedy when there has been a substantial breach or non-performance of a reciprocal obligation. Reciprocal obligations are those that arise from the same cause and are correlative of each other.

The injured (or aggrieved) party (ie the party who is not in breach and is ready to comply with his or her obligation) may choose between the alternative remedies of rescission or specific performance and claim damages in either case. This party may also waive the right to rescind. In case of rescission, the guilty party may be liable for damages, including actual, moral, nominal, temperate, liquidated, or exemplary damages. Good faith on the part of the guilty party may help limit or reduce the amount of the damages awarded.

An action for rescission may be carried out extrajudicially or judicially. Since the power of rescission is implied in reciprocal obligations, a party may extrajudicially rescind a contract even though there is no express stipulation granting such right in the contract. While judicial action is not required to rescind a contract, a party can go to court to either enforce or question the validity of a rescission. If or when the matter is brought before it, the court has the ultimate authority to decide whether rescission is proper. The court may even grant the guilty party a period to perform his or her obligation. However, the fixing of a grace period will only be allowed when there is just cause or under exceptional circumstances. A grace period will generally not be permitted when there has been a substantial breach of an essential term or condition of the contract that defeats its object.

When rescinding a contract, the injured party must give notice to the other party. Notice is necessary because it informs the parties of the extinction, or as the Civil Code of the Philippines (Civil Code) calls it, the 'extinguishment' of their obligations, and it determines when rescission takes effect. Rescission has a retroactive effect and abrogates the entire contract from the very beginning (ie from the moment of perfection). This is in accord with the principal aim of rescission, which is to restore the parties to their original status or position before they entered into the contract. As a natural consequence of this, the parties are subject to the obligation of mutual restitution for all of the property, rights, and benefits they received from the contract.

Michael Anthony C Dizon, *Rescission of Contracts in the Philippines* In: *Studies in the Contract Laws of Asia V: Ending and Changing Contracts*. Edited by: Mindy Chen-Wishart, Dora Neo, and Stefan Vogenauer, Oxford University Press.
 DOI: 10.1093/oso/9780198995814.003.0019

II. Ending Contracts

1. Grounds for Extinguishing Obligations

Under Philippine law, an obligation is 'a juridical necessity to give, to do or not to do'.[1] One of the five sources of obligations is contract.[2] A contract is defined as 'a meeting of minds between two persons whereby one binds himself, with respect to the other, to give something or to render some service'.[3] With regard to obligations arising from contracts, the Civil Code provides that they 'have the force of law between the contracting parties and should be complied with in good faith'.[4] Furthermore, 'the contract must bind both contracting parties; its validity or compliance cannot be left to the will of one of them', following the principle of mutuality of contract.[5] As explained by Tolentino, a contract's binding effect is founded on two principles: (i) 'obligations arising from contract have the force of law between the contracting parties' and (ii) 'mutuality between the parties based on their essential equality'.[6]

Compliance with or fulfilment by a contracting party of his or her obligation under a contract (eg 'by payment or performance') is one of the grounds for extinguishing obligations.[7] The opposite is also true. A party's breach or non-performance of the contract may also serve as a basis to extinguish obligations. As stated in Article 1231 of the Civil Code, rescission is one of the '[o]ther causes of extinguishment of obligations', aside from loss of the thing due; 'condonation' (or 'remission') of the debt; confusion or merger of the rights of obligee ('creditor') and obligor ('debtor'); compensation; novation; annulment; fulfilment of a resolutory condition; and prescription.[8] It should be noted that the list of enumerated grounds for extinguishing obligations under Article 1231 is not exclusive and there are other causes found in other parts of the Civil Code as well as in the case law (eg death of a party, mutual dissent, etc).[9]

Under Philippine law, a principal remedy for a breach or non-performance of an obligation is the rescission of the contract by the injured or innocent party. The general principles and rules on rescission of contracts are contained in Article 1191 of the Civil Code:

> The power to rescind obligations is implied in reciprocal ones, in case one of the obligors should not comply with what is incumbent upon him.
> The injured party may choose between the fulfillment and the rescission of the obligation, with the payment of damages in either case. He may also seek rescission, even after he has chosen fulfillment, if the latter should become impossible.

1 Civil Code, art 1156.
2 ibid art 1157 (the others being law, quasi-contracts, crimes or delicts, and quasi-delicts or torts).
3 ibid art 1305.
4 ibid art 1159.
5 ibid art 1308.
6 AM Tolentino, *Commentaries and Jurisprudence on the Civil Code of the Philippines, vol 4* (Central Lawbook Publishing Co 1987) 424. See also RF Balane, *Jottings and Jurisprudence in Civil Law (Obligations and Contracts)* (Central Book Supply 2018) 526.
7 Civil Code, art 1231(1).
8 ibid art 1231.
9 Balane (n 6) 302 and 308. See also HS de Leon and HM de Leon, Jr, *Comments and Cases on Obligations and Contracts* (Rex Book Store 2014) 295–96.

> The court shall decree the rescission claimed, unless there be just cause authorizing the fixing of a period.

Aside from Article 1191 and other relevant articles discussed below, there are no other detailed or specific rules under Philippine law on whether certain types of breaches or non-performance entitle a party to rescind a contract. The primary focus of this chapter is the rescission of contracts based on a party's breach or non-performance of his or her reciprocal obligations.

2. Rescission Contrasted with Termination

There are important distinctions between rescission and termination of a contract. The Supreme Court has noted that it is 'not unmindful of the fact that termination and rescission are terms that have been used loosely and interchangeably in the past. But distinctions ought to be made . . . [since] the terms mean differently and lead to equally different consequences.'[10] Rescission has been 'defined as the "unmaking of a contract, or its *undoing from the beginning, and not merely its termination*"', whereas termination 'refers to an "end in time or existence; a close, cessation or conclusion"'.[11] The basis for rescission is breach or non-performance of a reciprocal obligation, while termination can be based on other grounds such as novation, death of a party, or prescription. In terms of effect, the Supreme Court has held that 'rescission does not merely terminate the contract and release the parties from further obligations to each other, but abrogates the contract from its inception and restores the parties to their original positions as if no contract has been made'.[12] In contrast, when a contract is 'terminated, it is deemed valid at its inception. Prior to termination the contract binds the parties who are thus obliged to observe its provisions.'[13] The Supreme Court has also ruled that, unlike rescission,

> the parties in a case of termination are not restored to their original situation; neither is the contract treated as if it never existed. Prior to its termination, the parties are obliged to comply with their contractual obligations. Only *after* the contract has been cancelled will they be released from their obligations.[14]

With termination, a contract exists from the time of its perfection until it is terminated or ended. Any vested rights or benefits received by the parties under the contract are not affected by or before the termination. A party can therefore seek to enforce existing or demandable rights under the contract regardless of its cancellation (eg forfeiture of deposit). The Supreme Court explains that, as a result,

[10] *Pryce Corporation v Philippine Amusement and Gaming Corporation*, GR No 157480 (6 May 2005). See also de Leon and de Leon, Jr (n 9) 184.
[11] de Leon and de Leon, Jr (n 9) 184.
[12] *Gotesco Properties v Spouses Fajardo*, GR No 201167 (27 February 2013).
[13] de Leon and de Leon, Jr (n 9) 185.
[14] *Pryce Corporation v Philippine Amusement and Gaming Corporation* (n 10).

> [t]he termination or cancellation of a contract would necessarily entail enforcement of its terms prior to the declaration of its cancellation in the same way that before a lessee is ejected under a lease contract, he has to fulfill his obligations thereunder that had accrued prior to his ejectment.[15]

This is in contrast with rescission, where the contract is extinguished from the very beginning and any property or benefits obtained from the rescinded contract must be returned by the parties pursuant to the obligation of mutual restitution.

With regard to the nature of a rescinded contract, the Supreme Court has said:

> To rescind is to declare a contract *void* at its inception and to put an end to it as though it never was. It is not merely to terminate it and release the parties from further obligations to each other, but to abrogate it from the beginning and restore the parties to their relative positions as if no contract has been made.[16]

It should be noted that despite the mention of the word 'void' in describing the effects of rescission, a rescinded contract is not a void or inexistent contract.[17] A void contract is one where the cause or object is illegal or non-existent.[18] Balane explains that rescission:

> cancels or extinguishes the reciprocal contract. [Rescission] is a mode of extinguishment: the necessary assumption is that there was a valid contract which is abrogated by reason of unilateral breach. There was, in other words, a valid existing contract which is extinguished.[19]

Therefore, while the rescission 'of the contract has the effect of dissolving the obligation *ab initio*',[20] the rescinded contract is not itself 'inexistent or void from the beginning'.[21]

3. Rescission for Breach of Contract Distinguished from Rescissible Contracts

Although they use the same terms—'rescission' and 'rescind'—rescission due to breach or non-performance of a contract under Article 1191 is different from an action for rescission of a rescissible contract under Articles 1380–1382 of the Civil Code.[22] Rescission under Article 1191 is founded on a breach of reciprocal obligations, whereas an action to rescind a rescissible contract is based on the economic prejudice or injury suffered by a party or a third party.[23] Examples of rescissible contracts under Articles 1381 and 1382

[15] ibid.

[16] *Spouses Velarde v Court of Appeals*, GR No 108346 (11 July 2001) (emphasis added).

[17] A void contract is one of the four kinds of defective contracts. The others are voidable, unenforceable, and rescissible contracts.

[18] Civil Code, art 1409.

[19] Balane (n 6) 209.

[20] Tolentino (n 6) 184.

[21] Civil Code, art 1409.

[22] *The Wellex Group v U-Land Airlines*, GR No 167519 (14 January 2015). See also Balane (n 6) 206.

[23] Civil Code, arts 1380 and 1381. See also *Universal Food Corporation v Court of Appeals*, GR No L-29155 (13 May 1970). See also MAC Dizon and JJM Disini, 'Invalidity of Contracts in the Philippines: Grounds for

include: '[t]hose which are entered into by guardians whenever the wards whom they represent suffer lesion by more than one-fourth of the value of the things which are the object thereof', '[t]hose undertaken in fraud of creditors', '[t]hose which refer to things under litigation', and '[p]ayments made in a state of insolvency' that are not yet due.[24] Further, rescission for breach of contract under Article 1191 is a principal action, whereas an action to rescind a rescissible contract is subsidiary.[25]

It is worth noting that rescission for a breach of contract under Article 1191 could be more precisely called a 'resolution' of a contract following the original wording of the article under the prior Spanish Civil Code of 1889. Rather than using the original terms 'resolve' or 'resolution', the drafters of the Civil Code of 1949 decided to use the terms 'rescind' and 'rescission' instead. Balane considers that the 'change in terminology is unfortunate and causes unnecessary confusion' between the two disparate meanings of rescission.[26] The Supreme Court has similarly observed:

> the defective technique of the new Code that terms both instances as rescission without distinctions between them; unlike the previous Spanish Civil Code of 1889, that differentiated 'resolution' for breach of stipulations from 'rescission' by reason of *lesion or damage*.[27]

For present purposes, unless otherwise indicated, the terms 'rescind' and 'rescission' should be understood with reference to obligations being extinguished for breach of contract under Article 1191.

III. Rescission of Contracts

1. Breach or Non-performance

(a) Reciprocal obligations

The power to rescind reciprocal obligations is expressly recognized by law: '[t]he power to rescind obligations is implied in reciprocal ones, in case one of the obligors should not comply with what is incumbent upon him'.[28] This tacit or implied power exists even though the parties have not explicitly provided for it in their contracts.[29] Under this provision, the option to rescind is therefore read into every reciprocal contract: this power or right to rescind is triggered when 'one of the obligors should not comply with what is incumbent upon him'.[30] In other words, rescission is available to a contracting party when another contracting party is in breach or does not perform or fulfil his or her reciprocal obligation

Annulment Based on Defects of Intellect and Will' in M Chen-Wishart, H Sono, and S Vogenauer (eds), *Studies in the Contract Laws of Asia, vol IV: Invalidity* (OUP 2022) 323, 325–27.

[24] Civil Code, arts 1381 and 1382.
[25] Tolentino (n 6) 174 and 574.
[26] Balane (n 6) 169.
[27] *Universal Food Corporation v Court of Appeals* (n 23).
[28] Civil Code, art 1191.
[29] Tolentino (n 6) 175. See also de Leon and de Leon, Jr (n 9) 152; Balane (n 6) 170.
[30] Civil Code, art 1191.

under the contract. The power to rescind is therefore 'predicated on a breach of obligation by the other party that violates the reciprocity between them'.[31]

The Supreme Court has ruled that '[t]he breach contemplated in the said provision is the obligor's failure to comply with an existing obligation. When the obligor cannot comply with what is incumbent upon it, the obligee may seek rescission'.[32] According to de Leon and de Leon, there is a breach of obligation 'when there is a failure or refusal, by a party without legal reason or excuse to perform, in whole or in part, the obligation or undertaking which is incumbent upon him'.[33] It has been said that 'the breach or contravention of the obligation constitutes a resolutory condition the happening of which entitles the aggrieved party to set the obligation aside'.[34] Tolentino likewise believes that the breach or non-performance of one party is an 'implied or tacit resolutory condition' that serves as a ground for extinguishing the contract and its attendant obligations.[35] It is worth noting that, as has been seen above, rescission and 'fulfillment of a resolutory condition' are two of the stated grounds for extinguishing obligations under Article 1231.

It should be noted that Article 1191 only applies in cases of reciprocal obligations.[36] The Supreme Court has clarified that:

> For Article 1191 to be applicable, however, there must be reciprocal prestations as distinguished from mutual obligations between or among the parties. A prestation is the object of an obligation, and it is the conduct required by the parties to do or not to do, or to give. Parties may be mutually obligated to each other, but the prestations of these obligations are not necessarily reciprocal. The reciprocal prestations must necessarily emanate from the same cause that gave rise to the existence of the contract.[37]

The contracting parties must be 'mutually debtor and creditor of each other. . . . Both relations must arise from the same cause, such that one obligation is correlative to the other'.[38] In this way, 'the performance by one party of his [or her] obligation is designed to be the equivalent and the condition for the performance by the other of his [or] her own obligation'.[39] This is so because the reciprocity 'arise[s] from identity of cause, and necessarily the two obligations are created at the same time'.[40]

According to the Supreme Court, a loan is an example of a reciprocal obligation:

> as it arises from the same cause where one party is the creditor, and the other the debtor. The obligation of one party in a reciprocal obligation is dependent upon the obligation of the other, and the performance should ideally be simultaneous.[41]

31 de Leon and de Leon, Jr (n 9) 154.
32 *Fong v Duenas*, GR No 185592 (15 June 2015).
33 de Leon and de Leon, Jr (n 9) 155.
34 Balane (n 6) 167.
35 Tolentino (n 6) 175.
36 *Prudence Reality v Court of Appeals*, GR No 110274 (21 March 1994). See also Tolentino (n 6) 174.
37 *The Wellex Group v U-Land Airlines* (n 22).
38 Tolentino (n 6) 175. See also Balane (n 6) 168.
39 de Leon and de Leon, Jr (n 9) 152.
40 Tolentino (n 6) 175.
41 *Development Bank of the Philippines v Guariña Agricultural and Realty Development Corporation*, GR No 160758 (15 January 2014).

Tolentino is similarly of the opinion that reciprocal obligations are 'performed simultaneously, so that the performance of one [party] is conditioned upon the simultaneous fulfillment of the other'.[42] Balane, however, believes that while, '*as a general rule* ... this article applies to obligations with simultaneous reciprocal prestations', it is possible to have reciprocal obligations that do not have to be simultaneously performed.[43] He argues that 'simultaneity is not an essential element of rescission ... under this article' and cites the example of a contract of sale for goods where the payment of the purchase price is to be made a few days after delivery.[44] In case the seller fails to make the delivery on the specified date, the buyer can rescind the contract even though the obligation of the buyer to pay does not legally arise until a few days after the delivery. Balane concludes that '[t]he stipulation of the parties or the nature of the obligation may ... do away with the element of simultaneity' in relation to the performance of reciprocal obligations,[45] but this does not affect the reciprocal nature of the contract.

(b) Substantial or fundamental breach

To rescind a contract, there must be a substantial or fundamental breach. The Supreme Court has held that: '[a]s a contractual remedy, rescission is available when one of the parties substantially fails to do what he has obligated himself to perform. It aims to address the breach of faith and the violation of reciprocity between two parties in a contract.'[46] The breach must be serious because rescission 'will not be permitted for a slight or casual breach of the contract'.[47] The Supreme Court has held that 'substantial, unlike slight or casual breaches of contract, are fundamental breaches that defeat the object of the parties in entering into an agreement, since the law is not concerned with trifles'.[48] The breach or non-performance must then violate 'an essential condition of the contract as to warrant rescission for non-performance'.[49] According to de Leon and de Leon, '[t]he question of whether a breach is slight or substantial largely depends upon the attendant circumstances'.[50] The Supreme Court has ruled that a 'substantial breach of a reciprocal obligation, like failure to pay the price in the manner prescribed by the contract, entitled the injured party to rescind the obligation'.[51] On the other hand, '[w]here time is not of the essence of the agreement, a slight delay on the part of one party in the performance of his obligation is not a sufficient ground for the rescission of the agreement'.[52]

With respect to intention, the injured party has a right to rescind even though the substantial breach was committed unintentionally or negligently. The manner in which the breach is committed is not typically considered relevant by the courts. It is the fact or occurrence of the substantial breach that is controlling, albeit attendant circumstances will

42 Tolentino (n 6) 175; see *Ong v Court of Appeals*, GR No 97347 (6 July 1999).
43 Balane (n 6) 169.
44 ibid.
45 ibid: see *Solar Harvest v Davao Corrugated Carton Corporation*, GR No 176868 (26 July 2010).
46 *Fong v Duenas* (n 32).
47 Tolentino (n 6) 179.
48 *Maglasang v Northwestern University*, GR No 188986 (20 March 2013). See also Tolentino (n 6) 179; de Leon and de Leon, Jr (n 9) 174.
49 Tolentino (n 6) 180. See also *Fong v Duenas* (n 32).
50 de Leon and de Leon, Jr (n 9) 174.
51 *Spouses Velarde v Court of Appeals* (n 16).
52 de Leon and de Leon, Jr (n 9) 175.

be taken into account. Fraud, bad faith, or malice on the part of the guilty party would be relevant in providing the context of the breach as well as ascertaining the damages to be imposed (if any).[53] Whether the innocent party is a consumer or business is not normally a consideration in cases of rescission.

The requirement of substantial breach is illustrated in one of the hypothetical cases addressed in this volume.[54] Car Machinery & Co appointed Traders Ltd as its sole distributor of their car panel presses for a five-year period. A clause in the agreement required Traders Ltd to send their representatives to visit all six large car manufacturers in the country at least once every week for the purpose of soliciting orders for car panel presses. The clause also provided that '[f]ailure to comply with this obligation shall entitle Car Machinery to terminate the agreement with immediate effect'. In the second month of the contractual period, Trader Ltd missed two visits to car manufacturers. In this scenario, unless there are exceptional circumstances or just cause for Trader Ltd's non-compliance or it can show good faith and readiness to comply with its obligations, Car Machinery may rescind the agreement because Trader Ltd has committed a substantial breach. It is evident from the terms of the agreement and the relationship between the parties that weekly visits to car manufacturers by Traders Ltd was an essential term of the contract. As the exclusive distributor of Car Machinery's car panel presses, it was imperative for Traders Ltd to regularly visit car manufacturers to solicit orders. The importance of the obligation to visit the car manufacturers was further underscored in the agreement itself, which expressly states that failure to comply permits Car Machinery to cancel the agreement with immediate effect. The presence of an automatic rescission clause highlights the importance of the weekly visits to car manufacturers as this was one of the main objects of the contract.

A similar outcome would result in another of the hypothetical scenarios. Seven Seas was an importer of seafood. It agreed to sell two tons of mussels to Big Chef, a restaurant chain. Seven Seas delivered one ton of mussels, which, upon inspection, turned out to contain a concentration of cadmium (a substance toxic to humans) that was 2 per cent above the concentration permitted by national food regulations. In this situation, Big Chef is entitled to rescind the contract on the basis of Seven Seas' substantial breach. Big Chef has a right to expect that the mussels were safe for human consumption. Whether it was expressly stated in the agreement or not, Seven Seas had the obligation to deliver mussels that did not pose a danger to health. The requirements of law, including national food regulations, are read into every contract and must be complied with by the parties.[55] Non-compliance with these requirements is a substantial breach of the contract and entitles Big Chef to rescind.

In cases where both parties have committed a breach, Article 1192 of the Civil Code provides that 'the liability of the first infractor shall be equitably tempered by the courts. If it cannot be determined which of the parties first violated the contract, the same shall be deemed extinguished, and each shall bear his own damages.'[56]

[53] Civil Code, art 1170.

[54] The fact scenarios of the hypotheticals described in this section are taken from M Chen-Wishart, D Neo, and S Vogenauer, 'Introduction', ch 1 in this volume, 9.

[55] Civil Code, art 1315 (see text at n 58): see de Leon and de Leon, Jr (n 9) 554.

[56] Civil Code, art 1192. See also Tolentino (n 6) 176.

(c) Good faith or lack thereof

A substantive or fundamental breach is a ground for rescinding a contract because '[o]bligations arising from contracts have the force of law between the contracting parties and should be complied with in good faith'.[57] In the performance of their contractual obligations, parties 'are bound not only to the fulfillment of what has been expressly stipulated but also to all the consequences which, according to their nature, may be in keeping with *good faith*, usage and law'.[58] These are on top of the general duty that '[e]very person must, in the exercise of his rights and in the performance of his duties, act with justice, give everyone his due, and observe honesty and *good faith*'.[59] In this regard, the Supreme Court has held that:

> The contract has the force of law between the parties and they are expected to abide in good faith by their respective contractual commitments, not weasel out of them. Just as nobody can be forced to enter into a contract, in the same manner, once a contract is entered into, no party can renounce it unilaterally or without the consent of the other. It is a general principle of law that no one may be permitted to change his mind or disavow and go back upon his own acts, or to proceed contrary thereto, to the prejudice of the other party.[60]

While good faith is a nebulous concept, the Supreme Court defines it as:

> an intangible and abstract quality with no technical meaning or statutory definition, and it encompasses, among other things, an honest belief, the absence of malice and the absence of design to defraud or to seek an unconscionable advantage. An individual's personal good faith is a concept of his own mind[61] and, therefore, may not conclusively be determined by his protestations alone. It implies honesty of intention, and freedom from knowledge of circumstances which ought to put the holder upon inquiry. The essence of good faith lies in an honest belief in the validity of one's right, ignorance of a superior claim, and absence of intention to overreach another.[62]

Deficient or non-performance of a contractual obligation accompanied by lack of good faith or the presence of bad faith provides sufficient grounds to rescind a contract.

In general, good faith is a duty of a contracting party and it cannot be relied on as an excuse or defence by the guilty party. However, in some limited instances, courts may take into account good faith on the part of the party in breach when deciding whether to allow the rescission of a contract. As discussed in the section below on fixing a grace period, in case of judicial rescission, courts may grant a guilty party a period to comply with his or her obligation when there are exceptional circumstances or just cause to do so. As long as the breach is not serious or substantial, the non-performance is excusable, or the guilty party is ready and willing to perform, a party exhibiting good faith may be allowed time to comply with his or her obligation under the contract. In any event, it is worth noting that

[57] Civil Code, art 1159.

[58] ibid art 1315 (emphasis added).

[59] ibid art 19 (emphasis added).

[60] *Metropolitan Manila Development Authority v Jancom Environmental Corp*, GR No 147465 (30 January 2002).

[61] *Office of the Ombudsman v Torres*, GR No 168309 (29 January 2008) ('concept of his own mind' means it is concerned with a person's state of mind, eg subjective intent or motive).

[62] *Philippine National Bank v De Jesus*, GR No 149295 (23 September 2003).

an assertion of good faith compliance by the guilty party cannot undo or rectify a substantial breach. Good faith of the guilty party *by itself* will not preclude or bar rescission of the contract when there has already been a substantial breach. This is so because the key determinant for rescinding a contract is the occurrence of a substantial breach of an essential term or condition of the contract that defeats its object or purpose.

A guilty party's good faith may also have an effect on his or her liability for damages. A party acting in good faith will only be liable for 'the natural and probable consequences of the breach of the obligation, and which the parties have foreseen or could have reasonably foreseen at the time the obligation was constituted'; in contrast, in cases of 'fraud, bad faith, malice or wanton attitude', the guilty party 'shall be responsible for all damages which may be reasonably attributed to the non-performance of the obligation'.[63] Bad faith and fraud are the grounds most cited by courts for imposing damages in breach of contract cases.[64]

2. Remedies of an Injured Party

(a) Rescission or specific performance

Article 1191 of the Civil Code sets out the remedies available in case of a breach or non-fulfilment of reciprocal obligations: 'The injured party may choose between the fulfillment and the rescission of the obligation, with the payment of damages in either case. He may also seek rescission, even after he has chosen fulfillment, if the latter should become impossible.'[65] De Leon and de Leon explain that:

> [o]nly the injured party can rescind a contract without violating the principle of mutuality of contracts . . . which prohibits allowing the validity and performance of contracts to be left to the will of one of the parties.[66]

In order to exercise the right to rescind a contract, the injured party should be 'ready, willing and able to comply with his [or her] own [reciprocal] obligations thereunder'.[67] This is related to the general rule on delay or default in Article 1169, which states that '[i]n reciprocal obligations, neither party incurs in delay if the other does not comply or is not ready to comply in a proper manner with what is incumbent upon him'.[68] A contracting party may therefore withhold or discontinue his or her own performance when the other party is not ready to comply with their corresponding obligations or is in breach of the contract.

In case of breach or non-performance of reciprocal obligations, the injured party may choose between the alternative remedies of rescission or an action for specific performance.[69] As noted by Tolentino, 'these two remedies are alternative; the injured party cannot have both. Thus, where he asks for rescission, he cannot at the same time ask for specific

63 Civil Code, art 2201.
64 *Radio Communications of the Philippines Inc v Verches*, GR No 164349 (31 January 2006).
65 See also Tolentino (n 6) 176.
66 de Leon and de Leon, Jr (n 9) 156.
67 ibid 173.
68 Civil Code, art 1169.
69 de Leon and de Leon, Jr (n 9) 152 and 153. See also Tolentino (n 6) 176.

performance.'[70] These remedies are 'alternative and not cumulative'.[71] Further, a party 'cannot ask for partial rescission and partial fulfillment'.[72] This is, of course, subject to the qualification provided in the article that if the injured party has chosen fulfilment of the obligation but the performance has become impossible or 'there are insuperable and legal obstacles thereto',[73] the injured party may afterwards resort to rescission. There is also no prohibition against asking for rescission or specific performance as alternative reliefs in a court action. This is so because 'an alternative prayer in the complaint for fulfillment or rescission is permissible in the discretion of the court for in such a case it cannot be said that the plaintiff is availing of both remedies'.[74] From the wording of the article, however, it appears that the reverse is not permitted: the injured party cannot elect for rescission and thereafter change his or her mind and pursue specific performance. As de Leon and de Leon say, 'after choosing rescission of the obligation, he cannot thereafter demand its compliance, nor seek partial fulfillment under the guise of recovering damages'.[75]

With regard to the party in breach, he or she is not permitted to avail of the remedies provided in Article 1191 because '[u]nder the rule of *exceptio non adimpleti contractus*, the party who has not performed his [or her] part of the agreement is not entitled to sue'.[76] Moreover, it has been said that rescission, like '[a]n action for specific performance of a contract is an equitable proceeding, and he who seeks to enforce it must himself [or herself] be fair and reasonable, and do equity'.[77]

Despite having the power and prerogative of rescission, the injured party may nonetheless opt to disregard the other party's breach and waive the right to rescind. Tolentino explains that '[w]hile the right to rescind reciprocal obligations is implied, that is, that such right need not be expressly provided in the contract, nevertheless the contracting parties may waive the same'.[78] Such waiver of the right of rescission may be done expressly or impliedly.[79] For there to be a valid waiver, it 'must be certain and unequivocal, and intelligently made; such waiver follows only where liberty of choice has been fully accorded'.[80] As part of the options granted to the injured party, rescission 'is not mandatory on the creditor; he may still choose to require specific performance, unless the contrary is expressly stipulated'.[81] For example, there is a waiver of the right of rescission when '[t]he vendor has thereby chosen the remedy of specific performance or simple collection of debt'.[82] Also, '[a]cceptance by the creditor of delayed installment payment beyond the grace period amounts to a waiver of the right of rescission'.[83] In cases where the injured party is aware of the breach but does not exercise the right to rescind, the party may be estopped by his or her actions or

70 Tolentino (n 6) 181. See also *AFP Mutual Benefit Association v Court of Appeals*, GR No 104769 (3 March 2000).
71 de Leon and de Leon, Jr (n 9) 166.
72 Tolentino (n 6) 181.
73 ibid 182.
74 de Leon and de Leon, Jr (n 9) 166. See also Tolentino (n 6) 182.
75 de Leon and de Leon, Jr (n 9) 166.
76 ibid 155–56.
77 Tolentino (n 6) 176.
78 ibid 184.
79 de Leon and de Leon, Jr (n 9) 177.
80 *Palay v Clave*, GR No L-56076 (21 September 1983).
81 Tolentino (n 6) 184–85.
82 ibid 184.
83 ibid 184.

inactions from subsequently seeking to rescind the contract.[84] The Supreme Court has held that a 'respondent's failure to exercise her right of rescission after petitioner's alleged default constitutes a waiver of such right. Her continued acceptance of the installment payments places her in estoppel.'[85]

(b) Damages

In addition to seeking either rescission or specific performance, the injured party may also claim 'the payment of damages in either case' under Article 1191. It is worth noting that, in case of a breach of contract, the primary remedies of an injured party are the alternative actions for rescission or specific performance. The relief of damages is secondary in nature.[86] As the Supreme Court explains:

> The *rescission on account of breach of stipulations is not predicated on injury to economic interests of the party plaintiff but on the breach of faith by the defendant, that violates the reciprocity between the parties.* It is not a subsidiary action, and Article 1191 may be scanned without disclosing anywhere that the action for rescission thereunder is subordinated to anything other than the culpable breach of his obligations by the defendant. *This rescission is in principal action retaliatory in character, it being unjust that a party be held bound to fulfill his promises when the other violates his.* As expressed in the old Latin aphorism: '*Non servanti fidem, non est fides servanda.*' Hence, *the reparation of damages for the breach is purely secondary.*[87]

The right to claim damages under Article 1191 should be read together with Article 1170 of the Civil Code, which states: '[t]hose who in the performance of their obligations are guilty of fraud, negligence, or delay, and those who in any manner contravene the tenor thereof, are liable for damages.'[88] Further, the general rules on damages in the Civil Code apply to a rescission for breach of contract.[89] Depending of the facts and context of the case, the party in breach may be held liable for different kinds of damages,[90] including actual or compensatory, moral, nominal,[91] temperate or moderate,[92] liquidated,[93] or exemplary or corrective damages.[94]

Tolentino explains that '[i]n estimating the damages to be awarded in case of rescission . . . those elements of damages only can be admitted that are compatible with the idea of rescission.'[95] In accordance with the principle of rescission that the parties should be restored to their status *quo ante*, the grant of damages is meant to make the injured parties whole.

[84] de Leon and de Leon, Jr (n 9) 177.
[85] *Rapanut v Court of Appeals*, GR No 109680 (14 July 1995).
[86] *Universal Food Corporation v Court of Appeals* (n 23).
[87] ibid (emphases added).
[88] Civil Code, art 1170. See also ibid art 2199.
[89] ibid arts 2195, 2198, and 1157. See also *Cathay Pacific v Spouses Fuentebella*, GR No 188283 (20 July 2016).
[90] Civil Code, art 2197.
[91] ibid art 2222.
[92] ibid art 2224.
[93] ibid arts 2226 and 2228.
[94] ibid art 2232.
[95] Tolentino (n 6) 184. See also de Leon and de Leon, Jr (n 9) 171.

With respect to actual or compensatory damages, according to the Supreme Court, '[t]here are two kinds . . . one is the loss of what a person already possesses, and the other is the failure to receive as a benefit that which would have pertained to him'.[96] An injured party can claim actual or compensatory damages (ie 'adequate compensation . . . for such pecuniary loss suffered by him as he has duly proved').[97] The injured party may also seek indemnity not just for 'the value of the loss suffered . . . [but also] profits which [he or she] failed to obtain'.[98] In case of lost profits,

> the familiar rule is that damages consisting of unrealized profits, frequently referred as '*ganacias frustradas*' or '*lucrum cessans*,' are not to be granted on the basis of mere speculation, conjecture, or surmise, but rather by reference to some reasonably definite standard such as market value, established experience, or direct inference from known circumstances.[99]

In order to be awarded damages for lost profits, the aggrieved party 'must produce the best evidence of which his case is susceptible and if that evidence warrants the inference that he has been damaged by the loss of profits which he might with reasonable certainty have anticipated but for the defendant's wrongful act, he is entitled to recover'.[100] The Supreme Court explains,

> [w]hen the existence of a loss is established, absolute certainty as to its amount is not required. The benefit to be derived from a contract which one of the parties has absolutely failed to perform is of necessity to some extent, a matter of speculation, but the injured party is not to be denied for that reason alone.[101]

In the illustrative case of *Producers Bank v Court of Appeals*, the plaintiffs—Spouses Chua—deposited Philippine pesos (PHP) 960,000 to pay for their loans with the defendant bank. However, the amount was not actually credited to their account because the bank's branch manager absconded with the funds.[102] Because the plaintiffs' account was not credited, the bank subsequently dishonoured checks issued by the spouses, sought to foreclose a real estate mortgage over the plaintiffs' gasoline station, and cancelled their credit line. The Spouses Chua sought compensatory damages for unrealized profits from their gasoline station business. One of the spouses testified that '[b]ecause of the . . . [extrajudicial foreclosure] I did not have [a] credit line anymore. Since I have no capital I was forced to sell my right to operate [the gasoline station] to my relatives'.[103] In this case, the Supreme Court denied the award of compensatory damages because the plaintiffs did not provide the best evidence to support their claims, particularly 'documentary evidence which is necessary to substantiate their claim for actual or compensatory damages'. The Court ruled that '[t]he

[96] *Producers Bank v Court of Appeals*, GR No 111584 (17 September 2001). See also *Interphil Laboratories v OEP Philippines*, GR No 203697 (30 March 2019).
[97] Civil Code, art 2199.
[98] ibid art 2200.
[99] *Producers Bank v Court of Appeals* (n 96).
[100] ibid.
[101] ibid.
[102] ibid.
[103] ibid.

bare assertion of ... Salvador Chua that he lost an average of PHP18,000.00 per month is inadequate if not speculative and should be admitted with extreme caution especially because it is not supported by independent evidence'. According to the Supreme Court, the Spouses Chua should have provided evidence such as 'reports on the average actual profits earned by their gasoline business, their financial statements, and other evidence of profitability'. The Court noted that the plaintiffs also failed to 'present any instrument or deed evidencing their claim that they have transferred their right to operate their gasoline station to their relatives'.[104]

For obligations involving payment, the party in breach may also be liable to pay the stipulated interest rate in the contract, or, if none is provided, the legal rate of interest, which is 'the accepted measure of damages for detention of money'.[105] Courts are also given the discretionary power to order interest on 'damages awarded for breach of contract'.[106] Moral damages can be imposed in cases of breach of contract where the guilty party 'acted fraudulently or in bad faith'.[107] Exemplary damages may be awarded if the party in breach 'acted in a wanton, fraudulent, reckless, oppressive, or malevolent manner'.[108]

The Supreme Court has ruled that the injured party may also recover damages in relation to other interests for breach of contract:

> his '*expectation interest*,' which is his interest in having the benefit of his [or her] bargain by being put in as good a position as he [or she] would have been in had the contract been performed, or his '*reliance interest*,' which is his interest in being reimbursed for loss caused by reliance on the contract by being put in as good a position as he would have been in had the contract not been made; or his '*restitution interest*,' which is his interest in having restored to him any benefit that he has conferred on the other party.[109]

The above rules on damages can be applied in one of the hypothetical cases addressed in this volume.[110] Coco, a famous architect, agreed with David that he would landscape the garden in her next property development. David was scheduled to start work on 1 December, but on 1 October, Coco informed him that she was no longer interested in his services because the development would not include a garden after all. David had already purchased materials. He also estimated that his future earnings would be 10 per cent lower because he would not be able to benefit from having worked with Coco and make his name as a landscape gardener. In this scenario, David cannot demand specific performance because a garden is no longer needed for the development. Nevertheless, David can bring an action for rescission of the contract and demand damages from Coco. He can ask for reimbursement of the materials he has already purchased. He can also demand payment for any time he has spent on preparatory work. David can also request damages based on his potential loss of future earnings due to his expectation and reliance interests in the contract.

[104] ibid.
[105] Tolentino (n 6) 184; Civil Code, art 2209.
[106] Civil Code, art 2210.
[107] ibid art 2220.
[108] ibid arts 2232 and 2229.
[109] *FGU Insurance Corporation v GP Sarmiento Trucking Corporation*, GR No 141910 (6 August 2002). See also de Leon and de Leon, Jr (n 9) 59–60.
[110] The fact scenarios of the hypotheticals described in this section are taken from M Chen-Wishart, D Neo, and S Vogenauer, 'Introduction', ch 1 in this volume, 9.

In another of the hypothetical scenarios, Bob contracted to build a house for Sue for the price of $100,000. After completing a third of the work, Bob abandons the job and leaves materials worth $15,000. Sue uses the materials to finish the work. In this situation, Bob can claim the value of the work done and the materials. However, because Bob was in breach of the contract, he would be liable to Sue for damages in the amount of the additional costs and expenses she incurred to complete the house.

3. Action for Rescission

(a) Extrajudicial or judicial

Article 1191 of the Civil Code provides that '[t]he court shall decree the rescission claimed'. Despite the wording of the article, the injured party may rescind the contract either extra-judicially or judicially. According to Balane, '[t]he aggrieved party may, at his option, resolve either judicially ([through] recourse to the courts) or extrajudicially (without need of judicial recourse)'.[111] In general, rescission may be exercised unilaterally by the injured party or by mutual agreement of both parties.[112]

While there have been some conflicting cases as to whether rescission can be exercised extrajudicially without an express stipulation granting such right in the contract,[113] the current and controlling position is that judicial action is not required to rescind a reciprocal contract.[114] As the Supreme Court has ruled in the seminal case of *University of the Philippines v De Los Angeles*,

> *the party who deems the contract violated may consider it resolved or rescinded, and act accordingly, without previous court action*, but it proceeds at its own risk. For it is only the final judgment of the corresponding court that will conclusively and finally settle whether the action taken was or was not correct in law. But *the law definitely does not require that the contracting party who believes itself injured must first file suit and wait for a judgment before taking extrajudicial steps to protect its interest*. Otherwise, the party injured by the other's breach will have to passively sit and watch its damages accumulate during the pendency of the suit until the final judgment of rescission is rendered when the law itself requires that he should exercise due diligence to minimize its own damages.[115]

In other words, rescission in the first instance can be exercised without having to involve the courts. In a more recent case, the Supreme Court confirms that 'an aggrieved party is not prevented from extrajudicially rescinding a contract to protect its interests, even in the absence of any provision expressly providing for such right'.[116] The Court also states that 'an extrajudicial rescission based on grounds not specified in the contract would not preclude a party to treat the same as rescinded'.[117]

111 Balane (n 6) 184.
112 de Leon and de Leon, Jr (n 9) 184.
113 Balane (n 6) 170–73.
114 *University of the Philippines v De Los Angeles*, GR No L-28602 (29 September 1970).
115 ibid (emphases added).
116 *Nissan Car Lease v Lica Management*, GR No 176986 (13 January 2016).
117 ibid.

As Tolentino explains, 'rescission may take place by the declaration of the injured party; the rescission is a *power*, which does not require the previous declaration of rescission by the courts. Nothing in this article prohibits cancellation of contract by an injured party without judicial intervention.'[118] Balane is similarly of the view that '[t]he option to [rescind] extrajudicially is available even if such right is not expressly agreed upon by the parties'[119] since '[t]he right to resolve is inherent in reciprocal obligations. It exists without need of stipulation to that effect.'[120] Tolentino further points out that '[o]ur Code, like the Spanish Code, does not reproduce the requirement, contained in article 1184 of the French Code and article 1165 of the Italian Code, that the rescission "must be demanded judicially"'.[121] The Supreme Court similarly notes that:

> even without express provision conferring the power of cancellation upon one contracting party, the Supreme Court of Spain, in construing the effect of Article 1124 of the Spanish Civil Code (of which Article 1191 of our own Civil Code is practically a reproduction), has repeatedly held that a resolution of reciprocal or synallagmatic contracts may be made extrajudicially unless successfully impugned in court.[122]

In case of an extrajudicial rescission, the injured party 'may treat the obligation as resolved, and act accordingly'.[123] This is especially true in cases 'where the other party does not oppose or impugn the extra-judicial declaration of rescission, [and] such declaration produces legal effect'.[124] The guilty party's 'silence suggests an admission of the veracity and validity of the rescinding party's claim'.[125] Furthermore, extrajudicial rescission is particularly appropriate in cases of executory contracts or where the parties have not yet performed their respective reciprocal obligations. Tolentino explains, '[i]f the obligation has not yet been performed, extra-judicial declaration of resolution or rescission by the party who is ready and willing to perform would suffice; he can refuse to perform if the other party is not ready and willing to perform'.[126] The injured party can 'by his own declaration elect to [extrajudicially] rescind by not performing his own undertaking'.[127]

In any event, while the injured party may rescind the contract extrajudicially, the other party can always go to court to question or challenge the validity or propriety of the rescission (eg on grounds of abuse or error).[128] The Supreme Court explains that 'extrajudicial rescission has legal effect where the other party does not oppose it. Where it is objected to, a judicial determination of the issue is still necessary.'[129] This is so because '[t]he right to rescind by the injured party . . . is not absolute. It is always provisional, *i.e.*, contestable and subject to scrutiny and review by the courts.'[130] According to the Supreme Court,

118 Tolentino (n 6) 177.
119 Balane (n 6) 184.
120 ibid.
121 Tolentino (n 6) 177.
122 *University of the Philippines v De Los Angeles* (n 114).
123 Balane (n 6) 185.
124 Tolentino (n 6) 178. See also de Leon and de Leon, Jr (n 9) 172.
125 de Leon and de Leon, Jr (n 9) 183.
126 Tolentino (n 6) 178.
127 ibid 177.
128 de Leon and de Leon, Jr (n 9) 183.
129 *Palay v Clave* (n 80).
130 de Leon and de Leon, Jr (n 9) 172.

> in every case where the extrajudicial resolution is contested only the final award of the court of competent jurisdiction can conclusively settle whether the resolution was proper or not. It is in this sense that judicial action will be necessary, as without it, the extrajudicial resolution will remain contestable and subject to judicial invalidation, unless attack thereon should become barred by acquiescence, estoppel or prescription.[131]

The courts then have the ultimate authority to decide whether the rescission is valid or not. The Supreme Court also points out that, even though extrajudicial rescission is permissible, '[t]he rescinding party... by such course of action, subjects himself [or herself] to the risk of being held liable for damages when the extrajudicial rescission is questioned by the opposing party in court'.[132]

Recourse to judicial rescission is pertinent when the contract has already been partially performed. Tolentino explains that:

> where the injured party has already performed such as when property has already been delivered by him to the other party, he cannot by his own declaration rescind the contract and reacquire title to the property, if the other party opposed the rescission. In such a case, court action must be taken, and the function of the court is to declare the rescission as properly made, or to give a period to the debtor in which to perform.[133]

Seeking relief from the courts is necessary because the parties cannot take the law into their own hands. If the other party refuses to return what he or she had received in relation to the contract upon extrajudicial rescission, the other party must seek relief from the courts to enforce their respective rights. Balane states: 'Should the extrajudicial [rescission] involve the return of things already delivered by the aggrieved party to the offending party and the latter, even upon demand, refused to return them, the former will have to go to court to demand their return.'[134] De Leon and de Leon agree:

> Resort to courts may be necessary when the right involves the retaking of property which is not voluntarily surrendered by the other party. Permitting the use of unqualified force to repossess the property and without condition of notice would allow the lessor/owner to take the law into his [or her] own [hands].[135]

(b) Automatic rescission clauses

Related to extrajudicial rescission is the issue of the validity and effects of automatic rescission clauses. Under Philippine law, automatic rescission clauses are generally valid and enforceable. Such clauses are considered 'express resolutory condition[s]' that the contracting parties have agreed to.[136] The Supreme Court has held that '[t]he validity of the stipulation in the contract providing for automatic rescission upon non-payment cannot be doubted. It

[131] *University of the Philippines v De Los Angeles* (n 114).
[132] *Nissan Car Lease v Lica Management* (n 116).
[133] Tolentino (n 6) 178.
[134] Balane (n 6) 185.
[135] de Leon and de Leon, Jr (n 9) 169.
[136] Tolentino (n 6) 184.

is in the nature of an agreement granting a party the right to rescind a contract unilaterally in case of breach without need of going to court.'[137] Tolentino explains that '[t]he parties to a bilateral contract may validly stipulate that if one of them does not comply with his [or her] obligation, the contract shall be automatically resolved' as 'it is in the nature of a facultative resolutory condition'.[138] Similarly, according to de Leon and de Leon, the contracting parties 'may validly enter into an agreement that violation of the terms of the contract would cause cancellation thereof even without judicial intervention or permission or termination'.[139] The Supreme Court explains the acceptability of automatic rescission clauses:

> There is nothing in this law which prohibits the parties from entering into an agreement that a violation of the terms of the contract would cause its cancellation even without court intervention. The rationale for the foregoing is that in contracts providing for automatic revocation, judicial intervention is necessary not for purposes of obtaining a judicial declaration rescinding a contract already deemed rescinded by virtue of an agreement providing for rescission even without judicial intervention, but in order to determine whether or not the rescission was proper. Where such propriety is sustained, the decision of the court will be merely declaratory of the revocation, but it is not itself the revocatory act.[140]

Philippine courts respect these types of automatic rescission clauses whether they are in the form of standard terms (eg in insurance contracts) or individually negotiated.[141]

While a party may deem a contract to be automatically rescinded upon the triggering of an automatic rescission clause, such rescission should still be made known to the other party. De Leon and de Leon explain that:

> [j]udicial action for rescission is not necessary where the contract provides [an] automatic rescission in case of breach. But the act of a party treating a contract as cancelled should be made known to the other. For such act is always provisional. It is subject to review by the courts in case the alleged defaulter brings the matter to the proper courts.[142]

Furthermore, despite the presence of an automatic rescission clause, court action may also be necessary in cases where the contract has been partially performed. It has been said that:

> Resort to judicial action by the injured party is still necessary to recover whatever he may have delivered to the other party under the contract if the latter opposes the rescission. A contract between the parties providing for extrajudicial rescission and recovery of possession of property in case of breach has legal effect only where the other party does not

[137] *Calilap-Asmeron v Development Bank of the Philippines*, GR No 157330 (23 November 2011). See also de Leon and de Leon, Jr (n 9) 180.

[138] Tolentino (n 6) 184.

[139] de Leon and de Leon, Jr (n 9) 180.

[140] *Calilap-Asmeron v Development Bank of the Philippines* (n 137).

[141] *Spouses Labayen v Serafica*, GR No 178443 (6 October 2008): see the discussion of Philippine rules on unfair terms in MAC Dizon, 'Contract Terms in the Philippines: Incorporation, Interpretation, Implication, and Unfair Terms' in M Chen-Wishart and S Vogenauer (eds), *Studies in the Contract Laws of Asia, vol III: Contents of Contract and Unfair Terms* (OUP 2020) 308, 331–35.

[142] de Leon and de Leon, Jr (n 9) 181.

oppose the rescission. Where it is validly objected to, a judicial determination of the issue is still necessary.[143]

(c) Notice

Despite the absence of an express provision in the Civil Code, the injured party must give notice of the fact or act of rescission to the other party, both for extrajudicial and judicial rescission.[144] The Supreme Court has held that 'the act of [a] party in treating a contract as cancelled or resolved on account of infractions by the other contracting party must be made known to the other'.[145] According to Balane, '[t]he aggrieved party, having decided to resolve the obligation for justifiable grounds must furnish notice to the other party of the decision' to rescind.[146] De Leon and de Leon further explain that 'when parties to a contract expressly reserve an option to terminate or rescind a contract upon violation of a resolutory condition, notice of [rescission] must be given to the other party when such right is exercised'.[147]

Notice performs a crucial function because it informs the parties of the fact that the contract has been extinguished and it determines when the rescission takes effect. It also gives the other party the opportunity to question the validity of the rescission and seek judicial intervention. The notice requirement is connected to the principle of mutuality of contract, which provides that the validity of or compliance with a contract cannot be left to the will of one party.[148] The purpose of this principle is to prohibit contracts that make their 'fulfillment dependent exclusively upon the uncontrolled will of one of the contracting parties'.[149] A party cannot unilaterally rescind a contract without legal basis or justification.[150] While breach of contract provides the legal basis for an injured party to rescind a contract under Article 1191, the exercise of the power of rescission is not absolute and can be questioned in court. In short, rescission of a contract without notice would violate the principles of mutuality of contract and the essential equality of the contracting parties.[151]

In relation to effectivity, extrajudicial rescission, or rescission pursuant to an automatic rescission clause, 'produces its effects when the creditor notifies the debtor of his decision' to rescind.[152] In cases of judicially declared or confirmed rescissions, rescission is effective when notice of extrajudicial or judicial rescission is first 'made known to the breaching party, not upon the court decree'.[153]

Under the Civil Code, there are specific notice requirements for the rescission of a sale involving real or immovable property. Article 1592 provides that:

> In the sale of immovable property, even though it may have been stipulated that upon failure to pay the price at the time agreed upon the rescission of the contract shall of

143 ibid 181.
144 *Palay v Clave* (n 80). See also Balane (n 6) 210.
145 *University of the Philippines v De Los Angeles* (n 114).
146 Balane (n 6) 210.
147 de Leon and de Leon, Jr (n 9) 169; see *Palay v Clave* (n 80).
148 Civil Code, art 1308.
149 Tolentino (n 6) 424.
150 ibid 425. See also de Leon and de Leon, Jr (n 9) 513.
151 de Leon and de Leon, Jr (n 9) 512; Balane (n 6) 526.
152 Tolentino (n 6) 185.
153 Balane (n 6) 185.

> right take place, the vendee may pay, even after the expiration of the period, as long as no demand for rescission of the contract has been made upon him *either judicially or by a notarial act*. After the demand, the court may not grant him a new term.[154]

In this situation, formal notice of or demand for rescission must be made by way of judicial action for rescission or a notarial act.

It is important to stress though that the notice requirements in Article 1592 only apply to 'an absolute sale and not a contract to sell' of real property.[155] In a contract of sale (whether absolute or conditional), 'one of the contracting parties obligates himself to transfer the ownership of and to deliver a determinate thing, and the other to pay therefor a price certain in money or its equivalent'.[156] Furthermore, a contract of sale 'is perfected at the moment there is a meeting of minds upon the thing which is the object of the contract and upon the price . . . From that moment, the parties may reciprocally demand performance.'[157] The Supreme Court explains that '[u]pon perfection of the contract [of sale], the parties may reciprocally demand performance, *i.e.*, the vendee may compel transfer of ownership of the object of the sale, and the vendor may require the vendee to pay the thing sold'.[158] This is different from a contract to sell, which involves a reservation of title and is:

> defined as a bilateral contract whereby the prospective seller, while expressly reserving the ownership of the property despite delivery thereof to the prospective buyer, binds himself to sell the property exclusively to the prospective buyer upon fulfillment of the condition agreed upon, *i.e.*, the full payment of the purchase price.[159]

A contract to sell is also distinct from a *conditional contract of sale*. The Supreme Court explains the distinction:

> *A contract to sell . . . may not even be considered as a conditional contract of sale where the seller may likewise reserve title to the property subject of the sale until the fulfillment of a suspensive condition*, because in a conditional contract of sale, the first element of consent is present, although it is conditioned upon the happening of a contingent event which may or may not occur. If the suspensive condition is not fulfilled, the perfection of the contract of sale is completely abated. However, if the suspensive condition is fulfilled, the contract of sale is thereby perfected, such that if there had already been previous delivery of the property subject of the sale to the buyer, ownership thereto automatically transfers to the buyer by operation of law without any further act having to be performed by the seller.
>
> In a contract to sell, upon the fulfillment of the suspensive condition which is the full payment of the purchase price, *ownership will not automatically transfer to the buyer*

[154] Emphasis added; see also Realty Installment Buyer Act.
[155] *Padilla v Spouses Paredes*, GR No 124874 (17 March 2000).
[156] Civil Code, art 1458.
[157] ibid art 1475.
[158] *ACE Foods v Micro Pacific Technologies*, GR No 200602 (11 December 2013).
[159] ibid.

> *although the property may have been previously delivered to him. The prospective seller still has to convey title to the prospective buyer by entering into a contract of absolute sale.*[160]

The key factor that distinguishes a contract to sell from a contract of sale is the kind of condition imposed on the parties.[161] In a contract to sell, 'payment of the purchase price is a positive suspensive condition', whereas 'the non-payment of the price is a resolutory condition' in a contract of sale.[162] With respect to a contract to sell, the Supreme Court has said that:

> the failure of the private respondent to comply with the positive suspensive condition [i.e., payment of the purchase price] cannot even be considered a breach—casual or serious—but simply an event that prevented the obligation of petitioner corporation to convey title from acquiring binding force.[163]

The Supreme Court discusses at length the legal effects of a contract to sell vis-à-vis a contract of sale:

> in a contract to sell, title remains with the vendor and does not pass on to the vendee until the purchase price is paid in full. Thus, in contract to sell, the payment of the purchase price is a positive suspensive condition. Failure to pay the price agreed upon is not a mere breach, casual or serious, but a situation that prevents the obligation of the vendor to convey title from acquiring an obligatory force. This is entirely different from the situation in a contract of sale, where non-payment of the price is a negative resolutory condition. The effects in law are not identical. In a contract of sale, the vendor has lost ownership of the thing sold and cannot recover it, unless the contract of sale is rescinded and set aside. In a contract to sell, however, the vendor remains the owner for as long as the vendee has not complied fully with the condition of paying the purchase. If the vendor should eject the vendee for failure to meet the condition precedent, he is enforcing the contract and not rescinding it.[164]

Based on the above differences between a contract to sell and a contract of sale, the notice requirements for the sale of real property under Article 1592 do not apply to a contract to sell. The Supreme Court has confirmed that:

> Article 1592 speaks of nonpayment of the purchase price as a resolutory condition. It does not apply to a contract to sell. As to Article 1191, it is subordinated to the provisions of Article 1592 when applied to sales of immovable property. Neither provision is applicable in the present case [involving a contract to sell].[165]

160 *Reyes v Tuparan*, GR No 188064 (1 June 2011) (emphases added).
161 Civil Code, art 1182. See also de Leon and de Leon, Jr (n 9) 120.
162 de Leon and de Leon, Jr (n 9) 178.
163 *Visayan Sawmill Company v Court of Appeals*, GR No 83851 (3 March 1993).
164 *Spouses Santos v Court of Appeals*, GR No 120820 (1 August 2000).
165 ibid.

In a contract to sell where the buyer fails to pay the purchase price, rescission is not an option as no existing or demandable obligation has been breached. The Supreme Court states that '[t]he remedy of rescission is not available in contracts to sell'.[166] The Supreme Court further states that with a contract to sell:

> the obligation of the seller to sell becomes demandable only upon the happening of the suspensive condition. *The full payment of the purchase price is the positive suspensive condition, the failure of which is not a breach of contract, but simply an event that prevented the obligation of the vendor to convey title from acquiring binding force.* Thus, for its non-fulfilment, there is no contract to speak of, the obligor having failed to perform the suspensive condition which enforces a juridical relation. With this circumstance, there can be no rescission or fulfillment of an obligation that is still non-existent, the suspensive condition not having occurred as yet. Emphasis should be made that *the breach contemplated in Article 1191 of the New Civil Code is the obligor's failure to comply with an obligation already extant, not a failure of a condition to render binding that obligation.*[167]

The proper remedy for the non-fulfilment of an obligation in relation to a contract to sell is termination not rescission.

The above principles and rules can be applied in one of the hypothetical cases.[168] Prime Ltd agreed to sell a piece of land to Devil Corp. Under the contract, Devil Corp would pay a 10 per cent deposit, with the remainder of the purchase price due at 5 pm on 30 September, time being of the essence. The contract also contained Clause 12, which expressly provided that failure to meet the deadline would result in the deposit being forfeited and the agreement being terminated. Devil Corp was ten minutes late in tendering the completion money. Prime refused to continue with the sale. In this scenario, unless Devil Corp can cite exceptional circumstances that excuse its non-performance or show substantial performance on its part, Prime properly exercised its right to terminate the contract because Devil Corp failed to pay the rest of the purchase price by the agreed deadline. Prime could retain the deposit as this was expressly provided for in the contract. Even though the payment was only ten minutes late, Prime rightfully terminated the contract because not only was there a clear and explicit deadline in the agreement, but the parties knew that time was of the essence. The result would be the same even if there was no Clause 12. The contract between Prime Ltd and Devil Corp was a contract to sell since payment of the full purchase price was a positive suspensive condition before Prime Ltd would become obligated to sell and transfer ownership of the land to Devil Corp. Since the condition was not met, no obligation on the part of Prime Ltd to sell the land was created and Devil Corp has no right to sue for specific performance. Moreover, Devil Corp was aware that payment of the completion money before the stated deadline was an essential condition of the contract that it failed to comply with. Finally, given that the contract was a contract to sell, termination rather than rescission was the appropriate remedy. The notice requirements for rescission under Article 1592 do not apply.

[166] *Diego v Diego*, GR No 179965 (20 February 2013).

[167] *Reyes v Tuparan* (n 160) (emphases added).

[168] The fact scenario of this hypothetical is taken from M Chen-Wishart, D Neo, and S Vogenauer, 'Introduction', ch 1 in this volume, 9.

(d) Fixing a grace period

In cases of judicial action for rescission, Article 1191 of the Civil Code provides that '[t]he court shall decree the rescission claimed, unless there be just cause authorizing the fixing of a period'. De Leon and de Leon explain that '[t]he court has discretionary power to allow a period within which a person in default may be permitted to perform his [or her] obligation if there is a just cause for giving time to the debtor'.[169] The fixing of a grace period will only be ordered in exceptional circumstances because the general rule is that courts are 'not authorized to fix a period. The courts have no right to make contracts for the parties'.[170]

In the case of *Roman v Court of Appeals*, the vendor Sarangaya agreed to sell five parcels of land to Roman and two other vendees. Under the contract, the vendor was required to secure title over the properties within a year. The vendees agreed to pay the total purchase price within 60 days of notice of the issuance of titles. The vendor was able to secure titles over the subject properties. When the vendees failed to pay the purchase price within 60 days of receiving notice, the vendor filed a judicial action for rescission. During the court proceedings, the parties sought to settle the case. One of the vendees (Roman) offered to pay the original purchase price, but the vendor made a counter-offer that included payment of the original purchase price plus legal costs and attorney fees, interest, and other fees. Roman did not accept the counter-offer. After the case dragged on for six years, the trial court issued a decision ordering the vendor to sell the property to Roman under the terms of the counter-offer. The trial court ruled:

> Considering the said offer and counter-offer by the parties, which constitute a just cause for fixing the period within which the defendant can comply, in pursuance of the provision of Art. 1191, New Civil Code, the Court hereby grants him an opportunity to comply with his obligations.[171]

When the matter was appealed before it, the Supreme Court ruled that there was no just cause for fixing a period under Article 1191. The Court said that:

> [a]fter institution of the action against him, what [Roman] should have done, which he did not do, was to pay [the vendor] within 60 days after service of summons. It would not have been just to grant him an extension of more than six (6) years, from October 11, 1958 [date when notice was received] to January 9, 1965 [date of trial court decision], to comply with his 60-day obligation.[172]

It is worth mentioning that the exception allowing a grace period only applies when 'the guilty party is willing to comply with his [or her] obligation but needs time to do so and not where he [or she] refused to perform'.[173] The courts may also fix a period if the breach or non-performance is not serious or there has already been either substantial performance or excusable non-performance on the part of the guilty party.[174] For

169 de Leon and de Leon, Jr (n 9) 173.
170 ibid 204; see Civil Code, art 1197.
171 *Roman v Court of Appeals*, GR No L-37976 (16 July 1985).
172 ibid.
173 de Leon and de Leon, Jr (n 9) 165.
174 Civil Code, art 1170.

example, a period may be granted in cases of payment by instalment where the buyer has already paid a significant percentage of the purchase price and has only missed or been in delay on a few payments. A period may similarly be granted when 'the default incurred was not wilful or could be excused in view of the surrounding circumstances'.[175] Furthermore, fixing a period would not be warranted if the contract has an automatic rescission clause or time is of the essence in the contract. As Tolentino explains, when there is an automatic rescission clause, rescission 'takes place by force of law, and the court cannot grant the debtor a period within which to perform'.[176] Therefore, '[i]n absence of any just cause for the court to determine the period of compliance, the court shall decree the rescission'.[177]

Despite the power of the court to authorize the fixing of a period for the guilty party to perform his or her obligation, the general rule is that the injured party is not required to give the guilty party a second chance (eg a grace period) or provide an opportunity for supplementary performance as a precondition to rescind a contract. Once a substantial breach has occurred, the injured party is generally entitled to rescind the contract.

4. Effects of Rescission

(a) Retroactive effect

The main effect of rescission is to extinguish the reciprocal obligations between the parties. According to Tolentino, rescission is 'equivalent to invalidating and unmaking the juridical tie, leaving things in their status before the celebration of the contract'.[178] In this way, '[t]he exercise of the power to rescind extinguishes the obligatory relation as if it had never been created, the extinction having a retroactive effect' to the time of the perfection of the contract.[179] Further, 'rescission has the effect of abrogating the contract in all parts. The party seeking rescission cannot have performance as to a part and rescission as to the remainder.'[180]

(b) Mutual restitution

The Supreme Court has held that 'the ultimate effect of rescission is to restore the parties to their original status before they entered in a contract'.[181] Thus, a natural consequence of rescission is the obligation of mutual restitution.[182] According to the Supreme Court, mutual restitution 'is required in cases involving rescission under Article 1191. This means bringing the parties back to their original status prior to the inception of the contract.'[183] The rationale for this is that '[w]hen an agreement is rescinded, it is deemed inexistent and the parties are returned to their status *quo ante*. Hence there is mutual restitution of the

175 de Leon and de Leon, Jr (n 9) 173.
176 Tolentino (n 6) 184.
177 de Leon and de Leon, Jr (n 9) 173.
178 Tolentino (n 6) 180.
179 ibid 180.
180 ibid 181.
181 *Fong v Duenas* (n 32).
182 de Leon and de Leon, Jr (n 9) 174.
183 *Gotesco Properties v Spouses Fajardo* (n 12). See also *Pryce Corporation v Philippine Amusement and Gaming Corporation* (n 10); de Leon and de Leon, Jr (n 9) 157.

benefits received.'[184] The parties must return or surrender to each other the property and benefits they respectively received from the contract.[185]

Upon rescission, the parties have the primary 'obligation to return the object of the contract' as well as the fruits and interest thereon.[186] Because of the requirement of mutual restitution, rescission 'can be carried out only when the one who demands rescission can return whatever he may be obliged to restore'.[187] In relation to the rights of third parties, Article 1191 provides that rescission 'is understood to be without prejudice to the rights of third persons who have acquired the thing, in accordance with articles 1385 and 1388 and the Mortgage Law'. This means that 'if the thing, subject matter of the obligation, is in the hands of a third person who acted in good faith, rescission is not available as a remedy.... In such a case, the injured party may recover damages from the person responsible for the transfer.'[188] Aside from protecting third parties, Article 1385 on rescissible contracts is also applicable to rescissions for breach of contract under Article 1191.[189] Article 1385 states that '[r]escission creates the obligation to return the things which were the object of the contract, together with their fruits, and the price with its interest; consequently, it can be carried out only when he who demands rescission can return whatever he may be obliged to restore'.

It is worth noting that the obligation of mutual restitution does not prevent the injured party from enforcing a penalty clause in the rescinded contract. The Supreme Court has 'recognized the validity of a forfeiture or penalty clause which the parties stipulated in a contract that was eventually rescinded'.[190] The Court has clarified that '[i]f this Court recognized the right of the parties to stipulate on an extrajudicial rescission under Article 1191, there is no reason why this Court will not allow the parties to stipulate on the matter of damages in case of such rescission'.[191]

IV. Conclusion and Recommendations for Future Reform

Rescission for breach of contract is one of the grounds for extinguishing obligations under Philippine law. It is the primary remedy and most commonly used way to end contracts. Since the key issue in rescission is the occurrence of a substantial breach of an essential term or condition of the contract, most case law on rescission focuses on determining whether the breach committed is substantial or fundamental. As explained above, the rules for assessing whether there has been a substantial breach are plain and evident and can be applied to all manner of cases and situations. While the principles and rules of rescission are fairly straightforward, there are specific areas that are worth highlighting for possible further research and future reform.

Even though it may appear like mere semantics, it would be advantageous to amend the Civil Code and use the terms 'resolution' and 'resolve' rather than 'rescission' or 'rescind' in

184 de Leon and de Leon, Jr (n 9) 184–85.
185 ibid 157. See also Tolentino (n 6) 180–81.
186 de Leon and de Leon, Jr (n 9) 157.
187 ibid 157. See also Tolentino (n 6) 181.
188 de Leon and de Leon, Jr (n 9) 174.
189 *Gotesco Properties v Spouses Fajardo* (n 12).
190 *Heirs of Kim v Quicho*, GR No 249247 (15 March 2021).
191 *Laperal v Solid Homes*, GR No 130913 (21 June 2005).

the context of breach of contract. As discussed previously, while there is a clear distinction between rescission for breach of contract versus rescission of a rescissible contract, the use of the same term for two disparate legal concepts can lead to confusion. Since the enactment of the Civil Code, time and again the Supreme Court has had to explain the difference between these two types of rescission because the parties have confused one remedy for the other. A statutory change in the terms used for rescission for breach of contract would resolve this misunderstanding once and for all.[192]

Despite the fact that the Supreme Court has made numerous, unequivocal rulings on the matter, the question of whether judicial action is necessary to rescind a contract has remained a perennial issue in Philippine contract law and jurisprudence. To remove any doubt, Article 1191 of the Civil Code should be amended to reflect the current and controlling position that judicial action is not required to rescind a contract and extrajudicial rescission can be exercised even in the absence of an express contractual stipulation granting such right.

Rescission for breach of contract is so ingrained in legal parlance that people tend to use it synonymously or interchangeably with other seemingly related terms such as termination, cancellation, or invalidation. As clarified earlier, rescission is distinguishable from termination of contracts. While rescission retroactively abrogates the entire contract from the time of its perfection, termination has a prospective effect, and rights existing before the contract is terminated can be still enforced even after termination. Although the distinction between rescission and termination for breach of contract is quite notable, it appears that the remedy of termination in lieu of rescission has not been fully availed of by parties in contract disputes. People are so used to employing rescission by default even though termination would be the more appropriate remedy, particularly in cases where a party desires to enforce parts of the contract. There are many situations where a party would be better served terminating rather than rescinding a contract because the former will not result in the total abrogation of the contract *ab initio* or give rise to the obligation of mutual restitution. For instance, a party may wish to terminate a contract to release himself or herself from further obligations, yet still have the power to enforce existing rights under the contract (eg retain possession or ownership of property delivered under the contract, keep partial payments made, forfeit a deposit, or continue to demand non-disclosure obligations). There should be greater appreciation of the appropriateness and utility of termination as opposed to rescission in cases of breach of contract.

A final area for further research and future law reform is damages. While courts have recognized the protection of expectation, reliance, and restitution interests when there has been a contractual breach, there have only been a small number of cases where these interests have been explicitly mentioned. Fewer still are the cases that explain in greater detail how these interests are assessed and enforced. It would be beneficial if the courts elucidated further what these interests are, what they entail, and how they apply to a breach of contract. These interests are important not only because they help determine the kinds and amounts of the damages to be imposed, but also because they are essential for achieving one of the purposes of rescission, which is to make the injured party whole.

[192] ibid.

20

Contractual Obligations and Change of Circumstances in Singapore

Dora NEO

I. Introduction

In Singapore, the legal effect of a change of circumstances on contractual obligations is primarily governed by the common law doctrine of frustration.[1] If a contract is frustrated, both parties are automatically discharged from their obligations under the contract; if not, the obligations are binding despite the change in circumstances. Contracting parties may insert a *force majeure* clause in their contract to deal with changes in circumstances which make performance of the contract impossible or more onerous. The applicability and effect of a *force majeure* clause depends on the parties' intentions. In some cases, general contract law principles may be relevant to determine the rights of the contracting parties; for example, there might be an implied term dealing with the new circumstances.

This chapter will focus on the doctrine of frustration. It will also discuss *force majeure* clauses and the potential application of general contract law principles to situations of changed circumstances as well as the COVID-19 pandemic, the case law arising therefrom, and the temporary relief provided by the Singapore government. The legal principles applying to a change of circumstances are largely found in case law. This chapter will highlight Singapore cases, but a full account of the law must refer to a large extent to English cases, which remain highly influential because of Singapore's history as a British colony.

II. Frustration

1. General Principles and Juridical Basis

The main elements of the doctrine of frustration were summarized by the Court of Appeal in *Alliance Concrete Singapore Pte Ltd v Sato Kogyo (S) Pte Ltd* (*Alliance Concrete*)[2]: (i) there must be a supervening event occurring after the formation of the contract; (ii) the event occurred without the fault of either party; and (iii) the event renders the performance of the obligation radically or fundamentally different from what had been agreed in the contract.[3] This is consistent with the classic test for frustration formulated by Lord Reid in

[1] ABL Phang (ed), *The Law of Contract in Singapore, vol* 2 (2nd edn, Academy Publishing 2022) ch 19; ABL Phang and Y Goh, *Contract Law in Singapore* (Kluwer Law International BV 2012); B Ong and B Wong, *Contract Law in Singapore: Cases, Materials and Commentary* (2nd edn, Academy Publishing 2022).

[2] [2014] 3 SLR 857.

[3] *Alliance Concrete* (n 2) [33].

Dora Neo, *Contractual Obligations and Change of Circumstances in Singapore* In: *Studies in the Contract Laws of Asia V: Ending and Changing Contracts*. Edited by: Mindy Chen-Wishart, Dora Neo, and Stefan Vogenauer, Oxford University Press. © Dora Neo 2026. DOI: 10.1093/oso/9780198995814.003.0020

the English House of Lords case of *Davis Contractors Ltd v Fareham Urban District Council* (*Davis Contractors*),[4] which has been adopted in many cases in Singapore:

> [F]rustration occurs whenever the law recognises that without default of either party a contractual obligation has become incapable of being performed because the circumstances in which performance is called for would render it a thing radically different from that which was undertaken by the contract. . . . It was not this that I promised to do.[5]

Where a contract is frustrated, both parties are automatically discharged from the contract by operation of law.[6] Where it is not frustrated, the parties must perform their obligations. There is no possibility of adapting the contract unless there is a term to that effect. In applying the 'radical change in obligation' test, the court will take a multi-factorial approach and consider various factors.[7] An important question is whether the parties had allocated the risks of gains and losses arising from non-performance of the contract in the changed circumstances.[8] If they had, the allocation of risk will apply, and the contract will not be frustrated.

Juridical bases that have been suggested for the doctrine of frustration include 'an implied condition, the disappearance of the foundation of the contract, the intervention of the law to impose a just and reasonable solution, or the fact of a radical change in the character of the obligation'.[9] In Singapore, the courts have stated that the doctrine of frustration is based on construction of the contract. In *Lim Kim Som v Sheriffa Taibah bte Abdul Rahman* (*Lim Kim Som*),[10] the Court of Appeal quoted with approval Lord Reid's statement in *Davis Contractors* that 'frustration depends, at least in most cases, not on adding any implied term, but on the true construction of the terms which are in the contract read in light of the nature of the contract and of the relevant surrounding circumstances when the contract was made'.[11] The 'construction of the contract' basis is a broad one that could support other rationales for the doctrine of frustration, for instance that there has been a radical change in the character of the obligation[12] or that a party's consent has run out.[13] The starting point for the applicability of the latter two rationales is that the contract must first be construed to determine what obligations have been undertaken so as to assess whether the contract is wide enough to apply in the new situation[14] or whether performance in the new situation would be radically different from what had been agreed so that a party could say that this is not what he had consented to do.

4 [1956] AC 696, 729.

5 See eg the Court of Appeal decisions in *Lim Kim Som v Sheriffa Taibah bte Abdul Rahman* [1994] 1 SLR(R) 233 [12]; *Glahe International Expo AG v ACS Computer Pte Ltd* [1999] 1 SLR(R) 945 [27]; *RDC Concrete Pte Ltd v Sato Kogyo (S) Pte Ltd* [2007] 4 SLR(R) 413 [59]; *Alliance Concrete* (n 2) [34].

6 *Alliance Concrete* (n 2) [33].

7 *Alliance Concrete* (n 2) [37].

8 Phang (n 1) para 19.028.

9 *MTU Asia Pte Ltd v Brightside-Woh Hup* [1987] SLR(R) 419 [27]. The judge was quoting from *Halsbury's Laws of England, vol 9* (4th edn, Butterworths 1974) 314 para 450.

10 [1994] 1 SLR(R) 233.

11 [1956] AC 696, 720–21, quoted in *Lim Kim Som* (n 5) [25].

12 See n 9.

13 M Chen-Wishart, *Contract Law* (7th edn, OUP 2023) para 7.2.3.

14 [1956] AC 696, 720–21, quoted in *Lim Kim Som* [26].

2. Applicability of the Doctrine in Various Circumstances

In *Alliance Concrete*, the Court of Appeal highlighted that the doctrine of frustration 'is an exception to the norm of sanctity of contract and therefore is to be applied to discharge the parties from their contract in only exceptional circumstances'.[15] This strict approach is reflected in the case law, discussed below under various headings. These are just classifications of convenience. There are other ways of classifying frustration cases and there may be overlaps where the facts of a case can fall under more than one heading. The question is always whether the performance of the obligations in the new circumstances would be radically different from what had been agreed under the contract.

(a) Supervening 'impossibility'

The strongest ground for frustration of a contract is that its performance has become impossible. However, a range of situations may fall broadly under the heading of 'impossibility' of performance, and not all will frustrate the contract. These could range from clear-cut cases where the contract is physically impossible to perform to situations where, for example, the subject matter of the contract becomes unavailable; where the method of performance becomes impossible; where the source of the goods has failed; or where the purpose for which the contract was entered into becomes impossible to carry out. Not all will frustrate a contract; whether it does will depend on the construction of the contract and the type of 'impossibility' involved.

(1) Destruction of subject matter

The most famous example of destruction of the subject matter of the contract can be found in the English case of *Taylor v Caldwell*,[16] involving a rental of 'the Surrey Gardens and Music Hall' for a series of concerts. A fire destroyed the music hall before the concerts took place. The court decided that as the music hall ceased to exist without fault of either party, both parties were excused from performance of the contract. Although the word 'frustration' was not used in the judgment, this case is generally accepted as the starting point of the modern doctrine of frustration. The position is similar in the context of a sale of goods: where specific goods that have been sold are destroyed after the parties have made the contract but before the contract has been performed, both parties are discharged from their obligations under the contract.[17]

However, a destruction of what appears to be the subject matter of the contract may not always lead to frustration. In *Chiang Hong Pte Ltd v Lim Poh Neo (trading as Tai San Plastic Factory)*,[18] an occupier of a wooden building had entered into a compensation agreement with the owner of the premises to vacate the premises by a certain date. Before the date for handing over the premises, a fire completely destroyed the wooden structure. The owner claimed that the compensation agreement was frustrated as the fire had destroyed the subject matter of the contract. The Court of Appeal approved the judge's construction of the

[15] [2014] 3 SLR 857 [38].
[16] (1863) 3 B & S 826.
[17] Sale of Goods Act 1979, 2020 revised edition, s 7. This statute is based on the UK Sale of Goods Act 1979, UK 1979, c 54. It should be noted that s 7 also mentions the passing of risk: the contract would not be frustrated if the risk in the goods had passed to the buyer at the time of their destruction.
[18] [1983–1984] SLR(R) 346.

contract, that the owners were primarily, if not wholly, interested to recover vacant possession of the land, and that the structure was inconsequential to them.[19] Despite the destruction of the structure, the owner would get what it had bargained for, which was vacant possession of the land, and the contract was not frustrated.

(2) Death or incapacity of a contracting party

In a contract which requires the personal performance of one or both contracting parties, the death of one of the parties or an incapacity which renders performance of the contract impossible would frustrate the contract. Examples might be the death of the employee in an employment contract or an accident leading to the amputation of one of the legs of a dancer who has agreed to perform in a ballet.

(3) Legal impossibility: Illegality

Where there has been a change of circumstances after the contract has been concluded such that performance of the contract becomes illegal, public policy dictates that the contract should be frustrated. In the English House of Lords decision in *Denny, Mott & Dickson Ltd v James B Fraser & Co Ltd*, Lord Macmillan stated that '[i]t is plain that a contract to do what has become illegal to do cannot be legally enforceable. There cannot be a default in doing what the law forbids to be done.'[20] In this case, the contract was frustrated when war-time regulations prohibited transactions in the type of goods which formed the subject matter of the contract.

(4) Unavailability of subject matter

A contract may become impossible to perform because the subject matter of the contract, or an item that is essential to its performance, has become unavailable. Two examples in Singapore relate to compulsory acquisition of properties by the government, which led to the frustration of a contract for the sale of a house in one case[21] and of a tenancy agreement in another.[22] Another example relates to the exchange controls imposed by the Malaysian government on 1 September 1998. In *Shenyin Wangou-APS Management Pte Ltd v Commerzbank (South-East Asia) Ltd (Shenyin Wangou)*,[23] the High Court found that the subject matter of the deposit contract was Malaysian ringgit (MYR) in the offshore market and that the entire offshore market for MYR had been wiped out by the economic control measures of the Malaysian government in pursuing its legitimate national objectives. There was therefore no MYR available in the offshore market, due to no fault of either party, and the contract was frustrated.

(5) Impossibility of method of performance

When the contemplated method of performance specified in the contract becomes impossible, the contract will generally be frustrated. The legal position is less clear with a method that is contemplated but unspecified in the contract by the parties. A strict approach to this issue was taken in the English case of *Tsakiroglou & Co Ltd v Noblee Thorl GmbH*

[19] [1983–1984] SLR(R) 346 [16], [19].
[20] [1944] AC 265 at 272.
[21] *Lim Kim Som* (n 5).
[22] *Singapore Woodcraft Manufacturing Co (Pte) Ltd v Mok Ah Sai* [1979–1980] SLR(R) 159.
[23] [2001] 3 SLR(R) 108.

(*Tsakiroglou*),[24] where the House of Lords decided the closure of the Suez Canal did not frustrate a contract for the sale of goods from Port Sudan to Hamburg as shipment by the Cape of Good Hope was still possible. Although the Cape route was much longer and more expensive, this was not so onerous to the sellers as to make the performance of the contract fundamentally different from what they had promised.[25] An important finding in this case was that although both parties contemplated that the goods would be shipped by the Suez Canal, there was no evidence that the buyers cared what route was taken, or, within reasonable limits, when the goods arrived.[26] It is likely that a Singapore court will follow the approach taken in *Tsakiroglou* and decide that a contract would not be frustrated in similar circumstances where an alternative method of performance was available.

(6) *Failure of source*

A contract may become impossible to perform because of the failure of a particular source from which the subject matter of the contract is to be derived, for example, where a specific crop of potatoes is wiped out by disease[27] or a supply of timber is disrupted by war.[28] In such cases, if the source is referred to in the contract, the contract will generally be discharged by frustration.[29] If the source is not provided for in the contract and only one of the parties intends to use that particular source, the contract will generally not be frustrated.[30] In *Alliance Concrete*, the source was not specified in the contract, but both parties 'contemplated or could reasonably have contemplated that unspecified source'. The Court of Appeal stated that this could operate to frustrate the contract;[31] that is, the contract for the supply of ready-mixed concrete was frustrated by the Indonesian government's ban on sand exports as both parties contemplated that Indonesian sand would be used in the preparation of ready-mixed concrete by the supplier, and such sand was not available.[32]

The English case of *Howell v Coupland*[33] illustrates the situation of a partial failure of a source. Here, the seller agreed to sell 200 tons of regent potatoes grown on his land in Whaplode. Disease attacked the crop causing it to fail and only 80 tons were delivered to the buyer. The buyer sued for the shortfall in delivery but was unsuccessful. The English Court of Appeal upheld the High Court's decision and treated the contract as having been discharged. The decision in *Howell v Coupland* can be interpreted in two ways.[34] The first is that the duty to deliver was conditional upon the coming into existence and continued existence of the requisite quantity of potatoes from the specified location.[35] The second interpretation, preferred by the Singapore Court of Appeal in *Alliance Concrete*, is that 'a contract for the sale of goods will be discharged if that contract expressly provides for the goods to be taken from a particular source and that source fails without the fault of either

24 [1962] AC 93.
25 [1962] AC 93, Lord Hodson at 128.
26 [1962] AC 93 at 115.
27 *Howell v Coupland* (1876) 1 QBD 258.
28 *Blackburn Bobbin Co Ltd v TW Allen & Sons Ltd* [1918] 2 KB 467.
29 *Alliance Concrete* (n 2) [49]; *Howell v Coupland* (n 27).
30 *Blackburn Bobbin Co Ltd v TW Allen & Sons Ltd* (n 28). See also *Alliance Concrete* (n 2) [51].
31 [2014] 3 SLR 857 [55].
32 [2014] 3 SLR 857 [71], [79].
33 (1876) 1 QBD 258.
34 See the discussion in Phang and Goh (n 1) para 1383.
35 *In re Wait* [1927] 1 Ch 606, 631; *HR and S Sainsbury Ltd v Street* [1972] 1 WLR 834, 837, referred to in *Alliance Concrete* (n 2) [50].

contracting party'.[36] The Singapore Court of Appeal did not make a distinction between a partial and a complete failure of a source and it would seem from their discussion of *Howell v Coupland* that a partial failure can also frustrate a contract. However, this analysis does not explain the basis upon which the existing crop of 80 tons was delivered. If frustration involves the discharge of the entire contract, could the seller have refused to deliver the 80 tons of potatoes that were produced? Was there a new contract for the 80 tons that had been delivered, or was there a doctrine of partial frustration, leaving intact the obligation to deliver the part of the goods that had been produced? An implied condition approach would deal with this situation in a more principled way and support the argument that the contract was 'not an absolute contract of delivery under all circumstances, but a contract to deliver so many potatoes, of a particular kind, grown on a specific place, if deliverable from that place'.[37]

(7) *Impossibility of purpose*

A contract may be frustrated where the purpose for which one or both parties entered into the contract can no longer be achieved because of a change of circumstances. A famous example is the English case of *Krell v Henry*,[38] where a contract to rent a flat in Pall Mall overlooking the route of King Henry VII's coronation procession was frustrated by the cancellation of the procession due to the king's illness. Here, both parties considered the viewing of the procession as the main purpose of the contract. This was supported by the fact that the flat was unusually rented out in the daytime on the relevant dates and the price was higher than normal. *Krell v Henry* is often contrasted with another English coronation-related case, *Herne Bay Steamboat Co v Hutton*,[39] where the court decided that a contract to hire a boat to view the naval review and a day's cruise around the fleet was not frustrated by the cancellation of the naval review. This result can be explained by the fact that it was still possible to use the boat for sightseeing, and the naval review was just one of the purposes of the contract.

In impossibility of purpose cases, the court must decide whether the continued existence of a state of affairs was a necessary foundation of the contract. In *MTU Asia Pte Ltd v Brightside-Woh Hup*,[40] the defendant, a subcontractor for a development project (the 'Gateway project'), contracted with the plaintiff to supply equipment which the plaintiff intended to use for the subcontract. The Gateway project was subsequently cancelled, but the court rejected the defendant's argument that the contract was frustrated. The court found that although the plaintiffs were aware that the equipment was ordered for the Gateway project, the defendants had never informed them that the equipment was intended exclusively for the project or that the continuing existence of that project was to be the basis of the contract and that the plaintiffs would never have agreed to sell the equipment if that had been the stipulated basis.[41] A different result was reached in *Sheng Siong Supermarket Pte Ltd v Carilla Pte Ltd* (*Sheng Siong*),[42] where the plaintiffs rented

[36] *Alliance Concrete* (n 2) [50].
[37] (1876) 1 QBD 258, 261.
[38] [1903] 2 KB 740.
[39] [1903] 2 KB 683.
[40] [1987] SLR(R) 419.
[41] [1987] SLR(R) 419 [12].
[42] [2011] 4 SLR 1094.

a leasehold property from the defendant intending to use part of it as a supermarket but the proposal for such usage was subsequently rejected by the Housing and Development Board (HDB). The High Court found that the parties intended the lease to be conditional on the premises being permitted to be used as a supermarket and therefore that HDB's rejection of the proposed plans frustrated the contract.[43] Although this was not discussed in the *Sheng Siong* judgment, a possible alternative analysis could be that the contract was subject to a condition precedent which was not satisfied so that there was no contract between the parties.

(b) Impracticality of performance

The performance of a contract could become more burdensome or less profitable because of matters such as increased costs, inflation, an unfavourable exchange rate, higher taxation, loss of use, or decreased profitability. The Singapore courts have made it clear that a mere increase in the burden or a decrease in the profitability of a contract is unlikely to amount to frustration.

A good example is *Glahe International Expo AG v ACS Computer Pte Ltd (Glahe)*,[44] where the buyer of computers to be delivered to Moscow for the Russian market argued that the contract was frustrated due to increased taxation (imposition of 200 per cent *ad valorem* tax), severe inflation (up to 1,353 per cent in 1992), currency depreciation between US$ and Russian ruble (RUB) (from US$1:RUB0.57 to US$1:RUB40), and the turbulent and chaotic changes in the political situation which led to the dissolution of the Union of Soviet Socialist Republics (USSR). The Court of Appeal found that the contract was not frustrated as the obligations of the buyer under the contract were not fundamentally or radically altered. The contract price (in US dollars) had not changed, the computers were not prohibited from entering the USSR, it remained possible to ship computers to the USSR, and the buyer still had the ability to open a letter of credit. The only thing that had changed was the profitability of the contract to the buyer as it would be difficult to resell the computers, given the import tax and disadvantageous exchange rate. Examples and principles from well-known English cases have been considered and accepted in Singapore.[45] These include *Davis Contractors*,[46] where a builder contracted to build 78 house for a local authority for £94,000 but a labour shortage raised the cost to £115,000 and houses took 22 months to complete instead of 8 months as originally agreed; *National Carriers Ltd v Panalpina (Northern) Ltd*,[47] where in the fifth year of a ten-year lease, a warehouse had its only vehicular access blocked by the local authority for safety reasons for a period of 20 months; and *Tsakiroglou*,[48] discussed earlier. In all these cases, the plea of frustration failed as performance of the contract in the changed circumstances was not regarded as radically different from the original obligations.

The strict approach taken by the courts might lead one to ask whether a contract can ever be frustrated because performance has become more burdensome or the contract

43 [2011] 4 SLR 1094 [76], [77].
44 [1999] 1 SLR(R) 945. See also *MP Bilt Pte Ltd v Edy Yumianto* [1999] 2 SLR(R) 655; *Oversea-Chinese Banking Corp Ltd v Daewoo Singapore Pte Ltd* [2000] 2 SLR(R) 161.
45 See eg *Glahe* (n 5) [38]–[42].
46 [1956] AC 696.
47 [1981] AC 675.
48 [1962] AC 93.

has become less profitable. The answer, at least theoretically, seems to be yes. In *Glahe*, the Court of Appeal entertained the idea that 'there may well be cases where extreme onerousness would render a contract so unprofitable to perform that the contractual obligations may be considered to be fundamentally or radically different.'[49] Courts in the UK and Singapore have hinted that an 'astronomical' increase in costs might be sufficient to frustrate a contract,[50] but there has been no definite statement on this point and no guidance as to what would be considered 'astronomical'. The Singapore courts have also stated that inflation might possibly bring about frustration in 'very exceptional circumstances'.[51]

(c) Delay

For a delay to lead to frustration, it 'must be abnormal, in its cause, its effects, or its expected duration, so that it falls outside what the parties could reasonably contemplate at the time of contracting'.[52] There are hardly any Singapore frustration cases involving the effect of delay.[53] In *Premier Properties Pte Ltd v Tan Soo Tiong*,[54] the defendant agreed to sell their apartments to the plaintiff developers in an *en bloc* sale in exchange for a new apartment in the plaintiffs' new development. The new apartments were to be ready not more than 33 months after the handing over of the old apartments. There was in fact a delay of 12 months, but this, according to the court, did not so alter the nature of the bargain as to frustrate the contract.

Where the length of the delay is not immediately apparent, a court must assess whether it is likely to have a sufficiently serious effect on the performance of the contract or whether the effect is likely to be temporary.[55] The probable length of the delay 'must be assessed in relation to the nature of the contract, and to the expected duration of the contract after the delay is expected to end'.[56] In the English case of *Metropolitan Water Board v Dick Kerr & Co*,[57] a contract to build a reservoir in six years was interrupted when the outbreak of war led to an order by the Minister of Munitions one-and-a-half years after the contract had been concluded, prohibiting construction work on the reservoir. The House of Lords held that the contract had been discharged as a result of the Minister's order because the effect of the prohibition might be that the works could not be resumed until a good part of the six years were over, by which time the conditions regarding labour and materials might be completely different.[58]

49 [1999] 1 SLR(R) 945 [42].

50 *Tsakiroglou* (n 24) 118 and 128–29 (discussed in Phang and Goh (n 1) para 1397); *Glahe* (n 5) [24]. The question of an astronomical increase in costs was also discussed in the context of a *force majeure* clause in *Holcim (Singapore) Pte Ltd v Precise Development Pte Ltd* [2011] 2 SLR(R) 106 [53], [78].

51 *MP Bilt v Edy Yumianto* (n 44) [15].

52 AG Guest. *Chitty on Contracts* (27th edn, Sweet & Maxwell 1994) 1113, quoted with approval in *Premier Properties Pte Ltd v Tan Soo Tiong* [2000] SGHC 12 [17].

53 Guidance can be taken from the English cases on this point. See eg *Jackson v Union Marine Insurance Co Ltd* (1874) LR 10 CP 125; *Metropolitan Water Board v Dick, Kerr & Co* [1918] AC 119; *Bank Line Ltd v Arthur Capel Ltd* [1919] AC 435; *The Nema* [1982] AC 724.

54 [2000] SGHC 12, affirmed by the Court of Appeal in *Chua Chay Lee v Premier Properties Pte Ltd* [2000] 2 SLR(R) 464.

55 Phang (n 1) para 19.089.

56 *Chitty on Contracts* (n 52) 1113, quoted with approval in *Premier Properties Pte Ltd v Tan Soo Tiong* (n 52) [17].

57 [1918] AC 119.

58 [1918] AC 119, 126–27.

3. Limits to Frustration

(a) Foreseeability

Can a contract be frustrated by a supervening event that is foreseeable? One might argue that it should not because if one or both the parties had foreseen the change in circumstances and had not provided for it under the contract, the conclusion must be that they were willing to bear the risk of the changed circumstances. The answer to this question, according to the Singapore Court of Appeal in *Lim Kim Som*, 'is not free from doubt', and 'different judges have proffered different views on the subject'.[59] Nevertheless, the predominant view expressed by Singapore judges is that the doctrine of frustration will not apply where the supervening event is foreseeable. There have been express statements to this effect in a few cases[60] and the reasoning in several prominent decisions also supports this view. In *Glahe*, one reason given for the finding that the contract was not frustrated was that at the time of contract formation, 'significant changes in terms of rates of exchange, currency depreciation, inflation, imposition of taxes and political situations were already taking place in Russia'.[61] In *Alliance Concrete*, the court, in finding frustration, referred to the fact that the Indonesian sand ban was neither foreseen nor reasonably foreseeable.[62]

The authors of a popular local contract textbook have suggested that we should acknowledge that the issue of foreseeability is a matter of degree so that where 'either the alleged frustrating event is actually foreseen or where there is a high degree of foreseeability' the doctrine of frustration is excluded.[63]

(b) Self-induced frustration

A party who is affected by a frustrating event and could have avoided its negative effects but failed to do so will be prevented from claiming that the contract has been frustrated.[64] The rule that self-induced frustration cannot constitute frustration is consistent with the idea that a frustrating event cannot be due to the fault of either party. There has been no Singapore decision that rests squarely on this point,[65] but the principle is well accepted by the courts.[66]

59 [1994] 1 SLR 393 [48]. Here, the Court of Appeal discussed the contrasting views of English judges in several cases but did not mention any local cases.

60 *Win Supreme Investment (S) Pte Ltd v Joharah bte Abdul Wahab* [1996] 3 SLR(R) 583 [33]; *HDB v Microform Precision Industries* [2003] SGHC 214 [7]. In the UK, see eg *Walton Harvey Ltd v Walker & Humfrays Ltd* [1931] 1 Ch 274.

61 [1999] 1 SLR(R) 945 [34].

62 [2014] 3 SLR 857 [62].

63 Phang and Goh (n 1) para 1405.

64 The leading English cases are *Maritime National Fish v Ocean Trawlers Limited* [1935] AC 524; *The Super Servant Two* [1990] Lloyd's Rep 1 (Court of Appeal) and [1989] Lloyd's Rep 148 (Hobhouse J).

65 Although see the analysis in *Adani Wilmar Ltd v Cooperatieve Centrale Raiffeisen-Boerenleenbank BA* [2002] 2 SLR(R) 216 in Phang and Goh (n 1) para 1406. The judgment itself does not use the term 'self-induced frustration'.

66 See eg *Alliance Concrete* (n 2) [83]–[84]; *RDC Concrete Pte Ltd v Sato Kogyo (S) Pte Ltd* (n 5) [59]; and *Precise Development Pte Ltd v Holcim (Singapore) Pte Ltd* [2010] 1 SLR 1083, [52].

4. Effects of Frustration: The Frustrated Contracts Act 1959

When a contract is frustrated and comes to an end, all obligations arising before the frustrating event must be honoured and all future obligations are discharged. The effect of this under the common law could be unfair.[67] For example, if one of the parties had made an advance payment before the discharge of the contract but not yet received complete counter-performance, the payor could not get his money back unless there was a total failure of consideration.[68] Conversely, if the contract stipulated payment only on completion, and performance was interrupted midway by a frustrating event, the performing party would not get paid, even if the other party derived some benefit from this part performance.[69] These unsatisfactory common law principles have been modified by statute, and the position is now governed by the Frustrated Contracts Act 1959 (FCA).[70] It should be noted that the provisions of the FCA only come into play where a contract 'has become impossible of performance or been otherwise frustrated and the parties to the contract have for that reason been discharged from further performance'.[71] This means that before the provisions of the FCA can be applied, the court must first find that the contract is frustrated, and this is a question for the common law.

(a) Sums paid or payable and expenses incurred

Where a contract has been frustrated, section 2(2) FCA provides that all sums of money payable under the contract before the time of discharge cease to be payable, and any sums that have been paid are recoverable.[72] If the person to whom money was paid or is payable has incurred expenses for the performance of the contract before its discharge, section 2(3) provides that the court may, if it considers it just to do so having regard to all the circumstances of the case, allow him to retain or, as the case may be, recover the whole or any part of the sums so paid or payable, not being an amount in excess of the expenses so incurred. The amount to be awarded is at the discretion of the court, and the section only specifies the ceiling of the amount that can be retained or recovered by the claimant, being the lesser of (i) the expenses that had been incurred and (ii) the sum that is paid or payable. If the contract does not provide for any payment by one party before the time of discharge, no amount can be claimed by the other party for its expenses under section 2(3). In this situation, the party incurring expenses may nevertheless be able to claim a sum if he has provided a valuable benefit to the other party under the terms of section 2(4), as discussed below.

(b) Just sum awarded for the valuable benefit conferred

Section 2(4) applies where 'any party to the contract has, by reason of anything done by any other party to the contract in, or for the purpose of, the performance of the contract, obtained a valuable benefit (other than a payment of money to which subsection (2) applies) before the time of discharge'. This allows a contracting party who has partially performed

[67] Phang and Goh (n 1) paras 1415–1418.

[68] See the English case of *Fibrosa Spolka Akcyjna Appellants v Fairbairn Lawson Combe Barbour* [1943] 1 AC 32, overruling *Chandler v Webster* [1904] 1 KB 493.

[69] See eg the English case of *Appleby v Myers* (1867) LR 2 CP 651.

[70] 2020 rev edn. This is based on the English Law Reform (Frustrated Contracts) Act 1943, 1943 c 40.

[71] FCA, s 2(1).

[72] *Lim Kim Som* (n 5); *Sheng Siong* (n 42); *Dathena Science Pte Ltd v Justco (Singapore) Pte Ltd* [2021] SGHC 219.

his obligations before the frustrating event to claim a sum of money from the other party if the latter has benefited as a result of such performance. The court can award an amount that it considers just. Section 2(4) stipulates, inter alia, that the amount must not exceed the value of the benefit to the party obtaining it and that all the circumstances of the case must be taken into account. The court must also take into account any amount that the claimant had incurred in the performance of the contract before the frustrating event, including any sum paid by him and retained or recoverable by the other party under section 2(3). For example, if a contractor has done renovation work on the owner's premises and the contract is frustrated before payment is due, the court may award the contractor a sum which they think just under section 2(4) if the partially done renovation works have conferred a benefit to the owner. To prevent double recovery, if the contractor had been allowed to retain or recover a sum of money for his expenditure under section 2(3), the just sum awarded under section 2(4) may be reduced to offset this if the expenditure had been incurred for the purpose of the renovation works. So far, section 2(4) has not been discussed or applied by the Singapore courts. What if the frustrating event has wiped out any benefit received by the relevant party, for example, if a partially constructed building has been completely destroyed by fire? On a plain reading of section 2(4), it would seem that the valuable benefit to the building owner should be assessed before the fire because section 2(4) refers to a benefit obtained *before* the time of discharge.[73] However, since all the circumstances must be looked at when assessing the just sum, the total destruction by fire would be relevant. If the general approach of the FCA of preventing unjust enrichment rather than sharing losses[74] is applied in such assessment, the just sum in a case where the benefit has been completely wiped out should be zero.

III. *Force majeure* Clauses

The preceding discussion shows that it is difficult for contracting parties who are faced with changed circumstances to assess with certainty whether their contract has been discharged by frustration. Also, the doctrine of frustration not only operates within narrow limits but is also rigid in its effect. Either the contract comes to an end or it carries on as before; there is no room for varying the obligations of the parties. To avoid these potential issues, the parties can insert *force majeure* clauses in their contracts to deal with situations that might arise, over which the parties have little or no control, that might impede or obstruct the performance of the contract.[75] Such clauses are commonly used in Singapore. Whether a *force majeure* situation has arisen, and the rights and the obligations of the parties that might follow from this situation, will depend on the provisions of the clause.

The parties' definition of a *force majeure* event determines the circumstances that would trigger the operation of the clause. Deciding whether a *force majeure* clause is applicable to a particular situation requires a determination of the meaning of the clause as well as an

[73] However, see the analysis of s 1(3) of the UK Law Reform (Frustrated Contracts) Act 1943 (which is largely similar to s 2(4) of the Singapore FCA) in *BP Exploration Co (Libya) Ltd v Hunt (No 2)* [1979] 1 WLR 783, affirmed for the most part in [1981] 1 WLR 232 and [1983] 2 AC 352. See also the discussion in Phang (n 1) paras 19.110–19.123.

[74] *BP Exploration Co (Libya) Ltd v Hunt (No 2)* (n 73) 799.

[75] *Magenta Resources (S) Pte Ltd v China Resources (S) Pte Ltd* [1996] 2 SLR(R) 316 [60].

assessment of the situation that has taken place to see whether it falls within the clause. In *RDC Concrete Pte Ltd v Sato Kogyo (S) Pte Ltd* (*RDC Concrete*),[76] the *force majeure* event was defined as an act of God or a circumstance which arose 'due to any cause beyond the supplier's control'.[77] The Court of Appeal took the view that the shortage of raw materials which arose in the case did not fall within the *force majeure* clause because the supplier could still purchase these raw materials in the market, albeit at a higher price.[78] In *Holcim (Singapore) Pte Ltd v Precise Development Pte Ltd* (*Holcim*),[79] the *force majeure* clause would apply if supply had been 'disrupted' by a shortage of material. The Court of Appeal stated that a situation of 'disruption' or 'hindrance', unlike a situation of 'prevention', need not render performance impossible.[80] If a merchant was put in the commercially impracticable position of being unable to deliver the contracted goods unless he dislocated his business and broke his other contracts, this would be a situation that disrupted delivery.[81]

In *RDC Concrete*, the Court of Appeal stated that the principles relevant to the doctrine of frustration are also relevant to the construction of *force majeure* clauses as 'by their very nature and function, *force majeure* clauses would—in the ordinary course of events—be triggered only where there was a radical external event that supervened and that was not due to the fault of either of the contracting parties'.[82] Other parallels with the doctrine of frustration are also evident in the cases. For instance, in *Holcim*, the Court of Appeal highlighted that the increase in the cost of sand did not, in and of itself, constitute a 'disruption' within the meaning of a *force majeure* event,[83] in keeping with the common law doctrine of frustration where a mere increase in price would not generally constitute a frustrating event.[84]

The provisions of a *force majeure* clause can be wide-ranging. In addition to the definition of a *force majeure* event, the clause will typically provide for the effects of such event, and these can be more varied than under the doctrine of frustration and the FCA. For example, the parties may be given an extension of time, or they may be obliged to renegotiate to adapt the contract. A *force majeure* clause can also provide for specific procedures to be followed, such as the giving of notice to other party[85] or the obtaining of a certificate from a competent authority in country where the *force majeure* event took place.[86]

IV. Other Contractual Clauses

The principle of freedom of contract and the court's commitment to giving effect to the intention of the parties means that parties can, subject to the usual principles of contract

76 [2007] 4 SLR(R) 413.
77 [2007] 4 SLR(R) 413 [9].
78 [2007] 4 SLR(R) 413 [68]–[70].
79 [2011] 2 SLR 106.
80 [2011] 2 SLR 106 [56].
81 [2011] 2 SLR 106 [57] quoting Earl Loreburn in *Tennants (Lancashire) Limited v C S Wilson and Company, Limited* [1917] AC 495, 510–11.
82 *RDC Concrete* (n 5) [57].
83 [2011] 2 SLR 106 [54].
84 [2011] 2 SLR 106 [53]. However, the Court left open the question as to the legal position if the increase in price had been 'astronomical'.
85 *China Resources* [1997] 1 SLR(R) 1; *Glahe* (n 5).
86 *China Resources* (n 85) [41]; *Magenta Resources (S) Pte Ltd v China Resources (S) Pte Ltd* (n 75) [112].

law, include any provisions that they wish in their contract to deal with changes in circumstances and are not confined to *force majeure* clauses. An example might be a price adjustment clause triggered by defined events, with the adjustment fixed by reference to a reliable and well-established price index. This type of clause protects the parties against drastic price changes which would not usually constitute a *force majeure* event and would be particularly relevant in long term contracts to avoid the need for frequent renegotiation.

V. General Contractual Principles

1. Implied Term Analysis

A party who is unable to perform his contract because of a change of circumstances may try to argue that an implied term provides him with a lawful excuse. The Singapore law of implied terms was authoritatively set out in *Sembcorp Marine Ltd v PPL Holdings Pte Ltd*.[87] The Court of Appeal reiterated that an implied term is based on the presumed intention of the parties and set out the requirements for a term to be implied: there must be a true gap to be filled (one not contemplated by the parties), the implication of a term must be necessary (and not just desirable) to give business efficacy to contract, and the substance of the implied term must be one that the parties would have thought was obvious. While arguments based on an implied term are often raised in the courts, the relatively stringent requirements mean that it is not easy to succeed.[88]

2. Interpretation of Contractual Terms

Where circumstances have changed, the parties could try to argue that the contract should be interpreted in such a way that the parties are not bound to perform in the new circumstances. This will depend on the terms of the contract and the facts of the case. For example, the obligations of the parties may be subject to a condition precedent or a condition subsequent.[89] In the former situation, the contract does not come into existence if the condition is (or is not) satisfied, whereas in the latter, the contract comes to an end.

3. Mistake and Misrepresentation

The doctrines of mistake or misrepresentation could be applicable if their requisite elements are made out. However, mistake will not generally be relevant to changes in circumstances after the contract has been entered into. Unlike frustration, which deals with a supervening event, mistake focuses on the state of matters at the time of the contract. The law of misrepresentation is also unlikely to be applicable to a change of circumstances. Even if a person has said that he would act in a certain way but later changes his mind when

[87] [2013] SGCA 43 [75]–[101].
[88] See eg *Shenyin Wangou* (n 23).
[89] This is arguably an alternative justification for the result in *Sheng Siong* (n 42).

circumstances change, this does not necessarily mean that the earlier statement was false at the time that it was made.

VI. The COVID-19 Pandemic

1. Case Law

One of the first—if not the first—COVID-19-related contractual disputes to reach the Singapore courts was *Dathena Science Pte Ltd v Justco (Singapore) Pte Ltd* (*Dathena*).[90] This involved a two-year lease of business premises at OCBC Centre East. The defendant landlord was unable to deliver the premises by the agreed commencement date of 1 May 2020 because renovation work was delayed by the government 'circuit-breaker' measures. The plaintiff tenant sued for a return of its security deposit, arguing, inter alia, that the contract had been frustrated. The defendant argued, inter alia, that various terms in the agreement allowed it to replace the OCBC Centre East premises with other premises of a comparable size. The High Court found that the contract had been frustrated by the 'circuit-breaker' measures. In coming to this decision, the court took into account the four-month delay in delivering the premises, the fact that the alternative premises offered were not comparable to what had been agreed under the contract, and the incurrence of additional moving costs, all of which would have made the defendant's performance fundamentally different from what had been agreed under the contract.[91] The court therefore ordered the defendant to return the plaintiff's deposit under section 2(2) of the FCA.

In *Lachman's Emporium Pte Ltd v Kang Tien Kuan (trading as Lookers Music Café, a sole proprietorship)* (*Lachman's Emporium*),[92] the landlord of a nightclub sued the tenant for failure to pay rent and applied for summary judgment. The tenant argued that there was a frustration of purpose arising from the closure of night-time entertainment venues due to COVID-19-related government measures. The court dismissed the application for summary judgment because there was a triable issue whether using the premises as music lounge was a commonly held purpose shared by both parties. Although this was not explicitly expanded upon in the case, it would appear that the contract in *Lachman's Emporium* would be frustrated if such a common purpose could be found.

Dathena and *Lachmann's Emporium* confirm that the changes in circumstances brought about by the COVID-19 pandemic can qualify as supervening events that might give rise to the frustration of contracts. These cases also make clear that the happening of the pandemic did not in itself cause contracts to be frustrated. The 'radical change in obligation' test for frustration must still be satisfied. It is interesting that the judges in neither case discussed the potentially temporary nature of the pandemic and how this might limit the operation of the doctrine of frustration.

[90] [2021] SGHC 219. This case can be contrasted with the English case of *Bank of New York Mellon (International) Ltd v Cine-UK Ltd* [2021] EWHC 1013 (QB), where the judge decided that the leases in question were not frustrated by the pandemic. The English judge also expressed the view that there was no concept of 'temporary frustration' in the law.

[91] [2021] SGHC 291 [188].

[92] [2022] SGHC 19.

2. The COVID-19 Act

The COVID-19 pandemic caused unprecedented disruption to personal and commercial life globally. In Singapore, the government introduced the COVID-19 (Temporary Measures) Act 2020 (the COVID-19 Act)[93] on 17 April 2020 to deal with the health concerns and economic hardship associated with the pandemic. The Act provided for a 'circuit-breaker' period during which personal mobility and business activity were severely curtailed, social distancing rules were in place, and temporary relief for inability to perform contracts due to the pandemic was provided.[94] The types of contracts which qualified for relief are set out in the first schedule of the Act. These included leases of non-residential immovable property, tourism-related contracts, and construction contracts.[95] A party to a scheduled contract could apply for relief from performing the contract by serving a notice for relief on the other party.[96] Upon receiving such notice, the other party was temporarily prohibited from taking action to enforce the contract.[97] Applications for relief were heard by assessors appointed by the Ministry of Law, who were empowered to make various determinations relating to the rights of the parties so as to reach a just and equitable outcome.[98]

Interference with the sanctity of contracts and the alteration of performance obligations was not something undertaken lightly by the Singapore government. The need for these drastic measures was explained by the Minister for Law in Parliament: if the government did not intervene, most businesses would suffer bankruptcies and insolvencies, and there would be a complete destruction of the economic arena.[99] It would seem that the regulations were designed to, as far as possible in the circumstances, respect the contractual rights of the parties and to preserve the tenets of contract law. First, the relief for inability to perform contracts due to the pandemic was only temporary. These reliefs have now largely expired, and the contractual rights of the parties have been restored. Secondly, the time frames were carefully chosen to give relief only to those who were truly deserving. Relief only applied to contracts that were to be performed after 1 February 2020 (when the effects of COVID-19 began to be felt significantly in Singapore thereby affecting contractual performance) and that were entered into before 25 March 2020[100] (on 24 March, the Ministry of Health announced enhanced COVID-19 restrictions, so a person entering into a contract after that date with knowledge of the severity of the situation should not seek relief). Third, the temporary relief was expressed not to affect the taking of any other action, including an action pursuant to the FCA or a *force majeure* clause in the contract, where applicable.[101] In this author's view, this provision highlights that the COVID-19 contractual relief is directed at situations where the effect of the pandemic on the parties' ability to perform is not serious enough to frustrate the contract or where the situation does not fall within the coverage of a *force majeure* clause in the contract. Applying this principle, the COVID-19 Act does not prevent the frustration of a contract, and in the event of frustration, the rights of the parties

[93] No 14 of 2020 <https://sso.agc.gov.sg/act/covid19tma2020> accessed 23 May 2024.
[94] COVID-19 Act (n 93) div 2.
[95] COVID-19 Act (n 93) sch 1.
[96] COVID-19 Act (n 93) s 9.
[97] COVID-19 Act (n 93) s 5(3).
[98] COVID-19 Act (n 93) s 13.
[99] Singapore Parliamentary Debates, Official Report (4 April 2020) vol 94 (K Shanmugam, Minister for Law).
[100] COVID-19 Act (n 93) ss 4(a), 5(1)(a).
[101] COVID-19 Act (n 93) s 5(13).

would be decided under the FCA. Further, where the contract contains a *force majeure* clause and a particular pandemic-related situation falls within the definition of a *force majeure* event in the clause, the consequences set out in the clause will follow according to the parties' prior allocation of risk. In these two situations, there is no need for relief under the COVID-19 Act as the rights and obligations of the parties in the new situation are already provided for under the doctrine of frustration or by the law relating to *force majeure* clauses.

VII. The Hypotheticals

The following section will apply the principles of Singapore law to the hypothetical case scenarios proposed by the volume editors.[102]

1. Abraham and Bill

After more than 450 years (1567–2018), maintenance of the irrigation channel is now more onerous for Abraham's successors. However, this would not justify them in law asking Bill for a higher price. An argument that there was an implied term that the price should be reviewed periodically is unlikely to succeed if the price has not been reviewed since the time of the contract. As regards termination of the contract, it would be hard for Abraham's successors in law to argue that the contract had been frustrated as the fact that the contract has become more burdensome to perform because of increased costs and inflation does not make performance of the contract radically different from what the parties had agreed to do. Abraham's successors in law may have a better chance of success by arguing that there was an implied term in the contract that the agreement could be terminated by giving reasonable notice by either party. They could also argue, if the facts support this, that a right to terminate existed based on an interpretation of the terms of the contract.

2. Citi Corporation and Drive Bank

In this case, the rate of interest charged by Drive Bank cannot keep pace with the unusual rise in inflation from 1 to 6 per cent in the 20 years preceding the loan agreement to 50 per cent during the second year of a five-year loan contract. As the interest rate is fixed in the contract, the courts cannot vary it just because of the unprecedented rate of inflation. Although inflation could theoretically frustrate a contract, this would be highly exceptional, and a 50 per cent rise in inflation is unlikely to be sufficient to frustrate the contract. It is not easy to argue for an implication of a term to allow termination of the contract by reasonable notice or to permit an adjustment of the price. The contract is for five years and it is not clear that there is a lacuna in the contract, which would be necessary for the court to fill by implying a term.

[102] The fact scenarios of the hypothetical cases described in this section are taken from M Chen-Wishart, D Neo, and S Vogenauer, 'Introduction', ch 1, 7–8.

3. Easy and Frugle

Frugle finds that the rent that he is charging Easy for the lease of business premises has lagged behind the rise in rental values of comparable business premises, which have gone up 500 per cent. Frugle will not be able to adjust the rental upwards unless there is a provision in the contract allowing him to do so. Frugle is highly unlikely to be able to terminate the contract by arguing that it has been frustrated as there has not been a radical change in his obligations under the contract. However, Frugle may be able to terminate the contract if he succeeds in arguing that there is an implied term allowing termination by the giving of reasonable notice. The fact that Easy's profits are up 500 per cent is irrelevant.

4. George and Han

If the restaurant and the cellar are taken together as one entity, this would be a situation where the subject matter of the contract has been destroyed, and the contract would be frustrated. Even if the restaurant and the cellar are seen as two separate entities, it is likely that both Han and George regarded the continued existence of the restaurant as the foundation of their contract to refurbish the cellar so that the destruction of the restaurant would frustrate the contract. If so, Han is not required to pay the contract price nor to compensate George for his loss. However, George might try to argue that the existence of the restaurant and the purpose of the renovation did not matter to him as he only cared about refurbishing the cellar and getting paid for the job and that he could still proceed with the work despite the destruction of the restaurant.

5. Gina and H Hotel

Of the four situations set out in this hypothetical, Gina would most likely not be entitled to cancel her booking in the first three situations involving the cancellation of the exhibition, the terrorist threat, and the airport strike as these are of no concern to the hotel. These changes in circumstances do not make the performance of the contractual obligation—the booking of a hotel room—radically different from what was contracted for. However, in the fourth situation involving the cancellation of the inauguration proceedings, Gina will most likely be entitled to cancel her booking by arguing that the contract is frustrated. It is most likely that both Gina and the hotel regarded the happening of the inauguration procession as being the foundation of the contract: Gina had booked a room overlooking the street where the inauguration procession was to pass by, and the rental price of the room was ten times higher than normal.

6. Kris and Leila

As there was no express term regarding the use of the house, to succeed in an action for breach of contract, Kris has to argue that there was an implied term that the house would be dedicated to cultural use. However, the test for an implied term in Singapore law would be hard to satisfy as it requires that there must be a lacuna to be filled that had not been contemplated by the parties. On the facts, there was no lacuna as Kris and Leila had thought about the use of the house but did not provide for this in their contract. Kris is, therefore, unlikely to be able to claim the difference between the agreed price and the market value. Kris may be able to rescind the contract and claim restitution of the house if he succeeds in an action based on misrepresentation or mistake. But an action based on misrepresentation would not succeed if at the time of the contract, Leila genuinely had the intention to dedicate the house to cultural use, and an action based on mistake would fail if, as it seems on the facts, neither party had made a mistake at the time of contracting.

VIII. Conclusion

The law in Singapore will usually hold parties to their obligations under a contract even where there has been a change in circumstances unless the parties are absolved from performance by the terms of the contract. The main exception is where the contract has been frustrated because performance of the contract in the changed circumstances would be radically different from the obligations that the parties had undertaken at formation. The radical change in obligation test is a strict one, and it is not easy to successfully argue frustration. Even where the doctrine of frustration operates, it only allows the parties to discharge but not to adapt the contract. If parties want freedom to decide what their obligations should be in the event of changed circumstances, the best course of action would be to include a detailed and well-drafted *force majeure* clause setting out clearly the circumstances in which the clause will apply and the consequences of such application.

21

Termination under Singapore Law

Chee Ho THAM

I. Introduction

Up until fairly recently, readers of reports of decisions by the Singapore courts dealing with contract termination owing to non- or defective performance under Singapore law would be hard-pressed to spot any difference to the equivalent law in England. Seminal English authorities dealing with termination (ie 'discharge') of contracts for such reasons would frequently be cited without qualification by both Bench and Bar, signalling that in these areas, there was so little to distinguish between English and Singapore law as made no difference. This is not unexpected, given Singapore's reception of English law as a former British colony. However, since the 1990s and 2000s, Singapore contract law has been increasingly open to going its own way.

For example, in 2007, it appeared that the Singapore Court of Appeal had determined that Singapore law might possibly disregard the contracting parties' intention to bar discharge of a contract for breach of a particular term or terms in their contract, unless the effect of the breach was *not* so serious as to deprive the innocent party of substantially the whole of the benefit of the contract.[1] In other words, where the term breached was held not to be a 'condition' (being a term which, regardless of the severity of its breach, was intended by the parties to give rise to the power to discharge), the power to discharge for breach of such 'non-condition' would depend on the severity of the breach on the innocent party. Though subsequent decisions of the Singapore Court of Appeal since then have retreated somewhat, the law in Singapore on this point remains distinct from the English position, and the terminology which is used presently in Singapore courts to address these questions will be unfamiliar to an English lawyer. Additionally, in relation to particular areas of the law (eg the treatment of consumers[2] and the sale of land[3] under Singapore law), Singapore law has also developed in a distinctive way.

[1] *RDC Concrete Pte Ltd v Sato Kogyo (S) Pte Ltd* [2007] 4 SLR(R) 413 (SGCA). This case is discussed below in the main text to and following n 11.

[2] This is discussed in the main text to and following n 37.

[3] This is discussed in the main text to and following n 92.

Chee Ho Tham, *Termination under Singapore Law* In: *Studies in the Contract Laws of Asia V: Ending and Changing Contracts.* Edited by: Mindy Chen-Wishart, Dora Neo, and Stefan Vogenauer, Oxford University Press.
DOI: 10.1093/oso/9780198995814.003.0021

II. Principles, Requirements, and Effects of Discontinued Performance

1. When May Contract Parties Withhold or Discontinue Performance?

(a) Withholding performance

Singapore law allows contracting parties to stipulate the order by which their contractual obligations are to be performed.[4] Where preconditions to the promisor's obligation becoming due for performance are unfulfilled, performance may be suspended.[5]

(b) Discontinuation of performance through termination or discharge of contract

Besides suspension, performance may be discontinued prospectively. First, contracting parties may agree terms whereby one (or either) contracting party is empowered to unilaterally end the contract, prospectively[6] or retrospectively.[7] The operation of such provisions depends on their true construction.[8]

Second, the contractual promisee may be empowered to end or 'discharge' the contract, 'under common law following a repudiatory breach by the other party',[9] and when this power is exercised, all outstanding obligations of the contracting parties are brought to an end prospectively.[10]

2. When May the Innocent Party Terminate for Breach?

Where the breach by the 'party-in-breach' is 'non-repudiatory', the innocent party has no power to end the contract. Whether the breach is 'repudiatory' or not depends on application of the approaches set out in Situations 1, 2, 3(a), or 3(b), below.

3. When Is a Breach 'Repudiatory'?

(a) Nature of the term that has been breached

(1) The Singapore approach: Situations 1, 2, 3(a), and 3(b)

In *RDC v Sato Kogyo*, the Singapore Court of Appeal observed that:

[4] *Cutter v Powell* (1795) 6 TR 320, received as part of the general reception of English law pursuant to the Letters patent establishing the Court of Judicature at Prince of Wales Island, Singapore and Malacca, in the East Indies, dated 27 November 1826.

[5] This is a matter of construction: *Mizuho Corporate Bank Ltd v Woori Bank* [2004] SGHC 219 [37].

[6] *Piattchanine v Phosagro Asia Pte Ltd* [2015] 5 SLR 1257 (SGHC) [117] (reversed in part on appeal, but not on this point: [2016] 5 SLR 1052 (SGCA)).

[7] See eg the 'rescission' clause in *Tian Teck Construction Pte Ltd v Exklusiv Auto Pte Ltd* [1992] 1 SLR(R) 948 (SGCA).

[8] *Holcim (Singapore) Pte Ltd v Precise Development Pte Ltd a* [2011] 2 SLR 106 (SGCA) [49].

[9] *Piattchanine v Phosagro Asia Pte Ltd* (n 6) [117].

[10] *Isabel Redrup Agency Pte Ltd v A L Dakshnamoorthy* [2016] 2 SLR 634 (SGHC) [84] (affirmed on appeal: [2017] SGCA 11). See also discussion below in section II.8.

> The *first broad category* ('Situation 1') deals with the situation where the contract clearly and unambiguously states that, in the event of a certain event or events occurring, the innocent party will be entitled to terminate the contract.[11]

However, not all contracts make such provision, so three other broad categories were also prescribed, namely, 'Situation 2', 'Situation 3(a)', and 'Situation 3(b)'.[12]

Situation 2-type cases arise where 'a party, by his words or conduct, simply renounces its contract inasmuch as it clearly conveys to the other party to the contract that it will not perform its contractual obligations at all'.[13] Innocent parties receiving such renunciation are 'entitled to terminate the contract'.[14] No particular form of words need be used so long as the innocent party's intent to terminate is manifested clearly.[15] Using more traditional, English, terminology, Situation 2-type cases encompass anticipatory repudiatory breaches of contract.[16]

As for Situation 3(a), the Court of Appeal explained that:

> [T]he focus is on the nature of the term breached and, in particular, whether the intention of the parties to the contract was to designate that term as one that is so important that any breach, regardless of the actual consequences of such a breach, would entitle the innocent party to terminate the contract . . . In traditional legal terminology, such a term would be termed a 'condition'.
>
> If, however, the intention of the parties to the contract was to designate that term as one that is not so important so that no breach will ever entitle the innocent party to terminate the contract (even if the actual consequences of such a breach are extremely serious), then such a term would be termed a 'warranty'.[17]

The Court of Appeal then distinguished Situation 3(a)- and 3(b)-type cases from each other as follows:

> One main difference between the condition-warranty approach in Situation 3(a) and the *Hongkong Fir* approach in Situation 3(b) should be highlighted. Under the condition-warranty approach, the paramount aim of the court is to ascertain the parties' intention in relation to the nature of the contractual term *in advance, viz,* at the time of contracting. The innocent party's right to terminate the contract depends wholly on whether the term is classified as a 'condition' or a 'warranty'. In contrast, the *Hongkong Fir* approach requires

11 *RDC Concrete Pte Ltd v Sato Kogyo* (n 1) [91] (emphasis in original).

12 ibid [92].

13 ibid [93] (emphasis in original removed).

14 ibid [93].

15 *Vitol SA v Norelf Ltd (The Santa Clara)* [1996] AC 800 (HL) 810–11. The Singapore position is similar: see *Sintra Merchants Pte Ltd v Brown Noel Trading Pte Ltd (Donald & McArthy Pte Ltd, third party)* [1996] 1 SLR(R) 809 (SGHC) [58]; *Brown Noel Trading Pte Ltd v Donald & McArthy Pte Ltd* [1996] 3 SLR(R) 760 (SGCA) [30]; *Ng Chee Weng v Lim Jit Ming Bryan* [2015] 3 SLR 92 (SGCA) [76]; *BMO v BMP* [2017] SGHC 127 [94].

16 A Situation 2-type case may be broader than cases in which there had been an anticipatory renunciation where the contractual promisor had evinced his intention not to perform his outstanding obligations under the contract prior to their time of performance because 'Situation 2 can occur before or at the time performance is due': *The 'STX Mumbai'* [2014] 3 SLR 1116 [28] (reversed on appeal without addressing this point: [2015] 5 SLR 1).

17 *RDC Concrete Pte Ltd v Sato Kogyo* (n 1) [97]–[98].

> a confirmation of the right on the part of the innocent party to discharge the contract *after the fact* inasmuch as the parties have to 'wait and see' *what the nature and consequences of the breach actually are.*[18]

Hence, unlike Situation 3(a), the power to discharge under Situation 3(b) depends on the 'nature and consequences of the breach' on the promisee.

The *RDC* framework was refined in *Sports Connection Pte Ltd v Deuter Sports GmbH.* There, the court distinguished between two different types of 'warranty':

> The first situation is where the court finds that the term concerned is not a condition pursuant to the condition-warranty approach [ie, the Situation 3(a) approach]. If so, such a term must, ex hypothesi, be a warranty pursuant to that same approach. We assume that, in such a situation, the parties have not expressly stated that the term concerned is a warranty. We would characterise such a term as 'a warranty impliedly intended by the parties'.[19]

Such a 'non-condition' may be referred to as an 'implied warranty'. However, the court observed that there were terms which might be referred to as an 'express warranty':

> [W]here the term itself states expressly (as well as clearly and unambiguously) that any breach of it, regardless of the seriousness of the consequence that follow from that breach, will never entitle the innocent party to terminate the contract, then the court will give effect to this particular type of term (viz, a warranty expressly intended by the parties).[20]

Synthesizing *RDC v Sato Kogyo* with *Sports Connection*: where a term had been breached, and the facts reveal that the parties intended for that term to be a condition, the innocent party would have the power to discharge the contract within Situation 3(a). Where the facts do not show that the parties intended for that term to be a condition, the court would *presume* that they intended to allow for the innocent party to have the power to discharge the contract *if* the impact of the breach was so severe as to deprive the innocent party of substantially the whole of the benefit of the contract within Situation 3(b).[21] However, this presumption would be displaced if the term expressly, clearly, and unambiguously stated that any breach of it, regardless of the severity of its consequences, would *never* give rise to a power to discharge the contract (ie an 'express warranty'); the intention of the parties to preclude discharge so manifested would be given effect, and breach of such 'express warranty' would never empower the innocent party to discharge the contract.[22]

(2) Overlaps

Where parties had expressly provided that breach of a particular term by the contractual promisor would entitle the promisee to terminate the contract, applying the Situation 3(a)

[18] ibid [100] (emphasis in original).
[19] [2009] 3 SLR(R) 883 (SGCA) [31].
[20] ibid [57].
[21] *RDC Concrete Pte Ltd v Sato Kogyo* (n 1) [112].
[22] *Sports Connection Pte Ltd v Deuter Sports GmbH* (n 19) [57]. For guidance as to the factors indicating that the term breached is a 'condition', see *Man Financial (S) Pte Ltd v Wong Bark Chuan David* [2008] 1 SLR(R) 663 (SGCA) [160]–[174].

approach, such express provision could support a finding that parties had intended for that term to be a condition. However, in applying the Situation 1 approach, it could alternatively be said that the promisee had a contractually stipulated power to terminate the contract.

Situations 1 and 3 may thus overlap,[23] though not always. In a case where the contracting parties had stipulated that non-fulfilment of certain contractual terms by one party would entitle the counter-party to terminate the contract, the Singapore High Court adopted the distinction typified in English cases such as *Financings Ltd v Baldock*[24] and *Lombard North Central Plc v Butterworth*[25] and pointed out in *Tan Wee Fong v Denieru Tatsu F&B Holdings (S) Pte Ltd* that:

> a term is not automatically classified as a condition simply because the contracting parties have agreed to a right to terminate upon breach of a particular term; something more is required for the court to reach this conclusion . . . It bears repeating that the court will have to construe the term in context in order to determine whether it is a condition or a warranty.[26]

(3) The timing of the breach: Actual and anticipatory breaches

A term may be breached when its performance is due ('actual' breach) or in advance of that time ('anticipatory' breach).[27] So long as the breach is repudiatory (be it 'actual' or 'anticipatory'),[28] the innocent party to the breach is empowered to end the contract.

(b) Subjective intentions and/or motivations for the party-in-breach

Repudiatory breaches empower the innocent party to end the contract. The repudiatory intent behind such breaches is assessed objectively, and:

> [T]he test is to ascertain whether the action or actions of the party in default are such as to lead a reasonable person to conclude that he no longer intends to be bound by its provisions.[29]

Thus, if party A declines to perform its part of the bargain whilst honestly believing that it was entitled to do so because the counter-party, party B, had committed a repudiatory breach, if subsequent proceedings conclude that party A's belief was erroneous, party A's refusal to perform would amount to an anticipatory repudiatory breach.[30]

23 If the concern is merely over the discharge of a contract, it often does not matter which approach (Situation 1 or 3(b)) is adopted. However, adopting the Situation 1 approach can create complications over recovery of damages: it is unclear if damages for losses consequential upon termination pursuant to Situation 1 can be granted: see *Max Media FZ LLC v Nimbus Media Pte Ltd* [2010] 2 SLR 677; [2010] SGHC 30, [35]–[38].

24 [1963] 2 QB 104 (EWCA).

25 [1987] QB 527 (EWCA).

26 *Tan Wee Fong and others v Denieru Tatsu F&B Holdings (S) Pte Ltd* [2010] 2 SLR 298 (SGHC) [37]

27 *The 'STX Mumbai'* [2015] 5 SLR 1 (SGCA) [68]–[69].

28 ibid [64]–[78]. It is therefore now clear that, as a matter of Singapore law, it is also possible for there to be an 'anticipatory' repudiatory breach of a Situation 3(b)-type case in connection with an 'implied warranty'. In such a scenario, though the power to discharge depends on the severity of the impact of the breach, the Singapore Court of Appeal pointed out that, where necessary, it was open to the court to extrapolate what that impact might be, in advance of its actual occurrence.

29 *San International Pte Ltd v Keppel Engineering Pte Ltd* [1998] 3 SLR(R) 447 (SGCA) [20] (emphasis removed).

30 *GIB Automation Pte Ltd v Deluge Fire Protection (SEA) Pte Ltd* [2007] 2 SLR(R) 918 (SGHC) [77].

(c) Distinctions between consumer and non-consumer contracts

In general, Singapore contract law does not distinguish between consumer and non-consumer contracts. However, the general position in relation to contracts for the sale, supply, or hire-purchase of goods is supplemented by the Sale of Goods Act 1979[31] (SGA), the Supply of Goods Act 1982[32] (SGA 1982), and the Unfair Contract Terms Act 1977[33] (UCTA). These statutes distinguish between a party who 'deals as consumer'[34] when acquiring goods, and those who do not. Inter alia, where the party acquiring goods under contracts within the SGA or SGA 1982 deals other than as a consumer, powers to discharge the contract for breach,[35] or to reject the goods in question,[36] are more constrained.

The Consumer Protection (Fair Trading) Act 2003 (CPFTA)[37] also supplements the general contract law. For example, where an 'unfair practice'[38] is perpetrated on a 'consumer',[39] the consumer may[40] seek certain statutory remedies.[41]

The Consumer Protection (Fair Trading) (Cancellation of Contracts) Regulations 2009 (CCR 2009) also grant consumers in certain categories of contract[42] the power to 'cancel' such contract within a certain number of days from formation, independently of any 'unfair practice' or breach by the supplier.[43] If 'cancelled', 'the contract ceases to be enforceable'.[44] Sums paid by the consumer prior to cancellation are to be repaid,[45] goods supplied to the consumer prior to cancellation are to be returned,[46] and a 'reasonable compensation' is to be paid by the consumer for services received prior to cancellation.[47]

[31] 2020 rev edn. This act is based on the UK Sale of Goods Act 1979, ch 54.
[32] 2020 rev edn. This act is based on the UK Supply of Goods Act 1982, ch 29.
[33] 2020 rev edn. This act is based on the UK Unfair Contract Terms Act 1977, ch 50.
[34] Defined in the UCTA as:

> 12. (1) A party to a contract 'deals as consumer' in relation to another party if—
> (a) he neither makes the contract in the course of a business nor holds himself out as doing so;
> (b) the other party does make the contract in the course of a business; and
> (c) in the case of a contract governed by the law of sale of goods or hire-purchase, or by section 7, the goods passing under or in pursuance of the contract are of a type ordinarily supplied for private use or consumption.
> (2) But on a sale by auction or by competitive tender the buyer is not in any circumstances to be regarded as dealing as consumer.
> (3) Subject to this, it is for those claiming that a party does not deal as consumer to show that he does not.

[35] SGA, s 15A; SGA 1982, ss 5A, 10A.
[36] SGA, s 30(2A).
[37] 2020 rev edn.
[38] As defined in the CPFTA, s 4.
[39] ibid s 2(1) provides that:

> 'consumer' means an individual who, otherwise than exclusively in the course of business (a) receives or has the right to receive goods or services from a supplier; or (b) has a legal obligation to pay a supplier for goods or services that have been or are to be supplied to another individual.

[40] ibid s 6.
[41] These are set out at ibid s 7.
[42] That is, 'regulated contracts', as defined in the CCR 2009, reg 2(1).
[43] ibid reg 4.
[44] ibid reg 5(1)(a).
[45] ibid reg 5(1)(b).
[46] ibid reg 6(1), though the duty to return would not apply where the goods were perishable, had been consumed or been incorporated into any land or thing not comprised in the contract, or had been supplied to meet an emergency—in which case the consumer would have to pay a reasonable compensation for such goods as had been supplied: reg 6(2) read with 6(3).
[47] ibid reg 7.

Part III of the CPFTA also provides for additional entitlements for consumers who have entered into an 'applicable contract'.[48] If the goods acquired are 'non-conforming' (ie where there has been a breach of any express term or of certain terms implied by the relevant statute[49] in relation to the goods so acquired),[50] the consumer has a statutory power to 'rescind' the contract where 'repair or replacement' is impossible or has not taken place within a reasonable time and without causing significant inconvenience to the consumer.[51] If exercised, the non-conforming 'applicable contract' is treated as if it had never been formed in the first place.[52] The price for the goods in question (if paid) is to be reimbursed, and the goods are to be returned—with a monetary adjustment, if necessary, for usage of the goods in the interim.[53]

4. Is 'Supplementary Performance' Required before Termination?

Generally, once the party who had breached the contract manifests repudiatory intent, the innocent party may discharge the contract without having to give the party-in-breach a second chance to cure or make good the repudiation (ie to provide 'supplementary performance', by, say, performing, albeit at a later date, by providing a cure for the loss or injury occasioned by the non-performance, and so on and so forth). However, the power of a consumer to 'rescind' the contract under Part III of the CPFTA[54] is different since this statutory power only arises if repair or replacement of the good in question is impossible or the vendor has failed to repair or replace within a reasonable time and without causing significant inconvenience to the consumer.

5. Are Termination Clauses Effective?

Singapore law generally gives effect to party intentions in respect of these kinds of 'termination' clauses which have been individually negotiated,[55] if duly incorporated into the contract. No special rules are applied in relation to termination clauses like these unless the circumstances in which equitable relief against forfeiture arise. Some of these circumstances are mentioned in the discussion of the hypothetical case of *Prime Ltd v Devil Corp*, section III.2 below.

[48] That is, a contract for the sale, supply, or hire-purchase of goods: CPFTA, s 13(1).

[49] Namely, the SGA (for contracts for sale of goods) or the SGA 1982 (for contracts for the supply or hire-purchase of goods).

[50] CPFTA, s 13(4).

[51] ibid s 14(2)(b)(ii), read with s 16. From a plain reading of the statute, it would appear that the consumer's power to rescind the contract pursuant to s 14(2)(b)(ii) may be exercised without any prior order of court. See also the discussion in D Neo, 'Specific Remedies and the Performance Interest in Singapore Contract Law' in M Chen-Wishart, A Loke and B Ong (eds), *Studies in the Contract Law of Asia, vol I: Remedies for Breach of Contract* (OUP, 2016) 208–09 (referring to the equivalent provision, then numbered as s 12B(2)(b)(ii)).

[52] 'Rescind' is not statutorily defined in the CPFTA. But it was assumed in *Speedo Motoring Pte Ltd v Ong Gek Sing* [2014] 2 SLR 1398, [2014] SGHC 71 that, by using this language (as opposed to 'terminate' or 'discharge'), Parliament intended the consumer transaction in question to be terminated *ab initio* with retrospective effect.

[53] CPFTA, s 16(3).

[54] ibid.

[55] *RDC Concrete Pte Ltd v Sato Kogyo* (n 1) [91].

6. Are Court Orders Required for Termination?

A contracting party may discharge the contract once the requirements outlined in Situations 2, 3(a), or 3(b) are satisfied. There is no need to make any prior court application to invoke this power. As for Situation 1 cases, usually, the contractual terms giving rise to the power to terminate the contract will provide that the power is triggered without need for prior judicial proceedings.

7. When Might Entitlements to Terminate Be Lost?

Once exercised, a power to terminate comes to an end. But such power may be lost before it has been invoked because (i) it was given up or (ii) the contract was brought to an end for some other reason before it was exercised.

(a) Relinquishing powers to terminate

Where a contract breach results in a Situation 2, 3(a), or 3(b) case, the contract is discharged when the innocent party elects to do so[56] as opposed to leaving the contract in place. Such election becomes effective when:

> [An] unequivocal act or statement by [the electing party is] communicated to the person against whom the two mutually exclusive remedies are available[,] and showing that he intends to pursue one of them.[57]

However, the power to discharge a contract may be lost in a Situation 2,[58] 3(a), or 3(b)-type case if the innocent party 'affirms' the contract by words or conduct in 'clear and unequivocal terms'.[59]

Once made, the election to affirm is binding and irreversible.[60] Where the innocent party has adopted one of several alternative courses of action, the intention to affirm the contract can only be inferred where the course of action taken is inconsistent with the election to discharge.[61] Furthermore, an innocent party may only effectively affirm the contract 'with knowledge of his rights'.[62]

[56] *Vitol SA v Norelf Ltd (The Santa Clara)* (n 15) 810. The position in Singapore is similar: see *Lee Siong Kee v Beng Tiong Trading, Import and Export (1988) Pte Ltd* [2000] 3 SLR(R) 386 (SGCA) [18].

[57] *China National Foreign Trade Transportation Corporation v Evlogia Shipping Co ('The Miahlios Xilas')* [1979] 1 WLR 1018 (HL) 1086 (Lord Diplock).

[58] *Motor Oil Hellas (Corinth) Refineries SA v Shipping Corporation of India ('The Kanchenjunga')* [1990] 1 Lloyd's Rep 391 (HL) 399.

[59] ibid 398.

[60] *Hain Steamship Company v Tate & Lyle Ltd* [1936] 2 All ER 597, 601 (Lord Atkin) 615 (Lord Maugham); *Peyman v Lanjani* [1985] Ch 457 (EWCA) 488; *Yukong Line Ltd of Korea v Rendsburg Investments Corp of Liberia* [1996] 2 Lloyd's Rep 604 (EWHC) 607. There appears to be no Singapore case to the contrary.

[61] *Bolton MBC v Municipal Mutual Insurance Ltd* [2006] 1 WLR 1493 (EWCA) [31]–[34]; *State Trading Corp of India Ltd v M Golodetz Ltd* [1989] 2 Lloyd's Rep 277 (EWHC) 286. There appears to be no Singapore case to the contrary.

[62] *Hain Steamship Company, Ltd v Tate & Lyle Ltd* (n 60) 601. There appears to be no Singapore case to the contrary.

Neverheless, the innocent party's silence or omission may be taken to amount to affirmation. Where the innocent party is ignorant of facts pertaining to the power to discharge, non-exercise does not lead to its loss: the power may be invoked at that later point in time when the innocent party acquires knowledge of these facts.[63] However, failing to discharge a contract where the innocent party *was* aware that a repudiatory breach had occurred may indicate that the innocent party had decided to affirm the contract.[64] Hence, if not exercised within a 'reasonable' time, the power to discharge may be lost.[65]

Finally, the preceding discussion with regard to Situation 2- and 3-type cases is also generally true of an innocent party who has been given a contractual power to terminate the contract (a Situation 1-type case), unless the contract provides that the contract is to terminate immediately without the need for further steps.

(b) Where the contract has already been terminated

The power to end a contract may also be lost where the contract had already ended for 'other reasons', including (i) where the innocent party had also committed a repudiatory breach of its own, thereby giving the counter-party the power to discharge the contract, as well, and where the other party had already exercised its power;[66] (ii) where the preconditions permitting the counter-party to terminate the contract by reason of a contractual termination clause were also satisfied; or (iii) where a frustrating (or *force majeure*) event occurred in the interim, thereby causing the contract to come to an end by reason of the doctrine of frustration (or by operation of the *force majeure* clause, if present).[67]

8. What Is the Effect of Termination?

(a) What happens to the contract?

A contract which has been discharged pursuant to Situations 2, 3(a), or 3(b) will be ended prospectively from the time the innocent party exercises its power to discharge.[68] As for Situation 1-type cases, the contractual termination clause's effect depends on its wording: if the parties had provided for the contractual termination clause to operate with retrospective effect, such intention will be given effect to.[69]

[63] *Alliance Concrete Singapore Pte Ltd v Comfort Resources Pte Ltd* [2009] 4 SLR(R) 602 [63]; *Isabel Redrup Agency Pte Ltd v A L Dakshnamoorthy* (n 10) [84] (affirmed on appeal: [2017] 1 SLR 546).

[64] *Mardorf Peach & Co Ltd v Attica Sea Carriers Corporation of Liberia* [1977] AC 850 (HL) 872; *Scandinavian Trading Tanker Co AB v Flota Petrolera Ecuatoriana ('The Scaptrade')* [1981] 2 Lloyd's Rep 425 (EWHC) 430. There do not appear to be Singapore authorities adopting a contrary position.

[65] *Mardorf Peach & Co Ltd v Attica Sea Carriers Corporation of Liberia* (n 64) 872; *Motor Oil Hellas (Corinth) Refineries SA v Shipping Corp of India (The 'Kanchenjunga')* (n 58) 398 (Lord Goff). There appear to be no Singapore authorities to the contrary.

[66] This scenario is more fully explained in *Jet Holding Ltd v Cooper Cameron (Singapore) Pte Ltd* [2006] 3 SLR(R) 769 (SGCA) [98]–[99]. See also *Alliance Concrete Singapore Pte Ltd v Comfort Resources Ltd* (n 63) [46].

[67] As to which, see the contribution by D Neo on 'Contractual Obligations and Change of Circumstances in Singapore', ch 20 in this volume, 427–428.

[68] See section II.1(b).

[69] ibid.

(b) What happens to contracted-for benefits conferred prior to termination?

Whether the contract be brought to an end under Situation 1, 2, 3(a), or 3(b), unless contrary contractual provision was made, any benefit conferred pursuant to the contract prior to termination would not, as a matter of contract principles, have to be restored or returned to the party that had provided that benefit. However, the law of unjust enrichment may allow for restitutionary recovery (unless precluded by contract[70]).

Where a money benefit had been paid prior to discharge of the contract, an unjust enrichment claim based on the doctrine of total failure of consideration could be brought to recover the money benefit because that payment would have been made in exchange for a counter-performance of which nothing had, nor would now be, provided. As for non-money benefits provided by the innocent party, an analogous claim in *quantum meruit* could, in principle, be available.[71]

(c) Do restitutionary and damages claims following termination affect each other?

In a case where a claim for money damages had been made by a plaintiff against a defendant, if the defendant were to successfully bring a counter-claim for restitution against the plaintiff, the sums awarded in the claim and the counter-claim could be netted off against each other.

(d) Can the court give the party-in-breach additional time for performance?

Contractual terms should be performed strictly.[72] Where a contract provides that 'time is of the essence', a term stipulating a deadline for the performance of the contract will have been designated to be a condition. Breach would entitle the innocent party to discharge the contract without regard to the magnitude of the breach, even if the party-in-breach was in a position to carry on with its part of the bargain promptly. Furthermore, given such agreement, there would be little reason for the court to grant equitable relief to bar the innocent party from discharging the contract and so giving the party-in-breach more time—save, perhaps, in the circumstances as discussed in the hypothetical case of *Prime Ltd v Devil Corp* in the following section.

III. The Hypotheticals

1. Car Machinery & Co and Traders Ltd

Car Machinery & Co appoint Traders Ltd as sole distributors of their car panel presses for a period of five years. Clause 7(b) of the agreement provides that 'Distributors shall send their representatives to visit all six large car manufacturers in the country at least once in every week for the purpose of soliciting orders for car panel presses. Failure to comply with

[70] For example, when part of the purchase price for goods sold pursuant to a contract of sale is paid in advance by way of 'earnest money', that is, money which the parties intend to be paid to show that the payee is serious about performing the rest of its contractual obligations (namely, to pay the balance of the purchase price) and which may be forfeited if the payee fails to do so.

[71] See section III.5(a).

[72] *Arcos Ltd v E A Ronaasen & Son* [1933] AC 470 (HL) 479. The summary of *Arcos Ltd v E A Ronaasen* in M Bridge, *Benjamin's Sale of Goods* (8th edn, Sweet & Maxwell 2010) was cited with approval in *Chai Cher Watt v SDL Technologies Pte Ltd* [2012] 1 SLR 152 (SGCA) [21].

this obligation shall entitle Car Machinery to terminate the agreement with immediate effect.' Traders Ltd miss two visits to car manufacturers in the second month of the contractual period. Is Car Machinery entitled to terminate the agreement?[73]

Traders Ltd is obligated to 'visit all six large car manufacturers . . . at least once in every week'. When Traders Ltd fails to do so, Car Machinery is empowered to end the contract on various grounds.

First, Car Machinery could invoke the contractual power of termination as set out in the terms of the contract within Situation 1 since the precondition for its exercise had been satisfied. Second, if Traders Ltd's failure was a breach of a condition of the contract, Car Machinery could discharge the contract as a matter of the general law, without needing to assess the severity of Traders Ltd's breach. To support the proposition that this term was a condition, Traders Ltd could point to the term expressly providing that Car Machinery was empowered to end the contract once Traders Ltd failed to fulfil its obligation to visit all six large car manufacturers at least once every week: that wording could be construed as showing that the parties intended the term that Traders was to so visit to be a condition: it plainly cannot be construed to be an 'express warranty'.[74] If so, adopting a Situation 3(a) approach, breach of the said condition would empower Car Machinery to end the contract since breaches of conditions are always repudiatory. If, however, the term requiring Traders Ltd to visit the car manufacturers were construed to be other than a condition, and if it made no express provision indicating that discharge was never to be available, regardless of the severity of the breach (ie an 'express warranty), then a power to discharge the contract would arise, but only if the impact of the breach was so severe as to deprive Car Machinery of substantially the whole of the benefit of the contract within Situation 3(b).

2. Prime Ltd and Devil Corp

Prime Ltd sells a piece of land to Devil Corp. Under the terms of the contract, Devil pays a 10 per cent deposit, the remainder of the sum being due at 5:00 pm on 30 September, time being 'of the essence'. According to Clause 12, failure to meet the deadline would result in the deposit being forfeited and the agreement being terminated. Devil is ten minutes late in tendering the completion money and Prime refuses to accept performance. Can Devil sue for specific performance, arguing that Prime's reliance on the clause is unreasonable in some way?

(a) Contract includes a forfeiting clause

This hypothetical draws on facts taken from *Union Eagle Ltd v Golden Achievement Ltd*[75] where, in an appeal from the Hong Kong Court of Appeal, the Privy Council declined to grant equitable relief following late payment by the purchaser under a contract to purchase an interest in land (ie a 'land contract'), where time of payment had been made of the essence and where the contract incorporated an express clause empowering the vendor to 'rescind' the contract if the purchaser failed to comply with 'any of the terms' of the

[73] The fact scenarios of this and the other hypothetical cases discussed in this section are taken from M Chen-Wishart, D Neo, and S Vogenauer, 'Introduction', ch 1 in this volume, 9–10.

[74] See, in particular, *Sports Connection Pte Ltd v Deuter Sports GmbH* (n 19) [54].

[75] *Union Eagle Ltd v Golden Achievement Ltd* [1997] AC 514 (PC, on appeal from the Hong Kong Court of Appeal).

contract.[76] The Privy Council recognized that where a vendor had exercised its contractual entitlement to terminate a contract, the purchaser loses its right to specific performance, and:

> The purchaser's loss of the right to specific performance may be said to amount to a forfeiture of the equitable interest which the contract gave him in the land. . . . [T]he right to [terminate] the contract, though it involves termination of the purchaser's equitable interest, stands upon a rather different footing [from the issues concerning forfeiture of deposits or part payments]. Its purpose is, upon breach of an essential term, to restore to the vendor his freedom to deal with his land as he pleases. In a rising market, such a right may be valuable but volatile. Their Lordships think that in such circumstances a vendor should be able to know with reasonable certainty whether he may resell the land or not.[77]

Although *Union Eagle* has been discussed in other contexts by Singapore courts, its denial of equitable relief has yet to be discussed locally. Instead, *Pacific Rim Investments Pte Ltd v Lam Seng Tiong*[78] indicates that the Singapore response is not quite the same.

Clause 12 in this Hypothetical is a contractual termination clause in a land contract. Exercise of Clause 12 would lead to a Situation 1-type case. Alternatively, where Devil had breached the term requiring payment to be made by 5:00 pm on 30 September by tendering payment at 5:10 pm, Clause 12 could be taken to indicate that the parties had intended for the term as to time of payment to be a 'condition' within the ambit of Situation 3(a).

Furthermore, as 'time is of the essence', the term as to time of payment would be taken to have been intended by the parties as a condition in any event.[79] Thus, where Clause 12 is present, Prime, as vendor, could justify termination of the contract using a Situation 1, or 3(a), approach. Additionally, Clause 12 would entitle Prime to forfeit the 10 per cent deposit paid by Devil. But a complication arises because termination of the land contract would also 'forfeit' Devil's 'equitable proprietary interest' in the land arising from the equitable doctrine of conversion.[80]

Legal title to land sold under a valid[81] land contract can only be transferred upon conveyance. Land title conveyance typically requires registration[82] or, in some (now rare) cases, a deed of conveyance.[83] However, the purchaser in a land contract may acquire an 'equitable proprietary interest' in that legal title:[84]

[76] This case is discussed in KFK Low's contribution 'Termination of Contracts in Hong Kong', ch 6 in this volume, 122–123.

[77] *Union Eagle Ltd v Golden Achievement Ltd* (n 75) 520.

[78] *Pacific Rim Investments Pte Ltd v Lam Seng Tiong* [1995] 2 SLR(R) 643 (SGCA).

[79] See eg *Lee Seng Cheong v Seah Bak Seng* [2008] 2 SLR(R) 745 (SGHC) [29]. Conversely, where time to perform a particular term is *not* made of the essence, that term is possibly 'not so important that it is a condition of the contract': *Aero-Gate Pte Ltd v Engen Marine Engineering Pte Ltd* [2013] 4 SLR 409 (SGHC) [43].

[80] This complication only arises in connection with contracts for the sale of land. The extent to which the analysis below would apply to other kinds of contracts remains unclear.

[81] Civil Law Act (Cap 43, 1999 rev edn) s 6(d) provides that a contract for the sale of land must be in writing and be signed by the 'party to be charged' for it to be enforceable against that party.

[82] Land Titles Act (Cap 157, 2004 rev edn) s 45 provides that no instrument can transfer any estate or interest in land subject to the Land Titles Act until the instrument is registered, but the interest in question shall be transferred upon registration.

[83] A Singapore court would not regard a deed to be valid unless it was in the English language: Conveyancing and Law of Property Act (Cap 61, 1994 rev edn) s 53(1); and legal title would pass once it was 'signed, sealed, and delivered' by the vendor. Such deed would also only be admissible in court if registered in accordance with the Registration of Deeds Act (Cap 269, 1989 rev edn) s 45.

[84] HW Tang and KFK Low, *Tan Sook Yee's Principles of Singapore Land Law* (4th edn, LexisNexis 2019).

> The *locus classicus* is *Lysaght v Edwards*.[85] First, a purchaser of land is usually entitled to the equitable remedy of specific performance on the basis that since each piece of land is unique, damages will not be an adequate remedy. Second, the equitable maxim 'equity looks on as done which ought to be done'[86] accelerates in equity that which is inevitable at law so that completion is anticipated in equity.[87]

Or, to put it another way:

> [I]f there is a contract which is valid and enforceable, and in respect of which a court would grant a decree of specific performance, the purchaser is regarded as the equitable owner of the property.[88]

So far as the contract is validly formed, binding, and subsisting, those contractual obligations *ought* to be 'done' (ie performed). But if the contract is no more, then it is no longer tenable to say that those contractual obligations 'ought to be done'. Hence, if the land contract were terminated through invocation of Clause 12, the aspiration as to what *ought* to be done would fall away, and the equitable proprietary interest would fail.[89] In effect, Devil's equitable proprietary interest would have been 'forfeited'.

In *Union Eagle v Golden Achievement*, the Privy Council rejected the proposition that English (and Hong Kong) law countenanced a power to grant relief to prevent, in effect, the forfeiture of an equitable proprietary interest on an analogous set of facts:

> The principle that equity will restrain the enforcement of legal rights when it would be unconscionable to insist upon them has an attractive breadth. But the reasons why the courts have rejected such generalisations are founded not merely upon authority (see *per* Lord Radcliffe in *Campbell Discount Co Ltd v Bridge* [1962] AC 600, 626) but also upon practical considerations of business.
> [Hence,] for the past 80 years, the courts in England, although ready to grant restitutionary relief against penalties, have been unwilling to grant relief by way of specific performance against breach of an essential condition as to time.[90]

The Privy Council also declined to draw any distinction between land contracts in which time had been made of the essence and other 'commercial' contracts such as contracts for the hire of a ship; if no equitable relief was to be afforded in the latter context to preclude

[85] (1876) 2 Ch D 499, which was applied in *Lee Christina v Lee Eunice* [1993] 2 SLR(R) 644. Additionally, see *Chen Con-Ling Tony v Quay Properties Pte Ltd* [2004] 2 SLR(R) 181.

[86] Tang and Low (n 84) cite *Banks v Sutton* (1732) 2 P Wms 700, 715, 24 ER 922, 927 for this point.

[87] Tang and Low (n 84) cite *Oughtred v IRC* [1960] AC 206, 240 (Lord Jenkins) for this point.

[88] WJM Riquier, *Land Law* (4th edn, LexisNexis 2010) 96 (references omitted).

[89] *Jerome v Kelly* [2004] 1 WLR 1409 (HL) [32] (Lord Walker, emphasis added):

> It would . . . be wrong to treat an uncompleted contract for the sale of land as equivalent to an immediate, irrevocable declaration of trust (or assignment of beneficial interest) in the land. . . . Beneficial ownership of the land is in a sense split between the seller and buyer on the provisional assumptions that specific performance is available and that the contract will in due course be completed . . . *The provisional assumptions may be falsified by events, such as rescission of the contract (either under a contractual term or on breach)* [ie termination or discharge]. If the contract proceeds to completion the equitable interest can be viewed as passing to the buyer in stages, as title is made and accepted and the purchase price is paid in full.

[90] *Union Eagle Ltd v Golden Achievement Ltd* (n 75) 519 and 520.

withdrawal of the ship for late payment of hire, the same should be the case for a land contract since, '[l]and can also be an article of commerce and a flat in Hong Kong is probably as good an example as one could find'.[91]

The position in Singapore is less clear. In *EC Investment Holdings Pte Ltd v Ridout Residence Pte Ltd*,[92] the Singapore Court of Appeal declined to follow the departure in the court below from the 'orthodox position' that land ought to be treated, in general, as 'unique' such that damages would be an inadequate remedy where the vendor failed to complete performance under a land contract. Thus, in Singapore, land contracts are still distinguished from other kinds of contracts. However, in *Pacific Rim Investments Pte Ltd v Lam Seng Tiong*,[93] the Singapore Court of Appeal allowed equitable relief on facts similar to those in *Union Eagle*.

In *Pacific Rim*, Clause 5 of the land contract stipulated that non-payment of any instalment entitled the vendor to give the purchaser a further written notice to 'annul' the contract if the outstanding sum and late payment interest remained unpaid within the period stated in the notice. Clause 11 also provided that the vendors would pay liquidated damages if vacant possession was not delivered by 30 September 1993. The dispute arose when the vendor gave a Clause 5 notice demanding payment of outstanding sums and late payment interest within 14 days. The purchasers withheld payment of interest, claiming it could be set off by liquidated damages payable by the vendors under Clause 11. The vendors denied that set-off was permissible and claimed that the contract had been annulled. The purchasers then applied to the Singapore High Court[94] for specific performance.

The High Court held that the vendors were not entitled to rely on Clause 5 to end the land contract because the purchasers' liability for the late payment interest *could* be rightly set off against the vendors' liquidated damages liability. The vendors had thus breached the contract by refusing to complete their part of the contract. Consequently, the High Court allowed the purchasers' application and ordered the vendors to specifically perform the contract.[95]

The Singapore Court of Appeal affirmed the decision below[96] but also discussed whether equitable relief would still be awarded if the vendors had rightfully ended the contract for the purchasers' failure to make timely payment, where time was of the essence. The Court of Appeal reviewed[97] the English position in *Shiloh Spinners Ltd v Harding*,[98] as subsequently qualified by *Scandinavian Trading Tanker Co AB v Flota Petrolera Ecuatoriana ('The Scaptrade')*[99] and *Sport International Bussum BV v Inter-Footwear Ltd*.[100] It also reviewed Canadian,[101] Australian,[102] and New Zealand[103] authorities, before adopting the majority views of the High Court of Australia in *Legione v Hateley*:

[91] ibid 519.
[92] [2012] 1 SLR 32 [78] and [103] (SGCA).
[93] *Pacific Rim Investments Pte Ltd v Lam Seng Tiong* (n 78).
[94] [1994] 3 SLR(R) 387 (SGHC); alternatively, [1995] 2 SLR 194 (SGHC).
[95] [1994] 3 SLR(R) 387 (SGHC) [15], [20], and [22].
[96] *Pacific Rim Investments Pte Ltd v Lam Seng Tiong* (n 78) [38].
[97] ibid [42].
[98] [1973] AC 691 (HL) 722.
[99] [1983] 2 AC 694 (HL) 702.
[100] [1984] 1 WLR 776 (HL) 794.
[101] *Steedman v Drinkle* [1916] 1 AC 275 (PC, on appeal from the Supreme Court of Saskatchewan); followed in *Brickles v Snell* [1916] 2 AC 599 (PC, on appeal from the Supreme Court of Canada).
[102] *Legione v Hateley* (1982–1983) 152 CLR 406 (HCA); *Stern v McArthur* (1987–1988) 165 CLR 489 (HCA).
[103] *Location Properties Ltd v G H Lincoln Properties Ltd* [1988] 1 NZLR 307 (HC, Wellington, New Zealand).

> We accept that generally where a party to a contract has failed to perform his obligations in due time, in respect of which time is of the essence, the courts would not grant him specific performance. However, ... in a contract for the sale of land relief against forfeiture would be granted, notwithstanding a breach by the party seeking such relief of an obligation of which time was made of the essence.... The court, in essence, is asked to disregard the rescission or termination of the contract by the vendor as a form of relief prior to the grant of specific performance. The fundamental principle upon which equity acts is that a party having a legal right shall not be permitted to exercise it in such a way that the exercise amounts to unconscionable conduct (*per* Mason J and Dean J in *Legione* at 444)... Needless to say, such jurisdiction would only be exercised in exceptional circumstances since the courts would not ordinarily countenance a departure from contractual rights and obligations ... *In our judgment, in exceptional circumstances, relief against the forfeiture of an interest in land under a contract of sale may be granted where there is a breach of a provision as to payment, in respect of which time is of the essence.*[104]

Turning to the facts of the case, the Singapore Court of Appeal noted that the shortfall in the purchasers' payments as to interest (being around $1,000) was, 'a small and insignificant amount in relation to the liquidated damages [payable by the vendor] of $13,616.38[105] and the purchase price of $1m'.[106] Also:

> *[t]he breach by the purchasers ... arose because of a genuine dispute between the vendors and purchasers as to whether the purchasers were entitled to set off the interest owed against the liquidated damages.* There was no indication that the purchasers were in effect repudiating the agreement or were unable to perform their obligation under the agreement.... *The primary objective of the right to forfeiture is to ensure that the progress payments of the purchaser* [*sic*] *price are duly made.* In this case, an order for specific performance ... with appropriate provision for payment of interest, if necessary, would have given to the vendors all that the right of forfeiture aimed to achieve. In our judgment, this would be an appropriate case for such relief to be granted.[107]

On these facts, the Court of Appeal said it would have been prepared to grant equitable relief[108] but did not state if it regarded the vendor's right of termination based on exercise of the contractual power to 'annul' the contract in Clause 5 to be a case of discharge by agreement by exercise of the power to terminate arising from a termination clause (ie a Situation 1 case, using *RDC v Sato Kogyo* terminology) or if that clause showed that the parties had intended the term as to payment of interest to be a 'condition' whose breach would invariably entitle the innocent party to discharge the contract (ie a Situation 3(a)-type case, using *RDC v Sato Kogyo* terminology). Thus, it seems that the Court of Appeal's reasoning did not depend on the basis for contractual termination: so long as the land contract was

104 *Pacific Rim Investments Pte Ltd v Lam Seng Tiong* (n 78) [60] (emphasis added).

105 Clause 11 provided that the liquidated damages would be 10 per cent of the instalment payments which had been paid, to date.

106 *Pacific Rim Investments Pte Ltd v Lam Seng Tiong* (n 78) [61].

107 ibid (emphases added).

108 ibid.

rightfully terminated (whether under Situation 1 *or* 3(b)), and the Singapore position[109] set out in *Pacific Rim* seems to permit equitable relief against the vendor in 'exceptional' circumstances in either Situation.

Accordingly, Prime could bring the contract with Devil to an end using a Situation 1 or 3(b) approach. But equitable relief might be granted against forfeiture of Devil's equitable proprietary interest in the land[110] if the facts 'reveal[ed] elements of unconscionability and injustice'.[111]

This is a question of judgment. The court will consider whether the shortfall in performance was sufficiently 'trivial'. In *Pacific Rim*, the purchasers exceeded the 14 days from the receipt of the Clause 5 written notice within which they should have paid the late payment interest amounting to approximately $1,000 as compared with a purchase price of $1m (which the purchasers had paid in full before the lapse of the 14-day period). In comparison, Devil's lateness is in tendering the balance 90 per cent of the purchase price ten minutes late. Even if the court were to consider Devil's breach sufficiently trivial, it will probably also consider whether the purpose behind Clause 12 was to ensure that payments were duly made. If that was the intent, this might be met so long as the decree for specific performance was made on condition that the outstanding sum be paid to Prime, plus interest for losses occasioned by late payment.

But there remains a final point because:

> [S]pecific performance is an equitable and discretionary remedy, the court must . . . take into consideration all the circumstances of the case at hand in order to ensure that it would be just and equitable to grant the relief.[112]

The facts in this hypothetical case do not provide much to suggest that the court might decline to decree specific performance for discretionary reasons.[113] Thus, on the bare facts,

[109] The position reached in ibid on the availability of equitable relief remains good law. Equitable relief in accordance with *Pacific Rim* was granted in *Hua Khian Co (Pte) Ltd v Lee Eng Kiat* [1995] SGHC 252 (aff'd on appeal, but on other grounds: [1996] 2 SLR(R) 562 (SGCA)). *Pacific Rim* was also followed in *Yang Ming Jiann v Koh Lian Chye* [1996] SGHC 121 and in *Lim Lay Bee v Allgreen Properties Ltd* [1998] 3 SLR(R) 1028 (SGCA) (although relief in both these cases was declined owing to the lack of 'exceptional' circumstances). For more recent cases which accept that *Pacific Rim* remains good law on this point, see *TG Master Pte Ltd v Tung Kee Development (Singapore) Pte Ltd* [2022] SGHC 316 [111] (*obiter dicta*); and *Ethoz Capital Ltd v Im8ex Pte Ltd* [2023] 1 SLR 922 (SGCA) [115] (referred to without disapproval).

[110] '[R]elief against forfeiture has traditionally been available only to the forfeiture of interests in real property. Whether it is available in the context of forfeiture of deposits is a matter for another time': *Hon Chin Kong v Yip Fook Mun* [2018] 3 SLR 534 (SGHC) [143](e).

[111] *Pacific Rim Investments Pte Ltd v Lam Seng Tiong* (n 78) [60].

[112] *EC Investment Holding Pte Ltd v Ridout Estate Pte Ltd* (n 92) [103]. See also *Lee Chee Wei v Tan Hor Peow Victor* [2007] 3 SLR(R) 537 [52]–[53].

[113] For a short account of some of these discretionary grounds for denying equitable relief, see A Phang (ed), *The Law of Contract in Singapore, vol 2* (2nd edn, Academy Publishing 2022) paras 23.194–23.210. There remains some ambiguity as to whether the need to show that 'damages would be inadequate' before a decree of specific performance may be ordered is *only* a factor which goes towards the exercise of the court's discretion to grant specific performance or whether it is also a *jurisdictional* requirement to access what has, in earlier times, been referred to as the court's 'concurrent' jurisdiction in equity over breaches of contract. In *Lee Chee Wei v Tan Hor Peow Victor* (n 112) [53], the Singapore Court of Appeal asserted that in exercising its discretion to decree specific performance, it would consider whether damages would be an adequate remedy. Similar points appear to have been made by the Singapore Court of Appeal in *EC Investment Holding Pte Ltd v Ridout Residence Pte Ltd* (n 92) [103]–[106] and [111]. However, neither judgment explicitly denied that the inadequacy of damages also goes towards establishing the concurrent equitable jurisdiction of the court over contract breaches. The question, therefore, is arguably still open. See also Phang (above in this note) *vol 2*, fn 167 para 23.100.

Devil may well successfully obtain a decree of specific performance against Prime if the court concludes that Devil's breach was sufficiently trivial. If so, no question of refund of Devil's advance payments will arise.

(b) No forfeiting clause included

Even if the contract had not incorporated Clause 12, by providing that 'time [was] of the essence', the parties would have made the term stipulating that the balance 90 per cent was to be paid by 5:00 pm on 30 September into a condition, breach of which would bring Prime and Devil within Situation 3(a). However, equitable relief would still be possible according to *Pacific Rim*. As explained above, *Pacific Rim* followed *Legione v Hateley*[114] and granted equitable relief to a case of a land contract incorporating a contractual termination clause.[115] However, the Court of Appeal did not discriminate as to whether the contract before it had been terminated rightfully as a Situation 1- *or* a Situation 3(a)-type case: it seems the Court of Appeal was prepared to grant equitable relief in either Situation, so long as the facts revealed elements of unconscionability and injustice.[116] Consequently, even if the case between Prime and Devil had not included Clause 12 (so obviating the possibility of bringing Prime and Devil into Situation 1), since the contract between them would still fall within Situation 3(a), equitable relief to bar Prime from invoking its power to end the contract under Situation 3(a) would still be available. Accordingly, *Pacific Rim* may be read to support the proposition that equitable relief may also be possible (albeit exceptionally) where the contract fell solely within Situation 3(a).

3. Seven Seas and Big Chef

Seven Seas, an importer of seafood, sells two tons of mussels to Big Chef restaurant chain. After one ton has been delivered, it turns out that the concentration of cadmium in the mussels is 2 per cent above the concentration permitted by national food regulations. Can Big Chef terminate the contract?

This involves a contract for the sale of goods arising in the course of Seven Seas' business as a seafood importer. Section 14(2) SGA provides that it shall be a condition of every contract for the sale of goods that the goods shall be of 'satisfactory quality'. Section 14(2A) provides that goods are of 'satisfactory quality' if a reasonable person would regard them to be so, 'taking account of any description of the goods, the price . . . and all the other relevant circumstances'. Section 14(2B) then provides that the quality of goods includes their 'state and condition' and that, among others, the quality of goods encompasses their 'fitness for all the purposes for which goods of the kind in question are commonly supplied'.[117]

Assuming Big Chef purchased the mussels as an ingredient in its restaurant business, they would probably not be of 'satisfactory quality' without complying with national food standards: this would affect their fitness for the purpose for which they were 'commonly supplied'. Non-compliance with those standards would lead to a Situation 3(a)-type case,

[114] *Legione v Hateley* (n 102) 429 (Gibbs CJ and Murphy J) and 447 (Mason and Deane JJ).

[115] See text following n 93.

[116] See text following n 108.

[117] SGA, s 14(2B)(a).

empowering Big Chef to discharge the contract and to reject the already-delivered mussels.[118] However, the SGA constrains this power.

First, unless otherwise provided, the power to reject goods is lost once the goods are accepted.[119] However, even if Big Chef had not previously examined the first ton of mussels and immediately rejected them on delivery but had proceeded to use those mussels in a manner which was inconsistent with Seven Seas' ownership of the mussels (eg by cooking them), Big Chef would not be deemed to have accepted the goods until it had a reasonable opportunity of examining them to ascertain if they were in contractual conformity.[120]

Second, assuming Big Chef was not 'dealing as consumer'[121] but had purchased the mussels for its restaurant business, Big Chef's power to reject the goods by discharging the contract would be qualified by section 15A, where buyers who do not deal as consumers are to treat breaches of conditions implied by, inter alia, section 14, as breaches of warranty if 'the breach is so slight that it would be unreasonable for the buyer to reject them'.[122] Consequently, Big Chef's ability to reject the goods by discharging the contract because of Seven Seas' breach of condition may be barred if Seven Seas can show[123] that rejection would be 'unreasonable' in the circumstances of the case.

4. Coco and David

Coco, a famous architect, agrees with David that he will landscape the garden in her next development. He is due to start work on 1 December. For David, this is an important opportunity to make his name as a landscape gardener. On 1 October, she tells him that she is no longer interested because the development will not include a garden after all. David has already purchased materials. He estimates that his future earnings will be 10 per cent lower because he will not be able to benefit from having worked with Coco. Can he insist on doing the work? Can he bring an action for breach of contract?

Unless Coco excluded the garden owing to the doctrine of frustration, Coco's refusal to proceed with the contract and/or her acting in such a way as to make it impossible for David to perform his part of the bargain would amount to a form of anticipatory repudiatory breach: this would be a Situation 2-type case.

Assuming the contract had provided that David would only be paid after completion of the tasks set out in the contract, David would be unable to satisfy such preconditions to payment without Coco's cooperation. If Coco's non-cooperation persisted, there would be little economic purpose for David *not* to elect to discharge the contract and then sue for damages.

[118] The purchaser's power in ibid s 11(2) to reject goods is the corollary of the purchaser's being released from his duty to accept goods tendered in conformity with the terms in the sale of goods contract when that contract is discharged by the purchaser in light of the vendor's breach of condition.

[119] ibid s 11(3).

[120] ibid s 35(2)(a). For sales by sample, s 35(2)(b) would apply, instead.

[121] ibid 61(4A) provides that references to 'dealing as consumer' in the SGA must be construed in accordance with Part I of the UCTA (n 34).

[122] SGA, s 15A(1)(b).

[123] ibid s 15(A)(3).

There is also the question as to whether David might affirm the contract. In *White and Carter (Councils) Ltd v McGregor*,[124] Lord Reid suggested that an innocent party may only affirm the contract and go on to recover the contract price if it can be shown[125] that it has a 'legitimate interest' in performing the contract. This was assumed to be part of Singapore law in *MP-Bilt v Oey Widarto*,[126] although the court in that case noted that the doctrine is inapplicable in certain contexts, for example:

> [I]t does not apply where the innocent party can[not] reasonably perform his obligation without the co-operation of the contract-breaker. Illustrations: a contractor who has undertaken to repair a house for a lump sum cannot perform his obligation because the house owner can prevent him by denying access. The contractor will need an order of court to force the house owner to give him access which will ordinarily be refused as damages would suffice. The only remedy in such instance is to sue for damages and not the full contract price.[127]

Since David cannot complete his obligations under the contract without Coco's cooperation, it follows that he cannot affirm the contract and go on to claim the sums to be paid to him (assuming completion of those tasks on his part was a precondition to payment), even if he could establish that he had sufficient 'legitimate interest' in performing it.

5. Bob and Sue

Bob contracts to build a house for Sue for the price of $100,000. After doing a third of the work he abandons the job, leaving behind material worth $15,000 which Sue later uses to finish the works. Can Bob claim the value of the work done or of the materials?

The English case of *Sumpter v Hedges*[128] was cited in the Singapore case of *Trans-Link Exhibition Forwarding Pte Ltd v Wadkin Robinson Asia Pte Ltd* to stand for the proposition that, 'if a builder contracts to build a house and fails to finish the job, he is not entitled to any payment for the partial work'.[129] Hence, if the contract between Bob and Sue was such that Sue's obligation to pay Bob $100,000 was preconditioned on Bob's completion of all the building work on the house, Bob would not be entitled to be paid the contract price of $100,000 since he had only completed a third of the work on the house.

Bob's failure to complete the work is also likely to be a renunciation of the contract, bringing this within Situation 2. Alternatively, since Bob contracted to construct Sue *a* house (being an indivisible whole), Bob's leaving two thirds of the work undone probably

124 [1962] AC 413 (HL, on appeal from the Court of Session) 430–31.

125 The burden to demonstrate the lack of 'legitimate interest' appears to be on the party seeking to deny that the contract could be affirmed: ibid 431 (Lord Reid): 'Here the respondent did not set out to prove that the appellants had no legitimate interest in completing the contract and claiming the contract price rather than claiming damages.'

126 The concept of 'legitimate interest' was assumed in *MP-Bilt Pte Ltd v Oey Widarto* [1999] 1 SLR(R) 908 (SGHC) to be law in Singapore.

127 ibid [38].

128 [1898] 1 QB 673 (EWCA).

129 [1994] SGHC 197; reasoning upheld on appeal, although the quantification of the benefit which had been conferred by the party-in-breach on the innocent party was varied: [1996] 1 SLR(R) 424 (SGCA).

amounts to an actual breach which will have deprived Sue of substantially the whole of the benefit of the contract (being a *completed* house). If so, this would come within Situation 3(b). Sue would be empowered either way to discharge the contract: Sue's use of the materials left behind by Bob would likely be 'acceptance' of such breach since that would have made it impossible for Bob to perform his part of the bargain. But, leaving aside that a term requiring a reasonable or rateable sum be paid to Bob in respect of such work and materials as he had supplied might be successfully implied in fact,[130] might Bob rely on the law of unjust enrichment or, perhaps, the tort of conversion in connection with these matters?

(a) Work done and materials annexed to Sue's land before repudiatory breach

Where an innocent party has supplied goods and/or services in accordance with a contract which the innocent party has discharged due to the counter-party's repudiatory breach, such innocent party may make a *quantum meruit* claim in unjust enrichment against the party-in-breach in lieu of recovering damages for the innocent party's losses.[131] However, such claims are not open to the party-in-breach.

Citing a passage in *Luxor (Eastbourne) Ltd v Cooper*,[132] in *Lee Siong Kee v Beng Tiong Trading, Import and Export (1988) Pte Ltd*, the court concluded that:

> The crux of such a claim against a party for a quantum meruit on a restitutionary basis is the premise that the contract was terminated prematurely as a result of a breach of *that* party.[133]

This statement of the law has been repeatedly approved.[134] Consequently, Bob may not recover in *quantum meruit* for unjust enrichment for the work and materials he had supplied prior to Sue's discharge of the contract since Bob was the party-in-breach.

Bob will also find it difficult to claim in the tort of conversion. Although legal title in the relevant building materials would have been held initially by Bob, it was Bob who annexed them to Sue's land, prior to his abandonment of the project. Such annexation *by Bob* would have led Bob's legal title in those building materials to be lost given the law on fixtures.[135] But Sue would have had nothing to do with such annexation, and thus, she would not have 'converted' *those* goods to her own use.

(b) Materials annexed to Sue's land after repudiatory breach

Bob's position against Sue may be slightly better in relation to the materials which he had left on Sue's land after abandoning the contract and which Sue subsequently incorporated into her house.

[130] For an example, see *Gold Coin Ltd v Tay Kim Wee* [1985–1986] 2 SLR(R) 575 (SGCA). However, it is debatable whether the same result would be arrived at today, given the restrictive approach to implication of terms prescribed in *Sembcorp Marine Ltd v PPL Holdings Pte Ltd* [2013] 4 SLR 193 (SGCA) [101].

[131] See eg *Lee Siong Kee v Beng Tiong Trading, Import and Export (1988) Pte Ltd* (n 56) [35]–[37]. See also *Naughty G Pte Ltd v Fortune Marketing Pte Ltd* [2018] 5 SLR 1208 (SGHC).

[132] [1941] AC 108 (HL) 141.

[133] *Lee Siong Kee v Beng Tiong Trading, Import and Export (1988) Pte Ltd* (n 56) [37] (emphasis added).

[134] *Rabiah Bee bte Mohamed Ibrahim v Salem Ibrahim* [2007] 2 SLR(R) 655 (SGHC) [123]; *Grossner Jens v Raffles Holdings Ltd* [2004] 1 SLR(R) 202 (SGHC) [42]; *BMI Tax Services Pte Ltd v Heng Keok Meng* [2019] SGHC 9 [51].

[135] See the discussion of annexation on 455, below.

Unlike the position in respect of the materials which *Bob* had annexed to the land prior to abandonment of the contract,[136] here, the relevant materials were annexed through Sue's actions (or the actions of her agents), independently of Bob. Citing a passage in *Holland v Hodgson*[137] with approval, in *Pan-United Marine Ltd v Chief Assessor*[138] it was concluded that whether a chattel which became attached to land remained a chattel or had become a fixture depended on the degree and object of annexation to the land.

In Bob's and Sue's hypothetical, although the building materials had been placed on Sue's land with the intention that Bob would eventually annex them to Sue's land, Bob's leaving of the materials on Sue's land, without anything more on Bob's part, seems to satisfy neither requirement as to the degree or the object of annexation as would make them fixtures. If so, legal title to them would have been retained by Bob until *Sue* (or Sue's agents) annexed them to her land by using them to complete the construction of her house, thereby destroying Bob's legal title by reason of the law on fixtures. Thus, Bob may well recover in tort against Sue for conversion of those materials to her own use by affixing them to her land.

IV. Conclusion

Singapore's common law rules on termination of contracts draw on English common law. However, there are deviations, most evidently in relation to terminology. Although references to termination of contract for 'breach of "condition"', or for 'breach of "innominate terms" where the severity of the breach is sufficiently great' may still be encountered in the recent case law, one also encounters references to various 'Situations', ranging from Situation 1, 2, 3(a) and 3(b). Very approximately, these Situations map on to what English lawyers might refer to as instances of discharge by agreement, instances of anticipatory repudiatory breach, instances of actual breaches of conditions, and of actual breaches of innominate terms, respectively. Looking beyond the novel terminology, Singapore law on termination of contracts is also distinct from English law in light of Singapore developments in the realm of consumer law, and also, possibly, in connection with contracts for the sale of land (although the ramifications of such developments have yet to be fully explored in the cases).

136 See the discussion of alternative a above.

137 (1872) LR 7 CP 328 (Court of Exchequer Chamber, on appeal from the court of Common Pleas) 334–35 (Blackburn J).

138 [2008] 3 SLR(R) 569 (SGCA) [45].

22

The Doctrine of Change of Circumstances in Taiwanese Law

Tsung-fu CHEN

I. Introduction

The autonomy of private law and the principle that 'agreements must be kept' (*pacta sunt servanda*) are the foundations of Taiwanese contract law. The contracting parties have to follow the provisions stipulated in a contract since such provisions are determined and concluded freely by the parties. The doctrine of *clausula rebus sic stantibus*, which covers situations of a fundamental change of circumstances, is an exception to the *pacta sunt servanda* principle and can be applicable only in some special cases in which adherence to the original contractual obligations may lead to an obviously unfair and unjust outcome for one of the contracting parties. Only on such special occasions may the doctrine of change of circumstances intervene in the legal relationship between private contracting parties.

This chapter introduces the development of the doctrine of *clausula rebus sic stantibus* in Taiwanese civil law and the requirements for and the outcome of the application of change of circumstances. It also examines court cases concerning the doctrine of change of circumstances. Further, it explores the effects of contractual clauses that aim to override the provision of change of circumstances under the Taiwanese Civil Code (TCC).

II. Enactment of Provisions Covering Change of Circumstances

1. History and Theoretical Basis

Historically, in Taiwan the courts did not recognize the doctrine of change of circumstances due to strict adherence to *pacta sunt servanda*. Therefore, even if it was difficult for one of the parties to perform its duties because of war, disaster, or inflation of the price of materials, the courts decided that the contracting party still had to perform its obligations or to compensate the loss incurred by the other party. It was not until the Second World War that a provision on change of circumstances was enacted in the Supplemental Rules of Civil Procedure 1941 so as to deal with escalating cases concerning contract law disputes arising out of the extreme fluctuation of commodity prices and inflation.[1]

[1] 葉啟洲，台灣民法上之情事變更原則 (tai-wan min fa shang zhi qing shi bian geng yuan ze)，月旦民商法雜誌，第62期，第50, 51頁（2018年12月）[YE Qizhou, 'Change of Circumstances in the Taiwanese Civil Code' (2018) 62 Yudan Civil and Business Law Journal 50, 51].

Tsung-fu Chen, *The Doctrine of Change of Circumstances in Taiwanese Law* In: *Studies in the Contract Laws of Asia V: Ending and Changing Contracts*. Edited by: Mindy Chen-Wishart, Dora Neo, and Stefan Vogenauer, Oxford University Press.
 DOI: 10.1093/oso/9780198995814.003.0022

Article 20(2) of the Supplementary Rules of Civil Procedure 1941 provided that:

> in case there are no laws and rules governing this issue, if the legal relationships become obviously unfair in accordance with the original obligations due to a change of circumstances arising from a war that is unexpected at the time of the conclusion of contract, the court is allowed to increase or decrease the payment, delay the payment, or order payment by instalments, after reviewing the social economy, the parties' living situations, and the extent of the loss incurred by the war.[2]

It is evident that the doctrine of change of circumstances was adopted for dealing with the difficult cases produced by the war.

The provision on change of circumstances was later included in Article 397 of the Taiwanese Code of Civil Procedure in 1968 and, in the end, was revised and incorporated into Article 227-2(1) TCC in 2000, which provides:

> After the conclusion of a contract, where a change of circumstances occurred and it could not be predictable at the time of the conclusion of the contract, and where the performance of the original obligations arising therefrom would become obviously unfair, the party may apply to the court for a judgment to increase or reduce its payment, or to alter the original obligations.

In the revision commission for the law of obligations established by the Ministry of Justice in 2017, there was a proposal to supplement Article 227-2 TCC with a new paragraph to govern the 'interference with the basis of the transaction', as provided for in section 313(2) of the German Civil Code (BGB) as revised in 2002. The draft Article 227-2(2) TCC stipulated that '[w]here the parties make a mistake on the fundamental ideas of the basis of a juridical act, it is deemed to be a change of circumstances as provided in the preceding paragraph'.

The theoretical basis of the existing provision of change of circumstances under the TCC is good faith. The principle of good faith is stipulated in Article 148(2) TCC, which provides that '[t]he exercise of a right or performance of a duty has to follow the principle of honesty and credibility'. In terms of the theoretical justification for the doctrine of change of circumstances under Taiwanese law, all Taiwanese scholars agree that this doctrine arises from the principle of good faith and is a subordinate concept to this principle which aims to subsequently amend the adverse outcome of a change of circumstances.[3]

[2] Legal provisions cited in this chapter that are no longer in force have been translated by the author, while the existing provisions of laws are taken from a translation by the Ministry of Justice except where it is indicated otherwise. For further details on art 20(2), see 劉春堂，契約法總論 (Qi yue fa zong lun)，第278頁（台北：三民書局，2011年）[LIU Chungtang, *General Principles of Contract Law* (San-min Bookstore 2011) 278].

[3] 林誠二，債法總論新解（下）(Zhai fa zong lun)，第18頁（台北：瑞興圖書，2010年） [LIN Chenger, *New Comments on General Principles of Law of Obligations* (Riexing Books 2010) 18]; 鄭冠宇，民法債編總論(Min fa zhai bian zong lun)，第151頁（台北：新學林出版公司，2017年）[ZHENG Guanyu, *General Principles of Law of Obligations in the Civil Code* (Xinxuelin Publishing 2017) 151]; 楊芳賢，民法債編總論下(Min fa zhai bian zong lun)，第101頁（台北：三民書局，2017年） [YANG Fangxian, *General Principles of Law of Obligations, vol 2* (San-min Bookstore 2017) 101]; 邱聰智，新訂民法債編通則（下）(Xin ding min fa zhai bian tong ze)，第16頁（華太公司，2001年）[QIU Cong-zhi, *New Principles of the Law of Obligations in the Civil Code* (Hua-tai Company 2001) 16].

Indeed, the statement of legislative purpose of Article 227-2 TCC published in 2000 also states:

> The doctrine of *clausula rebus sic stantibus* is a basic principle of private law. . . . In current situations, the court relies on the principle of good faith to increase or decrease payments or to alter the original obligations under Article 397 of the Code of Civil Procedure. Nonetheless, whereas good faith is an overarching and abstract principle, it is more appropriate to have a specific and concrete provision [to govern it]. Accordingly, the first paragraph is added for application after taking reference of Article 397 of the Code of Civil Procedure.[4]

In the same vein, the Supreme Court has repeatedly held that:

> [t]he doctrine of change of circumstances provided for in Article 227-2(1) of the Civil Code is a general legal principle, which is produced through the embodiment of contents of the good-faith principle. This doctrine is a subordinate concept of the good-faith principle.[5]

2. Similar Provisions

In addition to the general provision on change of circumstances stipulated in Article 227-2, the TCC also provides some other, similar provisions. For instance, regarding lease contracts, Article 442 TCC provides that '[i]n case the thing leased is a real property, either party may apply to the court for an increase or reduction of its rental in proportion to the fluctuation of its value, unless the lease is made for a definite period'. In addition, Article 457 TCC stipulates that '[t]he lessee of an agricultural land may demand a reduction or release of the rental, if by reason of force majeure, the profits of the thing leased have decreased or totally failed'.

In one of the hypothetical scenarios that the editors of this volume asked contributors to resolve under their respective laws, Easy leased business premises from Frugle for a period of 15 years.[6] Shortly after the contract has been concluded, a nearby military airport is unexpectedly shut down for political reasons. The government invests an enormous amount of public funds in order to improve the commercial infrastructure in the area. As a result, Easy's profits are 500 per cent of what could reasonably have been expected at the time of making the contract. At the same time, the rental value of comparable business premises in the area rises to 500 per cent of the agreed rental price. Frugle requests that the rental price be adjusted accordingly or that the agreement be terminated.

In this case, the lease is made for a fixed period of 15 years. Therefore, Frugle is not entitled to apply for the court to increase the rental price under Article 442 TCC since this article is only applicable to leases without a fixed time period. This raises the question as to whether Article 227-2 TCC is applicable to a lease with a fixed time period in cases where Article 442 does not apply. All scholars agree that in the case of leases for a fixed time period,

[4] The *ratio legis* of the law and the court judgments described herein have been translated by the author.

[5] The Supreme Court 102 Tai-shang No 929 Civil Judgment (2013) and the Supreme Court 103 Tai-shang No 308 Civil Judgment (2014).

[6] The facts of this scenario are taken from M Chen-Wishart, D Neo, and S Vogenauer, 'Introduction', ch 1 in this volume, 7.

which are not covered by Article 442 TCC, Article 227-2 TCC is still applicable in order to achieve fairness between the contracting parties.[7] The Supreme Court 93 Tai-shang No 2446 Judgment took the same view, holding that Article 442 did not exclude the application of Article 227-2 TCC. In this case, the rental for an unspecified term was agreed upon on the basis of the original rental price plus 4 per cent annual increase of the interest of the price of the land as notified to the authorities. This rental had not been revised for more than 20 years, rendering it insufficient to pay the land and income taxes due. The court affirmed the claim for increased rental under Article 227-2 TCC.

In Easy's case, since the rental value of comparable business premises in the area has risen to 500 per cent of the agreed rental price, Easy is entitled to apply to the court for an adjustment of the rental price under Article 227-2 TCC.

III. Requirements under the Doctrine of Change of Circumstances

Under Article 227-2 TCC, a claimant is entitled to request the court to adjust a contract when the five elements specified in this article, as set out in the following, have been met. Since the doctrine of change of circumstances is an exceptional remedy in the law of contract, all these elements have to be examined carefully by the courts and tribunals.

1. Occurrence of Change of Circumstances

The 'circumstances' indicate all the facts that constitute the foundation, background, or prevailing circumstances of the contract at the time of its conclusion. In this regard, Taiwanese law deviates from German law, which has generally been very influential in the development of Taiwanese contract law. In Germany, section 313 BGB is based on Paul Oertmann's theory of the 'interference with the basis of the transaction' and deals with both the 'subjective' and 'objective basis of the contract'.[8] The 'subjective basis of the contract' includes the parties' shared 'material assumptions that have become the basis of the contract' and which may, at a later stage, turn out to have been incorrect. This may be illustrated with reference to a case decided by the Taiwanese Supreme Court in 2017 and discussed in section VII of this chapter: the parties to a construction contract assumed that the rocks that had to

[7] 鄭玉波，民法債編各論 (Min fa zhai bian gel un)，第210頁（台北：三民書局，1984年） [ZHEN Yubo, *The Law of Specific Obligations in the Civil Code* (San-min Bookstore 1984) 210]; 邱聰智，新訂債法各論（上）(Xin ding zhai fa ge ze)，第352頁（台北：元照出版公司，2002年）[QIU Cong-zhi, *New Principles of the Law of Specific Obligations* (Yuanzhao Publishing 2002) 352]; 吳秀明，租賃(Zhu lin)，收錄於黃立主編，《民法債編各論（上）》(Min fa zhai bian ge lun (shang))，第348頁（台北：元照出版公司，2002年）[WU Xiuming, 'Lease' in HUANG Li (ed), *The Law of Specific Obligations in the Civil Code* (Yuanzhao Publishing 2002) 348].

[8] H Beale, B Fauvarque-Cosson, J Rutgers, and S Vogenauer, *Ius Commune Casebooks for the Common Laws of Europe: Cases, Materials and Text on Contract Law* (3rd edn, Hart Publishing 2019) 1231; 吳從周，從工程承攬契約的兩個實務案型再思考情事變更原則之適用要件——以【物價漲跌型】及【工期展延型】之相關判決為中心 (Cong gong cheng cheng lan qi yue de liang ge shi wu an li zai si kao qing shi bian geng yuan ze zhi shi yong yao jian-yi wu jia zhang die xing ji gong qi yi zhan xing zhi xiang guan pan jue wei zhong xin)，政大法學評論，第153期，第1, 31–32頁（2018年6月）[WU Congzhou, 'Reconsideration of the Application of the Principle of Clausula Rebus Sic Stantibus from Two Practical Cases of Engineering Contracts: Focus on the Relevant Judgments of Price Fluctuation Type and Duration Extension Type' (2018) 153 Chengchi Law Review 1, 31–32].

be removed were of ordinary consistency; however, the rocks turned out to be much harder than usual so that their removal was more costly than originally envisaged.

Most Taiwanese scholars contend that such 'subjective circumstances' are not covered by Article 227-2 TCC, which merely includes 'objective circumstances'.[9] This is confirmed by the above-mentioned statement of legislative purpose for the amendment of the provision, which explains that 'such changes of circumstances are those of purely objective facts'.

The Supreme Court has unequivocally stated that:

> the doctrine of change of circumstances provided in Article 227-2 of the Civil Code is applicable only where the situations at the conclusion of a contract that constitute the basis, background, or prevailing circumstances [of the contract] have changed objectively without the parties having expected this and without the parties having been able to expect this. That is, the change is not attributable to either party. Where it is objectively foreseeable but is not foreseen by a party due to its negligence or mistake, the party has to be held responsible for it.[10]

Thus, when a contractor had adopted some kind of measure resulting in an increase in the price of transportation of earth, it was not a change of circumstances because the increase in price was attributable to the contractor.[11]

The Supreme Court also refused to consider an allegation of subjective circumstances as a change of circumstances. It stated that where business taxes were imposed on the appellant by the authority after the conclusion of the contract, it was only to perform a duty of public law and 'this was a burden subjectively unexpected by both parties due to their lack of knowledge of the tax law'. As a consequence, such imposition of business taxes was not a change of objective basis and thus the doctrine of change of circumstances was not applicable.[12] It is worthy of note, however, that the 2017 reform proposal for the addition of a new paragraph (2) to Article 227-1 TCC would change the outcome of this case by introducing the subjective element as in section 313(2) BGB.

The objective circumstances that constitute the doctrine of change of circumstances have to be 'materially changed' after the conclusion of the contract. That is, such a 'change' of circumstances has to be an 'extraordinary, tremendous, and obvious change', after taking into account the nature and purpose of a contract, the situation of the change, and the considerations in the contract etc, so as not to ruin *pacta sunt servanda*. In all other cases, the contracting parties have to assume the ordinary risk of performing the obligations of a contract in circumstances that include slight economic, social, and political changes.[13] In principle, like in German law, a change of circumstances is only 'tremendous' where the contracting parties would not have concluded the contract or would have concluded it on different terms if they could have foreseen that change at the time of contracting.[14]

9 LIN (n 3) 21; LIU (n 2) 279.

10 The Supreme Court 103 Tai-shang No 910 Civil Judgment (2015).

11 ibid.

12 The Supreme Court 106 Tai-shang No 2066 Civil Ruling (2017).

13 蔡晶瑩，情事變更原則之適用/最高院100台上1392號判決 (Qing shi bian geng yuan ze zhi shi yong/zui gao fa yuan 10 tai shang 1392 pan jue)，台灣本土法學雜誌，第215期，第236, 238頁（2013年1月）[TSAI Jingying, 'Application of the Doctrine of Change of Circumstances: Supreme Court 100 Tai-shang No 1392' (2013) 215 Taiwan Law Journal 236, 238]; LIU (n 2) 280.

14 WU (n 8) 37.

As such, the tremendous change of circumstances includes economic changes such as inflation, energy crisis, economic depression; and non-economic changes such as war, disaster, transportation interruption, widespread infection of disease, coup d'état, insurrection, or strikes.[15] The Supreme Court has stated that the change of contractual basis also includes inflation of commodity prices and the fluctuation of the value of money, as well as changes of the economic situation.[16]

In addition, a governmental act can be a change of circumstances. In the Supreme Court 97 Tai-shang No 60 Civil Judgment (2008), the government issued a ban on the collection of sand and rocks from rivers in the wake of the conclusion of a contract of construction. This ban brought about a tremendous increase in the price of sand and rocks of up to almost 50 per cent of the original price at the time of contracting. The Supreme Court held that the sharp rise in the price of sand and rocks due to the governmental ban was unforeseeable to the contracting parties under the consideration of normal market mechanisms, and thus the doctrine of change of circumstances was applicable in this case.

In some cases, the Supreme Court seems to interpret 'change of circumstances' quite broadly. For instance, in the Supreme Court 103 Tai-shang No 1363 Civil Judgment (2014), without fault a contractor took twice the agreed time to finish performance of a construction contract and thus incurred additional expenses and other losses. While in the case the claim was for reimbursement for the additional expenses and losses due to the extension of the work period, the Supreme Court decided that the work extension period was twice the agreed time due to 'the changed design of a bridge, the delay of acquiring the land for work, the delay of removing items and electronic poles on the site, and inhabitants' opposition to use the land'. Since such changes might be not expected by the contractor at the time of contracting, the doctrine of change of circumstances was applicable in this case.

Further, in the Supreme Court 96 Tai-shang No 482 Civil Judgment (2007), the claimant, a contractor, entered into a contract with the defendant to work on air conditioning facilities but delayed the completion of its work for over 1,000 days. The reason for the delayed work was that another contractor had suspended its work on the construction project, which was a prerequisite for the work on the air conditioning facilities. When the claimant sued for the increase of reimbursement because of the delay of over 1,000 days, the Court held that the extension of the period of time for the work due to another contractor's suspension of work was unforeseeable to the contractor and that it was unfair for the defendant to pay the price according to the original period of work. Thus, the doctrine of change of circumstances was applicable in this case.

In these two Supreme Court cases, the delayed completion of work was due to the acts of a third party. The court allowed the contractors to claim for extra reimbursement because such third-party acts were unforeseeable to the contractors. It was clear that the Taiwanese Supreme Court did not confine change of circumstances to specific incidents caused by *force majeure*, such as war or strikes.

Taiwanese scholars nonetheless stress that the doctrine of change of circumstances should be limited to such *force majeure*-type incidents because it is designed to exclude unfair outcomes of a contract and should be applicable only where no other remedies are available. Accordingly, where an unfairness of original performance is caused by a third

[15] LIN (n 3) 21; LIU (n 2) 280.

[16] The Supreme Court 87 Tai-shang No 876 Civil Judgment (1998).

party, the disadvantaged party is entitled to make a damages claim against the third party. As a result, the doctrine of change of circumstance is not applicable in such a case.[17]

2. Unexpected Change for the Contracting Party

For the doctrine of change of circumstances to apply, the objective change of circumstances has to have been unexpected and unforeseeable for both parties. If the contracting parties predict some kind of change of circumstances and enter into their contract accordingly, they have undertaken the risks occurring thereafter and the doctrine of change of circumstances is not applicable.

In practice, the Taiwanese Supreme Court 83 Tai-shang No 1190 Civil Judgment (1994) declared that 'the doctrine of change of circumstances is based on the concept of equity, and is a remedy merely for the tremendous change of circumstance that is unforeseeable to the parties'. Further, the Taiwanese Supreme Court 106 Tai-shang No 2052 Civil Judgment (2017) announced that '[i]f the parties had foreseen the change of circumstances at the time of the conclusion of the contract, and made an agreement on the ways of adjusting their performances, the doctrine of change of circumstances would not be applicable'. Provided that the parties had foreseen the change of circumstances but did not make any agreement on the adjustment of their performances, they had to fulfil their duties without the application of the doctrine of change of circumstances due to their negligence or mistake.[18]

Accordingly, an ordinary change of commodity prices or expected economic development do not constitute a change of circumstances under Article 227-2 TCC. Also, where a transaction is speculative in nature, such as an investment on the stock market, a futures contract, or sales of options, the investors have to take on the risks of the transaction with no application of the doctrine of change of circumstances. The reason is that such speculative transactions are extremely uncertain in nature, and this is known to the parties when engaging in them.[19]

3. Occurrence of Change after the Conclusion of the Contract and Application for Adjustment Prior to the End of the Contract

In German law, under section 313 BGB, the time of the change of circumstances is not an element to be considered. According to German scholars, both the changes prior to and those in the wake of conclusion of the contract can be seen as changed circumstances even if section 313 BGB stipulates 'after conclusion of the contract' in its wording. Therefore, relevant material changes of circumstances under the BGB include those changes that occurred prior to the conclusion of contract but appeared or were learned of by the parties after the conclusion of the contract.[20]

[17] LIN (n 3) 23–24; LIU (n 2) 281–82; WU (n 8) 33.

[18] LIU (n 2) 280–81. Where one of the contracting parties foresees the change of circumstances while the other party does not, only the other party who is bona fide is entitled to make a claim on the ground of change of circumstances. See LIN (n 3) 22.

[19] LIU (n 2) 281; ZHENG (n 3) 156.

[20] See the references to German literature in WU (n 8) 39.

In Taiwanese law, however, the common opinion is that in accordance with the wording of Article 227-2 TCC, the change of circumstances has to occur after the conclusion of the contract, and the provision does not include changes in circumstances that occur prior to the conclusion of the contract. Scholars have commented that any circumstances that changed prior to the conclusion of the contract have become the basis or conditions of the contract, and it was the parties' will to include them in a contract; therefore, the contracting parties deserve no special protection in the wake of the conclusion of the contract.[21]

Further, as has been emphasized with regard to the hardship rule in the UNIDROIT Principles of International Commercial Contracts (PICC), '[t]he change in the equilibrium must relate to obligations that remain to be performed; it cannot relate to obligations which have already been performed'.[22] In the same vein, Taiwanese scholars emphasize that the doctrine of change of circumstances is not applicable once the contract is extinguished, for example, due to the performance of the duties. That is, once a contract has come to an end, its effects may no longer be adapted by the court. As a result, where a change of circumstances occurs before the performance of a contract, but the debtor performs his or her duty as required in the contract without knowledge of such change or without requesting adaptation of the contract when he or she has learned of such change, the debtor is not allowed to make any claims under the doctrine of change of circumstances after his or her performance of the contract.[23] The Taiwanese Supreme Court has taken the same position, stating that:

> [t]he contracting party is allowed to claim for an increase or decrease of payments under the doctrine of change of circumstances provided for in Article 227-2 of the Civil Code only where the relationship of debt has not been extinguished due to repayments or any other acts. Other than that, no increase or decrease of payments is allowed.[24]

For instance, in the Supreme Court 71 Tai-shang No 32 Civil Judgment (1982), one party had acquired a piece of land and was ordered by a court to pay compensation to the other party. After the buyer deposited the payment for the seller with the court, the seller applied to the court for an increase in the payment because the price of the land had risen under the new scheme of land value issued by the authority. The court rejected the application since the payment of compensation had finished and thus the seller was not entitled to claim an increase in compensation under the doctrine of change of circumstances.

4. No Fault of the Contracting Party

The change of circumstances should not be attributable to the contracting parties; otherwise, the party that it can be attributed to bears responsibility for the losses incurred by the change of circumstances and must perform its duty as required by the contract. This can be illustrated by a comparison of two cases.

21 LIU (n 2) 280; WU (n 8) 38; YE (n 1) 56; LIN (n 3) 22.

22 E McKendrick in S Vogenauer (ed), *Commentary on the UNIDROIT Principles of International Commercial Contracts (PICC)* (2nd edn, OUP 2015) art 6.2.2 para 4.

23 LIN (n 3) 22; LIU (n 2) 280; YE (n 1) 56.

24 The Supreme Court 98 Tai-shang No 1822 Civil Judgment (2009).

In the Supreme Court 69 Tai-shang No 606 Civil Judgment (1980), the claimant sold a batch of steel to the defendant at a price of New Taiwan dollars (NT$) 4,600 per ton. The price of steel dramatically increased to NT$8,200 per ton in July 1973 and NT$14,500 per ton by the end of 1973 because of the energy crisis. The Court allowed the claimant's claim for an increase of the steel price under the doctrine of change of circumstances, stating that:

> [a]t that time, the market in our country was short of such commodity because of the ban on export in foreign countries. In such situation, it was difficult for the claimant to acquire the raw materials and thus it was unable to deliver its goods in time. [Such change] was a circumstance that was not attributable to the claimant and the rise of price was not foreseeable at the time of contracting.

Thus, the claimant's claim for an increase of the steel price was affirmed.

By contrast, in the case underlying the Supreme Court 98 Tai-shang No 59 Civil Judgment (2009), the Railroad Bureau prohibited its contractor from using some specific machinery in setting up cable lines, which resulted in an increase of expenses for the work because it had to be done by workers. When the contractor claimed for increase of its reimbursement for the work on the ground of the doctrine of change of circumstances, the Court held that:

> [w]here, after the conclusion of the contract, the cause of loss sustained by a party was attributable to another party, it was an issue as to damages upon non-performance but not a change of circumstances under Article 227-2 of the Civil Code.

Since the contractor's increased expenses were attributable to the Railroad Bureau, the doctrine of change of circumstances was not applicable.

5. Obvious Unfairness of the Original Obligations

The distribution of risks is the core value of the doctrine of change of circumstances. Any social and economic activities involve risks to a certain degree. Therefore, it is fair for the contracting parties to undertake reasonable risks occurring after the conclusion of the contract. The doctrine of change of circumstances governs only those incidents that alter the equilibrium of the contract and instances where the performance of the original obligations is obviously unfair to the contracting party in view of the principle of good faith.

There are several statements made by Taiwanese scholars to describe the obvious unfairness: (i) a contract cannot be expected to be performed in accordance with the original obligations,[25] (ii) the interests between the parties are tremendously altered with the result that the security of transaction is harmed,[26] and (iii) the balance between the performance and the counter-performance loses its adequacy to the parties. That is, the disadvantaged

[25] TSAI (n 13) 238.

[26] 鄭玉波，民法債編總論 (Min fa zhai bian zong lun)，第398頁（台北：三民書局，1998年） [ZHEN Yubo, *General Principles of the Law of Obligations* (San-min Bookstore 1998)].

party has to endure an extreme burden, while the other party has merely suffered slightly, and the equilibrium of the contract is affected unreasonably.[27]

To address obvious unfairness, the Supreme Court has focused on the equilibrium of the contract. Its 103 Tai-shang No 983 Civil Judgment (2014) laid out that:

> [u]nder the doctrine of change of circumstances, the change of the index price of a commodity is not the only basis for judgment; instead, the judgment has to follow an objective standard. It has to consider the losses suffered by one of the parties because of the change of circumstances, and the benefits gained by the other party because of the change of circumstances, together with any other factual situations, so as to determine the adequate amount of increased payment.

As a consequence, a lower court's decision that is based only on the losses suffered by one of the parties without considering the benefits to the other party should be overruled.

With regard to cases concerning the COVID-19 pandemic, the tenet of the Supreme Court 104 Tai-shang No 2413 Civil Judgment (2015) was cited frequently, stating that it was not a change of circumstances 'if the circumstances occurring did not go beyond the scope of risks that should be borne under the original outcome of a contract, taking into consideration the social-economic situations, common ideas, and any other objective affairs'. The two criteria declared by the Supreme Court (ie 'the circumstances going beyond the scope of risks' and 'the claimant's loss compared with the defendant's benefit') set up the basic rules for lower courts to deal with the cases where the COVID-19 pandemic was a factor.

The cases involving the COVID-19 pandemic in Taiwan were those of leases (except one case) where the claimants rented a building or a room to run a business such as hotels, restaurants, cinemas, karaoke theatres, and opticians. The lease terms were mostly between 5 and 15 years. After the COVID-19 pandemic, lessees sued lessors for a reduction of rentals under the doctrine of change of circumstances.

There were 19 district court cases in Taiwan involving the COVID-19 pandemic from 2020 to 2024, with only two court judgments affirming the claimants' requests for deduction of rentals, while the majority of courts refused to apply the doctrine of change of circumstances in these cases. For these two minority cases, in the case of a restaurant, the court allowed the reduction of rental fees on the ground that the claimant was completely unable to expect the government's order to ban the eating in a restaurant during the pandemic at the time of contracting.[28] In the case of a hotel, the court allowed the reduction of the rent because the number of foreign visitors to Taiwan dropped drastically (by 88.39 per cent) in 2020 and the claimant's turnover declined by 53 per cent.[29] The deduction rates allowed by the courts were 14 per cent and 10 per cent on the rental fees, respectively, in these two cases.

In the majority of the COVID-19 pandemic cases, the courts rebutted the assertion of the doctrine of change of circumstances on the grounds of there being no change of circumstances and/or no benefits gained by the lessors.

[27] ZHENG (n 3) 157; WU (n 8) 51.
[28] Taiwan Shilin District Court 111 Hujen No 261 Judgment (2022).
[29] Taiwan Taipei District Court 109 Jenshang No 494 Judgment (2020).

First, the courts held that under the principle of distribution of risks in a lease, a lessor undertakes the duty to provide a space or item for use and collecting profits, while a lessee undertakes the risk of a decrease of its revenue arising from a pandemic or from political issues such as the political relationship across the Taiwan Strait. In the long-term relational contract, since the lessee at issue had business experiences in the market, it had to be assumed that it had prudently assessed all subjective and objective facts before contracting and during performance and that it had considerable experiences in its business models, business operations, relevant risks, costs and benefits, profits, and market trends. It also had to be assumed that the lessee had the ability to evaluate and judge the risks. Accordingly, the lessee was not allowed to change its mind after the conclusion of a contract, given that its ability of performance and of taking measures of precautions had to be taken into account.[30] In addition, since rent is a business cost, it is the lessee who has to appropriately evaluate it and to take the risk of running a business. It is within the circumscription of the business to assume sole responsibility of its own profits and losses even if the change of market goes beyond the scope of its evaluation.[31]

Accordingly, the courts declared that in light of the fact that the lessee's revenue was merely influenced and decreased for a short period of time (ie several months) in a long-term lease with, for example, terms of 5 or 15 years, the COVID-19 pandemic was not a change of circumstances since such circumstances had not gone beyond the scope of the risks that should be borne under the original scenario of the contract.[32]

Secondly, the courts refused the application of the doctrine of change of circumstances in the COVID-19 pandemic cases on the ground that it is not obviously unfair to the lessee when performing the original obligations of the contract either because the lessee did not suffer large losses or because the lessor did not gain any benefits arising from the pandemic. For instance, in the case of a computer software services supply contract where the fees were charged monthly, the court stated that 'the so-called obvious unfairness indicates that the occurrence of the original legal effect is contradictory to the principle of good faith and fairness in light of the objective transaction order. That is, one of the parties should suffer inappropriate losses while the other party should gain unexpected benefits.' Since in this case the buyer did not suffer inappropriate losses and the seller did not enjoy unexpected benefits, the doctrine of change of circumstances was inapplicable.[33]

In another case, where a lessee (a cinema owner) was responsible to pay as rental a basic fee plus an extra fee that was counted on some percentage of the business profits of the cinema, the court stated that the lessor did not gain any benefits because it was merely entitled to the basic fee, while the extra fee was zero due to the pandemic, and thus the doctrine of change of circumstances was inapplicable.[34]

[30] Taiwan Taipei District Court 111 Beishu No 61 Judgment (2022); Taiwan Taipei District Court 111 Zhongsu No 379 Judgment (2022); Taiwan Taipei District Court 109 Zongshu No 603 Judgment (2020).

[31] Taiwan Taipei District Court 109 Zhongsu No 561 Judgment (2020).

[32] Taiwan Taipei District Court 109 Beijan No 22135 Judgment (2020); Taiwan Taipei District Court 109 Beizhongshu No 11 Judgment (2020); Taiwan Taipei District Court 109 Beijan No 12561 Judgment (2020); Taiwan Taipei District Court 110 Beijan No 12432 Judgment (2021); Taiwan Taipei District Court 109 Beijan No 10275 Judgment (2020); Taiwan Taipei District Court 110 Xiaoshang No 107 Judgment (2021).

[33] Taiwan Taipei District Court 109 Su No 5507 Judgment (2020).

[34] Taiwan Taipei District Court 109 Beizhongsu No 11 Judgment (2020). Other court judgments that disallowed the doctrine of change of circumstances on the ground of no benefits gained by the lessors are as follows: Taiwan Taipei District Court 110 Jenshang No 17166 Judgment (2021); Taiwan Taipei District Court 109 Beijan No 22135 Judgment (2020); Taiwan Taipei District Court 110 Beijan No 12432 Judgment (2021); Taiwan Taipei District Court 109 Zongshu No 603 Judgment (2020).

In one of the hypothetical scenarios for this volume, Abraham entered into a contract for an unlimited period of time with farmer Bill in 1567. Abraham promised to build and maintain an irrigation channel from which Bill could extract water at a fixed price. By 2018, inflation and the rise in the cost of maintenance and labour have made the price wholly inadequate. Abraham's successors in law ask for an increase in the price that would provide them with adequate compensation. Alternatively, they wish to terminate the contract.[35]

In the first place, Article 227-2 TCC is applicable to inflation after a long period of time. In the Supreme Court 98 Tai-shang No 1929 Civil Judgment (2009), the claimant bought a piece of land from the defendant in 1980, while the defendant resold the land and transferred the title of the land to a third party in 2003. The claimant sued for damages of NT$6 million, which corresponded to the actual loss incurred. However, the defendant sought to limit the amount by relying on the liquidated damages clause in the contract. This required that damages should amount to twice the money paid by the buyer of the land, that is, NT$1 million.

The Supreme Court held that the value of the land had increased to 43 times of the original price during the past 23 years, and this was not attributable to either party. The claimant could not foresee that the defendant might breach the contract 23 years later and thus did not include a clause to determine the payment for breach of contract as such. The alteration of the land value was viewed as a significant change of the contractual basis since the claimant would not have concluded this contract or would have concluded it in different terms if she could have foreseen such a change at the time of contracting. Also, it was unfair for the defendant to compensate the claimant on the basis of liquidated damages as agreed upon. Therefore, the doctrine of change of circumstances was applicable to this case. The increase of the price of the land equalled the benefit the defendant gained unexpectedly and the loss incurred by the claimant; therefore, the claimant was allowed to claim the NT$6 million as damages.[36]

In Abraham's case, Abraham's successors would be entitled to ask for an increase in the price under Article 227-1 TCC in accordance with the above-mentioned Supreme Court case since the value of the irrigation channel and its use must have increased to a large degree over the past four centuries. It was unfair for Bill to merely pay the price agreed upon centuries ago while Abraham's successors had to take the inadequately low price caused by inflation. However, according to the Taiwanese Supreme Court, the claim to the price that is adequate with a view to inflation can be made merely for that part of the price that has not been paid because the right to claim for the part of the price that has been paid is extinguished with the payments, and the increase in price should only be counted from the time when the claimant brought an action against the debtor.[37]

[35] The fact scenario of this hypothetical is taken from M Chen-Wishart, D Neo, and S Vogenauer, 'Introduction', ch 1 in this volume, 7.

[36] In a similar case, the Supreme Court 93 Tai-shang No 2503 Civil Judgment (2004), the claimant sold a piece of land to the defendant, who paid the price in 1961. The claimant seller terminated the contract in 1999 because of the defendant buyer's breach of contract. As a result, both parties had to return what they had received under the contract. The defendant buyer who could claim restitution of the purchase price demanded that the sum should be adjusted upwards in line with the rise of commodity prices that had occurred over the past decades. The Supreme Court allowed the claim for the adjusted sum.

[37] The Supreme Court 98 Tai-shang No 1822 Civil Judgment (2009) and the Supreme Court 71 Tai-shang No 32 Civil Judgment (1982); both are discussed in this chapter, section III.3.

Consequently, Abraham's successors would be entitled to apply to the court for an increase in the price of maintaining the irrigation channel for future payments under Article 227-1 TCC but could not claim for compensation for the use of the land during the past centuries under the law of unjustified enrichment. They also would not be entitled to terminate the contract since the adjustment of the price could be an appropriate way to achieve a balance of interests between both parties.

IV. Legal Effects of a Change of Circumstances

1. Application to the Court

Under Article 227-2 TCC, the disadvantaged party has to apply to the court for a judgment under the doctrine of change of circumstances so as to formulate a new legal relationship between the parties. Instead of filing a lawsuit to adapt the contract, the disadvantaged party is also allowed to make a defence on the ground of change of circumstances when he or she is sued by the other party before the court.[38]

It is controversial whether the court is allowed to adapt a contract under the doctrine of change of circumstances without a party's application.[39] Since party autonomy in court proceedings is a fundamental rule under the Taiwanese Code of Civil Procedure and also a basic principle of private law, it is not appropriate for the court to automatically adapt a contract, relying on the doctrine of change of circumstances, without a party's application.

2. Primary Effect and Secondary Effect

Based on the sanctity of contract, the contractual relationship should rather be maintained than terminated. Therefore, even when the doctrine of change of circumstances is applicable, the first measure of the court would be to adapt the contract so as to maintain the contractual relationship between the parties. Only when an adaptation of the contract cannot restore the equilibrium of the contract can the court resort to termination of the contract. The adaptation of contract is called 'the primary effect', while the termination of contract is 'the secondary effect' of the doctrine of change of circumstances.[40]

The primary effects include mainly the increase or decrease of payment, allowing payment in instalments, the delay of payment, and changes in the kinds of objects delivered. The primary effects are intended to alter the original contractual relationship as minimally as possible so that the equilibrium of the contract can be achieved again. Where the adaptation of the contract is impossible or unexpected in terms of elimination of unfairness, the court is allowed to terminate the contract so as to extinguish the contract. As to the primary and secondary effects, the Supreme Court held that:

[38] The Supreme Court 85 Tai-shang No 482 Civil Judgment (1996); the Supreme Court 90 Tai-shang No 1657 Civil Judgment (2001).

[39] For confirmation of this autonomous competence with regard to a change of circumstances, see QIU (n 3) 15; for denial of this competence, see LIU (n 2) 283–84; YE (n 1) 63.

[40] LIN (n 3) 26–27; LIU (n 2) 286–87; ZHENG (n 3) 158–59.

> the effect of the doctrine of change of circumstances is merely to increase or decrease the agreed payments of the contract (change of quantity of payments) or to alter its original effects (eg applying to the court for termination of the contract so as to extinguish the contractual relationships). It is not allowed to adjust the contents of a performance that is not provided for in the contract.[41]

For the factors to guide the adaptation of a contract, the court declared that:

> where a judgment on the increase of payment under the doctrine of change of circumstances is made, it cannot completely rely on the alteration of commodity prices, but shall follow the objectively fair standard. It has to consider the loss incurred by one party due to the change of circumstances and the benefits enjoyed by the other party due to the change of circumstances, and any other facts, so as to determine an appropriate amount of the increased payment.[42]

In another of the hypothetical scenarios for this volume, Citi Corporation received a loan from Drive Bank in 2015. The interest rate was fixed at 10 per cent for five years. In the 20 years preceding the agreement, the rate of inflation had been relatively stable within a range of 1 to 6 per cent. In 2017, the economic situation began to destabilize and inflation rose to 50 per cent. Drive Bank requested adjustment or termination of the contract.[43]

When Citi Corporation entered into the contract with Drive Bank, the inflation rate from 1 to 6 per cent was the basis of their agreement since it had been stable for the 20 years preceding the agreement. The destabilization of economy and its ensuing inflation was a tremendous alteration occurring after the making of the contract. Such inflation of up to 50 per cent was beyond the expectation of both parties. Therefore, in Taiwan, Drive Bank would be entitled to make a claim before a court to adjust the interest rate under the doctrine of change of circumstances (ie 'the primary effect'). Since an adjustment of the interest rate would be capable of restoring the balance of interests of both parties, it is not appropriate for the court to terminate the contract (ie 'the secondary effect').

Where a contract is terminated by a court decision based on the disadvantaged party's application, the other party is entitled to make a claim for restitution of the thing given and compensation for any loss incurred in the course of action. The liability for compensation levied on the disadvantaged party is not damages under the rule of non-performance of contract but is imposed on the grounds of the principle of good faith. As a result, the compensation includes only the actual loss of the other party but not the expected gains accumulated had the contract been performed.[44]

41 The Supreme Court 103 Tai-shang No 1142 Civil Judgment (2015).

42 The Supreme Court 66 Tai-shang No 2975 Civil Precedent (1977); the Supreme Court 100 Tai-shang No 290 Civil Judgment (2011); the Supreme Court 98 Tai-shang No 2351 Civil Judgment (2009).

43 This hypothetical is taken from M Chen-Wishart, D Neo, and S Vogenauer, 'Introduction', ch 1 in this volume, 7.

44 史尚寬，債法總論 (Zhai fa zong lun)，第442頁（自版，1980年）[SHI Shangkuan, *General Principles of the Law of Obligations* (1980) 442]; LIN (n 3) 27; LIU (n 2) 287.

3. Renegotiation?

Under Article 6.2.3 PICC, in case of hardship the disadvantaged party is entitled to request renegotiations, and upon failure to reach agreement within a reasonable time either party may resort to the court to terminate the contract or to adapt the contract. The renegotiation requirement has also been enacted in Article 1195 of the French Civil Code 2016. After the duty of renegotiation for change of circumstances was provided in the PICC and the French Civil Code, some Taiwanese scholars advocated its adoption in the revision of the TCC.

Those scholars alleged that the renegotiation requirement meets the principle of party autonomy on the distribution of risks, the principle of proportionality revealed in the primary and secondary effects of the doctrine of change of circumstances, and the protection of party autonomy in civil procedure that enhances the court's decision on the adaptation of the contract.[45] Nonetheless, this duty of renegotiation for change of circumstances was rejected in December 2018 by the Taiwanese Group of Research and Revision on the Law of Obligations of the Civil Code, established in the Ministry of Justice.

The members of this group reasoned that most existing provisions on renegotiation under the TCC do not have any practical function, that it was unclear what effect a violation of the duty of renegotiation would have, and that a provision on renegotiation was merely a declaration without any legal effect.[46] Indeed, in most cases where a change of circumstances occurred, the contracting parties had initiated negotiations in order to adapt their contracts before going to court for a judgment.[47] Thus, it was unnecessary for the law to require them to do so.

V. Contractual Clauses Overriding the Doctrine of Change of Circumstances

In principle, provision for adjustment of inflation on the basis of commodity price indices can be made by the parties to the contract at the time of contracting since such adjustment is a kind of management and control over the risks. For example, a construction contract can stipulate that if work is delayed due to the contractor's fault, remuneration is calculated on the basis of the lower price index between the price index determined at the date of planned completion of the work and that determined at the date of actual completion of the work. Since an indexation clause is binding on the basis of party autonomy and the freedom of contract, the doctrine of change of circumstances would be excluded from application.[48]

An indexation clause, however, may not exclude the application of the doctrine of change of circumstances if the change of circumstances is unexpected. For instance, in the Supreme

[45] 楊宏暉，論情事變更原則下重新協商義務之建構 (Lun Qing shi bian geng yuan ze xia cong xin xie shang yi wu zhi jian gou)，台北大學法學論叢，第97期，第1, 64–68頁（2016年3月） [YANG Honghui, 'On the Construction of the Duty of Renegotiations Under the Doctrine of Change of Circumstances' (2016) 97 Taipei University Law Review 1, 64–68]; YE (n 1) 65–68.

[46] 法務部民法債編研究修正小組第36次會議紀錄 (Fa wu bu min fa zhai bian yan jiu xiu zheng xiao zu di 36 ci hui yi ji lu)，第40–44頁（2018年12月27日） [The Ministry of Justice Research and Revision Groups on the Law of Obligations of the Civil Code, Record of the 36th Meeting (27 December 2018) 40–44].

[47] ZHENG (n 3) 158.

[48] The Supreme Court 102 Tai-shang No 231 Civil Judgment (2013).

Court 93 Tai-shang No 2446 Civil Precedent (2004), the contracting parties of a lease for an unlimited period of time made a clause about the calculation of the rental price in accordance with the fixed rate of land reporting prices issued by the authority. The Court held that:

> [a]lthough the agreed rental price was adjusted to increase or decrease according to the reporting prices of the land, where the circumstances have changed due to the nearby environment, degree of prosperity of business, economic value of the land, and the benefits of using the land enjoyed by the lessee, the lessor was entitled to resort to the court to adjust the rental price under Article 227-2 of the Civil Code if such change was unexpected at the time of contracting and it was unfair to calculate the rental price in accordance with the fixed rate of the reporting prices of the land.

Further, public construction contracts in Taiwan concluded between the government and the contractor usually include an indexation clause, stipulating, for example:

> This construction contract does not have any terms on the adjustment for the fluctuation of commodity prices, and the contractor agrees to estimate by itself the fluctuation of commodity prices occurring during the period of time for the work in its total bid price. The contractor agrees not to claim for compensation, damages, extension of contract, stop of work, or termination of contract.[49]

The binding force of such indexation clauses (which might rather be called 'non-indexation clauses') is fiercely disputed.

1. Freedom of Contract

Some scholars argue that based on the autonomy of private law and the freedom of contract, the doctrine of change of circumstances is not applicable where an indexation clause has been included in a construction contract since the contracting parties have taken into consideration the fluctuation of commodity prices in their contracts and their will has to be respected.[50]

One of the leading cases in this regard is the Supreme Court 100 Tai-shang No 1392 Civil Judgment (2011), which recognizes the binding force of an indexation clause concerning the rise of steel price. It states:

> Since clause 5.1.4 of the construction contract provides that 'the construction contract does not have any terms on the adjustment for the fluctuation of commodity prices', such clause excludes the application of Article 227-2 of the Civil Code concerning the doctrine

[49] Cited in the Supreme Court 101 Tai-shang No 813 Civil Judgment (2012).

[50] 鄭渼蓁，物價變動調整之情事變更原則適用(Wu jia bian dong tiao zheng zhi qing shi bian geng yuan ze shi yong)，萬國法律，第147期，第9, 14頁（2012年12月）[ZHEN Meizhen, 'Application of the Doctrine of Change of Circumstances to the Adjustment of Fluctuation of Commodity Prices' (2012) 147 Wanguo Law Review 9, 14].

> of change of circumstances. . . . In particular, the appellant is a professional construction company, and the price of this construction work is up to NT$204,000,000 dollars, demonstrating that the appellant is a professional construction company with large scale of business full of market experience. It is therefore endowed with capability of estimation and judgment on the change of commodity prices in the future. The commodity prices of construction work are greatly influenced by the uncertain elements arising from domestic and international markets in the open economic system; thus, the risks of costs for performance of the contract have to be taken into account. Since the market trend of increasing prices of construction materials could have been expected prior to the conclusion of the construction contract, and it was thus was not completely unforeseeable, the appellant should have been able to estimate the risks of costs for performance due to the increase of commodity prices prior to the conclusion of the contract . . . Otherwise, [if the doctrine of change of circumstances is applicable,] it is similar to encouraging the bid company not to correctly estimate the risks in advance and to bid the contract at a lower price, and then to claim for increase of the reimbursement of the work on the ground of the increase of commodity prices after concluding the contract. Such application is a violation of the purpose of Article 227-2 of the Civil Code.[51]

2. Reasonableness of Risk Distribution

The majority of scholars and courts do not fully accept the binding force of such indexation clauses. In principle, the contractual allocation of risk has to be followed by the court. Nonetheless, contractual clauses such as 'no adjustment of commodity prices' are interpreted to be an agreement on the distribution of foreseeable and reasonable risks between the parties at the time of conclusion of the contract. Where a risk is unforeseeable and unreasonable in terms of its occurrence and its scope of alteration, such risk is not covered by the indexation clause, and thus the doctrine of change of circumstances is still applicable. In addition, the government often has a monopoly, or at least very strong bargaining power, so it seems unfair that it should be allowed to shift the entire risk to private businesses. In any case, the provision of change of circumstances may not be excluded by a contract because it is a court measure to give the disadvantaged party relief in order to fulfil the court's function of achieving fairness and justice.[52]

The leading case of the majority opinion on contractual clauses concerning risk distribution between the parties is the Supreme Court 103 Tai-shang No 308 Civil Judgment (2014), which involved the following contractual clause:

[51] This court judgment is strongly criticized by scholars because, according to the Supreme Court, the inflation of the steel price was predictable for the contractor in this case, and thus the increase of the steel price is not a change of circumstances at all. See TSAI (n 13) 239; 姚志明，情事變更原則適用於工程糾紛問題之再探討—最高法院100年度台上字第1329號民事判決 (Qing shi bian geng yuan ze shi yong yu gong cheng jiuu fen wen ti zhi zai tan tao—zui gao fa yuan 100 nian du tai shang zi di 1329 hao min shi pan jue)，月旦裁判時報，第20期，第105, 106頁（2013年4月）[YAO Zhimin, 'Re-visiting the Issues of the Application of the Doctrine of Change of Circumstances on Construction Disputes: The Supreme Court 100 Tai-shang No 1329' (2013) 20 Yudan Judgment Times 105, 106].

[52] ZHENG (n 3) 158; YE (n 1) 57, 59; 謝哲勝、李金松，工程契約理論與實務 (Gon cheng qi yue li lun yu shi wu)，第350頁（台北：漢蘆出版公司，2005年）[XIE Zhesheng and L Jinsong, *Theory and Practice of Construction Contracts* (Hanlu Publishing 2005) 350].

> Commodity price index adjustment: where the commodity price inflates, the remuneration of the work has to be adjusted according to the price index of the construction materials issued by the Accounts Bureau.

In relation to the increase of the price of steel and metal products, the Court held:

> Where the contracting parties make an agreement in advance on the fair distribution of risk occurring thereafter, if such a risk is foreseeable at the time of contracting in terms of the occurrence of the risk and the scope of its alteration arising from the risk, after considering the parties' real intent, the contents and purposes of the contract, social and economic situations, and the general concepts, the contracting parties are limited to exercise their rights in accordance with the agreement in the contract and cannot claim for increase of payment on the ground of the doctrine of change of circumstances under '*pacta sunt servanda*' and 'the sanctity of contract'. Nevertheless, *where the occurrence of the risk and the scope of alteration is not a normal development of objective circumstances and goes beyond the basis or prevailing circumstances that is recognized by the parties at the time of the conclusion of contract, rendering it obviously not possible to be foreseeable, the contracting parties are allowed to claim for adjustment of the effects of the contract under the doctrine of change of circumstances on the basis of the function of the good-faith principle to govern the effects of a contract.* [Under such circumstances, the contracting parties] are not bound by the terms of the contract, so as to conform to the concept of fairness and contractual justice contained in the doctrine of change of circumstances.[53]

The Court has also indicated that:

> a contractual clause [concerning the exclusion of adjustment of the contract] governs merely the risks of ordinary and reasonable scope. The unexpected risks that exceed the reasonable scope are not governed by such a clause and therefore the doctrine of change of circumstances is still applicable.[54]

By and large, a contractual clause that distributes the risk concerning potential supervening circumstances will be respected by the courts only when the occurrence of the risk and the scope of its alteration are a normal development of objective circumstances and are foreseeable to the contracting parties. By contrast, such a contractual clause is not binding and the doctrine of change of circumstances is applicable where the occurrence of the risk and the scope of its alteration are not reasonable and are unforeseeable to the parties. In other words, unexpected risks are not governed by the indexation clause.

[53] Emphasis added. For similar findings, see the Supreme Court 104 Tai-shang No 132 Civil Judgment (2015); the Supreme Court 106 Tai-shang No 1866 Civil Judgment (2017); the Supreme Court 106 Tai-shang No 217 Civil Judgment (2017).

[54] The Supreme Court 103 Tai-shang No 308 Civil Judgment (2014). For similar findings, see the Supreme Court 103 Tai-shang No 1636 Civil Judgment (2014); the Supreme Court 101 Tai-shang No 813 Civil Judgment (2012).

VI. *Force majeure* Clauses

With regard to *force majeure* clauses in a contract, such clauses are designed to avoid contractual liability for non-performance based on fault. That is, where a debtor is liable for non-performance under a contract, he or she may avoid liability if his or her non-performance is due to *force majeure*. Therefore, the *force majeure* clause has nothing to do with the doctrine of change of circumstances in terms of non-performance of contract. Further, the objective incidents that are required for the doctrine of change of circumstances principally indicate the existence of an event amounting to *force majeure*. Thus, even if a *force majeure* clause is included in a contract, it cannot prevent the court from applying the doctrine of change of circumstances to adapt the contract or terminate it.

In Taiwan, only two High Court cases can be found that deal with *force majeure* clauses, even though such clauses are found in most international contracts. In one of these cases,[55] the defendant bid for a contract of repairs with the Ministry of Defence and thereafter concluded a contract of overseas services with the claimant, a German company, for the claimant to provide necessary technical services. Unfortunately, the defendant's bid with the Ministry of Defence, which was originally accepted, was later struck down by the relevant authority, and thus the defendant refused to pay the price for the services provided by the claimant on the ground that the annulment of the bid was *force majeure*.

The *force majeure* clause at issue stipulated the following:

> Force Majeure: A case for release from obligations (force majeure) is deemed to be caused by overwhelming and abnormal impediment or occurrence that delays or prevents the fulfillment of the Contract and which neither party had reason to take into account when entering into the Contract and which is independent of any action by either party and could not be averted or prevented without unreasonable expense or loss of time. Such cases may result from war, mutiny, high sea piracy, internal unrest, expropriation or confiscation for public needs, embargo, acts of God, discontinuation of public transportation or supply of energy, labor conflict, delayed granting of export license or fire or some other unusual event with equally drastic effects beyond both parties' control.

The court decided that although the bid was struck down by the authority after the conclusion of the contract of overseas services, the annulment was not an instance of *force majeure* as indicated in the *force majeure* clause since the annulment was based on the fact that the defendant had not provided the required documents to prove its past experience.

In another case,[56] which involved a contract of supply of Asymmetric Digital Subscriber Line (ADSL) components, the supplier failed to deliver the components specified in the contract. When the buyer claimed damages for non-performance, the supplier alleged that its failure to perform was due to the worldwide shortage of the goods at issue and that such worldwide shortage of the goods was a *force majeure* as stipulated in the contract.

[55] Taiwanese High Court 102 Zhong-shang No 214 Judgment (2013).
[56] Taiwanese High Court 90 Zhong-shang No 549 Judgment (2001).

The *force majeure* clause in this contract provided:

> Force Majeure: Neither Party shall be liable to the other for any delay or non-performance caused by any event beyond the reasonable control of the affected party, including but not limited to the following events: war, riot, civil unrest, action and inaction of government, strike, lock-out or other labour dispute, fire, earthquake, accident, transport damage, export restrictions, cessation or suspension or severe restrictions on national or international transport, general shortages of or delay in delivery of components, materials or utilities, natural disasters, and exceptional weather conditions.

The court held that the party could be exempted from its duty where the events stipulated in this clause occurred and such events caused the party's default. Nonetheless, the party could not be relieved from its duty if its ability to supply the goods was not influenced by the worldwide shortage. As a matter of fact, the supplier was able to deliver its goods to another Hong Kong buyer. Thus, its ability to supply was not influenced so that it could not perform its duty owed to the buyer. Accordingly, the *force majeure* clause was inapplicable.

VII. Common Mistake

1. A Shared Error in Motive

In German law, based on Oertmann's theory of the 'disappearance of the contractual basis' that includes both the subjective and the objective basis of the contract, section 313(2) BGB provides that 'if material assumptions that have become the basis of the contract subsequently turn out to be incorrect, they are treated in the same way as a change in circumstances'. This subsection concerns cases where both parties share incorrect assumptions at the stage of contracting. Such a 'shared error in motive' constitutes an initial absence of the basis of the transaction that is treated similarly to the subsequent failure or collapse of this basis.[57]

Unlike German law, the 'shared error in motive' is not governed by Article 227-2 TCC, which provides the doctrine of change of circumstances. Nonetheless, the 2017 reform proposal for the introduction of a new paragraph (2) in Article 227-2 TCC, which follows section 313(2) BGB, covers the 'shared error in motive'. Until this proposed new paragraph is actually enacted, the dispute continues as to how a shared error in motive should be dealt with under Taiwanese law.

2. Scholarly Opinion

All Taiwanese scholars opine that the disadvantaged party is entitled to apply to the court to adapt the contract due to a shared error in motive. With regard to the legal basis, some argue that Article 227-2 TCC is applicable by analogy based on the principle of good

[57] Beale and others (n 8) 1231.

faith where the substantial justice of the contract cannot be achieved due to the change of circumstances.[58]

Some scholars advocate that in the 'shared error in motive' cases, both parties enter into the contract on the basis of the occurrence or existence of certain facts. The risk of non-existence of the contractual basis has to be borne by both parties instead of the application of the doctrine of mistake in motive. Article 88 TCC concerning mistake cannot be applicable reasonably in the case of shared errors since the mistaken party is liable for damages for the loss incurred by the other party after avoiding or revoking his declaration.[59] Accordingly, 'shared error in motive' cannot be treated as a motive in mistake, whereby the contracting party has to be bound to the contract. In order to balance the interests of both parties, a better solution is to adjust the legal relationship between the parties on the basis of the principle of good faith.[60]

One scholar contends that the lack of a provision governing the 'shared error in motive' in the TCC is a legislative mistake and has to be supplemented through jurisprudence. Article 1 TCC provides that '[i]f there is no applicable act for a civil case, the case shall be decided according to custom. If there is no such custom, the case shall be decided according to the jurisprudence.' Foreign laws can be the 'jurisprudence' within the meaning of Article 1 TCC; therefore, section 313(2) BGB can be cited as jurisprudence and thus might be relevant in Taiwanese law to deal with the case of shared error in motive.[61]

3. Case Law

In some cases, the courts have rejected the application of the doctrine of change of circumstances because the facts underlying a contract at the time of its conclusion do not change. For instance, in the Supreme Court 100 Tai-shang No 471 Civil Judgment (2001), the contractor found waste under the land it was working on and additional costs were incurred to deal with the waste. When the contractor claimed for an increase in the costs for dealing with the extra waste, the Supreme Court decided that the waste at issue existed at the time of contracting and was not a change of circumstances after the conclusion of the contract; therefore, the doctrine of change of circumstances was not applicable.

[58] TSAI (n 13) 237.

[59] TCC, art 88(1):

> If the [expresser] was acting under a mistake as to the contents of his expression of intent, or had known the situation of affairs, he would not make the expression; he may revoke the expression; provided that the mistake or the ignorance of the affairs was not due to his own fault.

TCC, art 91:

> If an expression of intent is revoked according to Article 88 or Article 89, the expresser is bound to compensate for any injury which the other party or any third party may have sustained by relying upon the validity of the expression, except the injured party knew, or might know, of the ground on which the expression was revocable.

See also CHEN Tsung-fu, 'Mistake, Fraud, and Representation in Taiwanese Law' in M Chen-Wishart, H Sono, and S Vogenauer (eds), *Studies in the Contract Laws of Asia, vol IV: Invalidity* (OUP 2022) 395.

[60] 王澤鑑，民法總則 (Min fa zong ze)，第416頁（三民書局，2014年）[WAN Zejian, *General Principles of the Civil Code* (San-min Bookstore 2014) 416]; 陳自強，和解與計算錯誤 (He je yu ji suan cuo wu)，第184頁（元照出版公司，2014年）[CHEN Ziqiang, *Settlement and Mistakes on Calculation* (Yuanzhao Publishing 2014) 184].

[61] WU (n 8) 71.

Nonetheless, most court decisions confirm the application of the doctrine of change of circumstances in cases of shared error in motive. In the Supreme Court 106 Tai-shang No 39 Civil Judgment (2017), where the rocks were harder than expected in a construction contract, the Supreme Court reversed and remanded the lower court's judgment that rejected the doctrine of change of circumstances, stating that since the contractor encountered special layers of rocks and was allowed to revise the rate of its working process and its prices according to the contract, the contractor should have had a right to claim the increase of the payment under the contract or the doctrine of change of circumstances. In another similar case relating to a construction contract, where the layers of rocks changed unexpectedly, the Supreme Court reversed the lower court's decision, stating that the doctrine of change of circumstances might be applicable where it was unfair for the contractor to take all the risks under the principle of good faith.[62]

4. Hypothetical

In a further hypothetical scenario for this volume,[63] Gina booked a room for the weekend at the H hotel in X city, the capital of country Z. When the exhibition she intended to visit is cancelled at the very last moment, under Taiwanese law she would still have to pay the price for the room because her intention to visit the exhibition that is cancelled is an error in motive.

Under Taiwanese law, errors in motive generally do not affect the validity of a declaration under the principle that the declarant has to bear the risks that he produced. Even if the non-mistaken party was aware of the declarant's errors in motive, the risks borne by the declarant still cannot be shifted to the non-mistaken party, with the result that the declarant is not entitled to avoid his declaration.[64]

If Gina intends to terminate the contract because a terrorist group declares that it plans to launch attacks on tourists in X City, the terrorist attacks can be seen as *force majeure*. Gina is entitled to resort to the court to terminate the contract on the ground of the doctrine of change of circumstances. Moreover, even if Gina is not entitled to avoid the contract, she is not liable for damages for non-performance of the contract because she is not at fault, given that a debtor is merely liable at his or her fault under the TCC.

Similarly, where an unforeseeable strike by airport personnel prevents Gina from travelling to X City before Sunday afternoon, Gina is entitled to cancel the booking. An unforeseeable strike is also a kind of *force majeure* according to most Taiwanese commentators; therefore, Gina may resort to the court to terminate the contract under the doctrine of change of circumstances.

In the case where Gina booked a room overlooking the street where an inauguration procession was supposed to pass by, but the inauguration proceedings were cancelled (and due to the inauguration, the rental price of the room was ten times higher than the regular price), this scenario is a case of a 'shared error in motive'. Gina is entitled to resort to the

62 The Supreme Court 104 Tai-shang No 132 Civil Judgment (2015).

63 The fact scenarios of the hypotheticals described in this section VII are taken from M Chen-Wishart, D Neo, and S Vogenauer, 'Introduction', ch 1 in this volume, 8.

64 WAN (n 60) 415; 鄭冠宇，民法總則 (Min fa zong ze)，第378頁（學林出版公司，2016年）[ZHENG Guanyu, *General Principles of the Civil Code* (Xuelin Publishing 2016) 378].

court to terminate the contract on the ground of either the principle of good faith or Article 227-7 TCC applying the doctrine of change of circumstances by analogy.

In another hypothetical scenario, Kris sells his family home to Leila at 70 per cent of its market value because both parties assume that Leila will dedicate it to cultural use by the general public, without this assumption being expressly set out in the contract. After the sale, Leila changes her mind and gives the house to one of her sons instead.

In this case, the reason for Kris giving a discount price to sell his house to Leila is the assumption that Leila will dedicate it to cultural use. Leila has the same assumption when she buys the house. Thus, the common assumption that the house will be open for the public constitutes the basis of the sale of the house. Where the common assumption fails to come to existence, it is a shared error in motive for both parties. In Taiwanese law, Kris may claim for the adaptation of the contract or for termination under the good-faith principle or Article 227-2 TCC applying the doctrine of change of circumstances by analogy. Where the court adapts the contract, Kris may claim the difference between the agreed price and the market price. If the court terminates the contract, Kris is entitled to claim restitution of the house with the restitution, in turn, of Leila's payment.

VIII. Impossibility

1. Basic Rules

Similar to the traditional categories developed under German law, Taiwanese law distinguishes various categories of impossibility: initial, subsequent, objective, subjective, whole, and partial impossibility. Taiwanese law also makes a distinction between impossibility that is attributable or not attributable to the debtor.[65] What I discuss in the present section is subsequent impossibility not attributable to the debtor.

Subsequent impossibility not attributable to the debtor in a contract is governed mainly by two provisions of the TCC. Article 225 TCC prescribes that:

(1) The debtor will be released from his obligation to perform if the performance becomes impossible by reason of a circumstance to which he is not imputed.
(2) If the debtor is entitled to claim compensation for the injury against a third party in consequence of the impossibility of the performance under the preceding paragraph, the creditor may claim against the debtor for the transfer of the claim for the injury, or for the delivery of the compensation he has received.

Article 266 TCC stipulates:

(1) If none of the parties is imputed to the impossibility of one party's performance, the other party shall be released from his obligation to perform the counter-prestation.

[65] For the details, see JAN Sheng-Lin, 'Theory and Practice of Specific Performance in Taiwanese Contract Law' in M Chen-Wishart, A Loke, and B Ong (eds), *Studies in the Contract Laws of Asia, vol I: Remedies for Breach of Contract* (OUP 2016) 281, 282–85.

If the impossibility is only partial, the counter-prestation shall be reduced proportionately.

(2) In the case provided in the preceding paragraph, if the counter-prestation has been wholly or partially performed, it may be claimed for the reimbursement in accordance with the provisions concerning unjust enrichment.

The leading case in relation to Articles 225 and 266 TCC is the Supreme Court 30 Shang No 345 Civil Precedent (1941), which stated:

> Where the thing leased is destroyed, and this is not attributable to either of the parties, with the result that it cannot be used or profits therefrom collected, the legal relationship of the parties depends on whether the subject matter of the lease can be repaired. Where the subject matter of the lease cannot be repaired, the lessor is released from its obligation to provide the subject matter for the lessee to use and to collect profits therefrom, and the lessee is also released from its obligation to pay the rental price under Articles 225(1) and 266(1) of the Civil Code, which renders the legal relationship of a lease between the parties extinguished.
>
> Where the thing leased can be repaired, the lessor is released from its obligation to provide the subject matter for the lessee to use and to collect profits therefrom and the lessee is also released from its obligation to pay the rental prior to the repair of the subject matter under Articles 225(1) and 266(1) of the Civil Code. Nonetheless, the relationship of a lease is not extinguished therefrom under Article 430 of the TCC.[66] [Under this article], the lessee is entitled to terminate the contract by way of expressing its declaration, which renders the relationship of lease extinguished, after the lessor refuses to repair the thing leased during the period of time indicated in the notice given by the lessee, who had given a notice specifying a specific time of period for repair.

Accordingly, where the performance is definitively impossible and this is not attributable to either party, the debtor has no obligation to perform under Article 225(1) TCC and the creditor is released from its obligation to counter-perform under Article 266(1) TCC. As a result, once the performance is definitively impossible, the relationship in a contract is extinguished automatically. Neither party is liable in damages since neither of them is at fault. In such a case, if the creditor has wholly or partially performed the counter-performance, it is entitled to claim for reimbursement in accordance with unjustified enrichment under Article 266(2) TCC.

Nonetheless, similar to section 285 BGB, even if it has become impossible for the debtor to perform and the debtor is relieved from performing its obligations, the creditor may demand surrender of what has been received as substitute or assignment of the substitute claim if the debtor obtains a substitute or a substitute claim for the object

66 TCC, art 430 provides that:

> [i]f, for the duration of the lease, the thing leased is necessary for repairing incumbent on the lessor, the lessee may fix a reasonable deadline and notify the lessor to make such repairs. If the lessor fails to make such repairs within the deadline, the lessee may terminate the contract or make the repairs himself with demanding the lessor to return for any expenses incurred therefrom or deducting the said expenses from the rental.

owed under Article 225(2) TCC. Where the creditor exercises a right to substitute, the relationship in the contract is not extinguished and thus the creditor is responsible for its counter-performance.[67]

2. Hypothetical

In another hypothetical scenario for this volume, builder George agrees to refurbish the cellar of Han, the owner of a restaurant. The work is scheduled to start one month after the agreement. Before the work begins, the restaurant is completely destroyed by a storm that is much more violent than any other previous storm in the region. However, the cellar remains fully intact. Han immediately informs George of the situation and asks him not to start work. George insists on rendering performance because he has set aside two weeks to carry out the work and has already purchased the necessary materials.[68]

In this case, the first issue is whether George's performance has become impossible because of the destruction of the restaurant or whether Han is responsible for his failure to receive George's performance. Article 234 TCC provides that '[i]f the creditor refuses or fails to accept the performance tendered to him, he is responsible for the default from the moment when the performance has been tendered'. In practice, this sometimes raises an issue as to the difference between the impossibility of tendering performance by the debtor and the creditor's failure to receive performance.

For instance, a worker prepares to work in a factory or to conduct repairs of the factory but the factory is completely destroyed by fire; or a doctor prepares to undertake a surgery for a patient, who dies just moments before the surgery. It is impossible for both the worker and the doctor to render their performances, while at the same time both the owner of the factory and the patient are unable to receive the performance agreed upon. In such cases, since the possibility of performance is a prerequisite for the creditor's failure to receive performance, this constitutes an impossibility of performance where the fundamental elements of performance are not existent 'in accordance with social concepts'. Hence, both the worker's and the doctor's performances are impossible rather than it being a case of the creditor's failure to receive the performance.[69]

In the case of builder George, since the restaurant has been completely destroyed, it is an issue as to the impossibility of performance rather than an issue of failure to receive performance. The second issue here is as to whether it is possible for George to render his work because the cellar remains fully intact. The so-called impossibility of performance denotes 'any impossibility of performance in accordance with common social concepts'.[70] Since the restaurant has been completely destroyed except for the cellar, it would require excess expenses for Han to rebuild it in order to receive George's performance. Based on the principle of good faith, it is inappropriate for the law to request Han to rebuild the restaurant,

[67] 孫森焱，民法債編總論下冊(Min fa zhai bian zong lun xi ce)，第815頁（三民書局，2018年）。[SUN Senjan, *General Principles of the Law of Obligations, vol 2* (San-min Bookstore 2018) 815].

[68] The fact scenario of this hypothetical is taken from M Chen-Wishart, D Neo, and S Vogenauer, 'Introduction', ch 1 in this volume, 8.

[69] SUN (n 67) 545.

[70] ibid 495; QIU (n 3) 433.

and it is fully impossible for George to render his work on the cellar without rebuilding the restaurant since the cellar itself is useless for Han economically.

Because Han's restaurant is completely destroyed by a violent storm, the impossibility of George's performance is not attributable to either contracting party. George is released from his obligation to perform under Article 225(1) TCC, while Han is also released from his obligation to pay the contract price under Article 266(1) TCC.

IX. Conclusion

The doctrine of change of circumstances was enacted in Taiwanese law in response to the number of cases arising out of the social and economic turbulences in the wake of the war in the 1940s. Its theoretical basis is the principle of good faith as provided in the TCC. In addition to Article 227-2 TCC governing the doctrine of change of circumstances, some other similar articles, such as that concerning leases, are provided by the TCC to deal with a change of circumstances.

The doctrine of change of circumstances in Taiwan governs only the change of objective circumstances, such as disasters or strikes, while the change of subjective circumstances, such as the assumption of a certain quality of the rocks underneath the ground, is seen as a shared error in motive. The latter is governed by the good-faith principle or the doctrine of change of circumstances by analogy according to academics and by the change of circumstances directly under some court decisions.

A change of objective circumstances includes mainly *force majeure*-type events such as a war or energy crisis, while the courts also recognize the change of circumstances more broadly, including inflation over a long period of time, a third party's delay of work, a delay of acquiring the land for work, etc.

The change of circumstances must be unforeseeable to the party and has to occur after the time of contracting. The disadvantaged party has to apply to the court for adaptation of the contract prior to the end of the contract. Also, the change of circumstances cannot be attributable to either party and the performance of the original obligations must be obviously unfair to the disadvantaged party.

Where a change of circumstances occurs, the disadvantaged party may directly resort to the court for the adjustment of the contract, with no duty to renegotiate before the filing of the case. When dealing with a case concerning a change of circumstances, the court has to first adapt the contract in order to recover its equilibrium; only as a second option may it terminate the contract where adaptation is not feasible. Where the court adapts the contract, it mainly has to consider the loss incurred by one party and the benefits enjoyed by the other party due to the change of circumstances. Where the contract is terminated by the court, the other party may claim for damages and restitution against the disadvantaged party, with the damages being limited to actual loss instead of lost gains.

For contractual clauses that override the doctrine of change of circumstances, most court decisions hold that such clauses are binding merely for the foreseeable changes in the normal development of circumstances. Where the risks are not of an ordinary and reasonable nature, such contractual clauses are not binding on the court, which may then proceed to adapt the contract.

Where subsequent impossibility is not attributable to either party, the debtor has no obligation to perform and the creditor is released from its obligation to counter-perform, and thus the contract is extinguished. Nonetheless, if the creditor claims for the right to substitution, the contract at issue is not extinguished and thus the creditor is responsible for counter-performance.

23

Termination and Rescission under Taiwanese Contract Law

Sheng-Lin JAN

I. Introduction

Parties enter into reciprocal contracts in order to achieve their individual purposes. The achievement of contractual purposes depends on performance by the parties. Following German, Japanese, and most other civil law jurisdictions, the Taiwanese Civil Code (TCC) establishes the fundamental principle of *pacta sunt servanda* by providing explicitly in Article 199(1) that by virtue of an obligation, the obligee (commonly referred to as the 'creditor' in Taiwanese law) is entitled to claim performance from the obligor (or 'debtor').[1]

As a result, when one of the parties does not render performance in compliance with the contract, the other party shall be entitled to withhold the performance on his own side. Furthermore, when circumstances arise under which the contractual purposes can no longer be achieved, an innocent party may wish to be released from his own performance. According to the drafters of the TCC, the innocent party should in particular be entitled to walk away from the transaction if the breaching party is responsible for his non-performance.

To assist an innocent party in the two above situations, the TCC provides for the right to suspend performance and, in principle, depending on the nature of the contract, the right of termination or rescission, respectively.

II. Suspension and Refusal of Performance

Under the TCC, in the case of a reciprocal contract, unless obliged to perform in advance, a party is entitled to suspend or refuse his own contractual performance if the other party does not perform in line with the contract. This rule of the defence of unperformed contract (*exceptio non adimpleti contractus*), also referred to as the defence of simultaneous performance, is laid down in Article 264 TCC and is modelled on the provisions of section 320 of the German Civil Code (BGB) and Article 533 of the Japanese Civil Code (JCC).

In addition, Article 265 TCC deals with the scenario that it is agreed that one of the parties has to render performance first. If, after the conclusion of the contract, the financial position of the other party deteriorates significantly so that the first party's

[1] cf the German Civil Code, s 241(1) and the Japanese Civil Code, art 414.

Sheng-Lin Jan, *Termination and Rescission under Taiwanese Contract Law* In: *Studies in the Contract Laws of Asia V: Ending and Changing Contracts*. Edited by: Mindy Chen-Wishart, Dora Neo, and Stefan Vogenauer, Oxford University Press.
 DOI: 10.1093/oso/9780198995814.003.0023

claim for counter-performance is endangered, the first party may refuse to render his performance until the counter-performance has been rendered or security for the counter-performance has been provided. This rule of the defence of uncertainty was transplanted from the provisions of section 321(1) BGB and Article 83(1) Swiss Code of Obligations.[2]

Furthermore, each party is entitled to refuse to perform if the contract is terminated or rescinded.

III. Necessary Distinction between Termination and Rescission

Before going into more detail, it should be noted that, just as in German law where *Kündigung* has to be distinguished from *Rücktritt*,[3] in Taiwanese contract law a strict distinction must be drawn between what I will refer to as 'termination' (終止/*Chungzhi*) and 'rescission' (解除/*Jiechu*) in this chapter.

Under Taiwanese law, as will be elaborated, termination—equivalent to the German concept of *Kündigung*—only has prospective effect, whereas rescission—equivalent to the German notion of *Rücktritt*—has retrospective effect. In the case of termination, the parties are released from the duty to continue to perform, but what has been performed remains unaffected. In contrast, in the case of rescission, the parties are obliged to restore each other to the position before the conclusion of the contract; the performances and benefits received by one party have to be returned to the other.

In principle, a long-term contract—which creates continuing obligations for the parties—can only be subject to termination, while ordinary exchange contracts may either be rescinded or, although in far fewer cases, be terminated.[4] Under Taiwanese contract law,[5] typical long-term contracts include lease, employment, partnership, employment guarantee,[6] etc, whereas sale is an ordinary exchange contract.

IV. Requirements for Termination or Rescission

Under Taiwanese law, the entitlement of one of the parties—the 'innocent party'—to terminate or rescind the contract may arise either from statutory provisions or from contractual clauses. The former can be divided into two categories: provisions for specific types of contract and provisions for contracts in general.

[2] However, unlike s 321(2) BGB and art 83(2) Swiss Code of Obligations, the TCC does not explicitly provide that the party obliged to perform in advance is entitled to rescind the contract if, on demand, no security for the counter-performance is provided within a specified reasonable period set by that party.

[3] H Beale, B Fauvarque-Cosson, J Rutgers, and S Vogenauer, *Ius Commune Casebooks for the Common Law of Europe: Cases, Materials and Text on Contract Law* (3rd edn, Hart 2019) 984–86; H Kötz, *European Contract Law* (2nd edn, OUP 2017) 223.

[4] cf BS Markesinis, H Unberath, and AC Johnston, *The German Law of Contract: A Comparative Treatise* (2nd edn, Hart Publishing 2006) 419.

[5] As to the the notion of 'continuing obligations' in German contract law, cf Kötz (n 3) 223 n 24.

[6] Under art 756-1 TCC, an employment guarantee contract is a contract according to which one party shall be bound to compensate the damage that is suffered by the other party and has arisen from the performance of duties by the employee of that other party.

1. Statutory Provisions for Specific Types of Contract

Most provisions contained in the Special Part of the Law of Obligations of the TCC deal with the rights and obligations arising from certain types of contract, for example, sales, gifts, lease, loan, employment, contracts for works, mandate, transportation, guarantee, etc. Specific rules relating to the entitlement of one or both of the parties to terminate or rescind the contract are stipulated in those provisions governing sale, employment, lease, contracts for works, and mandate. Only a few important examples are illustrated here.

(a) Rescission or termination based on defects in goods sold, objects leased, or works completed

In the case of a sale or a 'contract for works' (where the contractor is under a duty to deliver a certain outcome, such as a building or a painting), the buyer or customer is entitled to rescind the contract if the relevant goods or works are defective. It does not matter whether the defect arises due to circumstances imputable to the seller or contractor (Articles 359, 494 TCC). Rescission is, however, not available to the buyer if such rescission would be obviously unfair. In this event, the buyer's remedy is confined to price reduction (Article 359 TCC). Rescission by the buyer is obviously unfair if the damage incurred by the seller as a result of the rescission significantly outweighs the buyer's damage caused by the defect.[7]

In the event of a lease contract, the lessee may terminate if the lessor, after being asked to do so by the lessee, refuses to remedy the defect in the leased object (Article 430 TCC). Furthermore, if the leased house or other property intended for habitation is so defective that the health or safety of the lessee or persons living with him is endangered, the lessee may terminate even though he knew of the defects at the time of concluding the contract or has waived his right of termination (Article 424 TCC).

(b) Termination in cases of a lease or service contract for an indefinite period

In those cases where a lease or services contract is entered into for an indefinite period of time, either party may terminate the contract at any time. If, however, custom is in favour of the lessee or the employee, such custom shall prevail (Articles 450(2), 488(2) TCC).

It should be noted that Article 488(2) TCC is not applicable to 'labour contracts' under the Labour Standards Act. According to Article 2 no 6 of this Act, a labour contract is 'an agreement that establishes an employee-employer relationship with subordination to authority'. An employer under a labour contract is entitled to terminate only under the circumstances specified in the provisions of the Act.[8]

(c) Termination at will in the event of a contract for works and mandate

Article 511 TCC confers on the customer of a contract for works an entitlement to terminate at his discretion (ie without the obligation to provide any reason) as long as the other party has not yet completed the outcome it promised.[9] However, the customer is liable for the

[7] cf Taiwanese Supreme Court 86 Tai-shang No 1182 Civil Judgment (1997); Taiwanese Supreme Court 107 Tai-shang No 76 Civil Judgment (2018).

[8] cf Taiwanese Labour Standards Act, arts 11 and 12 <https://law.moj.gov.tw/ENG/LawClass/LawAll.aspx?pcode=N0030001> accessed 3 January 2024.

[9] The rationale of art 511 TCC is that in the case of a contract for works the completion of the work is only for the contractual purpose of the customer. As a result, the customer shall have the discretion to terminate the

damages suffered by the contractor due to the termination. Rights and obligations that have already arisen from the contract are not affected by the termination. As a result, in addition to the above described compensation, the customer also has to pay the remuneration that is due prior to the termination.

In the case of a mandate contract, either party is free to terminate at any time without any reason. However, the party who terminates the contract at a time that is detrimental to the other party is liable for the damage suffered by the other party, unless the termination has occurred due to circumstances that are not attributable to the party terminating the contract (Article 549 TCC).[10]

2. Statutory Provisions for Contracts in General: Rescission or Termination for Non-performance

Where there are no provisions specified in the TCC's Special Part of the Law of Obligations, its general provisions governing non-performance contained in the General Part of the Law of Obligations determine the circumstances under which a right of termination or rescission arises.

(a) Rescission due to impossibility of performance

According to Articles 226 and 256 TCC, if the performance becomes impossible due to circumstances for which the obligor is responsible, the obligee may rescind the contract. Since the performance has become impossible, the right of termination is independent of the requirement of fixing a grace period for the obligor to effect performance.

(b) Rescission due to delay in performance

Delay in performance by the obligor also gives rise to the obligee's right of rescission. In this case, the TCC distinguishes between two situations: (i) where the defaulting obligor must be given a grace period to perform before the obligee may exercise the right to rescind and (ii) where the obligee is entitled to rescind the contract without giving the defaulting obligor additional time to perform.

According to Article 254 TCC, if the obligor is in default of performance, the obligee may set a reasonable period and notify the obligor to perform within that period. Failure to perform by the obligor within such period results in the obligee's right of termination.

Article 255 TCC, on the other hand, provides that if, according to the nature of the contract or the parties' declaration of intention, the purpose of the contract can be achieved only by performance at a fixed time, and if the obligor fails to perform at that fixed time, the obligee is entitled to rescind the contract without giving the notification specified in Article 254. Contracts dealt with under this provision are referred to as 'fixed transactions'.

completion of the work at any time, at the cost of compensating the loss incurred by the constructor as a result of the termination.

[10] Article 549 TCC mirrors art 651 JCC and art 404 Swiss Code of Obligations; cf also s 671 BGB, which entitles the mandator (principal) to revoke [*Widerruf*] at any time, while conferring on the mandatary (agent) the right of termination [*Kündigung*] at any time.

(c) Rescission due to malperformance

In Taiwanese contract law, performance which does not conform with what is required under the contract and is attributable to the obligor also gives the obligee the right to rescind. This is stipulated in Article 227(1) TCC. For example, in a case where goods delivered in due time are defective and the defect occurs due to a circumstance for which the seller is responsible, the buyer is entitled to rescind.

However, if the defect in performance can be cured, an additional period for curing malperformance must be given to the seller before the buyer exercises the right of rescission (Article 227(1) TCC in combination with the analogous application of Article 254 TCC). If, on the other hand, the defect in performance is incurable, the buyer may rescind the contract immediately (Article 227(1) TCC in combination with the analogous application of Article 256 TCC).

(d) Rescission due to breach of ancillary obligations

According to a recent decision of the Taiwanese Supreme Court, a breach of ancillary obligations also entitles the innocent party to rescind.[11] In such cases, the right to rescind, as in the case of the breach of primary obligations, is based on the provisions governing non-performance. However, while non-performance of primary obligations as such enables the aggrieved party to rescind, a breach of ancillary obligations gives rise to the right to rescind only if the breach is detrimental to the main interest of the innocent party and the achievement of the contractual purpose.[12]

Typical ancillary obligations include the seller's duty to instruct the buyer and the lessor's duty to provide assistance necessary for the achievement of the lessee's specific contractual purpose (eg use of the leased house as the place of a restaurant or a tutoring school).[13]

(e) No availability of rescission or termination for anticipatory breach

Unlike section 323(4) BGB 2002,[14] Article 72(1) of the United Nations Convention on Contracts for the International Sale of Goods (CISG), Article 9:304 of the UNIDROIT Principles of European Contract Law (PECL), and Article 7.3.3 of the Principles of International Commercial Contracts (PICC), the TCC does not lay down any provision stipulating that the obligee is entitled to rescind or terminate the contract if, prior to the

[11] Some decisions handed down by the Taiwanese Supreme Court before the beginning of 2000 held that a breach of ancillary obligations did not give rise to the innocent party's right of rescission. Nor was the innocent party entitled to specific performance. Instead, damages were the only available remedy; cf Taiwanese Supreme Court 86 Tai-shang No 440 Civil Judgment (1997); Taiwanese Supreme Court 91 Tai-shang No 438 Civil Ruling (2002).

[12] Taiwanese Supreme Court 91 Tai-shang No 2380 Civil Judgment (2002); Taiwanese Supreme Court 93 Tai-shang No 1488 Civil Judgment (2004); Taiwanese Supreme Court 100 Tai-shang No 2 Civil Judgment (2011); Taiwanese Supreme Court 104 Tai-shang No 799 Civil Judgment (2015). As for termination due to breach of an ancillary obligation in international contract law, cf P Huber in S Vogenauer (ed), *Commentary on the UNIDROIT Principles of International Commercial Contracts (PICC)* (2nd edn, OUP 2015) art 7.3.1 para 87.

[13] Taiwanese Supreme Court 107 Tai-shang No 1029 Civil Judgment (2018).

[14] The BGB 1900 did not explicitly contain provisions dealing with the obligee's right of termination due to the obligor's anticipatory non-performance. However, both legal scholarship and the German Federal Court of Justice (BGH) recognized that the obligee was entitled to immediately (ie without fixing any additional period for performance) exercise his right of termination [*Rücktritt*] in accordance with the provision of s 326 of the old BGB even before performance has fallen due; cf K Zweigert and H Kötz, *Introduction to Comparative Law* (3rd edn, Clarendon Press 1998) 493–94.

performance date, the obligor, by word or by action, renounces his readiness and willingness to perform (so-called anticipatory breach).[15]

In spite of fierce criticism from legal academics,[16] the Taiwanese Supreme Court, with very few exceptions,[17] has consistently held that the remedy of termination or rescission is not available in the event of an obligor's anticipatory breach. The Court bases its opinion on Article 316 TCC, which provides that if a time for performance is fixed, the obligee is not entitled to demand performance before such time is due; in the absence of an agreement to the contrary, the obligor may effect the performance prior to that time. The Taiwanese Supreme Court points out that, since pursuant to this provision the obligor is not obliged to perform before the performance is due, his renunciation does not constitute any kind of breach. As a result, the Supreme Court insists that even if the obligor renounces the contract before the time due for performance, the obligee still needs to wait until the breaching obligor is in default in order to avail himself of the right to rescind or terminate.[18]

The position of the Supreme Court that neither party may terminate or rescind the contract based on an anticipatory breach of the other party has a further consequence. If a party purports to terminate or rescind in that manner and, believing that he has released himself from his own counter-performance, subsequently refuses to comply with the other party's legitimate claim for counter-performance, the first party is deemed in breach of the contract. The other party who once evinced his intention not to perform is now entitled to every possible remedy, including damages and termination or rescission.

3. Rescission or Termination Clauses

Based on the principle of freedom of contract, as stipulated in Article 153 TCC,[19] Taiwanese courts usually respect contractual clauses providing that in the case of breach by one party the other party is entitled to terminate or rescind. This is particularly true when such clauses are individually negotiated by the parties.[20] Rescission or termination clauses contained in standard contracts are also, as a general rule, valid and enforceable if, according to such clauses, both parties are equally provided with the right to rescind or terminate.[21] Whilst standard rescission or termination clauses incorporated in contracts between businesses are usually held to be valid, standard clauses in consumer contracts which only enable the supplier (ie the enterprise) to rescind or terminate without conferring on the contracting

[15] Termination for anticipatory breach under the PICC; cf Huber (n 12) art 7.3.3 paras 1–2.

[16] S-L Jan, 'Non-conforming Performance: Development of the Supreme Court's Resolution and Decisions' (2002) 34 Taiwan Law Journal 23–50; CT Liu, *General Principles of the Law of Obligations, vol 1: General Introduction of Contract Law* (San-min Bookstore 2011) 376.

[17] cf Taiwanese Supreme Court 103 Tai-shang No 533 Civil Ruling (2014).

[18] Taiwanese Supreme Court 89 Tai-shang No 1871 Civil Judgment (2000); Taiwanese Supreme Court 104 Tai-shang No 816 Civil Judgment (2015); Taiwanese Supreme Court 105 Tai-shang No 1424 Civil Judgment (2016); cf Sun sen-yan, *General Principles of the Law of Obligations of the Civil Code, vol II* (San-min Bookstore 2018) 530.

[19] Article 153(1) TCC provides that when the parties have reciprocally declared their concordant intent, either expressly or impliedly, a contract shall be constituted.

[20] Taiwanese Supreme Court 104 Tai-shang No 1507 Civil Ruling (2015); Taiwanese Supreme Court 105 Tai-shang No 439 Civil Ruling (2016).

[21] Taiwanese Supreme Court 86 Tai-shang No 2665 Civil Judgment (1997).

consumer a right of rescission or termination shall be considered in violation of the principle of good faith and ineffective.[22]

V. Seriousness of Breach and Nature of the Relevant Obligation

First of all, it should be emphasized that the TCC does not specifically require that the breaching party's failure to perform has to amount to a fundamental non-performance in order to grant the innocent party a right of termination or rescission. Just as in German law,[23] Taiwanese contract law has no concept of a fundamental breach. This is different to Articles 49(1)(a), 51(2), 64(1)(a) CISG, Article 9:301(1) PECL, and Article 7.3.1(1) PICC.

In addition, unlike English law, where contract terms may be categorized either as 'conditions' or as 'warranties' and only the breach of a 'condition' creates a right to terminate,[24] the availability of termination or rescission under Taiwanese contract law exists irrespective of whether the contract term that is breached is considered a 'condition' or merely a 'warranty'.

As a matter of fact, the distinction between a 'condition' and a 'warranty' does not exist in Taiwanese contract law. Instead, if disputes as to the availability of termination or rescission arise, the resolution is dependent upon the nature of the obligations that are breached. While a breach of primary obligations automatically gives rise to a right of termination or rescission, a breach of ancillary obligations results in the right to terminate or rescind only when such breach prevents the aggrieved party from achieving his contractual purpose. In this regard, the breach of ancillary obligations under Taiwanese contract law seems to be comparable with breach of innominate or intermediate terms in the common law.[25]

In English law, the parties are free to agree that a particular term is to be considered a condition, with the result that the breach of such a term gives rise to the aggrieved party's right of termination.[26]

In Taiwanese law, contractual obligations that do not determine the characterization of the specific type of the contract[27] may also be classified by the parties as primary or merely secondary. In the absence of such a classification, the court will decide mainly in accordance with the nature of the disputed obligation and the purpose of the contract. The most essential factor for the decision is whether the breach of the obligation has substantially deprived the innocent party of his contractual interest in such a manner that it is unfair to expect him to be continuously connected to the contract.

For example, the lessee of a building is entitled to terminate if both parties agreed at the conclusion of the contract that the leased building is to be used as a cram school and, after the lessor has delivered the building to the lessee, due to circumstances attributable to the

[22] cf S-L Jan, 'Regulating Unfair Terms and Consumer Protection in Taiwan' in M Chen-Wishart and S Vogenauer (eds), *Studies in the Contract Laws of Asia, vol III: Contents of Contracts and Unfair Terms* (OUP 2020) 399.

[23] Kötz (n 3) 229.

[24] cf M Chen-Wishart, *Contract Law* (4th edn, OUP 2012) 463; J Cartwright, *Contract Law: An Introduction to the English Law of Contracts for the Civil Lawyer* (2nd edn, Hart Publishing 2013) 272; H Beale, *Chitty on Contracts, vol 1: General Principles* (33rd edn, Sweet & Maxwell 2018) para 13-019.

[25] cf S Rowan, *Remedies for Breach of Contract: A Comparative Analysis of the Protection of Performance* (OUP 2012) 73.

[26] E McKendrick, *Contract Law: Text, Cases, and Materials* (5th edn, OUP 2012) 761.

[27] For example, the seller's duty to transfer ownership and the buyer's duty to pay are typical obligations that characterize the contract as a sale and are always primary.

lessor the local government refused to grant the permit for the use of the building for the agreed purpose.[28] It is evident that the lessee has lost its interest of continuing with the performance of the contract although the lessor has fulfilled his primary duty to deliver the leased building.

In contrast, the customer in a contract for works may not rescind on the ground that the contractor breaches the duty to provide the security for the return of the pre-paid remuneration as the customer is still able to deduct the pre-paid amount from the payment of the future remunerations. In other words, the contractor's breach does not prejudice the contractual purpose of the customer and thus does not give rise to a right of rescission for the customer.[29]

VI. Fault

1. Rescission or Termination Based on Statutory Provisions

In the event of a rescission or termination arising from a defect in the objects sold or leased or work completed, it is irrelevant whether the defect occurs due to the intention or negligence of the seller, lessor, or constructor (Articles 359, 424, 494 TCC). This can be inferred from the plain wording of the provisions conferring on the buyer, lessee, or customer the right to rescind or terminate due to a defect in the delivered goods, leased property, or completed work.[30]

In contrast, termination or rescission based on the obligor's non-performance of contractual obligations (impossibility, delay, or non-conforming performance) is available only when the non-performance is attributable to the aggrieving party (Articles 226, 227, 230, 254, 255, 256 TCC).[31] In other words, intention or negligence on the part of the non-performing party is required in order to enable the innocent party to rescind or terminate the contract.

The requirement of fault for rescission or termination mirrors section 325 BGB 1900[32] and Article 543 JCC 1896.[33] However, under the new provisions of section 323 BGB 2002 and Article 541 JCC 2017, the remedy of termination is independent of any kind of fault of the breaching party. Article 9:301 PECL and Article 7.3.1 PICC do not set out the requirement of fault for the right of termination either. In light of this recent foreign and international legislation, it can be anticipated that in the future, Taiwanese contract law will ignore the obligor's fault when enabling the obligee to rescind or terminate the contract for non-performance.

[28] Taiwanese Supreme Court 89 Tai-shang No 699 Civil Judgment (2000).

[29] Taiwanese Supreme Court 108 Tai-shang No 57 Civil Judgment (2019).

[30] cf Taiwanese Supreme Court 87 Tai-shang No 261 Civil Judgment (1998); Taiwanese Supreme Court 93 Tai-shang No 1507 Civil Judgment (2004).

[31] cf also Taiwanese Supreme Court 80 Tai-shang No 2786 Civil Judgment (1991).

[32] Section 325(1) BGB 1900 provided that if the performance due from one party under a reciprocal contract became impossible owing to circumstances for which he was responsible, the other party was entitled to demand compensation for non-performance or rescind the contract.

[33] Article 543 JCC 1896 provided that if performance had become impossible, in whole or in part, the obligee was entitled to rescind the contract; however, this was not applicable if the failure to perform the obligation was due to reasons not attributable to the obligor.

2. Rescission or Termination Based on Contractual Clauses

In the case of termination or rescission based on contractual clauses, the clause itself may stipulate whether the conferred right to rescind or terminate is dependent on the intention or fault of the party in breach. If such stipulation is not contained in the clause, the decision as to the requirement of intention or fault shall be made in accordance with the above-described distinction between termination for defect and termination for non-performance.

3. Special Rules for Consumer Contracts

In the event of distance sales or door-to-door sales, consumers are entitled to rescind the contract without specifying any reason. However, rescission has to be effected within seven days upon receipt of the goods or services (Article 19 of the Taiwanese Consumer Protection Act). Rescission under this provision does not depend on any malicious or wrongful act of the enterprise that sells the goods or provides the services. Nor is it relevant whether the goods sold or the services provided are defective.

VII. Doctrine of *Nachfrist*: Setting of a Grace Period

1. Rescission or Termination for Non-performance

The German doctrine of *Nachfrist*, under which rescission or termination for non-performance is only available if the party in breach was given a second opportunity to provide 'supplementary performance', and which is also a feature of transnational commercial contract law, was transplanted into the TCC.[34]

As explained above, in the event of delay of a non-fixed transaction and in the case of a non-conforming performance that can be cured, the aggrieved obligee has to give the breaching obligor a notice granting him an additional reasonable period of time to perform at a later date or to cure the non-performance. Only if the obligor fails to make use of the second chance within such period is the obligee entitled to rescind or terminate (Article 254 TCC). The notice does not need to be in writing, although, for the sake of evidence, written notice is common in practice.

According to the Taiwanese Supreme Court, based on the good-faith principle, if a *Nachfrist* period is too short, the rescission or termination is still effective if the aggrieved party exercises his right to rescind or to terminate after a reasonable period has expired.[35]

For example, a seller who was only one of the 72 owners of a piece of land sold the entire land to the buyer in his own name. During the negotiation of the contract, the seller claimed that he was already in agreement with the other co-owners to sell the land and promised that he would be able to transfer the ownership to the buyer by 30 July 1995. The parties entered into the contract on 3 May 1995, and a clause of the contract stipulated that

[34] cf Markesinis, Unberath, and Johnston (n 4) 422; Huber (n 12) art 7.1.5 para 2.
[35] Taiwanese Supreme Court 90 Tai-shang No 1231 Civil Judgment (2001).

the seller was obliged to transfer the ownership to the buyer by 30 July 1995. As the seller failed to comply with the duty of transferring the ownership as stipulated in the contract, the buyer notified the seller on 6 October 1995 and requested the seller to perform by 12 October 1995. The seller remained in breach of the duty. On 24 August 1996, the buyer notified again and demanded that ownership be transferred within five days; the buyer also declared that in the event of the seller's failure to act in accordance with the demand the contract would be deemed rescinded.

The Taiwanese Supreme Court upheld the High Court's decision in favour of the buyer.[36] According to the High Court, given that there were 72 co-owners involved, both the 6-day *Nachfrist* of 6 October 1995 and the 5-day *Nachfrist* of 24 August 1996 were too short. The High Court pointed out, however, that since more than ten months had elapsed between the first and the second *Nachfrist* the buyer should be entitled to rescind the contract.

Setting a *Nachfrist* prior to rescinding or terminating the contract is not necessary if the right of rescission or termination arises from the impossibility of performance (Article 256 TCC), incurable non-conforming performance (Article 227(1) in combination with the analogous application of Article 256 TCC), or default in a fixed transaction (Article 255 TCC). In such cases, setting a grace period for performance or cure of malperformance would be meaningless.

The mere fact that a specific date or a period of time for performance is stipulated in the contract does not have the effect that the contract is to be considered as a 'fixed transaction' under Article 255 TCC. This is true in cases where a specific date for payment of the price,[37] the delivery of the goods,[38] the handing over and transfer in title of a flat,[39] or the completion of the work[40] is stated in the contract. Instead, it is required that the party obliged to render performance agrees to be strictly bound by the stipulated date or period for performance and has knowledge of the importance of such date or period for the achievement of the other party's contractual purposes.[41] This requirement is, in my view, very similar to the English doctrine of 'time is of the essence'.

2. Rescission or Termination for Defect in Goods Sold, Objects Leased, or Works Completed

According to the Taiwanese Supreme Court, in cases where the buyer rescinds the contract based on a defect in the goods as stipulated in Article 359 TCC, it is, pursuant to the plain language of this provision, not required that the buyer give the seller notice for curing the non-conforming performance prior to rescission.[42]

However, setting a *Nachfrist* for curing malperformance is a statutory requirement both for the lessee's right to terminate and the customer's right to rescind based on the defect in the object leased or the work completed (Articles 430, 493, 494 TCC).

36 Taiwanese Supreme Court 92 Tai-shang No 694 Civil Judgment (2003).
37 Taiwanese Supreme Court 64 Tai-zhai No 177 Civil Judgment (1975).
38 Taiwanese Supreme Court 103 Tai-shang No 898 Civil Judgment (2014).
39 Taiwanese Supreme Court 98 Tai-shang No 83 Civil Judgment (2009).
40 Taiwanese Supreme Court 88 Tai-shang No 1786 Civil Judgment (1999).
41 Taiwanese Supreme Court 64 Tai-zhai No 177 Civil Judgment (1975).
42 Taiwanese Supreme Court 85 Tai-shang No 486 Civil Judgment (1996); Taiwanese Supreme Court 95 Tai-shang No 2192 Civil Judgment (2006); Taiwanese Supreme Court 99 Tai-shang No 2443 Civil Judgment (2010).

3. *Nachfrist* Is Set by the Court

Unlike in English law, but very much like under French law,[43] Taiwanese courts have the power to give the party in breach additional time for performance. Article 318 TCC provides that the court may, taking into consideration the circumstances of the obligor, allow him to delay his performance in such reasonable time as may not substantially prejudice the interests of the obligee.

VIII. Exercise of the Right of Termination and Rescission

As in German and in Japanese law,[44] Article 258(1) TCC provides that rescission is effected by the aggrieved party's declaration to the party in breach. The aggrieved party may put an end to the contract by unilateral declaration. The involvement of a court is not necessary. This provision applies *mutatis mutandis* to termination based on statutory provisions (Article 263 TCC).

It should also be noted that, according to Articles 258(2) and 263 TCC, in cases where one party is constituted of two or more persons, the declaration of rescission or termination shall be effected by, or against, all of those persons.[45] Violation of the provision results in the invalidity of the declaration, and the contract remains in effect.[46]

In the event that the innocent party, without having rescinded the contract in advance, brings an action and sues the breaching party to return the performance received by the latter, this is usually interpreted as the innocent party's intention to rescind the contract, and the service of the complaint is deemed to be his declaration of rescission.[47]

1. Effect of Rescission and Termination

(a) Fate of the contract after rescission and termination

According to the Taiwanese Supreme Court, in the event of rescission, the contract is treated as if it has been annulled,[48] whereas in the event of termination, the contract ceases to exist beginning from the termination.[49]

[43] cf Beale and others (n 3) 1042–43; Rowan (n 25) 45, 79, 91.

[44] cf BGB, s 349 and JCC, art 540.

[45] cf BGB, s 351 and JCC, art 544.

[46] Taiwanese Supreme Court 95 Tai-shang No 2827 Civil Judgment (2006).

[47] If the innocent party sues for compensation in lieu of performance, it is not clear whether the innocent party wishes to rescind the contract because the exercise of the right of termination does not prejudice the claim of compensation (TCC, art 260).

[48] Taiwanese Supreme Court 40 Tai-shang No 1020 Civil Judgment (1951); Taiwanese Supreme Court 96 Tai-shang No 229 Civil Judgment (2007); Taiwanese Supreme Court 96 Tai-shang No 1240 Civil Judgment (2007); Taiwanese Supreme Court 104 Tai-shang No 799 Civil Judgment (2015). The opinion held by the Taiwanese Supreme Court is like French law under which *résolution* was traditionally also seen as retrospective and the contract was treated as if it had been annulled; cf Beale and others (n 3) 982–83 (also on the position of French law after the 2016 reforms).

[49] Taiwanese Supreme Court 85 Tai-shang No 2448 Civil Judgment (1996); Taiwanese Supreme Court 99 Tai-shang No 818 Civil Judgment (2010).

(b) Retrospective effect in the event of rescission: Restitution

In the case of rescission, the parties are released from the performance of all obligations save for those relating to dispute settlement. In addition, rescission under Taiwanese contract law is seen as retrospective and results in each party being liable to make restitution of any benefits received under the contract. This is clearly stipulated in Article 259 TCC.[50] Accordingly, the Taiwanese Supreme Court insists that in the event of rescission, all rights and obligations arising from the contract shall be eliminated retroactively; the parties are bound to return all the goods and services received from each other.[51] Benefits conferred in performance of the contract must also be restored. In this case, it does not matter whether the future and past performances can be separated from each other.

(c) Prospective effect in the event of termination

In contrast, termination under Taiwanese law is seen as prospective. Only the obligations that are due after termination are cancelled. Contractual performance rendered by either party prior to the termination is not affected.

The drafters of the TCC intentionally differentiated between the consequences of termination and those of rescission by specifying in Article 263 TCC that Article 259 TCC, which deals with restitution, cannot be applied *mutatis mutandis* to the case of termination. The parties' contractual relationship that existed before the termination remains unaffected. Insofar, termination under Taiwanese contract law has the same effect as that under English law and the European project of a Draft Common Frame of Reference (DFCR).[52]

(d) Relationship between rescission/termination and the remedy of damages

Just as in Article 545(3) JCC 2017, section 325 BGB 2002,[53] and Article 7.3.5(2) PICC, termination or rescission under the TCC does not preclude the aggrieved party from claiming damages for non-performance.

Article 260 TCC specifies that the exercise of the right of rescission does not prejudice the right to claim damages. In other words, the remedies of rescission and damages can be

[50] Article 259 TCC provides that in case of the rescission of a contract, each party shall, unless otherwise provided for by law or by the contract, restore the other party to its former condition in accordance with the following rules:

(1) Each party shall return the object received from the counter party.
(2) If the object received consisted of money, interest calculated from the time of receipt shall be added.
(3) If the performance received consisted of a service or the use of an object, the value of such service or use at the time of receipt shall be reimbursed in money.
(4) If the object to be returned has produced profits, such profits shall be restored.
(5) If necessary or beneficial expenses of the object to be returned have been made, the reimbursement of such expenses may be claimed, to the extent to which the opposite party has benefited at the time of return.
(6) If the object to be returned has been damaged or destroyed or cannot be returned due to any other causes, its value shall be reimbursed.

[51] Taiwanese Supreme Court 40 Tai-shang No 1020 Civil Judgment (1951); Taiwanese Supreme Court 104 Tai-shang No 799 Civil Judgment (2015).

[52] cf M Chen-Wishart and U Magnus, 'Termination, Price Reduction, and Damages' in G Dannemann and S Vogenauer (eds), *The Common European Sales Law in Context: Interaction with English and German Law* (OUP 2013) 648.

[53] Under the old BGB of 1900, the combination of the remedies of *Rücktritt* and damages for non-performance was not possible. For the current state of German law, cf Beale and others (n 3) 986, 993.

combined. According to Article 263 TCC, Article 260 TCC applies *mutatis mutandis* to termination.

As a result, the aggrieved party may choose either to rescind the contract and claim damages or only claim damages in lieu of performance. However, in the event of claiming damages in lieu of performance, the aggrieved party is obliged to provide the breaching party with its own counter-performance.

2. Loss of the Right of Termination or Rescission

The entitlement to termination or rescission can be lost under one of the circumstances listed in the following.

First: lapse of time. The right to terminate or rescind extinguishes after expiry of the period specifically stipulated by law. For example, the buyer's right of rescission based on a defect in the goods expires six months after the buyer notifies the seller of the defect, or, at the latest, five years after delivery of the goods (Article 365 TCC). The six-month period is, however, not applicable if the seller intentionally conceals the defect (Article 365 TCC). In addition, the customer's right to rescind based on a defect in the completed work is extinguished by prescription if it has not been exercised within one year from the discovery of the defect (Article 514(1) TCC). The period of defect discovery is one year commencing from delivery of the work or, if due to the nature of the work no delivery can take place, from completion of the work. Where the subject matter of the contract is the construction of a building or other works on land, or vital repairs to such buildings or works, the period of discovery is extended to five years. If the contractor intentionally conceals the defect, the periods of one year and five years shall be extended to five years and ten years, respectively (Articles 498, 499, 500 TCC).

Secondly: inaction after being requested to respond whether to exercise the right or not. In the case that no deadline for the exercise of the right to rescind is stipulated by law or in the contract, the other party may set a reasonable period of time and notify the entitled party to make a definite reply within such deadline whether he will rescind the contract or not. If no intention of rescission is declared after that period has expired, the right to rescind is extinguished (Article 257 TCC).

Thirdly: damage of the subject matter due to the fault of the obligee. The right to rescind is extinguished if the subject matter received by the entitled party has been damaged or destroyed or can no longer be returned due to circumstances attributable to that party; the same applies if the subject matter received has been converted into something else by processing or alteration (Article 262 TCC).

IX. The Hypotheticals

1. Car Machinery & Co and Traders Ltd

Car Machinery & Co appointed Traders Ltd as the sole distributor of their car panel presses for a period of five years. Clause 7(b) of the agreement provides that 'Distributors shall send their representatives to visit all six large car manufacturers in the country at least once every week for the purpose of soliciting orders for car panel presses. Failure to comply with this obligation shall entitle Car Machinery to terminate the agreement with immediate effect.' Traders Ltd missed two visits to car manufacturers in the second month of the contractual period. Is Car Machinery entitled to terminate the agreement?[54]

The sole distributorship agreement[55] in the example contains a termination clause. Clause 7(b) of the agreement confers on Car Machinery a right to terminate upon Traders Ltd's breach of the obligation to visit all six large car manufacturers in the country in a manner as stipulated in this clause.

Traders Ltd might contend that its breach of the obligation is not serious and that the contractual entitlement conferred on Car Machinery to terminate with immediate effect deviates from the basic statutory requirement of setting a grace period prior to terminating the contract as set out in Article 254 TCC.

However, according to the Taiwanese Supreme Court, in the event of termination under a termination clause, the entitled party may terminate the contract in accordance with the terms and conditions set forth by such clause. In other words, termination based on a termination clause is not subject to the rules governing termination rights that are provided by statute.[56] Given the plain wording of Clause 7(b) and the obvious breach of the obligation by Traders Ltd, it is unlikely that Taiwanese courts would sustain Traders Ltd's contention.

The last argument that Traders Ltd might be able to raise is that, unless its failure to comply with the obligation incurs significant loss to Car Machinery, the failure is so trivial that termination by Car Machinery would be in violation of good faith. It is difficult to predict whether such an argument would be accepted by the Taiwanese courts.

All things taken into account, Taiwanese courts would most likely decide in favour of Car Machinery and rule that it is entitled to terminate the agreement.

2. Prime Ltd and Devil Corp

Prime Ltd sold a piece of land to Devil Corp. Under the terms of the contract, Devil pays 10 per cent deposit, and the remainder of the payment is due at 5pm on 30 September, with time being 'of the essence'. According to Clause 12, failure to meet the deadline would result in the forfeiture of the deposit and the termination of the agreement. Devil is ten minutes late in tendering the final payment and Prime refuses performance. Can Devil sue for specific performance, arguing that Prime's reliance on the clause is unreasonable in some way? Would the result be different if the contract did not include Clause 12?

The example is based on the well-known case of *Union Eagle Ltd v Golden Achievement Ltd*.[57] In that case, the vendor terminated the contract on the grounds that the purchaser failed to strictly comply with the contract term stipulating the specific time for completion.

[54] The fact scenarios of the hypotheticals described in this section X are taken from M Chen-Wishart, D Neo, and S Vogenauer, 'Introduction', ch 1 in this volume 9–10.

[55] A sole distributorship agreement under Taiwanese contract law is regarded as a mandate contract, unless otherwise explicitly stipulated by the parties; cf Taiwanese Supreme Court 107 Tai-shang No 641 Civil Ruling (2018). In addition, according to art 549 TCC, a contract related to performance of services which does not belong to any kind of other contracts provided for by law is subject to the provisions governing mandate.

[56] Taiwanese Supreme Court 92 Tai-shang No 1988 Civil Judgment (2003); Taiwanese Supreme Court 94 Tai-shang No 990 Civil Judgment (2005).

[57] *Union Eagle Ltd v Golden Achievement Ltd* [1997] AC 514.

The purchaser sought specific performance, arguing that the vendor's reliance on such a right of termination was unconscionable. The purchaser's action failed in the Hong Kong courts and before the Privy Council. Lord Hoffman gave the only judgment and pointed out that '[t]he main question in the case is whether the court has, and should have exercised, an equitable power to absolve the purchaser from the contractual consequences of late payment, and to decree specific performance'.[58] Furthermore, '[t]he case illustrated the need for commercial certainty and to resist the temptation to allow equity to rewrite contracts in the name of fairness'.[59] Lord Hoffman concluded that '[t]he fact is that the purchaser was late. Any suggestion that relief can be obtained on the ground that he was only slightly late is bound to lead to arguments over how late is too late, which can be resolved only by litigation.'[60]

Interestingly, a very similar case was decided by the then Chinese Supreme Court in 1937.[61] The parties entered into a settlement agreement according to which the obligee agreed to reduce the original arrears to a certain amount and the obligor agreed to pay the reduced amount in ten instalments. In addition, the parties agreed that if the obligor paid all instalments on time, the original debts should be considered as paid, whereas in the event that the obligor delayed in any of the ten instalments, the obligee was entitled to claim the full payment of the original arrears. The obligor had paid the first eight instalments as scheduled, and the last two instalments were to take place before 12 pm on a specific day. At 11:32 am of the day, the obligor called the obligee and requested that the payment be postponed for a few minutes, but the obligee disagreed. The obligor paid at 12:30 pm; the obligee refused to accept the late payment and demanded the full amount of the original arrears as stipulated in the agreement. The Supreme Court held that since the delayed payment did not cause any damage to the obligee, his refusal to accept was in contradiction to the principle of good faith; he was therefore not entitled to claim the full payment.

Accordingly, if the hypothetical case were dealt with by a Taiwanese court, it is very likely that the court would apply the principle of good faith, stipulated in Article 148 TCC, to determine whether Prime may rely on Clause 12 to terminate the agreement. In the absence of proof of any considerable damage incurred by a payment that is ten minutes late, Prime's insistence on terminating the contract will be regarded as being in violation of the principle of good faith. Consequently, Prime cannot discharge itself from the contract by termination. Devil is entitled to sue for specific performance.

In the event that Clause 12 is not included in the agreement between Prime and Devil, Article 255 TCC is applicable. As explained above, this provision entitles the innocent party of a 'fixed transaction' to terminate without giving the breaching party an additional period for supplementary performance. The agreement between Prime and Devil clearly constitutes a 'fixed transaction' under Article 255 TCC. It is also evident that Devil has failed

[58] ibid 517.
[59] ibid 519.
[60] ibid 523.
[61] See 26 Hu-shang No 69 Civil Judgment of the then Chinese Supreme Court (1937). In this chapter, the term 'the Supreme Court' refers to the 'the Taiwan Supreme Court' when the author cites the court's judgments that are handed down after 1949. However, if its judgments were made before 1949 and cited by the author, this term refers to the 'then Chinese Supreme Court'. The Chinese Supreme Court was founded on 17 November 1927. As a consequence of the establishment of the People's Republic of China on 1 October 1949, this court was replaced by 'The Supreme People's Court of the People's Republic of China'.

to comply with the clearly specified time for performance. However, exercising the right arising from Article 255 TCC is also subject to the good-faith principle. As elaborated above, Prime cannot terminate without proving that the late payment of Devil has caused considerable damage. This applies not only to the case in which Prime's termination is based on Clause 12 but also to the case where the basis of Prime's termination is Article 255 TCC.

3. Seven Seas and Big Chef

Seven Seas, an importer of seafood, sells two tons of mussels to the Big Chef restaurant chain. After one ton has been delivered, it turns out that the concentration of cadmium in the mussels is 2 per cent above the concentration permitted by national food regulations. Can Big Chef terminate the contract?

In this hypothetical case, the delivery of the mussels contaminated with excessive cadmium constitutes not only a defect in the goods sold under Article 359 TCC but also non-conforming performance under Article 227 TCC. As a result, in relation to the first contract for one ton of mussels, Big Chef is entitled to rescind in accordance with these two provisions. Article 359 TCC permits Big Chef to rescind without giving a notice in advance requiring Seven Seas to cure its malperformance. Rescission based on Article 227 TCC does not require Big Chef to give Seven Seas an additional period for curing malperformance either if the excessive cadmium contained in the delivered mussels cannot be cured. Partial rescission or termination of contract is possible and permitted in Taiwanese law.[62]

As to the mussels that have not yet been delivered, Big Chef's entitlement to rescission is dependent on whether the non-conforming performance in relation to the first ton of mussels is so severe that Seven Seas cannot be expected to meet the contractual requirements for the performance of the rest of the mussels.

4. Coco and David

Coco, a famous architect, agrees with David that he will design the landscape for the garden in her next development. He is due to start work on 1 December. For David, this is an important opportunity to make his name as a landscape gardener. On 1 October, she tells him that she is no longer interested because the development will not include a garden after all. David has already purchased materials. He estimates that his future earnings will be 10 per cent lower because he will not be able to benefit from having worked with Coco. Can he insist on doing the work? Can he bring an action for breach of contract?

Under Taiwanese contract law, the agreement between Coco and David is categorized as a contract for works. As explained above, in the event of a contract for works, the customer is entitled to terminate before the completion of the works without any reason. He is, however, obliged to pay the remuneration in relation to the work that is completed before the

[62] cf Taiwanese Supreme Court 99 Tai-shang No 1049 Civil Judgment (2010).

termination. In addition, the customer is liable for any damage incurred by the constructor due to the termination (Article 511 TCC).

Consequently, David cannot insist on doing the work and sue for specific performance. He is, however, entitled to demand that Coco pay his expenses regarding purchase of materials. David may also claim compensation for the loss of future earnings. He bears the burden of proof for the recoverable amount.

5. Sue and Bob

Bob contracts to build a house for Sue for the price of $100,000. After completing a third of the work, he abandons the job, leaving behind material worth $15,000, which Sue later uses to finish the works. Can Bob claim the value of the work done or the materials?

Claim of the value of the work done: under the TCC, the agreement between Bob and Sue is a contract for works. Since Sue uses the material left behind by Bob to complete the work, it seems fair to consider that she, instead of rescinding the contract,[63] has chosen to accept the work that has been done by Bob. As a result, Sue is obliged to pay the remuneration for the work done by Bob. Bob can claim the remuneration as agreed by the parties when making the contract, but he cannot claim the total value of the work done if this differs from the agreed remuneration.

Claim of the value of the materials: provided that the materials belonged to Bob at the time when he abandoned the job, the use of the materials to finish the work constitutes a combination of movable things with immovable things through attachment under Article 811 TCC.[64] As a result, on one hand, Sue acquires the ownership of the materials and, on the other, in accordance with Article 816 TCC,[65] Bob is entitled to claim reimbursement of the value under the rules on unjustified enrichment.

X. Conclusion

In summary, the major features of termination and rescission under Taiwanese contract law are as follows.

In Taiwanese law, a strict distinction must be drawn between termination and rescission. Termination is similar to *Kündigung* under German law and only has prospective effect, while rescission is similar to the German notion of *Rücktritt*, and its effect is retrospective.

[63] Since Bob abandons the job without justified reason, Sue is entitled to rescind the contract in accordance with art 503 TCC. Under this provision, if completion or delivery of the work at a fixed deadline is of the essence to the contract and, due to circumstances for which the constructor is responsible, the work is delayed in such a manner that it can be foreseen that the work will not be completed within the deadline, the customer may rescind the contract and demand damages. If Sue rescinds the contract, she is not obliged to pay the remuneration for the work done by Bob irrespective of whether the work is valuable or not.

[64] Article 811 TCC provides that if a movable thing becomes an essential component part of a real property through attaching it to the latter, the owner of the real property acquires the ownership of such movable thing.

[65] Article 816 TCC provides that the person who, as a result of the provisions of the preceding five articles, suffers a loss is entitled to claim reimbursement of the value in accordance with the provisions governing unjust enrichment.

The right to terminate or rescind may be based either on mutual consent of the parties or on statutory provisions. Although not explicitly specified in the TCC, a mutually agreed right of termination or rescission is binding on the parties and, unless otherwise agreed upon, the same rules governing the statutory right to terminate or rescind are applicable.

The statutory right to terminate or rescind arises mainly from non-performance of primary contractual obligations, including impossibility of performance, delay in performance, and non-conforming performance. Termination or rescission arising from non-performance requires that the party in breach is at fault, which is the same as the provisions of the BGB 1900 and the JCC 1896 but differs from the BGB 2002, the JCC 2017, the CISG, the PECL, and the PICC.

As in German and in international contract law, the breach of ancillary obligations under Taiwanese contract law also triggers a right to terminate or rescind if the breach is so significant that the contractual purpose cannot be achieved.

Unlike in German law or in international contract law, an anticipatory breach neither dispenses with the requirement of a grace period nor gives rise to a right of termination or rescission.

Adopting the German doctrine of *Nachfrist*, the TCC entitles the aggrieved party to rescind the contract only if the breaching party was given a second chance to perform. However, this doctrine does not apply in the event of impossibility of performance and delay in a 'fixed transaction'.

In the case of sale or contracts for works, a defect in the goods or the work also gives the buyer or the customer a statutory right of rescission. Such a rescission, in contrast to the rescission arising from non-performance, does not depend on the fault of the seller or constructor.

The right of termination or rescission can be exercised without court involvement. The aggrieved party's declaration of the will to terminate or rescind suffices.

As under German and Japanese law, the primary effect of the rescission of a contract under the TCC is the release of the parties from the obligation to perform. Consequently, it is specified that one party is entitled to claim back from the other any performance that has been rendered. Also, as under the revised German law and international contract law, the aggrieved party is not prevented from combining the right of rescission and the remedy of damages.

24
A Change of Circumstances in Thai Law

Munin PONGSAPAN

I. Introduction

When a contract is formed, the contracting parties are entitled to performance in accordance with the terms of the contract. Specific performance is both the primary contractual right and the primary remedy for breach of contract under Thai law. This makes it hard for the parties to discharge or depart from the contract without mutual agreement.[1] In the absence of a mutual agreement, the Thai Civil and Commercial Code (TCCC) sets out certain circumstances where a party can unilaterally set aside the contract or where the contract will automatically come to an end.

When a contracting party faces a change of circumstances, there is no general provision in the TCCC that comprehensively deals with this. Neither is change of circumstances commonly recognized as a distinctive concept in Thai legal literature. This chapter will explain how Thai law copes with a change of circumstances in its statutory rules, judicial decisions, and scholarly opinions. It will furthermore examine how Thai law has dealt with the effects of the COVID-19 pandemic, especially in relation to contractual relationships.

II. Absence of the Concept of a Change of Circumstances in Thai Law

According to the general provisions of Thai contract law, a contracting party is permitted to depart from the contract when it is terminated either by mutual consent of both parties, or by a unilateral declaration of intention by the other party amounting to breach of contract, or when a specific condition of the contract is met. However, for certain types of contracts, the contractual relationship may end when a particular situation occurs. For example, a contract of hire ends when the subject matter of the contract is wholly lost.[2] A hire of work contract ends when the contractor dies.[3]

To understand why the concept of a change of circumstances is absent from Thai law, one needs to understand the historical origin of the TCCC, which was entirely copied from foreign legal rules, especially those of the German Civil Code of 1900 and the Japanese Civil Code of 1896. As a specific provision on change of circumstances is absent from both the German Civil Code of 1900 and the Japanese Civil Code of 1896, it is absent from the TCCC too. Although impossibility of performance is discussed by legal scholars in the context of

[1] M Pongsapan, 'Remedies for Breach of Contract in Thai Law' in M Chen-Wishart, A Loke, and B Ong (eds), *Studies in The Contract Laws of Asia: Remedies for Breach of Contract, vol I* (OUP 2016) 377–83.
[2] TCCC, s 567.
[3] TCCC, s 606.

Munin Pongsapan, *A Change of Circumstances in Thai Law* In: *Studies in the Contract Laws of Asia V: Ending and Changing Contracts*. Edited by: Mindy Chen-Wishart, Dora Neo, and Stefan Vogenauer, Oxford University Press.
 DOI: 10.1093/oso/9780198995814.003.0024

change of circumstances in most jurisdictions, in Thai law it is classified in the TCCC as a type of non-performance, that is, breach of contract. This is also true of the common law concept of hardship. In Thailand, the situations that are known to European judges or legal scholars as a change of circumstances are instead dealt with under the headings of impossibility of performance, good faith, contract interpretation, or mistake.

III. Impossibility of Performance and a Change of Circumstances

In one of the most recent cases concerning a situation which in European legal systems might be treated as a change of circumstances, the Supreme Court of Thailand clearly distinguished between impossibility of performance and hardship and precluded a contracting party from using the latter as a basis for departing from the contractual terms. In Case No 16469/2557 (2014), the defendant, which had entered into an agreement to sell apartments to the plaintiff, failed to complete the building and transfer their ownership at the agreed time. It denied contractual liability on the grounds of impossibility of performance and argued that it was not responsible for the failure to complete the building. Instead, it blamed the Ministry of Finance and the Bank of Thailand for ordering the discontinuation of the operation of 56 troubled financial institutions, 2 of which had provided credit of Thai baht (THB) 640,000,000 for it to complete the property development project in question. After the defendant received THB440,000,000 from the two financial institutions, provision of the remaining THB200,000,000 was prevented by the abovementioned order. The defendant claimed that this caused an insufficiency of funds which made it impossible to complete the project. The Supreme Court rejected the defendant's argument and took the opportunity to clarify the meaning of impossibility of performance by distinguishing it from hardship. It opined that impossibility of performance, which relieves the debtor from an obligation, must be 'definite and permanent'. Therefore, in the Court's view, the defendant's severe financial problems, which resulted from the discontinuation of the lenders' business, did not make performance impossible. In fact, it was merely a 'hardship' that might force the defendant to find a new source of funding and delay the completion of work, with an increase in expenses. But such change of circumstances did not entirely prevent it from performing the obligation.[4] The Court did not offer any solution for alleviating the hardship, probably because the defendant's defence was based solely on impossibility of performance.

Supreme Court Decision No 16469/2557 seems to follow the rationale of an earlier case decided in 2006, Supreme Court Decision No 1768/2549. In that case, the defendant, a financial institution which was struggling with severe difficulties as a result of Thailand's 1997 financial crisis, was unable to pay promissory notes given to the plaintiff due to an

[4] In its decision No 2934/2522 (1979), the Supreme Court viewed impossibility of performance as a circumstance which permanently prevents the debtor from performing the obligation. In this case, a sharp increase in the price of crude oil in the international market led to an increase in construction materials in the domestic market. The Supreme Court held that this unexpected change of circumstances did not make the debtor's duty to deliver construction materials to the plaintiff impossible to perform. In a similar case, a factory was temporarily shut down due to flooding and despite the fact that the owner of the factory successfully protected it from the water. The employer used this incident as an excuse for not paying the employees their wages. The Court viewed it as hardship, not as impossibility of performance which relieves the defendant from the obligation. Therefore, the employer was still responsible for paying the employees their wages. See Supreme Court Decision No 118/2525 (1982).

order of the Ministry of Finance. This order suspended its business and forced it to enter the reorganization process, which prevented it from making any debt repayment. The defendant consequently refused to repay the debt on the basis of impossibility of performance. However, the Supreme Court found that the reorganization did not legally and automatically relieve the debtor from the obligations, and the defendant's financial condition might improve after the process. In the Court's view, the defendant's financial problem was merely hardship that did not qualify as an impossibility of performance which would relieve it from the obligation to perform under section 219 TCCC.[5] However, according to the Supreme Court, the application of section 205 TCCC saved the debtor from being in default over the period of business suspension and reorganization because its inability to perform resulted from a circumstance for which it was not responsible.[6] From this decision, it can be observed that the reason the defendant was exempted from contractual liability was not hardship itself, but the official order of business suspension and reorganization.

A Supreme Court decision released in 2002 confirms that the 1998 Asian Financial Crisis,[7] which caused the collapse of most financial institutions and devastating damage to all business sectors in Thailand and which severely affected many debtors' ability to repay debts owed to financial institutions, did not automatically render the performance of contracts impossible. The Supreme Court needs to verify impossibility of performance on a case-by-case basis in order to determine whether the debtor is relieved from the obligation without liability. In this case, the defendant mortgaged a piece of land as security for his debt owed to the plaintiff but later refused to repay the debt on the grounds that the performance became impossible owing to the financial crisis. The Court rejected this argument as it found that it was still possible for the defendant to perform the obligation, though with great difficulty.[8]

The Thai Supreme Court regards a debtor's financial difficulties occurring over the course of its business operation as a normal incident. A debtor's inability to repay debt owed to the creditor does not *per se* render the debtor's performance impossible. In a case decided in 2002, the defendant argued that its failure to fully pay the price of the products purchased from the plaintiff was caused by a *force majeure*[9] which made it impossible to perform the obligation. The defendant had sold the products in question on to a third party and blamed the third party for failing to pay their price, causing the defendant to be unable to pay the outstanding debt owed to the plaintiff. The Supreme Court was not convinced by this argument as it saw the defendant's financial problems as a normal outcome of its business operation and thus not as a legitimate excuse.[10] This opinion is strengthened by a subsequent

[5] TCCC, s 219:

> The debtor is relieved from his obligation to perform if the performance becomes impossible in consequence of a circumstance, for which he is not responsible, occurring after the creation of the obligation. If the debtor, after the creation of the obligation, becomes unable to perform, it is equivalent to a circumstance rendering the performance impossible.

[6] TCCC, s 205: 'The debtor is not in default so long as the performance is not effected in consequence of a circumstance for which he is not responsible.'

[7] The 1997 Asian Financial Crisis which affected much of East Asia and Southeast Asia started in Thailand, where it is known as the *Tom Yum Goong* Crisis. It is one of the greatest financial disasters in the modern history of Thailand.

[8] Supreme Court Decision No 3506/2546 (2003).

[9] TCCC, s 8: '"*Force majeure*" denotes any event the happening or pernicious result of which could not be prevented even though a person against whom it happened or threatened to happen were to take such appropriate care as might be expected from him in his situation and in such condition.'

[10] Supreme Court Decision No 1678/2546 (2003).

Supreme Court decision of 2006. In this case, the plaintiff agreed to buy a piece of land and a house from the defendant. At the time the agreement was concluded, there was no house on the land, but the defendant agreed to build this. The agreement did not specify a time of performance but stated that the construction must be completed within a reasonable period of time. After more than three years from the conclusion of the contract, the plaintiff gave the defendant notice to fulfil the obligation, but the defendant, who had received full payment of the price from the plaintiff, ignored the notice. The plaintiff sued the defendant for breach of contract. The defendant denied liability and blamed a financial institution for breaking its promise to provide funds for the building project. The Supreme Court dismissed this argument as it was a matter between the defendant and the financial institution that could not be used as an excuse for breaching the contract with the plaintiff.[11] In other words, the defendant's financial difficulties did not allow it to depart from the contract or save it from contractual liability.

However, where the debtor is unable to perform an obligation due to an official order, it may be easier for the debtor to escape from contractual liability on the ground of impossibility of performance. In Supreme Court Decision No 4968–5050/2543, decided in 2000, a financial company agreed to undertake the duty to sell shares subscribed to by its former employees who, under the specific terms and conditions of the agreement, were unable to sell the shares by themselves. Before the company could sell the shares, due to its troubled financial situation, it was barred from operating its business, including equity trading, by an order of the Ministry of Finance. As a result, it was unable to fulfil its obligation to sell the shares. The Supreme Court viewed the official order as a circumstance which permanently prevented the debtor from performing the obligation and for which it was not responsible. Therefore, according to the Court's decision, the debtor's performance became impossible under section 219 TCCC and the debtor was relieved from its obligation. It is noteworthy that the facts of this case are different from those of the abovementioned Case No 1768/2549, where the debtor entered the reorganization process and had a chance to financially recover so as to be able to repay the debt. By comparison, in this case, the company's business came to an end and would never resume.

If the debtor's completion of the obligation depends on approval by a third party, the third party's failure to approve may render the debtor's performance impossible. In a case decided by the Supreme Court in 1989, the defendant transferred a lease to the plaintiff. Both parties had been aware of the fact that the transfer was subject to the approval of the owner of the property, which was a Buddhist temple. The transferor failed to receive this approval from the owner. The court held that the transferor's performance became impossible without this being any party's fault. It followed that the transferor was relieved from contractual liability arising from the impossibility of performance under section 219. However, the transferor was also not entitled to receive the transfer payment from the transferee under section 372 TCCC.[12]

Political unrest does not automatically render performance impossible and is not always treated as a *force majeure*. In a recent case decided in 2020, the Supreme Court rejected the employer's argument that political protest, which badly affected the event it had hired

[11] Supreme Court Decision No 3776/2549 (2006).

[12] Supreme Court Decision No 545/2532 (1989). The effects of impossibility of performance on the counter-performance will be discussed under section VII.

the contractor to organize, was a *force majeure* that rendered the contractor's performance impossible and that this impossibility of performance relieved the employer from the obligation to pay the contractor.[13] In the Court's view, the political protests did not entirely and permanently prevent the contractor from performing the obligation. It merely caused the contractor difficulty in achieving the results. The court held that the employer was liable to pay for the expenses incurred by the contractor for preparatory work. It should be observed that the term *force majeure* appears in pleadings of some cases concerning impossibility of performance because the party pleading *force majeure* believes that it makes their argument about impossibility of performance more convincing. However, it must be noted that *force majeure* is not an essential element of impossibility of performance. Impossibility of performance can be caused by any event, including a *force majeure*.

Temporary impossibility is not considered impossibility of performance that relieves the debtor from an obligation under section 219 TCCC. It can only give the debtor a defence against delayed performance. Under section 205 TCCC, the debtor is excused from liability arising from delayed performance if such is caused by an event for which the debtor is not responsible. The Supreme Court of Thailand is consistent in upholding this principle, as is evident in a number of its decisions discussed above.[14] In another clear example, the defendant entered into an agreement with the Military Communication Department, which permitted him to establish a radio station and have the exclusive right to advertise on the radio for eight years.[15] The defendant entered into a separate agreement with the plaintiff. Under the latter agreement, the plaintiff agreed to provide THB150,000 for the establishment of the radio station, and in return the defendant agreed to permit the plaintiff to advertise its products on the radio for two hours per day for six years or until the end of the agreement with the Military Communication Department, whichever ended earlier. The plaintiff was able to advertise for two years before the government issued an order to ban advertisements over the radio station in question. Three years later, the ban was lifted, but the defendant refused to allow the plaintiff to resume advertising, arguing that the ban made the defendant's duty to the plaintiff impossible to perform. However, the Supreme Court found that the agreement to establish the radio station between the defendant and the government department was still valid. As the plaintiff had so far exercised its right for just two years, it had the right to continue advertising until the completion of the period of six years. The defendant's refusal to perform the obligation after the ban was lifted amounted to breach of contract. Although section 205 TCCC was not raised by the parties or discussed by the Court, it is undoubtedly true that the defendant was not in default while the ban was in place as it prevented the defendant from performing the obligation and was a circumstance for which he was not responsible under section 205 TCCC.

Where hardship is attributable to some degree to the debtor's fault, he will not be able to benefit from section 205 TCCC. In a Supreme Court case decided in 2001, the defendant, a property developer, agreed to sell a house that was part of its publicly advertised property development project to the plaintiff at a time when it was not financially prepared to complete the project.[16] The defendant later failed to secure funding. The lack of funds resulted

[13] Supreme Court Decision No 65/2563 (2020).

[14] Supreme Court Decision Nos 1768/2549 (2006) and 4968–5050/2543 (2000).

[15] Supreme Court Decision No 1566/2518 (1965).

[16] Supreme Court Decision No 9047/2544 (2001).

in the delay of the project and a breach of contract. The defendant cited its hardship as a *force majeure* in order to escape from contractual liability. The Supreme Court disagreed as it believed that the defendant could have prevented or mitigated its financial troubles if it had made proper financial preparation before launching the project. The Court saw this as the defendant's own problem and therefore as constituting fault on its part. As a result, it was unable to benefit from section 205 TCCC to escape from becoming a debtor in default and to deny contractual liability.

From all the Supreme Court cases discussed above, it is safe to conclude that, in Thai law, hardship cannot relieve the debtor from contractual liability under section 219 TCCC or provide a legitimate defence against default under section 205 TCCC. Any attempt to use hardship or a change of circumstances as a basis of impossibility of performance or as a defence against contractual liability will most likely fail. As both sections 205 and 219 TCCC were copied from the German Civil Code of 1900, which relied heavily on the principle of fault, they only focus on saving the debtor who is not at fault for failing to perform the obligation, but they neglect the effect of this on the creditor. The applicability of section 205 TCCC is very broad and thus brings great uncertainty to business. Supreme Court Decision No 1566/2518 (1975 CE) is a striking illustration of a lengthy suspension of a contract and therefore of business uncertainty as a result of section 205 TCCC. This provision gives the court wide discretionary power to determine whether the debtor is responsible for the circumstance which prevents it from performing the obligation within or at the time of performance. If the circumstance meets the requirements of section 205 TCCC, the time of performance is reset. Some Thai scholars hold the opinion that the obligation will then be considered an obligation without an agreed time of performance. It follows that the creditor is required, under section 204 TCCC, to give the debtor a warning and grace period in order to put him in default.[17] Other scholars, including the author, hold the view that after the circumstance has passed, the debtor will have to perform the obligation by the earliest possible time, which should be considered a new fixed calendar time. If the debtor does not perform the obligation by the new time of performance, he will be in default immediately after the time passes. It needs to be stressed again that, in any event, the debtor is excused from breach of contract and the creditor is barred from claiming for any damage during the period when the debtor is temporarily prevented from performing the obligation.

IV. Interpretation of Contract and a Change of Circumstances

As a change of circumstances is not a valid ground in its own right for a party to be excused from a contractual obligation, the debtor may need to argue that, regardless of what appears at face value, based on interpretation of the contract, the situation is one of impossibility of performance. Sometimes, it is the court itself which invokes contract interpretation to find that there has been impossibility of performance. In a case decided by the Supreme Court

[17] TCCC, s 204:

> If the debtor does not perform after warning given by the creditor after maturity, he is in default through the warning. If a time by calendar is fixed for the performance, the debtor is in default without warning if he does not perform at the fixed time. The same rule applies if a notice is required to precede the performance, and the time is fixed in such manner that it may be reckoned by the calendar from the time of notice.

in 2010, the plaintiff hired the defendants, two separate shipping companies, to transport goods from Thailand to Chicago and Detroit in the United States. The contract stated that the goods should be transported to the destinations 'by sea or other modes of transportation'. The defendants had informed the plaintiff that they would transport them to Vancouver in Canada by sea and from there to the destinations in the United States by train. The goods successfully arrived in Canada, but the defendants chose to discontinue the transport because transporting goods of that kind by train between Canada and the United States was prohibited. The defendants denied liability for breach of contract on the ground of impossibility of performance. The Supreme Court interpreted the clause on the modes of transportation as an open-ended clause which suggested that the parties' true intention was to place more importance on the end result (ie the goods reaching the destinations) than on the modes of transportation. As it was proved in court that the defendants chose to stop performing the obligation despite being able to deliver the goods by car instead of train, the Court was not convinced by the defendants' argument of impossibility of performance. They were therefore held liable for breach of contract.[18]

The following hypothetical example will illustrate how contract interpretation can make a situation that might appear to be one of hardship become regarded as one of impossibility of performance instead, so as to relieve the debtor from the obligation to perform. A purchased 1,000 units of a specific type of product manufactured in Thailand from B at the market price of THB1,000 per unit. The parties agreed on general specifications of the products but did not specify where B would find them as products of this kind were abundant in the domestic market. However, before the time of delivery, the products suddenly disappeared from the domestic market as they were all exported to Singapore. In addition, the manufacturers closed down the production line in Thailand. As a result, Singapore became the only market where the products were available. It was still possible for B to import them back to Thailand, but B would have to sell them at the market price of THB20,000 to cover the costs. This would mean that at the time of delivery, the price of the product would be 20 times higher than at the time the contract was concluded. On the surface, this example seems to be a case of hardship or economic impossibility which is not accepted as impossibility of performance under section 219 TCCC. However, the case could be treated as one of impossibility of performance if B is able to identify the true intention of the parties as to the source of the product that they contracted for. B could argue that despite the absence of a clause on the source of the products, the contract price suggested that the parties intended to buy and sell products which were available in the domestic market. Therefore, it could be considered to be an implied term of the contract by applying the principles in sections 171 and 368 TCCC.[19] As it was impossible for B to find 1,000 units of the product domestically and deliver them to A, B's performance became impossible due to a circumstance for which B was not responsible. By virtue of section 219 TCCC, B was relieved from the obligation and did not breach the contract. In the absence of a rule dealing with a change of circumstances and hardship in Thai contract law, contract interpretation is a useful means of closing the loophole.

[18] Supreme Court Decision No 2587/2553 (2010).

[19] TCCC, s 171: 'In the interpretation of a declaration of intention, the true intention is to be sought rather than the literal meaning of the words or expressions.' TCCC, s 368: 'Contracts shall be interpreted according to the requirements of good faith, ordinary usage being taken into consideration.'

V. Good Faith and a Change of Circumstances

In Thai law, the principle of good faith[20] is often used to supplement the application of certain legal rules and principles, especially in contract interpretation, but has no direct role in helping the creditor to end the contract. As discussed in section IV above, when identifying and interpreting a contractual term, we need to discover the true intention of the parties (section 171 TCCC). This can be achieved with the help of the principle of good faith. In the example of buying 1,000 units of product discussed above, it could be argued that the parties' real intention was to buy products available in the domestic market because of the fact that the contract price appeared to be consistent with the market rate in the domestic market. This belief could be supported by the good-faith principle set out in section 368 TCCC as reasonably prudent persons who were in the same situation would not expect that the debtor's performance would cause him indebtedness or insolvency.

As the principle of good faith is already embedded in section 368 TCCC, which is one of the two essential rules of contract interpretation, its role in dealing with a change of circumstances is subsumed under that of contract interpretation.

VI. Mistake and a Change of Circumstances

There has so far been no example in judicial decisions and scholastic literature of using a mistake as a basis for attempting to escape liability following a change of circumstances. In principle, the argument that a mistake constituted a defect in consent in a case of change of circumstances would have no chance of success in Thai law. Consent is an essential condition for the validity of a contract in Thai law. However, to determine whether a contract is valid, consent is only relevant at the time the contract was concluded, while the nature of a change of circumstances suggests that the change occurred unexpectedly after the contract was formed. The TCCC recognizes two types of mistakes, namely, mistakes as to an essential element of the contract (section 156 TCCC) and mistakes as to an essential quality of a person or a thing in ordinary dealing (section 157 TCCC). Both types of mistakes concern an essential element of the contract and an essential quality of a person or a thing which exists at the time the contract is concluded. With reference to the example of buying 1,000 units of product discussed above, it is legally unsound for A or B to claim that they made a mistake at the time of the contract by assuming that there would be no change in circumstances (ie no extinction of products in the domestic market) after the contract was concluded. And even if they had made such a mistake, it would not have fallen under section 156 or section 157 TCCC.

VII. Legal Consequences of a Change of Circumstances

As discussed above, hardship has no place in the TCCC and receives little attention in Thai legal literature. By itself, it has no impact on the contractual relationship. When there is

[20] TCCC, s 5: 'Every person must, in the exercise of his rights and in the performance of his obligations, act in good faith.'

a change of circumstances which makes performance much more difficult, the debtor, in order to escape from the contract, must prove that this makes performance impossible and that he is not at fault in causing the impossibility. If these two conditions are satisfied, the debtor will be relieved from the obligation under section 219 TCCC. However, if the debtor is at fault for the impossibility of performance, he will be considered to have breached the contract and, hence, liable to compensate for the loss suffered by the creditor as a result of his breach of contract under section 218 TCCC.[21] In addition, the creditor will have the right to rescind the contract without the requirement of giving the debtor a grace period under section 389 TCCC.[22]

Contract interpretation seems to be the only means to turn what is at face value a situation of hardship into one of impossibility of performance. If this is unsuccessful, the debtor's last resort is section 205 TCCC, which can give the debtor an excuse for being in default during the time he was temporarily prevented from performing the obligation. The only question is how long he can be excused from breach of contract if the circumstance ends but his hardship continues. It is highly likely that the debtor will not be excused after the end of the circumstance as clearly stated in section 205 TCCC. The debtor's duty to perform the obligation will resume despite his continued hardship.

Where the debtor benefits from not being liable because of impossibility of performance under section 219 TCCC, or from having an excuse for default due to a circumstance for which he is not responsible under section 205 TCCC, the question arises as to what, in cases of reciprocal contracts, will happen to the counter-performance. For example, if the contractor debtor who has the obligation to make a product is relieved from contractual liability due to impossibility of performance under section 219, is he entitled to demand the remuneration from the employer creditor? This is determined by the rules on passing of risk. The relevant provisions are sections 370, 371, and 372[23] TCCC, which were copied from the Japanese Civil Code.

[21] TCCC, s 218:

> When the performance becomes impossible in consequence of a circumstance for which the debtor is responsible, the debtor shall compensate the creditor for any damage arising from the non-performance.
> In case of partial impossibility the creditor may, by declining the still possible part of the performance, demand compensation for non-performance of the entire obligation, if the still possible part of performance is useless to him.

[22] TCCC, s 389: 'If performance becomes wholly or partly impossible by a cause attributable to the debtor, the creditor may rescind the contract.'

[23] TCCC, s 370:

> If the object of a reciprocal contract is the creation or transfer of a real right in a specific thing, and such thing is lost or damaged by a cause which is not attributable to the debtor, the loss or damage falls upon the creditor.
> To a non-specific thing the provisions of the foregoing paragraph apply from the time when the thing has become specific in accordance with the provisions of Section 195 paragraph 2.

TCCC, s 371:

> The provisions of the foregoing section do not apply if the thing which forms the subject of a reciprocal contract depending upon a condition precedent is lost or destroyed while the condition is pending.
> If the thing is damaged by a cause not attributable to the creditor, the latter, when the condition is fulfilled, may at his option either demand performance with reduction of his counter-performance or rescind the contract, provided that in the case where the cause of the damage is attributable to the debtor, the creditor's right to compensate is not affected thereby.

TCCC, s 372:

> Except in the cases mentioned in the two foregoing sections, if an obligation becomes impossible of performance by a cause not attributable to either party, the debtor has no right to receive the counter-performance.

Sections 370 and 371 TCCC deal with a reciprocal contract that has the object of transferring ownership of a specific thing. Although the texts of the provisions seem to be unclear about which types of reciprocal contracts fall under their purview and this question has sparked debate among scholars, the Supreme Court has consistently made it clear that the two provisions apply mainly to sales contracts: section 370 TCCC applies when the ownership has already transferred from the debtor to the creditor while section 371 TCCC applies when the transfer of ownership is delayed by agreement. If impossibility of performance occurs after the ownership has been transferred from the seller to the buyer, the buyer who is the owner of the lost or totally damaged property will have to bear the loss, meaning that he will have to pay the full price despite the loss or destruction.

Section 372 TCCC applies to all cases which do not fall under sections 370 and 371 TCCC. These are mostly concerned with obligations to do something, notably agreements to sell and buy immovable property, hire of work contracts, and lease contracts. If the debtor was hired to make a product and the work was destroyed or damaged before it was completed, according to section 372 TCCC, the debtor will not be entitled to demand any remuneration from the creditor despite having done some of the work. The debtor will be entitled to demand the counter-performance (ie the full amount of remuneration) only if the impossibility of performance is attributable to the creditor.[24] However, the creditor may be able to demand a reduction, for example, if the impossibility of performance provides a chance for the debtor to work for someone else and generate income during the time of the contract with the creditor.[25]

Sections 370 and 372 TCCC do not recognize proportionality. This results in two extreme outcomes for the debtor, that is, getting all or nothing at all. In the case of hire of work contracts discussed above, the debtor will not receive any remuneration even if he has completed 95 per cent of the work. Fortunately, sections 370–372 TCCC are non-mandatory law and can be modified by contractual agreement.[26] It is, hence, normal practice for the parties in a hire of work contract to divide up the work into several phases in order to avoid the disproportionate outcomes of section 372 TCCC. These contracts provide that when the debtor completes a phase, he will be entitled to receive full payment for the completed phase even if the remaining phases subsequently become impossible to complete. Impossibility of performance will only affect the incomplete phases. This is the case with lease contracts where the rent for the term of lease is divided into equal instalments, for example, on a month-to-month basis. The lessee will have to pay the rent for the months in which performance was fully effected. For those months, the lessor completely performed his obligation, and the fulfilment of his obligation was not affected by the subsequent impossibility of performance. However, if performance becomes impossible before the lessee

> If performance becomes impossible by a cause attributable to the creditor, the debtor does not lose his right to the counter-performance. He must, however, deduct what he saves in consequence of release from the performance, or what he acquires or maliciously omits to acquire by a different application of his faculties. The same rule applies if the performance due from one party becomes impossible, in consequence of a circumstance for which he is not responsible, at the time when the other party is in default of acceptance.

[24] TCCC, ss 603 and 604, which are specific rules on the hire of work, are in line with the general provision under TCCC, s 372.

[25] TCCC, s 371(2).

[26] Supreme Court Decision No 3728/2535 (1992).

creditor takes possession of the property, he can recover the advance rent he paid to the lessor debtor.[27]

Where the circumstances temporarily prevent the debtor from performing the obligation, according to section 369 TCCC the debtor will not be able to receive the counter-performance, a reflection of the principle of withholding performance. According to section 369 TCCC, 'A party to a reciprocal contract may refuse to perform his obligation until the other party performs or tenders performance of his obligation. But this does not apply if the other party's obligation is not yet due.' For example, the debtor is hired to construct a house. The work and payment are divided up into phases and instalments, respectively. If the debtor fails to complete the work for a particular phase due to a change in circumstances, he will not be entitled to receive the remuneration agreed for that phase. In the 2020 Supreme Court case discussed above,[28] the employer's attempt to convince the court that political unrest was a *force majeure* and rendered the contractor's performance impossible under section 219 TCCC failed. This tactic was employed to try to benefit from section 372 TCCC, which may relieve the employer from the obligation to pay the contractor the remuneration in case of impossibility of performance. The court awarded the contractor a sum of money for the work it did before the event was cancelled. This is a fair result that is in accordance with section 369 TCCC.

VIII. Thai Law and the COVID-19 Pandemic

The COVID-19 pandemic is perhaps the most serious test of Thai law relating to a change of circumstances. It has badly affected contractual relationships in Thailand on an unprecedented scale. The absence of specific rules dealing with a change of circumstances forces Thai lawyers to work much harder to alleviate the effects of the pandemic and be more inventive in utilizing the existing law. As the Thai government prefers cooperative over legislative mechanisms to deal with the effects of the pandemic, there has been no comprehensive legislation like Singapore's COVID-19 (Temporary Measures) Act 2020. A few statutes focusing on helping small and medium enterprises (SMEs) and on taxation were introduced, while the Bank of Thailand, the country's central bank, forced Thai commercial banks to adopt some relief measures to temporarily save their customers, mainly borrowers. With the limited legislative mechanisms, most contracting parties have to rely heavily on the general provisions of the TCCC to determine their contractual rights and duties which are affected by the pandemic. Its catastrophic effects on both creditors and debtors make it even more difficult for Thai lawyers to determine which party should be protected.

The pandemic's direct and indirect effects on contractual relationships are mostly short-term ones, temporarily preventing the debtor from performing the obligation rather than

[27] Supreme Court Decision Nos 10514–10515/2558 (2015). In this case, the lessor agreed to remove the old building on the premises before the lessee took possession of it. The lessee paid the lessor an advance rent. However, the premise was subsequently declared a national heritage site by the government, rendering the lessor's performance impossible. The Supreme Court held that the lessor was relieved from contractual liability under TCCC, s 219. However, it would not be entitled to the counter-performance (ie the rent) under TCCC, s 372. Thus, the lessor had to return the advance rent to the lessee.

[28] Supreme Court Decision No 65/2563 (2020).

causing impossibility of performance. The pandemic may directly affect the contract if a contracting party contracts the disease and that temporarily stops him from completing the obligation within the agreed time. If the illness is not attributed to the debtor's own fault, he will be excused from being in default under section 205 TCCC. It is, however, evident that most people suffered from the indirect consequences of the pandemic, especially the temporary closure of business due to an official order, self-imposed prevention measures, or financial trouble. If an indirect consequence prevents the debtor from performing the obligation within the agreed time, the debtor may be saved from being in default under section 205 TCCC. For example, the debtor is hired to make a product, and in order to perform the obligation he needs to work at a specific workplace outside his home. However, due to the lockdown, he is unable to complete the work within the deadline. The debtor may be excused from being in default until the lockdown is lifted.

The debtor may be saved from being in default by section 205 TCCC. However, whether he is entitled to demand the counter-performance, usually a payment of money, is determined by the rule of reciprocal contracts under section 369 TCCC. Where the debtor fails to fulfil the obligation within the time agreed regardless of his fault, he is not entitled to receive the counter-performance. With reference to the example above, if the debtor is prevented from travelling to the workplace to complete the work due to the lockdown, he will not be entitled to demand the remuneration from the creditor. The debtor is not in default but will not receive payment until he properly fulfils the obligation. This makes sense. However, the applicability of section 369 TCCC is complicated when dealing with certain types of contracts, especially employment and lease contracts.

Employment contracts are governed by special legislation, namely the Labour Protection Act BE 2541, which overrides section 369 TCCC. The Act helps determine whether the employee will be entitled to receive a wage during the lockdown. Under section 75 of the Act, the employer will have to pay the employee 75 per cent of his normal wage if the business is suspended or closed down. However, if the closure is caused by a *force majeure*, the employer will be exempt from the obligation to pay wages during the suspension of business or after the business is closed down.[29] The latter result resembles that of section 369 TCCC. It is less controversial if the suspension is imposed by an official order, which is generally seen as a *force majeure*. But if the suspension or closure of business comes from the employer's own decision based on health and safety concerns or financial circumstances, the question arises as to whether the suspension or closure is caused by a *force majeure*. In the author's view, if the employer's decision to suspend or close down the business results from a reasonable self-imposed measure for protecting the health of the workers and people in the community, he can cite the pandemic as a *force majeure* causing the suspension or closure of business. However, if the pandemic financially affects his business, forcing him to suspend it or close it down, he should not be able to use the pandemic as a *force majeure*. This is because, unlike health issues, the financial problem is not a direct consequence of the pandemic and may be attributed to the employer's own mismanagement. The change of working mode (ie the change to working from home) is not a suspension or closure of business. Therefore, the creditor must continue paying the employees the normal wages unless the employment agreement states otherwise.

[29] Labour Protection Act, s 75.

The pandemic's impact on lease contracts makes the application of section 369 TCCC difficult. For example, A rents a retail unit in a shopping mall owned by B to run a café. The government temporarily closes most stores. A still has access to his café but cannot open it to customers. Does A have to pay rent during the closure? B may argue that he is performing his obligation properly by making the use of the leased premises available to A. This may be true but certainly causes unfairness to A. In the author's view, to determine the rights and duties of the parties in this kind of situation, contract interpretation is needed to search for the true intentions of the parties under sections 171 and 368 TCCC. In accordance with the principle of good faith and good commercial practice, the true intention of the parties is the use of the leased premise to run a business in a normally operating shopping mall. Therefore, the lessor's obligation is to make the leased premise in the normally operating shopping mall available to the lessee. As the shopping mall is almost entirely closed, the lessor fails to perform the obligation properly. He does not deserve the rent during the time the shopping mall is closed under section 369 TCCC. If the closure of the shopping mall continues until the lease expires, the lessor's performance becomes impossible. The result remains the same (ie the lessor has no right to receive the rent during the period of closure) but under a different provision, section 372 TCCC.

As discussed above, the financial impact of the pandemic does not make the monetary obligation impossible to be fulfilled. The TCCC provides no relief measures other than an excuse for being in default under section 205 TCCC. The only question Thai lawyers have to answer is how long the debtor can benefit from such excuse. Thai law does not allow a contracting party to unilaterally modify the contract or escape from the contractual obligations unless he can prove impossibility of performance. This is clearly reaffirmed by a number of Supreme Court decisions discussed above. Therefore, the suspension or closure of business does not relieve the debtor from the obligation to perform. It can only help delay performance or automatically postpone the time of performance by virtue of section 205 TCCC. The weakness of Thai law (ie the insufficiency of relief measures and specific provisions to deal with a change of circumstances) was embarrassingly revealed by the pandemic.

IX. The Hypotheticals

The principles of Thai law set out so far will now be applied to the hypothetical scenarios proposed by the volume editors.[30]

1. Abraham and Bill

In this hypothetical concerning the maintenance of an irrigation channel for an unlimited period of time, both inflation and the rise in the cost of maintenance and labour from 1567 to 2018 have made the price paid by Bill wholly inadequate. But this change in circumstances does not amount to an impossibility of performance under section 219 TCCC which can relieve Abraham's successors from the contractual obligation to maintain the

[30] The fact scenarios for the hypothetical cases in this section IX are taken from M Chen-Wishart, D Neo, and S Vogenauer, 'Introduction', ch 1, 7–8.

irrigation channel. It is still possible for them to perform the obligation, though with great financial difficulty. Abraham's successors can try to prove that the contract should be interpreted to show that the parties intended for Abraham's performance in exchange for a reasonable price which is adjustable in order to keep up with changing circumstances, for example, rising inflation. However, it is unlikely that Thai courts will be convinced by this argument as inflation is normally foreseeable and it is the parties' responsibility to bear the risk of uncertainty. There is also little chance of success in seeking to terminate the contract as there is no contractual term or specific provision permitting a contracting party to do so. In the absence of such a provision, the debtor's fault is a prerequisite for terminating a contract in Thai law unless the parties agree otherwise. In this hypothetical case, as there is no evidence of fault on the part of either party, there is no breach of contract. Therefore, neither party will have the right to terminate the contract. In conclusion, there is little chance of success for Abraham's successors to unilaterally end the contract or change its terms. In the author's view, their final resort is to argue that the contract has been void from the beginning on the grounds that its object to bind the parties forever caused great unfairness to the parties and is therefore contrary to public order and good morals, which renders the contract void under section 150 TCCC.

2. Citi Corporation and Drive Bank

In this hypothetical, the interest rate for the loan from Drive Bank to Citi Corporation in 2015 is fixed at 10 per cent for five years. In 2017, inflation rises to 50 per cent. Drive Bank wishes to request adjustment, or alternatively, termination of the contract. Presumably, this is because the interest rate on the loan makes it much less profitable or even unprofitable compared to at the time of the contract. According to Supreme Court Decisions Nos 118/2525, 3506/2546, and 1768/2549, hardship and even a national economic crisis will not relieve the debtor from contractual liability or give the parties the right to renegotiate the contract. The Court decided that hardship or a change in circumstances only raises the possibility of giving the debtor an excuse for not being in default under section 205 TCCC, which means that there is no breach of contract on the debtor's side. Therefore, Drive Bank as the creditor would not be entitled to seek any remedies against the debtor nor make any changes to the contract.

This case should be differentiated from hypothetical 1, where the obligation of Abraham's successors to provide the service for the fixed price lasted forever. In this case, the substantial increase in inflation may have only reduced Drive Bank's profits. The Thai Supreme Court makes it consistently clear that a financial crisis does not make the debtor's monetary performance impossible or give him the right to unilaterally end or change the contract.

3. Easy and Frugle

In this hypothetical involving a lease of business premises, the profits of the lessee, Frugle, have risen to 500 per cent more than what could be reasonably expected at the time of the contract. Further, the rental value of comparable business premises in the area have risen to 500 per cent of the agreed rental price. The lessor, Easy, requests to adjust the rental price or, alternatively, to terminate the contract. Under Thai law, an unexpected change in circumstances does not give a contracting party the right to renegotiate the contract. The creditor will acquire the right to terminate the contract only when there is breach of contract by the debtor. As discussed above, the debtor's fault is a prerequisite for breach of contract. The change of circumstances in this case is clearly not attributed to the debtor's fault. Therefore, Frugle has no right to terminate the contract or adjust the rental price without mutual agreement. The change of circumstances in this case gives the lessee a windfall and causes the lessor to lose out on the opportunity to make a greater profit than what had been agreed under the contract. This can be distinguished from hypothetical 2 where substantial, unprecedented rise in inflation erodes the money value of the agreed rental income, and from hypothetical 1, where Abraham's successors suffer from perpetually unfair contract terms.

4. George and Han

In this hypothetical, George agrees to refurbish the cellar of Han's restaurant but before the work begins, the restaurant is completely destroyed by a storm. This hypothetical is highly likely to be treated as a case of impossibility of performance in Thai law. In order to understand why this case should be treated as one of impossibility of performance, one needs to identify the parties' real intention (section 171 TCCC) and interpret the contract in accordance with the requirement of good faith (section 368 TCCC). A reasonably prudent person can accept that, although George's duty is to refurbish the cellar, not the restaurant, the former is a component of the latter. It is reasonable to believe that the parties did not envisage a refurbished standalone cellar but one which serves as an essential part of a specific thing, which is the restaurant building. Therefore, the object of this contract is to have the cellar of a specific thing refurbished. When the specific thing is completely destroyed, the object of the contract becomes impossible to fulfil. It is therefore impossible for George to refurbish the cellar at the specified restaurant. There is a Supreme Court case which may give a comparable example. In this case, the plaintiff gave the defendant a specific amount of unmilled rice for turning it into milled rice. The plaintiff agreed to give the defendant husk and bran in return. The rice was completely processed and kept at the mill, which was subsequently destroyed by fire. The Supreme Court regarded this contract as a mutual contract and held that the unmilled rice given to the defendant was a specific thing. As it was completely destroyed by an event which was not attributed to the defendant, he was relieved from the obligation under section 219 TCCC, meaning that the defendant did not breach the contract.[31] Where George's performance becomes impossible without this being Han's fault, he will not be entitled to receive any renumeration and compensation from Han according to the rule of the passing of risk under section 372 TCCC.[32] However, if the parties had agreed to divide George's work into phases and the payment into instalments in accordance with each completed phase, George will be entitled to receive payment for the completed phases.

31 Supreme Court Decision No 1074/2546 (2003).

32 TCCC, ss 603 and 604, which deal with the passing of risk for hires of work, provide the same outcome.

5. Gina and H Hotel

In this hypothetical, Gina books a room for the weekend at H Hotel in X City, the capital of country Z. For situation (i), where the exhibition Gina intended to visit is cancelled at the last moment, there is no chance of success in any attempt to prove impossibility of performance and to terminate the contract for the room. The hotel's obligation to let Gina occupy the room and Gina's obligation to pay rent are not affected by the cancellation of the exhibition. The performance of both parties is still possible. An attempt to avoid the contract on the basis of mistake will also fail because any mistake as to the availability of the exhibition will be treated as a mistake in Gina's motive, which is not recognized as a defect in consent that can make the contract invalid. Even if it is a mutual mistake, it will not render the contract voidable under section 157 TCCC because the availability of the exhibition is not normally an essential quality of a hotel room. Gina will not be able to terminate the contract as there is no breach of contract on the hotel's side. In summary, Gina cannot cancel the booking on the basis of the cancellation of the exhibition.

In situation (ii), a terrorist group declares that it plans to launch attacks on tourists in X. Like in situation (i), the incident does not directly affect the parties' performance. However, Gina may be able to argue that under the rules of contractual interpretation in sections 171 and 368 TCCC, the hotel has a contractual duty to provide its room and service in a safe environment for its customer. Services provided in an unsafe environment by the hotel would not be a proper performance and thus can be rejected by the customer under section 320 TCCC, which states that 'The creditor cannot be compelled to receive part performance or any other performance than that due to him.' Where the debtor's improper performance is rejected, the creditor can withhold his counter-performance (ie payment for the hotel room) according to the principle of reciprocal contract as reflected in section 369 TCCC. Therefore, Gina would be entitled to refuse to pay for her hotel room on the grounds that she did not receive a proper performance, that is, a safe service.

For situation (iii), where an unforeseeable strike by airport personnel prevents Gina from travelling to X, whether Gina can cancel the hotel booking depends on whether Gina lives in country Z at the time of the strike and whether there are other modes of transport available. If Gina lives in country Z and can travel to X City by train even though a train will take much more time than a plane, Gina will not be able to use the strike as an excuse for abandoning the booking. She still has the obligation to pay rent even though she did not stay in the hotel room. However, if Gina lives in a different country, and flying is the only mode of transport to country Z, the answer will be the same as that for situation (ii), that is, that Gina will be able to escape from breach of contract and will not be liable to pay rent.

Situation (iv) is perhaps the only situation where Gina can benefit from the law on impossibility of performance. Based on the rules of contractual interpretation in sections 171 and 369 TCCC, she can refer to the fact of the unusually high rental price of the room as proof of the parties' implied agreement that the hotel's obligation is to let her use the room for watching the inauguration proceedings. Where the event is cancelled, the debtor's performance becomes impossible under section 219 TCCC. The hotel will not be entitled to receive the rent under section 372 TCCC.

6. Kris and Leila

In this hypothetical, Kris sells his family home to Leila at 70 per cent of its market value. Both parties assume that Leila will dedicate it to cultural use by the general public. However, this assumption is not expressly set out in the contract. After the sale, Leila changes her mind and gives the house to one of her sons instead. To answer the question of whether Kris can claim the difference between the agreed price and the market value or, alternatively, restitution of the house, it is necessary to divide the analysis into two scenarios. First, if Kris wants the contract to continue but wants to seek compensation for the difference between the agreed price and the market value, he needs to prove that Leila breached the contract. Secondly, if Kris wants restitution of the house, he needs to set aside the contract. There are two possible ways to end the contract, namely, on the basis of termination of contract and on the basis of avoidance of contract. To terminate the contract, Kris will need to prove that Leila has breached the contract, which is also a requirement for claiming compensation, as mentioned above. Kris may need the rules of contractual interpretation, especially section 368 TCCC, to argue that Leila has an implied contractual duty in good faith to use the house for a cultural purpose. The second way of ending the contract is to prove that the contract was voidable from the time it was made. Fraud and mistake are two possible grounds which may render the contract voidable. Mistake may not be as convincing as fraud because it is hard to fit this case into one of the two categories: mistake as to an essential element and mistake as to an essential quality of a thing or a person. The ground of fraud will be made out successfully only if Kris was intentionally deceived by Leila at the time the contract was concluded. However, if Leila had an intention to dedicate the house to cultural use at the beginning but changed her mind later, this change does not give rise to mistake or fraud as it occurred after the contract was concluded.

X. Conclusion

Thai contract law adheres to the principle of *pacta sunt servanda*, as is evident from the absence of rules concerning a change of circumstances and the Supreme Court's reluctance to depart from contractual terms. This adherence does not seem to be an intentional design by the draftsmen of the TCCC but rather a mistake as a consequence of a rushed legal transplantation. It is an excusable and understandable mistake as the German and Japanese Civil Codes, the two principal models for Thai contract law, do not contain any provisions dealing specifically with a change of circumstances. In Thai law, a contract will end only when a condition for ending it is met as specified in the contract, when it is terminated under a specific term or by virtue of a specific provision of the TCCC, or when it is avoided. The debtor will also be released from his contractual obligation without the need to end the contract when his performance becomes impossible. Impossibility of performance seems to be the only channel for the limited relevance of change of circumstances to Thai contract law. However, most examples of change of circumstances and hardship do not qualify as impossibility of performance, and the exceptional cases qualify only with the help of contract interpretation. Section 205 TCCC may be able to temporarily save the debtor from being in default where non-performance is a result of a circumstance for which the debtor is not responsible, but the interpretation of this provision is dependent on judicial discretion. This is not good news for contract lawyers as well as businesses and consumers who are struggling to survive in Thailand's fast-changing economy and those who have been badly affected by the COVID-19 pandemic. It may be time to amend the TCCC in order to officially and expressly recognize the concept of change of circumstances in Thai law.

25

Termination of Contracts in Thai Law

Nadnaphas LEAKPECH

I. Introduction

Termination[1] is one of the three main remedies for a breach, or non-performance, of a contract under Thai law. The other two remedies are specific performance and damages.[2] Provisions concerning specific performance and damages are codified in 'Title I—General Provisions' of 'Book II: Obligations' of the Thai Civil and Commercial Code (TCCC), while the provisions on contract termination are cited in 'Title II—Contracts' of the same Book. These provisions concerning termination of contract are derived from both the Japanese Civil Code of 1896 and the German Civil Code of 1900. The majority of the provisions are a replica of the Japanese Civil Code, while a few of the provisions are modelled on the German Civil Code.

Remedies for a breach of contract are reminiscent of a fork in the road, in the sense that a creditor must choose between claiming specific performance or terminating the contract. If a creditor demands specific performance, she cannot exercise her right to terminate. Conversely, if contract termination is the preferred choice, the creditor will no longer be able to claim specific performance since the contractual relationship would have come to an end. However, a creditor can always claim compensatory damages, in addition to specific performance and termination of the contract, provided she can prove that she has suffered loss or damage as a result of the breach of contract.

Under Thai law, one must distinguish between termination and avoidance. The former operates as a remedy for non-performance, while the latter is a nullification of a voidable contract. The effects of both are similar in terms of restoring parties to their pre-contractual position. However, Thai contract law does not give the party who avoids the contract, nor the party who is affected by the avoidance, the right to claim compensatory damages since the contract is deemed to be void from the beginning. If they have suffered any loss arising from such avoidance, they would need to seek a remedy from another regime, that is, tort law.

This chapter provides an overview of Thai contract law with respect to termination of contracts. It is divided into five main sections, commencing with this introduction to familiarize readers with the basic concepts of termination. The second section describes the emergence of the right to terminate both by contract and by law and the loss thereof. Section III explains how this right is exercised once it is acquired. The effects of exercising the right to terminate are elaborated on in the fourth section, and the final section seeks to

[1] The terms 'termination' and 'rescission' are used interchangeably in this chapter as a remedy for a breach of contract.

[2] M Pongsapan, 'Remedies for Breach of Contract in Thai Law' in M Chen-Wishart, A Loke, and B Ong (eds), *Studies in the Contract Laws of Asia, vol I: Remedies for Breach of Contract* (OUP 2016) 370.

Nadnaphas Leakpech, *Termination of Contracts in Thai Law* In: *Studies in the Contract Laws of Asia V: Ending and Changing Contracts*. Edited by: Mindy Chen-Wishart, Dora Neo, and Stefan Vogenauer, Oxford University Press.
 DOI: 10.1093/oso/9780198995814.003.0025

draw conclusions regarding termination of a contract under Thai contract law based on the observations and analysis in the previous sections.

II. Right to Terminate

Under Thai law, there are two main ways to terminate a contract. Firstly, a contract is terminated by the consent of both parties, whereby one party makes an offer to terminate the contract and the other party accepts such offer. The acceptance can be either express or implied. The decision of the Supreme Court of Thailand in Case No 3090/2552 (2009) recognized an implied termination of contract. The case concerned the termination of a lease agreement, whereby the lessee had informed the lessor of his intention to end the agreement, despite having no right to terminate, either by contract or by law. The lessor, knowing of such intention, did not oppose but, instead, suspended all services to the lessee and returned the deposit. The Court held that both parties had voluntarily and implicitly terminated the contract.

Another instance of an implied termination is where considerable time has passed without any performance by either party or where one party has neglected to perform her obligation and the other party was too inattentive to claim for the performance. The Supreme Court, in its decisions in Cases Nos 4762/2549 (2006), 6990/2542 (1999), and 136/2509 (1966), deemed that, by abandoning the performance under the contract, the parties had implicitly terminated the contract.

Secondly, a contract can be terminated unilaterally. This occurs when one party terminates the contract without consent from the other party. In this case, such party must have the right to terminate the contract, either by the contract itself or by law, as specified in section 386 TCCC,[3] which states the following:

> If by contract or by the provisions of law one party has the right of rescission, such rescission is made by a declaration of intention to the other party.
> The declaration of intention mentioned in the foregoing paragraph cannot be revoked.[4]

If the party that is not entitled to terminate persists with the termination, the agreement is not terminated. The contractual relationship between the parties remains, and the rescinding party may be in breach of the agreement instead.

1. Termination Right Derived from the Contract

Under the principle of freedom of contract, parties can freely negotiate their termination clauses, provided they are not against the law relating to public order or good morals.[5] Since most provisions on the termination of contracts in the TCCC are not laws pertaining to

[3] This section was modelled on art 540 of the Japanese Civil Code 1896.

[4] For a translation of the TCCC, see K Sandhikshetrin, *The Civil and Commercial Code Book I-VI* (Nitibannagarn 2008).

[5] TCCC, s 151 states: 'An act is not void on account of its differing from a provision of any law, if such law does not relate to public order or good morals.'

public order or good morals, parties are at liberty to agree on termination clauses that are different from the legal provisions.

In Supreme Court Case Nos 4205/2548 (2005) and 9373/2538 (1995), the identical termination clause in the hire-purchase agreements under dispute read: 'In case the hirer is in default for payment of any monthly instalment, the agreement is deemed to be terminated without any notice from the owner.' Although the clause differed from both the hire-purchase provision of the TCCC[6] and general contract law—this will be discussed in more detail in section III—the Court upheld this clause on the ground that it was not against the law relating to public order or good morals. In contrast, a termination clause in an employment agreement cannot deviate from the legal provisions because it involves labour law, which concerns public order or good morals.[7]

Thai courts generally respect the parties' intentions as they are reflected in the negotiated clauses. However, in some cases, the courts tend also to consider the surrounding facts and circumstances when interpreting and enforcing the terms, as illustrated by the Supreme Court's decision in Case No 6184/2540 (1997). In this case, Clause 4 of a lease agreement imposed an obligation on the lessee not to modify the leased premises unless written consent from the lessor was obtained. Violating this provision resulted in the lessor having the right to claim for restoration at the expense of the lessee. In addition, Clause 12 granted the lessor the right to terminate if the lessee breached any provision in the agreement. The lessee subsequently violated Clause 4. The Court held that while Clause 12 applied as a general provision, liability for a breach of Clause 4 was a specific stipulation. Therefore, Clause 4 prevailed over Clause 12 and the termination clause did not apply in this case. The Court justified its reasoning by employing the principle of good faith and good commercial practice in interpreting the agreement. It considered the facts that (i) the lessee had contributed to the construction cost of the leased building, (ii) the modification did not cause damage to the building structure, (iii) the lessor had approved the same modification by other lessees in a neighbouring area, and (iv) the modification was in compliance with commercial practice with respect to renting a commercial building. The Court concluded that the lessor had no right to terminate, despite a breach of the agreement by the lessee.

Where one party is a consumer, the freedom of parties to negotiate their termination clauses is limited by two additional statutes governing the contractual relationship between consumers and business operators. The first is the Consumer Protection Act BE 2522 (1979) (CPA). The second is the Unfair Contract Terms Act BE 2550 (2007) (UCTA). Both laws aim to protect a party who is in an inferior bargaining position from being exploited by the other party. However, the scope of application of the UCTA is broader than that of the CPA.

The CPA provides safeguards to consumers at a pre-contracting stage. It grants power to the Contract Committee of the Consumer Protection Board to declare certain types of business in connection with the sale of any goods or the provision of services to be a 'controlled business' with respect to the contract. If a type of business is designated as a controlled business, the terms of the contract between the consumers and the business operators in such businesses shall be regulated. By virtue of section 35*bis* of the CPA, the Contract Committee is authorized to prescribe details of terms which are either required or

[6] TCCC, s 574(1) states: 'The owner may also terminate the contract in case of default of two successive payments, or breach of any material part of the contract; in which case all previous payments are forfeited to the owner who is entitled to resume possession of the property.'

[7] Supreme Court Decision No 1196–1218/2546 (2003).

prohibited. In principle, a contract must include terms the absence of which would cause consumers to be unreasonably disadvantaged. On the other hand, the contract shall not include terms that are unfair to consumers. For example, in a lease of property for accommodation which is a controlled business, a clause giving the lessee the right to terminate the contract by providing the lessor with thirty-day advance written notice shall be included in the contract. However, a termination clause granting a right to a business operator to terminate a lease without a breach of contract or a violation of any material terms by a lessee will not be allowed.[8] Under section 35 CPA, where there is a failure to include a clause required by law, the contract shall be deemed to include such clause. Conversely, if the contract stipulates prohibited terms, the same section provides that it shall be deemed that such terms do not exist. The CPA therefore operates as a compulsory supplement to a contract,[9] diminishing freedom of contract in exchange for the protection of consumers.

The UCTA protects consumers as well as any party who is in an inferior bargaining position at the stage of enforcing a contract. It applies not only to a contract made between consumers and business operators but also to a standard form contract[10] and a contract of sale with the right of redemption.[11] Under this Act, contract terms shall only be enforceable to the extent that they are fair and reasonable according to the circumstances (section 4(1) of the UCTA). The Act confers discretionary power on the courts to determine whether the term is unfair, and if it is unfair, to what extent it should be enforced.

Section 4(1) of the UCTA provides examples of terms that impose on one party greater burdens than would normally be expected by a reasonable person and, thus, may be regarded as unfair contract terms. Terms allowing the contract to be terminated without justifiable grounds, or granting the right to terminate the contract without the breach of an essential part of the contract by the other party, serve as examples. It is noteworthy that this type of termination clause is merely an example of a clause that confers an advantage over the other party. It is not automatically regarded as unfair.[12] A party alleging its unfairness has the burden to prove it,[13] and the court will decide whether or not it is unfair by considering the circumstances of the case. If a contract establishes the right to terminate for both parties equally, the clause allowing termination without cause is not deemed unfair.[14]

If potentially unfair termination terms are included in a contract, the court will determine to what extent the terms are enforceable as fair and reasonable. It shall take into consideration all the circumstances of the case, such as good faith, bargaining power, economic status, knowledge and understanding, the advantages and disadvantages of the contracting parties according to actual conditions, ordinary usages applicable to that kind of contract, and any potentially much heavier burden borne by one contracting party compared to the other party.[15]

[8] Announcement of the Contract Committee regarding the Business of Lease of a Property for Accommodation as a Controlled Business BE 2561 (2018).

[9] S Sotthibandhu, คำอธิบายนิติกรรมสัญญา [*Commentary on Juristic Acts and Contracts*] (22nd edn, Winyuchon 2018) 581

[10] UCTA, s 3 defines 'standard-form contract' as a written contract the material terms of which have been pre-formulated, which is used by either party in the operation of his business, whatever form in which it is made.

[11] A contract of sale with the right of redemption is a type of sales contract whereby the title of the property sold is transferred to the buyer, however, with an agreement between the parties that the seller can redeem that property (TCCC, s 491).

[12] Supreme Court Decision No 10657/2559 (2016).

[13] Supreme Court Decision No 2298/2553 (2010).

[14] Supreme Court Decisions Nos 933/2559 (2016) and 10300/2559 (2016).

[15] UCTA, s 10.

2. Termination Right Derived from Provisions of Law

Rights to terminate conferred by provisions of law can be found in both specific contract law and general contract law. Specific contract law is codified in Book III of the TCCC, and it is divided into 22 titles of contract. Some of these have specific termination provisions. Examples of the right to terminate, as stipulated in specific contract law, are as follows:

- In a lease of property, the lessor has the right to terminate the agreement if the lessee sublets, or transfers, her rights in the whole or part of the property to a third person.[16] A lessee may terminate the contract if the lessor delivers the leased property in a condition not suitable for the purpose of the lease.[17]
- In hire-purchase, a hirer may terminate an agreement at any time by returning the property to the owner at her own expense.[18] Conversely, if a hirer is in default of two consecutive payments, or breaches any material part of the contract, an owner is entitled to rescind the contract.[19]
- In a hire of work, an employer has the right to terminate a contract without any reason, provided the work has not yet been finished and upon making compensation to a contractor for any injury resulting from the termination of the contract.[20]
- In a loan for use, the law confers termination rights on a lender in the case where the borrower violates certain obligations, that is, where the borrower uses the borrowed property for purposes other than ordinary usage or outside the scope granted in an agreement, lets a third party use the borrowed property, keeps it longer than she ought to, or fails to properly maintain the property.[21]

If the provisions relating to specific contract law are not applicable to a case, then general contract law must be considered. Three provisions in general contract law lay down the rights to terminate. Section 387 operates as a general principle, while sections 388 and 389 apply as exceptions to this principle.

Section 387 TCCC states:

> If one party does not perform the obligation, the other party may fix a reasonable period and notify him to perform within that period. If he does not perform within that period, the other party may rescind the contract.[22]

Section 388 TCCC states:

> If the object of a contract according to its nature or to an intention declared by the parties can be accomplished only by performance at a fixed time or within a fixed period, and such

[16] TCCC, s 544.
[17] TCCC, s 548.
[18] TCCC, s 573.
[19] TCCC, s 574.
[20] TCCC, s 605.
[21] TCCC, s 645.
[22] This was modelled on art 541 of the Japanese Civil Code 1896.

> time or period has passed without one of the parties having performed, the other party may rescind the contract without the notification mentioned in the foregoing section.[23]

Section 389 TCCC states:

> If performance becomes wholly or partly impossible by a cause attributable to the debtor, the creditor may rescind the contract.[24]

A breach of contract does not automatically entitle the other party to terminate. If one party fails to perform her obligation, whether in whole or in part,[25] the other party must give her a second chance to perform within a reasonable period. Failure to perform within the grace period results in the right of the other party to terminate the contract. The courts have discretion to determine whether the time fixed by a party is reasonable. If it is not reasonable, the termination has no legal effect. However, the Supreme Court, in Cases Nos 6961/2550 (2007), 1188/2549 (2006), and 7732/2548 (2005), allowed the creditor to terminate the contract promptly without a notification fixing the period to perform. The reason provided was that it would have been futile to do so since the debtor did not intend to, or certainly could not, fulfil its obligation under the contract. In these cases, the seller in a real estate purchase agreement failed to transfer the property on the due date because the construction was not yet completed, and considerable time had elapsed without any progress towards meeting the required performance.

Sections 388 and 389 stipulate exceptional situations where the granting of a grace period is not required. There is one exception in section 388 where the time of performance is of the essence such that the aim of a contract, whether pursuant to the nature of a contract or the intentions of the parties, can only be fulfilled by the performance of a debtor at, or within, a specified time. When such time has passed, performance will be useless to the creditor. The law therefore allows the creditor to terminate the contract without having to provide the debtor with additional time to perform.

Although parties may specify in a contract that time is of the essence, practices between them may establish otherwise, for example, where an owner in a hire purchase agreement continues to accept late payments without any objection. In one such case, the Supreme Court held that the parties did not consider time to be essential. The creditor was not entitled to terminate the contract immediately under section 388 because whether time is of importance is determined by the intentions of parties, which in turn is exhibited through the conduct of the parties.[26]

The second exception, under section 389, is when the performance of an obligation becomes impossible, and such impossibility is attributable to the debtor. The creditor is then entitled to terminate the contract with immediate effect. If the debtor is not responsible for

[23] This was modelled on art 542 of the Japanese Civil Code 1896.

[24] This was modelled on art 543 of the Japanese Civil Code 1896.

[25] S Pramoj, ประมวลกฎหมายแพ่งและพาณิชย์ว่าด้วยนิติกรรมและหนี้ [*The Civil and Commercial Code on Juristic Acts and Obligations*] vol *1* (M Pongsapan ed, Winyuchon 2016) 394; and J Setthabutr, หลักกฎหมายแพ่งลักษณะนิติกรรมและสัญญา [*The Principle of Civil Law on Juristic Acts and Contracts*] (D Thirawat ed, 7th edn, Textbooks and Teaching Materials Scheme of Faculty of Law, Thammasat University 2013) 289–90.

[26] Supreme Court Decisions Nos 2677/2547 (2004) and 2556/2533 (1990).

the impossibility of the performance (eg the impossibility is caused by *force majeure*, a third party, or the creditor's fault), the creditor has no right to terminate the contract according to section 389.

The right to terminate a reciprocal contract is additionally laid down in section 371(2) TCCC. It governs a reciprocal contract that has a condition precedent and aims to create or transfer a right in a specific thing. If the thing is damaged by a cause not attributable to the creditor before the condition precedent takes effect, the creditor can elect, upon the fulfilment of the condition precedent, to either demand performance with a reduction of her counter-performance or rescind the contract. This provision is another exception where notification granting an additional period to perform is not required.

3. Seriousness of Breach and Fault of the Debtor

Only a material breach of contract or non-performance will give rise to the right to terminate.[27] The Thai Supreme Court has reaffirmed this concept in several decisions,[28] and the Court's decision in Case No 1094/2549 (2006) serves as a clear illustration. This case involved the sale of a room in a condominium. The seller had completed the construction of the condominium but had not yet completed building the wall in front of it, and the buyer put this forward as grounds for termination. The Court reasoned that the wall, by its nature, was only a supplement to facilitate the use of a room. Moreover, as the wall was not mentioned in the termination letter, the Court deemed that the buyer did not regard the wall as essential to the extent that she would not have entered into the contract if she was aware of the breach of this obligation. The buyer, therefore, did not have the right to terminate the contract because the breach was not material.

Whether the fault of a debtor is necessary in order for a creditor to terminate a contract is still under debate among Thai scholars. This refers to a situation where non-performance is attributable to the debtor, that is, wilfully or negligently caused by the debtor.[29] In determining whether the debtor is negligent, one must look into the standard of care required by the law. For instance, in a deposit contract, if the deposit is undertaken gratuitously, the depositary is bound to exercise as much care of the property deposited as she is accustomed to exercising in her own affairs. If the deposit is undertaken with remuneration, the standard of care is higher and the depositary must exercise such care which a person of ordinary prudence would exercise in the circumstances. Lastly, if the depositary is a professional, she is bound to exercise the degree of care and skill usual and requisite in such profession.[30] If the debtor fulfils the relevant standard, she is not deemed to be negligent, and the non-performance cannot be attributed to her.

While termination under section 389 states clearly that the fault of a debtor gives rise to the right of termination, the concept of fault is omitted from sections 387 and 388.

[27] Setthabutr (n 25) 290.

[28] Supreme Court Decisions Nos 2494/2553 (2010), 1998/2543 (2000), 1138/2542 (1999), 2295/2526 (1983), and 1803/2500 (1957).

[29] M Pongsapan, 'หลักความผิดในกฎหมายลักษณะสัญญาของไทย'['The Principle of Fault in Thai Contract Law'] (2014) 43(2) Thammasat Law Journal 289.

[30] TCCC, s 659.

Proponents of the fault principle opine that a non-performance which entitles a creditor to terminate a contract must be based on the debtor's fault.[31] It is argued that since Thai contract law has civil law origins, the principle of fault, which is a bedrock of the contract regime in the civil law system, should be applied in interpreting Thai contract law.[32] Consequently, a non-performance under section 387 must result from the debtor's fault. If there is no fault of the debtor (eg if the non-performance is caused solely by a third party, or by *force majeure*),[33] the creditor is not entitled to terminate a contract. However, in relation to section 388, since time is of the essence, it is fruitless to force parties to maintain their contractual relationship and accept late performance. Therefore, it is contended that non-performance under this section may be an exception to the principle of fault; that is, fault of the debtor is not required as a basis for termination.[34] Opponents of the principle of fault reach a different conclusion by examining German contract law, which is the main source of Thai contract law. They propose that the basis of contract termination is not the fault of a debtor but the uselessness of the performance by a debtor; that is, the breach renders the performance useless to a creditor. Consequently, the contractual relationship between the parties does not need to be preserved. The creditor can terminate a contract, even though the breach of contract is not caused by the debtor's fault.[35]

The Thai Supreme Court has not expressly discussed the principle of fault in contract termination. However, it can be observed from the Supreme Court's decisions that the Court has implicitly resorted to both views. In Case No 5908/2540 (1997), the Supreme Court implicitly applied the principle of fault. This case concerned the sale of telescopic sights imported from the UK. The seller failed to deliver the goods before the due date because the manufacturer did not receive an export permit from the UK government, which withheld the permit as Thailand was in turmoil. The Court held that the non-performance was not attributable to the seller, therefore the seller was not in default. Consequently, the buyer had no right to terminate the contract. Unfortunately, the Court failed to provide clear reasoning on why the buyer was not entitled to terminate the contract.

A different position was taken in Case No 8605/2552 (2009), where the Supreme Court did not apply the principle of fault. This case involved a construction agreement where the contractor failed to complete the construction of the building within the specified time because the hirer had modified the building plan several times while the construction was ongoing, thus resulting in a delay. The Court held that even though the delayed performance was not the fault of the contractor, the hirer was entitled to terminate the agreement because it had given the contractor notice fixing a reasonable period to perform according to section 387 TCCC. It can therefore be implied that the Court was of the view that fault of the debtor is not relevant in terminating a contract.

[31] Setthabutr (n 25) 289.

[32] Pongsapan (n 29) 293.

[33] TCCC, s 8 states: '"*Force majeure*" denotes any event the happening or pernicious result of which could not be prevented even though a person against whom it happened or threatened to happen were to take such appropriate care as might be expected from him in his situation and in such condition.'

[34] Pongsapan (n 29) 321.

[35] K Prokati, 'ปัญหาการวิเคราะห์โครงสร้างความรับผิดทางหนี้ และสิทธิบอกเลิกสัญญา' ['Analytical Issue on the Structure of Obligation Liability and Right to Terminate a Contract'] (2015) รวมบทความวิชาการ 60 ปี อาจารย์เงาะ [Compilation of Academic Articles 60 Years Ajarn Ngor] 225, 253.

4. Loss of Right to Terminate

When a party has the right to terminate a contract, she can choose whether to exercise this right. During the period when she has not asserted such right, the relationship between the parties is uncertain. Section 393 TCCC, which was modelled on Article 547 of the Japanese Civil Code 1896, helps alleviate such uncertainty by setting out a means to extinguish a termination right if it is not asserted within a reasonable time. Under section 393, where there is no time limit to exercise a termination right, the other party may fix a reasonable period and notify the party who has the right to terminate to invoke her right within such period. If the relevant time elapses without any termination notice being given, her right to terminate will be lost.

Another case where a party can lose her termination right is outlined in section 394 TCCC. This provision is a replica of Article 548 of the Japanese Civil Code 1896. The draftsmen did not provide clarification about the rationale behind this section. However, the concept of this provision is explained in relation to Japanese law as an implied waiver of the termination right.[36] Under section 394 TCCC, the right to terminate is lost if the party having the right has, by her own act or fault, made it more difficult, or impossible, to make restitution when the contract is rescinded. An example is where the party has materially damaged, or modified, the thing that is the subject of the contract or makes restitution of the thing impossible. However, such damage, modification, or impossibility must be caused by, or be attributable to, the party with the termination right. If the loss or damage to the thing does not result from an act of the party possessing the right, or is not the fault of such person, the termination right remains. In the author's view, this provision is based on the principle of good faith. Both parties have an obligation to make restitution when a contract is terminated. When the party who is entitled to terminate makes restitution impossible due to her own fault, it can be deemed that she does not act in good faith if she invokes the right to terminate. Therefore, the law does not allow her to terminate the contract and extinguishes her termination right.

5. The Hypotheticals

(a) Car Machinery & Co and Traders Ltd

Car Machinery & Co appoint Traders Ltd as sole distributors of their car panel presses for a period of five years. Clause 7(b) of the agreement provides that 'Distributors shall send their representatives to visit all six large car manufacturers in the country at least once in every week for the purpose of soliciting orders for car panel presses. Failure to comply with this obligation shall entitle Car Machinery to terminate the agreement with immediate effect.' Traders Ltd miss two visits to car manufacturers in the second month of the contractual period. Is Car Machinery entitled to terminate the agreement?[37]

According to section 386, the right to terminate is established by contract or by law. In this hypothetical case, the contract expressly confers the right to terminate on Car Machinery

[36] JE De Becker, *Annotated Civil Code of Japan, vol 2* (1st edn, Butterworth & Co 1909) 146.

[37] The fact scenarios of this and the other hypotheticals discussed in this section are taken from M Chen-Wishart, D Neo, and S Vogenauer, 'Introduction', ch 1 in this volume, 9.

if Traders Ltd fails to visit the car manufacturers as required. Thai Courts generally enforce termination clauses which have been negotiated by the parties, even if they allow termination for a trivial breach, unless the clause contradicts the true intentions of parties or their regular practices. Consequently, once Traders Ltd failed to comply with their contractual obligation, Car Machinery was entitled to terminate the agreement immediately, pursuant to Clause 7(b) of the agreement. However, if it is proved that although the contract provides a right of termination, the parties did not, in practice, regard this breach as fundamental enough to entitle termination of the agreement, the courts might not allow the termination as it would be against the parties' real intentions and the principle of good faith.

(b) Prime Ltd and Devil Corp

Prime Ltd sells a piece of land to Devil Corp. Under the terms of the contract, Devil pays a 10 per cent deposit, the remainder of the sum being due at 5:00 pm on 30 September, time being 'of the essence'. According to Clause 12, failure to meet the deadline would result in the deposit being forfeited and the agreement being terminated. Devil is ten minutes late in tendering the completion money and Prime refuses performance. Can Devil sue for specific performance, arguing that Prime's reliance on the clause is unreasonable in some way? Would the result be different if the contract did not include Clause 12?

The right to terminate is conferred by Clause 12 of the contract between the parties. By stating that failure to meet the deadline would result in the contract being terminated, Prime has expressed its intention to terminate the agreement in advance. If Devil does not perform by the due date, the contract is terminated by virtue of Clause 12. Prime's reliance on the clause is reasonable because the parties have agreed that punctual performance is of the essence of the contract, and no practices of the parties indicate otherwise. A late performance—even if is merely ten minutes late—is still a late performance, which fulfils the condition for the contract to be terminated under Clause 12. Consequently, Devil can no longer claim specific performance since the contract has come to an end.

This hypothetical case must be distinguished from the Supreme Court decision in Case No 8219/2544 (2001), although the facts may seem similar. The defendant in that case agreed to register the transfer of land at the land office on '22 March 1999 at 13:00', and the plaintiff agreed to pay the price on that day. The defendant arrived at the land office on time, while the plaintiff arrived at the land office twenty-five minutes late. The defendant then refused to register the transfer of land. The Court held that the plaintiff was not in default. It is noteworthy that, unlike the hypothetical case, there was no express contractual term stating that the time of the performance of the plaintiff was of the essence. In interpreting the contract, the Court therefore looked into the common intention of the parties and concluded that they intended to complete the transfer process, and for the defendant to receive the payment, that afternoon. The parties did not regard the time of the performance specified in the contract as being so essential that the defendant was entitled to terminate the contract without giving the plaintiff additional time to perform.

If the contract between Prime and Devil is a standard-form contract, the UCTA applies. In order for Clause 12 to be regarded as an unfair term, Devil must successfully prove that the clause causes Devil to perform or assume a burden greater than would be usually expected by a reasonable person. For example, if there are no justifiable reasons as to why time of the performance is so essential to the extent that the contract should be terminated, the termination clause can be deemed unfair.

If the contract between Prime and Devil did not include Clause 12, the right to terminate as specified by the law must be considered. Since the parties have agreed in the contract that the time of the performance is of the essence, and no practices of the parties indicate differently, the situation falls under section 388 TCCC. Applying this section, as Devil has not performed at the specified time, Prime has the right to terminate without having to provide Devil with additional time to perform. However, Prime must declare its intention to terminate to Devil in order for the termination to take effect in accordance with section 386(2). If Prime does not express its intention to terminate, the contract is still valid.

(c) Seven Seas and Big Chef

Seven Seas, an importer of seafood, sells two tons of mussels to Big Chef restaurant chain. After one ton has been delivered it turns out that the concentration of cadmium in the mussels is 2 per cent above the concentration permitted by national food regulations. Can Big Chef terminate the contract?

Since the contract does not provide the right to terminate, the right conferred by the law shall be considered. As Seven Seas delivers mussels that contain cadmium concentrations that are above the permitted standard, this is considered as a non-conforming performance. The degree of such non-conforming performance is serious because the purpose of this purchase is for Big Chef to serve mussels as food in the restaurant. Therefore, delivering poor-quality mussels that cannot be used in the restaurant undermines the objective of this contract and, thus, constitutes a fundamental breach. Big Chef is entitled to terminate the contract under section 387 TCCC, provided that a notice fixing a reasonable period for Seven Seas to perform is given to Seven Seas, and Seven Seas fails to deliver mussels of an acceptable quality within the fixed period. Section 388 does not apply to this case because time is not of the essence, either with respect to the intentions of the parties or the nature of the contract, and in any case, we are not told of any issues with the time of delivery in the hypothetical.

(d) Coco and David

Coco, a famous architect, agrees with David that he will landscape the garden in her next development. He is due to start work on 1 December. For David, this is an important opportunity to make his name as a landscape gardener. On 1 October, she tells him that she is no longer interested because the development will not include a garden after all. David has already purchased materials. He estimates that his future earnings will be 10 per cent lower because he will not be able to benefit from having worked with Coco. Can he insist on doing the work? Can he bring an action for breach of contract?

The right to terminate under the law shall be applied since the contract does not give the right to terminate. A contract between Coco and David is a hire of work under the law. Section 605 TCCC specifically confers a right on an employer to terminate a contract without cause, provided the work has not yet been finished, and compensation is made to the contractor for any injury resulting from the termination. Since David has not yet started the work, Coco is entitled to unilaterally terminate the contract without David's consent, upon making compensation to David. This is different from a repudiatory breach in common law, where the innocent party has an option whether to accept the repudiation, which will bring the contract to an end, or to carry on with performance (unless cooperation of the other party is necessary for performance), which will keep the contract alive.[38]

By telling David that she is no longer interested in hiring him, Coco has declared her intention to terminate to David. Consequently, the contract is terminated. Coco is obliged to compensate David for the price of materials that he has purchased. However, according to section 222 TCCC,[39] David cannot claim the loss of estimated future earnings as damages. The reason is that future earnings is merely an expectation, and it is not certain whether David will actually receive an expected amount of income.[40] To conclude, David can neither insist on doing the work nor bring an action for breach of contract because the termination of the contract by Coco is lawful.

III. Exercising the Right to Terminate

A contract does not terminate automatically when a party is entitled to rescind. The aggrieved party has the right and sole discretion to decide whether or not to end the contractual relationship. If she opts to terminate the contract, she must declare her intention to the other party according to section 386(1) TCCC. Such declaration of intention is sufficient to terminate the contract, and consent from the other party is not necessary.

There is no legal requirement as to the form of the declaration of intention to terminate. Thus, it can be expressed explicitly or implicitly. In Supreme Court Case No 1709/2520 (1977), the seller failed to transfer the purchased land to the buyer. The buyer then hired a lawyer to claim for the price already paid to the seller and demanded that the seller return her the land purchase agreement. The Supreme Court deemed that the buyer had implicitly terminated the agreement.[41]

In determining whether a declaration of intention takes effect, one must assess whether the expression of intention is made to the other contracting party in her presence. If it is made to a person who is present, it becomes effective from the time when the receiver knows of the intention. This includes when an expression is made via telephone, or by any other means, whereby the receiver can perceive the intention simultaneously.[42] In the case where the declaration is made to a person who is not physically present (eg by a letter or an email), it will take effect from the time it reaches the receiver. This declaration can only be withdrawn if the revocation of such intention reaches the receiver before the declaration of intention to terminate, or at the same time.[43] When the expression of an intention to terminate comes into force, the contract ends.

[38] *White & Carter (Councils) Ltd* v *McGregor* [1962] AC 413.

[39] TCCC, s 222(1) states: 'The claim of damages is for compensation for all such damage as usually arises from non-performance.' Paragraph 2 states: 'The creditor may demand compensation even for such damage as has arisen from special circumstances, if the party concerned foresaw or ought to have foreseen such circumstances.'

[40] Supreme Court Decisions Nos 6848/2540 (1997), 4826/2533 (1990), 2692/2529 (1986). In these cases, the Court ruled that estimated future earnings that are not certain cannot be claimed.

[41] See also Supreme Court Decision No 8722/2544 (2001) on very similar facts. In this case, the Court held that the buyer implicitly terminated the contract when she served the seller with a notice demanding the repayment of the price, and claiming for damages.

[42] TCCC, s 168.

[43] TCCC, s 169.

The expression of intention to terminate cannot be revoked.[44] However, in Case No 13145/2558 (2015) concerning an employment agreement, the Supreme Court allowed the parties to agree to revoke a declaration of an intention to terminate. After the employee sent a resignation email to the employer, the parties discussed the matter and agreed to cancel the resignation email. The Supreme Court held that the prohibition under section 386(2) applies only to a unilateral act of a party to withdraw his intention to terminate. It does not apply in a case where both parties agree to cancel, or renounce, a declaration of an intention to terminate. The resignation email was, therefore, revoked.

It should be observed from this decision that permitting a party to later renounce the intention to terminate, even with consent from the other party, creates instability in a relationship between parties.[45] Once the declaration of intention to terminate is effective, it triggers the consequences of the termination. Revoking a declaration of intention to terminate reverses the effects of the termination, leading to uncertainty as to the status of the parties involved. Therefore, in the author's view, even where the parties subsequently agree to withdraw the declaration of an intention to terminate, this should not be considered as a revocation of the declaration under the law but rather the execution of a new contract under the same terms and conditions.

It is recognized by the Supreme Court that an expression of intention to terminate can be made in advance, that is, before a party has a right to terminate. In Case No 4205/2548 (2005), a clause in the hire purchase agreement stipulated that 'In case a hirer makes default in payment of any monthly instalment, the agreement is deemed to be terminated without any notice from the owner.' The Supreme Court affirmed the enforceability of this clause and ruled that when the hirer was in default, the contract was terminated promptly without further notice given to the hirer.[46] It is noteworthy that this type of termination clause must be distinguished from a condition subsequent. A condition subsequent is a clause in an agreement that conditions the end of the effect of such agreement upon a future event that is uncertain (section 182 TCCC). Even though this type of termination clause has a similar effect to a condition subsequent (ie an agreement ends instantly when a specified event occurs), it should not be interpreted as a condition subsequent. A condition subsequent confers on parties the right to expect benefits when the condition is fulfilled.[47] Therefore, the law protects these expectation rights by imposing certain obligations on the parties, for example, an obligation not to do anything that will impair the benefit which the other party might derive from the fulfilment of the condition (section 184 TCCC). If this type of termination clause is regarded as a condition subsequent, obligations with respect to conditions subsequent would be imposed on the parties as well, resulting in unexpected restrictions on the parties. This would be against common practice as well as the intention of parties that intend to employ the clause as a remedy for non-performance. This type of clause should therefore be treated as a termination clause with an advance declaration of intention to terminate.

[44] TCCC, s 386(2).

[45] S Sanongchart, คำอธิบายประมวลกฎหมายแพ่งและพาณิชย์ นิติกรรมสัญญา [*Commentary on the Civil and Commercial Code: Juristic Acts and Contracts*] (11th edn, Nitibannagarn 2014) 519–20.

[46] See also Supreme Court Decisions Nos 9373/2538 (1995) and 914–927/2513 (1970), in which the Supreme Court delivered the same judgment as the decision in Case No 4205/2548 (2005).

[47] Pramoj (n 25) 192–93.

Termination rights are indivisible. In the case where one party to the contract consists of more than one person, section 390 TCCC states the means for such party to exercise the right to terminate, as follows:

> If in a contract there are several persons on the one or the other side, the right of rescission may be exercised only by all and against all. If the right of rescission is extinguished in respect of one of those persons entitled, it is extinguished also in respect of the others.[48]

One contract can only have one termination right, otherwise, it will create confusion among parties as to their contractual relationships. If several persons form one of the parties, the right to terminate cannot be exercised independently. It must be asserted only by all members of that party against all members of the other party. If such right is extinguished with respect to one of the members of the entitled party, it is also extinguished with respect to the others. For example, in a car purchase agreement, assume that the seller's side consists of *A*, *B*, and *C*, while *D* and *E* are on the buyer's side. If the car is completely destroyed due to a fault of *A*, the buyers *D* and *E* will have a right to terminate the agreement according to section 389. *D* and *E* must jointly exercise the termination right against *A*, *B*, and *C* all together. *D* cannot solely assert the termination right without *E*'s consent or claim it only against *A*.

IV. Effects of Termination

1. State of the Law

When a party has exercised the right to terminate by declaring such intention to the other party, and the declaration becomes effective, it brings about the effects of the termination, which are laid down in section 391 TCCC. However, the parties can agree otherwise as the provision is not related to public orders and good morals.[49] The Supreme Court in Case No 2165/2556 (2013) reaffirmed the freedom of parties in this respect. This case concerned the termination of an insurance agency agreement. Clause 26.2 of the agreement stipulated that 'When the agreement is terminated, the insurance company has the right to cease payments of compensation or any other benefits.' The insurance company later terminated the agreement. The agent demanded payment for her services already provided. The Court held that although section 391(3) affirms the right of an agent to claim payment for the services rendered, by agreeing to Clause 26.2, the agent had waived her right to claim such payment.

In the absence of specifically agreed contractual terms relating to the effects of the termination, section 391 shall apply. It states:

> If one party has exercised his right of rescission, each party is bound to restore the other to his former condition; but the right of the third person cannot be impaired.
> To money which is to be repaid in the case of the foregoing paragraph, interest is to be added from the time when it was received.

[48] It was modelled on art 356 of the German Civil Code 1900.
[49] Supreme Court Decisions Nos 1141/2550 (2007) and 3208/2565 (2022).

> For services rendered and for allowing the use of a thing, the restitution shall be made by paying the value, or, if in the contract a counter-payment in money is stipulated for, this shall be paid.
> The exercise of the right of rescission does not affect a claim for damages.[50]

When a contract is terminated, it brings the validity of the contract to an end. Even the courts cannot give a party in breach additional time to perform. The parties are discharged from their obligations under the contract. They can no longer demand specific performance. Unlike English law, where the termination is prospective only, under Thai law, termination has retroactive effect so that the contractual relationship of the parties not only ends for the future but also is cancelled from the beginning.[51] The parties must consequently be restored to their pre-contractual positions. In other words, each party returns all the benefits that she has received under the contract to the other party. For instance, in the case of a car purchase agreement, where the price has already been paid by the buyer, and the car has been transferred to the buyer, if there is a defect in the car and the buyer terminates the agreement, the buyer shall return the car to the seller, and the seller shall return the money to the buyer.

If money must be returned in order to restore the pre-contractual positions, interest at the rate of 3 per cent per year is added according to section 7 TCCC.[52] The interest is calculated from the time the money is received. From the previous example, the seller must return the price of the car, plus 3 per cent interest, calculated from the date the seller received the money.

In the case where a party has provided services under the agreement, the value of the services shall be paid in order to restore the pre-contractual positions. To illustrate, in Supreme Court Case No 3322/2528 (1985), the defendant drilled a water well in accordance with a contract. However, the supply capacity of the water well failed to meet the minimum requirements specified in the contract. The plaintiff terminated the agreement. The Court ordered the plaintiff to pay for the drilling that had been done. In Case No 7618/2552 (2009), the Supreme Court held that the payment for services shall be granted based on the actual value of the services rendered.

If a contract involves giving the other party the use of a thing, a payment for the use of it shall be made to restore the other party to its former condition. From the car purchase example that was previously mentioned, the buyer shall return the car and pay for the use of it from the day on which she received the car until she returns it to the seller. Supreme Court Case No 3849/2552 (2009) involves a real-estate hire-purchase agreement. The hirer terminated the contract because the total property area exceeded what he contracted for. The Supreme Court held that although the hirer did not settle in the house, he had obtained possession of the property. During that period, the owner could not make any use of such property. Consequently, in order to restore the pre-contractual positions according to section 391, the owner had the right to claim payment for the use of the property from the date the property was in the possession of the hirer until the date it was returned to the owner.

[50] This was modelled on art 545 of the Japanese Civil Code 1896 and art 346 of the German Civil Code 1900.
[51] Setthabutr (n 25) 298–99 and Sotthibandhu (n 9) 518–20.
[52] The interest rate was amended from 7.5 per cent per year to 3 per cent per year by the Emergency Decree on Amending the Civil and Commercial Code BE 2564 (2021).

Although the contractual relationship of the parties is wiped out as a result of the termination, the law shields a claim for damages from such effect. It allows a creditor to claim damages even when the contractual relationship no longer exists. Damages may result from non-performance of a debtor or a termination. If a creditor is entitled to claim for damages as a consequence of a debtor's non-performance before the contract is terminated, such right is not prejudiced by the termination of contract. However, damages suffered by a creditor must be proved before the court in order for the court to award damages.

The rights of a third person which have been acquired prior to the rescission of a contract are not impaired by the restoration of the parties to their pre-contractual positions following the termination. For example, A purchases a car from B. B has transferred the car to A, but A has not yet made a payment. A later sells the car to C. A eventually fails to pay the price. Hence, B invokes her right to terminate the contract. As a result, the contract ends. *A* must restore B to her former condition by returning the car to B and paying for the use of it. However, the car has been transferred to C. The right of C, who is a third person, is protected under section 391(1). A is unable to retrieve the car from C. A must then compensate B, by paying the price of the car, in order for the parties to be restored to their pre-contractual positions.

The performance of an obligation to make restitution is governed by section 392 TCCC, which states, 'The obligation of the parties resulting from rescission shall be performed according to the provision of section 369.'[53] The concept of performance in a reciprocal contract, according to section 369, is applied to an obligation to make restitution as well. Under section 369, a party may refuse to perform her obligation until the other party performs or tenders performance of her obligation, unless the other party's obligation is not yet due. Therefore, if one party does not return what she has received under the contract, the other party may refuse to perform an obligation to restitute on her part because the performance of one party is a condition for that party to demand the performance from the other party. The law does not specify which party has to perform its obligation first. Ideally, performance should be done concurrently; that is, both parties should be prepared to perform their respective obligations. The law merely allows the party who is ready to fulfil her obligation to refuse to perform when the other party does not intend to do so.

Thai contract law only provides for retroactive effect of termination pursuant to section 391. Unlike German contract law, there is no specific provision in Thai contract law that governs the termination of a continuing contract, that is, a contract that requires periodic performance, for example, a lease agreement or an employment agreement. However, it is widely accepted by Thai contract law scholars that the effects of the termination of a continuing contract shall not be retroactive. It should instead end the contractual relationship as from the time the contract is rescinded. Therefore, the relationship between parties before the termination remains intact. Unlike the effect specified in section 391, the party does not have an obligation to restore the other party to its former position.[54] However, it is observed from the Supreme Court's decisions[55] that even if a contract is a continuing contract, the Court applies section 391 by analogy to the termination thereof. To illustrate, in Case No 5753/2545 (2002), the Supreme Court held that when a lease agreement is terminated,

53 It was modelled on art 348 of the German Civil Code 1900.
54 Setthabutr (n 25) 302; Sotthibandhu (n 9) 528; Sanongchart (n 45) 508.
55 Supreme Court Decisions Nos 12803/2557 (2014) and 457/2553 (2010).

the parties must restore each other to their former condition, according to section 391(1). It can be understood that the effect of the termination in section 391 is applied in analogy to a lease agreement—a continuing contract—to make the lessee return the leased property to the lessor and to allow the lessor to claim for damages under paragraph 4 of the same section. Nevertheless, the Court did not demand that the lessor return all rental payments received.

2. Hypothetical: Bob and Sue

Bob contracts to build a house for Sue for the price of $100,000. After doing one-third of the work he abandons the job, leaving behind material worth $15,000 which Sue later uses to finish the works. Can Bob claim the value of the work done or of the materials?

By abandoning the job, Bob is in breach of contract. If Sue opts to terminate the contract, she must serve Bob a notice fixing a reasonable period and demand that Bob perform within such period. If Bob again fails to perform within the additional period, Sue has the right to terminate, pursuant to section 387 TCCC. When Sue exercises the right, the contract is rescinded. Bob and Sue must be restored to their pre-contractual positions. Since Bob has done a third of the work, Sue must pay Bob the value of the work done, according to section 391(3). In regard to the materials worth $15,000, Sue must also pay the price for such materials so that the parties can be restored to their pre-contractual positions. If Sue suffers from any damage that results from the non-performance or the termination, she can also claim damages according to section 391(4). To conclude, Bob can claim both the value of the work done and the price of materials. However, Bob and Sue can contractually provide for different effects of termination since section 391 is not a law relating to public order or good morals.

V. Conclusion

This chapter provides an overview of the termination of contracts in Thai law. In summary, a contract can be terminated by mutual consent of the parties or by a unilateral act of one party having the right to terminate. The right to terminate comes from either a contract or the law. If the contract does not provide the right to terminate, parties must seek the right under the law, that is, specific contract law and general contract law. Where provisions of specific contract law are not applicable, general contract law shall apply. The right to terminate under the general contract law consists of three main provisions: sections 387, 388, and 389 TCCC. Section 387 is a general provision which grants the right to terminate once a creditor has given a debtor a second chance to perform. Sections 388 and 389 operate as exceptions, where a second chance need not be given. Section 388 applies in cases where time of performance is of the essence, while section 389 applies to cases where performance becomes impossible, and such impossibility is attributable to a debtor. A party who has the right to terminate has a choice as to whether or not to end the contract. If the party opts for termination, she must declare her intention to terminate to the other party, according to section 386 TCCC. When the declaration takes effect, the contract ends with retroactive effect, whereby the parties must be restored to their pre-contractual positions. However, the right to claim for damages is not impaired, pursuant to section 391 TCCC. Given that these provisions on termination of contracts are a derivative of the old Japanese and German contract laws, Japanese and German law continue to have considerable influence on the interpretation of the provisions. As we have seen in the ongoing debate about the application of the principle of fault to Thai law, the sourced law is used to guide interpretation.

26

Change of Circumstances under Vietnamese Contract Law

DO Giang Nam

I. Introduction

It is well established under Vietnamese contract law that the doctrine of *force majeure* is a major exception to the principle of *pacta sunt servanda*. The doctrine of *force majeure* is concerned with the non-performance of the contract where the failure to perform is due to the occurrence of a supervening event but not the obligor's (or as Vietnamese lawyers would say with regard to all types of obligation, the 'debtor's') fault.[1] When the debtor can prove that a supervening event sufficiently constitutes a case of *force majeure* which makes his or her performance impossible, he or she can be exempted from civil liability. Apart from such *force majeure* events causing the impossibility of performance, it was, until recently, irrelevant under Vietnamese contract law whether a supervening event only made performance severely onerous to a contracting party. Thus, the position of Vietnamese contract law up until the introduction of the revised Vietnamese Civil Code (VCC) in 2015 can be referred to as an 'all-or-nothing' model: either performance is made impossible and the debtor is exempted from damages on the ground of *force majeure* or the contract has to be performed at whatever cost.[2]

However, it was argued that the traditional 'all-or-nothing' approach was too rigid to satisfy the demand of a modern economy where parties are frequently faced with an unforeseeable change of circumstances in comparison with the circumstances that existed at the time of contracting.[3] In early 2015, a historic public consultation was organized in Vietnam to gather people's opinions on ten major issues related to the revision of the VCC.[4] Number eight on the list of these issues was whether the new VCC should introduce the doctrine of

[1] Nông Quốc Bình, 'Một số vấn đề lý luận và thực tiễn đối với vấn đề bất khả kháng trong hợp đồng' (2012) 5 Tạp chí Luật học ['Several Theoretical and Practical Aspects of Force Majeure in Contracts' (2012) 5 The Journal of Legal Studies] 10.

[2] Lê Minh Hùng, *Hiệu lực của Hợp đồng* (Nhà Xuất Bản Hồng Đức 2015) [*Validity of Contract* (Hong Duc Press 2015)] 153.

[3] Phạm Duy Nghĩa, 'Điều Chỉnh Thông Tin Bất Cân Xứng và Quản Lý Rủi Ro trong Pháp Luật Hợp Đồng Việt Nam' in Nguyễn Như Phát and Lê Thị Thuy Thuỷ (eds), *Một Số Vấn Đề Lý Luận và Thực Tiễn về Pháp Luật Hợp Đồng Việt Nam Hiện nay* (Nhà Xuất Bản Công An Nhân Dân 2003) [Pham Duy Nghia, 'Regulating the Information Asymmetry and Governing the Risk in Vietnamese Contract Law' in Nguyen Nhu Phat and Le Thi Thu Thuy (eds), *A Number of Theoretical and Practical Issues in Vietnamese Contract Law* (The People's Police Press 2003)] 32.

[4] Quyết định số 1/QĐ-TTg ngày 2/1/2015 của Thủ Tướng ban hành Kế hoạch của Chính Phủ về việc tổ chức lấy ý kiến Nhân dân đối với dự thảo Bộ Luật Dân Sự (sửa đổi) [Decision No 1/QĐ-TTg dated 2 January 2015 of the prime minister declaring a plan for gathering People's Opinion about the Draft of the Civil Code (Amendment)].

Do Giang Nam, *Change of Circumstances under Vietnamese Contract Law* In: *Studies in the Contract Laws of Asia V: Ending and Changing Contracts*. Edited by: Mindy Chen-Wishart, Dora Neo, and Stefan Vogenauer, Oxford University Press.
 DOI: 10.1093/oso/9780198995814.003.0026

'change of circumstances' that would allow courts to modify contracts upon the occurrence of unforeseen circumstances which fundamentally affect the rights and interests of a party.[5] Consequently, the VCC 2015 introduced Article 420, entitled 'Performance of contract in the case of a fundamental change of circumstances'. As a result, the current Vietnamese contract law recognizes both the doctrine of *force majeure* and the doctrine of change of circumstances as core exceptions to the principle of *pacta sunt servanda*. The former aims to deal with legal effects of supervening events which make performance impossible, whereas the latter is concerned with mechanisms responding to supervening events which make performance more onerous.

Against this backdrop, the present chapter will examine the doctrine of change of circumstances in Vietnamese contract law. It consists of seven sections. After the introduction, sections II and III will be devoted to presenting the detailed discussions about the enactment of the provisions for a change of circumstances in the VCC 2015 and its position within the system of Vietnamese contract law. Then, sections IV and V will study the legal requirements and legal effects of the doctrine of change of circumstances in detail. Section VI will present the author's arguments regarding several hypotheticals set by the editors to lay the foundation for further functional comparison between Vietnamese law and other Asian jurisdictions. The final section will offer some concluding remarks.

II. Discussions Preceding the Introduction of the Doctrine of Change of Circumstances

On the occasion of re-codifying Vietnamese private law, the Vietnamese government made numerous efforts to establish a new doctrine of change of circumstances in order to protect the rights of the affected party in hardship. Nevertheless, the mere fact that the introduction of this doctrine was selected as one of the ten major issues submitted to a public opinion poll reveals that the Vietnamese legislators were particularly cautious with the content of the draft provision codifying the doctrine. Among numerous opinions collected from the public, the majority expressed their adherence to the government decision of introducing the doctrine of change of circumstances as a necessary legal mechanism to react to economic and social instability. Others who supported this doctrine in principle still forcefully expressed their concerns about the proposed design of the legal requirements and remedies for a fundamental change of circumstances. Specifically, they were worried that the unwise design of such a provision would lead to the undesired effect of thwarting legal certainty—one of the core values of Vietnamese contract law, which the Vietnamese legal community had been tirelessly struggling to achieve for more than 20 years.

[5] Bùi Đăng Hiếu, 'Góp Ý về 10 Vấn Đề Trọng Tâm Lấy Ý Kiến Nhân Dân Trong Dự Thảo Bộ Luật Dân Sự (Sửa Đổi)' (2015) 6 Tạp Chí Luật học [Bui Dang Hieu, 'Comments on 10 Fundamental Issues Gathering People's Opinions on the Draft of the Civil Code (Amendment)' (2015) 6 Journal of Legal Studies] 5–11.

1. Justifications for Introducing the Doctrine of Change of Circumstances

The *travaux préparatoires* of the VCC 2015 reveal three main reasons justifying the necessity to adopt the doctrine of change of circumstances: (i) this doctrine is needed to react to the distortion of the contractual equilibrium caused by unforeseen circumstances; (ii) this doctrine has its theoretical foundation in the principle of good faith; and (iii) it is in line with the general global trend of recognizing a separate doctrine of change of circumstances.[6]

First of all, this doctrine is necessary to mitigate the distortion of the contractual equilibrium when a change of circumstances makes the performance in the new situation completely different to that agreed upon when originally concluding the contract. Despite recognizing the fundamental role of the principle of *pacta sunt servanda*, the Vietnamese legislator opined that there should be exceptions to this principle in order to maintain the contractual equilibrium established by the parties.[7] In the event that a fundamental change of circumstances after the formation of a contract completely destroys this contractual equilibrium, the parties should not be obliged to continue with the performance of the contract if such performance causes serious damage to the affected party. Instead, so the argument went, the revised VCC should provide for an appropriate mechanism to make it easier for the parties to re-establish a contractual equilibrium that reflects the new situation.[8]

Secondly, the doctrine of change of circumstances is a concretization of the principle of good faith at the stage of contract performance. Under Vietnamese private law, good faith is regarded as the fundamental value governing the entire life of the contract, ranging from pre-contractual negotiations to the formation of the contract itself and eventually its performance.[9] In particular, it requires the parties to perform contractual obligations honestly, in the spirit of cooperation, and to the best benefits of both parties. As a shield of justice, the principle of good faith restricts the exercise of contractual rights if enforcing them would lead to the abuse of certain rights.[10] As a sword of justice, it plays a supplementary role which allows the court to fill the gaps left in the law.[11] To put it differently, the principle of

[6] Bộ Tư Pháp, *Những Điểm Mới Cơ Bản Của Bộ Luật Dân Sự 2015* (Nhà Xuất Bản Lao Động 2018) [Ministry of Justice, *On the Fundamental New Provisions of the 2015 Civil Code* (Labour Press 2018)] 184–85; Đỗ Văn Đại, *Bình Luận Khoa Học Những Điểm Mới Của Bộ Luật Dân Sự Năm 2015* (Xuất bản lần thứ 2, Nhà Xuất Bản Hồng Đức 2016) [Do Van Dai, *Commentary on New Provisions of the 2015 Civil Code* (2nd edn, Hong Duc Press 2016)] 385–86.

[7] In Vietnamese literature, in order to argue for the doctrine of change of circumstances, several authors also mentioned the classic idea of *rebus sic stantibus* ('the binding force of a contract is subject to the condition that the circumstances present at the formation of contract remain constant'). Nguyễn Thế Đức Tâm and Ngô Thu Trang, 'Thực hiện hợp đồng khi hoàn cảnh thay đổi cơ bản' (2017) 1 Tạp chí Nhà Nước và Pháp Luật [Nguyen The Duc Tam and Ngo Thu Trang, 'Performance of Contract in the Case of Fundamental Change of Circumstances' (2017) 1 Journal of State and Law] 60.

[8] Bộ Tư Pháp (n 6) 185.

[9] Different scholars have argued that the idea of good faith actually has its roots in Vietnamese traditional society where Confucian moral concepts such as benevolence played a central role in educating people. See Hoàng Thế Liên (ed), *Bình Luận Khoa Học Bộ Luật Dân Sự Năm 2005* (Nhà xuất bản chính trị quốc gia 2008) [Hoang The Lien (ed), *Scientific Commentary on the Civil Code of 2005, vol 1* (National Political Press 2008)] 29. Therefore, it is not surprising that the Central Civil Code promulgated in 1936 included a provision stipulating that '[t]he parties have an obligation of goodwill in their contractual relationships'. Following that legislative tradition, the 1995, 2005, and 2015 iterations of the Civil Code all recognized good faith as a central concept not only in contractual relationships but also concerning all civil juridical acts. For example, Civil Code 2005, art 6 states that in civil relations, the parties must act with 'goodwill and honesty' in the establishment and implementation of private law rights and obligations.

[10] Le Net, *Contract Law in Vietnam* (Kluwer Law International 2012) 62.

[11] ibid.

good faith under Vietnamese contract law does not merely mean that a party has a 'negative duty' not to deceive the other party; rather, by its very nature, it is a principle of cooperation which imposes a 'positive duty' on a party to take the legal rights and interests of other persons into account and then to assist and create the necessary conditions for each other to perform private law rights and obligations. Due to its adaptability, the concept of good faith enables judges to fill in legislative and doctrinal gaps in order to respond to the social developments in Vietnam.[12] Be that as it may, it has been commonly argued that it is for reasons of legal predictability and certainty that the legislator must present a separate doctrine of change of circumstances to specifically address the effects of unforeseen circumstances, instead of leaving such situations to be interpreted by judges according to the general principle of good faith.[13] To this extent, the introduction of the doctrine of change of circumstances is justified as a further concretization of the general principle of good faith and cooperation at the performance stage of a contract.

Last but not least, the introduction of the doctrine of change of circumstances is justified by the fact that many jurisdictions have successfully enacted relevant provisions. According to a report on comparative law in preparation for the reform of the VCC, the drafting committee concluded that the common trend of contract law in other jurisdictions was to recognize the doctrine of change of circumstances as a legal mechanism to protect the rights of a disadvantaged party who is severely affected by a fundamental change in social, political, or

[12] Although there were no separate legal grounds in general private law for the adaptation of a contract in case of a change of circumstances, it should be noted that in a limited number of cases, Vietnamese courts and arbitral tribunals have, in practice, invoked the general principle of good faith to do so. For instance, in a dispute relating to the sale of trucks, the two parties had agreed on the price of Vietnamese dong (vnd) 120,000,000 (equivalent to around US$4,500), and the buyer had transferred the amount of 20,000,000 as a deposit to the seller. However, the seller requested an increase of 30,000,000 in the price of the trucks because at the time of delivery a new regulation requiring a higher standard of gas emission control had been introduced, which forced the seller to adjust the price accordingly. The seller also gave notice that if the buyer did not agree, he would have to terminate the contract and willingly refund the deposit. The court held that although the promulgation of the new regulation occurred after the formation of the sales contract and was beyond the control of the parties, there was no *force majeure* because the event did not make the performance of the contract impossible. However, the court advised that the parties should negotiate to adjust the price in accordance with this change of circumstances. Apparently, the court applied the principle of good faith in a flexible manner in order to facilitate the reaching of a new agreement which would minimize the cost of performance on the part of the seller. This judgment of the Govap Court in 2008 is unpublished but has been made available by Professor Do Van Dai; since then it has been widely discussed by other authors: Đỗ Văn Đại, 'Bàn thêm về điều chỉnh hợp đồng khi hoàn cảnh thay đổi cơ bản' (2015) 13 Tạp chí Nghiên cứu Lập pháp [Do Van Dai, 'On the Adjustment of Contract in the Case of a Fundamental Change of Circumstances' (2015) 13 Journal of Legislative Studies] 31.

In another case relating to a five-year sales contract between a Vietnamese company (buyer) and a foreign company (seller), after two years of performance, the two sides argued about the price of goods in the third year as a significant decrease in the price of raw materials led to the decrease of the market price of the goods down to three times as compared to the agreed price. The arbitral tribunal constituted under the auspices of the Vietnam International Arbitration Center (VIAC) reasoned that since the two sides could not reasonably have foreseen the change of the price of raw materials, it would be unfair if the buyer alone had to bear the risks of market fluctuation. Hence, the arbitrators advised the parties to modify the contract in order to mutually share such risks: see VIAC, *Resolving the Contractual Disputes—Several Issues That the Trader Must Understand* (Youth Publisher 2019) 116.

Certainly, these two typical cases in Vietnamese practice highlighted that even though the court and arbitrators had wisely invoked the principle of good faith to base their decisions on, the difficulties arose from the fact that there was no clear, separate mechanism to address the effect of unforeseen circumstances which merely made the contract performance extremely difficult, but not impossible.

[13] Nguyễn Anh Thư, 'Đề Xuất Sửa Đổi Bổ Sung Quy Định Liên Quan Đến Nguyên Tắc Thiện Chí Trong Bộ Luật Dân Sự năm 2005' (2014) 3 Tạp Chí Khoa Học, Đại Học Quốc Gia Hà Nội: Luật Học [Nguyen Anh Thu, 'Proposals to Modify and Supplement Provisions Relating to the Principle of Good Faith in the Vietnamese Civil Code 2005' (2014) 3 The Journal of Science, Vietnam National University: Legal Studies] 61; Đỗ Văn Đại (n 12) 32.

economic conditions.[14] This is evidenced by the introduction of this doctrine, albeit under different names, in the 2002 reform of the German Civil Code (*Bürgerliches Gesetzbuch*, BGB) or the draft of the 2016 revision of the French Civil Code, as well as in soft law instruments such as the UNIDROIT Principles of International Commercial Contracts (PICC) and the Principles of European Contract Law (PECL).[15] Notably, the provisions on hardship in the PICC and the PECL have been used as a model to design the content of the doctrine of change of circumstances in the VCC 2015. In fact, the draft version of the new VCC submitted to the Vietnamese National Assembly in 2014 copied most of the provisions on hardship from the PECL and the PICC as follows:

1. In case the change of circumstances severely affects the rights of the disadvantaged party, the parties are entitled to adjust the contract.
2. A change of circumstances is proved when the occurrence of events fundamentally alters the equilibrium of the contract; furthermore, such change must meet the following requirements:
   (a) the change of circumstances occurred after the time of conclusion of the contract;
   (b) the change of circumstances could not have been reasonably foreseen at the time of conclusion of the contract;
   (c) the risks arising from the change of circumstances should not be assumed by the disadvantaged party.
3. In case the parties fail to reach agreement within a reasonable time, the court may:
   (a) terminate the contract at a date and on terms to be fixed by the court;
   (b) adapt the contract with a view to redistributing between the parties the losses and gains arising from the change of circumstances in a fair and equitable manner.

[14] Bộ Tư Pháp (n 6) 185; Nguyễn Văn Cừ and Trần Thị Huệ (eds), *Bình luận khoa học BLDS 2015* (Nhà Xuất Bản Công An Nhân Dân 2016) [Nguyen Van Cu and Tran Thi Hue (eds), *Scientific Commentary on the 2015 Civil Code* (The People's Police Press 2016)] 634.

[15] During the period 2014–2015, in order to improve the quality of the new Civil Code, the Vietnamese government consulted many international experts as to the contents of the draft revision, especially concerning ten major controversial issues. Among them was Professor Hannes Rösler, a well-known German expert on the topic of change of circumstances. He delivered two important lectures which comprehensively introduced the German doctrine of 'interference with the basis of the transaction' *(Störung der Geschäftsgrundlage)* and the contents of BGB, s 313 to the drafting committee. Arguably, his lectures partly led the drafting committee to revise the contents of the 2014 Draft, art 423. As will be discussed later, the current wording of art 420 seems to be influenced by BGB, s 313. The main evidence is that under the current law, the change of circumstances is relevant only if the claimant is able to show that the parties would not have entered into the contract or would have entered into it with different contents if they had foreseen this change. Certainly, this is not the language of the PICC but the BGB.

See H Rösler, 'Controversial Issues in the Drafted Revision of the Vietnamese Civil Code' (2014) International Workshop, GIZ-Projekt mit dem Regierungsbüro von Vietnam im Rahmen des deutsch-vietnamesischen Rechtsstaatsdialoges [Project run by the German GIZ in cooperation with the Vietnamese government as part of the Germany–Vietnam Rule of Law Dialogue], Hai Phong/Vietnam, 6–8 June; H Rösler, 'The Codification of Civil Law—Vietnam and the German Experience' (2015) International Workshop, GIZ-Projekt mit dem Regierungsbüro von Vietnam im Rahmen des deutsch-vietnamesischen Rechtsstaatsdialoges [Project run by the German GIZ in cooperation with the Vietnamese government as part of the Germany–Vietnam Rule of Law Dialogue], Ninh Binh/Vietnam, 2–3 April. Apart from learning from German law, at that time the drafting committee was fully aware of the contents of PECL, art 6:111 and PICC, arts 6.2.1–6.2.3 as well as of the fact that the French were preparing to introduce the doctrine of *imprévision* into their revised Code Civil.

The court may, in either case, order the party who refused to renegotiate or broke off the renegotiation process in bad faith to pay damages.[16]

2. Major Concerns: Desirability and Feasibility of Judicial Contract Modification

Although it was widely supported that a fundamental change of circumstances should constitute legal grounds for releasing the disadvantaged party from being bound to a performance which has become excessively onerous to him or her, various opinions raised in this regard showcased the serious concerns as to the desirability and feasibility of judicial modification of contract.

The first line of argument points out that a judicial modification of contract is undesirable because it is irreconcilable with the underlying value of party autonomy and the principle of *pacta sunt servanda*.[17] As mentioned above, at the heart of the first wave of codification of Vietnamese private law lay the tireless effort by the Vietnamese legal community to support private endeavours to pursue wealth maximization by conferring powers on private parties to freely decide on the content of their contracts and to enforce their transactions. Accordingly, respect for the freedom of contract, as one of the main manifestations of party autonomy, has been ensured in both positive and negative ways under Vietnamese contract law. While positive freedom of contract enables contracting parties to establish private law rights for themselves through their agreements, negative freedom of contract guarantees that the parties are free from any obligations unless those obligations are the legal consequence of their free will. Therefore, concern has been voiced extensively about whether the courts should be given the power to make a contract for the parties. Indeed, if the binding force of contract is justified on the basis of the free will of the contracting parties, judicial modification of contract would be considered as not only a threat to the freedom of contract and *pacta sunt servanda* but also an illegitimate interference with contractual arrangements.

A second argument against judicial modification of contracts was that judges lack the necessary expertise to supply the contractual terms for the parties.[18] In fact, the cases relating to the issue of a fundamental change of circumstances are usually concerned with complex long-term contracts, which makes it exceedingly challenging for judges to fully grasp the economic foundation of the contract. Hence, giving the courts wide discretion may lead to cases where a contract is adjusted in an inadequate and unsatisfactory manner. In the context of legal certainty, a judicial modification of contract without clear legislative guidance or a reliable system of case law may cause the risk of arbitrary court decisions.

Taking into account the two aforementioned criticisms, the Vietnamese legislator amended the provisional draft with regard to judicial modification of contracts as one of the remedies for a fundamental change of circumstances and adopted a more cautious position.

[16] Unless indicated otherwise, all translations of legislation and case law from Vietnamese into English are by the author.

[17] Bùi Đăng Hiếu (n 5) 10.

[18] Nguyễn Văn Cừ and Trần Thị Huệ (n 14) 634.

Indeed, the version that was eventually adopted deviated from the PICC model by allowing the judges to resort to a judicial modification of contract only in cases where a termination of the contract would lead to more severe damages compared to those potentially caused by judicial modification. This deviation is a distinctive element of the Vietnamese doctrine of change of circumstances in the sense that termination of the contract takes precedence over modification of contract.

III. The Doctrine of Change of Circumstances under Vietnamese Contract Law Today

As a result of these lively debates, the doctrine of change of circumstances was eventually incorporated into the VCC 2015 as Article 420, with the heading 'Performance of contract in the case of a fundamental change of circumstances':

1. Circumstances shall be deemed to change fundamentally when the following requirements are met:
   (a) a change of circumstances occurs for objective reasons and after the conclusion of the contract;
   (b) at the time of the conclusion of the contract, the parties could not have foreseen the change of circumstances;
   (c) the change of circumstances is so fundamental that the contract would not have been concluded or would have been concluded with a completely different content if the parties had foreseen such change;
   (d) the continued performance of the contract without adapting its contents will cause serious damage to one party;
   (e) the party whose benefits are affected has taken all necessary measures to the best of its ability and appropriate with the nature of the contract but is unable to prevent or mitigate the level to which the benefits are affected.
2. If circumstances change fundamentally, the disadvantaged party is entitled to request the other party to re-negotiate the contract within a reasonable time.
3. If the parties are unable to reach agreement on adaptation of the contract within a reasonable time, either party may request a court to:
   (a) terminate the contract at a date to be fixed;
   (b) adapt the contract with a view to rebalancing legitimate rights and benefits of the parties which were affected due to the fundamental change of circumstances.

   The court is only permitted to make a decision on adaptation of the contract in the case that termination of the contract will cause damage of an amount higher than the cost for performance of the contract if the contract is adapted.
4. During the process of negotiating an adaptation or termination of the contract and during the period the court resolves the case, the parties must continue to perform their obligations under the contract, unless otherwise agreed.

It must be very clear from the outset that under Vietnamese law the doctrine of change of circumstances is only an exception to the highly valued principle of *pacta sunt servanda*, which is embodied by Article 3(2) VCC 2015 as follows:

> Individuals and legal entities establish, perform and terminate their civil rights and obligations on the basis of free and voluntary commitments and agreements. Any commitment or agreement which does not violate a prohibition by law or is not contrary to social ethics is valid for performance by the parties and must be respected by other subjects.

Accordingly, contractual obligations which are lawfully created must be strictly performed by the contracting parties. Once the parties have expressed their intention to be legally bound to the contractual obligations, the principle of *pacta sunt servanda* implies that they cannot release themselves from the obligations, regardless of any burden the performance entails.[19] In this sense, the doctrine of change of circumstances must be applied in exceptional cases only, when the unforeseen circumstances make the performance not merely onerous but in fact onerous to an extreme degree.[20]

Moreover, as mentioned above, even before the introduction of the doctrine of change of circumstances, parties were not fully entitled to their rights as set out in the terms of the original contract if the non-performing party could prove that her failure to perform was justified by a *force majeure* event. However, a fundamental shift occurred with the introduction of the provision of 'changed circumstances' into the VCC 2015: the rigid approach of an 'all-or-nothing' solution based solely on the doctrine of *force majeure* gave way to the more flexible approach of the change of circumstances doctrine, which also covers situations where a supervening event merely causes contract performance to become excessively onerous.

While both change of circumstances and *force majeure* can have effects on the possibility of the non-performance of contractual obligations, in contrast to the newly developed doctrine of change of circumstances, the content of the doctrine of *force majeure* is well established in Vietnamese contract law. Its structure as set out in the VCC 2015 is complex, but it was already provided for in the two earlier Civil Codes and has thus been discussed extensively by legal scholars.[21] Under Vietnamese law, *force majeure* is largely understood

[19] Nguyễn Ngọc Điện, *Giáo Trình Luật Dân Sự Việt Nam, Tập 2* (Nhà Xuất Bản Đại Học Quốc Gia TP Hồ Chí Minh 2018) [Nguyen Ngoc Dien, *Textbook on Vietnam's Civil Law, vol II* (The Vietnam National University Ho Chi Minh Press 2018)] 107.

[20] Besides the 2015 version of the Civil Code, in several pieces of legislation governing specific fields of contracts such as insurance or construction contracts, Vietnamese law has also recognized the mechanism of modification of contract to react to supervening events. In the field of insurance contracts, the Law on Insurance Business 2000 has enshrined the right of disadvantaged parties to request an adaptation of price when there is a fundamental change of surrounding factors. Similarly, in the field of construction contracts, the Construction Law 2000 also provides that the content of a construction contract regarding state funds can be adjusted in cases of a change of circumstances.

[21] At present, both the VCC 2015 and the Commercial Law 2005 provide that *force majeure* is an exemption from the liability for non-performance of a contract. The complexity arises from the interplay of various rules: while the Commercial Law 2005 does not provide for a definition of *force majeure* as it frequently does with other important concepts under art 3 (on the interpretation of terms), the VCC 2015 only defines the meaning of an event of *force majeure* in art 156, located in the section dealing with limitation periods, which is contained in Part I: General Provisions. The main function of art 156 is thus not to address the doctrine of *force majeure* in contract law but to define time periods excluded from limitation periods for initiating legal action for civil cases. Certainly, by virtue of VCC 2015, art 6, it is always possible and necessary to apply art 156 analogously when ascertaining whether an event is qualified as an event of *force majeure*. However, the lack of a general concept of *force majeure* within contract law is still regrettable, especially taking into account the fact that the Commercial Law 1997 enshrined the concept of *force majeure* in art 77, which reads: 'Events of *force majeure* are unexpected external events occurring after the conclusion of contract which are unforeseeable and beyond the control of the parties.'

as an objective event that is unforeseeable and irresistible. Indeed, an event is only qualified as *force majeure* if it meets three requirements: (i) it must be an event that is objectively beyond the control of the debtor and occurred after the formation of contract; (ii) such event could not be reasonably taken into account by the parties; and (iii) such event and its effects are insurmountable.[22] Once the debtor provides evidence that meets the three requirements, she is excused from liability even if she fails to fully perform the contract.

Undoubtedly, the doctrines of *force majeure* and change of circumstances have different roles to play under the current Vietnamese contract law. The VCC 2015 deals with the doctrine of *force majeure* in the chapter on 'civil liability', whereas the doctrine of change of circumstances is positioned in the chapter on performance of contract. On the one hand, the doctrine of *force majeure* is considered an important subject within the question of legal remedies for non-performance. It deals with the issue of whether the occurrence of a supervening event can exempt the non-performing party from liability for damages. On the other hand, the doctrine of change of circumstances plays out in the context of contract performance. It concerns the question of what will happen if a fundamental change of circumstances makes the performance of a contract excessively onerous to the debtor.[23]

While the theory is clear, the distinction between the factual situations where each of those doctrines is applied proves more complicated. Some scholars emphasize the objective nature of the event and believe that *force majeure* usually concerns natural events happening beyond the parties' ability to predict, while the doctrine of change of circumstances usually applies when there is a fundamental change of policy or change of economic or social context affecting the performance of contract. However, it is widely held that under Vietnamese law, *force majeure* may not necessarily be connected to natural events, for instance a storm, but also to others, such as a work strike.[24] For this reason, the distinction between these two doctrines should not be based on the nature of events but on the impact of such events on the parties' ability to perform the contract in practice. Indeed, the concept of impossibility of performance distinguishes *force majeure* from change of circumstances: while under the former, unforeseeable events make performance impossible, under the latter, performance is only made exceptionally onerous, yet still making it unfair to hold the disadvantaged party to the originally agreed terms.

Additionally, once a ground for a fundamental change of circumstances can be established, the disadvantaged party will frequently request a modification of the contract; however, the other party, who maintains an interest in performance despite the change of circumstances, will often oppose such application and insist on specific performance of the contract. In this context, it must be noted that under Vietnamese law, contrary to

Nguyễn Ngọc Điện (n 19) 116; Đỗ Văn Đại, *Luật Hợp Đồng Việt Nam: Bản Án và Bình Luận Bản Án, Tập 2* (Nhà Xuất Bản Hồng Đức 2017) [Do Van Dai, *The Contract Law of Vietnam: Cases and Commentary, vol II* (6th edn, Hong Duc Press 2017)] 517; Khúc Thị Trang Nhung, 'Về miễn trách nhiệm bồi thường thiệt hại do vi phạm hợp đồng theo Bộ luật dân sự 2015' (2016) 1 Tạp chí Kiểm sát [Khuc Thi Trang Nhung, 'On the Exemption of Liability for Damages in the 2015 Civil Code' (2016) 1 Journal of Prosecution] 43.

[22] Đỗ Văn Đại (n 21) 517.
[23] Vũ Thị Lan Anh, 'Các vấn đề pháp lý đặt ra trong việc thực hiện hợp đồng khi hoàn cảnh thay đổi' (2016) 5 Tạp chí Nhà Nước và Pháp Luật [Vu Thi Lan Anh, 'On Legal Issues About the Performance of Contract in the Case of a Change of Circumstances' (2016) 5 Journal of State and Law] 32.
[24] Đỗ Văn Đại (n 21) 518.

various other jurisdictions,[25] the specific performance of contract is designed as an absolute regime without any exceptions. During the negotiating process of the VCC 2015, it was indicated that even in civil law jurisdictions where specific performance of contract is a primary remedy for breach of contract, some limitations of this remedy are still provided in order to protect the legitimate interests of the debtors.[26] In particular, it was proposed that Vietnamese law should learn from the PICC provisions which do not allow the obligee to request specific performance of contract if such performance results in unreasonable burdens or expenditure which is in gross disproportion to the debtor's interest.[27]

Certainly, a closer look at Vietnamese contract law reveals a number of possible solutions to this matter. For instance, the general limitations on exercising private law rights as provided for under Article 10 VCC 2015 (which prohibits abuse of rights by the parties) may be interpreted by the court so as to refuse applying the specific performance remedy if it creates excessive unfairness for one of the parties. However, interpreting and applying a general principle, such as the one codified in Article 10, rather than designing a new specific provision always bears the risk of uncertainty. Accordingly, the doctrine of fundamental change of circumstances as enshrined in Article 420 VCC 2015 is the most important and practicable mechanism for safeguarding the rights of the weaker parties from excessive unfairness during the performance of contract.

IV. Legal Requirements of the Doctrine of Fundamental Change of Circumstances

According to paragraph 1 of Article 420 VCC 2015, a disadvantaged party can only apply for the modification or termination of a contract if this party can prove the following five cumulative elements constituting a fundamental change of circumstances.

[25] By way of comparison, see BGB s 275(2), as translated in BS Markesinis, H Unberath, and A Johnston, *The German Law of Contract* (2nd edn, Hart Publishing 2006) 886:

> The debtor can refuse performance in so far as this requires expenditure which is in gross disproportion to the creditor's interest in performance, having regard to the content of the obligation relationship and the requirement of good faith. When determining the efforts to be expected of the debtor, consideration must also be given to whether the debtor is responsible for the hindrance to performance.

PECL, art 9:102 (Non-monetary Obligations): '(1) The aggrieved party is entitled to specific performance of an obligation other than one to pay money, including the remedying of a defective performance. (2) Specific performance cannot, however, be obtained where: . . . or (b) *performance would cause the obligor unreasonable effort or expense*; . . .' (emphasis added); PICC, art 7.2.2 (Performance of non-monetary obligation): 'Where a party who owes an obligation other than one to pay money does not perform, the other party may require performance, unless . . . (b) performance or, where relevant, enforcement is unreasonably burdensome or expensive.'

[26] Đỗ Văn Đại, *Biện pháp xử lý việc không thực hiện đúng hợp đồng trong pháp luật Việt Nam* (Nhà Xuất Bản Chính trị Quốc Gia 2012) [Do Van Dai, *Remedy for Non-performance of Contract under Vietnamese Contract Law* (National Politics Press 2012) 60.]; Nguyễn Thanh Tùng, 'Bất cập trong việc áp dụng chế tài buộc thực hiện đúng hợp đồng và tạm ngừng thực hiện hợp đồng trong thương mại: Một số kiến nghị' (2015) 7 Tạp chí Luật học [Nguyen Thanh Tung, 'On the Inadequacies of Practical Applications of Remedies of Specific Performance in Commercial Contracts: Several Recommendations' (2015) 7 Journal of Legal Studies] 67.

[27] Đỗ Văn Đại (n 26) 63. For a recent overview of the development of the remedy of specific performance, see Nguyễn Văn Hiển and Đỗ Giang Nam, 'Biện pháp xử lý việc không thực hiện đúng hợp đồng trong pháp luật Việt Nam' (2019) 5 Tạp chí Nghiên Cứu Lập Pháp [Nguyen Van Hien and Do Giang Nam, 'Remedy for Non-performance of Contract under Vietnamese Contract Law' (2019) 5 Journal of Legislative Studies] 15.

1. Objective Circumstance and the Time Factor

Under Article 420(1)(a) VCC 2015, the change of circumstances must occur objectively after the contract is concluded. Actually, the language of this paragraph demands two separate elements: (i) it requires that 'the change of circumstances must occur objectively', and (ii) the time of such event must be after the formation of the contract.

It is generally accepted that the requirement of externality must be interpreted broadly to include any events which are beyond the control of the disadvantaged party.[28] Such events can take the form of 'either natural catastrophes such as storm, flooding, drought, fire . . . or man-made calamities such as war and governmental actions'.[29] Although it remains to be seen whether a strike can be qualified as an external event for the sake of the applicability of Article 420, it is well established under the doctrine of *force majeure* that a strike is commonly considered as an event which is beyond the control of parties.[30] However, if the strike is caused by the obligor's employees, it has been commonly reasoned that the disadvantaged party in general can control it, and therefore it is not an external event.[31]

In this connection, in one of the few reported cases involving the doctrine of change of circumstances,[32] the Da Nang City People's Court reasoned that the loss of control over a company could not be regarded as a fundamental change of circumstances in accordance with Article 420 VCC 2015. In a case relating to the request for the termination of a mortgage contract due to a fundamental change of circumstances, the claimant argued that at the time of formation of the mortgage contract with the BIDV bank, he had used his private house as a guarantee for the loan of the S company from the bank because he believed that, as the director of the S company, he could effectively control the operation of the company and could reasonably expect to be able to pay for the loan on time. However, he was subsequently discharged from his position as a director and lost his managing power over the company. For this reason, he contended that when the company was operated inefficiently it prioritized other loans rather than the loan guaranteed by his asset, which resulted in the debt becoming overdue. As a consequence, the claimant argued that his discharge from the position as director was a fundamental change of circumstances, which must allow him to terminate the mortgage contract with the bank. The court declined his request and reasoned that an objective event should be understood as an event that did not occur due to the subjective intention of a party and beyond the control of the affected party. In this case, the discharge from his position as the director of the S company could not be regarded as an objective event, and the BIDV bank should not bear the risk of the customer's internal management affairs. Given the lack of cases applying the doctrine of change of circumstances, this case is not only one of the rare publicly available decisions discussing the requirements to apply Article 420 VCC 2015; it also contributes greatly to reaffirming that the benchmark to evaluate the externality of an event is to consider first whether it occurs beyond the control of the parties or not.

Taking inspiration from the German doctrine of 'the basis of the transaction', several authors even argued that the change of circumstances must include not only an objective

[28] Nguyễn Ngọc Điện (n 19) 123.
[29] ibid.
[30] Đỗ Văn Đại (n 21) 518.
[31] ibid.
[32] Judgment No 01/2018/KDTM-PT of 22 January 2018.

alteration but also a subjective alteration of circumstances.[33] This means that Article 420 would be applicable even if the circumstances underlying the contract remain constant, but the essential subjective preconceptions of the parties turn out to be wrong after concluding the contract.[34] A typical example relates to a German case when the buyer and seller have a common misunderstanding about the legal status of premises which later turn out to be, in fact, building grounds.[35] Arguably, this interpretation goes far beyond the spirit of Article 420, which explicitly limits its scope to change of circumstances 'for objective reasons'. Regarding the specific scenario, under Vietnamese law it is a matter of the doctrine of mistake, which aims to take care of erroneous assumptions by the contracting parties concerning the facts of the transaction at the time of the conclusion of contract.[36]

As far as the time factor is concerned, Vietnamese law requires that the external event must occur after the formation of contract. In this regard, Article 420 VCC 2015, as ultimately adopted, deviates from Article 6.2.2(a) PICC, where the events that lead to hardship may occur not only after contract formation but also at the time of contracting or even before then, provided that they 'become known to the disadvantaged party after the conclusion of the contract'.[37] Arguably, the Vietnamese legislator had a good reason for this deviation. The effect of Article 6.2.2(a) PICC is that it is difficult to distinguish the doctrine of hardship from the doctrine of mistake. However, as mentioned above, the position of the doctrine of fundamental change of circumstances, which is situated in the section on performance of contract, clearly shows an attempt by the Vietnamese legislator to provide separate regimes for regulating the validity of contract and its performance.

To illustrate the relevance of the time factor, let us see how Vietnamese law would approach the following hypothetical scenario:

> Kris sold his family home to Leila at 70 per cent of its market value. Both parties assumed that Leila would dedicate it to cultural use by the general public. However, this assumption was not expressly set out in the contract. After the sale, Leila changed her mind and gave the house to one of her sons instead. Can Kris claim the difference between the agreed price and the market value, or alternatively, restitution of the house?[38]

Obviously, the doctrine of change of circumstances would not be applicable in this hypothetical for the simple reason that the possibility that Leila might change her mind was reasonably foreseeable at the time of the formation of the contract. Rather, it is likely that Kris can invoke the doctrine of mistake to invalidate the agreement; as a result, Leila must return the house to Kris. Accordingly, the time factor is important: if the event is already present at

[33] Đàm Thị Diễm Hạnh and Lê Thị Kim Oanh, 'Nhận diện hoàn cảnh thay đổi cơ bản theo Bộ Luật Dân Sự Đức và bài học kinh nghiệm cho Việt Nam' (2019) 3 Tạp chí Nhà Nước và Pháp Luật [Dam Thi Diem Hanh and Le Thi Kim Oanh, 'On the Doctrine of Fundamental Change of Circumstances in the German Civil Code and Lessons Learnt for Vietnam' (2019) 3 Journal of State and Law] 9.

[34] ibid 10.

[35] ibid 11.

[36] For discussions about the doctrine of mistake, see Đỗ Văn Đại, *Luật Hợp Đồng Việt Nam: Bản Án và Bình Luận Bản Án, Tập 1* (Nhà Xuất Bản Hồng Đức 2017) [Do Van Dai, *The Contract Law of Vietnam: Cases and Commentary, vol 1* (6th edn, Hong Duc Press 2017)] 474.

[37] E McKendrick in S Vogenauer (ed), *Commentary on the UNIDROIT Principles for International Commercial Contracts (PICC)* (2nd edn, OUP 2015) art 6.2.2 para 10.

[38] For the fact scenario described here, see M Chen-Wishart, D Neo, and S Vogenauer, 'Introduction', ch 1 in this volume, 8.

the time when the contract is formed, the doctrine of change of circumstances is irrelevant, but relief may be sought on the ground of mistake.[39]

2. Circumstances Could Not Have Been 'Reasonably' Foreseeable

The second condition for invoking Article 420 is that the change of circumstances could not be foreseeable by the parties at the time of concluding the contract. The aim of such requirement is very clear: if the change of circumstances could have been taken into account by the parties, it can be expected that they would deal with this problem by inserting a specific clause in their contract to allocate the risks among themselves. In practice, unlike the rather popular *force majeure* clauses, it is rare to find hardship clauses in contracts in Vietnam. In a paper published in 2014, right before the promulgation of the VCC 2015, Tran and Nguyen conducted a survey of 29 big enterprises located in Ho Chi Minh City, the biggest city in Vietnam, about the practice of inserting a hardship clause in their commercial contracts. The result is that while only 3 out of 29 enterprises were apprised by their in-house lawyers about the function of hardship clauses (eg the International Chamber of Commerce (ICC) Hardship Clause 2003), none of these enterprises ever inserted such a clause into their commercial contracts. The interviews with their lawyers also indicate that the reasons that these enterprises decided not to insert hardship clauses into the contract are two-fold: (i) as there is no clear legal basis for including this clause into a contract in Vietnamese contract law, it would easily lead to misunderstandings and potential abuse of such a clause by the other party; (ii) the existence of a *force majeure* clause in the contract is sufficient to deal with the effects of supervening events.[40] After the introduction of the VCC 2015, which officially recognizes the doctrine of change of circumstances, it seems that enterprises have come to better understand the value of hardship clauses.[41] However, among the rare number of reported cases relating to Article 420 VCC 2015, there is no single case in which the contracting parties inserted a hardship clause in their contracts. Against this background, it is clear that Article 420 has an important function as a default rule permitting the renegotiation of contracts due to changes of circumstances that the parties could not have reasonably foreseen.

It should be noted that, unlike the PICC, Article 420 VCC 2015 does not explicitly consider the non-assumption of risk as a separate condition for applying the doctrine of change of circumstances.[42] One eminent member of the drafting team famously argued that, in contrast to the PICC, the requirement for hardship that 'the risk of the events was not assumed by the disadvantaged party' is redundant in light of the 'unforeseeability'

[39] Do Giang Nam and Tran Kien, 'Invalidity Due to Defects of Consent: Vietnam' in M Chen-Wishart, H Sono, and S Vogenauer (eds), *Studies in the Contract Laws of Asia, vol IV: Invalidity* (OUP 2022) 459.

[40] Trần Thanh Tâm and Nguyễn Minh Hiển, 'Điều khoản hardship trong hợp đồng mua bán hàng hoá quốc tế', (2015) 2 Tạp chí Kinh tế đối ngoại số 70 [Tran Thanh Tam and Nguyen Minh Hien, 'Hardship Clause in International Commercial Contracts' (2015) 2 Journal of Foreign Trade No 70] 50, 59.

[41] Trần Việt Dũng and Khưu Hồng Linh, 'Những vấn đề pháp lý trong soạn thảo điều khoản sự kiện bất khả kháng và điều khoản hoàn cảnh thay đổi cơ bản trong bối cảnh đại dịch COVID-19' (2022) 5 Tạp chí Nghiên cứu Lập pháp [Tran Viet Dung and Khuu Hong Linh, 'Legal Issues in the Drafting of the *Force Majeure* Clause and the "Fundamental Change of Circumstances" Clause in the Context of the COVID-19 Pandemic' (2022) 5 Legislative Studies Journal] 39.

[42] See the requirement set out in PICC, art 6.2.2(d): 'the risk of the events was not assumed by the disadvantaged party'; McKendrick (n 37) art 6.2.2 para 14.

condition.[43] Although this opinion has not found unanimous consent, it is a matter of fact that the requirement of risk allocation that was still present in the final draft submitted to the Vietnamese National Assembly is absent from the VCC 2015 as adopted. This seems to point to two characteristics of the doctrine of change of circumstances under Vietnamese law: first, the element of risk allocation is still relevant for hardship, and secondly, this element has not been explicitly spelt out but implicitly included through the unforeseeability element. Accordingly, the unforeseeability condition for hardship must be understood to exclude the foreseeable change of circumstances because once the disadvantaged party foresees or could have foreseen it and did not take any measures to shield itself, this party must be assumed to have taken on the risk of the changed circumstances.

It must also be noted that, as compared to the final draft, which was modelled on Article 6.2.2 PICC, the adopted language of Article 420 VCC 2015 does not keep the standard of 'reasonableness' to measure the foreseeability of the events. Although this is regrettable, a common understanding shared by numerous scholars is that the test for assessing the foreseeability of a supervening event is whether 'a reasonable person—a person acting with proper diligence and care—in the same situation as the obligor' could have foreseen it.[44] Indeed, these scholars have convincingly argued that a mere subjective assessment of the change of circumstances by way of analysing the particular circumstance of the obligor is undesirable; rather, the situation must be assessed objectively by asking what a reasonable person could have foreseen at the time of the conclusion of contract.[45] Arguably, this kind of objective interpretation of unforeseeability must be embraced. Not only does it bring the doctrine of change of circumstances in line with the doctrine of *force majeure*, which also treats the foreseeability condition objectively, but also, and more importantly, only an objective assessment of foreseeability can help the Vietnamese legislator to achieve the aim of implicitly incorporating the element of risk allocation into the unforeseeability requirement. Indeed, only when the standard of assessing foreseeability is an objective one can a party be considered by the courts to have assumed the risk implicitly by refraining from taking any positive action such as integrating a hardship clause to protect itself. For example, let us have a look at how Vietnamese law may deal with a case where a buyer of shares in a company refuses to pay the total agreed price on the ground that the value of shares has significantly diminished because the company had become insolvent between the time of conclusion of contract and the date for paying the balance.[46] Obviously, if the contract is governed by the PICC, the seller can easily argue that, since the risk must have been assumed by the buyer, he cannot successfully invoke the doctrine of hardship. The problem with Vietnamese law is that it does not explicitly provide for the requirement of risk assumption. To address this shortcoming, it is possible for the seller to invoke the test of foreseeability objectively and argue that—due to the nature of a contract to purchase shares, which is a speculative transaction—a reasonable buyer in similar circumstances must always foresee the risk of fluctuation in the price of shares.

In a judgment relating to a commercial franchising contract,[47] the Da Nang City People's Court rejected the defendant's invocation of a change of circumstances for the termination

43 Đỗ Văn Đại (n 12) 35.

44 ibid 40; Nguyễn Thế Đức Tâm and Ngô Thu Trang (n 7) 61.

45 Đỗ Văn Đại (n 12) 40; Nguyễn Thế Đức Tâm and Ngô Thu Trang (n 7) 61.

46 *G Brencius v Ukio investicine grupe*, Supreme Court of Lithuania, 19 May 2003, <www.unilex.info/principles/case/1183> accessed 25 January 2025.

47 Judgment No 02/2018/KDTM-PT of 26 January 2018.

of a contract to lease premises between the applicant and a third party. In this case, the defendant had entered into an exclusive commercial franchising contract with the claimant for a three-year period from 1 April 2016 until 1 May 2019 at the price of vnd3,375,000,000 (equivalent to US$150,000), and the defendant signed a contract to lease premises with a third party in order to run the franchising business. However, after performing the contract for some time, the third party terminated the contract for the premises, and consequently the cost of business operations increased significantly. On this ground, the defendant requested a decrease in the franchising price, which was rejected by the claimant. The court reasoned that at the time of the formation of contract, the defendant must have reasonably foreseen the difficulties and challenges during the performance of such a long-term contract, and thus the termination of the leasing contract with the third party could not be regarded as a fundamental change of circumstances in accordance with Article 420 VCC 2015. In this case, although the court did not explicitly mention the connection between the element of foreseeability and the requirement of risk assumption, it may be understood implicitly that according to the court, the increase in the cost of doing business arising out of the termination of the contract with the third party was a risk that the defendant had to foresee and assume.

On the basis of this objective approach, it is further argued that the foreseeability of the change of circumstances must be measured regarding not only its occurrence but also its intensity. To some extent, the occurrence of an event such as a war, a hurricane, a strike, or inflation is not unforeseeable in the abstract. What matters is the foreseeability of the intensity of this event. By way of illustration, although in a transitional economy like Vietnam, a considerable degree of fluctuation is hardly considered as unforeseeable, a surprising and extraordinary rise in the inflation rate might be considered as a fundamental change of circumstances. Therefore, the evaluation of foreseeability must be expanded to the factual consequences of the event on the obligations of the parties.

3. Reasonable Efforts of the Disadvantaged Party

A further requirement for the invocation of the doctrine of change of circumstances is that the disadvantaged party must show that it has taken all necessary measures to the best of its ability and appropriate with the nature of the contract but is unable to prevent or mitigate the level to which the benefits are affected. This requirement is rooted in the underlying principle of good faith. The suggested test to be applied in the case is whether a reasonable person in similar circumstances could be reasonably expected to take any actions to resist the event and its consequences.[48]

[48] As mentioned above, such requirement is similar to the requirement of irresistibility under the doctrine of *force majeure*. Therefore, it is logical to predict that the court is likely to apply the rules established for the doctrine of *force majeure* to measure whether the disadvantaged party applied all necessary and possible measures to avoid or overcome the effects of the changed circumstances. The disadvantaged party is expected to take preventive measures to avoid the event or its effects. So, in the case of an insurance contract in which the claimant's ship was sunk due to a major storm, it was reasoned that there was no *force majeure* because of the claimant's failure to undertake any precautionary measures to avoid the storm, which had been forecast.

4. Relevant Threshold for the Distortion of the Contractual Equilibrium

One of the biggest challenges for the Vietnamese legislator was to find a precise criterion for determining when the imbalance in the contracting parties' performance is unacceptable and thus calls for judicial intervention. The historical evidence reveals that Vietnamese law had initially paid particular attention to the objective approach of the PICC to define the concept of hardship. Under this objective approach, hardship is defined as a supervening event that constitutes a fundamental alteration of the contractual equilibrium. Furthermore, the PICC examine the state of contractual equilibrium through assessing whether there is an increase in the cost of a party's performance or a decrease in the value of the performance received by one party.[49] Initially, this pattern was followed by the version of Article 420 in the 2014 draft of the VCC, in which the legislator considered that an unexpected change in circumstances was only relevant if it fundamentally disrupted the contractual equilibrium which originally reflected the parties' intention. Thus, the relevant threshold for applying the rule of change of circumstances is whether such unforeseen change would result in a significant imbalance in their respective performance.[50]

Surprisingly, the official version of the VCC 2015 uses different language for the test of the relevant factual imbalance caused by a change of circumstances. Indeed, unlike the PICC, Article 420 VCC 2015 combines both objective and subjective elements to establish the threshold for the distortion of contractual equilibrium. Objectively, it directly concerns the state of onerousness of performance through assessing whether the continued performance of the contract without adapting its contents will cause serious damage to one party.[51] Subjectively, it examines the state of mind of the contracting parties by asking whether the change of circumstances is of such nature that the parties would not have concluded the contract, or would have concluded it with a completely different content, if they had foreseen such change.[52]

Certainly, the combination of objective and subjective elements to define the relevant threshold for a distortion of the contractual equilibrium reveals a restrictive approach by the Vietnamese legislator towards the doctrine. This in turn plays an important role in signalling to the stakeholders, including judges and contracting parties, the exceptional nature of the doctrine in comparison to the general principle of *pacta sunt servanda*. Indeed, the language of sub-paragraphs (1)(c) and (d) of Article 420 suggests that only if the performance of the contract has become extremely difficult for one party are the parties under a duty to renegotiate the contract. Such exceptional difficulty that the disadvantaged party is confronted with may be the direct consequence of increased performance costs, for example, the significantly increased transport costs in the well-known case of the closure of the Suez Canal, which forced a ship to sail around the Cape of Good Hope.[53] Alternatively, it may be the result of the depreciation of the performance received by one party; for instance, if the dramatic increase in inflation has decreased the value of an original price.

Be that as it may, the complicated language of sub-paragraphs 1(c) and (d) of Article 420 makes it exceedingly challenging for the courts to decide whether a fundamental change

[49] McKendrick (n 37) art 6.2.2 paras 2–9.
[50] Bùi Đăng Hiếu (n 5) 11.
[51] VCC 2015, art 420(1)(d).
[52] ibid art 420(1)(c).
[53] *Tsakiroglou & Co Ltd v Noblee Thorl GmbH* [1962] AC 93 (HL).

of circumstances exists. As a matter of fact, given the lack of certainty with the language of Article 420, several authors argued that the Supreme Court should provide guidance by indicating a quantitative figure for the threshold of 'seriously excessive' increase in performance costs, which would enable precise measurement in monetary terms.[54] Notably, they did so by opting for both a negative and positive figure. Indeed, referring to the fact that the figure of an alteration by 50 per cent or more of the cost or the value of the performance presented in the Official Comment to the 1994 edition of the PICC was dropped from the subsequent 2004 edition, they argued that an increase or decrease of less than 50 per cent is highly unlikely to qualify as a hardship.[55] In contrast, a higher threshold, such as an increase to 150–200 per cent, has been suggested with reference to arbitral decisions regarding the interpretation of Article 79(1) of the United Nations Convention on Contracts for the International Sale of Goods (CISG).[56] However, providing a specific figure always comes with the risk of arbitrariness; until now, a majority of authors have shared the view that instead of providing a rigid figure to assess the hardship, the courts should decide on a case-by-case basis regarding the specific threshold of 'seriously excessive' performance costs.

V. Legal Consequences of a Fundamental Change of Circumstances

According to paragraphs (2), (3), and (4) of Article 420 VCC 2015, as long as a fundamental change of circumstances is shown, the disadvantaged party may request the other party to renegotiate the contract within a reasonable time limit. If the parties cannot agree on a modification of the contract, either party may request a court to (i) terminate the contract at a specified time or (ii) modify the contract to balance the lawful rights and interests of the parties in the context of a fundamental change of circumstances.

1. Self-Enforcement: Renegotiation

The first legal effect of a fundamental change of circumstances under Vietnamese contract law is that the disadvantaged party is entitled to request the renegotiation of the contract within a reasonable time in order to alter its content to fit the new circumstances. A fundamental change of circumstances does not automatically lead to the effect that the court can adapt or terminate the contract; the renegotiation is constituted as a precondition for the commencement of court proceedings. This approach towards renegotiation has been widely supported by the Vietnamese legal community because it addresses the main concerns underlying the doctrine of change of circumstances in an ideal manner.[57] First, it absolutely corresponds to the idea of *favor contractus*, which puts emphasis on the value of a good-faith relationship and thus prefers maintaining the contract whenever possible to

[54] Vũ Thị Lan Anh (n 23) 33; Nguyễn Minh Hằng and Trần Thu Giang, 'Đề xuất diễn giải và áp dụng điều 420 Bộ Luật Dân sự 2015 về thực hiện hợp đồng khi hoàn cảnh thay đổi cơ bản' (2016) 86 Tạp chí Kinh tế Đối Ngoại [Nguyen Minh Hang and Tran Thu Giang, 'On the Proposal to Interpret and Apply Article 420 of the 2015 Civil Code: Performance of Contract in the Case of Fundamental Change of Circumstances' (2016) 86 Journal of Foreign Trade] 1.

[55] Nguyễn Minh Hằng and Trần Thu Giang (n 54) 2.

[56] Nguyễn Thế Đức Tâm and Ngô Thu Trang (n 7) 67.

[57] Vũ Thị Lan Anh (n 23) 39; Nguyễn Minh Hằng and Trần Thu Giang (n 54) 5.

terminating the contract. Secondly, it perfectly matches the presumption that the parties are always the best judges of their interests and thus the law should entrust the parties themselves rather than the court to rewrite their contracts.

Be that as it may, there are three major controversial issues regarding the remedy of renegotiation under Vietnamese law, namely: (i) whether the other party is obliged to renegotiate upon the request of the disadvantaged party; (ii) what the legal mechanisms necessary to warrant a successful renegotiation are; and (iii) how to interpret the requirement of 'reasonable time' for the affected party to request a renegotiation.

As far as the other party's duty to renegotiate is concerned, although the wording of Article 420 does not explicitly require it, such duty can be derived from the principle of good faith. Under the VCC 2015, the principle of good faith is expressed in various provisions governing the entire life of the contract, ranging from pre-contractual negotiations to the formation of the contract itself and eventually its performance. Particularly, the parties are required to perform contractual obligations honestly, in the spirit of cooperation. Accordingly, once the law gives the affected party the right to initiate the renegotiation, it is fair to argue that the other party is obliged to comply, and both parties must conduct the renegotiation process in good faith. Also, it is important to note that the duty to renegotiate a contract is, by its very nature, a duty of best efforts rather than a duty to achieve a specific result.[58] This means that the other party must honestly participate in the renegotiation process at the request of the disadvantaged party, but the other party is not obliged to reach a new agreement no matter what. On the other hand, in light of the principle of good faith, the requesting party must provide for a clear legal basis for the change of circumstances and evidence showing that such change of circumstances is fundamental and causes serious impact on the performance of the contract. If there is no such legal basis, the requested party is entitled to decline the request.

A further complicated issue is how to encourage the parties to successfully rewrite a contract under the premise of changed circumstances. Several authors have criticized that the VCC 2015 simply lacks feasible remedies to address the problem of renegotiating in bad faith. However, it should be noted that by establishing a duty to renegotiate in good faith, certain remedies may be triggered if one of the parties violates this duty by intentionally carrying out renegotiations in bad faith. Arguably, it is possible to apply, by way of analogy, the legal rules providing for compensation for losses incurred because one of the parties conducted the negotiations at the time of concluding the contract in bad faith (these include compensation for expenses incurred).[59] Furthermore, apart from allowing the parties to request renegotiation, Vietnamese law also provides the remedies of adaptation and termination of contract. The mere fact that the court is entitled to intervene in the contract is likely to act as further motivation for parties in gridlock to intensify their efforts and reach a deal by themselves.

As far as the third issue is concerned, the concept of 'reasonable time' is mentioned several times in the VCC 2015, for instance in Article 142: 'The principal knows but does not oppose within a reasonable time' or Article 300: 'Before the collateral is realized, the

[58] For the distinction between a duty of best efforts and a duty to achieve a specific result, see Nguyễn Ngọc Điện (n 19) 197.

[59] VCC 2015, art 387. See also Lê Trường Sơn, *Giai đoạn tiền hợp đồng trong pháp luật Việt Nam* (Nhà Xuất Bản Hồng Đức 2016) [Le Truong Son, *Pre-contractual Stage in Vietnamese Contract Law* (Hong Duc Publisher 2016)].

secured party must issue the notice in writing within a reasonable time.' Thus, in order to be consistent in the application of the provisions of the VCC 2015, the interpretation and application of the concept of 'reasonable time' in Article 420 must be put in the context of the general interpretation of this requirement across the VCC 2015 and take into account the nature of the transactions and the circumstances.[60] Normally, to ensure the objectivity standard, the reasonableness is evaluated by an objectivity test, according to which 'reasonable time' is the period of time within which a reasonable person, under similar circumstances, must raise the request in order to satisfy the requirement of good faith.

2. Judicial Remedies: Termination and/or Adaptation

One common structural trait of remedies for the change of circumstances is that, apart from the self-imposed remedy of renegotiation, the judicial remedies are designed to empower the courts to modify or terminate the contract.[61] Under Vietnamese law, termination and adaptation of contract are also listed as two legal consequences of a fundamental change of circumstances. Furthermore, Article 420(3) VCC 2015 establishes a clear hierarchy for judicial enforcement mechanisms, which prioritizes termination of contract as the first remedy and adaptation as merely a secondary judicial solution for a fundamental change of circumstances.[62] The former means that the contract is discharged, thus releasing the parties from performing any further obligations, whereas the latter has the effect of keeping the contract alive through adjusting the contractual terms to meet the new, changed circumstances. Termination, according to Vietnamese law, does not occur automatically upon notification of the party but must be made by means of a judicial decision. It means that even when the disadvantaged party can establish that there is sufficient ground for a fundamental change of circumstances, it is not entitled to be automatically relieved from the contract. As a result, paragraph (4) of Article 420 explicitly stipulates that the disadvantaged party is not allowed to suspend the performance of its obligation. However, it should be noted that contrary to termination as a remedy for a fundamental breach of contract, the court can terminate the contract at a date to be fixed.[63] Adaptation of a contract as a remedy laid down in Article 420 is generally understood as a modification of the contractual obligations of one or both parties with the aim to restore the balance of the parties' interests under the contract, which was substantially disrupted by the changed circumstances. In this sense, the judicial power is strictly confined to modifying rather than redrafting the whole contract or to change its nature. In this context, the task of the courts to modify the contract is closely related to the

[60] Nguyễn Minh Hằng and Trần Thu Giang (n 54) 6.

[61] R Momberg, *The Effect of a Change of Circumstances on the Binding Force of Contracts* (Intersentia 2011) 273–78.

[62] According to PICC, art 6.2.3(3), if the parties fail to reach an agreement within a reasonable time, either party may resort to the court, which may terminate the contract at a date and on terms to be fixed or adapt it with a view to restoring its equilibrium. The PICC do not provide a hierarchy between termination and adaptation and thus the application of these two remedies is essentially at the courts' discretion; the latter is the 'more likely solution in the majority of cases', McKendrick (n 37) art 6.2.3 para 7.

[63] For discussions about the effect of a fundamental breach of contract and the law on termination under Vietnamese law, see Võ Sỹ Mạnh, 'Vi phạm cơ bản hợp đồng trong pháp luật Việt Nam: Một số bất cập và định hướng hoàn thiện' (2014) 67 Tạp chí Kinh tế Đối Ngoại [Vo Sy Manh, 'Fundamental Breach of Contract in Vietnamese Contract Law: Several Shortcomings and Improving Orientation' (2014) 67 Journal of Foreign Trade] 1; Tran K, 'Termination of Contracts under Vietnamese Law', ch 27 in this volume, 585.

process of interpreting the contract. In order to successfully adapt the contract, it is certain that the courts must apply the techniques of interpretation to establish the parties' aims and expectations when they entered into the contractual agreement as well as external circumstances surrounding the agreement.[64]

From a comparative law perspective, one of the unique characteristics of the Vietnamese remedial system for a change of circumstances is that it sets up a clear hierarchy in which termination takes precedence over adaptation of contract. Initially, the Vietnamese approach was criticized as unwise because it limited the court's right to choose the remedy most appropriate to the circumstances of the case. Inspired by the approach of the PICC, several authors argued that the courts should be given the discretion to either terminate or adapt the contract as long as, after taking into consideration the circumstances of the case, the courts find which remedy is more reasonable.[65] Specifically, they preferred adaptation as the primary choice as a judicial remedy for a change of circumstances because it logically resulted from the principle of *favor contractus* that the courts must undertake their utmost efforts to keep the contract alive.

However, it should be observed that the adaptation of a contract is still possible as long as the courts can establish that 'termination of the contract will cause loss and damage of an amount higher than the costs for the performance of the contract if the contract is adapted'. This means that the remedy of adaptation should be granted in limited instances where the harm resulting from a termination of the contract would significantly exceed the expenditures necessary for the performance of the altered contract. As the historical evidence shows, the Vietnamese legislator's choice of preferring termination to adaptation seems to partly reflect the concern that judges are not well equipped with specialized knowledge and may find it difficult to amend the contract satisfactorily for the parties. Although it is true that the courts would face many challenges to carry out a cost–benefit assessment between the options of adaptation or termination, the language of Article 420 clearly requires that the court's decision to adapt the contract must be oriented towards and justified by efficiency-based considerations. To this effect, it must be noted that the Vietnamese approach in favour of termination seems to be in line with the recommendations of economists.[66]

It should also be noticed that Article 420(3) only mentions the court as the dispute settlement body granted power to alter or terminate the contract in the case of change of circumstances. This means that the provision does not address the possibility that arbitral tribunals—increasingly important and popular dispute settlement bodies—exercise their jurisdiction.[67] In reality, the contracting parties frequently insert an arbitration clause in

64 For recent discussions about how to interpret contracts under Vietnamese Law, see Hà Thị Mai Hiên and Hà Thị Thuý, 'Bàn về Chế định Giải Thích Hợp đồng trong dự thảo BLDS sửa đổi' (2015) 3 Tạp Chí Nhà Nước và Pháp Luật [Ha Thi Mai Hien and Ha Thi Thuy, 'On the Provisions on the Interpretation of Contracts in the Draft of the Revised Civil Code' (2015) 3 Journal of State and Law] 44; Nguyen Hung Quang and Nguyen Thuy Duong, 'Contract Interpretation and Unfair Terms in Vietnamese Contract Law' in M Chen-Wishart and S Vogenauer (eds), *Studies in the Contract Laws of Asia, vol III: Contents of Contracts and Unfair Terms* (OUP 2020) 447.

65 Nguyễn Minh Hằng and Trần Thu Giang (n 54) 5; Đàm Thị Diễm Hạnh and Lê Thị Kim Oanh, 'Một số bình luận về Điều 420 Bộ Luật Dân sự 2015: Thực hiện hợp đồng khi hoàn cảnh thay đổi cơ bản' (2018) 7 Tạp chí Nhà Nước và Pháp Luật [Dam Thi Diem Hanh and Le Thi Kim Oanh, 'Several Comments on Article 420 of the 2015 Civil Code: Performance of Contract in the Case of Fundamental Change of Circumstances' (2018) 7 Journal of State and Law] 19–24.

66 M Kovac, 'Frustration of Purpose and the French Contract Law Reform: The Challenge to the International Commercial Attractiveness of English Law?' (2018) 25 Maastricht Journal of European and Comparative Law 28.

67 Đỗ Văn Đại (n 12) 39; Đàm Thị Diễm Hạnh and Lê Thị Kim Oanh (n 65) 24.

their contracts, stipulating that any contract-related disputes between them must be settled through arbitration. The court then does not have the competence to settle the dispute, according to the Commercial Arbitration Law 2010.[68] However, under a strict interpretation of Article 420 VCC 2015, arbitral tribunals would not have jurisdiction to consider a fundamental change of circumstances. Accordingly, in order to avoid the case that no dispute settlement body is competent to settle the dispute, Article 420(3) should be broadly interpreted so that 'court' also includes an arbitral tribunal, and thus when the two parties agreed on an arbitration agreement, arbitrators should be able to invoke Article 420 to settle such dispute.[69]

VI. Factual Approach towards the Change of Circumstances under Vietnamese Contract Law

In order to comprehensively assess the applicability of Article 420 and other related provisions of the VCC 2015 to address the effect of a change of circumstances on the performance of contract, it may be helpful to discuss them in the light of representative fact situations.[70]

1. Inflation

Consider the following hypothetical situation:

> In 2015, Citi Corporation received a loan from Drive Bank with the fixed interest rate of 10 per cent for five years. In the 20 years preceding the agreement, the rate of inflation had been relatively stable within a range of 1 to 6 per cent. In 2017, the economic situation began to destabilize and inflation rose to 50 per cent. Drive Bank requests adjustment or, alternatively, termination of the contract.

Under Vietnamese law, it should be noted firstly that Drive Bank would not be exempt from civil liability on the ground of *force majeure* if the bank fails to continuously perform its obligations for the simple reason that inflation does not make performance impossible but only makes it more onerous to the bank. On this account, the key issue here is whether Drive Bank may invoke Article 420 VCC 2015 to request an adjustment or, alternatively, termination of the contract. Certainly, as a general rule, regular inflation does not constitute a change of circumstances in the spirit of Article 420 VCC 2015. Although Drive Bank can

[68] The Commercial Arbitration Law 2010, arts 5 and 6 provide that the dispute must be settled by arbitration if the two parties agree to do so by way of an arbitration agreement; in this case, if one of the parties still submits the dispute to the court, the court shall decline to hear the case, except for the case that the arbitration agreement is null and void or is impossible to be performed.

[69] From a comparative law perspective, some cases applying the PICC in proceedings before the ICC International Court of Arbitration show that the term 'court' here may be understood to include also arbitral tribunals, and thus an arbitral tribunal would still be permitted to hear the case in the event of hardship. For example, ICC International Court of Arbitration, Paris 7365/FMS <www.unilex.info/principles/case/653> and ICC International Court of Arbitration, Paris 8873 <www.unilex.info/case.cfm?id=641>, both accessed 25 January 2025. See also PICC, art 1.11: '"court" includes an arbitral tribunal.'

[70] The hypotheticals described in this section VI are taken from M Chen-Wishart, D Neo, and S Vogenauer, 'Introduction', ch 1 in this volume, 7–8.

easily prove that inflation is a supervening event occurring objectively after the time of the formation of the contract, it is extremely challenging for them to establish that the parties could not reasonably foresee this change. In the context of a transitional economy such as Vietnam, the parties must take into account the fluctuation in the value of currency; hence, they must bear the risk of regular inflation.

However, unlike the case of regular inflation, the above hypothetical (i) describes a case of extraordinary inflation when the economic situation began to destabilize and inflation rose to 50 per cent and (ii) this was not foreseen by the parties because 'in the 20 years preceding the agreement, the rate of inflation had been relatively stable within a range of 1 to 6 per cent'. For that reason, although in principle Article 420 is not applicable in the case of regular inflation, it is highly possible that it will be applied in this exceptional case. Accordingly, Drive Bank may request Citi Corporation to renegotiate a more reasonable interest rate if it can establish that it has made utmost effort to mitigate adverse effects but to no avail. In case the parties are not able to reach agreement, a court may intervene to terminate the contract or modify the contract to take account of the effect of extraordinary inflation.

2. Devaluation of the Price Agreement in a Long-Term Contract

Again, consider the following hypothetical situation:

> In 1567, Abraham entered into a contract for an unlimited period of time with farmer Bill under which Abraham promised to build and maintain an irrigation channel from which Bill could extract water at a fixed price. By 2018, inflation and the rise in the cost of maintenance and labour have made the price wholly inadequate. Abraham's successors in law ask for an increase in the price that would provide them with adequate compensation. Alternatively, they wish to terminate the contract.

In this case, Abraham's successors in law ask for an adjustment of price because the original price has become completely inadequate due to not only inflation but also the rise in the cost of maintenance of an irrigation channel. Applying similar reasoning as in the Drive Bank hypothetical, on the one hand, if the rate of inflation is only regular, the affected party can hardly invoke Article 420 VCC 2015 to request an adjustment of contract. On the other hand, Bill's successors in law may also argue that the increase in the cost of maintaining the irrigation channel is an event which must be reasonably foreseeable by the parties at the formation of contract. Thus, if Abraham's successors only based their arguments on the regular inflation and the rise in the normal costs of doing business, they could not successfully invoke Article 420 to request for an adjustment of price.

Nevertheless, it is highly likely that Abraham's successors may request termination of contract under Vietnamese law. In this hypothetical, the single important fact is that the contract has been concluded for an undefined period of time. In this case, if the nature of the contract is that of a leasing contract, the VCC 2015 clearly provides in Article 474 that if the leasing contract is for an undefined period of time, each party is entitled to terminate the contract at any time. On the other hand, if the contract is regarded as a service contract, the VCC 2015 unfortunately only gives the service users the right to unilaterally terminate the contract if they do not desire to use such service any longer; there is no provision for a similar right for the suppliers of the service.[71] However, there is a general trend among scholars that it is necessary to establish a general rule to regulate all kinds of contracts which are concluded for an undefined period of time in the manner that each party is entitled to terminate the contract any time as long as they provide notification within a reasonable time. It is obviously contrary to the principle of good faith if the service suppliers are forever bound by the contract even when they suffer considerable loss by providing the service.[72] Thus, it is highly possible that a court would recognize the right of the claimant to unilaterally terminate the contract on condition that the claimant notifies the other party within a reasonable time.

3. Extraordinary Increase of the Rental Value in a Long-Term Lease

Consider the following hypothetical scenario:

> Easy leases business premises from Frugle for a fixed period of 15 years. Shortly after the contract has been concluded, a nearby military airport is unexpectedly shut down for political reasons. The government invests an enormous amount of public funds in order to improve the commercial infrastructure in the area. As a result, Easy's profits are 500 per cent of what could reasonably have been expected at the time of making the contract. At the same time, the rental value of comparable business premises in the area rises to 500 per cent of the agreed rental price. Frugle requests that the rental price should be adjusted accordingly or, alternatively, that the agreement should be terminated.

In this case, unlike in the irrigation channel hypothetical, the lease is for a defined period of 15 years. Hence, Frugle could not invoke Article 474 VCC 2015 to terminate the leasing contract by just providing a notice to Easy within a reasonable period of time. Besides, Frugle may not invoke the doctrine of *force majeure* because the contract performance is completely possible, even though such performance may cause him considerable loss. In this context, the most feasible legal ground that Frugle may rely upon to request an increase in the rental price or, alternatively, to terminate the original agreement is Article 420 VCC 2015, a change of circumstances.

Obviously, Frugle can easily establish that the government's decision to shut down a nearby military airport and improve the commercial infrastructure in the area is an external circumstance that both parties could not reasonably foresee at the time of the formation of contract. The questions are whether such change of circumstances is so fundamental that both parties would not have concluded this contract, or only with a completely different content, if they had foreseen this change, and whether the continued performance of the contract without adapting its contents will cause serious damage to one party. As mentioned above, although there is no consensus as to a relevant quantitative figure, it is likely that the court will consider a change as fundamental if there is an increase to 150–200 per

[71] VCC 2015, art 520.

[72] Kiều Thị Thuỳ Linh, 'Hoàn thiện pháp luật về hợp đồng dịch vụ' (2017) 2 Tạp Chí Dân Chủ và Pháp Luật [Kieu Thi Thuy Linh, 'Improving the Law on Service Contracts' (2017) 2 Journal of Democracy and Law] 15.

cent of the cost or the value of the performance. Accordingly, since the rental value of comparable business premises in the area has risen to 500 per cent of the agreed rental price, the court would probably find that there is a fundamental change of circumstances in this hypothetical. As a result, Frugle is entitled to ask Easy to renegotiate the rental price. And if they fail to reach an agreement, Frugle can bring the case before the courts to request a termination or modification of contract.

4. Frustration of Purposes

Consider the final hypothetical as follows:

> Builder George agreed to refurbish the cellar of Han, the owner of a restaurant. The work was scheduled to start one month after the agreement. Before the work began, the restaurant was completely destroyed by a storm that was much more violent than any other previous storm in the region. However, the cellar remained fully intact. Han immediately informed George of the situation and asked him not to start work. George insisted on rendering performance because he had set aside two weeks to carry out the work and had already purchased the necessary materials.

Under Vietnamese law, a contract is terminable if it is impossible to perform due to the fact that the object of the contract is destroyed.[73] Unfortunately for Han, this rule is inapplicable in this hypothetical since although the restaurant was completely destroyed by the storm, the cellar, as the object of the contract, remained fully intact. However, since it is a service contract, Han may invoke Article 520 VCC 2015 to request the termination of the contract, for the reason that George's performance of service is no longer suitable to Han's interests. In this case, Han is under a duty to notify George within a reasonable period of time. According to Article 428 VCC 2015, George is in turn entitled to ask Han to pay damages.

Alternatively, Han may rely on the doctrine of change of circumstances. As discussed above, the Vietnamese legislator intended Article 420 to address distortions of the contractual equilibrium between parties due to not only the increase in the cost of performance but also the decrease in the value of the performance. The latter is exactly the legal issue that this hypothetical has raised. Undoubtedly, the value of performance that Han may receive from the refurbishment of the cellar is significantly diminished because his restaurant was destroyed by an unforeseeable storm. Accordingly, since the purpose of the contract has been frustrated by a change of circumstances, it is likely that Han is entitled to adjust or terminate the contract in accordance with Article 420 VCC 2015. The remaining issue is whether George could be entitled to claim damages for compensating losses incurred due to the purchase of the necessary materials. Although the VCC 2015 does not explicitly address the issue of whether losses should be distributed between the parties, it is reasonable to resolve this problem by analogously applying the relevant provisions on unilateral termination of contracts.[74] Thus, Han must compensate George for the cost of purchasing the

[73] VCC 2015, art 422(5).
[74] VCC 2015, art 428.

materials for refurbishing the cellar unless those materials can be reasonably used for other constructions.

VII. Conclusion

Including provisions on a fundamental change of circumstances in the VCC 2015 has been one of the most remarkable reforms of Vietnamese contract law since the promulgation of the first civil code in 1995. Speaking of legislative technique, the content of Article 420 clearly highlights that the provision is the fruit of comparative law and inspired more specifically from the provisions on hardship in the PICC and section 313 BGB. However, Article 420 VCC 2015 has its own unique features, which evidence the specific concerns of the Vietnamese legislator relating to the role and competence of the courts in the adaptation of contracts. This is proof that in the process of studying foreign experiences, the legislator learnt from and applied those experiences on a selective basis. Speaking of legal policy, by promoting the negotiation process to rebalance the contractual relationship between parties when supervening events have occurred without the fault of the contracting parties, the new doctrine of change of circumstances reaffirms that Vietnamese contract law has recognized the increasingly important role of the principle of good faith, which exists in parallel to the principle of freedom of contract, in regulating contractual relationships between parties.

Furthermore, the new doctrine of change of circumstances is a necessary supplement to the classic doctrine of *force majeure* to establish a robust legal framework equipped to deal with the impact of unforeseeable events on existing contracts. It is highly likely that the recent COVID-19 pandemic, which had profound effects on the possibility of performing existing contracts, will give rise to numerous post-pandemic disputes that will help clarify how these two doctrines are actually applied in practice. Actually, there have been several discussions among Vietnamese lawyers about whether the pandemic and the related governmental actions of imposing social distancing measures and restrictions of non-essential commercial activities[75] would be qualified as a *force majeure* event to release a contracting party who fails to perform its obligation from liabilities.[76] Indeed, there is no clear answer to this general question as it depends first and foremost on the construction of a *force majeure* clause, if such is inserted into the contract, to find out how the parties actually intended to allocate the contractual risk due to unforeseen events such as the COVID-19 pandemic; then it would require the consideration of the specific kinds of obligations arising out of the contract.[77] However, it should be noted that under current Vietnamese contract law, even

[75] Decree No 16/CT-TTg of 31 March 2020, issued by the Prime Minister, imposed social distancing measures and restrictions on non-essential commercial activities in the whole country for the duration of one month.

[76] Trương Nhật Quang and Ngô Thái Ninh, 'Vấn đề miễn trách nhiệm dân sự do vi phạm nghĩa vụ thanh toán trong trường hợp bất khả kháng—COVID-19' (2020) 4 Tạp chí Nghiên cứu lập pháp [Truong Nhat Quang and Ngo Thai Ninh, 'The Question of Possible Exemption from Civil Liability for Breach of Payment Obligations in the Case of COVID-19 as a *Force Majeure* Event' (2020) 4 Journal of Legislative Studies] 11; Ngô Quốc Chiến, 'Bất khả kháng và nghĩa vụ hoàn trả tài sản' (2020) 8 Tạp chí Nghiên cứu lập pháp [Ngo Quoc Chien, '*Force Majeure* and the Obligation of Restitution and Reimbursement' (2020) 8 Journal of Legislative Studies 51].

[77] For instance, as for the obligation of delivery of goods, the party who fails to deliver goods on time may easily prove that the government's prohibition to leave the city may make it impossible to perform the contract during the period when these restrictions are in place, and thus such government action may be considered to be a *force majeure* event. However, as for rental contracts, although it is true that the COVID-19 pandemic causes financial

when the reference to the doctrine of *force majeure* is fruitless due to the fact that performance would still be possible, but unduly onerous on one party only, this party could still rely on the doctrine of change of circumstances under Article 420 VCC 2015 to seek renegotiation of the contract and judicial support for an adaptation of the contractual terms.[78]

The application of the new provision on the fundamental change of circumstances will surely pose a number of challenges for the Vietnamese courts. The analysis in this contribution shows that Article 420 VCC 2015 still leaves a number of issues to be interpreted, and these issues may only be resolved by the incremental development of the case law in the future. However, there is little doubt that this provision must be interpreted on a narrow basis as an exception of the principle of *pacta sunt servanda*.

challenges for the obligor (debtor), it is very difficult to claim that it makes the obligation to pay the rental fee impossible. In Judgment No 133/2021/DS-PT of 8 July 2021 concerning the effect of the COVID-19 pandemic on the non-performance of obligations arising from a rental contract, Ca Mau Province People's Court rejected the defendant's claim that her failure to pay the rental fee was excused because the COVID-19 pandemic should be deemed a *force majeure* event.

[78] Đỗ Giang Nam and Trần Quang Cường, '"Thiên nga đen"—COVID-19 và cơ chế điều chỉnh của pháp luật hợp đồng Việt Nam' (2021) 13 Tạp chí Nghiên cứu Lập pháp [Do Giang Nam and Tran Quang Cuong, '"Black Swan"—COVID-19 and the Regulatory Mechanisms of Vietnamese Contract Law' (2021) 13 Legislative Studies Journal] 21; Đàm Thị Diễm Hạnh and Lê Thị Kim Oanh, 'Áp dụng quy định "hoàn cảnh thay đổi cơ bản" đối với hợp đồng thuê nhà trong bối cảnh đại dịch COVID-19' (2021) 21 Tạp chí Kiểm sát [Dam Thi Diem Hanh and Le Thi Kim Oanh, 'Application of the Doctrine of "Fundamental Change of Circumstances" to Rental Contracts in the Context of the COVID-19 Pandemic' (2021) 21 Journal of Prosecution] 46.

27

Termination of Contracts under Vietnamese Law

TRAN Kien

I. Introduction: Complex Web of Regulations

Two important observations should be made at the beginning of an introduction to the issue of termination of contracts under Vietnamese law. First, there is a complex web of regulations governing the termination of contracts in Vietnam that comprises at least five layers of rules. And secondly, the problem is significantly under-researched by both legal scholars and practitioners in Vietnam from a general perspective.

It should be noted that, taking the first observation into consideration, contracts in general and related issues on the termination of contracts in particular are governed by a wide range of statutory and regulatory provisions and now, to a certain extent, judicial decisions. These rules can be systematically structured into five layers. The first of these is a number of fundamental principles and general provisions that are laid down in the Vietnamese Constitution of 2013 and the Vietnamese Civil Code (VCC) of 2015. The first 15 articles of the VCC provide a foundation for the entire field of private law in Vietnam, including for contracts. Special attention should be given to the new Article 3 VCC, in which a set of five cardinal principles was established for the first time. Article 4 VCC canonizes these five principles when stipulating that 'Any relevant laws governing civil relations in specific sectors must not be inconsistent with the basic principles of civil law prescribed in Article 3 of this Code.'[1] The same article further prescribes: 'Where other relevant laws do not contain provisions [on civil relations] or contain provisions which are in breach of paragraph 2 of this article, the provisions of this Code shall apply.' This essentially annuls any provisions, including both other provisions in the VCC and provisions that are promulgated in specialized laws, which are contrary to the five basic principles.

The second layer of rules governing contracts is the corpus of provisions regulating civil transactions. Part I, Chapter VIII of the VCC 2015 deals with 'civil transactions'. It consists of 18 articles—Articles 116–133—governing general issues related to civil transactions. 'Civil transaction' is defined as a contract or a unilateral juristic act which gives rise to, changes, or terminates civil rights and civil obligations.[2] A civil transaction in this sense is

[1] Hà Hùng Cường, 'Bộ luật dân sự năm 2015: Một số nội dung mới, quan trọng, mang tính đột phá hướng tới phục vụ sự phát triển nhanh, bền vững của đất nước' (2016) Tạp chí cộng sản ['The 2015 Civil Code: Some New, Breakthrough, and Important Provisions Aiming at Accelerating the Rapid, Sustainable Development of the Country' (2016) Communist Review] 885 <https://phapluatdansu.edu.vn/2018/05/28/12/07/bo-luat-dan-su-nam-2015-mot-so-noi-dung-moi-quan-trong-mang-tinh-dot-pha-huong-toi-phuc-vu-su-phat-trien-nhanh-ben-vung-cua-dat-nuoc> accessed 10 February 2025.

[2] VCC 2015, art 116.

Tran Kien, *Termination of Contracts under Vietnamese Law* In: *Studies in the Contract Laws of Asia V: Ending and Changing Contracts*. Edited by: Mindy Chen-Wishart, Dora Neo, and Stefan Vogenauer, Oxford University Press.
DOI: 10.1093/oso/9780198995814.003.0027

essentially a juristic act that is well defined and applied in civil law.[3] Contract-related issues such as validity, nullity, restitution, and the rights of bona fide third parties are governed principally and generally by this corpus of provisions.

The third layer of rules setting important conditions for the operation of contracts in Vietnam is the law of obligations. Part III of the VCC 2015 devotes a total of 111 articles—Articles 274–384—to obligations in general. In this context, 'contract' is one, and surely the most important, of the sources giving rise to legal ties that bind two or more parties; others include unilateral juristic acts and delicts.[4] Among the most significant issues related to contracts in this framework of obligations are the provisions stipulating the termination of obligations in general. Article 372 VCC 2015 provides 11 causes for the rescission of an obligation. It is followed by 12 articles providing for detailed application of each cause. The significance of this layout is that, apart from the rules on 'civil transactions' in Part I, Chapter VIII, there is an additional body of provisions detailing cases in which a contract can be terminated. Generally speaking, if there are rules on the termination of obligations, there is no need for provisions on the termination of contract and vice versa, as demonstrated by the German Civil Code (BGB) and the French Code civil. The peculiarity of this arrangement, as will be discussed later, while being of extreme importance in relation to settling disputes about the termination of a contract, is neglected by both legal scholars and practitioners in Vietnam. Đỗ Văn Đại, for example, does not include any discussion on the termination of obligations in his popular two-volume work on the law of obligations in Vietnam. However, he devotes a great part to analysing issues substantively in relation to the termination of contracts in his other two-volume work on the law of contract in Vietnam.[5]

The fourth layer of rules is essentially provisions in the VCC 2015 that govern contracts directly. The VCC 2015 devotes its largest body of provisions—totalling 185 articles (Articles 385–569)—to dealing with contracts in general (Part III, Chapter XV, Section 7 and Part III, Chapter XVI).[6] In this body, one can find a number of important provisions setting a wide range of conditions and causes that can lead to the termination of a contract: more specifically Articles 422–429. However, it should be noted that these provisions only deal with issues of contract in general.

The fifth layer of rules, and also the largest, most diverse corpus, is an uncountable number of provisions governing contracts spread across specialized statutory and regulatory instruments and other sources of law in Vietnam. There are thousands of provisions containing specialized, customized rules to govern contracts in specific fields and relations such as commerce, labour, marriage and family, maritime undertakings, etc. Of these fields, commercial law and labour law stand out because they provide two unique sets of regulations in relation to the termination of contracts.

[3] C Sumner Lobingier, 'Juristic Acts in the Civil Law' (1949) 24 Tulane Law Review 178; Ngô Huy Cương, *Góp Phần Bàn về Cải Cách Pháp Luật ở Việt Nam Hiện Nay* [*Contribution to the Debate on Legal Reform in Vietnam Today* (Judicial Publishing House 2006)].

[4] VCC 2015, art 275.

[5] Van Đai Đo, *Luật nghĩa vụ dân sự và bảo đảm thực hiện nghĩa vụ dân sự Việt Nam: bản án và bình luận bản án Tập 2* (Nhà xuất bản Chính trị quốc gia 2014) [*Vietnamese Laws of Obligations and Security: Cases and Commentary, vol 2* (Political Publishing House 2014].

[6] Not to mention that it is still debatable whether promises of rewards and prize competitions are contracts or unilateral juristic acts. They used to be considered as a type of contract in the 2005 and 1995 Civil Codes but are separated from the provisions on contracts in the VCC 2015 as a standalone category. Nguyễn Xuân Quang, Lê Nết, and Nguyễn Hồ Bích Hằng, *Luật Dân Sự Việt Nam* (Nhà Xuất Bản Đại Học Quốc Gia Thành Phố Hồ Chí Minh 2007) [*Vietnam's Civil Law* (Viet Nam National University–Ho Chi Minh City Press 2007)] 351.

These five layers of rules constitute a comprehensive legal framework that governs contracts in general and termination of contracts in particular. It is imaginable that these different layers could create a complex situation, with different approaches, conflicting solutions, and heated disagreements when it comes to terminating a contract. In principle, however, these layers should work in a hierarchical manner: starting from the fifth layer up to the first one. In other words, provisions in specialized laws should be applied first and the general provisions including the five basic principles of the VCC 2015 should be applied last. This hierarchy of application seems to be in line with the agreed approach among the Vietnamese legal community, where specialized rules are given priority over general provisions.[7] However, when it comes to the conflict between general provisions or specialized provisions themselves, especially those within the same instrument, there is no settled solution.[8] For instance, layers two, three, and four contain rules on the termination of contracts within the VCC 2015, and they seem to conflict at some points. Which rule should be given priority? This problem, unfortunately, has not attracted appropriate and sufficient attention or discussion from either academia or practitioners in the country.[9] Much of the concern is just given to the provisions terminating an employment contract prescribed in labour law.[10] There have been publications discussing certain problems in a very general sense; recently, issues relating to a particular provision on the termination of a contract in a specific situation in commercial law and in the VCC 2015 have arisen in discussions. However, they fall short of creating a balanced, agreed approach to the problem, let alone solving it. For instance, if an obligation arising out of a contract has been set off in accordance with the provisions on the termination of obligations, does the contract itself also come to an end as provided for in the rules on the termination of contracts? The answer is different depending on which of the various ways and approaches is adopted in order to understand the relation between these five layers, as well as depending on the interpretation of the relevant provisions.

A candid remark should be given at the end of this introduction as an attempt to explain the coming into force of these layers and their intended function. In the author's opinion, the existence of these layers represents a complex amalgamation of legal transplantation and home-grown development that fits into the nation's social, economic, and political conditions at a particular time. The VCC 2015 in particular, and many other pieces of legislation in general are products of a prolonged history of mixed legal transplantation along with endless domestic reforms and adaptations to create a suitable legal system for the country at a specific period of time.[11] It is well evidenced that Vietnam has consistently received and learnt from foreign legal experiences to create its national legislation: from China during medieval times,[12] to French law during the colonial

[7] VCC 2015, art 4(2), (3), and (4); Commercial Law 2005, art 4.

[8] The Law on Promulgation of Legislative Acts of 2015 does provide solutions to settle conflicts between certain types of provisions, for example, between statutory and regulatory provisions or between old and new provisions. But it has not anticipated any solution for the conflict between provisions in the same instrument. Law on Promulgation of Legislative Acts 2015, art 156.

[9] So far only Nguyen Ngoc Dien and Ngo Huy Cuong have raised this issue but have not dealt with it substantially.

[10] A simple search on a number of online legal databases reveals that most of the journal articles, theses, and books that discuss in part or touch upon the problem of terminating a contract relate to labour law.

[11] Kien Tran, Nam Ho Pham, and Quynh-Anh Lu Nguyen, 'Negotiating Legal Reform through Reception of Law: The Missing Role of Mixed Legal Transplants' (2019) 14 Asian Journal of Comparative Law 175.

[12] Ngoc Huy Nguyễn and Van Tài Ta, *The Lê Code: Law in Traditional Vietnam: A Comparative Sino-Vietnamese Legal Study with Historical-Juridical Analysis and Annotations* (Ohio University Press 1987).

period,[13] to Soviet law from 1945 until the collapse of the Soviet Union.[14] From 1986 onwards, Vietnam has attempted to build a socialist rule-of-law state based on a socialism-orientated market economy that tolerates the existence of private ownership of the means of production. As such, it has reformed its economic and legal systems to match that of developed countries while resolving to maintain its political and ideological system of socialism.[15] In relation to law, it has created a 'system of everything'. In this system, one can find characteristics and flavours of major legal systems from all over the world, especially with regard to laws governing the private sphere.[16]

Take the VCC as an example: on the surface, the structure and arrangement of its provisions, especially in the 1995 iteration, look very similar to the Civil Code of the Russian Soviet Federated Socialist Republic (RSFSR) of 1964,[17] which in turn is said to have borrowed heavily from the BGB. The drafters of the 1995 version of the VCC publicly acknowledged that they based their code in part on the RSFSR Civil Code. However, they also stated that they learnt from the civil code models and experiences of Japan, Germany, and France.[18] Subsequently, they combined these different models and experiences to create a code that they thought would best suit the situation of Vietnam. The 2005 and 2015 versions of the VCC went through a similar process as well.[19]

This practice of mixed legal transplantation and reform, in the author's critical assessment, while seeming to create the best possible solutions as claimed, actually alienates the code from its most vital merit: its structural coherence and comprehensiveness. A civil code in its true sense is not an ordinary piece of legislation, a simple aggregate of rules. It is a codified work that reforms the entire field of private law in a coherent and structured way.[20] As such, attributable partly to the working and drafting method employed by Vietnamese

[13] Vũ Văn Mẫu, *Dân-Luật Khái Luận* (Bộ Quốc Gia Giáo Dục Xuất Bản 1961) [*General Introduction to Civil Law* (Ministry of Education Publication 1961)]; Vũ Văn Mẫu, *Cổ-Luật Việt Nam Thông-Khảo và Tư-Pháp Sử* [*Vietnamese Ancient Legal History, vol I* (Ministry of National Education 1974)].

[14] J Gillespie, 'Changing Concepts of Socialist Law in Vietnam' in J Gillespie and P Nicholson (eds), *Asian Socialism and Legal Change: The Dynamics of Vietnamese and Chinese Reforms* (Australian National University Press 2005); Pham Duy Nghia, 'Confucianism and the Conception of the Law in Vietnam' in Gillespie and Nicholson (this note) 76; Bui Ngoc Son, 'The Introduction of Constitutionalism in East Asian Confucian Context: The Case of Vietnam in the Early Twentieth Century' (2013) 7 National Taiwan University Law Review 429.

[15] J Gillespie, 'Transplanting Commercial Law Reform: Developing a Rule of Law in Vietnam' (DPhil thesis, Australian National University 2005); Pham Duy Nghia, 'Transplanted Law—An Ideological and Cultural Analysis of Industrial Property Law in Vietnam' in C Antons, M Blakeney, and C Heath (eds), *Intellectual Property Harmonisation within ASEAN and APEC* (Kluwer Law International 2004); Phạm Duy Nghĩa, 'Tiếp Nhận Pháp Luật Nước Ngoài—Thời Cơ và Thách Thức Mới Cho Nghiên Cứu Lập Pháp'n ['Receiving Foreign Laws—New Opportunities and Challenges for Legislative Research'] (2002) 5 Legislative Studies 50.

[16] Gillespie (n 15); J Gillespie and P Nicholson, *Law and Development and the Global Discourses of Legal Transfers* (CUP 2012). Submission of the Government on the 1995 draft of the Civil Code of the Socialist Republic of Vietnam <https://phapluatdansu.edu.vn/2018/04/29/00/36/to-trnh-cua-chnh-phu-ve-du-n-bo-luat-dn-su-nam-1995-cua-nuoc-cong-ha-x-hoi-chu-nghia-viet-nam> accessed 27 January 2025.

[17] W Gray and R Stults (trs), *Civil Code of the Russian Soviet Federated Socialist Republic: An English Translation* (University of Michigan Law School 1965).

[18] Submission of the Government on the 1995 draft of the Civil Code (n 16).

[19] The entire documentation concerning the preparation of the VCC 2015 can be found here <https://vibonline.com.vn/du_thao/du-thao-bo-luat-dan-su-sua-doi> accessed 27 January 2025.

[20] WY Wang (ed), *Codification in East Asia: Selected Papers from the 2nd IACL Thematic Conference* (Springer International 2016) 3–18; W Gray, 'Codification, Decodification and Recodification: History, Politics and Procedure in WY Wang, *Codification in International Perspective: Selected Papers from the 2nd IACL Thematic Conference* (Springer International 2014) 3–10; H Collins, *The European Civil Code: The Way Forward* (CUP 2008); L Chen and CH van Rhee, *Towards a Chinese Civil Code: Comparative and Historical Perspectives* (Brill Nijhoff 2012); C von Bar and others (eds), *Principles, Definitions and Model Rules of European Private Law: Draft Common Frame of Reference (DCFR)* (Sellier European Law Publishers 2009).

lawmakers, the legislators not only failed to capture the true meaning and inner coherent structure of a codified collection of civil law provisions but also created a failed arrangement of many of the related provisions.[21] There is now a code that is incoherent and loosely structured, with many provisions that are hard to comprehend in both their functions and relations to each other, of which the many different rules on the termination of contracts are a prime example.[22] This is not to mention that there were different drafting committees in charge of different laws whose members were often inspired by different foreign legal experiences and employed different practices and solutions that they deemed fit for their field. For example, the civil code often falls under the remit of the Ministry of Justice, while commercial law is attached to the authority of the Ministry of Industry and Trade, and labour law is supervised by the Ministry of Labour, Invalids, and Social Affairs.

II. The Concept of 'Termination': Causes for Termination and Their Classification

Having set out an introduction to the complex web of regulations administering the termination of contracts, this part will delve into analysing directly related provisions in detail. It starts with a deliberation on the concept of termination, causes for termination, and their classification. To begin with, the four principal provisions in the VCC 2015 on the termination of contracts in general (as shown in Table 27.1) and of commercial and employment contracts in particular (as displayed in Table 27.2) are discussed.[23]

1. VCC 2015 Provisions on Termination of Obligations and Contracts

Apart from the two important provisions that create grounds for termination of obligations and contracts in general, there are other provisions that establish individual grounds for termination of specialized contracts. They include provisions on the operation of a term in a contract which stipulates that the contract is ended upon the occurrence of an event—a condition. Article 120 VCC 2015 on conditional civil transactions provides that 'Where parties have an agreement on the conditions which will give rise to or which will rescind a civil transaction, such transaction shall arise or be rescinded upon occurrence of such conditions.' It should be noted here that this provision applies to civil transactions in general, including both unilateral juristic acts and contracts. However, another provision, Article 402 VCC 2015, seems to have a different approach to what is meant by a 'conditional contract' when stipulating that 'A conditional contract is a contract the performance of which

[21] Ngọc Điện Nguyễn, *Giáo Trình Luật Dân Sự Tập 2* (Nhà xuất bản Đại học Quốc gia Thành phố Hồ Chí Minh 2018) [*Textbook on Civil Law, vol 2* (Viet Nam National University–Ho Chi Minh City Press 2018)]; Ngô Huy Cương, *Giáo Trình Luật Hợp Đồng: Phần Chung* (NXB Đại học Quốc gia Hà Nội 2013) [*Textbook on Contract Law: General Part* (Viet Nam University Hanoi Press 2013)]. Nguyễn Ngoc Điện provides an analysis on the termination of obligations including on the termination of contracts. Ngô Huy Cương, in his work on the laws of obligations and contracts, analyses the termination of contracts only.

[22] The author of this chapter has not read any analysis or discussion that captures the complex relationship between provisions on the termination of obligations and the ones on the termination of contracts.

[23] An unofficial English translation of the VCC 2015 is provided by Economica Vietnam at <www.economica.vn/Content/files/LAW%20%26%20REG/91_2015_QH13%20Civil%20Code.pdf> accessed 27 January 2025.

Table 27.1 Termination of obligations and contracts

Article 372: Grounds for termination of obligations	**Article 422: Termination of contracts**
An obligation shall terminate in the following cases:	A contract shall terminate in the following cases:
(1) The obligation is fulfilled.	(1) The contract has been completed.
(2) The parties so agree.	(2) The parties so agree.
(3) The obligee waives performance of the obligation.	(3) Where a contract can only be performed by the particular individual or legal entity which entered into the contract, and that particular individual dies, or that legal entity ceases to exist.
(4) The obligation is substituted by another obligation.	(4) The contract is cancelled or unilaterally terminated.
(5) The obligation is offset.	(5) The contract cannot be performed because the subject matter of the contract no longer exists.
(6) The obligee and the obligor merge.	(6) The contract is terminated in accordance with Article 420 of this Code.
(7) The statutory period for release from the obligation has expired [matured].	(7) Other circumstances as provided by law.
(8) The obligor being an individual dies, or the obligor being a legal entity ceases to exist, and the obligation must be performed by that particular individual or legal entity.	
(9) The obligee being an individual dies and the right to demand does not form part of the bequeathed estate, or the obligee being a legal entity ceases to exist and the right to demand cannot be transferred to another legal entity.	
(10) The distinctive object which is the subject matter of the obligation no longer exists and is substituted by another civil obligation.	
(11) Other cases as provided by law.	

Source: Author.

depends on the occurrence, modification or termination of a specified event.'[24] In other words, while with Article 120 VCC 2015 we have conditions that give rise to or terminate a civil transaction (including contracts), Article 402 VCC 2015 describes a type of condition that does not give rise to or terminate a contract but rather relates to its performance. It is unclear whether they are two different types of conditions or whether actually Article 402 VCC 2015 is just the application of Article 120 VCC 2015 in the narrow scope of contract only. If the latter explanation has any merit, there is a conflicting situation here. Đỗ Văn Đại suggests that they are actually three distinctive conditions (for establishment, termination, and performance).[25]

Article 407(2) VCC 2015 is another peculiar provision on ending a contract, related to the invalidation of the principal contract and its effect on the ancillary contract. It stipulates:

[24] VCC 2015, art 402(6).

[25] Văn Đại Đỗ, *Luật Hợp Đồng Việt Nam: Bản Án và Bình Luận Bản Án Tập 2* [*The Contract Law of Vietnam: Cases and Commentary, vol 2*] (6th edn, Hong Duc Publishing House 2017) 697–98. See further Judgment No 42/2010/DS-ST of 15 June 2010 of the Chau Thanh District People's Court; Judgment No 122/2007/DS-ST of 11 September 2007 of the Chau Doc District People's Court.

Table 27.2 Termination of Specific Types of Contracts

Commercial Law of 2005[a] **Article 292: Types of commercial remedies**	**Labour Code of 2012**[b] **Article 36: Cases of termination of an employment contract**
(1) Specific performance of contracts. (2) Fines (or penalty clauses) for breaches. (3) Forcible payment of damages. (4) Suspension of performance of contracts. (5) Cessation of performance of contracts. (6) Cancellation of contracts. (7) Other remedies agreed upon by involved parties which are not contrary to the fundamental principles of Vietnamese law, treaties to which the Socialist Republic of Vietnam is a contracting party, and international commercial practices.	(1) The employment contract expires, except for the case regulated in Article 192 paragraph 6 of this Code. (2) The tasks stated in the employment contract have been completed. (3) Both parties agree to terminate the employment contract. (4) The employee fully meets the requirements of the qualified contribution period of social insurance and reaches the age of retirement stipulated in Article 187 of this Code. (5) The employee is sentenced to imprisonment or capital punishment or is prohibited from performing the work stipulated in the employment contract by an effective conviction or judgment of the court. (6) The employee dies or is declared by the court to have lost the capacity of civil acts, or as missing or dead. (7) The employer, who is an individual, dies or is declared by the court as dead or missing, or has lost the capacity of civil acts; the employer, who is not an individual, ceases operation. (8) The employee is dismissed in accordance with Article 125 paragraph 3 of this Code. (9) The employee unilaterally terminates the employment contract in accordance with Article 37 of this Code. (10) The employer unilaterally terminates the employment contract in accordance with Article 38 of this Code; the employer terminates the employment contract due to structural and technological changes or because of economic reasons, merger and acquisition, separation of the enterprise or the cooperative.

Note: [a] An English translation can be found at <https://www.wto.org/english/thewto_e/acc_e/vnm_e/WTACCVNM43_LEG_11.pdf> accessed 27 January 2025. [b] An English translation can be found at < https://vbpl.vn/TW/Pages/vbpqen-toanvan.aspx?ItemID=11135 > accessed 21 December 2025.

Source: Author.

> Invalidity of a principal contract shall terminate an ancillary contract, unless the parties agree that the ancillary contract replaces the principal contract. This provision shall not apply with respect to security for the performance of obligations.

Article 407(3) VCC 2015 continues, affirming that 'Invalidity of an ancillary contract shall not terminate the principal contract, unless the parties agree that the ancillary contract is an inseparable part of the principal contract.' This is a rather interesting solution not generally found elsewhere in comparative law.[26]

2. Specialized Provisions on Termination of Commercial and Employment Contracts

'Commercial contracts' are dealt with under the Commercial Law of Vietnam of 2005. Although there is no statutory definition provided in this statute, a commercial contract is understood to be a contract concluded between traders (either natural or juristic persons) and mostly regulates commercial activities stipulated by the Commercial Law 2005. As such, commercial contracts are contracts between for-profit traders and regulated principally by commercial law, although contractual issues not provided for in the Commercial Law 2005 such as offer, acceptance, and conditions of validity continue to be governed by the VCC 2015.

Following on from what has been presented in Table 27.2, it can be seen that the terms *chấm dứt* (termination) and *chấm dứt hợp đồng* (termination of contract) in the VCC are loose terms encompassing different grounds not only confined to contractual default but also covering grounds such as full performance, agreement, operation of a contractual condition, operation of the law, supervening impossibility, and so on.[27] In this sense, *chấm dứt hợp đồng* in Vietnamese law appears similar to *résolution* in the old French Code civil, where it includes both termination on the theory of risks and termination for contractual default.[28] This meaning seems to conform with the approach proposed by Mindy Chen-Wishart when she refers to the end of the life of a contract in a broad sense rather than just termination for breach of contract.[29] Nguyễn Ngọc Điện, a prominent civil law scholar and French trained jurist, adopts a similar approach to *chấm dứt nghĩa vụ* (termination of obligations) in his textbook on civil law.[30] Ngô Huy Cương, employing comparative law methodology, introduces a somewhat similar approach of classification in relation to grounds for termination.[31]

Thus, by adopting the approach proposed by Chen-Wishart, a classification of grounds for termination of contract under Vietnamese law can be discerned (Figure 27.1) and will be detailed in the following.

3. Classification of the Grounds for Terminating Contracts

One important aspect of the decision to terminate a contract due to breach that has not been fully examined by the Vietnamese legal community is whether to consider termination as a

[26] AT von Mehren, *Contracts in General* (Mohr Siebeck 2008); H Beale, B Fauvarque-Cosson, J Rutgers, and S Vogenauer, *Ius Commune Casebook for the Common Law of Europe: Cases, Materials and Text on Contract Law* (3rd edn, Hart Publishing 2019); M Chen-Wishart, *Contract Law* (OUP 2012).

[27] Beale and others (n 26) 981–82.

[28] von Mehren (n 26) para 143.

[29] Chen-Wishart (n 26) 453.

[30] Nguyễn (n 21) 395–429.

[31] Ngô Huy Cương (n 21) 370–79.

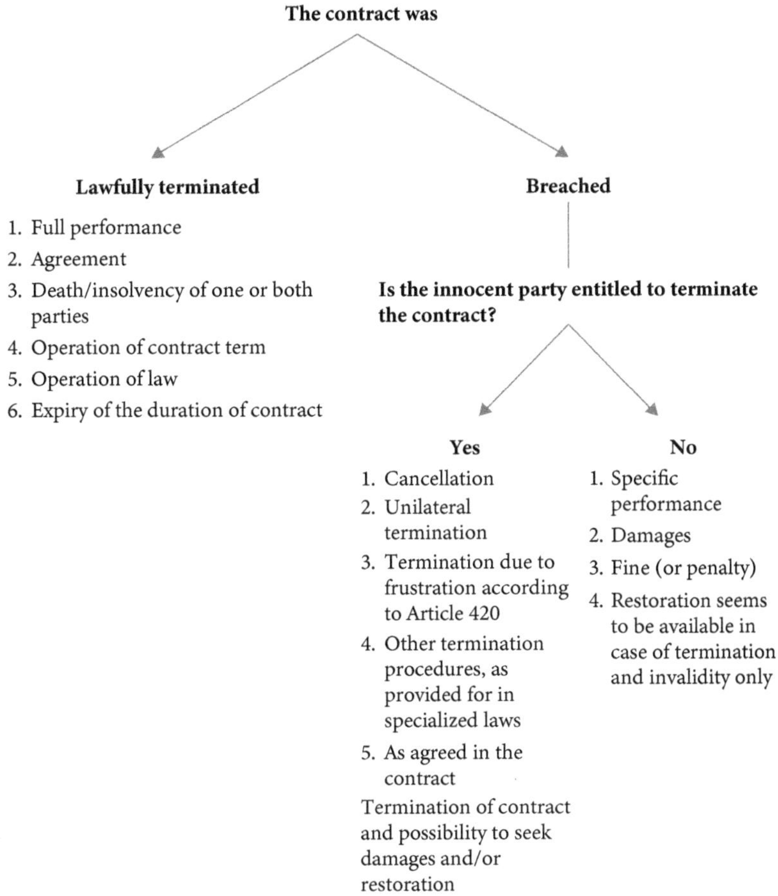

Figure 27.1 Grounds for terminating contracts
Source: Author.

remedy—as is the trend at the international level.[32] In Vietnamese legislation, termination is not a type of remedy available to the aggrieved party. Article 11 VCC 2015, which deals with civil remedies ('methods to protect civil rights'), does not mention termination per se. The language used in the VCC 2015 even makes the situation more complicated by using the terms 'right to terminate' and 'right to cancel'. Furthermore, termination as an umbrella term includes within its scope a number of remedies such as cancellation and unilateral termination. Given the fact that remedies are often supported and enforced by the threat of state power, it is expected that all remedies must be explicitly provided for in statutory provisions.[33] Parties to a contract cannot agree on a new remedy between themselves.[34]

[32] cf P Huber in S Vogenauer (ed), *Commentary on the UNIDROIT Principles of International Commercial Contracts ('PICC')* (2nd edn, OUP 2015) Introduction to ch 7.3 para 1.

[33] Đức Giang Bùi, 'Về việc thỏa thuận mức bồi thường thiệt hại cố định trong hợp đồng: Câu trả lời còn dang dở' (2015) 5 *Thời Báo Kinh Tế Sài Gòn* ['Liquidated Damages in the Law of Contract: Unanswered Questions' (2015) 5 *Sai Gon Times*] 54, 55.

[34] One notable example is liquidated damages, a type of remedy that has not been recognized in Vietnam. Some courts have declared the agreement on liquidated damages to be void because it infringes a statutory prohibition.

An interestingly divergent approach between the VCC 2015 and the Commercial Law 2005 can be raised in relation to this issue. The Commercial Law 2005 explicitly calls these grounds for termination 'remedies' and even goes further in allowing parties in commercial relationships to agree on new remedies between them, so far as they do not contradict basic principles of Vietnamese law.[35] As such, the Commercial Law 2005 appears to be more in line with international trends than the VCC 2015.[36]

There are two uncertain cases in the context of the termination of contracts. The first case relates to situations where the subject matter of a contract no longer exists, as foreseen by Article 422(5) VCC 2015. It is stipulated that such cases also lead to a termination of contract. The first major problem is that 'the subject matter of a contract' is not defined anywhere. Rather, there is only a definition of the subject matter of obligations. Article 276 VCC 2015 says that 'the subject matter of an obligation shall be property or acts which must be performed or acts which must not be performed'. Is the subject matter of an obligation also the subject matter of a contract? It might be, as in the case of Article 1163 of the French Code civil of 2016. However, this has not been settled in Vietnamese doctrine. The other problem is the interpretation of Article 422(5) VCC 2015 governing the termination of contracts due to the fact that the subject matter of a contract has ceased to exist. There are two scenarios related to this provision. The first scenario relates to the hypothesis that if, immediately from the time a contract is entered into, it is impossible to perform the subject matter of the contract, the contract shall be invalid (Article 408 VCC 2015). In this case, the contract will be declared void rather than being terminated. The second scenario envisages that if the subject matter becomes impossible or disappears after the contract has been entered into, it will be terminated rather than being declared void. There is a provision that seems to detail this second scenario: Article 426 VCC 2015 on the cancellation of contracts where property is lost or damaged. However, it is unlikely that Article 422(5) VCC 2015 has anything to do with Article 426 VCC 2015. In other words, they cover two separate situations. For example, Nguyễn Ngọc Điện seems to distinguish Article 422(5) from Article 426.[37] Đỗ Văn Đại, however, suggests otherwise. He posits that Article 426 VCC 2015 is the application of Article 422(5) VCC 2015.[38] If that is the case, Article 426 VCC 2015 fails to capture the full scope of application of Article 422(5) VCC 2015 because it only deals with one type of contractual subject matter: property. There are still other types of contractual subject matter, such as work and service. Furthermore, even if the property ceases to exist, the parties to the contract still have the right to replace it with other property, thus avoiding the termination of their contract. The language of Article 422(5) VCC 2015 is more general than the situations Article 426 VCC 2015 envisages. That is to say, in case the subject matter of a contract becomes unavailable or ceases to exist, the innocent contractual party should be entitled to terminate the contract. If this situation has come about due to the fault of one party, then the aggrieved party should be able to claim damages as well.

35 Mạnh Dũng Nguyễn and Vũ Minh Hà Đặng, 'Thiệt Hại Ước Tính' ['Liquidated Damages'] (2016) <http://dzungsrt.com/wp-content/uploads/2016/01/12312014-Liquidated-damages.pdf> accessed 27 January 2025.

36 H Kötz, *European Contract Law* (2nd edn, OUP 2017) 215–40.

37 Nguyễn (n 21) 403–05.

38 Văn Đại Đỗ, *Bình Luận Khoa Học Những Điểm Mới Của Bộ Luật Dân Sự Năm 2015 Xuất Bản Lần Thứ 2* (Nhà xuất bản Hồng Đức 2016) [*Commentary on New Provisions of the 2015 Civil Code* (2nd edn, Hong Duc Publishing House 2016)] 401–02.

The second uncertain case concerns a contract that has expired. In that case, the question is whether it will be possible to terminate even in cases where the contract has not been fully performed or discharged. This ground is not explicitly included in the two important general provisions on the termination of obligations and contracts cited above. However, there are several specialized provisions that stipulate that the expiry of the duration of the contract will terminate the contract itself.[39] Đỗ Văn Đại, quoting French experiences and provisions of the revised French Code civil of 2016, reasons that in principle the contract will be terminated once its duration has expired.[40] However, there are a number of exceptions to this principle. Some contracts will remain in force even though they have come to an end; they include employment contracts and service contracts.[41] In case the contract has expired but the contract's obligations have not been fully performed, the obligations shall remain binding and enforceable on the parties.[42]

It should also be noted that the death of a party to the contract generally does not end the contract. The personal rights and obligations arising out of the contract are inherited by the heirs of the deceased according to the law of succession stipulated in the VCC 2015. Article 615 VCC 2015 explicitly provides that 'a person entitled to an inheritance has the responsibility to perform the proprietary obligations within the scope of the estate left by the deceased'. This essentially means that the heirs must continue performing the contract instead of having any right to terminate it, except for rights and obligations related to the personality of the deceased as prescribed by Articles 365 and 370 VCC 2015.[43] The death of a party to the contract shall terminate the contract only in case the contract must be performed by the deceased party as agreed or prescribed by law.

A final note should be given to the distinction between invalid contracts and terminated contracts, especially in the case of cancellation or unilateral termination. In practice, it can be seen that lawyers and judges struggle with this distinction. One can find a number of decisions and judgments where a contract is cancelled because of invalidating reasons or *hợp đồng bị hủy bỏ do vô hiệu*.[44] In other words, they use the terminology for termination of contracts to invalidate a contract in dispute, which is clearly inappropriate. While there are some similarities between the two, there are significant differences. To demonstrate this, it helps to highlight the legal consequences of a termination of contract. In essence, Article 131 VCC 2015 acknowledges that 'An invalid civil transaction shall not give rise to civil rights and obligations with respect to the parties or to changes and termination of such rights and obligations as from the time the transaction is entered into.' Put differently, it means that there is no contract at all. On the other hand, to terminate a contract requires that such a contract must have been entered into.[45]

[39] VCC 2015, arts 140(3)(a), 554.

[40] Đỗ (n 25) 905.

[41] ibid 910–14.

[42] Judgment No 1508/2005/DSPT of 18 July 2005 of the Ho Chi Minh City People's Court; Decision No 09/2011/KDTM-GDT of 17 August 2008 of the Judicial Council of Supreme People's Court; Decision No 18/2013/LD-GDT of 4 July 2013 of the Labour Court of the Supreme People's Court.

[43] Văn Đại Đỗ, *Luật thừa kế Việt Nam: bản án và bình luận bản án* (Nhà xuất bản Chính trị quốc gia 2009) [*Vietnamese Succession Law: Cases and Commentary* (Political Publishing House 2009)] 521–38.

[44] Hồng Hải Nguyễn, 'Một Số Vấn Đề về Hợp Đồng vô Hiệu Trong Pháp Luật Tư Hiện Hành Của Việt Nam' ['Some Issues Related to Invalid Contracts in Vietnamese Private Law'] (2018) <https://phapluatdansu.edu.vn/2018/09/26/20/51/21724> accessed 27 January 2025.

[45] Chen-Wishart (n 26) 453–55; Beale and others (n 26) ch 25.2.

III. Requirements for Termination

1. Lawfully Terminated Contracts

The classification of grounds for the termination of contracts under Vietnamese law proposed above paves the way to engage more coherently and systematically with the requirements for termination of contracts in Vietnam. For contracts that are lawfully terminated, there seem to be no specific requirements that have to be adhered to. In practice, contracts falling within this group end based upon one of three grounds: (i) full performance; (ii) agreement to end the contract, including by operation of contractual conditions; and (iii) operation of law.

First, full performance is the most desirable result for *bona fide* parties to a contract for their agreement to end. In theory, when a contract has been fully performed, it should be terminated automatically without any formal notice. However, the reality might be more complicated because normally a contract creates more than one principal obligation that needs to be discharged. There are other ancillary obligations that might still continue after the principal obligation has been performed. Therefore, in practice, parties to a contract in Vietnam often sign a so-called 'contract liquidation' (*biên bản thanh lý hợp đồng*)—a written agreement to formally declare and put an end to a contract that has been fully performed.[46]

Secondly, agreement to end a contract is also a desirable result, even though in reality it means that the contract has not been fully performed. In this case, an agreement between the parties suffices to end the contract. The agreement itself constitutes a notice to both parties that the contract has been ended. Within this category, the author would include the operation of contract terms, most notably, conditional contracts or contracts with conditions. As discussed above, there are three types of contractual conditions in the VCC 2015: suspensive conditions (conditions that give rise to a contract), resolutive conditions (conditions that terminate a contract), and performing conditions (conditions to perform a contract). All conditions must be agreed by the parties. They can be included in the contract or exist in a separate agreement.[47] As an agreement, a type of civil transaction, this is subject to conditions and hence it must meet all requirements for it to be effective, binding, and legally enforceable.[48] If the event specified in a resolutive condition occurs, the contract will be terminated.

The third ground for lawful termination of a contract is by operation of law. The VCC 2015 provides several cases according to which a contract will be terminated by operation of law, such as the death of a party. Specialized provisions stipulate most cases where a contract can be terminated by this method. The most notable might be the Labour Code 2012 in relation to employment contracts. Paragraphs (4)–(8) of Article 36 of the Labour Code 2012 are the best examples of when an employment contract will be terminated as 'the employee fully meets the requirements of qualified contribution period of social insurance and reaches the age of retirement' or 'the employee is sentenced to imprisonment or capital

[46] Almost all written contracts are accompanied by a contract liquidation. Much of the statutory and regulatory legislation in Vietnam also explicitly requires a written contract liquidation as a proof of fully performing and discharging a contract under their stipulation.

[47] Đỗ (n 25) 693–715.

[48] ibid 704–15.

punishment or is prohibited from performing the work stipulated in the employment contract by an effective conviction or judgment of the court'.

2. Termination for Breach of Contract

A valid contract binds parties to the performance of the contract until their obligation has been fully discharged. Any breach would result in the imposition of a number of legal remedies that can be enforced with the support of an authority. However, remedies vary in terms of their severity, function, and procedure with which they are applied. Certain remedies are more severe and serious than others in relation to their legal consequences so that they invite careful consideration and conditions for their application. In the realm of the law of contract, invalidity and termination are the two most severe and serious remedies that can bring a contract to its end.[49] Unfortunately, the Vietnamese legal community has not come to a consensus on the range and types of civil remedies available. As mentioned earlier, the Commercial Law 2005 uses the term 'remedies' to describe certain grounds that the VCC 2015 stipulates as the termination of contracts. Nguyễn Ngọc Điện, for instance, strictly follows Article 11 VCC 2015 and divides civil remedies into two narrow sets of actions and self-help.[50] This approach would exclude all grounds for the termination of a contract provided for in Article 422 from the scope of statutory remedies. Đỗ Văn Đại, Phạm Duy Nghĩa, and Ngô Huy Cương appear to accept a broader scope of remedies that includes certain remedies laid down in Article 422 VCC 2015.[51] This approach is more in line with international trends and comparative law scholarship, especially concerning the termination of contracts.[52]

From this perspective, it is safe to argue that there are at least two important remedies provided for in Article 422 VCC 2015 that can terminate a breached contract. They are cancellation (*hủy bỏ*) and unilateral termination (*đơn phương chấm dứt*). These are dealt with in Articles 423 and 428, respectively.

Article 423. Cancellation of contracts

(1) A party has the right to cancel a contract and shall not be liable to compensate for loss and damage in the following cases:
    (a) The parties agree that a breach of contract by the other party gives rise to cancellation.
    (b) The other party commits a serious breach of contractual obligations.
    (c) Other circumstances as provided by law.

[49] H Beale (ed), *Chitty on Contracts: Second Cumulative Supplement to the Thirty-Second Edition, vol 1* (32nd edn, Sweet and Maxwell 2017) para 24-001.

[50] Ngọc Điện Nguyễn, *Giáo Trình Luật Dân Sự Tập 1* (Nhà xuất bản Đại học Quốc gia Thành phố Hồ Chí Minh 2018) [*Textbook on Civil Law, vol 1* (Viet Nam National University–Ho Chi Minh City Press 2018)] 29–33.

[51] Duy Nghĩa Phạm, *Giáo Trình Luật Kinh Tế* (Tái bản lần thứ 5, có chỉnh sửa, bổ sung, Nhà Xuất Bản Công An Nhân Dân 2015) [*Textbook of Economic Law* (Public Security Press 2015)] paras 432–38; Văn Đại Đỗ, *Các Biện Pháp Xử Lý Việc Không Thực Hiện Đúng Hợp Đồng Trong Pháp Luật Việt Nam* (Tái bản có sửa chữa, bổ sung, Nhà xuất bản Chính trị quốc gia 2013) [*Measures to Remedy Breach of Contract in Vietnamese Law* (Political Publishing House 2013)] 40–46; Huy Cương Ngô, *Giáo trình luật hợp đồng phần chung: Dùng cho đào tạo sau đại học* (Nhà xuất bản Đại học Quốc gia Hà Nội 2013) [*Textbook on General Contract Law: For Postgraduate Students* (Viet Nam National University–Hanoi Press 2013)] 389–412.

[52] Chen-Wishart (n 26) 457–81; Beale and others (n 26) 996–1011; von Mehren (n 26) paras 203–39; Huber (n 32).

(2) Serious breach means failure to fulfil correctly obligations by a party so that the other party is unable to achieve the purpose of entering into the contract.
(3) A party cancelling a contract must notify the other party immediately of the cancellation and must compensate if the failure to notify causes loss and damage.

Besides this over-arching rule, there are three other provisions that cover three specific cases for cancelling a contract: Article 424 VCC 2015 on cancellation of contracts due to late performance of obligations, Article 425 VCC 2015 on cancellation of contracts due to inability to implement the obligations undertaken by the obligor, and Article 426 VCC 2015 on cancellation of contracts where property is lost or damaged. Finally, Article 428 VCC 2015 is of particular importance:

Article 428. Unilateral termination of performance of contracts
(1) A party has the right to unilaterally terminate the performance of a contract and is not required to pay compensation for loss and damage if the other party commits a serious breach of the obligations stipulated in the contract or if so agreed by the parties or so provided by law.
(2) A party unilaterally terminating the performance of a contract must notify the other party immediately of its termination of the contract and must compensate if the failure to notify causes loss and damage.
(3) Where the performance of a contract is terminated unilaterally, it shall terminate from the time when the other party is notified of the termination. [In such case,] the parties do not have to continue to perform their obligations, except for the agreements on penalties for breach and compensation for loss and damage, and the agreements on dispute resolution. A party which has already performed its obligation may demand the other party to make payment for the portion of the obligation which has been fulfilled.
(4) The party suffering loss and damage caused by failure to correctly perform contractual obligations by the other party shall be compensated.
(5) In the case of unilateral termination of performance of a contract with no grounds provided in paragraph 1 of this Article, the party unilaterally terminating performance of the contract shall be determined as the party breaching obligations and must perform civil liabilities in accordance with this Code and other relevant laws due to failure to perform correctly the contractual obligations.

The Commercial Law 2005 does not use the term 'unilateral termination'. Instead, it uses the term *đình chỉ thực hiện hợp đồng*—'suspension of the performance of contract'. *Đình chỉ* and *đơn phương chấm dứt* are identical, as will be discussed later.

(a) Seriousness of the breach

The remedy in the Commercial Law 2005 was actually the inspiration for the reform that led to the 2015 version of the Civil Code, with some differences, and can serve as a starting point for comparison and discussion relating to the seriousness of breach or default.[53] This will now be applied to several hypothetical scenarios.[54]

[53] Đỗ (n 38) 396–407.
[54] The hypothetical scenarios described in this section are taken from M Chen-Wishart, D Neo, and S Vogenauer, 'Introduction', ch 1 in this volume, 9–10.

(1) Sue and Bob

Bob contracts to build a house for Sue for the price of $100,000. After doing a third of the work he abandons the job, leaving behind material worth $15,000 which Sue later uses to finish the works. Can Bob claim the value of the work done or of the materials?

Suppose that the contract is terminated by Sue due to the serious breach of incomplete performance by Bob. The consequences of the termination would depend on which mechanism Sue used to terminate: Article 423 VCC 2015 on cancelling or Article 428 VCC 2015 on unilateral termination. If Sue invoked Article 423 VCC 2015, then the contract would be deemed terminated at the time of its conclusion. Both parties have to restore what they have received so far. In this case, Sue has to return $15,000. However, Sue can initiate a lawsuit against Bob for damages caused by his failure to perform.

If Sue terminated the contract in accordance with Article 428 VCC 2015, the contract would be terminated at the time Bob receives a formal notice. There would be no restoration. Instead, both parties would be released from future performance. The obligor would be reimbursed for any past performance. However, the defaulting party would have to pay damages. As such, Bob could claim the value of his material, to the amount of $15,000. However, he would have to pay damages due to his breach.

One important point should be raised to emphasize a crucial aspect of these remedies. Cancellation and unilateral termination are two different remedies that can end a breached contract under Vietnamese law. They dictate two different sets of criteria for a breached contract to be terminated. They also envisage two distinctive legal consequences for the terminated contract. One is retrospective (in the case of cancellation). The other is prospective (in the in case of unilateral termination). This seems to be a specific feature of Vietnamese law of contract on the issues of termination. Although this distinction has been criticized as overlapping and unnecessary, it is still maintained in the 2015 version of the VCC.[55] The Principles of European Contract Law (PECL) and the UNIDROIT Principles of International Commercial Contracts (PICC) do not introduce such a distinction.[56]

The essential question in relation to the application of these two remedies is which type of breach will entitle the innocent party to cancel or unilaterally terminate the contract. As a starting point of discussion, Professor Treitel provides a delicate distinction between 'the nature of the obligation which is not performed' and 'the effect of the failure in performance'.[57] In theory it makes sense that a contract can create a bundle of obligations that need to be performed rather than just one obligation. Some obligations are vital and fundamental, and some are trivial. This leads to two possible solutions: either only the breach of important obligations—whether the breach is serious or not—can lead to the termination of a contract or it does not matter which obligation—be it vital or trivial—is breached; any breach that is serious will lead to termination.[58]

(2) Prime Ltd and Devil Corp

Prime Ltd sells a piece of land to Devil Corp. Under the terms of the contract, Devil pays a 10 per cent deposit, the remainder of the sum being due at 5:00 pm on 30 September, time being 'of the essence'. According to Clause 12, failure to meet the deadline would result in

55 Đỗ (n 38).

56 Beale and others (n 26) ch 25.1; Huber (n 32) art 7.3.1 paras 1–18; Kötz (n 36) 215–24.

57 As cited by von Mehren (n 26) para 167.

58 Huber (n 32) art 7.3.1 paras 12–18; Beale and others (n 26) ch 25.4.

the deposit being forfeited and the agreement being terminated. Devil is ten minutes late in tendering the completion money and Prime refuses performance. Can Devil sue for specific performance, arguing that Prime's reliance on the clause is unreasonable in some way? Would the result be different if the contract did not include Clause 12?

According to Article 11 VCC 2015, Devil cannot sue for specific performance because Devil is the defaulting party. Only defaulted parties can bring a lawsuit for the application of a specific remedy to protect their infringed rights and interests. In addition, as there is an agreement in the contract specifying that a party can terminate the contract in the said circumstance, the court would honour the agreement and Prime Ltd can terminate the contract if the specific agreement is breached.

If there were no Clause 12 in the contract, the case would be more difficult. The court would give some weight to the agreement that time was of the essence. However, it would have to rely on Article 423(2) VCC 2015 for the definition of 'serious breach'. Crucial weight would be given to assess whether time being of the essence in the contract is so important that its default would make the aggrieved party unable to achieve the purpose of entering into the contract. Given the nature of the contract, a conveyance related to real estate, often contracted after a prolonged negotiation, Vietnamese courts would be unwilling to recognize that a ten-minute delay in payment would be a serious breach that would entitle the aggrieved party to terminate the contract.

On this point, Vietnamese laws follow the international trend that the breach must attain a certain degree of seriousness for the aggrieved party to terminate the contract, with two important alternatives.[59] In general, the Commercial Law 2005 requires that there must be a 'fundamental breach' (*vi phạm cơ bản*), while the VCC 2015 dictates that only a 'serious breach' (*vi phạm nghiêm trọng*) will entitle the innocent party to terminate a contract. Fundamental breach is defined as a contractual breach by a party which causes damage to the other party to the extent that the other party cannot achieve the purpose for which the contract was originally entered into,[60] while the VCC 2015 defines serious breach as failure to correctly fulfil obligations by a party so that the other party is unable to achieve the purpose for which the contract was entered into.

(3) Seven Seas and Big Chef

Seven Seas, an importer of seafood, sells two tons of mussels to Big Chef restaurant chain. After one ton has been delivered it turns out that the concentration of cadmium in the mussels is 2 per cent above the concentration permitted by national food regulations. Can Big Chef terminate the contract?

In the absence of an agreement to terminate the contract due to defective goods and without a specific circumstance provided for by law, we have to rely on Article 423(2) VCC 2015 to assess whether the breach is serious in the sense that it makes the other party unable to achieve the purpose for which the contract was entered into. In this case, the author is of the opinion that it is a serious breach as it makes the contract meaningless from the side of the buyer; they cannot use the goods for their business. That is to

[59] Judgment No 16/2009/DS-ST of 7 July 2009 of District Four People's Court; Judgment No 02/2010/KDTM-ST of 12 January 2010 of the District Eleven People's Court.

[60] Commercial Law 2005, art 3(13).

say, applying either Articles 423(1)(b) or 428(1) VCC 2015, Big Chef can terminate the contract.

Interestingly, there is a mistaken perception in relation to the use of terminology in these above-mentioned provisions. Đỗ Văn Đại provides an insight that, when asked to make comments on the draft of the 2015 version of the VCC, he opposed the use of the term *vi phạm cơ bản*—'fundamental breach'—in the Commercial Law 2005 because the term is borrowed from English law and does not exist in the PECL, the PICC, or the United Nations Convention on Contracts for the International Sale of Goods (CISG). The more accepted term, according to Đỗ Văn Đại, is *vi phạm nghiêm trọng*—'serious breach'.[61] This is plainly wrong as Articles 25, 46(2), 49(1)(a), and other provisions in the CISG employ the notion of 'fundamental breach', whereas Article 7.3.1 PICC and Article 8:103 PECL use the term 'fundamental non-performance'.

Let us turn to another important issue related to what legally constitutes a breach under Vietnamese law. Commercial law mentions fundamental breach of a contractual obligation while the VCC speaks of serious breach of a contractual obligation. However, neither piece of legislation contains any provision detailing what constitutes a breach of a contractual obligation. The VCC 2015 instead has a provision on what constitutes a breach of an obligation in general. Article 351(1) VCC 2015 states that breach of obligation means an obligor fails to perform the obligation on time, does not perform the obligation fully, or performs the contents of the obligation incorrectly. This article suggests that there are three types of breach: late performance, partial performance, and defective performance.

Apart from the serious, fundamental breach of a contractual obligation that will entitle the innocent party to terminate the contract, one party to the contract can cancel or unilaterally terminate the contract if (i) there is a breach that the two parties have agreed will allow for the cancellation or unilateral termination of the contract and (ii) in other circumstances as provided for by law. Two accounts should be given in relation to these provisions. First, there is a divergence between Articles 423 and 428 VCC 2015 on the 'agreed right to termination'. It seems that Article 423 VCC 2015 on cancellation of contracts requires that the agreed right to terminate stipulated by Article 423(1) VCC 2015 must relate to a breach, whether serious or trivial, while Article 428 VCC 2015 on unilateral termination does not mention that the agreed right must relate to a breach. So, any event notwithstanding, the breach of a contractual obligation that the two parties agree upon and that later happens can entitle any party to unilaterally terminate the contract. Secondly, the agreed right to terminate a contract will take precedence over other cases. From this perspective, it looks like Vietnamese law aligns with the PICC rather than the PECL and other model laws in respecting and giving priority to freedom of contract and the principle of party autonomy.[62]

(4) Coco and David

Coco, a famous architect, agrees with David that he will landscape the garden in her next development. He is due to start work on 1 December. For David, this is an important opportunity to make his name as a landscape gardener. On 1 October, she tells him that she is

[61] Đỗ (n 38) 352.
[62] Huber (n 32) art 7.3.1 para 7.

no longer interested because the development will not include a garden after all. David has already purchased materials. He estimates that his future earnings will be 10 per cent lower because he will not be able to benefit from having worked with Coco. Can he insist on doing the work? Can he bring an action for breach of contract?

This is a very difficult case. Suppose that a contract has been made between Coco and David either verbally or in writing and David's performance is not due yet. Article 278(2) VCC 2015 prohibits the obligor to perform his obligation in advance with the only exception being where the obligee later affirms the performance, which does not happen in this case. That is to say, the purchase made by David to prepare for the performance of the contract would not have to be reimbursed by Coco. However, one also needs to take into consideration whether Coco knew or ought to have known that David had been making orders to prepare for his work. If she knew, the situation will be complicated further because she is breaching her obligation to act in good faith and with honesty, as dictated by Article 3 VCC 2015. If this is the case, she might be required to pay damages to David if David can establish that he suffers loss due to her breach.

Now, we can move to whether Coco can terminate the part of the contract on a landscape garden. If Coco does not have any lawful ground for termination, then she cannot terminate it and has to continue honouring the contract and let David complete his performance. However, in this case, it seems that there are two grounds that Coco can rely on to justify her termination. The first one is *force majeure*, as defined at Article 156(1) VCC 2015. However, in principle, this can only exempt her from civil liability according to Article 351(2) VCC 2015 on civil liability resulting from a breach of obligations. If there is a clause in the contract stipulating that one party can terminate the contract due to a *force majeure* event, which happens quite often in Vietnam, then Coco will be able to terminate the contract. The second ground that can entitle Coco to terminate the contract is frustration or hardship, as stipulated in Article 420 VCC 2015. These two grounds are only applicable if Coco can argue that a change of plans concerning the development is an event beyond her control.[63]

(5) Car Machinery & Co and Traders Ltd

Car Machinery & Co appoint Traders Ltd as sole distributors of their car panel presses for a period of five years. Clause 7(b) of the agreement provides that 'Distributors shall send their representatives to visit all six large car manufacturers in the country at least once in every week for the purpose of soliciting orders for car panel presses. Failure to comply with this obligation shall entitle Car Machinery to terminate the agreement with immediate effect.' Traders Ltd miss two visits to car manufacturers in the second month of the contractual period. Is Car Machinery entitled to terminate the agreement?

In this case, Car Machinery is entitled to terminate the agreement without having to give due regard to the seriousness of Traders Ltd's breach as this has been clearly agreed upon by the two parties. Car Machinery should make sure that they follow any process or conditions for terminating the contract set out between the two parties if they choose to exercise this right. However, as analysed above, because there are differences in terms of legal

[63] For these doctrines, see Do GN, 'Change of Circumstances under Vietnamese Law', ch 26 in this volume, 543–546.

consequences between cancellation and unilateral termination, it is desirable that the two parties should make clear in their contract whether Car Machinery is entitled to cancellation or unilateral termination.

(b) Fault

Does fault play any role in determining the right to terminate a contract? This question has become extremely complicated following the enactment of the 2015 version of the VCC. Professor Treitel includes fault in his treatment concerning grounds for termination.[64] There are also conflicting views worldwide on the role of fault in terminating a contract. *Résolution* in French law, for example, does not require fault on the part of the obligor.[65]

The VCC 2015, on the one hand, drops the requirement of fault in the constitutive elements of delict or tort. Article 584 VCC 2015 no longer includes the language of fault in its wording.[66] On the other hand, fault is still a requirement for the establishment of civil liability resulting from any breach of obligations. Article 364 VCC 2015 stipulates two types of fault: intentional and non-intentional (or negligent). This controversial reform has created a massive headache for the legal community of Vietnam in dealing with the question of liability, remedies, and so on. In principle, it could be argued that in order to terminate a contract, the aggrieved party must establish that the defaulting party has breached a contractual obligation. As such, it also has to establish the existence of fault on the part of the defaulting party. Phạm Duy Nghĩa, however, thinks otherwise. He argues that fault is presumed rather than must be proven. Thus, the aggrieved party does not have to prove the existence of fault on the part of the defaulting party.[67] Other authors argue that since the abolition of fault in tort in the 2015 version of the Civil Code, it is no longer relevant to take it into consideration when determining the termination of a contract.[68] There is an extremely interesting case in relation to fault and cancellation of contracts in the VCC 2015. Article 413 VCC 2015 envisages one of the more unusual cases when stipulating that:

> With respect to a bilateral contract, when one party is unable to perform its obligation due to the fault of the other party, the first party has the right to demand that the other party continue to perform its obligation with respect to the first party, or has the right to cancel the contract and demand compensation for loss and damage.

(c) Termination for delay in performance

If the obligor delays his performance, a number of questions tend to arise: 'How long does the obligee have to wait before terminating? Can he terminate right away? Must he show that the delay is very serious? Or must he at least give the obligor a warning so that, in effect, the obligor has a second chance?'[69] In the case of delay in performance, there are a number of

[64] As cited by von Mehren (n 26) paras 155–60.
[65] Beale and others (n 26) ch 25.2.
[66] Đỗ (n 38) 474–76.
[67] Phạm (n 51) para 433.
[68] Đỗ (n 25).
[69] Beale and others (n 26) ch 25.5.

options at the obligee's disposal under Vietnamese law. First, the obligor has to inform the obligee immediately about the delay and might ask the obligee to delay the performance of his obligation. The obligee has total freedom to grant the delay or take other actions because the delay in performance is clearly a breach of obligation as set out in Article 351 VCC 2015. If the obligee grants the delay, then the obligor will not be considered to have breached his obligation. The obligee can also delay the performance of his obligation until the obligor has the ability to perform or provide security.[70] Alternatively, the obligee can sue for specific performance, damages, or payment of a penalty. And lastly, the obligee can terminate the contract if the delay in performance meets the threshold laid down in Articles 423 or 428 VCC 2015, that is to say: (i) as agreed in advance; (ii) serious breach; (iii) as provided for by law.[71] If the performance is not yet due when the obligor informs the obligee about a potential delay, and the obligee wants to terminate the contract because of the delay, then he has to give notice of the termination of the contract, as stipulated by Articles 423 or 428. However, he does not have to give the obligor a second chance to perform within a reasonable time beyond the due date.

(d) Termination before performance is due

The issue of anticipatory non-performance in Vietnam is more complex and it is harder to provide a clear solution. In general, statutory provisions do not give the potentially aggrieved party the right to terminate a contract that is not yet due even if the obligor has announced that he is not going to perform his obligation under the contract.[72] Courts confirm this approach by denying the right of the seller to sell his goods to another party if the buyer has made it clear that he would not be able to receive them.[73] There seems to be a very narrow situation where an obligee can escape a contract that will not be performed when due.[74] On the other hand, comparative law scholarship has shown that such a termination is permitted under various foreign laws, with the BGB, the PECL, and French and English cases as prime examples.[75]

IV. The Mechanisms of Termination

1. The Option to Terminate

It should be made clear at the beginning of this part that the decision to terminate a contract resulting from a breach of contractual obligation resides entirely with the aggrieved party. In other words, it might choose not to terminate at all and pursue different paths such as specific performance, damages, penalty, and so on. As analysed earlier, because termination in Vietnamese law is a broad term encompassing different grounds for discharging parties from performing a contract, there are diverse mechanisms employed. Comparative law

[70] VCC 2015, art 411.

[71] Đỗ (n 25) 632–56. See also Judgment No 1350/2008/KDTM-PT of 17 November 2008 of the Ho Chi Minh City People's Court; Judgment No 1217/2011/KDTM-PT of 19 September 2011 of the Ho Chi Minh People's Court.

[72] Đỗ (n 25) 786–96.

[73] Judgment No 73/2005/KDTM-ST of 12 September 2005 of the Hanoi People's Court.

[74] Commercial Law 2005, art 313(2).

[75] Beale and others (n 26) ch 25.6; Kötz (n 36) 228.

scholarship suggests that there is divergence on this issue, with some countries requiring the intervention of the courts in terminating a contract, while other countries do not do so.[76] The VCC 2015 appears to have learned from both foreign experiences and domestic dynamics, especially through the practical adjudication of courts and arbitral tribunals, as well as from the Commercial Law 2005.[77]

2. Lawful Ending or Termination: No Specific Mechanism

There are no specific requirements that the aggrieved party must comply with if a contract is lawfully ended or terminated. This includes the cases of full performance, agreement of the parties to terminate the contract, death or insolvency of one or both parties, operation of contractual conditions, operation of law, and expiry of the duration of the contract.

3. Cancellation or Unilateral Termination: Required Mechanism

Both Articles 423 and 428 VCC 2015 on the cancellation and unilateral termination of contracts require that the aggrieved party send a formal notice to the obligor to terminate the contract. Failure to comply with this requirement might result in the aggrieved party having to pay damages to the obligor if the latter suffers any loss caused by the failure to send a formal notice.[78] This requirement, it is argued, provides a necessary safeguard for the legitimate interests of the obligor.[79] One unresolved question is the form of notice: does it have to be verbal, by conduct, or in writing?[80] This is actually a simple problem that can be solved easily if one looks at the substance of the issue rather than its outward appearance. The act of terminating a contract is also a unilateral juristic act. As such, it is a civil transaction in accordance with the VCC 2015. For a civil transaction, the person can choose any of the following forms: verbal notice, relevant conduct, or notice in writing.[81] In addition, parties to the contract can include a clause in their agreement on the form and method of terminating their contract. In such cases, the aggrieved party must follow the prescribed form or otherwise be deemed in breach of the contract.

When can the contract be considered terminated? At the time the aggrieved party sends the notice or at the time the defaulting party receives the notice? This question is actually not provided for in the VCC 2015. Employing analogous application of law and comparative law methodology, one can argue that the contract will be terminated at the time of reception of the notice by the defaulting party.[82]

[76] Beale and others (n 26) ch 25.8; von Mehren (n 26) paras 147–54.

[77] Đỗ (n 25) 720–21; Đỗ (n 51); Đỗ (n 38) 390–408.

[78] Judgment No 64/2006/KDTM-ST of 17 August 2006 of the Hanoi People's Court; Decision No 334/2012/DS-GDT of 24 July 2012 of the Civil Court of the People's Supreme Court.

[79] Đỗ (n 25) 721–22.

[80] Thế Liên Hoàng (ed), *Bình Luận Khoa Học Bộ Luật Dân Sự 2005 Tập 2* (Nhà Xuất Bản Chính Trị Quốc Gia 2013) [*Scientific Commentary on the 2005 Civil Code, vol 2* (National Publishing House 2013)] 275.

[81] VCC 2015, art 119.

[82] Đỗ (n 25) 724–25. VCC 2015, art 388 on the effective date of an offer chooses the reception theory.

There is one interesting hypothesis in relation to the failure of making a formal notice. If the aggrieved party fails to make a proper formal notice as stipulated by law, is the act of terminating the contract still valid? There are various opinions. Two authors hold the view that even in this case the contract is still terminated.[83] Practice before the courts seems to agree with this approach.[84] However, it remains to be seen whether this approach will be confirmed by the Supreme Court through precedent.

One note should be provided at the end of this discussion in relation to the intervention of the courts. As mentioned, several countries require the intervention of a court to terminate a contract. This is not a requirement in Vietnamese law. However, in practice, parties to a contract often bring their disputes regarding the termination of the contract to the courts. This essentially creates an informal mechanism of court intervention in the termination of contract.

V. Effects of Termination

Compared to other jurisdictions, Vietnamese law lacks the discussion of an important policy consideration concerning the effects of termination: the policy of balancing the interests of obligee and obligor.[85] This policy, in both theory and practice, would help to frame the proper, appropriate issues related to the termination of contracts, such as 'How to decide whether the non-performance allows termination? What are the mechanics of the claim for termination? Is it possible to terminate the contract before performance is due ("anticipatory breach")? What is the effect of termination? Can the obligee withhold performance?'[86] In the absence of such a policy, many important issues concerning termination of contract, especially the effects of termination, remain unresolved.

In addition, as discussed above, Vietnamese law provides two remedies to terminate a contract in the case of breach: cancellation and unilateral termination. Table 27.3 shows how each remedy dictates a different effect and legal consequences that each party to the contract has to bear.

This table gives an overview of the similarities and differences between cancellation and unilateral termination relating to the effects of terminating a contract. This is probably the most peculiar characteristic of the provisions on terminating contracts in Vietnam in comparison with other jurisdictions.[87] Both the new French Code civil of 2016 and English law accept that the termination of contract is prospective, while German law appears to be more complex.

On this matter, the VCC 2015 represents a reformed position based significantly on the experience of European countries and a number of model laws.[88] The lessons learnt have been combined with domestic experience, most notably in relation to the Commercial Law

[83] Minh Tuấn Nguyễn (ed), *Bình Luận Khoa Học Bộ Luật Dân Sự* (Nhà Xuất Bản Tư Pháp 2014) [*Scientific Commentary on the Civil Code* (Judicial Publishing House 2014)] 544–45; Đỗ (n 38) 726–27.

[84] Judgment No 13/2016/KDTM-PT of 28 June 2016 of the Long An Provincial People's Court.

[85] von Mehren (n 26) para 146; JM Smits, *Contract Law: A Comparative Introduction* (Edward Elgar 2017) 229–30.

[86] Smits (n 85) 230.

[87] Beale and others (n 26) ch 25.2; von Mehren (n 26) para 179.

[88] Đỗ (n 38) 355–58.

Table 27.3 Effects of termination of contracts

Issues	Cancellation	Unilateral termination
Consequence for contract	Terminated	Terminated
Effects	Retrospective Where a contract is cancelled, it shall be [deemed to have been] ineffective as from the time when it was entered into. The parties shall not be required to perform the agreed obligations (cf Article 427(1)).	Prospective Where the performance of a contract is terminated unilaterally, it shall terminate from the time when the other party is notified of the termination. The parties do not have to continue to perform their obligations (cf Article 428(3)).
Fine (penalty clause)	The relevant clause will still be applicable.	The relevant clause will still be applicable.
Damages	The party suffering loss and damage caused by a breach of obligations by the other party shall be compensated.	The party suffering loss and damage caused by failure of the other party to correctly perform contractual obligations shall be compensated.
Restitution	Yes Each party must return anything it has received from the other party upon deduction of reasonable costs during performance of the contract and costs for the preservation and development of property. The restitution shall be made in kind. If restitution cannot be made in kind, it must be valued in terms of money for the purpose of restitution. Where [all or both] the parties have an obligation to return, restitution must be implemented at the same time, unless otherwise agreed or unless otherwise provided by law.	No, but A party that has already performed its obligation may demand the other party make payment for the portions of the obligations which have been fulfilled.
Dispute settlement clauses	The relevant clause will still be applicable.	The relevant clause will still be applicable.

Source: Author.

2005 and courts' dispute settlement activities to create the above-mentioned effects of termination in two separate cases.[89]

First, a cancelled contract shall be deemed terminated from the time it was entered into,[90] while a unilaterally terminated contract shall be considered as such from the time the defaulting party receives a notice of termination.[91]

Secondly, in the case of a cancelled contract, both parties must restore what they have received from each other. The restoration shall be made in kind. If impossible, it can be

[89] Đỗ (n 25) 737–38.
[90] Decision No 91/2014/QDDS-GDT of 20 August 2014 of the Ho Chi Minh City People's Court.
[91] Judgment No 27/2011/KDTM-PT of 10 March 2011 of the Court of Appeal in Da Nang.

made in cash. However, contracts that are unilaterally terminated do not require restoration. In fact, they require reimbursement for the part of the obligation that has been performed.[92]

Thirdly, rights that have been acquired from the cancelled contract shall also be cancelled, while the rights acquired from a unilaterally terminated contract shall not be cancelled until the moment of termination, as its effect is prospective. Similarly, rights that have been transferred to other people through a cancelled contract shall be restored to its former rights' holder.[93] The same rule seems not to apply in the case of unilateral termination.

Agreements on dispute settlement, penalty clauses, and the right to claim damages are still maintained even after a contract has been terminated.[94]

The effects of termination would be complicated in case a contract is terminated in part or in whole. While the VCC 2015 does not have any explicit provision on this matter, the Commercial Law 2005 does.[95] This solution was applied in case law.[96] Vietnamese lawmakers were also aware of Article 9:302 PECL, which provides for a contract to be terminated in part or in whole.[97]

VI. Restrictions on and Loss of the Right to Terminate

The final important issue related to the right to terminate a contract is the question of restrictions on exercising this right. There are a number of ways in which the right to terminate a contract can be lost or restricted.[98]

1. Affirmation

A breached contract can be affirmed by the aggrieved party, a point that seems too obvious to deny. It is not only an application of the principle of freedom of contract that is enshrined in Article 3 VCC 2015; it is also expressed through a number of provisions that allow the defaulted party to accept late performance, replacement of property, continued performance, and so on.[99] The affirmation can be analysed from the perspective of a juristic act or a civil transaction as well: it is the manifestation of will of one party, and if it meets all the requirements laid down in Article 117 VCC 2015, then the affirmation will give rise to, alter, or terminate rights and obligations; in this case, the defaulted party terminates his right to cancel a contract.[100]

[92] Đỗ Văn Đại seems not to understand this difference in his analysis.

[93] Judgment No 01/2014/DS-ST of 14 January 2014 of the Bao Loc District People's Court.

[94] Sỹ Mạnh Võ, 'Hậu Quả Của Việc Hủy Bỏ Hợp Đồng Theo Bộ Luật Dân Sự 2015' (2017) 86 *Tạp chí kinh tế đối ngoại* ['Legal Consequences of Cancelling Contracts According to the 2015 Civil Code' (2017) 86 External Economics Review] 1–17.

[95] Commercial Law 2005, art 312(1)(2)(3).

[96] Judgment No 02/2010/KDTM-ST of 12 January 2010 of the District Eleven People's Court.

[97] Beale and others (n 26) ch 25.1; Dỗ (n 25) 689–90.

[98] Beale and others (n 26) ch 25.10; von Mehren (n 26) paras 185–87.

[99] VCC 2015, art 354; VCC 2015, arts 356–358.

[100] Beale and others (n 26) ch 25.10.

2. Lapse of Time

Vietnamese law does not have provisions setting out a period of time during which the aggrieved party must exercise its right to terminate a contract equivalent to those of the PICC and the PECL.[101] However, the right to cancel or unilaterally terminate a contract due to a breach of contractual obligations is subject to lapse of time or prescription in the VCC 2015.[102] Article 429 VCC 2015 explicitly states:

> The limitation period for initiating legal action to request a court to resolve a dispute relating to a contract is three years from the date on which the person with the right to make the request knew or should have known that his/her lawful rights and interests were infringed.

The three-year prescription starts from the moment the aggrieved party 'knows the fact that gives it the right to terminate'.[103] In practice, Vietnamese courts often make use of this provision to limit a contractual party's right to terminate.[104]

3. Restriction on the Cancellation of Contracts for the Benefit of Third Parties

There is another rather interesting provision that might limit the right to terminate a contract of the defaulted party. Article 417 VCC 2015 provides that 'Where a third person has agreed to receive a benefit, the parties to the contract may not amend or cancel the contract, even where the contract is yet to be performed, except with the consent of the third person.' Other national and transnational contract laws deal with this issue in their respective articles on contracts for the benefit of third parties.[105] There are two important issues in relation to this situation. The first is with regard to the ability to terminate the contract; the second relates to the effects of the terminated contract on the third party. In relation to the first issue, comparative law scholarship suggests that the contract can still be terminated even though it relates to a third party.[106] Concerning the second issue, the VCC 2015 envisages a similar situation in which a contract is declared void and there is a need to protect a bona fide third party at Article 133 that has actually been applied in adjudication.[107]

[101] PECL, art 9:303(2); PICC, art 7.3.2(2).
[102] Đỗ (n 25) 775–82.
[103] Beale and others (n 26) ch 25.10.B.
[104] Judgment No 1039/2009/KDTM-ST of 28 April 2009 of the Ho Chi Minh City People's Court; Decision No185/2014/DS-GDT of 13 May 2014 of the Civil Court of the Supreme People's Court; Judgment No 301/2015/DSST of 27 July 2015 of the Binh Tan District People's Court.
[105] cf S Vogenauer in Vogenauer (n 32) art 5.2.5 paras 1–9.
[106] Đỗ (n 25) 833–36.
[107] Judgment No 1610/2012/DS-PT of 27 December 2012 of the Ho Chi Minh City People's Court.

28

Ending and Changing Contracts

Comparative Conclusions

*Hugh BEALE**

I. Introduction

1. Overview of the Chapter

The chapters in this volume cover two situations in which a party may be permitted to depart from the terms agreed in the contract or to end its obligations to perform: when a change of circumstances after contract formation makes performance more difficult or impossible and when the other party repudiates or breaches the original terms.[1] In this concluding chapter, I will divide the situations a little differently and treat them in a different order. I will deal first with when one party may suspend its performance or bring an end to its obligations because of breach or repudiation by the other party (including cases in which performance has become impossible but the impossibility is attributable to one of the parties); secondly, when it may treat its obligations as at an end because, without the fault of either party, performance has become impossible (in a literal sense[2]) or illegal; and lastly, when the contract may be adjusted or ended because performance by one party, though not impossible, has become much more onerous for that party or of no value to the other party due to a change of circumstances.

Taking a purely functional approach, we will see that in cases of impossibility and of repudiation or breach, the contract laws covered in this volume reach broadly similar results, but where performance has become more difficult or valueless, there are very pronounced differences. The difference is especially marked as between those contract laws that have been heavily influenced by civil law systems and those that are derived from the common law, whether directly or indirectly via the Indian Contract Act 1872 (ICA) or the versions of that Act in force in Malaysia and Myanmar.

However, when we consider the mechanisms used to reach those results—if, in other words, we peer into the 'black box' represented by the functional approach to try to see how each law of contract reaches its outcome in a particular fact situation—we find that the systems may use very different reasoning. Moreover, even when systems use similar reasoning

* Other chapters in this volume are referred to by the name(s) of the author(s), the chapter number, and the jurisdiction concerned.

1 Chen-Wishart, Neo, and Vogenauer, ch 1—Introduction 6: variations or discharge agreed between the parties are not covered: ibid.

2 This is sometimes referred to as 'objective' impossibility, that is, no one could perform the relevant obligation, eg Bell, ch 9—Indonesia 179 and 185.

Hugh Beale, *Ending and Changing Contracts: Comparative Conclusions* In: *Studies in the Contract Laws of Asia V: Ending and Changing Contracts*. Edited by: Mindy Chen-Wishart, Dora Neo, and Stefan Vogenauer, Oxford University Press.
 DOI: 10.1093/oso/9780198995814.003.0028

and have ostensibly similar provisions or principles, we may find significant differences in the way that the provisions or principles are applied in practice. Some apparent friends may turn out to be false. The result is that the chapters in this book present a wonderful kaleidoscope, but the apparent patterns need careful examination.

2. General Preliminary Observations

(a) Terminology

A first general point is about terminology. A bewildering number of different words are used to describe the ending of a party's, or both parties', obligations under the contract in the different situations; and even a single system may use a variety of words to describe what seem to be identical processes. For example, in the common law, when one party has committed a serious breach of contract, it has been said that the other party has the right to 'put an end to the contract',[3] 'rescind' it, 'terminate' it, or 'treat the contract as repudiated';[4] and the ICA adds a further variation, that the contract 'becomes voidable'.[5] In the systems that were influenced by the civil law there are also variations in the way the process is described, particularly when it comes to the question whether the contract is ended with retroactive effect or only for the future.

As our Reporter for Myanmar remarks, a debate about terminology is essentially arid; what matters is the orientation and purpose of the legal remedies which are triggered by a certain event or non-event.[6] Nonetheless, if we are to compare the reasoning and the remedies in different systems, it is useful to adopt words to describe the remedy or outcome in general terms, while recognizing that this is done purely stipulatively. This is what I do in this conclusion. There is no implication that the word or phrase that I have chosen to use is the 'best' one or that systems that use other terms should change their ways.[7]

So, when the question is about the rights of the victim of a serious breach of contract, I will normally refer to the right to 'terminate' the contract (whether termination is for the future only or is in some sense retroactive). When, without the fault of either party, one party's performance has become partly or wholly impossible, with the result that the other party has a choice whether or not to end the contract, I will usually refer to a right to terminate; when there is no such choice, I will refer to 'automatic termination' or 'discharge'. When the question is whether the contract can be adjusted after it has become much more onerous to one party or useless to the other, I shall talk about a 'change of circumstances' that will sometimes give rise to 'adjustment' of the contract or its 'termination' by the court or the affected party.

3 See eg s 39 ICA (Effect of refusal of party to perform promise wholly).

4 See eg s 13 of the Hong Kong Sale of Goods Ordinance 2018.

5 See eg ss 53 (Liability of party preventing event on which the contract is to take effect) and 55 ICA (Effect of failure to perform at fixed time, in contract in which time is essential).

6 Briggs, ch 17—Myanmar 355.

7 A degree of standardization appears to be emerging; while the 1980 Vienna Convention on Contracts for the International Sale of Goods (CISG) refers to 'avoidance' for breach, both the Principles of European Contract Law (PECL) Parts I & II (O Lando and H Beale (eds) (Kluwer 2000)) and the UNIDROIT Principles of International Commercial Contracts 2016 (PICC) refer to avoidance for invalidity and termination for breach, and this usage is followed in recent European Directives, eg Directive (EU) 2019/771 of the European Parliament and of the Council of 20 May 2019 on certain aspects concerning contracts for the sale of goods, OJ L 136, 22 May 2019, 28.

(b) Scope of the study: 'Discharge' or 'termination' on other grounds

Although the focus of both the national reports and this comparative conclusion is on the three issues mentioned—termination for breach of contract, termination or discharge for impossibility, and adjustment or termination because of changed circumstances—it is instructive to note what other situations or doctrines Reporters mention as falling within their notions of 'discharge' or 'termination', if only to indicate clearly what this study does and does not focus on. For example, many of the reports point out that obligations may also be discharged or terminated not only by agreement[8] but also by such events as performance,[9] by the expiry of a fixed term, by avoidance or nullity on the ground of impaired consent, by the operation of a non-promissory condition, and by limitation (prescription).[10] Also it seems that in all the systems a contract for an indefinite period may be terminated by either party by giving notice,[11] though there may be exceptions such as employment contracts.[12] In a consumer contract the consumer may also have a right to escape the contract without a reason; this may be called a right of cancellation.[13] These other situations or doctrines fall outside the scope of this study and I will not cover them in the conclusion.

(c) Differences between mechanisms

I have said that even where systems reach broadly similar outcomes, the mechanisms by which they do so may differ markedly. Very broadly speaking, most systems seem to fit into one of four basic models, according to the laws that have influenced them most. I will call these the Napoleonic, the German, the common law, and the ICA models. But within these models there are many variations and quite a few 'crossovers', where a law appears to have adopted ideas from more than one model. And the two contract laws that have been fundamentally reformed most recently, the laws in China and in Vietnam, stand apart from any one of the four models.

(d) Differences in policy

We will see that there are also very interesting differences in attitude and between the policies that the laws seem to be pursuing. The differences are most obvious when a system from one 'family' is compared to a system that is based on another model, but even laws in the same family sometimes seem to have differences in the way that apparently similar rules are applied. These differences may reflect different understandings of how contractual risks should be distributed or, more broadly, of what contract law is trying to achieve.

[8] See n 1.

[9] In the ICA, the provisions on termination appear in Chapter IV, Of the Performance of Contracts: see Vardhan and Narayan, ch 8—India 159.

[10] See eg the forms of discharge or termination listed in Herliana, ch 10—Indonesia 203–204; Dizon, ch 19—Philippines 392; and Tran, ch 27—Vietnam 571.

[11] See eg Kamo, ch 12—Japan 234.

[12] Jan, ch 23—Taiwan 485.

[13] Tham, ch 21—Singapore 440; Jan, ch 23—Taiwan 491. Some systems recognize that if a buyer has paid earnest money, it may have a right to withdraw from the contract, forfeiting the earnest money: see eg Kamo, ch 12—Japan 238.

II. Withholding Performance and Termination for Repudiation or Breach

1. Introduction

In this section of the conclusion I will refer to the party which appears likely to break the contract, or who has done so, as A, and the other party as B.

On a functional approach, all the systems reach the results that:

(i) If A is to perform first and has not done so, or the parties were to perform simultaneously but A is not ready and willing to do so, B may withhold its performance until (respectively) A performs or is ready to do so.
(ii) If A persists in its non-performance, or performs in a way that is defective, B may have the right to terminate the contract, putting an end to both its own and A's obligations to perform for the future.
(iii) B may also have a right to terminate if, before A's performance is due, A makes it clear that it is unwilling or unable to perform.
(iv) The right to terminate is limited, either by a requirement that A's breach is sufficiently serious or one that A must be given a chance to perform correctly.
(v) If B terminates the contract, B may then claim damages for non-performance.
(vi) Alternatively, or sometimes in addition, B may have a claim in restitution for benefits it transferred under the contract before the date of termination. The extent of any restitutionary claim will depend on the nature of the contract.
(vii) B's right to terminate the contract may be lost, typically by affirmation or waiver.

Beyond those seven broad propositions, the outcomes are not uniform, but we will see that there are many similarities between the laws, including between laws that follow different basic models.

2. Withholding Performance

When A has failed to perform, or is not ready to perform, a contractual obligation that was due to be performed before B's reciprocal obligation, or where the obligations on each side are to be performed simultaneously, all the laws permit B to wait to perform until A does so or is ready to do so. In the civilian systems, this is most often conceptualized as a defence that may be raised by B, should A seek to enforce B's obligation when A has not performed itself. It is still often referred to by its Roman name, the *exceptio non adimpleti contractus*.

In Indonesia, as was the case in France before 2016,[14] there is no general text giving one party the right to withhold its performance when the other has failed to perform or is not ready and willing to do so: the only express provision is Article 1478 of the Indonesian Civil

[14] cf the position in France before 2016, when the old French Civil Code of 1804 (OFCC) provided for withholding of performance only in specific contracts, but during the twentieth century the courts allowed a general *exception d'inexécution*: see B Nicholas, *French Law of Contract* (OUP 1972) 213–16; S Rowan, *The New French Law of Contract* (OUP 2022) 194–95. See now art 1219 of the French Civil Code.

Code (ICC), which provides that a seller 'is not obligated to deliver the goods if the buyer has not paid the purchase price and if the seller has not granted him an extension of the period of payment'. However, writers argue for a general principle of *exceptio non adimpleti contractus* so that a party is excused from performing a contract if the other party has not fulfilled its obligations as set out in the contract.[15] In the Philippines, Article 1169 of the Civil Code (PCC) states that:

> [i]n reciprocal obligations, neither party incurs in delay if the other does not comply or is not ready to comply in a proper manner with what is incumbent upon him,

from which it is deduced that B may withhold its performance when A is not ready to comply with its corresponding obligations or is in breach of the contract.[16]

The laws of Japan,[17] South Korea,[18] and Taiwan[19] each have a specific provision allowing B to withhold its performance of a reciprocal obligation until A offers to perform. Like the provision of the German Civil Code (BGB)[20] from which they are derived, each provides that it does not apply when B is to perform first. In other words, it depends on the order of performance. However, we will see that the systems may also provide that in certain circumstances a party which was to perform first can suspend its performance if it has reason to doubt that the other will perform when its turn comes.[21]

In the traditional common law systems in Hong Kong and Singapore, a similar result is reached via the order in which the parties are to perform and the notion of conditions, that is, that where A is to perform first, its performance may be a 'condition precedent' to B's obligation to perform its reciprocal obligation; or where the parties are to perform simultaneously, their obligations are normally construed as 'concurrent conditions' so that neither need perform until the other is ready and willing to do so.[22] These notions are made explicit in the ICA, sections 51 (Promisor not bound to perform, unless reciprocal promisee ready and willing to perform) and 54 (Effect of default as to that promise which should be first performed, in contract consisting of reciprocal promises).[23] There is some question whether the common law and ICA systems really recognize withholding of performance as a distinct remedy; as the Reporter for Myanmar puts it, sections 51 and 54 have the effect that until A has performed or, as the case may be, is ready and willing to perform, B has no obligation to perform, so that there is nothing for B to withhold. But in practical terms, a party faced with non-performance by the other will often wish to suspend its performance as at least a temporary measure, both to protect itself and to put some pressure on the non-performer. At least in some of the civilian systems, the right to withhold performance is also seen as a matter of 'fairness in exchange of performances'.[24]

[15] Herliana, ch 10—Indonesia 204.

[16] Dizon, ch 19—Philippines 400.

[17] Article 533 of the Japanese Civil Code (JCC), see Jan, ch 23—Taiwan 483 (withholding performance is not discussed in Kamo, ch 12—Japan).

[18] Article 536 of the Korean Civil Code (KCC), see Ahn, ch 14—Korea 279.

[19] Article 264 of the Taiwanese Civil Code (TCC), see Jan, ch 23—Taiwan 457.

[20] See s 320 BGB.

[21] This is discussed under 'Suspension on Grounds of Insecurity', section II.3.

[22] Low, ch 6—Hong Kong 119; Tham, ch 21—Singapore 436.

[23] Vardhan and Narayan, ch 8—India 160; s 52 ICA provides that the parties must perform in the order fixed by the contract or, where the order is not fixed expressly, 'in that order which the nature of the transaction requires'.

[24] Ahn, ch 14—Korea 280.

Where there appears to be a difference between the common law systems and the civilian systems is that in the common law, although merely withholding performance is only temporary, and leaves it open to A to perform after all, the same notion of conditions is used to explain when B may go on to terminate the contract because of A's breach.[25] B's obligation to perform is not conditional on exact performance of every one of A's obligations. For example, if A has 'substantially performed' the work required, or the term that A has not performed is only a warranty,[26] B may neither withhold performance nor terminate the contract. In contrast, in some civilian traditions the exception of non-performance is seen as quite separate from that of termination.[27] The practical effect of this may be that in some civilian systems B may withhold its performance until A performs some relatively minor obligation, non-performance of which would not be sufficiently serious to justify B in terminating the contract.[28] Thus Article 264 of the Taiwanese Civil Code (TCC) provides that in the case of partial non-performance by A, B's right to withhold performance is qualified only by good faith. In the common law systems, however, the same degree of seriousness seems to be required for both withholding performance and termination.

The right to withhold performance is set out very clearly in two provisions of the Chinese Civil Code (CCC), Articles 525 (simultaneous obligations) and 526 (one party to perform before the other).[29] The Vietnamese Civil Code of 2015 (VCC 2015) also provides that a party due to perform second may postpone its performance until the party due to perform first has done so.[30]

3. Suspension on Grounds of Insecurity

It is quite common for laws on the sale of goods to allow a seller who has agreed to deliver on credit to withhold delivery if it discovers that the buyer is insolvent or in financial difficulties. At least two of the laws studied contain generalized provisions allowing a party who was due to perform first, but who discovers that the other may well not be able to perform when its turn comes, to suspend its performance and to demand that the other perform first or provide security or an assurance that it will perform.[31]

4. Termination

(a) Introduction

In all the laws of contract covered in this volume, if party A has broken its contract with party B, B may in some circumstances have the right to terminate the contract, in the sense that B's obligations to perform come to an end. Termination will also bring to an end A's

[25] ibid 279, referring to G Treitel, *Remedies for Breach of Contract—A Comparative Approach* (OUP 1988) 245, 300, 319.
[26] See section II.4(e).
[27] Ahn, ch 14—Korea.
[28] See the discussion of French law on this point in Rowan (n 14) 196–97.
[29] These articles are not discussed in Chen and Wu, ch 4—China.
[30] Article 411(2) VCC 2015: see Tran, ch 27—Vietnam 581.
[31] Jan, ch 23—Taiwan 457, citing art 265 TCC; Chen and Wu, ch 4—China 76, citing arts 527 and 528 CCC, which also allow termination if the insecurity continues and no assurance is given: see section II.4(g).

principal obligations[32] actually to perform, though they will normally be replaced by an obligation to pay B damages to compensate B for the non-performance. In many systems the same may apply if, before A's performance is due, A makes it clear that it is unwilling or unable to perform. I will refer to the latter situation as 'anticipatory repudiation'.[33] However, there is quite a variety in the conceptual mechanisms involved in termination for breach or anticipatory repudiation, and some difference in practical outcomes.

(b) A self-help remedy

In most of the laws covered in this volume, termination of a reciprocal contract is a 'self-help' remedy that B can exercise without obtaining a court order by giving notice to A.[34] The only exception to this is in Indonesia, which retains the traditional Napoleonic position[35] that termination requires a judicial decision.[36] In Indonesia, termination without an order has been held to constitute a tort.[37]

(c) Effect of notice when not justified

If B were to give notice of termination on the grounds of a breach when it had no justification for doing so (eg because the breach was not sufficiently serious),[38] the effect seems to vary. In most systems it seems that B will then be guilty of a wrongful breach or repudiation, and therefore A may terminate the contract and B will become liable to compensate A for non-performance.[39]

(d) Formalities

In most systems, the notice of termination can be informal; it need only clearly indicate that the contract is being terminated. In contrast, both Article 423 VCC 2015 on the cancellation of contracts and Article 428 of the same Code on their unilateral termination[40] require that

32 For obligations that may survive termination, see section II.4(m)(2).

33 See section II.4(g).

34 See eg Kamo, ch 12—Japan 255; Jan, ch 23—Taiwan 493; Leakpech, ch 25—Thailand 520; Low, ch 6—Hong Kong 133; Dizon, ch 19–Philippines 405; Tham, ch 21—Singapore 442; Vardhan and Narayan, ch 8—India (unusually, under s 27 of the Specific Relief Act 1963, anyone may ask the court to rescind the contract on the basis that it is voidable or terminable: Vardhan and Narayan, ch 8—India 171); Cheong and Lee, ch 16—Malaysia 331–332 (may be ordered by a court, though unusual). In some systems the parties may agree that the contract will terminate automatically in certain events: Cheong and Lee, ch 16—Malaysia 327; also Leakpech, ch 25—Thailand 531; Briggs, ch 17—Myanmar 369; Dizon, ch19—Philippines 407–408 (but subject to review by court); Chen and Wu, ch 4—China 81; Tran, ch 27—Vietnam 583.

35 See art 1184 OFCC. This system remains in place in some European countries, eg Italy. In France, termination without a court order was permitted if there was a clause allowing it (called a *pacte commissoire*) or in some cases of urgency: see Nicholas (n 14) 243–45, also referring to some legislative exceptions; also Herliana, ch 10—Indonesia 205. Since the reforms of 2016 B will have a general right to terminate by giving notice: see art 1224 of the French Civil Code.

36 Article 1266(2) ICC: see Herliana, ch 10—Indonesia 205. Article 1266(1) reflects art 1184 OFCC in basing the right to terminate on a resolutory condition: Herliana, ch 10—Indonesia 205. The JCC of 1890 would have required a court order but the provision was never brought into force: Kamo, ch 12—Japan 242.

37 Herliana, ch 10—Indonesia 206 and 212. Whether Indonesian law permits the parties to agree that the contract may be terminated by notice is debated: ibid 209–210.

38 See section II.4(e)(1).

39 For common law see eg Tham, ch 21—Singapore 439. For civil law see eg Dizon, ch 19—Philippines 407; it is not clear whether in a case of 'unjustified' termination the court has a power to reinstate the contract, as do the courts in France: see art 1228 of the French Civil Code.

40 The VCC 2015 has separate provisions for cancellation (termination with retroactive effect) (art 423) and 'unilateral termination' (which has only prospective effect) (art 428): see Tran, ch 27—Vietnam 577. On the effect of the distinction see section II.4(m)(3).

the aggrieved party send a formal notice to the obligor to terminate the contract. However, as the Reporter tells us that a formal notice may be oral or in any form of writing, it may be that this is really no more than a requirement that the notice is clear. It is debated whether giving a notice that is not sufficiently formal is ineffective or is effective to terminate the contract but results in B having to pay damages to A if A suffers any loss caused by the failure to send a formal notice.[41]

(e) Adequate grounds for termination

In what circumstances will a notice of termination be justified? A system in which termination requires a court order may leave the question to the court; this is the case in Indonesia.[42] Systems that allow the victim of a breach to terminate by notice need some restrictions to prevent contracts being terminated too readily as termination might be abusive.[43] We will see that there are two basic approaches to the problem. One is to require that the breach is of a certain seriousness. The other is to require that B give a warning to A that if A does not perform, or perform properly, within a stated period, B will terminate the contract; and if A does not perform properly within the time set, to allow B to terminate without having to show that the breach is particularly serious.[44] On occasions the two approaches lead to differing results, but we will see that when various qualifications to each approach are considered, the two are much closer than appears at first sight.

(1) A serious breach

The common law approach taken by Hong Kong[45] allows B to terminate the contract and then to recover damages[46] for non-performance if the breach was of a term that 'goes to the root of the contract' (a 'condition'[47]). If the term was merely a 'warranty', B has only a claim for damages.[48] Some terms, however, do not fall into either category (in which case they are often called 'innominate terms'). When the breach is of an innominate term, whether B has a right to terminate depends on whether the actual breach has such serious consequences that it deprives B of the substance of what was being contracted for. This may be one reason why the Court of Appeal in Singapore has adopted a somewhat different terminology ('is the breach "repudiatory"?') and method of classification by a series of numbered

[41] Tran, ch 27—Vietnam 584.
[42] Herliana, ch 10—Indonesia 206.
[43] See section II.4(l).
[44] Chen and Wu, ch 4—China 74.
[45] Low, ch 6—Hong Kong 120–121.
[46] The qualification as to damages is because the parties may agree that B shall have a right to terminate in circumstances which would not justify termination under the general law; but the contract is likely to be construed in such a way that if B exercises the right, it will not have a right to damages for non-performance: see section II.4(f).
[47] See section II.2. The requirement that the breach be serious is qualified by the fact that the contract may provide that any of the contractual obligations is a condition, breach of which will give rise to a right of termination. Provided the language is clear enough, the courts will give effect to the provision: see section II.4(e)(3). It is important to keep this use of the word 'condition', that is describing an obligation, distinct from another use of the same word that refers to an event on which the operation of the main obligations depends but which neither party is promising to bring about (an 'aleatory' or 'non-promissory' condition), eg where a sale is agreed on condition that the seller can obtain an export licence.
[48] There has been a debate over whether the 'warranty' category has any meaning now that it is recognized that a breach of a term that is not a condition will justify termination if it deprives B of the substance of what it was contracting for: see Low, ch 6—Hong Kong 120.

situations,[49] but it is not evident that the outcomes under the Singaporean approach differ from those under Hong Kong law.

The position under the ICA and its variants in Malaysia and Myanmar is less straightforward because of the wording used in the Acts. Section 39 ICA, which the Reporters for India describe as 'a go-to section in cases of breach',[50] on its face applies only where A has 'refused to perform, or disabled himself from performing his promise in its entirety'. Section 40 of the Malaysian Contracts Act 1950 (MCA) is identical. As the Reporters for both Malaysia and Myanmar point out, 'in its entirety' is ambiguous; it might mean that A must have refused to perform at all or that it suffices that A is unwilling or unable to perform exactly.[51] However, the courts in India have interpreted the section broadly so as to apply to cases of actual breach and to take into account the seriousness of the breach.[52] Similarly, the courts in Malaysia have treated section 40 MCA as incorporating the English law notion that a breach by A will justify termination by B if the breach is sufficiently serious. To decide this question, though they do not refer to conditions, warranties, and innominate terms, the courts have in effect adopted the English approach.[53] There is no case law in Myanmar; the Reporter suggests that whether the breach is '"serious enough" is the best test'.[54]

Articles 423 and 428 VCC 2015[55] both allow termination only if the breach is 'serious'.[56] In contrast, the Vietnamese Commercial Law of 2005 requires the breach to be 'fundamental', but both 'serious' and 'fundamental' are defined as breaches that mean that the other party cannot achieve the purpose for which the contract was originally entered into.[57]

(2) Warning

The laws that have been heavily influenced by the German model generally distinguish three types of non-performance: impossibility, delay, and defective (or incomplete) performance.[58] In cases of delay and defective performance, the basic rule is that B must give A a warning of a reasonable length, and A must have failed to comply with the notice, before B can terminate the contract.[59] Our Reporters for several systems refer to such a warning

[49] Tham, ch 21—Singapore 435 and 436–439.

[50] Vardhan and Narayan, ch 8—India 165. Another important section is s 55 ICA, which covers late performance: see section II.4(j).

[51] Cheong and Lee, ch 16—Malaysia 323; Briggs, ch 17—Myanmar 359.

[52] Vardhan and Narayan, ch 8—India 162–164.

[53] Cheong and Lee, ch 16—Malaysia 323–324. The Federal Court has said the breach must result in a total failure of consideration, in the sense that B has received no performance at all (a criterion for some claims in restitution, see further below), but this is not consistent with either other statements in the same case or other case law: Cheong and Lee, ch 16—Malaysia 324–325.

[54] Briggs, ch 17—Myanmar 362.

[55] See section II.4(d).

[56] Tran, ch 27—Vietnam 575 and 576.

[57] ibid 578, citing art 3(13) Commercial Law 2005.

[58] For instance, Taiwan: see TF Chen, 'Remedies for Non-Performance of Contract in the Taiwan Civil Code—A Comparative Perspective' in M Chen-Wishart, A Loke, and B Ong (eds), *Studies in the Contract Laws of Asia, vol I: Remedies for Breach of Contract* (OUP 2016) 301, 302. The Reporter for Vietnam points out that art 351(1) VCC 2015 states that 'breach of obligation' means an obligor fails to perform the obligation on time, does not perform the obligation fully, or performs the contents of the obligation incorrectly. This suggests that here too there are three types of breach: late performance, partial performance, and defective performance: Tran, ch 27—Vietnam 579. However, unlike the systems derived from German law, the VCC does not have separate provisions to deal with the three types of breach.

[59] Kamo, ch 12—Japan 248; Ahn, ch 14—Korea 285; Leakpech, ch 25—Thailand 523, citing s 387 of the Thai Civil and Commercial Code (TCCC); Jan, ch 23—Taiwan 486, art 254 TCC. Ahn, ch 14—Korea 286 stresses that in these cases a warning should be required even if the breach is fundamental.

notice by the German word *Nachfrist*.[60] When B has given A a warning which A has failed to comply with, these systems may allow B to terminate although the non-performance was not serious.

However, we find a number of qualifications to this basic rule which reduce the differences between it and systems that insist on a serious breach as a prerequisite for termination.

First, there are cases in which a prior warning is not required. A prior warning is not required if performance has become impossible for reasons for which A is responsible: then B may terminate the contract without more ado.[61] Where the impossibility is only partial, B may terminate the contract without serving a warning if performance of the remaining part is of no interest to him[62] or if '[the] purpose of the contract cannot be achieved by performance of the remaining part of the obligation'.[63] Nor is a warning required if the delay means that performance is no longer possible, or prompt performance was essential,[64] or if the defect (or incomplete performance) cannot be cured.[65] In most of these cases it is evident that either A has not performed at all or its non-performance will have a very serious effect.[66]

Secondly, even if A has failed to comply with B's warning, these systems impose limitations on B's right to terminate. Under the Japanese Civil Code (JCC), B cannot terminate if A's breach was 'minor'.[67] This seems to reflect the German rule that termination is not permitted for a breach that is *unerheblich*.[68] The translation provided by the German Federal Ministry of Justice[69] renders this as 'trivial', and the view of the Drafting Committee revising the JCC was that B should have the right to terminate the contract if A has failed to perform it properly after due warning, even though the breach is not 'fundamental' (to use the word used in the CISG, PICC,[70] and PECL[71]).[72]

In Taiwan, B has an unqualified right to terminate after giving notice only if the breach was of one of A's primary obligations.[73] Originally breach of a 'subsidiary' or 'ancillary' obligation gave rise only to a claim for damages. The Supreme Court has now recognized that B may terminate the contract for breach of a subsidiary obligation, but only if the breach is detrimental to the main interest of the innocent party and the achievement of the contractual

[60] See eg Chen and Wu, ch 4—China 76; Ahn, ch 14—Korea 285; Jan, ch 23—Taiwan 491.

[61] Leakpech, ch 25—Thailand 524, citing s 389 Thai Civil and Commercial Code (TCCC); Jan, ch 23—Taiwan 486, citing arts 226 and 256 TCC. Contracts that have become impossible for reasons that are not imputable to A are dealt with in section III.

[62] See art 226(2) TCC.

[63] Kamo, ch 12—Japan 251, citing art 542(1)(iii) JCC.

[64] Art 542(iv) JCC, 'the purpose of the contract cannot be achieved' if performance is late: see Kamo, ch 12—Japan 251; Leakpech, ch 25—Thailand 523, citing s 388 TCCC; Jan, ch 23—Taiwan 486, art 255.

[65] Jan, ch 23—Taiwan 486–465, arts 227(1), 254, and 256 TCC.

[66] Article 359 TCC allows a buyer who has been supplied with defective goods to terminate without giving a warning but not if termination would be obviously unfair: Jan, ch 23—Taiwan 485.

[67] This provision is criticized by the Reporter for Korea, who believes that termination should only be permitted if the breach (whether after a *Nachfrist* or not) prevents attainment of the purposes of the contract, a criterion that he regards as more predictable than the criterion of 'fundamental breach' or 'fundamental non-performance' used in the international instruments: Ahn, ch 14—Korea 286–288.

[68] See s 323(5)(2) BGB.

[69] See <www.gesetze-im-internet.de/englisch_bgb/englisch_bgb.html#p1216> accessed 11 April 2025.

[70] See art 7.3.1 PICC.

[71] See art 9:301(1) PECL.

[72] In Taiwan, a specific provision for defects in property sold or leased seems to lead to a similar result: a buyer or lessee may terminate the contract unless termination would be obviously unfair: Jan, ch 23—Taiwan 485, citing arts 359, 494 TCC, and see n 66.

[73] See next paragraph.

purpose.[74] Korean law also recognizes a distinction between major and only incidental obligations, allowing termination only for breach of the former. The distinction between the two types of term depends not only on the intentions of the parties at the time the contract was made but also on the consequences of the non-performance.[75] Thus the Taiwanese and Korean laws seem to impose a significantly tougher restriction on 'termination after notice' than does Japanese law. The Thai Supreme Court has held that termination is only possible if the breach was material.[76]

Chinese law is to similar effect. Under Article 563 CCC,[77] termination is permitted if the delay or breach renders the purpose of the contract impossible, or if a party delays performance after being given a warning of a reasonable length—but only if the delay is in performing a principal obligation.

Warnings are also normally required in Indonesia,[78] but here the purpose of the notice is different. Unless the contract provides otherwise, normally A will not be in breach at all unless B has previously served a notice on A demanding performance,[79] and damages for delay will run only from the date set by the notice.[80] It is usual for the creditor to serve a further notice before taking the debtor to court to seek performance, termination, and/or damages.[81]

Warnings have a function in the common law systems too, though their role is less prominent. We have seen that B may not terminate unless A's breach is a breach of condition or deprives B of the substance of what B was contracting for. But in addition, subject to a qualification that we will explore below,[82] B cannot terminate until the time for performance has expired. If time was of the essence, because of the nature of the contract or the circumstances, or because the contract so provided, B may terminate as soon as the date for performance has passed.[83] But if time was not of the essence, B cannot terminate until B, after suffering an unreasonable delay, has 'made time of the essence' by giving a notice setting a reasonable period in which A must perform, and A has failed to do so.[84]

It will be appreciated that this means that there is less difference between the common law and the systems influenced by German law than appears from first impressions. If A's breach was of an important term or had a serious effect, and any further delay will prevent the purpose of the contract being attained, B can terminate immediately; if timing is not critical, B may terminate only if it has given a warning to A that A must perform within a

[74] Jan, ch 23—Taiwan 487.

[75] Ahn, ch 14—Korea 283.

[76] Leakpech, ch 25—Thailand 525.

[77] Chen and Wu, ch 4—China 74.

[78] Herliana, ch 10—Indonesia 208–209. This seems to reflect the position in French law before 2016, when the creditor had to serve a *mise en demeure* on the debtor and the debtor's liability in damages would run only from the date the notice expired. However, the courts frequently held that the parties had implicitly waived the need for a *mise en demeure*: see Nicholas (n 14) 237.

[79] See art 1238 ICC.

[80] ibid art 1243.

[81] Herliana, ch 10—Indonesia 209. It will be recalled that in Indonesian law termination normally requires a court order: see section II.4(b).

[82] Anticipatory repudiation: see section II.4(g).

[83] Low, ch 6—Hong Kong 122; Tham, ch 21—Singapore 444.

[84] Low, ch 6—Hong Kong 123. The ICA does not provide for the case where time is not of the essence, and some courts have held that there is then no right to terminate, others that B may terminate after giving reasonable notice: Vardhan and Narayan, ch 8—India 168–169 argue that the latter view is preferable.

reasonable time, and A has failed to do so; but again, in most systems the breach must be of an important obligation or have a very serious effect.[85]

(3) Party agreement

It is also widely accepted that the parties may agree that a particular obligation is critical to the contract, or that the time for performance is essential,[86] although that would not otherwise follow from the nature of the contract or the circumstances, with the result that any breach of the relevant obligation by A will give B the right to terminate the contract.[87] In traditional common law parlance, such an obligation (common lawyers would normally say 'such a term') is a 'condition'.[88]

(f) Express right to terminate

It is quite common for the parties to agree that if certain events occur, one or either of the parties may terminate the contract: for example, in a contract under which A is to lease a machine from B, the contract may provide that B may terminate the contract if A dies or becomes insolvent. Neither death nor insolvency will be a breach of contract, or even amount to inability to perform, as A's heir, personal representative, or insolvency officer might well choose to pay. But it is not uncommon for the events that give B a right to terminate under the clause to include breaches of the contract by A that are not sufficiently serious to justify termination under the general rules. The hypothetical scenario involving Car Machinery & Co and Traders Ltd provides an example: a clause of the agreement provides that any failure by the distributor to visit entitles the other party to terminate the agreement with immediate effect. If A's breach does not have a serious effect on B, may B nonetheless terminate the contract, and may B then claim damages from A for non-performance of the agreement as a whole?

Reporters give a variety of answers to this. In some systems it seems that the clause will be taken to show that the parties regarded missing any visit as a very serious breach so that the effect is just as if the agreement had stated that explicitly (see section II.4(e)(3)).[89]

[85] Thus in considering the hypothetical case in which Traders Ltd had missed two visits, many Reporters seemed to doubt whether Car Machinery & Co would be able to terminate the contract had there been no express provision permitting it, as the missed visits might not have a serious effect. In contrast, in the hypothetical scenario of Seven Seas and Big Chef, most thought that the buyer could refuse to keep or pay for the defective mussels, though those from Japan, Korea, Thailand, and Taiwan considered that first the buyer must give the sellers a warning and thus a chance to cure the breach if that was still possible (Kamo, ch 12—Japan 254; Ahn, ch 14—Korea 295; Leakpech, ch 25—Thailand 529; Jan, ch 23—Taiwan 499, in relation to termination under art 227 TCC, whereas under art 359 TCC (applicable to sales and defective work) the buyer may terminate without first giving a warning). The fact scenarios of the hypotheticals described in this section II are taken from Chen-Wishart, Neo, and Vogenauer, ch 1—Introduction 9.

[86] On this, see section II.4(j).

[87] See eg Kamo, ch 12—Japan 253 (discussing the hypothetical case scenario Car Machinery & Co and Traders Ltd); Tran, ch 27—Vietnam 579; Leakpech, ch 25—Thailand 521.

[88] See section II.4(e)(1), and Low, ch 6—Hong Kong 125, points out that clear language will be needed. In Singapore, this is now referred to as 'Situation 3(a)': see Tham, ch 21—Singapore 437. In India and Malaysia, it seems the courts will also give effect to the parties' designation of performance of a particular obligation as essential (Vardhan and Narayan, ch 8—India 165 and Cheong and Lee, ch 16—Malaysia 327, both discussing the hypothetical of Car Machinery & Co and Traders Ltd). In Myanmar, there is no case law yet; Briggs, ch 17—Myanmar 362 reaches the same conclusions, though without referring necessarily to the term as a 'condition'.

[89] See eg Tran, ch 27—Vietnam 580; Kamo, ch 12—Japan 253 (but pointing out that such a wide clause might violate the principle of good faith); Herliana, ch 10—Indonesia 210 (but 'the principles of equity which are manifested in the principle of good faith, appropriateness, and correctness will come into play').

Others will give effect to the clause independently of the statutory rules on termination but point out that when the breach by A was trivial, termination might be treated as contrary to good faith.[90] Traditional common law systems, which lack a general doctrine of good faith, have developed other mechanisms to prevent or discourage the use of express termination clauses in cases of breaches that are not serious. First, the clause may be 'read down' (ie interpreted strictly) so as to apply only to breaches that are sufficiently serious as to justify termination under the normal rules.[91] Secondly, the clause may be held to give B only a right to terminate the contract and no right to claim damages for non-performance generally.[92]

(g) Anticipatory repudiation

(1) Refusal or inability to perform

Many of the laws covered in the book also accept that if, before A's performance is due, A makes it clear that it is unwilling or unable to perform, B may terminate the contract and claim damages for non-performance without waiting until the date for performance. If A is only unwilling or unable to perform part of its obligations, B may terminate only if that part is an essential term or its non-performance will prevent B from attaining the purpose of the contract. In the common law, this is known as the doctrine of anticipatory breach.[93] We have seen that in the ICA, 'refusal to perform' is the case that is addressed by section 39.[94] In most of the systems influenced by German law, the situation is covered by a statutory provision[95] or a similar outcome has been allowed by the courts.[96] But no such rule is found in Taiwan[97] or Vietnam.[98] Nor do the laws of either the Philippines or of Indonesia appear to recognize the doctrine; neither Reporter mentions it, even when discussing the hypothetical case of Coco and David in which an architect repudiates her obligation to employ a landscape gardener well before the date the gardener was to start work.[99]

(2) Insecurity

We saw earlier that some laws allow a party that was required by the terms of the contract to perform first, but who has good reason to doubt that the other party will perform when its turn comes, to suspend its performance or to demand that the other perform first or provide security. In China, the CCC provides that the other party may then provide appropriate assurance, in which case the first party's performance must be resumed; if the other

[90] Ahn, ch 14—Korea 295; Jan, ch 23—Taiwan 497 (the Supreme Court has held that termination under an express clause is not subject to the statutory rules). An express right to terminate will be enforced under the ICA also: see Vardhan and Narayan, —India 165 and Cheong and Lee, ch 16—Malaysia 327, though it is not stated whether the distributor will be liable for damages after termination by the other party in reliance on the clause; cf the text at the end of this paragraph.

[91] See the English cases cited by Low, ch 6—Hong Kong 136.

[92] Low, ch 6—Hong Kong 136; Tham, ch 21—Singapore 439.

[93] Low, ch 6—Hong Kong 132–133; Tham, ch 21—Singapore 437 ('Situation 2') and 439.

[94] And s 40 MCA. See section II.4(e)(1).

[95] Kamo, ch 12—Japan 251, citing art 542 JCC; Chen and Wu, ch 4—China 74, citing art 563(2) CCC.

[96] See eg Ahn, ch 14—Korea 285.

[97] Jan, ch 23—Taiwan 487–488, stating that the decision not to adopt a provision has been criticized.

[98] Tran, ch 27—Vietnam 582.

[99] It would not be surprising if the systems do not recognize anticipatory breach as it is not recognized as a general doctrine in French law (see S Whittaker, 'How Does French Law Deal with Anticipatory Breaches of Contract?' (1996) 45 International and Comparative Law Quarterly 662), even after the reforms of 2016–18, nor in the Spanish Civil Code. However, the doctrine has been recognized by the Spanish Supreme Court (see the judgments of 30 March 2010 (ECLI:ES:TS:2020:1930) and of 18 July 2013 (ECLI:ES:TS:2013:4245). I am grateful to Professor B Gregoraci for bringing these cases to my attention.

party fails to regain its ability to perform and fails to provide appropriate assurance within a reasonable period of time, the first party may terminate the contract and claim damages for non-performance.[100]

(h) Performance no longer wanted

Systems of contract law that have been influenced by German law normally make specific performance readily available. However, these systems often have specific provisions for contracts of work, allowing an employer that no longer wants the work it has contracted for[101] to escape having the work (or any further work) forced upon it. The employer may give notice to bring the counterparty contractor's obligation and right to perform to an end; instead, the employer must pay compensation to the contractor (as well as the price for any divisible parts of the performance that have been completed to date).[102] In the traditional common law countries,[103] where specific performance is seldom awarded and the normal remedy will be damages, an employer that no longer wants the work can simply repudiate the contract and pay damages in the normal way; the counterparty will not have any way to force the employer to allow completion of the work.[104]

(i) Instalment contracts

The contract may call for successive actions by A, for example, delivery of goods by instalments or the performance of services over a period of time. The effect if A fails to perform properly on one occasion (eg if one of the deliveries is defective) depends on whether the contract is divisible, in the sense that each delivery can have independent value, or indivisible because the effect of a breach in relation to one instalment is to make delivery of the remainder useless because the instalments are of no value on their own.

If the contract is indivisible, the fact that the performance was broken down into instalments (eg in a sales contract, to make it easier to deliver or receive the goods) will in effect be ignored. The systems seem to come to the same conclusion: if the effect of the breach is to make delivery of the remainder useless, and to prevent the buyer attaining the intended purpose, the buyer may terminate the contract as a whole and will be able to claim back payments made.[105]

Where the contract is divisible, three questions may arise: first, whether B can refuse to accept and pay for the defective delivery; secondly, whether B may refuse to accept any

[100] Chen and Wu, ch 4—China 76, citing art 528 CCC. See also art 411(1) VCC 2015.

[101] As in the hypothetical scenario of Coco and Daniel, see Chen-Wishart, Neo, and Vogenauer, ch 1—Introduction 9.

[102] See eg Kamo, ch 12—Japan 239–240, citing arts 641 and 634 JCC, while art 651 contains similar provisions for contracts of mandate: Kamo, ch 12—Japan 241; similarly Jan, ch 23—Taiwan 485–486.

[103] The same is true in Malaysia and Myanmar, but in India recent reforms to the Specific Relief Act 1963 mean that specific performance will normally be available: see Vardhan and Narayan, ch 8—India 170.

[104] In the UK, the question has arisen whether, if (exceptionally) the counterparty will be able to complete the work without the cooperation of the employer, the counterparty can ignore the employer's repudiation, complete the work, and claim the contract price. The traditional answer was yes, but more recently the courts have held that the worker may not do so if it has 'no legitimate interest' in completing the work. The UK cases have been considered in Hong Kong and Singapore but were held not to be relevant on the facts: Low, ch 6—Hong Kong 133; Tham, ch 21—Singapore 453.

[105] See eg Kamo, ch 12—Japan 254 and Jan, ch 23—Taiwan 499, both discussing the hypothetical case of Seven Seas and Big Chef involving a delivery of mussels that were contaminated: see Chen-Wishart, Neo, and Vogenauer, ch 1—Introduction 9.

future deliveries and terminate the contract as a whole; and thirdly, whether termination of the contract will merely affect the position for the future or will be retrospective in its effect so that, for example, B may recover payments that it has already made.

Those systems whose Reporters commented on whether B may reject the defective instalment seem to agree that B may do so if the defect is sufficiently serious that it would justify termination were this the only delivery to be made.[106]

Whether B can refuse future deliveries even though the later instalments might be useable on their own is a more difficult question. In the common law systems, this is answered traditionally by asking whether the defective performance amounts to a repudiation of the contract as a whole, either because of the proportion that is defective or because the breach is 'repudiatory' in that it shows that A is unwilling or unable to perform the rest of the contract properly.[107] This approach is explicitly embodied in section 38(2) of the Indian Sale of Goods Act 1930 and of the Malaysian Sale of Goods Act 1957,[108] and section 39 ICA has been interpreted as adopting the same approach.[109] A similar approach seems to be taken in Taiwan, where the test is said to be whether A cannot be expected to meet the contractual requirements for the performance of the rest of its obligations. The Reporters for the other civil law systems in this volume do not discuss the question.[110]

Where the instalments or other acts of performance have some value of their own, the question whether termination is retrospective or only prospective in its effect seems to depend again on whether the individual instalments or other acts of performance had an independent value. However, the issue is closely connected to the effects of termination and the availability of restitution and all these questions will be discussed later.[111]

(j) Late performance

We have already encountered the issue of delay in performance when discussing the need for a warning (or *Nachfrist*). We saw that, in all systems, if the nature of the contract or the circumstances mean that anything other than prompt performance by A will defeat the object of the contract, B may terminate as soon as the date for performance has passed. In systems influenced by German law, the date may be described as a 'fixed transaction';[112] in the common law and ICA systems, it will be said that 'time is of the essence'.[113] If prompt performance is not obviously essential, B may have first to serve a warning and can terminate only if A does not perform within the time set; but the parties may agree that the

[106] See eg Chen and Wu, ch 4—China 85; Herliana, ch 10—Indonesia 211; Ahn, ch 14—Korea 295; Dizon, ch 19—Philippines 398; Leakpech, ch 25—Thailand 529; Tran, ch 27—Vietnam 578; see further section II.4(e)(1).

[107] Low, ch 6—Hong Kong 129; Vardhan and Narayan, ch 8—India 164; Cheong and Lee, ch 16—Malaysia 329–330.

[108] Both provisions replicate what is now s 31 of the UK's Sale of Goods Act 1979, as do s 33 of the Hong Kong Sale of Goods Ordinance 2018 and s 31 of the Singapore Sale of Goods Act 1979.

[109] Vardhan and Narayan, ch 8—India 163.

[110] In discussing the hypothetical scenario of Seven Seas and Big Chef, Jan, ch 23—Taiwan 499 states:

> As to mussels that have not yet been delivered, Big Chef's entitlement to rescission is dependent on whether the non-conforming performance in relation to the first ton of mussels is so severe that Seven Seas cannot be expected to meet the contractual requirements for the performance of the rest of the mussels.

[111] See section II.4(m) and (o).

[112] Jan, ch 23—Taiwan 486.

[113] Low, ch 6—Hong Kong 122; Vardhan and Narayan, ch 8—India 166, citing s 55 ICA; Cheong and Lee, ch 16—Malaysia 325–326, citing s 56 MCA.

date for performance shall be a 'fixed transaction'[114] or 'of the essence' so that no warning is needed.[115]

It is possible that the traditional common law systems are readier to give effect to 'time-of-the-essence' clauses[116] than are some other systems. Thus in common law jurisdictions, 'time-of-the-essence' clauses will normally be taken at face value, whereas in Indonesia (where, of course, termination is judicial), the court will examine whether the creditor has a special interest in the timelines of performance even when the contract states that failure to meet a deadline will result in termination.[117] This is in part a question of how the clauses are interpreted and partly of additional controls, such as good faith, which will be discussed below.

(k) Debtor given extra time

Even when A has committed a serious breach and prima facie B is justified in terminating, some systems allow a court to give A a further period in which to perform. General provisions to this effect are found in systems influenced by the Napoleonic tradition,[118] such as Indonesia[119] and the Philippines,[120] and also in Taiwan.[121] In the common law systems, relief can be granted only if termination would result in A losing a proprietary or possessory interest in the subject matter of the contract, and it will not be given where time is of the essence of the contract, whether because of the nature of the contract or an express provision.[122] The doctrine of relief against forfeiture, as it is called, was not replicated in the ICA,[123] though our Reporters for India argue that a court is able to give extra time if time was not of the essence.[124]

(l) Other restrictions on termination

Laws of contract that embody the principle of good faith may employ it to prevent a party from terminating the contract when that seems unfair. For example, B might seek to terminate the contract on the grounds of A's breach when the breach did not have serious consequences for B and B is trying to escape the contract for other reasons, such as that the deal has turned out to be unprofitable. Opportunism of this kind is not a problem if the law requires a judicial declaration or that the breach have serious consequences for B before B

[114] In German terminology, such an express agreement would be an '*absolutes Fixgeschäft*': see H Beale, B Fauvarque-Cosson, J Rutgers, and S Vogenauer, *Ius Commune Casebooks for the Common Law of Europe: Cases, Materials and Text on Contract Law* (3rd edn, Hart Publishing 2019) 1015.

[115] Tran, ch 27—Vietnam 581. Article 542(1)(iv) JCC allows immediate termination if the purpose of the contract cannot be achieved 'due to the nature of the contract or a manifestation of intention by the parties': see Kamo, ch 12—Japan 251. Article 255 TCC is to similar effect: see Jan, ch 23—Taiwan 486.

[116] The same may be true of other 'express conditions' (see section II.4(e)(3)) but I did not find enough information to be sure.

[117] Herliana, ch 10—Indonesia 211.

[118] A French court may grant a *délai de grâce* of up to two years: see art 1343-5 of the French Civil Code.

[119] Herliana, ch 10—Indonesia 208, citing art 1266(4) ICC, which allows a grace period of up to a month.

[120] Dizon, ch 19—Philippines 391 and 413 (grace period is allowed only in exceptional circumstances).

[121] Jan, ch 23—Taiwan 493, citing art 318 TCC, under which the court may also allow the debtor to perform in parts, provided that the performance is divisible.

[122] Low, ch 6—Hong Kong 122 and 131; but in Singapore the law is less rigid over time, see Tham, ch 21—Singapore 449–50.

[123] Briggs, ch 17—Myanmar 369 (no sign of court having power to give additional time for performance). Section 55 ICA states that if time was not of the essence, the contract does not 'become voidable' as a result of a delay; but see n 84 for our Indian Reporters' argument that it may be ended after reasonable notice.

[124] Vardhan and Narayan, ch 8—India 169.

can terminate,[125] but it can be a problem where the contract provides that compliance with a particular obligation is 'a condition', although the breach in question does not have serious consequences, or that time is 'of the essence' when in fact a delay will not cause problems.

This was one reason why common law courts developed the notion of the innominate term: if obligations whose non-performance might have serious consequences were to be classified as conditions, the innocent party would have the right to terminate even if the particular breach that has occurred had little or no adverse effect.[126] A similar problem of opportunism may arise where a term is labelled by statute as a condition.[127] In Singapore, as in England, the latter problem has been tackled by specific legislation to prevent a non-consumer buyer of goods from rejecting them because of a defect or delivery of the wrong quantity if the defect, shortfall, or excess quantity is so slight that it would be 'unreasonable' to reject them.[128] It is very interesting to read that Hong Kong decided not to adopt these provisions and that the courts have made very little use of the concept of innominate terms. The Reporter for Hong Kong argues that this is because of the premium the law of Hong Kong places on certainty and also due to judicial conservatism.[129]

In Taiwan, termination of the contract when a 'fixed' time for performance has not been met[130] is subject to compliance with good faith. Thus in the hypothetical case of Prime Ltd and Devil Corp,[131] the purchaser of land who is ten minutes late in tendering the final instalment of the price, terminating will be seen as contrary to good faith unless the vendor can show that the delay caused considerable damage.[132] And in the contract for the sale of goods, the buyer may terminate if the goods are defective without giving a warning but not if termination would be obviously unfair.[133]

(m) Effects of termination

(1) Duties to perform primary obligations end

In all the systems studied, if A commits a serious breach of contract and B justifiably terminates the contract, broadly speaking, B's obligation to perform comes to an end; A's obligations may also come to an end and be replaced by an obligation (common lawyers would normally say 'liability') to pay damages. But this apparently simple statement needs qualification and explanation.

(2) Continuing ancillary obligations

The first point is that the parties may agree that some obligations will continue despite termination of the contract, for example, obligations not to deal with competitors; and some clauses will be presumed to continue to apply, such as arbitration clauses with their

125 Even when the law insists that the breach be serious, as in China, courts may use good faith (art 7 CCC) or abuse of rights (art 132 CCC) as reasons to prevent B terminating: see Chen and Wu, ch 4—China 70.

126 This was the situation in the leading English case, *Hong Kong Fir Shipping Co v Kawasaki Kisen Kaisha Ltd* [1962] 2 QB 26 (CA) (on which see Low, ch 6—Hong Kong 120). A time-chartered ship was not seaworthy and had to spend eight weeks in dry dock for repairs. The charterer, who was unable to find a profitable use for the ship in any event, in fact saved money as a result of the breach as the ship was 'off hire' for the period of repair.

127 *Arcos Ltd v EA Ronaasen & Son* [1933] AC 470 (HL).

128 See ss 15A and 30 of the relevant Sale of Goods Acts.

129 Low, ch 6—Hong Kong 130 and 129.

130 See section II.4(j).

131 Chen-Wishart, Neo, and Vogenauer, ch 1—Introduction 9.

132 Jan, ch 23—Taiwan 497–498.

133 ibid 485; see section II.4(e)(2).

associated obligations (essentially contractual) to comply with the directions of the arbitrator, etc.[134] So we have to distinguish between the primary obligations to perform, which may end, and the ancillary ones that may continue.

(3) Existing obligations

If the contract is indivisible, then termination will end the primary obligations of each party. But if the contract is divisible, termination may affect only those parts of it that were due to be performed in the future; each party may continue to have obligations in respect of the parts already due. For example, if a lease provides for rent to be paid monthly, termination by either party will end the tenant's right to occupy the premises, and the landlord's corresponding entitlement to rent for the future, but it will not affect the tenant's liability to pay the rent for each month completed before the date of termination.

In civilian systems, the difference is usually reflected in terms of two forms of termination, one that is only for the future[135] and one that has retrospective effect,[136] so that the parties may obtain restitution of benefits they have transferred to each other.[137] For example, Article 259 of the TCC provides for what the Ministry of Justice's translation and our Reporter call 'rescission', which will result in each party having to make restitution, and Article 263 TCC for 'termination', which does not.[138]

In traditional common law systems, termination is seen as merely prospective.[139] However, the practical outcomes do not seem to differ from those in the civil law-influenced systems. If A's performance to date is rendered useless, B may reject it (if it can be returned) and (even if it cannot be returned) refuse to pay for it. If the performance rendered and retained by B has some value, A may be able to obtain restitution, whether of money paid or of the value of what it has transferred.[140]

(n) Loss of right to terminate

Where performance of the contract or part of it remains possible despite a serious breach by A, B will have a choice as to whether or not to terminate the contract. The systems agree that B may lose that right by waiving it or affirming the contract.[141] Some systems also have fixed time limits. In China, the right is lost if it is not exercised within one year from the date when the right-holder knows or ought to have known about the cause for termination.[142] Other systems apply more general provisions; some set a period for notifying the other party of defects in goods or in building work[143] and in a number of jurisdictions, the right to

[134] eg Kamo, ch 12—Japan 256 n 96.

[135] Often referred to in Napoleonic systems as *résiliation*, in German-influenced systems as *Kündigung*.

[136] Referred to as *résolution* or *Rücktritt*, respectively.

[137] In Vietnam, the two processes are referred to as unilateral termination and cancellation: see section II.4(d).

[138] Jan, ch 23—Taiwan 484 and 494.

[139] Low, ch 6—Hong Kong 135; Tham, ch 21—Singapore 443.

[140] Low, ch 6—Hong Kong 136–137. See further section II.4(o).

[141] See eg Herliana, ch 10—Indonesia 213 (the ICC requires an explicit statement but one will be assumed from subsequent acceptance of further performance); Tran, ch 27—Vietnam 586 (application of art 3 VCC 2015 on freedom of contract); Dizon, ch 19—Philippines 401; Ahn, ch 14—Korea 294 (application of good faith and the so-called 'principle of forfeiture'); Low, ch 6—Hong Kong 134; Tham, ch 21—Singapore 442; Vardhan and Narayan, ch 8—India 171; Cheong and Lee, ch 16—Malaysia 332; Briggs, ch 17—Myanmar 369; Chen and Wu, ch 4—China 81 (probably); seemingly also in Japan, where the right may be waived in advance by a clause in the contract: see Kamo, ch 12—Japan 258.

[142] Chen and Wu, ch 4—China 81, citing art 564(2) CCC.

[143] See eg Kamo, ch 12—Japan 254 and Jan, ch 23—Taiwan 495 (defects in goods); these time limits apply to the rights to repair and to price reduction also.

terminate is lost at the end of a limitation period.[144] In contrast, in the traditional common law systems delay is not a bar, in and of itself, but may amount to evidence of affirmation or possibly give rise to an estoppel.[145] In Korea, Thailand, and China, A may ask whether B wishes to exercise the right of termination, and if B does not respond within a reasonable time, B will lose the right to terminate.[146]

A number of systems also bar termination if a deliberate or careless act by A means that property transferred under the contract cannot be returned[147] or if a third party has acquired rights over it.[148]

(o) Restitution after termination

In those systems in which one form of termination is seen as retrospective, a justified termination in that sense (rather than termination just for the future) will result in each party having to restore what they have recovered under the contract or, where it cannot be returned,[149] its monetary value.[150]

In contrast, the traditional common law approach differentiates claims by the victim of the breach (B) and claims by the party in breach (A). B may claim back money paid if there has been a 'total failure of consideration', in the sense that B has derived no benefit from the contract, or where there has been a total failure in relation to a divisible part of it. If B has delivered goods or performed services under the contract, B must claim the agreed price if the price has become due, otherwise it may claim their reasonable value.[151] A, the party in breach, may claim back any money paid, unless it was paid as a deposit or for work done by B under the contract. In respect of goods delivered or services performed under the contract, A may claim the price for them insofar as it has become payable under the terms of the contract; otherwise A may not claim the value of goods delivered or services performed except to the extent that goods that A had delivered could have been returned but were not.[152]

Section 64 ICA[153] provides explicitly that a person (in the designation used in this chapter, B) 'rescinding' a 'voidable' contract (which has been held to include cases of termination of

144 Kamo, ch 12—Japan 258; Jan, ch 23—Taiwan 495; Vardhan and Narayan, ch 8—India 171.

145 Low, ch 6—Hong Kong 134–135.

146 Chen and Wu, ch 4—China 81, citing art 564 CCC; Ahn, ch 14—Korea 294, citing art 552 KCC; Leakpech, ch 25—Thailand 527, citing s 393 TCCC; Jan, ch 23—Taiwan 495, citing art 257 TCC.

147 Kamo, ch 12—Japan 259, citing art 548 JCC; Jan, ch 23—Taiwan 495, citing art 262 TCC; Ahn, ch 14—Korea 294, citing art 553 KCC; Leakpech, ch 25—Thailand 527, citing s 394 TCCC; Vardhan and Narayan, ch 8—India 171, citing s 27(2)(b) of the Specific Relief Act 1963.

148 See eg Dizon, ch 19—Philippines 415; Vardhan and Narayan, ch 8—India 171, citing s 27(2)(c) of the Specific Relief Act 1963. This is considered below in relation to restitution: see section II.4(o).

149 This will include the case where a third party has acquired rights over the property but that is not treated as preventing termination. This is the case in Japan: see Kamo, ch 12—Japan 257, citing art 545(1) JCC, at least if the third-party buyer of an immoveable has registered its title; see also Ahn, ch 14—Korea 291; Leakpech, ch 25—Thailand 534.

150 Kamo, ch 12—Japan 257, citing art 545(1) JCC; Jan, ch 23—Taiwan 494; Ahn, ch 14—Korea 291 (including the value of any benefit a party got through using the property before it had to be returned); Leakpech, ch 25—Thailand 533, citing s 391 TCCC; Tran, ch 27—Vietnam 585. Indonesia 'does not have clear rules on restitution' but the Reporter argues that the same effects will follow termination: Herliana, ch 10—Indonesia 214. Article 566 CCC provides for the restoration of each party to its original state after termination, in addition to having a right to damages; whether this is a form of restitution, and whether general rules of restitution (such as the defence of change of position) apply, is debated: see Chen and Wu, ch 4—China 82.

151 Low, ch 6—Hong Kong 137; Tham, ch 21—Singapore 444.

152 Low, ch 6—Hong Kong 137; Tham, ch 21—Singapore 444 and 455.

153 And likewise ss 64 and 65 of the Myanmar Contract Act and ss 65 and 66 MCA.

the contract for breach[154]) who has received any benefit from the other party (A) must restore it; section 65 provides that any party who has received any advantage under a contract that has become void must restore it or make compensation for it. Both provisions have been held to apply to cases of termination of the contract for breach.[155] The results represent 'something of a departure' from the English position that is applied in Hong Kong and Singapore[156] and bring the ICA jurisdictions closer to the civil law-influenced systems.

III. Impossibility

1. Introduction

As explained in the Introduction to this chapter, impossibility—when it has become literally impossible for anyone to perform the contract or illegal to do so—is treated in this section, and change of circumstances—the doctrine under which a contract may be adjusted or ended because performance by one party, though not impossible, has become much more onerous for that party or of no value to the other party—is treated separately in section IV.

The systems covered by this volume that broadly follow the traditional common law approach do not recognize change of circumstances. The systems that do recognize it usually also treat it separately from impossibility.[157] Only in the CCC is there a single provision to deal with both situations.[158] However, we will see that the concept of impossibility is sometimes 'stretched' to cover what appear to be cases in which the contract was more difficult to perform or where the performance had less value but was not literally impossible.

All the systems recognize that if, after the contract was made, a change occurs which was unforeseen, was not the result of anything done by either party, and was outside the normal risks, and the change makes the contract factually impossible or legally impermissible to perform, a party who is unable to perform will neither be required to do so nor be liable to pay damages for breach of contract for failing to perform and that the counterparty may be released from its obligations also. However, once again, the mechanisms used to reach these results differ.

To give a brief overview, in the civilian systems a party will not be required to perform an obligation that is impossible. Nor will the non-performing party be liable to pay compensation for the non-performance if (in the Napoleonic models) it can show that its non-performance was caused by *force majeure* or (in the systems influenced by German law on this point) it can show that it was not at fault. If the impossibility is total and permanent, usually the parties are treated as being released from their contractual obligations automatically; if the impossibility is only partial or temporary, the creditor may have the right to terminate the contract if the effects of the non-performance are sufficiently serious.

[154] Cheong and Lee, ch 16—Malaysia 334.

[155] ibid 333.

[156] ibid 334–335, where Cheong and Lee criticize a decision to deny restitution to A on the grounds that this would allow it to take advantage of its own wrong, as ignoring the words of the statute and failing to take account of the fact that the other party will have an action for damages, which can be set off against any claim for restitution.

[157] Though in Japan it has been argued by one scholar that the rules on change of circumstances can be applied to cases of impossibility: see Taoka, ch 11—Japan 220 n 19.

[158] See section III.4.

The common law comes to the same result in cases of permanent and complete impossibility: the parties' obligations are discharged automatically under the doctrine of frustration, so again there will be no liability either way for future non-performance. The same is true under the ICA and its derivatives. But even in the eyes of many common lawyers, the common law doctrine is 'clunky' in that it does not cope easily with cases of partial or temporary impossibility; the courts have managed to reach sensible results but only by resorting to other doctrines, such as implied conditions, or by simply pronouncing the result without an explanation of how it fits with accepted doctrine. In practice, in cases of temporary impossibility the court's task may be made easier by the very common practice of including a *force majeure* clause in the contract; then the dispute will usually be over whether the clause applies to the events that have caused the impossibility.

If the contract is terminated or discharged, in most systems each party will be able to obtain restitution of benefits it had transferred to the other before the contract was terminated or discharged, or their value. In the traditional common law countries, and also in Malaysia, recovery is more limited.

2. Obligations Discharged or Terminated because Wholly Impossible

(a) Civil law systems

In Indonesia, the relevant provisions are derived almost word for word from the French Code Napoléon of 1804, via the Dutch Civil Code of 1838 (*Burgerlijk Wetboek*), in the Philippines, via the Spanish Civil Code. If one party's performance (again let us say, A's) becomes impossible because of *force majeure*, A cannot be required to perform and will be excused from liability in damages.[159] In Indonesian law, A can rely on *force majeure* if it can show that its performance has been made impossible by an event that was fortuitous, external to it, and that it could not have done anything about; A must also not have been acting in bad faith. The ICC does not require that the event be unforeseeable but a requirement to that effect is said to derive from French doctrine and jurisprudence.[160] In the Philippines, the Civil Code refers to events 'which could not be foreseen, or which, though foreseen, were inevitable'.[161] The VCC 2015 and the Vietnamese Commercial Law of 2005 likewise recognize *force majeure* as a defence, and there has been extensive discussion of it in doctrine.[162] *Force majeure* is only defined in the legislation in relation to limitation periods, but our Reporter suggests that the article can be applied analogously to impossibility of performance in general.[163]

Under Indonesian law, because A is no longer bound to perform, the other party (B) is also released from its obligations since they now lack *cause*.[164] The result is that the contract comes to an end automatically; it is not necessary for either party to give notice to the

[159] Bell, ch 9—Indonesia 183, citing arts 1244 and 1245 ICC; Chan-Gonzaga, ch 18—Philippines 371–372, citing arts 1174 and 1266 PCC. Both codes also have provisions dealing with the destruction or loss of a specific item that was to be transferred under the contract: see art 1244 ICC and art 1262 PCC.

[160] Bell, ch 9—Indonesia 183.

[161] Chan-Gonzaga, ch 18—Philippines 372.

[162] Do, ch 26—Vietnam 544 (see art 351 VCC 2015).

[163] Do, ch 26—Vietnam 544 n 21.

[164] Bell, ch 9—Indonesia 183.

other.[165] The Civil Code of the Philippines provides explicitly that the debtor in obligations to do is released when the prestation becomes legally or physically impossible without the fault of the obligor.[166] The VCC 2015 provides that if a contract cannot be performed because the subject matter of the contract no longer exists, the contract will terminate.[167]

In the systems that were heavily influenced by German law the concepts that apply in cases of impossibility are somewhat different from those in the Napoleonic systems. Evidently, a party will not be ordered to perform an obligation if its performance has become impossible, for whatever reason.[168] Where performance has become impossible for reasons that are not imputable to the debtor (A), neither party will be able to claim damages from the other because liability for damages is fault-based and in this situation neither party is at fault.[169] A will be released from its obligation to perform[170] and the other party (B) will be released from its counter-obligation.[171]

Under Article 542 of the JCC,[172] the parties are not released automatically, but if A's obligation has become wholly impossible, B may cancel the contract (without giving a warning)[173] unless the impossibility is attributable to B.[174] If A's obligation has become partially impossible, B may cancel that part of the contract[175] and, if the purpose of the contract cannot be achieved by the performance of the remaining part of A's obligation, B may cancel the whole.[176] Again, A will not be liable to pay damages to B if the impossibility was not attributable to A.[177]

Thus in the hypothetical scenario of builder George and Han,[178] where the contract is to refurbish the cellar of a restaurant that has subsequently been destroyed in a storm, Reporters who analyse the case as one in which the restaurant and its cellar must be treated as a single entity say that the parties are released without liability for non-performance on either side.[179]

165 Bell, ch 9—Indonesia 186.

166 Chan-Gonzaga, ch 18—Philippines 372, citing art 1266 PCC.

167 Tran, ch 27—Vietnam 568, citing art 422 VCC 2015, and also Tran, ch 27—Vietnam 572, discussing the difficulties in interpreting this article and its interrelationship to art 426 VCC 2015 on the cancellation of contracts where property is lost or damaged.

168 See eg art 441(1) JCC: see K Nakata, 'Performance and Monetary Remedies for Breach of Contract in Japan' in Chen-Wishart, Loke, and Ong (n 58) 107, 108; art 389(1) KCC: see TY Ahn, 'Specific Performance and Cure under Korean Law' in Chen-Wishart, Loke, and Ong (n 58) 140, 143; art 226 TCC: see SL Jan, 'Theory and Practice of Specific Performance in Taiwanese Contract Law' in Chen-Wishart, Loke, and Ong (n 58) 281, 287, and 294.

169 Chen, ch 22—Taiwan 479.

170 ibid 479, citing art 225 TCC and noting that if A can claim compensation from a third party, A may have to hand over its claim or the compensation received to B (art 225(2)) and the contract is not extinguished.

171 See art 266(1) TCC; art 537 KCC; Arts 219 and 372 TCCC, see Pongsapan, ch 24—Thailand 509–510.

172 Taoka, ch 11—Japan 220 n 19.

173 See art 542(1)(i) JCC.

174 ibid art 543.

175 ibid art 542(2)(i).

176 ibid art 542(1)(iii).

177 ibid art 415(1).

178 Chen-Wishart, Neo, and Vogenauer, ch 1—Introduction 8.

179 See eg Pongsapan, ch 24—Thailand 515; Chen, ch 22—Taiwan 480, arguing that the cellar is useless without the restaurant and as a matter of good faith the owner cannot be required to rebuild the restaurant. Other Reporters treat the work on the cellar as still possible and consider the case to be treated under change of circumstances: see Taoka, ch 11—Japan 223; Kwon, ch 13—Korea 276 (though reporting that there are few cases in which the doctrine has been applied to frustration of purpose); Bell, ch 9—Indonesia 196; Do, ch 26—Vietnam 560.

(b) Traditional common law-based systems

(1) Literal impossibility

The traditional common law-based systems in Hong Kong and Singapore reach similar results but by a different route. Both rely on the doctrine of frustration developed in English law, and both the relevant chapters cite English authorities extensively. If performance of the contract, or of one party's obligation, becomes factually impossible (i) because of a supervening event occurring after the formation of the contract, (ii) because the event occurred without the fault of either party, and (iii) because the event renders the performance of the obligation radically or fundamentally different from what had been agreed in the contract, the contract as a whole is 'frustrated' and the parties are automatically discharged from any further obligation to perform.[180] A contract will also be frustrated if a change in the law makes it illegal to perform.[181]

In both jurisdictions it is necessary to identify whether the risk of what has occurred was allocated to one or the other party, in which case the contract will not be frustrated. In both jurisdictions, the courts' approach is described as 'multi-factorial'. The court must consider:

> [1] the terms of the contract itself, its matrix or context, [2] the parties' knowledge, expectations, assumptions and contemplations, in particular as to risk, as at the time of contract, at any rate so far as these can be ascribed mutually and objectively, and then [3] the nature of the supervening event, and [4] the parties' reasonable and objectively ascertainable calculations as to the possibilities of future performance in the new circumstances.[182]

If the event was foreseeable, it will normally be assumed that the party affected was taking the risk of its occurrence, and in Singapore the predominant judicial opinion is that the doctrine of frustration will not apply where the supervening event was foreseeable,[183] but in Hong Kong it seems that a foreseeable event may frustrate a contract if the contract does not point to the risk being allocated one way or the other.[184] In both jurisdictions, it is accepted that a contract should be treated as frustrated only in exceptional circumstances,[185] and it is not enough that the contract has become much more difficult or expensive to perform.[186]

(2) Frustration of purpose

In both Hong Kong and Singapore it is recognized that the doctrine reaches beyond literal impossibility, to encompass cases in which the event has caused such a radical change from the point of view of both parties that the agreement no longer applies in the changed situation;[187] this is seen as a matter of construction (ie interpretation) of the

[180] Hall, ch 5—Hong Kong 92–100; Neo, ch 20—Singapore 417–425.

[181] Hall, ch 5—Hong Kong 95; Neo, ch 20—Singapore 420. Our Reporter for Singapore argues that in the hypothetical case of Builder George and Han, the restaurant and cellar should be treated as one entity so that the subject matter of the contract has been destroyed and the contract is therefore impossible to perform: see Neo, ch 20—Singapore 433.

[182] Hall, ch 5—Hong Kong 99, quoting *Edwinton Commercial Corp v Tsavliris Russ (Worldwide Salvage and Towage) Ltd (The Sea Angel)* [2007] EWCA Civ 547, [2007] 2 Lloyd's Rep 517 (Rix LJ) [111] (numbering added); Neo, ch 20—Singapore 418.

[183] Neo, ch 20—Singapore 425.

[184] Hall, ch 5—Hong Kong 96–97.

[185] ibid 97; Neo, ch 20—Singapore 419.

[186] Hall, ch 5—Hong Kong 97; Neo, ch 20—Singapore 423.

[187] See the examples given in Hall, ch 5—Hong Kong and Neo, ch 20—Singapore 422. These are discussed in section IV.2.

agreement.[188] It is necessary to identify 'the contractual venture'.[189] Thus in both systems, the fourth scenario of the hypothetical case of Gina and H Hotel,[190] in which a room was booked to watch a procession that was later cancelled, might fall within the doctrine of frustration.[191] Our Reporter for Hong Kong takes the hypothetical case of Builder George and Han as a case in which the restaurant's complete destruction renders achievement of the contractual adventure impossible, or makes further performance of the contract something radically different than that which the parties agreed, so that the contract will have terminated automatically.[192]

(c) Indian Contract Act-based systems

The ICA was enacted before the doctrine of frustration in the common law had been established in its modern form, and our Reporters for India tell us that the origins of section 56, which deals with subsequent impossibility, do not lie in English doctrine. Section 56(2) provides that:

> A contract to do an act which, after the contract is made, becomes impossible, or, by reason of some event which the promisor could not prevent, unlawful, becomes void when the act becomes impossible or unlawful.[193]

As far as cases of absolute impossibility are concerned, the outcomes seem very similar to those in the traditional common law systems. In Malaysia, the courts have applied the equivalent section in line with English authorities; a contract will be frustrated if it becomes factually or legally impossible to perform,[194] and the parties will then be discharged automatically;[195] but not if performance has merely become more onerous.[196] However, although English authorities have been relied on to identify the principles and factors that should lead to the contract 'becoming void',[197] in all three jurisdictions the section seems to apply to a narrower range of situations than the common law doctrine. The Indian Supreme Court has rejected the notion that the section will apply if, though performance is still possible, the foundation of the contract has ceased to exist; however, the contract might be held to have become void on the different basis that it was subject to a contingent condition.[198]

188 Hall, ch 5—Hong Kong 96–97; Neo, ch 20—Singapore 433. The hypothetical is based on the English 'Coronation' case of *Krell v Henry* [1903] 2 KB 740 (CA), in which the contract for a room overlooking the procession route was held to have been frustrated: see Neo, ch 20—Singapore 422.

189 Hall, ch 5—Hong Kong 96.

190 Gina books a room for the weekend at H Hotel in X City, the capital of country Z. However, (iv) the inauguration proceedings of the new head of state of Z that were scheduled for Saturday are cancelled. Gina had booked a room overlooking the street where the inauguration procession was supposed to pass by. Due to the inauguration, the rental price of the room was ten times higher than the regular price.

191 Hall, ch 5—Hong Kong 108; Neo, ch 20—Singapore 433.

192 Hall, ch 5—Hong Kong 107.

193 Section 57(2) MCA is identical, as is s 56(2) of the Myanmar Contract Act. The Acts also contain a section on contracts that are contingent on an event happening or not happening; s 32 ICA provides that if the event becomes impossible, the contract becomes void. The Reporters for India argue that this differs from a case of frustration because the event was foreseen by the parties and provided for in the contract (Narayan and Vardhan, ch 7—India 139, 141, and 144). But in Malaysia, it is unclear whether the equivalent section of the MCA also embodies the doctrine of frustration: Lee and Cheong, ch 15—Malaysia 299–300, and see section III.5.

194 Lee and Cheong, ch 15—Malaysia 300–301.

195 ibid 308; Briggs, ch 17—Myanmar 341.

196 Lee and Cheong, ch 15—Malaysia 303.

197 Narayan and Vardhan, ch 7—India 140.

198 Narayan and Vardhan, ch 7—India 145. Section 32 ICAdeals with contingent conditions. However, the Reporters say in their summary that 'Impossibility will be found where the whole purpose or basis of the contract

It has been said that the section can cover 'practical impossibility' as well as literal impossibility, but the section does not:

> absolve a party from the liability to perform his part of the contract, merely because on account of an uncontemplated turn of events, the performance of the contract may become onerous.[199]

In Malaysia, it is not clear that the courts would accept that the equivalent section can apply if the contract can still be performed but its purpose has gone.[200] In Myanmar also it is unclear that the section will be interpreted to cover frustration of purpose.[201] Thus our Reporters for both Malaysia and Myanmar doubt that the contract in the hypothetical scenario of Builder George and Han will be frustrated as the work on the cellar is still possible and may not be 'radically different', even if its purpose can no longer be fulfilled.[202]

3. Temporary or Partial Impossibility

Broadly speaking,[203] if it is temporarily impossible for A to perform, in the civil law systems A will not be liable for the delay, either because A can rely on the defence of *force majeure* (in the Napoleonic systems)[204] or because A will be able to show that the delay was not its fault (in the German-influenced systems).[205] If the delay is so long that the contract becomes impossible, then the parties will be released in the same way as in the case when an event immediately made the performance wholly impossible.

When A's obligations have become only partially impossible, and the impossibility does not defeat the whole purpose of the contract, it seems that courts in Indonesia will follow the French jurisprudence[206] in holding that the debtor is only relieved in part.[207] The Philippine Civil Code, departing from the Spanish model, includes an express provision on partial impossibility:

> Article 1264. The courts shall determine whether, under the circumstances, the partial loss of the object of the obligation is so important as to extinguish the obligation.[208]

was frustrated by the intrusion or occurrence of an unexpected event or change of circumstances which was beyond what was contemplated by the parties' (Narayan and Vardhan, ch 7—India 148), so it may be that in practice frustration of purpose is treated as frustrating the contract.

199 Narayan and Vardhan, ch 7—India 146.

200 Lee and Cheong, ch 15—Malaysia 305–306.

201 Briggs, ch 17—Myanmar 338.

202 Lee and Cheong, ch 15—Malaysia 316; Briggs, ch 17—Myanmar 353. Our Reporters for India appear to regard the contract as impossible to perform: Narayan and Vardhan, ch 7—India 156.

203 These issues were discussed only in some of the chapters, so this account will be incomplete.

204 It seems that in both systems temporary impossibility will merely excuse A for the period of the delay, and if and when it becomes possible for A to perform, both parties will be obliged to perform, but this issue is not discussed in either report.

205 Chen, ch 22—Taiwan 478–479, citing art 220 TCC.

206 The balance of opinion in French doctrine before 2016 took the view that B's obligations were wholly extinguished but the courts applied art 1184 OFCC and might hold that B's obligations were merely reduced: Nicholas (n 14) 206–08.

207 Bell, ch 9—Indonesia 183 n 13.

208 Chan-Gonzaga, ch 18—Philippines 373. This and other translations are taken from the relevant chapter, unless indicated otherwise.

The TCC provides that in the case in which A's performance becomes partially impossible, B's counter-obligation is reduced accordingly.[209] The new JCC allows B to terminate the contract if the performance of part of the obligation is impossible and the purpose of the contract cannot be achieved by the performance of the remaining part of the obligation.[210]

The English courts' approach in cases of partial or temporary impossibility has been unclear. The problem is that on a traditional view, either the contract is frustrated as a whole, and both parties are discharged, or the parties' obligations are not affected. The courts have tended to deal with cases of partial failure (eg when the contract is for the supply of a quantity of a crop to be grown on a particular piece of land, and the crop has partly failed, producing less than the contract quantity) by implying conditions into the particular contract; there is no recognized doctrine of partial frustration.[211] If there is a temporary delay, but it is so long that the contract becomes impossible to perform[212] or the contractual venture becomes wholly different, the contract will be frustrated as a whole;[213] but a lesser delay will not have that effect and the traditional position is that A will remain liable for it[214]—which is why contracts governed by English law so often contain a *force majeure* clause.

In India and Myanmar, however, the case of partial impossibility has been addressed in the Specific Relief Acts of 1963 and 1877, respectively. Section 12 provides that a party to a contract shall not be directed to perform a part of the contract except in the circumstances provided in that section. The section sets out rules for assessing if a part of a contract can still be performed and when specific performance of such part will be directed.

4. Adjustment of Contract

In all but one of the systems covered in this book, the effect of unforeseen impossibility for which neither is responsible, etc is that if the contract is wholly impossible, the parties are released from their obligations to perform, and there will be no liability for damages in either direction. If the contract becomes temporarily or partially impossible, at least in the civil law systems,[215] the party who has been prevented from performing will not be liable for non-performance, and the other will have the option to terminate the contract if the effects of the non-performance are sufficiently serious.

The one exception is in China. Article 533 CCC uniquely applies to both cases of *force majeure* and cases of changes of circumstances. This means that in cases of *force majeure* there is the possibility that the court may adjust the terms of the contract so as to 'return it to life'.[216]

[209] Chen, ch 22—Taiwan 479, citing art 266 TCC; cf Kamo, ch 12—Japan 252: if a divisible part of the contract becomes impossible, B may cancel in respect of that part, citing art 542(2) JCC.

[210] Kamo, ch 12—Japan 252, citing art 542(1)(iii) JCC.

[211] Neo, ch 20—Singapore 421. It is suggested that under the ICA this type of case might be dealt with under s 32: see section III.2(c).

[212] This may be because time was 'of the essence': see Hall, ch 5—Hong Kong 99.

[213] ibid 99; Neo, ch 20—Singapore 424.

[214] Neo, ch 20—Singapore 430 n 90.

[215] We have noted the difficulties with the common law in these cases: see section III.3.

[216] Wang, ch 3—China 57.

5. Remedies for Unjust Enrichment

In the systems influenced by German law, when a contract comes to an end because of unforeseen impossibility that is not the responsibility of either party, and either party has partly performed, it may claim reimbursement under the rules of unjustified enrichment.[217] One might expect something similar in the Napoleonic systems, given that termination is seen as retroactive,[218] so that the parties are to be returned to their pre-contractual position and therefore restitution of property transferred or, if the property itself cannot be returned, of its value, seems natural.[219] In the Philippines there must be mutual restitution.[220] However, the ICC does not recognize the concept of unjust enrichment and there is apparently no case law on the point.[221] The ICA also provides for the mutual restoration of benefits received under a contract that has become void.[222]

In contrast, English common law allows for restitution in more limited circumstances, and the outcomes were not considered fair in some situations.[223] In 1943, England adopted legislation on the effects of frustration, allowing recovery in a wider range of circumstances, and identical or essentially similar provisions have been adopted not only in Hong Kong[224] and Singapore[225] but also in Malaysia,[226] though our Reporters note that the courts in Malaysia rely on the Contracts Act more often than they apply the newer legislation.

IV. Change of Circumstances

1. Introduction

Where a party's performance has not been made impossible by an unforeseen change of circumstances, but performance has become very much more difficult, or will now be valueless to the other party, there are very pronounced differences between the systems described in the chapters of this volume. The difference is especially marked as between those contract laws that are derived from the common law, whether directly or indirectly via the

[217] See art 266(2) TCC; Kamo, ch 12—Japan 256, citing art 545 JCC. In Korea, it has been established by decisions of the Supreme Court that restitution must follow termination, irrespective of fault: Ahn, ch 14—Korea 290.

[218] Except where the contract is one requiring performance in stages, in which case termination may be only for the future: see section II.4(m)(3).

[219] See note 8 to arts 9:305–9:309 PECL, citing arts 1379 and 1380 read with art 1184 OFCC; Nicholas (n 14) 206.

[220] Chan-Gonzaga, ch 18—Philippines 372; Dizon, ch 19—Philippines 414.

[221] Herliana, ch 10—Indonesia 215.

[222] Section 65 ICA: see Narayan and Vardhan, ch 7—India 149; s 65 Myanmar Contract Act: see Briggs, ch 17—Myanmar 338; s 66 MCA: see Lee and Cheong, ch 15—Malaysia 311–312; but note the Malaysian Civil Law Act 1956, discussed at n 226.

[223] Hall, ch 5—Hong Kong 106; Neo, ch 20—Singapore 426.

[224] Law Amendment and Reform (Consolidation) Ordinance (Cap 23) s 16; Hall, ch 5—Hong Kong 106–107.

[225] Frustrated Contracts Act 1959: see Neo, ch 20—Singapore 426.

[226] Sections 15 and 16 Malaysian Civil Law Act 1956: see Lee and Cheong, ch 15—Malaysia 298 and 309–310. There is discussion of whether a contract that becomes void for failure of a condition under s 33 MCA is frustrated so that ss 15 and 16 of the Civil Law Act apply; our Reporters argue that the effect of s 33 is not to frustrate the contract: see Lee and Cheong, ch 15—Malaysia 300.

ICA, or the versions of that Act in force in Malaysia and Myanmar, and systems that have been heavily influenced by civil law systems.

It goes without saying that in this type of case the parties are free to renegotiate their contract or end it voluntarily, though in the common law jurisdictions there may be complications over consideration if a change in the terms of the contract benefits only one of the parties.[227] Moreover the parties are free to include in the contract provisions for it to be terminated or adjusted in such circumstances, and such clauses seem to be effective in all the jurisdictions. The difference between the systems is over whether the court may terminate the contract, or possibly adjust its terms to restore the equilibrium of the contract, when an unforeseen change of circumstances has made performance very much more difficult for one party or valueless to the other party.

2. Traditional Common Law Systems

In Hong Kong and Singapore, the fact that a contractual obligation, though still possible to perform, has become much more onerous, or its performance is now of little value to the other party, is not a ground for its compulsory adjustment or termination.

As we have seen, both laws recognize that if performance of the contract has become impossible or illegal to perform, it will be frustrated and the parties will be discharged from any further obligations to perform. I have often heard it said by civil lawyers that the common law doctrine covers situations that in Napoleonic systems, for example, would not be recognized as cases of *force majeure*.[228] It is true that in both Hong Kong and Singapore it is recognized that the doctrine of frustration reaches beyond literal impossibility, to encompass cases in which the event has caused such a radical change from the point of view of both parties that the agreement no longer applies in the changed situation;[229] this is seen as a matter of construction (ie interpretation) of the agreement.[230] It is necessary to identify the contractual venture.[231]

Certainly some of the cases of 'frustration of purpose',[232] or in which it has been held that the circumstances in which performance would now have to take place are so 'radically different' from what was contemplated that the contract has been frustrated,[233] might seem to involve changed circumstances rather than literal impossibility. Our Reporter from Singapore cites the English 'Coronation' cases, in one of which it was held that the cancellation of the coronation procession of King Edward VII resulted in the frustration of a contract to rent rooms overlooking the coronation route as the purpose of the contract could no longer be achieved.[234] Cases in Singapore do not seem to have developed this doctrine

[227] Hall, ch 5—Hong Kong 91. Renegotiations have sometimes given rise to issues of 'economic duress': see L Ho, 'Reprehensible Conduct: Threats and Unfair Exploitation in Hong Kong' in M Chen-Wishart, H Sono, and S Vogenauer (eds), *Studies in the Contract Laws of Asia, vol IV: Invalidity* (OUP 2022) 87, 88.

[228] See eg K Zweigert and H Kötz, *An Introduction to Comparative Law* (3rd edn, OUP 1998) 533.

[229] See the examples given in Hall, ch 5—Hong Kong and Neo, ch 20—Singapore 422.

[230] Hall, ch 5—Hong Kong 95–97; Neo, ch 20—Singapore 417.

[231] Hall, ch 5—Hong Kong 96.

[232] Neo, ch 20—Singapore 422.

[233] Hall, ch 5—Hong Kong 98; Neo, ch 20—Singapore 418.

[234] *Krell v Henry* [1903] 2 KB 740 (CA): see Neo, ch 20—Singapore 422.

any more widely.[235] The courts in Hong Kong seem to go a little further than the English judges. In one case, the vendor of land had to pay the government a charge based on the current value of the land; the officials who set the charge took so long to do so, and meanwhile the current value of the land increased so much, that the charge was almost twice the price agreed for the land. In another, flats in a block being built had been sold, under agreements requiring completion by a fixed date, when a landslip destroyed the site; rebuilding would take a very long time. In both cases it was held that performance in the new circumstances had become 'radically different' and the contracts were frustrated.[236] But in both Hong Kong and Singapore it seems to be accepted that the fact that one party will find it much more difficult to perform,[237] or that the buyer of goods now has no use for them,[238] cannot amount to frustration. There is no suggestion in either law that a contract might be adjusted to restore the contractual equilibrium.

3. The Contract(s) Acts of India, Malaysia, and Myanmar

We saw earlier that the section of these acts dealing with contracts to do an act afterwards becoming impossible or unlawful is interpreted as dealing only with literal impossibility, or possibly 'practical impossibility',[239] and not with frustration of purpose. There is no sign of relief being given merely because performance has become even very much more onerous.

4. Civil Law-Based Systems

(a) Systems influenced by German law

We have seen that some of the laws covered in this volume have been heavily influenced by German law, and so it is not surprising to find that most of them have adopted something broadly similar to the doctrine of change of circumstances that was developed by the German courts on the basis of good faith and is now incorporated into the BGB.[240] However, there was a strong attachment to the notion of *pacta sunt servanda*,[241] and change of circumstances was adopted later than in Germany. Taiwan introduced a provision in 1941 to deal with disputes arising out of the extreme fluctuation of commodity prices and inflation.[242] Now Article 227-2(1) of the TCC provides:

[235] In one case, it was held that a contract to lease land for the purpose of building a supermarket was frustrated when permission to build was refused, but our Reporter argues convincingly that this is better viewed as a case of a condition precedent which was not satisfied: see Neo, ch 20—Singapore 422.

[236] Hall, ch 5—Hong Kong 98–99.

[237] ibid 97; Neo, ch 20—Singapore 423, though in Singapore, there are dicta hinting that an 'astronomical' increase in costs, or inflation 'in exceptional circumstances', might bring about frustration (Neo, ch 20—Singapore 423).

[238] Neo, ch 20—Singapore 422.

[239] See section III.2(c).

[240] See s 313 BGB. An historical account of the development of the doctrine can be found in B Markesinis, H Unberath, and A Johnston, *The German Law of Contract* (2nd edn, Hart Publishing 2006) 320–33.

[241] Kwon, ch 13—Korea 261 and 265; Chen, ch 22—Taiwan 456.

[242] Chen, ch 22—Taiwan 456.

> After the conclusion of a contract, where a change of circumstances occurred and it could not be predictable at the time of the conclusion of the contract, and where the performance of the original obligations arising therefrom would become obviously unfair, the party may apply to the court for a judgment to increase or reduce its payment, or to alter the original obligations.[243]

In both Japan and Korea, the doctrine is recognized but it remains a matter of case law,[244] though termination or modification of specific types of contract is allowed by specific statutory provisions.[245] In Japan, adoption of a general doctrine was mooted in the 1920s but the earliest case cited by our Reporter, and the only one in which the Supreme Court has actually given relief on this basis, was decided in 1944.[246] In South Korea, the adoption was not mooted until 1957 and it was only taken up by the Supreme Court in 2007. Although it is widely accepted by scholarly and judicial opinion, in Korea it has seldom been applied by the courts.[247]

The contract law of the People's Republic of China has officially recognized the doctrine of change of circumstances since 2007, though it had appeared in a pioneering judgment in 1999. It is now incorporated into the Civil Code in Article 533.[248]

An exception to the adoption of change of circumstances is in Thailand. Our Reporter explains that the Thai Civil and Commercial Code, which was entirely copied from foreign legal rules, especially those of the BGB of 1900 and the JCC of 1896, does not have a provision on change of circumstances because neither of those Codes contained one.[249] More surprisingly, given the widespread influence the German doctrine has around the civil law world, the Supreme Court has maintained a strict division between hardship and impossibility, refusing to give relief except in cases of impossibility.[250]

(b) Napoleonic systems

Given that the doctrine of change of circumstances (*imprévision*) was only adopted definitively in French law when the Code civil was reformed in 2016,[251] and is not dealt with by the Spanish Civil Code,[252] it was interesting to find that it also has a foothold in systems

243 Translation on Ministry of Justice website <https://law.moj.gov.tw/ENG/LawClass/LawAll.aspx?pcode=B0000001> accessed 4 February 2025.

244 In Korea, there have been two attempts to incorporate the doctrine into the KCC; both failed for lack of legislative time: see Kwon, ch 13—Korea 267–268.

245 Taoka, ch 11—Japan 218 n 6, citing a number of specific statutes, including art 11 of the Act on Land and Building Leases (Act No 90 of October 4, 1991); Kwon, ch 13—Korea 263, citing art 286 KCC; Chen, ch 22—Taiwan 458, citing arts 442 (adjustment of rent of real property in accordance with changes in value, unless lease for fixed period) and 457 (reduction of agricultural rent if profit decreases or fails because of *force majeure*) TCC.

246 Taoka, ch 11—Japan.

247 Kwon, ch 13—Korea 261.

248 Wang, ch 3—China 51–52.

249 Pongsapan, ch 24—Thailand 501.

250 ibid 502–503.

251 See art 1195 of the French Civil Code. Before 2016, the civil courts had held occasionally that good faith required the renegotiation of a contract, eg Cass civ (1) 16 March 2004, D 2004, 1754, or even that a change might deprive the contract of *cause*: Cass com 29 June 2010, no 09-67369, unpublished.

252 Since the financial crisis of 2008, the Spanish courts have occasionally allowed revision on the basis of the doctrine of *rebus sic stantibus*: see C Jerez, M Kubica, and A Ruda, 'Force Majeure and Hardship in the Corona Crisis: Some Contract Law Reflections on ELI Principle no 13' in E Hondius and others, *Coronavirus and the Law in Europe* (Intersentia 2021) 603, 606–07.

influenced by the Code Napoleon. In the Philippines the new Civil Code adopted in 1950 provides that:

> When the service has become so difficult as to be manifestly beyond the contemplation of the parties, the obligor may also be released therefrom, in whole or in part.[253]

'Service' does not include the paying of rent but has been interpreted quite widely by the courts so as to include performances of other kinds.[254] However, there is some doubt and confusion over whether inflation or deflation of the currency can ever be grounds for relief.[255] There is no provision for change of circumstances in the ICC but scholars, influenced by the provisions of the 1992 Dutch Civil Code, the *Nieuw Burgerlijk Wetboek* (NBW),[256] have argued in favour of relief,[257] and though the courts have not recognized any doctrine of change of circumstances, they have sometimes relied on a wide discretion to revise contracts on the basis of equity and good faith when there has been a change of circumstances.[258]

In Vietnam, the doctrine of change of circumstances was incorporated into the Civil Code of 2015 after an extensive debate.[259] Our Reporter's account reveals the concerns that typically surround proposals to adopt the doctrine, such as its impact on party autonomy and the principle of *pacta sunt servanda*, and the capacity of judges to understand the context well enough to make informed decisions on revising contracts.[260] Ultimately the reform was adopted for three main reasons:

> (i) this doctrine is needed to react to the distortion of the contractual equilibrium caused by unforeseen circumstances; (ii) this doctrine has its theoretical foundation in the principle of good faith; and (iii) it is in line with the general global trend of recognizing a separate doctrine of change of circumstances.[261]

5. Conditions of Application

(a) General

According to the Korean Supreme Court ruling in 2007 (and in subsequent other cases),[262]

> termination or rescission of a contract for change of circumstances requires that: (i) the underlying fundamental circumstances of the contract have changed significantly;

[253] See art 1267 PCC. Previously contractual obligations had to be performed unless they had become impossible or performance would be so dangerous that it would be contrary to public policy: see Chan-Gonzaga, ch 18—Philippines 373–374.

[254] Chan-Gonzaga, ch 18—Philippines 377–379.

[255] ibid. Relief might be given on the basis of an absence of *cause*: see ibid 387.

[256] See art 6:258 NBW.

[257] Though the theory advocated would lead only to termination: see Bell, ch 9—Indonesia 174.

[258] ibid 179 and 194–196.

[259] See art 420 VCC 2015, quoted in n 265.

[260] Do, ch 26—Vietnam 542.

[261] ibid 539.

[262] Supreme Court Decision 2008Da44368 (24 June 2011); Supreme Court Decision 2012Da13637 (26 September 2013).

(ii) the change of circumstances occurred after execution of the contract; (iii) the parties to the contract were unable to anticipate such change of circumstances; (iv) the change of circumstances occurred due to a cause not attributable to the party who claims the termination right; and (v) if the original binding force of the contract were maintained, it would lead to a consequence that would violate the principle of trust and good faith.[263]

Our Reporter's formulation of the requirements in Japanese law is very similar in substance[264] and so, in most respects, is the explanation of the application of Article 227-2 of the TCC, of Article 533 of the CCC, and of Article 420 of the VCC 2015.[265] It is convenient to take the conditions point by point.

(b) Significant change in the underlying circumstances

The change in circumstances must make performance 'excessively onerous'; small-scale fluctuations will not suffice.[266] In Taiwanese law, it is said that there must be an 'extraordinary, tremendous, and obvious change', after taking into account the nature and purpose of a contract.[267]

The changed circumstance at issue must be expressly or implicitly shared by the parties as part of the foundation of the contract at issue; it may either be something on which the terms of the contract, such as the price, were based, or a shared purpose. The changed circumstances must relate to 'objective' circumstances, not merely to one party's subjective intention or personal circumstances.[268]

263 Kwon, ch 13—Korea 266.
264 Taoka, ch 11—Japan 217.
265 Article 420 VCC 2015 reads:

1. Circumstances shall be deemed to change fundamentally when the following requirements are met:
   (a) a change of circumstances occurs for objective reasons and after the conclusion of the contract;
   (b) at the time of the conclusion of the contract, the parties could not have foreseen the change of circumstances;
   (c) the change of circumstances is so fundamental that the contract would not have been concluded or would have been concluded with a completely different content if the parties had foreseen such change;
   (d) the continued performance of the contract without adapting its contents will cause serious damage to one party;
   (e) the party whose benefits are affected has taken all necessary measures to the best of its ability and appropriate with the nature of the contract but is unable to prevent or mitigate the level to which the benefits are affected.

266 Kwon, ch 13—Korea 268; Wang, ch 3—China 53; Chan-Gonzaga, ch 18—Philippines 376 ('extremely difficult but not impossible').

267 Chen, ch 22—Taiwan 460, but see section IV.7; cf art 420(1)(c) VCC 2015: 'the change of circumstances is so fundamental that the contract would not have been concluded or would have been concluded with a completely different content if the parties had foreseen such change': see Do, ch 26—Vietnam 543.

268 Kwon, ch 13—Korea 268; see similarly Taoka, ch 11—Japan 220; Chen, ch 22—Taiwan 460; art 420(1)(a) VCC 2015, quoted in n 265. See also the answers to the first fact situation in the hypothetical scenario of Gina and H Hotel (whether hotel booking may be cancelled when an exhibition the guest intended to view is cancelled); this was regarded as merely a matter of motive: see Chen, ch 22—Taiwan 477; Taoka, ch 11—Japan 222; Wang, ch 3—China 68. The fact scenarios of the hypotheticals described in this section IV are taken from Chen-Wishart, Neo, and Vogenauer, ch 1—Introduction 7–8.

The answers to one of the hypothetical situations that Reporters were asked to consider raised an interesting issue. The facts of the hypothetical were:

> Easy leases business premises from Frugle for a fixed period of 15 years. Shortly after the contract has been concluded, a nearby military airport is unexpectedly shut down for political reasons. The government invests an enormous amount of public funds in order to improve the commercial infrastructure in the area. As a result, Easy's profits are 500 per cent of what could reasonably have been expected at the time of making the contract. At the same time, the rental value of comparable business premises in the area rises to 500 per cent of the agreed rental price. Frugle requests that the rental price should be adjusted accordingly or, alternatively, that the agreement should be terminated.

This is not a case in which one party finds it more expensive to perform or in which its performance has ceased to be of value to the other. Rather, Frugle is missing out an opportunity to make a greater profit than what had been agreed under the contract, and Easy gets what may be regarded as a windfall.[269] Thus it does not fall within the description of the doctrine that I have used so far in this conclusion, and it was something of a surprise that Reporters for many of the jurisdictions that recognize change of circumstances say that in this case the rent payable by the tenant may be increased by the court,[270] though in Japan this would be on the basis of legislation applicable to land and building leases rather than under the doctrine of change of circumstances.[271] Where the doctrine is recognized in Asian jurisdictions, it is given a broad application.

(c) Change after the contract was made

The change in circumstances must have occurred after the contract was made.[272] Changes that occurred beforehand but were unknown to the parties are dealt with under mistake[273] (which in Korea is dealt with as a matter of 'supplemental interpretation'[274]). Further, in Taiwan some decisions have held that relief cannot be given if the contract has actually been performed before relief is sought, though others have allowed it.[275]

[269] Pongsapan, ch 24—Thailand 514.

[270] Wang, ch 3—China 67; Chen, ch 22—Taiwan 459; Do, ch 26—Vietnam 559. Relief would not be given in the Philippines as the case falls outside the reach of art 1267 PCC (see section IV.4(b)), nor in Korea, our Reporter remarking wryly that 'Changes due to governmental action are risks that are generally assumed and anticipated by the parties. This is even more so in a society where such governmental action or inaction happens frequently': Kwon, ch 13—Korea 275. There would be no relief in any of the systems derived from the common law.

[271] Taoka, ch 11—Japan 232; the legislation is quoted at ibid 218 n 6. There is similar legislation in Taiwan, but there it does not apply if the lease is for a fixed period; where the period is fixed, as in the hypothetical of Easy and Frugle, art 227-2 TCC (see section IV.4(a)) may be applied: see Chen, ch 22—Taiwan 458. In Indonesia, a court could review the contract on the basis of equity, fairness, and good faith: see Bell, ch 9—Indonesia 194–196.

[272] See eg art 420(1)(a) VCC 2015, quoted in n 265; Do, ch 26—Vietnam 548.

[273] Taoka, ch 11—Japan 219, referring to art 95 JCC; Wang, ch 3—China 53; Chen, ch 22—Taiwan 463 and 475 (noting that in 2017 it was proposed to add a provision equivalent to s 313(2) BGB so as to bring cases of shared mistake within the doctrine of change of circumstances).

[274] Kwon, ch 13—Korea 269. Supplementary interpretation is broadly equivalent to the implication of terms in the common law: see Beale and others (n 114) 797. In German law, the doctrine of change of circumstances is used in cases of shared mistake: Beale and others (n 114).

[275] Chen, ch 22—Taiwan 463.

(d) Change that could not have been anticipated

The change must be something that the parties could not have anticipated at the time of the contract;[276] if it could have been foreseen, it will normally be assumed that one or the other of the parties was taking the risk of it happening.[277]

(e) Change not attributable to either party

The change of circumstances must not be the fault of the party seeking relief.[278] In its decision in 2007,[279] the Korean Supreme Court stated non-attributability as a requirement but in 2017 it dropped it, seemingly subsuming the 'no-fault' requirement under questions of risk allocation or foreseeability.[280]

(f) Change not within the risk assumed by either party

The change must not be something of which the party seeking relief took the risk, expressly or by implication.[281] For example, in Japanese law, a party is assumed to carry the risk of events that fell within their sphere of control, even if the occurrence was not the party's fault.[282] In Taiwan, relief is not available when there has just been an ordinary change in commodity prices or if the contract was speculative in nature.[283] The question of whether a party should bear the risk of what took place is important also in the Chinese system—and difficult to decide.[284] Risk allocation is not mentioned in Article 420 VCC 2015 but it is understood that it is implicitly included through the unforeseeability element.[285]

(g) Enforcement of original terms contrary to good faith

In Taiwan,

> [t]he doctrine of change of circumstances governs only those incidents that alter the equilibrium of the contract and instances where the performance of the original obligations is obviously unfair to the contracting party in view of the principle of good faith.[286]

This requires the court to consider not only the losses suffered by the party seeking relief but also whether the other party benefited from the change of circumstances.[287]

276 Wang, ch 3—China 53; Chan-Gonzaga, ch 18—Philippines 375; Do, ch 26—Vietnam 549–550.

277 Kwon, ch 13—Korea 269; similarly Taoka, ch 11—Japan 219; Chen, ch 22—Taiwan 462; Do, ch 26—Vietnam 549.

278 Taoka, ch 11—Japan 219 (change must not be attributable to either party); Kwon, ch 13—Korea 269; Chen, ch 22—Taiwan 463–464 (noting that if one party's increased expense is caused by an unforeseen act by the other party, the case does not come under the doctrine but is one of breach of contract—see also Wang, ch 3—China 53); Chan-Gonzaga, ch 18—Philippines 375. Where the extra expense is caused by a third person, it has been argued that a remedy should be sought against that person, not the other party to the contract: see Chen, ch 22—Taiwan 461.

279 See section IV.4(a).

280 Kwon, ch 13—Korea 271.

281 See eg Chen, ch 22—Taiwan 462; Chan-Gonzaga, ch 18—Philippines 384 (discussing the hypothetical of Abraham and Bill).

282 Taoka, ch 11—Japan 220. See also Do, ch 26—Vietnam 547.

283 Chen, ch 22—Taiwan 462.

284 Wang, ch 3—China 55, drawing a parallel to the 'multi-factorial' approach used in the common law.

285 Do, ch 26—Vietnam 549.

286 Chen, ch 22—Taiwan 464. See similarly Wang, ch 3—China 53–54.

287 Chen, ch 22—Taiwan 464–465.

In Japanese law, enforcement of the original contract must be deemed significantly inequitable to one of the parties in light of the good faith principle, and opinion[288] is that this will be the cases when disruption of the known and agreed purpose of a contract means an impossibility of performance,[289] when one's performance of the contract has become economically 'impossible',[290] and when the values of the performances in a contract have become economically imbalanced to such a degree that its performance would be significantly inequitable to one of the parties in the light of good faith.[291] In Korean law, the Supreme Court first said that relief would be given if enforcement of the original terms of the contract would be so unfair as to be contrary to good faith.[292] This requirement was criticized as too vague, and in 2017, the Supreme Court replaced it with more concrete criteria: substantial imbalance between the parties and frustration of the purpose of the contract.[293]

In Vietnam, rather than adopt a criterion of whether the change of circumstances has caused a serious upset to the equilibrium of the contract, the legislation requires such a fundamental change of circumstances that the parties would not have concluded the contract, or would have concluded it with a completely different content, if they had foreseen such change and also that continued performance of the contract without adapting its contents will cause serious damage to one party.[294]

(h) Excluded cases

In Japan, it is considered that the doctrine of changed circumstance is inapplicable to a loan contract because an adjustment of the loaned amount or interest rate in response to inflation goes against the nominalism of an obligation to pay money.[295] We have seen that in the Philippines there is controversy over whether a contract can ever be adjusted because of inflation or deflation.[296]

(i) Mandatory?

In some European systems, it is not possible for the parties to exclude the operation of change of circumstances,[297] and in Taiwan the majority view among scholars and courts is

[288] Taoka, ch 11—Japan 220–221, indicating (at n 18) that the analysis is derived from K Larenz, *Geschäftsgrundlage und Vertragserfüllung: die Bedeutung 'veränderter Umstände' im Zivilrecht* (CH Beck 1957) 89–107.

[289] This clearly resembles the common law notion of frustration of purpose, but it seems that inability to achieve one party's purpose suffices if that purpose was known to and accepted by the other, whereas arguably frustration of purpose requires that the purpose of both parties has become impossible (see section III.2(b)(2)).

[290] The dividing line between change of circumstances and impossibility is unclear: see Taoka, ch 11—Japan 221.

[291] See eg when land had risen in value by 23 times, but not when the increase was lower: Taoka, ch 11—Japan 221.

[292] Kwon, ch 13—Korea 270, referring to the principle of trust and good faith stipulated by art 2 KCC.

[293] Kwon, ch 13—Korea 271.

[294] See art 420(1)(c) and (d) VCC, quoted in n 265 and Do, ch 26—Vietnam 552.

[295] Taoka, ch 11—Japan 224.

[296] Chan-Gonzaga, ch 18—Philippines 380–381; section IV.4(b).

[297] For instance, in the Netherlands, art 6:258 NBW is regarded as mandatory: see E Hondius and C Grigoleit (eds), *Unexpected Circumstances in European Contract Law* (CUP 2011) 73. In contrast, in French law, although the doctrine is based on good faith and the duty of good faith itself is seen as mandatory (art 1104(2) of the French Civil Code), the operation of the change of circumstances doctrine (art 1195 of the French Civil Code) can be excluded by agreement: O Deshayes, T Genicon, and Y Laithier, *Réforme du droits des contrats, du régime général et de la preuve des obligations* (2nd edn, LexisNexis 2018) 440, citing preparatory works and the discussion in the Senate.

that the provision of change of circumstances may not be excluded by a contract 'because it is a court measure to give the disadvantaged party relief in order to fulfil the court's function of achieving fairness and justice'.[298] Equally, in China, the courts will not respect any attempt to exclude the doctrine (now embodied in Article 533 CCC) because it is 'based on contractual justice and not contractual freedom'.[299] If the parties have agreed on a clause allowing for adaptation, that will be respected,[300] but where an abnormal change of circumstances goes beyond what could have been contemplated by the parties at the time the contract was made, the doctrine will still apply.[301]

6. The Conditions and Nature of Relief

(a) Renegotiation

When there has been a sufficiently serious change of circumstances to merit relief, one may hope that the parties will negotiate a settlement of some kind, and it has been suggested that the parties might come under a duty to renegotiate the contract,[302] but no duty or requirement to negotiate has been established in Korean law.[303] In Taiwan, it was debated whether to adopt a duty to renegotiate but the idea was rejected as unnecessary.[304] In China, however, if one party requests a renegotiation, the other must do so and the people's court actively guides the parties through the process of renegotiation and changing the contract. However, the only sanction for refusing to negotiate is the same as if the negotiations fail: the court may modify or terminate the contract.[305]

(b) Judicial adjustment of the contract terms

In Taiwan, the courts have regularly adjusted the terms of the contract in response to a change of circumstances;[306] but it seems that they are willing only to adjust the contract prices, not to change the other obligations under the contract.[307] In contrast, in Korea, there has been no Supreme Court decision so far that acknowledges judicial modification as one possible consequence.[308] Similarly in Japan, no consensus has been reached over whether the court may adjust the contract. In the Philippines, the Supreme Court has held that Article 1267 PCC[309] only allows for the release of the party in difficulty, not for modification or revision of the contract, though in a subsequent case in which termination of the

[298] Chen, ch 22—Taiwan 472.
[299] Wang, ch 3—China 51. We do not have information on this point for most systems.
[300] ibid.
[301] Chen, ch 22—Taiwan 473.
[302] Taoka, ch 11—Japan 225; Do, ch 26—Vietnam 554 (arguable that good faith imposes such a duty and that failure to negotiate in good faith might give rise to liability in damages). Compare art 6:111(2) PECL, cited in Kwon, ch 13—Korea 272, which would render a party who fails to negotiate in good faith liable in damages to the other party.
[303] Kwon, ch 13—Korea 272.
[304] Chen, ch 22—Taiwan 470.
[305] Wang, ch 3—China 54.
[306] e.g. Chen, ch 22—Taiwan 460–461. The affected party must have requested adjustment: see ibid. Article 420 VCC 2015 also allows for adjustment, but only if termination is inappropriate: see section IV.6(d).
[307] Chen, ch 22—Taiwan 468–469.
[308] Kwon, ch 13—Korea 272. The proposal for legislation in 2014 (see n 244) would have introduced judicial modification.
[309] See section IV.4.(b).

contract would have resulted in severe disruption to an essential public service, the court relied on its general equitable jurisdiction to modify the contract.[310]

(c) Termination

In Korea, termination for change of circumstances has seldom been permitted.[311] Scholarly opinion is that if adaptation of the contract is not possible or would not be fair to one party, the contract may be terminated for the future by the disadvantaged party rather than by the court.[312] In Vietnam, termination must be ordered by a court.[313]

(d) Primary and secondary remedies

In Taiwan, adjustment is considered to be the primary remedy; the contract should be terminated only if adjustment is not possible or would be unfair.[314] In Vietnam, in contrast, the priority is the other way around: the court may only adapt the contract if its termination 'will cause loss and damage of an amount higher than the costs for the performance of the contract if the contract is adapted'. This decision by the legislator is controversial.[315]

7. Differences in Application

Although the relief available varies from one system to another, on paper the doctrine of change of circumstances seems broadly similar in all the jurisdictions that have adopted it. However, it is much more developed in Taiwan than elsewhere. So it is not easy to make detailed comparisons. It is even harder to compare how the doctrine is or will be applied in the different systems. For example, how large must the change be for the doctrine to be triggered?

The doctrine is of course a legal transplant, and we know that legal transplants often develop very differently in the host soil.[316] This may be an example. In German law, it is said that the doctrine must be restricted to extreme cases:

> What is really required is such a fundamental and radical change in the relevant circumstances that it would be an intolerable result, quite inconsistent with law and justice, to hold the party to the contract.[317]

310 Chan-Gonzaga, ch 18—Philippines 379–380. In the light of articles of the PCC allowing the court to modify the contract in specific circumstances (such as mistake or where a clause is penal), it has been argued that generally relief should include modification: see Chan-Gonzaga, ch 18—Philippines 389–390.

311 The one case in which the Supreme Court permitted it was more akin to a failure of condition precedent: see n 235.

312 Kwon, ch 13—Korea 273. It seems that in Japan also, a party who can show that it should be excused under the doctrine has a right to terminate the contract: Taoka, ch 11—Japan 225.

313 Do, ch 26—Vietnam 555. Whether an arbitral tribunal has the same power is an open question: see ibid 556. In Taiwan also, termination must be ordered by the court: see Chen, ch 22—Taiwan 468.

314 Chen, ch 22—Taiwan 468–469.

315 Do, ch 26—Vietnam 556.

316 See eg M Chen-Wishart, 'Legal Transplant of Undue Influence: Lost in Translation or a Working Misunderstanding?' (2013) 62 International and Comparative Law Quarterly 1, 1–3.

317 Markesinis, Unberath, and Johnston (n 240) 325, quoting 14 October 1959, BGH NJW 1959, 2203–04.

Section 313 BGB and German cases restrict change of circumstances to cases where what has happened is outside the risk that the complaining party is normally expected to bear. Likewise in Taiwan, in principle a 'tremendous change' is required for the doctrine to be triggered,[318] one that is outside 'the scope of risks that should be borne under the original outcome of a contract, taking into consideration the social-economic situations, common ideas, and any other objective affairs'.[319] However, actual cases from Taiwan seem to present a marked contrast to those in Germany. The Taiwanese Supreme Court has applied change of circumstances to a construction contract when the government issued a ban on the collection of sand and rocks from rivers, which brought about a 50 per cent increase in the price of sand and rocks. The same court has indicated that the doctrine might apply when a construction contract was unexpectedly delayed by 'the changed design of a bridge, the delay of acquiring the land for work, the delay of removing things and electronic poles on the site, and inhabitants' opposition to use the land' and took twice the expected time;[320] and similarly when a contractor was delayed for over 1,000 days by another contractor unexpectedly suspending work.[321] It seems unlikely that a German court would consider such changes to be sufficiently serious to trigger section 313 BGB.

Our Reporter for Japan describes an even more radical view, one that would take the doctrine of change of circumstances even further than in Taiwan. She points out that the concept of contract that lies behind the traditional reluctance to adjust the contract in changed circumstances is a 'static' one, and that some scholars take a different approach, according to which:

> the concept of contract is no longer static, but rather fluid in the sense that 'contractual obligations are not finalized at the time of the formation of the contract, but rather changed and re-established through the parties' continuous negotiations'[322] even after the formation of the contract. Since a renegotiation, as well as an amendment of a contract, is a process of redefining the contractual obligations, the process is part of upholding a contract, or the principle of *pacta sunt servanda*. In consequence, the doctrine of changed circumstance becomes a rule facilitating the *pacta sunt servanda* principle, rather than an exception to it.

Professor Taoka links this to the idea of relational contracts, which 'also views the concept of contract as a fluid one, [so that] the doctrine of changed circumstances is viewed as a rule to support the *pacta sunt servanda* principle'.[323] She tells us that this relaxed view is not the predominant one[324] but that there is a 'prevalent' practice of including a term requiring negotiation in good faith when changes have made the terms originally agreed unreasonable. This limits the need for a broad doctrine of change of circumstances.[325]

318 Chen, ch 22—Taiwan 460.

319 Supreme Court 104 Tai-shang No 2413 Civil Judgment (2015), as reported and translated by Chen ch 22—Taiwan 465.

320 Supreme Court 103 Tai-shang No 1363 Civil Judgment (2014), cited and translated by Chen ch 22—Taiwan 461. I have not been able to find other translations of the decisions of the Supreme Court of Taiwan.

321 Supreme Court 96 Tai-shang No 482 Civil Judgment (2007), cited by Chen, ch 22—Taiwan 461.

322 Taoka, ch 11—Japan 229.

323 ibid.

324 ibid 233; see also the concerns over certainty and excessive interference with freedom of contract, voiced in the debate over whether to codify the doctrine: ibid 231.

325 ibid 228 and 231.

To my mind, the more relaxed approach advocated by some Japanese scholars might also be linked to the reportedly traditional approach of parties to contracts in Japan: that the contracts tend to be short, defining the rights of the parties in only broad terms and leaving the rest to negotiation between the parties should a conflict arise, while parties to a contract are not seen as having conflicting interests but a mutually beneficial and cooperative relationship, one of mutual trust.[326] It would be very interesting to know whether opinions and practices in Japan had any influence on Taiwanese attitudes and the approach its courts take to change of circumstances.

If it is correct that the courts in Taiwan apply the doctrine of change of circumstances much more freely than it is applied in Germany, this suggests different understandings of the kind and the degree of risk that a party to a particular type of contract is normally expected to bear. It would be interesting to compare typical (presumably standard form) construction contracts, and also actual contract practice, in the two jurisdictions. What makes it very hard for the comparatist is that even within a single system, approaches seem to vary from one context to another. It is very interesting to compare the court decisions in Taiwan over leases of premises that the tenant was unable to make use of because of governmental restrictions imposed during the recent pandemics.

8. COVID-19 Pandemic and Change of Circumstances

(a) Introduction

In countries across Asia, many contracts were affected either by the recent pandemics, first Severe Acute Respiratory Syndrome (SARS) in 2003 and then COVID-19 in 2020, or more widely by the restrictions that were imposed by governments to try to limit the spread of the diseases. Many contracts will have been rendered either factually or legally impossible to perform. Many more will have become much more expensive for one party to perform, or performance will have become much less valuable for the other party. For example, many business tenants were faced with paying rent on shop or office premises that they could not legally use or which were attracting almost no business.

The reports in this volume vary in the amount of information they provide on how the effects on contracts were handled in their jurisdiction and, in any event, space precludes more than a very brief discussion. We will leave aside cases in which performance was rendered impossible and look at just two issues. First, did systems that do not recognize the doctrine of change of circumstances feel it necessary to introduce special measures to deal with the impact on contracts? And second, in jurisdictions in which the doctrine of change of circumstances is recognized, what use of it was expected or actually made?

[326] H Oda, *Japanese Law* (4th edn, OUP 2021) 160–61, referring to works by Kawashima and Gray, and subsequent discussion by a number of authors. Oda himself seems doubtful how much difference there is between Japan and other countries in this respect: ibid. But see Taoka, ch 11—Japan 228 ('long-standing practice to insert a term in a contract to obligate the parties to negotiate in good faith for the purpose of adjusting the price in the event where the price has become unreasonable due to an increase or decrease in associated costs, and changes in law, values of the currency and other economic situations').

(b) Special measures

There were surprising variations between the measures adopted in systems which, under their general law, take very similar approaches. We have seen that the common law and ICA-based systems recognize impossibility but not change of circumstances, but some brought in special measures that provided broadly similar relief. Singapore's COVID-19 (Temporary Measures) Act 2020, which applied to a wide range of business-to-business contracts made before 1 February 2020, allowed contractual relief where the effect of the pandemic on the parties' ability to perform was not serious enough to frustrate the contract and did not fall within the coverage of a *force majeure* clause in the contract. It is quite true that, as our Reporter argues, the measures were only temporary and applied only to contracts made before the restrictions were announced,[327] but for a jurisdiction that does not recognize change of circumstances they were remarkable in their breadth.[328]

India and Malaysia also introduced special measures but of a much more limited kind. India's legislation allowed for a refund of 95 per cent of the performance security, earnest money, or liquidated damages forfeited by the enterprise as a result of default in performance where the period of completion was between 19 February 2020 and 31 March 2022, but this applied only to contracts with the government of India or government companies.[329] Malaysia's Coronavirus Disease (COVID-19) Act 2020 prevented enforcement of contractual rights against parties affected by specified disease control measures but only if they were actually prevented from performing.[330] Hong Kong did not adopt any special measures to provide relief.

(c) Use of the doctrine of change of circumstances

Several Reporters discuss the application of the doctrine of change of circumstances in relation to contracts whose performance was affected by the pandemic or disease-control measures.[331] Some suggest that it can be applied,[332] and in China the Supreme People's Court has issued guidance:

> If continuing performance of the contract makes it obviously unfair to one party, and the party requests to change the performance period, performance method, or price of the contract, the people's court shall, based on actual conditions of the case, decide whether to support such a request. If a party requests to dissolve the contract because the purpose of the contract cannot be achieved, the people's court shall support such a request.[333]

[327] Neo, ch 20—Singapore 431.

[328] They prevented not only the commencement of court or arbitral proceedings and execution of distress, etc in relation to the contract but also the repossession of any hired goods or the termination or forfeiture of leases or licences of immoveable property for a prescribed period. There were special provisions, for instance for inability to perform construction contracts or supply contracts, giving relief against the forfeiture of performance bonds and liquidated damages clauses; and interest charges were limited to the legal rate. To some extent, contract prices could be adjusted; for example, the contractor could require the employer to pay additional 'foreign manpower salary' costs.

[329] Narayan and Vardhan, ch 7—India 154.

[330] Lee and Cheong, ch 15—Malaysia 319.

[331] Our Reporter for Thailand, where the doctrine of change of circumstances is not recognized (see section IV.4.(a)), argues that in the light of good faith, the lease of premises in a shopping mall should be interpreted as requiring the lessor to make the premises available in a normally operating mall so that the case can be treated as one of impossibility: Pongsapan, ch 24—Thailand 513.

[332] Do, ch 26—Vietnam 561.

[333] Wang, ch 3—China 63.

However, in the systems for which we are given information about actual decisions, it seemed rare that relief was given. In Taiwan, for example, there have been 19 District Court cases in which tenants have sought relief from paying rent, but only two tenants were successful. In the other cases, relief was denied on one of a number of grounds: that a reduction on the tenant's income for a couple of months was not outside the normal risk taken by the tenant; that having to perform its original obligations was not obviously unfair to the tenant, either because the tenant did not suffer large losses or because the lessor did not gain any benefits arising from the pandemic; or that a two-month interruption was not severe enough or that there was no benefit to the lessor.[334]

Given that in other contexts, the courts in Taiwan seem fairly ready to give relief for change of circumstances (eg when a change has affected construction contracts),[335] the restrictive approach in the majority of COVID-19 cases is interesting. Perhaps the seemingly different approach in the COVID-19 cases was because the different countries have different ideas of what are 'normal' risks in various kinds of contract. Possibly, it merely reflects the fact that businesses in Taiwan were less seriously affected than businesses in many other countries, for example, in Europe.[336] Whatever the true explanation, the treatments of the effects of the pandemic seem to demonstrate just how hard it is to compare the actual application of apparently similar doctrines in different jurisdictions.

9. Hypothetical Cases of Change of Circumstances

That difficulty is reflected in the answers given to the hypothetical cases involving a change of circumstances.[337] The first case was as follows:

> In 1567, Abraham enters into a contract for an unlimited period of time with farmer Bill under which Abraham promises to build and maintain an irrigation channel from which Bill may extract water at a fixed price. By 2018, inflation and the rise in the cost of

[334] Chen, ch 22—Taiwan 465–466.

[335] See section IV.7.

[336] For a wide-ranging consideration of the way the impact of COVID-19 was handled in European jurisdictions, see Hondius and others (n 252). There is a particularly interesting contrast between what the courts in Taiwan did and what took place in Germany. Many German courts were refusing to give relief, but the legislator introduced a provision that where measures had resulted in significant restrictions on a tenant's use of non-residential premises, there should be a presumption that there has been a change in the basis of the contract within the meaning of s 313(1) BGB (art 240(7)(1) of the Act on Mitigation of the Consequences of the COVID-19 Pandemic in Civil, Insolvency and Criminal Proceedings, 27 March 2020, introducing art 240 into the Introductory Act to the Civil Code (*Einführungsgesetz zum Bürgerlichen Gesetzbuch*), amended to add para 7 with effect from 31 December 2020. A translation is available at <www.gesetze-im-internet.de/englisch_bgbeg/englisch_bgbeg.html#p0237> accessed 4 February 2025. Subsequently the Bundesgerichtshof ruled not only that s 313 BGB applies to this kind of case in principle but also that there is, and in the light of art 240 para 7 continues to be, a rebuttable presumption that the COVID-19 restrictions have changed the circumstances of the contract: there is no reason to believe that the lessee had assumed the sole risk of use were their retail business to be shut down owing to the pandemic, unless there are provisions in the contract showing otherwise: BGH 12 January 2022, BGHZ 232, 178.

[337] The hypothetical scenario of Builder George and Han (discussed earlier, section III.2(a)) was normally taken to be a case of impossibility rather than of change of circumstances (though see Taoka, ch 11—Japan 223); and similarly, the second and the third variants of the hypothetical case of Gina and H Hotel (government ban and strike, respectively, prevented hotel guest from getting to the hotel). The hypothetical of Easy and Frugle was discussed in section IV.5(b). It was generally agreed that the hypothetical scenario of Kris and Leila did not involve a change of circumstances; the outcome would depend on whether Leila had given a contractual undertaking to dedicate the property to cultural uses, and so the case is not discussed further in this conclusion.

> maintenance and labour have made the price wholly inadequate. Abraham's successors in law ask for an increase in the price that would provide them with adequate compensation. Alternatively, they wish to terminate the contract.

Given that it is not impossible for Abraham's successors to perform their obligations, merely ruinously expensive, it is not surprising that none of the common law or ICA-based jurisdictions would give relief,[338] save that the Reporter for India ingeniously suggested that as the ICA would not apply to a contract made over 300 years before the Act was passed, relief might be given in equity.[339] Relief will also be refused in Thailand, where the doctrine of change of circumstances has not been adopted.[340]

Among the jurisdictions that recognize the doctrine of change of circumstances, there was considerable variation.[341] In Taiwan[342] (and also in Indonesia, though by the court invoking the concepts of fairness and equity to modify the price,[343] and possibly in the Philippines[344]), the contract price would be adjusted to rebalance the contract, but in Japan and Vietnam, relief would probably be refused on the ground that the effects of normal inflation are predictable.[345] In Korea, the outcome is very hard to predict because though relief has been refused in a somewhat similar case, subsequently the Supreme Court has seemed more willing to grant relief.[346]

Answers to the hypothetical scenario of Citi Corporation and Drive Bank[347] broadly followed the same pattern,[348] save that relief would probably be denied in this case in Korea;[349] and also in the Philippines, on the ground that the case does not fall within the limited scope of Article 1267 PCC.[350] Possibly relief would be given in Vietnam in this case, as the inflation was abnormal;[351] and in China, the bank would have the right to request the people's court or arbitration institution to adjust the interest rate or to terminate the contract.[352]

The case of Gina and H Hotel, with the hotel guest who wanted to cancel her booking when the inauguration procession she was due to watch was unexpectedly cancelled, was also seen as one in which the guest might be released from the contract under the doctrine

[338] Hall, ch 5—Hong Kong 112–113; Neo, ch 20—Singapore 432; Lee and Cheong, ch 15—Malaysia 315; Briggs, ch 17—Myanmar 352.

[339] Narayan and Vardhan, ch 7—India 155.

[340] Pongsapan, ch 24—Thailand 501; see section IV.4(a).

[341] A number of Reporters argued that a contract 'for an unlimited period of time' might be treated as one for an indefinite duration, and therefore that it could be terminated on giving notice. Some therefore did not consider change of circumstances: see Wang, ch 3—China 66.

[342] Chen, ch 22—Taiwan 467–468.

[343] Bell, ch 9—Indonesia 194–196; see section IV.4(b).

[344] Chan-Gonzaga, ch 18—Philippines 385, though there, relief may be limited to allowing termination of the contract: see section IV.4(b).

[345] Taoka, ch 11—Japan 233; Do, ch 26—Vietnam 559.

[346] Kwon, ch 13—Korea 274, remarking that probably relief would be limited to termination as there is no clear legal doctrine permitting modification of the contract.

[347] The hypothetical facts were that in 2015, Citi Corporation receives a loan from Drive Bank. The interest rate is fixed at 10 per cent for five years. In the 20 years preceding the agreement, the rate of inflation had been relatively stable within a range of 1 to 6 per cent. In 2017, the economic situation begins to destabilize and inflation rises to 50 per cent. Drive Bank requests adjustment or, alternatively, termination of the contract.

[348] Adjustment: Chen, ch 22—Taiwan 469; no relief: Taoka, ch 11—Japan 224; Pongsapan, ch 24—Thailand 514; and also in all the systems derived from the common law.

[349] Kwon, ch 13—Korea 275, citing the Supreme Court's strict attitude towards change of circumstances to date.

[350] Chan-Gonzaga, ch 18—Philippines 385; on art 1267 PCC, see section IV.4(b).

[351] Do, ch 26—Vietnam 558.

[352] Wang, ch 3—China 66.

of change of circumstances[353] (or in Indonesia on the basis of equity, fairness, and good faith[354]). In the Philippines, the guest might cancel the contract on the basis that the contract now lacks '*cause*'. But the facts of this hypothetical are very close to those of the English 'Coronation' case, and accordingly our reports for both Hong Kong and Singapore argued that a court might regard the purpose of the contract as having been frustrated. In Malaysia, if Gina is able to persuade the court that first, it should adopt the English concept of frustration of purpose, and second, that the purpose of the contract between Gina and H Hotel was to enable Gina to view the inauguration procession, the same might apply.[355]

V. Conclusion

In the Introduction to this chapter I suggested that as far as withholding of performance and termination for breach or wrongful repudiation are concerned, in functional terms the various systems appear to reach broadly similar results. I think the detailed account that followed justifies that suggestion. Certainly, there are some cases in which the outcome will be substantively different under one system than in others—to take a single example, Taiwan does not have a doctrine on anticipatory breach.[356] What differs much more is the reasoning used to reach those results. So we saw that in the systems using or derived from the common law, termination is permitted only for a serious breach but does not require a prior warning; whereas in systems influenced by German law, the starting point is that termination is permitted only after a *Nachfrist* has been served and not complied with, but the seriousness of the breach does not matter.[357] But when we look in more detail, we see that often the common law systems do require a warning when time is not of the essence,[358] while the Germanic systems often dispense with a *Nachfrist* but prevent termination for breaches that are not serious.[359] Thus, in all the systems, if A's breach was of an important term or had a serious effect, and any further delay will prevent the purpose of the contract being attained, B can terminate immediately; if timing is not critical, generally B may terminate only if it has given a warning to A that A must perform within a reasonable time, and A has failed to do so; but in most systems, the breach must be of an important obligation or have a serious effect.[360]

What is much more difficult to tell is whether there are differences in when a breach—for example, missing a couple of weekly visits[361] or a brief delay in making a payment[362]—will be treated as sufficiently serious to justify termination and not fall foul of other control mechanisms such as good faith.[363] That would require a much more detailed examination

353 Chen, ch 22—Taiwan 477; Taoka, ch 11—Japan 223; Wang, ch 3—China 68; Kwon, ch 13—Korea 277 (though cautioning that the case might be seen as one on which only the guest's subjective purpose was frustrated so that relief would be denied (cf section IV.5(b)).

354 Bell, ch 9—Indonesia 194–196.

355 Our Reporters from India and for Myanmar both said there would not be frustration, on different grounds: either that the cancellation was foreseeable (Narayan and Vardhan, ch 7—India 157) or that it was still possible to perform the contract (Briggs, ch 17—Myanmar 354).

356 See section II.4(g)(1).

357 See section II.4(e).

358 See section II.4(j).

359 See section II.4(e)(2).

360 See section II.4(e).

361 As in the hypothetical scenario of Car Machinery & Co and Traders Ltd: see section II.4(f).

362 As in the hypothetical scenario of Prime Ltd and Devil Corp: see section II.4(l).

363 See section II.4(e) and (l).

of each jurisdiction's court decisions, and possibly doctrinal writing, than was possible in this study.

We see a similar pattern in relation to cases of impossibility that occur without the fault of either party. Though the mechanisms used to reach the results differ between systems, if the event making the contract impossible was unforeseeable, and the effect is considered to be outside the risk taken by either party, the parties will be released from their obligations without liability for non-performance.[364] There may then be mutual restitution of any benefits transferred under the contract before it ended, though legislation in Hong Kong, Malaysia, and Singapore applies a somewhat less generous system.

When the contract has become only partially or temporarily impossible, situations which do not fit easily within the common law doctrine, courts struggle but seem to produce results that are broadly similar to those of the civil law-based systems. On the face of it, the only real difference between the systems is that the traditional common law systems have adopted a slightly wider definition of impossibility that includes frustration of purpose, where the purpose of the contract from the point of view of both the parties has become impossible. But that is a situation which in most of the other systems will fall within change of circumstances—which the common law systems do not recognize.[365]

Again, however, without more detailed study than was possible for this volume, it is hard to know exactly how doctrines of impossibility or *force majeure* will be applied. In particular, in relation to change of circumstances we have seen that systems seem to take rather different views of what risks a party is expected to bear. It is very likely that there is a similar difference in cases of impossibility. In the traditional common law systems, courts are very reluctant to hold that a contract has been frustrated,[366] and often this is because the court considers that the risk of what happened was taken by one or other of the parties.[367]

It is when we consider change of circumstances that major differences in outcome become obvious. As we have seen, most of the civil law-based systems now recognize the doctrine or reach similar results through the application of principles of equity, fairness, and good faith. The degree to which the doctrine is accepted varies greatly. It seems most firmly established in Taiwan, where it has been incorporated into the Civil Code and there is a lot of case law.[368] Japan has not incorporated it into the Code but there are quite a number of court decisions,[369] whereas in Korea there are few.[370] There are also important differences between these systems, in particular over whether the contract can be adjusted by the court or only terminated.[371] There may also be significant differences in the readiness of different courts to grant relief, and this may vary from context to context even within a single system.[372] The chapters in this volume, excellent though they are, demonstrate only too vividly how much work is needed and how difficult it is to get into the mindset of judges and lawyers from other jurisdictions.

[364] See section III.2.
[365] See section III.5.
[366] See section III.2(b).
[367] A prime example is *Edwinton Commercial Corp v Tsavliris Russ (Worldwide Salvage and Towage) Ltd (The Sea Angel)* [2007] EWCA Civ 547, [2007] 2 Lloyd's Rep 517, cited by Hall, ch 5—Hong Kong 99.
[368] See section IV.4(a).
[369] ibid.
[370] ibid.
[371] See section IV.6.
[372] See section IV.7.

However, it seems evident that in nearly all the civil law systems studied in this volume, when there has been a fundamental change of circumstances, relief of some kind will be given in a far wider range of situations than in the common law and ICA jurisdictions, even taking into account frustration of purpose—which is not yet recognized in India, Malaysia, or Myanmar.[373]

Why is there this apparently stark difference? It seems to reflect differing notions of what the law of contract should be seeking to do. Systems that allow relief for change of circumstances do so in order to preserve the equilibrium of the contract.[374] In contrast, common law judges would normally say that their primary task is to hold the parties to their contract and will only allow one of them to escape from it without the other's consent if there is one of a narrow range of vitiating factors[375] or a serious breach by the other. I suspect that very few common law judges think that it is appropriate to give any relief just because performance has become much more onerous for that party or of no value to the other party, due to a change of circumstances, unless the parties have provided in the contract for adjustment of the terms or termination of the contract if one party is unexpectedly facing hardship.

That, of course, leaves the question, why do judicial attitudes vary so much between countries that are near neighbours? In the conclusion to volume IV of this series,[376] I suggested that one reason may be that the type of case that is typically coming before the courts varies from one system to another; and that in England, whose law still has great influence in the common law world, whether directly or through the various Contract(s) Acts, the senior courts are typically dealing with 'commercial' cases, usually involving high-value contracts between parties who are sophisticated or at least well advised. I suggested that this underlies the English judges' approach; such parties do not need the same degree of protection that may be needed by, for example, a small business that has little knowledge or experience of contracting and is less able to take risks. I think the argument may well apply also to the differences in approach to changes of circumstances.

Given the economic and social differences between England, on the one hand, and the countries represented in this volume that still use the common law or the ICA and its variants, on the other, it is perhaps surprising that there have not been more departures from the English model. It will be very interesting to see whether the picture changes over time. But equally it will be interesting to see whether ideas—for example, as to what risks a party should be expected to bear—percolate from the common law systems to others that are currently more ready to adjust the contract or give some other form of relief.

If there were to be any cross-fertilization of that kind, it quite likely would have been prompted by this volume and the others in the *Studies in the Contract Laws of Asia* series. The various national reports in this volume are not just really interesting accounts of each law; they are likely to prompt lawyers in each jurisdiction to ask, how else could we govern contracts? Would another rule be better or another approach to applying the rules better reflect modern conditions? The Reporters whose work is in the volume, and the organizers of the project, are to be congratulated on work that is certainly fascinating and quite possibly inspirational.

[373] See section III.2(b)(2).

[374] See sections IV.4(b) and IV.5(g).

[375] These are explored in Chen-Wishart, Sono, and Vogenauer (n 227).

[376] H Beale, 'Invalidity of Contracts in Asia: Comparative Conclusions', in Chen-Wishart, Sono, and Vogenauer (n 227), 489, 523–24.

Index

For the benefit of digital users, indexed terms that span two pages (e.g., 52–53) may, on occasion, appear on only one of those pages.

General references to a topic are found under the main heading for the topic.

Country-specific references to a topic are found under the main heading for the country.